THE LAW OF WAR
A DOCUMENTARY HISTORY

LEON FRIEDMAN is an attorney on the staff of the Association of the Bar of the City of New York. He is the author of *The Wise Minority* (1971), *Unquestioning Obedience to the President* (1972), and has co-edited and contributed to *The Justices of the United States Supreme Court: 1789–1969* (1969), which won the 1970 Scribes Award. His articles have appeared in the *American Scholar, Commentary*, the *New Republic* and numerous legal periodicals.

THE LAW OF WAR

A DOCUMENTARY HISTORY–Volume II

Edited by **Leon Friedman**

With a Foreword by Telford Taylor

Random House, New York

Reference Series Editors:

Fred L. Israel
William P. Hansen

 Published in the United States by Random House, Inc., New York, and simultaneously in Canada by Random House of Canada Limited, Toronto.

Library of Congress Cataloging in Publication Data

Friedman, Leon, comp. The law of war.

1. War (International law) 2. Treaties—Collections. I. Title.
JX4505.F7 341.6'026 72-765

Manufactured in the United States of America
ISBN 0-394-47240-3
First Edition

CONTENTS

VOLUME II

THE LAW OF WAR
A DOCUMENTARY HISTORY

MILITARY GOVERNMENT—GERMANY
UNITED STATES ZONE
ORDINANCE NO. 7

Effective Date: October 18, 1946

ORGANIZATION AND POWERS OF CERTAIN MILITARY TRIBUNALS

ARTICLE I

The purpose of this Ordinance is to provide for the establishment of military tribunals which shall have power to try and punish persons charged with offenses recognized as crimes in Article II of Control Council Law No. 10, including conspiracies to commit any such crimes. Nothing herein shall prejudice the jurisdiction or the powers of other courts established or which may be established for the trial of any such offenses.

ARTICLE II

(*a*) Pursuant to the powers of the Military Governor for the United States Zone of Occupation within Germany and further pursuant to the powers conferred upon the Zone Commander by Control Council Law No. 10 and Articles 10 and 11 of the Charter of the International Military Tribunal annexed to the London Agreement of 8 August 1945 certain tribunals to be known as "Military Tribunals" shall be established hereunder.

(*b*) Each such tribunal shall consist of three or more members to be designated by the Military Governor. One alternate member may be designated to any tribunal if deemed advisable by the Military Governor. Except as provided in subsection (*c*) of this Article, all members and alternates shall be lawyers who have been admitted to practice, for at least five years, in the highest courts of one of the United States or its territories or of the District of Columbia, or who have been admitted to practice in the United States Supreme Court.

(*c*) The Military Governor may in his discretion enter into an agreement with one or more other zone commanders of the member nations of the Allied Control Authority providing for the joint trial of any case or cases. In such cases the tribunals shall consist of three or more members as may be provided in the agreement. In such cases the tribunals may include properly qualified lawyers designated by the other member nations.

(*d*) The Military Governor shall designate one of the members of the tribunal to serve as the presiding judge.

(*e*) Neither the tribunals nor the members of the tribunals or the alternates may be challenged by the prosecution or by the defendants or their counsel.

(*f*) In case of illness of any member of a tribunal or his incapacity for some other reason, the alternate, if one has been designated, shall take his place as a member in the pending trial. Members may be replaced for reasons of health or for other good reasons, except that no replacement of a member may take place, during a trial, other than by the alternate. If no alternate has been designated, the trial shall be continued to conclusion by the remaining members.

(*g*) The presence of three members of the tribunal or of two members when authorized pursuant to subsection (*f*) *supra* shall be necessary to constitute a quorum. In the case of tribunals designated under (*c*) above the agreement shall determine the requirements for a quorum.

(*h*) Decisions and judgments, including convictions and sentences, shall be by majority vote of the members. If the votes of the members are equally divided, the presiding member shall declare a mistrial.

ARTICLE III

(*a*) Charges against persons to be tried in the tribunals established hereunder shall originate in the Office of the Chief of Counsel for War Crimes, appointed by the Military Governor pursuant to paragraph 3 of the Executive Order Numbered 9679 of the President of the United States dated 16 January 1946. The Chief of Counsel for War Crimes shall determine the persons to be tried by the tribunals and he or his designated representative shall file the indictments with the Secretary General of the tribunals (see Article XIV, *infra*) and shall conduct the prosecution.

(*b*) The Chief of Counsel for War Crimes, when in his judgment it is advisable, may invite one or more United Nations to designate representatives to participate in the prosecution of any case.

ARTICLE IV

In order to ensure fair trial for the defendants, the following procedure shall be followed:

(*a*) A defendant shall be furnished, at a reasonable time before his trial, a copy of the indictment and of all documents lodged with the indictment, translated into a language which he understands. The indictment shall state the charges plainly, concisely and with sufficient particulars to inform defendant of the offenses charged.

(*b*) The trial shall be conducted in, or translated into, a language which the defendant understands.

(*c*) A defendant shall have the right to be represented by counsel of his own selection, provided such counsel shall be a person qualified under existing regulations to conduct cases before the courts of defendant's country, or any other person who may be specially authorized by the tribunal. The tribunal shall appoint qualified counsel to represent a defendant who is not represented by counsel of his own selection.

(*d*) Every defendant shall be entitled to be present at his trial except that a defendant may be proceeded against during temporary absences if in the opinion of the tribunal defendant's interests will not thereby be impaired, and except further as provided in Article VI (*c*). The tribunal may also proceed in the absence of any defendant who has applied for and has been granted permission to be absent.

(*e*) A defendant shall have the right through his counsel to present evidence at the trial in support of his defense, and to cross-examine any witness called by the prosecution.

(*f*) A defendant may apply in writing to the tribunal for the production of witnesses or of documents. The application shall state where the witness or document is thought to be located and shall also state the facts to be proved by the witness or the document and the relevancy of such facts to the defense. If the tribunal grants the application, the defendant shall be given such aid in obtaining production of evidence as the tribunal may order.

Article V

The tribunals shall have the power

(*a*) to summon witnesses to the trial, to require their attendance and testimony and to put questions to them;

(*b*) to interrogate any defendant who takes the stand to testify in his own behalf, or who is called to testify regarding any other defendant;

(*c*) to require the production of documents and other evidentiary material;

(*d*) to administer oaths;

(*e*) to appoint officers for the carrying out of any task designated by the tribunals including the taking of evidence on commission;

(*f*) to adopt rules of procedure not inconsistent with this Ordinance. Such rules shall be adopted, and from time to time as necessary, revised by the members of the tribunal or by the committee of presiding judges as provided in Article XIII.

Article VI

The tribunals shall

(*a*) confine the trial strictly to an expeditious hearing of the issues raised by the charges;

(*b*) take strict measures to prevent any action which will cause unreasonable delay, and rule out irrelevant issues and statements of any kind whatsoever;

(*c*) deal summarily with any contumacy, imposing appropriate punishment, including the exclusion of any defendant or his counsel from some or all further proceedings, but without prejudice to the determination of the charges.

Article VII

The tribunals shall not be bound by technical rules of evidence. They shall adopt and apply to the greatest possible extent expeditious and nontechnical procedure, and shall admit any evidence which they deem to have probative value. Without limiting the foregoing general rules, the following shall be deemed admissible if they appear to the tribunal to contain information of probative value relating to the charges: affidavits, depositions, interrogations, and other statements, diaries, letters, the records, findings, statements and judgments of the military tribunals and the reviewing and confirming authorities of any of the United Nations, and copies of any document or other secondary evidence of the contents of any document, if the original is not readily available or cannot be produced without delay. The tribunal shall afford the opposing party such opportunity to question the authenticity or probative value of such evidence as in the opinion of the tribunal the ends of justice require.

Article VIII

The tribunals may require that they be informed of the nature of any evidence before it is offered so that they may rule upon the relevance thereof.

Article IX

The tribunals shall not require proof of facts of common knowledge but shall take judicial notice thereof. They shall also take judicial notice of official governmental documents and reports of any of the United Nations, including the acts and documents of the committees set up in the various Allied countries for the investigation of war crimes, and the records and findings of military or other tribunals of any of the United Nations.

Article X

The determinations of the International Military Tribunal in the judgment in Case No. 1 that invasions, aggressive acts, aggressive wars, crimes, atrocities or inhumane acts were planned or occurred, shall be binding on the tribunals established hereunder and shall not be questioned except insofar as the participation therein or knowledge thereof by any particular person may be concerned. Statements of the International Military Tribunal in the judgment in Case No. 1 constitute proof of the facts stated, in the absence of substantial new evidence to the contrary.

Article XI

The proceedings at the trial shall take the following course:

(*a*) The tribunal shall inquire of each defendant whether he has received and had an opportunity to read the indictment against him and whether he pleads "guilty" or "not guilty."

(*b*) The prosecution may make an opening statement.

(*c*) The prosecution shall produce its evidence subject to the cross examination of its witnesses.

(*d*) The defense may make an opening statement.

(*e*) The defense shall produce its evidence subject to the cross examination of its witnesses.

(*f*) Such rebutting evidence as may be held by the tribunal to be material may be produced by either the prosecution or the defense.

(*g*) The defense shall address the court.

(*h*) The prosecution shall address the court.

(*i*) Each defendant may make a statement to the tribunal.

(*j*) The tribunal shall deliver judgment and pronounce sentence.

Article XII

A Central Secretariat to assist the tribunals to be appointed hereunder shall be established as soon as practicable. The main office of the Secretariat shall be located in Nurnberg. The Secretariat shall consist of a Secretary General and such assistant secretaries, military officers, clerks, interpreters and other personnel as may be necessary.

Article XIII

The Secretary General shall be appointed by the Military Governor and shall organize and direct the work of the Secretariat. He shall be subject to the supervision of the members of the tribunals, except that when at least three tribunals shall be functioning, the presiding judges of the several tribunals may form the supervisory committee.

Article XIV

The Secretariat shall:

(*a*) Be responsible for the administrative and supply needs of the Secretariat and of the several tribunals.

(*b*) Receive all documents addressed to tribunals.

(*c*) Prepare and recommend uniform rules of procedure, not inconsistent with the provisions of this Ordinance.

(*d*) Secure such information for the tribunals as may be needed for the approval or appointment of defense counsel.

(*e*) Serve as liaison between the prosecution and defense counsel.

(*f*) Arrange for aid to be given defendants and the prosecution in obtaining production of witnesses or evidence as authorized by the tribunals.

(*g*) Be responsible for the preparation of the records of the proceedings before the tribunals.

(*h*) Provide the necessary clerical, reporting and interpretative services to the tribunals and its members, and perform such other duties as may be required for the efficient conduct of the proceedings before the tribunals, or as may be requested by any of the tribunals.

Article XV

The judgments of the tribunals as to the guilt or the innocence of any defendant shall give the reasons on which they are based and shall be final and not subject to review. The sentences imposed may be subject to review as provided in Article XVII, *infra.*

Article XVI

The tribunal shall have the right to impose upon the defendant, upon conviction, such punishment as shall be determined by the tribunal to be just, which may consist of one or more of the penalties provided in Article II, Section 3, of Control Council Law No. 10.

Article XVII

(*a*) Except as provided in (*b*) *infra,* the record of each case shall be forwarded to the Military Governor who shall have the power to mitigate, reduce or otherwise alter the sentence imposed by the tribunal, but may not increase the severity thereof.

(*b*) In cases tried before tribunals authorized by Article II (*c*), the sentence shall be reviewed jointly by the zone commanders of the nations involved, who may mitigate, reduce or otherwise alter the sentence by majority vote, but may not increase the severity thereof. If only two nations are represented, the sentence may be altered only by the consent of both zone commanders.

Article XVIII

No sentence of death shall be carried into execution unless and until confirmed in writing by the Military Governor. In accordance with Article III, Section 5, of Law No. 10, execution of the death sentence may be deferred by not to exceed one month after such confirmation if there is reason to believe that the testimony of the convicted person may be of value in the investigation and trial of other crimes.

Article XIX

Upon the pronouncement of a death sentence by a tribunal established thereunder and pending confirmation thereof, the condemned will be remanded to the prison or place where he was confined and there be segregated from the other inmates, or be transferred to a more appropriate place of confinement.

Article XX

Upon the confirmation of a sentence of death the Military Governor will issue the necessary orders for carrying out the execution.

Article XXI

Where sentence of confinement for a term of years has been imposed the condemned shall be confined in the manner directed by the tribunal imposing sentence. The place of confinement may be changed from time to time by the Military Governor.

Article XXII

Any property declared to be forfeited or the restitution of which is ordered by a tribunal shall be delivered to the Military Governor, for disposal in accordance with Control Council Law No. 10, Article II (3).

Article XXIII

Any of the duties and functions of the Military Governor provided for herein may be delegated to the Deputy Military Governor. Any of the duties and functions of the Zone Commander provided for herein may be exercised by and in the name of the Military Governor and may be delegated to the Deputy Military Governor.

Ordinance No. 11: Amendment to Military Government Ordinance No. 7 of 18 October 1946, Entitled "Organization and Powers of Certain Military Tribunals"

Article I

Article V of Ordinance No. 7 is amended by adding thereto a new subdivision to be designated "(g)," reading as follows:

"(*g*) The presiding judges, and, when established, the supervisory committee of presiding judges provided in Article XIII shall assign the cases brought by the Chief of Counsel for War Crimes to the various Military Tribunals for trial."

Article II

Ordinance No. 7 is amended by adding thereto a new article following Article V to be designated Article V-B, reading as follows:

"(*a*) A joint session of the Military Tribunals may be called by any of the presiding judges thereof or upon motion, addressed to each of the Tribunals, of the Chief of Counsel for War Crimes or of counsel for any defendant whose interests are affected, to hear argument upon and to review any interlocutory ruling by any of the Military Tribunals on a fundamental or important legal question either substantive or procedural, which ruling is in conflict with or is inconsistent with a prior ruling of another of the Military Tribunals.

"(*b*) A joint session of the Military Tribunals may be called in the same manner as provided in subsection (*a*) of this Article to hear argument upon and to review conflicting or inconsistent final rulings contained in the decisions or judgments of any of the Military Tribunals on a fundamental or important legal question, either substantive or procedural. Any motion with respect to such final ruling shall be filed within ten (10) days following the issuance of decision or judgment.

"(*c*) Decisions by joint sessions of the Military Tribunals, unless thereafter altered in another joint session, shall be binding upon all the Military Tribunals. In the case of the review of final rulings by joint sessions, the judgments reviewed may be confirmed or remanded for action consistent with the joint decision.

"(*d*) The presence of a majority of the members of each Military Tribunal then constituted is required to constitute a quorum.

"(*e*) The members of the Military Tribunals shall, before any joint session begins, agree among themselves upon the selection from their number of a member to preside over the joint session.

"(*f*) Decisions shall be by majority vote of the members. If the votes of the members are equally divided, the vote of the member presiding over the session shall be decisive."

ARTICLE III

Subdivisions (*g*) and (*h*) of Article XI of Ordinance No. 7 are deleted; subdivision (*i*) is relettered "(*h*)"; subdivision (*j*) is relettered "(*i*)"; and a new subdivision, to be designated "(*g*)," is added, reading as follows:

"(*g*) The prosecution and defense shall address the court in such order as the Tribunal may determine."

This Ordinance becomes effective 17 February 1947.

BY ORDER OF THE MILITARY GOVERNMENT:

THE NUREMBERG JUDGMENT
Nuremberg, 1945–46

TRIAL OF THE MAJOR WAR CRIMINALS BEFORE THE INTERNATIONAL MILITARY TRIBUNAL (1945–1946)

THE UNITED STATES of America, the French Republic, the United Kingdom of Great Britain and Northern Ireland, and the Union of Soviet Socialist Republics.

AGAINST

Hermann Wilhelm Göring, Rudolf Hess, Joachim Von Ribbentrop, Robert Ley, Wilhelm Keitel, Ernst Kaltenbrunner, Alfred Rosenberg, Hans Frank, Wilhelm Frick, Julius Streicher, Walter Funk, Hjalmar Schacht, Gustav Krupp Von Bohlen Und Halbach, Karl Dönitz, Erich Raeder, Baldur von Schirach, Fritz Sauckel, Alfred Jodl, Martin Bormann, Franz Von Papen, Arthur Seyss-Inquart, Albert Speer, Constantin Von Neurath, and Hans Fritzsche, Individually and as Members of Any of the Following Groups or Organizations to which They Respectively Belonged, Namely: Die Reichsregierung (Reich Cabinet); Das Korps Der Politischen Leither Der Nationalsozialistischen Deutschen Arbeiterpartei (Leadership Corps of the Nazi Party); Die Schutzstaffeln Der Nationalsozialistischen Deutschen Arbeiterpartei (commonly known as the "SS") and including Der Sicherheitsdienst (commonly known as the "SD"); Die Geheime Staatspolizei (Secret State Police, commonly known as the "Gestapo"); Die Sturmabteilungen Der Nsdap (commonly known as the "SA"); and the General Staff and High Command of the German Armed Forces, all as defined in Appendix B of the Indictment,

Defendants.

September 30, 1946

JUDGMENT

On 8 August 1945, the Government of the United Kingdom of Great Britain and Northern Ireland, the Government of the United States of America, the Provisional Government of the French Republic, and the Government of the Union of Soviet Socialist Republics entered into an agreement establishing this Tribunal for the trial of War Criminals whose offenses have no particular geographical location. In accordance with Article 5, the following Governments of the United Nations have expressed their adherence to the Agreement:

Greece, Denmark, Yugoslavia, the Netherlands, Czechoslovakia, Poland, Belgium, Ethiopia, Australia, Honduras, Norway, Panama, Luxembourg, Haiti, New Zealand, India, Venezuela, Uruguay, and Paraguay.

By the Charter annexed to the Agreement, the constitution, jurisdiction and functions of the Tribunal were defined.

The Tribunal was invested with power to try and punish persons who had committed Crimes against Peace, War Crimes, and Crimes against Humanity as defined in the Charter.

The Charter also provided that at the trial of any individual member of any group or organization the Tribunal may declare (in connection with any act of which the individual may be convicted), that the group or organization of which the individual was a member was a criminal organization.

In Berlin, on 18 October 1945, in accordance with Article 14 of the Charter, an indictment was lodged against the defendants named in the caption above, who had been designated by the Committee of the Chief Prosecutors of the signatory Powers as major war criminals.

A copy of the Indictment in the German language was served upon each defendant in custody at least 30 days before the Trial opened.

This Indictment charges the defendants with Crimes against Peace, by the planning, preparation, initiation and waging of wars of aggression, which were also wars in violation of international treaties, agreements, and assurances, with War Crimes and with Crimes against Humanity. The defendants are also charged with participating in the formulation or execution of a common plan or conspiracy to commit all these crimes. The Tribunal was further asked by the Prosecution to declare all the named groups or organizations to be criminal within the meaning of the Charter.

The Defendant Robert Ley committed suicide in prison on 25 October 1945. On 15 November 1945 the Tribunal decided that the Defendant Gustav Krupp von Bohlen and Halbach could not then be tried because of his physical and mental condition, but that the charges against him in the Indictment should be retained for trial thereafter, if the physical and mental condition of the defendant should permit. On 17 November 1945 the Tribunal decided to try the Defendant Bormann in his absence under the provisions of Article 12 of the Charter. After argument and consideration of full medical reports, and a statement from the defendant himself, the Tribunal decided on 1 December 1945 that no grounds existed for a postponement of the trial against the Defendant Hess because of his mental condition. A similar decision was made in the case of the Defendant Streicher.

In accordance with Articles 16 and 23 of the Charter, counsel were either chosen by the defendants in custody themselves, or at their request were appointed by the Tribunal. In his absence the Tribunal appointed counsel for the Defendant Bormann, and also assigned counsel to represent the named groups or organizations.

The Trial, which was conducted in four languages—English, Russian, French, and German—began on 20 November 1945, and pleas of "Not Guilty" were made by all the defendants except Bormann.

The hearing of evidence and the speeches of counsel concluded on 31 August 1946.

Four hundred and three open sessions of the Tribunal have been held. Thirty-three witnesses gave evidence orally for the Prosecution against the individual defendants, and 61 witnesses, in addition to 19 of the defendants, gave evidence for the Defense.

A further 143 witnesses gave evidence for the Defense by means of written answers to interrogatories.

The Tribunal appointed Commissioners to hear evidence relating to the organizations, and 101 witnesses were heard for the Defense before the Commissioners, and 1,809 affidavits from other witnesses were submitted. Six reports were also submitted, summarizing the contents of a great number of further affidavits.

Thirty-eight thousand affidavits, signed by 155,000 people, were submitted on behalf of the Political Leaders; 136,213 on behalf of the SS; 10,000 on behalf of the SA; 7,000 on behalf of the SD; 3,000 on behalf of the General Staff and OKW; and 2,000 on behalf of the Gestapo.

The Tribunal itself heard 22 witnesses for the organizations. The documents tendered in evidence for the prosecution of the individual defendants and the organizations numbered several thousands. A complete stenographic record of everything said in court has been made, as well as an electrical recording of all the proceedings.

Copies of all the documents put in evidence by the Prosecution have been supplied to the Defense in the German language. The applications made by the defendants for the production of witnesses and documents raised serious problems in some instances, on account of the unsettled state of the country. It was also necessary to limit the number of witnesses to be called, in order to have an expeditious hearing, in accordance with Article 18(c) of the Charter. The

Tribunal, after examination, granted all those applications which in their opinion were relevant to the defense of any defendant or named group or organization, and were not cumulative. Facilities were provided for obtaining those witnesses and documents, granted through the office of the General Secretary established by the Tribunal.

Much of the evidence presented to the Tribunal on behalf of the Prosecution was documentary evidence, captured by the Allied armies in German army headquarters, Government buildings, and elsewhere. Some of the documents were found in salt mines, buried in the ground, hidden behind false walls and in other places thought to be secure from discovery. The case, therefore, against the defendants rests in a large measure on documents of their own making, the authenticity of which has not been challenged except in one or two cases.

* * *

The Common Plan or Conspiracy and Aggressive War

The Tribunal now turns to the consideration of the Crimes against Peace charged in the Indictment. Count One of the Indictment charges the defendants with conspiring or having a common plan to commit crimes against peace. Count Two of the Indictment charges the defendants with committing specific crimes against peace by planning, preparing, initiating, and waging wars of aggression against a number of other states. It will be convenient to consider the question of the existence of a common plan and the question of aggressive war together, and to deal later in this Judgment with the question of the individual responsibility of the defendants.

The charges in the Indictment that the defendants planned and waged aggressive wars are charges of the utmost gravity. War is essentially an evil thing. Its consequences are not confined to the belligerent states alone, but affect the whole world.

To initiate a war of aggression, therefore, is not only an international crime; it is the supreme international crime differing only from other war crimes in that it contains within itself the accumulated evil of the whole.

The first acts of aggression referred to in the Indictment are the seizure of Austria and Czechoslovakia; and the first war of aggression charged in the Indictment is the war against Poland begun on 1 September 1939.

Before examining that charge it is necessary to look more closely at some of the events which preceded these acts of aggression. The war against Poland did not come suddenly out of an otherwise clear sky; the evidence has made it plain that this war of aggression, as well as the seizure of Austria and Czechoslovakia, was premeditated and carefully prepared, and was not undertaken until the moment was thought opportune for it to be carried through as a definite part of the preordained scheme and plan.

For the aggressive designs of the Nazi Government were not accidents arising out of the immediate political situation in Europe and the world; they were a deliberate and essential part of Nazi foreign policy.

From the beginning, the National Socialist movement claimed that its object was to unite the German people in the consciousness of their mission and destiny, based on inherent qualities of race, and under the guidance of the Führer.

For its achievement, two things were deemed to be essential; the disruption of the European order as it had existed since the Treaty of Versailles, and the creation of a Greater Germany beyond the frontiers of 1914. This necessarily involved the seizure of foreign territories.

War was seen to be inevitable, or at the very least, highly probable, if these purposes were to be accomplished. The German people, therefore, with all their resources, were to be organized as a great political-military army, schooled to obey without question any policy decreed by the State.

* * *

The Planning of Aggression

Evidence from captured documents has revealed that Hitler held four secret meetings to which the Tribunal proposes to make special reference because of the light they shed upon the question of the common plan and aggressive war.

These meetings took place on 5 November 1937, 23 May 1939, 22 August 1939, and 23 November 1939.

At these meetings important declarations were made by Hitler as to his purposes, which are quite unmistakable in their terms.

The documents which record what took place at these meetings have been subject to some criticism at the hands of defending counsel.

Their essential authenticity is not denied, but it is said, for example, that they do not purport to be verbatim transcripts of the speeches they record, that the document dealing with the meeting on 5 November 1937 was dated 5 days after the meeting had taken place, and that the two documents dealing with the meeting of 22 August 1939 differ from one another and are unsigned.

Making the fullest allowance for criticism of this kind, the Tribunal is of the opinion that the documents are documents of the highest value, and that their authenticity and substantial truth are established.

They are obviously careful records of the events they describe, and they have been preserved as such in the archives of the German Government, from whose custody they were captured. Such documents could never be dismissed as inventions, nor even as inaccurate or distorted; they plainly record events which actually took place.

Conferences of 23 November 1939 and 5 November 1937

It will perhaps be useful to deal first of all with the meeting of 23 November 1939, when Hitler called his supreme commanders together. A record was made of what was said, by one of those present. At the date of the meeting, Austria and Czechoslovakia had been incorporated into the German Reich, Poland had been conquered by the German armies, and the war with Great Britain and France was still in its static phase. The moment was opportune for a review of past events. Hitler informed the commanders that the purpose of the conference was to give them an idea of the world of his thoughts, and to tell them his decision. He thereupon reviewed his political task since 1919, and referred to the secession of Germany from the League of Nations, the denunciation of the Disarmament Conference, the order for rearmament, the introduction of compulsory armed service, the occupation of the Rhineland, the seizure of Austria, and the action against Czechoslovakia. He stated:

> One year later, Austria came; this step also was considered doubtful. It brought about a considerable reinforcement of the Reich. The next step was Bohemia, Moravia, and Poland. This step also was not possible to accomplish in one campaign. First of all, the western fortification had to be finished. It was not possible to reach the goal in one effort. It was clear to me from the first moment that I could not be satisfied with the Sudeten German territory. That was only a partial solution. The decision to march into Bohemia was made. Then followed the erection of the Protectorate and with that the basis for the action against Poland was laid, but I was not quite clear at that time whether I should start first against the East and then in the West or vice versa. . . . Basically I did not organize the Armed Forces in order not to strike. The decision to strike was always in me. Earlier or later I wanted to solve the problem. Under pressure it was decided that the East was to be attacked first.

This address, reviewing past events and reaffirming the aggressive intentions present from the beginning, puts beyond any question of doubt the character of the actions against Austria and Czechoslovakia, and the war against Poland.

For they had all been accomplished according to plan; and the nature of that plan must now be examined in a little more detail.

At the meeting of 23 November 1939 Hitler was looking back to things accomplished; at the earlier meetings now to be considered, he was looking forward, and revealing his plans to his confederates. The comparison is instructive.

The meeting held at the Reich Chancellery in Berlin on 5 November 1937 was attended by Lt. Col. Hossbach, Hitler's personal adjutant, who compiled a long note of the proceedings, which he dated 10 November 1937 and signed.

The persons present were Hitler, and the Defendants Göring, Von Neurath and Raeder, in their capacities as Commander-in-Chief of the Luftwaffe, Reich Foreign Minister, and Commander-in-Chief of the Navy respectively,

General Von Blomberg, Minister of War, and General Von Fritsch, the Commander-in-Chief of the Army.

Hitler began by saying that the subject of the conference was of such high importance that in other states it would have taken place before the Cabinet. He went on to say that the subject matter of his speech was the result of his detailed deliberations, and of his experiences during his four and a half years of government. He requested that the statements he was about to make should be looked upon in the case of his death as his last will and testament. Hitler's main theme was the problem of living space, and he discussed various possible solutions, only to set them aside. He then said that the seizure of living space on the continent of Europe was therefore necessary. . . .

* * *

The Aggression against Poland

By March 1939 the plan to annex Austria and Czechoslovakia, which had been discussed by Hitler at the meeting of 5 November 1937, had been accomplished. The time had now come for the German leaders to consider further acts of aggression, made more possible of attainment because of that accomplishment.

On 23 May 1939 a meeting was held in Hitler's study in the new Reich Chancellery in Berlin. Hitler announced his decision to attack Poland and gave his reasons, and discussed the effect the decision might have on other countries. In point of time, this was the second of the important meetings to which reference has already been made, and in order to appreciate the full significance of what was said and done, it is necessary to state shortly some of the main events in the history of German-Polish relations.

As long ago as the year 1925 an Arbitration Treaty between Germany and Poland had been made at Locarno, providing for the settlement of all disputes between the two countries. On 26 January 1934, a German-Polish declaration of non-aggression was made, signed on behalf of the German Government by the Defendant Von Neurath. On 30 January 1934, and again on 30 January 1937, Hitler made speeches in the Reichstag in which he expressed his view that Poland and Germany could work together in harmony and peace. On 20 February 1938 Hitler made a third speech in the Reichstag in the course of which he said with regard to Poland:

> And so the way to a friendly understanding has been successfully paved, an understanding which, beginning with Danzig, has today, in spite of the attempts of certain mischief-makers, succeeded in finally taking the poison out of the relations between Germany and Poland and transforming them into a sincere, friendly co-operation. Relying on her friendships, Germany will not leave a stone unturned to save that ideal which provides the foundation for the task which is ahead of us—peace.

On 26 September 1938, in the middle of the crisis over the Sudetenland,

Hitler made the speech in Berlin which has already been quoted, and announced that he had informed the British Prime Minister that when the Czechoslovakian problem was solved there would be no more territorial problems for Germany in Europe. Nevertheless, on 24 November of the same year, an OKW directive was issued to the German Armed Forces to make preparations for an attack upon Danzig; it stated:

> The Führer has ordered:
>
> (1) . . . preparations are also to be made to enable the Free State of Danzig to be occupied by German troops by surprise.

In spite of having ordered military preparations for the occupation of Danzig, Hitler, on 30 January 1939, said in a speech in the Reichstag:

> During the troubled months of the past year, the friendship between Germany and Poland has been one of the most reassuring factors in the political life of Europe.

Five days previously, on 25 January 1939, Ribbentrop said in the course of a speech in Warsaw:

> Thus Poland and Germany can look forward to the future with full confidence in the solid basis of their mutual relations.

Following on the occupation of Bohemia and Moravia by Germany on 15 March 1939, which was a flagrant breach of the Munich Agreement, Great Britain gave an assurance to Poland on 31 March 1939 that in the event of any action which clearly threatened Polish independence, and which the Polish Government accordingly considered it vital to resist with their national forces, Great Britain would feel itself bound at once to lend Poland all the support in its power. The French Government took the same stand. It is interesting to note in this connection that one of the arguments frequently presented by the Defense in the present case is that the defendants were influenced to think that their conduct was not in breach of international law by the acquiescence of other powers. The declarations of Great Britain and France showed, at least, that this view could be held no longer.

On 3 April 1939 a revised OKW directive was issued to the Armed Forces, which after referring to the question of Danzig made reference to Fall Weiss (the military code name for the German invasion of Poland) and stated:

> The Führer has added the following directions to Fall Weiss:
>
> (1) Preparations must be made in such a way that the operation can be carried out at any time from 1 September 1939 onwards.
>
> (2) The High Command of the Armed Forces has been directed to draw up a precise timetable for Fall Weiss and to arrange by conferences the synchronized timings between the three branches of the Armed Forces.

On 11 April 1939, a further directive was signed by Hitler and issued to the Armed Forces, and in one of the annexes to that document the words occur:

> Quarrels—with Poland—should be avoided. Should Poland . . . however adopt a threatening attitude towards Germany, "a final settlement" will be neces-

sary, notwithstanding the pact with Poland. The aim is then to destroy Polish military strength, and to create in the East a situation which satisfies the requirements of defense. The Free State of Danzig will be incorporated into Germany at the outbreak of the conflict at the latest. Policy aims . . . at limiting the war to Poland, and this is considered possible in view of the internal crisis in France, and British restraint as a result of this. . . .

In spite of the contents of these two directives, Hitler made a speech in the Reichstag on 28 April 1939 in which, after describing the Polish Government's alleged rejection of an offer he had made with regard to Danzig and the Polish Corridor, he stated:

I have regretted greatly this incomprehensible attitude of the Polish Government, but that alone is not the decisive fact; the worst is that now Poland, like Czechoslovakia a year ago, believes, under the pressure of a lying international campaign, that it must call up its troops, although Germany on her part has not called up a single man, and had not thought of proceeding in any way against Poland. . . . The intention to attack on the part of Germany which was merely invented by the international press. . . .

It was 4 weeks after making this speech that Hitler, on 23 May 1939, held the important military conference to which reference has already been made. Among the persons present were the Defendants Göring, Raeder, and Keitel. The adjutant on duty that day was Lt. Col. Schmundt, and he made a record of what happened, certifying it with his signature as a correct record.

The purpose of the meeting was to enable Hitler to inform the heads of the Armed Forces and their staffs of his views on the political situation and his future aims. After analyzing the political situation and reviewing the course of events since 1933, Hitler announced his decision to attack Poland. He admitted that the quarrel with Poland over Danzig was not the reason for this attack, but the necessity for Germany to enlarge her living space and secure her food supplies. He said:

The solution of the problem demands courage. The principle by which one evades solving the problem by adapting oneself to circumstances is inadmissible. Circumstances must rather be adapted to aims. This is impossible without invasion of foreign states or attacks upon foreign property.

Later in his address he added:

There is therefore no question of sparing Poland, and we are left with the decision to attack Poland at the first suitable opportunity. We cannot expect a repetition of the Czech affair. There will be war. Our task is to isolate Poland. The success of the isolation will be decisive. . . . The isolation of Poland is a matter of skillful politics.

Lt. Col. Schmundt's record of the meeting reveals that Hitler fully realized the possibility of Great Britain and France coming to Poland's assistance. If, therefore, the isolation of Poland could not be achieved, Hitler was of the opinion that Germany should attack Great Britain and France first, or at any rate should concentrate primarily on the war in the West, in order to defeat Great Britain and France quickly, or at least to destroy their effectiveness.

Nevertheless, Hitler stressed that war with England and France would be a life-and-death struggle which might last a long time, and that preparations must be made accordingly.

During the weeks which followed this conference, other meetings were held and directives were issued in preparation for the war. The Defendant Ribbentrop was sent to Moscow to negotiate a non-aggression pact with the Soviet Union.

On 22 August 1939 there took place the important meeting of that day, to which reference has already been made. The Prosecution have put in evidence two unsigned captured documents which appear to be records made of this meeting by persons who were present. The first document is headed: "The Führer's speech to the commanders-in-chief on 22 August 1939. . . ." The purpose of the speech was to announce the decision to make war on Poland at once, and Hitler began by saying:

> It was clear to me that a conflict with Poland had to come sooner or later. I had already made this decision in the spring, but I thought that I would first turn against the West in a few years, and only afterwards against the East. . . . I wanted to establish an acceptable relationship with Poland in order to fight first against the West. But this plan, which was agreeable to me, could not be executed since essential points have changed. It became clear to me that Poland would attack us in case of a conflict with the West.

Hitler then went on to explain why he had decided that the most favorable moment had arrived for starting the war. "Now," said Hitler, "Poland is in the position in which I wanted her. . . . I am only afraid that at the last moment some *Schweinhund* will make a proposal for mediation. A beginning has been made for the destruction of England's hegemony."

* * *

The Aggressive War against the Union of Soviet Socialist Republics

On 23 August 1939 Germany signed the non-aggression pact with the Union of Soviet Socialist Republics.

The evidence has shown unmistakably that the Soviet Union on their part conformed to the terms of this pact; indeed the German Government itself had been assured of this by the highest German sources. Thus, the German Ambassador in Moscow informed his Government that the Soviet Union would go to war only if attacked by Germany, and this statement is recorded in the German War Diary under the date of 6 June 1941.

Nevertheless, as early as the late summer of 1940, Germany began to make preparations for an attack on the U.S.S.R. in spite of the non-aggression pact. This operation was secretly planned under the code name "Case Barbarossa," and the former Field Marshal Paulus testified that on 3 September 1940, when he joined the German General Staff, he continued developing "Case Barbarossa," which was finally completed at the beginning of November

1940; and that even then, the German General Staff had no information that the Soviet Union was preparing for war.

On 18 December 1940 Hitler issued Directive Number 21, initialled by Keitel and Jodl, which called for the completion of all preparations connected with the realization of "Case Barbarossa" by 15 May 1941. This directive stated:

> The German Armed Forces must be prepared to crush Soviet Russia in a quick campaign before the end of the war against England. . . . Great caution has to be exercised that the intention of an attack will not be recognized.

Before the directive of 18 December had been made, the Defendant Göring had informed General Thomas, Chief of the Office of War Economy of the OKW, of the plan, and General Thomas made surveys of the economic possibilities of the U.S.S.R. including its raw materials, its power and transport system, and its capacity to produce arms.

In accordance with these surveys, an economic staff for the Eastern territories with many military-economic units (inspectorates, commandos, groups) was created under the supervision of the Defendant Göring. In conjunction with the military command, these units were to achieve the most complete and efficient economic exploitation of the occupied territories in the interest of Germany.

The framework of the future political and economic organization of the occupied territories was designed by the Defendant Rosenberg over a period of 3 months, after conferences with and assistance by the Defendants Keitel, Jodl, Raeder, Funk, Göring, Ribbentrop, and Frick or their representatives. It was made the subject of a most detailed report immediately after the invasion.

These plans outlined the destruction of the Soviet Union as an independent State, and its partition, the creation of so-called Reich Commissariats, and the conversion of Estonia, Latvia, Bielorussia and other territories into German colonies.

At the same time Germany drew Hungary, Romania, and Finland into the war against the U.S.S.R. In December 1940 Hungary agreed to participate on the promise of Germany that she should have certain territories at the expense of Yugoslavia.

In May 1941 a final agreement was concluded with Antonescu, the Prime Minister of Romania, regarding the attack on the U.S.S.R., in which Germany promised to Romania Bessarabia, Northern Bukovina, and the right to occupy Soviet territory up to the Dnieper.

On 22 June 1941, without any declaration of war, Germany invaded Soviet territory in accordance with the plans so long made.

* * *

War against the United States

Four days after the attack launched by the Japanese on the United States fleet in Pearl Harbor on 7 December 1941, Germany declared war on the United States.

The Tripartite Pact between Germany, Italy, and Japan had been signed on 27 September 1940, and from that date until the attack upon the U.S.S.R. the Defendant Von Ribbentrop, with other defendants, was endeavoring to induce Japan to attack British possessions in the Far East. This, it was thought, would hasten England's defeat, and also keep the United States out of the war.

The possibility of a direct attack on the United States was considered and discussed as a matter for the future. Major Von Falkenstein, the Luftwaffe liaison officer with the Operations Staff of the OKW, summarizing military problems which needed discussion in Berlin in October of 1940, spoke of the possibility "of the prosecution of the war against America at a later date." It is clear, too, that the German policy of keeping America out of the war, if possible, did not prevent Germany promising support to Japan even against the United States. On 4 April 1941, Hitler told Matsuoka, the Japanese Foreign Minister, in the presence of the Defendant Ribbentrop, that Germany would "strike without delay" if a Japanese attack on Singapore should lead to war between Japan and the United States. The next day Ribbentrop himself urged Matsuoka to bring Japan into the war.

On 28 November 1941, 10 days before the attack on Pearl Harbor, Ribbentrop encouraged Japan, through her Ambassador in Berlin, to attack Great Britain and the United States, and stated that should Japan become engaged in a war with the United States, Germany would join the war immediately. A few days later, Japanese representatives told Germany and Italy that Japan was preparing to attack the United States, and asked for their support. Germany and Italy agreed to do this, although in the Tripartite Pact, Italy and Germany had undertaken to assist Japan only if she were attacked. When the assault on Pearl Harbor did take place, the Defendant Ribbentrop is reported to have been "overjoyed," and later, at a ceremony in Berlin, when a German medal was awarded to Oshima, the Japanese Ambassador, Hitler indicated his approval of the tactics which the Japanese had adopted of negotiating with the United States as long as possible, and then striking hard without any declaration of war.

Although it is true that Hitler and his colleagues originally did not consider that a war with the United States would be beneficial to their interest, it is apparent that in the course of 1941 that view was revised, and Japan was given every encouragement to adopt a policy which would almost certainly bring the United States into the war. And when Japan attacked the United States fleet in Pearl Harbor and thus made aggressive war against the United States, the Nazi Government caused Germany to enter that war at once on the side of Japan by declaring war themselves on the United States.

* * *

Violations of International Treaties

The Charter defines as a crime the planning or waging of war, that is, a war of aggression or a war in violation of international treaties. The Tribunal has decided that certain of the defendants planned and waged aggressive wars against twelve nations, and were therefore guilty of this series of crimes. This makes it unnecessary to discuss the subject in further detail, or even to consider at any length the extent to which these aggressive wars were also "wars in violation of international treaties, agreements, or assurances."

These treaties are set out in Appendix C of the Indictment. Those of principal importance are the following.

Hague Conventions

In the 1899 Convention the signatory powers agreed: "before an appeal to arms . . . to have recourse, as far as circumstances allow, to the good offices or mediation of one or more friendly powers." A similar clause was inserted in the Convention for Pacific Settlement of International Disputes of 1907. In the accompanying Convention Relative to Opening of Hostilities, Article 1 contains this far more specific language:

> The Contracting Powers recognize that hostilities between them must not commence without a previous and explicit warning, in the form of either a declaration of war, giving reasons, or an ultimatum with a conditional declaration of war.

Germany was a party to these conventions.

Versailles Treaty

Breaches of certain provisions of the Versailles Treaty are also relied on by the Prosecution—not to fortify the left bank of the Rhine (Articles 42–44); to "respect strictly the independence of Austria" (Article 80); renunciation of any rights in Memel (Article 99); and in the Free City of Danzig (Article 100); the recognition of the independence of the Czechoslovak State; and the military, naval, and air clauses against German rearmament found in Part V. There is no doubt that action was taken by the German Government contrary to all these provisions, the details of which are set out in Appendix C. With regard to the Treaty of Versailles, the matters relied on are:

1. The violation of Articles 42 and 44 in respect of the demilitarized zone of the Rhineland;

2. The annexation of Austria on 13 March 1938, in violation of Article 80;

3. The incorporation of the district of Memel on 22 March 1939, in violation of Article 99;

4. The incorporation of the Free City of Danzig on 1 September 1939, in violation of Article 100;

5. The incorporation of the provinces of Bohemia and Moravia on 16 March 1939, in violation of Article 81;

6. The repudiation of the military, naval, and air clauses of the Treaty, in or about March of 1935.

On 21 May 1935 Germany announced that, whilst renouncing the disarmament clauses of the Treaty, she would still respect the territorial limitations, and would comply with the Locarno Pact. (With regard to the first five breaches alleged, therefore, the Tribunal finds the allegation proved.)

Treaties of Mutual Guarantee, Arbitration, and Non-Aggression

It is unnecessary to discuss in any detail the various treaties entered into by Germany with other powers. Treaties of mutual guarantee were signed by Germany at Locarno in 1925, with Belgium, France, Great Britain, and Italy, assuring the maintenance of the territorial *status quo*. Arbitration treaties were also executed by Germany at Locarno with Czechoslovakia, Belgium, and Poland.

Article I of the latter treaty is typical, providing:

> All disputes of every kind between Germany and Poland . . . which it may not be possible to settle amicably by the normal methods of diplomacy, shall be submitted for decision to an arbitral tribunal. . . .

Conventions of arbitration and conciliation were entered into between Germany, the Netherlands, and Denmark in 1926; and between Germany and Luxembourg in 1929. Non-aggression treaties were executed by Germany with Denmark and Russia in 1939.

Kellogg-Briand Pact

The Pact of Paris was signed on 27 August 1928 by Germany, the United States, Belgium, France, Great Britain, Italy, Japan, Poland, and other countries; and subsequently by other powers. The Tribunal has made full reference to the nature of this pact and its legal effect in another part of this Judgment. It is therefore not necessary to discuss the matter further here, save to state that in the opinion of the Tribunal this pact was violated by Germany in all the cases of aggressive war charged in the Indictment. It is to be noted that on 26 January 1934 Germany signed a Declaration for the Maintenance of Permanent Peace with Poland, which was explicitly based on the Pact of Paris, and in which the use of force was outlawed for a period of 10 years.

The Tribunal does not find it necessary to consider any of the other treaties referred to in the Appendix, or the repeated agreements and assurances of her peaceful intentions entered into by Germany.

The Law of the Charter

The jurisdiction of the Tribunal is defined in the Agreement and Charter, and the crimes coming within the jurisdiction of the Tribunal, for which there shall be individual responsibility, are set out in Article 6. The law of the Charter is decisive, and binding upon the Tribunal.

The making of the Charter was the exercise of the sovereign legislative power by the countries to which the German Reich unconditionally surrendered; and the undoubted right of these countries to legislate for the occupied territories has been recognized by the civilized world. The Charter is not an arbitrary exercise of power on the part of the victorious nations, but in the view of the Tribunal, as will be shown, it is the expression of international law existing at the time of its creation, and to that extent is itself a contribution to international law.

The Signatory Powers created this Tribunal, defined the law it was to administer, and made regulations for the proper conduct of the Trial. In doing so, they have done together what any one of them might have done singly; for it is not to be doubted that any nation has the right thus to set up special courts to administer law. With regard to the constitution of the Court, all that the defendants are entitled to ask is to receive a fair trial on the facts and law.

The Charter makes the planning or waging of a war of aggression or a war in violation of international treaties a crime; and it is therefore not strictly necessary to consider whether and to what extent aggressive war was a crime before the execution of the London Agreement. But in view of the great importance of the questions of law involved, the Tribunal has heard full argument from the Prosecution and the Defense, and will express its view on the matter.

It was urged on behalf of the defendants that a fundamental principle of all law—international and domestic—is that there can be no punishment of crime without a pre-existing law. "*Nullum crimen sine lege, nulla poena sine lege.*" It was submitted that *ex post facto* punishment is abhorrent to the law of all civilized nations, that no sovereign power had made aggressive war a crime at the time that the alleged criminal acts were committed, that no statute had defined aggressive war, that no penalty had been fixed for its commission, and no court had been created to try and punish offenders.

In the first place, it is to be observed that the maxim *nullum crimen sine lege* is not a limitation of sovereignty, but is in general a principle of justice. To assert that it is unjust to punish those who in defiance of treaties and assurances have attacked neighboring states without warning is obviously untrue, for in such circumstances the attacker must know that he is doing wrong, and so far from it being unjust to punish him, it would be unjust if his wrong were allowed to go unpunished. Occupying the positions they did in the Government of Germany, the defendants, or at least some of them, must have known of the treaties signed by Germany, outlawing recourse to war for the settlement of international disputes; they must have known that they were acting in defiance of all international law when in complete deliberation they carried out their designs of invasion and aggression. On this view of the case alone, it would appear that the maxim has no application to the present facts.

This view is strongly reinforced by a consideration of the state of international law in 1939, so far as aggressive war is concerned. The General Treaty for the Renunciation of War of 27 August 1928, more generally known as the Pact of Paris or the Kellogg-Briand Pact, was binding on 63 nations, including Germany, Italy, and Japan, at the outbreak of war in 1939. In the preamble, the signatories declared that they were:

> Deeply sensible of their solemn duty to promote the welfare of mankind; persuaded that the time has come when a frank renunciation of war as an instrument of national policy should be made to the end that the peaceful and friendly relations now existing between their peoples should be perpetuated . . . and all changes in their relations with one another should be sought only by pacific means . . . thus uniting civilized nations of the world in a common renunciation of war as an instrument of their national policy. . . .

The first two articles are as follows:

> Article I: The High Contracting Parties solemnly declare in the names of their respective peoples that they condemn recourse to war for the solution of international controversies and renounce it as an instrument of national policy in their relations to one another.
>
> Article II: The High Contracting Parties agree that the settlement or solution of all disputes or conflicts, of whatever nature or of whatever origin they may be, which may arise among them, shall never be sought except by pacific means.

The question is, what was the legal effect of this pact? The nations who signed the pact or adhered to it unconditionally condemned recourse to war for the future as an instrument of policy, and expressly renounced it. After the signing of the pact, any nation resorting to war as an instrument of national policy breaks the pact. In the opinion of the Tribunal, the solemn renunciation of war as an instrument of national policy necessarily involves the proposition that such a war is illegal in international law; and that those who plan and wage such a war, with its inevitable and terrible consequences, are committing a crime in so doing. War for the solution of international controversies undertaken as an instrument of national policy certainly includes a war of aggression, and such a war is therefore outlawed by the pact. As Mr. Henry L. Stimson, then Secretary of State of the United States, said in 1932:

> War between nations was renounced by the signatories of the Kellogg-Briand Treaty. This means that it has become throughout practically the entire world . . . an illegal thing. Hereafter, when nations engage in armed conflict, either one or both of them must be termed violators of this general treaty law. . . . We denounce them as law breakers.

But it is argued that the pact does not expressly enact that such wars are crimes, or set up courts to try those who make such wars. To that extent the same is true with regard to the laws of war contained in the Hague Convention.

The Hague Convention of 1907 prohibited resort to certain methods of waging war. These included the inhumane treatment of prisoners, the employment of poisoned weapons, the improper use of flags of truce, and similar matters. Many of these prohibitions had been enforced long before the date of the Convention; but since 1907 they have certainly been crimes, punishable as offenses against the laws of war; yet the Hague Convention nowhere designates such practices as criminal, nor is any sentence prescribed, nor any mention made of a court to try and punish offenders. For many years past, however, military tribunals have tried and punished individuals guilty of violating the rules of land warfare laid down by this Convention. In the opinion of the Tribunal, those who wage aggressive war are doing that which is equally illegal, and of much greater moment than a breach of one of the rules of the Hague Convention. In interpreting the words of the Pact, it must be remembered that international law is not the product of an international legislature, and that such international agreements as the Pact of Paris have to deal with general principles of law, and not with administrative matters of procedure. The law of war is to be found not only in treaties, but in the customs and practices of states which gradually obtained universal recognition, and from the general principles of justice applied by jurists and practiced by military courts. This law is not static, but by continual adaptation follows the needs of a changing world. Indeed, in many cases treaties do no more than express and define for more accurate reference the principles of law already existing.

The view which the Tribunal takes of the true interpretation of the pact is supported by the international history which preceded it. In the year 1923 the draft of a Treaty of Mutual Assistance was sponsored by the League of Nations. In Article I the treaty declared "that aggressive war is an international crime," and that the parties would "undertake that no one of them will be guilty of its commission." The draft treaty was submitted to 29 states, about half of whom were in favor of accepting the text. The principal objection appeared to be in the difficulty of defining the acts which would constitute "aggression," rather than any doubt as to the criminality of aggressive war. The preamble to the League of Nations 1942 Protocol for the Pacific Settlement of International Disputes ("Geneva Protocol"), after "recognizing the solidarity of the members of the international community," declared that "a war of aggression constitutes a violation of this solidarity and is an international crime." It went on to declare that the contracting parties were "desirous of facilitating the complete application of the system provided in the Covenant of the League of Nations for the pacific settlement of disputes between the states and of insuring the repression of international crimes." The Protocol was recommended to the members of the League of Nations by a unanimous resolution in the assembly of the 48 members of the League. These members included Italy and Japan, but Germany was not then a member of the League. Although the Protocol was never ratified, it was signed by the leading statesmen of the world, representing the vast majority of the civilized states and peoples, and may be regarded as strong evidence of the intention to brand aggressive war as an international crime.

At the meeting of the Assembly of the League of Nations on 24 September 1927, all the delegations then present (including the German, the Italian, and the Japanese) unanimously adopted a declaration concerning wars of aggression. The preamble to the declaration stated:

> The Assembly: Recognizing the solidarity which unites the community of nations; being inspired by a firm desire for the maintenance of general peace; being convinced that a war of aggression can never serve as a means of settling international disputes, and is in consequence an international crime. . . .

The unanimous resolution of 18 February 1928 of 21 American republics at the Sixth (Havana) Pan-American Conference, declared that "war of aggression constitutes an international crime against the human species."

All these expressions of opinion, and others that could be cited, so solemnly made, reinforce the construction which the Tribunal placed upon the Pact of Paris, that resort to a war of aggression is not merely illegal, but is criminal. The prohibition of aggressive war demanded by the conscience of the world finds its expression in the series of pacts and treaties to which the Tribunal has just referred.

It is also important to remember that Article 227 of the Treaty of Versailles provided for the constitution of a special Tribunal, composed of representatives of five of the Allied and Associated Powers which had been belligerents in the first World War opposed to Germany, to try the former German Emperor "for a supreme offense against international morality and the sanctity of treaties." The purpose of this trial was expressed to be "to vindicate the solemn obligations of international undertakings, and the validity of international morality." In Article 228 of the Treaty, the German Government expressly recognized the right of the Allied Powers "to bring before military tribunals persons accused of having committed acts in violation of the laws and customs of war."

It was submitted that international law is concerned with the actions of sovereign states and provides no punishment for individuals; and further, that where the act in question is an act of state, those who carry it out are not personally responsible, but are protected by the doctrine of the sovereignty of the state. In the opinion of the Tribunal, both these submissions must be rejected. That international law imposes duties and liabilities upon individuals as well as upon states has long been recognized. In the recent case of *ex parte* Quirin (1942–317, US-1), before the Supreme Court of the United States, persons were charged during the war with landing in the United States for purposes of spying and sabotage. The late Chief Justice Stone, speaking for the Court, said:

> From the very beginning of its history this Court has applied the law of war as including that part of the law of nations which prescribes for the conduct of war, the status, rights, and duties of enemy nations as well as enemy individuals.

He went on to give a list of cases tried by the courts, where individual offenders were charged with offenses against the laws of nations, and particularly the laws of war. Many other authorities could be cited, but enough has been said to show that individuals can be punished for violations of international law. Crimes against international law are committed by men, not by abstract entities, and only by punishing individuals who commit such crimes can the provisions of international law be enforced.

The provisions of Article 228 of the Treaty of Versailles, already referred to, illustrate and enforce this view of individual responsibility.

The principle of international law which, under certain circumstances, protects the representatives of a state, cannot be applied to acts which are condemned as criminal by international law. The authors of these acts cannot shelter themselves behind their official position in order to be freed from punishment in appropriate proceedings. Article 7 of the Charter expressly declares:

> The official position of defendants, whether as heads of state, or responsible officials in government departments, shall not be considered as freeing them from responsibility, or mitigating punishment.

On the other hand the very essence of the Charter is that individuals have international duties which transcend the national obligations of obedience imposed by the individual state. He who violates the laws of war cannot obtain immunity while acting in pursuance of the authority of the state, if the state in authorizing action moves outside its competence under international law.

It was also submitted on behalf of most of these defendants that in doing what they did they were acting under the orders of Hitler, and therefore cannot be held responsible for the acts committed by them in carrying out these orders. The Charter specifically provides in Article 8:

> The fact that the defendant acted pursuant to order of his Government or of a superior shall not free him from responsibility, but may be considered in mitigation of punishment.

The provisions of this article are in conformity with the law of all nations. That a soldier was ordered to kill or torture in violation of the international law of war has never been recognized as a defense to such acts of brutality, though, as the Charter here provides, the order may be urged in mitigation of the punishment. The true test, which is found in varying degrees in the criminal law of most nations, is not the existence of the order, but whether moral choice was in fact possible.

The Law As to the Common Plan or Conspiracy

In the previous recital of the facts relating to aggressive war, it is clear that planning and preparation had been carried out in the most systematic way at every stage of the history.

Planning and preparation are essential to the making of war. In the opinion of the Tribunal aggressive war is a crime under international law. The Charter defines this offense as planning, preparation, initiation or waging of a war of aggression "or participation in a Common Plan or Conspiracy for the accomplishment . . . of the foregoing." The Indictment follows this distinction. Count One charges the Common Plan or Conspiracy. Count Two charges the planning and waging of war. The same evidence has been introduced to support both Counts. We shall therefore discuss both Counts together, as they are in substance the same. The defendants have been charged under both Counts, and their guilt under each Count must be determined.

The "Common Plan or Conspiracy" charged in the Indictment covers 25 years, from the formation of the Nazi Party in 1919 to the end of the war in 1945. The Party is spoken of as "the instrument of cohesion among the defendants" for carrying out the purposes of the conspiracy—the overthrowing of the Treaty of Versailles, acquiring territory lost by Germany in the last war and "Lebensraum" in Europe, by the use, if necessary, of armed force, of aggressive war. The "seizure of power" by the Nazis, the use of terror, the destruction of trade unions, the attack on Christian teaching and on Churches, the persecution of Jews, the regimentation of youth—all these are said to be steps deliberately taken to carry out the common plan. It found expression, so it is alleged, in secret rearmament, the withdrawal by Germany from the Disarmament Conference and the League of Nations, universal military service, and seizure of the Rhineland. Finally, according to the Indictment, aggressive action was planned and carried out against Austria and Czechoslovakia in 1936–1938, followed by the planning and waging of war against Poland, and, successively, against 10 other countries.

The Prosecution says, in effect, that any significant participation in the affairs of the Nazi Party or Government is evidence of a participation in a conspiracy that is in itself criminal. Conspiracy is not defined in the Charter. But in the opinion of the Tribunal the conspiracy must be clearly outlined in its criminal purpose. It must not be too far removed from the time of decision and of action. The planning, to be criminal, must not rest merely on the declarations of a party program, such as are found in the 25 points of the Nazi Party, announced in 1920, or the political affirmations expressed in *Mein Kampf* in later years. The Tribunal must examine whether a concrete plan to wage war existed, and determine the participants in that concrete plan.

It is not necessary to decide whether a single master conspiracy between the defendants has been established by the evidence. The seizure of power by the Nazi Party, and the subsequent domination by the Nazi State of all spheres of economic and social life must of course be remembered when the later plans for waging war are examined. That plans were made to wage war as early as 5 November 1937, and probably before that, is apparent. And thereafter, such preparations continued in many directions, and against the peace of many countries. Indeed the threat of war—and war itself if necessary—was an integral part of the Nazi policy. But the evidence establishes with certainty the existence of many separate plans rather than a single conspiracy embracing them all. That Germany was rapidly moving to complete dictatorship from the moment that the Nazis seized power, and progressively in the direction of war, has been overwhelmingly shown in the ordered sequence of aggressive acts and wars already set out in this Judgment.

In the opinion of the Tribunal, the evidence establishes the common planning to prepare and wage war by certain of the defendants. It is immaterial to consider whether a single conspiracy to the extent and over the time set out in the Indictment has been conclusively proved. Continued planning, with aggressive war as the objective, has been established beyond doubt. The truth of the situation was well stated by Paul Schmidt, official interpreter of the German Foreign Office, as follows:

> The general objectives of the Nazi leadership were apparent from the start, namely the domination of the European continent, to be achieved first by the incorporation of all German-speaking groups in the Reich, and secondly, by territorial expansion under the slogan "Lebenstraum." The execution of these basic objectives, however, seemed to be characterized by improvisation. Each succeeding step was apparently carried out as each new situation arose, but all consistent with the ultimate objectives mentioned above.

The argument that such common planning cannot exist where there is complete dictatorship is unsound. A plan in the execution of which a number of persons participate is still a plan, even though conceived by only one of them; and those who execute the plan do not avoid responsibility by showing that they acted under the direction of the man who conceived it. Hitler could not make aggressive war by himself. He had to have the co-operation of statesmen, military leaders, diplomats, and business men. When they, with knowledge of his aims, gave him their co-operation, they made themselves parties to the plan he had initiated. They are not to be deemed innocent because Hitler made use of them, if they knew what they were doing. That they were assigned to their tasks by a dictator does not absolve them from responsibility for their acts. The relation of leader and follower does not preclude responsibility here any more than it does in the comparable tyranny of organized domestic crime.

Count One, however, charges not only the conspiracy to commit aggressive war, but also to commit War Crimes and Crimes against Humanity. But the Charter does not define as a separate crime any conspiracy except the one to commit acts of aggressive war. Article 6 of the Charter provides:

> Leaders, organizers, instigators and accomplices participating in the formulation or execution of a common plan or conspiracy to commit any of the foregoing crimes are responsible for all acts performed by any persons in execution of such plan.

In the opinion of the Tribunal these words do not add a new and separate crime to those already listed. The words are designed to establish the responsibility of persons participating in a common plan. The Tribunal will therefore disregard the charges in Count One that the defendants conspired to commit War Crimes and Crimes against Humanity, and will consider only the common plan to prepare, initiate and wage aggressive war.

* * *

War Crimes and Crimes against Humanity

The evidence relating to war crimes has been overwhelming in its volume and its detail. It is impossible for this Judgment adequately to review it, or to record the mass of documentary and oral evidence that has been presented. The truth remains that war crimes were committed on a vast scale, never before seen in the history of war. They were perpetrated in all the countries occupied by Germany, and on the high seas, and were attended by every conceivable circumstance of cruelty and horror. There can be no doubt that the majority of them arose from the Nazi conception of "total war," with which the aggressive wars were waged. For in this conception of "total war," the moral ideas underlying the conventions which seek to make war more humane are no longer regarded as having force or validity. Everything is made subordinate to the overmastering dictates of war. Rules, regulations, assurances, and treaties, all alike, are of no moment; and so, freed from the restraining influence of international law, the aggressive war is conducted by the Nazi leaders in the most barbaric way. Accordingly, war crimes were committed when and wherever the Führer and his close associates thought them to be advantageous. They were for the most part the result of cold and criminal calculation.

On some occassions, war crimes were deliberately planned long in advancc. In the case of the Soviet Union, the plunder of the territories to be occupied, and the ill-treatment of the civilian population, were settled in minute detail before the attack was begun. As early as the autumn of 1940, the invasion of the territories of the Soviet Union was being considered. From that date onwards, the methods to be employed in destroying all possible opposition were continuously under discussion.

Similarly, when planning to exploit the inhabitants of the occupied countries for slave labor on the very greatest scale, the German Government conceived it as an integral part of the war economy, and planned and organized this particular war crime down to the last elaborate detail.

Other war crimes, such as the murder of prisoners of war who had escaped and been recaptured, or the murder of Commandos or captured airmen, or the destruction of the Soviet commissars, were the result of direct orders circulated through the highest official channels.

The Tribunal proposes, therefore, to deal quite generally with the question of war crimes, and to refer to them later when examining the responsibility of the individual defendants in relation to them. Prisoners of war were ill-treated and tortured and murdered, not only in defiance of the well-established rules of international law, but in complete disregard of the elementary dictates of humanity. Civilian populations in occupied territories suffered the same fate. Whole populations were deported to Germany for the purposes of slave labor upon defense works, armament production and similar tasks connected with the war effort. Hostages were taken in very large numbers from the civilian populations in all the occupied countries and were shot as suited the German purposes. Public and private property was systematically plundered and pillaged in order to enlarge the resources of Germany at the expense of the rest of Europe. Cities and towns and villages were wantonly destroyed without military justification or necessity.

Murder and Ill-Treatment of Prisoners of War

Article 6 (b) of the Charter defines War Crimes in these words:

> War Crimes: namely, violations of the laws or customs of war. Such violations shall include, but not be limited to, murder, ill-treatment or deportation to slave labor or for any other purpose of civilian population of or in occupied territory, murder or ill-treatment of prisoners of war or persons on the seas, killing of hostages, plunder of public or private property, wanton destruction of cities, towns, or villages, or devastation not justified by military necessity.

In the course of the war, many Allied soldiers who had surrendered to the Germans were shot immediately, often as a matter of deliberate, calculated policy. On 18 October 1942, the Defendant Keitel circulated a directive authorized by Hitler, which ordered that all members of Allied "Commando" units, often when in uniform and whether armed or not, were to be "slaughtered to the last man," even if they attempted to surrender. It was further provided that if such Allied troops came into the hands of the military authorities after being first captured by the local Police, or in any other way, they should be handed over immediately to the SD. This order was supplemented from time to time, and was effective throughout the remainder of the war, although after the Allied landings in Normandy in 1944 it was made clear that the order did not apply to "Commandos" captured within the immediate battle area. Under the provisions of this order, Allied "Commando" troops, and other military units operating independently, lost their lives in Norway, France, Czechoslovakia, and Italy. Many of them were killed on the spot, and in no case were those who were executed later in concentration camps ever given a trial of any kind. For example, an American military mission which landed behind the German front in the Balkans in January 1945, numbering about 12 to 15 men and wearing uniform, were taken to Mauthausen under the authority of this order, and according to the affidavit of Adolf Zutte, the adjutant of the Mauthausen Concentration Camp, all of them were shot.

In March 1944 the OKH issued the "Kugel," or "Bullet," decree, which directed that every escaped officer and NCO prisoner of war who had not been put to work, with the exception of British and American prisoners of war, should on recapture be handed over to the Sipo and SD. This order was distributed by the Sipo and SD to their regional offices. These escaped officers and NCO's were to be sent to the concentration camp at Mauthausen, to be executed upon arrival by means of a bullet shot in the neck.

In March 1944 50 officers of the British Royal Air Force, who escaped from the camp at Sagan where they were confined as prisoners, were shot on recapture, on the direct orders of Hitler. Their bodies were immediately cremated, and the urns containing their ashes were returned to the camp. It was not contended by the defendants that this was other than plain murder, in complete violation of international law.

When Allied airmen were forced to land in Germany, they were sometimes killed at once by the civilian population. The Police were instructed not to interfere with these killings, and the Ministry of Justice was informed that no one should be prosecuted for taking part in them.

The treatment of Soviet prisoners of war was characterized by particular inhumanity. The death of so many of them was not due merely to the action of individual guards, or to the exigencies of life in the camps. It was the result of systematic plans to murder. More than a month before the German invasion of the Soviet Union, the OKW were making special plans for dealing with political representatives serving with the Soviet Armed Forces who might be captured. One proposal was that "political commissars of the Army are not recognized as prisoners of war, and are to be liquidated, at the latest in the transient prisoners-of-war camps." The Defendant Keitel gave evidence that instructions incorporating this proposal were issued to the German Army.

On 8 September 1941, regulations for the treatment of Soviet prisoners of war in all prisoners-of-war camps were issued, signed by General Reinecke, the head of the prisoner-of-war department of the High Command. These orders stated:

> The Bolshevist soldier has therefore lost all claim to treatment as an honorable opponent, in accordance with the Geneva Convention. . . . The order for ruthless and energetic action must be given at the slightest indication of insubordination, especially in the case of Bolshevist fanatics. Insubordination, active or passive resistance, must be broken immediately by force of arms (bayonets, butts, and firearms). . . . Anyone carrying out the order who does not use his weapons, or does so with insufficient energy, is punishable. . . . Prisoners of war attempting escape are to be fired on without previous challenge. No warning shot must ever be fired. . . . The use of arms against prisoners of war is as a rule legal.

The Soviet prisoners of war were left without suitable clothing; the wounded without medical care; they were starved, and in many cases left to die.

On 17 July 1941, the Gestapo issued an order providing for the killing of all Soviet prisoners of war who were or might be dangerous to National Socialism. The order recited:

> The mission of the commanders of the Sipo and SD stationed in Stalags is the political investigation of all camp inmates, the elimination and further treatment) (a) of all political, criminal, or in some other way unbearable elements among them, (b) of those persons who could be used for the reconstruction of the occupied territories. . . . Further, the commanders must make efforts from the beginning to seek out among the prisoners elements which appear reliable, regardless of whether there are Communists concerned or not, in order to use them for intelligence purposes inside of the camp, and if advisable, later in the

occupied territories also. By use of such informers, and by use of all other existing possibilities, the discovery of all elements to be eliminated among the prisoners must proceed step by step at once. . . .

"Above all, the following must be discovered: all important functionaries of State and Party, especially professional revolutionaries . . . all Political Commissars in the Red Army, leading personalities of the State . . . leading personalities of the business world, members of the Soviet Russian Intelligence, all Jews, all persons who are found to be agitators or fanatical Communists. . . . Executions are not to be held in the camp or in the immediate vicinity of the camp. . . . The prisoners are to be taken for special treatment if possible into the former Soviet Russian territory.

The affidavit of Warlimont, Deputy Chief of Staff of the Wehrmacht, and the testimony of Ohlendorf, former Chief of Amt III of the RSHA, and of Lahousen, the head of one of the sections of the Abwehr, the Wehrmacht's intelligence service, all indicate the thoroughness with which this order was carried out.

The affidavit of Kurt Lindow, a former Gestapo official, states:

. . . There existed in the prisoner-of-war camps on the Eastern Front small screening teams (Einsatzkommandos), headed by lower-ranking members of the Secret Police (Gestapo). These teams were assigned to the camp commanders and had the job to segregate the prisoners of war who were candidates for execution according to the orders that had been given, and to report them to the office of the Secret Police.

On 23 October 1941 the camp commander of the Gross-Rosen Concentration Camp reported to Müller, Chief of the Gestapo, a list of the Soviet prisoners of war who had been executed there on the previous day.

An account of the general conditions and treatment of Soviet prisoners of war during the first 8 months after the German attack upon Russia was given in a letter which the Defendant Rosenberg sent to the Defendant Keitel on 28 February 1942:

The fate of the Soviet prisoners of war in Germany is on the contrary a tragedy of the greatest extent. . . . A large part of them has starved, or died because of the hazards of the weather. Thousands also died from spotted fever. . . .

. . . the camp commanders have forbidden the civilian population to put food at the disposal of the prisoners, and they have rather let them starve to death. . . .

. . . in many cases, when prisoners of war could no longer keep up on the march because of hunger and exhaustion, they were shot before the eyes of the horrified population, and the corpses were left.

In numerous camps no shelter for the prisoners of war was provided at all. They lay under the open sky during rain or snow. Even tools were not made available to dig holes or caves.

In some cases Soviet prisoners of war were branded with a special permanent mark. There was put in evidence the OKW order dated 20 July 1942 which laid down that:

The brand is to take the shape of an acute angle of about 45 degrees, with the long side to be 1 cm. in length, pointing upwards and burnt on the left buttock . . . This brand is made with the aid of a lancet available in any military unit. The coloring used is Chinese ink.

The carrying-out of this order was the responsibility of the military authorities, though it was widely circulated by the Chief of the Sipo and the SD to German police officials for information.

Soviet prisoners of war were also made the subject of medical experiments of the most cruel and inhuman kind. In July 1943 experimental work was begun in preparation for a campaign of bacteriological warfare; Soviet prisoners of war were used in these medical experiments, which more often than not proved fatal. In connection with this campaign for bacteriological warfare, preparations were also made for the spreading of bacterial emulsions from planes, with the object of producing widespread failures of crops and consequent starvation. These measures were never applied, possibly because of the rapid deterioration of Germany's military position.

The argument in defense of the charge with regard to the murder and ill-treatment of Soviet prisoners of war, that the U.S.S.R. was not a party to the Geneva Convention, is quite without foundation. On 15 September 1941 Admiral Canaris protested against the regulations for the treatment of Soviet prisoners of war signed by General Reinecke on 8 September 1941. He then stated:

> The Geneva Convention for the treatment of prisoners of war is not binding in the relationship between Germany and the U.S.S.R. Therefore only the principles of general international law on the treatment of prisoners of war apply. Since the 18th century these have gradually been established along the lines that war captivity is neither revenge nor punishment, but solely protective custody, the only purpose of which is to prevent the prisoners of war from further participation in the war. This principle was developed in accordance with the view held by all armies that it is contrary to military tradition to kill or injure helpless people. . . . The decrees for the treatment of Soviet prisoners of war enclosed are based on a fundamentally different viewpoint.

This protest, which correctly stated the legal position, was ignored. The Defendant Keitel made a note on this memorandum:

> The objections arise from the military concept of chivalrous warfare. This is the destruction of an ideology. Therefore I approve and back the measures.

Murder and Ill-Treatment of Civilian Population

Article 6 (b) of the Charter provides that "ill-treatment of civilian population of or in occupied territory . . . killing of hostages . . . wanton destruction of cities, towns or villages . . ." shall be a War Crime. In the main, these provisions are merely declaratory of the existing laws of war as expressed by the Hague Convention, Article 46, which stated: "Family honor and rights, the lives of persons and private property, as well as religious convictions and practices, must be respected."

The territories occupied by Germany were administered in violation of the laws of war. The evidence is quite overwhelming of a systematic rule of violence, brutality, and terror. On 7 December 1941 Hitler issued the directive since known as the "Nacht und Nebel Erlass" (Night and Fog Decree), under which persons who committed offenses against the Reich or the German forces in occupied territories, except where the death sentence was certain, were to be taken secretly to Germany and handed over to the Sipo and SD for trial or punishment in Germany. This decree was signed by the Defendant Keitel. After these civilians arrived in Germany, no word of them was permitted to reach the country from which they came, or their relatives; even in cases when they died awaiting trial the families were not informed, the purpose being to create anxiety in the minds of the family of the arrested person. Hitler's purpose in issuing this decree was stated by the Defendant Keitel in a covering letter, dated 12 December 1941, to be as follows:

> Efficient and enduring intimidation can only be achieved either by capital punishment or by measures by which the relatives of the criminal and the population do not know the fate of the criminal. This aim is achieved when the criminal is transferred to Germany.

Even persons who were only suspected of opposing any of the policies of the German occupation authorities were arrested, and on arrest were interrogated by the Gestapo and the SD in the most shameful manner. On 12 June 1942 the Chief of the Sipo and SD published, through Müller, the Gestapo Chief, an order authorizing the use of "third degree" methods of interrogation, where preliminary investigation had indicated that the person could give information on important matters, such as subversive activities, though not for the purpose of extorting confessions of the prisoner's own crimes. This order provided:

> . . . Third degree may, under this supposition, only be employed against Communists, Marxists, Jehovah's Witnesses, saboteurs, terrorists, members of resistance movements, parachute agents, anti-social elements, Polish or Soviet Russian loafers or tramps; in all other cases my permission must first be obtained. . . . Third degree can, according to circumstances, consist amongst other methods of very simple diet (bread and water), hard bunk, dark cell, deprivation of sleep, exhaustive drilling, also in flogging (for more than 20 strokes a doctor must be consulted).

The brutal suppression of all opposition to the German occupation was not confined to severe measures against suspected members of resistance movements themselves, but was also extended to their families. On 19 July 1944, the Commander of the Sipo and SD in the district of Radom, in Poland, published an order, transmitted through the Higher SS and Police Leaders, to the effect that in all cases of assassination or attempted assassination of Germans, or where saboteurs had destroyed vital installations, not only the guilty person, but also all his or her male relatives should be shot, and female relatives over 16 years of age put into a concentration camp.

In the summer of 1944 the Einsatzkommando of the Sipo and SD at Luxembourg caused persons to be confined at Sachsenhausen Concentration Camp because they were relatives of deserters, and were therefore "expected to endanger the interest of the German Reich if allowed to go free."

The practice of keeping hostages to prevent and to punish any form of civil disorder was resorted to by the Germans; an order issued by the Defendant Keitel on 16 September 1941 spoke in terms of fifty or a hundred lives from the occupied areas of the Soviet Union for one German life taken. The order stated that "it should be remembered that a human life in unsettled countries frequently counts for nothing and a deterrent effect can be obtained only by unusual severity." The exact number of persons killed as a result of this policy is not known, but large numbers were killed in France and the other occupied territories in the West, while in the East the slaughter was on an even more extensive scale. In addition to the killing of hostages, entire towns were destroyed in some cases; such massacres as those of Oradour-sur-Glane in France and Lidice in Czechoslovakia, both of which were described to the Tribunal in detail, are examples of the organized use of terror by the occupying forces to beat down and destroy all opposition to their rule.

One of the most notorious means of terrorizing the people in occupied territories was the use of concentration camps. They were first established in Germany at the moment of the seizure of power by the Nazi Government. Their original purpose was to imprison without trial all those persons who were opposed to the Government, or who were in any way obnoxious to German authority. With the aid of a secret police force, this practice was widely extended, and in the course of time concentration camps became places of organized and systematic murder, where millions of people were destroyed.

In the administration of the occupied territories the concentration camps were used to destroy all opposition groups. The persons arrested by the Gestapo were as a rule sent to concentration camps. They were conveyed to the camps, in many cases without any care whatever being taken for them, and great numbers died on the way. Those who arrived at the camp were subject to systematic cruelty. They were given hard physical labor, inadequate food, clothes, and shelter, and were subject at all times to the rigors of a soulless regime, and the private whims of individual guards. In the report of the War Crimes Branch of the Judge Advocate's Section of the 3d US Army, under date 21 June 1945, the conditions at the Flossenbürg Concentration Camp were investigated, and one passage may be quoted:

> Flossenbürg Concentration Camp can best be described as a factory dealing in death. Although this camp had in view the primary object of putting to work the mass slave labor, another of its primary objects was the elimination of human lives by the methods employed in handling the prisoners. Hunger and starvation rations, sadism, inadequate clothing, medical neglect, disease, beatings, hangings, freezings, forced suicides, shooting, *et cetera,* all played a major role in obtaining their object. Prisoners were murdered at random; spite killings against Jews were common, injections of poison and shooting in the neck were everyday occurrences; epidemics of typhoid and spotted fever were permitted to run rampant as a means of eliminating prisoners; life in this camp meant nothing. Killing became a common thing, so common that a quick death was welcomed by the unfortunate ones.

A certain number of the concentration camps were equipped with gas chambers for the wholesale destruction of the inmates, and with furnaces for the burning of the bodies. Some of them were in fact used for the extermination of Jews as part of the "final solution" of the Jewish problem. Most of the non-Jewish inmates were used for labor, although the conditions under which they worked made labor and death almost synonymous terms. Those inmates who became ill and were unable to work were either destroyed in the gas chambers or sent to special infirmaries, where they were given entirely inadequate medical treatment, worse food if possible than the working inmates, and left to die.

The murder and ill-treatment of civilian populations reached its height in the treatment of the citizens of the Soviet Union and Poland. Some four weeks before the invasion of Russia began, special task forces of the Sipo and SD, called Einsatzgruppen, were formed on the orders of Himmler for the purpose of following the German armies into Russia, combating partisans and members of resistance groups, and exterminating the Jews and Communist leaders, and other sections of the population. In the beginning, four such Einsatzgruppen were formed, one operating in the Baltic states, one toward Moscow, one toward Kiev, and one operating in the south of Russia. Ohlendorf, former Chief of Amt III of the RSHA, who led the fourth group, stated in his affidavit:

> When the German Army invaded Russia, I was leader of Einsatzgruppe D, in the southern sector, and in the course of the year during which I was leader of the Einsatzgruppe D it liquidated approximately 90,000 men, women, and children. The majority of those liquidated were Jews, but there were also among them some Communist functionaries.

In an order issued by the Defendant Keitel on 23 July 1941, and drafted by the Defendant Jodl, it was stated that:

> In view of the vast size of the occupied areas in the East, the forces available for establishing security in these areas will be sufficient only if all resistance is punished, not by legal prosecution of the guilty, but by the spreading of such terror by the Armed Forces as is alone appropriate to eradicate every inclination to resist among the population. . . . Commanders must find the means of keeping order by applying suitable draconian measures.

The evidence has shown that this order was ruthlessly carried out in the territory of the Soviet Union and in Poland. A significant illustration of the measures actually applied occurs in the document which was sent in 1943 to the Defendant Rosenberg by the Reich Commissioner for Eastern Territories, who wrote:

> It should be possible to avoid atrocities and to bury those who have been liquidated. To lock men, women, and children into barns and set fire to them does not appear to be a suitable method of combating bands, even if it is desired to exterminate the population. This method is not worthy of the German cause, and damages our reputation severely.

The Tribunal has before it an affidavit of one Hermann Graebe, dated 10 November 1945, describing the immense mass murders which he witnessed. He was the manager and engineer in charge of the branch of the Solingen firm of Joseph Jung in Sdolbunov, Ukraine, from September 1941 to January 1944. He first of all described the attack upon the Jewish ghetto at Rovno:

> . . . Then the electric floodlights which had been erected all round the ghetto were switched on. SS and militia details of four to six members entered, or at least tried to enter, the houses. Where the doors and windows were closed, and the inhabitants did not open upon the knocking, the SS men and militia broke the windows, forced the doors with beams and crowbars, and entered the dwellings. The owners were driven on to the street just as they were, regardless of whether they were dressed or whether they had been in bed. . . . Car after car was filled. Over it hung the screaming of women and children, the cracking of whips and rifle shots.

Graebe then described how a mass execution at Dubno, which he witnessed on 5 October 1942, was carried out:

> Now I heard shots in quick succession from behind one of the earth mounds. The people who had got off the trucks, men, women, and children of all ages, had to undress upon the orders of an SS man, who carried a riding or dog whip. . . . Without screaming or crying, these people undressed, stood around by families, kissed each other, said farewells, and waited for the command of another SS man, who stood near the excavation, also with a whip in his hand. . . . At that moment the SS man at the excavation called something to his comrade. The latter counted off about 20 persons, and instructed them to walk behind the earth mound. . . . I walked around the mound and stood in front of a tremendous grave; closely pressed together, the people were lying on top of each other so that only their heads were visible. The excavation was already two-thirds full; I estimated that it contained a thousand people. . . . Now already the next group approached, descended into the excavation, lined themselves up against the previous victims and were shot.

The foregoing crimes against the civilian population are sufficiently appalling, and yet the evidence shows that at any rate in the East, the mass murders and cruelties were not committed solely for the purpose of stamping out opposition or resistance to the German occupying forces. In Poland and the Soviet Union these crimes were part of a plan to get rid of whole native populations by expulsion and annihilation, in order that their territory could be used for colonization by Germans. Hitler had written in *Mein Kampf* on these lines, and the plan was clearly stated by Himmler in July 1942, when he wrote:

> It is not our task to germanize the East in the old sense, that is to teach the people there the German language and the German law, but to see to it that only people of purely Germanic blood live in the East.

In August 1942 the policy for the Eastern Territories as laid down by Bormann was summarized by a subordinate of Rosenberg as follows:

> The Slavs are to work for us. Insofar as we do not need them, they may die. Therefore, compulsory vaccination and German health services are superfluous. The fertility of the Slavs is undesirable.

It was Himmler again who stated in October 1943:

> What happens to a Russian, a Czech, does not interest me in the slightest. What the nations can offer in the way of good blood of our type, we will take. If necessary, by kidnapping their children and raising them here with us. Whether nations live in prosperity or starve to death interests me only insofar as we need them as slaves for our culture, otherwise it is of no interest to me. . . .

Slave Labor Policy

Article 6 (b) of the Charter provides that the "ill-treatment or deportation to slave labor or for any other purpose, of civilian population of or in occupied territory" shall be a War Crime. The laws relating to forced labor by the inhabitants of occupied territories are found in Article 52 of the Hague Convention, which provides:

> Requisition in kind and services shall not be demanded from municipalities or inhabitants except for the needs of the army of occupation. They shall be in proportion to the resources of the country, and of such a nature as not to involve the inhabitants in the obligation of taking part in military operations against their own country.

The policy of the German occupation authorities was in flagrant violation of the terms of this convention. Some idea of this policy may be gathered from the statement made by Hitler in a speech on 9 November 1941:

> The territory which now works for us contains more than 250,000,000 men, but the territory which works indirectly for us now includes more than 350,000,000. In the measure in which it concerns German territory, the domain which we have taken under our administration, it is not doubtful that we shall succeed in harnessing the very last man to this work.

The actual results achieved were not so complete as this, but the German occupation authorities did succeed in forcing many of the inhabitants of the occupied territories to work for the German war effort, and in deporting at least 5,000,000 persons to Germany to serve German industry and agriculture.

In the early stages of the war, manpower in the occupied territories was under the control of various occupation authorities, and the procedure varied from country to country. In all the occupied territories compulsory labor service was promptly instituted. Inhabitants of the occupied countries were conscripted and compelled to work in local occupations to assist the German war economy. In many cases they were forced to work on German fortifications and military installations. As local supplies of raw materials and local industrial capacity became inadequate to meet the German requirements, the system of deporting laborers to Germany was put into force. By the middle of April 1940 compulsory deportation of laborers to Germany had been ordered in the Government General; and a similar procedure was followed in other eastern territories as they were occupied. A description of this compulsory deportation from Poland was given by Himmler. In an address to SS officers he recalled how in weather 40 degrees below zero they had to "haul away thousands, tens of thousands, hundreds of thousands." On a later occasion Himmler stated:

> Whether 10,000 Russian females fall down from exhaustion while digging an anti-tank ditch interests me only insofar as the anti-tank ditch for Germany is finished. . . . We must realize that we have 6 or 7 million foreigners in Germany . . . They are none of them dangerous so long as we take severe measures at the merest trifles.

During the first 2 years of the German occupation of France, Belgium, Holland, and Norway, however, an attempt was made to obtain the necessary workers on a voluntary basis. How unsuccessful this was may be seen from the report of the meeting of the Central Planning Board on 1 March 1944. The respresentative of the Defendant Speer, one Kehrl, speaking of the situation in France, said: "During all this time a great number of Frenchmen were recruited, and voluntarily went to Germany."

He was interrupted by the Defendant Sauckel: "Not only voluntarily, some were recruited forcibly."

To which Kehrl replied: "The calling up started after the recruitment no longer yielded enough results."

To which the Defendant Sauckel replied: "Out of the five million workers who arrived in Germany, not even 200,000 came voluntarily."

And Kehrl rejoined: "Let us forget for the moment whether or not some slight pressure was used. Formally, at least, they were volunteers."

Committees were set up to encourage recruiting, and a vigorous propaganda campaign was begun to induce workers to volunteer for service in Germany. This propaganda campaign included, for example, the promise that a prisoner of war would be returned for every laborer who volunteered to go to Germany. In some cases it was supplemented by withdrawing the ration cards of laborers who refused to go to Germany, or by discharging them from their jobs and denying them unemployment benefit or an opportunity to work elsewhere. In some cases workers and their families were threatened with reprisals by the Police if they refused to go to Germany. It was on 21 March 1942 that the Defendant Sauckel was appointed Plenipotentiary General for the Allocation of Labor, with authority over "all available manpower, including that of workers recruited abroad, and of prisoners of war."

The Defendant Sauckel was directly under the Defendant Göring as Delegate of the Four Year Plan, and a Göring decree of 27 March 1942 transferred all his authority over manpower to Sauckel. Sauckel's instructions, too, were that foreign labor should be recruited on a voluntary basis, but also provided that "where, however, in the occupied territories, the appeal for volunteers does not suffice, obligatory service and drafting must under all circumstances be resorted to." Rules requiring labor service in Germany were published in all the occupied territories. The number of laborers to be supplied was fixed by Sauckel, and the local authorities were instructed to meet these requirements by conscription if necessary. That conscription was the rule rather than the exception is shown by the statement of Sauckel, already quoted, on 1 March 1944.

The Defendant Sauckel frequently asserted that the workers belonging to foreign nations were treated humanely, and that the conditions in which they lived were good. But whatever the intention of Sauckel may have been, and however much he may have desired that foreign laborers should be treated humanely, the evidence before the Tribunal establishes the fact that the conscription of labor was accomplished in many cases by drastic and violent methods. The "mistakes and blunders" were on a very great scale. Manhunts took place in the streets, at motion picture houses, even at churches and at night in private houses. Houses were sometimes burnt down, and the families taken as hostages, practices which were described by the Defendant Rosenberg as having their origin "in the blackest periods of the slave trade." The methods used in obtaining forced labor from the Ukraine appear from an order issued to SD officers which stated:

> It will not be possible always to refrain from using force. . . . When searching villages, especially when it has been necessary to burn down a village, the whole population will be put at the disposal of the commissioner by force. . . . As a rule no more children will be shot. . . . If we limit harsh measures through the above orders for the time being, it is only done for the following reason. . . . The most important thing is the recruitment of workers.

The resources and needs of the occupied countries were completely disregarded in carrying out this policy. The treatment of the laborers was governed by Sauckel's instructions of 20 April 1942 to the effect that: "All the men must be fed, sheltered, and treated in such a way as to exploit them to the highest possible extent, at the lowest conceivable degree of expenditure."

The evidence showed that workers destined for the Reich were sent under guard to Germany, often packed in trains without adequate heating, food, clothing, or sanitary facilities. The evidence further showed that the treatment of the laborers in Germany in many cases was brutal and degrading. The evidence relating to the Krupp Works at Essen showed that punishments of the most cruel kind were inflicted on the workers. Theoretically at least the workers were paid, housed, and fed by the DAF, and even permitted to transfer their savings and to send mail and parcels back to their native country; but restrictive regulations took a proportion of the pay; the camps in which they were housed were insanitary; and the food was very often less than the minimum necessary to give the workers strength to do their jobs. In the case of Poles employed on farms in Germany, the employers were given authority to inflict corporal punishment and were ordered, if possible, to house them in stables, not in their own homes. They were subject to constant supervision by the Gestapo and the SS, and if they attempted to leave their jobs they were sent to correction camps or concentration camps. The concentration camps were also used to increase the supply of labor. Concentration camp commanders were ordered to work their prisoners to the limits of their physical power. During the latter stages of the war the concentration camps were so productive in certain types of work that the Gestapo was actually instructed to arrest certain classes of laborers so that they could be used in this way. Allied prisoners of war were also regarded as a possible source of labor. Pressure was exercised on non-commissioned officers to force them to consent to work, by transferring to disciplinary camps those who did not consent. Many of the prisoners of war were assigned to work directly related to military operations, in violation of Article 31 of the Geneva Convention. They were put to work in munition factories and even made to load bombers, to carry ammunition, and to dig trenches, often under the most hazardous conditions. This condition applied particularly to the Soviet prisoners of war. On 16 February 1943, at a meeting of the Central Planning Board, at which the Defendants Sauckel and Speer were present, Milch said:

> We have made a request for an order that a certain percentage of men in the Ack-Ack artillery must be Russians; 50,000 will be taken altogether. 30,000 are already employed as gunners. This is an amusing thing, that Russians must work the guns.

And on 4 October 1943, at Posen, Himmler, speaking of the Russian prisoners captured in the early days of the war, said:

> At that time we did not value the mass of humanity as we value it today, as raw material, as labor. What, after all, thinking in terms of generations, is not to be regretted, but is now deplorable by reason of the loss of labor, is that the prisoners died in tens and hundreds of thousands of exhaustion and hunger.

The general policy underlying the mobilization of slave labor was stated by Sauckel on 20 April 1942. He said:

> The aim of this new gigantic labor mobilization is to use all the rich and tremendous sources conquered and secured for us by our fighting Armed Forces under the leadership of Adolf Hitler, for the armament of the Armed Forces, and also for the nutrition of the homeland. The raw materials, as well as the fertility of the conquered territories and their human labor power, are to be used completely and conscientiously to the profit of Germany and her allies. . . . All prisoners of war from the territories of the West, as well as the East, actually in Germany, must be completely incorporated into the German armament and nutrition industries. . . . Consequently it is an immediate necessity to use the human reserves of the conquered Soviet territory to the fullest extent. Should we not succeed in obtaining the necessary amount of labor on a voluntary basis, we must immediately institute conscription or forced labor. . . . The complete employment of all prisoners of war, as well as the use of a gigantic number of new foreign civilian workers, men and women, has become an indisputable necessity for the solution of the mobilization of the labor program in this war.

Reference should also be made to the policy which was in existence in Germany by the summer of 1940, under which all aged, insane, and incurable people, "useless eaters," were transferred to special institutions where they were killed, and their relatives informed that they had died from natural causes. The victims were not confined to German citizens, but included foreign laborers who were no longer able to work, and were therefore useless to the German war machine. It has been estimated that at least some 275,000 people were killed in this manner in nursing homes, hospitals, and asylums, which were under the jurisdiction of the Defendant Frick in his capacity as Minister of the Interior. How many foreign workers were included in this total it has been quite impossible to determine.

Persecution of the Jews

The persecution of the Jews at the hands of the Nazi Government has been proved in the greatest detail before the Tribunal. It is a record of consistent and systematic inhumanity on the greatest scale. Ohlendorf, Chief of Amt III in the RSHA from 1939 to 1943, and who was in command of one of the Einsatzgruppen in the campaign against the Soviet Union, testified as to the methods employed in the extermination of the Jews. He said that he employed firing squads to shoot the victims in order to lessen the sense of individual guilt on the part of his men; and the 90,000 men, women, and children who were murdered in one year by his particular group were mostly Jews.

When the witness Von dem Bach-Zelewski was asked how Ohlendorf could admit the murder of 90,000 people, he replied: "I am of the opinion that when for years, for decades, the doctrine is preached that the Slav race is an inferior race, and Jews not even human, then such an outcome is inevitable."

But the Defendant Frank spoke the final words of this chapter of Nazi history when he testified in this court:

> We have fought Jewry, we have fought against it for years; and we have allowed ourselves to make utterances, and my own diary has become a witness against me in this connection—utterances which are terrible. . . . A thousand years will pass and this guilt of Germany will still not be erased.

The anti-Jewish policy was formulated in Point 4 of the Party Program which declared: "Only a member of the race can be a citizen. A member of the race can only be one who is of German blood, without consideration of creed. Consequently, no Jew can be a member of the race." Other points of the program declared that Jews should be treated as foreigners, that they should not be permitted to hold public office, that they should be expelled from the Reich if it were impossible to nourish the entire population of the state, that they should be denied any further immigration into Germany, and that they should be prohibited from publishing German newspapers. The Nazi Party preached these doctrines throughout its history. *Der Stürmer* and other publications were allowed to disseminate hatred of the Jews, and in the speeches and public declarations of the Nazi leaders the Jews were held up to public ridicule and contempt.

With the seizure of power, the persecution of the Jews was intensified. A series of discriminatory laws were passed, which limited the offices and professions permitted to Jews; and restrictions were placed on their family life and their rights of citizenship. By the autumn of 1938, the Nazi policy towards the Jews had reached the stage where it was directed towards the complete exclusion of Jews from German life. Pogroms were organized, which included the burning and demolishing of synagogues, the looting of Jewish businesses, and the arrest of prominent Jewish business men. A collective fine of one billion marks was imposed on the Jews, the seizure of Jewish assets was authorized, and the movement of Jews was restricted by regulations to certain specified districts and hours. The creation of ghettos was carried out on an extensive scale, and by an order of the Security Police Jews were compelled to wear a yellow star to be worn on the breast and back.

It was contended for the Prosecution that certain aspects of this anti-Semitic policy were connected with the plans for aggressive war. The violent measures taken against the Jews in November 1938 were nominally in retaliation for the killing of an official of the German Embassy in Paris. But the decision to seize Austria and Czechoslovakia had been made a year before. The imposition of a fine of one billion marks was made, and the confiscation of the financial holdings of the Jews was decreed, at a time when German armament expenditure had put the German treasury in difficulties, and when the reduction of expenditure on armaments was being considered. These steps were taken, moreover, with the approval of the Defendant Göring, who had been given responsibility for economic matters of this kind, and who was the strongest advocate of an extensive rearmament program notwithstanding the financial difficulties.

It was further said that the connection of the anti-Semitic policy with aggressive war was not limited to economic matters. The German Foreign Office circular, in an article of 25 January 1939, entitled "Jewish question as a factor in German foreign policy in the year 1938," described the new phase in the Nazi anti-Semitic policy in these words:

> It is certainly no coincidence that the fateful year 1938 has brought nearer the solution of the Jewish question simultaneously with the realization of the idea of Greater Germany, since the Jewish policy was both the basis and consequence of the events of the year 1938. The advance made by Jewish influence and the destructive Jewish spirit in politics, economy, and culture paralyzed the power and the will of the German people to rise again, more perhaps even than the power policy opposition of the former enemy Allied powers of the first World War. The healing of this sickness among the people was therefore certainly one of the most important requirements for exerting the force which, in the year 1938, resulted in the joining together of Greater Germany in defiance of the world.

The Nazi persecution of Jews in Germany before the war, severe and repressive as it was, cannot compare, however, with the policy pursued during the war in the occupied territories. Originally the policy was similar to that which had been in force inside Germany. Jews were required to register, were forced to live in ghettos, to wear the yellow star, and were used as slave laborers. In the summer of 1941, however, plans were made for the "final solution" of the Jewish question in all of Europe. This "final solution" meant the extermination of the Jews, which early in 1939 Hitler had threatened would be one of the consequences of an outbreak of war, and a special section in the Gestapo under Adolf Eichmann, as head of Section B 4 of the Gestapo, was formed to carry out the policy.

The plan for exterminating the Jews was developed shortly after the attack on the Soviet Union. Einsatzgruppen of the Security Police and SD, formed for the purpose of breaking the resistance of the population of the areas lying behind the German armies in the East, were given the duty of exterminating the Jews in those areas. The effectiveness of the work of the Einsatzgruppen is shown by the fact that in February 1942 Heydrich was able to report that Estonia had already been cleared of Jews and that in Riga the number of Jews had been reduced from 29,500 to 2,500. Altogether the Einsatzgruppen operating in the occupied Baltic states killed over 135,000 Jews in 3 months.

Nor did these special units operate completely independently of the German Armed Forces. There is clear evidence that leaders of the Einsatzgruppen obtained the co-operation of army commanders. In one case the relations between an Einsatzgruppe and the military authorities was described at the time as being "very close, almost cordial"; in another case the smoothness of an Einsatzkommando operation was attributed to the "understanding for this procedure" shown by the army authorities.

Units of the Security Police and SD in the occupied territories of the East, which were under civil administration, were given a similar task. The planned and systematic character of the Jewish persecutions is best illustrated by the original report of SS Brigadier General Stroop, who was in charge of the destruction of the ghetto in Warsaw, which took place in 1943. The Tribunal received in evidence that report, illustrated with photographs, bearing on its title page: "The Jewish ghetto in Warsaw no longer exists." The volume records a series of reports sent by Stroop to the Higher SS and Police Führer East. In April and May of 1943, in one report, Stroop wrote:

> The resistance put up by the Jews and bandits could only be suppressed by energetic actions of our troops day and night. The Reichsführer SS ordered therefore on 23 April 1943 the cleaning out of the ghetto with utter ruthlessness and merciless tenacity. I therefore decided to destroy and burn down the entire ghetto, without regard to the armament factories. These factories were systematically dismantled and then burnt. Jews usually left their hideouts, but frequently remained in the burning buildings, and jumped out of the windows only when the heat became unbearable. They then tried to crawl with broken bones across the street into buildings which were not afire. . . . Life in the sewers was not pleasant after the first week. Many times we could hear loud voices in the sewers. . . . Tear gas bombs were thrown into the manholes, and the Jews driven out of the sewers and captured. Countless numbers of Jews were liquidated in sewers and bunkers through blasting. The longer the resistance continued, the tougher became the members of the Waffen-SS, Police, and Wehrmacht, who always discharged their duties in an exemplary manner.

Stroop recorded that his action at Warsaw eliminated "a proved total of 56,065 people. To that we have to add the number of those killed through blasting, fire, *et cetera,* which cannot be counted." Grim evidence of mass murders of Jews was also presented to the Tribunal in cinematograph films depicting the communal graves of hundreds of victims which were subsequently discovered by the Allies.

These atrocities were all part and parcel of the policy inaugurated in 1941, and it is not surprising that there should be evidence that one or two German officials entered vain protests against the brutal manner in which the killings were carried out. But the methods employed never conformed to a single pattern. The massacres of Rovno and Dubno, of which the German engineer Graebe spoke, were examples of one method, the systematic extermination of Jews in concentration camps was another. Part of the "final solution" was the gathering of Jews from all German-occupied Europe in concentration camps. Their physical condition was the test of life or death. All who were fit to work were used as slave laborers in the concentration camps; all who were not fit to work were destroyed in gas chambers and their bodies burnt. Certain concentration camps, such as Treblinka and Auschwitz, were set aside for this main purpose. With regard to Auschwitz, the Tribunal heard the evidence of Hoess, the commandant of the camp from 1 May 1940 to 1 December 1943. He estimated that in the camp of Auschwitz alone in that time 2,500,000 persons were exterminated, and that a further 500,000 died from disease and starvation. Hoess described the screening for extermination by stating in evidence:

> We had two SS doctors on duty at Auschwitz to examine the incoming transports of prisoners. The prisoners would be marched by one of the doctors who would make spot decisions as they walked by. Those who were fit for work were sent into the camp. Others were sent immediately to the extermination plants. Children of tender years were invariably exterminated since by reason of their youth they were unable to work. Still another improvement we made over Treblinka was that at Treblinka the victims almost always knew that they were to be exterminated, and at Auschwitz we endeavored to fool the victims into thinking that they were to go through a delousing process. Of course, frequently they realized our true intentions and we sometimes had riots and difficulties due to that fact. Very frequently, women would hide their children under their clothes, but of course when we found them we would send the children in to be exterminated.

He described the actual killing by stating:

> It took from three to fifteen minutes to kill the people in the death chamber, depending upon climatic conditions. We knew when the people were dead because their screaming stopped. We usually waited about one-half hour before we opened the doors and removed the bodies. After the bodies were removed our special commandos took off the rings and extracted the gold from the teeth of the corpses.

Beating, starvation, torture, and killing were general. The inmates were subjected to cruel experiments at Dachau in August 1942, victims were immersed in cold water until their body temperature was reduced to 28° centigrade, when they died immediately. Other experiments included high altitude experiments in pressure chambers, experiments to determine how long human beings could survive in freezing water, experiments with poison bullets, experiments with contagious diseases, and experiments dealing with sterilization of men and women by X-rays and other methods.

Evidence was given of the treatment of the inmates before and after their extermination. There was a testimony that the hair of women victims was cut off before they were killed, and shipped to Germany, there to be used in the manufacture of mattresses. The clothes, money, and valuables of the inmates were also salvaged and sent to the appropriate agencies for disposition. After the extermination the gold teeth and fillings were taken from the heads of the corpses and sent to the Reichsbank.

After the cremation the ashes were used for fertilizer, and in some instances attempts were made to utilize the fat from the bodies of the victims in the commercial manufacture of soap. Special groups traveled through Europe to find Jews and subject them to the "final solution." German missions were sent to such satellite countries as Hungary and Bulgaria to arrange for the shipment of Jews to extermination camps, and it is known that by the end of 1944, 400,000 Jews from Hungary had been murdered at Auschwitz. Evidence has also been given of the evacuation of 110,000 Jews from part of Romania for "liquidation." Adolf Eichmann, who had been put in charge of this program by Hitler, has estimated that the policy pursued resulted in the killing of 6,000,000 Jews, of which 4,000,000 were killed in the extermination institutions.

The Law Relating to War Crimes and Crimes against Humanity

Article 6 of the Charter provides:

> (b) War Crimes: namely, violations of the laws or customs of war. Such violations shall include, but not be limited to, murder, ill-treatment, or deportation to slave labor or for any other purpose of civilian population of or in occupied territory, murder or ill-treatment of prisoners of war or persons on the seas, killing of hostages, plunder of public or private property, wanton destruction of cities, towns or villages, or devastation not justified by military necessity;
>
> (c) Crimes against Humanity; namely, murder, extermination, enslavement, deportation, and other inhumane acts committed against any civilian population, before or during the war; or persecutions on political, racial, or religious grounds in execution of or in connection with any crime within the jurisdiction of the Tribunal, whether or not in violation of the domestic law of the country where perpetrated.

As heretofore stated, the Charter does not define as a separate crime any conspiracy except the one set out in Article 6(a), dealing with Crimes against Peace.

The Tribunal is of course bound by the Charter, in the definition which it gives both of War Crimes and Crimes against Humanity. With respect to War Crimes, however, as has already been pointed out, the crimes defined by Article 6, section (b) of the Charter were already recognized as War Crimes under international law. They were covered by Articles 46, 50, 52, and 56 of the Hague Convention of 1907, and Articles 2, 3, 4, 46, and 51 of the Geneva Convention of 1929. That violations of these provisions constituted crimes for which the guilty individuals were punishable is too well settled to admit of argument.

But it is argued that the Hague Convention does not apply in this case, because of the "general participation" clause in Article 2 of the Hague Convention of 1907. That clause provided:

> The provisions contained in the regulations (Rules of Land Warfare) referred to in Article I, as well as in the present convention, do not apply except between contracting powers, and then only if all the belligerents are parties to the convention.

Several of the belligerents in the recent war were not parties to this convention.

In the opinion of the Tribunal it is not necessary to decide this question. The rules of land warfare expressed in the convention undoubtedly represented an advance over existing international law at the time of their adoption. But the convention expressly stated than it was an attempt "to revise the general laws and customs of war," which it thus recognized to be then existing, but by 1939 these rules laid down in the convention were recognized by all civilized nations, and were regarded as being declaratory of the laws and customs of war which are referred to in Article 6(b) of the Charter.

A further submission was made that Germany was no longer bound by the rules of land warfare in many of the territories occupied during the war, because Germany had completely subjugated those countries and incorporated them into the German Reich, a fact which gave Germany authority to deal with the occupied countries as though they were part of Germany. In the view of the Tribunal it is unnecessary in this case to decide whether this doctrine of subjugation, dependent as it is upon military conquest, has any application where the subjugation is the result of the crime of aggressive war. The doctrine was never considered to be applicable so long as there was an army in the field attempting to restore the occupied countries to their true owners, and in this case, therefore, the doctrine could not apply to any territories occupied after 1 September 1939. As to the war crimes committed in Bohemia and Moravia, it is a sufficient answer that these territories were never added to the Reich, but a mere protectorate was established over them.

With regard to crimes against humanity, there is no doubt whatever that political opponents were murdered in Germany before the war, and that many of them were kept in concentration camps in circumstances of great horror and cruelty. The policy of terror was certainly carried out on a vast scale, and in many cases was organized and systematic. The policy of persecution, repression and murder of civilians in Germany before the war of 1939, who were likely to be hostile to the Government, was most ruthlessly carried out. The persecution of Jews during the same period is established beyond all doubt. To constitute crimes against humanity, the acts relied on before the outbreak of war must have been in execution of, or in connection with, any crime within the jurisdiction of the Tribunal. The Tribunal is of the opinion that revolting and horrible as many of these crimes were, it has not been satisfactorily proved that they were done in execution of, or in connection with, any such crime. The Tribunal therefore cannot make a general declaration that the acts before 1939 were Crimes against Humanity within the meaning of the Charter, but from the beginning of the war in 1939 war crimes were committed on a vast scale, which were also crimes against humanity; and insofar as the inhumane acts charged in the Indictment, and committed after the beginning of the war, did not constitute war crimes, they were all committed in execution of, or in connection with, the aggressive war, and therefore constituted crimes against humanity.

* * *

The Accused Organizations

Article 9 of the Charter provides:

At the trial of any individual member of any group or organization the

> Tribunal may declare (in connection with any act of which the individual may be convicted) that the group or organization of which the individual was a member was a criminal organization.
>
> After receipt of the Indictment the Tribunal shall give such notices as it thinks fit that the Prosecution intends to ask the Tribunal to make such declaration, and any member of the organization will be entitled to apply to the Tribunal for leave to be heard by the Tribunal upon the question of the criminal character of the organization. The Tribunal shall have power to allow or reject the application. If the application is allowed, the Tribunal may direct in what manner the applicants shall be represented and heard.

Article 10 of the Charter makes clear that the declaration of criminality against an accused organization is final, and cannot be challenged in any subsequent criminal proceedings against a member of that organization. Article 10 is as follows:

> In cases where a group or organization is declared criminal by the Tribunal, the competent national authority of any Signatory shall have the right to bring individuals to trial for membership therein before national, military, or occupation courts. In any such case the criminal nature of the group or organization is considered proved and shall not be questioned.

The effect of the declaration of criminality by the Tribunal is well illustrated by Law Number 10 of the Control Council of Germany, passed on 20 December, 1945, which provides:

> Each of the following acts is recognized as a crime:
>
> (d) Membership in categories of a criminal group or organization declared criminal by the International Military Tribunal. . . .
>
> (3) Any person found guilty of any of the crimes above mentioned may upon convection be punished as shall be determined by the Tribunal to be just. Such punishment may consist of one or more of the following:
>
> (a) Death.
> (b) Imprisonment for life or a term of years, with or without hard labor.
> (c) Fine, and imprisonment with or without hard labor, in lieu thereof.
> (d) Forfeiture of property.
> (e) Restitution of property wrongfully acquired.
> (f) Deprivation of some or all civil rights.

In effect, therefore, a member of an organization which the Tribunal has declared to be criminal may be subsequently convicted of the crime of membership and be punished for that crime by death. This is not to assume that international or military courts which will try these individuals will not exercise appropriate standards of justice. This is a far-reaching and novel procedure. Its application, unless properly safeguarded, may produce great injustice.

Article 9, it should be noted, uses the words: "The Tribunal may declare," so that the Tribunal is vested with discretion as to whether it will declare any organization criminal. This discretion is a judicial one and does not permit arbitrary action, but should be exercised in accordance with well-settled legal principles, one of the most important of which is that criminal guilt is personal, and that mass punishments should be avoided. If satisfied of the criminal guilt of any organization or group, this Tribunal should not hesitate to declare it to be criminal because the theory of "group criminality" is new, or because it might be unjustly applied by some subsequent tribunals. On the other hand, the Tribunal should make such declaration of criminality so far as possible in a manner to insure that innocent persons will not be punished.

A criminal organization is analogous to a criminal conspiracy in that the essence of both is co-operation for criminal purposes. There must be a group bound together and organized for a common purpose. The group must be formed or used in connection with the commission of crimes denounced by the Charter. Since the declaration with respect to the organizations and groups will, as has been pointed out, fix the criminality of its members, that definition should exclude persons who had no knowledge of the criminal purposes or acts of the organization and those who were drafted by the state for menbership, unless they were personally implicated in the commission of acts declared criminal by Article 6 of the Charter as members of the organization. Membership alone is not enough to come within the scope of these declarations.

Since declarations of criminality which the Tribunal makes will be used by other courts in the trial of persons on account of their membership in the organizations found to be criminal, the Tribunal feels it appropriate to make the following recommendations:

1. That so far as possible throughout the four zones of occupation in Germany the classifications, sanctions, and penalties be standardized. Uniformity of treatment so far as practical should be a basic principle. This does not, of course, mean that discretion in sentencing should not be vested in the Court; but the discretion should be within fixed limits appropriate to the nature of the crime.

2. Law Number 10, to which reference has already been made, leaves punishment entirely at the discretion of the trial court, even to the extent of inflicting the death penalty.

The Denazification Law of 5 March 1946, however, passed for Bavaria, Greater Hesse, and Württemberg-Baden, provides definite sentences for punishment in each type of offense. The Tribunal recommends that in no case should punishment to be imposed under Law Number 10 upon any members of an organization or group declared by the Tribunal to be criminal exceed the punishment fixed by the Denazification Law. No person should be punished under both laws.

3. The Tribunal recommends to the Control Council that Law Number 10 be amended to prescribe limitations on the punishment which may be imposed for membership in a criminal group or organization so that such punishment shall not exceed the punishment prescribed by the Denazification Law.

The Indictment asks that the Tribunal declare to be criminal the following organizations: The Leadership Corps of the Nazi Party; the Gestapo; the SD; the SS; the SA; the Reich Cabinet; and the General Staff and High Command of the German Armed Forces.

* * *

Conclusion

The Leadership Corps was used for purposes which were criminal under the Charter and involved the Germanization of incorporated territory, the persecution of the Jews, the administration of the slave labor program, and the mistreatment of prisoners of war. The Defendants Bormann and Sauckel, who were members of this organization, were among those who used it for these purposes. The Gauleiter, the Kreisleiter, and the Ortsgruppenleiter participated, to one degree or another, in these criminal programs. The Reichsleitung as the staff organization of the Party is also responsible for these criminal programs as well as the heads of the various staff organizations of the Gauleiter and Kreisleiter. The decision of the Tribunal on these staff organizations includes only the Amtsleiter who were heads of offices on the staffs of the Reichsleitung, Gauleitung, and Kreisleitung. With respect to other staff officers and party organizations attached to the Leadership Corps other than the Amtsleiter referred to above, the Tribunal will follow the suggestion of the Prosecution in excluding them from the declaration.

The Tribunal declares to be criminal within the meaning of the Charter the group composed of those members of the Leadership Corps holding the positions enumerated in the preceding paragraph who became or remained members of the organization with knowledge that it was being used for the commission of acts declared criminal by Article 6 of the Charter, or who were personally implicated as members of the organization in the commission of such crimes. The basis of this finding is the participation of the organization in war crimes and crimes against humanity connected with the war; the group declared criminal cannot include, therefore, persons who had ceased to hold the positions enumerated in the preceding paragraph prior to 1 September 1939.

* * *

Gestapo and SD

The Gestapo and SD were used for purposes which were criminal under the Charter, involving the persecution and extermination of the Jews, brutalities and killings in concentration camps, excesses in the administration of occupied territories, the administration of the slave labor program and the mistreatment and murder of prisoners of war. The Defendant Kaltenbrunner, who was a member of this organization, was among those who used it for these purposes. In dealing with the Gestapo the Tribunal includes all executive and administrative officials of Amt IV of the RSHA, or concerned with Gestapo administration in other departments of the RSHA, and all local Gestapo officials serving both inside and outside of Germany, including the members of the Frontier Police, but not including the members of the Border and Customs Protection or the Secret Field Police, except such members as have been specified above. At the suggestion of the Prosecution the Tribunal does not include persons employed by the Gestapo for purely clerical, stenographic, janitorial, or similar unofficial routine tasks. In dealing with the SD the Tribunal includes Amter III, VI, and VII of the RSHA and all other members of the SD, including all local representatives and agents, honorary or otherwise, whether they were technically members of the SS or not.

The Tribunal declares to be criminal within the meaning of the Charter the group composed of those members of the Gestapo and SD holding the positions enumerated in the preceding paragraph who became or remained members of the organization with knowledge that it was being used for the commission of acts declared criminal by Article 6 of the Charter, or who were personally implicated as members of the organization in the commission of such crimes. The basis for this finding is the participation of the organization in war crimes and crimes against humanity connected with the war; this group declared criminal cannot include, therefore, persons who had ceased to hold the positions enumerated in the preceding paragraph prior to 1 September 1939.

* * *

The SS

The SS was utilized for purposes which were criminal under the Charter involving the persecution and extermination of the Jews, brutalities and killings in concentration camps, excesses in the administration of occupied territories, the administration of the slave labor program, and the mistreatment and murder of prisoners of war. The Defendant Kaltenbrunner was a member of the SS implicated in these activities. In dealing with the SS the Tribunal includes all persons who had been officially accepted as members of the SS, including the members of the Allgemeine SS, members of the Waffen-SS, members of the SS Totenkopfverbände, and the members of any of the different police forces who were members of the SS. The Tribunal does not include the so-called SS riding units. The Sicherheitsdienst des Reichsführer SS (commonly known as the SD) is dealt with in the Tribunal's judgment on the Gestapo and SD.

The Tribunal declares to be criminal within the meaning of the Charter the group composed of those persons who had been officially accepted as members of the SS as enumerated in the preceding paragraph, who became or remained members of the organization with knowledge that it was being used for the commission of acts declared criminal by Article 6 of the Charter, or who were personally implicated as members of the organization in the commission of such crimes, excluding, however, those who were drafted into membership by the State in such a way as to give them no choice in the matter, and who had committed no such crimes. The basis of this finding is the participation of the organization in war crimes and crimes against humanity connected with the war; this group declared criminal cannot include, therefore, persons who had ceased to belong to the organizations enumerated in the preceding paragraph prior to 1 September 1939.

The SA

* * *

Until the purge beginning on 30 June 1934, the SA was a group composed in large part of ruffians and bullies who participated in the Nazi outrages of that period. It has not been shown, however, that these atrocities were part of a specific plan to wage aggressive war, and the Tribunal therefore cannot hold that these activities were criminal under the Charter. After the purge, the SA was reduced to the status of a group of unimportant Nazi hangers-on. Although in specific instances some units of the SA were used for the commission of war crimes and crimes against humanity, it cannot be said that its members generally participated in or even knew of the criminal acts. For these reasons the Tribunal does not declare the SA to be a criminal organization within the meaning of Article 9 of the Charter.

The Reich Cabinet

The Prosecution has named as a criminal organization the Reich Cabinet (Die Reichsregierung) consisting of members of the ordinary Cabinet after 30 January 1933, members of the Council of Ministers for the Defense of the Reich and members of the Secret Cabinet Council. The Tribunal is of opinion that no declaration of criminality should be made with respect to the Reich Cabinet for two reasons:

(1) because it is not shown that after 1937 it ever really acted as a group or organization;

(2) because the group of persons here charged is so small that members could be conveniently tried in proper cases without resort to a declaration that the Cabinet of which they were members was criminal. . . .

October 1, 1946

MORNING SESSION

THE PRESIDENT: There is a correction which the Tribunal wishes to make in the Judgment pronounced yesterday at Page 159, with reference to the SD.

The Tribunal's attention has been drawn to the fact that the Prosecution expressly excluded honorary informers who were not members of the SS and members of the Abwehr who were transferred to the SD. In view of that exclusion by the Prosecution, the Tribunal also excludes those persons from the SD, which was declared criminal.

Article 26 of the Charter provides that the Judgment of the Tribunal as to the guilt or innocence of any defendant shall give the reasons on which it is based.

The Tribunal will now state those reasons in declaring its Judgment on such guilt or innocence.

Göring

Göring is indicted on all four Counts. The evidence shows that after Hitler he was the most prominent man in the Nazi regime. He was Commander-in-Chief of the Luftwaffe, Plenipotentiary for the Four Year Plan, and had tremendous influence with Hitler, at least until 1943, when their relationship deteriorated, ending in his arrest in 1945. He testified that Hitler kept him informed of all important military and political problems.

Crimes against Peace

From the moment he joined the Party in 1922 and took command of the street-fighting organization, the SA, Göring was the adviser, the active agent of Hitler, and one of the prime leaders of the Nazi movement. As Hitler's political deputy he was largely instrumental in bringing the National Socialists to power in 1933 and was charged with consolidating this power and expanding German armed might. He developed the Gestapo and created the first concentration camps, relinquishing them to Himmler in 1934, conducted the Röhm purge in that year, and engineered the sordid proceedings which resulted in the removal of Von Blomberg and Von Fritsch from the Army. In 1936 he became Plenipotentiary for the Four Year Plan and in theory and in practice was the economic dictator of the Reich. Shortly after the Pact of Munich, he announced that he would embark on a five-fold expansion of the Luftwaffe and speed up rearmament with emphasis on offensive weapons.

Göring was one of the five important leaders present at the Hossbach conference of 5 November 1937, and he attended the other important conferences already discussed in this Judgment. In the Austrian Anschluss he was indeed the central figure, the ringleader. He said in court: "I must take 100 percent responsibility. . . . I even overruled objections by the Führer and brought everything to its final development." In the seizure of the Sudetenland, he played his role as Luftwaffe chief by planning an air offensive which proved unnecessary, and his role as a politician by lulling the Czechs with false promises of friendship. The night before the invasion of Czechoslovakia and the absorption of Bohemia and Moravia, at a conference with Hitler and President Hacha, he threatened to Bomb Prague if Hacha did not submit. This threat he admitted in his testimony.

Göring attended the Reich Chancellery meeting of 23 May 1939, when Hitler told his military leaders "there is, therefore, no question of sparing

Poland," and was present at the Obersalzberg briefing of 22 August 1939. And the evidence shows he was active in the diplomatic maneuvers which followed. With Hitler's connivance, he used the Swedish businessman, Dahlerus, as a go-between to the British, as described by Dahlerus to this Tribunal, to try to prevent the British Government from keeping its guarantee to the Poles.

He commanded the Luftwaffe in the attack on Poland and throughout the aggressive wars which followed.

Even if he opposed Hitler's plans against Norway and the Soviet Union, as he alleged, it is clear that he did so only for strategic reasons; once Hitler had decided the issue, he followed him without hesitation. He made it clear in his testimony that these differences were never ideological or legal. He was "in a rage" about the invasion of Norway, but only because he had not received sufficient warning to prepare the Luftwaffe offensive. He admitted he approved of the attack: "My attitude was perfectly positive." He was active in preparing and executing the Yugoslavian and Greek campaigns and testified that "Plan Marita," the attack on Greece, had been prepared long beforehand. The Soviet Union he regarded as the "most threatening menace to Germany," but said there was no immediate military necessity for the attack. Indeed, his only objection to the war of aggression against the U.S.S.R. was its timing; he wished for strategic reasons to delay until Britain was conquered. He testified: "My point of view was decided by political and military reasons only."

After his own admissions to this Tribunal, from the positions which he held, the conferences he attended, and the public words he uttered, there can remain no doubt that Göring was the moving force for aggressive war second only to Hitler. He was the planner and prime mover in the military and diplomatic preparation for war which Germany pursued.

War Crimes and Crimes against Humanity

The record is filled with Göring's admissions of his complicity in the use of slave labor. "We did use this labor for security reasons so that they would not be active in their own country and would not work against us. On the other hand, they served to help in the economic war." And again: "Workers were forced to come to the Reich. That is something I have not denied." The man who spoke these words was Plenipotentiary for the Four Year Plan charged with the recruitment and allocation of manpower. As Luftwaffe Commander-in-Chief he demanded from Himmler more slave laborers for his underground aircraft factories: "That I requested inmates of concentration camps for the armament of the Luftwaffe is correct and it is to be taken as a matter of course."

As plenipotentiary, Göring signed a directive concerning the treatment of Polish workers in Germany and implemented it by regulations of the SD, including "special treatment." He issued directives to use Soviet and French prisoners of war in the armament industry; he spoke of seizing Poles and Dutch and making them prisoners of war if necessary, and using them for work. He agrees Russian prisoners of war were used to man anti-aircraft batteries.

As plenipotentiary, Göring was the active authority in the spoliation of conquered territory. He made plans for the spoliation of Soviet territory long before the war on the Soviet Union. Two months prior to the invasion of the Soviet Union, Hitler gave Göring the overall direction for the economic administration in the territory. Göring set up an economic staff for this function. As Reich Marshal of the Greater German Reich, "the orders of the Reich Marshal cover all economic fields, including nutrition and agriculture." His so-called "Green" folder, printed by the Wehrmacht, set up an "Economic Executive Staff East." This directive contemplated plundering and abandonment of all industry in the food deficit regions and, from the food surplus regions, a diversion of food to German needs. Göring claims its purposes have been misunderstood, but admits "that as a matter of course and a matter of duty we would have used Russia for our purposes" when conquered.

And he participated in the conference of 16 July when Hitler said the National Socialists had no intention of ever leaving the occupied countries, and that "all necessary measures—shooting, resettling, *et cetera*" should be taken.

Göring persecuted the Jews, particularly after the November 1938 riots, and not only in Germany, where he raised the billion-mark fine as stated elsewhere, but in the conquered territories as well. His own utterances then and his testimony now shows this interest was primarily economic—how to get their property and how to force them out of the economic life of Europe. As these countries fell before the German Army, he extended the Reich anti-Jewish laws to them; the *Reichsgesetzblatt* for 1939, 1940, and 1941 contains several anti-Jewish decrees signed by Göring. Although their extermination was in Himmler's hands, Göring was far from disinterested or inactive, despite his protestations in the witness box. By decree of 31 July 1941 he directed Himmler and Heydrich to "bring about a complete solution of the Jewish question in the German sphere of influence in Europe."

There is nothing to be said in mitigation. For Göring was often, indeed almost always, the moving force, second only to his leader. He was the leading war aggressor, both as political and as military leader; he was the director of the slave labor program and the creator of the oppressive program against the Jews and other races, at home and abroad. All of these crimes he has frankly admitted. On some specific cases there may be conflict of testimony, but in terms of the broad outline his own admissions are more than sufficiently wide to be conclusive of his guilt. His guilt is unique in its enormity. The record discloses no excuses for this man.

Conclusion

The Tribunal finds the Defendant Göring guilty on all four Counts of the Indictment.

Hess

Hess is indicted under all four Counts. He joined the Nazi Party in 1920 and participated in the Munich Putsch on 9 November 1923. He was imprisoned with Hitler in the Landsberg fortress in 1924 and became Hitler's closest personal confidant, a relationship which lasted until Hess' flight to the British Isles. On 21 April 1933, he was appointed Deputy to the Führer, and on 1 December 1933 was made Reich Minister without Portfolio. He was appointed member of the Secret Cabinet Council on 4 February 1938, and a member of the Ministerial Council for the Defense of the Reich on 31 August 1939. In September 1939, Hess was officially announced by Hitler as successor designate to the Führer after Göring. On 10 May 1941, he flew from Germany to Scotland.

Crimes against Peace

As Deputy to the Führer, Hess was the top man in the Nazi Party with responsibility for handling all Party matters and authority to make decisions in Hitler's name on all questions of Party leadership. As Reich Minister without Portfolio he had the authority to approve all legislation suggested by the different Reich Ministers before it could be enacted as law. In these positions, Hess was an active supporter of preparations for war. His signature appears on the law of 16 March 1935, establishing compulsory military service. Throughout the years he supported Hitler's policy of vigorous rearmament in many speeches. He told the people that they must sacrifice for armaments, repeating the phrase, "Guns instead of butter." It is true that between 1933 and 1937 Hess made speeches in which he expressed a desire for peace and advocated international economic co-operation. But nothing which they contained can alter the fact that of all the defendants none knew better than Hess how determined Hitler was to realize his ambitions, how fanatical and violent a man he was, and how little likely he was to refrain from resort to force, if this was the only way in which he could achieve his aims.

Hess was an informed and willing participant in German aggression against Austria, Czechoslovakia, and Poland. He was in touch with the illegal Nazi Party in Austria throughout the entire period between the murder of Dollfuss and the Anschluss and gave instructions to it during that period. Hess was in Vienna on 12 March 1938, when the German troops moved in; and on 13 March 1938 he signed the law for the reunion of Austria within the German Reich. A law of 10 June 1939 provided for his participation in the administration of Austria. On 24 July 1938, he made a speech in commemoration of the unsuccessful Putsch by Austrian National Socialists which had been attempted 4 years before, praising the steps leading up to the Anschluss and defending the occupation of Austria by Germany.

In the summer of 1938 Hess was in active touch with Henlein, Chief of the Sudeten German Party in Czechoslovakia. On 27 September 1938, at the time of the Munich crisis, he arranged with Keitel to carry out the instructions of Hitler to make the machinery of the Nazi Party available for a secret mobilization. On 14 April 1939, Hess signed a decree setting up the Government of the Sudetenland as an integral part of the Reich; and an ordinance of 10 June 1939 provided for his participation in the administration of the Sudetenland. On 7 November 1938, Hess absorbed Henlein's Sudeten German Party into the Nazi Party and made a speech in which he emphasized that Hitler had been prepared to resort to war if this had been necessary to acquire the Sudetenland.

On 27 August 1939, when the attack on Poland had been temporarily postponed in an attempt to induce Great Britain to abandon its guarantee to Poland, Hess publicly praised Hitler's "magnanimous offer" to Poland and attacked Poland for agitating for war and England for being responsible for Poland's attitude. After the invasion of Poland Hess signed decrees incorporating Danzig and certain Polish territories into the Reich and setting up the Government General (Poland).

These specific steps which this defendant took in support of Hitler's plans for aggressive action do not indicate the full extent of his responsibility. Until his flight to England, Hess was Hitler's closest personal confidant. Their relationship was such that Hess must have been informed of Hitler's aggressive plans when they came into existence. And he took action to carry out these plans whenever action was necessary.

With him on his flight to England, Hess carried certain peace proposals which he alleged Hitler was prepared to accept. It is significant to note that this flight took place only 10 days after the date on which Hitler fixed 22 June 1941 as the time for attacking the Soviet Union. In conversations carried on after his arrival in England, Hess wholeheartedly supported all Germany's aggressive actions up to that time and attempted to justify Germany's action in connection with Austria, Czechoslovakia, Poland, Norway, Denmark, Belgium, and the Netherlands. He blamed England and France for the war.

War Crimes and Crimes against Humanity

There is evidence showing the participation of the Party Chancellery, under Hess, in the distribution of orders connected with the commission of War Crimes; that Hess may have had knowledge of, even if he did not participate in, the crimes that were being committed in the East, and proposed laws discriminating against Jews and Poles; and that he signed decrees forcing certain groups of Poles to accept German citizenship. The Tribunal, however, does not find that the evidence sufficiently connects Hess with these crimes to sustain a finding of guilt.

As previously indicated the Tribunal found, after a full medical examination of and report on the condition of this defendant, that he should be tried, without any postponement of his case. Since that time further motions have been made that he should again be examined. These the Tribunal denied, after having had a report from the prison psychologist. That Hess acts in an abnormal manner, suffers from loss of memory, and has mentally deteriorated during this Trial, may be true. But there is nothing to show that he does not realize the nature of the charges against him, or is incapable of defending himself. He was ably represented at the Trial by counsel, appointed for that purpose by the Tribunal. There is no suggestion that Hess was not completely sane when the acts charged against him were committed.

Conclusion

The Tribunal finds the Defendant Hess guilty on Counts One and Two; and not guilty on Counts Three and Four.

Von Ribbentrop

Ribbentrop is indicted under all four Counts. He joined the Nazi Party in 1932. By 1933 he had been made foreign policy adviser to Hitler, and in the same year the representative of the Nazi Party on foreign policy. In 1934 he was appointed Delegate for Disarmament Questions and in 1935 Minister Plenipotentiary at Large, a capacity in which he negotiated the Anglo-German Naval Agreement in 1935 and the Anti-Comintern Pact in 1936. On 11 August 1936 he was appointed Ambassador to England. On 4 February 1938, he succeeded Von Neurath as Reich Minister for Foreign Affairs as part of the general reshuffle which accompanied the dismissal of Von Fritsch and Von Blomberg.

Crimes against Peace

Ribbentrop was not present at the Hossbach conference held on 5 November 1937, but on 2 January 1938, while still Ambassador to England, he sent a memorandum to Hitler indicating his opinion that a change in the *status quo* in the East in the German sense could only be carried out by force and suggesting methods to prevent England and France from intervening in a European war fought to bring about such a change. When Ribbentrop became Foreign Minister, Hitler told him that Germany still had four problems to solve: Austria, Sudetenland, Memel, and Danzig, and mentioned the possibility of "some sort of show-down" or "military settlement" for their solution.

On 12 February 1938, Ribbentrop attended the conference between Hitler and Schuschnigg at which Hitler, by threats of invasion, forced Schuschnigg to grant a series of concessions designed to strengthen the Nazis in Austria, including the appointment of Seyss-Inquart as Minister of Security and Interior, with control over the Police. Ribbentrop was in London when the occupation of Austria was actually carried out and, on the basis of information supplied him by Göring, informed the British Government that Germany had not presented

Austria with an ultimatum, but had intervened in Austria only to prevent civil war. On 13 March 1938, Ribbentrop signed the law incorporating Austria into the German Reich.

Ribbentrop participated in the aggressive plans against Czechoslovakia. Beginning in March 1938, he was in close touch with the Sudeten German Party and gave them instructions which had the effect of keeping the Sudeten German question a live issue which might serve as an excuse for the attack which Germany was planning against Czechoslovakia. In August 1938 he participated in a conference for the purpose of obtaining Hungarian support in the event of a war with Czechoslovakia. After the Munich Pact he continued to bring diplomatic pressure with the object of occupying the remainder of Czechoslovakia. He was instrumental in inducing the Slovaks to proclaim their independence. He was present at the conference of 14 and 15 March 1939, at which Hitler, by threats of invasion, compelled President Hacha to consent to the German occupation of Czechoslovakia. After the German troops had marched in, Ribbentrop signed the law establishing a protectorate over Bohemia and Moravia.

Ribbentrop played a particularly significant role in the diplomatic activity which led up to the attack on Poland. He participated in a conference held on 12 August 1939 for the purpose of obtaining Italian support if the attack should lead to a general European war. Ribbentrop discussed the German demands with respect to Danzig and the Polish Corridor with the British Ambassador in the period from 25 August to 30 August 1939, when he knew that the German plans to attack Poland had merely been temporarily postponed in an attempt to induce the British to abandon their guarantee to the Poles. The way in which he carried out these discussions makes it clear that he did not enter into them in good faith in an attempt to reach a settlement of the difficulties between Germany and Poland.

Ribbentrop was advised in advance of the attack on Norway and Denmark and of the attack on the Low Countries and prepared the official Foreign Office memoranda attempting to justify these aggressive actions.

Ribbentrop attended the conference on 20 January 1941, at which Hitler and Mussolini discussed the proposed attack on Greece, and the conference in January 1941, at which Hitler obtained from Antonescu permission for German troops to go through Romania for this attack. On 25 March 1941, when Yugoslavia adhered to the Axis Tri-Partite Pact, Ribbentrop had assured Yugoslavia that Germany would respect its sovereignty and territorial integrity. On 27 March 1941 he attended the meeting, held after the *coup d'état* in Yugoslavia, at which plans were made to carry out Hitler's announced intention to destroy Yugoslavia.

Von Ribbentrop attended a conference in May 1941 with Hitler and Antonescu relating to Romanian participation in the attack on the U.S.S.R. He also consulted with Rosenberg in the preliminary planning for the political exploitation of Soviet territories and in July 1941, after the outbreak of war, urged Japan to attack the Soviet Union.

War Crimes and Crimes against Humanity

Ribbentrop participated in a meeting of 6 June 1944, at which it was agreed to start a program under which Allied aviators carrying out machine gun attacks should be lynched. In December 1944 Ribbentrop was informed of the plans to murder one of the French generals held as a prisoner of war and directed his subordinates to see that the details were worked out in such a way as to prevent its detection by the protecting powers. Ribbentrop is also responsible for War Crimes and Crimes against Humanity because of his activities with respect to occupied countries and Axis satellites. The top German official in both Denmark and Vichy France was a Foreign Office representative, and Ribbentrop is therefore responsible for the general economic and political policies put into effect in the occupation of these countries. He urged the Italians to adopt a ruthless occupation policy in Yugoslavia and Greece.

He played an important part in Hitler's "final solution" of the Jewish question. In September 1942 he ordered the German diplomatic representatives accredited to various Axis satellites to hasten the deportation of Jews to the East. In June 1942 the German Ambassador to Vichy requested Laval to turn over 50,000 Jews for deportation to the East. On 25 February 1943, Ribbentrop protested to Mussolini against Italian slowness in deporting Jews from the Italian occupation zone of France. On 17 April 1943, he took part in a conference between Hitler and Horthy on the deportation of Jews from Hungary and informed Horthy that the "Jews must either be exterminated or taken to concentration camps." At the same conference Hitler had likened the Jews to "tuberculosis bacilli" and said if they did not work they were to be shot.

Ribbentrop's defense to the charges made against him is that Hitler made all the important decisions, and that he was such a great admirer and faithful follower of Hitler that he never questioned Hitler's repeated assertions that he wanted peace or the truth of the reasons that Hitler gave in explaining aggressive action. The Tribunal does not consider this explanation to be true. Ribbentrop participated in all of the Nazi aggressions from the occupation of Austria to the invasion of the Soviet Union. Although he was personally concerned with the diplomatic rather than the military aspect of these actions, his diplomatic efforts were so closely connected with war that he could not have remained unaware of the aggressive nature of Hitler's actions. In the administration of territories over which Germany acquired control by illegal invasion, Ribbentrop also assisted in carrying out criminal policies, particularly those involving the extermination of the Jews. There is abundant evidence, moreover, that Ribbentrop was in complete sympathy with all the main tenets of the National Socialist creed, and that his collaboration with Hitler and with other defendants in the commission of Crimes against Peace, War Crimes and Crimes against Humanity was whole-hearted. It was because Hitler's policy and plans coincided with his own ideas that Ribbentrop served him so willingly to the end.

Conclusion

The Tribunal finds that Ribbentrop is guilty on all four Counts.

KEITEL

Keitel is indicted on all four Counts. He was Chief of Staff to the then Minister of War Von Blomberg from 1935 to 4 February 1938; on that day Hitler took command of the Armed Forces, making Keitel Chief of the High Command of the Armed Forces. Keitel did not have command authority over the three Wehrmacht branches which enjoyed direct access to the Supreme Commander. OKW was in effect Hitler's military staff.

Crimes against Peace

Keitel attended the Schuschnigg conference in February 1938 with two other generals. Their presence, he admitted, was a "military demonstration," but since he had been appointed OKW chief just one week before, he had not known why he had been summoned. Hitler and Keitel then continued to put pressure on Austria with false rumors, broadcasts, and troop maneuvers. Keitel made the military and other arrangements and Jodl's diary noted "the effect is quick and strong." When Schuschnigg called his plebiscite, Keitel that night briefed Hitler and his generals, and Hitler issued "Case Otto" which Keitel initialed.

On 21 April 1938 Hitler and Keitel considered making use of a possible "incident," such as the assassination of the German Minister at Prague, to preface the attack on Czechoslovakia. Keitel signed many directives and memoranda on "Fall Grün," including the directive of 30 May, containing Hitler's statement: "It is my unalterable decision to smash Czechoslovakia by military action in the near future." After Munich, Keitel initialed Hitler's directive for the attack on Czechoslovakia and issued two supplements. The second supplement said the attack should appear to the outside world as "merely an act of pacification, and not a warlike undertaking." The OKW chief attended Hitler's negotiations with Hacha when the latter surrendered.

Keitel was present on 23 May 1939 when Hitler announced his decision "to attack Poland at the first suitable opportunity." Already he had signed the directive requiring the Wehrmacht to submit its "Fall Weiss" timetable to OKW by 1 May.

The invasion of Norway and Denmark he discussed on 12 December 1939 with Hitler, Jodl, and Raeder. By directive of 27 January 1940 the Norway plans were placed under Keitel's "direct and personal guidance." Hitler had said on 23 May 1939 he would ignore the neutrality of Belgium and the Netherlands, and Keitel signed orders for these attacks on 15 October, 20

November, and 28 November 1939. Orders postponing this attack 17 times until spring 1940 all were signed by Keitel or Jodl.

Formal planning for attacking Greece and Yugoslavia had begun in November 1940. On 18 March 1941 Keitel heard Hitler tell Raeder that complete occupation of Greece was a prerequisite to settlement, and also heard Hitler decree on 27 March that the destruction of Yugoslavia should take place with "unmerciful harshness."

Keitel testified that he opposed the invasion of the Soviet Union for military reasons, and also because it would constitute a violation of the Non-Aggression Pact. Nevertheless he initialed "Case Barbarossa," signed by Hitler on 18 December 1940, and attended the OKW discussion with Hitler on 3 February 1941. Keitel's supplement of 13 March established the relationship between the military and political officers. He issued his timetable for the invasion on 6 June 1941 and was present at the briefing of 14 June when the generals gave their final reports before attack. He appointed Jodl and Warlimont as OKW representatives to Rosenberg on matters concerning the Eastern territories. On 16 June he directed all Army units to carry out the economic directives issued by Göring in the so-called "Green Folder" for the exploitation of Russian territory, food, and raw materials.

War Crimes and Crimes against Humanity

On 4 August 1942 Keitel issued a directive that paratroopers were to be turned over to the SD. On 18 October Hitler issued the Commando Order, which was carried out in several instances. After the landing in Normandy, Keitel reaffirmed the order, and later extended it to Allied missions fighting with partisans. He admits he did not believe the order was legal, but claims he could not stop Hitler.

When, on 8 September 1941, OKW issued its ruthless regulations for Soviet prisoners of war, Canaris wrote to Keitel that under international law that SD should have nothing to do with this. On this memorandum, in Keitel's handwriting, dated 23 September and initialed by him, is the statement: "The objections arise from the military concept of chivalrous warfare. This is the destruction of an ideology. Therefore I approve and back the measures." Keitel testified that he really agreed with Canaris and argued with Hitler, but lost. The OKW chief directed the military authorities to co-operate with the Einsatzstab Rosenberg in looting cultural property in occupied territories.

Lahousen testified that Keitel told him on 12 September 1939, while aboard Hitler's headquarters train, that the Polish intelligentsia, nobility, and Jews were to be liquidated. On 20 October, Hitler told Keitel that intelligentsia would be prevented from forming a ruling class, the standard of living would remain low, and Poland would be used only for labor forces. Keitel does not remember the Lahousen conversation, but admits there was such a policy and that he had protested without effect to Hitler about it.

On 16 September 1941, Keitel ordered that attacks on soldiers in the East should be met by putting to death 50 to 100 Communists for one German soldier, with the comment that human life was less than nothing in the East. On 1 October he ordered military commanders always to have hostages to execute when German soldiers were attacked. When Terboven, the Reich Commissioner in Norway, wrote Hitler that Keitel's suggestion that workmen's relatives be held responsible for sabotage, could work only if firing squads were authorized, Keitel wrote on this memorandum in the margin: "Yes, that is the best."

On 12 May 1941, five weeks before the invasion of the Soviet Union, the OKW urged upon Hitler a directive of the OKH that political commissars be liquidated by the Army. Keitel admitted the directive was passed on to field commanders. And on 13 May Keitel signed an order that civilians suspected of offenses against troops should be shot without trial, and that prosecution of German soldiers for offenses against civilians was unnecessary. On 27 July all copies of this directive were ordered destroyed without affecting its validity. Four days previously he had signed another order that legal punishment was inadequate and troops should use terrorism.

On 7 December 1941, as already discussed in this opinion, the so-called "Nacht and Nebel" decree, over Keitel's signature, provided that in occupied territories civilians who had been accused of crimes of resistance against the army of occupation would be tried only if a death sentence was likely; otherwise they would be handed over to the Gestapo for transportation to Germany.

Keitel directed that Russian prisoners of war be used in German war industry. On 8 September 1942 he ordered French, Dutch, and Belgian citizens to work on the Atlantic Wall. He was present on 4 January 1944 when Hitler directed Sauckel to obtain 4 million new workers from occupied territories.

In the face of these documents Keitel does not deny his connection with these acts. Rather, his defense relies on the fact that he is a soldier and on the doctrine of "superior orders," prohibited by Article 8 of the Charter as a defense.

There is nothing in mitigation. Superior orders, even to a soldier, cannot be considered in mitigation where crimes so shocking and extensive have been committed consciously, ruthlessly, and without military excuse or justification.

Conclusion

The Tribunal finds Keitel guilty on all four Counts.

KALTENBRUNNER

Kaltenbrunner is indicted under Counts One, Three, and Four. He joined the Austrian Nazi Party and the SS in 1932. In 1935 he became leader of the SS in Austria. After the Anschluss he was appointed Austrian State Secretary for Security and, when this position was abolished in 1941, he was made Higher SS and Police Leader. On 30 January 1943, he was appointed Chief of the Security Police and SD and head of the Reich Security Head Office (RSHA), a position which had been held by Heydrich until his assassination in June 1942. He held the rank of Obergruppenführer in the SS.

Crimes against Peace

As leader of the SS in Austria Kaltenbrunner was active in the Nazi intrigue against the Schuschnigg Government. On the night of 11 March 1938, after Göring had ordered Austrian National Socialists to seize control of the Austrian Government, 500 Austrian SS men under Kaltenbrunner's command surrounded the Federal Chancellery and a special detachment under the command of his adjutant entered the Federal Chancellery while Seyss-Inquart was negotiating with President Miklas. But there is no evidence connecting Kaltenbrunner with plans to wage aggressive war on any other front. The Anschluss, although it was an aggressive act, is not charged as an aggressive war, and the evidence against Kaltenbrunner under Count One does not, in the opinion of the Tribunal, show his direct participation in any plan to wage such a war.

War Crimes and Crimes against Humanity

When he became Chief of the Security Police and SD and head of the RSHA on 30 January 1943, Kaltenbrunner took charge of an organization which included the main offices of the Gestapo, the SD, and the Criminal Police. As Chief of the RSHA, Kaltenbrunner had authority to order protective custody to and release from concentration camps. Order to this effect were normally sent over his signature. Kaltenbrunner was aware of conditions in concentration camps. He had undoubtedly visited Mauthausen, and witnesses testified that he had seen prisoners killed by the various methods of execution, hanging, shooting in the back of the neck, and gassing, as part of a demonstration. Kaltenbrunner himself ordered the execution of prisoners in those camps and his office was used to transmit to the camps execution orders which originated in Himmler's office. At the end of the war Kaltenbrunner participated in the arrangements for the evacuation of inmates of concentration camps, and the liquidation of many of them, to prevent them from being liberated by the Allied armies.

During the period in which Kaltenbrunner was head of the RSHA, it was engaged in a widespread program of War Crimes and Crimes against Humanity. These crimes included the mistreatment and murder of prisoners of war. Einsatzkommandos operating under the control of the Gestapo were engaged in the screening of Soviet prisoners of war. Jews, commissars, and others who were thought to be ideologically hostile to the Nazi system were reported to the RSHA, which had them transferred to a concentration camp and murdered. An

RSHA order issued during Kaltenbrunner's regime established the "Bullet Decree," under which certain escaped prisoners of war who were recaptured were taken to Mauthausen and shot. The order for the execution of Commando troops was extended by the Gestapo to include parachutists while Kaltenbrunner was chief of the RSHA. An order signed by Kaltenbrunner instructed the Police not to interfere with attacks on bailed-out Allied fliers. In December 1944 Kaltenbrunner participated in the murder of one of the French generals held as a prisoner of war.

During the period in which Kaltenbrunner was head of the RSHA, the Gestapo and SD in occupied territories continued the murder and ill-treatment of the population, using methods which included torture and confinement in concentration camps, usually under orders to which Kaltenbrunner's name was signed.

The Gestapo was responsible for enforcing a rigid labor discipline on the slave laborers and Kaltenbrunner established a series of labor reformatory camps for this purpose. When the SS embarked on a slave labor program of its own, the Gestapo was used to obtain the needed workers by sending laborers to concentration camps.

The RSHA played a leading part in the "final solution" of the Jewish question by the extermination of the Jews. A special section under the Amt IV of the RSHA was established to supervise this program. Under its direction approximately 6 million Jews were murdered, of which 2 million were killed by Einsatzgruppen and other units of the Security Police. Kaltenbrunner had been informed of the activities of these Einsatzgruppen when he was a Higher SS and Police Leader, and they continued to function after he had become Chief of the RSHA.

The murder of approximately 4 million Jews in concentration camps has heretofore been described. This part of the program was also under the supervision of the RSHA when Kaltenbrunner was head of that organization, and special missions of the RSHA scoured the occupied territories and the various Axis satellites arranging for the deportation of Jews to these extermination institutions. Kaltenbrunner was informed of these activities. A letter which he wrote on 30 June 1944 described the shipment to Vienna of 12,000 Jews for that purpose and directed that all who could not work would have to be kept in readiness for "special action," which meant murder. Kaltenbrunner denied his signature to this letter, as he did on a very large number of orders on which his name was stamped or typed, and in a few instances, written. It is inconceivable that in matters of such importance his signature could have appeared so many times without his authority.

Kaltenbrunner has claimed that when he took office as Chief of the Security Police and SD and as head of the RSHA he did so pursuant to an understanding with Himmler under which he was to confine his activities to matters involving foreign intelligence and not to assume overall control over the activities of the RSHA. He claims that the criminal program had been started before his assumption of office; that he seldom knew what was going on; and that when he was informed he did what he could to stop them. It is true that he showed a special interest in matters involving foreign intelligence. But he exercised control over the activities of the RSHA, was aware of the crimes it was committing, and was an active participant in many of them.

Conclusion

The Tribunal finds that Kaltenbrunner is not guilty on Count One. He is guilty under Counts Three and Four.

Rosenberg

Rosenberg is indicted on all four Counts. He joined the Nazi Party in 1919, participated in the Munich Putsch of 9 November 1923, and tried to keep the illegal Nazi Party together while Hitler was in jail. Recognized as the Party's ideologist, he developed and spread Nazi doctrines in the newspapers *Völkischer Beobachter* and *NS Monatshefte,* which he edited, and in the numerous books he wrote. His book *Myth of the Twentieth Century* had a circulation of over a million copies.

In 1930 Rosenberg was elected to the Reichstag and he became the Party's representative for Foreign Affairs. In April 1933 he was made Reichsleiter and head of the Office of Foreign Affairs of the NSDAP (The APA). Hitler, in January 1934, appointed Rosenberg his deputy for the supervision of the entire spiritual and ideological training of the NSDAP. In January 1940, he was designated to set up the "Hohe Schule," the center of National Socialist ideological and educational research, and he organized the "Einsatzstab Rosenberg" in connection with this task. He was appointed Reich Minister for the Occupied Eastern Territories on 17 July 1941.

Crimes against Peace

As head of the APA, Rosenberg was in charge of an organization whose agents were active in Nazi intrigue in all parts of the world. His own reports, for example, claim that the APA was largely responsible for Romania's joining the Axis. As head of the APA, he played an important role in the preparation and planning of the attack on Norway.

Rosenberg, together with Raeder, was one of the originators of the plan for attacking Norway. Rosenberg had become interested in Norway as early as June 1939, when he conferred with Quisling. Quisling had pointed out the importance of the Norwegian coast in the event of a conflict between Germany and Great Britain and stated his fears that Great Britain might be able to obtain Norwegian assistance. As a result of this conference Rosenberg arranged for Quisling to collaborate closely with the National Socialists and to receive political assistance by the Nazis.

When the war broke out Quisling began to express fear of British intervention in Norway. Rosenberg supported this view and transmitted to Raeder a plan to use Quisling for a coup in Norway. Rosenberg was instrumental in arranging the conferences in December 1939 between Hitler and Quisling which led to the preparation of the attack on Norway and at which Hitler promised Quisling financial assistance. After these conferences Hitler assigned to Rosenberg the political exploitation of Norway. Two weeks after Norway was occupied, Hitler told Rosenberg that he had based his decision to attack Norway "on the continuous warnings of Quisling as reported to him by Reichsleiter Rosenberg."

Rosenberg bears a major responsibility for the formulation and execution of occupation policies in the Occupied Eastern Territories. He was informed by Hitler, on 2 April 1941, of the coming attack against the Soviet Union, and he agreed to help in the capacity of a "Political Adviser." On 20 April 1941 he was appointed Commissioner for the Central Control of Questions Connected with the East European Region. In preparing the plans for the occupation, he had numerous conferences with Keitel, Raeder, Göring, Funk, Ribbentrop, and other high Reich authorities. In April and May 1941 he prepared several drafts of instructions concerning the setting up of the administration in the Occupied Eastern Territories. On 20 June 1941, two days before the attack on the U.S.S.R., he made a speech to his assistants about the problems and policies of occupation. Rosenberg attended Hitler's conference of 16 July 1941, in which policies of administration and occupation were discussed. On 17 July 1941, Hitler appointed Rosenberg Reich Minister for the Occupied Eastern Territories and publicly charged him with responsibility for civil administration.

War Crimes and Crimes against Humanity

Rosenberg is responsible for a system of organized plunder of both public and private property throughout the invaded countries of Europe. Acting under Hitler's orders of January 1940 to set up the "Hohe Schule," he organized and directed the "Einsatzstab Rosenberg," which plundered museums and libraries, confiscated art treasures and collections, and pillaged private houses. His own reports show the extent of the confiscations. In "Aktion-M" (Möbel), instituted in December 1941 at Rosenberg's suggestion, 69,619 Jewish homes were plundered in the West, 38,000 of them in Paris alone, and it took 26,984 railroad cars to transport the confiscated furnishings to Germany. As of 14 July 1944, more than 21,903 art objects, including famous paintings and museum pieces, had been seized by the Einsatzstab in the West.

With his appointment as Reich Minister for the Occupied Eastern Territories on 17 July 1941, Rosenberg became the supreme authority for those areas. He helped to formulate the policies of Germanization, exploitation, forced labor, extermination of Jews and opponents of Nazi rule, and he set up the administration which carried them out. He took part in the conference of 16 July 1941, in which Hitler stated that they were faced with the task of "cutting up the giant cake according to our needs in order to be able: first, to dominate it, second, to administer it, and third, to exploit it," and he indicated that ruthless action was contemplated. Rosenberg accepted his appointment on the following day.

Rosenberg had knowledge of the brutal treatment and terror to which the Eastern people were subjected. He directed that the Hague Rules of Land Warfare were not applicable in the Occupied Eastern Territories. He had knowledge of and took an active part in stripping the Eastern territories of raw materials and foodstuffs, which were sent to Germany. He stated that feeding the German people was first on the list of claims on the East, and that the Soviet people would suffer thereby. His directives provided for the segregation of Jews, ultimately in ghettos. His subordinates engaged in mass killings of Jews, and his civil administrators in the East considered that cleansing the Eastern Occupied Territories of Jews was necessary. In December 1941, Rosenberg made the suggestion to Hitler that in a case of shooting 100 hostages, Jews only be used. Rosenberg had knowledge of the deportation of laborers from the East, of the methods of "recruiting" and the transportation horrors, and of the treatment Eastern laborers received in the Reich. He gave his civil administrators quotas of laborers to be sent to the Reich, which had to be met by whatever means necessary. His signature of approval appears on the order of 14 June 1944, for the "Heu Aktion," the apprehension of 40,000 to 50,000 youths, aged 10–14, for shipment to the Reich.

Upon occasion Rosenberg objected to the excesses and atrocities committed by his subordinates, notably in the case of Koch, but these excesses continued and he stayed in office until the end.

Conclusion

The Tribunal finds that Rosenberg is guilty on all four Counts.

Frank

Frank is indicted under Counts One, Three, and Four. Frank joined the Nazi Party in 1927. He became a member of the Reichstag in 1930, the Bavarian State Minister of Justice in March 1933, and when this position was incorporated into the Reich Government in 1934, Reich Minister without Portfolio. He was made a Reichsleiter of the Nazi Party in charge of legal affairs in 1933, and in the same year President of the Academy of German Law. Frank was also given the honorary rank of Obergruppenführer in the SA. In 1942 Frank became involved in a temporary dispute with Himmler as to the type of legal system which should be in effect in Germany. During the same year he was dismissed as Reichsleiter of the Nazi Party and as President of the Academy of German Law.

Crimes against Peace

The evidence has not satisfied the Tribunal that Frank was sufficiently connected with the common plan to wage aggressive war to allow the Tribunal to convict him on Count One.

War Crimes and Crimes against Humanity

Frank was appointed Chief Civil Administration Officer for occupied Polish territory and, on 12 October 1939, was made Governor General of the occupied Polish territory. On 3 October 1939, he described the policy which he intended to put into effect by stating: "Poland shall be treated like a colony; the Poles will become the slaves of the Greater German World Empire." The evidence establishes that this occupation policy was based on the complete destruction of Poland as a national entity, and a ruthless exploitation of its human and economic resources for the German war effort. All opposition was crushed with the utmost harshness. A reign of terror was instituted, backed by summary police courts which ordered such actions as the public shootings of groups of 20 to 200 Poles and the widespread shooting of hostages. The concentration camp system was introduced in the Government General by the establishment of the notorious Treblinka and Maidanek camps. As early as 6 February 1940, Frank gave an indication of the extent of this reign of terror by his cynical comment to a newspaper reporter on Von Neurath's poster announcing the execution of the Czech students: "If I wished to order that one should hang up posters about every seven Poles shot, there would not be enough forests in Poland with which to make the paper for these posters." On 30 May 1940, Frank told a police conference that he was taking advantage of the offensive in the West, which diverted the attention of the world from Poland, to liquidate thousands of Poles who would be likely to resist German domination of Poland, including "the leading representatives of the Polish intelligentsia." Pursuant to these instructions the brutal AB Action was begun, under which the Security Police and SD carried out these exterminations which were only partially subjected to the restraints of legal procedure. On 2 October 1943, Frank issued a decree under which any non-German hindering German construction in the Government General was to be tried by summary courts of the Security Police and SD and sentenced to death.

The economic demands made on the Government General were far in excess of the needs of the army of occupation and were out of all proportion to the resources of the country. The food raised in Poland was shipped to Germany on such a wide scale that the rations of the population of the occupied territories were reduced to the starvation level, and epidemics were widespread. Some steps were taken to provide for the feeding of the agricultural workers who were used to raise the crops, but the requirements of the rest of the population were disregarded. It is undoubtedly true, as argued by counsel for the Defense, that some suffering in the Government General was inevitable as a result of the ravages of war and the economic confusion resulting therefrom. But the suffering was increased by a planned policy of economic exploitation.

Frank introduced the deportation of slave laborers to Germany in the very early stages of his administration. On 25 January 1940, he indicated his intention of deporting a million laborers to Germany, suggesting on 10 May 1940 the use of police raids to meet this quota. On 18 August 1942, Frank reported that he had already supplied 800,000 workers for the Reich and expected to be able to supply 140,000 more before the end of the year.

The persecution of the Jews was immediately begun in the Government General. The area orginally contained from 2,500,000 to 3,500,000 Jews. They were forced into ghettos, subjected to discriminatory laws, deprived of the food necessary to avoid starvation, and finally systematically and brutally exterminated. On 16 December 1941, Frank told the Cabinet of the Government General: "We must annihilate the Jews wherever we find them and wherever it is possible in order to maintain there the structure of the Reich as a whole." By 25 January 1944, Frank estimated that there were only 100,000 Jews left.

At the beginning of his testimony, Frank stated that he had a feeling of "terrible guilt" for the atrocities committed in the occupied territories. But his defense was largely devoted to an attempt to prove that he was not in fact responsible; that he ordered only the necessary pacification measures; that the excesses were due to the activities of the Police which were not under his control; and that he never even knew of the activities of the concentration camps. It has also been argued that the starvation was due to the aftermath of the war and policies carried out under the Four Year Plan; that the forced labor program was under the direction of Sauckel; and that the extermination of the Jews was by the Police and SS under direct orders from Himmler.

It is undoubtedly true that most of the criminal program charged against Frank was put into effect through the Police, that Frank had jurisdictional difficulties with Himmler over the control of the Police, and that Hitler resolved many of these disputes in favor of Himmler. It therefore may well be true that some of the crimes committed in the Government General were committed without the knowledge of Frank, and even occasionally despite his opposition. It may also be true that some of the criminal policies put into effect in the Government General did not originate with Frank but were carried out pursuant to orders from Germany. But it is also true that Frank was a willing and knowing participant in the use of terrorism in Poland; in the economic exploitation of Poland in a way which led to the death by starvation of a large number of people; in the deportation to Germany as slave laborers of over a million Poles; and in a program involving the murder of at least 3 million Jews.

Conclusion

The Tribunal finds that Frank is not guilty on Count One but is guilty under Counts Three and Four.

Frick

Frick is indicted on all four Counts. Recognized as the chief Nazi administrative specialist and bureaucrat, he was appointed Reich Minister of the Interior in Hitler's first cabinet. He retained this important position until August 1943, when he was appointed Reich Protector of Bohemia and Moravia. In connection with his duties at the center of all internal and domestic administration, he became the Prussian Minister of the Interior, Reich Director of Elections, General Plenipotentiary for the Administration of the Reich, and a member of the Reich Defense Council, the Ministerial Council for Defense of the Reich, and the "Three Man College." As the several countries incorporated into the Reich were overrun, he was placed at the head of the central offices for their incorporation.

Though Frick did not officially join the Nazi Party until 1925, he had previously allied himself with Hitler and the National Socialist cause during the Munich Putsch, while he was an official in the Munich Police Department. Elected to the Reichstag in 1924, he became a Reichsleiter as leader of the National Socialist faction in that body.

Crimes against Peace

An avid Nazi, Frick was largely responsible for bringing the German nation under the complete control of the NSDAP. After Hitler became Reich Chancellor, the new Minister of the Interior immediately began to incorporate local governments under the sovereignty of the Reich. The numerous laws he drafted, signed, and administered, abolished all opposition parties and prepared the way for the Gestapo and their concentration camps to extinguish all individual opposition. He was largely responsible for the legislation which suppressed the trade unions, the Church, the Jews. He performed this task with ruthless efficiency.

Before the date of the Austrian aggression Frick was concerned only with domestic administration within the Reich. The evidence does not show that he participated in any of the conferences at which Hitler outlined his aggressive intentions. Consequently the Tribunal takes the view that Frick was not a member of the common plan or conspiracy to wage aggressive war as defined in this Judgment.

Six months after the seizure of Austria, under the provisions of the Reich Defense Law of 4 September 1938, Frick became Plenipotentiary General for the Administration of the Reich. He was made responsible for war administration, except the military and economic, in the event of Hitler's proclaiming a state of defense. The Reich Ministries of Justice, Education, Religion, and the Office of Spatial Planning were made subordinate to him. Performing his allotted duties, Frick devised an administrative organization in accordance with wartime standards. According to his own statement, this was actually put into operation after Germany decided to adopt a policy of war.

Frick signed the law of 13 March 1938, which united Austria with the Reich, and he was made responsible for its accomplishment. In setting up German administration in Austria, he issued decrees which introduced German law, the Nuremberg Decrees, the Military Service Law, and he provided for police security by Himmler.

He also signed the laws incorporating into the Reich the Sudetenland, Memel, Danzig, the Eastern territories (West Prussia and Posen), and Eupen, Malmedy, and Moresnet. He was placed in charge of the actual incorporation and of the establishment of German administration over these territories. He signed the law establishing the Protectorate of Bohemia and Moravia.

As the head of the central offices for Bohemia and Moravia, the Government General, and Norway, he was charged with obtaining close co-operation between the German officials in these occupied countries and the supreme authorities of the Reich. He supplied German civil servants for the administrations in all occupied territories, advising Rosenberg as to their assignment in the Occupied Eastern Territories. He signed the laws appointing Terboven Reich Commissioner to Norway and Seyss-Inquart to Holland.

War Crimes and Crimes against Humanity

Always rabidly anti-Semitic, Frick drafted, signed, and administered many laws designed to eliminate Jews from German life and economy. His work formed the basis of the Nuremberg Decrees, and he was active in enforcing them. Responsible for prohibiting Jews from following various professions and for confiscating their property, he signed a final decree in 1943, after the mass destruction of Jews in the East, which placed them "outside the law" and handed them over to the Gestapo. These laws paved the way for the "final solution," and were extended by Frick to the incorporated territories and to certain of the occupied territories. While he was Reich Protector of Bohemia and Moravia, thousands of Jews were transferred from the Terezin ghetto in Czechoslovakia to Auschwitz where they were killed. He issued a decree providing for special penal laws against Jews and Poles in the Government General.

The Police officially fell under the jurisdiction of the Reich Minister of the Interior. But Frick actually exercised little control over Himmler and police matters. However, he signed the law appointing Himmler Chief of the German Police, as well as the decrees establishing Gestapo jurisdiction over concentration camps and regulating the execution of orders for protective custody. From the many complaints he received, and from the testimony of witnesses, the Tribunal concludes that he knew of atrocities committed in these camps. With knowledge of Himmler's methods, Frick signed decrees authorizing him to take necessary security measures in certain of the incorporated territories. What these "security measures" turned out to be has already been dealt with.

As the supreme Reich authority in Bohemia and Moravia, Frick bears general responsibility for the acts of oppression in that territory after 20 August 1943, such as terrorism of the population, slave labor, and the deportation of Jews to the concentration camps for extermination. It is true that Frick's duties as Reich Protector were considerably more limited than those of his predecessor, and that he had no legislative and limited personal executive authority in the Protectorate. Nevertheless, Frick knew full well what the Nazi policies of occupation were in Europe, particularly with respect to Jews, at that time, and by accepting the office of Reich Protector he assumed responsibility for carrying out those policies in Bohemia and Moravia.

German citizenship in the occupied countries as well as in the Reich came under his jurisdiction while he was Minister of the Interior. Having created a racial register of persons of German extraction, Frick conferred German citizenship on certain groups of citizens of foreign countries. He is responsible for Germanization in Austria, Sudetenland, Memel, Danzig, Eastern Territories (West Prussia and Posen), and in the territories of Eupen, Malmedy, and Moresnet. He forced on the citizens of these territories German law, German courts, German education, German police security, and compulsory military service.

During the war nursing homes, hospitals, and asylums in which euthanasia was practiced as described elsewhere in this Judgment, came under Frick's jurisdiction. He had knowledge that insane, sick, and aged people, "useless eaters," were being systematically put to death. Complaints of these murders reached him, but he did nothing to stop them. A report of the Czechoslovak War Crimes Commission estimated that 275,000 mentally deficient and aged people, for whose welfare he was responsible, fell victim to it.

Conclusion

The Tribunal finds that Frick is not guilty on Count One. He is guilty on Counts Two, Three and Four.

STREICHER

Streicher is indicted on Counts One and Four. One of the earliest members of the Nazi Party, joining in 1921, he took part in the Munich Putsch. From 1925 to 1940 he was Gauleiter of Franconia. Elected to the Reichstag in 1933, he was an honorary general in the SA. His persecution of the Jews was notorious. He was the publisher of *Der Stürmer,* an anti-Semitic weekly newspaper, from 1923 to 1945 and was its editor until 1933.

Crimes against Peace

Streicher was a staunch Nazi and supporter of Hitler's main policies. There is no evidence to show that he was ever within Hitler's inner circle of advisers;

nor during his career was he closely connected with the formulation of the policies which led to war. He was never present, for example, at any of the important conferences when Hitler explained his decisions to his leaders. Although he was a Gauleiter there is no evidence to prove that he had knowledge of these policies. In the opinion of the Tribunal, the evidence fails to establish his connection with the conspiracy or common plan to wage aggressive war as that conspiracy has been elsewhere defined in this Judgment.

Crimes against Humanity

For his 25 years of speaking, writing, and preaching hatred of the Jews, Streicher was widely known as "Jew-Baiter Number One." In his speeches and articles, week after week, month after month, he infected the German mind with the virus of anti-Semitism and incited the German people to active persecution. Each issue of *Der Stürmer,* which reached a circulation of 600,000 in 1935, was filled with such articles, often lewd and disgusting.

Streicher had charge of the Jewish boycott of 1 April 1933. He advocated the Nuremberg Decrees of 1935. He was responsible for the demolition on 10 August 1938 of the synagogue in Nuremberg. And on 10 November 1938, he spoke publicly in support of the Jewish pogrom which was taking place at that time.

But it was not only in Germany that this defendant advocated his doctrines. As early as 1938 he began to call for the annihilation of the Jewish race. 23 different articles of *Der Stürmer* between 1938 and 1941 were produced in evidence, in which extermination "root and branch" was preached. Typical of his teachings was a leading article in September 1938 which termed the Jew a germ and a pest, not a human being, but "a parasite, an enemy, and evil-doer, a disseminator of diseases who must be destroyed in the interest of mankind." Other articles urged that only when world Jewry had been annihilated would the Jewish problem have been solved, and predicted that 50 years hence the Jewish graves "will proclaim that this people of murderers and criminals has after all met its deserved fate." Streicher, in February 1940, published a letter from one of *Der Stürmer's* readers which compared Jews with swarms of locusts which must be exterminated completely. Such was the poison Streicher injected into the minds of thousands of Germans which caused them to follow the National Socialist policy of Jewish persecution and extermination. A leading article of *Der Stürmer,* in May 1939, shows clearly his aim:

> A punitive expedition must come against the Jews in Russia, a punitive expedition which will provide the same fate for them that every murderer and criminal must expect. Death sentence and execution. The Jews in Russia must be killed. They must be exterminated root and branch.

As the war in the early stages proved successful in acquiring more and more territory for the Reich, Streicher even intensified his efforts to incite the

Germans against the Jews. In the record are 26 articles from *Der Stürmer,* published between August 1941 and September 1944, 12 by Streicher's own hand, which demanded annihilation and extermination in unequivocal terms. He wrote and published on 25 December 1941:

> If the danger of the reproduction of that curse of God in the Jewish blood is finally to come to an end, then there is only one way—the extermination of that people whose father is the devil.

And in February 1944 his own article stated:

> Whoever does what a Jew does is a scoundrel, a criminal. And he who repeats and wishes to copy him deserves the same fate: annihilation, death.

With knowledge of the extermination of the Jews in the Occupied Eastern Territories, this defendant continued to write and publish his propaganda of death. Testifying in this Trial, he vehemently denied any knowledge of mass executions of Jews. But the evidence makes it clear that he continually received current information on the progress of the "final solution." His press photographer was sent to visit the ghettos of the East in the spring of 1943, the time of the destruction of the Warsaw ghetto. The Jewish newspaper, *Israelitisches Wochenblatt,* which Streicher received and read, carried in each issue accounts of Jewish atrocities in the East, and gave figures on the number of Jews who had been deported and killed. For example, issues appearing in the summer and fall of 1942 reported the death of 72,729 Jews in Warsaw, 17,542 in Lodz, 18,000 in Croatia, 125,000 in Romania, 14,000 in Latvia, 85,000 in Yugoslavia, 700,000 in all of Poland. In November 1943 Streicher quoted verbatim an article from the *Israelitisches Wochenblatt* which stated that the Jews had virtually disappeared from Europe, and commented: "This is not a Jewish lie." In December 1942, referring to an article in the London *Times* about the atrocities aiming at extermination, Streicher said that Hitler had given warning that the second World War would lead to the destruction of Jewry. In January 1943 he wrote and published an article which said that Hitler's prophecy was being fulfilled, that world Jewry was being extirpated, and that it was wonderful to know that Hitler was freeing the world of its Jewish tormentors.

In the face of the evidence before the Tribunal it is idle for Streicher to suggest that the solution of the Jewish problem which he favored was strictly limited to the classification of Jews as aliens, and the passing of discriminatory legislation such as the Nuremberg Laws, supplemented if possible by international agreement on the creation of a Jewish state somewhere in the world, to which all Jews should emigrate.

Streicher's incitement to murder and extermination at the time when Jews in the East were being killed under the most horrible conditions clearly constitutes persecution on political and racial grounds in connection with War Crimes, as defined by the Charter, and constitutes a Crime against Humanity.

Conclusion

The Tribunal finds that Streicher is not guilty on Count One, but that he is guilty on Count Four.

FUNK

Funk is indicted under all four Counts. Funk, who had previously been a financial journalist, joined the Nazi Party in 1931, and shortly thereafter became one of Hitler's personal economic advisers. On 30 January 1933, he was made Press Chief in the Reich Government, and on 11 March 1933 became Under Secretary in the Ministry of Propaganda and shortly thereafter a leading figure in the various Nazi organizations which were used to control the press, films, music, and publishing houses. Funk took office as Minister of Economics and Plenipotentiary General for War Economy in early 1938, and as President of the Reichsbank in January 1939. He succeeded Schacht in all three of these positions. He was made a member of the Ministerial Council for the Defense of the Reich in August 1939, and a member of the Central Planning Board in September 1943.

Crimes against Peace

Funk became active in the economic field after the Nazi plans to wage aggressive war had been clearly defined. One of his representatives attended a conference on 14 October 1938, at which Göring announced a gigantic increase in armaments and instructed the Ministry of Economics to increase exports to obtain the necessary exchange. On 28 January 1939, one of Funk's subordinates sent a memorandum to the OKW on the use of prisoners of war to make up labor deficiencies which would arise in case of mobilization. On 30 May 1939, the Under Secretary of the Ministry of Economics attended a meeting at which detailed plans were made for the financing of the war.

On 25 August 1939, Funk wrote a letter to Hitler expressing his gratitude that he was able to participate in such world-shaking events; that his plans for the "financing of the war," for the control of wage and price conditions and for the strengthening of the Reichsbank had been completed; and that he had inconspicuously tranferred into gold all foreign exchange resources available to Germany. On 14 October 1939, after the war had begun, he made a speech in which he stated that the economic and financial departments of Germany working under the Four Year Plan had been engaged in the secret economic preparation for war for over a year.

Funk participated in the economic planning which preceded the attack on the U.S.S.R. His deputy held daily conferences with Rosenberg on the economic problems which would arise in the occupation of Soviet territory. Funk himself participated in planning for the printing of rouble notes in Germany prior to the attack to serve as occupation currency in the U.S.S.R. After the attack he made a speech in which he described plans he had made for the economic exploitation of the "vast territories of the Soviet Union" which were to be used as a source of raw material for Europe.

Funk was not one of the leading figures in originating the Nazi plans for aggressive war. His activity in the economic sphere was under the supervision of Göring as Plenipotentiary of the Four Year Plan. He did, however, participate in the economic preparation for certain of the aggressive wars, notably those against Poland and the Soviet Union, but his guilt can be adequately dealt with under Count Two of the Indictment.

War Crimes and Crimes against Humanity

In his capacity as Under Secretary in the Ministry of Propaganda and Vice-Chairman of the Reich Chamber of Culture. Funk had participated in the early Nazi program of economic discrimination against the Jews. On 12 November 1938, after the pogroms of November, he attended a meeting held under the chairmanship of Göring to discuss the solution of the Jewish problem and proposed a decree providing for the banning of Jews from all business activities, which Göring issued the same day under the authority of the Four Year Plan. Funk has testified that he was shocked at the outbreaks of 10 November, but on 15 November he made a speech describing these outbreaks as a "violent explosion of the disgust of the German people, because of a criminal Jewish attack against the German people," and saying that the elimination of the Jews from economic life followed logically their elimination from political life.

In 1942 Funk entered into an agreement with Himmler under which the Reichsbank was to receive certain gold and jewels and currency from the SS and instructed his subordinates, who were to work out the details, not to ask too many questions. As a result of this agreement the SS sent to the Reichsbank the personal belongings taken from the victims who had been exterminated in the concentration camps. The Reichsbank kept the coins and bank notes and sent the jewels, watches, and personal belongings to Berlin municipal pawn shops. The gold from the eyeglasses and gold teeth and fillings were stored in the Reichsbank vaults. Funk has protested that he did not know that the Reichsbank was receiving articles of this kind. The Tribunal is of the opinion that he either knew what was being received or was deliberately closing his eyes to what was being done.

As Minister of Economics and President of the Reichsbank, Funk participated in the economic exploitation of occupied territories. He was President of the Continental Oil Company which was charged with the exploitation of the oil resources of occupied territories in the East. He was responsible for the seizure of the gold reserves of the Czechoslovakian National Bank and for the liquidation of the Yugoslavian National Bank. On 6 June 1942, his deputy sent a letter to the OKW requesting that funds from the French occupation cost fund be made available for black market purchases. Funk's knowledge of German occupation policies is shown by his presence at the meeting of 8 August 1942, at which Göring addressed the various German occupation chiefs, told them of the products required from their territories, and added: "It makes no difference to me in this connection if you say that your people will starve."

In the fall of 1943, Funk was a member of the Central Planning Board which determined the total number of laborers needed for German industry and required Sauckel to produce them, usually by deportation from occupied territories. Funk did not appear to be particularly interested in this aspect of the forced labor program and usually sent a deputy to attend the meetings, often SS General Ohlendorf, the former chief of the SD inside of Germany and the former commander of Einsatzgruppe D. But Funk was aware that the board of which he was a member was demanding the importation of slave laborers and allocating them to the various industries under its control.

As President of the Reichsbank, Funk was also indirectly involved in the utilization of concentration camp labor. Under his direction the Reichsbank set up a revolving fund of 12,000,000 Reichsmarks to the credit of the SS for the construction of factories to use concentration camp laborers.

In spite of the fact that he occupied important official positions, Funk was never a dominant figure in the various programs in which he participated. This is a mitigating fact of which the Tribunal takes notice.

Conclusion

The Tribunal finds that Funk is not guilty on Count One but is guilty under Counts Two, Three, and Four.

Schacht

Schacht is indicted under Counts One and Two of the Indictment. Schacht served as Commissioner of Currency and President of the Reichsbank from 1923 to 1930; was reappointed President of the bank on 17 March 1933; Minister of Economics in August 1934; and Plenipotentiary General for War Economy in May 1935. He resigned from these two positions in November 1937 and was appointed Minister without Portfolio. He was reappointed as President of the Reichsbank for a one-year term on 16 March 1937, and for a four-year term on 9 March 1938, but was dismissed on 20 January 1939. He was dismissed as Minister without Portfolio on 22 January 1943.

Schacht was an active supporter of the Nazi Party before its accession to power on 30 January 1933 and supported the appointment of Hitler to the post of Chancellor. After that date he played an important role in the vigorous rearmament program which was adopted, using the facilities of the Reichsbank to the fullest extent in the German rearmament effort. The Reichsbank, in its traditional capacity as financial agent for the German Government, floated long-term Government loans, the proceeds of which were used for rearmament. He devised a system under which five-year notes, known as "mefo" bills, guaranteed by the Reichsbank and backed, in effect, by nothing more than its position as a bank of issue, were used to obtain large sums for rearmament from the short-term money market. As Minister of Economics and as Plenipotentiary General for the War Economy he was active in organizing the German economy for war. He made detailed plans for industrial mobilization and the co-ordination of the Army with industry in the event of war. He was particularly concerned with shortages of raw materials and started a scheme of stockpiling, and a system of exchange control designed to prevent Germany's weak foreign exchange position from hindering the acquisition abroad of raw materials needed for rearmament. On 3 May 1935, he sent a memorandum to Hitler stating that "the accomplishment of the armament program with speed and in quantity is the problem of German politics, that everything else therefore should be subordinated to this purpose."

Schacht, by April 1936, began to lose his influence as the central figure in the German rearmament effort when Göring was appointed co-ordinator for raw materials and foreign exchange. Göring advocated a greatly expanded program for the production of synthetic raw materials, which was opposed by Schacht on the ground that the resulting financial strain might involve inflation. The influence of Schacht suffered further when on 16 October 1936, Göring was appointed Plenipotentiary for the Four Year Plan with the task of putting "the entire economy in a state of readiness for war within 4 years." Schacht had opposed the announcement of this plan and the appointment of Göring to head it, and it is clear that Hitler's action represented a decision that Schacht's economic policies were too conservative for the drastic rearmament policy which Hitler wanted to put into effect.

After Göring's appointment, Schacht and Göring promptly became embroiled in a series of disputes. Although there was an element of personal controversy running through these disputes, Schacht disagreed with Göring on certain basic policy issues. Schacht, on financial grounds, advocated a retrenchment in the rearmament program, opposed as uneconomical much of the proposed expansion of production facilities, particularly for synthetics, urged a drastic tightening on Government credit, and a cautious policy in dealing with Germany's foreign exchange reserves. As a result of this dispute and of a bitter argument in which Hitler accused Schacht of upsetting his plans by his financial methods. Schacht went on leave of absence from the Ministry of Economics on 5 September 1937, and resigned as Minister of Economics and as Plenipotentiary General for War Economy on 16 November 1937.

As President of the Reichsbank, Schacht was still involved in disputes. Throughout 1938, the Reichsbank continued to function as the financial agent for the German Government in floating long-term loans to finance armaments. But on 31 March 1938, Schacht discontinued the practice of floating short-term notes guaranteed by the Reichsbank for armament expenditures. At the end of 1938, in an attempt to regain control of fiscal policy through the Reichsbank, Schacht refused an urgent request of the Reichsminister of Finance for a special credit to pay the salaries of civil servants which were not covered by existing funds. On 2 January 1939, Schacht held a conference with Hitler at which he urged him to reduce expenditures for armaments. On 7 January 1939, Schacht submitted to Hitler a report signed by the Directors of the Reichsbank which urged a drastic curtailment of armament expenditures and a balanced budget as the only method of preventing inflation. On 19 January, Hitler dismissed Schacht as President of the Reichsbank. On 22 January 1943, Hitler dismissed Schacht as Reich Minister without Portfolio because of his "whole attitude during the present fateful fight of the German nation." On 23 July 1944, Schacht was arrested by the Gestapo and confined in a concentration camp until the end of the war.

It is clear that Schacht was a central figure in Germany's rearmament program, and the steps which he took, particularly in the early days of the Nazi regime, were responsible for Nazi Germany's rapid rise as a military power. But rearmament of itself is not criminal under the Charter. To be a Crime against Peace under Article 6 of the Charter it must be shown that Schacht carried out this rearmament as part of the Nazi plans to wage aggressive wars.

Schacht has contended that he participated in the rearmament program only because he wanted to build up a strong and independent Germany which would carry out a foreign policy which would command respect on an equal basis with other European countries; that when he discovered that the Nazis were rearming for aggressive purposes he attempted to slow down the speed of rearmament; and that after the dismissal of Von Fritsch and Von Blomberg he participated in plans to get rid of Hitler, first by deposing him and later by assassination.

Schacht, as early as 1936, began to advocate a limitation of the rearmament program for financial reasons. Had the policies advocated by him been put into effect, Germany would not have been prepared for a general European war. Insistence on his policies led to his eventual dismissal from all positions of economic significance in Germany. On the other hand, Schacht, with his intimate knowledge of German finance, was in a peculiarly good position to understand the true significance of Hitler's frantic rearmament and to realize that the economic policy adopted was consistent only with war as its object.

Moreover Schacht continued to participate in German economic life and even, in a minor way, in some of the early Nazi aggressions. Prior to the occupation of Austria he set a rate of exchange between the mark and the schilling. After the occupation of Austria he arranged for the incorporation of the Austrian National Bank into the Reichsbank and made a violently pro-Nazi speech in which he stated that the Reichsbank would always be Nazi as long as he was connected with it, praised Hitler, defended the occupation of Austria, scoffed at objections to the way it was carried out, and ended with "to our

Führer, a triple 'Sieg Heil'." He has not contended that this speech did not represent his state of mind at the time. After the occupation of the Sudetenland, he arranged for currency conversion and for the incorporation into the Reichsbank of local Czech banks of issue. On 29 November 1938, he made a speech in which he pointed with pride to his economic policy which had created the high degree of German armament, and added that this armament had made Germany's foreign policy possible.

Schacht was not involved in the planning of any of the specific wars of aggression charged in Count Two. His participation in the occupation of Austria and the Sudetenland (neither of which is charged as aggressive war) was on such a limited basis that it does not amount to participation in the common plan charged in Count One. He was clearly not one of the inner circle around Hitler which was most closely involved with this common plan. He was regarded by this group with undisguised hostility. The testimony of Speer shows that Schacht's arrest on 23 July 1944 was based as much on Hitler's enmity towards Schacht growing out of his attitude before the war as it was on suspicion of his complicity in the bomb plot. The case against Schacht therefore depends on the inference that Schacht did in fact know of the Nazi aggressive plans.

On this all-important question evidence has been given for the Prosecution, and a considerable volume of evidence for the Defense. The Tribunal has considered the whole of this evidence with great care, and comes to the conclusion that this necessary inference has not been established beyond a reasonable doubt.

Conclusion

The Tribunal finds that Schacht is not guilty on this Indictment, and directs that he shall be discharged by the Marshal, when the Tribunal presently adjourns.

DÖNITZ

Dönitz is indicted on Counts One, Two, and Three. In 1935 he took command of the first U-Boat flotilla commissioned since 1918, became in 1936 commander of the submarine arm, was made Vice-Admiral in 1940, Admiral in 1942, and on 30 January 1943 Commander-in-Chief of the German Navy. On 1 May 1945 he became the Head of State, succeeding Hitler.

Crimes against Peace

Although Dönitz built and trained the German U-Boat arm, the evidence does not show he was privy to the conspiracy to wage aggressive wars or that he prepared and initiated such wars. He was a line officer performing strictly tactical duties. He was not present at the important conferences when plans for aggressive wars were announced, and there is no evidence he was informed about the decisions reached there. Dönitz did, however, wage aggressive war within the meaning of that word as used by the Charter. Submarine warfare which began immediately upon the outbreak of war, was fully co-ordinated with the other branches of the Wehrmacht. It is clear that his U-boats, few in number at the time, were fully prepared to wage war.

It is true that until his appointment in January 1943 as commander-in-chief he was not an "Oberbefehlshaber." But this statement underestimates the importance of Dönitz' position. He was no mere army or division commander. The U-Boat arm was the principal part of the German fleet and Dönitz was its leader. The high seas fleet made a few minor, if spectacular, raids during the early years of the war, but the real damage to the enemy was done almost exclusively by his submarines, as the millions of tons of allied and neutral shipping sunk will testify. Dönitz was solely in charge of this warfare. The Naval War Command reserved for itself only the decision as to the number of submarines in each area. In the invasion of Norway, for example, he made recommendations in October 1939 as to submarine bases, which he claims were no more than a staff study, and in March 1940 he made out the operational orders for the supporting U-boats, as discussed elsewhere in this Judgment.

That his importance to the German war effort was so regarded is eloquently proved by Raeder's recommendation of Dönitz as his successor and his appointment by Hitler on 30 January 1943 as Commander-in-Chief of the Navy. Hitler too knew that submarine warfare was the essential part of Germany's naval warfare.

From January 1943, Dönitz was consulted almost continuously by Hitler. The evidence was that they conferred on naval problems about 120 times during the course of the war.

As late as April 1945 when he admits he knew the struggle was hopeless, Dönitz as its commander-in-chief urged the Navy to continue its fight. On 1 May 1945 he became the Head of State and as such ordered the Wehrmacht to continue its war in the East, until capitulation on 9 May 1945. Dönitz explained that his reason for these orders was to insure that the German civilian population might be evacuated and the Army might make an orderly retreat from the East.

In the view of the Tribunal, the evidence shows that Dönitz was active in waging aggressive war.

War Crimes

Dönitz is charged with waging unrestricted submarine warfare contrary to the Naval Protocol of 1936, to which Germany acceded, and which reaffirmed the rules of submarine warfare laid down in the London Naval Agreement of 1930.

The Prosecution has submitted that on 3 September 1939 the German

U-Boat arm began to wage unrestricted submarine warfare upon all merchant ships, whether enemy or neutral, cynically disregarding the Protocol, and that a calculated effort was made throughout the war to disguise this practice by making hypocritical references to international law and supposed violations by the Allies.

Dönitz insists that at all times the Navy remained within the confines of international law and of the Protocol. He testified that when the war began, the guide to submarine warfare was the German Prize Ordinance, taken almost literally from the Protocol; that pursuant to the German view, he ordered submarines to attack all merchant ships in convoy and all that refused to stop or used their radio upon sighting a submarine. When his reports indicated that British merchant ships were being used to give information by wireless, were being armed and were attacking submarines on sight, he ordered his submarines on 17 October 1939 to attack all enemy merchant ships without warning on the ground that resistance was to be expected. Orders already had been issued on 21 September 1939 to attack all ships, including neutrals, sailing at night without lights in the English Channel.

On 24 November 1939, the German Government issued a warning to neutral shipping that, owing to the frequent engagements taking place in the waters around the British Isles and the French coast between U-Boats and Allied merchant ships which were armed and had instructions to use those arms as well as to ram U-Boats, the safety of neutral ships in those waters could no longer be taken for granted. On 1 January 1940, the German U-Boat command, acting on the instructions of Hitler, ordered U-Boats to attack all Greek merchant ships in the zone surrounding the British Isles which was banned by the United States to its own ships and also merchant ships of every nationality in the limited area of the Bristol Channel. Five days later a further order was given to U-Boats "to make immediately unrestricted use of weapons against all ships" in an area of the North Sea, the limits of which were defined. Finally on 18 January 1940, U-Boats were authorized to sink, without warning, all ships "in those waters near the enemy coast in which the use of mines can be pretended." Exceptions were to be made in the cases of United States, Italian, Japanese, and Soviet ships.

Shortly after the outbreak of war the British Admiralty, in accordance with its *Handbook of Instructions* of 1938 to the merchant navy, armed its merchant vessels, in many cases convoyed them with armed escort, gave orders to send position reports upon sighting submarines, thus integrating merchant vessels into the warning network of naval intelligence. On 1 October 1939, the British Admiralty announced British merchant ships had been ordered to ram U-Boats if possible.

In the actual circumstances of this case, the Tribunal is not prepared to hold Dönitz guilty for his conduct of submarine warfare against British armed merchant ships.

However, the proclamation of operational zones and the sinking of neutral merchant vessels which enter those zones presents a different question. This practice was employed in the war of 1914–1918 by Germany and adopted in retaliation by Great Britain. The Washington Conference of 1922, the London Naval Agreement of 1930 and the Protocol of 1936 were entered into with full knowledge that such zones had been employed in that war. Yet the Protocol made no exception for operational zones. The order of Dönitz to sink neutral ships without warning when found within these zones was, in the opinion of the Tribunal, therefore a violation of the Protocol.

It is also asserted that the German U-Boat arm not only did not carry out the warning and rescue provisions of the Protocol but that Dönitz deliberately ordered the killing of survivors of shipwrecked vessels, whether enemy or neutral. The Prosecution has introduced much evidence surrounding two orders of Dönitz, War Order Number 154, issued in 1939, and the so-called *Laconia* order of 1942. The Defense argues that these orders and the evidence supporting them do not show such a policy and introduced much evidence to the contrary. The Tribunal is of the opinion that the evidence does not establish with the certainty required that Dönitz deliberately ordered the killing of shipwrecked survivors. The orders were undoubtedly ambiguous, and deserve the strongest censure.

The evidence further shows that the rescue provisions were not carried out and that the defendant ordered that they should not be carried out. The argument of the Defense is that the security of the submarine is, as the first rule of the sea, paramount to rescue and that the development of aircraft made rescue impossible. This may be so, but the Protocol is explicit. If the commander cannot rescue, then under its terms he cannot sink a merchant vessel and should allow it to pass unharmed before his periscope. These orders, then, prove Dönitz is guilty of a violation of the Protocol.

In view of all of the facts proved, and in particular of an order of the British Admiralty announced on 8 May 1940, according to which all vessels should be sunk at night in the Skagerrak, and the answer to interrogatories by Admiral Nimitz that unrestricted submarine warfare was carried on in the Pacific Ocean by the United States from the first day that nation entered the war, the sentence of Dönitz is not assessed on the ground of his breaches of the international law of submarine warfare.

Dönitz was also charged with responsibility for Hitler's Commando Order of 18 October 1942. Dönitz admitted he received and knew of the order when he was Flag Officer of U-Boats, but disclaimed responsibility. He points out that the order by its express terms excluded men captured in naval warfare, that the Navy had no territorial commands on land, and that submarine commanders would never encounter Commandos.

In one instance, when he was Commander-in-Chief of the Navy, in 1943, the members of the crew of an Allied motor torpedo boat were captured by German naval forces. They were interrogated for intelligence purposes on behalf of the local admiral, and then turned over by his order to the SD and shot. Dönitz said that if they were captured by the Navy their execution was a violation of the Commando Order, that the execution was not announced in the Wehrmacht communiqué, and that he was never informed of the incident. He pointed out that the admiral in question was not in his chain of command, but was subordinate to the Army general in command of the Norway occupation. But Dönitz permitted the order to remain in full force when he became commander-in-chief, and to that extent he is responsible.

Dönitz, in a conference of 11 December 1944, said "12,000 concentration camp prisoners will be employed in the shipyards as additional labor."

At this time he had no jurisdiction over shipyard construction and claims that this was merely a suggestion at the meeting that the responsible officials do something about producing ships, that he took no steps to get these workers, since it was not a matter for his jurisdiction, and that he does not know whether they ever were procured. He admits he knew of concentration camps. A man in his position must necessarily have known that citizens of occupied countries in large numbers were confined in the concentration camps.

In 1945 Hitler requested the opinion of Jodl and Dönitz whether the Geneva Convention should be denounced. The notes of the meeting between the two military leaders on 20 February 1945 show that Dönitz expressed his view that the disadvantages of such an action outweighed the advantages. The summary of Dönitz' attitude shown in the notes taken by an officer, included the following sentence:

> It would be better to carry out the measures considered necessary without warning; and at all costs to save face with the outer world.

The Prosecution insisted that "the measures" referred to meant that the Convention should not be denounced, but should be broken at will. The Defense explanation is that Hitler wanted to break the Convention for two reasons: to take away from German troops the protection of the Convention, thus preventing them from continuing to surrender in large groups to the British and Americans; and also to permit reprisals against Allied prisoners of war because of Allied bombing raids. Dönitz claims that what he meant by "measures" were disciplinary measures against German troops to prevent them from surrendering and had no reference to measures against the Allies; that this was merely a suggestion, and that in any event no such measures were ever taken, either against Allies or Germans. The Tribunal, however, does not believe this explanation. The Geneva Convention was not, however, denounced by Germany. The Defense has introduced several affidavits to prove that British naval prisoners of war in camps under Dönitz' jurisdiction were treated strictly according to the Convention, and the Tribunal takes this fact into consideration and regards it as a mitigating circumstance.

The Tribunal finds Dönitz is not guilty on Count One of the Indictment, and is guilty on Counts Two and Three.

RAEDER

Raeder is indicted on Counts One, Two, and Three. In 1928 he became Chief of Naval Command and in 1935 Oberbefehlshaber der Kriegsmarine (OKM); in 1939 Hitler made him Grossadmiral. He was a member of the Reich Defense Council. On 30 January 1943, Dönitz replaced him at his own request, and he became Admiral Inspector of the Navy, a nominal title.

Crimes against Peace

In the 15 years he commanded it, Raeder built and directed the German Navy; he accepts full responsibility until retirement in 1943. He admits the Navy violated the Versailles Treaty, insisting it was "a matter of honor for every man" to do so, and alleges that the violations were for the most part minor, and Germany built less than her allowable strength. These violations, as well as those of the Anglo-German Naval Agreement of 1935, have already been discussed elsewhere in this Judgment.

Raeder received the directive of 24 June 1937 from Von Blomberg requiring special preparations for war against Austria. He was one of the five leaders present at the Hossbach conference of 5 November 1937. He claims Hitler merely wished by this conference to spur the Army to faster rearmament, insists he believed the questions of Austria and Czechoslovakia would be settled peacefully, as they were, and points to the new naval treaty with England which had just been signed. He received no orders to speed construction of U-Boats, indicating that Hitler was not planning war.

Raeder received directives on "Fall Grün" and the directives on "Fall Weiss" beginning with that of 3 April 1939; the latter directed the Navy to support the Army by intervention from the sea. He was also one of the few chief leaders present at the meeting of 23 May 1939. He attended the Obersalzberg briefing of 22 August 1939.

The conception of the invasion of Norway first arose in the mind of Raeder and not that of Hitler. Despite Hitler's desire, as shown by his directive of October 1939, to keep Scandinavia neutral, the Navy examined the advantages of naval bases there as early as October. Admiral Carls originally suggested to Raeder the desirable aspects of bases in Norway. A questionnaire, dated 3 October 1939, which sought comments on the desirability of such bases, was circulated within SKL. On 10 October Raeder discussed the matter with Hitler; his war diary entry for that day says Hitler intended "to give the matter consideration." A few months later Hitler talked to Raeder, Quisling, Keitel, and Jodl; OKW began its planning and the Naval War Staff worked with OKW staff officers. Raeder received Keitel's directive for Norway on 27 January 1940 and the subsequent directive of 1 March, signed by Hitler.

Raeder defends his actions on the ground it was a move to forestall the British. It is not necessary again to discuss this defense, which has heretofore been treated in some detail, concluding that Germany's invasion of Norway and Denmark was aggressive war. In a letter to the Navy, Raeder said: "The operations of the Navy in the occupation of Norway will for all time remain the great contribution of the Navy to this war."

Raeder received the directives, including the innumerable postponements, for the attack in the West. In a meeting of 18 March 1941 with Hitler he urged the occupation of all Greece. He claims this was only after the British had landed and Hitler had ordered the attack, and points out the Navy had no interest in Greece. He received Hitler's directive on Yugoslavia.

Raeder endeavored to dissuade Hitler from embarking upon the invasion of the U.S.S.R. In September 1940 he urged on Hitler an aggressive Mediterrenean policy as an alternative to an attack on Russia. On 14 November 1940 he urged the war against England "as our main enemy" and that submarine and naval air force construction be continued. He voiced "serious objections against the Russian campaign before the defeat of England," according to notes of the German Naval War Staff. He claims his objections were based on the violation of the non-aggression pact as well as strategy. But once the decision had been made, he gave permission 6 days before the invasion of the Soviet Union to attack Russian submarines in the Baltic Sea within a specified warning area and defends this action because these submarines were "snooping" on German activities.

It is clear from this evidence that Raeder participated in the planning and waging of aggressive war.

War Crimes

Raeder is charged with war crimes on the high seas. The *Athenia,* an unarmed British passenger liner, was sunk on 3 September 1939, while outward bound to America. The Germans 2 months later charged that Mr. Churchill deliberately sank the *Athenia* to encourage American hostility to Germany. In fact, it was sunk by the German U-Boat *U-30.* Raeder claims that an inexperienced U-Boat commander sank it in mistake for an armed merchant cruiser, that this was not known until the *U-30* returned several weeks after the German denial and that Hitler then directed the Navy and Foreign Office to continue denying it. Raeder denied knowledge of the propaganda campaign attacking Mr. Churchill.

The most serious charge against Raeder is that he carried out unrestricted submarine warfare, including sinking of unarmed merchant ships, of neutrals, non-rescue and machine-gunning of survivors, contrary to the London Protocol of 1936. The Tribunal makes the same finding on Raeder on this charge as it did as to Dönitz, which has already been announced, up until 30 January 1943 when Raeder retired.

The Commando Order of 18 October 1942 which expressly did not apply to naval warfare was transmitted by the Naval War Staff to the lower naval commanders with the direction it should be distributed orally by flotilla leaders and section commanders to their subordinates. Two Commandos were put to death by the Navy, and not by the SD, at Bordeaux on 10 December 1942. The comment of the Naval War Staff was that this was "in accordance with the Führer's special order, but is nevertheless something new in international law, since the soldiers were in uniform." Raeder admits he passed the order down through the chain of command and he did not object to Hitler.

Conclusion

The Tribunal finds that Raeder is guilty on Counts One, Two and Three.

VON SCHIRACH

Von Schirach is indicted under Counts One and Four. He joined the Nazi Party and the SA in 1925. In 1929 he became the Leader of the National Socialist Students' Union. In 1931 he was made Reich Youth Leader of the Nazi Party with control over all Nazi youth organizations including the Hitler Jugend. In 1933, after the Nazis had obtained control of the Government, Von Schirach was made Leader of Youth in the German Reich, originally a position within the Ministry of the Interior, but, after 1 December 1936, an office in the Reich Cabinet. In 1940, Von Schirach resigned as head of the Hitler Jugend and Leader of Youth in the German Reich, but retained his position as Reichsleiter with control over Youth Education. In 1940 he was appointed Gauleiter of Vienna, Reich Governor of Vienna, and Reich Defense Commissioner for that territory.

Crimes against Peace

After the Nazis had come to power Von Schirach, utilizing both physical violence and official pressure, either drove out of existence or took over all youth groups which competed with the Hitler Jugend. A Hitler decree of 1 December 1936 incorporated all German youth within the Hitler Jugend. By the time formal conscription was introduced in 1940, 97 percent of those eligible were already members.

Von Schirach used the Hitler Jugend to educate German youth "in the spirit of National Socialism" and subjected them to an intensive program of Nazi propaganda. He established the Hitler Jugend as a source of replacements for the Nazi Party formations. In October 1938 he entered into an arrangement with Himmler under which members of the Hitler Jugend who met SS standards would be considered as the primary source of replacements for the SS.

Von Schirach also used the Hitler Jugend for premilitary training. Special units were set up whose primary purpose was training specialists for the various branches of the service. On 11 August 1939, he entered into an agreement with Keitel under which the Hitler Jugend agreed to carry out its premilitary activities under standards laid down by the Wehrmacht, and the Wehrmacht agreed to train 30,000 Hitler Jugend instructors each year. The Hitler Jugend placed particular emphasis on the military spirit, and its training program stressed the importance of return of the colonies, the necessity for Lebensraum, and the noble destiny of German youth to die for Hitler.

Despite the warlike nature of the activities of the Hitler Jugend, however, it does not appear that Von Schirach was involved in the development of Hitler's plan for territorial expansion by means of aggressive war, or that he participated in the planning or preparation of any of the wars of aggression.

Crimes against Humanity

In July 1940, Von Schirach was appointed Gauleiter of Vienna. At the same time he was appointed Reich Governor for Vienna and Reich Defense Commissioner, originally for Military District 17, including the Gaue of Vienna, Upper Danube, and Lower Danube and, after 17 November 1942, for the Gau of Vienna alone. As Reich Defense Commissioner, he had control of the civilian war economy. As Reich Governor he was head of the municipal administration of the City of Vienna and, under the supervision of the Minister of the Interior, was in charge of the governmental administration of the Reich in Vienna.

Von Schirach is not charged with the commission of War Crimes in Vienna, only with the commission of Crimes against Humanity. As has already been seen, Austria was occupied pursuant to a common plan of aggression. Its occupation is, therefore, a "crime within the jurisdiction of the Tribunal," as that term is used in Article 6(c) of the Charter. As a result, "murder, extermination, enslavement, deportation, and other inhumane acts" and "persecutions on political, racial, or religious grounds" in connection with this occupation constitute a Crime against Humanity under that Article.

As Gauleiter of Vienna, Von Schirach came under the Sauckel decree dated 6 April 1942, making the Gauleiter Sauckel's plenipotentiaries for manpower with authority to supervise the utilization and treatment of manpower within their Gaue. Sauckel's directives provided that the forced laborers were to be fed, sheltered, and treated so as to exploit them to the highest possible degree at the lowest possible expense.

When Von Schirach became Gauleiter of Vienna the deportation of the Jews had already been begun, and only 60,000 out of Vienna's original 190,000 Jews remained. On 2 October 1940, he attended a conference at

Hitler's office and told Frank that he had 50,000 Jews in Vienna which the Government General would have to take over from him. On 3 December 1940, Von Schirach received a letter from Lammers stating that after the receipt of the reports made by Von Schirach, Hitler had decided to deport the 60,000 Jews still remaining in Vienna to the Government General because of the housing shortage in Vienna. The deportation of the Jews from Vienna was then begun and continued until the early fall of 1942. On 15 September 1942, Von Schirach made a speech in which he defended his action in having driven "tens of thousands upon tens of thousands of Jews into the ghetto of the East" as "contributing to European culture."

While the Jews were being deported from Vienna, reports, addressed to him in his official capacity, were received in Von Schirach's office from the office of the Chief of the Security Police and SD, which contained a description of the activities of Einsatzgruppen in exterminating Jews. Many of these reports were initialed by one of Von Schirach's principal deputies. On 30 June 1944, Von Schirach's office also received a letter from Kaltenbrunner informing him that a shipment of 12,000 Jews was on its way to Vienna for essential war work and that all those who were incapable of work would have to be kept in readiness for "special action."

The Tribunal finds that Von Schirach, while he did not originate the policy of deporting Jews from Vienna, participated in this deportation after he had become Gauleiter of Vienna. He knew that the best the Jews could hope for was a miserable existence in the ghettos of the East. Bulletins describing the Jewish extermination were in his office.

While Gauleiter of Vienna, Von Schirach continued to function as Reichsleiter for Youth Education and in this capacity he was informed of the Hitler Jugend's participation in the plan put into effect in the fall of 1944 under which 50,000 young people between the ages of 10 and 20 were evacuated into Germany from areas recaptured by the Soviet forces and used as apprentices in German industry and as auxiliaries in units of the German Armed Forces. In the summer of 1942, Von Schirach telegraphed Bormann urging that a bombing attack on an English cultural town be carried out in retaliation for the assassination of Heydrich which, he claimed, had been planned by the British.

Conclusion

The Tribunal finds that Von Schirach is not guilty on Count One. He is guilty under Count Four.

Sauckel

Sauckel is indicted under all four Counts. Sauckel joined the Nazi Party in 1923, and became Gauleiter of Thuringia in 1927. He was a member of the Thuringian legislature from 1927 to 1933, was appointed Reichsstatthalter for

Thuringia in 1932, and Thuringian Minister of the Interior and head of the Thuringian State Ministry in May 1933. He became a member of the Reichstag in 1933. He held the formal rank of Obergruppenführer in both the SA and the SS.

Crimes against Peace

The evidence has not satisfied the Tribunal that Sauckel was sufficiently connected with the common plan to wage aggressive war or sufficiently involved in the planning or waging of the aggressive wars to allow the Tribunal to convict him on Counts One or Two.

War Crimes and Crimes against Humanity

On 21 March 1942, Hitler appointed Sauckel Plenipotentiary General for the Utilization of Labor, with authority to put under uniform control "the utilization of all available manpower, including that of workers recruited abroad and of prisoners of war." Sauckel was instructed to operate within the fabric of the Four Year Plan, and on 27 March 1942, Göring issued a decree as Delegate for the Four Year Plan transferring his manpower sections to Sauckel. On 30 September 1942, Hitler gave Sauckel authority to appoint commissioners in the various occupied territories and "to take all necessary measures for the enforcement" of the decree of 21 March 1942.

Under the authority which he obtained by these decrees, Sauckel set up a program for the mobilization of the labor resources available to the Reich. One of the important parts of this mobilization was the systematic exploitation, by force, of the labor resources of the occupied territories. Shortly after Sauckel had taken office, he had the governing authorities in the various occupied territories issue decrees establishing compulsory labor service in Germany. Under the authority of these decrees Sauckel's commissioners, backed up by the police authorities of the occupied territories, obtained and sent to Germany the laborers which were necessary to fill the quotas given them by Sauckel. He described so-called "voluntary" recruiting by "a whole batch of male and female agents just as was done in the olden times for shanghaiing." That real voluntary recruiting was the exception rather than the rule is shown by Sauckel's statement on 1 March 1944, that "out of five million foreign workers who arrived in Germany not even 200,000 came voluntarily." Although he now claims that the statement is not true, the circumstances under which it was made, as well as the evidence presented before the Tribunal, leave no doubt that it was substantially accurate.

The manner in which the unfortunate slave laborers were collected and transported to Germany, and what happened to them after they arrived, has already been described. Sauckel argues that he is not responsible for these excesses in the administration of the program. He says that the total number of workers to be obtained was set by the demands from agriculture and from industry; that obtaining the workers was the responsibility of the occupation authorities, transporting them to Germany that of the German railways, and taking care of them in Germany that of the Ministries of Labor and Agriculture, the German Labor Front, and the various industries involved. He testifies that insofar as he had any authority he was constantly urging humane treatment.

There is no doubt, however, that Sauckel had over-all responsibility for the slave labor program. At the time of the events in question he did not fail to assert control over the fields which he now claims were the sole responsibility of others. His regulations provided that his commissioners should have authority for obtaining labor, and he was constantly in the field supervising the steps which were being taken. He was aware of ruthless methods being taken to obtain laborers and vigorously supported them on the ground that they were necessary to fill the quotas.

Sauckel's regulations also provided that he had responsibility for transporting the laborers to Germany, allocating them to employers and taking care of them, and that the other agencies involved in these processes were subordinate to him. He was informed of the bad conditions which existed. It does not appear that he advocated brutality for its own sake, or was an advocate of any program such as Himmler's plan for extermination through work. His attitude was thus expressed in a regulation:

> All the men must be fed, sheltered, and treated in such a way as to exploit them to the highest possible extent at the lowest conceivable degree of expenditure.

The evidence shows that Sauckel was in charge of a program which involved deportation for slave labor of more than 5,000,000 human beings, many of them under terrible conditions of cruelty and suffering.

Conclusion

The Tribunal finds that Sauckel is not guilty on Counts One and Two. He is guilty under Counts Three and Four.

Jodl

Jodl is indicted on all four Counts. From 1935 to 1938 he was Chief of the National Defense Section in the High Command. After a year in command of troops, in August 1939 he returned to become Chief of the Operations Staff of the High Command of the Armed Forces. Although his immediate superior was Defendant Keitel, he reported directly to Hitler on operational matters. In the strict military sense, Jodl was the actual planner of the war and responsible in large measure for the strategy and conduct of operations.

Jodl defends himself on the ground he was a soldier sworn to obedience, and not a politician; and that his staff and planning work left him no time for other matters. He said that when he signed or initialed orders, memoranda, and letters, he did so for Hitler and often in the absence of Keitel. Though he claims that as a soldier he had to obey Hitler, he says that he often tried to obstruct certain measures by delay, which occasionally proved successful as when he resisted Hitler's demand that a directive be issued to lynch Allied "terror fliers."

Crimes against Peace

Entries in Jodl's diary of 13 and 14 February 1938 show Hitler instructed both him and Keitel to keep up military pressure against Austria, begun at the Schuschnigg conference, by simulating military measures, and that these achieved their purpose. When Hitler decided "not to tolerate" Schuschnigg's plebiscite, Jodl brought to the conference the "old draft," the existing staff plan. His diary for 10 March shows Hitler then ordered the preparation of "Case Otto," and the directive was initialed by Jodl. Jodl issued supplementary instructions on 11 March, and initialed Hitler's order for the invasion on the same date.

In planning the attack on Czechoslovakia, Jodl was very active, according to the Schmundt notes. He initialed Items 14, 17, 24, 36, and 37 in the notes. Jodl admits he agreed with OKH that the "incident" to provide German intervention must occur at the latest by 1400 hours on X-1 Day, the day before the attack, and said it must occur at a fixed time in good flying weather. Jodl conferred with the propaganda experts on "imminent common tasks" such as German violations of international law, exploitation of them by the enemy, and refutations by the Germans, which "task" Jodl considered "particularly important."

After Munich, Jodl wrote:

> Czechoslovakia as a power is out. . . . The genius of the Führer and his determination not to shun even a world war have again won the victory without the use of force. The hope remains that the incredulous, the weak, and the doubtful people have been converted and will remain that way.

Shortly after the Sudeten occupation, Jodl went to a post command and did not become Chief of the Operations Staff in OKW until the end of August 1939.

Jodl discussed the Norway invasion with Hitler, Keitel, and Raeder on 12 December 1939; his diary is replete with later entries on his activities in preparing this attack. Jodl explains his comment that Hitler was still looking for an "excuse" to move meant that he was waiting for reliable intelligence on the British plans, and defends the invasion as a necessary move to forestall them. His testimony shows that from October 1939 Hitler planned to attack the West through Belgium, but was doubtful about invading Holland until the middle of November. On 8 February 1940, Jodl, his deputy Warlimont, and Jeschonnek, the air forces planner, discussed among themselves the "new idea" of attacking Norway, Denmark, and Holland, but guaranteeing the neutrality of Belgium. Many of the 17 orders postponing the attack in the West for various reasons, including weather conditions, until May 1940, were signed by Jodl.

He was active in the planning against Greece and Yugoslavia. The Hitler order of 11 January 1941 to intervene in Albania was initialed by Jodl. On 20 January, 4 months before the attack, Hitler told a conference of German and Italian generals in Jodl's presence that German troops concentrations in Romania were to be used against Greece. Jodl was present on 18 March when Hitler told Raeder all Greece must be occupied before any settlement could be reached. On 27 March, when Hitler told the German High Command that the destruction of Yugoslavia should be accomplished with "unmerciful harshness," and the decision was taken to bomb Belgrade without a declaration of war, Jodl was also there.

Jodl testified that Hitler feared an attack by Russia and so attacked first. This preparation began almost a year before the invasion. Jodl told Warlimont as early as 29 July 1940 to prepare the plans since Hitler had decided to attack; and Hitler later told Warlimont he had planned to attack in August 1940 but postponed it for military reasons. He initialed Hitler's directive on 12 November 1940 that preparations verbally ordered should be continued and also initialed "Case Barbarossa" on 18 December. On 3 February 1941, Hitler, Jodl, and Keitel discussed the invasion, and he was present on 14 June when final reports of "Case Barbarossa" were made.

War Crimes and Crimes against Humanity

On 18 October 1942 Hitler issued the Commando Order, and a day later a supplementary explanation to commanding officers only. The covering memorandum was signed by Jodl. Early drafts of the order were made by Jodl's staff, with his knowledge. Jodl testified he was strongly opposed on moral and legal grounds but could not refuse to pass it on. He insists he tried to mitigate its harshness in practice by not informing Hitler when it was not carried out. He initialed the OKW memorandum of 25 June 1944 reaffirming the order after the Normandy landings.

A plan to eliminate Soviet commissars was in the directive for "Case Barbarossa." The decision whether they should be killed without trial was to be made by an officer. A draft contains Jodl's handwriting suggesting this should be handled as retaliation, and he testified this was his attempt to get around it.

When in 1945 Hitler considered denouncing the Geneva Convention, Jodl argued the disadvantages outweighed the advantages. On 21 February he told Hitler adherence to the Convention would not interfere with the conduct of the war, giving as an example the sinking of a British hospital ship as a reprisal and calling it a mistake. He said he did so because it was the only attitude Hitler would consider, that moral or legal arguments had no effect, and argues he thus prevented Hitler from denouncing the Convention.

There is little evidence that Jodl was actively connected with the slave labor program, and he must have concentrated on his strategic planning function. But in his speech of 7 November 1943 to the Gauleiter he said it was necessary to act "with remorseless vigor and resolution" in Denmark, France, and the Low Countries to compel work on the Atlantic Wall.

By teletype of 28 October 1944, Jodl ordered the evacuation of all persons in northern Norway and the burning of their houses so they could not help the Russians. Jodl says he was against this, but Hitler ordered it and it was not fully carried out. A document of the Norwegian Government says such an evacuation did take place in northern Norway and 30,000 houses were damaged. On 7 October 1941, Jodl signed an order that Hitler would not accept an offer of surrender of Leningrad or Moscow, but on the contrary he insisted that they be completely destroyed. He says this was done because the Germans were afraid those cities would be mined by the Russians as was Kiev. No surrender was ever offered.

His defense, in brief, is the doctrine of "superior orders," prohibited by Article 8 of the Charter as a defense. There is nothing in mitigation. Participation in such crimes as these has never been required of any soldier and he cannot now shield himself behind a mythical requirement of soldierly obedience at all costs as his excuse for commission of these crimes.

Conclusion

The Tribunal finds that Jodl is guilty on all four Counts.

Von Papen

Von Papen is indicted under Counts One and Two. He was appointed Chancellor of the Reich on 1 June 1932, and was succeeded by Von Schleicher on 2 December 1932. He was made Vice Chancellor in the Hitler Cabinet on 30 January 1933, and on 13 November 1933, Plenipotentiary for the Saar. On 26 July 1934, he was appointed Minister to Vienna, and was recalled on 4 February 1938. On 29 April 1939, he was appointed Ambassador to Turkey. He returned to Germany when Turkey broke off diplomatic relations with Germany in August 1944.

Crimes against Peace

Von Papen was active in 1932 and 1933 in helping Hitler to form the Coalition Cabinet and aided in his appointment as Chancellor on 30 January 1933. As Vice Chancellor in that Cabinet he participated in the Nazi consolidation of control in 1933. On 16 June 1934, however, Von Papen made a speech at Marburg which contained a denunciation of the Nazi attempts to supress the free press and the Church, of the existence of a reign of terror, and of "150 percent Nazis" who were mistaking "brutality for vitality." On 30 June 1934, in the wave of violence which accompanied the so-called Röhm Purge, Von Papen was taken into custody by the SS, his office force was arrested, and two of his associates, including the man who had helped him work on the Marburg speech, were murdered. Von Papen was released on 3 July 1934.

Notwithstanding the murder of his associates, Von Papen accepted the position of Minister to Austria on 26 July 1934, the day after Dollfuss had been assassinated. His appointment was announced in a letter from Hitler which instructed him to direct relations between the two countries "into normal and friendly channels" and assured him of Hitler's "complete and unlimited confidence." As Minister to Austria, Von Papen was active in trying to strengthen the position of the Nazi Party in Austria for the purpose of bringing about the Anschluss. In early 1935 he attended a meeting in Berlin at which the policy was laid down to avoid everything which would give the appearance of German intervention in the internal affairs of Austria. Yet he arranged for 200,000 marks a month to be transmitted to "the persecuted National Socialist sufferers in Austria." On 17 May 1935, he reported to Hitler the results of a conference with Captain Leopold, the leader of the Austrian Nazis, and urged Hitler to make a statement recognizing the national independence of Austria, and predicting that the result might be to help the formation of a coalition between Schuschnigg's Christian Socialists and the Austrian Nazis against Starhemberg. On 27 July 1935, Von Papen reported to Hitler that the union of Austria and Germany could not be brought about by external pressure but only by the strength of the National Socialist movement. He urged that the Austrian Nazi Party change its character as a centralized Reich German Party and become a rallying point for all national Germans.

Von Papen was involved in occasional Nazi political demonstrations, supported Nazi propaganda activities, and submitted detailed reports on the activities of the Nazi Party, and routine reports relating to Austrian military defenses. His Austrian policy resulted in the agreement of 11 July 1936, which nominally restored relations between Germany and Austria to "normal and friendly form," but which had a secret supplement providing for an amnesty for Austrian Nazis, the lifting of censorship on Nazi papers, the resumption of political activities by Nazis, and the appointment of men friendly to the Nazis in the Schuschnigg Cabinet.

After the signing of this agreement Von Papen offered to resign but his resignation was not accepted. Thereafter he proceeded to bring continued pressure on the Austrian Government to bring Nazis into the Schuschnigg Cabinet and to get them important positions in the Fatherland Front, Austria's single legal party. On 1 September 1936, Von Papen wrote Hitler advising him that anti-Nazis in the Austrian Ministry of Security were holding up the infiltration of the Nazis into the Austrian Government and recommended bringing "slowly intensified pressure directed at changing the regime."

On 4 February 1938, Von Papen was notified of his recall as Minister to Austria, at the same time that Von Fritsch, Von Blomberg, and Von Neurath were removed from their positions. He informed Hitler that he regretted his recall because he had been trying since November 1937 to induce Schuschnigg to hold a conference with Hitler, and Schuschnigg had indicated his willingness to do so. Acting under Hitler's instructions, Von Papen then returned to Austria and arranged the conference which was held at Berchtesgaden on 12 February 1938. Von Papen accompanied Schuschnigg to that conference, and at its conclusion advised Schuschnigg to comply with Hitler's demands. On 10 March 1938, Hitler ordered Von Papen to return to Berlin. Von Papen was in the Chancellery on 11 March when the occupation of Austria was ordered. No evidence has been offered showing that Von Papen was in favor of the decision to occupy Austria by force, and he has testified that he urged Hitler not to take this step.

After the annexation of Austria Von Papen retired into private life and there is no evidence that he took any part in politics. He accepted the position of Ambassador to Turkey in April 1939 but no evidence has been offered concerning his activities in that position implicating him in crimes.

The evidence leaves no doubt that Von Papen's primary purpose as Minister to Austria was to undermine the Schuschnigg regime and strengthen the Austrian Nazis for the purpose of bringing about the Anschluss. To carry through this plan he engaged in both intrigue and bullying. But the Charter does not make criminal such offenses against political morality, however bad these may be. Under the Charter Von Papen can be held guilty only if he was a party to the planning of aggressive war. There is no evidence that he was a party to the plans under which the occupation of Austria was a step in the direction of further aggressive action, or even that he participated in plans to occupy Austria by aggressive war if necessary. But it is not established beyond a reasonable doubt that this was the purpose of his activity, and therefore the Tribunal cannot hold that he was a party to the common plan charged in Count One or participated in the planning of the aggressive wars charged under Count Two.

Conclusion

The Tribunal finds that Von Papen is not guilty under this Indictment, and directs that he shall be discharged by the Marshal, when the Tribunal presently adjourns.

Seyss-Inquart

Seyss-Inquart is indicted under all four Counts. Seyss-Inquart, an Austrian attorney, was appointed State Councillor in Austria in May 1937 as a result of German pressure. He had been associated with the Austrian Nazi Party since 1931, but had often had difficulties with that party and did not actually join the Nazi Party until 13 March 1938. He was appointed Austrian Minister of

Security and Interior with control over the police pursuant to one of the conditions which Hitler had imposed on Schuschnigg in the Berchtesgaden conference of 12 February 1938.

Activities in Austria

Seyss-Inquart participated in the last stages of the Nazi intrigue which preceded the German occupation of Austria and was made Chancellor of Austria as a result of German threats of invasion.

On 12 March 1938, Seyss-Inquart met Hitler at Linz and made a speech welcoming the German forces and advocating the reunion of Germany and Austria. On 13 March, he obtained the passage of a law providing that Austria should become a province of Germany and succeeded Miklas as President of Austria when Miklas resigned rather than sign the law. Seyss-Inquart's title was changed to Reich Governor of Austria on 15 March 1938, and on the same day he was given the title of a general in the SS. He was made a Reich Minister without Portfolio on 1 May 1939.

On 11 March 1939, he visited the Slovakian Cabinet in Bratislava and induced them to declare their independence in a way which fitted in closely with Hitler's offensive against the independence of Czechoslovakia.

As Reich Governor of Austria, Seyss-Inquart instituted a program of confiscating Jewish property. Under his regime Jews were forced to emigrate, were sent to concentration camps, and were subject to pogroms. At the end of his regime he co-operated with the Security Police and SD in the deportation of Jews from Austria to the East. While he was governor of Austria, political opponents of the Nazis were sent to concentration camps by the Gestapo, mistreated, and often killed.

Criminal Activities in Poland and the Netherlands

In September 1939, Seyss-Inquart was appointed Chief of Civil Administration of South Poland. On 12 October 1939, Seyss-Inquart was made Deputy Governor General of the Government General of Poland under Frank. On 18 May 1940, Seyss-Inquart was appointed Reich Commissioner for Occupied Netherlands. In these positions he assumed responsibility for governing territory which had been occupied by aggressive wars and the administration of which was of vital importance in the aggressive war being waged by Germany.

As Deputy Governor General of the Government General of Poland, Seyss-Inquart was a supporter of the harsh occupation policies which were put in effect. In November 1939, while on an inspection tour through the Government General, Seyss-Inquart stated that Poland was to be so administered as to exploit its economic resources for the benefit of Germany. Seyss-Inquart also advocated the persecution of Jews and was informed of the beginning of the AB Action which involved the murder of many Polish intellectuals.

As Reich Commissioner for Occupied Netherlands, Seyss-Inquart was ruthless in applying terrorism to suppress all opposition to the German occupation, a program which he described as "annihilating" his opponents. In collaboration with the local Higher SS and Police Leaders he was involved in the shooting of hostages for offenses against the occupation authorities and sending to concentration camps all suspected opponents of occupation policies, including priests and educators. Many of the Dutch police were forced to participate in these programs by threats of reprisal against their families. Dutch courts were also forced to participate in this program, but when they indicated their reluctance to give sentences of imprisonment because so many prisoners were in fact killed, a greater emphasis was placed on the use of summary police courts.

Seyss-Inquart carried out the economic administration of the Netherlands without regard for rules of the Hague Convention, which he described as obsolete. Instead, a policy was adopted for the maximum utilization of the economic potential of the Netherlands, and executed with small regard for its effect on the inhabitants. There was widespread pillage of public and private property which was given color of legality by Seyss-Inquart's regulations and assisted by manipulations of the financial institutions of the Netherlands under his control.

As Reich Commissioner for the Netherlands, Seyss-Inquart immediately began sending forced laborers to Germany. Until 1942, labor service in Germany was theoretically voluntary, but was actually coerced by strong economic and governmental pressure. In 1942 Seyss-Inquart formally decreed compulsory labor service, and utilized the services of the Security Police and SD to prevent evasion of his order. During the occupation over 500,000 people were sent from the Netherlands to the Reich as laborers, and only a very small proportion were actually volunteers.

One of Seyss-Inquart's first steps as Reich Commissioner of the Netherlands was to put into effect a series of laws imposing economic discriminations against the Jews. This was followed by decrees requiring their registration, decrees compelling them to reside in ghettos and to wear the star of David, sporadic arrests and detention in concentration camps, and finally, at the suggestion of Heydrich, the mass deportation of almost 120,000 of Holland's 140,000 Jews to Auschwitz and the "final solution." Seyss-Inquart admits knowing that they were going to Auschwitz, but claims that he heard from people who had been to Auschwitz that the Jews were comparatively well-off there, and that he thought that they were being held there for resettlement after the war. In the light of the evidence and on account of his official position it is impossible to believe his claim.

Seyss-Inquart contends that he was not responsible for many of the crimes committed in the occupation of the Netherlands because they were either ordered from the Reich, committed by the Army, over which he had no control, or by the German Higher SS and Police Leader who, he claims, reported directly to Himmler. It is true that some of the excesses were the responsibility of the Army, and that the Higher SS and Police Leader, although he was at the disposal of Seyss-Inquart, could always report directly to Himmler. It is also true that in certain cases Seyss-Inquart opposed the extreme measures used by these other agencies, as when he was largely successful in preventing the Army from carrying out a scorched earth policy, and urged the higher SS and Police Leaders to reduce the number of hostages to be shot. But the fact remains that Seyss-Inquart was a knowing and voluntary participant in War Crimes and Crimes against Humanity which were committed in the occupation of the Netherlands.

Conclusion

The Tribunal finds that Seyss-Inquart is guilty under Counts Two, Three, and Four; Seyss-Inquart is not guilty on Count One.

Speer

Speer is indicted under all four Counts. Speer joined the Nazi Party in 1932. In 1934 he was made Hitler's architect and became a close personal confidant. Shortly thereafter he was made a department head in the German Labor Front and the official in charge of capital construction on the staff of the Deputy to the Führer, positions which he held through 1941. On 15 February 1942, after the death of Fritz Todt, Speer was appointed Chief of the Organization Todt and Reich Minister for Armaments and Munitions (after 2 September 1943, for Armaments and War Production). The positions were supplemented by his appointments in March and April 1942 as Plenipotentiary General for Armaments and as a member of the Central Planning Board, both within the Four Year Plan. Speer was a member of the Reichstag from 1941 until the end of the war.

Crimes against Peace

The Tribunal is of opinion that Speer's activities do not amount to initiating, planning, or preparing wars of aggression, or of conspiring to that end. He became the head of the armament industry well after all of the wars had been commenced and were under way. His activities in charge of German armament production were in aid of the war effort in the same way that other productive enterprises aid in the waging of war; but the Tribunal is not prepared to find that such activities involve engaging in the common plan to wage aggressive war as charged under Count One, or waging aggressive war as charged under Count Two.

War Crimes and Crimes against Humanity

The evidence introduced against Speer under Counts Three and Four relates entirely to his participation in the slave labor program. Speer himself had no direct administrative responsibility for this program. Although he had advocated the appointment of a Plenipotentiary General for the Utilization of Labor because he wanted one central authority with whom he could deal on labor matters, he did not obtain administrative control over Sauckel. Sauckel was appointed directly by Hitler, under the decree of 21 March 1942, which provided that he should be directly responsible to Göring, as Plenipotentiary of the Four Year Plan.

As Reich Minister for Armaments and Munitions and Plenipotentiary General for Armaments under the Four Year Plan, Speer had extensive authority over production. His original authority was over construction and production of arms for the OKH. This was progressively expanded to include naval armaments, civilian production, and finally, on 1 August 1944, air armament. As the dominant member of the Central Planning Board, which had supreme authority for the scheduling of German production and the allocation and development of raw materials, Speer took the position that the board had authority to instruct Sauckel to provide laborers for industries under its control and succeeded in sustaining this position over the objection of Sauckel. The practice was developed under which Speer transmitted to Sauckel an estimate of the total number of workers needed; Sauckel obtained the labor and allocated it to the various industries in accordance with instructions supplied by Speer.

Speer knew when he made his demands on Sauckel that they would be supplied by foreign laborers serving under compulsion. He participated in conferences involving the extension of the slave labor program for the purpose of satisfying his demands. He was present at a conference held during 10 and 12 August 1942 with Hitler and Sauckel, at which it was agreed that Sauckel should bring laborers by force from occupied territories where this was necessary to satisfy the labor needs of the industries under Speer's control. Speer also attended a conference in Hitler's headquarters on 4 January 1944, at which the decision was made that Sauckel should obtain "at least 4 million new workers from occupied territories" in order to satisfy the demands for labor made by Speer, although Sauckel indicated that he could do this only with help from Himmler.

Sauckel continually informed Speer and his representatives that foreign laborers were being obtained by force. At a meeting of 1 March 1944, Speer's deputy questioned Sauckel very closely about his failure to live up to the obligation to supply 4 million workers from occupied territories. In some cases Speer demanded laborers from specific foreign countries. Thus, at the conference of 10 and 12 August 1942, Sauckel was instructed to supply Speer with "a further million Russian laborers for the German armament industry up to and including October 1942." At a meeting of the Central Planning Board on 22 April 1943, Speer discussed plans to obtain Russian laborers for use in the coal mines and flatly vetoed the suggestion that this labor deficit should be made up by German labor.

Speer has argued that he advocated the reorganization of the labor program to place a greater emphasis on utilization of German labor in war production in Germany and on the use of labor in occupied countries in local production of consumer goods formerly produced in Germany. Speer took steps in this direction by establishing the so-called "blocked industries" in the occupied territories which were used to produce goods to be shipped to Germany. Employees of these industries were immune from deportation to Germany as slave laborers and any worker who had been ordered to go to Germany could avoid deportation if he went to work for a blocked industry. This system, although somewhat less inhumane than deportation to Germany, was still illegal. The system of blocked industries played only a small part in the over-all slave labor program, and Speer urged its co-operation with the slave labor program, knowing the way in which it was actually being administered. In an official sense, he was its principal beneficiary and he constantly urged its extension.

Speer was also directly involved in the utilization of forced labor as chief of the Organization Todt. The Organization Todt functioned principally in the occupied areas on such projects as the Atlantic Wall and the construction of military highways, and Speer has admitted that he relied on compulsory service to keep it adequately staffed. He also used concentration camp labor in the industries under his control. He originally arranged to tap this source of labor for use in small out-of-the-way factories; and later, fearful of Himmler's jurisdictional ambitions, attempted to use as few concentration camp workers as possible.

Speer was also involved in the use of prisoners of war in armament industries, but contends that he only utilized Soviet prisoners of war in industries covered by the Geneva Convention.

Speer's position was such that he was not directly concerned with the cruelty in the administration of the slave labor program, although he was aware of its existence. For example, at meetings of the Central Planning Board he was informed that his demands for labor were so large as to necessitate violent methods in recuiting. At a meeting of the Central Planning Board on 30 October 1942, Speer voiced his opinion that many slave laborers who claimed to be sick were malingerers and stated: "There is nothing to be said against SS and Police taking drastic steps and putting those known as slackers into concentration camps." Speer, however, insisted that the slave laborers be given adequate food and working conditions so that they could work efficiently.

In mitigation it must be recognized that Speer's establishment of blocked industries did keep many laborers in their homes and that in the closing stages of the war he was one of the few men who had the courage to tell Hitler that the war was lost and to take steps to prevent the senseless destruction of production facilities, both in occupied territories and in Germany. He carried out his opposition to Hitler's scorched earth program in some of the Western countries and in Germany by deliberately sabotaging it at considerable personal risk.

Conclusion

The Tribunal finds that Speer is not guilty on Counts One and Two, but is guilty under Counts Three and Four.

Von Neurath

Von Neurath is indicted under all four Counts. He is a professional diplomat who served as German Ambassador to Great Britain from 1930 to 1932. On 2 June 1932, he was appointed Minister of Foreign Affairs in the Von Papen Cabinet, a position which he held under the Cabinets of Von Schleicher and Hitler. Von Neurath resigned as Minister of Foreign Affairs on 4 February 1938, and was made Reich Minister without Portfolio, President of the Secret Cabinet Council, and a member of the Reich Defense Council. On 18 March 1939, he was appointed Reich Protector for Bohemia and Moravia and served in this capacity until 27 September 1941. He held the formal rank of Obergruppenführer in the SS.

Crimes against Peace

As Minister of Foreign Affairs, Von Neurath advised Hitler in connection with the withdrawal from the Disarmament Conference and the League of Nations on 14 October 1933; the institution of rearmament; the passage, on 16 March 1935, of the Law for universal military service; and the passage, on 21 May 1935, of the secret Reich Defense Law. He was a key figure in the negotiation of the Naval Accord entered into between Germany and England on 18 June 1935. Von Neurath played an important part in Hitler's decision to reoccupy the Rhineland on 7 March 1936, and predicted that the occupation could be carried through without any reprisals from the French. On 18 May 1936, he told the American Ambassador to France that it was the policy of the German Government to do nothing in foreign affairs until "the Rhineland had been digested," and that as soon as the fortifications in the Rhineland had been constructed and the countries of central Europe realized that France could not enter Germany at will, "all those countries will begin to feel very differently about their foreign policies and a new constellation will develop."

Von Neurath took part in the Hossbach conference of 5 November 1937. He has testified that he was so shocked by Hitler's statements that he had a heart attack. Shortly thereafter, he offered to resign, and his resignation was accepted on 4 February 1938, at the same time that Von Fritsch and Von Blomberg were dismissed. Yet with knowledge of Hitler's aggressive plans he retained a formal relationship with the Nazi regime as Reich Minister without Portfolio, President of the Secret Cabinet Council, and a member of the Reich Defense Council. He took charge of the Foreign Office at the time of the occupation of Austria, assured the British Ambassador that this had not been caused by a German ultimatum, and informed the Czechoslovakian Minister that Germany intended to abide by its arbitration convention with Czechoslavakia. Von Neurath participated in the last phase of the negotiations preceding the Munich Pact but contends that he entered these discussions only to urge Hitler to make every effort to settle the issues by peaceful means.

Criminal Activities in Czechoslovakia

Von Neurath was appointed Reich Protector of Bohemia and Moravia on 18 March 1939. Bohemia and Moravia were occupied by military force. Hacha's consent, obtained as it was by duress, cannot be considered as justifying the occupation. Hitler's decree of 16 March 1939, establishing the Protectorate, stated that this new territory should "belong henceforth to the territory of the German Reich," an assumption that the Republic of Czechoslovakia no longer existed. But it also went on the theory that Bohemia and Moravia retained their sovereignty subject only to the interests of Germany as expressed by the Protectorate. Therefore, even if the doctrine of subjugation should be considered to be applicable to territory occupied by aggressive action, the Tribunal does not believe that this proclamation amounted to an incorporation which was sufficient to bring the doctrine into effect. The occupation of Bohemia and Moravia must therefore be considered a military occupation covered by the rules of warfare. Although Czechoslovakia was not a party to the Hague Convention of 1907, the rules of land warfare expressed in this Convention are declaratory of existing international law and hence are applicable.

As Reich Protector, Von Neurath instituted an administration in Bohemia and Moravia similar to that in effect in Germany. The free press, political parties, and trade unions were abolished. All groups which might serve as opposition were outlawed. Czechoslovakian industry was worked into the structure of German war production, and exploited for the German war effort. Nazi anti-Semitic policies and laws were also introduced. Jews were barred from leading positions in government and business.

In August 1939 Von Neurath issued a proclamation warning against any acts of sabotage and stating that "the responsibility for all acts of sabotage is attributed not only to individual perpetrators but to the entire Czech population." When the war broke out on 1 September 1939, 8,000 prominent Czechs were arrested by the Security Police in Bohemia and Moravia and put into protective custody. Many of this group died in concentration camps as a result of mistreatment.

In October and November 1939, Czechoslovakian students held a series of demonstrations. As a result, on Hitler's orders all universities were closed, 1,200 students imprisoned, and the nine leaders of the demonstration shot by Security Police and SD. Von Neurath testified that he was not informed of this action in advance, but it was announced by proclamation over his signature posted on placards throughout the Protectorate, which he claims, however, was done without his authority.

On 31 August 1940 Von Neurath transmitted to Lammers a memorandum which he had prepared dealing with the future of the Protectorate, and a memorandum with his approval prepared by Karl Hermann Frank on the same subject. Both dealt with the question of Germanization and proposed that the majority of the Czechs might be assimilated racially into the German nation. Both advocated the elimination of the Czechoslovakian intelligentsia and other groups which might resist Germanization, Von Neurath's by expulsion, Frank's by expulsion or "special treatment."

Von Neurath has argued that the actual enforcement of the repressive measures was carried out by the Security Police and SD who were under the control of his state secretary, Karl Hermann Frank, who was appointed at the suggestion of Himmler and who, as Higher SS and Police Leader, reported directly to Himmler. Von Neurath further argues that anti-Semitic measures and those resulting in economic exploitation were put into effect in the Protectorate as the result of policies decided upon in the Reich. However this may be, he served as the chief German official in the Protectorate when the administration of this territory played an important role in the wars of aggression which Germany was waging in the East, knowing that war crimes and crimes against humanity were being committed under his authority.

In mitigation it must be remembered that he did intervene with the Security Police and SD for the release of many of the Czechoslovaks who were arrested on 1 September 1939, and for the release of students arrested later in the fall. On 23 September 1941 he was summoned before Hitler and told that he was not being harsh enough and that Heydrich was being sent to the Protectorate to combat the Czechoslovakian resistance groups. Von Neurath attempted to dissuade Hitler from sending Heydrich, and when he was not successful offered to resign. When his resignation was not accepted he went on leave, on 27 September 1941, and refused to act as Protector after that date. His resignation was formally accepted in August 1943.

Conclusion

The Tribunal finds that Von Neurath is guilty under all four Counts.

FRITZSCHE

Fritzsche is indicted on Counts One, Three, and Four. He was best known as a radio commentator, discussing once a week the events of the day on his own program, "Hans Fritzsche Speaks." He began broadcasting in September 1932; in the same year he was made the head of the Wireless News Service, a Reich Government agency. When on 1 May 1933, this agency was incorporated by the National Socialist into their Reich Ministry of Popular Enlightenment and Propaganda, Fritzsche became a member of the Nazi Party and went to that Ministry. In December 1938 he became head of the Home Press Division of the Ministry; in October 1942 he was promoted to the rank of Ministerial Director. After serving briefly on the Eastern Front in a propaganda company, he was, in November 1942, made head of the Radio Division of the Propaganda Ministry and Plenipotentiary for the Political Organization of the Greater German Radio.

Crimes against Peace

As head of the Home Press Division, Fritzsche supervised the German press of 2,300 daily newspapers. In pursuance of this function he held daily press conferences to deliver the directives of the Propaganda Ministry to these papers. He was, however, subordinate to Dietrich, the Reich Press Chief, who was in turn a subordinate of Goebbels. It was Dietrich who received the directives to the press of Goebbels and other Reich Ministers, and prepared them as instructions which he then handed to Fritzsche for the press.

From time to time, the "Daily Paroles of the Reich Press Chief," as these instructions were labelled, directed the press to present to the people certain themes, such as the leadership principle, the Jewish problem, the problem of living space, or other standard Nazi ideas. A vigorous propaganda campaign was carried out before each major act of aggression. While Fritzsche headed the Home Press Division, he instructed the press how the actions or wars against Bohemia and Moravia, Poland, Yugoslavia, and the Soviet Union should be dealt with. Fritzsche had no control of the formulation of these propaganda policies. He was merely a conduit to the press of the instructions handed him by Dietrich. In February 1939 and before the absorption of Bohemia and Moravia, for instance, he received Dietrich's order to bring to the attention of the press Slovakia's efforts for independence, and the Anti-Germanic policies and politics of the existing Prague Government. This order to Dietrich originated in the Foreign Office.

The Radio Division, of which Fritzsche became the head in November 1942, was one of the 12 divisions of the Propaganda Ministry. In the beginning Dietrich and other heads of divisions exerted influence over the policies to be followed by radio. Towards the end of the war, however, Fritzsche became the sole authority within the Ministry for radio activities. In this capacity he formulated and issued daily radio "paroles" to all Reich propaganda offices, according to the general political policies of the Nazi regime, subject to the directives of the Radio-Political Division of the Foreign Office, and the personal supervision of Goebbels.

Fritzsche, with other officials of the Propaganda Ministry, was present at Goebbels' daily staff conferences. Here they were instructed in the news and propaganda policies of the day. After 1943 Fritzsche himself occasionally held these conferences, but only when Goebbels and his state secretaries were absent. And even then his only function was to transmit Goebbels' directives relayed to him by telephone.

This is the summary of Fritzsche's positions and influence in the Third Reich. Never did he achieve sufficient stature to attend the planning conferences which led to aggressive war; indeed according to his own uncontradicted testimony he never even had a conversation with Hitler. Nor is there any showing that he was informed of the decisions taken at these conferences. His activities cannot be said to be those which fall within the definition of the common plan to wage aggressive war as already set forth in this Judgment.

War Crimes and Crimes against Humanity

The Prosecution has asserted that Fritzsche incited and encouraged the commission of war crimes, by deliberately falsifying news to arouse in the German people those passions which led them to the commission of atrocities under Counts Three and Four. His position and official duties were not sufficiently important, however, to infer that he took part in originating or formulating propaganda campaigns.

Excerpts in evidence from his speeches show definite anti-Semitism on his part. He broadcast, for example, that the war had been caused by Jews and said their fate had turned out "as unpleasant as the Führer predicted." But these speeches did not urge persecution or extermination of Jews. There is no evidence that he was aware of their extermination in the East. The evidence moreover shows that he twice attempted to have publication of the anti-Semitic *Der Stürmer* suppressed, though unsuccessfully.

In these broadcasts Fritzsche sometimes spread false news, but it was not proved he knew it to be false. For example, he reported that no German U-Boat was in the vicinity of the *Athenia* when it was sunk. This information was untrue; but Fritzsche, having received it from the German Navy, had no reason to believe it was untrue.

It appears that Fritzsche sometimes made strong statements of a propagandistic nature in his broadcasts. But the Tribunal is not prepared to hold that they were intended to incite the German people to commit atrocities on conquered peoples, and he cannot be held to have been a participant in the crimes charged. His aim was rather to arouse popular sentiment in support of Hitler and the German war effort.

Conclusion

The Tribunal finds that Fritzsche is not guilty under this Indictment, and directs that he shall be discharged by the Marshal when the Tribunal presently adjourns.

Bormann

Bormann is indicted on Counts One, Three, and Four. He joined the National Socialist Party in 1925, was a member of the Staff of the Supreme Command of the SA from 1928 to 1930, was in charge of the Aid Fund of the Party, and was Reichsleiter from 1933 to 1945. From 1933 to 1941 he was Chief of Staff in the office of the Führer's Deputy and, after the flight of Hess to England, became Head of the Party Chancellery on 12 May 1941. On 12 April 1943 he became Secretary to the Führer. He was political and organizational head of the Volkssturm and a general in the SS.

Crimes against Peace

Bormann, in the beginning a minor Nazi, steadily rose to a position of power and, particularly in the closing days, of great influence over Hitler. He was active in the Party's rise to power and even more so in the consolidation of that power. He devoted much of his time to the persecution of the Churches and of the Jews within Germany.

The evidence does not show that Bormann knew of Hitler's plans to prepare, initiate, or wage aggressive wars. He attended none of the important conferences when Hitler revealed piece by piece these plans for aggression. Nor can knowledge be conclusively inferred from the positions he held. It was only when he became head of the Party Chancellery in 1941, and later in 1943 Secretary to the Führer, when he attended many of Hitler's conferences, that his positions gave him the necessary access. Under the view stated elsewhere which the Tribunal has taken of the conspiracy to wage aggressive war, there is not sufficient evidence to bring Bormann within the scope of Count One.

War Crimes and Crimes against Humanity

By decree of 29 May 1941 Bormann took over the offices and powers held by Hess; by decree of 24 January 1942 these powers were extended to give him control over all laws and directives issued by Hitler. He was thus responsible for laws and orders issued thereafter. On 1 December 1942, all Gaue became Reich defense districts, and the Party Gauleiter responsible to Bormann were appointed Reich Defense Commissioners. In effect, this made them the administrators of the entire civilian war effort. This was so not only in Germany, but also in those territories which were incorporated into the Reich from the absorbed and conquered territories.

Through this mechanism Bormann controlled the ruthless exploitation of the subjected populace. His order of 12 August 1942 placed all Party agencies at the disposal of Himmler's program for forced resettlement and denationalization of persons in the occupied countries. Three weeks after the invasion of Russia, he attended the conference of 16 July 1941 at Hitler's field quarters with Göring, Rosenberg, and Keitel; Bormann's report shows that there were discussed and developed detail plans of enslavement and annihilation of the population of these territories. And on 8 May 1942 he conferred with Hitler and Rosenberg on the forced resettlement of Dutch personnel in Latvia, the extermination program in Russia, and the economic exploitation of the Eastern territories. He was interested in the confiscation of art and other properties in the East. His letter of 11 January 1944 called for the creation of a large-scale organization to withdraw commodities from the occupied territories for the bombed-out German populace.

Bormann was extremely active in the persecution of the Jews not only in Germany but also in the absorbed or conquered countries. He took part in the discussions which led to the removal of 60,000 Jews from Vienna to Poland in co-operation with the SS and the Gestapo. He signed the decree of 31 May 1941 extending the Nuremberg Laws to the annexed Eastern territories. In an order of 9 October 1942 he declared that the permanent elimination of Jews in Greater German territory could no longer be solved by emigration, but only by applying "ruthless force" in the special camps in the East. On 1 July 1943 he signed an ordinance withdrawing Jews from the protection of the law courts and placing them under the exclusive jurisdiction of Himmler's Gestapo.

Bormann was prominent in the slave labor program. The Party leaders supervised slave labor matters in the respective Gaue, including employment, conditions of work, feeding, and housing. By his circular of 5 May 1943 to the Leadership Corps, distributed down to the level of Ortsgruppenleiter, he issued directions regulating the treatment of foreign workers, pointing out they were subject to SS control on security problems, and ordered the previous mistreatment to cease. A report of 4 September 1942 relating to the transfer of 500,000 female domestic workers from the East to Germany showed that control was to be exercised by Sauckel, Himmler, and Bormann. Sauckel by decree of 8 September directed the Kreisleiter to supervise the distribution and assignment of these female laborers.

Bormann also issued a series of orders to the Party leaders dealing with the treatment of prisoners of war. On 5 November 1941 he prohibited decent burials for Russian prisoners of war. On 25 November 1943 he directed Gauleiter to report cases of lenient treatment of prisoners of war. And on 13 September 1944 he ordered liaison between the Kreisleiter with the camp commandants in determining the use to be made of prisoners of war for forced labor. On 29 January 1943 he transmitted to his leaders OKW instructions allowing the use of fire arms and corporal punishment on recalcitrant prisoners of war contrary to the rules of land warfare. On 30 September 1944 he signed a decree taking from the OKW jurisdiction over prisoners of war and handing them over to Himmler and the SS.

Bormann is responsible for the lynching of Allied airmen. On 30 May 1944 he prohibited any police action or criminal proceedings against persons who had taken part in the lynching of Allied fliers. This was accompanied by a

Goebbels propaganda campaign inciting the German people to take action of this nature, and the conference of 6 June 1944 where regulations for the application of lynching were discussed.

His counsel, who has labored under difficulties, was unable to refute this evidence. In the face of these documents which bear Bormann's signature it is difficult to see how he could do so even were the defendant present. Counsel has argued that Bormann is dead and that the Tribunal should not avail itself of Article 12 of the Charter which gives it the right to take proceedings *in absentia.* But the evidence of death is not conclusive, and the Tribunal, as previously stated, determined to try him *in absentia.* If Bormann is not dead and is later apprehended, the Control Council for Germany may, under Article 29 of the Charter, consider any facts in mitigation, and alter or reduce his sentence, if deemed proper.

Conclusion

The Tribunal finds that Bormann is not guilty on Count One, but is guilty on Counts Three and Four.

THE PRESIDENT: Before pronouncing sentence on any of the defendants, and while all the defendants are present, the Tribunal takes the occasion to advise them that any application to the clemency of the Control Council must be lodged with the General Secretary of this Tribunal within 4 days from today. . . .

AFTERNOON SESSION

In accordance with Article 27 of the Charter, the International Military Tribunal will now pronounce the sentences on the defendants convicted on this Indictment:

"Defendant *Hermann Wilhelm Göring,* on the Counts of the Indictment on which you have been convicted, the International Military Tribunal sentences you to death by hanging.

"Defendant *Rudolf Hess,* on the Counts of the Indictment on which you have been convicted, the Tribunal sentences you to imprisonment for life.

"Defendant *Joachim von Ribbentrop,* on the Counts of the Indictment on which you have been convicted, the Tribunal sentences you to death by hanging.

"Defendant *Wilhelm Keitel,* on the Counts of the Indictment on which you have been convicted, the Tribunal sentences you to death by hanging.

"Defendant *Ernst Kaltenbrunner,* on the Counts of the Indictment on which you have been convicted, the Tribunal sentences you to death by hanging.

"Defendant *Alfred Rosenberg,* on the Counts of the Indictment on which you have been convicted, the Tribunal sentences you to death by hanging.

"Defendant *Hans Frank,* on the Counts of the Indictment on which you have been convicted, the Tribunal sentences you to death by hanging.

"Defendant *Wilhelm Frick,* on the Counts of the Indictment on which you have been convicted, the Tribunal sentences you to death by hanging.

"Defendant *Julius Streicher,* on the Count of the Indictment on which you have been convicted, the Tribunal sentences you to death by hanging.

"Defendant *Walter Funk,* on the Counts of the Indictment on which you have been convicted, the Tribunal sentences you to imprisonment for life.

"Defendant *Karl Dönitz,* on the Counts of the Indictment on which you have been convicted, the Tribunal sentences you to ten years' imprisonment.

"Defendant *Erich Raeder,* on the Counts of the Indictment on which you have been convicted, the Tribunal sentences you to imprisonment for life.

"Defendant *Baldur von Schirach,* on the Count of the Indictment on which you have been convicted, the Tribunal sentences you to twenty years' imprisonment.

"Defendant *Fritz Sauckel,* on the Counts of the Indictment on which you have been convicted, the Tribunal sentences you to death by hanging.

"Defendant *Alfred Jodl,* on the Counts of the Indictment on which you have been convicted, the Tribunal sentences you to death by hanging.

"Defendant *Arthur Seyss-Inquart,* on the Counts of the Indictment on which you have been convicted, the Tribunal sentences you to death by hanging.

"Defendant *Albert Speer,* on the Counts of the Indictment on which you have been convicted, the Tribunal sentences you to twenty years' imprisonment.

"Defendant *Konstantin von Neurath,* on the Counts of the Indictment on which you have been convicted, the Tribunal sentences you to fifteen years' imprisonment.

The Tribunal sentences the Defendant *Martin Bormann,* on the Counts of the Indictment on which he has been convicted, to death by hanging.

I have an announcement to make. The Soviet member of the International Military Tribunal desires to record his dissent from the decisions in the cases of the Defendants Schacht, Von Papen, and Fritzsche. He is of the opinion that they should have been convicted and not acquitted.

He also dissents from the decisions in respect to the Reich Cabinet and the General Staff and High Command, being of the opinion that they should have been declared to be criminal organizations.

He also dissents from the decision in the case of the sentence on the Defendant Hess and is of the opinion that the sentence should have been death, and not life imprisonment.

This dissenting opinion will be put into writing and annexed to the Judgment, and will be published as soon as possible.

RESOLUTION AFFIRMING THE PRINCIPLES OF INTERNATIONAL LAW RECOGNIZED BY THE CHARTER OF THE NUREMBERG TRIBUNAL

United Nations, December, 1946

General Assembly Resolution 95

The General Assembly,

Recognizes the obligation laid upon it by Article 13, paragraph 1, subparagraph a of the Charter, to initiate studies and make recommendations for the purpose of encouraging the progressive development of international law and its codification; and

Takes note of an Agreement for the establishment of an International Military Tribunal for the prosecution and punishment of the major war criminals of the European Axis signed in London on 8 August 1945, and of the Charter annexed thereto, and of the fact that similar principles have been adopted in the Charter of the International Military Tribunal for the trial of the major war criminals in the Far East, proclaimed at Tokyo on 19 January 1946;

Therefore,

Affirms the principles of international law recognized by the Charter of the Nürnberg Tribunal and the judgment of the Tribunal;

Directs the Committee on codification of international law established by the resolution of the General Assembly of 11 December 1946, to treat as a matter of primary importance plans for the formulation, in the context of a general codification of offences against the peace and security of mankind, or of an International Criminal Code, of the principles recognized in the Charter of the Nürnberg Tribunal and in the judgment of the Tribunal.

[Shortly after the Nuremberg judgment was rendered, President Harry S Truman addressing the United Nations General Assembly, gave high praise to the principles of law applied at Nuremberg. He said it pointed the "path along which agreement might be sought, with hope of success," among the people of all countries "upon principles of law and justice." The Secretary General of the UN, Trygve Lie, endorsed the idea that the Nuremberg principles be made a permanent part of international law: "In the interests of peace and in order to protect mankind against future wars, it will be of decisive significance to have the principles which were implied in the Nuremberg trials . . . made a permanent part of the body of international law as quickly as possible." On November 15, 1946 the United States delegation introduced a resolution to that effect before the General Assembly, and after some modifications, it was adopted unanimously in the above language on December 11, 1946.]

THE TOKYO WAR CRIMES TRIAL
November, 1948

INTERNATIONAL MILITARY TRIBUNAL FOR THE FAR EAST

THE UNITED STATES of America, The Republic of China, The United Kingdom of Great Britain and Northern Ireland, The Union of Soviet Socialist Republics, The Commonwealth of Australia, Canada, The Republic of France, The Kingdom of the Netherlands, New Zealand, India, and The Commonwealth of the Philippines.

AGAINST

Sadao Araki; Kenji Dohihara; Kingoro Hashimoto; Shunroku Hata; Kiichiro Hiranuma; Koki Hirota; Naoki Hoshino; Seishiro Itagaki; Okinori Kaya, Koichi Kido, Heitaro Kimura, Kuniaki Koiso; Iwane Matsui; Yosuke Matsuoka; Jiro Minami; Akira Muto; Osami Nagano; Takasumi Oka; Shumei Okawa; Hiroshi Oshima; Kenryo Sato; Mamoru Shigemitsu; Shigetaro Shimada; Toshio Shiratori; Teiichi Suzuki; Shigenori Togo; Hideki Tojo; Yoshijiro Umezu.

PART A—CHAPTER I. ESTABLISHMENT AND PROCEEDINGS OF THE TRIBUNAL

The Tribunal was established in virtue of and to implement the Cairo Declaration of the 1st of December, 1943, the Declaration of Potsdam of the 26th of July, 1945, the Instrument of Surrender of the 2nd of September, 1945, and the Moscow Conference of the 26th of December, 1945.

The Cairo Declaration was made by the President of the United States of America, the President of the National Government of the Republic of China, and the Prime Minister of Great Britain. It reads as follows:

The several military missions have agreed upon future military operations against Japan. The Three Great Allies expressed their resolve to bring unrelenting pressure against their brutal enemies by sea, land, and air. This pressure is already rising.

The Three Great Allies are fighting this war to restrain and punish the aggression of Japan. They covet no gain for themselves and have no though of territorial expansion. It is their purpose that Japan shall be stripped of all the islands in the Pacific which she had seized or occupied since the beginning of the first World War in 1914, and that all the territories Japan has stolen from the Chinese, such as Manchuria, Formosa, and the Pescadores, shall be restored to the Republic of China, Japan will also be expelled from all other territories which she has taken by violence and greed. The aforesaid Three Great Powers, mindful of the enslavement of the people of Korea, are determined that in due course Korea shall become free and independent.

With these objects in view the three Allies, in harmony with those of the United Nations at war with Japan, will continue to persevere in the serious and prolonged operations necessary to procure the unconditional surrender of Japan.

The Declaration of Potsdam was made by the President of the United States of America, the President of the National Government of the Republic of China, and the Prime Minister of Great Britain and later adhered to by the Union of Soviet Socialist Republics. Its principal relevant provisions are:

Japan shall be given an opportunity to end this war.

There must be eliminated for all time the authority and influence of those who have deceived and misled the people of Japan into embarking on world conquest, for we insist that a new order of peace, security and justice will be impossible until irresponsible militarism is driven from the world.

The terms of the Cairo Declaration shall be carried out and Japanese sovereignty shall be limited to the islands of Honshu, Kokkaido, Kyushu, Shikoku and such minor islands as we determine.

We do not intend that the Japanese people shall be enslaved as a race or destroyed as a nation, but stern justice shall be meted out to all war criminals including those who have visited cruelties upon our prisoners.

The Instrument of Surrender was signed on behalf of the Emperor and Government of Japan and on behalf of the nine Allied Powers. It contains inter alia the following proclamation, undertaking, and order:

We hereby proclaim the unconditional surrender to the Allied Powers of the Japanese Imperial General Headquarters and all Japanese armed forces and all armed forces under Japanese control wherever situated.

We hereby undertake for the Emperor, the Japanese Government, and their successors, to carry out the provisions of the Potsdam Declaration in good faith, and to issue whatever orders and take whatever action may be required by the Supreme Commander for the Allied Powers or by any other designated representatives of the Allied Powers for the purpose of giving effect to the Declaration.

The authority of the Emperor and the Japanese Government to rule the State shall be subject to the Supreme Commander for the Allied Powers who will take such steps as he deems proper to effectuate these terms of surrender. We hereby command all civil, military, and naval officials to obey and enforce all proclamations, orders, and directives deemed by the Supreme Commander for the Allied

Powers to be proper to effectuate this surrender and issued by him or under his authority.

By the Moscow Conference it was agreed by and between the Governments of the United States of America, Great Britain, and the Union of Soviet Socialist Republics with the concurrence of China that:

> The Supreme Commander shall issue all orders for the implementation of the Terms of Surrender, the occupation and control of Japan and directives supplementary thereto.

Acting on this authority on the 19th day of January, 1946, General MacArthur, the Supreme Commander for the Allied Powers, by Special Proclamation established the Tribunal for "the trial of those persons charged individually or as members of organizations or in both capacities with offences which include crimes against peace." The constitution, jurisdiction, and functions of the Tribunal were by the Proclamation declared to be those set forth in the Charter of the Tribunal approved by the Supreme Commander on the same day. Before the opening of the Trial the Charter was amended in several respects.

On the 15th day of February, 1946, the Supreme Commander issued an Order appointing the nine members of the Tribunal nominated respectively by each of the Allied Powers. This Order also provides that "the responsibilities, powers, and duties of the Members of the Tribunal are set forth in the Charter thereof. . . ."

By one of the amendments to the Charter the maximum number of members was increased from nine to eleven to permit the appointment of members nominated by India and the Commonwealth of the Philippines. By subsequent Orders the present members from the United States and France were appointed to succeed the original appointees who resigned and the members from India and the Philippines were appointed.

Pursuant to the provisions of Article 9(c) of the Charter each of the accused before the opening of the Trial appointed counsel of his own choice to represent him; each accused being represented by American and Japanese counsel.

On the 29th of April, 1946, an indictment, which had previously been served on the accused in conformity with the rules of procedure adopted by the Tribunal, was lodged with the Tribunal.

The Indictment is long, containing fifty-five counts charging twenty-eight accused with Crimes against Peace, Conventional War Crimes, and Crimes against Humanity during the period from the 1st of January, 1928, to the 2nd of September, 1945.

It may be summarized as follows:

In Count 1 all accused are charged with conspiring as leaders, organisers, instigators or accomplices between 1st January 1928 and 2nd September 1945 to have Japan, either alone or with other countries, wage wars of aggression against any country or countries which might oppose her purpose of securing the military, naval, political and economic domination of East Asia and of the Pacific and Indian oceans and their adjoining countries and neighbouring islands.

Count 2 charges all accused with conspiring throughout the same period to have Japan wage aggressive war against China to secure complete domination of the Chinese provinces of Liaoning, Kirin, Heilungkiang, and Jehol (Manchuria).

Count 3 charges all accused with conspiracy over the same period to have Japan wage aggressive war against China to secure complete domination to China.

Count 4 charges all accused with conspiring to have Japan, alone or with other countries, wage aggressive war against the United States, the British Commonwealth, France, the Netherlands, China, Portugal, Thailand, the Philippines and the Union of Soviet Socialist Republics to secure the complete domination of East Asia and the Pacific and Indian Oceans and their adjoining countries and neighbouring islands.

Count 5 charges all accused with conspiring with Germany and Italy to have Japan, Germany and Italy mutually assist each other in aggressive warfare against any country which might oppose them for the purpose of having these three nations acquire complete domination of the entire world, each having special domination in its own sphere, Japan's sphere to cover East Asia and the Pacific and Indian Oceans.

Counts 6 to 17 charge all accused except Seiratori with having planned and prepared aggressive war against named countries.

Counts 18 to 26 charge all accused with initiating aggressive war against named countries.

Counts 27 to 36 charge all accused with waging aggressive war against named countries.

Count 37 charges certain accused with conspiring to murder members of the armed forces and civilians of the United States, the Philippines, the British Commonwealth, the Netherlands and Thailand by initiating unlawful hostilities against those countries in breach of the Hague Convention No. III of 18th October 1907.

Count 38 charges the same accused with conspiring to murder the soldiers and civilians by intiating hostilities in violation of the agreement between the United States and Japan of 30th November 1908, the Treaty between Britain, France, Japan and the United States of 13th December 1921, the Pact of Paris of 27th August 1928, and the Treaty of Unity between Thailand and Japan of 12th June 1940.

Counts 39 to 43 charge the same accused with the commission on 7th and 8th December 1941 of murder at Pearl Harbour (Count 39) Kohta Behru (Count 40) Hong Kong (Count 41) on board *H. M. S. Petrel* at Shanghai (Count 42) and at Davao (Count 43).

Count 44 charges all accused with conspiring to murder on a wholesale scale prisoners of war and civilians in Japan's power.

Counts 45 to 50 charge certain accused with the murder of disarmed soldiers and civilians at Nanking (Count 45) Canton (Count 46) Hankow (Count 47) Changsha (Count 48) Hengyang (Count 49) and Kweilin and Luchow (Count 50).

Count 51 charges certain accused with the murder of members of the armed forces of Mongolia and the Soviet Union in the Khalkin-Gol River area in 1939.

Count 52 charges certain accused with the murder of members of the armed forces of the Soviet Union in the Lake Khasan area in July and August 1938.

Counts 53 and 54 charge all the accused except Okawa and Shiratori with having conspired to order, authorize or permit the various Japanese Theatre Commanders, the officials of the War Ministry and local camp and labour unit officials to frequently and habitually commit breaches of the laws and customs of war against the armed forces, prisoners of war, and civilian internees of complaining powers and to have the Government of Japan abstain from taking adequate steps to secure the observance and prevent breaches of the laws and customs of war.

Count 55 charges the same accused with having recklessly disregarded their legal duty by virtue of their offices to take adequate steps to secure the observance and prevent breaches of the laws and customs of war.

During the course of the Trial two of the accused, Matsuoka and Nagano, died and the accused Okawa was declared unfit to stand his trial and unable to defend himself. Matsuoka and Nagano were therefore discharged from the Indictment. Further proceedings upon the Indictment against Okawa at this Trial were suspended.

On the 3rd and 4th of May the Indictment was read in open court in the presence of all the accused, the Tribunal then adjourning till the 6th to receive the pleas of the accused. On the latter date pleas of "not guilty" were entered by all the accused now before the Tribunal.

The Tribunal then fixed the 3rd of June following as the date for the commencement of the presentation of evidence by the Prosecution.

In the interval the Defence presented motions challenging the jurisdiction of the Tribunal to hear and decide the charges contained in the Indictment. On the 17th of May, 1946, after argument, judgment was delivered dismissing all the said motions "for reasons to be given later." These reasons will be given in dealing with the law of the case in Chapter II of this part of the judgment.

The Prosecution opened its case on the 3rd of June, 1946, and closed its case on the 24th of January 1947.

The presentation of evidence for the Defence opened on the 24th of February, 1947, and closed on the 12th of January, 1948, an adjournment having been granted from the 19th of June to the 4th of August, 1947, to permit Defence Counsel to coordinate their work in the presentation of evidence common to all the accused.

Prosecution evidence in rebuttal and Defence evidence in reply were permitted; the reception of evidence terminating on the 10th of February, 1948. In all 4336 exhibits were admitted in evidence, 419 witnesses testified, in court, 779 witnesses gave evidence in depositions and affidavits, and the transcript of the proceedings covers 48,412 pages.

Closing arguments and summations of Prosecution and Defence opened on the 11th of February and closed on the 16th of April, 1948.

Having regard to Article 12 of the Charter which requires "an expeditious hearing of the issues" and the taking of "strict measures to prevent any "action which would cause any unreasonable delay", the length of the present trial requires some explanation and comment.

In order to avoid unnecessary delay which would have been incurred by adopting the ordinary method of translation by interrupting from time to time evidence, addresses and other matters which could be prepared in advance of delivery, an elaborate public address system was installed. Through this system whenever possible a simultaneous translation into English or Japanese was given and in addition when circumstances required from or into Chinese, Russian, and French. Without such aids the trial might well have occupied a very much longer period. Cross-examination and extempore argument on objections and other incidental proceedings had, however, to be translated in the ordinary way as they proceeded.

Article 13(a) of the Charter provides that "the Tribunal shall not be bound by technical rules of evidence. It shall . . . admit any evidence which it deems to have probative value. . . ." The application of this rule to the mass of documents and oral evidence offered inevitably resulted in a great expenditure of time. Moreover, the charges in the Indictment directly involved an inquiry into the history of Japan during seventeen years, the years between 1928 and 1945. In addition our inquiry has extended to a less detailed study of the earlier history of Japan, for without that the subsequent actions of Japan and her leaders could not be understood and assessed.

* * *

PART A—CHAPTER II. THE LAW

(A) JURISDICTION OF THE TRIBUNAL

In our opinion the law of the Charter is decisive and binding on the Tribunal. This is a special tribunal set up by the Supreme Commander under authority conferred on him by the Allied Powers. It derives its jurisdiction from the Charter. In this trial its members have no jurisdiction except such as is to be found in the Charter. The Order of the Supreme Commander, which appointed the members of the Tribunal, states: "The responsibilities, powers, and duties of the members of the Tribunal are set forth in the Charter thereof . . ." In the result, the members of the Tribunal, being otherwise wholly without power in respect to the trial of the accused, have been empowered by the documents, which constituted the Tribunal and appointed them as members, to try the accused but subject always to the duty and responsibility of applying to the trial the law set forth in the Charter.

The foregoing expression of opinion is not to be taken as supporting the view, if such view be held, that the Allied Powers or any victor nations have the right under international law in providing for the trial and punishment of war criminals to enact or promulgate laws or vest in their tribunals powers in conflicts with recognised international law or rules or principles thereof. In the exercise of their right to create tribunals for such a purpose and in conferring powers upon such tribunals belligerent powers may act only within the limits of international law.

The substantial grounds of the defence challenge to the jurisdiction of the Tribunal to hear and adjudicate upon the charges contained in the Indictment are the following:

(1) The Allied Powers acting through the Supreme Commander have no authority to include in the Charter of the Tribunal and to designate as justiciable "Crimes against Peace" (Article 5(a));

(2) Aggressive war is not per se illegal and the Pact of Paris of 1928 renouncing war as an instrument of national policy does not enlarge the meaning of war crimes nor constitute war a crime;

(3) War is the act of a nation for which there is no individual responsibil ity under international law;

(4) The provisions of the Charter are "ex post facto" legislation and therefore illegal;

(5) The Instrument of Surrender which provides that the Declaration of Potsdam will be given effect imposes the condition that Conventional War Crimes as recognised by international law at the date of the Declaration (26 July, 1945) would be the only crimes prosecuted;

(6) Killings in the course of belligerent operations except in so far as they constitute violations of the rules of warfare or the laws and cutoms of war are the normal incidents of war and are not murder;

(7) Several of the accused being prisoners of war are triable by court martial as provided by the Geneva Convention of 1929 and not by this Tribunal.

Since the law of the Charter is decisive and binding upon it this Tribunal is formally bound to reject the first four of the above seven contentions advanced for the Defence but in view of the great importance of the questions of law involved the Tribunal will record its opinion on these questions.

After this Tribunal had in May 1946 dismissed the defence motions and upheld the validity of its Charter and its jurisdiction thereunder, stating that the reasons for this decision would be given later, the International Military Tribunal sitting at Nuremberg delivered its verdicts on the first of October 1946. That Tribunal expressed inter alia the following opinions:

"The Charter is not an arbitrary exercise of power on the part of the victorious nations but is the expression of international law existing at the time of its creation;

"The question is what was the legal effect of this pact (Pact of Paris, August 27, 1928)? The Nations who signed the pact or adhered to it unconditionally condemned recourse to war for the future as an instrument of policy and expressly renounced it. After the signing of the pact any nation resorting to war as an instrument of national policy breaks the pact. In the opinion of the Tribunal, the solemn renunciation of war as an instrument of national policy necessarily involves the proposition that such a war is illegal in international law; and that those who plan and wage such a war, with its inevitable and terrible consequences, are committing a crime in so doing.

"The principle of international law which under certain circumstances protects the representative of a state cannot be applied to acts which are condemned as criminal by international law. The authors of these acts cannot shelter themselves behind their official position in order to be freed from punishment in appropriate proceedings.

"The maxim 'nullum crimen sine lege' is not a limitation of sovereignty but is in general a principle of justice. To assert that it is unjust to punish those who in defiance of treaties and assurances have attacked neighbouring states without warning is obviously untrue for in such circumstances the attacker must know that he is doing wrong, and so far from it being unjust to punish him, it would be unjust if his wrong were allowed to go unpunished.

"The Charter specifically provides . . . 'the fact that a defendant acted pursuant to order of his Government or of a superior shall not free him from responsibility but may be considered in mitigation of punishment.' This provision is in conformity with the laws of all nations . . . The true test which is found in varying degrees in the criminal law of most nations is not the existence of the order but whether moral choice was in fact possible."

With the foregoing opinions of the Nuremberg Tribunal and the reasoning by which they are reached this Tribunal is in complete accord. They embody complete answers to the first four of the grounds urged by the defence as set forth above. In view of the fact that in all material respects the Charters of this Tribunal and the Nuremberg Tribunal are identical, this Tribunal prefers to express its unqualified adherence to the relevant opinions of the Nuremberg Tribunal rather than by reasoning the matters anew in somewhat different language to open the door to controversy by way of conflicting interpretations of the two statements of opinions.

The fifth ground of the Defence challenge to the Tribunal's jurisdiction is that under the Instrument of Surrender and the Declaration of Potsdam the only crimes for which it was contemplated that proceedings would be taken, being the only war crimes recognized by international law at the date of the Declaration of Potsdam, are Conventional War Crimes as mentioned in Article 5(b) of the Charter.

Aggressive war was a crime at international law long prior to the date of the Declaration of Potsdam, and there is no ground for the limited interpretation of the Charter which the defense seek to give it.

A special argument was advanced that in any event the Japanese Government, when they agreed to accept the terms of the Instrument of Surrender, did not in fact understand that those Japanese who were alleged to be responsible for the war would be prosecuted.

There is no basis in fact for this argument. It has been established to the satisfaction of the Tribunal that before the signature of the Instrument of Surrender the point in question had been considered by the Japanese Government and the then members of the Government, who advised the acceptance of the terms of the Instrument of Surrender, anticipated that those alleged to be responsible for the war would be put on trial. As early as the 10th of August, 1945, three weeks before the signing of the Instrument of Surrender, the Emperor said to the accused Kido, "I could not bear the sight . . . of those responsible for the war being punished . . . but I think now is the time to bear the unbearable."

The sixth contention for the Defence; namely, that relating to the charges which allege the commission or murder will be discussed at a later point.

The seventh of these contentions is made on behalf of the four accused who surrendered as prisoners of war—Itagaki, Kimura, Muto and Sato. The submission made on their behalf is that they, being former members of the armed forces of Japan and prisoners of war, are triable as such by court martial under the articles of the Geneva Convention of 1929 relating to prisoners of war, particularly Articles 60 and 63, and not by a tribunal constituted otherwise than under that Convention. This very point was decided by the Supreme Court of the United States of America in the Yamashita case. The late Chief Justice Stone, delivering the judgment for the majority of the Court said: "We think it clear from the context of these recited provisions that Part 3 and Article 63, which it contains, apply only to judicial proceedings directed against a prisoner of war for offences committed while a prisoner of war. Section V gives no indication that this part was designated to deal with offences other than those referred to in Parts 1 and 2 of Chapter 3." With that conclusion and the reasoning by which it is reached the Tribunal respectfully agrees.

The challenge to the jurisdiction of the Tribunal wholly fails.

(b) Responsibility for War Crimes Against Prisoners

Prisoners taken in war and civilian internees are in the power of the Government which captures them. This was not always the case. For the last two centuries, however, this position has been recognised and the customary law to this effect was formally embodied in the Hague Convention No. IV in 1907 and repeated in the Geneva Prisoner of War Convention of 1929. Responsibility for the care of prisoners of war and of civilian internees (all of whom we will refer to as "prisoners") rests therefore with the Government having them in possession. This responsibility is not limited to the duty of mere maintenance but extends to the prevention of mistreatment. In particular, acts of inhumanity to prisoners which are forbidden by the customary law of nations as well as by conventions are to prevented by the Government having responsibility for the prisoners.

In the discharge of these duties to prisoners Governments must have resort to persons. Indeed the Governments responsible, in this sense, are those persons who direct and control the functions of Government. In this case and in the above regard we are concerned with the members of the Japanese Cabinet. The duty to prisoners is not a meaningless obligation cast upon a political abstraction. It is a specific duty to be performed in the first case by those persons who constitute the Government. In the multitude of duties and tasks involved in modern government there is of necessity an elaborate system of subdivision and delegation of duties. In the case of the duty of Governments to prisoners held by them in time of war those persons who constitute the Government have the principal and continuing responsibility for their prisoners, even though they delegate the duties of maintenance and protection to others.

In general the responsibility for prisoners held by Japan may be stated to have rested upon:

(1) Members of the Government;

(2) Military or Naval Officers in command of formations having prisoners in their possession;

(3) Officials in those departments which were concerned with the well-being of prisoners;

(4) Officials, whether civilian, military, or naval, having direct and immediate control of prisoners.

It is the duty of all those on whom responsibility rests to secure proper treatment of prisoners and to prevent their ill-treatment by establishing and securing the continuous and efficient working of a system appropriate for these purposes. Such persons fail in this duty and become responsible for ill-treatment of prisoners if:

(1) They fail to establish such a system.

(2) If having established such a system, they fail to secure its continued and efficient working.

Each of such persons has a duty to ascertain that the system is working and if he neglects to do so he is responsible. He does not discharge his duty by merely instituting an appropriate system and thereafter neglecting to learn of its application. An Army Commander or a Minister of War, for example, must be at the same pains to ensure obedience to his orders in this respect as he would in respect of other orders he has issued on matters of the first importance.

Nevertheless, such persons are not responsible if a proper system and its continuous efficient functioning be provided for and conventional war crimes be committed unless:

(1) They had knowledge that such crimes were being committed, and having such knowledge they failed to take such steps as were within their power to prevent the commission of such crimes in the future, or

(2) They are at fault in having failed to acquire such knowledge.

If, such a person had, or should, but for negligence or supineness, have had such knowledge he is not excused for inaction if his Office required or permitted him to take any action to prevent such crimes. On the other hand it is not enough for the exculpation of a person, otherwise responsible, for him to show that he accepted assurances from others more directly associated with the control of the prisoners if having regard to the position of those others, to the frequency of reports of such crimes, or to any other circumstances he should have been put upon further enquiry as to whether those assurances were true or untrue. That crimes are notorious, numerous and widespread as to time and place are matters to be considered in imputing knowledge.

A member of a Cabinet which collectively, as one of the principal organs of the Government, is responsible for the care of prisoners is not absolved from responsibility if, having knowledge of the commission of the crimes in the sense already discussed, and omitting or failing to secure the taking of measures to prevent the commission of such crimes in the future, he elects to continue as a member of the Cabinet. This is the position even though the Department of which he has the charge is not directly concerned with the care of prisoners. A Cabinet member may resign. If he has knowledge of ill-treatment of prisoners, is powerless to prevent future ill-treatment, but elects to remain in the Cabinet thereby continuing to participate in its collective responsibility for protection of prisoners he willingly assumes responsibility for any ill-treatment in the future.

Army or Navy Commanders can, by order, secure proper treatment and prevent ill-treatment of prisoners. So can Ministers of War and of the Navy. If crimes are committed against prisoners under their control, of the likely occurrence of which they had, or should have had knowledge in advance, they are responsible for those crimes. If, for example, it be shown that within the units under his command conventional war crimes have been committed of which he knew or should have known, a commander who takes no adequate steps to prevent the occurrence of such crimes in the future will be responsible for such future crimes.

Departmental officials having knowledge of ill-treatment of prisoners are not responsible by reason of their failure to resign; but if their functions included the administration of the system of protection of prisoners and if they had or should have had knowledge of crimes and did nothing effective, to the extent of their powers, to prevent their occurrence in the future then they are responsible for such future crimes.

(c) The Indictment

Under the heading of "Crimes Against Peace" the Charter names five separate crimes. These are planning, preparation, initiation and waging aggressive war or a war in violation of international law, treaties, agreements or assurances: to these four is added the further crime of participation in a common plan or conspiracy for the accomplishment of any of the foregoing. The Indictment was based upon the Charter and all the above crimes were charged in addition to further charges founded upon other provisions of the Charter.

A conspiracy to wage aggressive or unlawful war arises when two or more persons enter into an agreement to commit that crime. Thereafter, in furtherance of the conspiracy, follows planning and preparing for such war. Those who participate at this stage may be either original conspirators or later adherents. If the latter adopt the purpose of the conspiracy and plan and prepare for its fulfillment they become conspirators. For this reason, as all the accused are charged with the conspiracies, we do not consider it necessary in respect of those we may find guilty of conspiracy to enter convictions also for planning and preparing. In other words, although we do not question the validity of the charges we do not think it necessary in respect of any defendants who may be found guilty of conspiracy to take into consideration nor to enter convictions upon counts 6 to 17 inclusive.

A similar position arises in connection with the counts of initiating and waging aggressive war. Although initiating aggressive war in some circumstances may have another meaning, in the Indictment before us it is given the meaning of commencing the hostilities. In this sense it involves the actual waging of the aggressive war. After such a war has been initiated or has been commenced by some offenders others may participate in such circumstances as to become guilty of waging the war. This consideration, however, affords no reason for registering convictions on the counts of initiating as well as of waging aggressive war. We propose therefore to abstain from consideration of Counts 18 to 26 inclusive.

Counts 37 and 38 charge conspiracy to murder. Article 5, sub-paragraphs (b) and (c) of the Charter, deal with Conventional War Crimes and Crimes against Humanity. In sub-paragraph (c) of Article 5 occurs this passage: "Leaders, organizers, instigators and accomplices participating in the formulation or execution of a common plan or conspiracy to commit any of the foregoing crimes are responsible for all acts performed by any person in execution of such plan." A similar provision appeared in the Nuremberg Charter although there it was an independent paragraph and was not, as in our Charter incorporated in sub-paragraph (c). The context of this provision clearly relates it exclusively to sub-paragraph (a), Crimes against Peace, as that is the only category in which a "common plan or conspiracy" is stated to be a crime. It has no application to Conventional War Crimes and Crime against Humanity as conspiracies to commit such crimes are not made criminal by the Charter of the Tribunal. The Prosecution did not challenge this view but submitted that the counts were sustainable under Article 5 (a) of the Charter. It was argued that the waging of aggressive war was unlawful and involved unlawful killing which is murder. From this it was submitted further that a conspiracy to wage war unlawfully was a conspiracy also to commit murder. The crimes triable by this Tribunal are those set out in the Charter. Article 5 (a) states that a conspiracy to commit the crimes therein specified is itself a crime. The crimes, other than conspiracy, specified in Article 5(a) are "planning, preparation, initiating or waging" of a war of aggression. There is no specification of the crime of conspiracy to commit murder by the waging of aggressive war or otherwise. We hold therefore that we have no jurisdiction to deal with charges of conspiracy to commit murder as contained in Counts 37 and 38 and decline to entertain these charges.

In all there are 55 counts in the Indictment charged against the 25 defendants. In many of the counts each of the accused is charged and in the remainder 10 or more are charged. In respect to Crimes against Peace alone there are for consideration no less than 756 separate charges.

This situation springs from the adoption by the Prosecution of the common practice of charging all matters upon which guilt is indicated by the evidence it proposes to adduce even though some of the charges are cumulative or alternative.

The foregoing consideration of the substance of the charges shows that this reduction of the counts for Crimes against Peace upon which a verdict need be given can be made without avoidance of the duty of the Tribunal and without injustice to defendants.

Counts 44 and 53 charge conspiracies to commit crimes in breach of the laws of war. For reasons already discussed we hold that the Charter does not confer any jurisdiction in respect of a conspiracy to commit any crime other than a crime against peace. There is no specification of the crime of conspiracy to commit conventional war crimes. This position is accepted by the Prosecution and no conviction is sought under these counts. These counts, accordingly, will be disregarded.

Insofar as the opinion expressed above with regard to Counts 37, 38, 44, and 53 may appear to be in conflict with the judgment of the Tribunal of the 17th May, 1946, whereby the motions going to the Tribunal's jurisdiction were dismissed, it is sufficient to say that the point was not raised at the hearing on the motions. At a much later date, after the Nuremberg judgment had been delivered, this matter was raised by counsel for one of the accused. On this topic the Tribunal concurs in the view of the Nuremberg Tribunal. Accordingly, upon those counts, it accepts the admission of the Prosecution which is favorable to the defendants.

Counts 39 to 52 inclusive (omitting Count 44 already discussed) contain charges of murder. In all these counts the charge in effect is that killing resulted from the unlawful waging of war at the places and upon the dates set out. In some of the counts the date is that upon which hostilities commenced at the place named, in others the date is that upon which the place was attacked in the course of an alleged illegal war already proceeding. In all cases the killing is alleged as arising from the unlawful waging of war, unlawful in respect that there had been no declaration of war prior to the killings (Counts 39 to 43, 51, and 52) or unlawful because the wars in the course of which the killings occurred were commenced in violation of certain specified Treaty Articles (Counts 45 to 50). If, in any case, the finding be that the war was not unlawful then the charge of murder will fall with the charge of waging unlawful war. If, on the other hand, the war, in any particular case, is held to have been unlawful then this involves unlawful killings not only upon the dates and at the places stated in these counts but at all places in the theater of war and at all times throughout the period of the war. No good purpose is to be served, in our view, in dealing with these parts of the offences by way of counts for murder when the whole offence of waging those wars unlawfully is put in issue upon the counts charging the waging of such wars.

The foregoing observations relate to all the counts enumerated; i.e., Counts 39 to 52 (omitting 44). Counts 45 to 50 are stated obscurely. They charge murder at different places upon the dates mentioned by unlawfully ordering, causing, and permitting Japanese armed forces to attack those places and to slaughter the inhabitants thereby unlawfully killing civilians and disarmed soldiers. From the language of these counts it is not quite clear whether it is intended to found the unlawful killings upon the unlawfulness of the attack or upon subsequent breaches of the laws of war or upon both. If the first is intended then the position is the same as in the earlier counts in this group. If breaches of the laws of war are founded upon then that is cumulative with the charges in Counts 54 and 55. For these reasons only and without finding it necessary to express any opinion upon the validity of the charges of murder in such circumstances we have decided that it is unnecessary to determine Counts 39 to 43 inclusive and Counts 45 to 52 inclusive.

* * *

Laws of Belligerency

The law governing the entrance of States into, as well as their conduct while in, belligerency received further restatement during the two decades immediately preceding the period covered by the Indictment and during the years 1928 and 1929. In 1907, the second Peace Conference at The Hague produced thirteen Conventions and one Declaration, all signed on 18 October 1907. The Kellogg-Briand Pact (Pact of Paris) condemning aggressive war was signed at Paris on 27 August 1928. Then on 27 July 1929, two important Conventions were signed at Geneva, namely: the Convention Relative to the Treatment of Prisoners of War, and the Convention for the Amelioration of the Condition of the Wounded and Sick of Armies in the Field. These Agreements not only impose direct treaty obligations upon the Contracting Powers, but also delineate more precisely the customary law. The effectiveness of some of the Conventions signed at The Hague on 18 October 1907 as direct treaty obligations was considerably impaired by the incorporation of a so-called "general participation clause" in them, providing that the Convention would be binding only if all the Belligerents were parties to it. The effect of this clause is, in strict law, to deprive some of the Conventions of their binding force as direct treaty obligations, either from the very beginning of a war or in the course of it as soon as a non-signatory Power, however insignificant, joins the ranks of the Belligerents. Although the obligation to observe the provisions of the Convention as a binding treaty may be swept away by operation of the "general participation clause," or otherwise, the Convention remains as good evidence of the customary law of nations, to be considered by the Tribunal along with all other available evidence in determining the customary law to be applied in any given situation.

First Hague Convention

The First Convention agreed upon by the Conference at The Hague in 1907 was the Convention for the Pacific Settlement of International Disputes. (Annex No. B-14). The Convention was signed by, or on behalf of, Japan and each of the Powers bringing the Indictment, and ratified by, or on behalf of, all of them, except Great Britain, Australia, Canada, India and New Zealand. Twenty-one other Powers also signed and ratified the Convention, and five additional Powers later acceded to it. The Powers bringing the Indictment, who did not ratify this Convention, remained bound, in so far as their relations with Japan were concerned, by the Convention for the Pacific Settlement of International Disputes signed at The Hague on 29 July 1899; since that Convention was signed and ratified by, or on behalf of, Japan and each of these Powers. Neither of the Conventions mentioned under this title contained a "general participation clause"; they were, therefore, binding upon Japan as direct treaty obligations at all relevant times mentioned in the Indictment. Japan, as well as the other Contracting Powers, among other things agreed:

(1) That, in order to obviate as far as possible recourse to force in her relations with other States, she would use her best efforts to insure the pacific settlement of international differences; and,

(2) That in case of serious disagreement or dispute, before an appeal to arms, she would have recourse to the good offices or mediation of one or more friendly Powers.

Kellogg-Briand Pact

The Kellogg-Briand Pact or Pact of Paris, which was signed at Paris on 27 August 1928, condemned aggressive war and restated the law evidenced by the First Hague Convention of 18 October 1907 for the Pacific Settlement of International Disputes. (Annex No. B-15). The Treaty was signed and ratified by, or on behalf of, Japan and each of the Powers bringing the Indictment, except the Union of Soviet Socialist Republics, China and the Netherlands. Japan ratified the Treaty on 24 July 1929, and China adhered to the Treaty on 8 May 1929. The Netherlands adhered to the Treaty on 12 July 1929, and the Union of Soviet Socialist Republics adhered on 27 September 1928. Therefore, Japan and each of the Powers bringing the Indictment had definitely acceded to the Treaty by 24 July 1929; in addition, eight other Powers had signed and ratified the Treaty; and forty-five additional Powers, at one time or another, adhered to it. The Treaty was binding upon Japan at all relevant times mentioned in the Indictment.

The Contracting Powers, including Japan, declared that they condemn recourse to war for the solution of international controversies, and renounce it as an instrument of national policy in their relations with one another.

The Contracting Powers then agreed that the settlement or solution of all disputes or conflicts of whatever nature or of whatever origin they may be, which might arise among them, would never be sought except by pacific means.

Prior to ratification of the Pact, some of the Signatory Powers made declarations reserving the right to wage war in self-defence including the right to judge for themselves whether a situation requires such action. Any law, international or municipal, which prohibits recourse to force, is necessarily limited by the right of self-defence. The right of self-defence involves the right of the State threatened with impending attack to judge for itself in the first instance whether it is justified in resorting to force. Under the most liberal interpretation of the Kellogg-Briand Pact, the right of self-defence does not confer upon the State resorting to war the authority to make a final determination upon the justification for its action. Any other interpretation would nullify the Pact; and this Tribunal does not believe that the Powers in concluding the Pact intended to make an empty gesture.

Third Hague Convention

The Third Convention concluded by the Powers in Conference at The Hague in 1907 was the Convention Relative to the Opening of Hostilities. The Convention was signed and ratified by, or on behalf of, Japan and each of the Powers bring the Indictment, except China; but China adhered to the Convention in 1910. A total of twenty-five Powers signed and ratified the Convention, including Portugal and Thailand, and six Powers later adhered to it. This Convention does not contain a "general participation clause". It provides that it shall take effect in case of war between two or more of the Contracting Powers, it was binding upon Japan at all relevant times mentioned in the Indictment. By ratifying this Convention, Japan agreed, among other things: That hostilities between her and any other Contracting Power must not commence without previous and explicit warning, in the form either of a declaration of war, giving reasons, or of an ultimatum with conditional declaration of war.

Fifth Hague Convention

The Fifth Hague Convention of 1907 was the Convention Respecting the Rights and Duties of Neutral Powers and Persons in War on Land. The Convention was signed and ratified by, or on behalf of, Japan and each of the Powers bringing the Indictment, except Great Britain, Australia, Canada, New Zealand, India and China. However, China adhered to the Convention in 1910. A total of twenty-five Powers signed and ratified the Convention, including Thailand and Portugal; and three Powers later adhered to it. Great Britain and sixteen other Powers, who signed the Convention, have not ratified it.

This is one of the Hague Conventions which contains a "general participation clause"; although it ceased to be applicable in the recent war as a direct treaty obligation of Japan upon the entry of Great Britain into the war on 8 December 1941, it remained as good evidence of the customary law of nations to be considered along with all other available evidence in determining the customary law to be applied in any given situation, to which the principles stated in the Convention might be applicable.

By this Convention, Japan agreed, among other things:

(1) That the territory of neutral Powers is inviolable;

(2) That Belligerents are forbidden to move troops or convoys of either munitions of war or supplies across the territory of a neutral Power; and,

(3) That a neutral Power is not called upon to prevent the export or transport, on behalf of one or the other of the Belligerents, of arms, munitions of war, or, in general of anything which can be of use to an army or a fleet.

Fourth Hague Convention

The Fourth Hague Convention of 1907 is the Convention Respecting the Laws and Customs of War on Land. Regulations Respecting the Laws and Customs of War on Land were annexed to and made a part of this Convention. The Convention was signed and ratified by, or on behalf of, Japan and each of the Powers bringing the Indictment, except China. Nineteen additional Powers, including Thailand and Portugal, also signed and ratified this Convention; and two other Powers later adhered to it.

This is another of the Hague Conventions which contains "general participation clause." What we have said respecting this clause applies equally well here.

As stated in the Preamble to this Convention, the Contracting Powers were animated by the desire, even in the extreme case, to serve the interests of humanity and the needs of civilization by diminishing the evils of war and adopted the Convention and the Regulations thereunder which were intended to serve as a general rule of conduct for Belligerents. Realizing that it was not possible at the time to concert regulations covering all circumstances that might arise in practice, the Powers declared that they did not intend that unforeseen cases should be left to the arbitrary judgment of military commanders; and that until a more complete code should be issued, they declared that in cases not included in the Regulations the inhabitants and belligerents remained under the protection and principles of the laws of nations as they resulted from the usages of civilized peoples, the laws of humanity, and the dictate of the public conscience.

By this Convention, Japan agreed, among other things:

(1) That prisoners of war are in the power of the hostile Government, but not of the individuals or corps who capture them; that they must be humanely treated; and all their personal belongings, except arms, horses, and military papers, remain their property;

(2) That in case of capture of any of the armed forces of a Belligerent, whether they consisted of combatants or non-combatants, they would be treated as prisoners of war.

(3) That although she might utilize the labor of prisoners of war, officers excepted, the task would not be excessive and would not be connected with the operation of war; and that she would pay to the prisoners compensation for all work done by them;

(4) That as regards board, lodging, and clothing, in the absence of a special agreement between the Belligerents, she would treat prisoners of war on the same footing as the troops who captured them;

(5) That prisoners of war in her power would be subject to the laws governing her own army and entitled to the benefits thereof;

(6) That she would institute at the commencement of hostilities an inquiry office. That it would be the function of this office to reply to all inquiries about the prisoners and to keep up to date an individual return for each prisoner of war in which would be recorded all necessary vital statistics and other useful information pertaining to such prisoners.

(7) That relief societies for prisoners of war would receive every facility from her for the efficient performance of their humane task and their agents would be admitted to places of internment for the purpose of administering relief, etc.;

(8) That it was forbidden: (a) To employ poison or poisoned weapons; (b) To kill or wound treacherously individuals belonging to the hostile Nation or Army; (c) To kill or wound an enemy, who having laid down his arms, or having no longer means of defence, has surrendered at discretion; (d) To declare that no quarter will be given; (e) To make improper use of a flag of truce, of the national flag or of the military insignia and uniform of the enemy, or of the distinctive badges of the Geneva Convention; or (f) To destroy or seize the enemy's property, unless such destruction or seizure be imperatively demanded by the necessities of war;

(9) That in sieges and bombardments all necessary steps would be taken by her to spare buildings dedicated to religion, art, science and charitable purpose, historic monuments and hospitals and places where the sick and wounded are collected;

(10) That the pillage of a town or other place, even when taken by assault, was prohibited; and,

(11) That family honor and rights, the lives of persons, and private property, as well as religious convictions and practice would be respected by her during war.

Geneva Prisoner of War Convention

The Convention Relative to the Treatment of Prisoners of War was signed at Geneva on 27 July 1929. (Annex No. B–20). Forty-seven Powers signed the Convention; and thirty-four Powers either ratified it or adhered to it. Excepting Australia, China and the Union of Soviet Socialist Republics, the Convention was signed and ratified by, or on behalf of, each of the Powers bringing the Indictment.

Japan sent plenipotentiaries, who participated in the Conference and signed the Convention; but Japan did not formally ratify the Convention before the opening of hostilities on 7 December 1941. However, early in 1942 the United States, Great Britain and other Powers informed Japan that they proposed to abide by the Convention and sought assurances from Japan as to her attitude towards the Convention. Japan acting through her Foreign Minister, who was the Accused Togo, declared and assured the Powers concerned that, while she was not formally bound by the Convention, she would apply the Convention, "mutatis mutandis", toward American, British, Canadian, Australian and New Zealand prisoners of war. Under this assurance Japan was bound to comply with the Convention save where its provisions could not be literally complied with owing to special conditions known to the parties to exist at the time the assurance was given, in which case Japan was obliged to apply the nearest possible equivalent to literal compliance. The effect of this assurance will be more fully considered at a later point in this judgment.

This Convention is the "more complete code of the laws of war" contemplated by the Powers signatory to the Hague Convention Respecting the Laws and Customs of War concluded on 18 October 1907; and the Convention provides by its terms that it will be considered to be Chapter II of the Regulations annexed to that Hague Convention. The Convention does not contain a "general participation clause"; but it does contain a provision that it shall remain in force as between the Belligerents who are parties to it even though one of the Belligerents is not a Contracting Power.

The Convention provides, among other things:

(1) That prisoners of war are in the power of the hostile Power, but not of the individuals or corps who have captured them; that they must be humanely treated and protected, particularly against acts of violence, insults and public curiosity; that they have the right to have their person and honor respected; that women shall be treated with all regard to their sex; and that all prisoners of war must be maintained by the detaining Power;

(2) That prisoners of war shall be evacuated as quickly as possible to depots removed from the zone of combat; but that the evacuation, if on foot, shall only be effected by stages of 20 kilometers a day, unless the necessity of reaching water and food requires longer stages;

(3) That prisoners of war may be interned; but they may not be confined or imprisoned, except as an indispensible measure of safety or sanitation; that if captured in unhealthful regions or climates, they will be transported to a more favorable region; that all sanitary measure will be taken to insure cleanliness and healthfulness of camps; that medical inspections shall be arranged at least once a month to ensure the general health of the prisoners; that collective disciplinary measures affecting food are prohibited; that the food ration shall be equal in quantity and quality to that of troops in base camp; that prisoners shall be furnished facilities together with a sufficiency of potable water for preparing additional food for themselves; that they shall be furnished clothing, linen and footwear as well as work clothes for those who labor; and that every camp shall have an infirmary, where prisoners of war shall receive every kind of attention needed;

(4) That although prisoners of war are required to salute all officers of the detaining Powers, officers who are prisoners are bound to salute only officers of a higher or equal rank of that Power;

(5) That Belligerents may utilize the labor of able prisoners of war, officers excepted, and provided that non-commissioned officers are used only for supervisory work; that no prisoner may be employed at labors for which he is physically unfit; that the length of the day's work shall not be excessive, and every prisoner shall be allowed a rest of twenty-four consecutive hours each week; that prisoners shall not be used at unhealthful or dangerous work, and labor detachments must be conducted similar to prisoner-of-war camps, particularly with regard to sanitary conditions, food, medical attention, etc.; that prisoners must be paid wages for their labor; and that the labor of prisoners of war shall have no direct relation with war operations, particularly the manufacture and transportation of munitions, or the transportation of material for combat units;

(6) That prisoners of war must be allowed to receive parcels by mail intended to supply them with food and clothing; and that relief societies for prisoners of war shall receive from the detaining Power every facility for the efficient performance of their humane tasks;

(7) That prisoners of war have the right to make requests and register complaints regarding the conditions of their captivity; that in every place where there are prisoners of war they have the right to appoint agents to represent them directly with the military authorities of the detaining Power; and that such agent shall not be transferred without giving him time to inform his successors about affairs under consideration;

(8) That although prisoners of war are subject to the laws, regulations, and orders in force in the armies of the detaining Power, punishments other than those provided for the same acts for soldiers of the armies of the detaining Power may not be imposed upon them; and that corporal punishment, imprisonment in quarters without daylight, and in general any form of cruelty, is forbidden, as well as collective punishment for individual acts or omissions;

(9) That escaped prisoners of war who are retaken shall be liable only

to disciplinary punishment; and that the comrades who assisted his escape may incur only disciplinary punishment;

(10) That at the opening of judicial proceedings against a prisoner of war, the detaining Power shall advise the representative of the protecting Power thereof at least before the opening of the trial; that no prisoner shall be sentenced without having an opportunity to defend himself, and shall not be required to admit himself guilty of the act charged; that the representative of the protecting Power shall be entitled to attend the trial; that no sentence shall be pronounced against a prisoner except by the same courts and according to the same procedure as in the case of trial of persons belonging to the armed forces of the detaining Power, that the sentence pronounced shall be immediately communicated to the protecting Power; and that in the case of death sentences, the sentence must not be executed before the expiration of three months after such communication;

(11) That Belligerents are bound to send back to their own country, regardless of rank or number, seriously sick and seriously injured prisoners of war, after having brought them to a condition where they can be transported;

(12) That Belligerents shall see that prisoners of war dying in captivity are honorably buried and that their graves bear all due information and are respected and maintained;

(13) That upon outbreak of hostilities each Belligerent shall institute a prisoner of war information bureau, which shall prepare and preserve an individual return upon each prisoner showing certain vital information prescribed, and which shall furnish such information as soon as possible to the interested Power.

Japan also assured the Belligerents that she would apply this Convention to civilian internees and that in applying the Convention she would take into consideration the national and racial manners and customs of prisoners of war and civilian internees under reciprocal conditions when supplying clothing and provisions to them.

Geneva Red Cross Convention

The Geneva Red Cross Convention for the Amelioration of the Condition of the Wounded and Sick of Armies in the Field was also signed on 27 July 1929. (Annex No. B–21). The Convention was signed and ratified by, or on behalf of, Japan and each of the Powers bringing the Indictment as well as thirty-two other Powers. It was binding upon Japan and her subjects at all relevant times mentioned in the Indictment, as a direct treaty obligation. The Convention contains a provision to the effect that it must be respected by the Contracting Powers under all circumstances; and if in time of war, one of the Belligerents is not a party to the Convention, its provisions shall remain in force between the Belligerents who are parties to it.

By signing and ratifying the Convention, Japan, as well as the other Signatory Powers, agreed, among other things:

(1) That officers, soldiers, and other persons officially attached to the

armies, who are wounded or sick, shall be respected and protected in all circumstances; and that they shall be humanely treated and cared for without distinction of nationality by the Belligerent in whose power they are;

(2) That after every engagement, the Belligerent who remains in possession of the field of battle shall search for the wounded and dead and protect them from robbery and ill-treatment; and that those wounded and sick who fall into the power of the enemy shall become prisoners of war to whom the general rules of international law respecting prisoners of war shall be applicable;

(3) That all personnel charged exclusively with the removal, transportation, and treatment of the wounded and sick, including administration personnel of sanitary formations and establishments and chaplains, shall be respected and protected, and when they fall into the hands of the enemy they shall not be treated as prisoners of war, and shall not be detained, but will be returned as soon as possible to their own army along with their arms and equipment;

(4) That mobile sanitary formations, and fixed sanitary establishments shall be respected and protected; and if they fall into the hands of the enemy, they shall not be deprived of their buildings, transport and other equipment which may be needed for the treatment of the sick and wounded;

(5) That only those personnel, formations and establishments entitled to respect and protection under the Convention shall display the distinctive emblem of the Geneva Convention; and,

(6) That it is the duty of commanders-in-chief of belligerent armies to provide for the details of execution of the provisions of the Convention, as well as unforeseen cases conformable to the general principles of the Convention.

Tenth Hague Convention

The Tenth Convention agreed upon at the Conference at The Hague and signed on 18 October 1907 was the Convention for the Adaption to Naval War of the Principles of the Geneva Convention of 6 July 1906. (Annex No. B–22). The Convention was signed and ratified by, or on behalf of, Japan and each of the Powers bringing the Indictment, except Great Britain, Australia, Canada, India and New Zealand. The Convention was signed and ratified by twenty-seven Powers and later five other Powers adhered to it. The Indicting Powers who did not ratify this Convention and also Japan are parties to the Convention which was signed at The Hague on 29 July 1899; and, therefore, as between them, they are bound by the Convention of 1899, which contains most of the provisions found in the later Convention of 1907.

This, also, is one of the Hague Conventions, which contains a "general participation clause," and, therefore, it ceased to be applicable upon Japan as a direct treaty obligation when a non-signatory Power joined the ranks of the Belligerents. What we have said regarding this clause applies equally well here.

The Convention provides, among other things;

(1) That after every engagement the Belligerents shall take steps to look for the shipwrecked, sick and wounded, and protect them and the dead from pillage and ill treatment; those falling into the power of the enemy shall become

prisoners of war; the detaining Power shall send to their country as soon as possible a description of those picked up by him, and shall treat the sick and wounded and bury the dead;

(2) That hospital ships shall be respected and cannot be captured; but these ships may not be used for military purposes and shall be distinguished by markings and flags displaying the emblem of the Geneva Convention; and that the distinguishing markings prescribed for hospital ships shall not be used for protecting any ships other than those entitled to protection under the Convention.

JAPAN WAS A MEMBER OF THE FAMILY OF NATIONS.

Thus for many years prior to the year 1930, Japan had claimed a place among the civilized communities of the world and had voluntarily incurred the above obligations designed to further the cause of peace, to outlaw aggressive war, and to mitigate the horrors of war. It is against that background of obligations that the actings of the Accused must be viewed and judged.

* * *

[Editor's note: A detailed account of the Japanese government's preparation for war is given in the judgment.]

Conclusions

It remains to consider the contention advanced on behalf of the defendants that Japan's acts of aggression against France, her attack against the Netherlands, and her attacks on Great Britain and the United States of America were justifiable measures of self-defence. It is argued that these Powers took such measures to restrict the economy of Japan that she had no way of preserving the welfare and prosperity of her nationals but to go to war.

The measures which were taken by these Powers to restrict Japanese trade were taken in an entirely justifiable attempt to induce Japan to depart from a course of aggression on which she had long been embarked and upon which she had determined to continue. Thus the United States of America gave notice to terminate the Treaty of Commerce and Navigation with Japan on 26th July 1939 after Japan had seized Manchuria and a large part of the rest of China and when the existence of the treaty had long ceased to induce Japan to respect the rights and interests of the nationals of the United States in China. It was given in order that some other means might be tried to induce Japan to respect these rights. Thereafter the successive embargoes which were imposed on the export of materials to Japan were imposed as it became clearer and clearer that Japan had determined to attack the territories and interests of the Powers. They were imposed in an attempt to induce Japan to depart from the aggressive policy on which she had determined and in order that the Powers might no longer supply Japan with the materials to wage war upon them. In some cases, as for example in the case of the embargo on the export of oil from the United States of America to Japan, these measures were also taken in order to build up the supplies which were needed by the nations who were resisting the aggressors. The argument is indeed merely a repetition of Japanese propaganda issued at the time she was preparing for her wars of aggression. It is not easy to have patience with its lengthy repetition at this date when documents are at length available which demonstrate that Japan's decision to expand to the North, to the West and to the South at the expense of her neighbors was taken long before any economic measures were directed against her and was never departed from. The evidence clearly establishes contrary to the contention of the defense that the acts of aggression against France, and the attacks on Britain, the United States of America and the Netherlands were prompted by the desire to deprive China of any aid in the struggle she was waging against Japan's aggression and to secure for Japan the possessions of her neighbors in the South.

The Tribunal is of opinion that the leaders of Japan in the years 1940 and 1941 planned to wage wars of aggression against France in French Indo-China. They had determined to demand that France cede to Japan the right to station troops and the right to air bases and naval bases in French Indo-China, and they had prepared to use force against France if their demands were not granted. They did make such demands upon France under threat that they would use force to obtain them, if that should prove necessary. In her then situation France was compelled to yield to the threat of force and granted the demands.

The Tribunal also finds that a war of aggression was waged against the Republic of France. The occupation by Japanese troops of portions of French Indo-China, which Japan had forced France to accept, did not remain peaceful. As the war situation, particularly in the Philippines, turned against Japan the Japanese Supreme War Council in February 1945 decided to submit the following demands to the Governor of French Indo-China: (1) that all French troops and armed police be placed under Japanese command, and (2) that all means of communication and transportation necessary for military action be placed under Japanese control. These demands were presented to the Governor of French Indo-China on 9th March 1945 in the form of an ultimatum backed by the threat of military action. He was given two hours to refuse or accept. He refused, and the Japanese proceeded to enforce their demands by military action. French troops and military police resisted the attempt to disarm them. There was fighting in Hanoi, Saigon, Phnom-Penh, Nhatrang, and towards the Northern frontier. We quote the official Japanese account, "In the Northern frontiers the Japanese had considerable losses. The Japanese army proceeded to suppress French detachments in remote places and contingents which had fled to the mountains. In a month public order was re-established except in remote places". The Japanese Supreme War Council had decided that, if Japan's demands were refused and military action was taken to enforce them, "the two countries will not be considered as at war." This Tribunal finds that Japanese actions at that time constituted the waging of a war of aggression against the Republic of France.

The Tribunal is further of opinion that the attacks which Japan launched on 7th December 1941 against Britain, the United States of America and the Netherlands were wars of aggression. They were unprovoked attacks, prompted by the desire to seize the possessions of these nations. Whatever may be the difficulty of stating a comprehensive definition of "a war of aggression," attacks made with the above motive cannot but be characterised as wars of aggression.

It was argued on behalf of the defendants that, in as much as the Netherlands took the initiative in declaring war on Japan, the war which followed cannot be described as a war of aggression by Japan. The facts are that Japan had long planned to secure for herself a dominant position in the economy of the Netherlands East Indies by negotiation or by force of arms if negotiation failed. By the middle of 1941 it was apparent that the Netherlands would not yield to the Japanese demands. The leaders of Japan then planned and completed all the preparations for invading and seizing the Netherlands East Indies. The orders issued to the Japanese army for this invasion have not been recovered, but the orders issued to the Japanese navy on 5th November 1941 have been adduced in evidence. This is the Combined Fleet Operations Order No. 1 already referred to. The expected enemies are stated to be the United States, Great Britain and the Netherlands. The order states that the day for the outbreak of war will be given in an Imperial General Headquarters order, and that *after 0000 hours on that day a state of war will exist* and the Japanese forces will commence operations according to the plan. The order of Imperial General Headquarters was issued on 10th November and it fixed 8th December (Tokyo time), 7th December (Washington time) as the date on which a state of war would exist and operations would commence according to the plan. In the very first stage of the operations so to be commenced it is stated that the Southern Area Force will annihilate enemy fleets in the Philippines, British Malaya and the Netherlands East Indies area. There is no evidence that the above order was ever recalled or altered in respect to the above particulars. In these circumstances we find in fact that orders declaring the existence of a state of war and for the execution of a war of aggression by Japan against the Netherlands were in effect from the early morning of 7th December 1941. The fact that the Netherlands, being fully apprised of the imminence of the attack, in self-defence declared war against Japan on 8th December and thus officially recognised the existence of a state of war which had been begun by Japan cannot change that war from a war of aggression on the part of Japan into something other than that. In fact Japan did not declare war against the Netherlands until 11th January 1942 when her troops landed in the Netherlands East Indies. The Imperial Conference of 1st December 1941 decided that "Japan will open hostilities against the United States, Great Britain and the

Netherlands." Despite this decision to open hostilities against the Netherlands, and despite the fact that orders for the execution of hostilities against the Netherlands were already in effect, Tojo announced to the Privy Council on 8th December (Tokyo time) when they passed the Bill making a formal declaration of war against the United States of America and Britain that war would not be declared on the Netherlands in view of the future strategic convenience. The reason for this was not satisfactorily explained in evidence. The Tribunal is inclined to the view that it was dictated by the policy decided in October 1940 for the purpose of giving as little time as possible for the Dutch to destroy oil wells. It has no bearing, however, on the fact that Japan launched a war of aggression against the Netherlands.

The position of Thailand is special. The evidence bearing upon the entry of Japanese troops into Thailand is meagre to a fault. It is clear that there was complicity between the Japanese leaders and the leaders of Thailand in the years 1939 and 1940 when Japan forced herself on France as mediator in the dispute as to the border between French Indo-China and Thailand. There is no evidence that the position of complicity and confidence between Japan and Thailand, which was then achieved, was altered before December 1941. It is proved that the Japanese leaders planned to secure a peaceful passage for their troops through Thailand into Malaya by agreement with Thailand. They did not wish to approach Thailand for such an agreement until the moment when they were about to attack Malaya, lest the news of the imminence of that attack should leak out. The Japanese troops marched through the territory of Thailand unopposed on 7th December 1941 (Washington time). The only evidence the prosecution has adduced as to the circumstances of that march is (1) a statement made to the Japanese Privy Council between 10 a.m. and 11 a.m. on 8th December 1941 (Tokyo time) that an agreement for the passage of the troops was being negotiated, (2) a Japanese broadcast announcement that they had commenced friendly advancement into Thailand on the afternoon of the 8th December (Tokyo time) (Washington time, 7th December), and that Thailand had facilitated the passage by concluding an agreement at 12.30 p.m., and (3) a conflicting statement, also introduced by the prosecution, that Japanese troops landed at Singora and Patani in Thailand at 3.05 in the morning of 8th December (Tokyo time). On 21st December 1941 Thailand concluded a treaty of alliance with Japan. No witness on behalf of Thailand has complained of Japan's actions as being acts of aggression. In these circumstances we are left without reasonable certainty that the Japanese advance into Thailand was contrary to the wishes of the Government of Thailand and the charges that the defendants initiated and waged a war of aggression against the Kingdom of Thailand remain unproved.

Count 31 charges that a war of aggression was waged against the British Commonwealth of Nations. The Imperial Rescript which was issued about 12 noon on 8th December 1941 (Tokyo time) states "We hereby declare war on the United States of America and the British Empire." There is a great deal of lack of precision in the use of terms throughout the many plans which were formulated for an attack on British possessions. Thus such terms as "Britain," "Great Britain," and "England" are used without discrimination and apparently used as meaning the same thing. In this case there is no doubt as to the entity which is designated by "the British Empire." The correct title of that entity is "the British Commonwealth of Nations." That by the use of the term "the British Empire" they intended the entity which is more correctly called "the British Commonwealth of Nations" is clear when we consider the terms of the Combined Fleet Operations Order No. I already referred to. That order provides that a state of war will exist after 0000 hours X-Day, which was 8th December 1941 (Tokyo time), and that, the Japanese forces would then commence operations. It is provided that in the very first phase of the operations the "South Seas Force" will be ready for the enemy fleet in the Australia area. Later it was provided that "The following are areas expected to be occupied or destroyed as quickly as operational conditions permit, a, Eastern New Guinea, New Britain." These were governed by the Commonwealth of Australia under mandate from the League of Nations. The areas to be destroyed or occupied are also stated to include "Strategic points in the Australia area." Moreover, "important points in the Australian coast" were to be mined. Now the Commonwealth of Australia is not accurately described as being part of "Great Britain," which is the term used in the Combined Fleet Secret Operations Order No. I, nor is it accurately described as being part of "the British Empire," which is the term used in the Imperial Rescript. It is properly designated as part of "the British Commonwealth of Nations." It is plain therefore that the entity against which hostilities were to be directed and against which the declaration of war was directed was "the British Commonwealth of Nations," and Count 31 is well-founded when it charges that a war of aggression was waged against the British Commonwealth of Nations.

It is charged in Count 30 of the Indictment that a war of aggression was waged against the Commonwealth of the Philippines. The Philippines during the period of the war were not a completely sovereign state. So far as international relations were concerned they were part of the United States of America. It is beyond doubt that a war of aggression was waged against the people of the Philippines. For the sake of technical accuracy we shall consider the aggression against the people of the Philippines as being a part of the war of aggression waged against the United States of America.

Part B. Chapter VIII: Conventional War Crimes

Atrocities

After carefully examining and considering all the evidence we find that it is not practicable in a judgment such as this to state fully the mass of oral and documentary evidence presented; for a complete statement of the scale and character of the atrocities reference must be had to the record of the trial.

The evidence relating to atrocities and other Conventional War Crimes presented before the Tribunal establishes that from the opening of the war in China until the surrender of Japan in August 1945 torture, murder, rape and other cruelties of the most inhumane and barbarous character were freely practiced by the Japanese Army and Navy. During a period of several months the Tribunal heard evidence, orally or by affidavit, from witnesses who testified in detail to atrocities committed in all theaters of war on a scale so vast, yet following so common a pattern in all theaters, that only one conclusion is possible—the atrocities were either secretly ordered or wilfully permitted by the Japanese Government or individual members thereof and by the leaders of the armed forces.

Before proceeding to a discussion of the circumstances and the conduct of the accused in relation to the question of responsibility for the atrocities it is necessary to examine the matters charged. In doing so we will in some cases where it may be convenient refer to the association, if any, of the accused with the happenings under discussion. In other cases and generally, as far as it is practicable, circumstances having relevance to the issue of responsibility will be dealt with later.

At the beginning of the Pacific War in December 1941 the Japanese Government did institute a system and an organization for dealing with prisoners of war and civilian internees. Superficially, the system would appear to have been appropriate; however, from beginning to end the customary and conventional rules of war designed to prevent inhumanity were flagrantly disregarded.

Ruthless killing of prisoners by shooting, decapitation, drowning, and other methods; death marches in which prisoners including the sick were forced to march long distances under conditions which not even well-conditioned troops could stand, many of those dropping out being shot or bayonetted by the guards; forced labor in tropical heat without protection from the sun; complete lack of housing and medical supplies in many cases resulting in thousands of deaths from disease; beatings and torture of all kinds to extract information or confessions or for minor offences; killing without trial of recaptured prisoners after escape and for attempt to escape; killing without trial of captured aviators; and even cannibalism: these are some of the atrocities of which proof was made before the Tribunal.

The extent of the atrocities and the result of the lack of food and medical supplies is exemplified by a comparison of the number of deaths of prisoners of war in the European Theater with the number of deaths in the Pacific Theater. Of United States and United Kingdom forces 235,473 were taken prisoners by the German and Italian Armies; of these 9,348 or 4 per cent died in captivity. In the Pacific Theater 132,134 prisoners were taken by the Japanese from the United States and United Kingdom forces alone of whom 35,756 or 27 per cent died in captivity.

Allegation That the Laws of War Did Not Apply to the Conduct of the War in China

From the outbreak of the Mukden Incident till the end of the war the successive Japanese Governments refused to acknowledge that the hostilities in China constituted a war. They persistently called it an "Incident". With this as an excuse the military authorities persistently asserted that the rules of war did not apply in the conduct of the hostilities.

This war was envisaged by Japan's military leaders as a punitive war, which was being fought to punish the people of China for their refusal to acknowledge the superiority and leadership of the Japanese race and to cooperate with Japan. These military leaders intended to make the war so brutal and savage in all its consequences as to break the will of the Chinese people to resist.

As the Southern movement advanced to cut off aid to Generalissimo Chiang Kai-shek, the Chief-of-Staff of the Central China Expeditionary Force on 24 July 1939 sent an estimate of the situation to War Minister Itagaki. In that estimate of the situation, he said:

> The Army Air Force should carry out attacks upon strategic points in the hinterland in order to terrorize the enemy forces and civilians, and so develop among them an anti-war, pacifist tendency. What we expect of offensive operations against the interior is the mental terror they will create among the enemy forces and civilians rather than the material damage inflicted direct upon enemy personnel and equipment. We will wait and see them falling into nervous prostration in an excess of terror and madly starting anti-Chiang and pacifist movements.

Government and military spokesmen alike from time to time stated that the purpose of the war was to make the Chinese people "seriously reflect" upon the error of their ways, which in effect meant acceptance of Japanese domination.

Hirota in February, 1938, speaking in the House of Peers said "Japan has been endeavoring to make the Chinese Nationalist Government make reflections, if possible, while chastising their mistaken ideas by armed force . . . ." In the same speech he said "Since they were facing Japan with very strong anti-Japanese feeling, we decided on a policy whereby we had to necessarily chastise them."

Hiranuma began his "stimulation of the national morale" by a speech to the Diet on 21 January 1939 in which he said:

> In regard to the China Incident upon which both the Cabinet and the people are concentrating their endeavors, there exists an immutable policy for which Imperial Sanction was obtained by the previous Cabinet. The present Cabinet is of course committed to the same policy. I hope the intention of Japan will be understood by the Chinese so that they may cooperate with us. As for those who fail to understand, we have no other alternative than to exterminate them.

Formulation of Military Policy

Before discussing the nature and extent of atrocities committed by the Japanese armed forces it is desirable to state, very shortly, the system under which such conduct should have been controlled.

Those having authority in the formulation of military policy were the Army and Navy Ministers, the Chiefs of the Army and Navy General Staffs, the Inspector-General of Military Education, the Supreme War Council of Field Marshals and Fleet Admirals, and the War Council. The Army and Navy Ministers administered; the Inspector-General of Military Education supervised training; and the Chiefs of the Army and Navy General Staffs directed operations of the armed forces. The two war councils were advisory groups. The Army enjoyed special prerogatives. One of these was the exclusive right to nominate the successor of the War Minister. By the exercise of this power the Army was able to enforce continued adherence to the policies advocated by it.

In the War Ministry the policy initiating agency was the Military Affairs Bureau, which after consultation with the Army General Staff, other Bureaux of the War Ministry and other departments of the government concerned, announced the policy of the Japanese Military, usually in the form of regulations issued over the signature of the War Minister. This was the Bureau which formed the policy and issued regulations governing the conduct of war in general and the treatment of civilian internees and prisoners of war in particular. Such administration of prisoners of war as there was during the war in China was conducted by this Bureau. Until the opening of hostilities in the Pacific War, the administration of civilian internees and prisoners of war was retained by this Bureau when a special Division was created in the Bureau to perform that function. Three of the accused served as Chiefs of this powerful Military Affairs Bureau; they were Koiso, Muto and Sato. Koiso served at the beginning of the war in China between the dates of 8 January 1930 and 29 February 1932. Muto served before and after the commencement of the Pacific War; he became Chief of the Bureau on 30 September 1939 and served until 20 April 1942. Sato was employed in the Bureau before the beginning of the Pacific War, having been appointed on 15 July 1938; when Muto was transferred to command troops in Sumatra, Sato became Chief of the Bureau and served in that capacity from 20 April 1942 to 14 December 1944.

The corresponding Bureau in the Navy Ministry was the Naval Affairs Bureau. The Naval Affairs Bureau formed and promulgated regulations for the Navy and prescribed the policy of the Navy in conducting war at sea, occupied islands and other territory under its jurisdiction, and administered such prisoners of war and civilian internees as came under its power. The accused Oka served as Chief of this Bureau before and during the Pacific War from 15 October 1940 to 31 July 1944.

In the War Ministry, the Vice-Minister of War was the operating chief of the War Ministry Office and was responsible for coordination of the various Bureaux and other agencies under the Ministry. He received reports and suggestions from commanders in the field, advised the War Minister on the affairs under the Ministry and often issued orders and directives. Three of the accused served as Vice-Minister of War during the period prior to the Pacific War. Koiso served from 29 February 1932 to 8 August 1932. Umezu occupied the position from 23 March 1936 to 30 May 1938. Tojo became Vice-Minister of war on 30 May 1938 and served until 10 December 1938. Kimura was Vice-Minister of War before and after the commencement of the Pacific War; he was appointed on 10 April 1941 and served until 11 March 1943.

Lastly, of course, the commanders in the field were responsible for the maintenance of the discipline and the observance of the laws and customs of war by the troops under their command.

Captives Taken in the China War Were Treated As Bandits

The Japanese Delegate at Geneva in accepting the resolution of the League of Nations of 10 December 1931 setting up the Lytton Commission and imposing a virtual truce, stated that his acceptance was based on the understanding that the resolution would not preclude the Japanese Army from taking action against "bandits" in Manchuria. It was under this exception to the resolution that the Japanese Military continued hostilities against the Chinese troops in Manchuria. They maintained that no state of war existed between Japan and China; that the conflict was a mere "incident" to which the laws of war did not apply; and that those Chinese troops who resisted the Japanese Army were not lawful combatants but were merely "bandits." A ruthless campaign for the extermination of these "bandits" in Manchuria was inaugurated.

Although the main Chinese Army withdrew within the Great Wall at the end of 1931, resistance to the Japanese Army was constantly maintained by widely dispersed units of Chinese volunteers. The Kwantung Army Intelligence Service listed a large number of so-called Chinese route-armies, which in 1932 formed the subdivisions of the volunteer armies. These volunteer armies were active in the areas around Mukden, Haisheng and Yingkow. In August 1932, fighting broke out in the immediate vicinity of Mukden. At the height of the fighting at Mukden on 8 August 1932 Vice-Minister of War Koiso was appointed Chief-of-Staff of the Kwantung Army and also Chief of its Intelligence Service. He served in that capacity until 5 March 1934. On 16 September 1932 the Japanese forces in pursuit of defeated Chinese volunteer units arrived at the towns of Pingtingshan, Chienchinpao and Litsekou in the vicinity of Fushun. The inhabitants of these towns were accused of harboring the volunteers or "bandits" as they were called by the Japanese. In each town the Japanese troops assembled people along ditches and forced them to kneel; they then killed these civilians, men, women and children, with machine guns; those who survived the machine-gunning being promptly bayoneted to death. Over 2,700 civilians perished in this massacre, which the Japanese Kwantung Army claimed to be justified under its program of exterminating "bandits." Shortly thereafter, Koiso sent to the Vice-Minister of War an "Outline for Guiding Manchukuo" in which he said: "Racial struggle between Japanese and Chinese is to be expected. Therefore, we must never hesitate to wield military power in case of necessity." In this spirit, the practice of massacring, or "punishing" as the Japanese termed it, the inhabitants of cities and towns in retaliation for actual or supposed aid rendered to Chinese troops was applied. This practice continued throughout the China War; the worst example of it being the massacre of the inhabitants of Nanking in December 1937.

Since the Government of Japan officially classified the China War as an "Incident" and considered Chinese soldiers in Manchuria as "bandits", the Army refused to accord to captives taken in the fighting the status and the rights of Prisoners of War. Muto says that it was officially decided in 1938 to continue to call the war in China an "Incident" and to continue for that reason to refuse to apply the rules of war to the conflict. Tojo told us the same.

Many of the captured Chinese were tortured, massacred, placed in labor units to work for the Japanese Army, or organized into army units to serve the puppet governments established by Japan in the conquered territory in China. Some of these captives who refused to serve in these armies were transported to Japan to relieve the labor shortage in the munitions industries. At the camp at Akita, on the northwest shore of Honshu Island, 418 Chinese out of a group of 981 so transported to Japan died from starvation, torture or neglect.

The Policy Remained Unchanged after the Marco Polo Bridge Incident

Both the League of Nations and the meeting at Brussels of the signatories of the Nine-power Treaty failed to stop Japan's pursuing this "punitive" war on China after the outbreak of hostilities at the Marco Polo Bridge in 1937. This policy of Japan to treat the China war as an "incident" remained unchanged. Even after the establishment of the Imperial General Headquarters which was considered appropriate only in the case of an "incident" of such an extent as to require a declaration of war, as suggested by the War Minister at the Cabinet meeting held on 19th November 1937, no additional effort was made to enforce the laws of war in the conduct of the hostilities in China. Although the Government and the fighting services were organized on a full wartime basis, the China war was still treated as an "incident" with the consequent disregard of the rules of war.

The Rape of Nanking

As the Central China Expeditionary Force under command of Matsui approached the city of Nanking in early December 1937, over one-half of its one million inhabitants and all but a few neutrals who remained behind to organize an International Safety Zone, fled from the city. The Chinese Army retreated, leaving approximately 50,000 troops behind to defend the city. As the Japanese forces stormed the South Gate on the night of 12 December 1937, most of the remaining 50,000 troops escaped through the North and West Gates of the city. Nearly all the Chinese soldiers had evacuated the city or had abandoned their arms and uniforms and sought refuge in the International Safety Zone and all resistance had ceased as the Japanese Army entered the city on the morning of 13 December 1937. The Japanese soldiers swarmed over the city and committed various atrocities. According to one of the eyewitnesses they were let loose like a barbarian horde to desecrate the city. It was said by eyewitnesses that the city appeared to have fallen into the hands of the Japanese as captured prey, that it had not merely been taken in organized warfare, and that the members of the victorious Japanese Army had set upon the prize to commit unlimited violence. Individual soldiers and small groups of two or three roamed over the city murdering, raping, looting, and burning. There was no discipline whatever. Many soldiers were drunk. Soldiers went through the streets indiscriminately killing Chinese men, women and children without apparent provocation or excuse until in places the streets and alleys were littered with the bodies of their victims. According to another witness Chinese were hunted like rabbits, everyone seen to move was shot. At least 12,000 non-combatant Chinese men, women and children met their deaths in these indiscriminate killings during the first two or three days of the Japanese occupation of the city.

There were many cases of rape. Death was a frequent penalty for the slightest resistance on the part of a civilian or the members of her family who sought to protect her. Even girls of tender years and old women were raped in large numbers throughout the city, and many cases of abnormal and sadistic behavior in connection with these rapings occurred. Many women were killed after the act and their bodies mutilated. Approximately 20,000 cases of rape occurred within the city during the first month of the occupation.

Japanese soldiers took from the people everything they desired. Soldiers were observed to stop unarmed civilians on the road, search them, and finding nothing of value then to shoot them. Very many residential and commercial properties were entered and looted. Looted stocks were carried away in trucks. After looting shops and warehouses, the Japanese soldiers frequently set fire to them. Taiping Road, the most important shopping street, and block after block of the commercial section of the city were destroyed by fire. Soldiers burned the homes of civilians for no apparent reason. Such burning appeared to follow a prescribed pattern after a few days and continued for six weeks. Approximately one-third of the city was thus destroyed.

Organized and wholesale murder of male civilians was conducted with the apparent sanction of the commanders on the pretense that Chinese soldiers had removed their uniforms and were mingling with the population. Groups of Chinese civilians were formed, bound with their hands behind their backs, and marched outside the walls of the city where they were killed in groups by machine gun fire and with bayonets. More than 20,000 Chinese men of military age are known to have died in this fashion.

The German Government was informed by its representative about "atrocities and criminal acts not of an individual but of an entire Army, namely, the Japanese," which Army, later in the Report, was qualified as a "bestial machinery."

Those outside the city fared little better than those within. Practically the same situation existed in all the communities within 200 li (about 66 miles) of Nanking. The population had fled into the country-side in an attempt to escape from the Japanese soldiers. In places they had grouped themselves into fugitive camps. The Japanese captured many of these camps and visited upon the fugitives treatment similar to that accorded the inhabitants of Nanking. Of the civilians who had fled Nanking over 57,000 were overtaken and interned. These were starved and tortured in captivity until a large number died. Many of the survivors were killed by machine gun fire and by bayoneting.

Large parties of Chinese soldiers laid down their arms and surrendered outside Nanking; within 72 hours after their surrender they were killed in groups by machine gun fire along the bank of the Yangtze River. Over 30,000 such prisoners of war were so killed. There was not even a pretence of trial of these prisoners so massacred.

Estimates made at a later date indicate that the total number of civilians and prisoners of war murdered in Nanking and its vicinity during the first six weeks of the Japanese occupation was over 200,000. That these estimates are not exaggerated is borne out by the fact that burial societies and other organizations counted more than 155,000 bodies which they buried. They also reported that most of those were bound with their hands tied behind their backs. These figures do not take into account those persons whose bodies were destroyed by burning or by throwing them into the Yangtze River or otherwise disposed of by Japanese.

Japanese Embassy officials entered the city of Nanking with the advance elements of the Army; and on 14 December an official of the Embassy informed the International Committee for the Nanking Safety Zone that the "Army was determined to make it bad for Nanking, but that the Embassy officials were going to try to moderate the action." The Embassy officials also informed the members of the Committee that at the time of the occupation of the city no more than 17 military policemen were provided by the Army commanders to maintain order within the city. When it transpired that complaints to the Army officials did not have any result, those Japanese embassy officials suggested to the foreign missionaries that the latter should try and get publicity in Japan, so that the Japanese Government would be forced by public opinion to curb the Army.

Dr. Bates testified that the terror was intense for two and one-half to three weeks, and was serious six to seven weeks following the fall of the city.

Smythe, the Secretary of the Int. Committee for the Safety Zone, filed two protests a day for the first six weeks.

Matsui, who had remained in a rear area until 17 December, made a triumphal entry into the city on that day and on 18 December held a religious service for the dead, after which he issued a statement in the course of which he said:

> I extend much sympathy to millions of innocent people in the Kiangpei and Chekiang districts, who suffered the evils of war. Now the flag of the rising sun is floating high over Nanking, and the Imperial Way is shining in the southern parts of the Yangtze-Kiang. The dawn of the renaissance of the East is on the verge of offering itself. On this occasion, I hope for reconsideration of the situation by the 400 million people of China.

Matsui remained in the city for nearly a week.

Muto, then a colonel, had joined Matsui's staff on 10 November 1937 and was with Matsui during the drive on Nanking and participated in the triumphal entry and occupation of the city. Both he and Matsui admit that they heard of the atrocities being committed in the city during their stay at rear headquarters after the fall of the city. Matsui admits that he heard that foreign governments were protesting against the commission of these atrocities. No effective action was taken to remedy the situation. Evidence was given before the Tribunal by an eye witness that while Matsui was in Nanking on the 19th of December the business section of the city was in flames. On that day the witness counted fourteen fires in the principal business street alone. After the entry of Matsui and Muto into the city, the situation did not improve for weeks.

Members of the Diplomatic Corps and Press and the Japanese Embassy in Nanking sent out reports detailing the atrocities being committed in and around Nanking. The Japanese Minister-at-Large to China, Ito Nobofumi, was in Shanghai from September 1937 to February 1938. He received reports from the Japanese Embassy in Nanking and from members of the Diplomatic Corps and Press regarding the conduct of the Japanese troops and sent a resume of the reports to the Japanese Foreign Minister, Hirota. These reports as well as many others giving information of the atrocities committed at Nanking, which were forwarded by members of the Japanese diplomatic officials in China, were forwarded by Hirota to the War Ministry of which Umezu was Vice-Minister. They were discussed at Liaison Conferences, which were normally attended by the Prime Minister, War and Navy Ministers, Foreign Minister Hirota, Finance Minister Kaya, and the Chiefs of the Army and Navy General Staffs.

News reports of the atrocities were widespread. Minami, who was serving as Governor-General of Korea at the time, admits that he read these reports in the Press. Following these unfavorable reports and the pressure of public opinion aroused in nations all over the world, the Japanese Government recalled Matsui and approximately 80 of his officers but took no action to punish any of them. Matsui, after his return to Japan on 5 March 1938, was appointed a Cabinet Councillor and on 29 April 1940 was decorated by the Japanese Government for "meritorious services" in the China War. Matsui, in explaining his recall, says that he was not replaced by Hata because of the atrocities committed by his troops at Nanking but because he considered his work ended at Nanking and wished to retire from the Army. He was never punished.

The barbarous behavior of the Japanese Army cannot be excused as the acts of a soldiery which had temporarily gotten out of hand when at last a stubbornly defended position had capitulated—rape, arson and murder continued to be committed on a large scale for at least six weeks after the city had been taken and for at least four weeks after Matsui and Muto had entered the city.

The new Japanese Garrison Commander at Nanking, General Amaya, on 5 February 1938, at the Japanese Embassy in Nanking made a statement to the Foreign diplomatic corps criticizing the attitude of the foreigners who had been sending abroad reports of Japanese atrocities at Nanking and upbraiding them for encouraging anti-Japanese feeling. This statement by Amaya reflected the attitude of the Japanese Military toward foreigners in China, who were hostile to the Japanese policy of waging an unrestrained punitive war against the people of China.

The War Was Extended to Canton and Hankow

When Shanghai capitulated on 12 November 1937 and Matsui began his advance on Nanking, the National Government of China under Generalissimo Chiang Kai-shek abandoned its capital city, moved to Chungking with interim headquarters at Hankow and continued the resistance. After the capture of Nanking on 13 December 1937 the Japanese Government established a puppet government at Peiping.

The program designed to "pacify" the inhabitants of this occupied area and "make them rely on the Japanese Army" and force "self-examination" on the part of the National Government of China, which was adopted at Shanghai and Nanking and proclaimed by Matsui at Nanking, indicated settled policy. In December 1937 at Hsing Tai District on the Peiping-Hankow Railway Gendarmes under the command of a Japanese Warrant Officer seized seven civilians, who were suspected of being Chinese Irregulars, tortured and starved them for three days, then bound them to a tree and bayoneted them to death. Soldiers from this Army had appeared at the village of Tung Wang Chia, in Hopeh Province, earlier in October 1937 and committed murder, rape and arson, killing 24 of the inhabitants and burning about two-thirds of the homes. Another village in the same province known as Wang-Chia-To was visited by a Japanese unit in January 1938 and more than 40 of the civilian inhabitants were murdered.

Many of the inhabitants of the area around Shanghai fared no better than those in Nanking and other parts of North China. After the fighting had ceased at Shanghai, observers found around the ashes of farm houses in the suburban areas of Shanghai the bodies of farmers and their families with their hands tied behind them and bayonet wounds in their backs. As Matsui's troops occupied village after village on their march to Nanking they plundered and murdered and terrorized the population. Soochow was occupied in November 1937 and a number of residents who had not fled from the advancing troops were murdered.

Hata's troops entered Hankow and occupied the city on 25 October 1938. The next morning a massacre of prisoners occurred. At the customs wharf, the Japanese soldiers collected several hundred prisoners. They then selected small groups of three or four at a time, marched them to the end of the gangplanks reaching out to deep water; pushed them into the river and shot them. When the Japanese saw that they were being observed from the American gunboats anchored in the river off Hankow, they stopped and adopted a different method. They continued to select small groups, put them into motor launches and took them out in the stream where they threw them into the water and shot them.

It was during the Third Konoye Cabinet that the massacre at the town of Powen, on the Chinese Island of Hainan, occurred. In August 1941 during a punitive operation, a Japanese Naval Unit passed through the town of Powen without opposition. The next day, as a Detachment from that Unit returned to Powen, they found the dead body of a sailor of the Japanese Navy who had apparently been dead for several days. Under the assumption that the sailor had been killed by the residents of Powen, the Detachment burned the native houses and the church of the town. They killed the French missionary and 24 natives and burned their bodies. This incident is important because the wide circulation given the report of the massacre must have informed the members of the Cabinet and its subordinate officials of the method of warfare continuing to be employed by the Japanese military forces. The Chief-of-Staff of the Japanese occupation forces on Hainan Island made a complete report of this matter to Vice-Minister of War Kimura on 14 October 1941. Kimura at once circulated the report for the information of all concerned to the various bureaux of the War Ministry and then sent it to the Foreign Ministry. It received wide circulation both in and out of the Army.

An indication that the ruthless methods of the Japanese Army in waging war continued is revealed by the conduct of a Detachment of soldiers from Umezu's Army in Manchukuo in the campaign designed to stifle all resistance to the puppet regime under Emperor Pu Yi. This Detachment visited the village of Si-Tu-Ti in Jehol Province one night in August 1941. It captured the village, killed the members of more than 300 families and burned the village to the ground.

Even long after the occupation of Canton and Hankow, the Japanese, while carrying on campaigns into the farther interior, committed large-scale atrocities there. Toward the end of 1941, Japanese troops entered the city of Wei-Yang, in Kwantung Province. They indulged in a massacre of Chinese civilians, bayoneting male and female, old and young without discrimination. One eye-witness, who survived a bayonet wound in the abdomen, told of the slaughter of more than 600 Chinese civilians by Japanese troops. In July 1944,

Japanese troops arrived at the Tai Shan District in the Kwantung Province. They committed arson, robbery, slaughter and numerous other atrocities. As a result thereof, 559 shops were burnt, and more than 700 Chinese civilians killed.

From Hankow, the Japanese troops carried on their campaign southward to Changsha. In September 1941, the Japanese troops of the Sixth Division forced more than 200 Chinese prisoners of war to plunder large quantities of rice, wheat and other commodities. Upon their return, the Japanese soldiers, to conceal these crimes, massacred them by artillery fire. After the Japanese forces had occupied Changsha, they also freely indulged in murder, rape, incendiarism and many other atrocities throughout the district. Then they drove further down southward to Kweilin and Liuchow in Kwangsi Province. During the period of Japanese occupation of Kweilin, they committed all kinds of atrocities such as rape and plunder. They recruited woman labour on the pretext of establishing factories. They forced the women thus recruited into prostitution with Japanese troops. Prior to their withdrawal from Kweilin in July 1945, the Japanese troops organized an arson corps and set fire to buildings in the entire business district of Kweilin.

Returning Soldiers Told of Atrocities Committed by Them

After the occupation of Hankow, Japanese soldiers returning from China told stories of the army's misdeeds in China and displayed loot which they had taken. This conduct on the part of the soldiers returning to Japan apparently became so general that the War Ministry under Itagaki, in an effort to avoid unfavorable criticism at home and abroad, issued special orders to the commanders in the field to instruct returning officers and men upon the proper conduct to be followed by them upon reaching Japan. These special orders were prepared in the Military Service Section of the Military Service Bureau of the War Ministry, classified as "Top Secret" and issued by Itagaki's Vice-Minister of War in February 1939. They were transmitted by the Vice-Chief of the Army General Staff to the Japanese Army Commanders in China. These secret orders detailed the objectionable conduct of returning soldiers which was to be corrected. It was complained that the soldiers told stories of atrocities committed by them on Chinese soldiers and civilians; some of the stories commonly heard were cited as follows: "One company commander unofficially gave instructions for raping as follows: 'In order that we will not have problems, either pay them money or kill them in some obscure place after you have finished' "; "If the army men who participated in the war were investigated individually, they would probably all be guilty of murder, robbery or rape.' "; ' 'The thing I like best during the battle is plundering. In the front lines the superiors turn a blind eye to plundering and there were some who plundered to their heart's content. At . . . we captured a family of four. We played with the daughter as we would with a harlot. But as the parents insisted that the daughter be returned to them we killed them. We played with the daughter as before until the unit's departure and then killed her."; "In the half year of battle, about the only things I learned are rape and burglary."; "The plundering by our army in the battle area is beyond imagination."; and "The Prisoners taken from the Chinese Army were sometimes lined up in one line and killed to test the efficiency of the machine-gun." Concerning loot brought back to Japan by returning soldiers, it was noted that some commanders distributed among the men license cards authorized by the stamp of the Unit Commander permitting the soldiers to transport their loot to Japan. These orders stated: "Not only does the improper talk of the returned officers and men become the cause of rumors, but also impairs the trust of the people in the Army, disrupts the unity of the people supporting the Army, etc. I repeat the order again to make the control of instruction even more strict and consequently glorify the meritorious deeds, raise the Japanese Army's military reputation and insure that nothing will impair the accomplishment of the object of the Holy War."

Murder of Captured Aviators

Japanese leaders feared that aerial warfare might be waged against the cities and towns of Japan. One of the reasons given by the Japanese Military for opposing ratification of the Geneva Prisoner of War Convention of 1929 was that such ratification would double the range of enemy planes making raids on Japan in that the crews could land on Japanese territory after completing their mission and be secure in the knowledge that they would be treated as prisoners of war.

The fear that Japan would be bombed was realized on 18 April 1942 when American planes under the command of Colonel Doolittle bombed Tokyo and other cities in Japan. This was the first time Japan had been subjected to a bombing raid; and in the words of Tojo, it was an awful "shock" to the Japanese. Sugiyama, the Chief of the Japanese General Staff, demanded the death penalty for all aviators who bombed Japan. Although there had been no law or regulation of the Japanese Government prior to this raid under which the death penalty could be administered, Prime Minister Tojo ordered regulations issued to be retroactive to the time of the raid which would permit the death penalty to be imposed upon the Doolittle fliers. Tojo later admitted that he took this action as a deterrent to prevent future raids.

These regulations which were dated 13 August 1942 were made applicable to "enemy fliers who have raided" Japan, Manchukuo or Japanese operational areas "and have come within the jurisdiction of the Japanese Expeditionary Forces in China." Thus they were directly and retrospectively aimed at the United States airmen already in the hands of the Japanese in China.

The offences were air attacks

(1) upon ordinary people,

(2) upon private property of a non-military nature,
(3) against other than military objectives, and
(4) "Violations of war time international law."

The punishment prescribed was death or imprisonment for ten years or more.

Conduct defined as offences 1, 2, and 3 were such as the Japanese themselves had regularly practiced in China. It will be remembered that in July 1939 the Chief-of-Staff of the Central China Expeditionary Force reported to War Minister Itagaki that a policy of indiscriminate bombing in order to terrorize the Chinese had been adopted. The fourth, violations of the laws of war, required no such regulations. Their breach was punishable in any event, but, of course, only upon proper trial and within the limits of punishment permitted by international law.

The crews of two of the Doolittle planes which had been forced to land in China were taken prisoner by the Japanese occupation forces under the command of Hata. These eight fliers composing the crews were treated as common criminals, being handcuffed and bound. The members of one crew were taken to Shanghai and the members of the other crew were taken to Nanking; at each place they were interrogated under torture. On 25 April 1942 the fliers were taken to Tokyo and were kept blindfolded and handcuffed until they were inside the Military Police Headquarters in Toyko. They were then placed in solitary confinement, from which they were taken out and questioned again under torture for eighteen days. At the end of this period the fliers to avoid further torture signed statements written in Japanese, the contents of which were unknown to them.

The fliers were returned to Shanghai on 17 June 1942 where they were incarcerated, starved, and otherwise ill-treated. On 28 July 1942 Vice-Minister of War Kimura transmitted Tojo's orders to Hata who was the Supreme Commander of all Japanese Forces in China at that time. Tojo's orders were to the effect that the fliers were to be punished under the new regulations. On orders from the Chief of the General Staff, Hata instructed that the fliers be put on trial. At this "trial" some of the airmen were too ill to take part in the proceedings, there was no translation of the matters charged, and they were given no opportunity to defend themselves. The trial was a mere mockery. This trial was held on 20 August 1942 when all of the fliers were sentenced to death. Upon review in Tokyo, and on the recommendation of Tojo, five of the sentences were reduced to life imprisonment and the remaining three death sentences were approved. On 10 October 1942 Hata ordered the sentences to be executed and reported his action to the Army Chief of Staff. The death sentences were carried out as ordered.

In this manner was begun the policy of killing Allied fliers who fell into the hands of the Japanese. This was done not only in Japan, but in occupied territories during the remainder of the Pacific War. The usual practice was to starve and torture captured aviators before their murder. Even the formality of a trial was often omitted. Where a court-martial was held prior to their being killed it appears that the court-martial was a mere formality.

As an illustration we cite the case of two American B-29 fliers at Osaka on 18 July 1945, who were charged with violation of the regulations. Prior to the trial, their case was investigated by an officer appointed to perform that duty, who recommended the death penalty. The recommendation was approved by the Commander of the Central Military District and by General Hata, who was at that time the Commander of the Second Army Corps at Hiroshima. The recommendation of the Investigating Officer, with the approval of the Military Commanders, was sent to the War Ministry for final approval; and that approval was obtained. At the trial, the report and recommendation of the Investigating Officer and the approval of General Hata and others were read to the court-martial by the prosecutor, who demanded the death penalty based upon those documents. The accused were asked a few routine questions and the death penalty was imposed. They were executed the same day.

In the Tokai Military District, prior to May 1945, eleven Allied airmen were subjected to trials in which their interests were not safeguarded, sentenced to death and executed. However, the Commandant of Military Police for Japan considered this procedure imposed an unnecessary delay in the killing of captured Allied fliers; consequently in June 1945, he sent a letter to each of the Military Police Headquarters Commandants of the several military districts in Japan complaining of the delay in the disposition of captured Allied airmen, stating that it was impossible to dispose of them immediately by courts-martial, and recommending that the Military Police in the military districts dispense with courts-martial after securing the approval of the Commander of the Military District. In the Tokai Military District 27 Allied fliers were killed without trial after this letter was received. In the Central Military District over which Hata exercised administrative command, 43 Allied airmen were killed without having been tried by courts-martial or otherwise. At Fukuoka eight Allied airmen were killed without trial on 20 June 1945, eight more in the same manner on 12 August 1945, and three days later on 15 August 1945 the third group of eight, making a total of 24 Allied airmen killed at Fukuoka without being given a trial after the above-mentioned letter recommending this procedure was sent out from Tokyo by the Commandant of Military Police.

The killing of Allied airmen in the Tokai, Central and Western Districts of Japan was done by firing squads; in the Eastern District, which embraced Tokyo, more inhumane methods were used. Allied airmen captured in that district were detained in the Military Police Headquarters Guard House, pending a so-called investigation to determine whether they had violated the Regulations. This investigation consisted of interrogation under torture in an effort to coerce the victim into confessing to facts which would subject him to the death penalty under the regulations. No less than 17 airmen died in this guard house as a result of torture, starvation and lack of medical care. Those who survived this torture were victims of a more dreadful death. The Tokyo Army Prison was located on the edge of the Yoyogi Military Parade Ground. This prison was a disciplinary barracks in which were confined Japanese soldiers serving sentences. The prison grounds were small and surrounded by a brick wall approximately 12 feet high. The prison buildings were of wood and were constructed so close together as to occupy all of the ground available within the brick wall except for necessary alley-ways and courts. One of the cell blocks was set apart by a wooden wall seven feet high. On 25 April 1945, five Allied fliers were placed in that cell block; on 9 May, 29 more were added; and on 10 May, 28 others were confined there. On the night of 25 May 1945 Tokyo was heavily bombed. On that night there were 62 Allied fliers confined in this cell block. There were 464 Japanese Army prisoners confined in other buildings within the prison. The wooden buildings of the prison, as well as the highly inflammable dwellings surrounding it, were hit and set on fire by incendiary bombs. The prison was completely demolished; and after the fire, it was found that all of the 62 Allied fliers had perished. It is significant that none of the 464 Japanese or any of their jailors suffered a similar fate. The evidence shows that the fate of the Allied airmen was deliberately planned.

In the occupied territories, one of the methods of killing captured airmen was by decapitation with a sword, and at the hands of a Japanese officer. Captured airmen were killed this way at Singapore, Malaya (June-July 1945); Samarinda, Borneo (January 1945); Palembang, Sumatra (March 1943); Batavia, Java (April 1942); Menada, Celebes (June 1945); Tomohon, Celebes (September 1944); Toli Toli, Celebes (October 1944); Kendari, Celebes (November 1944) (January 1945) (February 1945); Beo, Talaud Islands (March 1945); Rainis, Talaud Islands (January 1945); Singkang, Celebes (July 1945); Çarara, Ambon Island (August 1944); New Guinea (October 1944); Totabil, New Britain (November 1944); Porton Island (December 1943); Kwajalein Island (October 1942); and Cebu City, Philippines (March 1945).

Another method of murdering Allied fliers was used at Hankow, China, in December 1944. Three American fliers, who had been forced down and captured sometime before, were paraded through the streets and subjected to ridicule, beating and torture by the populace. When they had been weakened by the beatings and torture, they were saturated with gasoline and burned alive. Permission for this atrocity was granted by the Commander of the 34th Japanese Army.

The cruelty of the Japanese is further illustrated by the treatment of an Allied airman, who was captured at Rabaul on the Island of New Britain. He was bound with a rope on which fish-hooks had been attached so that when he moved the hooks dug into his flesh. He ultimately died of malnutrition and dysentery.

Massacres

Massacres of prisoners of war, civilian internees, sick and wounded, patients and medical staffs of hospitals and civilian population were common throughout the Pacific War. Prisoners of war and civilian internees were massacred in some instances shortly after capture.

A massacre at Balikpapan in Borneo occurred in the following circumstances: On January 20, 1942, two Dutch POW officers were ordered by the Japanese to Balikpapan to transmit an ultimatum to the Dutch commandant in which it was demanded to surrender Balikpapan intact. In case of noncompliance, all Europeans were to be killed. The ultimatum was read in the presence of a Japanese Major General and five other Japanese officers to the Dutch officers who had to deliver it to the commander at Balikpapan. Reply was sent by the Commander of Balikpapan to the Japanese to the effect that the Commander at Balikpapan had had from the Dutch authorities the necessary instructions with regard to demolition, which, therefore, had to be carried out.

When the Japanese approached Balikpapan, the oil fields were set on fire. In an affidavit of an eyewitness, the Tribunal was given a description of the massacre of the white population of Balikpapan numbering between 80 and 100, who were executed in a cruel manner on 24 February 1942 by being driven into the sea and subsequently shot after some had been killed by having arms and legs lopped off with swords, as is described later.

In this relation, it is interesting to note that there was produced, in this trial, a Foreign Affairs document, marked "very secret," containing a "tentative draft of Japan's policies toward the Southern Regions," dated October 4, 1940. In this draft it states with regard to the Dutch East Indies:

> If any of the important natural resources should be destroyed, all the persons connected with the raw material, ten government officials concerned, shall be severely punished as being the responsible persons.

It was of vital importance for Japan to take the NEI oil fields intact. The oil question was a decisive element in the move to the South, and the Japanese Government was very much afraid lest, in case of war, the oil fields would be set on fire. Matsuoka gave expression to this fear to von Ribbentrop on March 29, 1941, when he stated:

> If at all avoidable, he would not touch the Netherlands East Indies, since he was afraid that in the event of a Japanese attack on this area the oil fields would be set on fire. They could be brought into operation again only after one or two years.

In view of this, and remembering the fact that the Japanese Government officially ordered the destruction of all harmful documents, this Foreign Office draft obtains a special significance. Yamamoto, a former high official in the Foreign Office, when asked for the reason why most of the things planned in the "tentative draft" actually did occur, in spite of the fact that this draft was, according to him, made only by a junior secretary, cynically replied that "these secretaries were very good students."

Taking all these facts together, the result justifies the inference that the plan proposed in the draft of October 4, 1940, was accepted as government policy, the more so because a massacre of male personnel also occurred at Blora, apparently in relation to the demolition of the oil fields at Tjepu, Java. Women in this place were not killed, but were all raped several times in the presence of the commanding officer.

Instances of such massacres occurred at: Hong Kong, China (December 1941); Ipoh, Malaya (December 1941); between Parit Sulong and Maur, Malaya (January 1942); Parit Sulong, Malaya (January 1942); Katonga, Malaya (January 1942); Alexander Hospital, Malaya (January 1942); Singapore, Malaya (February-March 1942); Panjang, Malaya (February 1942); Maur, Malaya (February 1942); Jampong Job, Thailand (December 1941); Longnawa, Borneo (August 1942); Tarakan, Borneo (January 1942); Banka Island, Netherlands East Indies (February 1942); Kota Radja, Sumatra (March 1942); Rembang, Java (March 1942); Lembang, Java (March 1942); Soebang, Java (March 1942); Tjiatar Pass, Java (March 1942); Bandoeng, Java (March 1942); Laha, Ambon Island, Moluccas (February 1942); Okabeti, Dutch Timor (February 1942); Oesapa Besar, Dutch Timor (April 1942); Tatu Meta, Portuguese Timor (February 1942); Milne Bay, British New Guinea (August 1942); Buna, British New Guinea (August 1942); Tol, New Britain (February 1942); Tarawa Island (October 1942); Camp O'Donnell, Philippines (April 1942); and Santa Cruz, Manila, Philippines (April 1942). Massacres occurred in this manner in French Indo-China in the hostilities against the Free French organizations there. Prisoners of war and detained civilians were massacred at such places as: Langson (March 1945); Dinh Lap (March 1945); Thakhek (March 1945); Tong (March 1945); Tan Qui (March 1945); Loas (March 1945); Dong Dang (March 1945); Hagiang (March 1945); and Tonkin (March 1945).

Citizens of the U.S.S.R. at Hailar in Manchuria were massacred on 9 August 1945. This was done at the instance of the Commander of the Kwantung Army. Those murdered were not charged with any offense, but the reason given for the murders was that they might carry on espionage or sabotage against the Japanese Army.

After the Japanese forces had occupied territory and fighting had ceased, massacres were freely committed as a means of terrorizing the civilian population and subjecting them to the domination of the Japanese. Massacres of this type were committed against the civilian population at the following places: Shanywa, Burma (1945); Tharrawaddy, Burma (May 1945); Ongun, Burma (May 1945); Ebaing, Burma (June 1945); Kalagon, Burma (July 1945); Mantanani Island (February 1944); Sulug Island (October 1943); Udar Island (Early 1944); Dinawan Island (July 1944); Pontianak, Borneo (October 1943–June 1944); Singkawang, Borneo (August 1944); Buitenzorg, Java (1943); Java (The "Koo" Incident) (July 1943–March 1944); Lautem, Portuguese Timor (January 1943); Moa Island (September 1944); Semata Island (September 1944); Aileu, Portuguese Timor (September 1942); Nauru Island (March 1943); Hopevale, Philippines (December 1943); Alaminos, Philippines (March 1944); San Carlos, Philippines (February 1943); Barrio Angad, Philippines (November 1944); Palo Beach, Philippines (July 1943); Tigbuan, Philippines (August 1943); Calbayog, Philippines (July 1943); Ranao-Pilayan, Philippines (June 1944); Bogo, Philippines (October 1944); Barrio Umagos,

Philippines (October 1944); Lipa Airport, Philippines (1944); Santa Catalina, Philippines (August 1944); and Sitio Canugkay, Pilar, Philippines (December 1944). There were massacres of prisoners of war and civilian internees or conscripted laborers during the occupation which were committed because they had become starved, diseased or otherwise disabled and were no longer of use or for other reasons had become a burden to the Japanese occupation force. Such massacres were committed at the following places: Chaymoga Labor Camp, Siam (February 1944); Hsipaw, Burma (January 1945); Port Blair, Andaman Islands (August 1945); Kota Tjane, Sumatra (May 1943); Sibolga, Sumatra (April 1942); Djombang, Java (April 1942); Amboina, Ambon Island (July 1943); Wewak, British New Guinea (May 1944); Aitape, New Guinea (October 1943) But, New Guinea (June 1944); Rabaul, New Britain (January 1943); Bouganville (August 1944); Wake Island (October 1943); and in the labor camps along the Burma-Siam Railroad Project (1943–1944). There were some massacres which were intended to discourage general violation of regulations such as that at the labor camp on Hainan Island (May 1943) in an effort to prevent smuggling; that at Saigon, French Indo-China (December 1943) intended to prevent illegal use of the radio; and that of civilians and prisoners of war at Amboina, Ambon Island (July 1943) where the civilians were killed for giving, and the prisoners for receiving, food. In addition to those referred to were other massacres and murders, such as that aboard the Nitta Maru (December 1941) where American prisoners of war were beheaded; and that on New Guinea which involved the killing of two American prisoners of war (October 1944). In the latter case, the Japanese officer responsible said, "I asked if I could get an American prisoner of war and kill him." The Commander of the 36th Japanese Division promptly granted the request and delivered two prisoners to be killed. They were blindfolded, tied and stabbed in the back with bayonets and then decapitated with shovels.

There were massacres perpetrated in anticipation of a Japanese withdrawal or of an Allied attack. These were not limited to prisoners of war, although many prisoners were massacred under these circumstances, apparently to prevent them from being liberated by the Allied forces. Civilian internees and members of the civilian population were also massacred under such circumstances. Massacres of this type occurred in the following places: Hailar, China (August 1945); Malacca, Nicobar Islands (July 1945); Sandakan, British Borneo (June–July 1945); Ranau, British Borneo (August 1945); Kuala Belat, British Borneo (June 1945); Miri, British Borneo (June 1945); Labuan, British Borneo (June 1945); Laeluta, Portuguese Timor (September 1945); Ballah Island (January 1943); Ocean Island (September 1943); Puerto Princesa, Philippines (December 1944); Irisan Area, Philippines (April 1945); Calambya, Philippines (February 1945); Panghulo, Philippines (February 1945); Tapel, Philippines (July 1945); and Barrio Dinwiddie, Philippines (August 1945). Massacres of this kind were very numerous in Batangas Province of the Philippines. They were committed among others at the following places: Barrio San Indres (January 1945); Bauan (February 1945); Santo Tomas (February 1945); Lippa (February and March 1945); Taal (February 1945); Tanauan (February 1945); and Rosario (March 1945). When it became apparent that Manila would be liberated massacres of this type were committed all over the city as well as rape and arson.

We have not mentioned massacres of prisoners of war at sea, to be discussed later, nor those that occurred in "death marches". These also we shall mention later. Apart from the massacres already mentioned there were many individual murders. Many of them were committed in horrible fashion; many were committed in connection with other crimes such as rape, robbery and arson, while others were committed apparently for no other purpose than to gratify the cruel instincts of the perpetrators.

Some of the massacres call for further description, especially those of patients and medical personnel in military hospitals which were clearly marked with the Geneva insignia and entitled to protection under that convention as well as the general laws of war. During the massacres at Hong Kong, Japanese troops entered the Military Hospital at St. Stephens College and bayoneted the sick and wounded in their beds, and raped and murdered nurses who were on duty there. During the battle of Northwestern Jehore in Malaya (January 1942), an ambulance convoy containing sick and wounded was captured by Japanese soldiers. The personnel and wounded were removed from the ambulances and killed by shooting, bayoneting and burning alive after being saturated with oil. At Katonga in Malaya (January 1942), an ambulance convoy was fired upon by Japanese machine gunners. The personnel and wounded were taken from the convoy, tied together and shot in the back. The Alexandra Hospital at Singapore, Malaya was captured by the Japanese forces on 13 February 1942. The Japanese troops went through the first floor of the hospital and bayoneted everyone on that floor. They entered the operating room where a soldier was under chloroform undergoing an operation and bayoneted the patient, the surgeon and the anesthetist. They then went to the second floor and other parts of the building and removed the patients and medical personnel and massacred them. When the Japanese troops entered Soebang, Java, in March 1942, they removed a nurse and her patients from the Military Hospital and massacred them with women and children of the civilian population. These massacres in disregard of the laws of war respecting the treatment to be accorded to military hospitals and their personnel and patients illustrate the attitude of Japanese soldiers and their officers towards the laws of war.

There is a similarity of method to be found in most of the massacres. The victims were first bound and then shot, bayoneted or decapitated with swords. In most instances, the victims were shot and then bayoneted by Japanese soldiers who went among the wounded killing those who still lived. In a number of cases they were gathered on a beach with the water to their backs or on the edge of a cliff and there killed.

In some places even more dreadful methods were employed. At the Manila German Club and at Fort Santiago the victims were gathered together in a building, which was set on fire; and those who attempted to escape were shot or bayoneted as they emerged from the flames.

In evidence upon the atrocity committed at the German Club in Manila in February 1945, it was disclosed that fugitives took shelter under the Club from bombardment and shell-fire then proceeding. Japanese soldiers surrounded the Club by a barricade of inflammable material, then poured gasoline over this barricade and ignited it. Thus the fugitives were forced to attempt to escape through the flaming barricade. Most of them were bayoneted and shot by the waiting Japanese soldiers. Some of the women were raped and their infants bayoneted in their arms. After raping the women the Japanese poured gasoline on their hair and ignited it. The breasts of some of the women were cut off by Japanese soldiers.

A massacre took place at St. Paul's College in Manila in the following manner: Approximately 250 people were placed in the building and the doors and windows solidly shut and barred. While so confined it was noticed that the three hanging chandeliers were wrapped in blackout paper and that strings or light wires ran from inside these wrappings to the outside of the building. Later the Japanese brought in biscuits, candy and liquor of some sort, placed them in the centre of the room and told the captives that they were safe where they were and that they might have the food and drink which had been brought to them. Accordingly they went to the food as deposited and within a matter of moments there were three explosions. The covered chandeliers had contained explosives. Many were thrown to the floor and a panic ensued. Japanese outside the building began firing machine guns into it and threw grenades. The explosions had blown out the windows and a portion of the wall, through which those who were able endeavoured to escape. Many of these were killed as they tried to do so.

At a prisoner of war camp above Puerto Princesa Bay on the Philippine Island of Palawan there occurred a particularly cruel and premeditated massacre of American prisoners. There were some 150 prisoners in this camp. They had been told previously by their captors that if Japan won the war they would be returned to America but that they would be killed if Japan were defeated. Before the massacre there had been some raiding of the island by American aircraft. In the camp a number of shallow and lightly covered airraid shelters had been dug. At about 2 p.m. on 14 December 1944, the prisoners were ordered to go to these shelters. Japanese soldiers armed with rifles and machine guns were posted around the camp. When the prisoners were all in the shelters, gasoline was thrown into them from buckets and then this was followed by lighted torches. Explosions followed and those prisoners who were not too badly burnt struggled to escape. These were killed by fire from the rifles and machine guns placed in position for the purpose. In some cases they were killed by bayonet thrusts. Five only of the 150 survived this dreadful experience. They did so by swimming out into the bay whence after nightfall they escaped into the jungle and eventually joined up with Philippines guerillas.

Mass drowning was used at Port Blair, Andaman Islands (August 1945), where the civilian internees were placed aboard ship, taken to sea, and forced into the water. A combination of drowning and shooting, similar to that employed at Hankow, was used at Kota Radja (March 1942), where Dutch prisoners of war were placed in sloops, towed to sea, shot and thrown into the sea. At Tarakan, Borneo (January 1942), Dutch prisoners of war were taken aboard a Japanese light cruiser, taken to the spot where a Japanese destroyer had been fired upon by them, decapitated and thrown into the sea.

Massacres Were Ordered

The evidence shows that most of these massacres were ordered by commissioned officers, that some of them were ordered by high-ranking generals and admirals, that in many cases commissioned officers were actually present during their commission, observing, directing or actually doing the killing. Japanese orders were captured which gave directions for killing Filipinos. The file of orders issued by the Manila Navy Defence Force between December 1944 and February 1945 was captured. It contained this order: "Be careful to make no mistake in the time of exploding and burning when the enemy invades. When killing Filipinos, assemble them together in one place as far as possible thereby saving ammunition and labor." Diaries of Japanese soldiers were captured indicating that their owners had been ordered to massacre and had done so pursuant to such orders. Battle reports of military units and police reports of military police, which were captured, contained reports to superior authorities relating to massacres which had been committed, together with the number of rounds of ammunition expended and the number of victims killed. Prisoners of war from many camps in Japan and the occupied areas have testified that they were informed by their Japanese, Formosan and Korean guards that they would be killed in case the Allies invaded the locality or if Japan should lose the war. We have referred to cases where these threats were carried out. In one camp, at least, written evidence of an order from higher authority to kill the prisoners of war was found. The captured journal from a camp in Formosa contained an entry showing that a reply had been sent to an inquiry from the Chief-of-Staff of the 11th Military Police Unit of the Kiirun Fortified Area Headquarters regarding "extreme measures" for prisoners of war. The method to be employed in carrying out these "extreme measures" was detailed as follows: "Whether they are destroyed individually or in groups, or however it is done, with mass bombing, poisonous smoke, poisons, drowning, decapitation, or what, dispose of them as the situation dictates. In any case, it is the aim not to allow the escape of a single one, to annihilate them all, and not to leave any traces." This annihilation was, *inter alia,* prescribed in all cases "where escapes from the camp may turn into a hostile fighting force."

A general order was issued by Vice-Minister of War Shibayama on 11 March 1945. The order stated: "The handling of prisoners of war in these times when the state of things is becoming more and more pressing and the evils of war extend to the Imperial Domain, Manchuria and other places, is in the enclosed summary. We hope you follow it, making no mistakes." The enclosed summary to which reference was made began: "The Policy: With the greatest efforts prevent the prisoners of war falling into the hands of the enemy. Further for this purpose carry out a transfer of the place of confinement for those prisoners of war for whom it is necessary." The Ranau Death Marches, which began at about this time between Sandakan and Ranau in Borneo to which we will refer presently, conformed to the policy indicated by the order just quoted.

Death Marches

The Japanese Army did not observe the laws of war in the movement of prisoners of war from one place to another. Prisoners were forced to march long distances without sufficient food and water and without rest. Sick and wounded were forced to march in the same manner as the able. Prisoners who fell behind on such marches were beaten, tortured and murdered. We have been furnished evidence of many such marches.

The Bataan March is a conspicuous example. When General King surrendered his forces on Bataan on 9 April 1942, he was assured by Japanese General Homma's Chief-of-Staff that his soldiers would be treated humanely. General King had saved sufficient trucks from demolition to move his men from Bataan to the prisoner of war camp. The American and Filipino soldiers on Bataan had been on short rations and the sick and wounded were numerous. However, when General King suggested the use of the trucks, he was forbidden to do so. The prisoners were marched in intense heat along the highway to San Fernando, Pampanga, which is a distance of 120 kilometers or 75 miles. The sick and wounded were forced to march. Those who fell by the roadside and were unable to continue were shot or bayoneted. Others were taken from the ranks, beaten, tortured and killed. The march continued for nine days, with the Japanese guards being relieved at five kilometer intervals by fresh guards who had been transported in the American trucks. During the first five days the prisoners received little or no food or water. Thereafter, the only water available was that from an occasional artesian well or caribou wallow. When the prisoners grouped around a well in an attempt to get water the Japanese fired upon them. Shooting and bayoneting of prisoners were commonplace. Dead bodies littered the side of the road. Murata, who had been sent to the Philippines in February 1942 by War Minister Tojo as a civilian advisor to General Homma, drove along this highway and saw the dead bodies along the highway in such great numbers that he was prompted to ask General Homma about the situation. Murata testified that, "I merely saw it; I did not complain about it; I just asked questions." At San Fernando, the prisoners were crowded into railway freight cars to be transported to Camp O'Donnell. They were forced to stand through lack of space and many died in the cars from exhaustion and lack of ventilation. It is not clear how many died in this movement from Bataan to Camp O'Donnell. The evidence indicates that there were approximately 8,000 deaths of American and Filipino prisoners. At Camp O'Donnell, the evidence shows that from April to December 1942 no less than 27,500 Americans and Filipinos died.

Tojo admitted that he heard of this march in 1942 from many different sources. He said that his information was to the effect that the prisoners had been forced to march long distances in the heat and that many deaths had occurred. Tojo also admitted that the United States Government's protest against the unlawful treatment of these prisoners had been received and discussed at the bi-weekly meetings of the Bureaux Chiefs in the War Ministry soon after the death march occurred, but that he left the matter to the discretion of the Bureau Chiefs. Tojo said that the Japanese forces in the Philippines were not called upon for a report on the incident and that he did not even discuss the matter with General Homma when that General visited Japan in early 1943. Tojo said that he first inquired into this subject when he visited the Philippines in May 1943; and at that time he discussed it with General Homma's Chief-of-Staff, who informed him of the details. Tojo explained his failure to take action to prevent a repetition of similar atrocities as follows: "It is Japanese custom for a commander of an expeditionary army in the field to be given a mission in the performance of which he is not subject to specific orders from Tokyo, but has considerable autonomy." This can mean only that under the Japanese method of warfare such atrocities were expected to occur, or were at least permitted, and that the Government was not concerned to prevent them.

Such atrocities were repeated during the Pacific War which it is reasonable to assume resulted from the condonation of General Homma's conduct at Bataan.

Other Forced Marches

On the march from the port to Koepang prisoner of war camp on Dutch Timor in February 1942 the prisoners suffering from wounds, hunger, malaria and dysentery were marched for five days with their hands tied behind their backs, and were driven and beaten along by their Japanese and Korean guards like a herd of cattle. Similar marches were imposed upon Indian prisoners between Wewak, But and Aitape in British New Guinea during 1943 and 1944. On those marches the prisoners who became ill and were unable to keep up with the main body were shot. There was evidence of other similar happenings. Those mentioned show the accepted and common practice followed by the Japanese Army and Prisoner of War Administration when moving prisoners of war from one place to another under harsh conditions enforced by the beating and murdering of stragglers.

The Ranau marches are in a different category. They began early in 1945, when the Japanese feared that the Allies were preparing a landing at Kuching;

the purpose of these marches was to remove the prisoners to prevent their liberation. The village of Ranau is in a jungle over 100 miles west of Sandakan in Borneo on the eastern slope of Mt. Kinabalu. The trail from Sandakan to Ranau lies through dense jungle and is too narrow for vehicles. The first 30 miles are marshy and heavy with mud and slush. The next 40 miles are in higher country over short, steep hills. The next 20 miles are over a mountain. The last 26 miles are all uphill and mountainous. Australian prisoners of war were moved along this jungle trail in a series of marches. The prisoners were suffering from malaria, dysentery, beri-beri and malnutrition before they were taken from the camp at Sandakan. The test to determine whether a prisoner was fit to make the march was to beat and torture him to make him stand; if he did stand, he was considered fit for the march. The prisoners were forced to carry food and ammunition for their guards as well as their own scanty rations. One party of 40 prisoners was forced to subsist for three days on this march upon six cucumbers divided among them. Those who fell out of the marching column were shot or bayoneted to death. The marches continued until the first part of April 1945. The trail was littered with the corpses of those who perished along the way. Less than one-third of the prisoners of war who began these marches at Sandakan ever reached Ranau. Those who did reach Ranau were starved and tortured to death or died of disease or were murdered. Only six out of more than two thousand who were prisoners at Sandakan are known to have survived. These did so by escaping from the camp at Ranau. Those who were too sick to begin the marches at Sandakan died of disease or were murdered by their guards.

Burma-Siam Railway

A flagrant example of atrocities over an extended period in one area is found in the treatment of prisoners of war and native workmen employed in the construction of the Burma-Siam Railway. Prior to and during the work prisoners were constantly subjected to ill-treatment, torture and privation of all kinds, commencing with a forced march of 200 miles to the area under almost indescribable hardships. As a result in eighteen months 16,000 prisoners out of 46,000 died.

To further their strategic plans in Burma and India, Japanese Imperial General Headquarters early in 1942 considered the question of communications. The shortest convenient line of communications at that time was through Thailand. It was decided to link the railroad running from Bangkok in Siam with that from Moulmein in Burma, the distance of the gap being about 250 miles (400 kil.). Thus communication with the Japanese armies in Burma would be facilitated.

For that purpose, on the advice of Tojo, it was decided to use prisoners of war and orders were issued to the Southern Army then stationed in Malaya to proceed with the work with all possible speed, November 1943 being fixed as the completion date. Pursuant to these orders two groups of prisoners were sent from the Singapore area commencing in August 1942; one group known as "A" Force being sent by sea and the second group, composed of "F" and "H" Forces by rail to Bangpong. From Bangpong they were made to march to the various camps along the line of the projected construction.

Before "F" and "H" Forces left Singapore, the Japanese general in charge of the prisoner of war administration informed the prisoners that they were being sent to rest camps in the mountains where the food situation was better because so many of them were sick and suffering from malnutrition, caused by lack of food and insanitary conditions in the Singapore camps. He therefore insisted that the sick be included in those to be sent to the labor camps. The prisoners were crowded into railway freight cars with the men sitting cross-legged on the floor without sufficient space to lie down. They had been told that it would not be necessary to carry along their cooking utensils as they would be replaced. However, they were not replaced. Furthermore, the only food furnished the prisoners was thin vegetable stew, and for the last twenty-four hours of the trip by rail no food or water was available.

After four days and four nights the prisoners were detrained and required to surrender their baggage and what cooking gear they had brought, as well as all drugs and medical equipment. They were then required to march 200 miles on foot in two and one-half weeks. The march would have taxed fit soldiers, as the route lay over rough jungle tracks in mountainous country. The march was accomplished in fifteen night stages in the rain and mud of the monsoon. The weakened condition of the prisoners, together with the necessity of carrying some 2,000 non-walking sick, made this march almost beyond human endurance. Some of those who became sick or too weak to march were beaten and driven by their guards.

In the camps established along the projected railway, which lay in virgin jungle, no cover was provided; sanitary facilities were almost non-existent, medical care and drugs were not provided, clothing was not furnished, rations were completely inadequate, while the constant driving and daily beating of the prisoners added to the ever-mounting toll of dead and disabled. Those who tried to escape were killed. Other groups of prisoners of war from Singapore followed "F" and "H" Forces and were accorded similar treatment.

Tojo told the Tribunal that he had received reports of the poor condition of the prisoners employed on this project and that he sent the Chief of the Prisoner of War Information Bureau to investigate in May 1943. He admits that the only action which he took as a result of that investigation was to court-martial a certain company commander who had dealt unfairly with the prisoners of war, and to relieve from duty the Commanding General of Railway Construction. However, we find from other evidence that the Commanding General was not removed because of the ill-treatment of prisoners of war. The first Commanding General of Railway Construction, who was in charge of this project, was killed by an Allied air raid. The second Commanding General in charge of the project was transferred because he was too sick to attend to his duties, and because the work was not progressing fast enough for the Imperial General Headquarters. The inspector, who recommended the removal of the second Commanding General was not, as stated by Tojo, the Chief of the Prisoner of War Information Bureau, but Wakamatsu, the Director of the Third Division of the Army General Staff in charge of transportation and communication. He reported to the Chief of the Army General Staff that the work was not making sufficient progress and recommended that the General in command of the railroad units in Malaya be placed in charge of the construction and that he be allowed a two-months extension of the date set for the completion of the road.

The court-martial of one company commander was so insignificant and inadequate as a corrective measure in view of the general disregard of the laws of war by those in charge of prisoners of war on this project and the inhumane treatment to which they were subjecting the prisoners as to amount to condonation of their conduct. One of the principal concerns of the Government and the Japanese Imperial General Staff in 1943 was that the railway should be completed in time to use it in resisting the advance of the Allied forces which was making progress in Burma. No concern appears to have been shown for the cost in sick, wounded and dead Allied prisoners of war caused by the constant driving, beating torturing and murdering at the hands of their Japanese and Korean guards and the insanitary conditions in which the prisoners were required to live and work and the failure of the Japanese Government to furnish the barest necessities of life and medical care.

The lack of proper accommodation, the treatment of the sick, and the inhumane treatment of prisoners engaged in connection with construction of the railway, which is typical of Japanese treatment of prisoners of war, is described by the witness, Colonel Wild, who was kept on this project until November 1943. Colonel Wild; who, by reason of his knowledge of Japanese, acted as liaison officer between the prisoners of war and the Japanese officers, visited many of the camps in which the prisoners were kept and had a first-hand knowledge of the treatment accorded them. The following extract from his evidence graphically describes conditions:

Q: Substantially, was there any difference between the living conditions and treatment of prisoners of war in these various camps?

A: None.

Q: Will you describe one of them as an example?

A: When I entered Songkrei camp on the third of August 1943, I went first to a very large hut accommodating about 700 men. The hut was of the usual pattern. On each side of an earthen gangway there was a 12-foot wide sleeping platform made of split bamboo. The roof was inadequately made with an insufficient quantity of palm leaves which let the rain through almost everywhere. There were no walls, and a stream of water was running down the earthen gangway. The framework of the hut was bamboo tied with creeper.

In this hut were 700 sick men. They were lying two deep along each side of the hut on the split bamboo platform. Their bodies were touching one another down the whole length of the hut. They were all very thin and practically naked. In the middle of the hut were about 150 men suffering from tropical ulcers. These commonly stripped the whole of the flesh from a man's leg from the knee to the ankle. There was an almost overwhelming smell of putrefaction. The only dressings available were banana leaves tied around with puttees, and the only medicine was hot water. There was another hut further up the hill of similar design in which so-called fit men were kept, and one-well-roofed and better constructed hut occupied by the Japanese guards.

Q: Was any bedding supplied?

A: None whatever.

Q: What did they have to cover them from the rain?

A: When we first entered these working camps none of them were roofed at all for the first few weeks. The monsoon had already broken, and during those weeks the men had nothing whatever to cover themselves from the rain except banana leaves. If they were strong enough each man cut a couple of banana leaves and put them over this own body.

Q: Was any roofing material ever received?

A: In my own camp of which I was in command, Lower Niki, we got a lorry load of atap palm, which was enough to roof half the hut in which the worst of the sick were lying. In Niki Camp no atap palm was ever received, but we got some rotten, leaking canvas. In the other four camps after a few weeks about enough atap palm was supplied to roof all the huts with about half the amount that was necessary. Again, this does not apply to the Japanese and Korean guards, who always had a proper roof over them.

Q: By the middle of July 1934, that is, ten weeks after you had left Singapore, what was the state of '"F" Force as a whole?

A: We had 1700 deaths by that time, and 700 men out of the 7,000 were going out to work. Of these 700, we British officers considered that 350 should have been lying down sick.

The account of the construction of this railway would be incomplete without reference to the treatment of the conscripted native labour employed.

To supplement the prisoners of war employed on the work native labourers, Burmese, Tamils, Javanese, Malayans and Chinese were recruited sometimes on promises of varying kinds and at others by force for labour in occupied areas. In all about 150,000 of these labourers were employed on the railway work. The treatment given them and the conditions under which they existed were, if anything, worse than those already described. At least 60,000 of the 150,000 died during the period of construction.

We shall deal later in some detail with protests made by the Allies against ill-treatment of prisoners and shall refer to knowledge of atrocities on the part of the General Staff and the Government. It is, however, pertinent at this stage to refer to the evidence establishing that before the railway project was begun the Army was advised of the terrible conditions under which the work would be done; that the Government had knowledge of the casualties and failed to remedy these conditions.

In 1942 before the work began the Southern Army Headquarters was advised of the danger of prisoners contracting the various tropical diseases, and from time to time the death rate was reported. Confirmation of the knowledge of the danger to the health of the prisoners and the insufficiency of food, shelter and medical supplies is found in a report dated 6 October 1944 from the Chief-of-Staff of the Southern Army to the Chief of the Prisoner of War Information Bureau, reading in part: "For strategic reasons the completion of the railway was most urgent. Since the proposed site of this railway line was a virgin jungle, shelter, food, provisions and medical supplies were far from adequate and much different from normal conditions for prisoners of war."

In July 1943, when thousands of prisoners had died or were incapacitated by disease, Foreign Minister Shigemitsu in reply to a protest said that the prisoners were equitably treated and that all sick received medical attention. Yet, even according to Japanese figures, within a month of the sending of Shigemitsu's message the total of prisoners who had died in Thailand alone was 2,909. According to the same source the death rate had increased enormously month by month from 54 in November 1942 to 800 in August 1943.

In the summer of 1943 Wakamatsu on his return to Tokyo from his inspection of the area, previously referred to, reported personally to Sugiyama, Chief of the General Staff, that he had seen many cases of beri-beri and dysentery and that the quality of the food was not of the required standard.

It is claimed that many of the deaths occurred because the Allied Forces interfered with the regular supply of food and drugs. However, for the very reason of this interference with shipping the order was given in February 1943 to shorten the terms by which the work had to be finished, by four months. Since that order the commanders became reckless. POWS were told: Men are of no importance, the railroad has to be built irrespective of any suffering or death, or, "the construction of the railway had to go on without delay as it was required for operational purposes, and had to be finished within a certain time at all costs, irrespective of the loss of lives of British and Australian prisoners".

Finally we refer to one of the monthly reports, dated 3 September 1943, received by the Prisoner of War Information Bureau from the Prisoner of War Commandant in Thailand, which stated that of a total of 40,314 prisoners 15,064 were sick. In view of the practice of forcing beri-beri and dysentery cases to continue to work the number of sick, if these had been included, would have been much greater.

Torture and Other Inhumane Treatment

The practice of torturing prisoners of war and civilian internees prevailed at practically all places occupied by Japanese troops, both in the occupied territories and in Japan. The Japanese indulged in this practice during the entire period of the Pacific War. Methods of torture were employed in all areas so uniformly as to indicate policy both in training and execution. Among these tortures were the water treatment, burning, electric shocks, the knee spread, suspension, kneeling on sharp instruments and flogging.

The Japanese Military Police, the Kempeitai, was most active in inflicting these tortures. Other Army and Navy units, however, used the same methods as the Kempeitai. Camp guards also employed similar methods. Local police forces organized by the Kempeitai in the occupied territories also applied the same methods of torture.

We will show how the Chiefs of Camps were instructed in Tokyo before assuming their duties. We will also show that these Chiefs of Camps were under the administrative control and supervision of the Prisoner of War Administration Section of the Military Affairs Bureau of the War Ministry to which they rendered monthly reports. The Kempeitai were administered by the War Ministry. A Kempeitai training school was maintained and operated by the War Ministry in Japan. It is a reasonable inference that the conduct of the Kempeitai and the camp guards reflected the policy of the War Ministry.

To indicate the prevalence of torture and the uniformity of the methods employed we give a brief summary of these methods.

The so-called "water treatment" was commonly applied. The victim was bound or otherwise secured in a prone position; and water was forced through his mouth and nostrils into his lungs and stomach until he lost consciousness. Pressure was then applied, sometimes by jumping upon his abdomen to force the water out. The usual practice was to revive the victim and successively repeat the process. There was evidence that this torture was used in the following places: China, at Shanghai, Peiping and Nanking; French Indo-China, at Hanoi and Saigon; Malaya, at Singapore; Burma, at Kyaikto; Thailand, at Chumporn; Andaman Islands, at Port Blair; Borneo, at Jesselton; Sumatra, at Medan, Tadjong Karang and Palembang; Java, at Batavia, Bandung, Soerabaja and Buitenzong; Celebes, at Makassar; Portuguese Timor, at Ossu and Dilli; Philippines, at Manila, Nichols Field, Palo Beach and Dumaguete; Formosa, at Camp Haito; and in Japan, at Tokyo.

Torture by burning was practiced extensively. This torture was generally inflicted by burning the body of the victim with lighted cigarettes, but in some instances burning candles, hot irons, burning oil and scalding water were used. In many of these cases, the heat was applied to sensitive parts of the body, such as the nostrils, ears, abdomen, sexual organs, and in the case of women, to the breasts. We have evidence of specific instances in which this form of torture was employed in the following places: China, at Hankow, Peiping, Shanghai and Nomonhan; French Indo-China, at Haiphong, Hanoi, Vinh and Saigon; Malaya, at Singapore, Victoria Point, Ipoh and Kuala Lumpur; Burma, at Kyaikto; Thailand, at Chumporn; Andaman Islands, at Port Blair; Nicobar Islands, at Kakana; Borneo, at Jesselton; Sumatra, at Palembang and Pakan Baru; Java, at Batavia, Bandung and Semarang; Moluccas Islands, at Amboina; Portuguese Timor, at Ossu; Solomon Islands, at Buin; Philippine Islands, at Manila, Iloilo City, Palo, Bataan and Dumaguete; and in Japan, at Kawasaki.

The electric shock method was also common. Electric current was applied to a part of the victim's body so as to produce a shock. The point of application was generally a sensitive part of the body such as the nose, ears, sexual organs or breasts. The evidence shows specific instances of the use of this method of torture at the following places: China, at Peiping and Shanghai; French Indo-China, at Hanoi and Mytho; Malaya, at Singapore; Thailand, at Chumporn; Java, at Bandung, Buitenzorg and Semarang; and in the Philippine Islands, at Davao.

The so-called knee spread was a frequent method of torture. The victim, with his hands tied behind his back, was forced to kneel with a pole, sometimes as much as three inches in diameter, inserted behind both knee joints so as to spread those joints as pressure was applied to his thighs, at times by jumping on his thighs. The result of this torture was to separate the knee joints and so cause intense pain. The evidence shows specific instances of this torture being used at the following places: China, at Shanghai and Nanking; Burma, at Tavoy; Andaman Islands, at Port Blair; Borneo, at Sandakan; Sumatra, at Pakan Baru; Moluccas Islands, at Halmahera Island; Portuguese Timor, at Dilli; Philippine Islands, at Manila, Nichols Field and Pasay Camp; and in Japan, at Tokyo.

Suspension was another common form of torture. The body of the victim was suspended by the wrists, arms, legs or neck, and at times in such manner as to strangle the victim or pull joints from their sockets. This method was at times combined with flogging during suspension. Specific instances of the employment of this method of torture occurred in the following places: China, at Shanghai and Nanking; French Indo-China, at Hanoi; Malaya, at Singapore, Victoria Point, Ipoh and Kuala Lumpur; Thailand, at Chumporn; Burma, at Kyaikto; Borneo, at Sandakan; Sumatra, at Brastagi; Java, at Bandung, Soerabaja and Buitenzorg; Moluccas Islands, at Amboina; Portuguese Timor, at Dilli; Philippine Islands, at Manila, Nichols Field, Palo, Iloilo City and Dumaguete; and in Japan, at Tokyo and Yokkaichi.

Kneeling on sharp instruments was another form of torture. The edges of square blocks were mostly used as the sharp instruments. The victim was forced to kneel on these sharp edges for hours without relief; if he moved he was flogged. Specific instances of the use of this method have been shown to us to have occurred at the following places: French Indo-China, at Hanoi; Malaya, at Singapore; Andaman Islands, at Port Blair, Moluccas Islands, on Halmahera Island; Philippine Islands, at Davao; and in Japan, at Fukuoka and Omuta.

Removal of the nails of the fingers and toes also occurred. Instances of this method of torture are found at the following places: China, at Shanghai; Celebes, at Menado; Philippines, at Manila, Iloilo City; and in Japan, at Yamani.

Underground dungeons were used as torture chambers at the following places: French Indo-China, at Hanoi, Malaya, at Singapore; and in Java, at Bandung.

Flogging was the most common of the cruelties of the Japanese. It was commonly used at all prisoner of war and internee camps, prisons, Kempeitai headquarters and at all work camps and on all work projects as well as aboard prison ships. It was indulged in freely by the guards with the approval and often at the direction of the Camp Commandant or some other officer. Special instruments were issued for use in flogging at camps; some of these were billets of wood the size of a baseball bat. On occasions prisoners were forced to beat their fellow prisoners under the supervision of the guards. Prisoners suffered internal injuries, broken bones, and lacerations from these beatings. In many instances they were beaten into unconsciousness only to be revived in order to suffer a further beating. The evidence shows that on occasions prisoners were beaten to death.

Mental torture was commonly employed. An illustration of this form of torture is to be found in the treatment to which the Doolittle fliers were subjected. After having been subjected to the various other forms of torture, they were taken one at a time and marched blindfolded a considerable distance. The victim could hear voices and marching feet, then the noise of a squad halting and lowering their rifles as if being formed to act as a firing squad. A Japanese officer then came up to the victim and said: "We are Knights of the Bushido of the Order of the Rising Sun. We do not execute at sundown; we execute at sunrise." The victim was then taken back to his cell and informed that unless he talked before sunrise, he would be executed.

On 5 December 1944, the Swiss Legation in Tokyo delivered to Foreign Minister Shigemitsu a Note of Protest from the British Government. In that note Shigemitsu was informed that a copy of a book entitled, "Notes for the Interrogation of Prisoners of War", and issued by the Japanese Hayashi Division in Burma on 6 August 1943, had been captured. The note gave Shigemitsu direct quotations from that book as follows:

> Care must be exercised when making use of rebukes, invectives or torture as it will result in his telling falsehoods and making a fool of you. The following are the methods normally to be adopted: (a) Torture which includes kicking, beating and anything connected with physical suffering. This method to be used only when everything else fails as it is the most clumsy one. [This passage was specially marked in the copy captured.] Change the interrogating officer when using violent torture, and good results can be had if the new officer questions in a sympathetic manner. (b) Threats. (1) Hints of future physical discomforts, for instance: torture, murder, starving, solitary-confinement, deprivation of sleep. (2) Hints of future mental discomforts, for instance: he will not be allowed to send letters, he will not be given the same treatment as the other prisoners of war, he will be kept till the last in the event of an exchange of prisoners, etc.

The note then continued:

> The Government of the United Kingdom has requested that the attention of the Japanese Government be drawn to the foregoing. It recalls that the Japanese

Government has recently strongly denied that Imperial Japanese authorities make use of torture. See the letter from Shigemitsu to the Swiss Minister of 1 July 1944.

We have no evidence that any action was taken to stop this practice of torturing Allied prisoners of war; on the other hand, the practice continued to the time of the surrender of Japan and, when the surrender came, orders were issued to assist the criminals in avoiding just punishment for their crimes. In addition to ordering all incriminating evidence in the form of documents to be destroyed, the following order was issued by the Chief of Prisoner of War Camps of the Prisoner of War Administration Section of the Military Affairs Bureau on 20 August 1945: "Personnel who mistreated prisoners of war and internees or are held in extremely bad sentiment by them are permitted to take care of it by immediately transferring or by fleeing without trace." This order was sent to various prisoner of war camps, including those in Formosa, Korea, Manchuria, North China, Hong Kong, Borneo, Thailand, Malaya and Java.

Vivisection and Cannibalism

Vivisection was practiced by Japanese Medical Officers upon prisoners in their hands. There were also cases of dismemberment of prisoners by Japanese who were not Medical Officers. In addition to the incidents stated below other dismembered bodies of dead captives were found in circumstances indicating that the mutilation had occurred before death.

There was evidence that at Khandok a prisoner of war described as "healthy, unwounded" was treated as follows: "The man was tied to a tree outside the Hikari Kikan Office. A Japanese doctor and four Japanese medical students stood around him. They first removed the finger nails, then cutting open his chest removed his heart, on which the doctor gave a practical demonstration."

The captured diary of a Japanese, apparently an officer, recorded an incident on Guadalcanal.

> 26 September—Discovered and captured the two prisoners who escaped last night in the jungle, and let the Guard Company guard them. To prevent their escaping a second time, pistols were fired at their feet, but it was difficult to hit them. The two prisoners were dissected while still alive by Medical Officer Yamaji and their livers were taken out, and for the first time I saw the internal organs of a human being. It was very informative.

A case of mutilation of a living captive, this time not by a medical but by a combatant Japanese officer, was deposed to from Canangay, in the Philippines. The evidence was:

> A young woman . . . about 24 years old, was caught hiding in the grass. The officer in charge of the entire patrol tore off her clothes, while two soldiers held her. He then had her taken to a small nipa hut, without walls . . . . and there the officer in charge of the patrol used his sabre to cut her breasts and womb.

Soldiers held her while the officer did this. At first, the girl was screaming. She finally lay still and silent. The Japanese then set fire to the nipa hut.

At Manila an eye witness described how his house boy was tied to a pillar. The Japanese then cut off his genitals and thrust his severed penis in his mouth.

Other instances of the mutilation of prisoners in the hands of Japanese soldiers occurred at Balikpapan in Borneo. The incident was related by an eye witness as follows:

> I saw a district-officer in uniform and a Police Inspector in uniform. A Japanese officer started a conversation with that district-officer. . . . I saw that during that conversation that officer was ill-treating the district-officer by blows in his face with the hand, and further with the scabbard over his body. . . . The Japanese officer who had started the talk with the [Dutch] district-officer, drew his sword and hewed off both the district-officer's arms, a little above his elbows, and then his two legs at the height of the knees. The district-officer was also taken to a cocoanut tree, bound to it and stabbed to death with a bayonet. . . . After this, the same officer went over to the Policeman in uniform; . . . he was kicked and beaten with the hand and with the sword in the scabbard. After this, that [Japanese] officer hewed off his arms under the elbow and his legs near the knees; I heard him shout once more "God save the Queen". With bayonet thrusts and kicks the Policeman was made to stand up, and standing on his leg stumps, he was stabbed to death with a bayonet.

Towards the end of the Pacific War the Japanese Army and Navy descended to cannibalism, eating parts of the bodies of Allied prisoners whom they had unlawfully killed. This practice was not unnoticed nor even disapproved by the Japanese Army. A Japanese prisoner upon interrogation said: "On 10 December 1944 an order was issued from 18 Army Headquarters that troops were permitted to eat the flesh of Allied dead but must not eat their own dead." This statement was confirmed by a captured memorandum upon discipline found in the possession of a Major General. In this memorandum occurs the passage: "Although it is not prescribed in the criminal code, those who eat human flesh (except that of the enemy), knowing it to be so, shall be sentenced to death as the worst kind of criminal against mankind."

At times this consumption of the flesh of their enemies was made into something of a festive occasion at officers' quarters. Even officers of the rank of General and Rear-Admiral took part. Flesh of murdered prisoners or soup made from such flesh was served at meals of Japanese below the rank of officers. The evidence indicates that this cannibalism occurred when there was other food available. That is to say, on such occasions, this horrible practice was indulged in from choice and not of necessity.

Prison Ships Were Subjected to Attack

The Japanese practices in the movement of prisoners of war by sea was in line with equally unlawful and inhumane methods of movement by land. The prisoners were crowded into holds and coal bunkers of ships with inadequate sanitary facilities and insufficient ventilation, and were given no medical service. They were forced to remain below decks during long voyages and to subsist on meager rations of food and water. These prison ships were unmarked and subjected to Allied attacks in which thousands of prisoners perished.

The method employed to conserve space was generally as follows: Wooden stages or temporary decks were built in empty coal bunkers and holds with a vertical distance of three feet between them. The space allotted to prisoners on these temporary decks was an area six feet by six feet for 15 prisoners. They were compelled to sit corss-legged during the entire voyage. Space was conserved also by the elimination of proper sanitary facilities. The sanitary facilities provided consisted of buckets or boxes which were lowered into the hold or bunker with ropes and were removed in the same manner for emptying over the side. Drippings from these containers added to the general insanitary conditions. Many prisoners were suffering from dysentery when taken on board; and their excreta fell freely through the cracks of the wooden stages upon the prisoners below. To save space for the preparation of food, the prisoners were served uncooked food or food that had been prepared before sailing. For the same reason, an inadequate supply of water was carried. To add to the horrible conditions which prevailed prisoners were not allowed on deck. This method of transportation by sea of prisoners of war prevailed generally during the entire period of the Pacific War. It has been defended as necessary because of a shortage of tonnage possessed by Japan. This is not a good defence; for the Japanese Government was not entitled to move prisoners if it was unable to do so under the conditions prescribed by the laws of war.

This method of transportation was used in August 1942 in moving the first group of British prisoners from Singapore to Moulmein to labor on the Burma-Siam Railroad. It occurred again when the "Nitta Maru" called at Wake Island in January 1942 to remove 1,235 American prisoners of war and civilian internees to Yokohoma and Shanghai. In this case as in others, the prisoners and internees were forced to run the gauntlet of Japanese soldiers in which they were beaten and kicked as they went aboard. It was in connection with this voyage that our attention was first called to the "Regulations for Prisoners" which were in force aboard prison ships. Those regulations among other things provided as follows:

> The prisoners disobeying the following orders will be punished with immediate death: (a) those disobeying orders and instructions; (b) those showing a motion of antagonism and raising a sign of opposition; . . . (d) those talking without permission and raising loud voices; (e) those walking and moving without order; . . . (i) those climbing ladder without order; . . . the Navy of the Great Japanese Empire will not try to punish you all with death. Those obeying all the rules of the Japanese Navy, cooperating with Japan in constructing the "New Order of Great Asia" will be well treated.

On some voyages the prisoners were crowded into bunkers not fitted with temporary decks and forced to range themselves around the coal so long as standing room remained. On other voyages, highly inflammable cargo was packed in the hold with the prisoners. In addition to the many obvious discomforts and dangers to health to which this method of packing prison ships subjected the prisoners, it made their escape from the ship in case of sinking almost impossible.

The prison ships were often attacked in the same manner as other Japanese ships by the Allied forces who could not distinguish them from other ships. A large number of sinkings resulted and thousands of Allied prisoners of war were lost. It was the practice in some cases, when these attacks occurred, to fasten down the hatches to prevent the escape of the prisoners and to station Japanese soldiers armed with rifles and machine guns with orders to kill those prisoners who might overcome these obstacles and escape from the sinking ship. This happened on the "Libson Maru" which was sunk in October 1942 on a voyage out of Hong Kong with British prisoners aboard. In other cases, the prisoners were shot or otherwise murdered after the sinking and while in the water. This was done in the case of the "Oryoku Maru", which was sunk on a voyage from Manila in December 1944 with American prisoners of war aboard. The same thing occurred in the case of the sinking of the "Van Waerwyck" in the Malacca Straits in June 1944. This occurred again in the sinking of the "Junior Maru" in September 1944 off the east coast of Sumatra with large numbers of Ambonese prisoners of war and conscripted Indonesian laborers aboard.

Many prisoners of war died on these voyages from suffocation, disease and starvation; those who survived were so weakened from the ordeal of the voyage that they were unable to labor upon arriving at their destination. This impairment of the ability of the prisoners of war to perform labor caused the War Ministry to issue "Despatch, Army Asia Secret Order No. 1504" dated 10 December 1942. In that order it was stated that, "Recently during the transportation of the prisoners of war to Japan many of them have taken ill or have died and quite a few of them have been incapacitated for further work due to the treatment on the way, which at times was inadequate." Instructions were then given to insure the arrival of the prisoners at their destination in condition to perform labor. The condition of the prisoners transported by sea was not materially improved by the issuance of this order, however; and on 3 March 1944, Tojo's Vice-Minister of War, Tominaga, issued another order to "the Units concerned in which, among other things, he said:

> In the Prisoner of War Administration, the use of prisoners for labor has been stressed heretofore. Although this has directly helped to increase our fighting strength, the average prisoner of war's health condition is hardly satisfactory. Their high death rate must be brought to our attention. In the light of the recent intensified enemy propaganda warfare, if the present condition continues to exist, it will be impossible for us to expect the world opinion to be what we wish it to be. Such will cause an obstacle to our prosecution of moral warfare. Not only that, it is absolutely necessary to improve the health condition of prisoners of war from the standpoint of using them satisfactorily to increase our fighting strength. It should be added that, although efforts must be exerted to utilize spaces on ships in transporting war prisoners, it is necessary that the purport of the Despatch, Army Asia Secret No. 1504 of 1942 be thoroughly understood in handling war prisoners at this juncture.

Members of the Government and many government officials were aware of the effect of these methods upon the prisoners. Such corrective measures as were taken by them, which were totally inadequate, were designed to preserve the ability of the prisoners to perform labor for use in the prosecution of the war, not to insure the enforcement of the laws of war relating to the movement of prisoners of war.

SUBMARINE WARFARE

Inhumane, illegal warfare at sea was waged by the Japanese Navy in 1943 and 1944. Survivors of passengers and crews of torpedoed ships were murdered.

Ambassador Oshima was empowered by the Tojo Cabinet to discuss the prosecution of the war with the Reich Foreign Minister; and although technical questions were to be discussed directly by members of the Mixed Commission, it was Oshima's expressed opinion that it was of the greatest importance that questions of policy should be discussed exclusively by Oshima and Ribbentrop, the German Foreign Minister. Oshima had a conference with Hitler on 3 January 1942. Hitler explained his policy of submarine warfare, which he was conducting against Allied shipping, and said that although the United States might build ships very quickly, her chief problem would be the personnel shortage since the training of seafaring personnel took a long time. Hitler explained that he had given orders for his submarines to surface after torpedoing merchant ships and to shoot up the life-boats, so that the word would get about that most seamen were lost in torpedoings and the United States would have difficulty in recruiting new crews. Oshima, in replying to Hitler, approved this statement of policy and stated that the Japanese, too, would follow this method of waging submarine warfare.

An order issued by the Commander of the First Submarine Force at Truk on 20 March 1943, contained this command:

> All submarines shall act together in order to concentrate their attacks against enemy convoys and shall totally destroy them. Do not stop with the sinking of enemy ships and cargoes; at the same time, you will carry out the complete destruction of the crews of the enemy's ships; if possible, seize part of the crew and endeavor to secure information about the enemy.

This order for inhumane warfare at sea was followed by the Japanese submarine commanders. Between 13 December 1943 and 29 October 1944, Japanese submarines, after sinking eight British, American and Dutch merchant vessels in the Indian Ocean and one American vessel in the Pacific Ocean, surfaced after firing their torpedoes, attempted to or did take on board the master of the ship, and then proceeded to destroy the life-boats and murder the survivors.

Repeated protests were made by the Allied Governments in which they stated the exact date and position of the sinkings and the details of the atrocities committed upon the passengers and crews of the torpedoed vessels. No satisfactory answer was made to these protests and the sinkings continued without modification of the treatment of survivors.

The action taken by the Japanese Navy in the sinking of the British Merchant Ship "Behar" by gunfire on 9 March 1944 is illustrative. One hundred and fifteen survivors were picked up by the cruiser "Tone". Later in the day, the "Tone" reported the sinking and capture to the Flagship "Aoba". Orders were immediately signalled to the "Tone" from the "Aoba" to kill the survivors. It was later decided to place fifteen of the survivors, including two women and one Chinese in a civilian internee camp and to kill the remaining one hundred. On orders of the captain of the "Tone" these hundred survivors were killed aboard the "Tone."

The massacre of survivors of the American ship "Jean Nicolet" is another example of methods employed by the Japanese Navy. This ship was travelling from Australia to Ceylon in July 1944 when she was torpedoed at night by a Japanese submarine while some 600 miles from land. Her ship's company was about 100 of whom about 90 were taken aboard the submarine. The ship was sunk and her boats were also smashed by gun fire although all did not sink. The hands of the survivors were tied behind their backs. A few of the officers were taken below and their fate is not known to the Tribunal. The remainder were made to sit on the forward deck of the submarine as she cruised searching for survivors. During this time some were washed overboard and others were beaten with wooden and metal bludgeons and robbed of personal property such as watches and rings. Then they were required to proceed singly towards the stern between lines of Japanese who beat them as they passed between their ranks. Thus they were forced into the water to drown. Before all the prisoners had been forced to run the gauntlet the vessel submerged leaving the remaining prisoners on her deck to their fate. Some, however, did survive by swimming. These and their comrades whom they kept afloat were discovered the next day by aircraft which directed a rescuing ship to them. Thus twenty-two survived this terrible experience, from some of whom this Tribunal received testimony of this inhumane conduct of the Japanese Navy.

Illegal Employment, Starvation, and Neglect of Prisoners and Internees

General Uemura, Director of the Prisoner of War Administration Section of the Military Affairs Bureau of the War Ministry, only a few weeks after the agreement with the Allies to apply the provisions of the Geneva Prisoner of War Convention to prisoners of war and civilian internees, advised the Chief-of-Staff of the Japanese Army in Formosa on 2 April 1942 that "Plans are now being pushed for the use of prisoners of war in production," and requested an immediate report upon the number that might be utilized for that purpose in Formosa.

On 6 May 1942, the Vice-Minister of War informed the Chief-of-Staff of the Army in Formosa of the policy governing employment of prisoners of war. He said that it had been decided that:

> Prisoners of war can be used for the enlargement of our production and as military labor, white prisoners of war will be confined successively in Korea, Formosa and Manchuria. Superior technicians and high ranking officers—Colonels and above—will be included among the prisoners of war confined in Formosa. Those who are not suitable for use in enlargement of our production will be confined in prisoner of war camps which will be built immediately on the spot.

General Uemura on 5 June 1942 directed the Chief-of-Staff of the Army in Formosa as follows:

> Although the working of prisoner of war officers and warrant officers is forbidden by the Regulations of 1903, the policy of the control authorities is that under the situation of our country where not one person now eats without working they want them to get to work. It is desired that you give proper orders on this.

These instructions were also sent to all other Army units concerned. This directive originated within the Cabinet for on 30 May 1942, Prime Minister Tojo issued instructions to the Commander of a Division, which had a prisoner of war camp under its jurisdiction in which he said:

> The present situation of affairs in this country does not permit anyone to lie idle doing nothing but eating freely. With that in view, in dealing with prisoners of war, I hope you will see that they may be usefully employed.

On 25 June 1942, Tojo issued his instructions to newly appointed Chiefs of Prisoner of War camps. He said:

> In Japan, we have our own ideology concerning prisoners of war, which should naturally make their treatment more or less different from that in Europe and America. In dealing with them, you should, of course, observe the various Regulations concerned, aim at an adequate application of them . . . At the same time, you must not allow them to lie idle doing nothing but eating freely for even a single day. Their labor and technical skill should be fully utilized for the replenishment of production, and contribution rendered toward the prosecution of the Greater East Asiatic War for which no effort ought to be spared.

The application of these instructions account at least in part for the constant driving, beating and prodding of the sick and wounded prisoners and those suffering from malnutrition to force them to labor upon military works until they died from disease, malnutrition and exhaustion. These instructions were repeated on 26 June 1942 by Tojo to another group of newly appointed prisoner of war camp chiefs and again to another such group on 7 July 1942.

That the Cabinet supported Tojo in his program to employ prisoners of war to aid in the prosecution of the war is shown by the "Foreign Affairs Monthly Report" of the Foreign Section of the Police Bureau of the Home Ministry issued for the month of September 1942. The report showed that due to the labor shortage in Japan, the Cabinet Planning Board with the concurrence of the Prisoner of War Administration Section of the Military Affairs Bureau of the War Ministry held a conference on 15 August 1942 at which it was decided to transfer prisoners of war to Japan and employ them to mitigate the labor shortage in the industries in the National Mobilization Plan. According to the report, it had been decided to employ the prisoners of war in mining, stevedoring, and on engineering and construction works for national defense. A complete plan had been agreed upon whereby the prefectural governors cooperating with the Welfare Ministry and the Army would take charge of the supervision of the prisoners of war and their employment. With members of the Government, Hoshino and Suzuki participated in this decision. Hoshino had been selected as Chief Secretary of the Cabinet by Tojo because of his long experience in economic planning and had been charged by Tojo to devote his main efforts to such activities in cooperation with Suzuki, whom he had selected to head the Cabinet Planning Bureau. Hoshino became Chief Secretary of the Cabinet on 18 October 1941 and served until the fall of the Tojo Cabinet on 19 July 1944. Suzuki became a Councillor of the Planning Bureau on 30 May 1939 and when Hoshino was relieved as President of the Cabinet Planning Bureau and as Minister without Portfolio on 4 April 1941, Suzuki succeeded him and continued to serve as Minister without Portfolio and President of the Cabinet Planning Bureau in the Third Konoye Cabinet and the Tojo Cabinet until the Tojo Cabinet resigned on 19 July 1944.

Consideration for Racial Needs
Food and Clothing

The Japanese Government promised early in 1942 to take into consideration the national customs and racial habits of the prisoners of war and civilian internees in supplying them with food and clothing. This was never done. Regulations in force at the time this promise was made required that camp commandants in supplying prisoners of war and internees with food and clothing should be guided by the Table of Basic Allowances governing the supply of the Army. The commandants were authorized to determine the amount of the allowance to be made to the inmates of the camps but were directed to make such determination within the limits prescribed in the Table of Allowances. These Regulations, insofar as they affected diet, were interpreted as forbidding the prisoners and internees sufficient food, even when other food existed in the vicinity of the camps. This rule was followed even when the inmates of the camps were dying in large numbers from malnutrition. The amount and kind of food prescribed by the Table of Allowances was not materially changed during the war, except to reduce the amount prescribed, although it soon became apparent to those in command that due to different national dietary customs and habits, the prisoners and internees could not subsist on the food supplied. On 29 October 1942, orders were issued to all camp commandants that "in view of the consumption of rice and barley by workers in heavy industries in Japan," the ration for prisoners of war and civilian internees who were officers or civil officials should be cut so as not to exceed 420 grams per day. In

January 1944, this ration of rice was further cut to a maximum of 390 grams per day. As the inmates of the camps began to suffer from malnutrition, they fell easy prey to disease and were quickly exhausted by the heavy labor forced upon them. Regardless of this, the commandants of the camps enforced Tojo's instructions that those who did not labor should not eat and still further reduced the ration and in some cases withdrew it entirely from those who were unable to labor because of illness or injury.

The Regulations provided that the prisoners of war and civilian internees should wear the clothing formerly worn by them, that is to say the clothing they were wearing when captured or interned. This Regulation was enforced by the camp commandants with the result that in many of the camps the inmates were in rags before the war ended. It is true that the Regulation allowed the camp commandants to lend certain items of clothing in cases where the clothing formerly worn by the prisoners or internees was unfit, but this appears to have been used only in rare cases.

Medical Supplies

The Japanese Army and Navy were required by their regulations to keep on hand and in storage a supply of medicine and medical equipment sufficient for one year's use. This was done in many instances by confiscating Red Cross drugs and medical supplies, but the supplies were kept in storage or used mostly for the benefit of Japanese troops and camp guards. The prisoners of war and civilian internees were rarely furnished medicines and equipment from these warehouses. At the time of surrender, large quantities of these supplies were found stored in and around prisoner of war and civilian internee camps in which prisoners and internees had been dying at an alarming rate for lack of such supplies.

Suzuki, Kunji, who served as a staff officer of the Eastern Military District on Honshu Island under Dohihara and other Commanders, testified before this Tribunal. Suzuki admitted that he authorized chiefs prisoners of war and civilian internees were detained were located near the place of employment without regard to their safety, in consequence they were subjected to unnecessary danger from air raids both on and off their work. There is evidence that in some instances the camps were so located deliberately with the intention of deterring the Allies from raiding the military works or factories concerned.

Native Labor

Having decided upon a policy of employing prisoner of war and civilian internees on work directly contributing to the prosecution of the war, and having established a system to carry that policy into execution, the Japanese went further and supplemented this source of manpower by recruiting laborers from the native population of the occupied territories. This recruiting of laborers was accomplished by false promises, and by force. After being recruited, the laborers were transported to and confined in camps. Little or no distinction appears to have been made between these conscripted laborers on the one hand and prisoners of war and civilian internees on the other hand. They were all regarded as slave laborers to be used to the limit of their endurance. For this reason, we have included these conscripted laborers in the term "civilian internees" whenever that term is used in this chapter. The lot of these conscripted laborers was made worse by the fact that generally they were ignorant of the principles of hygiene applicable to their unusual and crowded conditions and succumbed more readily to the diseases resulting from the insanitary conditions of confinement and work forced upon them by their Japanese captors.

Prisoners and Internees Forced to Sign Parole

To reduce the number of guards necessary for prisoners of war and civilian internees, regulations in defiance of the Rules of War were issued by the War Ministry early in 1943 providing, "As soon as prisoners of war have been imprisoned, they shall be administered an oath forbidding them from making an escape. Prisoners of war who refuse to take the oath mentioned in this paragraph shall be deemed to have intentions of escaping and shall be placed under strict surveillance." This "strict surveillance" in practice meant solitary confinement on reduced rations or subjection to torture until they took the oath required. At Singapore in August 1942, 16,000 prisoners, who had refused to give the parole demanded, were herded into a barrack square and kept there without food or latrine facilities for four days to force them to sign the parole. The resulting conditions are too disgusting to describe. Some of the prisoners of war at Hong Kong, who refused to sign the parole, were confined in a prison without food and forced to kneel all day. If they moved they were beaten. The senior prisoner of war at the camp at Sandakan, who, with his men, refused to sign was immediately seized and beaten. A firing squad paraded. He was saved from death only when his men agreed to sign. Prisoners of war in camps in Batavia and Java were beaten and deprived of food until they signed the parole. At Zentsuji Camp on Shikoku Island, 41 prisoners were kept in confinement from 14 June 1942 until 23 September 1942 for refusing to take the oath and were finally threatened with death if they persisted in their refusal. As already stated, the Prisoner of War Regulations also applied to civilian internees by virtue of another regulation which we have quoted. To enforce this parole, which was obtained by coercion, the regulations further provided,

> Persons on parole, who break the parole, shall be subject to either the death penalty, or hard labor, or imprisonment for life or for a minimum of seven years. When the persons mentioned offer armed resistance, they shall be subject to the death penalty. . . . Those persons, who violate any other oath, shall be subject to a maximum of ten years imprisonment. . . . Before a commandant of a prisoner of

> war camp dispatches prisoners of war (i.e. sends prisoners of war to work details or to work camps from the prisoner of war camp), he shall endeavor to prevent escapes and unexpected disturbances, investigating thoroughly the characters, mental attitudes, past histories, as well as the abilities of the prisoners of war, and in addition he shall administer a solemn oath on other matters of importance.

Itagaki, as Commander of the Korean Army, informed War Minister Tojo by a message dated 4 September 1942, that he intended to force all prisoners of war, including officers and warrant officers under his jurisdiction to work; as he put it, "Not one prisoner of war must be left to time in idleness". He stated that one of the regulations he had issued was that "It is important to guard against destruction by the prisoners of war; if necessary, make them give an oath and establish severe penalties." On 1 September 1942, Tojo received a message from the Commander of the Formosa Army that

> 399 prisoners of war, including Lt. General Percival, 6 Major-Generals, or Rear Admirals 27 Brigadier-Generals, or Commodores, 25 Colonels, or Navy Captains, 130 officers of the rank of Lt. Colonel, or Commander or below, and 210 non-commissioned officer together with 6 civil officials, who had been transferred from the Tomi group, were interned on 31 August 1942 in the Formosa Prisoner of War Camp. At first Lt. General Percival and others refused to make an oath, but finally all but three (1 Brigadier-General, 1 Navy Captain and 1 Engineering Lieutenant) signed their names.

This system of regulations issued and enforced by the Japanese Government to compel prisoners of war and civilian internees by duress to give an oath not to escape and not to violate other regulations and orders of the Japanese Government violated the general laws of war. The system was devised, instituted and maintained as part of the policy of the Japanese Government in disregard and violation of the laws of war.

Excessive and Unlawful Punishment was Imposed

Tojo, in his instructions to chiefs of prisoner of war and civilian internee camps told those officials to tighten their control over their subordinates and to supervise the prisoners rigidly; he said, "It is necessary to put them under strict discipline." He repeated this charge in his instructions to the Commander of the Zentsuji Division on 30 May 1942, when he said:

> Prisoners of war must be placed under strict discipline as far as it does not contravene the law of humanity. It is necessary to take care not to be obsessed with the mistaken idea of humanitarianism or swayed by personal feelings towards those prisoners of war which may grow in the long time of their imprisonment.

The Geneva Prisoner of War Convention of 1929 provided with respect to punishment of prisoners of war for offenses committed while they were prisoners:

> Any corporal punishment, any imprisonment in quarters without daylight, and, in general any form whatever of cruelty is forbidden, and Collective punishment for individual acts is also forbidden.

Other important limitations upon punishments that might be inflicted upon prisoners of war were included. All of them were designed to insure humane treatment of the prisoners. One of these limitations was contained in a provision of the Convention which dealt with escapes and attempts to escape; that provision reads:

> Escaped prisoners of war who are retaken before being able to rejoin their own army or to leave the territory occupied by the army which captured them shall be liable only to disciplinary punishment. After an attempted or accomplished escape, the comrades of the person escaping who assisted in the escape may incur only disciplinary punishment on this account. Arrest is the most severe summary punishment which may be imposed on a prisoner of war. The duration of a single punishment may not exceed 30 days.

In this connection disciplinary punishment and summary punishment were used as synonymous terms. It was also provided that,

> Attempted escape, even if it is not a first offense, shall not be considered as an aggravating circumstance in case the prisoner of war should be given over to the courts on account of crimes or offenses against persons or property committed in the course of that attempt.

That the Japanese truly understood the Convention is shown by their objection in 1934 to its ratification. They said that under the Convention

> Prisoners of war could not be so severely punished as Japanese soldiers and this would involve a revision of Japanese Military and Naval Disciplinary Codes to put them on an equal footing, a revision which was undesirable in the interests of discipline.

The real objection to the ratification of the Convention was that the Military desired to avoid any express commitments which would hinder their policy of ill-treatment of prisoners of war.

Early in the Pacific War and after the Japanese Government had given its promise to apply the provisions of the Convention to Allied prisoners of war and civilian internees, ordinances and regulations were made contrary to that promise. In 1943, this regulation was published:

> In case a prisoner of war is guilty of an act of insubordination, he shall be subject to imprisonment or arrest; and any other measures deemed necessary for the purpose of discipline may be added.

Under this regulation, corporal punishment as well as torture and mass punishment was administered. It was common practice in all areas in which prisoner of war and civilian internee camps were located to inflict corporal punishment for the slightest offence or for no offence. This punishment in its mildest forms was beating and kicking the victim. The victim if he became unconscious was often revived with cold water or by other means, only to have the process repeated. Thousands died as a result of this punishment. In some cases death was hastened by weakness due to starvation and disease. Other forms of cruel punishments frequently employed were: exposing the victim to the hot tropical sun for long hours without headdress or other protection; suspension of the victim by his arms in such a manner as at times to force the arms from their sockets; binding the victim where he would be attacked by insects; confining the victim in a cramped cage for days without food; confining the victim in an underground cell without food, light or fresh air for weeks; and forcing the victim to kneel on sharp objects in a cramped position for long periods of time.

In direct defiance of the rules of war mass punishments were commonly employed as punishment for individual acts, especially when the Japanese were unable to discover the offender. The usual form of mass punishment was to force all members of the group involved to assume a strained position such as sitting with the legs folded under the body and the hands on the knees with the palm turned upward, or kneeling, and to remain in that position during daylight hours for days. Other forms of mass punishment were also employed such as that used at Havelock Road Camp in Malaya where the prisoners were forced to run in a circle without shoes over broken glass while being spurred on by Japanese soldiers who beat them with rifle butts. On 9 March 1943 an ordinance was issued providing the death penalty, or life imprisonment, or confinement for ten years or more for a number of offences; the novel feature of this ordinance was that in the case of each offence it provided for the death penalty or other severe penalty to be imposed upon the so-called "leader" of any group action resulting in the commission of the offence named and the same punishment, or a slightly less severe penalty, for all others who might be involved. Under this ordinance, mass punishment was often inflicted upon groups of prisoners of war or civilian internees for what at the most amounted to no more than an individual act. This ordinance also provided the death penalty for "prisoners of war who defy or disobey the orders of persons supervising, guarding, or escorting them"; it also provided imprisonment for five years for "prisoners of war who privately or publicly insult persons supervising, guarding or escorting them." This is an example, of which there are a number, where the Japanese Government departed from its undertaking in respect of the Geneva Convention by altering its laws concerning prisoners of war.

During the Pacific War, contrary to its undertaking already referred to, the Japanese Prison of War regulations were amended to permit an escaping prisoner to be punished in the same way as a deserter from the Japanese Army. The ordinance of 9 March 1943 contained the following provision:

> The leader of a group of persons, who have acted together in effecting an escape, shall be subject to either death or to hard labor or to imprisonment for life or for a minimum of ten years. The other persons involved shall be subject to either the death penalty, or to hard labor or to imprisonment for life or for a minimum of one year.

This provision taken together with the regulations governing paroles not to escape, which prisoners of war were forced to give, constituted the regulations governing escapes which were enforced in all camps. These regulations were in direct violation of international law and, as we have just pointed out, were contrary to the Convention which Japan had promised to apply. Under these regulations, the death penalty was imposed almost without exception upon all prisoners who attempted to escape or escaped and were recaptured. Also, under these regulations, those comrades who assisted a prisoner to escape were also punished, frequently by the death penalty. In some camps, the prisoners were divided into groups and the practice was to kill all members of the group if one member attempted to escape or was successful in escaping. Even the formality of a trial was dispensed with in many instances. The death penalty is proved to have been imposed for attempt to escape at the following camps: Mukden in Liaoning Province of China (July 1943); Hong Kong, China (July 1943); Singapore, Malaya (March 1942); Mergui, Burma (1942);Tarakan, Borneo (1942 and 1945); Pontianak, Borneo (June 1942); Bandjermasin, Borneo (July 1942); Samarinda, Borneo (January 1945); Palembang, Sumatra (March 1942); Djati Nanggor, Java (March 1942); Bandung, Java (April); Batavia, Java (April 1942); Soekaboemi, Java (May 1942); Jogjakarta, Java (May 1942); Tjimahi, Java (May 1942); Makassar, Celebos (September 1942); Amboina, Moluccas Islands (November 1942) (April 1945); Oesapa Besar, Dutch Timor (February 1942); Cabanatuan, Philippines (June 1942) Motoyama, Japan (November 1942); Fukuoka, Japan (May 1944); Wake Island (October 1943); and Ranau, Borneo (August 1945).

Prisoners of War Humiliated

The Japanese maintained a policy of submitting allied prisoners of war to violence, insults and public humiliation to impress other peoples of Asia with the superiority of the Japanese race.

On 4 March 1942, Vice-Minister of War Kimura received a telegram from the Chief-of-Staff of the Korean Army, of which Itagaki was Commander, stating that:

> As it would be very effective in stamping out the respect and admiration of the Korean people for Britain and America, and also in establishing in them a strong faith in victory, and as the Governor-General and the Army are both strongly desirous of it, we wish you would intern 1,000 British and 1,000 American prisoners of war in Korea. We wish you would give us special consideration regarding this matter.

The Governor-General of Korea at that time was Minami. On 5 March 1942, Kimura replied that about 1,000 white prisoners of war were to be sent to Fusan, Korea. On 23 March 1942, Itagaki sent a message to War Minister Tojo informing him of the plans to use the prisoners of war for psychological purposes; he said:

> It is our purpose by interning American and British prisoners of war in Korea to make the Koreans realize positively the true might of our Empire as well as to contribute to psychological propaganda work for stamping out any ideas of worship of Europe and America which the greater part of Korea still retains at bottom.

Itagaki went on to say that the first camp would be located at Seoul, Korea, in the abandoned Iwamure Silk Reeling Warehouse; his former plan to confine the prisoners in the theological school in Fusan having been abandoned when Kimura objected that those buildings were too good for prisoners of war. Among the main points of his plan, Itagaki stated that the prisoners of war would be used on various works in the principal cities of Korea, especially where psychological conditions were not good, in order to achieve his purpose stated at the beginning of his message; and that the equipment of the camps would be cut to a minimum and that the internment, supervision and guarding of the prisoners would be carried out so as to leave nothing to be desired in the accomplishment of the purpose for which the prisoners of war were being transported to Korea.

On 2 April 1942, the Chief-of-Staff of the Army in Formosa informed the Prisoner of War Information Bureau that he planned to use prisoners of war not only for labor to increase production for war but also "as material for education and guidance."

Thus was applied the plan to use prisoners in violation of the laws of war as pro-Japanese propaganda. On 6 May 1942, the Vice-Minister of War informed the Chief-of-Staff of the Formosa Army that "white prisoners of war will be confined successively in Korea, Formosa, and Manchuria". He added, "for the purpose of control and security it is planned to assign special units organized of Koreans and Formosans". The psychological effect was to be attained by allowing Koreans and Formosans to take part in the plan to submit Allied prisoners of war to insult and public curiosity!

On 16 May 1942, Vice-Minister of War Kimura notified the Commander-in-Chief of the Southern Area Army, whose headquarters were at Singapore, that between May and August the white prisoners of war at Singapore should be handed over to the Formosan and Korean Armies.

The white prisoners of war were handed over and sent to Korea. About 1,000 prisoners captured in the fighting in Malaya arrived in Korea and were marched through the streets of Seoul, Fusan, and Jinsen where they were paraded before 120,000 Koreans and 57,000 Japanese. These prisoners had previously been subjected to malnutrition, ill-treatment and neglect so that their physical condition would elicit contempt from those who saw them. Itagaki's Chief-of-Staff in reporting to Kimura on what he considered the great success of this demonstration of Japanese superiority quoted a Korean bystander who had remarked: "When we look at their frail and unsteady appearance, it is no wonder that they lost to the Japanese forces"; he also quoted another Korean bystander who remarked: "When I saw young Korean soldiers, members of the Imperial Army, guarding the prisoners, I shed tears of joy!" Itagaki's Chief-of-Staff concluded his message with the observation that, "As a whole, it seems that the idea was very successful in driving all admiration for the British out of the Koreans' minds and in driving into them an understanding of the situation."

As far away as in Moulmein, in Burma, this practice of parading prisoners of war was followed. In February 1944, 25 Allied prisoners of war were paraded through the streets of that city. They were in an emaciated condition and were forced to carry notices in Burmese, falsely stating that they had been recently captured on the Arakan front. They were ridiculed and held up to contempt by a Japanese officer who accompanied the parade.

The System

Certain changes made regarding the enforcement of the laws of war and the administration of prisoners of war and civilian internees by Japan after the outbreak of the Pacific War were nominal only; they did not secure the enforcement of the laws of war. The attitude of the Japanese Government toward the enforcement of the laws of war, as demonstrated in its prosecution of the China War, did not really change with the commencement of the Pacific War. Certain changes in governmental organizations and methods of procedure were made, but no real effort was made to secure the enforcement of the laws of war. In fact, as has been shown in the Regulations affecting attempts to escape, changes were made which enjoined the commission of grave breaches of the laws of war. During the China War no special agency had been created by the Japanese Government for the administration of prisoners of war and civilian internees and no Prisoner of War Information Bureau was maintained as required by The Hague and Geneva Conventions. Muto said that "the question of whether Chinese captives would be treated as prisoners of war or not was quite a problem, and it was finally decided in 1938 that because the Chinese conflict was officially known as an 'incident' although it was really a war that Chinese captives would not be regarded as prisoners of war". Tojo said that this was true; and that after the commencement of hostilities in the Pacific War, he considered that Japan was bound to abide by The Hague and Geneva Conventions; and for that reason, he caused a Prisoner of War Information Bureau to be created. This statement by Tojo that he considered that Japan was bound to abide by The Hague and Geneva Conventions in the prosecution of the Pacific War must be interpreted in the light of his statement made during a meeting of the Investigation Committee of the Privy Council on 18 August 1943. He then said: "International Law should be interpreted from the view point of executing the war according to our own opinions." This idea was the basis upon which the policy of the Japanese Government for its treatment of prisoners of war and civilian internees was developed.

Japan Agreed to Apply the Geneva Convention, 1929

The Secretary of State of the United States directed the American Legation in Switzerland, on 18 December 1941, to request the Government of Switzerland to inform the Japanese Government that the Government of the United States intended to abide by the Geneva Prisoner of War Convention and the Geneva Red Cross Convention, both of which had been signed on 27 July 1929, that it further intended to extend and apply the provisions of the Geneva Prisoner of War Convention to any civilian enemy aliens that it might intern, that it hoped that the Japanese Government would apply the provisions of these conventions reciprocally as indicated, and that the Government of the United States would appreciate an expression of intention by the Japanese Government in that respect. The inquiry was delivered to the Japanese Foreign Minister Tojo on 27 December 1941 by the Minister for Switzerland.

The Governments of Great Britain and the Dominions of Canada, Australia and New Zealand also inquired through the Argentine Ambassador in Tokyo on 3 January 1942. In that inquiry, those Governments said that they would observe the terms of the Geneva Prisoner of War Convention of 1929 towards Japan and asked if the Japanese Government was prepared to make a similar declaration.

On 5 January 1942, the Argentine Ambassador delivered another note on behalf of Great Britain, Canada, Australia and New Zealand, proposing that in the application of Articles 11 and 12 of the Convention relative to the provision of food and clothing to prisoners, both parties take into consideration the national and racial customs of the prisoners.

Upon receipt of these inquiries, Togo called upon the War Ministry, Navy Ministry, Ministry for Home Affairs and Ministry of Overseas Affairs for their opinion. At that time Tojo was concurrently Prime Minister and War Minister; Muto was Chief of the Military Affairs Bureau of the War Ministry; Sato was Muto's assistant in the Military Affairs Bureau, Kimura was Vice-Minister of War; Shimada was Navy Minister; Oka was Chief of the Naval Affairs Bureau in the Naval Ministry; and Hoshino was Chief Secretary of the Cabinet.

Togo was concerned for the safety of the Japanese living in Allied countries and for that reason desired to give a favorable answer to the inquiries and so instructed the Bureau of Treaties, pointing out that the fate of Japanese residents, amounting to several hundred thousands, in the enemy countries would be affected by the treatment by Japan of the prisoners of war and civilian internees who might be in her power. The War Ministry agreed with Togo. On 23 January 1942, Kimura told Togo: "In view of the fact that the Geneva Convention relating to prisoners of war was not ratified by His Majesty, we can hardly announce our observance of the same. But it would be safe to notify the world that we have no objection to acting in accordance with the Convention in the treatment of prisoners of war. As regards providing prisoners of war with food and clothing, we have no objection to giving due consideration to the national or racial habits and customs of the prisoners."

Togo answered the American and British inquiries on 29 January 1942. His note to the Government of the United States read as follows:

> Japan strictly observes the Geneva Convention of July 27, 1929, relative to the Red Cross, as a signatory of that Convention. The Imperial Government has not yet ratified the Convention relating to treatment of prisoners of war of 27 July

> 1929. It is therefore not bound by the said Convention. Nevertheless it will apply *mutatis mutandis* the provisions of that Convention to American prisoners of war in its power.

The note addressed to the Governments of Great Britain, Canada, Australia and New Zealand on the same date was as follows:

> The Imperial Government has not ratified the agreement concerning the treatment of prisoners of war dated 27 July 1929, and therefore, it would not be bound to any extent by the said agreement, but would apply *mutatis mutandis* the provisions of the said agreement toward the British, Canadian, Australian and New Zealand prisoners of war under Japanese control. The Imperial Government would consider the national and racial manners and customs under reciprocal conditions when supplying clothing and provisions to prisoners of war.

The same assurances were given to the other allied powers.

As the War Ministry had not agreed to extend these provisions to civilian internees, Togo through his Vice-Minister inquired of the War Ministry on 27 January 1942 regarding the application of the Prisoner of War Convention to non-combatant internees. After conferences, the War Ministry acquiesced further in Togo's plan to protect Japanese nationals in Allied countries, and on 6 February 1942 Kimura told Togo:

> The 1929 Convention relating to prisoners of war has no binding power whatsoever on Japan. But this Ministry has no objection to applying the principles of the Convention to non-combatant internees within such limits as it is applicable, provided, however, that no person be subjected to labor against his will.

Togo informed the Government of the United States on 13 February 1942 that,

> The Imperial Government will apply for the duration of the war under conditions of reciprocity of provisions of the Convention relating to treatment of prisoners of war of 27 July 1929 to enemy civilian internees, in so far as they are applicable and provided that they are not made to work without their consent.

Taking note of the assurance Togo had addressed the British countries on 29 January 1942 that Japan would take into consideration the national and racial customs of the prisoners of war in supplying them with clothing and provisions, the United States addressed another inquiry on that subject. That inquiry was dated 20 February 1942 and stated that the Government of the United States would be bound by the same provisions for prisoners of war as for civilian internees in conformity with Articles 11 and 12 of the Geneva Convention and expected in consequence that the Japanese Government would equally conform to those provisions in the treatment of prisoners of war and civilian internees. Togo answered this inquiry on 2 March 1942 in the following manner: "The Imperial Government intends to take into consideration, with regard to provisions and clothing to be distributed, the racial and national customs of American prisoners of war and civilian internees placed under Japanese power."

This exchange of assurances constituted a solemn agreement binding the

Government of Japan as well as the Governments of the other combatants to apply the provisions of the Geneva Prisoner of War Convention of 27 July 1929 to prisoners of war and civilian internees alike, to take into consideration the national and racial customs of those prisoners and internees when supplying them with food and clothing as required by that Convention and not to force internees to work. The agreement provided that the Convention was to be applied in a spirit of reciprocity, that is to say equally by both sides, each performing in kind and in return for that done by the other. The only exception to this rule established by the agreement were such as might be justified under the reservation *mutatis mutandis*. That the agreement did not allow an exception to be made by reason of conflict with the municipal law of Japan is plain upon construction and is shown by Togo's testimony as follows:

> The inquiries from the United States and Britain were therefore referred in the normal course by the Foreign Ministry Treaty Bureau, which managed such matters, to the War Ministry, as the ministry empowered to decide the question. The answer which came back was that we should undertake to apply the terms of the Geneva Convention *mutatis mutandis,* and it was therefore so replied to the Governments inquiring.
>
> Although the prosecution seems to consider that by the giving of this answer Japan became bound by the Convention to the same extent as if she had ratified it, I assumed (and still assume) that we were binding ourselves only to apply the Convention so far as *circumstances permitted. Mutatis mutandis,* then, I supposed to imply that in the absence of serious hindrances the Covention would be applied; I assumed also (although this was only assumption on my part) that where the requirements of the Convention came into conflict with the provisions of domestic law the former would prevail.

The Director of the Bureau of Treaties, who conducted the conferences with the other Ministries regarding the answer to be given the Allied inquiries, further confirmed this.

Although when it was made the members of the Tojo Cabinet intended that the Allied Powers should understand the agreement as we have interpreted it, they did not abide by the agreement. Instead it was used as a means to secure good treatment for Japanese who might become prisoners of war or be interned by the Allied Powers. When Vice-Minister Kimura answered Togo's request for his opinion regarding the answer to be made to the Allied inquiries, he said that "it would be safe to notify the world" that Japan would observe the Convention, but he prefaced that statement with the remark that the Government could hardly afford to announce an intention to observe the Convention in view of the fact that the Emperor had not ratified it. The successive Japanese governments did not enforce the Convention, for although the Ministers of State considered these assurances to the Allies to be a promise to perform new and additional duties for the benefit of prisoners of war and internees, they never issued any new orders or instructions to their officers in charge of prisoners of war and internees to carry this new promise into execution and never set up any system which secured performance of the promise. Instead of making an effort to perform this agreement they made efforts to conceal from the Allies their guilty non-performance by denying access to the prisoner of war and internee camps; by limiting the length, contents and number of letters which a prisoner or internee might mail; by suppressing all news regarding such prisoners and internees; and by neglecting to answer or by making false answers to protests and inquiries addressed to them regarding the treatment of prisoners and internees.

Reference has been made in an earlier part of this judgment to the effect of the various conventions in relation to the treatment of prisoners of war and civilian internees and to the obligations of belligerents in that respect. Whatever view may be taken of the assurance or undertaking of the Japanese Government to comply with the Geneva Prisoner of War Convention *mutatis mutandis* the fact remains that under the customary rules of war, acknowledged by all civilized nations, all prisoners of war and civilian internees must be given humane treatment. It is the grossly inhumane treatment by the Japanese military forces as referred to in this part of the judgment that is particularly reprehensible and criminal. A person guilty of such inhumanities cannot escape punishment on the pleas that he or his government is not bound by any particular convention. The general principles of the law exist independently of the said conventions. The conventions merely reaffirm the pre-existing law and prescribe detailed provisions for its application.

As to the effect of the undertaking by the Japanese Government to observe the convention *mutatis mutandis,* counsel for the Defence submitted *inter alia* that the insufficiency of food and medical supplies in many of the instances established was due to disorganization and lack of transport facilities resulting from the Allied offensives. Whatever merit that argument has in its narrow application it loses effect in face of the proof that the Allied Powers proposed to the Japanese Government that they should send, for distribution among prisoners of war and internees, the necessary supplies; which offer was refused by the Japanese Government.

It is not necessary to enter into a precise definition of the condition *mutatis mutandis* for at no stage in the defence was anything said or even suggested to the effect that these words justified the atrocities and other grossly inhumane acts of Japanese forces nor was it argued that these words could justify the looting, pillaging and arson which has been clearly established. On those points the accused who gave evidence, for the most part, did no more than plead complete ignorance of the happenings deposed to.

Any interpretation placed on the condition which attempted to justify the atrocities would amount to nothing more than a submission that by the insertion of the words "*mutatis mutandis*" the Japanese military forces would be permitted with impunity to behave with gross barbarity under the guise of complying with a Convention which prescribed humane treatment as its cardinal principle. Such a submission could not be accepted.

Ill-Treatment of Prisoners of War a Policy

The Japanese Government signed and ratified the Fourth Hague Convention of 1907 Respecting the Laws and Customs of War on Land, which provided for humane treatment of prisoners of war and condemned treacherous and inhumane conduct of war. The reason for the failure of the Japanese Government to ratify and enforce the Geneva Prisoner of War Convention which it signed at Geneva in 1929 is to be found in the fundamental training of the Japanese Soldier. Long before the beginning of the period covered by the Indictment, the young men of Japan had been taught that "The greatest honor is to die for the Emperor," a precept which we find Araki repeating in his speeches and propaganda motion pictures. An additional precept was taught that it is an ignominy to surrender to the enemy.

The combined effect of these two precepts was to inculcate in the Japanese soldier a spirit of contempt for Allied soldiers who surrendered, which, in defiance of the rules of war, was demonstrated in their ill-treatment of prisoners. In this spirit they made no distinction between the soldier who fought honorably and courageously up to an inevitable surrender and the soldier who surrendered without a fight. All enemy soldiers who surrendered under any circumstances were to be regarded as being disgraced and entitled to live only by the tolerance of their captors.

Ratification and enforcement of the Geneva Convention of 1929 it was thought would involve abandonment of this view of the Military. The Convention had been signed by the Japanese Plenipotentiaries at Geneva in 1929; but when the Convention came up for ratification in 1934, both the Japanese Army and Navy petitioned against ratification; and by that time they had sufficient political power to prevent ratification. They gave as some of their reasons for resisting ratification, that the obligations imposed by the Convention were unilateral, that the Convention imposed new and additional burdens on Japan, but that Japan could not gain anything by ratifying it, for no Japanese soldier would ever surrender to the enemy.

In this connection it is interesting to note that Tojo giving instructions to chiefs of prisoner of war camps said: "In Japan we have our own ideology concerning prisoners of war, which should naturally make their treatment more or less different from that in Europe and America."

Japanese Purpose Was to Protect Japanese Nationals

The decision to create a Prisoner of War Information Bureau was prompted by an inquiry from the International Red Cross in Geneva, which was forwarded to the War Ministry from the Foreign Ministry on 12 December 1941. The International Red Cross had telegraphed the Japanese Foreign Ministry that in view of the fact that the war had extended to the Pacific its

Committee had placed the services of the Central Prisoner of War Bureau at the disposal of the belligerent States and inquiring whether the Japanese Government was disposed to exchange by the intermediary of the Central Bureau of Geneva lists of information on prisoners of war and in so far as possible on civilian internees. Conferences were held by the officials in the War Ministry; and on 28 December 1941, Vice-Minister of War Kimura informed Foreign Minister Togo that the War Ministry was ready to exchange information, but that "it is not that we declare that we are prepared to apply in practice the provisions of the Prisoner of War Convention of 1929, but that we utilize them for the convenience of transmission of information." By 12 January 1942, the International Red Cross had received replies from Japan and the United States declaring that they were ready to proceed with the transmission of information.

Creation of the Prisoner of War Information Bureau

The Prisoner of War Information Bureau was created by Imperial Ordinance on 27 December 1941. The Bureau was charged with making investigations of the following subjects: internments, removals, releases on parole, exchanges, escapes, admissions to hospitals and deaths of prisoners of war. It was also given the duty of maintaining records for each prisoner of war and managing the communications and correspondence regarding prisoners of war, and of collecting information pertaining to the condition of prisoners of war. The ordinance provided that the Bureau should have a Director and four Secretaries. This Prisoner of War Information Bureau was placed under the supervision and control of the War Minister and was organized as a section of the Military Affairs Bureau, where at different times it came under the control and supervision of Muto and Sato. All personnel of the Prisoner of War Information Bureau were appointed on the recommendation of the War Minister. Tojo appointed Lieutenant General Uemura as the first Director of the Bureau.

Creation of the Prisoner of War Administration Section

On 31 March 1942, "Regulations for the Treatment of Prisoners of War" were promulgated, creating what was called the "Prisoner of War Administration Section" in the Military Affairs Bureau of the War Ministry under the supervision and control of Tojo as War Minister. Tojo exercised this control and supervision through Muto as Chief of the Military Affairs Bureau. The regulations provided that the Section should have a Director and other personnel to be appointed upon the recommendation of the War Minister. Tojo appointed Lieutenant General Uemura as the First Director of the Section, thereby combining in one person the administration of the Prisoner of War Information Bureau and the Prisoner of War Administration Section. The Prisoner of War

Information Bureau was only an information and records office created, as Kimura said, to use the provisions of the Prisoner of War Convention of 1929 for the purpose of gaining information; it had no power of control or supervision over prisoners of war and civilian internees. The Prisoner of War Administration Section on the other hand was given authority to "conduct all affairs relative to the treatment of prisoners of war and civilian internees in the theater of war."

The Military Affairs Bureau Retained Control

The Military Affairs Bureau of the War Ministry under Muto and later under Sato retained control of the system set up for enforcement of the Laws of War during the Pacific War. Although the ordinance creating the Prisoner of War Information Bureau provided: "In regard to matters falling within his jurisdiction, the Director may demand information from any military or naval unit concerned," General Uemura and the Directors following him were required to transmit all inquiries and other communications through the office of the Chief of the Military Affairs Bureau. They had no power to take any action without the approval of the Chief of the Military Affairs Bureau.

According to Tojo, all orders and directives relating to prisoners of war and civilian internees were issued by the War Minister. He also says that these orders and directives were drafted by the Military Affairs Bureau after the Chief of that Bureau had held conferences with the General Staff and other agencies of the Government concerned.

As we will discuss presently, bi-weekly conferences of all Bureau Chiefs in the War Ministry were held and attended by the War Minister and Vice-Minister of War, Tojo and Kimura attended most of these conferences. Kimura was Vice-Minister of War from 10 April 1941 to 11 March 1943. Matters relating to prisoners of war and civilian internees were discussed at these conferences, with Tojo and Kimura at times attending. Orders and regulations were formulated and forwarded to all agencies of the Government concerned with the treatment of prisoners of war and civilian internees.

Detention Camps and Their Administration

Detention camps for prisoners of war were authorized by Imperial Ordinances and Regulations issued by the War Ministry on 23 December 1941. These regulations provided that prisoner of war camps were to be administered by a commander of an Army or a commander of a garrison under the general supervision of the Minister of War. As we have stated, however, all these camps were not under the Army commanders; in those areas under the jurisdiction of the Navy, the camps were administered by Navy officers of corresponding rank and authority.

Detention camps for civilian internees were authorized by regulations issued by the War Ministry on 7 November 1943. The regulations provided:

> When the commander of an army, which term shall herein include persons of the equivalent status as a commander of an army, has interned enemy nationals or neutrals at the front, he shall establish an army internment camp as soon as possible. The commander of an army that establishes the army internment camp shall administer the same.

General regulations were issued providing for the administration of civilian internees, which were not materially different from those providing for the administration of prisoners of war. All regulations applicable to prisoners of war were made applicable to civilian internees, except in those cases where specific regulations were issued applicable to civilian internees alone. These regulations also provided that, "The commander of an army that establishes the army internment camp shall administer the same."

The following accused administered detention camps as military commanders during the Pacific War, namely: Dohihara as Commander of the Eastern Military District in Japan and as Commander of the 7th Area Army at Singapore; Hata as commander of all Japanese Expeditionary Forces in China and as Commander of the military districts in Central and Western Honshu in Japan; Itagaki as Commander of the Korean Army and as Commander of the 7th Area Army at Singapore; Kimura as Commander of the Army in Burma; Muto as Commander of the Japanese Army in Northern Sumatra; Sato as Commander of the Army in French Indo-China; and Umezu as Commander of the Kwantung Army in Manchuria.

The regulations provided that,

> A commander of an army or a commander of a garrison may, whenever necessary, delegate his subordinates to assist in the management of a prisoner of war or civilian internee camp. Persons delegated according to these provisions shall be under the supervision and command of the Commandant.

Special supervisors or chiefs were selected and trained in Tokyo to manage prisoner of war and civilian internee camps; and after careful and detailed instruction, which was completed by a personal message from Prime Minister Tojo, these chiefs of camps were sent out from Japan to all places where prisoner of war and civilian internee camps were located to take charge of those camps and manage them under the command of the Army and Navy commanders. These chiefs of camps were required by regulations to make monthly reports to the Prisoner of War Administration Section in the Military Affairs Bureau of the War Ministry. These reports were discussed at the bi-weekly conferences of the Bureau Chiefs in the War Ministry, which were usually attended by the War Minister and Vice-Minister of War. These reports included statistics relative to the high death rate in the camps due to malnutrition and other causes. Tojo said that this item received his particular attention. A summary of the monthly reports from the chiefs of camps was filed in the office of the Prisoner of War Information Bureau, which was under the same director as the Prisoner of War Administration Section.

The Navy Participated in the System

It was contemplated that the Navy would deliver to the Army for detention and administration all prisoners of war taken and civilian internees interned by it, but in many cases this was not done or was delayed for a long time. Also, in some areas the Navy exercised jurisdicition for administration of occupied areas. For instance, the Navy occupied such islands as Borneo, the Celebes, the Moluccas, Timor and other islands east of a line through Bali. It also occupied other islands, such as Wake Island. In those areas occupied by the Navy, the prisoners of war and civilian internees were administered by the Navy Minister and the enforcement of the laws of war in those areas became the responsibility of the Navy, under the directions of Shimada and Oka.

Administration of the System in Japan Proper

Prisoners of war detained in Japan were under the War Ministry in the same manner as prisoners in other areas, but it is said that the Home Ministry was in charge of the police in Japan and was therefore considered to be the proper Ministry to administer all matters relating to civilian internees in Japan proper. It will be noted that Tojo served as Home Minister from 18 October 1941 to 17 February 1942 and from 25 November 1942 to 6 January 1943. Tojo said that "there was a separate body under the Home Ministry to deal with civilian internees, but I don't know what the name of that was."

For the purpose of defence and military administration, Japan was divided into eight military districts. Each military district was occupied by an army, the commander of which was also the military administrator of the district and in charge of all prisoner of war camps within his district. The Eastern District embraced the Tokyo-Yokohama Area and was occupied by the 12th Area Army. Dohihara commanded that army and administered the district from 1 May 1943 to 22 March 1944 and again from 25 August 1945 to the time of the surrender on 2 September 1945. The Chugoku Military District embraced the Hiroshima Area and the western tip of Honshu Island and was garrisoned by the Second Army Corps. Hata commanded that Corps from 7 April 1945 until the surrender on 2 September 1945.

Administration of the System in Formosa, Korea, and Sakhalin

In the overseas possessions of Japan, which were not in a theater of operations, such as Formosa, Korea and Sakhalin, civilian internees were under the administration of the Ministry of Overseas Affairs, but prisoners of war in those possessions were under the administration of the War Ministry in the same manner as prisoners in other areas. The Ministry of Overseas Affairs was established by Imperial Ordinance of 10 June 1929. That Ordinance provided that this Ministry was to control all affairs relating to the Korea Governor-General's Office, the Formosa Governor-General's Office, the Kwantung Administration Office and the South Seas Administration Office. To provide for the major wartime reorganization of the Japanese Government, this Ministry was abolished in 1943 and its functions divided and transferred to the Ministry of Home Affairs, and the Ministry of Greater East Asia. Togo was Minister of Overseas Affairs from 18 October 1941 to 2 December 1941.

Administration of the System in the Occupied Territories

The Ministry of Greater East Asia was created by Imperial Ordinance on 1 November 1942. That Ordinance directed that

> the Minister of Greater East Asiatic Affairs shall administer the execution of various political affairs, excepting purely diplomatic affairs, concerning Greater East Asia, which is hereinafter defined as excluding Japan proper, Korea, Formosa and Sakhalin. The Minister of Greater East Asiatic Affairs shall superintend affairs concerning the Kwantung Bureau and of the South Seas Government Office. There shall be instituted in the Ministry of Greater East Asiatic Affairs the following four Bureaux: The General Affairs Bureau, the Manchurian Affairs Bureau, The Chinese Affairs Bureau and the Southern Area Affairs Bureau.

This Ministry was organized to govern all areas which had fallen or might fall under the military power of Japan, except Korea, Formosa and Sakhalin. The Ordinance further provided, "To extend cooperation to the Army and the Navy, the Ministry of Greater East Asiatic Affairs shall conduct affairs concerning administration of the occupied areas within the Greater East Asia Area." The first Minister was Aoki, who was followed by Shigemitsu who took over this Ministry on 20 July 1944 and served in that capacity until 7 April 1945, when he was succeeded by Togo who held the office until 16 August 1945.

Accused Who Administered the System in the Occupied Territories

Umezu became Commander-in-Chief of the Kwantung Army on 7 September 1939 and served in that capacity until 18 July 1944. He was the virtual ruler of Manchukuo and was directly responsible for the treatment of prisoners of war and civilian internees in Manchuria. Hata was Commander-in-Chief of the Japanese Expeditionary Force in China from 1 March 1941 to 22 November 1944. On 11 March 1943, Kimura resigned as Vice-Minister of War; he was appointed Commander-in-Chief of the Japanese Army in Burma on 30 August 1944 and served in that position until the surrender. During his tour of duty in Burma he put into practice the policies which he helped to develop during his term of office as Vice-Minister of War. He first established his headquarters at Rangoon. At this time atrocities occurred in that area, at Hsipaw, Moksokwin Reserve Forest, Henzada, Ongun Cemetery, Tharrawaddy and at the Kempeitai Jail in Rangoon. At the end of April 1945, Kimura moved his headquarters to Moulmein. Thereafter atrocities occurred at or near Moulmein. The entire population of Kalagon, a village 10 miles from Kimura's headquarters, was massacred on 7 July 1945 under order of his field officers. Massacres occurred in Moulmein after Kimura's arrival; the Kempeitai became more inhumane in their treatment of Burmese and the internees in the camp at Tavoy were starved and beaten.

Muto made an inspection trip to the southern Regions from 20 March 1942 to 12 April 1942; he visited Formosa, Saigon, Bangkok, Rangoon, Singapore, Palembang, Java, Manila and other places. He returned to Tokyo and was appointed Commander of the Imperial Guards Division on 20 April 1942 and stationed in Northern Sumatra. He was the Japanese military commander in Northern Sumatra, with his headquarters at Medan until 12 October 1944, when he was transferred to the Philippine Islands. During his term of office as such commander, he put into practice the policies which he advocated as Chief of the Military Affairs Bureau of the War Ministry in Tokyo. In the area occupied by his troops in Northern Sumatra, some of the most disgraceful atrocities of the war were committed. Prisoners of war and civilian internees were starved, neglected, tortured, murdered and otherwise mistreated and civilians were massacred. The laws of war were ignored. Muto further demonstrated his disregard for the laws of war upon his transfer on 12 October 1944 to become Chief-of-Staff of the 14th Japanese Army in the Philippine Islands under General Yamashita. On the night of 20 October 1944, Muto arrived at Fort McKinley in the Philippines to assume his duties as Chief-of-Staff to General Yamashita. He held that assignment until the Japanese surrender in September 1945. During his tenure as such Chief-of-Staff, a campaign massacre, torture and other atrocities was waged by the troops under Yamashita and Muto on the civilian population of the Philippines including the massacres in Batangas and massacres and other atrocities at Manila. These bore the same features and followed the pattern set eight years earlier at Nanking when Muto was a member of Matsui's staff. During this period prisoners of war and civilian internees were starved, tortured and murdered.

Dohihara commanded the 7th Area Army at Singapore from 22 March 1944 until he was relieved by Itagaki on 7 April 1945 to become Inspector-General of Military Education. During his period of command prisoners of war were treated as common criminals, starved, tortured and otherwise ill-treated. After Itagaki assumed the command of the 7th Area Army at Singapore, there was no improvement in the condition of the prisoners of war under the jurisdiction of that Army. During June and July 1945, while he was in command, no less than 17 Allied airmen were taken from their cells in the Outram Road Gaol and murdered.

Allied Protests

Formal and informal protests and warnings against violations of the laws of war lodged by the Allied Powers and the Protecting Power during the Pacific War were ignored; or when they were answered, the commission of the offenses was denied, or untruthful explanations were given.

The procedure followed in Tokyo was described to us as follows: Formal protests from the Allied Powers and the Protecting Power were regularly delivered to the Foreign Ministry. The Foreign Ministry then circulated copies of these protests to the Ministries and Bureaux of the Japanese Government concerned. All protests concerning matters under the jurisdiction of the War Ministry and the Prisoner of War Information Bureau were first delivered to the Secretariat of the War Ministry. The Secretariat forwarded the protests to the Military Affairs Section of the Military Affairs Bureau. Muto was Chief of this bureau from 30 September 1939 to 20 April 1942. Sato was Chief of this Section from 15 July 1938 until he replaced Muto as Chief of the Military Affairs Bureau in 1942. Sato served as Chief of the Military Affairs Bureau until 14 December 1944. The Military Affairs Section discussed the protest with the various sections of the Military Affairs Bureau concerned, such as the Prisoner of War Administration Section or the Prisoner of War Information Bureau. The protest was then taken up and discussed at the bi-weekly meetings of the Bureaux Chiefs of the War Ministry which were usually attended by the War Minister and Vice-Minister of War. At these meetings, it was decided whether a reply would be made to the protest and the nature of the reply to be made. The Director of the Prisoner of War Administration Section, who was also the Director of the Prisoner of War Information Bureau, attended these discussions and received orders on important matters direct from the War Minister and the Vice-Minister; he furnished copies of the protests and the replies to be made thereto to the Prisoner of War Information Bureau for filing. This was the practice even when the copies of the protests were addressed to the War Minister or the Prisoner of War Information Bureau.

In addition to formal protests, radio broadcasts were regularly made over Allied stations detailing the atrocities and other violations of the laws of war being committed by the Japanese armed forces and warning the Japanese Government that it would be held responsible for these offenses. These broadcasts were monitored by the Japanese Foreign Ministry and distributed to all ministries, bureaux and officials concerned. Lord Keeper of the Privy Seal Kido recorded in his diary on 19 March 1942 that: "The Imperial Household Minister came to the office and told me about Eden's address in Parliament concerning our soldiers' atrocities at Hong Kong, and we exchanged opinions."

The formal protests delivered were too numerous for detailed mention here. In general, it may be said that these protests related to the violations of the laws of war which we have mentioned as well as to many others. In each case, specific and detailed facts were stated which permitted complete investigation. The same thing may be said of the protests and warnings delivered over the radio.

We will mention here, by way of illustration only, some of those protests and warnings. As early as 14 February 1942, the United States Government delivered a note through the Swiss Government stating that it had received reports that the Japanese authorities in the occupied areas of the Philippines were subjecting American civilians to an extremely rigid and harsh regime involving abuse and humiliation and that the American Government desired assurances that immediate steps had been taken to remedy the situation and to accord to Americans in the Philippines moderate treatment similar to that being extended to Japanese nationals in the territories of the United States. Foreign Minister Togo replied on 24 February 1942 that, "conditions applied to American Nationals in the Philippines by the Japanese authorities are more favorable than contemplated by the Geneva Convention of 1929". This statement was false. He denied that American nationals were being subjected to unfavorable treatment and said that the "Apprehensions of the American Government were based on unknown sources and cited no exact facts and therefore were without foundation."

On 12 December 1942, the United States Government delivered another formal protest. It stated that it had learned of gross ill-treatment suffered by American civilians and prisoners of war in violation of the commitment of the Japanese Government to apply the provisions of the Geneva Prisoner of War Convention of 1929 to American prisoners of war and, in so far as they might be applicable, to civilian internees. The United States stated that it was evident that Japan had failed to fulfill its undertaking and that some Japanese officers and agencies had violated the principles of that Convention not only by positive ill-treatment but by failure to provide for those American nationals the necessities of life. The United States then lodged an emphatic protest and stated that it expected this inhumane and uncivilized treatment of American prisoners of war and civilian internees to be made a matter of immediate investigation, that it expected those responsible to be disciplined immediately, and that it expected an assurance that ill-treatment of prisoners of war and civilian internees would be discontinued. Specific instances were cited, giving dates and other facts to support this protest. No reply was made to this protest until 28 May 1943, when Foreign Minister Shigemitsu replied that an investigation was being made and that he would communicate "in due course" when the results of the investigation were known.

In the meantime, on 5 April 1943, the United States had filed another protest against the ill-treatment of the Doolittle fliers. The United States Government warned: "The American Government also solemnly warns the Japanese Government that for any other violations of its undertakings as regards American prisoners of war or for any other acts of criminal barbarity inflicted upon American prisoners in violation of the laws of warfare, accepted and practiced by civilized nations, as military operations now in progress draw to their inexorable and inevitable conclusion, the American Government will visit upon the officers of the Japanese Government responsible for such uncivilized and inhumane acts the punishment they deserve."

A large number of specific protests was lodged by the United States with Foreign Minister Shigemitsu before he finally answered, on 24 April 1944, the protest of the United States which had been made on 12 December 1942. In that reply, he indicated that the investigation, which he had mentioned in his Note of 28 May 1943, had been completed, and that he had a report thereon. He accused the Government of the United States of "distorting and exaggerating the facts" and rejected the protest; he went to great length to set out what he claimed to be the facts as disclosed by the so-called investigation. The United States replied to this accusation on 1 March 1945 by a note reading: "The United States Government cannot accept a statement by the Japanese Government impugning its veracity. The United States Government's protest concerning treatment accorded by Japanese authorities to American nationals in Japan and Japanese occupied territory is based on documentary evidence, which cannot be refuted in such an arbitrary fashion by the Japanese Government. The statements contained in the Japanese Government's reply of 24 April 1944 are so far removed from the facts as known to the United States Government that it can only conclude that the Japanese Government has permitted itself to be misled by fabricated reports of local officials and had not made an independent investigation of the matters protested in the United States Government's Note of 12 December 1942. The United States Government therefore considers the reply unsatisfactory and will continue to hold the Japanese Government answerable."

British protests were treated in the same fashion as those from the Government of the United States. An illustration is afforded by the protests and answer regarding the treatment of prisoners of war in Rangoon Gaol. On 8 July 1942, the British Government caused a protest to be delivered to Foreign Minister Togo in which it was stated that a photograph had appeared in the Japan Times and Advertiser, a newspaper published in Tokyo, which showed British prisoners of war cleaning the streets of Rangoon under the amused eyes of the public. The protest was renewed on 1 August 1942. On 15 September 1942, the British Government further protested that the prisoners in Rangoon Gaol were furnished insufficient rations, that they were forced to sleep on the bare floors of the prison and that their boots had been confiscated. Tojo acted as Foreign Minister from 1 September 1942 to 17 September 1942; and while occupying that office received a Note calling his attention to the foregoing protests. On 9 February 1943, Foreign Minister Tani, who had replaced Tojo as Foreign Minister replied, "the competent authorities have stated after having made a full inquiry that the facts stated in said letters never happened."

The protests of the British Government against the treatment of British prisoners of war in Burma and Siam received similar treatment. The British Government protested on 4 July 1944 in a Note delivered to Shigemitsu that it had learned from postcards printed by the Japanese authorities that about twenty thousand British prisoners of war had been transferred to the vicinity of Moulmein without notification. It also protested against the unfavorable conditions and ill-treatment to which these prisoners were subjected. Shigemitsu replied on 26 August 1944 that the "majority of British and Allied prisoners of war, who were in Burma on 4 July 1944 were prisoners who had been attached to camps in Thailand and Malaya and had been provisionally transferred to Burma". Shigemitsu replied on 3 October 1944 to further protests from the British Government relative to the health of prisoners laboring in Burma and Siam. In that reply he said: "The Imperial Government, by exercising great vigilance as to the health and hygiene of prisoners of war, takes added measures, such as monthly medical examination of each prisoner of war camp, to enable sickness to be treated in the first stage." He then detailed the medical aid which he claimed had been given to the prisoners on the Burma-Siam Railway. The facts stated were entirely false as the prisoners had not received medical attention and had been dying by thousands from beri-beri, cholera, maleria and other tropical diseases. The true facts were learned when the Rakuyo Maru was torpedoed and sunk in the South China Sea on 12 September 1944. There had been 1300 prisoners of war aboard that unmarked Japanese prison ship. The Japanese picked up the Japanese survivors, but deliberately left the prisoners to their fate. Approximately 100 Australian and United Kingdom survivors were later rescued and taken to Australia and Great Britain. From these prisoners it was learned that all available prisoners of war in Singapore and Java were moved early in 1942 to Burma and Thailand to work on the Burma-Siam Railway project. We have already described the conditions under which they traveled and the terrible conditions during the construction of the railway. Shigemitsu was informed of the facts learned from these rescued prisoners of war in a Note from the British Government dated 4 December 1944, renewing the British protests. Forced at last to reply, Togo, who had succeeded Shigemitsu as Foreign Minister, made a belated reply to these protests on 15 May 1945. He said that it was regretted that the situation was such that "the concerted efforts of all the sanitary services of the Japanese troops cannot prevent the spread of diseases of the digestive system, etc." He denied that atrocities had been committed by Japanese troops in Burma and as to the protest against the parading of British prisoners of war in Moulrein, which we have mentioned, he gave the conventional Japanese answer that it "never happened".

In addition to the disregard shown these formal protests, the many protests and warnings given over the radio were completely ignored although these had been regularly recorded in the Japanese Foreign Office and distributed to the various ministries. On 24 January 1944, a report from the United States Government giving the details and results of the Bataan March was broadcast over the British Broadcasting Corporation's network and recorded in the Japanese Foreign Office. Again on 29 January 1944 radio station KWID at San Francisco, California, broadcast White House Secretary Stephen Early's disclosure that the Japanese would not permit the United States Government to send food and supplies to United States and Filipino prisoners. Early said, "The time has come for releasing the factual reports which have been carefully investigated and authenticated because we cannot expect to get further relief to our prisoners now in the hands of the Japanese." This broadcast was recorded in the Japanese Foreign Office. KWID again broadcast on 29 January 1944 statements by United States Secretary of State Cordell Hull and British Foreign Secretary Anthony Eden. Mr. Hull in speaking of the treatment of prisoners of war in Japanese hands stated:

> According to the reports of cruelty and inhumanity, it would be necessary to summon the representatives of all the demons available anywhere and combine their fiendishness with all that is bloody in order to describe the conduct of those who inflicted those unthinkable atrocities on the Americans and Filipinos.

The vigor of this language was fully justified by the evidence given before the Tribunal. Mr. Eden had stated before the House of Commons that British protests had drawn unsatisfactory results from Japan. He said that the Japanese were violating not only international law but all human, decent civilized conduct. He warned the Japanese Government that in time to come the record of their military atrocities in the war would not be forgotten. Mr. Hull had closed his statement with the remark that the United States Government was assembling all possible facts concerning Japanese treatment of prisoners of war and that it intended to seek full punishment of the responsible Japanese authorities. General MacArthur's General Headquarters issued a warning on 22 October 1944 to the Japanese Commander of the 7th Area Army at Singapore, who had jurisdiction over the Philippine Islands as well as a large segment of the Pacific Area. General MacArthur warned that he would hold the enemy leaders immediately responsible for any failure to accord prisoners of war and civilian internees proper treatment. He said that although the Americans and Filipinos who surrendered in the Philippines believed they would be treated with the dignity, honor and protection to which prisoners of war were entitled under the laws of war, unimpeachable evidence had been received of the degradation and even brutality to which they had been subjected in violation of the most sacred code of martial honor. All of these broadcasts were recorded in the Japanese Foreign Office and given a wide circulation among the Japanese Ministries.

Ill-Treatment of Prisoners of War and Civilian Internees was Condoned and Concealed

The Japanese Government condoned ill-treatment of prisoners of war and civilian internees by failing and neglecting to punish those guilty of ill-treating them or by prescribing trifling and inadequate penalties for the offence. That Government also attempted to conceal the ill-treatment and murder of prisoners and internees by prohibiting the representatives of the Protecting Power from visiting camps, by restricting such visits as were allowed, by refusing to forward to the Protecting Power complete lists of prisoners taken and civilians interned, by censoring news relating to prisoners and internees, and ordering the destruction of all incriminating documents at the time of the surrender of Japan.

The following are examples of inadequate sentences imposed for ill-treatment of prisoners. For flogging the punishment imposed was admonition or a few days confinement in quarters or a few days extra duty. A guard guilty of torturing prisoners of war was admonished. A guard who was guilty of frequently lynching prisoners of war was admonished. Several guards were found guilty of lynching prisoners of war; the most severe punishment imposed was discharge. The penalty imposed on the officer responsible for the burning alive of 62 Allied fliers during an air raid on the Tokyo Army Prison was an admonition. These cases are evidence that the War Ministry knew there was ill-treatment of prisoners. The trifling nature of the punishments imposed implies condonation.

The Government actively concealed the ill-treatment to which prisoners of war and civilian internees were being subjected by refusing visits by representatives of the Protecting Power designated by the Allies. The Swiss Minister in Tokyo, as early as 12 February 1942, delivered a note to Foreign Minister Togo in which he said:

> I have the honor to bring to the knowledge of Your Excellency that the Government of the United States is prepared to facilitate, at the request of the representative of the Protecting Power, their visits to Japanese subjects who are temporarily detained, interned, or at liberty on parole. I would be greatly obliged to Your Excellency if you would facilitate in part the task of my Legation so far as it concerns visits to internees.

He delivered another note to Foreign Minister Togo on 17 February 1942 in which he said:

> The Government of the United States of America has already informed the Spanish Ambassador, protecting Japanese interests in the United States, that he is at liberty to visit prisoner of war camps as well as places where civilian internees are detained. The Government of the United States requests, in conformity with the Geneva Prisoner of War Convention, that the Swiss representatives in Japan and in the territories occupied by Japanese forces be authorized as soon as possible to commence their visits of inspection to places where American citizens, who are prisoners of war or civilian internees, are located.

He delivered other notes to Togo in March and June 1942 repeating those requests. During June 1942 he requested the same permission to visit the subjects of Great Britain and the Dominions, who were detained as prisoners or internees. Togo at last replied to these requests on 30 July 1942 by a note in which he said: "I desire to inform Your Excellency that the Imperial Government having in principle refused to recognize the representation of any interests in the occupied territories comprising the Philippine Islands, Hong Kong, Malaya and the Netherlands East Indies, it follows that permission cannot be given to your delegates to visit American prisoners of war and civilian internees in the above-mentioned territories; but that in respect of Shanghai only, in occupied China, the competent authorities can give this permission." The Governments of the United States and Great Britain protested immediately and renewed their requests. The correspondence between the Swiss Minister and Foreign Minister Tani, who succeeded Togo, reflects that this policy of refusing permission to visit prisoners and internees detained in the occupied territories and in Japan's overseas possessions was continued. The Swiss Minister continued to press for permission, however; and on 22 April 1943, Shigemitsu, who had become Foreign Minister, delivered a Note Verbal to the Swiss Minister in which he said: "As the Foreign Minister has communicated to the Swiss Minister by Note dated 20 July 1942, the Imperial Government shall not permit visits to prisoners of war and civilian internee camps in occupied territories." Although the Swiss Minister had been informed by Foreign Minister Togo that representatives of the Protecting Power would be allowed to visit camps at Shanghai, the visits were not made because the so-called "competent authorities", to which Togo referred the Swiss Minister, refused to give permission for the visits and the permission was not forthcoming from the Tojo Cabinet in Tokyo. Shigemitsu was informed of this in a note from the Swiss Minister dated 12 May 1943. In response to these persistent and repeated requests from the Swiss Government for permission to visit prisoners of war and civilian internees, a few selected camps, which had been prepared for the occasion, were allowed to be visited in Japan. The Swiss Minister, on 2 June 1943 requested permission from Shigemitsu to visit the remaining camps in Japan as well as the camps in the occupied territories, and inquired when a second visit might be made to the camps which had been visited in Japan. Foreign Minister Shigemitsu replied on 23 July 1943 and said:

> As regards prisoner of war camps in the occupied areas, a notification will be made to Your Excellency if the time comes when permission can be granted; and as regards prisoner of war camps in Japan proper, which have not yet been visited, permission will be granted gradually at a favorable opportunity. Permission for periodic visits to those camps, that have already been visited, shall not be granted in advance; but in case a visit is desired, consideration will be given to applications made on all such occasions.

However, consideration was not given to these applications; and on 12 February 1944, the Swiss Minister complained to Shigemitsu that no reply had been made to requests to visit detention camps between August 1943 and February 1944. This complaint was repeated in a note to Shigemitsu on 30 March 1944, in which the Swiss Minister said:

> You know that I am not satisfied with my activities as representative of foreign interests in Japan. The results do not correspond to the efforts. I can see this in a concrete fashion as shown by the statistics of my services and requests which have been made by my Government at the request of the Governments who have confided their interests in us. I desire to confine myself for the moment to my requests to visit prisoner of war camps. Reviewing my requests made over more than two years, I find that from 1 February 1942 to 15 March 1944, I have intervened 134 times in writing. These 134 notes have brought exactly 24 replies from the Foreign Ministry. Most of these replies are either negative or forward to me decisions made by competent authorities. I have received three replies in nine months.

It was not until 13 November 1944 that he was notified by Shigemitsu's Foreign Ministry that the time had come when permission could be granted to visit prisoners of war and internees in the occupied territories; and then the visits were limited to Manila, Shonan and Bangkok. In a note addressed to the Swiss Minister in Tokyo on 17 November 1944, Shigemitsu informed the Swiss Minister that visits would be allowed to prisoner of war camps in the occupied territories on condition of reciprocity if they did not interfere with military operations. The Swiss Minister in a note dated 13 January 1945, asked Shigemitsu when these visits could be commenced. It was not until 7 April 1945, that Togo, who had succeeded Shigemitsu as Foreign Minister, replied to the many urgent requests to visit detention camps in the occupied territories. In that reply, Togo stated that Japan "would lose no time" in making preparations for visits in Thailand. By the use of one excuse or another, visits were never freely allowed throughout the war.

In the few cases where the representatives of the Protecting Power were allowed to visit detention camps, the camps were prepared for the visit, and the visits were strictly supervised. Regulations issued by the Tojo Cabinet early in the Pacific War provided that when an interview with a prisoner of war was authorized restrictions regarding the time and place of the interview and the range within which the conversation was to be conducted would be imposed and that a guard would be present during the interview. These regulations were enforced notwithstanding the repeated objections of the Protecting Power. In a note to the Swiss Minister, dated 22 April 1943, Shigemitsu said: "The Imperial Government shall not allow delegates of the Protecting Power to interview prisoners of war without the presence of a guard." The Swiss Minister protested and Shigemitsu replied on 24 June 1943: "The Ministry hastens to inform the Legation that Article 13 of our country's detailed regulations stipulates that a guard shall be present when prisoners of war are interviewed, and that it is not possible to modify our treatment of prisoners of war practiced in conformity with the said Article." After a visit to the prisoner of war camp at Motoyama in Japan in the spring of 1943, the senior prisoner at the camp, who had dared to complain of the working conditions to which the prisoners had been subjected, was tortured. He was forced to kneel for five hours before a Japanese guard. The next time this camp was visited, this senior prisoner was placed in confinement and was not allowed to speak to the representative although that representative demanded to interview him.

The fate of prisoners of war and civilian internees was further concealed by refusal to forward to the Protecting Power a list of the names of prisoners of war and civilian internees detained. An example of the refusal to supply such lists is the case of the prisoners of war and civilian internees detained after the capture of Wake Island. The Swiss Minister on 27 May 1942 requested of Togo the names of the prisoners of war and civilian internees captured on Wake Island and their present whereabouts. On 6 October 1942, the Swiss Minister informed the Foreign Minister, then Tani, that the United States Government was still without report on approximately 400 American civilians who were on Wake Island at the time of its capture. On 8 April 1943, the list not having been furnished, the Swiss Minister informed Foreign Minister Tani that the

United States Government was insisting upon being furnished the names and location of the remaining 400. Foreign Minister Tani replied on 19 April 1943 that all information to be furnished had already been given. On 21 August 1943, the Swiss Minister furnished the new Foreign Minister Shigemitsu a list of 432 American civilians who should have been on Wake Island at the time of its occupation by the Japanese forces, but whose names were not found on the lists furnished to the International Red Cross Bureau by the Japanese, and requested information regarding those civilians. On 15 May 1945, the Swiss Minister informed Foreign Minister, now Togo, that no answer had been received to the request for information regarding the remaining 432 civilians from Wake Island. The information was not obtained until after the surrender of Japan. In truth, all these unfortunate people were murdered by the Japanese Navy in October 1943.

News reports and mail were specially censored, no doubt to prevent disclosure of the ill-treatment to which prisoners of war were being subjected. Censorship regulations issued by the Information Bureau of the War Ministry on 20 December 1943, while Tojo was War Minister, provided among other things the following:

> Care should be taken to avoid issuing twisted reports of our fair attitude which might give the enemy food for evil propaganda and bring harm to our interned brothers. For this reason, any reports including photographs, pictures, etc., which come under the following categories are prohibited: Anything that gives the impression that prisoners of war are too well treated or are cruelly treated; any concrete information concerning facilities, supplies, sanitary conditions, or other matters pertaining to living conditions within prisoner of war camps; any information giving the names of any location of prisoner of war camps other than the following:

Then followed twelve general names such as Tokyo, Korea, Borneo, etc. The mail which prisoners of war were allowed to send was restricted almost to the point of prohibition. Prisoners in some camps, such as those at Singapore, were told by their guards that unless they reported favorably on conditions at the camp their cards would not be sent. This appears to have been the general rule.

When it became apparent that Japan would be forced to surrender, an organized effort was made to burn or otherwise destroy all documents and other evidence of ill-treatment of prisoners of war and civilian internees. The Japanese Minister of War issued an order on 14 August 1945 to all Army headquarters that confidential documents should be destroyed by fire immediately. On the same day, the Commandant of the Kempeitai sent out instructions to the various Kempeitai Headquarters detailing the methods of burning large quantities of documents efficiently. The Chief of the Prisoner of War Camps under the Prisoner of War Administration Section of the Military Affairs Bureau sent a circular telegram to the Chief-of-Staff of the Formosan Army on 20 August 1945 in which he said: "Documents which would be unfavorable for us in the hands of the enemy are to be treated in the same way as secret documents and destroyed when finished with." This telegram was sent to the Korean Army, Kwantung Army, North China Army, Hong Kong, Mukden, Borneo, Thailand, Malaya and Java. It was in this telegram that the Chief of Prisoner of War Camps made this statement: "Personnel who ill-treated prisoners of war and internees or who are held in extremely bad sentiment by them are permitted to take care of it by immediately transferring or by fleeing without trace."

PART C. CHAPTER IX: FINDINGS ON COUNTS OF THE INDICTMENT

In Count 1 of the Indictment it is charged that all the defendants together with other persons participated in the formulation or execution of a common plan or conspiracy. The object of that common plan is alleged to have been that Japan should secure the military, naval, political and economic domination of East Asia and of the Pacific and Indian Oceans, and of all countries and islands therein or bordering thereon, and for that purpose should, alone or in combination with other countries having similar objects, wage a war or wars of aggression against any country or countries which might oppose that purpose.

There are undoubtedly declarations by some of those who are alleged to have participated in the conspiracy which coincide with the above grandiose statement, but in our opinion it has not been proved that these were ever more than declarations of the aspirations of individuals. Thus, for example, we do not think the conspirators ever seriously resolved to attempt to secure the domination of North and South America. So far as the wishes of the conspirators crystallised into a concrete common plan we are of opinion that the territory they had resolved that Japan should dominate was confined to East Asia, the Western and South Western Pacific Ocean and the Indian Ocean, and certain of the islands in these oceans. We shall accordingly treat Count 1 as if the charge had been limited to the above object.

We shall consider in the first place whether a conspiracy with the above object has been proved to have existed.

Already prior to 1928 Okawa, one of the original defendants, who has been discharged from this trial on account of his present mental state, was publicly advocating that Japan should extend her territory on the Continent of Asia by the threat or, if necessary, by use of military force. He also advocated that Japan should seek to dominate Eastern Siberia and the South Sea Islands. He predicted that the course he advocated must result in a war between the East and the West, in which Japan would be the champion of the East. He was encouraged and sided in his advocacy of this plan by the Japanese General Staff. The object of this plan as stated was substantially the object of the conspiracy, as we have defined it. In our review of the facts we have noticed many subsequent declarations of the conspirators as to the object of the conspiracy. These do not vary in any material respect from this early declaration by Okawa.

Already when Tanaka was premier, from 1927 to 1929, a party of military men, with Okawa and other civilian supporters, was advocating this policy of Okawa's that Japan should expand by the use of force. The conspiracy was now in being. It remained in being until Japan's defeat in 1945. The immediate question when Tanaka was premier was whether Japan should attempt to expand her influence on the continent—beginning with Manchuria—by peaceful penetration, as Tanaka and the members of his Cabinet wished, or whether that expansion should be accomplished by the use of force if necessary, as the conspirators advocated. It was essential that the conspirators should have the support and control of the nation. This was the beginning of the long struggle between the conspirators, who advocated the attainment of their object by force, and those politicians and latterly those bureaucrats, who advocated Japan's expansion by peaceful measures or at least by a more discreet choice of the occasions on which force should be employed. This struggle culminated in the conspirators obtaining control of the organs of government of Japan and preparing and regimenting the nation's mind and material resources for wars of aggression designed to achieve the object of the conspiracy. In overcoming the opposition the conspirators employed methods which were entirely unconstitutional and at times wholly ruthless. Propaganda and persuasion won many to their side, but military action abroad without Cabinet sanction or in defiance of Cabinet veto, assassination of opposing leaders, plots to overthrow by force of arms Cabinets which refused to cooperate with them, and even a military revolt which seized the capital and attempted to overthrow the government were part of the tactics whereby the conspirators came ultimately to dominate the Japanese polity.

As and when they felt strong enough to overcome opposition at home and latterly when they had finally overcome all such opposition the conspirators carried out in succession the attacks necessary to effect their ultimate object, that Japan should dominate the Far East. In 1931 they launched a war of aggression against China and conquered Manchuria and Jehol. By 1934 they had commenced to infiltrate into North China, garrisoning the land and setting up puppet governments designed to serve their purposes. From 1937 onwards they continued their aggressive war against China on a vast scale, overrunning and occupying much of the country, setting up puppet governments on the above model, and exploiting China's economy and natural resources to feed the Japanese military and civilian needs.

In the meantime they had long been planning and preparing a war of aggression which they proposed to launch against the U.S.S.R. The intention was to seize that country's Eastern territories when a favourable opportunity occurred. They had also long recognized that their exploitation of East Asia and their designs on the islands in the Western and South Western Pacific would bring them into conflict with the United States of America, Britain, France and the Netherlands who would defend their threatened interests and territories. They planned and prepared for war against these countries also.

The conspirators brought about Japan's alliance with Germany and Italy, whose policies were as aggressive as their own, and whose support they desired both in the diplomatic and military fields, for their aggressive actions in China had drawn on Japan the condemnation of the League of Nations and left her friendless in the councils of the world.

Their proposed attack on the U.S.S.R. was postponed from time to time for various reasons, among which were (1) Japan's preoccupation with the war in China, which was absorbing unexpectedly large military resources, and (2) Germany's pact of nonaggression with the U.S.S.R. in 1939, which for the time freed the U.S.S.R. from threat of attack on her Western frontier, and might have allowed her to devote the bulk of her strength to the defence of her Eastern territories if Japan had attacked her.

Then in the year 1940 came Germany's great military successes on the continent of Europe. For the time being Great Britain, France and the Netherlands were powerless to afford adequate protection to their interests and territories in the Far East. The military preparations of the United States were in the initial stages. It seemed to the conspirators that no such favourable opportunity could readily recur of realising that part of their objective which sought Japan's domination of Southwest Asia and the islands in the Western and South Western Pacific and Indian Oceans. After prolonged negotiations with the United States of America, in which they refused to disgorge any substantial part of the fruits they had seized as the result of their war of aggression against China, on 7th December 1941 the conspirators launched a war of aggression against the United States and the British Commonwealth. They had already issued orders declaring that a state of war existed between Japan and the Netherlands as from 00.00 hours on 7th December 1941. They had previously secured a jumping-off place for their attacks on the Philippines, Malaya and the Netherlands East Indies by forcing their troops into French Indo-China under threat of military action if this facility was refused to them. Recognising the existence of a state of war and faced by the imminent threat of invasion of her Far Eastern territories, which the conspirators had long planned and were now about to execute, the Netherlands in self-defence declared war on Japan.

These far-reaching plans for waging wars of aggression, and the prolonged and intricate preparation for and waging of these wars of aggression were not the work of one man. They were the work of many leaders acting in pursuance of a common plan for the achievement of a common object. That common object, that they should secure Japan's domination by preparing and waging wars of aggression, was a criminal object. Indeed no more grave crimes can be conceived of than a conspiracy to wage a war of aggression or the waging of a war of aggression, for the conspiracy threatens the security of the peoples of the world, and the waging disrupts it. The probable result of such a conspiracy, and the inevitable result of its execution is that death and suffering will be inflicted on countless human beings.

The Tribunal does not find it necessary to consider whether there was a conspiracy to wage wars in violation of the treaties, agreements and assurances specified in the particulars annexed to Count 1. The conspiracy to wage wars of aggression was already criminal in the highest degree.

The Tribunal finds that the existence of the criminal conspiracy to wage wars of aggression as alleged in Count 1, with the limitation as to object already mentioned, has been proved.

The question whether the defendants or any of them participated in that conspiracy will be considered when we deal with the individual cases.

The conspiracy existed for and its execution occupied a period of many years. Not all of the conspirators were parties to it at the beginning, and some of those who were parties to it had ceased to be active in its execution before the end. All of those who at any time were parties to the criminal conspiracy or who at any time with guilty knowledge played a part in its execution are guilty of the charge contained in Count 1.

In view of our finding on Count 1 it is unnecessary to deal with Counts 2 and 3, which charge the formulation or execution of conspiracies with objects more limited than that which we have found proved under Count 1, or with Count 4, which charges the same conspiracy as Count I but with more specification.

Count 5 charges a conspiracy wider in extent and with even more grandiose objects than that charged in Count 1. We are of opinion that although some of the conspirators clearly desired the achievements of these grandiose objects nevertheless there is not sufficient evidence to justify a finding that the conspiracy charged in Count 5 has been proved.

For the reasons given in an earlier part of this judgment we consider it unnecessary to make any pronouncement on Counts 6 to 26 and 37 to 53. There remain therefore only Counts 27 to 36 and 54 and 55, in respect of which we now give our findings.

Counts 27 to 36 charge the crime of waging wars of aggression and wars in violation of international law, treaties, agreements and assurances against the countries named in those counts.

In the statement of facts just concluded we have found that wars of aggression were waged against all those countries with the exception of the Commonwealth of the Philippines (Count 30) and the Kingdom of Thailand (Count 34). With reference to the Philippines, as we have heretofore stated, that Commonwealth during the period of the war was not a completely sovereign State and so far as international relations were concerned it was a part of the United States of America. We further stated that it is beyond doubt that a war of aggression was waged in the Philippines, but for the sake of technical accuracy we consider the aggressive war in the Philippines as being a part of the war of aggression waged against the United States of America.

Count 28 charges the waging of a war of aggression against the Republic of China over a lesser period of time than that charged in Count 27. Since we hold that the fuller charge contained in Count 27 has been proved we shall make no pronouncement on Count 28.

Wars of aggression having been proved, it is unnecessary to consider whether they were also wars otherwise in violation of international law or in violation of treaties, agreements and assurances. The Tribunal finds therefore that it has been proved that wars of aggression were waged as alleged in Counts 27, 29, 31, 32, 33, 35 and 36.

Count 54 charges ordering, authorising and permitting the commission of Conventional War Crimes. Count 55 charges failure to take adequate steps to secure the observance and prevent breaches of conventions and laws of war in respect of prisoners of war and civilian internees. We find that there have been cases in which crimes under both these Counts have been proved.

Consequent upon the foregoing findings, we propose to consider the charges against individual defendants in respect only of the following Counts: Numbers 1, 27, 29, 31, 32, 33, 35, 36, 54 and 55.

PART C. CHAPTER X: VERDICTS

The Tribunal will now proceed to render its verdict in the case of each of the accused.

Article 17 of the Charter requires that the judgment shall give the reasons on which it is based. Those reasons are stated in the recital of facts and the statement of findings the reading of which has just been completed. Therein the Tribunal has examined minutely the activities of each of the accused concerned in relation to the matters in issue. Consequently, the Tribunal does not propose in the verdicts now to be read to repeat the many particular findings on which the verdicts are based. It will give its reasons in general terms for its findings in respect of each accused, such general reasons being based on the particular statements and findings in the recital already referred to.

ARAKI, SADAO

The defendant Araki, Sadao is charged under Count 1 with conspiracy to wage aggressive wars and wars in violation of international law, treaties, agreements and assurances. He is charged also under Counts 27, 29, 31, 32, 33, 35 and 36 with waging such wars. Under Counts 54 and 55 he is charged with responsibility for war crimes committed in China. At all material times he was a Military Officer of high rank. He became a Lieutenant-General in 1927 and a General in 1933. Throughout he was prominent in the hierarchy of the Army.

He was an energetic proponent of the Army policy of political domination at home and of military aggression abroad. He was in fact and was recognised as being one of the prominent leaders of that Army movement. As a member of different Cabinets he advanced the Army policy to prepare for wars of aggression by stimulating the warlike spirit of the young men of Japan, by mobilizing Japan's material resources for war and by speeches and by control of the press inciting and preparing the Japanese people for war. Both in and out of political office he helped to formulate and was a vigorous advocate of the policy of the military party to enrich Japan at the expense of her neighbours. He both approved and actively supported the policies undertaken by the Japanese Army in Manchuria and Jehol to separate that territory politically from China, to create a Japanese-controlled government and to place its economy under the domination of Japan. The Tribunal finds him to have been one of the leaders of the conspiracy set out in Count 1 and he is adjudged guilty under that Count.

Araki assumed office as Minister of War in December 1931 after the aggressive war against the Republic of China in Manchuria had commenced. He continued as Minister of War until January 1934. Throughout that period he took a prominent part in the development and the carrying out of the military and political policies pursued in Manchuria and Jehol. He gave all possible support to the successive military steps taken for the occupation of that portion of the territories of China. Araki from May 1938 until August 1939 was Minister of Education, in which capacity he approved and collaborated in military operations in other parts of China. We have found that the war in China was from 1931 onwards a war of aggression and we find that this defendant participated in the waging of that war. Accordingly we find him guilty under Count 27.

There is no evidence that he took any active part in the wars referred to in Counts 29, 31, 32, 33, 35 and 36, on all of which we find him not guilty. As to war crimes there is no evidence of his responsibility for such crimes and we find him not guilty under Counts 54 and 55.

Dohihara, Kenji

The defendant Dohihara, Kenji is charged under Counts 1, 27, 29, 31, 32, 33, 35, 36, 54 and 55.

At the commencement of the period under review Dohihara was a Colonel in the Japanese army and by April 1941 had attained the rank of General. Before the Manchurian Affair he had been in China for about eighteen years and had come to be regarded in the Army as a specialist on China. He was intimately involved in the initiation and development of the war of aggression waged against China in Manchuria and in the subsequent establishment of the Japanese-dominated state of Manchukuo. As the aggressive policy of the Japanese military party was pursued in other areas in China Dohihara took a prominent part in its development by political intrigue, by threat of force and by the use of force.

Dohihara acted in close association with other leaders of the military faction in the development, preparation, and execution of their plans to bring East and South East Asia under Japanese domination.

When his special knowledge of China and his capacity for intrigue there were no longer required he was employed as a General Officer in the field in pursuit of the aims for which he had conspired. He took part in the waging of aggressive war not only against China but also against the U.S.S.R. and against those countries against whom also Japan waged aggressive war from 1941 until 1945 excepting the Republic of France. As to the wars waged against the U.S.S.R. in 1938 and 1939, Dohihara was a Lieutenant General on the General Staff which had overhead control of the Lake Khassan fighting. At Nomonhan elements of the Army he commanded took part in that fighting.

As to the waging of war against the Republic of France (Count 33) the decision to wage this war was made by the Supreme Council for the Direction of War in February 1945. The accused was not a party to that decision and the evidence does not establish that he took part in the waging of that war.

We find him to be guilty of conspiracy to wage aggressive war under Count I and of waging aggressive wars as charged under Counts 27, 29, 31, 32, 35 and 36. He is not guilty under Count 33.

Dohihara commanded the 7th Area Army from April 1944 until April 1945. This command included Malaya, Sumatra, Java and for a time Borneo. The evidence as to the extent of his responsibility for protecting prisoners of war within the area of his command from murder and torture is conflicting. At least he was responsible for their supplies of food and medicine. The evidence is clear that they were grossly ill-treated in respect of these supplies. Prisoners were starved and deaths from malnutrition and food deficiency diseases occurred at an appalling rate. These conditions applied only to prisoners of war and did not occur among their captors. It was urged in defence that the deterioration of Japan's war position in those areas and the severance of communications made it impossible to maintain better supplies for prisoners. The evidence shows that food and medicine was available which could have been used to relieve the terrible conditions of the prisoners. These supplies were withheld upon a policy for which Dohihara was responsible. Upon these findings of fact Dohihara's offence falls rather within Count 54 than Count 55. Accordingly he is found guilty under Count 54 and we make no finding under Count 55.

HASHIMOTO, KINGORO

Hashimoto is indicted under counts 1, 27, 29, 31, 32, 54 and 55.

He was an Army officer and early joined the conspiracy. He thereafter furthered the achievement of its objects by all the means in his power. None of the conspirators held more extreme views than he did; none was more outspoken in his statement of these views. In the beginning he advocated the expansion of Japan through the seizure of Manchuria by force of arms. As time went on he advocated the use of force against all Japan's neighbours for the accomplishment of the aims of the conspirators.

He was an ardent admirer of government by military dictatorship. He detested the political parties, which played some part in the government of Japan and opposed the schemes of conquest which the conspirators were determined to effect. He was a principal in many of the activities by which the conspirators came ultimately to suppress the opposition of the democratic elements in Japan and to control the government. Without this control their aggressive schemes could not have been accomplished. Thus, for example, he was one of the principals in the plots of March and October 1931 which were designed to overthrow the existing cabinets and to establish cabinets in their place which would support the conspirators. He was also a party to the plot of May 1932 of which the object and result was the assassination of Premier Inukai who had championed democracy and opposed the policies of the conspirators. His publications and the activities of the societies he founded or supported were largely devoted to the destruction of democracy and the establishment of a form of government more favourable to the use of war for achieving the expansion of Japan.

He played some part in planning the occurrence of the Mukden Incident so as to give the Army a pretext for seizing Manchuria. He claimed some of the credit for the seizure of Manchuria and for Japan leaving the League of Nations.

After its early years it was mainly as a propagandist that he figured in the execution of the conspiracy. He was a prolific publicist and contributed to the success of the conspiracy by inciting the appetite of the Japanese people for the possessions of Japan's neighbours, by inflaming Japanese opinion for war to secure these possessions, by his advocacy of an alliance with Germany and Italy which were bent on similar schemes of expansion, by his denunciation of treaties by which Japan had bound herself to refrain from the schemes of aggrandisement which were the aims of the conspiracy, and by his fervent support of the agitation for a great increase in the armaments of Japan so that she might secure these aims by force or the threat of force.

He was a principal in the formation of the conspiracy and contributed largely to its execution.

As to Count 27, having first plotted the seizure of Manchuria by force of arms he there-after played some part in the planning of the Mukden Incident so that it might serve as a pretext for the seizure of Manchuria. Being thus fully apprised that the war against China was a war of aggression and being one of those who had conspired to bring about that war he did everything within his power to secure its success. For a time he was, in fact, a military commander in the field. He thereby waged a war of aggression against China as charged in Count 27.

There is no evidence directly connecting Hashimoto with any of the crimes charged in Counts 29, 31, 32, 54 or 55. The Tribunal finds him not guilty on these Counts.

The Tribunal finds Hashimoto guilty on Counts 1 and 27.

HATA, SHUNROKO

Hata is charged under Counts 1, 27, 29, 31, 32, 35, 36, 54, and 55.

On the formation of the Abe Cabinet in August 1939 Hata assumed the post of War Minister which he held continuously until July 1940 when the Yonai Cabinet fell. Though holding Cabinet rank for less than one year Hata contributed substantially to the formulation and execution of the aggressive plans. As War Minister he exerted considerable influence on Government policy. The war in China was waged with renewed vigor; the Wang Ching Wei Government was established at Nanking; the plans for control of French Indo-China were developed and the negotiations with the Netherlands in relation to matters concerning the Netherlands East Indies were conducted.

Hata favored Japanese domination of East Asia and the areas to the South. To achieve this object he, for example, approved the abolition of political parties to be replaced by the Imperial Rule Assistance Association, and in collaboration with and after consulting other high military authorities he precipitated the fall of the Yonai Cabinet, thereby making way for the full alliance with Germany and the establishment of a virtual totalitarian state in Japan.

Thereafter from March 1941 as Commander-in-Chief of the expeditionary forces in China he continued to wage war in that country until November 1944.

He continued to wage war against China and the Western Powers as Inspector General of Military Education, one of the highest active military posts in the Japanese Army.

When the Lake Khassan hostilities occurred Hata was in Central China and at the time of the Nomonhan Incident he was Aide-de-Camp to the Emperor, becoming War Minister a little more than a week before the conclusion of that Incident. The Tribunal is of the opinion that Hata did not participate in the waging of either of these wars.

War Crimes

In 1938 and again from 1941 to 1944 when Hata was in command of expeditionary forces in China atrocities were committed on a large scale by the troops under his command and were spread over a long period of time. Either Hata knew of these things and took no steps to prevent their occurrence, or he was indifferent and made no provision for learning whether orders for the humane treatment of prisoners of war and civilians were obeyed. In either case he was in breach of his duty as charged and under Count 55.

The Tribunal finds Hata guilty under Counts 1, 27, 29, 31, 32, and 55. He is not guilty under Counts 35, 36 and 54.

HIRANUMA, KIICHIRO

Hiranuma is indicted under Counts 1, 27, 29, 31, 32, 33, 35, 36, 54 and 55. He became a member of the conspiracy if not at the beginning, shortly afterwards. He was a member and from 1936 President of the Privy Council until 1939, when he became Prime Minister; later he served in succession as Minister Without Portfolio and Home Minister in the second and third Konoye Cabinets.

During the period when he was a member of the Privy Council he supported the various measures coming before that body which involved the carrying out of the aggressive plans of the militarists. As Prime Minister and as Minister he continued to support these plans.

From 17 October 1941 until 19 April 1945, the accused was one of the Senior Statesmen. At the meeting of Senior Statesmen held on 29 November 1941 to advise the Emperor on the question of peace or war with the Western Powers, the accused accepted the opinion that war was inevitable and advised the strengthening of public opinion against the possibility of a long war.

At the meeting of the Senior Statesmen held on 5 April 1945 the accused strongly opposed any overtures for peace and advocated that Japan should fight to the end.

At all times covered by the Indictment Hiranuma was not only a supporter of the policy of the domination of Japan in East Asia and the South Seas by force when necessary, but he was one of the leaders of the conspiracy and an active participant in furthering its policy. In carrying out that policy he waged war against China, the United States of America, the British Commonwealth of Nations, the Netherlands, and in 1939 against the U.S.S.R.

The Tribunal finds the accused Hiranuma guilty on Counts 1, 27, 29, 31, 32 and 36.

There is no evidence directly connecting him with the crimes charged in Counts 33, 35, 54 and 55. We, therefore, find him not guilty on these counts.

HIROTA, KOKI

Hirota is indicted under Counts 1, 27, 29, 31, 32, 33, 35, 54, and 55.

Hirota was Foreign Minister from 1933 until March 1936 when he became Prime Minister. From the fall of his Cabinet in February 1937 for four months he held no public office. He was Foreign Minister again in the First Konoye Cabinet until May 1938. From that time forward his relation with public affairs was limited to attending meetings of the Senior Statesmen (Jushin) from time to time to advise on the appointment of Prime Ministers and on other important questions submitted.

From 1933 to 1938, when Hirota held these high offices, the Japanese gains in Manchuria were being consolidated and turned to the advantage of Japan and the political and economic life of North China was being "guided" in order to separate it from the rest of China in preparation for the domination by Japan of the Chinese political and economic life. In 1936 his cabinet formulated and adopted the national policy of expansion in East Asia and the Southern Areas. This policy of far-reaching effect was eventually to lead to the war between Japan and the Western Powers in 1941. Also in 1936 the Japanese aggressive policy with regard to the U.S.S.R. was reiterated and advanced, in the Anti-Comintern Pact.

From the 7th of July 1937 when the war in China was revived, throughout Hirota's tenure of office, the military operations in China received the full support of the Cabinet. Early in 1938, also, the real policy towards China was clarified and every effort made to subjugate China and abolish the Chinese National Government and to replace it with a government dominated by Japan.

In early 1938 the plan and legislation for mobilization of man power, industrial potential, and natural resources was adopted. This plan with little change in essentials was the basis on which the preparations to continue the China War and for waging further aggressive wars were carried out during the succeeding years. All these plans and activities were fully known to and supported by Hirota.

Thus during his tenure of office Hirota, apparently a very able man and a forceful leader, was at times the originator and at other times a supporter of the aggressive plans adopted and executed by the military and the various Cabinets.

On his behalf Counsel in final argument urged the Tribunal to consider Hirota's consistent advocacy of peace and peaceful or diplomatic negotiation of disputed questions. It is true that Hirota, faithful to his diplomatic training, consistently advocated attempting firstly to settle disputes through diplomatic channels. However, it is abundantly clear that in so doing he was never willing to sacrifice any of the gains or expected gains made or expected to be made at the expense of Japan's neighbours and he consistently agreed to the use of force if diplomatic negotiations failed to obtain fulfilment of the Japanese demands. The Tribunal therefore cannot accept as exculpating this accused the defense offered on this point.

The Tribunal consequently finds that at least from 1933 Hirota participated in the common plan or conspiracy to wage aggressive wars. As Foreign Minister he also participated in the waging of war against China.

As to Counts 29, 31 and 32 Hirota's attitude and advice as one of the Senior Statesmen in 1941 is quite consistent with his being opposed to the opening of hostilities against the Western Powers. He held no public office after 1938 and played no part in the direction of the wars referred to in these Counts. The Tribunal holds that the evidence offered does not establish his guilt on these Counts.

As to Counts 33 and 35, there is no proof of Hirota's participation in or support of the military operations at Lake Khassan, or in French Indo-China in 1945.

With regard to War Crimes there is no evidence of Hirota's having ordered, authorized, or permitted the commission of the crimes as alleged in Count 54.

As to Count 55 the only evidence relating him to such crimes deals with the atrocities at Nanking in December 1937 and January and February 1938. As Foreign Minister he received reports of these atrocities immediately after the entry of the Japanese forces into Nanking. According to the Defence evidence credence was given to these reports and the matter was taken up with the War Ministry. Assurances were accepted from the War Ministry that the atrocities would be stopped. After these assurances had been given reports of atrocities continued to come in for at least a month. The Tribunal is of opinion that Hirota was derelict in his duty in not insisting before the Cabinet that immediate action be taken to put an end to the atrocities, failing any other action open to him to bring about the same result. He was content to rely on assurances which he knew were not being implemented while hundreds of murders, violations of women, and other atrocities were being committed daily. His inaction amounted to criminal negligence.

The Tribunal finds Hirota guilty under Counts 1, 27, and 55. He is not guilty under Counts 29, 31, 32, 33, 35, and 54.

HOSHINO, NAOKI

Hoshino is charged under Counts 1, 27, 29, 31, 32, 33, 35, 54 and 55.

Until the accused Hoshino went to Manchuria in 1932 he was employed in the Japanese Department of Finance. He was sent to Manchuria by his Government to become a Senior Official of the Manchukuo Finance Ministry and of the Manchukuo General Affairs Bureau. By 1936 he had become Vice Chief of the Finance Ministry of Manchukuo and Chief of the General Affairs Section of the National Affairs Board of Manchukuo. In these positions he was able to exercise a profound influence upon the economy of Manchukuo and did exert that influence towards Japanese domination of the commercial and industrial development of that country. He operated in close co-operation with the Commander of the Kwantung Army, the virtual ruler of Manchukuo. In effect, if not in name, he was a functionary of that Army whose economic policy was directed to making the resources of Manchukuo serve the warlike purposes of Japan.

Although he was nominally a servant of the Government of Manchukuo and had been so for eight years he was recalled to Japan in 1940 to become a Minister without Portfolio and President of the Planning Board. In this position he was the leader in the special steps then being taken to equip Japan for the continuation of the aggressive war then being waged in China and for wars of aggression then contemplated against other countries with possessions in East Asia.

From April 1941, when he left the Cabinet, his official functions in connection with warlike preparations were reduced but not entirely abandoned.

Upon the accession of the accused Tojo as Prime Minister in October 1941 Hoshino became the Chief Secretary of the Cabinet and soon after a Councillor of the Planning Board. From this time he was in close association with all the preparations for the aggressive war already determined upon and now shortly to be waged against those countries attacked by Japan in December 1941.

Throughout all the period from 1932 to 1941 he was an energetic member of the conspiracy alleged in Count 1 of the Indictment and is accordingly adjudged guilty under that Count.

Not only did he conspire to wage aggressive war but in his successive official positions he took a direct part in the waging of aggressive wars as set out in Counts 27, 29, 31 and 32, under all of which also he is adjudged guilty.

He has not been proved to have participated in the wars charged in Counts 33 and 35 and of those is found not guilty.

There is no evidence connecting him with the crimes charged in Counts 54 and 55 and of those also he is found not guilty.

* * *

Itagaki, Seishiro

The accused is charged under Counts 1, 27, 29, 31, 32, 33, 35, 36, 54 and 55.

By the year 1931 Itagaki, then a Colonel on the Staff of the Kwantung Army, had joined the conspiracy the immediate object of which then was that Japan should seize Manchuria by force of arms. He fanned the agitation in support of this aim: he helped to engineer the so-called "Mukden Incident" as a pretext for military action; he suppressed several attempts to prevent that military action; he authorised and directed that military action.

He next played a principal part in the intrigues which fostered the sham movement for the independence of Manchuria and which resulted in the establishment of the puppet state of Manchukuo.

He became Vice-Chief of Staff of the Kwantung Army in December 1934 and thereafter was active in setting-up puppet regimes in Inner Mongolia and North China. He wished to extend Japan's military occupation into Outer Mongolia to serve as a threat to the territories of the U.S.S.R. He was one of the coiners of the phrase "Anti-Communism" to serve as a pretext for Japanese aggression in North China.

When fighting broke out at Marco Polo Bridge in July 1937 he was sent from Japan to China where he took part in the fighting as a Divisional Commander. He favoured the expansion of the area of aggression there.

He became Minister of War in the Konoye Cabinet in May 1938. Under him the attacks on China were intensified and extended. He was a party to the important ministerial conferences which decided to attempt to destroy the National Government of China and to set up a puppet regime in its stead. He then was largely responsible for the preliminary arrangements which resulted in the setting-up of the puppet regime of Wang Ching-Wei. He took part in the arrangements for the exploitation of the occupied areas of China for the benefit of Japan.

As Minister of War in the Hiranuma Cabinet he was again responsible for the prosecution of the war against China, and for the expansion of Japan's armaments. In the Cabinet he was a strong advocate of an unrestricted military alliance among Japan, Germany and Italy.

As War Minister he tried by a trick to obtain the consent of the Emperor to the use of force against the U.S.S.R. at Lake Khassan. Subsequently at a Five Ministers Conference he obtained authority to use such force. He was still War Minister during the fighting at Nomonhan.

He was a strong supporter of the declaration of Japan's so-called "New Order" in Last Asia and the South Seas. He recognised that the attempt to set up the New Order must lead to war with the U.S.S.R., France and Great Britain who would defend their possessions in these areas.

From September 1939 to July 1941 he carried on the war against China as Chief of Staff of the China Expeditionary Army.

From July 1941 to April 1945 he was Commander-in-Chief of the Army in Korea.

From April 1945 to the date of the Surrender he commanded the 7th Area Army with Headquarters in Singapore. His subordinate armies defended Java, Sumatra, Malaya, the Andaman and Nicobar Islands, and Borneo.

Having conspired to wage wars of aggression against China, the United States of America, the British Commonwealth, the Netherlands, and the U.S.S.R., he took an active and important part in waging these wars which he knew were wars of aggression.

The Tribunal finds Itagaki guilty on Counts 1, 27, 29, 31, 32, 35 and 36. He is not guilty under Count 33.

War Crimes

The area which Itagaki commanded from April 1945 to the Surrender included Java, Sumetra, Malay, the Andaman and Nicobar Islands, and Borneo. Many thousands of prisoners of war and internees were held in camps in these areas during the above period.

According to the evidence which he adduced these camps, save those in Singapore, were not under his direct command but he was responsible for the supply of food, medicines and hospital facilities to them.

During this period the conditions in these camps were unspeakably bad. The supply of food, medicines and hospital facilities was grossly inadequate. Deficiency diseases were rampant and as a result many persons died every day. Those who survived to the date of the Surrender were in a pitiable condition. When the camps were visited after the Surrender no such conditions prevailed among the guards.

Itagaki's excuse for this atrocious treatment of the prisoners and internees is that the attacks of the Allies on Japanese shipping had made the transportation of supplies to these areas very difficult and that he did the best he could with the supplies he had. After the Surrender, however, supplies of food and medicine were made available by Itagaki's Army to the camps in Singapore, Borneo, Java and Sumatra. The explanation tendered in evidence and argument for Itagaki is that the Japanese were expecting a long war and were conserving supplies. This amounts to a contention that Itagaki was justified under the prevailing circumstances in treating the prisoners and internees with gross inhumanity. The Tribunal has no hesitation in rejecting the defense. If Itagaki, being responsible for supplies to many thousands of prisoners and internees, found himself unable to maintain them for the future, his duty under the laws of War was to distribute such supplies as he had and meantime to inform his superiors that arrangements must be made, if necessary with the Allies, for the support of the prisoners and internees in the future. By the policy which he adopted he is responsible for the deaths or sufferings of thousands of people whose adequate maintenance was his duty.

The Tribunal finds Itagaki guilty on Count 54. As in the case of Dohihara, the Tribunal makes no finding on Count 55.

Kaya, Okinori

The accused Kaya is charged under Counts 1, 27, 29, 31, 32, 54 and 55.

Kaya was a civilian.

In 1936 he was appointed a Councillor of the Manchurian Affairs Bureau and in February 1937 he became Vice Minister of Finance. In June 1937 he was appointed Finance Minister in the first Konoye Cabinet, which position he held until May 1938. In July 1938 he became Advisor to the Finance Ministry. In July 1939 he was appointed a member of the Asia Development Committee, and in August of that year President of the North China Development Company, in which position he remained until October 1941, when he became Finance Minister in the Tojo Cabinet. He resigned as Finance Minister in February 1944, but again became Adviser to the Finance Ministry.

In these positions he took part in the formulation of the aggressive policies of Japan and in the financial, economic and industrial preparation of Japan for the execution of those policies.

Throughout this period, particularly as Finance Minister in the first Konoye and Tojo Cabinets, and as President of the North China Development Company, he was actively engaged in the preparation for and the carrying out of aggressive wars in China and against the Western Powers. He was an active member of the conspiracy alleged in Count 1 and is adjudged guilty under that Count.

In the various positions held by him Kaya took a principal part in the waging of aggressive wars as alleged in Counts 27, 29, 31 and 32 of the Indictment. He is, therefore, adjudged guilty under those Counts.

The evidence does not disclose Kaya's responsibility for war crimes and accordingly he is found not guilty under Counts 54 and 55.

KIDO, KOICHI

The accused Kido, Koichi is charged under Counts 1, 27, 29, 31, 32, 33, 35, 36, 54 and 55.

From 1930 until 1936 Kido was a member of the Emperor's household in the position of Chief Secretary to the Lord Keeper of the Privy Seal. During this period he was aware of the true nature of the military and political ventures in Manchuria. At this time, however, he was not associated with the conspiracy which had been instituted by the military and their supporters.

In 1937 Kido joined the first Konoye Cabinet as Education Minister and for a period was Welfare Minister. On the accession of Hiranuma as Prime Minister in 1939 Kido continued as a member of the Cabinet until August 1939 with the portfolio of Home Affairs. In this period from 1937 to 1939 Kido adopted the views of the conspirators and devoted himself wholeheartedly to their policy. The war in China had entered into its second phase. Kido was zealous in the pursuit of that war, even resisting the efforts of the General Staff to shorten the war by making terms with China. He was intent on the complete military and political domination of China.

Not only did Kido thus support the plans of the conspirators in China but as Education Minister he applied himself to the development of a strong warlike spirit in Japan.

Between August 1939 and June 1940 when he became Lord Keeper of the Privy Seal, Kido was active with Konoye in the development of a scheme to replace the existing political parties by a single party of which Konoye was to be President and Kido Vice President. This one-party system was expected to give Japan a totalitarian system and thus remove political resistance to the plans of the conspirators.

As Lord Keeper of the Privy Seal Kido was in a specially advantageous position to advance the conspiracy. His principal duty was to advise the Emperor. He kept in close touch with political events and was on terms of intimate political and personal relationship with those most concerned. His position was one of great influence. He used that influence, not only with the Emperor but also by political intrigue so as to further the aims of the conspiracy. He shared those aims which involved the domination of China and the whole of East Asia as well as the areas to the South.

As the time approached for the commencement of war against the Western Powers Kido displayed some degree of hesitation because doubts of complete success were entertained within the Navy. Even in this state of timidity Kido was determined to pursue the aggressive war against China and lent himself, although now with less confidence, to the projected war against Great Britain and the Netherlands and in case of need against the United States of America.

When the doubts of the Navy had been overcome Kido's doubts seem also to have been removed. He resumed his pursuit of the full purposes of the conspiracy. He was largely instrumental in securing the office of Prime Minister for Tojo who until now had been a determined advocate of immediate war with the Western Powers. In other ways he used his position in support of such a war or purposely refrained from action which might have prevented it. He refrained from advising the Emperor to take any stand against war either at the last or earlier when it might have been more effective.

The Prosecution has tendered no evidence pointing to guilt in Kido for the wars referred to in Counts 33, 35 and 36.

As to war crimes Kido was a member of the Cabinet when the atrocities were committed at Nanking. The evidence is not sufficient to attach him with responsibility for failure to prevent them. During the war against the Western Powers in 1941 and thereafter Kido's position was such that he cannot be held responsible for the atrocities committed.

Kido is found guilty of the charges in Counts 1, 27, 29, 31, and 32, and not guilty under Counts 33, 35, 36, 54 and 55.

KIMURA, HEITARO

Kimura is indicted under Counts 1, 27, 29, 31, 32, 54 and 55.

Kimura, an army officer, during the greater part of the period under consideration was engaged in administrative work in the War Ministry, culminating in his becoming Vice Minister of War in April 1941. Later he was appointed Councillor of the Planning Board and Councillor of the Total War Research Institute. In March 1943 he was relieved of the post of Vice War Minister and in August 1944 he became Commander-in-Chief of the Burma Area Army which post he held until the surrender of Japan in 1945.

During his service as Vice War Minister in almost daily contact with the War Minister and other Ministers, Vice Ministers, and Bureau Chiefs he was in a position to learn and was kept fully informed of all government decisions and action during the crucial negotiations with the U.S.A. He had full knowledge of the plans and preparations for the Pacific War and the hostilities in China. Throughout, he collaborated and cooperated with the War Minister and the other Ministries from time to time giving advice based on his wide experience, wholeheartedly supporting the aggressive plans.

Though not a leader, he took part in the formulation and development of policies which were either initiated by himself or proposed by the General Staff or other bodies and approved and supported by him. In this way he was a valuable collaborator or accomplice in the conspiracy to wage aggressive wars.

Concurrently with his activities as one of the conspirators as Commander of a division in 1939 and 1940, then as Chief of Staff of the Kwantung Army and later as Vice War Minister he played a prominent part in the conduct of the war in China and in the Pacific War. Possessed with full knowledge of the illegality of the Pacific War, in August 1944 he took command of the Burma Area Army and so continued until the Surrender.

In a positive way he was a party to breaches of the Rules of War in that he approved the employment of prisoners in many instances in work prohibited by the Rules and in work under conditions resulting in the greatest hardship and the deaths of thousands of prisoners. An example of the latter case is the employment of prisoners in the construction of the Burma-Siam Railway, the orders for which were approved and passed on my Kimura.

Furthermore with knowledge of the extent of the atrocities committed by Japanese troops in all theaters of war, in August 1944 Kimura took over command of the Burma Area Army. From the date of his arrival at his Rangoon Headquarters and later when his headquarters was moved to Moulmein the atrocities continued to be committed on an undiminished scale. He took no disciplinary measures or other steps to prevent the commission of atrocities by the troops under his command.

It has been urged in Kimura's defence that when he arrived in Burma he issued orders to his troops to conduct themselves in a proper soldierly manner and to refrain from ill-treating prisoners. In view of the nature and extent of the ill-treatment of prisoners, in many cases on a large scale within a few miles of his headquarters, the Tribunal finds that Kimura was negligent in his duty to enforce the rules of war. The duty of an army commander in such circumstances is not discharged by the mere issue of routine orders, if indeed such orders were issued. His duty is to take such steps and issue such orders as will prevent thereafter the commission of war crimes and to satisfy himself that such orders are being carried out. This he did not do. Thus he deliberately disregarded his legal duty to take adequate steps to prevent breaches of the laws of war.

The Tribunal finds Kimura guilty under Counts 1, 27, 29, 31, 32, 54 and 55.

Koiso, Kuniaki

Koiso is charged under Counts 1, 27, 29, 31, 32, 36, 54, and 55.

He joined the conspiracy in 1931 by participating as one of the leaders of the March Incident the purpose of which was to overthrow the Hamaguchi Government and put in office a government favourable to the occupation of Manchuria. Thereafter he played a leading role in the development of the Japanese plans for expansion from August 1932 when he was appointed Chief-of-Staff of the Kwantung Army.

As Chief-of-Staff of the Kwantung Army from August 1932 to March 1934 he prepared or concurred in proposals and plans submitted to the Government through the War Ministry for the political and economic organization of Manchukuo according to the policy of the conspirators as adopted by the Japanese Government. It is urged in his defense that in forwarding proposals and plans to Tokyo he did so merely as Chief-of-Staff and that such action did not import his personal approval. In view of his knowledge of the aggressive plans of Japan the Tribunal cannot accept this plea. He went beyond the scope of the normal duties of a Chief-of-Staff in advising on political and economic matters to further these plans.

While he was Chief-of-Staff there also occurred the military invasion of Jehol and renewed fighting in Manchuria.

Later as Overseas Minister in the Hiranuma and Yonai Cabinets Koiso supported and took part in the direction of the war in China, the beginning of the occupation of French Indo-China and the negotiations intended to obtain concessions from and eventual economic domination of the Netherlands East Indies.

During the same period he advocated the plan for Japan to advance "in all directions".

In July 1944 Koiso was recalled from his post of Governor of Korea to become Prime Minister. In that capacity he urged and directed the waging of the war against the Western Powers. He retired as Prime Minister to make way for the Suzuki Cabinet in April 1945 when it became clear that the war was lost for Japan.

There is no evidence that he played any part in the hostilities at Nomonhan either by organizing or directing them.

War Crimes

When Koiso became Prime Minister in 1944 atrocities and other war crimes being committed by the Japanese troops in every theater of war had become so notorious that it is improbable that a man in Koiso's position would not have been well-informed either by reason of their notoriety or from interdepartmental communications. The matter is put beyond doubt by the fact that in October 1944 the Foreign Minister reported to a meeting of the Supreme Council for the Direction of War, which Koiso attended, that according to recent information from enemy sources it was reported that the Japanese treatment of prisoners of war "left much to be desired". He further stated that this was a matter of importance from the point of view of Japan's international reputation and future relations. He asked that directions be issued to the competent authorities so that the matters might be fully discussed. Thereafter Koiso remained Prime Minister for six months during which the Japanese treatment of prisoners and internees showed no improvement whatever. This amounted to a deliberate disregard of his duty.

The Tribunal finds Koiso guilty under Counts 1, 27, 29, 31, 32 and 55. He is not guilty under Counts 36 and 54.

MATSUI, IWANE

The accused Matsui is charged under Counts 1, 27, 29, 31, 32, 35, 36, 54 and 55.

Matsui was a senior Officer in the Japanese Army and attained the rank of General in 1933. He had a wide experience in the Army, including service in the Kwantung Army and in the General Staff. Although his close association with those who conceived and carried out the conspiracy suggests that he must have been aware of the purposes and policies of the conspirators, the evidence before the Tribunal does not justify a finding that he was a conspirator.

His military service in China in 1937 and 1938 cannot be regarded, of itself, as the waging of an aggressive war. To justify a conviction under Count 27 it was the duty of the prosecution to tender evidence which would justify an inference that he had knowledge of the criminal character of that war. This has not been done.

In 1935 Matsui was placed on the retired list but in 1937 he was recalled to active duty to command the Shanghai Expeditionary Force. He was then appointed Commander-in-Chief of the Central China Area Army, which included the Shanghai Expeditionary Force and the Tenth Army. With these troops he captured the city of Nanking on 13th December 1937.

Before the fall of Nanking the Chinese forces withdrew and the occupation was of a defenceless city. Then followed a long succession of most horrible atrocities committed by the Japanese Army upon the helpless citizens. Wholesale massacres, individual murders, rape, looting and arson were committed by Japanese soldiers. Although the extent of the atrocities was denied by Japanese witnesses the contrary evidence of neutral witnesses of different nationalities and undoubted responsibility is overwhelming. This orgy of crime started with the capture of the City on the 13th December 1937 and did not cease until early in February 1938. In this period of six or seven weeks thousands of women were raped, upwards of 100,000 people were killed and untold property was stolen and burned. At the height of these dreadful happenings on 17th December, Matsui made a triumphal entry into the City and remained there from five to seven days. From his own observations and from the reports of his staff he must have been aware of what was happening. He admits he was told of some degree of misbehaviour of his Army by the Kempeitai and by Consular Officials. Daily reports of these atrocities were made to Japanese diplomatic representatives in Nanking who in turn reported them to Tokyo. The Tribunal is satisfied that Matsui knew what was happening. He did nothing, or nothing effective, to abate these horrors. He did issue orders before the capture of the City enjoining propriety of conduct upon his troops and later he issued further orders to the same purport. These orders were of no effect as is now known and as he must have known. It was pleaded in his behalf that at this time he was ill. His illness was not sufficient to prevent his conducting the military operations of his command nor to prevent his visiting the City for days while these atrocities were occurring. He was in command of the Army responsible for these happenings. He knew of them. He had the power as he had the duty to control his troops and to protect the unfortunate citizens of Nanking. He must be held criminally responsible for his failure to discharge this duty.

The Tribunal holds the accused Matsui guilty under Count 55 and not guilty under Counts 1, 27, 29, 31, 32, 35, 36 and 54.

MINAMI, JIRO

Minami is charged under Counts 1, 27, 29, 31, 32, 54 and 55.

In the year 1931 Minami was a General and from April to December he was Minister of War. Prior to the Mukden Incident he had already associated himself with the conspirators in their advocacy of militarism, of the expansion of Japan, and of Manchuria as "the lifeline of Japan". He was forewarned of the likelihood of the incident occurring. He was ordered to prevent it. He took no adequate steps to prevent it. When the incident happened he described the action of the Army as "righteous self-defence". The Cabinet at once decided that the incident must not be expanded and Minami agreed to put the policy of the Cabinet into effect, but day after day the area of the operations expanded and Minami took no adequate steps to restrain the Army. In the Cabinet he supported the steps taken by the Army. He early advocated Japan's withdrawal from the League of Nations, if that body should oppose the actions Japan had taken in China. The Cabinet decided that there should be no occupation of Manchuria and no military administration. Minami knew that the Army was taking steps to carry both those measures into effect but did nothing to stop it. His failure to support the Premier and Foreign Minister by taking steps to control the Army led to the downfall of the Cabinet. Thereafter he advocated that Japan should take over the defence of Manchuria and Mongolia. He had already advocated that a new state must be founded in Manchuria.

From December 1934 to March 1936 he was Commander-in-Chief of the Kwantung Army, completed the conquest of Manchuria, and aided in the exploitation of that part of China for the benefit of Japan. He was responsible for setting-up puppet governments in North China and Inner Mongolia under the threat of military action.

He was in part responsible for the development of Manchuria as a base for an attack on the U.S.S.R. and for plans for such an attack.

He became Governor-General of Korea in 1936 and in 1938 supported the prosecution of the war against China which he called "the Holy War", and the destruction of the National Government of China.

The Tribunal finds Minami guilty on Counts 1 and 27. He is not guilty of the charges contained in Counts 29, 31, 32, 54, and 55.

MUTO, AKIRA

The accused is indicted under Counts 1, 27, 29, 31, 32, 33, 36, 54 and 55.

He was a soldier and prior to holding the important post of Chief of the Military Affairs Bureau of the Ministry of War he held no appointment which involved the making of high policy. Further, there is no evidence that in this earlier period he, alone or with others, tried to affect the making of high policy.

When he became Chief of the Military Affairs Bureau he joined the conspiracy. Concurrently with this post he held a multiplicity of other posts from September 1939 to April 1942. During this period planning, preparing and waging wars of aggression on the part of the conspirators was at its height. He played the part of a principal in all these activities.

When he became Chief of the Military Affairs Bureau the fighting at Nomonhan was over. He had no part in the waging of this war.

He was Chief-of-Staff in the Philippines when Japan attacked France in French Indo-China in March 1945. He had no part in the waging of this war.

The Tribunal finds Muto guilty on Counts 1, 27, 29, 31 and 32. He is not guilty on Counts 33 and 36.

War Crimes

Muto was an officer on the Staff of Matsui from November 1937 to July 1938. It was during this period that shocking atrocities were committed by the Army of Matsui in and about Nanking. We have no doubt that Muto knew, as Matsui knew, that these atrocities were being committed over a period of many weeks. His superior took no adequate steps to stop them. In our opinion Muto, in his subordinate position, could take no steps to stop them. Muto is not responsible for this dreadful affair.

From April 1942 to October 1944 Muto commanded the Second Imperial Guards Division in Northern Sumatra. During this period in the area occupied by his troops widespread atrocities were committed for which Muto shares responsibility. Prisoners of war and civilian internees were starved, neglected, tortured and murdered, and civilians were massacred.

In October 1944 Muto became Chief-of-Staff to Yamashita in the Philippines. He held that post until the Surrender. His position was now very different from that which he held during the so-called "Rape of Nanking". He was now in a position to influence policy. During his tenure of office as such Chief-of-Staff a campaign of massacre, torture and other atrocities was waged by the Japanese troops on the civilian population, and prisoners of war and civilian internees were starved, tortured and murdered. Muto shares responsibility for these gross breaches of the Laws of War. We reject his defence that he knew nothing of these occurrences. It is wholly incredible. The Tribunal finds Muto guilty on Counts 54 and 55.

OKA, TAKASUMI

Oka is charged in Counts 1, 27, 29, 31, 32, 54, and 55 of the Indictment.

Oka was an officer in the Japanese Navy. In October 1940 he was promoted to Rear Admiral and became Chief of the Naval Affairs Bureau of the Navy Ministry.

Oka was an active member of the conspiracy during his tenure of office as Chief of the Naval Affairs Bureau from October 1940 to July 1944. In this office he was an influential member of the Liaison Conference at which the policy of Japan was largely decided. He participated in the formation and execution of the policy to wage aggressive war against China and the Western Powers.

War Crimes

There is some evidence tending to show that Oka knew or ought to have known that war crimes were being committed by naval personnel against prisoners of war with whose welfare his department was concerned but it falls short of the standard of proof which justifies a conviction in criminal cases.

The Tribunal finds Oka not guilty on Counts 54 and 55, and guilty on Counts 1, 27, 29, 31 and 32.

Oshima, Hiroshi

Oshima is indicted under Counts 1, 27, 29, 31, 32, 54 and 55.

Oshima, an Army officer, was engaged during the period under review in the diplomatic field. He was first Military Attache of the Japanese Embassy in Berlin, later being promoted to the post of Ambassador. Holding no diplomatic post for about one year from 1939 he returned to Berlin as Ambassador where he remained till the Surrender of Japan.

A believer in the success of the Hitler Regime, from his first appointment in Berlin Oshima exerted his full efforts to advance the plans of the Japanese military. At times, going over the head of the Ambassador, he dealt directly with Foreign Minister Ribbentrop, in an endeavour to involve Japan in a full military alliance with Germany. Upon his appointment as Ambassador he continued his efforts to force the acceptance by Japan of a treaty which would align Japan with Germany and Italy against the Western Powers and thus open the way for putting into execution the Hirota policy. In furtherance of the aggressive policy of the Army faction he repeatedly pursued a policy in opposition to and in defiance of that of his Foreign Minister.

The Soviet-German Neutrality Pact temporarily blocked his schemes. He then returned to Tokyo and there supported the proponents of war by articles in newspapers and magazines and by closely cooperating with the German Ambassador.

Oshima was one of the principal conspirators and consistently supported and promoted the aims of the main conspiracy.

He took no part in the direction of the war in China or the Pacific War and at no time held any post involving duties or responsibility in respect of prisoners.

Oshima's special defence is that in connection with his activities in Germany he is protected by diplomatic immunity and is exempt from prosecution.

Diplomatic privilege does not import immunity from legal liability, but only exemption from trial by the Courts of the State to which an Ambassador is accredited. In any event this immunity has no relation to crimes against international law charged before a tribunal having jurisdiction. The Tribunal rejects this special defence.

The Tribunal finds Oshima guilty under Count 1. He is not guilty under Counts 27, 29, 31, 32, 54 and 55.

SATO, KENRYO

The accused Sato, Kenryo, is charged under Counts 1, 27, 29, 31, 32, 54 and 55.

In 1937 Sato, then a member of the Military Affairs Bureau, was promoted to the rank of Lieutenant Colonel. In that year he was appointed an Investigator of the Planning Board. Thereafter in addition to his duties in the Military Affairs Bureau he had other duties, not only with the Planning Board, of which for a time he was Secretary, but also with other bodies in greater or less degree connected with Japan's war in China and its contemplated wars with other countries.

The Konoye Cabinet presented the General Mobilization Law to the Diet in February 1938. Sato was employed as an "explainer" and made a speech before the Diet in support of the measure.

In February 1941 Sato was appointed Chief of the Military Affairs Section of the Military Affairs Bureau. He was promoted to Major General in October 1941. In April 1942 he became Chief of the Military Affairs Bureau, a position of considerable importance in the Japanese Army. This position he held until 1944. Concurrently he held a variety of other appointments mostly concerned with other departments of state whose activities he linked with the Ministry of War.

It was thus not until 1941 that Sato attained a position which by itself enabled him to influence the making of policy, and no evidence has been adduced that prior to that date he had indulged in plotting to influence the making of policy. The crucial question is whether by that date he had become aware that Japan's designs were criminal, for thereafter he furthered the development and execution of these designs so far as he was able.

The matter is put beyond reasonable doubt by a speech which Sato delivered in August 1938. He states the Army point of view on the war in China. He shows complete familiarity with the detailed terms, never revealed to China, upon which Japan was prepared to settle the war against China. These on the face of them plainly involved the abolition of the legitimate government of China, recognition of the puppet state of Manchukuo whose resources had been by this time largely exploited for Japan's benefit, regimentation of the economy of China for Japan's benefit, and the stationing of Japanese troops in China to ensure that these illicit gains would not be lost. He states that North

China would be put completely under Japan's control and its resources developed for national defence, i.e. to aid in Japan's military preparations. He predicts that Japan will go to war with the U.S.S.R., but says she will select a chance when her armaments and production have been expanded.

This speech shows that Sato did not believe that Japan's actions in China had been dictated by the wish to secure protection for Japan's legitimate interests in China as the Defence would have us believe. On the contrary he knew that the motive for her attacks on China was to seize the wealth of her neighbour. We are of opinion that Sato, having that guilty knowledge, was clearly a member of the conspiracy from 1941 onwards.

Thereafter in important posts in the Government and as an Army Commander he waged wars of aggression as charged in Counts 27, 29, 31, and 32.

War Crimes

There is no doubt that Sato knew of the many protests against the behaviour of Japan's troops, for these protests came to his Bureau and they were discussed at the bi-weekly meetings of Bureau Chiefs in the War Ministry. Tojo presided at these meetings and he it was who decided that action or inaction should be taken in regard to the protests. Sato, his subordinate, could not initiate preventive action against the decision of his chief.

The Tribunal finds Sato guilty on Counts 1, 27, 29, 31, and 32. He is not guilty on Counts 54 and 55.

SHIGEMITSU, MAMORU

The accused is charged under Counts 1, 27, 29, 31, 32, 33, 35, 54, and 55.

As to Count 1, his actions are challenged when he was Minister to China in 1931 and 1932; when he was Councillor of the Board of Manchurian Affairs; when he was Ambassador to the U.S.S.R. from 1936 to 1938; when he was Ambassador to Great Britain from 1938 to 1941; and when he was Ambassador to China during the years 1942 and 1943. There is no evidence that he played any part in the making of policy as Councillor of the Board of Manchurian Affairs. For the rest we find that Shigemitsu, as Minister and Ambassador, never exceeded the functions proper to these offices. During the years above mentioned he was not one of the conspirators. Indeed he repeatedly gave advice to the Foreign Office which was opposed to the policies of the conspirators.

By the year 1943, when he became Foreign Minister, the policy of the conspirators to wage certain wars of aggression had been settled and was in course of execution. Thereafter there was no further formulation nor development of that policy.

The Tribunal finds Shigemitsu not guilty on Count 1.

In 1943 his country was engaged in the war in the Pacific. He was fully aware that so far as Japan was concerned that war was a war of aggression, for he knew of the policies of the conspirators which had caused the war and indeed had often advised that they should not be put into effect. Nevertheless he now played a principal part in waging that war until he resigned on 13th April, 1945.

The Tribunal finds Shigemitsu guilty on Counts 27, 29, 31, 32, and 33. He is not guilty on Count 35.

War Crimes

During the period from April 1943 to April 1945, when Shigemitsu was Foreign Minister, the Protecting Powers transmitted to the Japanese Foreign Office protest after protest which it had received from the Allies. These were grave protests forwarded to the Protecting Powers by responsible agencies of state and in many cases accompanied by a wealth of detail. The matters of protest were (1) inhumane treatment of prisoners, (2) refusal to permit the Protecting Powers to inspect all save a few prisoners' camps, (3) refusal to permit the representatives of the Protecting Powers to interview prisoners without the presence of a Japanese witness, and (4) failure to provide information as to the names and location of prisoners. The protests were dealt with in the Foreign Ministry in the first place. Where necessary they were passed to other ministries with requests for information to enable the Foreign Minister to reply to them.

One cannot read the long correspondence between the Japanese Foreign Office and the Protecting Powers without suspecting that there was a sinister reason for the failure of the Japanese military to supply their Foreign Office with satisfactory answers to these protests, or at the least that there was a case for an independent inquiry by an agency other than the military, whose conduct was in question. Protest after protest went unanswered or was only answered after months of unexplained delay. Reminder after reminder by the Protecting Powers went unnoticed. Those protests which were answered were met without exception by a denial that there was anything to complain of.

Now it was the highest degree unlikely that every one of the complaints made by responsible people and accompanied by circumstance and detail was completely unjustified. Moreover the refusal of the military to permit inspection of camps, their refusal to permit the representatives of the Protecting Powers to interview prisoners without the presence of a Japanese witness, and their failure to provide details of the prisoners in their hands gave rise to the suspicion that they had something to hide.

We do no injustice to Shigemitsu when we held that the circumstances, as he knew them, made him suspicious that the treatment of the prisoners was not as it should have been. Indeed a witness gave evidence for him to that effect. Thereupon he took no adequate steps to have the matter investigated, although he, as a member of the government, bore overhead responsibility for the welfare of the prisoners. He should have pressed the matter, if necessary to the point of resigning, in order to quit himself of a responsibility which he suspected was not being discharged.

There is no evidence that Shigemitsu ordered, authorized, or permitted the commission of war, crimes or crimes against humanity. The Tribunal finds Shigemitsu not guilty on Count 54.

The Tribunal finds Shigemitsu guilty on Count 55.

In mitigation of sentence we take into account that Shigemitsu was in no way involved in the formulation of the conspiracy; that he waged no war of aggression until he became Foreign Minister in April 1943, by which time his country was deeply involved in a war which would vitally effect its future; and in the matter of war crimes that the military completely controlled Japan while he was Foreign Minister so that it would have required great resolution for any Japanese to condemn them.

SHIMADA, SHIGETARO

The accused is charged under Counts 1, 27, 29, 31, 32, 54 and 55.

Until October 1941 Shimada played nothing but the role of a naval officer carrying out his duties as such and until that date had no part in the conspiracy.

In October 1941 he was a Senior Naval Officer eligible for the post of Navy Minister. He became Navy Minister in the Tojo Cabinet and held that office until August 1944. For a period of six months from February to August 1944 he was also Chief of the Navy General Staff.

From the formation of the Tojo Cabinet until the Western Powers were attacked by Japan on 7th December 1941 he took part in all the decisions made by the conspirators in planning and launching that attack. He gave as his reason for adopting this course of conduct that the freezing orders were strangling Japan and would gradually reduce her ability to fight; that there was economic and military "encirclement" of Japan; that the United States of America was unsympathetic and unyielding in the negotiations; and that the aid given by the Allies to China had raised bitter feeling in Japan. This defence leaves out of account the fact that the gains to retain which he was determined to fight were, to his knowledge, gains Japan had acquired in years of aggressive war. The Tribunal has already fully examined this defence and rejected it.

After war was declared he played a principal part in waging it.

The Tribunal finds Shimada guilty on Counts 1, 27, 29, 31 and 32.

War Crimes

Some most disgraceful massacres and murders of prisoners were committed by members of the Japanese Navy in the islands of the Pacific Ocean and on the survivors of torpedoed ships. Those immediately responsible ranged in rank from Admirals downwards.

The evidence, however, is insufficient to justify a finding that Shimada is responsible for these matters, that he ordered, authorized or permitted the commission of war crimes, or that he knew they were being committed and failed to take adequate steps to prevent their commission in the future.

The Tribunal finds Shimada not guilty on Counts 54 and 55.

SHIRATORI, TOSHIO

The accused is indicted under Counts 1, 27, 29, 31, and 32.

He entered the Japanese diplomatic service in 1914. He first comes into prominence as Chief of the Information Bureau of the Foreign Office, which post he held from October 1930 to June 1933. In that position he justified Japan's seizure of Manchuria to the Press of the world. No doubt it was dictated to him that he should do so, but it is characteristic of the accused's activities then and thereafter that he was not content to perform whatever might be his duties at the moment. Thus early he was expressing views on matters of policy, views which received consideration in high quarters. He early advocated that Japan should withdraw from the League of Nations. He supported the setting-up of a puppet government in Manchuria. From this period dates his support of the aims of the conspiracy, a support which he continued to afford for many years and by all the means in his power.

He was Minister to Sweden from June 1933 to April 1937. Certain letters of his show his views at this time. In his opinion Russian influence should be expelled from the Far East by force, if necessary, and before she became too strong to be attacked. He was further of opinion that such foreign influences as might be thought to be harmful to Japanese interests should be excluded from China, and that Japanese diplomats should support the policy of the militarists. He showed himself a whole-hearted believer in aggressive war.

Returning to Japan he published articles advocating a totalitarian form of government for Japan and an expansionist policy for Japan, Germany and Italy.

When the negotiations for an alliance among Japan, Germany and Italy had commenced he was appointed Ambassador to Rome in September 1938. In these negotiations he collaborated with the accused Oshima, then Ambassador to Berlin, in support of the conspirators, who insisted on a general military alliance among these countries. He went so far as to refuse to comply with the instructions of the Foreign Minister, who wished a more limited alliance only. He and Oshima threatened to resign if the wishes of the conspirators were not met.

When Japan delayed too long and Germany signed a non-aggression pact with the U.S.S.R. the negotiations broke down, for Japanese opinion commonly regarded this as a breach of the Anti-Comintern Pact. Shiratori returned to Japan where he carried on propaganda designed to excuse Germany's action and to prepare the way for the general military alliance with Germany and Italy which he still thought necessary to support Japanese expansionist aims. In his propaganda at one time or another he advocated all the objects of the conspirators: that Japan should attack China, that Japan should attack Russia, that Japan should ally herself with Germany and Italy, that she should take determined action against the Western Powers, that she should establish the "New Order", that she should seize the chance offered by the European War to advance to the South, that she should attack Singapore, and so on. This propaganda was continued while he was advisor to the Foreign Office from August 1940 to July 1941.

He became ill in April 1941 and resigned the position of advisor to the Foreign Office in July of that year. Thereafter he plays no important part in events. The Tribunal finds Shiratori guilty on Count 1.

He never occupied such a position as would justify a finding that he waged any war of aggression. The Tribunal finds Shiratori not guilty on Counts 27, 29, 31 and 32.

SUZUKI, TEIICHI

Suzuki, Teiichi, is charged in Counts 1, 27, 29, 31, 32, 35, 36, 54 and 55 of the Indictment.

Suzuki was a soldier. As a Lieutenant Colonel and Member of the Military Affairs Bureau in 1932, he was an active member of the conspiracy. After the assassination of Premier Inukai in May 1932 he said that similar acts of violence would occur if new Cabinets were organized under political leadership and he favored the formation of a coalition government. The object was to secure a government which would support the schemes of the conspirators against China.

During his service with the Bureau he insisted that the U.S.S.R. was the absolute enemy of Japan and assisted in the preparations then being made to wage aggressive war against that Power.

There is no evidence that Suzuki participated in waging war against the U.S.S.R. at Lake Khassan and there is no evidence that he participated in waging war against the U.S.S.R. or the Mongolian Peoples' Republic at Nomonhan.

In November 1937, Suzuki became a Major-General. He was one of the organizers and head of the political and administrative division of the Asia Development Board. As such he actively furthered the exploitation of the parts of China occupied by Japan.

When the Second Konoye Cabinet was formed to complete the military domination of Japan, and to prosecute the move to the South, Suzuki became Minister Without Portfolio and one of the Councillors of the Total War Research Institute. Konoye replaced Hoshino by Suzuki as President of the Planning Board. Suzuki continued in that position until the fall of the Tojo Cabinet on 19 July 1944.

As President of the Planning Board and Minister Without Portfolio, Suzuki regularly attended the meetings of the Liaison Conference, the virtual policy making body for Japan. Suzuki was present at most of the important conferences leading to the initiating and waging of aggressive wars against the Allied Powers. At those conferences he actively supported the conspiracy.

There is no evidence that the accused was responsible for the commission of atrocities.

We find Suzuki guilty as charged in Counts 1, 27, 29, 31, and 32, and not guilty of Counts 35, 36, 54 and 55.

Togo, Shigenori

The accused Togo is indicted under Counts 1, 27, 29, 31, 32, 36, 54 and 55.

Togo's principal association with the crimes charged against him was as Foreign Minister in the Tojo Cabinet from October 1941 until September 1942 when he resigned and later in the Suzuki Cabinet of 1945 in which he also acted as Foreign Minister. During the interval between his resignation and reappointment he played no part in public life.

From the date of his first appointment until the outbreak of the Pacific War he participated in the planning and preparing for the war. He attended Cabinet meetings and conferences and concurred in all decisions adopted.

As Foreign Minister he played a leading role in the negotiations with the United States immediately preceding the outbreak of the war and lent himself to the plans of the proponents of war. The duplicity employed in those negotiations has been dealt with earlier.

After the outbreak of the Pacific War he collaborated with other members of the Cabinet in its conduct as well as in the waging of the war in China.

In addition to the defence common to all the accused of encirclement and economic strangulation of Japan, which has been dealt with elsewhere, Togo pleads specially that he joined the Tojo Cabinet on the assurance that every effort would be made to bring the negotiations with the United States to a successful conclusion. He states further that from the date of his taking office he opposed the Army and was successful in obtaining from them concessions which enabled him to keep the negotiations alive. However, when the negotiations failed and war became inevitable, rather than resign in protest he continued in office and supported the war. To do anything else he said would have been cowardly. However his later action completely nullifies this plea. In September 1942 he resigned over a dispute in the Cabinet as to the treatment of occupied countries. We are disposed to judge his action and sincerity in the one case by the same considerations as in the other.

There is no proof of any criminal act on Togo's part as alleged in Count 36. His only part in relation to that count was to sign the post war agreement between the U.S.S.R. and Japan settling the boundary between Manchuria and Outer Mongolia.

War Crimes

Up to his resignation in 1942 Togo appears to have endeavored to see to the observance of the Rules of War. He passed on such protests as came to him for investigation and in several instances remedial measures were taken. At the time of his resignation atrocities committed by the Japanese troops had not become so notorious as to permit knowledge to be imputed to him.

In the spring of 1945 when he returned as Foreign Minister there was then an accumulation of protests which he passed on to the proper authorities. The Tribunal is of opinion that there is not sufficient proof of Togo's neglect of duty in connection with war crimes.

The Tribunal finds Togo guilty on Counts 1, 27, 29, 31 and 32. He is not guilty on Counts 36, 54, and 55.

TOJO, HIDEKI

The accused is charged under Counts 1, 27, 29, 31, 32, 33, 36, 54 and 55.

Tojo became Chief-of-Staff of the Kwantung Army in June 1937 and thereafter was associated with the conspirators as a principal in almost all of their activities.

He planned and prepared for an attack on the U.S.S.R.; he recommended a further onset on China in order to free the Japanese Army from anxiety about its rear in the projected attack on the U.S.S.R.; he helped to organize Manchuria as a base for that attack; never at any time thereafter did he abandon the intention to launch such an attack if a favourable chance should occur.

In May 1938 he was recalled from the field to become Vice-Minister of War. In addition to that office he held a great number of appointments so that he played an important part in almost all aspects of the mobilisation of the Japanese people and economy for war. At this time he opposed suggestions for a peace of compromise with China.

He became Minister of War in July 1940 and thereafter his history is largely the history of the successive steps by which the conspirators planned and waged wars of aggression against Japan's neighbours, for he was a principal in the making of the plans and in the waging of the wars. He advocated and furthered the aims of the conspiracy with ability, resolution and persistency.

He became Prime Minister in October 1941 and continued in that office until July 1944.

As War Minister and Premier he consistently supported the policy of conquering the National Government of China, of developing the resources of China in Japan's behalf, and of retaining Japanese troops in China to safeguard for Japan the results of the war against China.

In the negotiations which preceded the attacks of 7th December 1941 his resolute attitude was that Japan must secure terms which would preserve for her the fruits of her aggression against China and which would conduce to the establishment of Japan's domination of East Asia and the Southern Areas. All his great influence was thrown into the support of that policy. The importance of the leading part he played in securing the decision to go to war in support of that policy cannot be overestimated. He bears major responsibility for Japan's criminal attacks on her neighbours.

In this trial he defended all these attacks with hardihood, alleging that they were legitimate measures of self-defense. We have already dealt fully with that plea. It is wholly unfounded.

As to Count 36 there is no evidence that Tojo occupied any official position which would render him responsible for the war in 1939 as charged in Count 36.

The Tribunal finds Tojo guilty on Counts 1, 27, 29, 31, 32 and 33, and not guilty on Count 36.

War Crimes

Tojo was head of the War Ministry which was charged with the care of prisoners of war and of civilian internees in the theatre of war and with the supply of billets, food, medicines and hospital facilities to them. He was head of the Home Ministry which was charged with a similar duty towards civilian internees in Japan. Above all he was head of the Government which was charged with continuing responsibility for the care of prisoners and civilian internees.

The barbarous treatment of prisoners and internees was well known to Tojo. He took no adequate steps to punish offenders and to prevent the commission of similar offences in the future. His attitude towards the Bataan Death March gives the key to his conduct towards these captives. He knew in 1942 something of the conditions of that march and that many prisoners had died as a result of these conditions. He did not call for a report on the incident. When in the Philippines in 1943 he made perfunctory inquiries about the march but took no action. No one was punished. His explanation is that the commander of a Japanese Army in the field is given a mission in the performance of which he is not subject to specific orders from Tokyo. Thus the head of the Government of Japan knowingly and wilfully refused to perform the duty which lay upon that Government of enforcing performance of the Laws of War.

To cite another outstanding example, he advised that prisoners of war should be used in the construction of the Burma-Siam Railway, designed for strategic purposes. He made no proper arrangements for billeting and feeding the prisoners, or for caring for those who became sick in that trying climate. He learned of the poor condition of the prisoners employed on the project, and sent an officer to investigate. We know the dreadful conditions that investigator must have found in the many camps along the railway. The only step taken as a result of that investigation was the trial of one company commander for ill-treatment of prisoners. Nothing was done to improve conditions. Deficiency diseases and starvation continued to kill off the prisoners until the end of the project.

Statistics relative to the high death rate from malnutrition and other causes in prisoners of war camps were discussed at conferences over which Tojo presided. The shocking condition of the prisoners in 1944, when Tojo's Cabinet fell, and the enormous number of prisoners who had died from lack of food and medicines is conclusive proof that Tojo took no proper steps to care for them.

We have referred to the attitude of the Japanese Army towards Chinese prisoners of war. Since the Japanese Government did not recognise the "Incident" as a war, it was argued that the Rules of War did not apply to the fighting and that Chinese captives were not entitled to the status and rights of prisoners of war. Tojo knew and did not disapprove of that shocking attitude.

He bears responsibility for the instruction that prisoners who did not work should not eat. We have no doubt that his repeated insistence on this instruction conduced in large measure to the sick and wounded being driven to work and to the suffering and deaths which resulted.

We have fully referred to the measures which were taken to prevent knowledge of the ill-treatment of prisoners reaching the outside world. Tojo bears responsibility for these measures.

The Tribunal finds Tojo guilty under Count 54. We make no finding under Count 55.

UMEZU, YOSHIJIRO

The accused Umezu is charged under Counts 1, 27, 29, 31, 32, 36, 54, and 55.

Umezu was an Army officer. While he was in command of Japanese troops in North China from 1934 to 1936 he continued the Japanese aggression in that country against the northern provinces, he set up a pro-Japanese local government, and under threat of force compelled the Chinese to enter into the Ho-Umezu agreement of June 1935. This for a time limited the power of legitimate government of China.

Umezu was Vice-Minister of War from March 1936 to May 1938 while the National Policy Plans of 1936 and the Plan for Important Industries of 1937 were decided upon. These were Army plans and were one of the prime causes of the Pacific War.

In January 1937, when the Imperial Mandate to form a new Cabinet was given to General Ugaki, Umezu played an important part in the Army's refusal to countenance Ugaki as Hirota's successor. Because of this opposition Ugaki was unable to form a Cabinet.

When the fighting in China broke out anew in July 1937 at Marco Polo Bridge this accused knew and approved of the plans of the conspirators to carry on the war. Umezu was a member of the Cabinet Planning Board as well as of many other boards and commissions which largely contributed to the formulation of the aggressive plans of conspirators and to preparations necessary for the execution of these plans.

In December 1937, Tojo, as Chief-of-Staff of the Kwantung Army, sent to Umezu plans for preparation for the attack on the U.S.S.R. and later plans for the strengthening of the Kwantung Army and plans for installations in Inner Mongolia which Tojo stated were of vital importance both in the preparation for war with the U.S.S.R. and in connection with the war with China.

While Umezu was Commander of the Kwantung Army from 1939 to 1944 he continued the direction of the economy of Manchukuo so as to serve the purposes of Japan; plans were made for the occupation of Soviet territories, and plans were also made for the military administration of the Soviet areas to be occupied and officers were sent to the occupied areas in the south to study the military administration there with a view to using the information thus obtained in the Soviet territories.

The evidence is overwhelming that the accused was a member of the conspiracy.

With reference to Count 36, the fighting at Nomonhan had began before he took command of the Kwantung Army. He was in command only a very few days before the fighting ceased.

Umezu served as Chief of the Army General Staff from July 1944 until the Surrender. He thereby played a principle part in the waging of the war against China and the Western Powers.

War Crimes

There is not sufficient evidence that Umezu was responsible for the commission of atrocities.

The Tribunal finds Umezu guilty on Counts 1, 27, 29, 31, and 32. He is not guilty on Counts 36, 54, and 55.

Under the Charter the Judgment I have read is the Judgment of the Tribunal.

The Member for India dissents from the majority Judgment and has filed a statement of his reasons for such dissent.

The members for France and the Netherlands dissent as to part only from the majority Judgment and have filed statements of their reasons for such dissents.

The Member for the Philippines has filed a separate opinion concurring with the majority.

Generally, I share the view of the majority as to the facts, but without recording any dissent, I have filed a brief statement of my reasons for upholding the Charter and the jurisdiction of the Tribunal and of some general considerations that influenced me in deciding on the sentences.

These documents will be part of the Record and will be available to the

Supreme Commander, to Defense Counsel and to others who may be concerned. Defense Counsel have applied for a reading in court of these separate opinions, but the Tribunal had already considered this matter and decided that they would not be so read.

The Tribunal adheres to this decision.

The accused will be removed from the dock and then returned singly for sentence in the order in which their names appear in the title of the Indictment.

The three accused who are too ill to attend the trial today will be sentenced in their absence after those accused who are present have been sentenced.

To enable the accused who are present to be presented for sentence in the order stated, we will adjourn for fifteen minutes.

(Whereupon, at 15th 30, a recess was taken until 15th 55, after which the proceedings were resumed as follows:)

MARSHAL OF THE COURT: The International Military Tribunal for the Far East is now resumed.

THE PRESIDENT: In accordance with Article 15-h of the Charter, the International Military Tribunal for the Far East will now pronounce the sentences on the accused convicted on this Indictment.

Accused ARAKI, Sadao, on the Counts of the Indictment on which you have been convicted, the International Military Tribunal for the Far East sentences you to imprisonment for life.

Accused DOHIHARA, Kenji, on the Counts of the Indictment on which you have been convicted, the International Military Tribunal for the Far East sentences you to death by hanging.

Accused HASHIMOTO, Kingoro, on the Counts of the Indictment on which you have been convicted, the International Military Tribunal for the Far East sentences you to imprisonment for life.

Accused HATA, Shunroku, on the Courts of the Indictment on which you have been convicted, the International Military Tribunal for the Far East sentences you to imprisonment for life.

Accused HIRANUMA, Kingoro, on the Counts of the Indictment on which you have been convicted, the International Military Tribunal for the Far East sentences you to imprisonment for life.

Accused HIROTA, Koki, on the Counts of the Indictment on which you have been convicted, the International Military Tribunal for the Far East sentences you to death by hanging.

Accused HOSHINO, Naoki, on the Counts of the Indictment on which you have been convicted, the International Military Tribunal for the Far East sentences you to imprisonment for life.

Accused ITAGAKI, Seichiro, on the Counts of the Indictment on which you have been convicted, the International Military Tribunal for the Far East sentences you to death by hanging.

Accused KIDO, Koichi, on the Counts of the Indictment on which you have been convicted, the International Military Tribunal for the Far East sentences you to imprisonment for life.

Accused KIMURA, Heitaro, on the Counts of the Indictment on which you have been convicted, the International Military Tribunal for the Far East sentences you to death by hanging.

Accused KOISO, Kuniaki, on the Counts of the Indictment on which you have been convicted, the International Military Tribunal for the Far East sentences you to imprisonment for life.

Accused MATSUI, Iwane, on the Counts of the Indictment on which you have been convicted, the International Military Tribunal for the Far East sentences you to death by hanging.

Accused MINAMI, Jiro, on the Counts of the Indictment on which you have been convicted, the International Military Tribunal for the Far East sentences you to imprisonment for life.

Accused MUTO, Akira, on the Counts of the Indictment on which you have been convicted, the International Military Tribunal for the Far East sentences you to death by hanging.

Accused OKA, Takazumi, on the Counts of the Indictment on which you have been convicted, the International Military Tribunal for the Far East sentences you to imprisonment for life.

Accused OSHIMA, Hiroshi, on the Counts of the Indictment on which you have been convicted, the International Military Tribunal for the Far East sentences you to imprisonment for life.

Accused SATO, Kenryo, on the Counts of the Indictment on which you have been convicted, the International Military Tribunal for the Far East sentences you to imprisonment for life.

Accused SHIGEMITSU, Mamoru, on the Counts of the Indictment on which you have been convicted, the International Military Tribunal for the Far East sentences you to imprisonment for seven years as from the date of arraignment.

Accused SHIMADA, Shigetaro, on the Counts of the Indictment on which you have been convicted, the International military Tribunal for the Far East sentences you to imprisonment for life.

Accused SUZUKI, Teiichi, on the Counts of the indictment on which you have been convicted, the International Military Tribunal for the Far East sentences you to imprisonment for life.

Accused TOGO, Shigenori, on the Counts of the Indictment on which you have been convicted, the International Military Tribunal for the Far East sentences you to imprisonment for twenty years as from the date of arraignment.

Accused TOJO, Hideki, on the Counts of the Indictment on which you have been convicted, the International Military Tribunal for the Far East sentences you to death by hanging.

The Tribunal sentences the accused KAYA, SHIRATORI and UMEZU on the

Counts on which they have been convicted to imprisonment for life in each case.

The Tribunal adjourns.

(Whereupon, at 16: 12, 12 November 1948, the Tribunal adjourned.)

Dissentient Judgement of Justice R. B. Pal

I sincerely regret my inability to concur in the judgement and decision of my learned brothers. Having regard to the gravity of the case and of the questions of law and of fact involved in it, I feel it my duty to indicate my view of the questions that arise for the decision of this Tribunal.

On April 29, 1946 the eleven prosecuting nations named above filed their indictment against twenty-eight persons. Accused Matsuoka, Yosuke and Nagano, Osami died during the pendency of this trial and accused Okawa, Shumei was discharged from the present proceeding because of his mental incompetency. The remaining twenty-five persons are now arraigned as accused before us to take their trial for what has been stated to be the major war-crimes.

Evidence has been given in this case connecting each of the accused with the Government of Japan during the relevant period. Details showing this connection will be given as occasion arises.

The charges against these accused persons are laid in fifty-five counts grouped in three categories:

1. Crimes against Peace. (Count 1 to Count 36)
2. Murder. (Count 37 to Count 52)
3. Conventional War Crimes and Crimes against Humanity. (Count 53 to Count 55).

The counts of charges are prefaced by an introductory summary amply indicating the nature of the prosecution case and are appended with five appendices in the nature of bills of particulars.

In the language of the prosecution itself—

"*In Group One,* Crimes against Peace as defined in the Charter are charged in thirty-six counts. In the first five counts the accused are charged with conspiracy to secure the military, naval, political and economic demination of certain areas, by the waging of declared or undeclared war or wars of aggression and of war or wars in violation of international law, treaties, agreements and assurances. Count 1 charges that the conspiracy was to secure the domination of East Asia and of the Pacific and Indian Oceans; Count 2, domination of Manchuria; Count 3, domination of all China; Count 4, domination of the same areas named in Count 1, by waging such illegal war against sixteen specified countries and peoples. In Count 5, the accused are charged with conspiring with Germany and Italy to secure the domination of the world by the waging of such illegal wars against any opposing countries. The prosecution charges in the next twelve counts (6 to 17) that all or certain accused *planned and prepared* such illegal wars against twelve nations or people attacked pursuant thereto. In the next nine counts (18 to 26) it is charged that all or certain accused *initiated* such illegal wars against eight nations or peoples, identifying in a separate count each nation or people so attacked. In the next ten counts (27 to 36) it is charged that the accused *waged* such illegal wars against nine nations or peoples, identifying in a separate count each nation or people so warred upon.

"*In Group Two,* murder or conspiracy to murder is charged in sixteen counts (37 to 52). It is charged, in Count 37, that certain accused conspired unlawfully to kill and murder people of the United States, the Philippines, the British Commonwealth, the Netherlands, and Thailand (Siam), by ordering, causing and permitting Japanese armed forces, *in time of peace,* to attack those people in violation of Hague Convention III, and in Count 38, in violation of numerous treaties other than Hague Convention III.

"It is charged in the next five counts (39 to 43) that the accused unlawfully killed and murdered the persons indicated in Counts 37 and 38 by ordering, causing and permitting, *in time of peace,* armed attacks by Japanese armed forces, on December 7 and 8, 1941, at Pearl Harbour, Kota Bahru, Hong Kong, Shanghai and Davao. The accused are charged in the next count (44) with conspiracy to procure and permit the murder of prisoners of war, civilians and crews of torpedoed ships.

"The charges in the last eight counts (45 to 52) of this group are that certain accused, by ordering, causing and permitting Japanese armed forces unlawfully to attack certain cities in China (Counts 45 to 50) and territory in Mongolia and of the Union of Soviet Socialist Republics (Counts 51 and 52), unlawfully killed and murdered large numbers of soldiers and civilians.

"*In Group Three,* the final group of counts (53 to 55), other conventional War Crimes and Crimes against Humanity, are charged. Certain specified accused are charged in Count 53 with having conspired to order, authorize and permit Japanese commanders, War Ministry officials, police and subordinates to violate treaties and other laws by committing atrocities and other crimes against many thousands of prisoners of war and civilians belonging to the United States, the British Commonwealth, France, Netherlands, the Philippines, China, Portugal and the Union of Soviet Socialist Republics.

"*Certain specified accused* are directly charged in Count 54 with having ordered, authorized and permitted the persons mentioned in Count 53 to commit offences mentioned in that Count. The same specified accused are charged in the final count (55) with having violated the laws of war by deliberately and recklessly disregarding their legal duty to take adequate steps to secure the observance of conventions, assurances and the laws of war for the protection of prisoners of war and civilians of the nations and peoples named in Count 53."

* * *

In presenting its case at the hearing the prosecution offered what it characterized to be "the well-recognized conspiracy method of proof". It undertook to prove:

1. (*a*) that there was an over-all conspiracy;
   (*b*) that the said conspiracy was of a comprehensive character and of a continuing nature;
   (*c*) that this conspiracy was formed, existed and operated during the period from 1 January, 1928 to 2 September, 1945;
2. that the object and purpose of the said conspiracy consisted in the complete domination by Japan of all the territories generally known as Greater East Asia described in the indictment;
3. that the design of the conspiracy was to secure such domination by—
   (*a*) war or wars of aggression;
   (*b*) war or wars in violation of—
      (*i*) international law,
      (*ii*) treaties,
      (*iii*) agreements and assurances;
4. that each accused was a member of this over-all conspiracy at the time any specific crime set forth in any count against him was committed.

The prosecution claimed that as soon as it would succeed in proving the above matters, the guilt of the accused would be established without anything more and that it would not matter whether any particular accused had actually participated in the commission of any specified act or not.

In counts one to five the accused are charged with having participated in the formulation or execution of a common plan or conspiracy, the *object* of such plan or conspiracy being the military, naval, political and economic domination of certain territories and the means designed for achieving this object being:

1. declared or undeclared war or wars of aggression;
2. war or wars in violation of—
   (*a*) international law,
   (*b*) treaties,
   (*c*) agreements and assurances.

It is implied in these charges that acts in execution of such plan were performed. The accused are sought to be made criminally liable for such acts.

In these counts the questions that would arise for our decision are:

1. Whether military, naval, political and economic domination of one nation by another is a crime in international life;
2. Whether war or wars

(*a*) of aggression,
or
(*b*) in violation of
(*i*) international law,
(*ii*) treaties,
(*iii*) agreements and assurances
are crimes in international life and whether their legal character would in any way depend upon their being initiated with or without declaration.

Counts six to seventeen charge the accused only with having planned and prepared wars of the categories mentioned above. In order to sustain these charges it is essential that such wars must be criminal or illegal.

Counts eighteen to twenty-four relate to initiation of wars of the same categories and would, therefore, stand or fall according as such wars are or are not crime in international life.

Counts twenty-five to thirty-six charge the accused or some of them with having waged wars of the same categories and would thus fail if such wars are not crime in international life.

Counts thirty-seven to fifty-two contain charges on the footing that hostilities started in breach of treaties would not have the legal character of war and did not therefore confer on the Japanese forces any right of lawful belligerents.

I shall examine these several counts in detail later on. It is obvious that they all involve the question whether wars of the categories mentioned above became crime in international life.

The prosecution case is that these accused persons did the acts alleged in course of working the machinery of the Government of Japan taking advantage of their position in that Government. Grounds of individual responsibility for the alleged crimes are set out in Appendix E of the Indictment thus:

> It is charged against each of the accused that he used the power and prestige of the position which he held and his personal influence in such a manner that he promoted and carried out the offences set out in each Count of this Indictment in which his name appears.
>
> It is charged against each of the accused that during the periods hereinafter set out against his name he was one of those responsible for all the acts and omissions of the various governments of which he was a member, and of the various civil, military or naval organizations in which he held a position of authority.
>
> It is charged against each of the accused, as shown by the numbers given after his name, that he was present at and concurred in the decision taken at some of the conferences and cabinet meetings held on or about the following dates in 1941, which decisions prepared for and led to unlawful war on 7 and 8 December, 1941.

The acts alleged are, in my opinion, all *acts of state* and whatever these accused are alleged to have done, they did that in working the machinery of the government, the duty and responsibility of working the same having fallen on them in due course of events.

Several serious questions of international law would thus arise for our consideration in this case. We cannot take up the questions of fact without coming to a decision on these questions.

The material questions of law that arise for our decision are the following:

1. Whether military, naval, political and economic domination of one nation by another is crime in international life.
2. (a) Whether wars of the alleged character became criminal in international law during the period in question in the indictment.

If not,

(b) Whether any *ex post facto law* could be and was enacted making such wars criminal so as to affect the legal character of the acts alleged in the indictment.

3. Whether individuals comprising the government of an alleged aggressor state can be held criminally liable in international law in respect of such acts.

Several subsidiary questions of law will also fall to be decided before we can justly take up the evidence in this case. These questions will be indicated in their proper places in course of the decision of the main questions specified above. But before all this, I must dispose of some preliminary matters concerning ourselves.

The accused at the earliest possible opportunity expressed their apprehension of injustice in the hands of the Tribunal as at present constituted.

The apprehension is that the Members of the Tribunal being representatives of the nations which defeated Japan and which are accusers in this action, the accused cannot expect a fair and impartial trial at their hands and consequently the Tribunal as constituted should not proceed with this trial.

Regarding the Constitution of the Court for the trial of persons accused of war crimes, the Advisory Committee of Jurists which met at The Hague in 1920 to prepare the statute for the Permanent Court of International Justice expressed a "vocu" for the establishment of an International Court of Criminal Justice. This, in principle, appears to be a wise solution of the problem, but the plan has not as yet been adopted by the states. Hall suggests that "it should be possible for both the victor and the vanquished in war to be able to bring to trial before an impartial Court persons who are accused of violating the laws and usages of war."

I feel tempted in this connection to quote the views of Professor Hans Kelsen of the University of California which may have the effect of turning our eyes to one particular side of the picture likely to be lost sight of in a "floodlit court house where only one thing is made to stand out clear for all men to see, namely that the moral conscience of the world is there reasserting the moral dignity of the human race."

The learned Professor says: "It is the jurisdiction of the victorious states over the war criminals of the enemy which the Three Power Declaration signed in Moscow demands . . . . It is quite understandable that during the war the peoples who are the victims of the abominable crimes of the Axis Powers wish *to take the law in their own hands* in order to punish the criminals. But after the war will be over our minds will be open again to the consideration that criminal jurisdiction exercised by the injured states over enemy subjects is considered by the peoples of the delinquents *as vengeance rather than justice,* and is consequently not the best means to guarantee the future peace. The punishment of war criminals should be an act of international justice, not the satisfaction of a thirst for revenge. It does not quite comply with the idea of international justice that only the vanquished states are obliged to surrender their own subjects to the jurisdiction of an international tribunal for the punishment of war crimes. The victorious states too should be willing to transfer their jurisdiction over their own subjects who have offended the laws of warfare to the same independent and impartial international tribunal."

The learned Professor further says: "As to the question—what kind of tribunal shall be authorized to try war criminals, national or international, there can be little doubt that an international court is much more fitted for this task than a national, civil, or military court. Only a court established by an international treaty, to which not only the victorious but also the vanquished states are contracting parties, will not meet with certain difficulties which a national court is confronted with. . . ."

Though not constituted in the manner suggested by the learned Professor, here is an international tribunal for the trial of the present accused.

The judges are here no doubt from the different victor nations, but they are here in their personal capacities. One of the essential factors usually considered in the selection of members of such tribunals is moral integrity. This of course embraces more than ordinary fidelity and honesty. It includes "a measure of freedom from prepossessions, a readiness to face the consequences of views which may not be shared, a devotion to judicial processes, and a willingness to make the sacrifices which the performance of judicial duties may involve." The accused persons here have not challenged the constitution of the tribunal on the ground of any shortcoming in any of the members of the tribunal in these respects. The Supreme Commander seems to have given careful and anxious thought to this aspect of the case and there is a provision in the Charter itself permitting the judges to decline to take part in the trial if for any reason they consider that they should not do so.

Ordinarily, on an objection like the one taken in this connection, the judges themselves might have expressed their unwillingness to take upon themselves the responsibility. Administration of justice demands that it should be conducted in such a way as not only to assure that justice is done but also to create the impression that it is being done. In the classic language of Lord Hewart, Lord Chief Justice of England, "It is not merely of *some* importance, but it is of *fundamental importance* that justice should not only be done but should manifestly and undoubtedly be *seen* to be done . . . . Nothing is to be done which creates even a suspicion that there has been an improper interference with the course of justice." The fear of miscarriage of justice is constantly in the mind of all who are practically or theoretically concerned with the law and especially with the dispensation of criminal law. The special difficulty as to the rule of law governing this case, taken with the ordinary uncertainty as to how far our means are sufficient to detect a crime and coupled further with the awkward possibilities of bias created by racial or political factors, makes our position one of very grave responsibility. The accused cannot be found fault with, if, in these circumstances, they entertain any such apprehension, and I, for myself, fully appreciate the basis of their fear. We cannot condemn the accused if they apprehend, in their trial by a body as we are, any possible interference of emotional factors with objectivity.

We cannot overlook or underestimate the effect of the influence stated above. They may indeed operate even unconsciously. We know how unconscious processes may go on in the mind of anyone who devotes his interest and his energies to finding out how a crime was committed, who committed it, and what were the motives and psychic attitude of the criminal. Since these processes may remain unobserved by the conscious part of the personality and may be influenced only indirectly and remotely by it, they present permanent pitfalls to objective and sound judgment—always discrediting the integrity of human justice. But in spite of all such obstacles it is human justice with which the accused must rest content. We, on our part, should always keep in view the words of the Supreme Commander for the Allied Powers with which Mr. Keenan closed his opening statement and avoid the eagerness to accept as real anything that lies in the direction of the unconscious wishes, that comes dangerously near to the aim of the impulses.

With these observations I persuade myself to hold that this objection of the accused need not be upheld.

The defense also took several other objections to the trial; of these *the substantial ones* may be subdivided under two heads:

1. Those relating strictly to the jurisdiction of the Tribunal.
2. Those which, while assuming the jurisdiction of the Tribunal, call on the Tribunal to discharge the accused of the charges contained in several counts on the ground that they do not disclose any offence at all.

Some of these objections even related to war crimes *stricto sensu* alleged to have been committed during the war which ended in the surrender. As preliminary objections, these are of no substance.

A war, whether legal or illegal, whether aggressive or defensive, is still a war to be regulated by the accepted rules of warfare. No pact, no convention has in any way abrogated *jus-in-bello.*

So long as States, or any substantial number of them, still contemplate recourse to war, the principles which are deemed to regulate their conduct as belligerents must still be regarded as constituting a vital part of international law. There is a persistent tendency on the part of the belligerents to shape their conduct according to what they consider to be their own needs rather than the requirements of international justice. Strong measures are required to curb this tendency in the belligerent conduct.

War crimes *stricto sensu,* as alleged here, refer to acts ascribable to individuals concerned in their individual capacity. These are not acts of State and consequently the principle that no State has jurisdiction over the acts of another State does not apply to this case.

Oppenheim says: "The right of the belligerent to punish, during the war, such war criminals as fall into his hands is a well-recognized principle of international law. It is a right of which he may effectively avail himself as he has occupied all or part of enemy territory, and is thus in the position to seize war criminals who happen to be there. He may, as a condition of the armistice, impose upon the authorities of the defeated state the duty to hand over persons charged with having committed war crimes, regardless of whether such persons are present in the territory actually occupied by him or in the territory which, at the successful end of hostilities, he is in the position to occupy. For in both cases the accused are, in effect, in his power. And, although normally the Treaty of Peace brings to an end the right to prosecute war criminals, no rule of international law prevents the victorious belligerent from imposing upon the defeated State the duty, as one of the provisions of the armistice or of the Peace Treaty, to surrender for trial persons accused of war crimes."

Similar views are expressed by Hall and Garner.

"The principle," says Garner, "that the individual soldier who commits acts in violation of the laws of war, when these acts are at the same time offences against the general criminal law, should be liable to trial and punishment, not only by the courts of his own state, but also by the courts of the injured adversary in case he falls into the hands of the authorities thereof, has long been maintained . . . ."

Hall says: "A belligerent, besides having the rights over his enemy which flow directly from the right to attack, possesses also the right of punishing persons who have violated the laws of war, if they afterwards fall into his hands . . . . To the exercise of the first of the above-mentioned rights no objection can be felt so long as the belligerent confines himself to punishing breaches of universally acknowledged laws."

It should only be remembered that this rule applies only where the crime in question is not an *act of state.* The statement that if an act is forbidden by international law as a war crime, the perpetrator may be punished by the injured state if he falls in its hands is correct only with this limitation that the act in question is not an act of the enemy state.

In my judgment, it is now well-settled that mere high position of the parties in their respective states would not exonerate them from criminal responsibility in this respect, if, of course, the guilt can otherwise be brought home to them. Their position in the State does not make every act of theirs *an act of state* within the meaning of international law.

The first substantial objection relating to the jurisdiction of the Tribunal is that the crimes triable by this tribunal must be limited to those committed in or in connection with the war which ended in the surrender on 2 September, 1945. In my judgment this objection must be sustained. It is preposterous to think that defeat in a war should subject the defeated nation and its nationals to trial for all the delinquencies of their entire existence. There is nothing in the Potsdam Declaration and in the Instrument of Surrender which would entitle the Supreme Commander or the Allied Powers to proceed against the persons who might have committed crimes in or in connection with any other war.

The prosecution places strong reliance on the Cairo Declaration read with paragraph 8 of the Potsdam Declaration and urges that the Cairo Declaration by expressly referring to all the acts of aggression by Japan since the First World War in 1914 vested the Allied Powers with all possible authority in respect to those incidents. The relevant passage in the Cairo Declaration runs thus: "It is their purpose that Japan shall be stripped of all the islands in the Pacific which she has seized or occupied since the beginning of the First World War in 1914, and that all the territories Japan has stolen from the Chinese, such as Manchuria, Formosa, and the Pescadores, shall be restored to the Republic of China. Japan will also be expelled from all other territories which she has taken by violence and greed. The aforesaid three great powers, mindful of the enslavement of the people of Korea, are determined that in due course Korea shall become free and independent."

The Potsdam Declaration in paragraph 8 says: "The terms of the Cairo Declaration shall be carried out and Japanese sovereignty shall be limited to the islands of Honshu, Hokkaido, Kyushu, Shikoku and such minor islands as we determine."

These Declarations are mere announcements of the intention of the allied powers. They have no legal value. They do not by themselves give rise to any legal right in the United Nations. The Allied Powers themselves disown any contractual relation with the vanquished on the footing of these Declarations: Vide paragraph 3 of the Authority of the Supreme Commander.

As I read these Declarations I do not find anything in them which will amount even to an announcement of intention on the part of the declarants to try and punish war criminals in relation to these incidents. I am prepared to go further. In my judgment, even if we assume that these Declarations can be read so as to cover such cases, that would not carry us far. The Allied Powers by mere declaration of such an intention would not acquire in law any such authority. In my view, if there is any international law which is to be respected by the nations, that law does not confer any right on the conqueror in a war to try and punish any crime committed by the vanquished not in connection with the war lost by him but in any other unconnected war or incident.

The Cairo Declaration referred to in the Potsdam Declaration rather goes against the contention of the prosecution. That Declaration expressly refers to certain specified past matters and proclaims what steps should be taken in respect to them. I do not find anything in that Declaration which would suggest any trial or punishment of any individual war criminal in connection with those past events. Nor do I find anything in the Charter which would entitle us to extend our jurisdiction to such matters.

In my opinion, therefore, crimes alleged to have been committed in or in connection with any conflict, hostility, incident or war not forming part of the war which ended in the surrender of the 2nd September, 1945 are outside the jurisdiction of the Tribunal.

* * *

After careful consideration of the question I come to the conclusion:

1. That the Charter has not defined the crime in question;
2. (*a*) That it was not within the competence of its author to define any crime;
   (*b*) That even if any crime would have been defined by the Charter that definition would have been *ultra vires* and would not have been binding on us.
3. That it is within our competence to question its authority in this respect.
4. That the law applicable to this case is the international law to be found by us.

The principal question which thus ultimately arises for our decision is whether the acts alleged in the indictment under the category of "Crimes against Peace" constituted any crime under the international law.

The acts alleged are "the planning, preparation and initiation" of wars of specified characters.

It is not the prosecution case that "war," irrespective of its character, became a crime in international law. Their case is that a war possessing the alleged character was made illegal and criminal in international law and that consequently persons provoking such criminal war by such acts of planning, etc., committed a crime under international law.

Two principal questions therefore arise here for our decision, namely;

1. Whether the wars of the alleged character became criminal in international law.
2. Assuming wars of the alleged character to be criminal in international law, whether the individuals functioning as alleged here would incur any criminal responsibility in international law.

I would take up the first of these questions first.

For the sake of convenience the question may be considered with reference to four distinct periods, namely:

1. That up to the First World War of 1914;
2. That between the First World War and the date of the Pact of Paris (27 August 1928);

3. That from the date of the Pact of Paris to the commencement of the World War under consideration;
4. That since the Second World War.

So far as the first of the above four periods is concerned it seems to be generally agreed that no war became crime in international life, though it is sometimes asserted that a distinction between "just" and "unjust" war had always been recognized. It may be that international jurists and philosophers sometimes used these distinctive expressions in their learned discourses. But international life itself never recognized this distinction and no such distinction was ever allowed to produce any practical result. At any rate an "unjust" war was not made "crime" in international law. In fact any interest which the western powers may now have in the territories in the Eastern Hemisphere was acquired mostly through armed violence during this period and none of these wars perhaps would stand the test of being "just war."

* * *

My own view is that war in international life remained, as before, outside the province of law, its conduct alone having been brought within the domain of law. The Pact of Paris did not come within the category of law at all and consequently failed to introduce any change in the legal position of a belligerent state or in the jural incidents of belligerency.

If the Pact of Paris thus failed to affect the legal character of war, either directly or indirectly, the next question is whether any category of war became crime or illegal thing in international life in any other way.

Dr. Glueck answers this question in the affirmative and says that a customary international law developed making an aggressive war a crime in international life.

For this purpose Dr. Glueck relies on the following data:

1. The time has arrived in the life of civilized nations when an international custom should be taken to have developed to hold aggressive war to be an international crime.
2. It is familiar law in the international field that custom may, in the words of Article 38 of the statute of the Permanent Court of International Justice, be considered "as evidence of a general practice accepted as law."
   (*a*) All that is necessary to show is that during the present century a widespread custom has developed among the civilized states to enter into agreements expressive of their solemn *conviction* that unjustified war is so dangerous a threat to the survival of mankind and mankind's law that it must be branded and treated as criminal.
3. In addition to the Pact of Paris, the following solemn international pronouncements may be mentioned as the evidence of this custom and of this conviction:

(*a*) The agreements limiting the nature of the deeds permissible in the extreme event of war: The Hague Conventions of 1899 and 1907 and the Geneva Conventions of 1929 regulating the treatment of prisoners of war;

(*b*) The draft of a treaty of mutual assistance sponsored by the League of Nations in 1923, solemnly declaring (Article 1) that aggressive war is an international crime, and that the parties would undertake that no one of them will be guilty of its commission.

(*c*) The preamble to the League of Nations 1924 Protocol for the Pacific Settlement of International Disputes (Geneva Protocol) referring to aggressive war as crime.

(*d*) The declarations made at the Eighteenth Plenary meeting of the Assembly of the League of Nations held on September 24, 1927.

(*e*) The unanimous resolution, February 18, 1928, of the twenty-one American Republics at the Sixth (Havana) Pan American Conference declaring that "War of aggression constitutes an international crime against the human species."

(*f*) The preamble of the general convention signed by the representatives of all the republics at the international conference of American states on conciliation and arbitration held at Washington in December 1928, containing the statement that the signatories desired "to demonstrate that the condemnation of war as an instrument of national policy in their mutual relations set forth in the Havana Resolution constitutes one of the fundamental bases of inter-American relations . . . ."

(*g*) The preamble of the Anti-war Treaty of Non-Aggression and conciliation signed at Rio de Janeiro, October 10, 1933, stating that the parties were entering into the agreement "to the end of condemning wars of aggression and territorial acquisitions . . . ."

(*h*) Article 1 of the notable Draft Treaty of Disarmament and Security prepared by an American group and carefully considered by the Third Committee on Disarmament of the Assembly of the League of Nations 1924, providing that "The High Contracting Parties solemnly declare that aggressive war is an international crime . . ."

(*i*) Senator Borah's Resolution introduced on December 12, 1927.

As evidence of the suggested custom Dr. Glueck refers to a few solemn international pronouncements noticed above. These pronouncements, it may be observed, are mostly in agreements between states.

* * *

After a careful consideration of all these facts and circumstances I am of the opinion that no international customary law could develop through the pronouncements referred to by Dr. Glueck and relied on by the prosecution.

The pronouncements at most only amounted to expressions of the conviction of persons making them. But these are not yet attended by any act on the part of any of the states. Custom as a source of law presupposes two essential elements:

1. The juristic sentiments of a people.

2. Certain external, constant and general *acts* by which it is shown. It is indicated by identical conduct under similar external circumstances. The conduct of national states during the period in question rather goes the other way.

It may be that Dr. Glueck is thinking of "customary law" in a specific sense. It cannot be denied that in one sense customary law, statute and juristic law are all shoots from the same slip, namely, popular consciousness. In this sense the center of gravity of the development of all law—not only of customary law—can be placed into the legal consciousness, "the natural harmony of the conviction of a people, which is a popular universal conviction." For this purpose its emergence in usage is not essential to the origin of law. In this *sense* there need be no other prerequisites to the origination of customary law than a common popular conviction. We are, however, not much concerned with customary law in this specific sense. No doubt it has its own scientific value. But we are concerned with customary law in a sense in which it becomes applicable by a judge. There are prerequisites to its applicability by the judge. Puchta was not concerned with such prerequisites in his scientific evaluation of customary law, but he recognized them: "But if we take prerequisites to mean something else, *e.g.*, if we take it in the sense of a prerequisite to the application by the judge, to his acceptance of customary law, then that whereof we are speaking no longer is a prerequisite to customary law itself. In this case the question to be answered is: What must the judge take into account when a party litigant appeals to customary law or when for any other reason he is called upon to consult this source of law? What are the presuppositions under which customary law can actually be assumed to exist?" *There is thus a sharp distinction between the question as to the origin of customary law in the mere popular conviction and as to its applicability by a court.* There may be customary law in the sense that it exists in the conviction of the people; yet it may not be law applicable by a court because the prerequisites to its applicability by the court are lacking. Herein comes the usage which is wanting in the present case. The people should not merely be conscious of their law but they must live their law,—they must act and conduct themselves according to it.

This living according to law is required not as a mere form of manifestation but also as a means of cognition of customary law. When the conduct of the nations is taken into account the law will perhaps be found to be that only a lost war is a crime.

I may mention here in passing that within four years of the conclusion of the Pact there occurred three instances of recourse to force on a large scale on the part of the signatories of the Pact. In 1929 Soviet Russia conducted hostilities against China in connection with the dispute concerning the Chinese

Eastern Railway. The occupation of Manchuria by Japan in 1931 and 1932 followed. Then there was the invasion of the Colombian Province of Leticia by Peru in 1932. Thereafter, we had the invasion of Abyssinia by Italy in 1935 and of Finland by Russia in 1939. Of course there was also the invasion of China by Japan in 1937.

Dr. Lauterpacht points out that it is arguable that a war or a succession of wars between a considerable number of important signatories would remove altogether (*i.e.,* also for other signatories) the basis of a Pact in which a substantial degree of universality may appropriately be regarded as being of the essence. But we may leave this question alone for the present.

In my opinion, no category of war became illegal or criminal either by the Pact of Paris or as a result of the same. Nor did any customary law develop making any war criminal.

* * *

I cannot leave the subject without referring to another line of reasoning in which reference is made to the various doctrines of natural law and a conclusion is drawn therefrom that "the dictates of the public, common, or universal conscience profess the natural law which is promulgated by man's conscience and thus universally binds all civilized nations even in the absence of the statutory enactment." A wealth of authority, both ancient and modern, is requisitioned to establish that public international law is derived from natural law. The authorities cited for this purpose range from Aristotle to Lord Wright. That this natural law is not a mere matter of history but is an essential part of the living international law is sought to be established by reference to the preamble of the Hague Convention of 1907 (Convention No. 4) as also to the text of the American Declaration of Independence. The Hague Convention in its preamble, it is pointed out, refers to the laws of humanity and the dictates of the public conscience. The American Declaration of Independence refers to "the laws of nature and nature's God". From these and various other authorities it is concluded "that public international law" is based on natural law: It is said "the principles of international law are based on the very nature of man and are made known to man by his reason, hence we call them the dictates of right reason. They are, therefore, not subject to the arbitrary will of any man or nation. Consequently, the world commonwealth of nations forms one natural organic, moral, juridical and political unity." It is further said, "From what has been said so far it follows that the world commonwealth must needs enjoy an inherent authority to enact positive law for the promotion of the common good. For, on the one hand, the dictates of right reason are only general provisions that must be applied and determined according to the particular circumstances of any given case. Thus, the positive legal enactments or agreements which govern international relations represent the political interpretations and applications of the general principles of the natural and moral law . . . . On the other hand, unified cooperation of all can only be obtained by issuing binding rules."

It is not for me to question the relevancy of this appeal to natural law. There may be deep-seated reason that in all ages and countries the idea of natural law, that is, one founded on the very reality of things and not on the simple "placet" of the legislature has been cultivated. There have no doubt been fundamental divergencies in the doctrine of natural law. The relations between the dictates of natural justice and juridical norms have also been variously conceived, depending upon diverse speculative tendencies and historical phases. Often a wide and impassable separation arose between the two systems of determination, while at other times the difference seemed one of genus and species, or two views of the same object. These divergencies however should not prevent the recognition of the deep-seated unity of the conception containing all the characteristics of a phychological necessity. What is a source of difficulty for science does not cease to exist in reality; and it would be a vain illusion to ignore a need because we cannot satisfy it.

The war against natural law, which many have declared in our day, is a reaction against the errors and omissions of the philosophical systems of the past. Indeed "for many the term 'natural law' still has about it a rich, deep odor of the witches' caldron, and the mere mention of it suffices to unloose a torrent of emotions and fears." It would certainly be unjust and irrational, if, under the pretext of correcting errors and omissions, this hostility is carried to the destruction of the very object of these systems.

* * *

It remains only to consider the cumulative effect of the entire evidence led before us so far as this question of over-all conspiracy is concerned.

I would again emphasize that, for our present purpose, it is not for us to see whether or not the events and their spread could be justified. We are now only to see whether the happenings could be explained otherwise than by the existence of a conspiracy or design of the character specified in Count 1 of the indictment.

As I have already pointed out, there is no direct evidence of this conspiracy or design. The factum of this alleged conspiracy, design or plan has not been attested to directly by any witness, thing, or document. By evidence the prosecution has sought to establish certain *intermediate facts* which, according to it, are sufficiently proximate to the principal fact to be proved, so as to be receivable as evidentiary of it. The evidentiary facts thus brought in are only of presumptive value; the connection between them and the principal fact to be proved is not of any necessary consequence of the laws of nature; their connection is only such as to make the inference of the principal fact a *probable one* from these evidentiary facts.

Absolute certainty amounting to demonstration is seldom to be had in the affairs of life. We are, therefore, obliged to act on degrees of probability which may fall short of certainty. But the degree of such probability must be so high as to justify one in regarding it as certainty. Conjecture or suspicion must not be confused with this probability. We must not start with a pre-occupied mind. It will be a very valuable aid to recall the warning words of Baron Alderson where he said: "the mind was apt to take a pleasure in adopting circumstances to one another, and even in straining them a little, if need be, to force them to form parts of one connected whole, and the more ingenious the mind of the individual, the more likely was it, considering such matters, to overreach and mislead itself, to supply some link that is wanting, to take for granted some fact consistent with its previous theories and necessary to render them complete."

The evidentiary facts relied upon by the prosecution must have such a bearing upon the principal fact as would make them inconsistent with any result other than the truth of the *factum probandum.*

I have considered above the several evidentiary facts relied on by the prosecution as leading to the establishment of the conspiracy, design or plan as alleged in Count 1 of the indictment and have shown how they could be well explained without any such conspiracy, design or plan.

It may be contended that although each event may thus be explained away, they all taken together can best be explained only by the existence of such an over-all conspiracy, design or plan.

In my opinion, that will not be the effect of the evidence.

But even assuming that that would be the case, there is a big assumption involved in this approach, and, in my opinion, thereby we beg the whole question. Why should we assume that all these events had one, single determining cause? If each event is completely explained otherwise, why should we think of connecting it with another at all, or adapting them to one another? Perhaps in doing this we will only be entertaining our mind with the pleasure which Baron Alderson thinks it is apt to seek.

Even if we are to find out any single cause, we are not necessarily driven to the alleged conspiracy. Foreign policy of no nation in the world indicates a conspiracy. Even when several nations form themselves into a group, and adopt a particular policy against any particular ideology prevailing somewhere in the international society, we do not characterize this as conspiracy. Whatever that be, circumstances certainly developed in such a way during the relevant period as to lead Japan to adopt certain policies in her foreign relations, which as a matter of fact she did adopt from time to time.

I have already indicated on several occasions how several diverse factors of diverse origin influenced the development of Japan's Manchurian policy, policy towards the rest of China and foreign policy in general. I have noticed in that connection that even the resumption of the so-called positive policy in respect of Manchuria was not of conspiratorial origin. The Lytton Commission itself mentioned several facts as preparing the way for the resumption of that policy. In deciding upon their policy, from time to time, the responsible statesmen of Japan could not and did not ignore the requirements and difficulties of their people as understood by them, and these must have operated as the determining factors. It is easy to impute particular motives to those controlling the foreign policy of any state. But such responsible statesmen are not always actuated by mere sinister design. Even in the case of the statesmen of a state which we do not like we must not forget that their functions involved responsibility to the people of their nation. As I have already noticed, these statesmen may not afford to ignore any difficulty even though such difficulties might have been their own creation or the creation of their predecessor. Even such origin of the difficulty would not make their policy a conspiracy when such policy is adopted to face such difficulty.

I would again emphasize here that it is immaterial for our present purpose to see whether any policy adopted at any particular time, or any action taken by Japan pursuant to that policy, was justifiable in law; perhaps it was not. All that we are concerned with here is to see if the circumstances can explain the adaptation of the policy or the action without the existence of the alleged conspiracy.

I believe I have already given enough materials in the foregoing pages of this judgment to satisfy any but a pre-occupied mind that these events happened without the alleged conspiracy. The statesmen, diplomats and politicians of Japan were perhaps wrong, and perhaps they misled themselves. But they were not conspirators. They did not conspire.

* * *

The prosecution contended that the offenses which are here sought to be punished under the international doctrine of conspiracy, are also punishable or approximately so, besides the Anglo-American systems, in the French, German, Dutch, Spanish, Chinese, Japanese and Russian legal orders. Consequently, the prosecution urged, the doctrine of conspiracy became a rule of international law being grounded on juridical notions existing in the French, German, Japanese, Chinese and Anglo-American legal orders and on a Russian juristic philosophy.

I do not think this would be of any avail to the prosecution case unless we accept the proposition that "the general principles of law recognized by civilized nations" became a source of international law even for the purposes of introducing individual criminal responsibility in international life. I have already given my reason why I cannot accept this proposition.

The basic principle of this crime as recognized by the various national systems is that every state has a right to evolve legal institutions to *suppress by force*, as criminal, certain agreements for the ultimate commission of acts which are at least *mala in se* and irrevocably involve grave social evils. Every state has a right to anticipate the ultimate commission of the act and suppress the combination by force.

The only general principle which these various systems will yield is that it is legitimate and expedient to evolve legal institutions for the prevention and suppression of potential crimes of certain categories. Such crimes are generally those endangering the very existence of the state.

Strictly speaking, in the present stage of the international society, there is no such organization at all whose security would attract the operation of this principle. There is no international superstate as yet. The national states are only individual members of that society occupying the position of individuals in a national state.

Even apart from these considerations, if we carefully examine the principles of the law of conspiracy as prevailing in the several civilized countries, we cannot fail to see that the essential principle underlying that law is the desirability and possibility of prevention. In my opinion, this object cannot be achieved in international life as at present constituted.

Conspiracy is fundamentally a mental offense.

The Prosecution says that in order to constitute conspiracy there must be a crossing of the line of mere meditation. The essence of the offense is the joint agreement, the joint undertaking. The crossing of the line of meditation may require some overt act. But "the act required does not amount to the dignity of the act required to sustain a conviction for an attempt to commit a crime. It is any act which is in furtherance of the conspiracy. It need not be a criminal act; it need not be an illegal act; it need not be an act of any importance; it need not be performed by more than one of the conspirators; . . . the sole purpose of requiring the overt act is to ensure that there is sufficient evidence that a conspiracy has actually been entered into. Any single one of the thousands of acts by any one of these defendants or by any one of their co-conspirators would meet the requirements of an overt act necessary to establish a conspiracy in those jurisdictions where it is required."

Activity in the external forum is relevant for determining whether there has been a conspiracy only in so far as it establishes the existence of the internal elements sufficient to constitute the crime. The two factors of will and reason, which enter into the making of any agreement, are the starting points in any analysis of the nature of the conspiratorial agreement.

Basically "conspiracy is an inchoate act for which the essential act is *slight*. It involves an intent to commit a further act. It is the commission of that act *which the state desires to prevent.*"

The essential element in the principle of the law of conspiracy is thus the desirability as also the possibility of prevention of the design contemplated by the conspirators.

Manifestly, there is grave danger where conviction and punishment can be based purely on intent. This has been recognized. The commissioners, on behalf of the Legislature of New York, in revising the conspiracy statutes of New York, in the introduction to the section which required an overt act before one could be convicted of conspiracy observed as follows:

> By a metaphysical train of reasoning, which has never been adopted in any other case in the whole criminal law, the offense of conspiracy is made to consist in the intent, in an act of the mind; and to prevent the shock to commonsense, which such a proposition would be sure to produce, the formation of this intent by the interchange of thoughts, is made itself an overt act, done in pursuance of the interchange of agreement. Surely an opportunity for repentance should be allowed to all human beings; and he who has conspired to do a criminal act, should be encouraged to repent and abandon it. Acts and deeds are subjects of human laws; not thoughts and intents, unless accompanied by acts.

Professor Sayre of the Harvard Law School is more outspoken in his denunciation of the doctrine of criminal conspiracy in the Anglo-American system. He says:

> Under such a principle every one who acts in co-operation with another may some day find his liberty dependent upon the innate prejudices or social bias of an unknown judge. It is the very antithesis of justice according to law.
>
> A doctrine so vague in its outlines and uncertain in its fundamental nature as criminal conspiracy lends no strength or glory to the law; it is veritable quicksand of shifting opinion and ill considered thought.
>
> It is a doctrine which has proved itself the evil genius of our law wherever it has touched it. May the time not be long delayed in coming when it will be nothing more than a shadow stalking through past cases.

Thus even in national systems conspiracy as constituting a crime has not gone unchallenged. Its only justification is the prevention and suppression of potential danger. It can have no place in a community which has not as yet organized any preventive means. Even if fully discovered at the conspiracy stage, the international community, as it now stands, has no means of punishing the offense and consequently the punishment provided in view of its potentiality is *brutum fulmen.* The law must wait till the potentiality becomes an actuality and then again till the favourable contingency happens, that is, till the conspirators lose the war.

On the other hand, if completed conspiracy by itself is a crime in international law, once certain parties enter into this conspiracy, there remains no scope for *locus penetentiae* for them. They gain nothing by desisting from further act so far as a conspiracy for aggressive war is concerned. They have already completed their offense. I do not think there is any justification for introducing such a crime in international life at the stage where it now stands.

We must also remember that in transposing the law of conspiracy in the international system we are really not seeking to prevent any dangerous combination, because, as I have shown above, such prevention is impossible at this stage of international life. The proposed extension may only give a dangerous weapon in the hands of an unscrupulous victor. Nations while making preparations for war would never think or admit that they are making such preparation for aggressive purposes. I should not repeat it here, but we have seen how statesmen in very high positions were claiming openly very wide and extensive right of self-defense. Every nation, for itself and for the nation which it likes, would take self-defense in such extensive sense, while at the same time, it would never appreciate its opponent's similarly wide definition. In order to make aggressive war a crime in international life, it would be necessary for us to hold that whether or not a measure taken by a state was in self-defense, the decision of the state concerned would not be final. The ultimate decision as to the lawfulness of the action claimed as taken in self-defense may not lie with the state concerned. But, in the absence of any international agency or court with compulsory jurisdiction competent to decide whether or not any right of self-defense was involved, it becomes the right of the victor to decide whether or not any right of self-defense was involved, it becomes the right of the victor to decide whether or not the vanquished resorted to war in self-defense. The application of the rule which we are now seeking to introduce will thus necessarily be in the hands of the opponent who would happen to be the victor, and who could never appreciate its defensive character. We can well imagine what may be the consequence. In my opinion, while serving no useful purpose, it would be introducing a dangerous principle in the international system, further retarding the peaceful relations in that life.

There is yet another consideration against the introduction of conspiracy as a crime in international life. The international society even now recognizes the compulsive means of settlement of differences between states. Even now it is permissible to a state to take to measures containing a certain amount of compulsion for the purpose of making another state consent to such settlement of a difference as is required by the former: See Oppenheim's International Law, Chapter II. These compulsive means remain legitimate even after the Pact of Paris. "The question," says Dr. Lauterpacht, "whether the Paris Pact by forbidding resort to war has also prohibited resort to force short of war is a controversial one. Article 2 of the Pact refers to the obligation of the contracting parties not to solve disputes by any other except *pacific* means; and in the Preamble the contracting parties express their conviction that 'all changes in their relations with one another should be sought only by pacific means and be the result of a peaceful and orderly process'. In the view of some writers these provisions must be interpreted as meaning that the Pact prohibits recourse to force short of war. But the last-quoted passage refers only to changes in relations, not to the enforcement of existing legal relations; as to Article 2, it must be borne in mind that *although measures of force short of war are compulsive means, they are still pacific means.*" Compulsive means are in theory and practice considered peaceable, although not amicable, means of settling international differences. I need not stop here to examine in detail the various compulsive means in contradistinction to war. All that I want to point out in this connection is that in the preparatory stages the line between the two may be very thin and a preparation ultimately to serve only the purposes of a legitimate compulsive measure may be mistaken for a preparation for war. The same outward manifestation of mind may thus be indicative of two different mental states—one of them being legitimate in international life and the other criminal, if conspiracy be introduced as a crime. While serving no practical useful purpose, the introduction of this mental crime in international life would bring with it this difficulty of ascertaining the particular criminal state of the mind.

After giving my anxious thought to the question I have come to the conclusion that "conspiracy" by itself is not yet a crime in international law.

* * *

For the reasons given in the foregoing pages, I would hold that each and everyone of the accused must be found not guilty of each and every one of the charges in the indictment and should be acquitted of all those charges.

I have not considered whether or not any of the wars against any of the nations covered by the indictment was aggressive. The view of law that I take as to the criminality or otherwise of any war makes it unnecessary for me to enter into this question. Further, I have indicated the difficulty that I feel in defining "aggressive war", keeping in view the generally prevalent behaviour of the powers in international life.

There is indeed one possible approach to the case, which I have, as yet, left unexplored. It is said that the victor nations, as military occupants of Japan, can take action under Article 43 of the Hague Convention IV of 1907 in order to 'ensure public order and safety' and that this power entitles them to define the circumstances in which they would proceed to take such action and the action which they would consider requisite for the purpose.

Reference is made to the case of Napoleon Bonaparte and thence to Article 43 of the Hague Convention of 1907, and it is contended that the victor powers would have every right, for the sake of ensuring public order and safety of the world, to remove any of the accused from any sphere of life where there would be any possibility of his doing any future mischief.

I believe this is really an appeal to the political power of the victor nations with a pretense of legal justice. It only amounts to "piecing up want of legality with matter of convenience."

I have already noticed the case of Napoleon Bonaparte and have pointed out how, even in those days, a good deal of difficulty was felt and doubts entertained as to the exact legal position arising in his case. Those who took the final step of detention of Napoleon realized that it was necessary for them to equip themselves with some authority for this purpose from their national legislature. 56 George III chapters 22 and 23 were enacted to furnish this authority.

At the Congress of Aix-la-Chapelle in 1818, the Allied Powers, in their measures against Napoleon, proceeded on the assumption that the case was not covered by international law and they gave their reasons for saying so. I do not see what productive principle we can derive from his case for the purposes of international law. The case only yields a particular rule having a very narrow sphere of attraction and, in my opinion, a strictly limited field of projection. We may no doubt sometimes apply even such a rule beyond the field covered by its original logical content. But such a projection must not be allowed to take it to a field essentially and fundamentally different from its field of origin. I do not know the position of the Hitler group. Perhaps it might have been possible to liken their case to the case of Napoleon.

The Allied Powers thought that they were justified by the law of nations in using force to prevent Bonaparte from usurping the governorship of France, and that with this justification they made war upon him and his adherents as enemies to the Allies when France was no enemy to them. Bonaparte was designated as merely "the chief of a shapeless force without recognized political character," and, consequently, without any right to claim the advantages and the courtesies due to public power by civilized nations. That might have been the position of the Hitler group also, if that group stifled altogether the German constitutional life, and usurped power in the manner in which, and, to the extent to which, it is brought out in evidence in that case. In either case perhaps, the so-called state, if it could be called a state at all, succeeded in withdrawing from the influence of the social tendency and placing itself consciously into opposition to the society concerned.

The case of the accused before us cannot in any way be likened to the case either of Napoleon or of Hitler. The constitution of Japan was fully working. The Sovereign, the Army and the civil officials, all remained connected as usual and in normal ways with the society. The constitution of the State remained fashioned as before in relation to the will of the society. The public opinion was in full vigour. The society was not in the least deprived of any of its means to make its will effective. These accused came into power constitutionally and only to work the machinery provided by the constitution. They remained all along amenable to public opinion, and even during war the public opinion truly and vigorously functioned. The war that took place in the Pacific was certainly war with Japan. These persons did not usurp any power, and certainly they were only working the machinery of the internationally recognized state of Japan as parts of the Japanese force which was at war with the Allied Powers.

An appeal to Article 43 of the Hague Convention IV of 1907 may indeed look like seeking a pretext for the trial of these persons. We are told that the starting point for a discussion of the punishment of war criminals must be the Hague Convention IV of 18 October 1907. This convention, it is said, is essentially the handiwork of modern European scholarship and as such essentially reflects the tradition of modern Roman law and of modern Romanist codification. We are then told that it will be distorted or misunderstood, if it is conceived of exclusively in accordance with Anglo-American conceptions of legal or juridical method, and if it is conceived of without recognizing modern juristic theories concerning the role of purpose in law. It will be ineffectual and distorted if it is not interpreted and administered in accordance with Romanist conceptions relating to juridical method, as well as in accordance with the purposes or goals stated in the very text of the convention itself.

The purposes or goals said to be "stated in the very text of the Convention itself" are referred to in order to bring within Article 43 the right and power of the victors to make law declaring aggressive war a crime and a crime for individuals. I believe "the purposes and goals" of the convention would not take us to the determination of the character of the war itself. The whole purpose was to give the laws and customs of war, assuming the pre-existence of the war condition.

The Covenanting Powers, "Seeing that, while seeking means to preserve peace and prevent armed conflicts between nations, it is likewise necessary to bear in mind the case where the appeal to arms has been brought about by events which their care was unable to avert;

"Animated by the desire to serve, even in this extreme case the interests of humanity and the ever progressive needs of civilization;

"Thinking it important, with this object, to revise the general laws and customs of war, either with a view to defining them with greater precision or to confining them with such limits as would mitigate their severity as far as possible;

"Have deemed it necessary to complete and explain in certain particulars the work of the First Peace Conference, which, following on the Brussels Conference of 1874, and inspired by the ideas dictated by a wise and generous forethought, adopted provisions intended to define and govern the usages of war on land."

While so doing, they gave certain rules relating to "military authority over the territory of the hostile state" in Section III of the Annex to the Covenant, and Article 43 found a place in that section. The Article stands thus: "The authority of the legitimate power having in fact passed into the hands of the occupant, the latter shall take all the measures in his power to restore, and ensure, as far as possible, public order and safety, while respecting, unless absolutely prevented, the laws in force in the country." Its provisions would apply when a territory is occupied during belligerency by a hostile army. If the construction sought to be put on Article 43 be correct, then an army, in such occupation of a territory during war would be entitled to declare the war, conducted by the government of that territory as aggressive and criminal, and, if it succeeds in getting hold of any personnel of that government, would be competent to create a charter defining law for the trial of that personnel and get them tried and convicted. I shall not, for a moment, think that that was "the purpose and goal" of the Powers who covenanted themselves into the Hague Convention of 1907.

I am not prepared to strain and twist Article 43 of the Hague Convention to cull any such purpose and goal out of it. I am not also prepared to project the Napoleon case to the present. I have already pointed out, how even after this war, the charter of the United Nations, which was promulgated by the peoples of the United Nations avowedly "to save succeeding generations from the scourge of war" and expressly announced "the purposes of the United Nations" to be "to maintain international peace and security and to that end: to take corrective measures for the prevention and removal of threats to the peace, and for the suppression of acts of aggression or other breaches of the peace . . . . ," did not introduce any such measure against the individual members of any offending state.

Chapter VII of that Charter provides for "action with respect to threats to the peace, breaches of the peace, and acts of aggression." The provisions of this chapter do not contemplate any steps against individuals. It may safely be asserted that the coercive actions envisaged by chapter VII would not be invoked individually against those who might be responsible for the functioning of the offending collective entity.

As a judicial tribunal, we cannot behave in any manner which may justify the feeling that the setting up of the tribunal was only for the attainment of an objective which was essentially political though cloaked by a juridical appearance.

It has been said that a victor can dispense to the vanquished everything from mercy to vindictiveness; but the one thing the victor cannot give to the vanquished is justice. At least, if a tribunal be rooted in politics as opposed to law, no matter what its form and pretenses, the apprehension thus expressed would be real, unless "justice is really nothing else than the interest of the stronger."

Had we been openly called upon to decide such political issues, the entire proceedings would have assumed a different appearance altogether and the scope of our enquiry would have been much wider than what we allowed it to assume. The past conduct of the persons under trial in such a case would have simply furnished some evidentiary facts; the real ultimate *probandum* would have been the future threat to the 'public order and safety' of the world. There is absolutely no material before us to judge of any such future menace. The parties were never called upon to adduce any evidence in this respect. The matter would certainly involve extensive investigation of facts perhaps hitherto undisclosed to the world. When the Nazi aggressors are all eliminated and the Japanese conspirators are well secure in prison, we are still authoritatively told that "never before in history has the world situation been more threatening to our ideals and interests." So, it may be that the world's attention has not yet been directed in the right direction. "The depressing aspect of the situation," the world is told, "is the duplication of the high-handed, calculated procedure of the Nazi regime." This may be so; or it may also be that we are only being betrayed by what is false within,—the incipient failure of will and wisdom.

It is indeed a common experience that, in times of trial and stress like those the international world is now passing through, it is easy enough to mislead the people's mind by pointing to false causes as the fountains of all ills and thus persuading it to attribute all the ills to such causes. For those who want thus to control the popular mind, these are the opportune times; no other moment is more propitious for whispering into the popular ear the means of revenge while giving it the outward shape of the only solution demanded by the nature of the evils. A judicial tribunal, at any rate, should not contribute to such delusion.

The name of Justice should not be allowed to be invoked only for the prolongation of the pursuit of vindictive retaliation. The world is really in need of generous magnanimity and understanding charity. The real question arising in a genuinely anxious mind is, "can mankind grow up quickly enough to win the race between civilization and disaster?"

It is very true that "we must change our accustomed ways of thinking far more rapidly than we have ever had to change them before. We must begin systematically to reduce and eliminate all chief causes of war." Such causes do not lie in the war potentialities of a nation's industries. To look at the problem thus is only to visualize our present day problems as mere reproductions of old ones. We must not fail to realize that "they are in principle a new kind of problem. They are not merely national problems with world implications. They are indisputably world problems and humanity problems." We must cease to "grapple with these tremendous matters with the thought that they are only more complex reproductions of problems which have plagued us since 1914."

Let not "the implication of atomic explosion" fail to "spur men of judgment . . . . to seek a method whereby the peoples of the earth can live in peace and justice." But the course of action signified in the trial and punishment of the leaders of a defeated nation does not indicate much appreciation of this implication. Perhaps it has been truly said that "the turbulent emotions aroused by watching trials of hated enemy leaders . . . . will leave little room for consideration of the fundamentals of world union. . . ." "Public understanding of the real condition of peace would not be increased, but rather confused, by all the emphasis upon one detail, the trials. . . ."

The trials should not be allowed to use up the precious little thought that a peace-bound public may feel inclined to spare in order to find the way "to conquer the doubts and the fears, the ignorance and the greed, which made this horror possible." "The vindictive and oratorial pleas of the prosecutors in the language of emotionalized generalities did entertain rather than educate." We may not altogether ignore the possibility that perhaps the responsibility did not lie only with the defeated leaders. Perhaps the guilt of the leaders was only their misconception, probably founded on illusions. It may indeed be that such illusions were only egocentric. Yet we cannot overlook the fact that even as such egocentric illusions these are ingrained in human minds everywhere. It is very likely that "*When time shall have softened passion and prejudice, when* Reason *shall have stripped the mask from misrepresentation, then justice, holding evenly her scales, will require much of past censure and praise to change places.*"

HIROTA, DOHIHARA, AND KIDO *vs.* GENERAL MACARTHUR

Washington, D.C., December, 1948*

THE CHIEF JUSTICE, Mr. Justice REED, Mr. Justice FRANKFURTER, and Mr. Justice BURTON are of the Opinion that there is want of jurisdiction. U.S. Constitution, Article III, Sec. 2, Clause 2.

Mr. Justice JACKSON has filed a memorandum stating his views.

Mr. Justice JACKSON.

Four members of this Court feel that the Japanese convicted of war crimes should have some form of relief, at least tentative, from this Court. The votes of these are not enough to grant it but, if I refrain from voting, they constitute one-half of the sitting Court. As I understand it, these Justices do not commit themselves as to whether there is any constitutional power in this Court to entertain these proceedings but only feel that they would like to hear argument to enlighten them in reaching a determination of that issue. They feel it so strongly that they not only favored grant of relief in conference, but, having failed, announce their dissent to the public—an interested section of which consists of our late enemies and allies in the Orient. This perhaps is all that these Justices could do consistently with the course that they have already taken in several German cases. This is their right, and I point it out not to question the right but as one of the facts which confronts me in deciding my own course.

On the other hand, four other Justices are convinced, from their study of the question, that there is no constitutional jurisdiction whatever in this Court over the subject matter. To interfere and assume to review it would in that view constitute an unwarranted interference with delicate affairs that are in no way committed to the jurisdiction of this Court. These four Justices, having satisfied themselves that this Court is without lawful power, have consistently refused to take action which would usurp it, even tentatively, in the German cases. Of

*335 U.S. 876 (1948)

course, they could not consistently, with equal justice under law, apply a different jurisdictional rule to these cases than they have to those of the Germans.

By reason of nonparticipation in the German cases, for reasons which are obvious, I remain uncommitted on the jurisdictional issues. My nonparticipation has prevented their resolution heretofore and I must decide whether another nonparticipation will prevent it now. The issue transcends the particular litigation.

This public division of the Court, equal if I do not participate, puts the United States before the world, and particularly before Oriental peoples, in this awkward position: Having major responsibility for the capture of these Japanese prisoners, it also has considerable responsibility for their fate. If their plea ends in stalemate in this Court, the authorities have no course but to execute sentences which half of this Court tells the world are on so doubtful a legal foundation that they favor some kind of provisional relief and fuller review. The fact that such a number of men so placed in the United States are of that opinion would for all time be capitalized in the Orient, if not elsewhere, to impeach the good faith and to discredit the justice of this country, and to comfort its critics and enemies.

The other possible course is to assert tentatively a jurisdiction in this Court to stay and order hearings in these proceedings. This is likewise bound to embarrass the United States. On American initiative, under direction of the President as Commander-in-Chief, this country invited our Pacific allies, on foreign soil, to cooperate in conducting a grand inquest into the alleged crimes, including the war guilt, of these defendants. Whatever its real legal nature, it bears the outward appearance of an international enterprise, undertaken on our part under the war powers and control of foreign affairs vested in the Executive. For this Court now to call up these cases for judicial review under exclusively American law can only be regarded as a warning to our associates in the trials that no commitment of the President or of the military authorities, even in such matters as these, has finality or validity under our form of government until it has the approval of this Court. And since the Court's approval or disapproval cannot be known until after the event—usually long after—it would substantially handicap our country in asking other nations to rely upon the word or act of the President in affairs which only he is competent to conduct.

In this equal division each side's position is taken after long and frequent consideration and repeated public announcement in the German cases. The one group of Justices can hardly fail to proffer to the Japanese an opportunity to argue reviewability which they have consistently announced should be allowed to the Germans. Neither can the other side extend to the Japanese opportunities which they have consistently denied to the Germans. The fact that neither side in good grace can retreat puts to me disagreeable alternatives as to whether I should break the deadlock or permit it to continue.

I do not regard myself as under a legal disqualification in these Japanese cases under the usages as to disqualification which prevail in this Court. While I negotiated the international Charter under which the Nazi war criminals were tried and also represented the United States in that Four-Power trial, the Japanese were not tried under that Charter but under a later and, in respects relevant to the present controversy, a somewhat different charter, promulgated by different authority. Of course, I participated in formulating basic rules on the subject of war crimes. But it is not the custom of this Court that a Justice disqualifies from passing on a particular case because he actively participated as a Senator or Representative in making the law under which it was tried. Nor has it been considered necessary to disqualify himself because he had handled cases which involved the same law or crimes as those involved in the case before him. I have had no participation either in the basic decision to hold war crimes trials in the Orient or as to the manner in which they should be conducted. Nevertheless, I have been so identified with the subject of war crimes that, if it involved my personal preferences alone, I should not sit in this case.

But the issues here are truly great ones. They only involve decision of war crimes issues secondarily, for primarily the decision will establish or deny that this Court has power to review exercise of military power abroad and the President's conduct of external affairs of our Government. The answer will influence our Nation's reputation for continuity of policy for a long time to come. For these reasons I decided at Saturday's conference to break the tie in the Japanese cases. The horns between which I must choose in the dilemma are such, as I have pointed out, that it is a choice between evils. The reasons which guide me to a choice are these:

If I add my vote to those who favor denying these applications for want of jurisdiction, it is irrevocable. The Japanese will be executed and their partisans will forever point to the dissents of four members of the Court to support their accusation that the United States gave them less than justice. This stain, whether deserved or not, would be impressed upon the record of the United States in Oriental memory. If, however, I vote with those who would grant temporary relief, it may be that fuller argument and hearing will convert one or more of the Justices on one side or the other from the views that have equally divided them in the German cases. In those cases I did not feel at liberty to cast the deciding vote and there was no course to avoid leaving the question unresolved. But here I feel that a tentative assertion of jurisdiction, which four members of the Court believe does not exist, will not be irreparable if they ultimately are right. To let the sentences be executed against the dissent of four members will be irreparably injurious even if they are wrong, and if their minds are open, as it is understood, to further persuasion, I would not want to be responsible for eliminating even a faint chance of avoiding dissents in this matter. Our allies are more likely to understand and to forgive any assertion of excess jurisdiction against this background than our enemies would be to understand or condone any excess of scruple about jurisdiction to grant them a hearing.

It is fair to counsel to say that I intend to sit and hear argument at the hearing which I am voting to grant. I shall hope not to participate in the final decision but as to that, I reserve full freedom of decision.

For the present, it is enough that I vote with Justices BLACK, DOUGLAS, MURPHY and RUTLEDGE, who have consistently noted their dissent in war crimes cases, for whatever temporary restraints or writs they see fit to grant for the purpose of bringing on any hearings or arguments they want to hear as a basis for reaching their final decision on the merits. Needless to say, in doing this I express neither approval nor disapproval of the course they have taken and intimate no views on the constitutional issues involved. I have thought, however, that a candid disclosure of the considerations which influence me is due, not only to the litigants in these cases and to those in the previous German cases, but in justice to the Court and to myself.

Time is important in these cases. I notified the full Court of my position on December 4, as soon as I knew the positions others took on this case, in order that no delay may be chargeable to my indecisions. I hope these cases will now be set for the earliest possible hearing. I also indulge the hope that argument will produce a majority decision of the Court without further intervention from one who has been so identified with controversial phases of war crimes law that he cannot expect others to consider him as detached and dispassionate on the subject as he thinks himself to be.

PER CURIAM*

The petitioners, all residents and citizens of Japan, are being held in custody pursuant to the judgments of a military tribunal in Japan. Two of the petitioners have been sentenced to death, the others to terms of imprisonment. They filed motions in this Court for leave to file petitions for *habeas corpus*. We set all the motions for hearing on the question of our power to grant the relief prayed, 335 U.S. 876, and that issue has now been fully presented and argued.

We are satisfied that the tribunal sentencing these petitioners is not a tribunal of the United States. The United States and other allied countries conquered and now occupy and control Japan. General Douglas MacArthur has been selected and is acting as the Supreme Commander for the Allied Powers. The military tribunal sentencing these petitioners has been set up by General MacArthur as the agent of the Allied Powers.

Under the foregoing circumstances the courts of the United States have no power or authority to review, to affirm, set aside or annul the judgments and sentences imposed on these petitioners and for this reason the motions for leave to file petitions for writs of *habeas corpus* are denied.

*338 U.S. 197 (1949)

Mr. Justice DOUGLAS concurs in the result for reasons to be stated in an opinion.

See 338 U.S. 197.

Mr. Justice MURPHY dissents.

Mr. Justice RUTLEDGE reserves decision and the announcement of his vote until a later time.

Mr. Justice JACKSON took no part in the final decision on these motions.

Mr. Justice DOUGLAS, concurring.

These cases present new, important and difficult problems.

Petitioners are citizens of Japan. They were all high officials of the Japanese Government or officers of the Japanese Army during World War II. They are held in custody pursuant to a judgment of the International Military Tribunal for the Far East. They were found guilty by that tribunal of various so-called war crimes against humanity.

Petitioners at the time of argument of these cases were confined in Tokyo, Japan, under the custody of respondent Walker, Commanding General of the United States Eighth Army who held them pursuant to the orders of respondent MacArthur, Supreme Commander for the Allied Powers. Other respondents are the Chief of Staff of the United States Army, the Secretary of the Department of the Army, and the Secretary of Defense.

First. There is an important question of jurisdiction that lies at the threshold of these cases. Respondents contend that the Court is without power to issue a writ of *habeas corpus* in these cases. It is argued that the Court has no original jurisdiction as defined in Art. III, §2, CI. 2 of the Constitution, since these are not cases affecting an ambassador, public minister, or consul; nor is a State a party. And it is urged that appellate jurisdiction is absent (1) because military commissions do not exercise judicial power within the meaning of Art. III, §2 of the Constitution and hence are not agencies whose judgments are subject to review by the Court; and (2) no court of the United States to which the potential appellate jurisdiction of this Court extends has jurisdiction over this cause.

It is to the latter contention alone that consideration need be given. I think it is plain that a District Court of the United States does have jurisdiction to entertain petitions for *habeas corpus* to examine into the cause of the restraint of liberty of the petitioners.

The question now presented was expressly reserved in Ahrens v. Clark, 335 U.S. 188, 192, note 4, 68 S.Ct. 1443, 1444, 92 L.Ed. 1898. In that case aliens detained at Ellis Island sought to challenge by *habeas corpus* the legality of their detention in the District Court for the District of Columbia. It was argued that that court had jurisdiction because the Attorney General who was responsible for their custody was present there. We rejected that view, holding that it was the District Court where petitioners were confined that had jurisdiction to issue the writ. It is now argued that no District Court can act in these cases because if in one case their jurisdiction under the *habeas corpus* statute is limited to inquiries into the causes of restraints of liberty of those confined within the territorial jurisdictions of those courts, it is so limited in any other.

That result, however, does not follow. In Ahrens v. Clark, supra, we were dealing with the distribution of judicial power among the several District Courts. There was an explicit legislative history, indicating disapproval of a practice of moving prisoners from one district to another in order to grant them the hearings to which they are entitled. We held that the court at the place of confinement was the court to which application must be made. But it does not follow that where that place is not within the territorial jurisdiction of any District Court, judicial power to issue the writ is rendered impotent.

Habeas corpus is an historic writ and one of the basic safeguards of personal liberty. See Bowen v. Johnston, 306 U.S. 19, 26, 59 S.Ct. 442, 445, 83 L.Ed. 455. There is no room for niggardly restrictions when questions relating to its availability are raised. The statutes governing its use must be generously construed if the great office of the writ is not to be impaired. In Ahrens v. Clark, supra, denial of a remedy in one District Court was not a denial of a remedy in all of them. There was a District Court to which those petitioners could resort. But in these cases there is none if the jurisdiction of the District Court is in all respects restricted to cases of prisoners who are confined within their geographical boundaries.

Such a holding would have grave and alarming consequences. Today Japanese war lords appeal to the Court for application of American standards of justice. Tomorrow or next year an American citizen may stand condemned in Germany or Japan by a military court or commission. If no United States court can inquire into the lawfulness of his detention, the military have acquired, contrary to our traditions (see Ex parte Quirin, 317 U.S. 1, 63 S.Ct. 1, 87 L.Ed. 3; In re Yamashita, 327 U.S. 1, 66 S.Ct. 340, 90 L.Ed. 499) a new and alarming hold on us.

I cannot agree to such a grave and startling result. It has never been deemed essential that the prisoner in every case be within the territorial limits of the district where he seeks relief by way of *habeas corpus.* In Ex parte Mitsuye Endo, 323 U.S. 283, 304–306, 65 S.Ct. 208, 219–220, 89 L.Ed. 243, a prisoner had been removed, pending an appeal, from the district where the petition had been filed. We held that the District Court might act if there was a respondent within reach of its process who had custody of the prisoner. The aim of the statute is the practical administration of justice. The allocation of jurisdiction among the District Courts, recognized in Ahrens v. Clark, is a problem of judicial administration not a method of contracting the authority of the courts so as to delimit their power to issue the historic writ.

The place to try the issues of this case is in the district where there is a respondent who is responsible for the custody of petitioners. That district is obviously the District of Columbia. That result was reached by the Court of Appeals for the District of Columbia in Eisentrager v. Forrestal, D.C.Cir., 174 F. 2d 961. It held, in the case of a German national confined in Germany in the custody of the United States Army, that the court having jurisdiction over those who have directive power over the jailer outside the United States could issue the writ. In my view that is the correct result. For we would have to conclude that the United States Generals who have custody of petitioners are bigger than our government to hold that the respondent-officials of the War Department have no control or command over them. That result would raise grave constitutional questions, as Eisentrager v. Forrestal, supra, suggests.

It is therefore clear to me that the District Court of the District of Columbia is the court to hear these motions. The appropriate course would be to remit the parties to it, reserving any further questions until the cases come here by certiorari. But the Court is unwilling to take that course, apparently because it deems the cases so pressing and the issues so unsubstantial that the motions should be summarily disposed of.

Second. The Court in denying leave to file states:

"We are satisfied that the tribunal sentencing these petitioners is not a tribunal of the United States. The United States and other allied countries conquered and now occupy and control Japan. General Douglas MacArthur has been selected and is acting as the Supreme Commander for the Allied Powers. The military tribunal sentencing these petitioners has been set up by General MacArthur as the agent of the Allied Powers.

"Under the foregoing circumstances the courts of the United States have no power or authority to review, to affirm, set aside or annul the judgments and sentences imposed on these petitioners. . . ."

But that statement does not in my opinion adequately analyze the problem. The formula which it evolves to dispose of the cases is indeed potentially dangerous. It leaves practically no room for judicial scrutiny of this new type of military tribunal which is evolving. It leaves the power of those tribunals absolute. Prisoners held under its mandates may have appeal to the conscience or mercy of an executive; but they apparently have no appeal to law.

The fact that the tribunal has been set up by the Allied Powers should not of itself preclude our inquiry. Our inquiry is directed not to the conduct of the Allied Powers but to the conduct of our own officials. Our writ would run not to an official of an Allied Power but to our own official. We would want to know not what authority our Allies had to do what they did but what authority our officials had.

If an American General holds a prisoner, our process can reach him wherever he is. To that extent at least the Constitution follows the flag. It is no defense for him to say that he acts for the Allied Powers. He is an American citizen who is performing functions for our government. It is our Constitution which he supports and defends. If there is evasion or violation of its obligations, it is no defense that he acts for another nation. There is at present no group or confederation to which an official of this Nation owes a higher obligation than he owes to us.

I assume that we have no authority to review the judgment of an international tribunal. But if as a result of unlawful action, one of our Generals holds prisoner in his custody, the writ of *habeas corpus* can effect a release from that custody. It is the historic function of the writ to examine into the cause of restraint of liberty. We should not allow that inquiry to be thwarted merely because the jailer acts not only for the United States but for other nations as well.

Let me illustrate the gravity and seriousness of the conclusion of the Court.

(1) Suppose an American citizen collaborated with petitioners in plotting a war against the United States. The laws of the United States provide severe penalties for such conduct. May that citizen be tried and convicted by an international tribunal and have no access to our courts to challenge the legality of the action of our representatives on it? May he, in the face of the safeguards which our Constitution provides even for traitors, have no protection against American action against him?

(2) Suppose an American citizen on a visit to Japan during the occupation commits murder, embezzlement, or the like. May he be tried by an international tribunal and have no recourse to our courts to challenge its jurisdiction over him?

(3) What about any other civilian so tried and convicted for such a crime committed during the occupation?

These are increasingly important questions as collaboration among nations at the international level continues. They pose questions for which there is no precedent. But we sacrifice principle when we stop our inquiry once we ascertain that the tribunal is international.

I cannot believe that we would adhere to that formula if these petitioners were American citizens. I cannot believe we would adhere to it if this tribunal or some other tribunal were trying American citizens for offenses committed either before or during the occupation. In those cases we would, I feel, look beyond the character of the tribunal to the persons being tried and the offenses with which they were charged. We would ascertain whether, so far as American participation is concerned, there was authority to try the defendants for the precise crimes with which they are charged. That is what we should do here.

(1) General Douglas MacArthur is the Supreme Commander for the Allied Powers. The Potsdam Declaration (July 26, 1945) provided for occupation of Japan by the Allies. The Instrument of Surrender (September 2, 1945) accepted the terms of the Potsdam Declaration. By the Moscow Agreement (December 27, 1945) the Supreme Commander was recognized as "the sole executive authority for the Allied Powers in Japan." It also established a Far Eastern Commission composed of representatives of eleven nations. It was vested with broad powers (a) to formulate policies, principles and standards by which Japan will fulfill its obligations under the Terms of Surrender and (b) to review directives issued to the Supreme Commander or any action taken by him involving policy decisions within its jurisdiction. All directives embodying policy

decisions of the Commission are to be prepared by the United States and it transmits them to the Supreme Commander. And the Commission is enjoined to respect "the chain of command from the United States Government to the Supreme Commander and the Supreme Commander's command of occupation forces."

The war crimes policy of the Allied Powers as respects Japan seems to have been first suggested in the Cairo Declaration (December 1, 1943). The Potsdam Declaration promised that "stern justice" would be meted out "to all war criminals."

The Far Eastern Commission on April 3, 1946, adopted a policy decision which defined "war crimes" as including "Planning, preparation, initiation or waging of a war of aggression or a war in violation of international treaties, agreements and assurances, or participation in a common plan or conspiracy for the accomplishment of any of the foregoing." It provided that the Supreme Commander for the Allied Powers should have power to appoint special international military courts to try war criminals. Prior to this time the Supreme Commander had constituted a court for that purpose and had appointed judges from various nations to it. On receipt of the directive based on the Commission's war crimes policy decision he provided a new court—the one before which petitioners were tried. To this court the Supreme Commander appointed from names submitted by the respective nations eleven judges—one each from the United States, China, United Kingdom, Russia, Australia, Canada, France, The Netherlands, New Zealand, India, and the Philippines.

So I think there can be no serious doubt that though the arrangement is in many respects amorphous and though the tribunal is dominated by American influence it is nonetheless international in character. But it should be noted that the chain of command from the United States to the Supreme Commander is unbroken. It is he who has custody of petitioners. It is through that chain of command that the writ of *habeas corpus* can reach the Supreme Commander.

(2) The Constitution gives Congress the power to define and punish "Offenses against the Law of Nations . . . ." Art. I, §8, Cl. 10. It is argued that Congress here has not made aggressive war a crime nor provided individual punishment for waging it. It is therefore argued that these petitioners cannot be tried by United States officials for any such crime. We do not need to consider a case where the definition given by Congress conflicts with what a President does. There is no conflict here. The grant of power to the Congress does not necessarily preclude exercise of authority by the President. The Constitution makes the President the "Commander in Chief of the Army and Navy of the United States . . . ." Art. II, §2. His power as such is vastly greater than that of troop commander. He not only has full power to repel and defeat the enemy; he has the power to occupy the conquered country, New Orleans v. Steamship Co., 20 Wall. 387, 394, 22 L.Ed. 354, and to punish those enemies who violated the law of war. Ex parte Quirin, supra, 317 U.S. at pages 28–29, 63 S.Ct. at pages 10–11, 87 L.Ed. 3; In re Yamashita, supra, 327

U.S. at pages 10–11, 66 S.Ct. at page 345, 90 L.Ed. 499. We need not consider to what extent, if any, the President, in providing that justice be meted out to a defeated enemy, would have to follow as he did in Ex parte Quirin, supra, and In re Yamashita, supra, the procedure that Congress had prescribed for such cases. Here the President did not utilize the conventional military tribunals provided for by the Articles of War. He did not act alone but only in conjunction with the allied Powers. This tribunal was an international one arranged for through negotiation with the Allied Powers.

The President is the sole organ of the United States in the field of foreign relations. See United States v. Curtiss-Wright Corp., 299 U.S. 304, 318–321, 57 S.Ct. 216, 220–221, 81 L.Ed. 255. Agreements which he has made with our Allies in furtherance of our war efforts have been legion. Whether they are wise or unwise, necessary or improvident are political questions, not justiciable ones. That is particularly true of questions relating to the commencement and conduct of the war. Agreement with foreign nations for the punishment of war criminals, insofar as it involves aliens who are the officials of the enemy or members of its armed services, is a part of the prosecution of the war. It is a furtherance of the hostilities directed to a dilution of enemy power and involving retribution for wrongs done. It falls as clearly in the realm of political decisions as all other aspects of military alliances in furtherance of the common objective of victory. Cf. Georgia v. Stanton, 6 Wall. 50, 71, 18 L.Ed. 721.

After the escape of Napoleon from Elba where he had voluntarily retired, he was by agreement among the Powers entrusted to the custody of Great Britain. Then followed his banishment to St. Helena. I have no doubt that our President could have done the same as respects these petitioners. Or he could have made arrangements with other nations for their custody and detention. When the President moves to make arrangements with other nations for their trial, he acts in a political role on a military matter. His discretion cannot be reviewed by the judiciary.

The political nature of the decision which brought these petitioners before the International Military Tribunal is emphasized by the rulings which that tribunal made. The Charter of the Tribunal was constituted by an order of the Supreme Commander. It established the tribunal, determined its procedure, and described its jurisdiction. It described the "crimes" that came within the jurisdiction of the tribunal and the standard of responsibility of the accused.

Justice Pal of India who dissented from the judgments of conviction claimed that the Allied Powers as victors did not have the legal right under international law to treat petitioners as war criminals. He wrote at length, contending that the Pact of Paris, 46 Stat. 2343, to which Japan was a signatory, did not affect the pre-existing legal position of war in international life. He rejected the argument that international customary law had developed under the Pact, or that there was individual responsibility for the waging of aggressive war even assuming it to be a crime under international law.

He called on the Tribunal to rule on these questions. He stated: "We have been set up as an International Military Tribunal. The clear intention is that we are to be 'a judicial tribunal' and not 'a manifestation of power.' The intention is that we are to act as a court of law and act under international law. We are to find out, by the application of the appropriate rules of international law, whether the acts constitute any crime under the already existing law, *dehors* the Declaration, the Agreement or, the Charter. Even if the Charter, the Agreement or the Declaration schedules them as crimes, it would only be the decision of the relevant authorities that they are crimes under the already existing law. But the Tribunal must come to its own decision. It was never intended to bind the Tribunal by the decision of these bodies, for otherwise the Tribunal will not be a 'judicial tribunal' but a mere tool for the manifestation of power.

"The so-called trial held according to the definition of crime *now* given by the victors obliterates the centuries of civilization which stretch between us and the summary slaying of the defeated in a war. A trial with law thus prescribed will only be a sham employment of legal process for the satisfaction of a thirst for revenge. It does not correspond to any idea of justice. Such a trial may justly create the feeling that the setting up of a tribunal like the present is much more a political than a legal affair, an essentially political objective having thus been cloaked by a juridical appearance. Formalized vengeance can bring only an ephemeral satisfaction, with every probability of ultimate regret; but vindication of law through *genuine legal process* alone may contribute substantially to the re-establishment of order and decency in international relations."

But the Tribunal, though expressing disagreement with Justice Pal on the point, did not rule on the question. It ruled that "the law of the Charter is decisive and binding" upon it. It said: "This is a special tribunal set up by the Supreme Commander under authority conferred on him by the Allied Powers. It derives its jurisdiction from the Charter. In this trial its members have no jurisdiction except such as is to be found in the Charter. The Order of the Supreme Commander, which appointed the members of the Tribunal, states: "The responsibilities, powers, and duties of the members of the Tribunal are set forth in the Charter thereof. . . . In the result, the members of the Tribunal, being otherwise wholly without power in respect to the trial of the accused, have been empowered by the documents, which constituted the Tribunal and appointed them as members, to try the accused but subject always to the duty and responsibility of applying to the trial the law set forth in the Charter."

The President of the Tribunal, Sir William Flood Webb of Australia, in a separate opinion stated:

"The Charter is binding as it is International Law, the Potsdam Declaration and the Instrument of Surrender put into operation by the martial law of the Supreme Commander of the Allied Powers in occupation of Japan.

"The Supreme Commander stated in his proclamation of the Tribunal and Charter—the martial law referred to—that he acted in order to implement the term of surrender that stern justice should be meted out to war criminals.

* * *

"Under International Law belligerents have the right to punish during the war such war criminals as fall into their hands. The right accrues after occupation of the enemy territory. As a condition of the armistice a victorious belligerent may require the defeated state to hand over persons accused of war crimes. The Potsdam Declaration and the Instrument of Surrender contemplate the exercise of this right. But guilt must be ascertained before punishment is imposed; hence the provision for trials.

"The occupying belligerent may set up military courts to try persons accused of war crimes; and to assure a fair trial may provide among other things for civilian judges, the right of appeal, and publicity. (Oppenheim on International Law, 6th Edn. Vol. II, p. 456.)"

The conclusion is therefore plain that the Tokyo Tribunal acted as an instrument of military power of the Executive branch of government. It responded to the will of the Supreme Commander as expressed in the military order by which he constituted it. It took its law from its creator and did not act as a free and independent tribunal to adjudge the rights of petitioners under international law. As Justice Pal said, it did not therefore sit as a judicial tribunal. It was solely an instrument of political power. Insofar as American participation is concerned, there is no constitutional objection to that action. For the capture and control of those who were responsible for the Pearl Harbor incident was a political question on which the President as Commander-in-Chief, and as spokesman for the nation in foreign affairs, had the final say.

THE JUSTICE CASE

Nuremberg, December, 1947*

Opinion and Judgment of United States Military Tribunal at Nuremberg in United States *vs.* Josef Altstoetter, et al.

Military Tribunal III was established on 14 February 1947 under General Order No. 11, issued by command of the United States Military Governor for Germany. The indictment was filed with the Secretary General of Military Tribunals on 4 January 1947, and the case was assigned to Tribunal III for trial. A copy of the indictment in the German language was served upon each defendant at least 30 days before the commencement of the trial. The defendants were arraigned on 17 February 1947, each defendant entering a plea of "not guilty" to all charges preferred against him. German counsel selected by the defendants were approved by the Tribunal and have represented the respective defendants throughout the trial.

The presentation of evidence in support of the charges was commenced on 6 March 1947 and was followed by evidence for the defendants. The taking of evidence was concluded on 13 October 1947. Copies of the exhibits tendered by the prosecution were furnished in the German language to the defendants prior to the time of the reception of the exhibits in evidence. The Tribunal has heard the oral testimony of 138 witnesses. In addition it has received 641 documentary exhibits for the prosecution and 1,452 for defendants, many of them of considerable length. Some affidavits have been presented by the prosecution, but they are few in comparison with the hundreds offered by the defense.

Whenever possible, and in substantially all cases, applications of defense counsel for the production in open court of persons who had made affidavits in support of the prosecution have been granted and the affiants have appeared for cross-examination. Affiants for the defense were cross-examined orally by the prosecution in comparatively few cases.

The defendant Carl Westphal died before the commencement of the trial.

* *Trial of War Criminals,* Vol. 3, p. 954 (Washington, D.C., 1947).

On 22 August 1947, the Tribunal entered an order declaring a mistrial as to the defendant, Karl Engert, who has been able to attend court for only 2 days since 5 March 1947. The action was rendered necessary under the provisions of article IV (*d*) of Military Government Ordinance No. 7, and by reason of the serious and continuing illness of said defendant.

The trial was conducted in two languages with simultaneous translations of German into English and English into German throughout the proceedings.

* * *

The trial has been continued before the Tribunal as thus reconstituted. The evidence has been submitted, final arguments of counsel have been concluded, and the Tribunal has heard a personal statement from each defendant who desired to address it.

In rendering this judgment it should be said that the case against the defendants is chiefly based upon captured German documents, the authenticity of which is unchallenged.

The indictment contains four counts, as follows:

(1) Conspiracy to commit war crimes and crimes against humanity. The charge embraces the period between January 1933 and April 1945.

(2) War crimes, to wit: violations of the laws and customs of war, alleged to have been committed between September 1939 and April 1945.

(3) Crimes against humanity as defined by Control Council Law No. 10, alleged to have been committed between September 1939 and April 1945.

(4) Membership of certain defendants in organizations which have been declared to be criminal by the judgment of the International Military Tribunal in the case against Goering, et al.

The sufficiency of count one of the indictment was challenged by the defendants upon jurisdictional grounds, and on 11 July 1947, the Tribunal made and entered the following order:

> Count one of the indictment in this case charges that the defendants, acting pursuant to a common design, unlawfully, willfully and knowingly did conspire and agree together to commit war crimes and crimes against humanity as defined in Control Council Law No. 10, article II. It is charged that the alleged crime was committed between January 1933 and April 1945.
>
> It is the ruling of this Tribunal that neither the Charter of the International Military Tribunal nor Control Council Law No. 10 has defined conspiracy to commit a war crime or crime against humanity as a separate substantive crime; therefore, this Tribunal has no jurisdiction to try any defendant upon a charge of conspiracy considered as a separate substantive offense.
>
> Count one of the indictment, in addition to the separate charge of conspiracy, also alleged unlawful participation in the formulation and execution of plans to commit war crimes and crimes against humanity which actually involved the commission of such crimes. We, therefore, cannot properly strike the whole of count one from the indictment, but, in so far as count one charges the commission of the alleged crime of conspiracy as a separate substantive offense, distinct from any war crime or crime against humanity, the Tribunal will disregard that charge.

This ruling must not be construed as limiting the force or effect of article II, paragraph 2, of Control Council Law No. 10, or as denying to either prosecution or defense the right to offer in evidence any facts or circumstances occurring either before or after September 1939, if such facts or circumstances tend to prove or to disprove the commission by any defendant of war crimes or crimes against humanity as defined in Control Council Law No. 10.

* * *

Source of Authority of C.C. Law 10

Having identified the instruments which purport to establish the jurisdiction of this Tribunal, we next consider the legal basis of those instruments. The unconditional surrender of Germany took place on 8 May 1945. The surrender was preceded by the complete disintegration of the central government and was followed by the complete occupation of all of Germany. There were no opposing German forces in the field; the officials who during the war had exercised the powers of the Reich Government were either dead, in prison, or in hiding. On 5 June 1945 the Allied Powers announced that they "hereby assume supreme authority with respect to Germany, including all the powers possessed by the German Government, the High Command, and any state, municipal or local government or authority," and declared that "there is no central government or authority in Germany capable of accepting responsibility for the maintenance of order, the administration of the country, and compliance with the requirements of the victorious powers." The Four Powers further declared that they "will hereafter determine the boundaries of Germany or any part thereof and the status of Germany or of any area at present being a part of German territory."

On 2 August 1945 at Berlin, President Truman, Generalissimo Stalin, and Prime Minister Attlee, as heads of the Allied Powers, entered into a written agreement setting forth the principles which were to govern Germany during the initial control period. Reference to that document will disclose the wide scope of authority and control which was assumed and exercised by the Allied Powers. They assumed "supreme authority" and declared that it was their purpose to accomplish complete demilitarization of Germany; to destroy the National Socialist Party, to prevent Nazi propaganda; to abolish all Nazi laws which "established discrimination on grounds of race, creed, or political opinion . . . whether legal, administrative, or otherwise;" to control education; to reorganize the judicial system in accordance with the principles of democracy and of equal rights; to accomplish the decentralization of the political structure. The agreement provided that "for the time being no central German government shall be established." In the economic field they assumed control of "German industry and all economic and financial international transactions." Finally, the Allies reaffirmed their intention to bring the Nazi war criminals to swift and sure justice.

It is this fact of the complete disintegration of the government in Germany, followed by unconditional surrender and by occupation of the territory, which explains and justifies the assumption and exercise of supreme governmental power by the Allies. The same fact distinguishes the present occupation of Germany from the type of occupation which occurs when, in the course of actual warfare, an invading army enters and occupies the territory of another state, whose government is still in existence and is in receipt of international recognition, and whose armies, with those of its allies, are still in the field. In the latter case the occupying power is subject to the limitations imposed upon it by the Hague Convention and by the laws and customs of war. In the former case (the occupation of Germany) the Allied Powers were not subject to those limitations. By reason of the complete breakdown of government, industry, agriculture, and supply, they were under an imperative humanitarian duty of far wider scope to reorganize government and industry and to foster local democratic governmental agencies throughout the territory.

* * *

We have considered it proper to set forth our views concerning the nature and source of the authority of C. C. Law 10 in its aspect as substantive legislation. It would have been possible to treat that law as a binding rule regardless of the righteousness of its provisions, but its justification must ultimately depend upon accepted principles of justice and morality, and we are not content to treat the statute as a mere rule of thumb to be blindly applied. We shall shortly demonstrate that the IMT Charter and C. C. Law 10 provide for the punishment of crimes against humanity. As set forth in the indictment, the acts charged as crimes against humanity were committed before the occupation of Germany. They were described as racial persecutions by Nazi officials perpetrated upon German nationals. The crime of genocide is an illustration. We think that a tribunal charged with the duty of enforcing these rules will do well to consider, in determining the degree of punishment to be imposed, the moral principles which underlie the exercise of power. For that reason we have contrasted the situation when Germany was in belligerent occupation of portions of Poland, with the situation existing under the Four-Power occupation of Germany since the surrender. The occupation of Poland by Germany was in every sense belligerent occupation, precarious in character, while opposing armies were still in the field. The German occupation of Poland was subject to the limitations imposed by the Hague Convention and the laws and customs of land warfare. In view of these limitations we doubt if any person would contend that Germany, during that belligerent occupation, could lawfully have provided tribunals for the punishment of Polish officials who, before the occupation by Germany, had persecuted their own people, to wit: Polish nationals. Now the Four Powers are providing by C. C. Law 10 for the punishment of German officials who, before the occupation of Germany, passed and enforced laws for the persecution of German nationals upon racial grounds. It appears that it would be equally difficult to justify such action of the Four Powers if the situation here were the same as the situation which existed in Poland under German occupation and if consequently the limitations of the Hague Convention were applicable. For this reason it seems appropriate to point out the distinction between the two situations. As we have attempted to show, the moral and legal justification under principles of international law which authorizes the broader scope of authority under C. C. Law 10 is based on the fact that the Four Powers are not now in belligerent occupation or subject to the limitations set forth in the rules of land warfare. Rather, they have justly and legally assumed the broader task in Germany which they have solemnly defined and declared, to wit: the task of reorganizing the German Government and economy and of punishing persons who, prior to the occupation, were guilty of crimes against humanity committed against their own nationals. We have pointed out that this difference in the nature of the occupations is due to the unconditional surrender of Germany and the ensuing chaos which required the Four Powers to assume provisional supreme authority throughout the German Reich. We are not attempting to pass judicially upon a question which is solely within the jurisdiction of the political departments of the Four Powers. The fixing of the date of the formal end of the war and similar matters will, of course, be dependent upon the action of the political departments. We do not usurp their function. We merely inquire, in the course of litigation when the lives of men are dependent upon decisions which must be both legal and just, whether the great objectives announced by the Four Powers are themselves in harmony with the principles of international law and morality.

In declaring that the expressed determination of the victors to punish German officials who slaughtered their own nationals is in harmony with international principles of justice, we usurp no power; we only take judicial notice of the declarations already made by the chief executives of the United States and her former Allies. The fact that C. C. Law 10 on its face is limited to the punishment of German criminals does not transform this Tribunal into a German court. The fact that the four powers are exercising supreme legislative authority in governing Germany and for the punishment of German criminals does not mean that the jurisdiction of this Tribunal rests in the slightest degree upon any German law, prerogative, or sovereignty. We sit as a Tribunal drawing its sole power and jurisdiction from the will and command of the Four occupying Powers.

Examination will disclose that C. C. Law 10 possesses a dual aspect. In its first aspect and on its face it purports to be a statute defining crimes and providing for the punishment of persons who violate its provisions. It is the legislative product of the only body in existence having and exercising general lawmaking power throughout the Reich. The first International Military Tribunal in the case against Goering, et al., recognized similar provisions of the IMT Charter as binding legislative enactments. We quote:

> The making of the Charter was the exercise of the sovereign legislative power by the countries to which the German Reich unconditionally surrendered; and the

undoubted right of these countries to legislate for the occupied territories has been recognized by the civilized world.

These provisions are binding upon the Tribunal *as the law to be applied to the case.*

Since the IMT Charter and C. C. Law 10 are the products of legislative action by an international authority, it follows of necessity that there is no national constitution of any one state which could be invoked to invalidate the substantive provisions of such international legislation. It can scarcely be argued that a court which owes its existence and jurisdiction solely to the provisions of a given statute could assume to exercise that jurisdiction and then, in the exercise thereof, declare invalid the act to which it owes its existence. Except as an aid to construction, we cannot and need not go behind the statute. This was discussed authoritatively by the first International Military Tribunal in connection with the contention of defendants that the IMT Charter was invalid because it partook of the nature of *ex post facto* legislation. That Tribunal said: "The Charter makes the planning or waging of a war of aggression or a war in violation of international treaties a crime; and it is, therefore, not strictly necessary to consider whether and to what extent aggressive war was a crime before the execution of the London Agreement."

As recently said by an American authority: The Charter was, of course, binding upon the Tribunal in the same way that a constitutional statute would bind a domestic court.

In its aspect as a statute defining crime and providing punishment the limited purpose of C. C. Law 10 is clearly set forth. It is an exercise of supreme legislative power in and for Germany. It does not purport to establish by legislative act any new crimes of international applicability. The London Agreement refers to the trial of "those German officers and men and members of the Nazi Party who have been responsible for . . . atrocities." C. C. Law 10 recites that it was enacted to establish a "uniform legal basis in Germany" for the prosecution of war criminals.

Military Government Ordinance No. 7 was enacted pursuant to the powers of the Military Government for the United States Zone of Occupation "within Germany."

We concur in the view expressed by the first International Military Tribunal as quoted above, but we observe that the decision was supported on two grounds. The Tribunal in that case did not stop with the declaration that it was bound by the IMT Charter as an exercise of sovereign legislative power. The opinion went on to show that the IMT Charter was also "the expression of international law existing at the time of its creation." All of the war crimes and many, if not all, of the crimes against humanity as charged in the indictment in the case at bar were, as we shall show, violative of preexisting principles of international law. To the extent to which this is true, C. C. Law 10 may be deemed to be a codification rather than original substantive legislation. Insofar as C. C. Law 10 may be thought to go beyond established principles of international law, its authority, of course, rests upon the exercise of the "sovereign legislative power" of the countries to which the German Reich unconditionally surrendered.

We have discussed C. C. Law 10 in its first aspect as substantive legislation. We now consider its other aspect. Entirely aside from its character as substantive legislation, C. C. Law 10, together with Ordinance No. 7, provides procedural means previously lacking for the enforcement within Germany of certain rules of international law which exist throughout the civilized world independently of any new substantive legislation. (Ex parte Quirin, 317 U.S. 1; 87 L. ed. 3; 63 S. Ct. 2.) International law is not the product of statute. Its content is not static. The absence from the world of any governmental body authorized to enact substantive rules of international law has not prevented the progressive development of that law. After the manner of the English common law it has grown to meet the exigencies of changing conditions.

It must be conceded that the circumstance which gives to principles of international conduct the dignity and authority of law is their general acceptance as such by civilized nations, which acceptance is manifested by international treaties, conventions, authoritative textbooks, practice, and judicial decisions.

It does not, however, follow from the foregoing statements that general acceptance of a rule of international conduct must be manifested by express adoption thereof by all civilized states.

* * *

For the reasons stated by Lord Wright, this growth by accretion has been greatly accelerated since the First World War. The IMT Charter, the IMT judgment, and C. C. Law 10 are merely "great new cases in the book of international law." They constitute authoritative recognition of principles of individual penal responsibility in international affairs which, as we shall show, had been developing for many years. Surely C. C. Law 10, which was enacted by the authorized representatives of the four greatest Powers on earth, is entitled to judicial respect when it states, "Each of the following acts is recognized as a crime." Surely the requisite international approval and acquiescence is established when 23 states, including all of the great powers, have approved the London Agreement and the IMT Charter without dissent from any state. Surely the IMT Charter must be deemed declaratory of the principles of international law in view of its recognition as such by the General Assembly of the United Nations. We quote:

> The General Assembly recognizes the obligation laid upon it by article 13, paragraph 1 (a) of the Charter, to initiate studies and make recommendations for the purpose of encouraging the progressive development of international law and its codification;
>
> Takes note of the agreement for the establishment of an International Military Tribunal for the prosecution and punishment of the major war criminals of the European Axis, signed in London on 8 August 1945, and of the Charter

annexed thereto and of the fact that similar principles have been adopted in the Charter of the International Military Tribunal for the trial of the major war criminals in the Far East, proclaimed at Tokyo on 19 January 1946;
Therefore—

Affirms the principles of international law recognized by the Charter of the Nuernberg Tribunal and the judgment of the Tribunal;

Directs the Committee on Codification of International Law established by the resolution of the General Assembly of . . . December 1946, to treat as a matter of primary importance plans for the formulation, in the text of a general codification of offenses against the peace and security of mankind, or of an International Criminal Code, of the principles recognized in the Charter of the Nuernberg Tribunal and in the judgment of the Tribunal.

Before the International Military Tribunal had convened for the trial of Goering, et al., the opinion had been expressed that through the process of accretion the provisions of the IMT Charter and consequently of C. C. Law 10 had already, in large measure, become incorporated into the body of international law. . . .

We are empowered to determine the guilt or innocence of persons accused of acts described as "war crimes" and "crimes against humanity" under rules of international law. At this point, in connection with cherished doctrines of national sovereignty, it is important to distinguish between the rules of common international law which are of universal and superior authority on the one hand, and the provisions for enforcement of those rules which are by no means universal on the other. As to the superior authority of international law, we quote:

> If there exists a body of international law, which states, from a sense of legal obligation do in fact observe in their relations with each other, and which they are unable individually to alter or destroy, that law must necessarily be regarded as the law of each political entity deemed to be a state, and as prevailing throughout places under its control. This is true although there be no local affirmative action indicating the adoption by the individual state of international law.
>
> International law, as the local law of each state, is necessarily superior to any administrative regulation or statute or public act at variance with it. There can be no conflict on an equal plane.

This universality and superiority of international law does not necessarily imply universality of its enforcement. As to the punishment of persons guilty of violating the laws and customs of war (war crimes in the narrow sense), it has always been recognized that tribunals may be established and punishment imposed by the state into whose hands the perpetrators fall. These rules of international law were recognized as paramount, and jurisdiction to enforce them by the injured belligerent government, whether within the territorial boundaries of the state or in occupied territory, has been unquestioned. (*Ex parte Quirin, supra;* In re: Yamashita, 327 U.S. 1, 90 L. ed.) However, enforcement of international law has been traditionally subject to practical limitations. Within the territorial boundaries of a state having a recognized, functioning government presently in the exercise of sovereign power throughout its territory, a violator of the rules of international law could be punished only by the authority of the officials of that state. The law is universal, but such a state reserves unto itself the exclusive power within its boundaries to apply or withhold sanctions. Thus, notwithstanding the paramount authority of the substantive rules of common international law, the doctrines of national sovereignty have been preserved through the control of enforcement machinery. It must be admitted that Germans were not the only ones who were guilty of committing war crimes; other violators of international law could, no doubt, be tried and punished by the state of which they were nationals, by the offended state if it can secure jurisdiction of the person, or by an international tribunal if of competent authorized jurisdiction.

Applying these principles, it appears that the power to punish violators of international law in Germany is not solely dependent on the enactment of rules of substantive penal law applicable only in Germany. Nor is the apparent immunity from prosecution of criminals in other states based on the absence there of the rules of international law which we enforce here. Only by giving consideration to the extraordinary and temporary situation in Germany can the procedure here be harmonized with established principles of national sovereignty. In Germany an international body (the Control Council) has assumed and exercised the power to establish judicial machinery for the punishment of those who have violated the rules of the common international law, a power which no international authority without consent could assume or exercise within a state having a national government presently in the exercise of its sovereign powers.

Construction of C. C. Law 10 War Crimes and Crimes Against Humanity

We next approach the problem of the construction of C. C. Law 10, for whatever the scope of international common law may be, the power to enforce it in this case is defined and limited by the terms of the jurisdictional act.

The first penal provision of C. C. Law No. 10, with which we are concerned is as follows:

Article II

1.—Each of the following acts is recognized as a crime:

* * *

(*b*) *War Crimes.* Atrocities or offences against persons or property constituting violations of the laws or customs of war, including but not limited to, murder, ill treatment or deportation to slave labour or for any other purpose, of civilian population from occupied territory, murder or ill treatment of prisoners of war or persons on the seas, killing of hostages, plunder of public or private property, wanton destruction of cities, towns or villages, or devastation not justified by military necessity.

Here we observe the controlling effect of common international law as such, for the statutes by which we are governed have adopted and incorporated the rules of international law as the rules by which war crimes are to be identified. This legislative practice by which the laws or customs of war are incorporated by reference into a statute is not unknown in the United States. (See cases cited in *Ex parte Quirin, supra.*)

* * *

It is therefore clear that the intent of the statute on crimes against humanity is to punish for persecutions and the like, whether in accord with or in violation of the domestic laws of the country where perpetrated, to wit: Germany. The intent was to provide that compliance with German law should be no defense. Article III of C. C. Law 10 clearly demonstrates that acts by Germans against German nationals may constitute crimes against humanity within the jurisdiction of this Tribunal to punish. That article provides that each occupying authority within its zone of occupation shall have the right to cause persons suspected of having committed a crime to be arrested and "(*d*) shall have the right to cause all persons so arrested . . . to be brought to trial . . . . Such Tribunal may, in the case of crimes committed by persons of German citizenship or nationality against other persons of German citizenship or nationality, or stateless persons, be a German court, if authorized by the occupying authorities."

As recently asserted by General Telford Taylor before Tribunal IV, in the case of the United States *vs.* Flick, et al.:

> This constitutes an explicit recognition that acts committed by Germans against other Germans are punishable as crimes under Law No. 10, according to the definitions contained therein, since only such crimes may be tried by German courts, in the discretion of the occupying power. If the occupying power fails to authorize German courts to try crimes committed by Germans against other Germans (and in the American Zone of Occupation no such authorization has been given), then these cases are tried only before non-German tribunals, such as these military tribunals.

Our jurisdiction to try persons charged with crimes against humanity is limited in scope, both by definition and illustration, as appears from C. C. Law 10. It is not the isolated crime by a private German individual which is condemned, nor is it the isolated crime perpetrated by the German Reich through its officers against a private individual. It is significant that the enactment employs the words "against any civilian population" instead of "against any civilian individual." The provision is directed against offenses and inhumane acts and persecutions on political, racial, or religious grounds systematically organized and conducted by or with the approval of government.

The opinion of the first International Military Tribunal in the case against Goering, et al., lends support to our conclusion. That opinion recognized the distinction between war crimes and crimes against humanity, and said:

> . . . insofar as the inhumane acts charged in the indictment, and committed after the beginning of the war, did not constitute war crimes, they were all committed in execution of, or in connection with, the aggressive war, and therefore constituted crimes against humanity.

The evidence to be later reviewed establishes that certain inhumane acts charged in count three of the indictment were committed in execution of, and in connection with, aggressive war and were therefore crimes against humanity even under the provisions of the IMT Charter, but it must be noted that C. C. Law 10 differs materially from the Charter. The latter defines crimes against humanity as inhumane acts, etc., committed, "in execution of, or in connection with, any crime within the jurisdiction of the tribunal," whereas in C. C. Law 10 the words last quoted are deliberately omitted from the definition.

The Ex Post Facto Principle

The defendants claim protection under the principle *nullum crimen sine lege,* though they withheld from others the benefit of that rule during the Hitler regime. Obviously the principle in question constitutes no limitation upon the power or right of the Tribunal to punish acts which can properly be held to have been violations of international law when committed. By way of illustration, we observe that C. C. Law 10, article II, paragraph 1 (*b*), *"War Crimes,"* has by reference incorporated the rules by which war crimes are to be identified. In all such cases it remains only for the Tribunal, after the manner of the common law, to determine the content of those rules under the impact of changing conditions.

Whatever view may be held as to the nature and source of our authority under C. C. Law 10 and under common international law, the *ex post facto* rule, properly understood, constitutes no legal nor moral barrier to prosecution in this case.

Under written constitutions the *ex post facto* rule condemns statutes which define as criminal, acts committed before the law was passed, but the *ex post facto* rule cannot apply in the international field as it does under constitutional mandate in the domestic field. Even in the domestic field the prohibition of the rule does not apply to the decisions of common law courts, though the question at issue be novel. International law is not the product of statute for the simple reason that there is as yet no world authority empowered to enact statutes of universal application. International law is the product of multipartite treaties, conventions, judicial decisions and customs which have received international acceptance or acquiescence. It would be sheer absurdity to suggest that the *ex post facto* rule, as known to constitutional states, could be applied to a treaty, a custom, or a common law decision of an international tribunal, or to the international acquiescence which follows the event. To have attempted to apply the *ex post facto* principle to judicial decisions of common international law would have been to strangle that law at birth. As applied in the field of international law, the principle *nullum crimen sine lege* received its true interpretation in the opinion of the IMT in the case versus Goering, et al. The question arose with reference to crimes against the peace, but the opinion expressed is equally applicable to war crimes and crimes against humanity. The Tribunal said:

> In the first place, it is to be observed that the maxim *nullum crimen sine lege* is not a limitation of sovereignty, but is in general a principle of justice. To assert that it is unjust to punish those who in defiance of treaties and assurances have attacked neighboring states without warning is obviously untrue, for in such circumstances the attacker must know that he is doing wrong, and so far from it being unjust to punish him, it would be unjust if his wrong were allowed to go unpunished.

To the same effect we quote the distinguished statesman and international authority, Henry L. Stimson—

> A mistaken appeal to this principle has been the cause of much confusion about the Nuremberg trial. It is argued that parts of the Tribunal's Charter, written in 1945, make crimes out of what before were activities beyond the scope of national and international law. Were this an exact statement of the situation we might well be concerned, but it is not. It rests on a misconception of the whole nature of the law of nations. International law is not a body of authoritative codes or statutes; it is the gradual expression, case by case, of the moral judgements of the civilized world. As such, it corresponds precisely to the common law of Anglo-American tradition. We can understand the law of Nuremberg only if we see it for what it is—a great new case in the book of international law, and not a formal enforcement of codified statutes. A look at the charges will show what I mean.
>
> It was the Nazi confidence that we would never chase and catch them, and not a misunderstanding of our opinion of them, that led them to commit their crimes. Our offense was thus that of the man who passed by on the other side. That we have finally recognized our negligence and named the criminals for what they are is a piece of righteousness too long delayed by fear.

That the conception of retrospective legislation which prevails under constitutional provisions in the United States does not receive complete recognition in other enlightened legal systems is illustrated by the decision in Phillips *vs.* Eyre, L.R. 6 Q.B. 1 [27 (1870–71)] described by Lord Wright as "a case of great authority." We quote:

> In fine, allowing the general inexpediency of retrospective legislation, it cannot be pronounced naturally or necessarily unjust. There may be occasions and circumstances involving the safety of the state, or even the conduct of individual subjects, the justice of which, prospective laws made for ordinary occasions and the usual exigencies of society for want of prevision fail to meet, and in which . . . the inconvenience and wrong, *summum jus summa injuria.*

We quote with approval the words of Sir David Maxwell-Fyfe:

> With regard to "crimes against humanity", this at any rate is clear. The Nazis, when they presecuted and murdered countless Jews and political opponents in Germany, knew that what they were doing was wrong and that their actions were

> crimes which had been condemned by the criminal law of every civilized state. When these crimes were mixed with the preparation for aggressive war and later with the commission of war crimes in occupied territories, it cannot be a matter of complaint that a procedure is established for their punishment.

Concerning the mooted *ex post facto* issue, Professor Wechsler of Columbia University writes:

> These are, indeed, the issues that are currently mooted. But there are elements in the debate that should lead us to be suspicious of the issues as they are drawn in these terms. For, most of those who mount the attack on one or another of these contentions hasten to assure us that their plea is not one of immunity for the defendants; they argue only that they should have been disposed of politically, that is, dispatched out of hand. This is a curious position indeed. A punitive enterprise launched on the basis of general rules, administered in an adversary proceeding under a separation of prosecutive and adjudicative powers is, in the name of law and justice, asserted to be less desirable than an *ex parte* execution list or a drumhead court martial constituted in the immediate aftermath of the war. I state my view reservedly when I say that history will accept no conception of law, politics or justice that supports a submission in these terms.

Again, he says:

> There is, indeed, too large a disposition among the defenders of Nuremberg to look for stray tags of international pronouncements and reason therefrom that the law of Nuremberg was previously fully laid down. If the Kellogg-Briand Pact or a general conception of international obligation sufficed to authorize England, and would have authorized us, to declare war on Germany in defense of Poland—and in this enterprise to kill countless thousands of German soldiers and civilians—can it be possible that it failed to authorize punitive action against individual Germans judicially determined to be responsible for the Polish attack? To be sure, we would demand a more explicit authorization for punishment in domestic law, for we have adopted for the protection of individuals a prophylactic principle absolutely forbidding retroactivity that we can afford to carry to that extreme. International society, being less stable, can afford less luxury. We admit that in other respects. Why should we deny it here?

Many of the laws of the Weimar era which were enacted for the protection of human rights have never been repealed. Many acts constituting war crimes or crimes against humanity as defined in C. C. Law 10 were committed or permitted in direct violation also of the provisions of the German criminal law. It is true that this Tribunal can try no defendant merely because of a violation of the German penal code, but it is equally true that the rule against retrospective legislation, as a rule of justice and fair play, should be no defense if the act which he committed in violation of C. C. Law 10 was also known to him to be a punishable crime under his own domestic law.

As a principle of justice and fair play, the rule in question will be given full effect. As applied in the field of international law that principle requires proof before conviction that the accused knew or should have known that in matters of international concern he was guilty of participation in a nationally organized system of injustice and persecution shocking to the moral sense of mankind, and that he knew or should have known that he would be subject to punishment if caught. Whether it be considered codification or substantive legislation, no person who knowingly committed the acts made punishable by C. C. Law 10 can assert that he did not know that he would be brought to account for his acts. Notice of intent to punish was repeatedly given by the only means available in international affairs, namely, the solemn warning of the governments of the states at war with Germany. Not only were the defendants warned of swift retribution by the express declaration of the Allies at Moscow of 30 October 1943. Long prior to the Second World War the principle of personal responsibility had been recognized.

The Commission on Responsibility of Authors of the War found that—

> The war was carried on by the central empires, together with their allies, Turkey and Bulgaria, by barbarous or illegitimate methods in violation of the established laws and customs of war and the elementary laws of humanity.
>
> As its conclusion, the Commission solemnly declared:
>
> All persons belonging to enemy countries, however high their position may have been, without distinction of rank, including Chiefs of States, who have been guilty of offences against the laws and customs of war or the laws of humanity, are liable to criminal prosecution.

The American members of that Commission, though in substantial accord with the finding, nevertheless expressed a reservation as to "the laws of humanity." The express wording of the London Charter and of C. C. Law 10 constitutes clear evidence of the fact that the position of the American Government is now in harmony with the Declaration of the Paris Commission concerning the "laws of humanity." We quote further from the report of the Paris Commission:

> Every belligerent has, according to international law, the power and authority to try the individuals alleged to be guilty of the crimes of which an enumeration has been given in chapter II on Violations of the Laws and Customs of War, if such persons have been taken prisoners or have otherwise fallen into its power. Each belligerent has, or has power to set up, pursuant to its own legislation, an appropriate tribunal, military or civil, for the trial of cases.

According to the Treaty of Versailles, article 228, the German Government itself "recognized the right to the Allied and associated powers to bring before military tribunals persons accused of offenses against the laws and customs of war. Such persons who might be found guilty were to be sentenced to punishments 'laid down by law'." Some Germans were, in fact, tried for the commission of such crimes.

The foregoing considerations demonstrate that the principle *nullum crimen sine lege,* when properly understood and applied, constitutes no legal or moral barrier to prosecution in the case at bar.

Crimes Against Humanity As Violative of International Law

C. C. Law 10 is not limited to the punishment of persons guilty of violating the laws and customs of war in the narrow sense; furthermore, it can no longer be said that violations of the laws and customs of war are the only offenses recognized by common international law. The force of circumstance, the grim fact of world-wide interdependence, and the moral pressure of public opinion have resulted in international recognition that certain crimes against humanity committed by Nazi authority against German nationals constituted violations not alone of statute but also of common international law. We quote:

> If a state is unhampered in its activities that affect the interests of any other, it is due to the circumstances that the practice of nations has not established that the welfare of the international society is adversely affected thereby. Hence that society has not been incited or aroused to endeavor to impose restraints; and by its law none are imposed. The Covenant of the League of Nations takes exact cognizance of the situation in its reference to disputes "which arise out of a matter which by international law is solely within the domestic jurisdiction" of a party thereto. It is that law which as a product of the acquiescence of states permits the particular activity of the individual state to be deemed a domestic one.
>
> In as much as changing estimates are to be anticipated, and as the evolution of thought in this regard appears to be constant and is perhaps now more obvious than at any time since the United States came into being, the circumstance that at any given period the solution of a particular question is by international law deemed to be solely within the control or jurisdiction of one state, gives frail assurance that it will always be so regarded.
>
> The family of nations is not unconcerned with the life and experience of the private individual in his relationships with the state of which he is a national. Evidence of concern has become increasingly abundant since World War I, and is reflected in treaties through which that conflict was brought to a close, particularly in provisions designed to safeguard the racial, linguistic and religious minorities inhabiting the territories of certain states, and in the terms of part XIII of the Treaty of Versailles, of June 28, 1919, in respect to labour, as well as in article XXIII of that treaty embraced in the Covenant of the League of Nations.
>
> The nature and extent of the latitude accorded a state in the treatment of its own nationals has been observed elsewhere. It has been seen that certain forms or degrees of harsh treatment of such individuals may be deemed to attain an international significance because of their direct and adverse effect upon the rights and interests of the outside world. For that reason it would be unscientific to declare at this day that tyrannical conduct, or massacres, or religious persecutions are wholly unrelated to the foreign relations of the territorial sovereign which is guilty of them. If it can be shown that such acts are immediately and necessarily injurious to the nationals of a particular foreign state, grounds for interference by it may be acknowledged. Again, the society of nations, acting collectively, may not unreasonably maintain that a state yielding to such excesses renders itself unfit to perform its international obligations, especially in so far as they pertain to the protection of foreign life and property within its domain. The property of interference obviously demands in every case a convincing showing that there is in fact a causal connection between the harsh treatment complained of, and the outside state that essays to thwart it.

The international concern over the commission of crimes against humanity has been greatly intensified in recent years. The fact of such concern is not a recent phenomenon, however. England, France, and Russia intervened to end the atrocities in the Greco-Turkish warfare in 1827.

President Van Buren, through his Secretary of State, intervened with the Sultan of Turkey in 1840 in behalf of the persecuted Jews of Damascus and Rhodes.

The French intervened and by force undertook to check religious atrocities in Lebanon in 1861.

Various nations directed protests to the governments of Russia and Rumania with respect to pogroms and atrocities against Jews. Similar protests were made to the government of Turkey on behalf of the persecuted Christian minorities. In 1872 the United States, Germany, and five other powers protested to Rumania; and in 1915, the German Government joined in a remonstrance to Turkey on account of similar persecutions.

In 1902 the American Secretary of State, John Hay, addressed to Rumania a remonstrance "in the name of humanity" against Jewish persecutions, saying, "This government cannot be a tacit party to such international wrongs."

Again, in connection with the Kishenef [Kishinev] and other massacres in Russia in 1903, President Theodore Roosevelt stated:

> Nevertheless there are occasional crimes committed on so vast a scale and of such peculiar horror as to make us doubt whether it is not our manifest duty to endeavor at least to show our disapproval of the deed and our sympathy with those who have suffered by it. The cases must be extreme in which such a course is justifiable. . . . The cases in which we could interfere by force of arms as we interfered to put a stop to intolerable conditions in Cuba are necessarily very few.

Concerning the American intervention in Cuba in 1898, President McKinley stated:

> First. In the cause of humanity and to put an end to the barbarities, bloodshed, starvation, and horrible miseries now existing there, and which the parties to the conflict are either unable or unwilling to stop or mitigate. It is no answer to say this is all in another country, belonging to another nation, and therefore none of our business. It is specially our duty, for it is right at our door.

The same principle was recognized as early as 1878 by a learned German professor of law, who wrote: "States are allowed to interfere in the name of international law if 'humanity rights' are violated to the detriment of any single race."

Finally, we quote the words of Sir Hartley Shawcross, the British Chief Prosecutor at the trial of Goering, et al.:

> The rights of humanitarian intervention on behalf of the rights of man trampled upon by a state in a manner shocking the sense of mankind has long been considered to form part of the [recognized] law of nations. Here, too, the Charter merely develops a preexisting principle.

We hold that crimes against humanity as defined in C. C. Law 10 must be strictly construed to exclude isolated cases of atrocity or persecution whether committed by private individuals or by governmental authority. As we construe it, that section provides for punishment of crimes committed against German nationals only where there is proof of conscious participation in systematic government organized or approved procedures amounting to atrocities and offenses of the kind specified in the act and committed against populations or amounting to persecutions on political, racial, or religious grounds.

Thus, the statute is limited by construction to the type of criminal activity which prior to 1939 was and still is a matter of international concern. Whether or not such atrocities constitute technical violations of laws and customs of war, they were acts of such scope and malevolence, and they so clearly imperiled the peace of the world that they must be deemed to have become violations of international law. This principle was recognized although it was misapplied by the Third Reich. Hitler expressly justified his early acts of aggression against Czechoslovakia on the ground that the alleged persecution of racial Germans by the government of that country was a matter of international concern warranting intervention by Germany. Organized Czechoslovakian persecution of racial Germans in Sudetenland was a fiction supported by "framed" incidents, but the principle invoked by Hitler was the one which we have recognized, namely, that government organized racial persecutions are violations of international law.

As the prime illustration of a crime against humanity under C. C. Law 10, which by reason of its magnitude and its international repercussions has been recognized as a violation of common international law, we cite "genocide" which will shortly receive our full consideration. A resolution recently adopted by the General Assembly of the United Nations is in part as follows:

> Genocide is a denial of the right of existence of entire human groups, as homicide is a denial of the right to live of individual human beings; such denial of the right of existence shocks the conscience of mankind, results in great losses to humanity in the form of cultural and other contributions represented by these human groups, and is contrary to moral law and to the spirit and aims of the United Nations.
>
> Many instances of such crimes of genocide have occurred when racial, religious, political, and other groups have been destroyed, entirely or in part.
>
> The punishment of the crime of genocide is a matter of international concern.
>
> The General Assembly therefore—
>
> Affirms that genocide is a crime under international law which the civilized world condemns, and for the commission of which principals and accomplices—whether private individuals, public officials, or statesmen, and whether the crime is committed on religious, racial, political or any other grounds—are punishable. . . .

The General Assembly is not an international legislature, but it is the most authoritative organ in existence for the interpretation of world opinion. Its recognition of genocide as an international crime is persuasive evidence of the fact. We approve and adopt its conclusions. Whether the crime against humanity is the product of statute or of common international law, or, as we believe, of both, we find no injustice to persons tried for such crimes. They are chargeable with knowledge that such acts were wrong and were punishable when committed.

The defendants contend that they should not be found guilty because they acted within the authority and by the command of German laws and decrees. Concerning crimes against humanity, C. C. Law 10 provides for punishment whether or not the acts were in violation of the domestic laws of the country where perpetrated (C. C. Law 10, art. II, par. 1(*c*)). That enactment also provides "the fact that any person acted pursuant to the order of his Government or of a superior does not free him from responsibility for a crime, but may be considered in mitigation." (C. C. Law 10, art. II, par. 4(*b*).)

The foregoing provisions constitute a sufficient, but not the entire, answer to the contention of the defendants. The argument that compliance with German law is a defense to the charge rests on a misconception of the basic theory which supports our entire proceedings. The Nuernberg Tribunals are not German courts. They are not enforcing German law. The charges are not based on violation by the defendants of German law. On the contrary, the jurisdiction of this Tribunal rests on international authority. It enforces the law as declared by the IMT Charter and C. C. Law 10, and within the limitations on the power conferred, it enforces international law as superior in authority to any German statute or decree. It is true, as defendants contend, that German courts under the Third Reich were required to follow German law (i.e., the expressed will of Hitler) even when it was contrary to international law. But no such limitation can be applied to this Tribunal. Here we have the paramount substantive law, plus a Tribunal authorized and required to apply it notwithstanding the inconsistent provisions of German local law. The very essence of the prosecution case is that the laws, the Hitlerian decrees and the Draconic, corrupt, and perverted Nazi judicial system themselves constituted the substance of war crimes and crimes against humanity and that participation in the enactment and enforcement of them amounts to complicity in crime. We have pointed out that governmental participation is a material element of the crime against humanity. Only when official organs of sovereignty participated in atrocities and persecutions did those crimes assume international proportions. It can scarcely be said that governmental participation, the proof of which is necessary for conviction, can also be a defense to the charge.

Frank recognition of the following facts is essential. The jurisdictional enactments of the Control Council, the form of the indictment, and the judicial procedure prescribed for this Tribunal are not governed by the familiar rules of American criminal law and procedure. This Tribunal, although composed of American judges schooled in the system and rules of the common law, is sitting by virtue of international authority and can carry with it only the broad principles of justice and fair play which underlie all civilized concepts of law and procedure.

No defendant is specifically charged in the indictment with the murder or abuse of any particular person. If he were, the indictment would, no doubt, name the alleged victim. Simple murder and isolated instances of atrocities do not constitute the gravamen of the charge. Defendants are charged with crimes of such immensity that mere specific instances of criminality appear insignificant by comparison. The charge, in brief, is that of conscious participation in a nation-wide government-organized system of cruelty and injustice, in violation of the laws of war and of humanity, and perpetrated in the name of law by the authority of the Ministry of Justice, and through the instrumentality of the courts. The dagger of the assassin was concealed beneath the robe of the jurist. The record is replete with evidence of specific criminal acts, but they are not the crimes charge in the indictment. They constitute evidence of the intentional participation of the defendants and serve as illustrations of the nature and effect of the greater crimes charged in the indictment. Thus it is that the apparent generality of the indictment was not only necessary but proper. No indictment couched in specific terms and in the manner of the common law could have encompassed within practicable limits the generality of the offense with which these defendants stand charged.

The prosecution has introduced evidence concerning acts which occurred before the outbreak of the war in 1939. Some such acts are relevant upon the charges contained in counts two, three, and four, but as stated by the prosecution, "None of these acts is charged as an independent offense in this particular indictment." We direct our consideration to the issue of guilt or innocence after the outbreak of the war in accordance with the specific limitations of time set forth in counts two, three, and four of the indictment. In measuring the conduct of the individual defendants by the standards of C. C. Law 10, we are also to be guided by article II, paragraph 2 of that law, which provides that a person "is deemed to have committed a crime as defined in paragraph 1 of this article, if he was (*a*) a principal or (*b*) was an accessory to the commission of any such crime or ordered or abetted the same or (*c*) took a consenting part therein or (*d*) was connected with plans or enterprises involving its commission or (*e*) was a member of any organization or group connected with the commission of any such crime."

* * *

Although the process by which the Hitler regime came into power was tainted with illegality and duress, nevertheless the power thus seized was later consolidated and the regime thereafter did receive the organized support of the German people and recognition by foreign powers. On 30 January 1934, more than 10 months after the enactment of the enabling act, and subsequent to the Reichstag election of 12 November 1933, the Reichstag passed an act by unanimous vote providing that "the sovereign powers of the Laender are transferred to the Reich," and further providing that "the Reich government may issue new constitutional laws." The act was regularly signed by Reich President von Hindenburg, and by Reich Chancellor Hitler, and Minister Frick. The provisions of the Enabling Act were renewed by acts of the Reichstag on 30 January 1937 and again on 30 January 1939.

On 14 June 1942, Dr. Lammers, Reich Minister and Chief of the Reich Chancellery, stated that they would "stress the fact that the Fuehrer himself and the Reich cabinet should not be eliminated from the powers of legislation."

The conduct of the defendants must be seen in a context of preparation for aggressive war, and must be interpreted as within the framework of the criminal law and judicial system of the Third Reich. We shall, therefore, next consider the legal and judicial process by which the entire judicial system was transformed into a tool for the propagation of the National Socialist ideology, the extermination of opposition thereto, and the advancement of plans for aggressive war and world conquest. Though the overt acts with which defendants are charged occurred after September 1939, the evidence now to be considered will make clear the conditions under which the defendant acted and will show knowledge, intent, and motive on their part, for in the period of preparation some of the defendants played a leading part in molding the judicial system which they later employed.

Beginning in 1933, there developed side by side two processes by which the Ministry of Justice and the courts were equipped for terroristic functions in support of the Nazi regime. By the first, the power of life and death was ever more broadly vested in the courts. By the second, the penal laws were extended in such inconclusive and indefinite terms as to vest in the judges the widest discretion in the choice of law to be applied, and in the construction of the chosen law in any given case. In 1933, by the law for the "Protection against Violent Political Acts," the death sentence was authorized, though not required, as to a number of crimes "whenever milder penalty has been prescribed hitherto."

On 24 April 1934, the definition of high treason was greatly expanded and the death sentence was authorized, though not required, in numerous instances. The manner in which this law was applied renders it all-important. The following provisions, among others, illustrate the scope of the amended law and the discretionary power of the judge:

> 83. Whoever publicly incites to or solicits an undertaking of high treason shall be punished by confinement in a penitentiary not to exceed 10 years.
>
> Whoever prepares an undertaking of high treason in any other way shall be punished in like manner.
>
> The death penalty, or confinement in a penitentiary for life, or for not less than 2 years, shall be inflicted:
>
> (1) if the act was directed toward establishing or maintaining an organized combination for the preparation of high treason or . . .
>
> (3) if the act was directed toward influencing the masses by making or distributing writings, recordings, or pictures, or by the installation of wireless telegraph or telephone, or
>
> (4) if the act was committed abroad or was committed in such a manner that the offender undertook to import writings, recordings, or pictures from abroad or for the purpose of distribution within the country.

On 20 December 1934, the government promulgated the following enactment "Law on Treacherous Acts against State and Party and for the Protection of Party Uniforms," which provided in part as follows:

Chapter 1. Article 1. (1) Unless heavier punishment is sanctioned under the authority of a law previously established, imprisonment not to exceed 2 years shall be imposed upon anybody deliberately making false or grievous statements, fit to injure the welfare or the prestige of the government of the Reich, the National Socialist Workers' Party, or its agencies. If such statements are made or circulated in public, imprisonment for not less than 3 months shall be imposed.

Article 2. (1) Anyone who makes or circulates statements proving a malicious, baiting or low-minded attitude toward leading personalities of the State or the NSDAP, or toward orders issued by them or toward institutions created by them—fit to undermine the confidence of the people in its political leadership—shall be punished with imprisonment.

(2) Statements of this kind which are not made in public shall warrant the same punishment—provided the offender figures on his statements eventually being circulated in public.

A decisive step was taken by the "Law to Change the Penal Code," which was promulgated on 28 June 1935 by Adolf Hitler as Fuehrer and Reich Chancellor, and by Dr. Guertner as Reich Minister of Justice. Article 2 of that enactment is as follows:

Article 2. Whoever commits an act which the law declares as punishable or which deserves punishment according to the fundamental idea of a penal law and the sound concept of the people, shall be punished. If no specific penal law can be directly applied to this act, then it shall be punished according to the law whose underlying principle can be most readily applied to the act.

In substance, this edict constituted a complete repudiation of the rule that criminal statutes should be definite and certain and vested in the judge a wide discretion in which Party political ideology and influence were substituted for the control of law as the guide to judicial decision.

Section 90 (f) of the Penal Code, as enacted on 24 April 1934, provided:

Whoever publicly, or as a German staying abroad, causes serious danger to the reputation of the German nation by an untrue or grossly inaccurate statement of a factual nature, shall be punished by confinement in a penitentiary.

The act was amended on 20 September 1944 as follows:

In especially serious cases a German may be punished by death.

By the act of 28 June 1935 it was provided:

Whoever publicly profanes the German National Socialist Labor Party, its subdivisions, symbols, standards, and banners, its insignia or decorations, or maliciously and with premeditation exposes them to contempt shall be punished by imprisonment.

The offense shall be prosecuted only upon order of the Reich Minister of Justice who shall issue such order in agreement with the Fuehrer's deputy.

By the law of 28 June 1935 it was provided:

If the main proceedings show that the defendant committed an act which deserves punishment according to the common sense of the people but which is not declared punishable by the law, then the court must investigate whether the underlying principle of a penal law applies to this act and whether justice can be helped to triumph by the proper application of this penal law. (Article 2 of the Penal Code.)

* * *

By the decree of 5 May 1944, the judges were substantially freed from all restrictions as to the penalty to be invoked in criminal cases. That decree reads as follows:

> With regard to all offenders who are guilty of causing serious prejudice or seriously endangering the conduct of war, or the security of the Reich, through an intentional criminal act, a penalty may be imposed in excess of the regular penal limits up to the statutory maximum for a given type of punishment, or hard labor for a term or for life, or death, if the regular statutory maximum limits are insufficient for expiation of the act according to the sentiment of the people. The same shall also apply to all offenses committed by negligence by which one made himself guilty of a particularly grave prejudice or a particularly serious danger to the conduct of war, or to the security of the Reich.

On 20 August 1942 Hitler issued the famous decree which marks the culmination of his systematic campaign to change the German judicial system into an instrumentality of the NSDAP. The decree was as follows:

> A strong administration of Justice is necessary for the fulfillment of the tasks of the great German Reich. Therefore, I commission and empower the Reich Minister of Justice to establish a National Socialist Administration of Justice and to take all necessary measures in accordance with my directives and instructions made in agreement with the Reich Minister and Chief of the Reich Chancellery and the Leader of the Party Chancellery. He can hereby deviate from any existing law.

The statutes which we have reviewed were merely steps in the process of increased severity of the criminal law and in the development of a loose concept concerning the definition of crime. The latter concept was especially evident in the statutes concerning the "sound sentiment of the people," crime by analogy, and undermining the military efficiency of the nation. In place of the control of law there was substituted the control of National Socialist ideology as a guide to judicial action.

The Draconic laws to which we have referred were upon their face, of general applicability. The discriminations on political, racial, and religious grounds are to be found not in the text, but in the application of the text.

But the Nazis were not content with statutes of a non-discriminatory nature even in view of the discriminatory manner in which they were enforced. Coincidentally with the development of these laws and decrees there arose another body of substantive law which expressly discriminated against minority groups both within and without the Reich, and which formed the basis for racial, religious, and political persecution on a vast scale. On 7 April 1933, a decree by the Reich government provided in part that—

Article 2. Persons who, according to the Law for the Restoration of the Professional Civil Service of 7 April 1933, are of non-Aryan descent, may be refused permission to practice law, even if there exists none of the reasons enumerated in the Regulations for Lawyers. The same rule applies in cases, as where a lawyer described in section 1, clause 2, wishes to be admitted to another court. . . .

Article 3. Persons who are active in the Communistic sense are excluded from the admission to the bar. Admissions already given have to be revoked.

The act was implemented by the power of injunction. The fact that the license to practice law had been canceled was also stated as a ground for the cancellation of employment contracts and office leases.

On 15 September 1935, the Reichstag enacted the "Law for the Protection of German Blood and Honor." We quote—

Article 1. (1) Marriages of Jews and citizens of German or related blood are prohibited. Marriages which are concluded nevertheless, are void even if they were concluded abroad in order to circumvent this law.

(2) Only the district attorney can sue for nullification of marriage.

Article 2. Sexual intercourse (except in marriage) between Jews and German nationals of German or German-related blood is forbidden.

By other laws, as amended from time to time, non-Aryans were almost completely expelled from public service. The number of non-Aryans in schools and higher institutions of learning was restricted. Jews were excluded from the homestead law concerning peasantry. Jewish religious communities were regulated. Jews were excluded from certain industrial enterprises and their rights as tenants were restricted.

By the act of 2 November 1942 it was provided—

Section 1. A Jew who has his domicile abroad cannot be a citizen of the Protectorate of Bohemia and Moravia. Domicile abroad is established if a Jew was abroad under circumstances which indicated that his tenure there is not of a temporary nature.

Section 2. A Jew loses his citizenship status in the Protectorate if—

(a) As of the effective date of this decree, he has an established domicile abroad;

(b) At a date subsequent to the effective date of this decree, he establishes a domicile abroad.

* * *

Pursuant to a decree of the Fuehrer of 16 March 1939, the defendant Schlegelberger, as Reich Minister of Justice in charge, together with the Minister of the Interior and the Chief of the Armed Forces, Keitel, issued a decree which reads in part as follows:

Section 1. In case of direct attack by a non-German citizen against the SS or the German Police or against any of their members, the Reich Leader of the SS and the Chief of the German Police in the Reich Ministry of the Interior may establish the jurisdiction of a combined SS court and police court, by declaring that special interests of parts of the SS or of the Police require that judgment be given by an SS and police court.

This declaration shall be sent to the Reich Protector of Bohemia and Moravia. The SS and police court, which shall have jurisdiction in individual cases, shall be specified by the Reich Leader of the SS and Chief of the German Police in the Reich Ministry of the Interior.

Section 2. If the offense directly injures the interests of the armed forces, the Reich Leader of the SS and chief of the German Police in the Reich Ministry of the Interior, and the chief of the Supreme Command of the Armed Forces shall reach an agreement as to whether the case shall be prosecuted by an SS and police court or by a military court.

Article II. Exemption of the Reich court from being bound to precedent sentence: The Reich Court as the highest German tribunal must consider it its duty to effect an interpretation of the law which takes into account the change of ideology and of legal concepts which the new State has brought about. In order to be able to accomplish this task without having to show consideration for the jurisdiction of the past brought about by other ideology and other legal concepts, it is ruled as follows:

When a decision is made about a legal question, the Reich Court can deviate from a decision laid down before this law went into effect.

The Law in Action

We pass now from the foregoing incomplete summary of Nazi legislation to a consideration of the law in action, and of the influence of the "Fuehrer principle" as it affected the officials of the Ministry of Justice, prosecutors, and judges. Two basic principles controlled conduct within the Ministry of Justice. The first concerned the absolute power of Hitler in person or by delegated authority to enact, enforce, and adjudicate law. The second concerned the incontestability of such law. Both principles were expounded by the learned Professor Jahrreiss, a witness for all of the defendants. Concerning the first principle, Dr. Jahrreiss said:

> If now in the European meaning one asks about legal restrictions, and first of all one asks about restrictions of the German law, one will have to say that restrictions under German law did not exist for Hitler. He was *legibus solutus* in the same meaning in which Louis XIV claimed that for himself in France. Anybody who said something different expresses a wish that does not describe the actual legal facts.

Concerning the second principle, Jahrreiss supported the opinion of Gerhard Anschuetz, "crown jurist of the Weimar Republic," who holds that if German laws were enacted by regular procedure, judicial authorities were without power to challenge them on constitutional or ethical grounds. Under the Nazi system, and even prior thereto, German judges were also bound to apply German law even when in violation of the principles of international law. As stated by Professor Jahrreiss:

> To express it differently, whether the law has been passed by the State in such

a way that it was inconsistent with international law on purpose or not, that could not play any part at all; and that was the legal state of affairs, regrettable as it may be.

This, however, is not to deny the superior authority of international law. Again we quote a statement of extraordinary candor by Professor Jahrreiss:

> On the other hand, certainly there were legal restrictions for Hitler under international law. . . . He was bound by international law. Therefore, he could commit acts violating international law. Therefore, he could issue orders violating international law to the Germans.

The conclusion to be drawn from the evidence presented by the defendants themselves is clear: In German legal theory Hitler's law was a shield to those who acted under it, but before a tribunal authorized to enforce international law, Hitler's decrees were a protection neither to the Fuehrer himself nor to his subordinates, if in violation of the law of the community of nations.

In German legal theory, Hitler was not only the supreme legislator, he was also the supreme judge. On 26 April 1942 Hitler addressed the Reichstag in part as follows:

> I do expect one thing: That the nation gives me the right to intervene immediately and to take action myself wherever a person has failed to render unqualified obedience. . . .
>
> I therefore ask the German Reichstag to confirm expressly that I have the legal right to keep everybody to his duty and to cashier or remove from office or position without regard for his person, or his established rights, whoever, in my view and according to my considered opinion, has failed to do his duty.
>
> . . . From now on, I shall intervene in these cases and remove from office those judges who evidently do not understand the demand of the hour.

On the same day the Greater German Reichstag resolved in part as follows:

> . . . the Fuehrer must have all the rights postulated by him which serve to further or achieve victory. Therefore—without being bound by existing legal regulations—in his capacity as leader of the nation, Supreme Commander of the Armed Forces, governmental chief and supreme executive chief, as supreme justice, and leader of the Party—the Fuehrer must be in a position to force with all means at his disposal every German, if necessary, whether he be common soldier or officer, low or high official or judge, leading or subordinate official of the Party, worker or employee, to fulfill his duties. In case of violation of these duties, the Fuehrer is entitled after conscientious examination, regardless of so-called well-deserved rights, to mete out due punishment, and to remove the offender from his post, rank and position, without introducing prescribed procedures.

The assumption by Hitler of supreme governmental power in all departments did not represent a new development based on the emergency of war. The declaration of the Reichstag was only an echo of Hitler's declaration of 13 July 1934. After the mass murders of that date (the Roehm purge) which were committed by Hitler's express orders, he said:

> Whenever someone reproaches me with not having used the ordinary court for their sentencing, I can only say: "In this hour I am responsible for the fate of the German nation and hence the supreme law lord of the German people."

The conception of Hitler as the supreme judge was supported by the defendant Rothenberger. We quote (*NG–075*, *Pros. Ex. 27*):

> However, something entirely different has occurred; with the Fuehrer a man has risen within the German people who awakens the oldest, long forgotten times. Here is a man who in his position represents the ideal of the judge in its perfect sense, and the German people elected him for their judge—first of all, of course, as "judge" over their fate in general, but also as "supreme magistrate and judge."

* * *

In operation the Nazi system forced the judges into one of two categories. In the first we find the judges who still retained ideals of judicial independence and who administered justice with a measure of impartiality and moderation. Judgments which they rendered were set aside by the employment of the nullity plea and the extraordinary objection. The defendants they sentenced were frequently transferred to the Gestapo on completion of prison terms and were then shot or sent to concentration camps. The judges themselves were threatened and criticized and sometimes removed from office. In the other category were the judges who with fanatical zeal enforced the will of the Party with such severity that they experienced no difficulties and little interference from party officials. To this group the defendants Rothaug and Oeschey belonged.

We turn to a consideration and classification of the evidence. The prosecution has introduced captured documents in great number which establish the Draconic character of the Nazi criminal laws and prove that the death penalty was imposed by courts in thousands of cases. Cases in which the extreme penalty was imposed may in large measure be classified in the following groups:

1. Cases against habitual criminals.
2. Cases of looting in the devastated areas of Germany; committed after air raids and under cover of black-out.
3. Crimes against the war economy—rationing, hoarding, and the like.
4. Crimes amounting to an undermining of the defensive strength of the nation; defeatist remarks, criticisms of Hitler, and the like.
5. Crimes of treason and high treason.
6. Crimes of various types committed by Poles, Jews, and other foreigners.
7. Crimes committed under the Nacht und Nebel program, and similar procedures.

Consideration will next be given to the first four groups as above set forth. The Tribunal is keenly aware of the danger of incorporating in the judgment as law its own moral convictions or even those of the Anglo-American legal world. This we will not do. We may and do condemn the Draconic laws and express abhorrence at the limitations imposed by the Nazi regime upon freedom of speech and action, but the question still remains unanswered: "Do those

Draconic laws or the decisions rendered under them constitute war crimes or crimes against humanity?"

Concerning the punsihment of habitual criminals, we think the answer is clear. In many civilized states statutory provisions require the courts to impose sentences of life imprisonment upon proof of conviction of three or more felonies. We are unable to say in one breath that life imprisonment for habitual criminals is a salutary and reasonable punishment in America in peace times, but that the imposition of the death penalty was a crime against humanity in Germany when the nation was in the throes of war. The same considerations apply largely in the case of looting. Every nation recognizes the absolute necessity of more stringent enforcement of the criminal law in times of great emergency. Anyone who has seen the utter devastation of the great cities of Germany must realize that the safety of the civilian population demanded that the werewolves who roamed the streets of the burning cities, robbing the dead, and plundering the ruined homes should be severely punished. The same considerations apply, though in a lesser degree, to prosecutions to hoarders and violators of war economy decrees.

Questions of far greater difficulty are involved when we consider the cases involving punishment for undermining military efficiency. The limitations on freedom of speech which were imposed in the enforcement of these laws are revolting to our sense of justice. A court would have no hesitation in condemning them under any free constitution, including that of the Weimar republic, if the limitations were applied in time of peace; but even under the protection of the Constitution of the United States a citizen is not wholly free to attack the Government or to interfere with its military aims in time of war. In the face of a real and present danger, freedom of speech may be somewhat restricted even in America. Can we then say that in the throes of total war and in the presence of impending disaster those officials who enforced these savage laws in a last desperate effort to stave off defeat were guilty of crimes against humanity?

It is persuasively urged that the fact that Germany was waging a criminal war of aggression colors all of these acts with the dye of criminality. To those who planned the war of aggression and who were charged with and were guilty of the crime against the peace as defined in the IMT Charter, this argument is conclusive, but these defendants are not charged with crimes against the peace nor has it been proven here that they knew that the war which they were supporting on the home front was based upon a criminal conspiracy or was *per se* a violation of international law. The lying propaganda of Hitler and Goebbels concealed even from many public officials the criminal plans of the inner circle of aggressors. If we should adopt the view that by reason of the fact that the war was a criminal war of aggression every act which would have been legal in a defensive war was illegal in this one, we would be forced to the conclusion that every soldier who marched under orders into occupied territory or who fought in the homeland was a criminal and a murderer. The rules of land warfare upon which the prosecution has relied would not be the measure of conduct and the pronouncement of guilt in any case would become a mere formality. In the opinion of the Tribunal the territory occupied and annexed by Germany after September 1939 never became a part of Germany, but for that conclusion we need not rest upon the doctrine that the invasion was a crime against the peace. Such purported annexations in the course of hostilities while armies are in the field are provisional only, and dependent upon the final successful outcome of the war. If the war succeeds, no one questions the validity of the annexation. If it fails, the attempt to annex becomes abortive. In view of our clear duty to move with caution in the recently charted field of international affairs, we conclude that the domestic laws and judgments in Germany which limited free speech in the emergency of war cannot be condemned as crimes against humanity merely by invoking the doctrine of aggressive war. All of the laws to which we have referred could be and were applied in a discriminatory manner and in the case of many, the Ministry of Justice and the courts enforced them by arbitrary and brutal means, shocking to the conscience of mankind and punishable here. We merely hold that under the particular facts of this case we cannot convict any defendant merely because of the fact, without more, that laws of the first four types were passed or enforced.

A different situation is presented when we consider the cases which fall within types 5, 6, and 7.

* * *

Crimes Under the Night and Fog Decree [Nacht und Nebel Erlass]

Paragraph 13 of count two of the indictment charges in substance that the Ministry of Justice participated with the OKW and the Gestapo in the execution of the Hitler decree of Night and Fog whereby civilians of occupied countries accused of alleged crimes in resistance activities against German occupying forces were spirited away for secret trial by special courts of the Ministry of Justice within the Reich; that the victim's whereabouts, trial, and subsequent disposition were kept completely secret, thus serving the dual purpose of terrorizing the victim's relatives and associates and barring recourse to evidence, witnesses, or counsel for defense. If the accused was acquitted, or if convicted, after serving his sentence, he was handed over to the Gestapo for "protective custody" for the duration of the war. These proceedings resulted in the torture, ill treatment, and murder of thousands of persons. These crimes and offenses are alleged to be war crimes in violation of certain established international rules and customs of warfare and as recognized in C. C. Law 10.

Paragraph 25 of count three of the indictment incorporates by reference paragraph 13 of count two of the indictment and alleges that the same acts, offenses, and crimes are crimes against humanity as defined by C. C. Law 10. The same facts were introduced to prove both the war crimes and crimes against humanity and the evidence will be so considered by us.

Paragraph 13 of count two of the indictment which particularly describes the Hitler NN plan or scheme, charges the defendants Altstoetter, von Ammon, Engert, Joel Klemm, Mettgenberg, and Schlegelberger with "special responsibility for the participation in these crimes," which are alleged to be war crimes.

Paragraph 8 of count two of the indictment charges all of the defendants with having committed the war crimes set forth in paragraphs 9 to 18 inclusive of count two, in that they were principals in, accessories to, ordered, abetted, took a consenting part in, and were connected with plans and enterprises involving the commission of atrocities and offenses against persons, including but not limited to murder, illegal imprisonment, brutalities, atrocities, transportation of civilians, and other inhumane acts which were set out in paragraphs 9 to 18 inclusive of the indictment as war crimes against the civilian population in occupied territories.

Paragraph 20 of count three of the indictment charges all of the defendants with having committed the same acts as contained in paragraph 8 of count two as being crimes against humanity. Paragraphs 21 to 30 inclusive of count three refer to and adopt the facts alleged in paragraphs 9 to 18 inclusive of count two, and thus all defendants are charged with having committed crimes against humanity upon the same allegations of facts as are contained in paragraphs 9 to 18 inclusive of count two.

In the foregoing manner all of the defendants are charged with having participated in the execution or carrying out of the Hitler NN decree and procedure either as war crimes or as crimes against humanity, and all defendants are charged with having committed numerous other acts which constitute war crimes and crimes against humanity against the civilian population of occupied countries during the war period between 1 September 1939 and April 1945.

* * *

Concentration Camps

The use of concentration camps for NN prisoners was shown by a letter dated 18 August 1942, signed by Gluecks, SS Brigade-fuehrer and General Major of the SS, which contained enclosures for information and execution by officials in charge of concentration camps, including Mauthausen, Auschwitz, Flossenbuerg, Dachau, Ravensbrueck, Buchenwald, and numerous others. The letter states that such prisoners will be transferred under the Keitel decree from the occupied countries to Germany for transfer to Special Courts. Should that for any reason be impossible, the accused will be put into one of the above-named concentration camps. Those in charge of the camps were instructed that absolute secrecy of such prisoners' detention was to be maintained including the prevention of any means of communication with the outside world either before or after the trial.

The following is illustrative of inhumane prison conditions for NN prisoners. The affidavit of Ludwig Schirmer, warden in the prison at Ebrach, confirmed by his oral testimony, states:

> The Ebrach prison which was used for criminal convicts had a capacity of 595 prisoners. In 1944, however, the prison became overcrowded and finally held a maximum of from 1,400 to 1,600 prisoners in 1945.
>
> This crowding had been caused by numerous NN prisoners from France and Belgium. Among them was the French General Vaillant who died in the prison of old age and of a heart disease. Owing to the overcrowding of the penitentiary, it was impossible to avoid the frequent outbreak of diseases, such as pulmonary tuberculosis, consumption, and, of course many cases of undernourishment. The very poor medical care was a serious disadvantage; the doctor showed up only two or three times a week. Sixty-two inmates died during the last months of the war. Many of them, of course, came in already sick. During the last months, a criminal convict was employed as physician. He was a morphinomaniac and a man of very low character.
>
> Although there were stocks of food at hand, the feeding of prisoners was bad; people got only soup and turnips for weeks. NN prisoners were crowded together, four in a single cell. From time to time a certain number of the prisoners was transferred to the concentration camp.

The affidavit of Josef Prey, head guard at the Amberg prison, confirmed by his oral testimony, states that foreigners, Jews, and NN prisoners at Amberg prison, which had a capacity of 900 to 1,100 were incarcerated there. Yet shortly before the collapse there were 2,000 prisoners of whom 800 to 900 prisoners were Polish, and NN prisoners who included Frenchmen, Dutchmen, and Belgians. From time to time by secret decree prisoners were transferred to the concentration camps at Mauthausen. Defendant Engert, the official representative of the department of justice, visited and officially inspected the prison and knew of these conditions.

By his affidavit Engert states that Thierack told him the Night and Fog prisoners had to be treated with special precaution, not allowed any correspondence, locked up hermetically from the outer world, and that care should be taken that their real names remain unknown to the lower prison personnel. Engert further states that these orders were the result of the Fuehrer decree of 7 December 1941 and that Thierack told him the Night and Fog prisoners were accused of resistance and violence against the armed forces. He did not know what became of these NN prisoners at the various prison camps. He did know that an agreement existed with the Gestapo that the bodies of Night and Fog prisoners should be given to them for secret burial. It was shown by other testimony that defendant Engert was ministerial director, who handled and investigated the Night and Fog prisoners and that he was in charge of the task of transferring prisoners and knew their nationality and the character of crime charged against them.

On 14 June 1944 defendant von Ammon wrote Bormann, Chief of the Party Chancellery, a letter sent by way of defendant Mettgenberg, requesting permission of the Fuehrer to inform NN women held under death sentence of the fact that such sentence has been reprieved, since he considers it to be unnecessarily cruel to keep these "condemned women" in suspense for years as to whether their death sentence will be carried out.

Mrs. Solf, the widow of a former distinguished German cabinet officer and ambassador, testified that she was tried and held as a political prisoner of the Nazi regime for several years in Ravensbrueck concentration camp and other prisons where a large number of foreign women were imprisoned. Concerning the ill-treatment of these women and the prison conditions under which they were incarcerated, Mrs. Solf testified:

> As to the prisoners who were with me at Ravensbrueck, as far as I can remember there was only an Italian woman of Belgian descent who was treated well, better than we were. However, in the penitentiary of Cottbus, as well as in the prison of Moabit, I met many foreigners. In the penitentiary of Cottbus, there alone were 300 French women who were sentenced to death, and five Dutch women sentenced to death who after a week or two were pardoned to penitentiary terms and whom I saw in the courtyard. The 300 French women sentenced to death were sent to Ravensbrueck at the end of November 1944. The night before they were transported they had to sleep on a bare stone floor. One of the auxiliary wardens, who was also an interpreter for them and who had a great deal of courage and a kind heart, came to me in order to ask us political prisoners to give them our blankets, which we certainly did.

She further testified:

> I know and have seen for myself that, for instance, in Moabit, some of the brutal wardens kicked them and shouted at them for reasons which seemed very, very unjust because these women did not understand what they were supposed to do.

The Night and Fog decree was from time to time implemented by several plans or schemes, which were enforced by the defendants. One plan or scheme was the transfer of alleged resistance prisoners or persons from occupied territorties who had served their sentences or had been acquitted to concentration camps in Germany where they were held incommunicado and were never heard from again. Another scheme was the transfer of the inhabitants of occupied territories to concentration camps in Germany as a substitute for a court trial. Defendant Engert made such an order.

Trials under NN Decree

The evidence establishes beyond a reasonable doubt that in the execution of the Hitler NN decree the Nazi regime's Ministry of Justice, Special Courts, and public prosecutors agreed to and acted together with the OKW and Gestapo in causing to be arrested, transported to Germany, tried, sentenced to death and executed or imprisoned under the most cruel and inhumane conditions in prisons and concentration camps, thousands of the civilian population of the countries overrun and occupied by the Nazi regime's military forces during the prosecution of its criminal and aggressive war.

* * *

Racial Persecution

The record contains innumerable acts of persecution of individual Poles and Jews, but to consider these cases as isolated and unrelated instances of perversion of justice would be to overlook the very essence of the offense charged in the indictment. The defendants are not now charged with conspiracy as a separate and substantive offense, but it is alleged that they participated in carrying out a governmental plan and program for the persecution and extermination of Jews and Poles, a plan which transcended territorial boundaries as well as the bounds of human decency. Some of the defendants took part in the enactment of laws and decrees the purpose of which was the extermination of Poles and Jews in Germany and throughout Europe. Others, in executive positions, actively participated in the enforcement of those laws and in atrocities, illegal even under German law, in furtherance of the declared national purpose. Others, as judges, distorted and then applied the laws and decrees against Poles and Jews as such in disregard of every principle of judicial behavior. The overt acts of the several defendants must be seen and understood as deliberate contributions toward the effectuation of the policy of the Party and State. The discriminatory laws themselves formed the subject matter of war crimes and crimes against humanity with which the defendants are charged. The material facts which must be proved in any case are (1) the fact of the great pattern or plan of racial persecution and extermination; and (2) specific conduct of the individual defendant in furtherance of the plan. This is but an application of general concepts of criminal law. The person who persuades another to commit murder, the person who furnishes the lethal weapon for the purpose of its commission, and the person who pulls the trigger are all principals or accessories to the crime.

We turn to the national pattern or plan for racial extermination.

Fundamentally, the program was one for the actual extermination of Jews and Poles, either by means of killing or by confinement in concentration camps, which merely made death slower and more painful. But lesser forms of racial persecution were universally practiced by governmental authority and constituted an integral part in the general policy of the Reich. We have already noted the decree by which Jews were excluded from the legal profession. Intermarriage between Jews and persons of German blood was prohibited. Sexual intercourse between Jews and German nationals was punished with extreme severity by the courts. By other decrees Jews were almost completely expelled from public service, from educational institutions, and from many business enterprises.

* * *

Former defendant Engert as vice president of the People's Court, and Thierack, the president of the People's Court, protested in July and August 1940 against the trial of minor cases in the People's Court as not being compatible with the dignity of the tribunal and suggested that the defendants in such cases should be transferred to a concentration camp. As Thierack put it—

> However right it is to exterminate harshly and uproot all the seeds of insurrection, as for example we see them in Bohemia and Moravia, it is wrong for every follower, even the smallest, to be given the honor of appearing for trial and being judged for high treason before a People's Court or, failing that, before an appellate court. In order to deal with these small cases and even with the smallest, the culprits should surely be shown that German sovereignty will not put up with their behavior and that it will take action accordingly. But that can also be done in a different way and I think in a more advantageous one, than through the tedious and also very expensive and ponderous channels of court procedure. I have therefore no objection whatsoever, if all the small hangers-on who are somehow connected with the high treason plans which have been woven by others are brought to their senses by being transferred to a concentration camp for some time.

As early as 29 January 1941 the senior public prosecutor at Hamm wrote to the Reich Minister of Justice, for the attention of State Secretary Schlegelberger (*NG–685*, *Pros. Ex. 259*):

> Upon inquiry, the Reich Trustee for Labor for the economic territory of Westphalia-Lower Rhine has informed me that "in accordance with an agreement between the Reich Minister for Labor and the Reich Leader SS as Chief of the German Police, breach of work contracts by Poles are to be punished by the Secret State Police with protective custody or concentration camps. The meaning of this step"—so writes this Reich trustee—"is that in the case of Poles the strictest measures are to be taken at once . . . ." For this reason we made it a point in my office to transfer the cases involving breaches of work contracts by Polish civilian workers, to the Gestapo (Secret State Police) for further action.

The same letter informs the defendant Schlegelberger of uncertainty which has arisen in the treatment of Polish civilians because in some cases the courts would sentence to 2 or 3 years imprisonment while the State Police may pronounce the death sentence for the same crime.

While the part played by the Ministry of Justice in the extermination of Poles and Jews was small compared to the mass extermination of millions by the SS and Gestapo in concentration camps, nevertheless the courts contributed greatly to the "final solution" of the problem. From a secret report from the office of the Reich Minister of Justice to the judges and prosecutors, including the defendant Lautz, it appears that 189 persons were sentenced under the law for the protection of German blood and honor in 1941, and 109 in 1942. In the year 1942, 61,836 persons were convicted under the law against Poles and Jews. This figure includes persons convicted in the Incorporated Eastern Territories, and also convictions for crimes committed in "other districts of the German Reich by Jews and Poles who on 1 September 1939 had their residence or permanent place of abode in territory of the former Polish state." These figures, of course, do not include any cases in which Jews were convicted of other crimes in which the law of 4 December 1941 was not involved.

The defendants contend that they were unaware of the atrocities committed by the Gestapo and in concentration camps. This contention is subject to serious question. Dr. Behl testified that he considered it impossible that anyone, particularly in Berlin, should have been ignorant of the brutalities of the SS and the Gestapo. He said: "In Berlin it would have been hardly possible for anybody not to know about it, and certainly not for anybody who was a lawyer and who dealt with the administration of justice." He testified specifically that he could not imagine that any person in the Ministry of Justice, or in the Party Chancellery, or as a practicing attorney or a judge of a Special (or) People's Court could be in ignorance of the facts of common knowledge concerning the treatment of prisoners in concentration camps. It has been repeatedly urged by and in behalf of various defendants that they remained in the Ministry of Justice because they feared that if they should retire, control of the matters pertaining to the Ministry of Justice would be transferred to Himmler and the Gestapo. In short, they claim that they were withstanding the evil encroachments of Himmler upon the justice administration, and yet we are asked to believe that they were ignorant of the character of the forces which they say they were opposing. We concur in the finding of the first Tribunal in the case of United States et al. *vs.* Goering, et al., concerning the use of concentration camps. We quote:

> Their original purpose was to imprison without trial all those persons who were opposed to the government, or who were in any way obnoxious to German authority. With the aid of a secret police force, this practice was widely extended, and in course of time concentration camps became places of organized and systematic murder where millions of people were destroyed.
>
> * * *
>
> A certain number of the concentration camps were equipped with gas chambers for the wholesale destruction of the inmates, and with furnaces for the burning of the bodies. Some of them were in fact used for the extermination of Jews as part of the "final solution" of the Jewish problem.
>
> * * *
>
> In Poland and the Soviet Union these crimes were part of a plan to get rid of whole native populations by expulsion and annihilation, in order that their territory could be used for colonization by Germans. Hitler had written in "Mein Kampf" on these lines, and the plan was clearly stated by Himmler in July 1942, when he wrote: "It is not our task to Germanize the East in the old sense, that is to teach

the people there the German language and the German law, but to see to it that only people of purely Germanic blood live in the East."

A large proportion of all of the Jews in Germany were transported to the east. Millions of persons disappeared from Germany and the occupied territory without a trace. They were herded into concentration camps within and without Germany. Thousands of soldiers and members of the Gestapo and SS must have been instrumental in the processes of deportation, torture, and extermination. The mere task of disposal of mountainous piles of corpses (evidence of which we have seen) became a serious problem and the subject of disagreement between the various organizations involved. The thousands of Germans who took part in the atrocities must have returned from time to time to their homes in the Reich. The atrocities were of a magnitude unprecedented in the history of the world. Are we to believe that no whisper reached the ears of the public or of those officials who were most concerned? Did the defendants think that the nation-wide pogrom of November 1938 officially directed from Berlin and Hilter's announcement to the Reichstag threatening the obliteration of the Jewish race in Europe were unrelated? At least they cannot plead ignorance concerning the decrees which were published in their official organ, "The Reichsgesetzblatt." Therefore, they knew that Jews were to be punished by the police in Germany and in Bohemia and Moravia. They knew that the property of Jews was confiscated on death of the owner. They knew that the law against Poles and Jews had been extended to occupied territories, and they knew that the Chief of the Security Police was the official authorized to determine whether or not Jewish property was subject to confiscation. They could hardly be ignorant of the fact that the infamous law againt Poles and Jews of 4 December 1941 directed the Reich Minister of Justice himself, together with the Minister of the Interior, to issue legal and administrative regulations for "implementation of the decree." They read *The Stuermer.* They listened to the radio. They received and sent directives. They heard and delivered lectures. This Tribunal is not so gullible as to believe these defendants so tupid that they did not know what was going on. One man can keep a secret, two men may, but thousands, never.

The evidence conclusively establishes the adoption and application of systematic government-organized and approved procedures amounting to atrocities and offenses of the kind made punishable by C. C. Law 10 and committed against "populations" and amounting to persecution on racial grounds. These procedures when carried out in occupied territory constituted war crimes and crimes against humanity. When enforced in the Alt Reich against German nationals they constituted crimes against humanity.

The pattern and plan of racial persecution has been made clear. General knowledge of the broad outlines thereof in all its immensity has been brought home to the defendants. The remaining question is whether or not the evidence proves beyond a reasonable doubt in the case of the individual defendants that they each consciously participated in the plan or took a consenting part therein.

THE DEFENDANT SCHLEGELBERGER

The defendant Franz Schlegelberger was born on 23 October 1875 in Koenigsberg. He received the degree of doctor of law at the University of Leipzig in 1899 and passed the higher state law examination in 1901. He is the author of several law books. His first employment was as an assistant judge at the local court in Koenigsberg. In 1904 he became judge at the district court at Lyck. In 1908 he was appointed judge of the local court in Berlin and in the fall of the same year was appointed as an assistant judge of the Berlin Court of Appeals. He was then appointed councillor of the Berlin Court of Appeals in 1914, where he worked until 1918. During the First World War, on 1 April 1918 he became an assistant to the Reich Board of Justice. On 1 October 1918 he was appointed Privy Government Councillor and department chief. In 1927 he was appointed ministerial director in the Reich Ministry of Justice. On 10 October 1931 he was appointed Secretary of State in the Reich Ministry of Justice under Minister of Justice Guertner, which position he held until Guertner's death. Upon Guertner's death on 29 January 1941 Schlegelberger was put in charge of the Reich Ministry of Justice as administrative Secretary of State. When Thierack became the new Minister of Justice on 20 August 1942, Schlegelberger resigned from the Ministry.

In 1938 Hitler ordered Schlegelberger to join the NSDAP. Schlegelberger testified that he made no use of the Party, that he never attended a Party meeting, that none of his family belonged to the Party, and that Party attitudes often rendered his position difficult. However, upon his retirement as Acting Minister of Justice on 20 August 1942, Schlegelberger received a letter of appreciation from Hitler together with a gift of 100,000 RM.

Later in 1944 Hitler gave Schlegelberger the special privilege to use the 100,000 RM to purchase a farm, which under the rule then prevailing could have been purchased only by an expert agriculturist. Schlegelberger states that the 100,000 RM were on deposit in a Berlin German bank to his account when the collapse came. Thus, it is shown that Hitler and Schlegelberger were not too objectionable to each other. These transactions also show that Hitler was at least attempting to reward Schlegelberger for good and faithful service rendered in the performance of some of which Schlegelberger committed both war crimes and crimes against humanity as charged in the indictment.

We have already adverted to his speech at the University of Rostock on 10 March 1936, on the subject, "A Nation Beholds Its Rightful Law." In this speech Schlegelberger declared:

> In the sphere of criminal law the road to a creation of justice in harmony with the moral concepts of the new Reich has been opened up by a new wording of section 2 of the criminal code, whereby a person is also [to] be punished even if his deed is not punishable according to the law, but if he deserves punishment in accordance with the basic concepts of criminal law and the sound instincts of the people. This new definition became necessary because of the rigidity of the norm in force hitherto.

As amended, section 2 remained in effect until repealed by Law No. 11 of the Allied Control Council. The term "the sound people's sentiment" as used in amended section 2 has been the subject of much discussion and difference of view as to both its proper translation and interpretation. We regard the statute as furnishing no objective standards "by which the people's sound sentiment may be measured." In application and in fact this expression became the "healthy instincts" of Hitler and his coconspirators.

What has been said with regard to the amendment to section 2 of the criminal code is equally true of the amendment of section 170a of the code by the decree of Hitler of 28 June 1935, which is also signed by Minister Guertner and which provides:

> If an act deserves punishment according to the common sense of the people but is not declared punishable in the code, the prosecution must investigate whether the underlying principle of a penal law can be applied to the act and whether justice can be helped to triumph by the proper application of this penal law.

This new conception of criminal law was a definite encroachment upon the rights of the individual citizen because it subjected him to the arbitrary opinion of the judge as to what constituted an offense. It destroyed the feeling of legal security and created an atmosphere of terrorism. This principle of treating crimes by analogy provided an expedient instrumentality for the enforcement of Nazi principles in the occupied countries. German criminal law was therefore introduced in the incorporated areas and also in the nonincorporated territories, and German criminal law was thereafter applied by German courts in the trial of inhabitants of occupied countries though the inhabitants of those countries could have no possible conception of the acts which would constitute criminal offenses.

In the earlier portions of this opinion we have repeatedly referred to the actions of the defendant Schlegelberger. Repetition would serve no good purpose. By way of summary we may say that Schlegelberger supported the pretension of Hitler in his assumption of power to deal with life and death in disregard of even the pretense of judicial process. By his exhortations and directives, Schlegelberger contributed to the destruction of judicial independence. It was his signature on the decree of 7 February 1942 which imposed upon the Ministry of Justice and the courts the burden of the prosecution, trial, and disposal of the victims of Hitler's Night and Fog. For this he must be charged with primary responsibility.

He was guilty of instituting and supporting procedures for the wholesale persecution of Jews and Poles. Concerning Jews, his ideas were less brutal than those of his associates, but they can scarcely be called humane. When the "final solution of the Jewish question" was under discussion, the question arose as to the disposition of half-Jews. The deportation of full Jews to the East was then in full swing throughout Germany. Schlegelberger was unwilling to extend the system to half-Jews. He therefore proposed to Reich Minister Lammers, by secret letter on 5 April 1942 (*4055–PS, Pros. Ex. 401*):

> The measures for the final solution of the Jewish question should extend only to full Jews and descendants of mixed marriages of the first degree, but should not apply to descendants of mixed marriages of the second degree. [First degree presumably those with two non-Aryan grandparents, and second degree with only one.]
>
> With regard to the treatment of Jewish descendants of mixed marriages of the first degree, I agree with the conception of the Reich Minister of the Interior which he expressed in his letter of 16 February 1942, to the effect that the prevention of propagation of these descendants of mixed marriages is to be preferred to their being thrown in with the Jews and evacuated. It follows therefrom that the evacuation of those half-Jews who are no more capable of propagation is obviated from the beginning. There is no national interest in dissolving the marriages between such half-Jews and a full-blooded German.
>
> Those half-Jews who are capable of propagation should be given the choice to submit to sterilization or to be evacuated in the same manner as Jews.

Schlegelberger knew of the pending procedures for the evacuation of Jews and acquiesced in them. As to half-Jews his only suggestion was that they be given the free choice of either one of the impaling horns of a dilemma. On 17 April 1941 Schlegelberger wrote to Lammers as follows (*NG–144*, *Pros. Ex. 199*):

> On being informed of the Fuehrer's intention to discriminate in the sphere of penal law between the Poles (and probably the Jews as well), and the Germans, I prepared, after preliminary discussions with the presidents of the courts of appeal and the attorneys general of the annexed eastern territories, the attached draft concerning the administration of the penal laws against Poles and Jews in the annexed eastern territories and in the territory of the former Free City of Danzig.

The draft of a proposed ordinance "concerning the administration of justice regarding Poles and Jews in the Incorporated Eastern Territories" was attached to his letter and is in evidence. A comparison of its phraseology with the phraseology contained in the notorious law against Poles and Jews of 4 December 1941 discloses beyond question that Schlegelberger's draft constituted the basis on which, with certain modifications and changes, the law against Poles and Jews was enacted. In this respect he was not only guilty of participation in the racial persecution of Poles and Jews; he was also guilty of violation of the laws and customs of war by establishing that legislation in the occupied territories of the East. The extension of this type of law into occupied territories was in direct violation of the limitations imposed by the Hague Convention, which we have previously cited.

It is of interest to note that on 31 January 1942 Schlegelberger issued a decree providing that the provisions of the law against Poles and Jews "will be equally applicable with the consent of the public prosecutor to offenses committed before the decree came into force." We doubt if the defendant would contend that the extension of this discriminatory and retroactive law into occupied territory was based on military necessity.

Schlegelberger divorced his inclinations from his conduct. He disapproved "of the revision of sentences" by the police, yet he personally ordered the murder of the Jew Luftgas on the request of Hitler, and assured the Fuehrer that he would, himself, take action if the Fuehrer would inform him of other sentences which were disapproved.

Schlegelberger's attitude toward atrocities committed by the police must be inferred from his conduct. A milking-hand, Bloedling, was sentenced to death in October 1940, and during the trial he insisted his purported confession had been obtained as a result of beatings imposed upon him by the police officer Klinzmann. A courageous judge tried Klinzmann and convicted him of brutality and sentenced him to a few months imprisonment. Himmler protested against the sentence of Klinzmann and stated that he was going "to take the action of the Hauptwachtmeister of the police Klinzmann as an occasion to express gratitude for his farsighted conduct which was only beneficial to the community." He said further: "I must reward his action because otherwise the joy of serving in the police would be destroyed by such verdicts. But finally K. has to be rehabilitated in public because his being sentenced by a court is known in public."

On 10 December 1941 Schlegelberger wrote to the Chief of the Reich Chancellery stating that he was unable to understand the sentence passed against Klinzmann. We quote:

> No sooner had the verdict passed on Klinzmann become known here, orders were for this reason given to the effect that the sentence in case of its validation should not be carried out for the time being. Instead, reports concerning the granting of a pardon should be made as soon as possible. In the meantime, however, the sentence passed on Klinzmann became valid, by decision of the Reich [Supreme] Court of 24 November 1941 which abandoned the procedure of revision as apparently unfounded. Taking into regard also the opinion you expressed on the sentence, Sir, I now ordered the remission of the sentence and of the costs of proceedings by way of pardon as well as the striking out of the penalty note in the criminal records.

On 24 December 1941 Schlegelberger wrote to Lammers that he had quashed the proceedings. In February 1942 Himmler wrote expressing appreciation of the efforts in quashing the proceedings against Klinzmann and stated that he had since promoted him to Meister of the municipal police.

Schlegelberger presents an interesting defense, which is also claimed in some measure by most of the defendants. He asserts that the administration of justice was under persistent assault by Himmler and other advocates of the police state. This is true. He contends that if the functions of the administration of justice were usurped by the lawless forces under Hitler and Himmler, the last state of the nation would be worse than the first. He feared that if he were to resign, a worse man would take his place. As the event proved, there is much truth in this also. Under Thierack the police did usurp the functions of the administration of justice and murdered untold thousands of Jews and political prisoners. Upon analysis this plausible claim of the defense squares neither with the truth, logic, or the circumstances.

The evidence conclusively shows that in order to maintain the Ministry of Justice in the good graces of Hitler and to prevent its utter defeat by Himmler's police, Schlegelberger and the other defendants who joined in this claim of justification took over the dirty work which the leaders of the State demanded, and employed the Ministry of Justice as a means for exterminating the Jewish and Polish populations, terrorizing the inhabitants of occupied countries, and wiping out political opposition at home. That their program of racial extermination under the guise of law failed to attain the proportions which were reached by the pogroms, deportations, and mass murders by the police is cold comfort to the survivors of the "judicial" process and constitutes a poor excuse before this Tribunal. The prostitution of a judicial system for the accomplishment of criminal ends involves an element of evil to the State which is not found in frank atrocities which do not sully judicial robes.

Schlegelberger resigned. The cruelties of the system which he had helped to develop were too much for him, but he resigned too late. The damage was done. If the judiciary could slay their thousands, why couldn't the police slay their tens of thousands? The consequences which Schlegelberger feared were realized. The police, aided by Thierack, prevailed. Schlegelberger had failed. His hesitant injustices no longer satisfied the urgent demands of the hour. He retired under fire. In spite of all that he had done he still bore an unmerited reputation as the last of the German jurists and so Hitler gave him his blessing and 100,000 RM as a parting gift. We are under no misapprehension. Schlegelberger is a tragic character. He loved the life of an intellect, the work of the scholar. We believe that he loathed the evil that he did, but he sold that intellect and that scholarship to Hitler for a mess of political pottage and for the vain hope of personal security. He is guilty under counts two and three of the indictment.

The Defendant Klemm

Herbert Klemm, formerly State Secretary of the Reich Ministry of Justice, was born in Leipzig on 15 May 1903. After normal schooling, he passed his first legal state examination in 1925, his second legal state examination in 1929. From 1929 to 1933, he was court assessor of the prosecution authority of Dresden. From March 1933 to March 1935 he was the personal Referent and adjutant of Thierack, Minister of Justice, Saxony. In 1935, at the time of the centralization of the administration of justice, he was transferred to the Reich Ministry of Justice where he remained until he was mobilized for war service on 23 June 1940. On 20 April 1939 he was promoted to the office of Ministerialrat. In July of 1940 he was assigned to the Reich Commissioner for the Occupied Dutch Territories, upon the request of the Plenipotentiary for Occupied Dutch Territories. On 17 March 1941 he was transferred to the staff of the deputy of the Fuehrer, which later became the Party Chancellery, in Munich. He remained with the Party Chancellery until 4 January 1944, when he became state secretary of the Reich Ministry of Justice under Thierack. He remained in this capacity until the surrender.

Klemm's Party connections were as follows: he applied for membership in the NSDAP on 4 November 1930; his membership card, 405576, was received 1 January 1931. On 30 June 1933 he joined the SA; the highest rank which he received in the SA was that of Oberfuehrer. When in Saxony he was the legal advisor of the SA for Saxony and liaison officer between the SA for Saxony and the Minister of Justice for Saxony. When he was transferred to Berlin, he was the liaison officer between the Reich Ministry of Justice and the SA Chief of Staff for Germany and the legal advisor to the Chief of Staff of the SA for Germany.

He was a member of the National Socialist Jurists' League from 1933. In September of 1944 he was appointed deputy chief of the National Socialist Jurists' League by Thierack, who was at that time chief.

* * *

Klemm's career under the Third Reich moved smoothly from comparative insignificance to the position of State Secretary in the Ministry of Justice. His ascent was marked by no serious differences as to Party policies. He was close to both Bormann and Thierack and ascended by their favor. Under the circumstances it is not credible that he was ignorant of the policies and methods of these ruthless figures.

The defendant lays great stress on an order of Hitler as to secrecy and states that in connection with this order he adhered strictly to it; that he did not attempt to hear anything outside of his official duties. Such orders as to secrecy were not confined to Germany during the war; they were standard procedure in other countries and by no means excluded knowledge of secret matters derived from normal human contacts, particularly friends and acquaintances in the higher levels of state affairs. Further, the confidential position held by the defendant gave him a wide scope as to secret matters within the sphere of his official duties. As State Secretary of the Ministry of Justice and deputy of the minister in his absence, the defendant's official duties required knowledge of the higher spheres of State policy.

More specifically, Klemm knew of abuses in concentration camps. He knew of the practice of severe interrogations. He knew of the persecution and oppression of the Jews and Poles and gypsies. He must be assumed to have known, from the evidence, the general basis of Nacht und Nebel procedure under the Department of Justice. Therefore, it becomes important to consider his connection with the carrying out of these crimes alleged in the indictment and established by the evidence in this case.

It is clear from the evidence, heretofore outlined in part, that when the defendant Klemm was in Holland he knew of the persecution of Jews and he was connected to some extent with that persecution.

While he was in the Party Chancellery he wrote the letter, heretofore pointed out, denying the application of the German juvenile law to Poles, Jews, and gypsies. This Tribunal does not construe that letter as a legal opinion but as an expression of Party policy, submitted through the Party Chancellery to the Ministry of Justice to the effect that minors of the prescribed races must be subject to the merciless provisions of the decree against Poles and Jews. The argument that they were necessarily excluded because they were foreigners, and that the German Juvenile Act contemplated entrance into the Hitler Youth, and similar provisions applicable only to Germans has little significance when the letter itself expressly states that there were no objections to applying the German Criminal Code for juveniles to foreign juveniles, unless they were Poles, Jews, or gypsies. Further, it can hardly be construed as a legal opinion as to gypsies in view of the statement therein made that a special regulation will come into effect which will prevent the German Criminal Code for juveniles from applying to gypsies and those of gypsy descent merely because a definite regulation is lacking.

While in the Party Chancellery, Klemm took part in drafting the law to make treason retroactive and applying it to annexed territories, and this draft bears his signature.

As State Secretary he knew of the NN procedure and was connected therewith, particularly as to the approximately 123 NN prisoners sentenced to death who were denied clemency while he sat in conference with Thierack, and in the eight cases where he denied clemency as deputy for Thierack.

As State Secretary in the Ministry of Justice, he necessarily exercised supervision over the enforcement of the decree against Poles and Jews and dealt with clemency matters pertaining to cases tried under that decree.

In connection with the defendant Klemm, two other transactions constituting crimes charged in the indictment are of particular significance. The first of these is charged under the second count of the indictment as a war crime against all the defendants and, particularly under paragraph 18 of the indictment, charging the defendant Klemm with special responsibility and participation. This pertains to the inciting of the German population to murder Allied airmen forced down within the Reich.

Evidence of this plan of the leaders of the German State is found as follows: First in the correspondence relative to the treatment of so-called "enemy terrorist airmen." As part of this correspondence from the deputy chief of the operations staff of the armed forces, entitled "Secret matter," dated 6 June 1944, and signed by General Warlimont, the following sentence is significant: "Lynch justice should be considered as being the rule."

Upon the evidence in this case it is the judgment of this Tribunal that the defendant, Klemm, is guilty under counts two and three of the indictment.

The Defendant Rothenberger

From his own sworn statements we derive the following information concerning the defendant Rothenberger. He joined the NSDAP on 1 May 1933 "for reasons of full conviction." From 1937 until 1942 he held the position of Gau Rechtsamtleiter. He states: "As such I also belonged to the Leadership Corps." Parenthetically, it should be stated that the organization within the Leadership Corps to which he belonged has been declared criminal by the judgment of the first International Military Tribunal, and that membership therein with knowledge of its illegal activities is a punishable crime under C. C. Law 10. We consider the interesting fact of his membership in the Leadership Corps no further, solely because defendant Rothenberger was not charged in the indictment with membership in a criminal organization. He was a Dienstleiter in the NSDAP during 1942 and 1943. From 1934 to 1942 he was Gaufuehrer in the National Socialist Jurists' League. In 1931 he became Landgerichtsdirektor, and in 1933 Justiz-Senator in Hamburg. From 1935 to 1942 he was president of the district court of appeals in Hamburg. In 1942 he was appointed Under Secretary in the Ministry of Justice under Thierack. He remained in that office until he left the Ministry in December 1943, after which he served as a notary in Hamburg. Thus, it is established by his own evidence that while serving as president of the district court of appeals he was also actively engaged as a Party official. Other evidence discloses the wide extent to which the interests and demands of the Ministry of Justice, the Party, the Gau Leadership, the SS, the SD, and the Gestapo affected his conduct in matters pertaining to the administration of justice. Rothenberger took over the Gau Leadership of the National Socialist Lawyers' League at the request of Gauleiter Kauffmann, who was the representative of German sovereignty in the Gau and who was, for all intents and purposes, a local dictator. As Gaufuehrer during the period following the seizure of power, Rothenberger had ample opportunity to learn of the corruption which permeated the administration of justice. He testified:

> It has been emphasized here time and again how during the first period, after the revolution of 1933, every Kreisleiter attempted to interfere in court proceedings; the Gestapo tried to revise sentences, and it is known how the NSRB, the National Socialist Jurists' League, tried to gain influence with the Gauleiter or the Reichsstatthalter in order to act against the administration of justice.

Concerning the dual capacity in which he served, he said:

> On account of the identity, of course, between president of the district court of appeals and Gaufuehrer, I was envied by all other district courts of appeal because they continually had to struggle against the Party while I was saved this struggle.

In August 1939, on the eve of war, Rothenberger was in conference with officials of the SS and expressed to them the wish to be able to fall back on the information apparatus of the SD, and offered to furnish to the SD copies of "such sentences as are significant on account of their importance for the carrying-out of the National Socialist ideas in the field of the administration of justice." Rothenberger testified that during the first few years after the seizure of power, there was the usual system of SD informers in Hamburg. The unsatisfactory personnel in the SD was removed by Reichsstatthalter Kauffmann, and the defendant Rothenberger nominated in their place individuals who, he said, "were judges and who I knew would never submit reports which were against the administration of justice." He states also:

> In the meantime, the directive had been sent down from the Reich Ministry of Justice to the effect that the SD should be considered and used as a source of information of the State by agencies of the administration of justice.

While he was president of the district court of appeals at Hamburg, and during the war, this ardent advocate of judicial independence was not adverse to acting as the agent of Gauleiter Kauffmann. On 19 September 1939 Kauffmann, as Reichsstatthalter and defense commissioner, issued an order as follows:

> The president of the Hanseatic Court of Appeals, Senator Dr. Rothenberger, is acting on my order and is entitled to demand information in matters concerning the special courts and to inspect documents of every kind. All administrative offices as well as the offices of the NSDAP are requested to assist him in his work.

On 26 September 1939 Rothenberger, as president of the Hanseatic Court of Appeals, notified the Prosecutor General of Kauffmann's order and requested that a copy of the indictment "in all politically important cases or cases which are of special interest to the public should be sent to him." In a report to Schlegelberger of 11 May 1942 he spoke of the "crushing effect" of the Fuehrer's speech of 26 April 1942 and of the feeling of consequent insecurity on the part of the judges, and said: "I have therefore assumed responsibility for each verdict which the judges discuss with me before passing it."

In the same report he states that on 6 May 1942 he made arrangements with all senior police officers, senior SS, senior officers of the criminal police, of the Secret State Police, and of the SD "to the effect that every complaint about juridical measures taken by judges was to be referred to me before the police would take action (especially regarding execution of sentence)."

In June 1942 Rothenberger reported to the defendant Schlegelberger that he had made similar arrangements in Bremen with the Kreisleiter, president of the police, leader of the Secret State Police (Gestapo), and the leader of the SD. He reported to Schlegelberger: "In view of the present situation, I am intensifying the internal direction and control of jurisdiction which I have considered to be my main task since 1933."

On 7 May 1942 Rothenberger issued an order in which he stated his intention to inform himself prior to the proceedings on cases which are of political significance "or which involve the possibility of a certain conflict between formal law and the instinctive reactions of the people or National Socialist ideology." He directed that reports be submitted to him which must be in sufficient detail in order, as he said, "to enable my deputy to judge the necessity of my intervention."

By reference to his own words we have already set forth Rothenberger's expressed convictions as to the duty of a judge as the "vassal" of the Fuehrer to decide cases as the Fuehrer would decide. The conclusion which we are compelled to draw from a great mass of evidence is not that Rothenberger objected to the exertion of influence upon the courts by Hitler, the Party leaders, or the Gestapo, but that he wished that influence to be channeled through him personally rather than directed in a more public way at each individual judge. On the one hand he established liaison with the Party officials and the police, and on the other he organized the system of guidance of the judges who were his subordinates in the Hamburg area. He testifies that he considered the system of conferences between judges and prosecutors before trial, during trial and sometimes after trial, but before the consultation of the judges, to be wrong, and states that he considered it more correct, in view of the situation, that such a discussion should take place a long time before the trial and not between individual judges and the prosecutor, "but on a higher level, namely, between the chiefs of the offices, so that there would be no possibility to exert an influence on the individual judge in any way." Concerning his dictatorial attitude toward the other judges, Rothenberger testified: "Of course, guidance is guidance, and absolute and complete independence of the judge is possible only in normal conditions of peace, and we did not have these conditions after the Hitler speech."

The guidance system instituted by the defendant Rothenberger was not limited to conferences concerning pending cases of political importance before trial. We are convinced from the evidence that he used his influence with the subordinate judges in his district to protect Party members who had been charged or convicted of crime, that on occasions he severely criticized judges for decisions rendered against Party officials, and on at least one occasion was instrumental in having a judge removed from his position because he had insisted upon proceeding with a criminal case against a Party official.

As further illustration of the character of control which was exercised by Rothenberger over the other judges in his district, reference is made to his letter of 7 May 1942 addressed to the judges in Hamburg and Bremen in which he announced that a conference would be held for the discussion of cases fixed for the following week. We quote (*NG–389, Pros. Ex. 76*): "A few cues to matters which will come up will be given, file numbers quoted, and comments made in a few key words."

He especially required of the judges that they report to him concerning penal cases against Poles, Jews, and other foreigners, and "penal and civil cases in which persons are involved who are State or Party officials, or NSDAP functionaries, or who hold some other eminent position in public life."

* * *

The defendant Rothenberger testified that various judges reported to him "that they had heard rumors to the effect that everything was not quite all right in the concentration camps" and that they wished to inspect one. Accordingly,

Rothenberger and the other judges visited the concentration camp at Neuengamme. He testified that they inquired about food conditions, accommodations, and the methods of work, and spoke to some inmates, and he asserts that they did not discover any abuses. This was in 1941. Again in 1942, according to his own testimony, the defendant visited Mauthausen concentration camp in company with Kaltenbrunner, who was later in charge of all concentration camps in Germany and has since suffered death by hanging. At Mauthausen concentration camp the defendant Rothenberger again inspected installations, conferred with inmates, and inquired as to the cause of detention of the inmates with whom he had talked. He states that from his spot checks he "could not find out that there was any case of a sentence being 'corrected.'" Upon inquiry as to what the defendant meant by the "correction of sentences," he answered:

> By correcting of a sentence we mean that when the court had pronounced a sentence, for example, had condemned somebody to be imprisoned for a term of 5 years—if the police now, after these 5 years had been served, if the police arrested this man and put him into a concentration camp—this is only an example of a correction. Or even if, and this is clearer, it happened that a person was acquitted by a court, and in spite of that the police put this man into a concentration camp. These are examples of correction of sentences.

* * *

The defendant Rothenberger is guilty of taking a minor but consenting part in the Night and Fog program. He aided and abetted in the program of racial persecution, and notwithstanding his many protestations to the contrary he materially contributed toward the prostitution of the Ministry of Justice and the courts and their subordination to the arbitrary will of Hitler, the Party minions, and the police. He participated in the corruption and perversion of the judicial system. The defendant Rothenberger is guilty under counts two and three of the indictment.

THE DEFENDANT VON AMMON

From his own sworn statements we gain the following information concerning the defendant von Ammon. He joined the SA in December 1933, in which organization he held the rank of Scharfuehrer. He joined the NSDAP in May 1937. He was called to the Reich Ministry of Justice as of 1 January 1935, became a Landgerichtsrat on 1 February 1935, and Landgerichtsdirektor on 1 July 1937. His main activity in the Ministry during that period concerned "questions of international legal usage in penal matters."

After the Austrian Anschluss he was employed as liaison officer of Department III (penal matters) in connection with Department VIII (Austria), in the Reich Ministry of Justice. He was consultant in the department for the administration of penal law under Ministerialdirektor Crohne. He was transferred to the Munich Court of Appeals as Oberlandesgerichtsrat where he served until

June 1940, at which time he was recalled to the Reich Ministry of Justice. As of 1 March 1943 he was appointed Ministerial Counsellor in the Ministry of Justice. He states (*NG-852, Pros. Ex. 55*):

> From 1942 onward I dealt mainly with Nacht und Nebel cases in the occupied territories. In my capacity as consultant for Nacht und Nebel cases I made several duty trips to the occupied territories and took part in discussions in Paris and Holland which dealt with questions of Nacht und Nebel proceedings.

The broad scope and the variety of the official activities of von Ammon may be illustrated by reference to reports which he made to officials of the Ministry of Justice during the year 1944. On 14 January 1944 he reported at the Ministry upon "jurisdiction of Denmark." On 10 February he reported to the minister on "Competence for Prosecution of NN Cases." On 31 May, under the heading "Submissions to the State Secretary" (Klemm), he reported on "Action Against Stateless Jews, Admission of Legal Procedure." Under the heading "Reports to the State Secretary" for 21 June 1944, he reported on "Pastoral Service for NN Prisoners," after which in handwriting appears the word "rejection." Under the heading "Submissions to the Minister" for 26 July, he reported on "Proceedings of State Police in Lower Styria." Under the heading "Reports to the Ministers" of 5 October, he reported on "Taking Over of Criminal Proceedings from the Eastern Districts." Under the heading "Formal Verbal Reports to the Minister" of 3 November 1944, he reported on "Liquidation of Offenses from the Eastern Territories." On 10 January 1945 it appears that he made a verbal report on the "Taking Over Administration of Penal Justice of the Minister for the East."

The prosecution introduced in evidence a captured document of 142 pages in length, containing lists of many hundreds of death sentences which were submitted to the Minister of Justice and at times to State Secretary Klemm for final disposition. The cases were classified as "clear" or as "doubtful." The former, "clear," outnumbered the latter. An examination of the document discloses that between 14 January 1944 and 16 November of the same year the defendant von Ammon made twenty-four reports on cases in which persons from the occupied territories had been sentenced to death under the Nacht und Nebel procedure. The death sentences averaged more than one for every 3 days of the entire period.

In a notice addressed to Under Secretary Rothenberger, and to Minister Thierack, von Ammon reported that on 1 September 1942, in Kiel, Essen, and Cologne cases were pending against 1,456 persons charged under the Night and Fog decree.

In view of the fact that von Ammon was in charge of Nacht und Nebel procedure from 1942 until the end of the war, it is clear that we have in evidence only incomplete records of the activities of this defendant in connection with the Night and Fog decree. The fragmentary character of the captured documents which have been submitted renders it impossible to give a complete picture of this criminal activity. The illustrations which we have given and which cover only a portion of the time involved will, however, serve as an indication of the scope of the activities which were under the direction of the defendants Mettgenberg and von Ammon. Von Ammon also participated in a lengthy secret correspondence concerning the transfer of NN cases to the Special Court at Oppeln and the necessity of allocating additional judges and public prosecutors to that court in view of the resultant increase in the volume of work.

The defendant von Ammon held an executive position of responsibility involving the exercise of personal discretion. Within the ministry he was in charge of the section which handled Night and Fog cases. The defendant Mettgenberg stated that the Night and Fog section within his subdivision was headed by von Ammon and that whenever von Ammon had doubts concerning the handling of individual cases joint discussions were held. We quote: "When he had no doubts he could decide on matters himself."

We have already set forth at length the statement of von Ammon concerning his knowledge and activities and his misgivings concerning the entire procedure. The defendants von Ammon and Mettgenberg were the representatives of the Reich Ministry of Justice at a conference at The Hague on 2 November 1943 concerning "New Regulations for Dealing with Night and Fog Cases from the Netherlands." Von Ammon states that assurance was given by Mettgenberg and himself that close connection would be maintained between the judicial authorities at Essen and the German authorities in the Netherlands in the handling of NN cases. We have already quoted a note signed by von Ammon wherein he remarked that it was "rather awkward" that the defendants should learn the details of their charges only during the trial and commented on the insufficiency of the translation facilities in the trial of French NN prisoners. Von Ammon is chargeable with actual knowledge concerning the systematic abuse of the judicial process in these cases.

In respect to his other activities we refer to our general discussion under the heading "Night and Fog." We find the defendant von Ammon guilty of war crimes and crimes against humanity under counts two and three of the indictment.

The Defendant Rothaug

Oswald Rothaug was born 17 May 1897. His education was interrupted from 1916 to 1918 while he was in the army. He passed the final law examination in 1922 and the State examination for the higher administration of justice in 1925.

He joined the NSDAP in the spring of 1938 and the membership was made effective from May 1937.

Rothaug was a member of the National Socialist Jurists' League and the National Socialist Public Welfare Association. In his affidavit he denies belonging to the SD. However, the testimony of Elkar and his own admission on the witness stand establishes that he was an "honorary collaborator" for the SD on legal matters.

In December 1925 he began his career as a jurist, first as an assistant to an attorney in Ansbach and later as assistant judge at various courts. In 1927 he became public prosecutor in Hof in charge of criminal cases. From 1929 to 1933 he officiated as counsellor at the local court in Nuernberg. In June 1933 he became senior public prosecutor in the public prosecution in Nuernberg. Here he was the official in charge of general criminal cases, assistant of the Chief Public Prosecutor handling examination of suspensions of proceedings and of petitions for pardon. From November to April 1937 he officiated as counsellor of the district court in Schweinfurt. He was legal advisor in the civil and penal chamber and at the Court of Assizes, as well as chairman of the lay assessors' court. From April 1937 to May 1943 he was director of the district court in Nuernberg, except for a period in August and September of 1939 when he was in the Wehrmacht. During this time he was chairman of the Court of Assizes, of a penal chamber, and of the Special Court.

From May 1943 to April 1945 he was public prosecutor of the public prosecution at the People's Court in Berlin. Here, as head of Department I he handled for a time cases of high treason in the southern Reich territory, and from January 1944 cases concerning the undermining of public morale in the Reich territory.

Crimes charged in the indictment, as heretofore stated in this opinion, have been established by the evidence in this case. The questions, therefore, to be determined as to the defendant Rothaug are: first, whether he had knowledge of any crime so established; and second, whether he was a participant in or took a consenting part in its commission.

Rothaug's sources of knowledge have, with those of all the defendants, already been pointed out. But Rothaug's knowledge was not limited to those general sources. Rothaug was an official of considerable importance in Nuernberg. He had many political and official contacts; among these—he was the friend of Haberkern, Gau inspector of the Gau Franconia; he was the friend and associate of Oeschey, Gau legal advisor for the Gau Franconia; and was himself Gauwalter of the Lawyers' League. He was the "honorary collaborator" for the SD. According to the witness Elkar, [he was] the agent of the SD for Nuernberg and vicinity, this position was more important than that of a confidential agent, and an honorary collaborator was active in SD affairs. He testifies that Rothaug took the SS oath of secrecy.

Whether Rothaug knew of all the aspects of the crimes alleged, we need not determine. He knew of crimes as established by the evidence, and it is the function of this Tribunal to determine his connection, if any, therewith.

The defendant is charged under counts two, three, and four of the indictment. Under count four he is charged with being a member of the Party Leadership Corps. He is not charged with membership in the SD. The proof as to count four establishes that he was Gauwalter of the Lawyers' League. The

Lawyers' League was a formation of the Party and not a part of the Leadership Corps as determined by the International Military Tribunal in the case against Goering, et al.

As to counts two and four of the indictment, from the evidence submitted, the Tribunal finds the defendant not guilty. The question of the defendant's guilt as to count three of the indictment remains to be determined.

The evidence as to the character and activities of the defendant is voluminous. We shall confine ourselves to the question as to whether or not he took a consenting part in the plan for the persecution, oppression, and extermination of Poles and Jews.

His attitude of virulent hostility toward these races is proved from many sources and is in no wise shaken by the affidavits he has submitted on his own behalf.

The evidence in this regard comes from his own associates—the judges, prosecutors, defense counsel, medical experts, and others with whom he dealt. Among, but not limited to these, we cite the evidence of Doebig, Ferber, Bauer, Dorfmueller, Elkar, Engert, Groben, and Markl. In particular the testimony of Father Schosser is important. He testified as to many statements made by the defendant Rothaug during the trial of his own case, showing the defendant's hostility to Poles and his general attitude toward them. He stated that concerning the Poles in general, Rothaug expressed himself in the following manner:

> If he [Rothaug] had his way, then no Pole would be buried in a German cemetery, and then he went on to make the remark which everybody heard in that courtroom—that he would get up from his coffin if there was a Pole being buried near to him. Rothaug himself had to laugh because of this mean joke, and he went on to say, "You have to be able to hate, because according to the Bible, God is a hating God."

The testimony of Elkar is even more significant. He testifies that Rothaug believed in severe measures against foreigners and particularly against Poles and Jews, whom he felt should be treated differently from German transgressors. Rothaug felt there was a gap in the law in this respect. He states that Rothaug asserted that in his own court he achieved this discrimination by interpretation of existing laws but that other courts failed to do so. Such a gap, according to Rothaug, should be closed by singling out Poles and Jews for special treatment. Elkar testifies that recommendations were made by the defendant Rothaug, through the witness, to higher levels and that the subsequent decree of 1941 against Poles and Jews conformed to Rothaug's ideas as expressed and forwarded by the witness Elkar through SD channels to the RSHA.

This animosity of the defendant to these races is further established by documents in this case which show that his discrimination against these races encompassed others who he felt lacked the necessary harshness to carry out the policy of the Nazi State and Party toward these people.

In this connection the communication of Oeschey to Deputy Gauleiter

Holz, concerning Doebig, is worthy of note. In this communication many charges were made against Doebig for his failure to take action against officials under him who had failed to carry out the Nazi programs against Jews and Poles. Oeschey testified that these charges were copied from a letter submitted to him by the defendant Rothaug and that the defendant assumed responsibility for these charges. Rothaug denies that he assumed responsibility or had anything to do with the charges made, except in one immaterial instance. However, in the light of the circumstances themselves, the Tribunal accepts Oeschey's testimony in this regard, particularly in view of the unimpeached affidavit of Oeschey's secretary to the effect that these charges were copied directly by her from a letter of Rothaug's.

Documentary proof of Rothaug's attitude in this respect is further found in the records of cases tried by him which hereafter will be considered.

* * *

The third case to be considered is that of Leo Katzenberger. The record in this case shows that Lehmann Israel Katzenberger, commonly called Leo Katzenberger, was a merchant and head of the Jewish community in Nuernberg; that he was "sentenced to death for an offense under paragraph 2, legally identical with an offense under paragraph 4 of the decree against public enemies in connection with the offense of racial pollution." The trial was held in the public session on 13 March 1942. Katzenberger's age at that time was over 68 years.

The offense of racial pollution with which he was charged comes under article 2 of the Law for the Protection of German Blood and Honor. This section reads as follows:

> Sexual intercourse (except in marriage) between Jews and German nationals of German or German-related blood is forbidden.

The applicable sections of the Decree Against Public Enemies reads as follows:

Section 2

"Crimes During Air Raids"

> Whoever commits a crime or offense against the body, life, or property, taking advantage of air raid protection measures, is punishable by hard labor of up to 15 years, or for life, and in particularly severe cases, punishable by death.

* * *

Section 4

"Exploitation of the State of War a Reason for More Severe Punishment"

> Whoever commits a criminal act exploiting the extraordinary conditions caused by war is punishable beyond the regular punishment limits with hard labor

of up to 15 years, or for life, or is punishable by death if the sound common sense of the people requires it on account of the crime being particularly despicable.

The evidence in this case, aside from the record, is based primarily upon the testimony of Hans Groben, the investigating judge who first investigated the case; Hermann Markl, the official who prosecuted the case; Karl Ferber, who was one of the associate judges in the trial; Heinz Hoffmann, who was the other associate judge in the trial; Armin Baur, who was medical expert in the trial; Georg Engert, who dealt with clemency proceedings; and Otto Ankenbrand, another investigating judge.

The salient facts established in connection with this case are in substance as follows: Sometime in the first half of the year 1941 the witness Groben issued a warrant of arrest against Katzenberger, who was accused of having had intimate relations with the photographer Seiler. According to the results of the police inquiry, actual intercourse had not been proved, and Katzenberger denied the charge. Upon Groben's advice, Katzenberger agreed that he would not move against the warrant of arrest at that time but would await the results of further investigation. These further investigations were very lengthy, although Groben pressed the public prosecutor for speed. The police, in spite of their efforts, were unable to get further material evidence, and it became apparent that the way to clarify the situation was to take the sworn statement of Seiler, and this was done.

In her sworn statement she said that Katzenberger had known both her and her family for many years before she had come to Nuernberg and that his relationship to her was a friendly and fatherly one and denied the charge of sexual intercourse. The evidence also showed that Katzenberger had given Seiler financial assistance on various occasions and that he was administrator of the property where Seiler lived, which was owned by a firm of which he was a partner. Upon Seiler's statement, Groben informed Dr. Herz, counsel for Katzenberger, of the result and suggested that it was the right time to move against the warrant of arrest.

When this was done, Rothaug learned of it and ordered that the Katzenberger case be transferred from the criminal divisional court to the Special Court. The first indictment was withdrawn, and another indictment was prepared for the Special Court.

The witness Markl states that Rothaug dominated the prosecution, especially through his close friendship with the senior public prosecutor, Dr. Schroeder, who was the superior of Markl.

The indictment before the Special Court was prepared according to the orders of Rothaug, and Katzenberger was not charged only with race defilement in this new indictment, but there was also an additional charge under the decree against public enemies, which made the death sentence permissible. The new indictment also joined the Seiler woman on a charge of perjury. The effect of joining Seiler in the charge against Katzenberger was to preclude her from being a witness for the defendant, and such a combination was contrary to established practice. Rothaug at this time told Markl that there was sufficient proof of sexual intercourse between Seiler and Katzenberger to convince him, and that he was prepared to condemn Katzenberger to death. Markl informed the Ministry of Justice of Rothaug's intended procedure against Katzenberger and was told that if Rothaug so desired it the procedure would be approved.

Prior to the trial, the defendant Rothaug called on Dr. Armin Baur, medical counsellor for the Nuernberg Court, as the medical expert for the Katzenberger case. He stated to Baur that he wanted to pronounce a death sentence and that it was, therefore necessary for the defendant to be examined. This examination, Rothaug stated, was a mere formality since Katzenberger "would be beheaded anyhow." To the doctor's reproach that Katzenberger was old, and it seemed questionable whether he could be charged with race defilement, Rothaug stated: "It is sufficient for me that the swine said that a German girl had sat upon his lap."

The trial itself, as testified to by many witnesses, was in the nature of a political demonstration. High Party officials attended, including Reich Inspector Oexle. Part of the group of Party officials appeared in uniform.

During the proceedings, Rothaug tried with all his power to encourage the witnesses to make incriminating statements against the defendants. Both defendants were hardly heard by the court. Their statements were passed over or disregarded. During the course of the trial, Rothaug took the opportunity to give the audience a National Socialist lecture on the subject of the Jewish question. The witnesses found great difficulty in giving testimony because of the way in which the trial was conducted, since Rothaug constantly anticipated the evaluation of the facts and gave expression to his own opinions.

Because of the way the trial was conducted, it was apparent that the sentence which would be imposed was the death sentence.

After the introduction of evidence was concluded, a recess was taken, during which time the prosecutor Markl appeared in the consultation room and Rothaug made it clear to him that he expected the prosecution to ask for a death sentence against Katzenberger and a term in the penitentiary for Seiler. Rothaug at this time also gave him suggestions as to what he should include in his arguments.

The reasons for the verdict were drawn up by Ferber. They were based upon the notes of Rothaug as to what should be included. Considerable space is given to Katzenberger's ancestry and the fact that he was of the Mosaic faith, although that fact was admitted by Katzenberger. Such space is also given to the relationship between Katzenberger and Seiler. That there was no proof of actual sexual intercourse is clear from the opinion. The proof seems to have gone little farther than the fact that the defendant Seiler had at times sat upon Katzenberger's lap and that he had kissed her, which facts were also admitted. Many assumptions were made in the reasons stated which obviously are not borne out by the evidence. The court even goes back to the time prior to the passage of the law for the protection of German Blood and Honor, during which Katzenberger had known Seiler. It draws the conclusion apparently without evidence, that their relationship for a period of approximately 10 years, had always been of a sexual nature. The opinion undertakes to bring the case under the decision of the Reich Supreme Court that actual sexual intercourse need not be proved, provided the acts are sexual in nature.

Having wandered far afield from the proof to arrive at this conclusion as to the matter of racial pollution, the court then proceeds to go far afield in order to bring the case under the decree against public enemies. Here the essential facts proved were that the defendant Seiler's husband was at the front and that Katzenberger, on one or possibly two occasions, had visited her after dark. On both points the following paragraphs of the opinion are enlightening (*NG-154, Pros. Ex. 152*):

> Looked at from this point of view, Katzenberger's conduct is particularly contemptible. Together with his offense of racial pollution he is also guilty of an offense under paragraph 4 of the ordinance against people's parasites. It should be noted here that the national community is in need of increased legal protection from all crimes attempting to destroy or undermine its inner cohesion.
>
> On several occasions since the outbreak of war the defendant Katzenberger crept into Seiler's flat after dark. In those cases the defendant exploited the measures taken for the protection in air raids. His chances were further improved by the absence of the bright street lighting which exists in the street along Spittlertorgraben in peacetime. He exploited this fact fully aware of its significance because thus he instinctively escaped during his excursions being observed by people in the street.
>
> The visits paid by Katzenberger to Seiler under the protection of the black-out served at least the purpose of keeping relations going. It does not matter whether during these visits extra-marital sexual relations took place or whether they only conversed as when the husband was present, as Katzenberger claims. The request to interrogate the husband was therefore overruled. The court holds the view the defendant's actions, done with a purpose within a definite plan, amount to a crime against the body according to paragraph 2 of the ordinance against people's parasites. The law of 15 September 1935 has been passed to protect German blood and German honor. The Jew's racial pollution amounts to a grave attack on the purity of German blood, the object of the attack being the body of a German woman. The general need for protection therefore makes appear as unimportant the behavior of the other partner in racial pollution who anyway is not liable to prosecution. The fact that racial pollution occurred up to at least 1939–1940 becomes clear from statements made by the witness Zeuschel to whom the defendant repeatedly and consistently admitted that up to the end of 1939 and the beginning of 1940 she was used to sitting on the Jew's lap and exchanging caresses as described above.
>
> Thus, the defendant committed an offense also under paragraph 2 of the ordinance against people's parasites.
>
> The personal character of the male defendant also stamps him as a people's parasite. The racial pollution practiced by him through many years grew, by exploiting wartime conditions, into an attitude inimical to the nation, into an attack on the security of the national community, during an emergency.
>
> This was why the defendant Katzenberger had to be sentenced both on a charge of racial pollution and of an offense under paragraphs 2 and 4 of the

ordinance against people's parasites, the two charges being taken in conjunction according to paragraph 73 of the criminal code.

* * *

In passing sentence the court was guided by these considerations: The political life of the German people under national socialism is based on the community. One fundamental factor of the life of the national community is race. If a Jew commits racial pollution with a German woman, this amounts to polluting the German race and, by polluting a German woman, to a grave attack on the purity of German blood. The need for protection is particularly strong.

Katzenberger has been practicing pollution for years. He was well acquainted with the point of view taken by patriotic German men and women as regards racial questions, and he knew that by this conduct he insulted the patriotic feelings of the German people. Nor did he mend his ways after the National Socialist revolution of 1933, after the passing of the law for the protection of German blood, in 1935, after the action against Jews in 1938, or the outbreak of war in 1939.

The court therefore regards it as indicated, as the only feasible answer to the frivolous conduct of the defendant, to pass death sentence, as the heaviest punishment provided by paragraph 4 of the decree against public enemies. His case takes on the complexion of a particularly grave crime as he was to be sentenced in connection with the offense of committing racial pollution, under paragraph 2 of the Decree Against Public Enemies, especially if one takes into consideration the defendant's character and the accumulative nature of commission. This is why the defendant is liable to the death penalty which the law provides for only such cases. Dr. Baur, the medical expert, describes the defendants fully responsible.

We have gone to some extent into the evidence of this case to show the nature of the proceedings and the animus of the defendant Rothaug. One undisputed fact, however, is sufficient to establish this case as being an act in furtherance of the Nazi program to persecute and exterminate Jews. That fact is that nobody but a Jew could have been tried for racial pollution. To this offense was added the charge that it was committed by Katzenberger through exploiting war conditions and the black-out. This brought the offense under the ordinance against public enemies and made the offense capital. Katzenberger was tried and executed only because he was a Jew. As stated by Elkar in his testimony, Rothaug achieved the final result by interpretations of existing laws as he boasted to Elkar he was able to do.

This Tribunal is not concerned with the legal incontestability under German law of these cases above discussed. The evidence establishes beyond a reasonable doubt that Katzenberger was condemned and executed because he was a Jew; and Durka, Struss, and Lopata met the same fate because they were Poles. Their execution was in conformity with the policy of the Nazi State of persecution, torture, and extermination of these races. The defendant Rothaug was the knowing and willing instrument in that program of persecution and extermination.

From the evidence it is clear that these trials lacked the essential elements of legality. In these cases the defendant's court, in spite of the legal sophistries which he employed, was merely an instrument in the program of the leaders of the Nazi State of persecution and extermination. . . .

This Tribunal has held that it has no jurisdiction to try any defendant for the crime of conspiracy as a separate substantive offense, but we recognize that there are allegations in count one of the indictment which constitute charges of direct commission of war crimes and crimes against humanity. However, after eliminating the conspiracy charge from count one, we find that all other alleged criminal acts therein set forth and committed after 1 September 1939 are also charged as crimes in the subsequent counts of the indictment. We therefore find it unnecessary to pass formally upon the remaining charges in count one. Our pronouncements of guilt or innocence under counts two, three, and four dispose of all issues which have been submitted to us.

Concerning those defendants who have been found guilty, our conclusions are not based solely upon the facts which we have set forth in the separate discussions of the individual defendants. In the course of 9 months devoted to the trial and consideration of this case, we have reached conclusions based upon evidence and observation of the defendants which cannot fully be documented within the limitations of time and space allotted to us. As we have said, the defendants are not charged with specific overt acts against named victims. They are charged with criminal participation in government-organized atrocities and persecutions unmatched in the annals of history. Our judgments are based upon a consideration of all of the evidence which tends to throw light upon the part which these defendants played in the entire tragic drama. We shall, in pronouncing sentence, give due consideration to circumstances of mitigation and to the proven character and motives of the respective defendants.

[Signed] JAMES T. BRAND
Presiding Judge
MALLORY B. BLAIR
Judge
JUSTIN W. HARDING
Judge

SENTENCES

THE MARSHALL: The Tribunal is again in session.

PRESIDING JUDGE BRAND: The Tribunal is informed that the defendant Schlegelberger is in a condition of illness rendering it impossible for his attendance and that his counsel desires that sentence be pronounced in his absence; in other words, that he waive the presence of the defendant Schlegelberger at the time of sentence.

Is our understanding correct, Dr. Kubuschok?

DR. KUBUSCHOK: Yes, Your Honor.

PRESIDING JUDGE BRAND: The Tribunal will now impose sentence upon those defendants who have been adjudged guilty in these proceedings.

This Tribunal has adjudged the defendant FRANZ SCHLEGELBERGER guilty on counts two and three of the indictment filed in this case. For the crimes of which he has been convicted, this Tribunal sentences him to imprisonment for life.

The Marshall will produce before the Tribunal the defendant Klemm.

HERBERT KLEMM, on the counts of the indictment on which you have been convicted, this Tribunal sentences you to imprisonment for life.

The Marshal will produce before the Tribunal the defendant Rothenberger.

CURT ROTHENBERGER, on the counts of the indictment on which you have been convicted, this Tribunal sentences you to seven years' imprisonment. You will receive credit upon your sentence for the time already spent in confinement awaiting and pending trial.

The Marshal will being before the Tribunal the defendant Ernst Lautz.

ERNST LAUTZ, on the counts of the indictment on which you have been convicted, this Tribunal sentences you to ten years' imprisonment. You will receive credit upon your sentence for the time already spent in confinement awaiting and pending trial.

The Marshal will produce the defendant Wolfgang Mettgenberg.

WOLFGANG METTGENBERG, on the counts of the indictment on which you have been convicted, this Tribunal sentences you to ten years' imprisonment. You will receive credit upon your sentence for the time already spent in confinement awaiting and pending trial.

The Marshal will remove this defendant from the court and produce the defendant Wilhelm von Ammon.

Defendant WILHELM VON AMMON, on the counts of the indictment on which you have been convicted, this Tribunal sentences you to ten years' imprisonment. You will receive credit upon your sentence for the time already spent in confinement awaiting and pending trial.

The Marshal will remove this defendant from the court and will produce the defendant Guenther Joel.

GUENTHER JOEL, on the counts of the indictment on which you have been convicted, this Tribunal sentences you to ten years' imprisonment. You will receive credit upon your sentence for the time already spent in confinement awaiting and pending trial.

The Marshal will remove this defendant from the court and will produce the defendant Oswald Rothaug.

Defendant OSWALD ROTHAUG, on the count of the indictment on which you have been convicted, this Tribunal sentences you to imprisonment for life.

The Marshal will remove this defendant from the court and will produce the defendant Rudoif Oeschey.

RUDOLF OESCHEY, on the counts of the indictment on which you have been convicted, this Tribunal sentences you to imprisonment for life.

The Marshall will remove this defendant from the court and will produce the defendant Josef Altstoetter.

JOSEF ALTSTOETTER, on the count of the indictment on which you have been convicted, this Tribunal sentences you to five years' imprisonment, You will receive credit upon your sentence for the time already spent in confinement awaiting and pending trial.

The Marshal will remove the defendant from the courtroom.

The Tribunal now stands adjourned without day.

THE MARSHAL: This Tribunal now adjourns without day.

(At 1745 hours, 4 December 1947, the Tribunal was adjourned.)

THE POHL CASE

Nuremberg, November, 1947*

OPINION AND JUDGMENT OF THE UNITED STATES MILITARY TRIBUNAL AT NUREMBERG IN UNITED STATES *vs.* OSWALD POHL ET AL.

UNITED STATES MILITARY Tribunal II was established on the 14th day of December 1946 by General Order No. 85 of the United States Military Governor for Germany. It was the second of several Military Tribunals constituted in the United States Zone of Occupation pursuant to Military Government Ordinance No. 7, for the trial of offenses defined as crimes by Law No. 10 of the Control Council for Germany.

Under the order which established the Tribunals and designated the undersigned as members thereof, Military Tribunal II was ordered to convene at the Palace of Justice, Nuernberg, Germany, and to hear and determine such cases as might be filed by the Chief of Counsel for War Crimes.

Telford Taylor, Brigadier General, U. S. Army, Chief of Counsel for War Crimes, on 13 January 1947, filed an indictment against the defendants herein named, in the Office of the Secretary General of Military Tribunals.

A copy of said indictment in the German language was served on each defendant on 13 January 1947, except for the defendant Georg Loerner, who was served on 14 January 1947. More than thirty days after said indictment was served on each defendant, Military Tribunal II arraigned the defendants in the Palace of Justice, Nuernberg, Germany, on 10 March 1947. Upon arraignment, each defendant entered a plea of "not guilty" to all the charges preferred against him. Prior to the arraignment, each defendant was assigned German counsel of his own selection and each defendant was represented by his counsel during the arraignment.

On 8 April 1947, the prosecution began its presentation of evidence. At the conclusion of the prosecution's case in chief the defendants began the presentation of their evidence. The submission of evidence and the arguments of counsel were concluded on 20 September 1947. The personal statements of all of the defendants were heard on 22 September 1947.

During the trial of the case, the Tribunal sat for 101 sessions, (on 101

* *Trial of War Criminals,* Vol. 5, p. 958 (Washington, D.C., 1950).

different dates, including date of arraignment; also, including one-half day joint session with all Tribunals in bank).

During the trial the prosecution offered 21 witnesses, the Tribunal itself called one witness, and the defendants offered 45 witnesses, including the 18 defendants themselves, a total of 67 witnesses.

In addition, the prosecution put in evidence as exhibits, a total of 742 documents; the defendants put in evidence as exhibits a total of 614 documents, making a grand total of 1356 documents received in evidence. The entire record of the case consists of more than 9,000 pages.

Copies of all exhibits offered in evidence by the prosecution in its case in chief were furnished in the German language to the defendants before the same were offered in evidence.

During the entire proceedings each defendant was present in Court, except when a defendant was absent for a short time upon his own motion, owing to illness, or other reasons.

Counsel for the defendants made numerous applications to the Tribunal for the purpose of procuring the personal attendance of persons who had made affidavits on behalf of the prosecution. If at all possible, the Tribunal granted such applications and procured the personal attendance of such persons in order that they could be interrogated or cross-examined by defense counsel.

The trial was conducted generally along the lines usually followed by the trial courts of the various States of the United States, except as to the rules of evidence. In compliance with the provisions of Article VII of Ordinance No. 7, great latitude in presenting evidence was allowed prosecution and defense counsel, even to the extent at times of receiving in evidence certain matters of but scant probative value.

The trial was conducted in English and German with an adequate sound system for conveying either language to all participants and listeners. All proceedings on the trial were reduced to writing in English and German, and an electrical recording of all proceedings was also made.

The Tribunal was most diligent in its efforts to allow each defendant to present his defense completely, in accordance with the spirit and intent of Military Government Ordinance No. 7. Counsel for each defendant was permitted to cross-examine witnesses of the prosecution and other defense witnesses and to offer in evidence all matters deemed of probative value.

The Jurisdiction of the Tribunal

The jurisdiction of Military Tribunal II is determined by Law No. 10 of the Control Council for Germany. The pertinent parts of this Law with which we are concerned provide as follows: . . .

Count one—The Common Design or Conspiracy

The first count of the indictment charges that the defendants, between

January 1933 and April 1945, acting pursuant to a common design, unlawfully, wilfully, and knowingly did conspire and agree together, and with each other, and with divers other persons, to commit war crimes and crimes against humanity as defined in Control Council Law No. 10, Article II.

During the trial each of the defendants challenged this count of the indictment, and moved that the same be quashed and stricken from the indictment. The defendants alleged in their motions that under the basic law the Tribunal did not have jurisdiction to try the charge of conspiracy as a separate substantive offense. The motion to quash was argued by counsel for the prosecution and defense and thereafter the Tribunal granted the motion. In order that this judgment may be complete, the ruling of the Tribunal is incorporated in this judgment:

> It is the ruling of this Tribunal that neither the charter of the International Military Tribunal nor Control Council Law No. 10 has defined conspiracy to commit a war crime or crime against humanity as a separate substantive crime; therefore, this Tribunal has no jurisdiction to try any defendant upon a charge of conspiracy considered as a separate substantive offense.
>
> Count one of the indictment, in addition to the separate charge of conspiracy, also alleges unlawful participation in the formulation and execution of plans to commit war crimes and crimes against humanity which actually involved the commission of such crimes. We, therefore, cannot properly strike the whole of count one from the indictment, but, insofar as count one charges the commission of the alleged crimes of conspiracy as a separate substantive offense, distinct from any war crime or crime against humanity, the Tribunal will disregard that charge.
>
> This ruling must not be construed as limiting the force or effect of Article II, paragraph 2 of Control Council Law No. 10, or as denying to either prosecution or defense the right to offer in evidence any facts or circumstances occurring either before or after September 1939, if such facts or circumstances tend to prove or to disprove the commission by any defendant of war crimes or crimes against humanity as defined in Control Council Law No. 10.

Inasmuch as the offenses charged in the unstricken part of count one are repeated in substance in counts two and three, the entire first count may for purposes of this judgment be disregarded without detracting from the contents of the indictment as a whole.

Counts Two and Three—War Crimes and Crimes Against Humanity

The second and third counts of the indictment charge the commission of war crimes and crimes against humanity. The counts are identical in content, except that in count two the acts which are made the basis for the charges are alleged to have been "committed against the civilian populations of occupied territories and prisoners of war," whereas in count three the criminal acts are alleged to have been "committed against German civilians and nationals of other countries." With this distinction observed, both counts will be treated as one and discussed together.

Counts two and three allege, in substance, that between September 1939 and April 1945 all of the defendants herein named, "were principals in, accessories to, ordered, abetted, took a consenting part in, and were connected with plans and enterprises involving the commission of atrocities and offenses, including but not limited to plunder of public property, murder, torture, illegal imprisonment and enslavement, and deportation to slave labor of, and brutalities, atrocities, and other inhumane and criminal acts against thousands of persons."

The indictment further avers that all of the defendants were associated with the Economic and Administrative Main Office, commonly known as the "WVHA" which was one of the twelve main departments of the SS.

The indictment more specifically charges the defendants with war crimes and crimes against humanity, as follows:

The defendant Oswald Pohl was the head of the WVHA and the defendants August Frank and Georg Loerner were his deputies. The WVHA was divided into Amtsgruppen [office groups or divisions], which were interrelated in their operations, purposes, and functions.

Amtsgruppe A, among other things, was responsible for financial matters of the SS, including those relating to its concentration camps. This Amtsgruppe was subdivided into five offices or Aemter, which were charged with responsibility for certain parts of the entire financial administration. The defendants Frank and Fanslau were, successively, heads of Amtsgruppe A. The defendants Hans Loerner, Frank, Vogt, and Fanslau were heads of offices or Aemter within this Amtsgruppe A.

Amtsgruppe B, among other things, was responsible for the supply of food and clothing for inmates of the concentration camps, and of food, uniforms, equipment, billets, and camp quarters for the members of the SS. It was subdivided into five offices or Aemter. The defendant Georg Loerner was the chief of Amtsgruppe B, and the defendant Tschentscher was his deputy and chief of one of the offices or Aemter within this Amtsgruppe B. The defendant Scheide was head of Amt B V [5] within Amtsgruppe B.

Amtsgruppe C, among other things, was charged with the construction and maintenance of houses, buildings, and structures of the SS, and German police, and of the concentration camps and prisoner of war camps. It was subdivided into six offices or Aemter. The defendants Kiefer and Eirenschmalz were heads of Aemter or offices within this Amtsgruppe C.

Amtsgruppe D, which prior to March 1942 was known as the Inspectorate of Concentration Camps, was responsible, among other things, for the administration of the concentration camps and of the concentration camp inmates. It was responsible for the food, clothing, housing, sanitation, and medical care of the concentration camp inmates, and of the order, discipline, and regulation of the lives of the inmates. It was charged with the supply of the forced services and labor of the concentration camp inmates to public and private employers throughout Germany and the occupied countries. It was subdivided into six

[four] offices or Aemter. The defendant Sommer was the deputy chief of one of the offices or Aemter of Amtsgruppe D, responsible for the supply of the services and labor of concentration camp inmates. The defendant Pook was in charge of matters relating to dentistry affecting the concentration camp inmates.

Amtsgruppe W, among other things, was responsible for the operation and maintenance of various industrial, manufacturing, and service enterprises throughout Germany and the occupied countries. In the operation of the enterprises under its control, this Amtsgruppe employed many concentration camp inmates. It was subdivided into eight offices or Aemter. The defendant Pohl was the head of Amtsgruppe W; the defendant Georg Loerner was his deputy; and the defendants Hohberg and Baier were his executive assistants. The defendant Volk was personal adviser on the staff of Oswald Pohl and head of the legal section of the executive office of Amtsgruppe W, and the defendants Mummenthey, Bobermin, and Klein were heads of offices or Aemter within this Amtsgruppe.

The indictment then goes on to charge that these defendants, acting concertedly within the framework of WVHA and in pursuance of a common criminal design, perpetrated, aided and abetted in the perpetration of atrocities and offenses against persons and property, including plunder of public and private property, murder, extermination, enslavement, deportation, unlawful imprisonment, torture, persecutions on political, racial, and religious grounds, ill-treatment of, and other inhumane and unlawful acts against thousands of persons, including German civilians, nationals of other countries, and prisoners of war. The indictment then relates in detail the means and methods by which the above criminal acts were accomplished.

Counts two and three of the indictment conclude with the averment that these crimes and atrocities "constitute violations of international conventions . . . , the laws and customs of war, the general principles of criminal law as derived from the criminal laws of all civilized nations, the internal penal laws of the countries in which such crimes were committed, and of Article II of Control Council Law No. 10."

Count Four—Membership in Criminal Organization

The fourth count of the indictment avers that all of the defendants herein except defendant Hohberg were members subsequent to 1 September 1939, of the SS, declared to be criminal by the International Military Tribunal and paragraph 1 (*d*), Article II of Control Council Law No. 10.

The law, as pronounced by the International Military Tribunal with reference to membership in an organization declared criminal, is as follows.

> In dealing with the SS the Tribunal includes all persons who had been officially accepted as members of the SS including the members of the Allgemeine SS, members of the Waffen SS, members of the SS Totenkopf Verbaende, and the

members of any of the different police forces who were members of the SS. The Tribunal does not include the so-called riding units. . . .

The Tribunal declares to be criminal within the meaning of the Charter the group composed of those persons who had been officially accepted as members of the SS as enumerated in the preceding paragraph who became or remained members of the organization with knowledge that it was being used for the commission of acts declared criminal by Article 6 of the Charter, or who were personally implicated as members of the organization in the commission of such crimes, excluding, however, those who were drafted into membership by the State in such a way as to give them no choice in the matter, and who had committed no such crimes. The basis of this finding is the participation of the organization in war crimes and crimes against humanity connected with the war; this group declared criminal cannot include, therefore, persons who had ceased to belong to the organizations enumerated in the preceding paragraph prior to 1 September 1939.

Under the American concept of liberty, and under the Anglo-Saxon system of jurisprudence, every defendant in a criminal case is presumed to be innocent until the prosecution by competent and credible proof has shown his guilt to the exclusion of every reasonable doubt. This presumption of innocence follows him throughout the trial until such degree of proof has been adduced. Beyond a reasonable doubt, does not mean beyond a vain, imaginary, or fanciful doubt, but means that the defendant's guilt must be fully proved to a moral certainty, before he is condemned. Stated differently, it is such a doubt as, after full consideration of all the evidence, would leave an unbiased, reflective person charged with the responsibility of decision, in such a state of mind that he could not say that he felt an abiding conviction amounting to a moral certainty of the truth of the charge.

If any defendant is to be found guilty under counts two or three of the indictment, it must only be because the evidence in the case has clearly shown beyond a reasonable doubt that such defendant participated as a principal in, accessory to, ordered, abetted, took a consenting part in, or was connected with plans or enterprises involving the commission of at least some of the war crimes and crimes against humanity with which the defendants are charged in the indictment. Only under such circumstances may he be convicted.

If any defendant is to be found guilty under count four of the indictment, it must be because the evidence has shown beyond a reasonable doubt that such defendant was a member of an organization or group subsequent to 1 September 1939, declared to be criminal by the International Military Tribunal, as contained in the judgment of said Tribunal.

The defendants are charged in the indictment as officials of the Wirtschafts- und Verwaltungshauptamt (commonly called the WVHA) of the Schutzstaffeln der Nationalsozialistischen Deutschen Arbeiterpartei (commonly known as the SS). The whole sordid history of the SS and its criminal activities has been told in detail in the judgment of the International Military Tribunal and need not be repeated here. In this case, the Tribunal is concerned only with the members of the WVHA, or Economic Administrative Main Office, and its predecessors, the Hauptamt Verwaltung und Wirtschaft, or Main Office Administration and Economy, and the Hauptamt Hauschalt und Bauten, or Main Office Budget and Buildings.

Early in 1942, the WVHA was organized under Himmler's order to coordinate and consolidate the administrative work of the SS. The organization of the former Administrative Department and Department of Budget and Buildings of the SS was taken over intact, and, in addition, another Main Office of the SS was incorporated into the WVHA, namely, the Inspekteur der Konzentrationslager, or Inspector of Concentration Camps. Of this revamped organization, the defendant Pohl was continued as chief and was in supreme command. The WVHA was divided into five Amtsgruppen, or departments [office groups or divisions], namely:

Amtsgruppe A—budget, law and administration.
Amtsgruppe B—supply, billeting, and equipment.
Amtsgruppe C—works and buildings.
Amtsgruppe D—concentration camps.
Amtsgruppe W—economic enterprises.

Each Amtsgruppe was headed by a chief and was, in turn, divided into Aemter or offices. For example, Amtsgruppe A was subdivided into Amt A I to Amt A V, Amtsgruppe B was likewise subdivided while Amtsgruppe W was subdivided into Amts W I to Amt W VIII. Each Amt or office was charged with some specialized phase of the general field covered by its Amtsgruppe.

The WVHA, as one of the twelve main offices of the SS central organization, was charged with the administrative needs of the entire SS, including supplies of every kind, billeting, transportation, and also the administration of the entire system of concentration camps. This did not involve the maintenance and administration of the camps and the use of the inmates as a source of forced labor.

In addition to its functions as an administrative agency, WVHA managed and controlled a vast number of economic enterprises which were either owned or controlled by the SS. These enterprises embraced an extensive industrial empire, extending from Holland to Poland and Hungary, and were operated almost entirely by the use of concentration camp labor. The operation and administration of these enterprises was the task of Amtsgruppe W, of which defendant Pohl was the chief and defendant George Loerner the deputy chief. Ancillary to Amtsgruppe W was an amorphous organization called staff W, headed by the chief of staff W, or chief W. This staff exercised general administrative supervision of the W industries, negotiated for and procured new enterprises, arranged financing, floated loans, negotiated financial matters with the Reich Minister of Finance, and in other ways performed broad coordinating functions within the framework of the SS industries. The chief of staff W was at one time the defendant Hohberg and later the defendants Volk and Baier.

More than 25 of the SS industries were controlled, through stock ownership, by a parent holding company, known as Deutsche Wirtschaftsbetriebe, or

DWB, of which defendant Pohl was the chief officer. These industries included a wide range of projects: stone quarries, brick manufacturing plants, cement mills, pharmaceutical factories, real estate, housing, building materials, book printing and binding, porcelain and ceramics, mineral water and fruit juices, furniture, foodstuffs, textiles and leather, etc. For the purposes of this case, four of these industries are of particular significance:

(1) The Deutsche Erd- und Steinwerke, known as DEST, which operated five granite quarries, six brick and tile plants, and a stone-cutting plant.

(2) The Klinker-Zement, manufacturing brick and cinder block, fireproof products, ceramics, lime, and chalk. This company had large subsidiaries at Golleschau, Prague, Lvov, and Bialystok.

(3) Ostindustrie, or OSTI, organized in March 1943 and dissolved a year later, which operated and later liquidated all the confiscated Jewish industries in the Government General, including foundries, textile plants, quarries, glass works, and others. Enforced Jewish labor was employed in these enterprises.

(4) The Deutsche Ausruestungswerke, or DAW, the German Equipment Works, which operated various industries in seven concentration camps, using forced inmate labor.

The freedom of man from enslavement by his fellow men is one of the fundamental concepts of civilization. Any program which violates that concept, whether prompted by a false feeling of superiority or arising from desperate economic needs, is intolerable and criminal. We have been told many times, "Germany was engaged in total war. Our national life was endangered. Everyone had to work." This cannot mean that everyone must work for Germany in her waging of criminal aggressive war. It certainly cannot mean that Russian, and Polish, and Dutch, and Norwegian noncombatants, including women and children, could be forced to work as slaves in the manufacture of war material to be used against their own countrymen and to destroy their own homelands. It certainly cannot mean, in spite of treaties and all rules of civilized warfare (if warfare can ever be said to be civilized), that prisoners taken in battle can be reduced to the status of slaves. Even Germany prior to 1939 had repudiated any such fallacious position. And yet, under the hypnotism of the Nazi ideology, the German people readily became complaisant to this strange and inhuman system. Under the spell of National Socialism, these defendants today are only mildly conscious of any guilt in the kidnaping and enslavement of millions of civilians. The concept that slavery is criminal *per se* does not enter into their thinking. Their attitude may be summarized thus: "We fed, clothed, and housed these prisoners as best we could. If they were hungry or cold, so were the Germans. If they had to work long hours under trying conditions, so did the Germans. What is wrong in that?" When it is explained that the Germans were free men working in their own homeland for their own country, they fail to see any distinction. The electrically charged wire, the armed guards, the vicious dogs, the sentinel towers—all those are blandly explained by saying, "Why, of course. Otherwise the inmates would have run away." They simply cannot realize that the most precious word in any language is "liberty." The Germans had become so accustomed to regimentation and government by decree that the protection of individual human rights by law was a forgotten idea. The fact that the people of the Eastern territories were torn from their homes, families divided, property confiscated, and the able-bodied herded into concentration camps, to work without pay for the perpetrators of these outrages—all this was complaisantly justified because a swollen tyrant in Berlin had scribbled "HH" on a piece of paper. And these are the men who now keep repeating, "*nulla poena sine lege.*"

This Tribunal, in its judgment in the case of United States *vs.* Erhard Milch, had occasion to say:

> The German nation, before the ascendancy of the NSDAP, had repeatedly recognized the rights of civilians in occupied countries. At the Hague Peace Conference in 1907, an amendment was submitted by the German delegate, Major General von Guendell, which read: "A belligerent is likewise forbidden to compel the nationals of the adverse party to take part in the operations of war directed against their country, even when they have been in his service before the commencement of the war." The German manual for war on land (*Kriegsbrauch im Landkriege,* Edition 1902) stated: "The inhabitants of an invaded territory are persons endowed with rights . . . subject to certain restrictions . . . but who otherwise may live free from vexations and, as in time of peace, under the protection of the laws.

A faint effort has been made to show that, although no formal judicial proceeding in the nature of an accusation and trial was had in each case, nevertheless each commitment to a concentration camp was preceded by a sort of "cabinet trial" by the Gestapo and that this complied with German Law. To put it bluntly, the Tribunal does not believe a word of it. Commitments to concentration camps did not depend upon individual conduct but were the carrying out of a broad categorical Nazi political policy, frankly announced by Himmler. We can hardly be expected to believe that the thousands of Eastern women in Ravensbrueck and the boys and girls who were liberated from the concentration camps by the Allied Armies were accorded even a "cabinet trial." When whole villages were deported en masse, it is ridiculous to believe that each of the inhabitants was accused of some infraction of German Law, given a hearing of even the "cabinet" variety, and then solemnly found guilty and committed. Could any rational person believe that this or any comparable procedure accompanied the annihilation of the ghetto at Warsaw?

Far from making any attempt at formal accusation and determination of guilt, a conscious effort was made to evade embarrassing steps which slowed up the program of extermination. On 13 October 1942, Thierack, Reich Minister of Justice, wrote to Martin Bormann, stating (*NO-558, Pros. Ex. 335*):

> I intend to turn over criminal proceedings against Poles, Russians, Jews and gypsies to the Reichsfuehrer SS. In so doing I base myself on the principle that the administration of justice can only make a small contribution to the extermination of members of these peoples. The Justice Administration undoubtedly pronounces

very severe sentences on such persons, but that is not enough to constitute any material contribution towards the realization of the above-mentioned aim. . . . I am . . . of the opinion that considerably better results can be accomplished by surrendering such persons to the police, who can then take the necessary measures *unhampered by any legal criminal evidence.* . . . The police may prosecute Jews and gypsies irrespective of these conditions."

This specious and shallow excuse has been offered seriously in justification of a nation-wide policy of deportation and slavery. We have witnessed a strange anomaly in this case. Defendants and their witnesses have bowed their heads in profound shame at the evidence of mass murder and wholesale extermination, but as to the cruel enslavement of whole races, they evidence little or no feeling of guilt or culpability whatsoever. They spoke freely and made voluminous records of "prisoner labor" and "inmate labor." They made elaborate industrial plans and wrote without shame, "We have been promised 8,000 Jewish laborers for this enterprise." They planned and started pretentious monuments adopted to dispose of the insane, but it was expanded to include the incurables, the aged, the "idle caters", the habitual criminals, and finally the political irreconcilables. It was a national Reich-approved plan for deliberate and premeditated murder on a large scale. Elaborate case histories of inmates were prepared and screened at the camps by travelling physicians, who by a process of snap judgment determined whether men and women should live or die. Those whose records happened to fall in the extermination file were shipped, like cattle to market, to an institution at Bernburg where "Action 14 f 13" was applied. This often was done by the injection of phenol or gasoline into the bloodstream, causing immediate death. After the extermination, the victim's personal effects, including the gold in his teeth, were shipped back to the concentration camp, and a report of "death from natural causes" was made out. This program was also extensively carried out directly in the concentration camps by the camp physicians.

Treatment of Concentration Camp Prisoners

The only interest which the SS and the Reich had in concentration camp inmates was as productive units. They were regarded as so many machines, not as human beings. The only concern with the collapse or death of an inmate was with the loss of a productive laborer. Their arrogant attitude that all non-Germans were subhumans made them wholly indifferent to the fate of those whose right to live out their lives was as sacred as that of any German. This attitude was epitomized by Himmler when he said:

> Whether ten thousand Russian females fall down from exhaustion while digging an antitank ditch interests me only in so far as the antitank ditch for Germany is finished.

And later, at Posen [Poznan], in October 1943, he said:

> At that time we did not value the mass of humanity as we value it today, as raw material, as labor. What, after all, thinking in terms of generations, is not to

> be regretted, but is now deplorable by reason of the loss of labor, is that the prisoners died in tens and hundreds of thousands of exhaustion and hunger.

When grinders or lathes broke down under hard use, they were scrapped; when inmates collapsed from exhaustion or hunger, they were shot or gassed. There was nothing incongruous in this to the twisted Nazi psychology. They talked and wrote frankly and volubly about it. True, there were some who professed a humanitarian interest in the welfare and comfort of the inmates, and who made some effort to alleviate their intolerable condition, but they still kept them hard at work. Tasks were found even for the bedridden, while they awaited their turn at the gas chambers. The ghastly story of Germany's mistreatment of the millions of slaves who filled her concentration camps to bursting—the endless hours of exhausting labor, the beatings and killings, the starvation, the degradation—this has become stale from retelling. That's the pity of it. It can be so soon forgotten. But let it be recorded here once more, for generations unborn to read and ponder, that millions of human beings between 1939 and 1945 were cast into slavery and treated with inhuman cruelty by a nation whose only excuse was economic need—the Nazi creed of "the state above humanity."

The story has come to the Tribunal from the lips of witnesses who personally experienced the horrors of the concentration camps—

Victor Abend—Polish inmate of three camps.
Bernhard Lauber—Polish inmate of two camps.
Jerzy Bielski—Polish inmate of two camps.
Albert Kruse—German inmate at Neuengamme.
Chaim Balizki—Polish inmate of two camps.
Herbert Engler—German inmate of Sachsenhausen.
Eugen Kogon—Austrian inmate of Buchenwald.
Josef Ackerman—German inmate of two camps.
Wolfgang Sanner—German inmate of Mauthausen.
Franz Mis—Yugoslav inmate of Dachau.
Helmut Bickel—German inmate of two camps.

We have had proof from camp commanders and physicains—

Karl Kahr—doctor at Dachau, Buchenwald, and Nordhausen.
Otto Barnewald—administrative chief at Mauthausen, Neuengamme, and Buchenwald.
Hermann Pister—commandant at Buchenwald.
Gerhard Schiedlausky—doctor at Mauthausen, Natzweiler, and Buchenwald.
Max Pauly—commandant at Neuengamme.
Rudolf Hoess—commandant at Auschwitz.
Philipp Grimm—commandant at Buchenwald.

We have seen the motion pictures of the frightful conditions in some of the camps when they were captured by the Allies—conditions so ghastly that they defy description. The proof is overwhelming that in the administration of the concentration camps the German war machine, and first and foremost the SS, resorted to practices which would shame the most primitive race of savage barbarians. All the instincts of human decency which distinguished men from beasts were forgotten, and the law of the jungle took command. If there is such a thing as a crime against humanity, here we have it repeated a million times over.

Treatment of the Jews

This disgraceful chapter in the history of Germany has been vividly portrayed in the judgment of the International Military Tribunal (*pp. 247-253 and 303, Official Edition*). Nothing can be added to that comprehensive finding of facts, in which this Tribunal completely concurs. From it we see the unholy spectacle of six million human beings deliberately exterminated by a civilized state whose only indictment was that its victims had been born in the wrong part of the world of forbears whom the murderers detested. Never before in history has man's inhumanity to man reached such depths. Had Germany rested content with the exclusion of Jews from her own territory, with denying them German citizenship, with excluding them from public office, or any like domestic regulation, no other nation could have been heard to complain. But such prejudice and hatred, once fanned into flame, is difficult to control. And so, when the Nuernberg decrees against the Jews were pronounced, the fuse was lighted and soon the program of world-wide extermination of Jews was launched. Had Germany not been checked, one wonders what race, or creed, or nation would next have been branded as subhuman and marked for extermination.

In his own affidavit of 1 April 1947 (*NO-2616, Pros. Ex. 523*), Pohl states:

> The liquidation of Jews in the Auschwitz concentration camp in the years 1942 and 1943, when Rudolf Hoess was commander, was known to me through Himmler's speech, and I myself also saw the gas chambers and the crematorium in Auschwitz in the summer of 1944.

The most lurid descriptions of the Jewish extermination program are found in the reports of German officers themselves, in which, it can be assumed, the cruelties and atrocities are not exaggerated. Major General of Police Katzmann, reporting with evident pride in June 1943 on progress in murder in Galicia, writes:

> I report that the District of Galicia with the exception of those Jews in the camps under the control of the SS and Police is free from Jews. Jews still caught in small numbers are given special treatment by the competent detachments of police.
>
> Up to June 1943, 434,329 Jews have been evacuated. 21,156 are still in concentration camps. This number is being reduced "currently."
>
> Since we received more and more alarming reports on the Jews becoming armed in an ever increasing manner, we started during the last fortnight in June 1943 an action throughout the whole of the district of Galicia with the intent to

use strongest measures to destroy the Jewish gangsterdom. Special measures were found necessary during the action to dissolve the ghetto in Lwow [Lvov] where the dugouts mentioned above had been established. Here we had to act brutally from the beginning, in order to avoid losses on our side; we had to blow up or to burn down several houses. On this occasion the surprising fact arose that we were able to catch about 20,000 Jews instead of 12,000 Jews who had registered. We had to pull at least 3,000 Jewish corpses out of every kind of hiding place; they had committed suicide by taking poison.

The "special treatment" referred to, means slaughter on the spot. The periodic reports of Stroop, SS Brigadefuehrer and brigadier general of police, who was charged with the destruction of the Warsaw ghetto, portrayed an astounding adventure in wholesale murder and robbery, ending with the terse statement, "There is no Jewish ghetto in Warsaw any more." The action terminated, he says, by blowing up the Warsaw synagogue. He then submits an inventory of his victims: 56,065 Jews exterminated plus an estimated 5,000 to 6,000 destroyed by being blown up or dying in burning buildings, 4,400,000 Zlotys (Polish units of currency) seized and counted, with five to six million more uncounted. Also gold and paper money and large amounts of jewelry are listed. What strange mental twist induces this man to constantly refer to the inmates of the ghetto as "bandits"? The German inspector of armament in the Ukraine reports in December 1941:

Later specially detached formations of the police executed a planned shooting of Jews. It was done entirely in public . . . and in many instances with members of the armed forces taking part voluntarily. The way these actions, which included men, old men, women, and children of all ages, were carried out was horrible. So far about fifteen to twenty thousand Jews have been executed in the part of the Ukraine belonging to the Reich.

In October 1941, Reich Commissioner Carl for the territory of Slutsk, reports:

The town itself offered a picture of horror during the action. With indescribable brutality . . . the Jewish people were taken out of their dwellings and herded together. Everywhere in the town, shots were to be heard, and in different streets the corpses of shot Jews accumulated. . . . The police battalion has looted during the action in an unheard of manner . . . . Everything of use such as boots, leather, cloth, gold, and other valuables has been taken away.

The Tribunal is quite willing to accept these statements of these high-ranking German officers, who were eye-witnesses, as conclusive proof of the facts related.

Looting of Public and Private Property

The story of systematic pillage of occupied countries is related in the judgment of the International Military Tribunal (*pp. 238-243, Official Edition*), which this Tribunal adopts as findings of fact in this case. It is a tale of ruthless depravity unequalled in history. It was not confined to looting by individuals or isolated detachments. It was the carrying out of a general military policy, announced by the top command at the outset of the war. As early as October 1939, Goering issued the following directive:

> The task for the economic treatment of the various administrative regions is different, depending on whether the country which is involved will be incorporated politically into the German Reich, or whether we will deal with the Government General, which in all probability will not be made a part of Germany. In the first mentioned territories, the . . . safeguarding of all their productive facilities and supplies must be aimed at, as well as a complete incorporation into the greater German economic system, at the earliest possible time. On the other hand, there must be removed from the territories of the Government General all raw materials, scrap materials, machines, etc., which are of use for the German war economy. Enterprises which are not absolutely necessary for the meager maintenance of the naked existence of the population must be transferred to Germany.

In pursuance of this policy of deliberate plunder, Poland, the Ukraine, and the occupied parts of Russia were stripped of agricultural supplies, food, raw materials, manufactured articles and such machinery as could not be used for German purposes where it stood. Obviously, this left large numbers of the population of these countries to starve, a fact which did not concern the German forces in the least. Alfred Rosenberg, Reich Minister for the occupied Eastern territories, bluntly stated in 1941 that the produce of Southern Russian and the Northern Caucasus should be taken to the Reich to feed the German people. He said:

> We see absolutely no reason for any obligation on our part to feed also the Russian people with the products of that surplus territory. We know that this is a harsh necessity, bare of any feelings.

To call such inhuman policy, "a harsh necessity," is the acme of understatement. It was deliberate murder by starvation, nothing less. To show that the policy of plunder was not prompted by economic needs alone or the necessity of supplying the German Army and population with necessities, we find that churches, libraries, art galleries, and museums, not only in the East but in France, Belgium, and Holland, were systematically looted of their treasures. This thievery was ordered, as the decree of Himmler put it, "for the strengthening of Germanism." The connection between the avowed purpose and the crime is not entirely clear. The experience of Prince Max Lobkowicz of Bohemia is typical. In his affidavit (*NO-4942, Pros. Ex. 733*) he states:

> I am the owner of landed property, situated in several districts of Bohemia. . . . Over two-thirds of this property came under German rule in October 1938 as a result of the occupation by the Germans after Munich.
>
> The rest of my property, including my chief residence at Rondnice and my house at Prague, came under German rule in March 1939, just after I had escaped with my family (wife and three sons) to London.
>
> I remained in the Czechoslovak diplomatic service, which I had entered in 1920 in London and during the war was appointed first Minister and later Ambassador to the Court of St. James. In February 1947, I was transferred from London to the Ministry of Foreign Affairs at Prague, to which I am attached now.
>
> The whole of my property was confiscated by the Germans.
>
> This confiscation included farm land, forests, vineyards, etc., as well as natural

mineral spring, breweries, saw mills and several large houses, with old family collections (over 1,000 pictures, furniture, a library of over 100,000 volumes, historical archives, etc.).

ACTION REINHARDT

The extermination and deportation of the Jews in the East produced a vast amount of valuable property, both real and personal, which the Reich was quick to recognize and seize. To marshal these resources, the Action Reinhardt was instituted, named approximately enough, for Reinhard Heydrich, formerly chief of the Security Police and SD, who met his death—and this, too, appropriately enough—in Czechoslovakia in 1942. The purpose of the action was to gather into the Reich all the Jewish manpower and wealth which could be reached. It was an ambitious and profitable undertaking for Germany. The Jews themselves were herded into concentration camps as slaves and their entire worldly possessions confiscated. The real property, where possible, was put to German use (largely through the WVHA agency of OSTI) and the movable property was shipped to WVHA, where it was inventoried, appraised, and distributed through prescribed channels. The thoroughness of this program of looting is evidenced by the articles listed: featherbeds, quilts, blankets, woolen yardage, shawls, umbrellas, canes, thermos bottles, flasks, baby carriages, combs, handbags, belts, pipes, sun glasses, mirrors, table silver, luggage, linens, pillows, eye glasses, furs, watches, clocks, and jewelry. Everything that could be lifted was moved. The defendant Frank listed as received up to 30 April 1943, 94,000 men's watches, 33,000 women's watches, and 25,000 fountain pens. Currency and precious metals seized reached a total value of 60,000,000 Reichsmarks. About 2,000 carloads of textiles reached Germany as a result of this plunder, and in all a grand total of over 100 million Reichsmarks in personal property was thus acquired. When Jews died in concentration camps, additional loot became available. The clothing was stripped from their bodies and, after being carefully searched for hidden valuables and the distinguishing Jewish Star removed, was distributed to still living inmates or to German civilians. Camp commandants were cautioned not to ship clothing which was stained with blood or showed bullet holes. To complete the desecration, the hair was shorn from the heads of the dead (one report showed a carload of 3,000 kilograms) and all the dental gold was extracted and deposited through WVHA in the vaults of the Reich Bank. It was ordered by the defendant Frank that all property originating from Action Reinhardt be called, "goods originating from thefts, receiving of stolen goods, and hoarded goods." In the true sense, this description is more accurate than Frank intended.

In the *Southern German Legal Gazette,* March 1947, crimes against humanity are defined as acts involving "cruelty against human life, degradation of the dignity of man or destruction of human civilization." The Tribunal is quite content to use this German concept as a standard in deciding whether or not the facts heretofore found constitute crimes against humanity. Only one conclusion is possible. These facts establish beyond a reasonable doubt the wholesale commission of both war crimes and crimes against humanity. It next becomes necessary to determine to what extent, if any, the several defendants are criminally responsible therefore, by reason of actual perpetration, participation, or taking a consenting part therein.

A defense which has been almost universally advanced is that all the criminal acts of the Reich were conducted under a cloak of secrecy which prevented the defendants from knowing about them. Hitler's famous secrecy order has been offered by nearly every defendant. It has been urged that there was strict censorship of the press, that listening to foreign broadcasts was prohibited, that concentration camp prisoners were required upon their release to be sworn to secrecy as to events which they had observed or experienced, and that the German people generally were kept in complete ignorance of what was going on. All these facts are true. But in the very nature of things, it was impossible to maintain complete secrecy or anything like it. It was impossible to keep hidden from public view the huge transports which carried the slave laborers from the East to the concentration camps. It was impossible to keep secret the public demonstrations against the Jews. Streicher's infamous, "Der Stuermer," had a circulation of 600,000 copies. Himmler spoke openly about "the final solution of the Jewish problem" at Poznan, Krakow [Kharkov], and Mctz. When prisoners were liberated from concentration camps, it is impossible to think that they maintained the complete secrecy to which they were bound. Soldiers returning on leave from Poland, Russia, and the Ukraine must have talked to some extent. The pall of smoke from the crematory at Auschwitz could not be kept hidden. In spite of decrees, foreign broadcasts were heard. The systematic murder of millions of human beings, extending over 5 years, could not by reason of its very magnitude be kept secret. It is undoubtedly true that millions of obscure and unimportant German citizens had no way of knowing and did not know of the horrible wrongs which were being perpetrated. But if high-ranking officers of the SS, whose daily tasks for years brought them into immediate contact with the operation of the camps, claim that they had no suspicion of the events occurring within the barbed wire, that defense cannot be believed. Undoubtedly some knew more than others, and some limited few knew nothing. With this conclusion Pohl himself agrees. In his interrogation of 13 June 1946 (*NO-4728, Pros. Ex. 693*), Pohl was confronted by Kaltenbrunner's testimony before the International Military Tribunal that, "there were only a handful of people in the WVHA who had any control or knew anything about concentration camps," to which Pohl commented:

> Well, that is complete nonsense. I described to you how these were handled in the WVHA. As for instance, in the case of the use of textiles and turning in of valuables, and also from Gluecks and Loerner right on down to the last little clerk, must have known what went on in the concentration camps, and it is complete nonsense for him to speak of just a handful of men.

In Liebehenschel's letter of 25 February 1943, written as chief of Amtsgruppe D [Amt D I] of the WVHA and addressed to all the concentration camp commanders, he states that the population in the East is beginning to be startled by the frequent casualties in the concentration camps. Apparently, in some areas at least, the secret was beginning to leak out.

The Tribunal is convinced that the ignorance professed by many of the defendants is the ignorance of convenience.

At the outset of the testimony, the Tribunal realized the necessity of guarding against assuming criminality, or even culpable responsibility, solely from the official titles which the several defendants held. It became apparent that, in conformity with the ancient German passion for high-sounding titles, many purely ministerial officers, performing perfunctory or even menial tasks, were designated by sonorous names which did not necessarily connote substantial power or authority. In some instances minor officers, engaged in purely routine tasks, were designated on the elaborate tables of organization by lengthy and awe-inspiring titles, which upon closer inspection were found to cover nothing more than a few desks in a remote corner. The Tribunal has been especially careful to discover and analyze the actual power and authority of the several defendants, and the manner and extent to which they were exercised, without permitting itself to be unduly impressed by the official designations on letterheads or office doors.

Oswald Pohl

Prior to 1934, defendant Pohl was chief disbursing officer of the German Navy. On a visit by Himmler to the naval base at Kiel in 1934, he met Pohl and persuaded him to sever his connection with the navy and assume an administrative position with the SS Main Office. Pohl had been a member of the National Socialist Party since 1926 and of the SA since 1929. At Himmler's insistence he became chief of the administrative department of the SS Central Office in February 1934. In 1939 that office was organized into two Main Offices under the names, "Main Office Budget and Buildings," and "Main Office Administration and Economy." These offices were in complete charge of all administrative matters affecting the fast growing SS. On 1 February 1942, these two Main Offices were united and renamed, "SS [Economic] Administrative Main Office," known as, "WVHA," to which was also added the Main Office of Inspector of Concentration Camps, which became Amtsgruppe D.

For 11 years Pohl was continuously the administrative head of the entire SS organization. His only superior within his field was Himmler. At the beginning of the war he became a member of the "Freundeskreis" or, "Circle of Himmler's Friends," a small select group of intimates who enjoyed Himmler's confidence. As chief of the WVHA he was in absolute control of an organization composed of 5 Amtsgruppen and 28 Aemter, with a personnel at the peak of over 1,700 employees. He not only directed and administered the fiscal affairs of the entire SS but he was in charge of the administrative aspects of all concentration camps and was head of the tremendous industrial empire which the SS built up under Amtsgruppe W. It is obvious that his duties were not perfunctory or formal but that he was an experienced, active, and dominant head of one of the largest branches of the German military machine. Although he had no actual military duties in the field, he attained the military rank of Obergruppenfuehrer, which is equivalent to the rank of lieutenant general.

Concentration Camps

Three months after the outbreak of the war, Himmler ordered that "the supervision of the economic matters of these institutions and their application to work is the responsibility of SS Obergruppenfuehrer Pohl." The change in Reich policy by which concentration camps were converted from places of mere detention to places of productive free labor was announced in April 1942, and the ruthless plan of extracting from concentration camp inmates their last ounce of energy in furtherance of the Reich's war plans became operative. It became Pohl's task to implement this policy and to make it work effectively for the Reich. Neither Pohl nor the WVHA had anything to do with the commitment of inmates to concentration camps nor with their release, except by death. Neither Pohl nor any other member of the WVHA had authority to order the execution of concentration camp prisoners. Nor is there any evidence that he or they attempted to exercise any such prerogative. The order for executions originated between the Secret State Police and Himmler personally. The greater part of the task of procuring inmates fell upon the Security Police and the SD, although it is quite evident that the SS and the Wehrmacht in the field rendered no little assistance. Pohl's jurisdiction began when the inmates reached the gates of the concentration camps. Pohl has contended that the inclusion in WVHA of Amtsgruppe D, which was concerned exclusively with concentration camp matters, was more a formal than an actual subordination; and that this Amtsgruppe, under Gluecks and Maurer, continued to operate more or less independently of Pohl, taking most of their orders directly from Himmler. It is probably true to some degree that the heads of Amtsgruppe D, which had formerly been an SS Main Office, resented somewhat their subordination to Pohl and continued to look to Himmler for orders. The fact remains, however, that Pohl as head of the WVHA was the superior of Gluecks and Maurer and was in a position to exercise and did exercise substantial supervision and control over Amtsgruppe D Pohl himself, in his affidavit of April 3, 1947 (*NO-2736, Pros. Ex. 525*), states:

> Gluecks was Chief of Amtsgruppe D and was subordinate to me in my capacity as Main Office Chief. Thus I became authority for the administration of concentration camps within the sphere of activity of the WVHA. The camp commanders were nominated by the SS Personnel Office on my recommendation and appointed by me.

As chief judicial officer of the SS, he had full disciplinary power over all guards who served in the concentration camps. All judgments arising in disciplinary proceedings against SS guards were submitted to Pohl for modification or confirmation.

One of the purposes in organizing the WVHA was to centralize and concentrate administrative authority and to reduce the number of independent administrative offices. In view of the fact that the SS enterprises administered under Amtsgruppe W were manned by concentration camp inmates and in many instances operated in concentration camps themselves, it was inevitable that the administrative affairs of the camps should be placed in the hands of Pohl, who was also the head of the enterprises. The camps and the enterprises were so inseparable that a unified control of both had to be fixed, and this control was imposed on Pohl.

Armed with this power, Pohl energetically set about driving the inmates to the limit of endurance in order to further the economic and war efforts of the Reich. In April 1942, he wrote to Himmler:

> The custody of prisoners for the sole reasons of security, education, or prevention is no longer the main consideration. The mobilization of all prisoners who are fit for work, for purposes of the war now, *and for purposes of construction in the forthcoming peace,* come to the foreground more and more.

In the affidavit of Philipp Grimm (*NO-2126, Pros. Ex. 298*), who in 1942 was labor assignment officer at Sachenhausen and later was transferred to office D II of WVHA, it is stated:

> Through my activity as labor assignment officer I know that in 1942 an order by Pohl was sent to the concentration camps, which authorized the camp commanders to retain prisoners who had been released for discharge by the Reich Security Main Office, but were important for the organization of labor in the camp. The duration of this illegal imprisonment could be extended to the end of the war.

To the very end of the war, Pohl kept a tight rein on all aspects of concentration camp administration. He constantly fought for longer hours, more intense effort, more production, selection of specialized skills, less loafing, and more strict supervision. As of July 1944 there were 20 concentration camps and 165 labor camps supervised by his Main Office. There was no phase of the administration of these camps in which he was not intensely interested, and this interest manifested itself at times in the smallest details. In some instances he recommended appointments and transfers of camp commanders, who were the slave drivers in the camps. In January 1943, in a letter to all camp commanders, he directed that the working hours of prisoners be kept at 11 hours per day during the winter, 6 days per week, and a half day on Sunday. In May 1941, when he found that half of a shipment of Jews from Hungary were women, he asked Himmler's approval for putting them to work on construction projects. Needless to say, Himmler consented. In December 1943, Pohl wrote to all camp commanders, complaining that SS guards were not urging prisoners to work sufficiently, stating, "Please instruct detachment leaders every Monday on this obvious duty of the guards."

In 1942, Gluecks, chief of Amtsgruppe D, in writing to the camp commanders, stated that Pohl had ordered that punishment by beating was to be executed by prisoners in concentration camps for men, but that it was forbidden to have foreign prisoners execute the punishment on German prisoners. This letter is significant because it recognizes Pohl's superior authority to issue such an order. If Gluecks enjoyed the degree of independence which Pohl attributes to him, he would have issued this order in person without attributing it to Pohl. On several occasions Pohl's interest led him to inspect concentration camps in person. He visited Ravensbrueck, Auschwitz, Dachau, and Oranienburg. During his visit to Auschwitz in 1943, Pohl was shown the plans for the enlargement of the camp, including the construction of four new crematories with modern gas chambers His solicitude for the inmates led him to order that specially hardworking prisoners be granted additional rations of food and tobacco and permission to patronize the camp brothel. For this last service Pohl fixed the charge and prescribed the method of dividing the income between the female inmates, the woman manager, and the WVHA. He also held periodic conferences with concentration camp commanders in Berlin. It was part of his duty to select new sites for concentration camps and to determine their economic potentialities. When a new camp was proposed, he determined its size, capacity, and the number of inmates which would be utilized in it.

There is no need to further elaborate upon the proof on this point although much more could be adduced. From all the evidence, it becomes clear to the Tribunal that Pohl at all times had an intimate and detailed knowledge of happenings in any way connected with the concentration camps. He made it his special business to know these facts. It is futile for him to say that he was not aware of the crematories when the plans were drawn and the construction supervised in his own organization and he visited the camps where they were installed. Nearly every Amt chief testified that he reported frequently to Pohl, in person, concerning events and problems arising in his immediate sphere. According to his own testimony and correspondence, he kept a running inventory, classified as to nationalities, of the labor supply of inmates in every camp. He knew how many prisoners died; he knew how many were unfit for work; and he knew what mass transfers were made from camp to camp. There was doubtless no other one person in Germany who knew as much about all the details of the concentration camps as Pohl. At least this much can be said and cannot be denied, that Pohl knew that hundreds of thousands of men and women had been cast into concentration camps and compelled to work, without remuneration and under the most rigid confinement, for the country which had devastated their homelands and abducted them into bondage. When these slaves died from exhaustion, starvation, or from the abuse of the SS overseers, Pohl cannot escape the fact that he was the administrative head of the agency which brought about these tragedies. His was more than a mere consenting part. It was active participation. Leaving all other considerations aside, Pohl stands before this Tribunal as an admitted slave driver on a scale never before known. On this count if no other he is guilty of direct participation in a war crime and a crime against humanity.

The mistreatment of prisoners of war, especially Russian and Polish prisoners, in the concentration camps, must also be laid at the door of Pohl. On 30 September 1944, Martin Bormann, head of the Party Chancellory, sent out an order from Hitler, which said in part:

> The mobilization of labor of the prisoners of war will be organized with the present labor mobilization office in joint action between SS Obergruppenfuehrer Berger and SS Obergruppenfuehrer Pohl.

On 28 September 1944, Himmler ordered that the question of the labor allocation of prisoners of war was to be submitted to Pohl. Not since the Roman Caesars brought back their prisoners of war, chained to their chariot wheels, has such inhuman treatment been accorded captives in battle as is shown by the record in this case. They, too, were simply grist for Germany's mill. By her treatment of these prisoners, Germany made the honorable profession of a soldier a by-word and a slur.

In the fall of 1942, Himmler's plans for the complete subjugation of Poland reached a pinnacle. The Jewish ghetto at Warsaw covered a total area of approximately 320 hectares or 800 acres. It comprised a large residential area and, in addition, housed a great number of industrial enterprises, principally textile and fur manufacturing plants. The ghetto had a population of nearly 60,000 persons. In October, Himmler ordered that the entire Jewish population of the ghetto was to be gathered together in concentration camps in Warsaw and Lublin to be used as an immense labor pool for armament purposes. After the round-up was completed, the Jews were to be deported to large concentration camps in the East and Polish labor substituted in the Warsaw industries. Himmler added: "Of course, there, too, the Jews shall someday disappear in accordance with the Fuehrer's wishes." All private Jewish firms were to be eliminated and no Jew was to be employed in private industry. This order raised a strong protest from the armament firms in Warsaw, in which a large number of Jews were employed, but Himmler was obdurate and insisted on the letter of his order being carried out. The Jewish residents of the ghetto, however, resisted deportation vigorously, and a pitched battle, lasting over a week, was necessary to uproot them. In February 1943, Himmler directed that after the removal of the concentration camp the ghetto be completely demolished. In his order he stated:

> A master plan for the pulling down of the ghetto has to be submitted to me. It has to be accomplished in any case that the living space, which accommodated 500,000 subhumans and was never suitable for Germans, will completely disappear, and that the city of Warsaw, with its one million inhabitants, will be reduced in size, having always been a dangerous center of rebellion.

This gigantic task of destruction and deportation was committed to Pohl as chief of the WVHA. Himmler directed that the "city center of the former ghetto is to be flattened completely and every cellar and every canal is to be filled in. After the work is finished, the area is to be covered up with earth, and a large park is to be planted."

By an order dated 23 June 1943, addressed to the Higher SS and Police Leader in the East and to Pohl, Himmler ordered the erection of a concentration camp in the vicinity of Riga, to which the largest possible number of the male Jews were to be transferred. Surplus Jews from the ghetto were to be evacuated to the East which meant ultimate starvation or extermination. In the summer of 1943. Pohl set to work to carry out Himmler's order. The concentration camp in the Warsaw ghetto was established and Pohl appointed Goecke, a veteran of Mauthausen, as commandant. Pohl reported to Himmler that at first there were only 300 prisoners in the camp but that this number would be increased as speedily as possible. In October, Pohl reported that Amtsgruppe C of the WVHA had been charged with the technical execution of the demolition order and Amtsgruppe D with the placing of the prisoners. Pohl engaged four private contracting firms, who guaranteed to pull down and remove 4,500 cubic meters daily. He advised that 1,500 prisoners were being used as laborers at the end of October, but that upon securing additional mechanical equipment 2,000 more prisoners would be needed at once. In February 1944, Pohl reported that 3,750,000 cubic meters of buildings had been demolished, and that 2,040 prisoners were being used. By April, 6,750,000 cubic meters had been "pulled down and blasted," and 2,180 prisoners were being used. By June, 10,000,000 cubic meters had been destroyed and the concentration camp had been completed. Thus was accomplished the most complete task of destruction of a modern city since Carthage met its fate many centuries ago, and in this nefarious undertaking Pohl stood hand in glove with Himmler and Stroop in accomplishing the task of total destruction. This was not a city taken in battle; it had long before been captured and occupied by the German armed forces. It was the deliberate and intentional destruction of a large modern city and its entire civilian population. It was wholesale murder, pillage, thievery, and looting, and Pohl's part in accomplishing this abominable project is recorded in his own handwriting. He cannot free himself from his share in Brigadefuehrer Stroop's shameful boast—"The total number of Jews dealt with is 56,065, including Jews caught, and Jews whose extermination can be proved."

Medical Experiments

Pohl's connection with the medical experiments, which have already been described, consisted only in supplying the subjects from the inmates of the concentration camps. It is not claimed that he actually participated in the performance of the experiments or did anything more than make them possible by supplying victims from his inmate pool. Here, again, his own writings convict him. In his own affidavit, dated 23 June 1946 (*NO-065, Pros. Ex. 183,* Pohl outlines his part in these experiments. He states that he was aware that experiments were being performed from April 1942 until the end of 1944; that Dr. Schilling continually asked for prisoners, but that he does not know the exact number that were sent; that at Himmler's request prisoners were sent to Dachau for the purpose of experimentation; that he accompanied Himmler to Dachau on one occasion and observed a high-altitude experiment; he received reports from Dr. Lolling of the number of prisoners used in experiments, totalling 350 to 400; he knew of Dr. Clauberg's experiments in sterilization; he knew that about 40 different experiments were performed. He states (*NO-407, Pros. Ex. 184*):

> The inmates were simply picked out and assigned for the experiments. Sometimes Himmler specified that inmates condemned to death should be used, but this was not always the case. There was no requirement that the subjects volunteer. We conducted no campaigns in the camp for volunteers; if these doctors were experimenting on volunteers, they need not have gone to Himmler and the concentration camps. It was for the very reason that they could not get volunteer subjects . . . that they went to Himmler and got him to consent to experiments on concentration camp inmates. This was a fact well known to anyone connected with those experiments. . . . In accordance with Himmler's racial policies, non-German nationals were essentially used in preference to German nationals.

Further proof of Pohl's connection with these outrageous experiments would seem unnecessary, but there is plenty in addition. The affidavit of Rudolf Brandt, Himmler's adjutant, states:

> Subjects for experiments were selected by Pohl. Himmler or I used to inform Pohl that a certain number of prisoners should be supplied for a particular experiment. Certain groups were usually specified.

Concerning the warming experiments at Auschwitz and Dachau, Himmler wrote to Dr. Rascher: "I am sending this letter to Pohl, whom I request to order the execution of your experiments."

Himmler wrote to Dr. Grawitz approving the use of eight Jews of the Polish Resistance Movement for experiments in epidemic jaundice at Auschwitz and sent a copy to Pohl, with the notation—"Request that you duly note."

Dr. Sievers wrote to Pohl as follows:

> In compliance with our request of 30 September 1943, you approved the carrying out of experiments for the production of a new type of spotted fever vaccine, and for this purpose transferred 100 suitable prisoners to Natzweiler.

Pohl was particularly interested in the production of Schweigrohr, a plant to be used in producing wholesale sterilization. Pohl wrote to Himmler in June 1942, stating that experiments with this plant were at a standstill because the plant was obtainable only from North America and the proposed process for growing the plant in Germany in hot houses would not yield sufficient drug to permit large-scale experiments. Continuing, Pohl stated that he had informed

Dr. Koch that he would attempt to obtain permission to build a large hot house for cultivation of the plant. Pohl arranged to put Dr. Lolling, whom he refers to as "chief of my office D III," in touch with a Vienna biologist for further study, looking toward the large-scale production of Schweigrohr. Rudolf Brandt sent to Dr. Clauberg Himmler's order to first confer with Pohl and then go to Ravensbrueck to pursue the sterilization program on Jewesses in that camp. Brandt inquires how long it would take to sterilize a thousand Jewesses by X-ray without their knowing it. Further proof could be accumulated, but it is unnecessary. Pohl's participation in the medical experiments was intimate and direct, and he must share the responsibility for their criminality.

The Tribunal finds that the food experiments in which Pohl was greatly interested did not involve the use of poisons but were simply legitimate experiments in the nutritional values of food. As such, of course, they had no element of criminality.

Action Reinhardt

This action, as has been indicated, involved a plan for draining the Eastern occupied countries of their last vestige of wealth. It had the two-fold purpose of reducing the East to abject poverty so that starvation would be the inevitable result to the population and, at the same time, filling the Reich Treasury. It was a program of deliberate wholesale brigandage which was, at the same time, an added aspect of the extermination program.

In the execution of this program, Pohl's WVHA played a major role. His organization was the clearing house for all the booty. All of the stolen property was routed through WVHA, where it was inventoried, appraised, and distributed. That Pohl knew of the criminal source of this property is evidenced by his letter of 9 February 1944, to Maurer, directing that valuables found in clothing were to be delivered in sealed boxes to Amtsgruppe D, and directing further, that nothing in the shipment should reveal its origin. The money which was stolen was secreted in the Reich Bank under the assumed name of Max Heiliger. On 4 July 1944, Pohl, in a communication to the Main Office chiefs, announced the names of officers responsible for the property seized in several areas, and stated: "As a matter of principle, it has to be kept in mind that the entire Jewish property is to be incorporated into the Reich property." Property from the Action Reinhardt which had been delivered to the Reich Main Treasury was kept in a separate account, appropriately called, "Department Booty."

Moved by the Christian spirit of Christmas, Pohl on 6 November 1943, wrote to Himmler, stating that he intended to make gifts of watches and fountain pens to SS units, and asked whether the gifts should be made in Himmler's name. Himmler approved Pohl's generous plan and added that 15,000 ladies' watches should be distributed to Germans coming from Russia for resettlement. Pohl thought it would be a generous gesture to distribute 3,000 clocks which had been repaired to guards at the concentration camps and to Berlin inhabitants who had been bombed. As an after-thought, he suggested to Himmler that 16 extra-fine gold precision wrist watches, valued at 300 Reichsmarks each, which had been repaired, be distributed among commanders of technical units.

Pohl's own statement as to his knowledge of the operation of Action Reinhardt and of his participation in the distribution of the loot is again quite sufficient. In his affidavit of 2 April 1947 (*NO-2714, Pros. Ex. 535*), he states that the action was instituted in 1941 or 1942 and was in direct charge of SS Gruppenfuehrer Globocnik; that by Himmler's direction he contacted the president of the Reich Bank to arrange for delivery of the valuables; these transactions were to be carried out in extreme secrecy. Together with Georg Loerner, Frank, and others, he visited the Reich Bank and was shown the accumulated valuables in the bank vaults. "It was never doubted," he said, "that this loot was taken from Jews exterminated in the concentration camps. . . . As I learned in 1943, gold teeth and crowns of inmates of concentration camps were broken out of their mouths after liquidation. This gold was melted down and delivered to the Reich Bank. . . . When I received all the vouchers, setting out the economic assets received, I realized the extent of the operation. I realized that the greatest part of the textile goods listed in these reports had been taken from people who had been violently put to death and that the purpose of the operation had been the extermination of the Jews."

In another affidavit, 15 July 1946 (*4045-PS, Pros. Ex. 536*), Pohl further indicates his knowledge of, and participation in the ghoulish scramble. The facts stated therein are cumulative and need not be specifically referred to.

The fact that Pohl himself did not actually transport the stolen goods to the Reich or did not himself remove the gold from the teeth of dead inmates, does not exculpate him. This was a broad criminal program, requiring the cooperation of many persons, and Pohl's part was to conserve and account for the loot. Having knowledge of the illegal purposes of the action and of the crimes which accompanied it, his active participation even in the afterphases of the action make him *particeps criminis* in the whole affair.

OSTI [EASTERN INDUSTRY]

Eastern Industries, known as "OSTI," was a running-mate of Action Reinhardt in the so-called final solution of the Jewish problem in the East. OSTI was organized 1 March 1943, and was dissolved one year later. The whole history of this project is clearly described in the report of Johann Sebastian Fischer in a final audit, 21 June 1944 (*NO-1271, Pros. Ex. 491*). It was impossible to completely strip the Eastern territories of all Jewish property. Some because of its nature could not be removed and some could be operated best by the Reich on the spot. To utilize this unremovable property, OSTI was organized, with a capital of 100,000 Reichsmarks. Of this Pohl held 75,000 and defendant Georg Loerner 25,000. Pohl was chairman of the Aufsichtsrat, or supervisory board, of which Georg Loerner was also a member. Globocnik and Dr. Max Horn were the active managers. Fischer describes the corporate purposes as follows: "OSTI had to administer all Jewish property within the territory of the Government General except cash, jewelry, and clothing; and in particular to utilize the manpower of the Jews living in the Government General for tasks benefiting the Reich."

This involved—

(1) Utilization of the working capacity of the Jews by erecting industrial plants in the Government General in connection with the Jewish labor camps.

(2) Taking over commercial enterprises which had previously been maintained by the SS in the Government General.

(3) Taking possession of movable property which was formerly Jewish, especially machines and raw materials. The machines were to be installed in plants and the raw materials to be used.

(4) Utilization of machines, tools, and merchandise formerly Jewish property which had been transferred to non-Jewish ownership.

A partial list of the industries thus administered included a glass works in Wolomin, a peat-cutting plant near Lublin, an iron foundry, a large textile factory, a plant for the manufacture of brushes, and a stone quarry. Globocnik states that the entire manpower was brought together and kept in closed camps into which the manufacture of essential items for war had been transferred. "All together 18 establishments had been built up and still more were to be added. About 52,000 laborers were available."

The project continued as long as the supply of Jewish concentration camp labor was available, but when, due to the exigencies of the war, in the fall of 1943 this labor supply was withdrawn, it was determined to liquidate OSTI, and Dr. Horn was designated as liquidating officer.

As will be observed, OSTI was simply another manifestation of the policy of slave labor and appropriation of private property. Linked with Action Reinhardt, it was the consummation of the Reich plan to leave the occupied Eastern countries as vast stretches of scorched earth. In the OSTI phase of this plan, Pohl had even a more direct connection than he had with Action Reinhardt. Here he was the directing head and the chief executive of the project. As an original incorporator, he was in it from its inception and he actively participated in every phase of it until its liquidation. This being true, he was guilty of war crimes and crimes against humanity.

Under a plan which was perhaps devised to give some semblance of legality to this inherently lawless plan, Pohl was designated as a trustee of the properties seized in the East and operated by OSTI. This was a strange species of trusteeship. All of the interests of the trustee were violently opposed to those of the *cestius qui trustent.* The recognized concept of a trustee is that he stands in the shoes of his beneficiaries and acts for their benefit and in opposition to any encroachment on their rights. Here, however, the trustee was in the service of adverse interests and acted at all times under an impelling motive to serve those interests at the expense of his benficiaries. Actually, the trusteeship was pure fiction. It cannot be believed that it was ever the plan of the Reich to return any of the confiscated property to its former Jewish owners, most of whom had fled and disappeared, or had been exterminated. The only probative value of this fictitious trusteeship is to furnish another cord to bind Pohl closer to OSTI's criminal purposes.

In an attempt at partial exculpation, Pohl has submitted in evidence (*Pohl 3, Pohl Ex. 2*) a decree, dated 28 February 1933, signed by Reich President von Hindenburg and Chancellor Hitler, suspending the provisions of the Weimar Constitution, which guaranteed personal freedom, freedom of speech and of the press, the right of assembly, privacy of communication, and immunity from search. The Secret State Police were given almost unlimited power over persons and property, independent of any obligations and free from restraint or review. They became the supreme authority of the land. This tyrannical agency was the partner of WVHA in the administration of the concentration camps. Upon the promulgation of this decree, Germany became a police state and the liberty and lives of all German citizens were dependent upon the whims of men like Heydrich and Kaltenbrunner. It is to be assumed that if this is the kind of national government the people of Germany preferred, they were entitled to it. If they consented to surrender their human liberties to a police force, that was their privilege, and any outsider who intruded could well be told to mind his own affairs. But when the attempt is made to make the provisions of such a decree extra-territorial in their effect and to apply their totalitarian and autocratic police measures to non-Germans and in non-German territory, they thereby invaded the domain of international law, where reason still rules. The Nazi leaders, drunk with power, could abuse and deceive the German people just as long as the German people submitted, but when they extended their tyranny into foreign lands and attempted to justify it by the provisions of local German Law, their arrogance became over-extended and a power superior to Hitler's came into play to stop them.

In recapitulation and upon the findings of fact heretofore made, the Tribunal determines that the defendant Pohl is guilty of war crimes and crimes against humanity, as alleged in counts two and three of the indictment.

Count Four

The Tribunal finds that the defendant Pohl was a member of a criminal organization, that is, the SS, under the conditions defined by the judgment of the International Military Tribunal, and is therefore guilty under count four of the indictment.

[Pohl was sentenced to death by hanging.]

THE FLICK CASE

Nuremberg, February, 1948*

OPINION AND JUDGMENT OF THE UNITED STATES
MILITARY TRIBUNAL AT NUREMBERG IN
UNITED STATES *vs.* FRIEDRICH FLICK ET AL.

PRESIDING JUDGE SEARS: At the close of the proceedings on 8 November, the defendants jointly and severally made a series of motions, among other things attacking the jurisdiction of this Tribunal and asking for the dismissal of the various counts of the indictment as to the defendants charged therein, and seeking to strike from the record hearsay testimony and affidavits on various grounds, and on 12 November defendant Flick moved to strike documents offered by prosecution on rebuttal, and on 14 November defendant Steinbrinck made a further motion.

We have examined all of these motions with care and hereby deny them all except the motion to dismiss the third count which we will determine in that part of the judgment itself which relates to that count. We find the motions otherwise fully and conclusively answered in the brief interposed by the prosecution in objection to the motion.

In order to avoid any misunderstanding, however, we make these summary statements.

As to the Tribunal, its nature, and competence: The Tribunal is not a court of the United States as that term is used in the Constitution of the United States. It is not a court martial. It is not a military commission. It is an international tribunal established by the International Control Council, the high legislative branch of the four Allied Powers now controlling Germany *(Control Council Law No. 10, 20 Dec. 1945)*. The judges were legally appointed by the Military Governor and the later act of the President of the United States in respect to this was nothing more than a confirmation of the appointments by the Military Governor. The Tribunal administers international law. It is not bound by the general statutes of the United States or even by those parts of its Constitution which relate to courts of the United States.

* *Trial of War Criminals,* Vol. 6, p. 1187 (Washington, D.C., 1952).

Some safeguards written in the Constitution and statutes of the United States as to persons charged with crime, among others such as the presumption of innocence, the rule that conviction is dependent upon proof of the crime charged beyond a reasonable doubt, and the right of the accused to be advised and defended by counsel, are recognized as binding on the Tribunal, as they were recognized by the International Military Tribunal (IMT). This is not because of their inclusion in the Constitution and statutes of the United States but because they are deeply ingrained in our Anglo-American system of jurisprudence as principles of a fair trial. In committing to the occupying authorities of the various zones the duty to try war criminals, it is implicit therein that persons charged with crime are to be given a fair trial according to the jurisprudence prevalent in the courts of the power conducting the trials.

As to hearsay evidence and affidavits.—A fair trial does not necessarily exclude hearsay testimony and *ex parte* affidavits, and exclusion and acceptance of such matters relate to procedure and procedure is regulated for the Tribunal by Article VII of Ordinance 7 issued by order of the Military Government and effective 18 October 1946. By this Article, the Tribunal is freed from the restraints of the common law rules of evidence and given wide power to receive relevant hearsay and *ex parte* affidavits as such evidence was received by IMT. The Tribunal has followed that practice here.

As to counsel and witnesses.—The defendants have not been denied the right to be advised and defended by counsel of their own choice. Defendants have not been denied the right to call any witness to give relevant testimony nor has the production of any available relevant document been denied by the Court.

As to the law administered.—The Tribunal is giving no *ex post facto* application to Control Council Law No. 10. It is administering that law as a statement of international law which previously was at least partly uncodified. Codification is not essential to the validity of law in our Anglo-American system. No act is adjudged criminal by the Tribunal which was not criminal under international law as it existed when the act was committed.

Now I will read the opinion and judgment as to Case 5.

Facing this Tribunal are private citizens of a conquered state being tried for alleged international crimes. Their judges are citizens of one of the victor states selected by its war department. There may well be misgivings as to the fairness of such a trial. These considerations have made the judges of the Tribunal keenly aware of their grave responsibility and of the danger to the cause of justice if the conduct of the trial and the conclusions reached should even seem to justify these misgivings. To err is human, but if error must occur it is right that the error must not be prejudicial to the defendants. That, we think, is the spirit of the law of civilized nations. It finds expression in the following principles well-known to students of Anglo-American criminal law.

1. There can be no conviction without proof of personal guilt.
2. Such guilt must be proved beyond a reasonable doubt.

3. The presumption of innocence follows each defendant throughout the trial.

4. The burden of proof is at all times upon the prosecution.

5. If from credible evidence two reasonable inferences may be drawn, one of guilt and the other of innocence, the latter must be taken.

We cannot imagine that German law contains concepts more favorable to defendants. Any less favorable, we, as American judges trained in Anglo-American criminal jurisprudence, would be reluctant to apply even though this is not an American court but a special tribunal constituted pursuant to a four-power agreement administering public international law.

To the extent required by article 10 of Military Government Ordinance No. 7 the Tribunal is bound by the judgment of the International Military Tribunal (hereinafter referred to as IMT) in Case 1 against Goering *et al.*, but we shall indulge no implications therefrom to the prejudice of the defendants against whom the judgment would not be *res judicata* except for this article. There is no similar mandate either as to findings of fact or conclusions of law contained in judgments of coordinate Tribunals. The Tribunal will take judicial notice of the judgments but will treat them as advisory only.

The indictment is in five counts. The first charges all six defendants, but in different capacities, with participation in the slave-labor program of the Third Reich and the use of prisoners of war in armament production. The second accuses all defendants except Terberger of spoliation of public and private property in occupied territories. In count three, Flick, Steinbrinck, and Kaletsch are accused of crimes against humanity in compelling by means of anti-Semitic economic pressure the owners of certain industrial properties to part with title thereto. The fourth count alleges that Flick and Steinbrinck, as members of the Keppler Circle or Friends of Himmler, with knowledge of its criminal activities, contributed large sums to the financing of Die Schutzstaffen der Nationalsozialistischen Deutschen Arbeiterpartei (hereinafter called the SS). In the last count Steinbrinck's membership in the SS is claimed to incriminate him under the ruling of IMT that it was a criminal organization. The theories upon which the several counts proceed will be elaborated as each is discussed.

* * *

It is noteworthy that defendants were not charged with planning, preparation, initiation, or waging a war of aggression or with conspiring or cooperating with anyone to that end. Except as to some of Steinbrinck's activities the defendants were not officially connected with the Nazi government but were private citizens engaged as businessmen in the heavy industry of Germany. Their counsel, and Flick in his closing unsworn statement, contended that in their persons industry itself is being persecuted. They have some shade of justification for so believing since the prosecution at the very beginning of the case made this statement—

> The defendants in this case are leading representatives of one of the two principal concentrations of power in Germany. In the final analysis, Germany's capacity for conquest derived from its heavy industry and attendant scientific techniques, and from its millions of able-bodied men, obedient, amenable to discipline, and overly susceptible to panoply and fanfare. Krupp, Flick, Thyssen, and a few others swayed the industrial group; Beck, Fritsch, Rundstedt, and other martial exemplars ruled the military clique. On the shoulders of these groups Hitler rode to power, and from power to conquest.

But the prosecution made no attempt to prove this charge and when the defendants, presenting their case, proposed to call witnesses to disprove it, upon the prosecution's objection that it was not in issue, the Tribunal excluded the testimony.

The question of the responsibility of individuals for such breaches of international law as constitute crimes has been widely discussed and is settled in part by the judgment of IMT. It cannot longer be successfully maintained that international law is concerned only with the actions of sovereign states and provides no punishment for individuals.

> That international law imposes duties and liabilities upon individuals as well as upon states has long been recognized. In the recent case of *ex parte Quirin* (1942, 317 U.S. 1, 63 S Ct. 2, 87 L. Ed. 3), before the Supreme Court of the United States, persons were charged during the war with landing in the United States for purposes of spying and sabotage. The late Chief Justice Stone, speaking for the Court, said:
>
> "From the very beginning of its history this Court has applied the law of war as including that part of the law of nations which prescribed for the conduct of war, the status, rights and duties of enemy nations as well as enemy individuals."

But IMT was dealing with officials and agencies of the State, and it is urged that individuals holding no public offices and not representing the State, do not, and should not come within the class of persons criminally responsible for a breach of international law. It is asserted that international law is a matter wholly outside the work, interest, and knowledge of private individuals. The distinction is unsound. International law, as such, binds every citizen just as does ordinary municipal law. Acts adjudged criminal when done by an officer of the government are criminal also when done by a private individual. The guilt differs only in magnitude, not in quality. The offender in either case is charged with personal wrong and punishment falls on the offender in *propria persona.* The application of international law to individuals is no novelty. There is no justification for a limitation of responsibility to public officials.

As background for all of the counts, the counts, the following brief history of the Flick organization with its personnel will suffice. The industrial career of defendant Flick had small beginnings. His first employment was as Prokurist or confidential clerk in a foundry. His first major capital acquisition was in the Charlottenhuette, a steel rolling mill, in 1915. Since then steel has been his principal interest, though he extended his organization to include iron and coal mining companies as foundation for steel production. Incidentally plants have been acquired for the further fabrication of the steel. His genius for corporate organization enabled him to obtain voting control of numerous companies in which he did not have a majority capital interest. At the height of his career, through the Friedrich Flick Kommanditgesellschaft, the top holding company, he had voting control of a dozen companies employing at least 120,000 persons engaged in mining coal and iron, making steel and building machinery and other products which required steel as raw material.

He has always been an advocate of individual enterprise and concerned in maintaining as his own against socialization the industries so acquired. As companies came under his voting domination, it was his policy to leave in charge the management which had proved itself and until the end of the war the Vorstaende (managing boards) of the different companies were in a large degree autonomous. There were no central buying, selling, or accounting agencies. Each company was administered by its own Vorstand. He was not a member of the Vorstand of any of the companies but confined his activities to the Aufsichtsraete (supervisory boards) which dealt chiefly with financial questions. As chairman of the Aufsichtsrat of several companies, he had a voice beyond that of the ordinary member in the selection of members of the Vorstand. These companies were scattered over Germany. For the purpose of coordinating the companies into one system, he established offices in Berlin where he spent most of his time. The total office force did not exceed 100 persons including secretaries, statisticians, file clerks, drivers, and messengers.

Until 1940 defendant Steinbrinck was Flick's chief assistant with defendants Burkart and Kaletsch having lesser roles but not necessarily subordinate to Steinbrinck. When Steinbrinck resigned in December 1939 defendant Weiss, who is a nephew of Flick, was called to the Berlin office as Flick's assistant but with permission to devote about one-fourth of his time to his own company, Siegener Maschinenbau A.G. (Siemag), in the Siegerland with about 2000 employees. Thereafter Weiss, Burkart, and Kaletsch, each in his own field, acted as assistants to Flick in the Berlin office. Weiss supervised the hard [soft] coal mining companies and finishing plants; Burkart the soft [brown] coal mining companies and steel plants, while Kaletsch acted as financial expert. Defendant Terberger was not in the Berlin office but was a part of a local administration as a member of the Vorstand of Eisenwerk Gesellschaft Maximilianshuette, A.G., commonly called Maxhuette, an important subsidiary operating plant in Bavaria and through stock ownership controlling other plants in Thuringia and south Germany.

The record comprises 10,343 pages. Not included therein are those portions of documents which were admitted without reading. The Court sat 5 days a week for 6 full months exclusive of recesses. Objection to evidence was rare until the prosecution was engaged in rebuttal. It is not too much to say that practically all the substantial evidence was received without objection.

Few of the legal questions in this case were suggested, much less argued and briefed, until the evidence had all been received. Arguments occupied the whole of the last week of November. Only since then has the Tribunal been able to obtain a comprehensive view of the evidence in the light of the legal principles sought to be applied by counsel. In reaching its conclusions, therefore, the Tribunal has been compelled to rely upon authority presented in the arguments and briefs, supplemented by such independent research as is possible with very inadequate library facilities. All of these Tribunals, no doubt, have suffered from the same handicap. This recital will serve to explain, if not to excuse, the lack of cited authority and the general summarization of the evidence.

Count One

Judge Christianson: The allegations in this count are substantially as follows: between September 1939 and May 1945 all the defendants committed war crimes and crimes against humanity as defined by Article II [paragraph 2] of Control Council Law No. 10, in that they were principals in, accessories to, ordered, abetted, took a consenting part in, were connected with plans and enterprises involving, and were members of organizations or groups connected with, enslavement and deportation to slave labor on a gigantic scale of members of the civilian populations of countries and territories under the belligerent occupation of or otherwise controlled by Germany. This charge also involved the enslavement of concentration camp inmates, including German nationals, and the use of prisoners of war in war operations and work having a direct relation to war operations. More specifically, it is alleged that between the dates above-mentioned the defendants sought and utilized such slave labor program [by using] tens of thousands of slave laborers, including concentration camp inmates and prisoners of war, in the industrial enterprises and establishments owned, controlled, or influenced by them.

It is asserted that defendant Flick, as a member of the Praesidium of the Reichsvereinigung Eisen, commonly referred to as RVE (May 1942–45), and of the Praesidium of the Reichsvereinigung Kohle, commonly referred to as RVK (Mar. 1941–Apr. 1945), and as a member of the Beirat (advisory council) of the Wirtschaftsgruppe Eisenschaffende Industrie (Economic Group of the Iron Producing Industry) (Sept. 1939 to Apr. 1945), participated in the formulation and execution of such slave-labor program. It is further alleged that Flick's influence and control over policies and actions of these organizations were extended through officials of his companies who also held positions in RVE and RVK.

It is further claimed that defendant Steinbrinck also was a member of the Praesidium of RVE (1941–45) and in that capacity exerted extensive influence upon the formulation and administration of the slave-labor program and that between September 1939 and April 1945 defendant Steinbrinck held the position of Beauftragter Kohle-West, also known as Bekowest (Plenipotentiary for Coal in the Occupied Western Territories) of France, Holland, Belgium, and Luxembourg and the position of Generalbeauftragter fuer die Stahlindustrie (Plenipotentiary General for the Steel Industry) in northern France, Belgium, and Luxembourg, and that by virtue of these positions, he exercised wide authority over the procurement, use, treatment, allocation, and transportation of thousands of slave laborers and prisoners of war.

It is further alleged that between September 1939 and May 1945, in the utilization of tens of thousands of slave laborers and prisoners of war in the industrial enterprises and establishments owned, controlled, and influenced by them, the defendants exploited such laborers under inhumane conditions with respect to their personal liberty, shelter, food, pay, hours of work, and health, and that the defendants used prisoners of war in work having a direct relation with war operations, including the manufacture and transportation of armament and munitions. It must here be noted that the defendants Flick, Burkart, Kaletsch, and Weiss are charged with the inhumane and repressive acts referred to in this paragraph with respect to the plants generally making up what is called the Flick Concern and that defendant Terberger is charged with such acts only insofar as they relate to one company in the Flick Concern known as Eisenwerk Gesellschaft Maximilianshuette A.G., commonly referred to as Maxhuette. The defendant Weiss is further charged with such acts as they relate to Siegener Maschinenbau A.G., commonly referred to as Siemag, a concern owned and controlled by him.

Count one then concludes,

> 7. The acts and conduct of the defendants set forth in this count were committed unlawfully, wilfully, and knowingly and constitute violations of international conventions, particularly of Articles 3–7, 14, 18, 23, 43, 46, and 52 of the Hague Regulations, 1907, and of Articles 2–4, 6, 9–15, 23, 25, 27–34, 46–48, 50, 51, 54, 56, 57, 60, 62, 63, 65–68, and 76 of the Prisoners of War Convention (Geneva, 1929), of the laws and customs of war, of the general principles of criminal law as derived from the criminal laws of all civilized nations, of the internal penal laws of the countries in which such crimes were committed, and of Article II of Control Council Law No. 10.

A great deal of oral and documentary evidence was adduced by both the prosecution and defense with respect to the charges in this count. Although all of this evidence has had the Tribunal's close scrutiny and consideration, it is neither practicable nor necessary that a detailed discussion of this great mass of evidence be included in this opinion. We will make only such general references to the evidence as may be necessary to explain and justify the conclusions reached by the Tribunal.

It is not necessary that we dwell at length upon the origin and extent of the notorious slave-labor program, as it is treated fully in the judgment of IMT. It is important to note, however, that on the basis of the proof submitted, it is clear that the slave-labor program had its origin in Reich governmental circles and was a governmental program, and that the defendants had no part in creating or launching this program. It should be observed also that for a considerable period of time prior to the institution of the slave-labor program here under consideration, the employment of labor in German industry had been directed and implemented by the Reich government.

The evidence with respect to this count clearly establishes that laborers procured under Reich regulations, including voluntary and involuntary foreign civilian workers, prisoners of war and concentration camp inmates, were employed in some of the plants of the Flick Concern and similarly some foreign workers and a few prisoners of war in Siemag. It further appears that in some of the Flick enterprises prisoners of war were engaged in work bearing a direct relation to war operations.

The evidence indicates that the defendants had no actual control of the administration of such program even where it affected their own plants. On the contrary, the evidence shows that the program thus created by the State was rigorously detailed and supervised by the State, its supervision even extending into prisoner-of-war labor camps and concentration camp inmate labor camps, established and maintained near the plants to which such prisoners of war and concentration camp inmates had been allocated. Such prisoner-of-war camps were in charge of the Wehrmacht [Armed Forces], and the concentration camp inmate labor camps were under the control and supervision of the SS. Foreign civilian labor camps were under camp guards appointed by the plant management subject to the approval of State Police officials. The evidence shows that the managers of the plants here involved did not have free access to the prisoner-of-war labor camps or the concentration labor camps connected with their plants, but were allowed to visit them only at the pleasure of those in charge.

The evacuation by the SS of sick concentration camp laborers from the concentration labor camp at the Groeditz plant for the purpose of "liquidating" them was done despite the efforts of the plant manager to frustrate the perpetration of the atrocity and illustrates all too graphically the extent and supremacy of the control and supervision vested in and exercised by the SS over concentration labor camps and their inmates.

With the specific exception hereinafter referred to and discussed, the following appears to have been the procedure with respect to the procurement and allocation of workers. Workers were allocated to the plants needing labor through the governmental labor offices. No plant management could effectively object to such allocation. Quotas for production were set for industry by the Reich authorities. Without labor, quotas could not be filled. Penalties were provided for those who failed to meet such quotas. Notification by the plant management to the effect that labor was needed resulted in the allocation of workers to such plant by the governmental authorities. This was the only way workers could be procured.

With the specific exception above alluded to and as hereinafter discussed, it appears that the defendants here involved were not desirous of employing foreign labor or prisoners of war. It further appears, however, that they were conscious of the fact that it was both futile and dangerous to object to the allocation of such labor. It was known that any act that could be construed as tending to hinder or retard the war economy programs of the Reich would be construed as sabotage and would be treated with summary and severe penalties, sometimes resulting in the imposition of death sentences. Numerous proclamations and decrees of the Reich kept such threats and penalties before the people. There were frequent examples of severe punishment imposed for infractions. Of this, all of the defendants were ever conscious. Moreover, the prosecution admits that the defendants were justified in their fear that the Reich authorities would take drastic action against anyone who might refuse to submit to the slave-labor program, for, in its final brief on this phase of the case, the prosecution states,

> It is undoubtedly true that if Flick had suddenly said in so many words, "I will shut down all my plants immediately because I don't like this idea of using forced foreign labor," the result would at least have been that management of his plants would have been taken away from him, and there was a possibility that he might even have been sent to a concentration camp.

Under such compulsion, despite the misgivings which it appears were entertained by some of the defendants with respect to the matter, they submitted to the program and, as a result, foreign workers, prisoners of war, or concentration camp inmates became employed in some of the plants of the Flick Concern and in Siemag. Such written reports and other documents as from time to time may have been signed or initialed by the defendants in connection with the employment of foreign slave labor and prisoners of war in their plants were for the most part obligatory and necessary to a compliance with the rigid and harsh Reich regulations relative to the administration of its program.

The exception to the foregoing, to which exception we have hereinbefore alluded, was the active participation of defendant Weiss, with the knowledge and approval of defendant Flick, in the solicitation of increased freight car production quota for the Linke-Hofmann Werke, a plant in the Flick Concern. This indisputably appears from the evidence. It likewise appears that Weiss took an active and leading part in securing an allocation of Russian prisoners of war for use in the work of manufacturing such increased quotas. It appears that in both efforts the defendants were successful.

The proof fails to show that defendant Flick, as a member of the Praesidiums of RVE and RVK or as a member of the Beirat of the Economic Group of the Iron Producing Industry, exerted any influence or took any part in the formation, administration or furtherance of the slave-labor program. The same may be said with respect to defendant Steinbrinck's membership on the Praesidium of RVK. With respect to defendant Steinbrinck's activities and participation in the slave-labor program as Bekowest and as Plenipotentiary General or Commissioner for the Steel Industry in northern France, Belgium, and Luxembourg, it must be borne in mind that he entered these positions long after the slave-labor program had been created and put in operation by the Reich. His duties and activities in these positions insofar as they involved the slave-labor program were obligatory. His only alternative to complying was to refuse to carry out the policies and programs of the government in the course of his duties, which, as hereinbefore indicated, would have been a desperately hazardous choice. It appears, however, that his actions in these positions as they affected labor were characterized by a distinctly humane attitude.

The charges in this count to the effect that the laborers thus employed in the defendant's plants were exploited by the defendants under inhuman conditions with respect to their personal liberty, shelter, food, pay, hours of work, and health are not sustained by the proof. The evidence offered in support of these charges was sketchy and far outweighed by the substantial and impressive evidence submitted by the defendants to the contrary. We must conclude that the cruel and atrocious practices which are known to have characterized the slave labor program in many places where it was employed did not prevail in the plants and establishments under the control of the defendants. Isolated instances of ill treatment or neglect shown by the evidence were not the result of a policy of the plants' managements, but were in direct opposition to it.

This is true even though, as hereinbefore indicated, the defendants did not have actual control and supervision over the labor camps connected with their plants. It clearly appears that the duties of defendants as members of the governing boards of various companies in the Flick Concern required their presence most of the time in the general offices of the Concern at Berlin. Thus they were generally quite far removed from day to day administration and conduct of such plants and labor conditions therein. It is equally clear, however, that the defendants authorized and caused to be carried out measures conducive to humane treatment and good working conditions for all laborers in their plants. This is strongly evidenced by the fact that it was the policy and practice of the managers of the plants with which defendants were associated to do what was within their power to provide healthful housing for such laborers, to provide them with not only better but more food than permitted by governmental regulations, to give them adequate medical care and necessary recreation and amusement. That such efforts generally bore fruit is clear from the evidence.

Following the collapse of Germany and the liberation of the slave laborers within the plants here under consideration, there were a number of striking demonstrations of gratitude by them toward the management of such plants for the humane treatment accorded while they were there employed. It thus appears that the charges of exploitation and mistreatment of the laborers allocated to the plants with which defendants were associated are not sustained by the proof.

Recognizing the criminality of the Reich labor program as such, the only question remaining for our decision with respect to this count is whether the defendants are guilty of having employed conscripted foreign workers, concentration camp inmates or prisoners of war allocated to them through the slave-labor program of the Reich under the circumstances of compulsion under which such employment came about. The circumstances have hereinbefore been discussed. The prosecution has called attention to the fact that defendants Walther Funk and Albert Speer were convicted by IMT because of their participation in the slave-labor program. It is clear, however, that relation of Speer and Funk to such program differs substantially from the nature of the participation in such program by the defendants in this case. Speer and Funk were numbered among the group of top public officials responsible for the slave-labor program.

We are not unmindful of the provision of paragraph 2 of Article II of Control Council Law No. 10 which states that—

> 2. Any person without regard to the nationality or the capacity in which he acted, is deemed to have committed a crime as defined in paragraph 1 of this Article, if he was (*a*) a principal or (*b*) was an accessory to the commission of any such crime or ordered or abetted the same or (*c*) took a consenting part therein or (*d*) was connected with plans or enterprises involving its commission.

Nor have we overlooked the provision in paragraph 4(*b*) of Article II of such Control Council Law No. 10 which states—

> (*b*) The fact that any person acted pursuant to the order of his Government or of a superior does not free him from responsibility for a crime, but may be considered in mitigation.

In our opinion, it is not intended that these provisions are to be employed to deprive a defendant of the defense of necessity under such circumstances as obtained in this case with respect to defendants Steinbrinck, Burkart, Kaletsch, and Terberger. This Tribunal might be reproached for wreaking vengeance rather than administering justice if it were to declare as unavailable to defendants the defense of necessity here urged in their behalf. This principle has had wide aceptance in American and English courts and is recognized elsewhere.

Wharton's Criminal Law, volume I, chapter III, subdivision VII, paragraph 126, contains the following statement with respect to the defense of necessity citing cases in support thereof:

> Necessity is a defense when it is shown that the act charged was done to avoid an evil both serious and irreparable; that there was no other adequate means of escape; and that the remedy was not disproportioned to the evil.

A note under paragraph 384 in chapter XIII, Wharton's Criminal Law, volume I, gives the underlying principle of the defense of necessity as follows:

> Necessity forcing a man to do an act justifies him, because no man can be guilty of a crime without the will and intent in his mind. When a man is absolutely, by natural necessity, forced, his will does not go along with the act. Lord Mansfield in Stratton's Case, 21 How. St. Tr. (Eng.) 1046–1223.

The prosecution, on final argument, contended that the defendants are barred from interposing the defense of necessity. In the course of its argument, the prosecution referred to paragraph 4 (*b*), of Article II of Control Council Law No. 10 and stated:

> This principle has been most frequently applied and interpreted in military cases.

Further on in the argument, it was said:

> The defendants in this case, as they have repeatedly and plaintively told us, were not military men or government officials. None of the acts with which they are charged under any count of the indictment were committed under "orders" of the type we have been discussing. By their own admissions, it seems to us they are in no position to claim the benefits of the doctrine of "superior orders" even by way of mitigation.

The foregoing statement was then closely followed by another, as follows:

> The defense of "coercion" or "duress" has a certain application in ordinary civilian jurisprudence. But despite the most desperate efforts, the defendants have not, we believe, succeeded in bringing themselves within the purview of these concepts.

The prosecution then asserted that this defense has no application unless the defendants acted under what is described as "clear and present danger." Reference was made to certain rules and cases in support of such position.

The evidence with respect to defendants Steinbrinck, Burkart, Kaletsch, and Terberger in our opinion, however, clearly established that there was in the instant case "clear and present danger" within the contemplation of that phrase. We have already discussed the Reich reign of terror. The defendants lived within the Reich. The Reich, through its hordes of enforcement officials and secret police, was always "present," ready to go into instant action and to mete out savage and immediate punishment against anyone doing anything that could be construed as obstructing or hindering the carrying out of governmental regulations or decrees.

In considering the application of rules to the defense of necessity, attention may well be called to the following statement:

> The law of cases of necessity is not lilely to be well furnished with precise rules; necessity creates the law, it supersedes rules, and whatever is reasonable and just in such cases is likewise legal. It is not to be considered as matter of surprise, therefore, if much instituted rule is not to be found on such subject. [Wharton's Criminal Law, vol. I, ch. III, subdivision VII, par. 126, and cases cited.]

In this case, in our opinion, the testimony establishes a factual situation which makes clearly applicable the defense of necessity as urged in behalf of the defendants Steinbrinck, Burkart, Kaletsch, and Terberger.

The active steps taken by Weiss with the knowledge and approval of Flick to procure for the Linke-Hofmann Works increased production quota of freight cars which constitute military equipment within the contemplation of the Hague Convention, and Weiss' part in the procurement of a large number of Russian prisoners of war for work in the manufacture of such equipment deprive the defendants Flick and Weiss of the complete defense of necessity. In judging the conduct of Weiss in this transaction, we must, however, remember that obtaining more materials than necessary was forbidden by the authorities just as falling short in filling orders was forbidden. The war effort required all persons involved to use all facilities to bring the war production to its fullest capacity.

The steps taken in this instance, however, were initiated not in governmental circles but in the plant management. They were not taken as a result of compulsion or fear, but admittedly for the purpose of keeping the plant as near capacity production as possible.

It is, accordingly, adjudged that the defendants Steinbrinck, Burkart, Kaletsch, and Terberger are not guilty on count one and that defendants Flick and Weiss are guilty on this count.

COUNT TWO

There is no necessity for detailing the averments of count two which deals with spoliation and plunder of occupied territories. It follows the pattern of count one with general recitals of facts as to the over-all Nazi program described in the IMT judgment followed by charges that defendants participated therein. Specific instances of the alleged participation are then cited. The count concludes with the accusation, in substance, that these activities were violations of the laws and customs of war, Articles 45–56 of the Hague Regulations of 1907, general principles of criminal law, internal penal laws of countries where the acts were committed and of Article II of Control Council Law No. 10.

After giving effect to the prosecution's withdrawal of certain charges, there remain the following. Flick and his assistants Weiss, Burkart and Kaletsch are accused of exploiting properties which for convenience during the trial have been called Rombach, in Lorraine; Vairogs, in Latvia; and Dnjepr Stahl [Dnepr Steel], in the Ukraine. Steinbrinck's activities as Plenipotentiary General for the Steel Industry and Plenipotentiary for Coal in certain occupied western territories are also claimed to be criminal. Flick and Steinbrinck are accused of participating in spoliation plans and programs through connections with RVE, RVK and their predecessor and subsidiary organizations. This accusation is not sustained by the evidence. Flick alone is charged with participation in the spoliation plans and program in Russia through his position as a member of the Verwaltungsrat (supervisory board of the Berg und Huettenwerke Ost (BHO). His influence therein, if any, was negligible.

IMT dealt with spoliation under the title "Pillage of Public and Private Property." Much that is said therein has no application to this case. No defendant is shown by the evidence to have been responsible for any act of pillage as that word is commonly understood. There were moveables brought from Latvia and the Ukraine upon the approach of the returning Russian armies. A large part thereof had been taken there from Germany to equip industrial plants which had been stripped by the Russians in their retreat. What movables the Russians left were doubtless of little value. It is not established with any certainty that they were shipped to Germany. But of more importance is the fact that the evidence does not connect any of these defendants with responsibility for the evacuation. The ten barges that disappeared from the plant at Rombach were all found by the French owners upon their return. Some had been used and sunk or damaged in the retreat of the fleeing German Army but for this defendants cannot be held [responsible]. Steinbrinck was responsible for no such pillage but may be credited with its prevention in several instances shown by the evidence.

The important questions center in Steinbrinck's activities directing the production of coal and steel in the western territories, the Flick administration of the Rombach plant and the occupation and use of the Vairogs and Dnjepr Stahl plants in the East.

No crimes against humanity are here involved. Nor are war crimes except as they may be embodied in the Hague Regulations. The prosecution so admits in its concluding brief, saying: "Thus, the charge amounts to, and it need only be proved, that the defendants participated in the systematic plunder of property which was held to be in violation of the Hague Regulations." The words "systematic plunder" came from the IMT judgment. They are not very helpful in enabling us to point to the specific regulations which defendants' acts are supposed to violate.

* * *

Prior to the First World War when Lorraine was German, a large plant was built by German capital near the town of Rombach. After that war it was expropriated by France from whom the title was acquired by a French corporation dominated by the Laurent family. The enterprise consisted in 1940 principally of blast furnaces, Thomas works, rolling mills and cement works. It furnished employment and the means of livelihood for a large indigenous population. When the German Army invaded Lorraine in 1940, the management fled but many of the workers including technicians remained. Key installations had been removed or destroyed so that the plant was inoperable until extensive repairs had been made. In the meanwhile the workers were idle except as they were employed to renovate the plant. After occupation of western territories, the Supreme Commander of the German Army issued a "Decree concerning the orderly management and administration of enterprises and concerns in the occupied territories" dated 23 June 1940. It stated that should an orderly management or administration of enterprises, including concerns dedicated to industry, not be insured owing to the absence of the persons authorized or for other compelling reasons, public commissioners should be appointed during whose administration the powers of the property holders or owners were to be suspended. The costs of the administration were to be borne by the enterprise. The commissioner was obligated to exercise the care of a prudent business man in the conduct of the enterprise. He was "not empowered to transfer his administration to a third party." On 27 July 1940, the same commander issued a directive for compliance with the decree of 23 June 1940. We do not find this directive in the record but an affidavit states that the appointment of "administrators had to take place exclusively through the chief for the civil administration." There seem to have been other directives which also are not in evidence. In any event a public commissioner or administrator was appointed for the Rombach plant and ultimately executed a contract with the Friedrich Flick Kommanditgesellschaft called "use of enterprise conveyance agreement" dated 15 December 1942 but effective as of 1 March 1941 when the Flick group took possession. The agreement recites an order of the Plenipotentiary for the Four Year Plan to the effect that the iron foundries situated in Lorraine are "in the name of the Reich to be controlled, managed, and operated by single individuals or enterprises on their own account." However, the contract designates the Flick Kommanditgesellschaft as trustee, not grantee. Prior to taking possession the Flick group had learned through governmental agencies that a number of plants in Lorraine were to be parceled out for administration by German firms. These firms, including Flick, had the hope of ultimately acquiring title to the respective properties and this trusteeship was sought to that end. There are provisions in the contract providing terms of purchase and also providing for remuneration for capital investment by the lessee in the event the purchase should not materialize. At no time, however, was there any definite sale commitment and of course the hope of its realization was frustrated by the fortunes of war. Charles Laurent as a witness testified that he was expelled from Lorraine in 1940 and that the Flick administration had nothing to do therewith. It does not appear that he tried to regain possession of the plant but he may have deemed futile such an attempt. A corporation called Rombacher Huettenwerke, G.m.b.H., was organized by Flick to operate the plant. Operations continued from March 1941 until the Allied invasion about 1 September 1944. All the profits were invested in repairs, improvements and new installations. As the Allied armies approached Rombach, the German military authorities gave orders to destroy the plants which were disobeyed by the officials of the trustee. When the French management returned, the plants were intact. There was conflicting testimony as to their condition in early 1941 and again in September 1944. The evidence satisfied us that the trustee left the properties in better condition than when they were taken over. Approximately one-third of the production of the blast furnaces in this district went to Germany, the rest to France, Belgium, and other countries. This general ratio of exports existed before the war. There are no separate figures for the Rombach plant.

The seizure of Rombach in the first instance may be defended upon the ground of military necessity. The possibility of its use by the French, the absence of responsible management and the need for finding work for the idle population are all factors that the German authorities may have taken into consideration. Military necessity is a broad term. Its interpretation involves the exercise of some discretion. If after seizure the German authorities had treated their possession as conservatory for the rightful owners' interests, little fault could be found with the subsequent conduct of those in possession.

But some time after the seizure, the Reich government in the person of

Goering, Plenipotentiary for the Four Year Plan, manifested the intention that it should be operated as the property of the Reich. This is clearly shown by the quoted statement in the contract which Flick signed. It was, no doubt, Goering's intention to exploit it to the fullest extent for the German war effort. We do not believe that this intent was shared by Flick. Certainly what was done by his company in the course of its management falls far short of such exploitation.

Flick was interested in extending his organization through the acquisition of additional steel plants. Lorraine was German territory before the First World War and many Germans felt that in its seizure Germany would be getting back merely what was already her own. In many respects during the occupation Germany treated Lorraine as Reich territory. Flick saw the possibilities resulting from the invasion and sought to add the Rombach property to his concern. But governmental policy was otherwise. It does not appear upon what grounds this decision was based. There may have been thought of the Hague Regulations under which private property must be respected and cannot be confiscated. But we recall no hint in the evidence that Flick or his associates gave any thought to the international law affecting the transaction. The Flick management of Rombach was conservative, not, however, with the intent of benefiting the French owners. It was suggested at one time that French management be included to which Flick did not agree. He knew that he did not have title and might never acquire it. Anticipating this possibility he inserted provisions by which he would be protected against the loss of any of his own capital that might be invested in the course of the company's operations. His expectation of ownership caused him to plow back into the physical property the profits of operation. This policy ultimately resulted to the advantage of the owners. In all of this we find no exploitation either for Flick's present personal advantage or to fulfill the aims of Goering.

Obviously the formula taken from the IMT judgment cannot apply to any part of the transaction except the distribution of the steel. There are no figures in the record showing the needs of the army of occupation. There are no Rombach statistics tending to show the effect of its production and distribution on the French economy. Therefore, criminal liability must be tested by a different rule.

While the original seizure may not have been unlawful, its subsequent detention from the rightful owners was wrongful. For this and other damage they may be compensated. Laurent, as a witness, told of his intention to claim reparations. For suggesting an element of damage of which he had not thought, he thanked one of defendants' counsel. It may be added that he agreed with counsel that the factory had not been "mismanaged or ransacked."

But there may be both civil and criminal liability growing out of the same transaction. In this case Flick's acts and conduct contributed to a violation of Hague Regulation 46, that is, that private property must be respected. Of this there can be no doubt. But his acts were not within his knowledge intended to contribute to a program of "systematic plunder" conceived by the Hitler regime and for which many of the major war criminals have been punished. If they added anything to this program of spoliation, it was in a very small degree.

The purpose of the Hague Convention, as disclosed in the preamble of chapter II, was "to revise the general laws and customs of war, either with a view to defining them with greater precision or to confine them within such limits as would mitigate their severity so far as possible." It is also stated that "these provisions, the wording of which has been inspired by a desire to diminish the evils of war, as far as military requirements will permit, are intended to serve as a general rule of conduct for the belligerents in their mutual relations and in their relations with the inhabitants." This explains the generality of the provisions. They were written in a day when armies traveled on foot, in horse-drawn vehicles and on railroad trains; the automobile was in its Ford model-T stage. Use of the airplane as an instrument of war was merely a dream. The atomic bomb was beyond the realms of imagination. Concentration of industry into huge organizations transcending national boundaries had barely begun. Blockades were the principal means of "economic warefare." "Total warfare" only became a reality in the recent conflict. These developments make plain the necessity of appraising the conduct of defendants with relation to the circumstances and conditions of their environment. Guilt, or the extent thereof, may not be determined theoretically or abstractly. Reasonable and practical standards must be considered.

It was stated in the beginning that responsibility of an individual for infractions of international law is not open to question. In dealing with property located outside his own state, he must be expected to ascertain and keep within applicable law. Ignorance thereof will not excuse guilt but may mitigate punishment. The Tribunal will find defendant Flick guilty in respect to the Rombach matter but will take fully into consideration in fixing his punishment all the circumstances under which he acted.

* * *

In summation the Tribunal finds Flick alone guilty on count two. Steinbrinck, Weiss, Burkart, and Kaletsch each is acquitted.

Count Three

Count three attempts to charge crimes against humanity. The evidence deals exclusively with four separate transactions by which the Flick interests acquired industrial property formerly owned or controlled by Jews. Three were outright sales of controlling shares in manufacturing and mining corporations. In the fourth, involving the Ignaz Petschek brown coal mines in central Germany, there was an expropriation by the Third Reich, from which afterward the Flick interests and others ultimately acquired the substance of the properties. There is no contention that the defendants in any way participated in the Nazi persecution of Jews other than in taking advantage of the so-called Aryanization program by seeking and using State economic pressure to obtain from the owners, not all of whom were Jewish, the four properties in question.

These transactions were completed prior to the war. Concerning the first three, there can be no controversy. The Ignaz Petschek property was expropriated by a general governmental decree dated 3 December 1938, pursuant to which trustees therefore were appointed 19 January 1939 and given power to sell 1 March 1939. That the written instrument of sale to a governmental holding company bears date of 8 September 1939, and that later there were sales through which Flick acquired some of the property, we do not regard as conflicting with our view that the expropriation, if not effective by the decree, certainly was completed by the appointment of the trustees.

In the IMT trial the Tribunal declined to take jurisdiction of crimes against humanity occurring before 1 September 1939, basing its ruling on the modifying phrase "in execution of or in connection with any crime within the jurisdiction of the Tribunal" found in Article 6 (a) of the Charter attached to the London Agreement of 8 August 1945. It is argued that the omission of this phrase from Control Council Law No. 10 evidences an intent to broaden the jurisdiction of this Tribunal to include such crimes. We find no support for the argument in express language of Law No. 10. To reach the desired conclusion its advocates must resolve ambiguity by a process of statutory construction. Jurisdiction is not to be presumed. A court should not reach out for power beyond the clearly defined bounds of its chartering legislation.

Law No. 10 was enacted 20 December 1945, but not all of its content was written at that time. Article 1 expressly states:

> The Moscow Declaration of 30 October 1943 "Concerning Responsibility of Hitlerites for Committed Atrocities" and the London Agreement of 8 August 1945 "Concerning Prosecution and Punishment of Major War Criminals of the European Axis" are made integral parts of this law.

The Charter was not merely attached to the London Agreement, but by Article 2 thereof, was incorporated therein as an "integral part." The construction placed on the Charter by IMT can hardly be separated therefrom. These documents constitute the chartering legislation of this Tribunal. The only purpose of the London Agreement was to bring to trial "war criminals."

I am quoting the words "war criminals," found in many sections of the London Agreement.

The only purpose of the Charter was to bring to trial "major war criminals." We conceive the only purpose of this Tribunal is to bring to trial war criminals that have not already been tried. Implicit in all of this chartering legislation is the purpose to provide for punishment of crimes committed during the war or in connection with the war. We look in vain for language evincing any other purpose. Crimes committed before the war and having no connection therewith were not in contemplation.

To try war crimes is a task so large, as the numerous prosecutions prove, that there is neither necessity nor excuse for expecting this Tribunal to try persons for offenses wholly unconnected with the war. So far as we are advised no one else has been prosecuted to date in any of these courts including IMT for crimes committed before and wholly unconnected with the war. We can see no purpose nor mandate in the chartering legislation of this Tribunal requiring it to take jurisdiction of such cases.

There was no pleading questioning jurisdiction until the conclusion of the evidence. During the long trial the conduct of defendants claimed to incriminate them under count three was explored meticulously and exhaustively by prosecution and defense. Hundreds of documents and volumes of oral testimony are before the Tribunal. Under these circumstances we make the following statements on the merits relating to this count with full appreciation that statements as to the merits are pure *dicta* where a finding of lack of jurisdiction is also made.

The law existing when the defendants acted is controlling. To the extent that Law No. 10 declares or codifies that law, and no further, is this Tribunal willing to go. Under the basic law of many states the taking of property by the sovereign, without just compensation, is forbidden, but usually it is not considered a crime. A sale compelled by pressure or duress may be questioned in a court of equity, but, so far as we are informed, such use of pressure, even on racial or religious grounds, has never been thought to be a crime against humanity. A distinction could be made between industrial property and the dwellings, household furnishings, and food supplies of a persecuted people. In this case, however, we are only concerned with industrial property, a large portion of which (ore and coal mines) constitutes natural resources in which the state has a peculiar interest.

Jurists and legal writers have been and are presently groping for an adequate inclusive definition of crimes against humanity. Donnedieu de Vabres recently said: "The theory of 'crimes against humanity' is dangerous: dangerous for the peoples *by the absence of precise definition*, dangerous for the States because it offers a pretext to intervention by a State in the internal affairs of weaker States." (Our emphasis.)

The seventh Conference for the Unification of Penal Law held at Brussels, 10 and 11 July 1947, in which the United States of America took part, endeavored to formulate a definition. In none of the drafts presented was deprivation of property included. Eugene M. Arroneau's definition, referred to in the report of the proceedings, specified, ". . . harm done on racial, national, religious, or political grounds to *liberty or the life of a person or group of persons, etc.*" (Our emphasis.) Mentioned in the proceedings was a section from a Brazilian law decree of 18 May 1938 to the effect that it is an offense "to incite or prepare an attempt upon the life of a person or upon his goods, for doctrinaire, political or religious motives," with penalty from 2 to 5 years imprisonment. The Brazilian representative, ignoring the purport of the phrase "or upon his goods," himself submitted a definition to the conference reading:

"Any act or omission which involves a serious threat of violence, moral or physical, against anyone by reason of his nationality, race, or his religion, philosophical or political opinions, is considered as a crime against humanity." A resolution was adopted evidencing agreement that—

> Any manslaughter or act which can bring about death, committed in peacetime as well as in wartime, against individuals, or groups of individuals, because of their race, nationality, religion, or opinions, constitutes a crime against humanity and must be punished as murder.

But from the report of the conference proceedings this seems to have been the extent of agreement.

In the opening statement of the prosecution are listed numerous instances of foreign intervention or diplomatic representations objecting to mistreatment of a population by its own rulers. It may be that incidental to these persecutions the oppressed peoples lost their homes, household goods, and investments in industrial property but so far as we are aware the outcry by the other nations was against the personal atrocities, not the loss of possessions. We believe that the proof does not establish a crime against humanity recognized as such by the law of nations when defendants were engaged in the property transactions here under scrutiny.

The prosecution in its concluding argument contends that the contrary has been decided in the IMT judgment. We find nothing therein in conflict with our conclusion. That Tribunal mentioned economic discrimination against the Jews as one of numerous evidentiary facts from which it reached the conclusion that the Leadership Corps was a criminal organization. Similarly when dealing with the question of Flick's guilt of war crimes and crimes against humanity, it mentioned anti-Semitic laws drafted, signed and administered by Flick. These led up to his final decree placing Jews "outside the law" and handing them over to the Gestapo which was the equivalent to an order for their extermination. Likewise in the cases of Funk and Seyss-Inquart, anti-Semitic economic discrimination is cited as one of several facts from which it is concluded that he was a war criminal. But it nowhere appears in the judgment that IMT considered, much less decided, that a person becomes guilty of a crime against humanity merely by exerting anti-Semitic pressure to procure by purchase or through state expropriation industrial property owned by Jews.

Not even under a proper construction of the section of Law No. 10 relating to crimes against humanity, do the facts warrant conviction. The "atrocities and offenses" listed therein "murder, extermination," etc., are all offenses against the person. Property is not mentioned. Under the doctrine of *ejusdem generis* the catch-all words "other persecutions" must be deemed to include only such as affect the life and liberty of the oppressed peoples. Compulsory taking of industrial property, however reprehensible, is not in that category. It may be added that the presence in this section of the words "against any civilian population," recently led Tribunal III to "hold that crimes against humanity as defined in Control Council Law No. 10 must be strictly construed to exclude isolated cases of atrocity or persecution whether committed by private individuals or by governmental authority." United States vs. Altstoetter, *et al.*, decided 4 December 1947. The transactions before us, if otherwise within the contemplation of Law No. 10 as crimes against humanity, would be excluded by this holding.

Whether we hold that we have not jurisdiction or whether we assume jurisdiction and hold that no crime against humanity has been proved, the result so far as these defendants are concerned is the same. They cannot be convicted on the fact that the evidence submitted on this count relates to subject matter not within its jurisdiction. Accordingly, count three is dismissed.

Counts Four and Five

Presiding Judge Sears: We consider together counts four and five. The latter charges Steinbrinck with membership subsequent to 1 September 1939 in the SS. The gist of count four is that as members of the Himmler Circle of Friends, Flick and Steinbrinck with knowledge of the criminal activities of the SS contributed funds and influence to its support.

The basis of liability of members of the SS, as declared by IMT, is that after 1 September 1939 they "became or remained members of the organization with knowledge that it was being used for the commission of acts declared criminal by Article 6 of the Charter, or who were personally implicated as members of the organization in the commission of such crimes, excluding, however, those who were drafted into membership by the State in such a way as to give them no choice in the matter and who had committed no such crimes." Steinbrinck was a member of the SS from 1933 to the time of the German collapse. There is no evidence that he was personally implicated in the commission of its crimes. It is not contended that he was drafted into membership in such a way as to give him no choice. His liability therefore must be predicated on the fact that he remained a member after 1 September 1939 with knowledge that "it was being used for the commission of acts declared criminal. . . ."

Sentences

The Marshal: The Tribunal is again in session.

Presiding Judge Sears: The Tribunal will now impose sentence upon those defendants who have been adjudged guilty in these proceedings.

The Marshal will produce defendant *Flick* before the Tribunal.

Friedrich Flick, on the counts of the indictment on which you have been convicted, the Tribunal sentences you to imprisonment for seven (7) years. The period already spent by you in confinement before and during the trial is to be credited on the term already stated and to this end the term of your imprisonment, as now adjudged, shall be deemed to begin on the 13th day of June 1945.

The Marshal will remove defendant *Flick*.

The Marshal will produce before the Tribunal defendant Steinbrinck.

Otto Steinbrinck, on the counts of the indictment on which you have been convicted, the Tribunal sentences you to imprisonment for five (5) years. The period already spent by you in confinement before and during the trial is to be credited on the term already stated, and to this end the term of your imprisonment, as now adjudged, shall be deemed to begin on the 30th day of August 1945.

The Marshal will remove defendant *Steinbrinck*.

The Marshal will produce before the Tribunal defendant *Weiss.*

Bernhard Weiss, on the count of the indictment on which you have been convicted, the Tribunal sentences you to imprisonment for two and one-half (2½) years. The periods already spent by you in confinement before and during the trial are to be credited on the term already stated and to this end the term of your imprisonment, as now adjudged, shall be deemed to begin on the 8th day of June 1946.

The Marshal will remove the defendant *Weiss.*

The defendants *Odilo Burkart*, *Konrad Kaletsch,* and *Hermann Terberger,* and each of them, having been acquitted, shall be discharged from custody by the Marshal when the Tribunal presently adjourns.

The Tribunal is about to adjourn.

The Tribunal now adjourns without date.

THE HOSTAGE CASE

Nuremberg, February, 1948*

OPINION AND JUDGMENT OF THE UNITED STATES MILITARY TRIBUNAL AT NUREMBERG IN UNITED STATES *vs.* WILHELM LIST ET AL.

PRESIDING JUDGE WENNERSTRUM: Judge Carter will read the first portion of the opinion.

JUDGE CARTER: In this case, the United States of America prosecutes each of the defendants on one or more of four counts of an indictment charging that each and all of said defendants unlawfully, willfully, and knowingly committed war crimes and crimes against humanity as such crimes are defined in Article II of the Control Council Law No. 10. They are charged with being principals in and accessories to the murder of thousands of persons from the civilian population of Greece, Yugoslavia, Norway, and Albania between September 1939 and May 1945 by the use of troops of the German armed forces under the command of and acting pursuant to orders issued, distributed, and executed by the defendants at the bar. It is further charged that these defendants participated in a deliberate scheme of terrorism and intimidation, wholly unwarranted and unjustified by military necessity, by the murder, ill-treatment and deportation to slave labor of prisoners of war and members of the civilian populations in territories occupied by the German armed forces; by plundering and pillaging public and private property and wantonly destroying cities, towns, and villages for which there was no military necessity. Upon these charges, each of the defendants except the defendant Boehme has been formally arraigned and a plea of not guilty accepted.

The indictment alleges that the defendants committed the acts charged while occupying the positions hereafter shown during the periods of time indicated—

The defendant Wilhelm List was a Generalfeldmarschall [Field Marshal] (General of the Army) of the German armed forces, serving as commander in chief, 12th Army, from April 1941 to October 1941; Armed Forces Commander Southeast from June 1941 to October 1941; and as commander in chief, Army Group A, from July 1942 to September 1942.

***Trial of War Criminals,* Vol. 11, p. 1230 (Washington D.C., 1950).

The defendant Maximilian von Weichs was a Generalfeldmarschall [Field Marshal] (General of the Army) of the German armed forces, serving as commander in chief, 2d Army, from April 1941 to July 1942; commander in chief, Army Group B, from July 1942 to February 1943; and commander in chief, Army Group F, and Supreme Commander Southeast from August 1943 to March 1945.

The defendant Lothar Rendulic was a Generaloberst (General) in the German armed forces, serving as commander in chief, 2d Panzer Army, from August 1943 to June 1944; commander in chief, 20th Mountain Army, from July 1944 to January 1945; Armed Forces Commander North from December 1944 to January 1945; commander in chief, Army Group North, from January 1945 to March 1945; commander in chief, Army Group Courland, from March 1945 to April 1945; and commander in chief, Army Group South, from April 1945 to May 1945.

The defendant Walter Kuntze was a General der Pioniere (Lieutenant General, Engineers) in the German armed forces, serving as acting commander in chief, 12th Army, from October 1941 to August 1942, and Deputy Armed Forces Commander Southeast during the same period.

The defendant Hermann Foertsch was a General der Infanterie (Lieutenant General, Infantry) in the German armed forces, serving as chief of staff, 12 Army, from May 1941 to August 1942; chief of staff, Army Group E, from August 1942 to August 1943; and chief of staff, Army Group F, from August 1943 to March 1944.

The defendant Franz Boehme was a General der Gebirgstruppen (Lieutenant General, Mountain Troops) in the German armed forces, serving as commander, XVIII Mountain Army Corps, from April 1941 to December 1941; Plenipotentiary Commanding General in Serbia from September 1941 to December 1941; and commander in chief, 2d Panzer Army, from June 1944 to July 1944.

The defendant Helmuth Felmy was a General der Flieger (Lieutenant General, Air Force) in the German armed forces, serving as commander, Southern Greece, from June 1941 to August 1942; and commander, LXVIII Army Corps, from June 1943 to October 1944.

The defendant Hubert Lanz was a General der Gebirgstruppen (Lieutenant General, Mountain Troops) in the German armed forces, serving as commander, 1st Mountain Division, from October 1940 to January 1943; and commander, XXII Mountain Army Corps, from August 1943 to October 1944.

The defendant Ernst Dehner was a General der Infanterie (lieutenant General, Infantry) in the German armed forces, serving as commander, LXIX Army Reserve Corps, from August 1943 to March 1944.

The defendant Ernst von Leyser was a General der Infanterie (Lieutenant General, Infantry) in the German armed forces, serving as commander, XV Mountain Army Corps, from November 1943 to July 1944; and commander, XXI Mountain Army Corps, from July 1944 to April 1945.

The defendant Wilhelm Speidel was a General der Flieger (Lieutenant General, Air Force) in the German armed forces, serving as commander, Southern Greece, from October 1942 to September 1943; and Military Commander Greece from September 1943 to June 1944.

The defendant Kurt von Geitner was a Generalmajor (Brigadier General) in the German armed forces, serving as chief of staff to the commanding general in Serbia from July 1942 to August 1943; and chief of staff to the Military Commander of Serbia and Military Commander Southeast from August 1943 to October 1944.

It is alleged in the indictment that the acts charged were violative of Control Council Law No. 10, duly enacted by the Allied Control Council on 20 December 1945. The portions of the law applicable to this case provide as follows [Article II]: . . .

Pursuant to the provisions of Control Council Law No. 10, the pertinent parts of which are herein set out, the United States of America filed its indictment charging the defendants in four counts with war crimes and crimes against humanity in accordance with the definitions thereof contained. Reduced to a minimum of words, these four counts charge—

1. That defendants were principals or accessories to the murder of hundreds of thousands of persons from the civilian populations of Greece, Yugoslavia, and Albania by troops of the German armed forces; that attacks by lawfully constituted enemy military forces, and attacks by unknown persons, against German troops and installations, were followed by executions of large numbers of the civilian population by hanging or shooting without benefit of investigation or trial; that thousands of noncombatants, arbitrarily designated as "partisans," "Communists," "Communist suspects," "bandit suspects" were terrorized, tortured, and murdered in retaliation for such attacks by lawfully constituted enemy military forces and attacks by unknown persons; and that defendants issued, distributed, and executed orders for the execution of 100 "hostages" in retaliation for each German soldier killed and 50 "hostages" in retaliation for each German soldier wounded.

2. That defendants were principals or accessories to the plundering and looting of public and private property, the wanton destruction of cities, towns, and villages, frequently together with the murder of the inhabitants thereof, and the commission of other acts of devastation not warranted by military necessity in the occupied territories of Greece, Yugoslavia, Albania, and Norway by troops of the German armed forces acting at the direction and order of these defendants; that defendants ordered troops under their command to burn, level, and destroy entire villages and towns and thereby making thousands of peaceful noncombatants homeless and destitute; thereby causing untold suffering, misery, and death to large numbers of innocent civilians without any recognized military necessity for so doing.

3. That defendants were principals or accessories to the drafting, distribution, and execution of illegal orders to the troops of the German armed forces

which commanded that enemy troops be refused quarters and be denied the status and rights of prisoners of war and surrendered members of enemy forces be summarily executed; that the defendants illegally ordered that regular members of the national armies of Greece, Yugoslavia, and Italy be designated as "partisans," "rebels," "Communists," and "bandits," and that relatives of members of such national armies be held responsible for such members' acts of warfare, resulting in the murder and ill-treatment of thousands of soldiers, prisoners of war, and their noncombatant relatives.

4. That defendants were principals or accessories to the murder, torture, and systematic terrorization, imprisonment in concentration camps, forced labor on military installations, and deportation to slave labor of the civilian populations of Greece, Yugoslavia, and Albania by troops of the German armed forces acting pursuant to the orders of the defendants; that large numbers of citizens—democrats, Nationalists, Jews, and gypsies—were seized, thrown into concentration camps, beaten, tortured, ill-treated, and murdered while other citizens were forcibly conscripted for labor in the Reich and occupied territories.

The acts charged in each of the four counts are alleged to have been committed willfully, knowingly, and unlawfully and constitute violations of international conventions, the Hague Regulations, 1907, the laws and customs of war, the general principles of criminal law as derived from the criminal laws of all civilized nations, the internal penal laws of the countries in which such crimes were committed, and were declared, recognized, and defined as crimes by Article II of Control Council Law No. 10 adopted by the representatives of the United States of America, Great Britain, the Republic of France, and the Soviet Union.

The defendant Franz Boehme committed suicide prior to the arraignment of the defendants, and the Tribunal has ordered his name stricken from the list of defendants contained in the indictment. The defendant Maximilian von Weichs became ill during the course of the trial and it having been conclusively ascertained that he is physically unfit and unable to appear in Court before the conclusion of the trial, his motion that the proceedings be suspended as to him was sustained. This holding is without prejudice to a future trial of this defendant on the charges herein made against him if and when his physical condition permits.

Before venturing into a discussion of specific issues, it seems advisable to briefly state the general nature of international law and the sources from which its principles can be ascertained. No attempt will be made here to give an all inclusive definition of international law, in fact, there is justification for the assertion that it ought not to be circumscribed by strict definition in order that it may have ample room for growth. Any system of law that is obviously subject to growth by the crystalization of generally prevailing custom and practice into law under the impact of common acceptance or consent must not be confined within the limits of formal pronouncement or complete unanimity. For our purposes it is sufficient to say that international law consists of the principles which control or govern relations between nations and their nationals. It is much more important to consider the sources from which these principles may be determined. . . .

The defendants invoke the defensive plea that the acts charged as crimes were carried out pursuant to orders of superior officers whom they were obliged to obey. This brings into operation the rule just announced. The rule that superior order is not a defense to a criminal act is a rule of fundamental criminal justice that has been adopted by civilized nations extensively. It is not disputed that the municipal law of civilized nations generally sustained the principle at the time the alleged criminal acts were committed. This being true, it properly may be declared as an applicable rule of international law.

It cannot be questioned that acts done in time of war under the military authority of an enemy cannot involve any criminal liability on the part of officers or soldiers if the acts are not prohibited by the conventional or customary rules of war. Implicit obedience to orders of superior officers is almost indispensable to every military system. But this implies obedience to lawful orders only. If the act done pursuant to a superior's orders be murder, the production of the order will not make it any less so. It may mitigate but it cannot justify the crime. We are of the view, however, that if the illegality of the order was not known to the inferior, and he could not reasonably have been expected to know of its illegality, no wrongful intent necessary to the commission of a crime exists and the interior will be protected. But the general rule is that members of the armed forces are bound to obey only the lawful orders of their commanding officers and they cannot escape criminal liability by obeying a command which violates international law and outrages fundamental concepts of justice. In the German War Trials (1922), the German Supreme Court of Leipzig in The Llandovery Castle case said:

> Patzig's order does not free the accused from guilt. It is true that, according to paragraph 47 of the Military Penal Code, if the execution of an order in the ordinary course of duty involves such a violation of the law as is punishable, the superior officer issuing such an order is alone responsible. According to No. 2, however, the subordinate obeying such an order is liable to punishment, if it was known to him that the order of the superior involved the infringement of civil or military law.

It is true that the foregoing rule compels a commander to make a choice between possible punishment by his lawless government for the disobedience of the illegal order of his superior officer, or that of lawful punishment for the crime under the law of nations. To choose the former in the hope that victory will cleanse the act of its criminal characteristics manifests only weakness of character and adds nothing to the defense.

We concede the serious consequences of the choice especially by an officer in the army of a dictator. But the rule becomes one of necessity, for otherwise the opposing army would in many cases have no protection at all against criminal excesses ordered by superiors.

* * *

International law has never approved the defensive plea of superior order as a mandatory bar to the prosecution of war criminals. This defensive plea is not available to the defendants in the present case, although, if the circumstances warrant, it may be considered in mitigation of punishment under the express provisions of Control Council Law No. 10.

* * *

We conclude that pre-existing international law has declared the acts constituting the crimes herein charged and included in Control Council Law No. 10 to be unlawful, both under the conventional law and the practices and usages of land warfare that had ripened into recognized customs which belligerents were bound to obey. Anything in excess of existing international law therein contained is a utilization of power and not of law. It is true, of course, that courts authorized to hear such cases were not established nor the penalties to be imposed for violations set forth. But this is not fatal to their validity. The acts prohibited are without deterrent effect unless they are punishable as crimes.

* * *

It is true, of course, that customary international law is not static. It must be elastic enough to meet the new conditions that natural progress brings to the world. It might be argued that this requires a certain amount of retroactive application of new rules and that by conceding the existence of a customary international law, one thereby concedes the legality of retroactive pronouncements. To a limited extent the argument is sound, but when it comes in conflict with a rule of fundamental right and justice, the latter must prevail. The rule that one may not be charged with crime for committing an act which was not a crime at the time of its commission is such a right. The fact that it might be found in a constitution or bill of rights does not detract from its status as a fundamental principle of justice. It cannot properly be changed by retroactive action to the prejudice of one charged with a violation of the laws of war.

An international crime is such an act universally recognized as criminal, which is considered a grave matter of international concern and for some valid reason cannot be left within the exclusive jurisdiction of the state that would have control over it under ordinary circumstances. The inherent nature of a war crime is ordinarily itself sufficient justification for jurisdiction to attach in the courts of the belligerent into whose hands the alleged criminal has fallen.

Some war crimes, such as spying, are not common law crimes at all; they being pure war crimes punishable as such during the war and, in this particular case, only if the offender is captured before he rejoins his army. But some other crimes, such as mass murder, are punishable during and after the war. But such crimes are also war crimes because they were committed under the authority or orders of the belligerent who, in ordering or permitting them, violated the rules of warfare. Such crimes are punishable by the country where the crime was committed or by the belligerent into whose hands the criminals have fallen, the jurisdiction being concurrent. There are many reasons why this must be so, not the least of which is that war is usually followed by political repercussions and upheavals which at times place persons in power who are not, for one reason or another, inclined to punish the offenders. The captor belligerent is not required to surrender the alleged war criminal when such surrender is equivalent to a passport to freedom. The only adequate remedy is the concurrent jurisdictional principle to which we have heretofore adverted. The captor belligerent may therefore surrender the alleged criminal to the state where the offense was committed, or, on the other hand, it may retain the alleged criminal for trial under its own legal processes.

It cannot be doubted that the occupying powers have the right to set up special courts to try those charged with the commission of war crimes as they are defined by international law. *Ex Parte Quirin, 317 U.S. 1, In Re Yamashita, 327 U.S. 1.* Nor can it be said that the crimes herein charged are invalid as retroactive pronouncements, they being nothing more than restatements of the conventional and customary law of nations governing the rules of land warfare, restricted by charter provisions limiting the jurisdiction of the Tribunal by designating the class of cases it is authorized to hear. The elements of an *ex post facto* act or a retroactive pronouncement are not present insofar as the crimes charged in the instant case are concerned.

The argument that the defendants cannot be tried before this Tribunal is without force. It is urged they can only be properly tried in accordance with the international principles laid down in Article 63 of the Geneva Convention of 1929 relative to the treatment of prisoners of war. We submit that the provision applies only to crimes and offenses committed while occupying the status of a prisoner of war, and confers no jurisdiction over a violation of international law committed prior to the time of becoming such.

In the recent case of *In Re Yamashita, 327 U.S. 1, 66 Sup. Ct. 348,* the Supreme Court of the United States arrived at this conclusion in the following language: "But we think examination of article 63 in its setting in the Convention plainly shows that it refers to sentence 'pronounced against a prisoner of war' for an offense committed while a prisoner of war, and not for a violation of the law of war committed while a combatant."

The defendants at bar are charged only with crimes alleged to have been committed as combatants before they became prisoners of war. We hold, therefore, that no rights under Article 63 of the Geneva Convention of 1929 can accrue to them in the present case. The jurisdictional question raised is without merit.

It is essential to a proper understanding of the issues involved in the present case, that the status of Yugoslavia, Greece, and Norway be determined during the periods that the alleged criminal acts of these defendants were committed. The question of criminality in many cases may well hinge on whether an invasion was in progress or an occupation accomplished. Whether an invasion has developed into an occupation is a question of fact. The term invasion implies a military operation while an occupation indicates the exercise of governmental authority to the exclusion of the established government. This presupposes the destruction of organized resistance and the establishment of an administration to preserve law and order. To the extent that the occupant's control is maintained and that of the civil government eliminated, the area will be said to be occupied.

The evidence shows that the invasion of Yugoslavia was commenced on 6 April 1941. Nine days later the Yugoslav Government capitulated and on 16 April 1941, large scale military operations had come to an end. The powers of government passed into the hands of the German armed forces and Yugoslavia became an occupied country. The invasion of Yugoslavia followed through into Greece. On 22 April 1941, the Greek armed forces in the north were forced to surrender and on 28 April 1941, Athens fell to the invader. On and after that date Greece became an occupied country within the meaning of existing international law.

The evidence shows that the population remained peaceful during the spring of 1941. In the early summer following, a resistance movement began to manifest itself. It increased progressively in intensity until it assumed the appearance of a military campaign. Partisan bands, composed of members of the population, roamed the territory doing much damage to transportation and communication lines. German soldiers were the victims of surprise attacks by an enemy which they could not engage in open combat. After a surprise attack, the bands would hastily retreat or conceal their arms and mingle with the population with the appearance of being harmless members thereof. Ambushing of German troops was a common practice. Captured German soldiers were often tortured and killed. The terrain was favorable to this type of warfare and the inhabitants most adept in carrying it on.

It is clear that the German armed forces were able to maintain control of Greece and Yugoslavia until they evacuated them in the fall of 1944. While it is true that the partisans were able to control sections of these countries at various times, it is established that the Germans could at any time they desired assume physical control of any part of the country. The control of the resistance forces was temporary only and not such as would deprive the German armed forces of its status of an occupant.

These findings are consistant with Article 42 of the Hague Regulations of 1907 which provide—"Territory is considered occupied when it is actually placed under the authority of the hostile army. The occupation extends only to the territory where such authority has been established and can be exercised."

It is the contention of the defendants that after the respective capitulations a lawful belligerency never did exist in Yugoslavia or Greece during the period here involved. The prosecution contends just as emphatically that it did. The evidence on the subject is fragmentary and consists primarily of admission contained in the reports, orders, and diaries of the German Army units involved. There is convincing evidence in the record that certain band units in both Yugoslavia and Greece complied with the requirements of international law entitling them to the status of a lawful belligerent. But the greater portion of the partisan bands failed to comply with the rules of war entitling them to be accorded the right of a lawful belligerent. The evidence fails to establish beyond a reasonable doubt that the incidents involved in the present case concern partisan troops having the status of lawful belligerents.

The evidence shows that the bands were sometimes designated as units common to military organization. They, however, had no common uniform. They generally wore civilian clothes although parts of German, Italian, and Serbian uniforms were used to the extent they could be obtained. The Soviet star was generally worn as insignia. The evidence will not sustain a finding that it was such that it could be seen at a distance. Neither did they carry their arms openly except when it was to their advantage to do so. There is some evidence that various groups of the resistance forces were commanded by a centralized command, such as the partisans of Marshal Tito, the Chetniks of Draja Mihailovic and the Edes of General Zervas. It is evident also that a few partisan bands met the requirements of lawful belligerency. The bands, however, with which we are dealing in this case were not shown by satisfactory evidence to have met the requirements. This means, of course, that captured members of these unlawful groups were not entitled to be treated as prisoners of war. No crime can be properly charged against the defendants for the killing of such captured members of the resistance forces, they being *francs-tireurs*.

The status of an occupant of the territory of the enemy having been achieved, international law places the responsibility upon the commanding general of preserving order, punishing crime, and protecting lives and property within the occupied territory. His power in accomplishing these ends is as great as his responsibility. But he is definitely limited by recognized rules of international law, particularly the Hague Regulations of 1907. Article 43 thereof imposes a duty upon the occupant to respect the laws in force in the country. Article 46 protects family honor and rights, the lives of individuals and their private property as well as their religious convictions and the right of public worship. Article 47 prohibits pillage. Article 50 prohibits collective penalties. Article 51 regulates the appropriation of properties belonging to the state or private individuals which may be useful in military operations. There are other restrictive provisions not necessary to mention here. It is the alleged violation of these rights of the inhabitants thus protected that furnish the basis of the case against the defendants.

The evidence is clear that during the period of occupation in Yugoslavia and Greece, guerrilla warfare was carried on against the occupying power. Guerrilla warfare is said to exist where, after the capitulation of the main part of the armed forces, the surrender of the government and the occupation of its territory, the remnant of the defeated army or the inhabitants themselves continue hostilities by harassing the enemy with unorganized forces ordinarily not strong enough to meet the enemy in pitched battle. They are placed much in the same position as a spy. By the law of war it is lawful to use spies. Nevertheless, a spy when captured, may be shot because the belligerent has the right, by means of an effective deterrent punishment, to defend against the grave dangers of enemy spying. The principle therein involved applies to guerrillas who are not lawful belligerents. Just as the spy may act lawfully for his country and at the same time be a war criminal to the enemy, so guerrillas may render great service to their country and, in the event of success, become heroes even, still they remain war criminals in the eyes of the enemy and may be treated as such. In no other way can an army guard and protect itself from the gadfly tactics of such armed resistance. And, on the other hand, members of such resistance forces must accept the increased risks involved in this mode of fighting. Such forces are technically not lawful belligerents and are not entitled to protection as prisoners of war when captured. The rule is based on the theory that the forces of two states are no longer in the field and that a contention between organized armed forces no longer exists. This implies that a resistance not supported by an organized government is criminal and deprives participants of belligerent status, an implication not justified since the adoption of chapter I, Article I of the Hague Regulations of 1907. In determining the guilt or innocence of an army commander when charged with a failure or refusal to accord a belligerent status to captured members of the resistance forces, the situation as it appeared to him must be given the first consideration. Such commander will not be permitted to ignore obvious facts in arriving at a conclusion. One trained in military science will ordinarily have no difficulty in arriving at a correct decision and, if he willfully refrains from so doing for any reason, he will be held criminally responsible for wrongs committed against those entitled to the rights of a belligerent. Where room exists for an honest error in judgment, such army commander is entitled to the benefit thereof by virtue of the presumption of his innocence.

We think the rule is established that a civilian who aids, abets, or participates in the fighting is liable to punishment as a war criminal under the laws of war. Fighting is legitimate only for the combatant personnel of a country. It is only this group that is entitled to treatment as prisoners of war and incurs no liability beyond detention after capture or surrender.

It is contended by the prosecution that the so-called guerrillas were in fact irregular troops. A preliminary discussion of the subject is essential to a proper determination of the applicable law. Members of a militia or a volunteer corps, even though they are not a part of the regular army, are lawful combatants if (*a*) they are commanded by a responsible person, (*b*) if they possess some distinctive insignia which can be observed at a distance, (*c*) if they carry arms openly, and (*d*) if they observe the laws and customs of war. (See chapter I, Article I, Hague Regulations of 1907.) In considering the evidence adduced on this subject, the foregoing rules will be applied. The question whether a captured fighter is a guerrilla or an irregular is sometimes a close one that can be determined only by a careful evaluation of the evidence before the Court.

The question of the right of the population of an invaded and occupied country to resist has been the subject of many conventional debates. (Brussels Conference of 1874; Hague Peace Conference of 1899.) A review of the positions assumed by the various nations can serve no useful purpose here for the simple reason that a compromise (Hague Regulations, 1907) was reached which has remained the controlling authority in the fixing of a legal belligerency. If the requirements of the Hague Regulation, 1907, are met, a lawful belligerency exists; if they are not met, it is an unlawful one.

The prosecution advances the contention that since Germany's wars against Yugoslavia and Greece were aggressive wars, the German occupation troops were there unlawfully and gained no rights whatever as an occupant. It is further asserted as a corollary, that the duties owed by the populace to an occupying power which are normally imposed under the rules of international law, never became effective in the present case because of the criminal character of the invasion and occupation.

For the purposes of this discussion, we accept the statement as true that the wars against Yugoslavia and Greece were in direct violation of the Kellogg-Briand Pact and were therefore criminal in character. But it does not follow that every act by the German occupation forces against person or property is a crime or that any and every act undertaken by the population of the occupied country against the German occupation forces thereby became legitimate defense. The prosecution attempts to simplify the issue by posing it in the following words:

> The sole issue here is whether German forces can with impunity violate international law by initiating and waging wars of aggression and at the same time demand meticulous observance by the victims of these crimes of duties and obligations owed only to a lawful occupant.

At the outset, we desire to point out that international law makes no distinction between a lawful and an unlawful occupant in dealing with the respective duties of occupant and population in occupied territory. There is no reciprocal connection between the manner of the military occupation of territory and the rights and duties of the occupant and population to each other after the relationship has in fact been established. Whether the invasion was lawful or criminal is not an important factor in the consideration of this subject.

It must not be overlooked that international law is prohibitive law. Where the nations have affirmatively acted, as in the case of the Hague Regulations, 1907, it prohibits conduct contradictory thereto. Its specific provisions control over general theories, however reasonable they may seem. We concur in the views expressed in the following text on the subject:[1] "Whatever may be the

[1]Oppenheim, *op. cit. supra*, p. 79.

cause of a war that has broken out, and whether or no the cause be a so-called just cause, the same rules of international law are valid as to what must not be done, may be done, and must be done by the belligerents themselves in making war against each other, and as between the belligerents and neutral states. This is so, even if the declaration of war is *ipso facto* a violation of international law, as when a belligerent declares war upon a neutral state for refusing passage to its troops, or when a state goes to war in patent violation of its obligations under the Covenant of the League or of the General Treaty for the Renunciation of War[1] To say that, because such a declaration of war is *ipso facto* a violation of neutrality and international law, it is 'inoperative in law and without any judicial significance' is erroneous. The rules of international law apply to war *from whatever cause it originates."*

The major issues involved in the present case gravitate around the claimed right of the German armed forces to take hostages from the innocent civilian population to guarantee the peaceful conduct of the whole of the civilian population and its claimed right to execute hostages, members of the civil population, and captured members of the resistance forces in reprisal for armed attacks by resistance forces, acts of sabotage and injuries committed by unknown persons.

We wholly exclude from the following discussion of the subject of hostages the right of one nation to take them, to compel the armed forces of another nation to comply with the rules of war or the right to execute them if the enemy ignores the warning. We limit our discussion to the right to take hostages from the innocent civilian population of occupied territory as a guaranty against attacks by unlawful resistance forces, acts of sabotage and the unlawful acts of unknown persons, and the further right to execute them if the unilateral guaranty is violated.

Neither the Hague Convention of 1907, nor any other conventional law for that matter, says a word about hostages in the sense that we are to use the term in the following discussion. But certain rules of customary law and certain inferences legitimately to be drawn from existing conventional law lay down the rules applicable to the subject of hostages. In former times prominent persons were accepted as hostages as a means of insuring observance of treaties, armistices, and other agreements, the performance of which depended on good faith. This practice is now obsolete. Hostages under the alleged modern practice of nations are taken (*a*) to protect individuals held by the enemy, (*b*) to force the payment of requisitions, contributions, and the like, and (*c*) to insure against unlawful acts by enemy forces or people. We are concerned here only with the last provision. That hostages may be taken for this purpose cannot be denied.

The question of hostages is closely integrated with that of reprisals. A reprisal is a response to an enemy's violation of the laws of war which would otherwise be a violation on one's own side. It is a fundamental rule that a

[1] Ibid.

reprisal may not exceed the degree of the criminal act it is designed to correct. Where an excess is knowingly indulged, it in turn is criminal and may be punished. Where innocent individuals are seized and punished for a violation of the laws of war which has already occurred, no question of hostages is involved. It is nothing more than the infliction of a reprisal. Throughout the evidence in the present case, we find the term hostage applied where a reprisal only was involved.

Under the ancient practice of taking hostages they were held responsible for the good faith of the persons who delivered them, even at the price of their lives. This barbarous practice was wholly abandoned by a more enlightened civilization. The idea that an innocent person may be killed for the criminal act of another is abhorrent to every natural law. We condemn the injustice of any such rule as a barbarous relic of ancient times. But it is not our province to write international law as we would have it; we must apply it as we find it.

For the purposes of this opinion the term "hostages" will be considered as those persons of the civilian population who are taken into custody for the purpose of guaranteeing with their lives the future good conduct of the population of the community from which they were taken. The term "reprisal prisoners" will be considered as those individuals who are taken from the civilian population to be killed in retaliation for offenses committed by unknown persons within the occupied area.

An examination of the available evidence on the subject convinces us that hostages may be taken in order to guarantee the peaceful conduct of the populations of occupied territories and, when certain conditions exist and the necessary preliminaries have been taken, they may, as a last resort, be shot. The taking of hostages is based fundamentally on a theory of collective responsibility. The effect of an occupation is to confer upon the invading force the right of control for the period of the occupation within the limitations and prohibitions of international law. The inhabitants owe a duty to carry on their ordinary peaceful pursuits and to refrain from all injurious acts toward the troops or in respect to their military operations. The occupant may properly insist upon compliance with regulations necessary to the security of the occupying forces and for the maintenance of law and order. In the accomplishment of this objective, the occupant may only, as a last resort, take and execute hostages.

Hostages may not be taken or executed as a matter of military expediency. The occupant is required to use every available method to secure order and tranquility before resort may be had to the taking and execution of hostages. Regulations of all kinds must be imposed to secure peace and tranquility before the shooting of hostages may be indulged. These regulations may include one or more of the following measures: (1) the registration of the inhabitants, (2) the possession of passes or identification certificates, (3) the establishment of restricted area, (4) limitations of movement, (5) the adoption of curfew regulations, (6) the prohibition of assembly, (7) the detention of suspected persons, (8) restrictions on communication, (9) the imposition of restrictions on food supplies, (10) the evacuation of troublesome areas, (11) the levying of monetary contributions, (12) compulsory labor to repair damage from sabotage, (13) the destruction of property in proximity to the place of the crime, and any other regulation not prohibited by international law that would in all likelihood contribute to the desired result.

If attacks upon troops and military installations occur regardless of the foregoing precautionary measures and the perpetrators cannot be apprehended, hostages may be taken from the population to deter similar acts in the future provided it can be shown that the population generally is a party to the offense, either actively or passively. Nationality or geographic proximity may under certain circumstances afford a basis for hostage selection, depending upon the circumstances of the situation. This arbitrary basis of selection may be deplored but it cannot be condemned as a violation of international law, but there must be some connection between the population from whom the hostages are taken and the crime committed. If the act was committed by isolated persons or bands from distant localities without the knowledge or approval of the population or public authorities, and which, therefore, neither the authorities nor the population could have prevented, the basis for the taking of hostages, or the shooting of hostages already taken, does not exist.

It is essential to a lawful taking of hostages under customary law that proclamation be made, giving the names and addresses of hostages taken, notifying the population that upon the recurrence of stated acts of war treason the hostages will be shot. The number of hostages shot must not exceed in severity the offenses the shooting is designed to deter. Unless the foregoing requirements are met, the shooting of hostages is in contravention of international law and is a war crime in itself. Whether such fundamental requirements have been met is a question determinable by court martial proceedings. A military commander may not arbitrarily determine such facts. An order of a military commander for the killing of hostages must be based upon the finding of a competent court martial that necessary conditions exist and all preliminary steps have been taken which are essential to the issurance of a valid order. The taking of the lives of innocent persons arrested as hostages is a very serious step. The right to kill hostages may be lawfully exercised only after a meticulous compliance with the foregoing safeguards against vindictive or whimsical orders of military commanders.

We are also concerned with the subject of reprisals and the detention of members of the civilian population for the purpose of using them as the victims of subsequent reprisal measures. The most common reason for holding them is for the general purpose of securing the good behavior and obedience of the civil population in occupied territory. The taking of reprisals against the civilian population by killing members thereof in retaliation for hostile acts against the armed forces or military operations of the occupant seems to have been originated by Germany in modern times. It has been invoked by Germany in the Franco-Prussian War, World War I, and in World War II. No other nation has resorted to the killing of members of the civilian population to secure peace and order insofar as our investigation has revealed. The evidence offered in this case on that point will be considered later in the opinion. While American, British, and French manuals for armies in the field seem to permit the taking of such reprisals as a last resort, the provisions do not appear to have been given effect. The American manual provides in part—

> The offending forces or populations generally may lawfully be subjected to appropriate reprisals. Hostages taken and held for the declared purpose of insuring against unlawful acts by the enemy forces or people may be punished or put to death if the unlawful acts are nevertheless committed.

The British field manual provides in part—

> Although collective punishment of the population is forbidden for the acts of individuals for which it cannot be regarded as collectively responsible, it may be necessary to resort to reprisals against a locality or community, for same act committed by its inhabitants, or members who cannot be identified.

In two major wars within the last 30 years, Germany has made extensive use of the practice of killing innocent members of the population as a deterrent to attacks upon its troops and acts of sabotage against installations essential to its military operations. The right to so do has been recognized by many nations including the United States, Great Britain, France, and the Soviet Union. There has been complete failure on the part of the nations of the world to limit or mitigate the practice by conventional rule. This requires us to apply customary law. That international agreement is badly needed in this field is self-evident.

International law is prohibitive law and no conventional prohibitions have been invoked to outlaw this barbarous practice. The extent to which the practice has been employed by the Germans exceeds the most elementary notions of humanity and justice. They invoke the plea of military necessity, a term which they confuse with convenience and strategical interests. Where legality and expediency have coincided, no fault can be found insofar as international law is concerned. But where legality of action is absent, the shooting of innocent members of the population as a measure of reprisal is not only criminal but it has the effect of destroying the basic relationship between the occupant and the population. Such a condition can progressively degenerate into a reign of terror. Unlawful reprisals may bring on counter reprisals and create an endless cycle productive of chaos and crime. To prevent a distortion of the right into a barbarous method of repression, international law provides a protective mantle against the abuse of the right.

Generally, it can be said that the taking of reprisal prisoners, as well as the taking of hostages, for the purpose of controlling the population involves a previous proclamation that if a certain type of act is committed, a certain number of reprisal prisoners will be shot if the perpetrators cannot be found. If the perpetrators are apprehended, there is no right to kill either hostages or reprisal prisoners.

As in the case of the taking of hostages, reprisal prisoners may not be shot unless it can be shown that the population as a whole is a party to the offense, either actively or passively. In other words, members of the population of one community cannot properly be shot in reprisal for an act against the occupation forces committed at some other place. To permit such a practice would conflict with the basic theory that sustains the practice in that there would be no deterrent effect upon the community where the offense was committed. Neither may the shooting of innocent members of the population as a reprisal measure exceed in severity the unlawful acts it is designed to correct. Excessive reprisals are in themselves criminal and guilt attaches to the persons responsible for their commission.

It is a fundamental rule of justice that the lives of persons may not be arbitrarily taken. A fair trial before a judicial body affords the surest protection against arbitrary, vindictive, or whimsical application of the right to shoot human beings in reprisal. It is a rule of international law, based on these fundamental concepts of justice and the rights of individuals, that the lives of persons may not be taken in reprisal in the absence of a judicial finding that the necessary conditions exist and the essential steps have been taken to give validity to such action. The possibility is great, of course, that such judicial proceedings may become ritualistic and superficial when conducted in wartime but it appears to be the best available safeguard against cruelty and injustice. Judicial responsibility ordinarily restrains impetuous action and permits principles of justice and right to assert their humanitarian qualities. We have no hesitancy in holding that the killing of members of the population in reprisal without judicial sanction is itself unlawful. The only exception to this rule is where it appears that the necessity for the reprisal requires immediate reprisal action to accomplish the desired purpose and which would be otherwise defeated by the invocation of judicial inquiry. Unless the necessity for immediate action is affirmatively shown, the execution of hostages or reprisal prisoners without a judicial hearing is unlawful. The judicial proceeding not only affords a measure of protection to innocent members of the population, but it offers, if fairly and impartially conducted, a measure of protection to the military commander, charged with making the final decision.

It cannot be denied that the shooting of hostages or reprisal prisoners may under certain circumstances be justified as a last resort in procuring peace and tranquility in occupied territory and has the effect of strengthening the position of a law abiding occupant. The fact that the practice has been tortured beyond recognition by illegal and inhuman application cannot justify its prohibition by judicial fiat.

Military necessity has been invoked by the defendants as justifying the killing of innocent members of the population and the destruction of villages and towns in the occupied territory. Military necessity permits a belligerent, subject to the laws of war, to apply any amount and kind of force to compel the complete submission of the enemy with the least possible expenditure of time, life, and money. In general, it sanctions measures by an occupant necessary to protect the safety of his forces and to facilitate the success of his operations. It permits the destruction of life of armed enemies and other persons whose destruction is incidentally unavoidable by the armed conflicts of the war; it allows the capturing of armed enemies and others of peculiar danger, but it does not permit the killing of innocent inhabitants for purposes of revenge or the satisfaction of a lust to kill. The destruction of property to be lawful must be imperatively demanded by the necessities of war. Destruction as an end in itself is a violation of international law. There must be some reasonable connection between the destruction of property and the overcoming of the enemy forces. It is lawful to destroy railways, lines of communication, or any other property that might be utilized by the enemy. Private homes and churches even may be destroyed if necessary for military operations. It does not admit the wanton devastation of a district or the willful infliction of suffering upon its inhabitants for the sake of suffering alone.

The issues in the present case raise grave questions of international law. Military men the world over debate both the law and the policy involved in the prosecution for war crimes of the high ranking commanders of defeated armies. This is partially brought about by the possibility of future wars and the further possibility that the victors of the present may be the vanquished of the future. This only serves to impress the Tribunal with the absolute necessity of affording the defendants a fair and impartial trial under the rules of international law as they were at the time the alleged offenses were committed. Unless this be done, the hand of injustice may fall upon those who so vindictively contend for more far reaching pronouncements, sustained by precedents which we would hereby establish.

Strict discipline is necessary in the organization of an army, and it becomes hard for many to believe that a violation of the orders of a superior may bring about criminal liability. Love of country and adherence to duty intervene to palliate unlawful conduct. The passage of time and the thankfulness for a return to peaceful pursuits tend to lessen the demand that war criminals answer for their crimes. In addition thereto, there is a general feeling that excesses occur in all armies, no matter how well disciplined, and that military trials are held to convict the war criminals of the vanquished while those of the victor are cleansed by victory. Unless civilization is to give way to barbarism in the conduct of war, crime must be punished. If international law as it applies to a given case is hopelessly inadequate, such inadequacy should be pointed out. If customary international law has become outmoded, it should be so stated. If conventional international law sets forth an unjust rule, its enforcement will secure its correction. If all war criminals are not brought to the bar of justice under present procedures, such procedures should be made more inclusive and more effective. If the laws of war are to have any beneficent effect, they must be enforced.

The evidence in this case recites a record of killing and destruction seldom exceeded in modern history. Thousands of innocent inhabitants lost their lives by means of a firing squad or hangman's noose, people who had the same inherent desire to live as do these defendants. Wherever the German armed forces were found, there also were the SS (Die Schutzstaffeln der Nationalsozialistischen Deutschen Arbeiterpartei), the SD (Der Sicherheitsdienst des Reichsfuehrer SS), the Gestapo (Die Geheime Staatspolizei), the SA (Die Sturmabteilungen der Nationalsozialistischen Deutschen Arbeiterpatei), the administrators of Goering's Four Year Plan, and the Einsatzstab Rosenberg, all participating in the administration of the occupied territories in varying degrees. Mass shootings of the innocent population, deportations for slave labor, and the indiscriminate destruction of public and private property, not only in Yugoslavia and Greece but in many other countries as well, lend credit to the assertion that terrorism and intimidation was the accepted solution to any and all opposition to the German will. It is clear, also, that this had become a general practice and a major weapon of warfare by the German Wehrmacht. The German attitude seems to be reflected in the introduction to the German War Book, as translated by J. H. Morgan [John Murray, London, 1915] on pages 53–55 wherein it is stated:

> If therefore, in the following work the expression "the law of war" is used, it must be understood that by it is meant not a *lex scripta* introduced by international agreements, but only a reciprocity of mutual agreement; a limitation of arbitrary behaviour, which custom and conventionality, human friendliness and a calculating egotism have erected, but for the observance of which there exists no express sanction, but only "the fear of reprisals" decides. . . . Moreover the officer is a child of his time. He is subject to the intellectual tendencies which influence his own nation; the more educated he is the more will this be the case. The danger that, in this way, he will arrive at false views about the essential character of war must not be lost sight of. The danger can only be met by a thorough study of war itself. By steeping himself in military history an officer will be able to guard himself against excessive humanitarian notions, it will teach him that certain severities are indispensable to war, nay more, that the only true humanity very often lies in a ruthless application of them. It will also teach him how the rules of belligerent intercourse in war have developed, how in the course of time they have solidified into general usages of war, and finally it will teach him whether the governing usages of war are justified or not, whether they are to be modified or whether they are to be observed.

It is apparent from the evidence of these defendants that they considered military necessity, a matter to be determined by them, a complete justification of their acts. We do not concur in the view that the rules of warfare are anything less than they purport to be. Military necessity or expediency do not justify a violation of positive rules. International law is prohibitive law. Articles 46, 47 and 50 of the Hague Regulations of 1907 make no such exceptions to its enforcement. The rights of the innocent population therein set forth must be respected even if military necessity or expediency decree otherwise. We have hereinbefore pointed out that it is the duty of the commanding general in occupied territory to maintain peace and order, punish crime, and protect lives and property. This duty extends not only to the inhabitants of the occupied territory but to his own troops and auxiliaries as well. The commanding general of occupied territory, having executive authority as well as military command, will not be heard to say that a unit taking unlawful orders from someone other than himself was responsible for the crime and that he is thereby absolved from responsibility. It is here claimed, for example, that certain SS units under the direct command of Heinrich Himmler committed certain of the atrocities herein charged without the knowledge, consent, or approval of these defendants. But this cannot be a defense for the commanding general of occupied territory. The duty and responsibility for maintaining peace and order, and the prevention of crime rests upon the commanding general. He cannot ignore obvious facts and plead ignorance as a defense. The fact is that the reports of subordinate units almost without exception advised these defendants of the policy of terrorism and intimidation being carried out by units in the field. They requisitioned food supplies in excess of their local need and caused it to be shipped to Germany in direct violation of the laws of war. Innocent people were lodged in collection and concentration camps where they were mistreated to the everlasting shame of the German nation. Innocent inhabitants were forcibly taken to Germany and other points for use as slave labor. Jews, gypsies, and other racial groups were the victims of systematized murder or deportation for slave labor for no other reason than their race or religion, which is in violation of the express conventional rule of the Hague Regulations of 1907. The German theory that fear of reprisal is the only deterrent in the enforcement of the laws of war cannot be accepted here. That reprisals may be indulged to compel an enemy nation to comply with the rules of war must be conceded.

It is not, however, an exclusive remedy. If it were, the persons responsible would seldom, if ever, be brought to account. The only punishment would fall upon the reprisal victims who are usually innocent of wrongdoing. The prohibitions of the Hague Regulations of 1907 contemplate no such system of retribution. Those responsible for such crimes by ordering or authorizing their commission, or by a failure to take effective steps to prevent their execution or recurrence, must be held to account if international law is to be anything more than an ethical code, barren of any practical coercive deterrent.

That the acts charged as crimes in the indictment occurred is amply established by the evidence. In fact, it is evident that they constitute only a portion of the large number of such acts which took place as a part of a general plan for subduing the countries of Yugoslavia and Greece. The guilt of the German occupation forces is not only proved beyond a reasonable doubt but it casts a pall of shame upon a once highly respected nation and its people. The defendants themselves recognize this situation when they decry the policies of Hitler and assert that they continually protested against orders of superiors issued in conformity with the plan of terrorism and intimidation.

It is the determination of the connection of the defendants with the acts charged and the responsibility which attaches to them therefor, rather than the commission of the acts, that poses the chief issue to be here decided.

Objection has been made that the documents offered in evidence by the prosecution are not the original instruments but photostatic copies only. No objection of this character was made at the time the exhibits were offered and received in evidence. In view of the fact that this objection was not timely made, it cannot receive the consideration of the Tribunal.

The record is replete with testimony and exhibits which have been offered and received in evidence without foundation as to their authenticity and, in many cases, where it is secondary in character, without proof of the usual conditions precedent to the admission of such evidence. This is in accordance with the provisions of Article VII, Ordinance No. 7, Military Government, Germany.

* * *

We find that the "Commissar Order" of 6 June 1941 (*NOKW-484, Pros. Ex. 13*) requiring the killing of all captured commissars was not issued, distributed or executed in the occupied territory under the command of List while he held the position of Armed Forces Commander Southeast. The charge that such order was issued, distributed, and executed by him while serving on the Russian front as commander in chief of Army Group A, is not established by the record. The evidence fails to show beyond a reasonable doubt that List was in any way responsible for the killing of commissars merely because they were such. Consequently, the defendant List is found to be not guilty of any crime in connection with the Commissar Order.

The defendant List contends that he never signed an order for the killing of hostages or other inhabitants, or fixed a ratio determining the number of persons to be put to death for each German soldier killed or wounded. The record sustains this contention. It will be observed, however, that as a high ranking commanding general no such act was ordinarily within the scope of his duties. It discloses, however, that List caused the Keitel order of 16 September 1941 (*NOKW-258, Pros. Ex. 53*)* containing the 100:1 ratio to be distributed to his subordinate commanders. This order provided, among other things, that 100 reprisal prisoners should be shot for each German soldier killed and 50 killed for each German soldier wounded. It is urged that the order was worded in such a way that literal compliance was not required. We do not deem it material whether the order was mandatory or directory. In either event, it authorized the killing of hostages and reprisal prisoners to an extent not permitted by international law. An order to take reprisals at an arbitrarily fixed ratio under any and all circumstances constitutes a violation of international law. Such an order appears to have been made more for purposes of revenge than as a deterrent to future illegal acts which would vary in degree in each particular instance. An order, directory or mandatory, which fixes a ratio for the killing of hostages or reprisal prisoners, or requires the killing of hostages or reprisal prisoners for every act committed against the occupation forces

*Ibid.

is unlawful. International law places no such unrestrained and unlimited power in the hands of the commanding general of occupied territory. The reprisals taken under the authority of this order were clearly excessive. The shooting of 100 innocent persons for each German soldier killed at Topola, for instance, cannot be justified on any theory by the record. There is no evidence that the population of Topola were in any manner responsible for the act. In fact, the record shows that the responsible persons were an armed and officered band of partisans. There is nothing to infer that the population of Topola supported or shielded the guilty persons. Neither does the record show that the population had previously conducted themselves in such a manner as to have been subjected to previous reprisal actions. An order to shoot 100 persons for each German soldier killed under such circumstances is not only excessive but wholly unwarranted. We conclude that the reprisal measure taken for the ambushing and killing of 22 German soldiers at Topola were excessive and therefore criminal. It is urged that only 449 persons were actually shot in reprisal for the Topola incident. The evidence does not conclusively establish the shooting of more than 449 persons although it indicates the killing of a much greater number. But the killing of 20 reprisal prisoners for each German soldier killed was not warranted under the circumstances shown. Whether the number of innocent persons killed was 2,200 or 449, the killing was wholly unjustified and unlawful.

The reprisal measures taken for the Topola incident were unlawful for another reason. The reprisal prisoners killed were not taken from the community where the attack on the German soldiers occurred. The record shows that 805 Jews and gypsies were taken from the collection camp at Sabac and the rest from the Jewish transit camp at Belgrade to be shot in reprisal for the Topola incident. There is no evidence of any connection whatever, geographical, racial, or otherwise between the persons shot and the attack at Topola. Nor does the record disclose that judicial proceedings were held. The order for the killing in reprisal appears to have been arbitrarily issued and under the circumstances shown is nothing less than plain murder.

It is further contended that the basic order for the taking of reprisals was issued by the High Command of the Armed Forces to whom the defendant List was subordinate and that this has the effect of relieving him of responsibility. Such a defense is not available to him. An officer is duty bound to carry out only the lawful orders that he receives. One who distributes, issues, or carries out a criminal order becomes a criminal if he knew or should have known of its criminal character. Certainly, a field marshal of the German Army with more than 40 years of experience as a professional soldier knew or ought to have known of its criminal nature. That he did know of it is evidenced by the fact that he opposed its issuance and, according to his own statement, did what he could to ameliorate its effect.

The defendant List also asserts that he had no knowledge of many of the unlawful killings of innocent inhabitants which took place because he was absent from his headquarters where the reports came in and that he gained no knowledge of the acts. A commanding general of occupied territory is charged with the duty of maintaining peace and order, punishing crime, and protecting lives and property within the area of his command. His responsibility is coextensive with his area of command. He is charged with notice of occurrences taking place within that territory. He may require adequate reports of all occurrences that come within the scope of his power and, if such reports are incomplete or otherwise inadequate, he is obliged to require supplementary reports to apprize him of all the pertinent facts. If he fails to require and obtain complete information, the dereliction of duty rests upon him and he is in no position to plead his own dereliction as a defense. Absence from headquarters cannot and does not relieve one from responsibility for acts committed in accordance with a policy he instituted or in which he acquiesced. He may not, of course, be charged with acts committed on the order of someone else which is outside the basic orders which he has issued. If time permits he is required to rescind such illegal orders, otherwise he is required to take steps to prevent a recurrence of their issue.

Want of knowledge of the contents of reports made to him is not a defense. Reports to commanding generals are made for their special benefit. Any failure to acquaint themselves with the contents of such reports, or a failure to require additional reports where inadequacy appears on their face, constitutes a dereliction of duty which he cannot use in his own behalf.

The reports made to the defendant List as Armed Forces Commander Southeast charge him with notice of the unlawful killing of thousands of innocent people in reprisal for acts of unknown members of the population who were not lawfully subject to such punishment. Not once did he condemn such acts as unlawful. Not once did he call to account those responsible for these inhumane and barbarous acts. His failure to terminate these unlawful killings and to take adequate steps to prevent their recurrence constitutes a serious breach of duty and imposes criminal responsibility. Instead of taking corrective measures, he complacently permitted thousands of innocent people to die before the execution squads of the Wehrmacht and other armed units operating in the territory. He contends further that many of these executions were carried out by units of the SS, the SD, and local police units which were not tactically subordinated to him. The evidence sustains this contention but it must be borne in mind that in his capacity as commanding general of occupied territory, he was charged with the duty and responsibility of maintaining order and safety, the protection of the lives and property of the population, and the punishment of crime. This not only implies a control of the inhabitants in the accomplishment of these purposes, but the control and regulation of all other lawless persons or groups. He cannot escape responsibility by a claim of a want of authority. The authority is inherent in his position as commanding general of occupied territory. The primary responsibility for the prevention and punishment of crime lies with the commanding general; a responsibility from which he cannot escape by denying his authority over the perpetrators.

The record shows that after the capitulation of Yugoslavia and Greece, the defendant List remained as the commanding general of the occupied territory. As the resistance movement developed, it became more and more apparent that the occupying forces were insufficient to deal with it. Repeated appeals to the High Command of the Armed Forces for additional forces were refused with the demand for a pacification of the occupied territory by more draconic measures. These orders were protested by List without avail. He contends that although such orders were in all respects lawful, he protested from a humanitarian viewpoint. It is quite evident that the High Command insisted upon a campaign of intimidation and terrorism as a substitute for additional troops. Here again the German theory of expediency and military necessity (Kriegsraeson geht vor Kriegsmanier) superseded established rules of international law. As we have previously stated in this opinion, the rules of international law must be followed even if it results in the loss of a battle or even a war. Expediency or necessity cannot warrant their violation. What then was the duty of the Armed Forces Commander Southeast? We think his duty was plain. He was authorized to pacify the country with military force; he was entitled to punish those who attcked his troops or sabotaged his transportation and communication lines as *franc-tireurs;* he was entitled to take precautions against those suspected of participation in the resistance movement, such as registration, limitations of movements, curfew regulations, and other measures hereinbefore set forth in this opinion. As a last resort, hostages and reprisal prisoners may be shot in accordance with international custom and practice. If adequate troops were not available or if the lawful measures against the population failed in their purpose, the occupant could limit its operations or withdraw from the country in whole or in part, but no right existed to pursue a policy in violation of international law.

The record establishes that List was an officer of the "old school" which quite generally resented the control of the National Socialist Party over the Wehrmacht. That Adolf Hitler in his capacity as Commander in Chief of the Armed Forces was generally considered a rank amateur in military matters by this group seems to be quite well established. The subsequent retirement of List "by request" because of a difference of opinion with Hitler on tactical matters during the Russian campaign further sustains his claimed viewpoint with respect to his relations with Hitler and the National Socialist Party. List states that his views on political matters were not inconsistent with his subsequent military service. It was his opinion that Hitler came to power in a lawful manner and that his obligation as a soldier and his loyalty to his country required him to continue in military service. That he was not in accord with many of the orders of the High Command of the Armed Forces with reference to the pacification of Yugoslavia and Greece is shown by the record. That his appeals for more troops for the subjugation of the growing resistance movement were met with counterdirectives and orders by Hitler and Keitel to accomplish it by a campaign of terrorism and intimidation of the population is amply established. That his orders and directives were more moderate than those of his superiors cannot be questioned. It is clear also that he was continually plagued with the operations of organizations receiving orders direct from superiors in Berlin, such as the SS, the SD, the SA, and emissaries of Goering in the administration of his Four Year Plan.

That German prisoners captured by the resistance forces were tortured, mutilated, and killed is shown by the evidence. In this connection, we point out the extent to which unlawful reprisals and counterreprisals may lead. Excesses on the part of troops are bound to occur in any way but certainly they will be more vicious and barbarous if cruelty and harshness constitute the policy of the commanding officers. It is almost inevitable that the murder of innocent members of the population, including the relatives and friends of the *francs-tireurs,* would generate a hatred that was bound to express itself in counterreprisals and acts of atrocity. As the severity of the draconic measures of the Wehrmacht were stepped up, so also were the reprisals in answer thereto. There could be but one result, a completely chaotic condition with an absolute disregard of the laws of war on the part of the fighters of both forces with acts of atrocity progressively increasing. The situation provides adequate proof for the necessity of enforcing the laws of war if torture and barbarity are to be restrained. The failure of the nations of the world to deal specifically with the problem of hostages and reprisals by convention, treaty, or otherwise, after the close of World War I, creates a situation that mitigates to some extent the seriousness of the offense. These facts may not be employed, however, to free the defendant from the responsibility for crimes committed. They are material only to the extent that they bear upon the question of mitigation of punishment.

We conclude therefore that the evidence establishes the guilt of the defendant List beyond a reasonable doubt on counts one and three.

On or about 24 October 1941, the defendant Kuntze was appointed Deputy Armed Forces Commander Southeast and commander in chief of the 12th Army. It is evident from the record that the appointment was intended as a temporary one for the period of the illness of Field Marshal List. He assumed the command on his arrival in the Balkans on 27 October 1941. He was superseded by General Alexander Loehr in June 1942, but remained in the position until the arrival of General Loehr on 8 August 1942.

The record shows that in June 1940, before coming to the Balkans, the defendant Kuntze became the commander of the XLII Army Corps. In June 1941, this corps was transferred to East Prussia where it was subordinated to the 9th Army in the fighting against the Russians. From the middle of July 1941 to October 1941, the corps was subordinated to the 18th Army. Pursuant to orders previously received, the corps, on or about 8 October 1941, commenced operations for its transfer to the Crimea which were concluded on 20 October 1941. It was upon the arrival of Kuntze in the Crimea that he received the order to report to Hitler that resulted in his appointment as Deputy Armed Forces Commander Southeast.

The defendant Kuntze is charged with issuing, distributing, and executing the Commissar Order of 6 June 1941, wherein Hitler ordered the killing of captured commissars. In this connection, evidence was offered that from 1 July 1942 to 4 July 1942 captured commissars were killed by the 217th Infantry Division. The evidence shows that this division was subordinated to the XLII Corps from August 1941 until the corps was transferred to the Crimea. Consequently, the defendant Kuntze is not chargeable with the acts of the 217th Infantry Division that occurred prior to August 1941. Evidence was also offered showing that units of the 61st Infantry Division killed a number of captured commissars between 26 September 1941 and 28 October 1941. It is evident that the killing of political commissars after 6 October 1941 cannot be charged to the defendant Kuntze for the reason that the XLII Corps was on that date moving to the Crimea. The 61st Infantry Division remained behind and in the very nature of things was no longer subordinate to the XLII Corps. There appears in the war diary of the 61st Infantry Division, however, under date of 26 September 1941, a recitation of the shooting to death of saboteurs and commissars by the Field Gendarme Squad 161a, a unit subordinate to the 61st Infantry Division. The defendant Kuntze admits that the 61st Infantry Division was subordinate to him from the middle of September 1941 to the first part of October, of the same year. He denies that he ordered any such action or authorized anyone to carry it out. He states that he had never heard of this incident and had no knowledge of the shooting of any commissar by any unit subordinate to him. He states further that the army commander to whom he was subordinate had specifically directed him to treat commissars as prisoners of war and that he complied in all respects with that order. We do not think the foregoing evidence is sufficient to hold the defendant criminally responsible for the issuance, distribution, or execution of the Commissar Order. Nor does the evidence establish that the Commissar Order was made effective in the Balkan area. It will not sustain a finding that this order was issued, distributed, or executed by the defendant Kuntze during the time he was Deputy Armed Forces Commander Southeast.

This defendant is also charged with issuing, distributing, and executing the Commando Order of 18 October 1942, (*C–81, Pros. Ex. 225*) during the period of his command in the Balkans. By this order, issued by Hitler in person, all sabotage troops generally referred to as commandos were to be shot immediately upon capture. The record shows that Kuntze was relieved of his command by General Loehr on 8 August 1942. Consequently, the order was not issued until after Kuntze had left the southeastern area. The prosecution has not attempted to disprove this fact and it must be treated as established. The defendant Kuntze has not been shown to have violated any duty with reference to his treatment of commandos or other groups mentioned in the Commando Order.

We hold also that the resistance forces with which we are here concerned were not entitled to be classed as lawful belligerents during the period the defendant Kuntze was Deputy Armed Forces Commander Southeast. The reasons stated in the treatment of this subject in its relation to the defendant List apply as well to the defendant Kuntze and they will not be repeated here. No criminal responsibility can therefore attach to him because of the killing of captured members of the resistance forces, they being *francs-tireurs* subject to such punishment.

The defendant Kuntze contends that a right exists to take reprisals by killing hostages and reprisal prisoners in retaliation for the criminal acts of the resistance forces and other unknown persons. He asserts also that members of bands and those supporting them were used for reprisal purposes and that he knew of no instance where a contrary course was pursued. He denies that excessive and disproportionate reprisals were taken and claims to have had little or no knowledge of the harsh measures taken as shown by the war diaries, orders, and reports offered in evidence. He further contends that the measures taken were prescribed by superiors whose orders he was bound to follow. The legal questions thus raised have been dealt with in disposing of the case against the defendant List and will not for reasons of brevity be repeated here. The factual situation will however be examined.

The defendant Kuntze assumed command in the Southeast on 27 October 1941, a month which exceeded all previous monthly records in killing innocent members of the population in reprisal for the criminal acts of unknown persons. On 9 October 1941, 2,200 Communists and Jews were shot in reprisal for 22 German soldiers of the 521st Army Signal Communication Regiment murdered at Topola; on 18 October 1941, 1,736 men and 19 Communist women were shot in reprisal for German losses sustained in the fight for Kraljevo; on 19 October 1941, 182 men were shot to death in Meckovac and 1,600 men from Valjevo were shot to death in reprisal for 16 Germans killed and 24 wounded; on 21 October 1941, 2,300 Serbs of various ages and professions were shot to death; on 27 October 1941, 101 arrestees were shot to death with further killings to be carried out after more arrestees had been turned in; and on 28 October 1941, 2,200 Serbs were shot for 10 German soldiers killed and 24 wounded in action. It seems highly improbable that Kuntze could step into the command in the Southeast in the midst of the carrying out and reporting of these reprisal actions without gaining knowledge and approval. Reports made to the defendant Kuntze, shown in the evidence, reveal that on 29 October 1941, 76 persons were shot in reprisal in Serbia; on 2 November 1941, 20 persons were shot to death near Loznica; on 2 November 1941, 125 persons were shot to death at Valjevo; and on 27 November 1941, 265 Communists were shot as a reprisal measure at Valjevo. Under date of 31 October 1941, the commanding general in Serbia, General Boehme, recapitulated the shootings in Serbia in a report to Kuntze as follows: "Shootings—405 hostages in Belgrade (total up to now in Belgrade 4,750), 90 Communists in Camp Sabac, 2,300 hostages in Kragujevac, 1,700 hostages in Kraljevo." In a similar report under date of 30 November 1941, General Boehme reported to Kuntze as follows: "Shot as hostages (total) 534 (500 of these by Serbian auxiliary police)." Many other similar shootings are shown by the record. Included was a report covering the whole period of the resistance movement up to and including 5 December 1841, wherein it is shown that 31,338 reprisal prisoners were to be shot on the basis of the 100 to 1 order, that 11,164 had been shot and that 20,-174 remained to be shot in reprisal to fulfill the quota fixed on the 100 to 1 basis.

On 5 December 1941, the new commanding general in Serbia, General Bader, ordered the basic reprisal ration reduced to 50 reprisal prisoners for each German killed and 25 for each German wounded. The defendant Kuntze asserts that this reduction of ratio was in a large part due to his insistence and effort in that direction. Thereafter, the killing of hostages and reprisal prisoners continued. In a daily report to the defendant Kuntze, General Bader stated that 449 reprisal prisoners were shot to death in January 1942, and the 3,484 additional shootings had been ordered to commence immediately to balance the reprisal killings against the Germans killed and wounded on the fixed ratio. On 21 February 1942, General Bader reported the shooting of 570 Communists by the Serbian auxiliary Gendarmerie, on 23 February 1942, the shooting of 403 reprisal prisoners, and on 25 February 1942, the shooting of 110 Communists in reprisal.

On 19 March 1942, the defendant Kuntze issued an order regarding the combating of insurgents which stated in part (*NOKW–835, Pros. Ex. 184*):

> I expect troop leaders of all ranks to show special energy and ruthless action as well as to commit fully their own person for the duty with which they are charged, which is to preserve quiet, order, and security by all means. All soldiers who do not follow orders and who do not act decisively are to be called to account.
>
> By means of brutal police and secret police measures, the formation of insurgent bands is to be recognized in its inception and to be burnt out. Captured insurgents are to be hanged or to be shot to death as a matter of principle; if they are being used for reconnaissance purposes, it merely means a slight delay in their death.

In the directives accompanying the foregoing order, it was stated:

> The more unequivocal and the harder reprisal measures are applied from the beginning the less it will become necessary to apply them at a later date. No false sentimentalities! It is preferable that 50 suspects are liquidated than one German soldier lose his life. . . . Villages with Communist administration are to be destroyed and men are to be taken along as hostages. If it is not possible to produce the people who have participated in any way in the insurrection or to seize them, reprisal measures of a general kind may be deemed advisable, for instance the shooting to death of all male inhabitants from the nearest villages, according to a definite ratio (for instance, 1 German dead—100 Serbs; 1 German wounded—50 Serbs).

The shooting of large numbers of reprisal prisoners and hostages was reported to Kuntze after the issuance of the foregoing order and directive.

Although he was advised of all these killings of innocent persons in reprisal for the actions of bands or unknown members of the population, Kuntze not only failed to take steps to prevent their recurrence but he urged more severe action upon his subordinate commanders. Not once did he attempt to halt these disproportionate reprisals. He directed the burning down of all villages having a Communist administration and the taking of all the male inhabitants as hostages. He directed the taking of reprisal measures against the population generally such as the shooting to death of all the male inhabitants of the nearest village on the basis of 100 for each German killed and 50 for each German wounded. In many cases persons were shot in reprisal who were being held in collecting camps without there being any connection whatever with the crime committed, actual, geographical, or otherwise. Reprisal orders were not grounded on judicial findings. The order and directives which brought about the killing of these innocent members of the population constitute violations of international law which are punishable as crimes. The orders he issued and his subsequent failure to take steps to end these unlawful killings after they had been reported to him makes him criminally responsible under the law previously announced and applied in this opinion to the defendant List.

With reference to the alleged mistreatment of Jews and other racial groups within the area commanded by the defendant Kuntze during the time he was Deputy Armed Forces Commander Southeast, the record shows the following: On 3 November 1941, the chief of the administrative staff, an official subordinate to General Boehme, who was in turn subordinate to the defendant Kuntze, ordered the immediate arrest of all Jews and gypsies as hostages and the deportation of their wives and children to an assembly camp near Belgrade. On 4 November 1941, a detailed report concerning the shooting of Jews and gypsies between 27 and 30 October 1941, is shown in the war diary of the 433d Infantry Regiment [704th Infantry Division]. (*NOKW-905, Pros. Ex. 143.*)* The lurid details of the shooting of these 2,200 persons is graphically recited in this report. A report under date of 5 December 1941 containing the notes of the Armed Forces Commander Southeast (Kuntze) made on a tour of inspection says in part: "All Jews and gypsies are to be transferred into a concentration çamp at Semlin (at present there are about 16,000 people there). They were proved to be the bearers of the communication service of the insurgents." On 4 February 1942, the 704th Infantry Division reported to General Bader that it had delivered 161 partisans, 17 Jews, and 2 Jewesses to the SD-Belgrade. On 19 March 1942, General Bader reported to the defendant Kuntze that 500 Jews had been transported from Metrovica to Semlin. On 10 March 1942, General Bader reported to Kuntze that in the Jewish camp of Semlin there were 5,780 persons, mostly women and children. On 20 April 1942, General Bader reported to the defendant Kuntze that in the concentration camps there were 182 hostages, 3,266 reprisal prisoners, and 4,005 Jews.

The foregoing evidence shows the collection of Jews in concentration camps and the killing of one large group of Jews and gypsies shortly after the

*Ibid.

defendant assumed command in the Southeast by units that were subordinate to him. The record does not show that the defendant Kuntze ordered the shooting of Jews or their transfer to a collecting camp. The evidence does show that he had notice from the reports that units subordinate to him did carry out the shooting of a large group of Jews and gypsies as hereinbefore mentioned. He did have knowledge that troops subordinate to him were collecting and transporting Jews to collecting camps. Nowhere in the reports is it shown that the defendant Kuntze acted to stop such unlawful practices. It is quite evident that he acquiesced in their performance when his duty was to intervene to prevent their recurrence. We think his responsibility for these unlawful acts is amply established by the record.

There is some evidence in the record that portions of the population were being deported for labor service in Germany, Norway, and other territories subjected to German influence. We are of the opinion that Kuntze's responsibility therefore, if such deportations were in fact carried out, has not been established beyond a reasonable doubt.

There is also some evidence concerning an improper use of the population in labor service in clearing mines and building military establishments. In this respect, the language of the reports is not definite and the testimony offered is not clear that such alleged acts were unlawful ones for which this defendant could be held responsible.

The defendant Kuntze denies that he was in any way responsible for the commission of unlawful acts by troops subordinate to him. While the record does not show that he ever ordered a ratio to be applied in the execution of reprisal measures, the record does show that he urged more severe measures and a direction that a ratio of 100:1 for each German killed and 50:1 for each German wounded be applied where the perpetrators could not be found. Reports made to him show that he was not without knowledge of the reprisals being taken and the ratios being applied. His claim of a lack of knowledge of the crimes being committed cannot be sustained.

* * *

The defendant Felmy had two assignments in Greece. He was appointed Commander Southern Greece about the middle of June 1941, and continued in the position until August 1942. During this period he had only three battalions of security and police troops subordinate to him. On 10 May 1943, the defendant became commander of the LXVIII Corps and continued in that position until the corps withdrew from Greece, an operation which was completed on 22 October 1944. In addition thereto on 9 September 1943, he assumed command of Army Group Southern Greece. He had subordinate to him the 1st Panzer Division, 117th Light Division, and a number of fortress battalions. Until the collapse of Italy, two Italian divisions were subordinate to him.

The defendant is charged with responsibility for the unlawful killing of innocent members of the population and the wanton destruction of villages and towns without military necessity existing therefor.

The defendant admits ordering reprisal measures but denies that they were unlawful. A brief review of some of these acts for which the defendant is responsible is therefore necessary. To begin with the defendant admits receiving the basic order of 16 September 1941 relative to reprisal measures up to 100 to 1 which has been often referred to in this opinion. He also received the Keitel order of 28 September 1941, relative to the taking of hostages from all sections of the population which has likewise been quoted herein. He also received and passed on the order of General Loehr, Commander in Chief Southeast, dated 10 August 1943, which states in part (*NOKW–155, Pros. Ex. 306*):

> In territories infested by the bandits, in which surprise attacks have been carried out, the arrest of hostages from *all* strata of the population remains a successful means of intimidation. Furthermore, it may be necessary to seize the entire male population, insofar as it does not have to be shot or hung on account of participation in or support of the bandits, and insofar as it is incapable of work, and bring it to the prisoner collecting points for further transport into the Reich. Surprise attacks on German soldiers and damage to German property must be retaliated in every case with shooting or hanging of hostages, destruction of the surrounding localities, etc. Only then will the population announce to the German offices the collections of the bandits, in order to remain protected from reprisal measures.

The defendant also received and passed on the order regarding reprisal measures issued by General Loehr, deputizing for Field Marshal von Weichs as Commander in Chief Southeast, under date of 22 December 1943, an order which has been previously quoted in this opinion. It says in part (*NOKW–172, Pros. Ex. 379*):

> Reprisal quotas are not fixed. The orders previously decreed concerning them are to be rescinded. The extent of the reprisal measures is to be established in advance in each individual case. . . . The procedure of carrying out reprisal measures after a surprise attack or an act of sabotage at random on persons and dwellings in the vicinity, close to the scene of the deed, shakes the confidence in the justice of the occupying power and also drives the loyal part of the population into the woods. This form of execution of reprisal measures is accordingly forbidden. If, however, the investigation on the spot reveals concealed collaboration or a conscientiously passive attitude of certain persons concerning the perpetrators, then these persons above all are to be shot as bandit helpers and their dwellings destroyed. . . . Such persons are co-responsible first of all who recognize communism.

The records show the following actions by troops subordinate to this defendant: On 9 September 1943, during mopping up operations of Levadeia "as reprisal measures for one murdered German soldier, 10 Greeks hanged." On 7 November 1943, the LXVIII Corps reports: "18 Communists were shot in Tripolis as reprisal for railroad sabotage committed lately." On 29 November 1943, the LXVIII Corps reports: "As reprisal for band attack on Tripolis-Sparta road, 100 hostages shot at the place of attack." On 5 December 1943, the LXVIII Corps reported "50 hostages were shot in Aighion for attacks committed lately," and on 6 December 1943, "for attack on railroad strong hold east of Tripolis, 50 hostages were hanged." On 6 December 1943, operation "Kalavritha" was commenced. In reprisal for the killing of 78 German soldiers, the 117th Division under the command of General von Le Suire carried out this attack. More than 25 villages were destroyed, and 696 Greeks are admitted to have been shot in reprisal. There is evidence of an eyewitness that approximately 1,300 Greeks were killed in reprisal. The defendant admits that this reprisal measure was excessive and says that he orally reprimanded General von Le Suire for the severity of this reprisal measure. No reprimand or complaint as to Le Suire's conduct appears in the documentary evidence before the Tribunal.

The diary of the LXVIII Corps reports the following reprisal measures: on 17 January 1944, "In retaliation for an attack on one officer in the Rhizaes area, 20 Communists executed"; on 22 April 1944, "In Tripolis 12 well known Communists were shot as a retaliation measure for the murder of a rural police officer"; on 23 February 1944, "Shooting of 200 hostages from the Tripolis hostage camp at the place of attack." This reprisal was for two truck convoy attacks resulting in 33 German dead and nine wounded. On 11 March 1944, for an attack on an armed German convoy, General Le Suire asked and was granted permission by this defendant to shoot "200 hostages (Communists) to be taken out of all hostage camps." Defendant contends that only 141 hostages were actually shot. The extent of the reprisals taken in the area of the LXVIII Corps is shown by the testimony of the defendant who says that between July and December 1943, 91 acts of sabotage occurred and 60 reprisals taken, and from January to June 1944 there was a monthly average of 55 acts of sabotage and engagements with bands.

It hardly seems necessary for us to point out that many of these reprisal killings were excessive and many were unlawful because there was no connection between the inhabitants shot and the offense committed. Reprisals were taken against special groups, such as "Communists" and "bandit suspects" without any relationship to the offense being established. The Kalavritha Operation can only be described as plain murder and a wanton destruction of property. The assertion of the defendant that he orally reprimanded General von Le Suire for the severity of this operation does not appear too convincing in view of the recommendations later made by defendant for the advancement of Le Suire to a higher command. Reprisal measures were carried out in the corps area without rhyme or reason. They became a part of the tactical campaign for the suppression of the bands in the first instance rather than as a last resort. It is plain that deterring the local population at the scene of the offense was not the primary objective. Reprisal prisoners were taken from hostage camps generally and at points distant from the place where the offenses occurred. It was more the case of an eye for an eye than an honest attempt to restrain the population by a use of hostage and reprisal measures as a last resort.

On 5 April 1944, the notorious "blood bath" at Klissura occurred. (*NOKW–469, Pros. Ex. 482.*) The facts are: On the date in question an engagement between bands and German troops occurred about 2½ kilometers outside the village of Klissura. After the retreat of the bands, the troops moved into the village and began searching for evidence of band support. None was found. Later in the afternoon, units of the 7th SS Panzer Grenadier Regiment entered the village and began almost immediately to kill the inhabitants. At least 215 persons, and undoubtedly more, were killed. Among these killed were 9 children less than 1 year old, 6 between 1 and 2 years of age, 8 between 2 and 3 years, 11 between 3 and 4 years, and 4 between 4 and 5 years. There were 72 massacred who were less than 15 years of age, and 7 people in excess of 80 years. No justification existed for this outrage. It was plain murder.

On 10 June 1944, troops of this same regiment carried out a reprisal measure against the inhabitants of the village of Distomon. (*NOKW–467, Pros. Ex. 484.*) It seems that bands were first engaged near Stiri, 5 kilometers southeast of Distomon. After the defeat of the bands, the troops returned to Distomon and shot approximately 300 of the population, including men, women, and children. It also was plain calculated murder.

A complaint was voiced by the Plenipotentiary of the Foreign Office and an investigation demanded. The defendant Felmy was charged with the duty of having the investigation made. He denies that this regiment was subordinate to him or that he had any disciplinary control over it. For the purpose of this discussion, we will accept his statement as true even though the order to investigate and report through Wehrmacht channels indicates the contrary. The point that is material here is that the investigation was made, the battle report of the commanding officer was found to be false, and the action of the regimental commander found to be in excess of existing orders. Upon the discovery of these facts the defendant Felmy recommended that disciplinary action (the method of trying minor offenses) be taken against the officer in charge in consideration of the sacrifices of the regiment in the combat area at the time. The defendant testified that he never knew what punishment, if any, was assessed against this guilty officer. He seems to have had no interest in bringing the guilty officer to justice. Two of the most vicious massacres of helpless men, women, and children appear to have met with complete indifference on his part. The falsification of the battle report by the regimental commander seems to have been deemed the major offense.

War at its best is a business but under no circumstances can cold-blooded mass murder such as these two cases establish be considered as related remotely even to the exigencies of war. The defendant's attitude toward the innocent population is reflected in his indifference to these unjustified and brutal murders which took place within the area of his command. It is a matter that goes to the question of the defendant's character, intent, and purpose in carrying out the facts for which he is charged. The responsibility of the defendant for the killing of innocent members of the population by the exercise of unlawful hostage and reprisal practices is clearly established. We find the defendant Felmy guilty on counts one and two.

The defendant Lanz was appointed to command XXII Mountain Corps on 25 August 1943 and actually assumed the position on 9 September 1943. The corps command was, generally speaking, the Epirus area of Greece. This consisted of the area between the Gulf of Corinth and Albania lying west of the Pindus Mountains. The corps headquarters was in Ioannina. The defendant is charged with the responsibility for killing hostages and reprisal prisoners in violation of international law and with the unlawful killing of Italian officers after the Italian capitulation.

A brief summarization of the evidence against the defendant is required. On 13 September 1943, General Stettner, commander of the 1st Mountain Division, a unit subordinate to the defendant and whose headquarters was at the time also in Ioannina, issued an order in part as follows (*NOKW–1104, Pros. Ex. 451*): "In order to oppose energetically the continued raids on convoys and members of the Wehrmacht, it is ordered that from 20 September 1943 onward for every German soldier wounded or killed by insurgents or civilians, 10 Greeks from all classes of the population are to be shot to death. This order must be carried out consistently in order to achieve a deterrent effect." On 29 September 1943, the XXII Corps reported: "Telephone sabotage in the area of Arta. Poles sawed off at two places. Thirty male civilian suspects arrested and shot." On 3 October 1943, the defendant issued an order reading in part as follows: "On account of the repeated cable sabotage in the area of Arta 30 distinguished citizens (Greeks) from Arta and 10 distinguished citizens (Greeks) from Filipias are to be arrested and kept as hostages. The population is to be notified that for every further cable sabotage 10 of these 40 hostages will be shot to death." The defendant denies that any of these hostages were shot and there is no evidence in the record to the contrary. On 4 October 1943, the 1st Mountain Division reported to the XXII Corps as follows: "Mopping up operations Eisl continue beyond Alomotros. Villages destroyed as reprisal measure. All civilians shot to death." On 18 October 1943, the 1st Mountain Division reported to the XXII Corps as follows: "Shot to death: Paramythia—reprisal measure for 6 murdered German soldiers, 58. Thereakision—reprisal measure for murder of Lieutenant Colonel Salminger, 14. Arta, Klissura—Suspicious elements near the localities where attacks had occurred (about), 30. Ioannina City—4." On 25 October 1943, the 1st Mountain Division issued a special directive to its subordinate units which stated in part: "If a member of the German Wehrmacht is killed by either attack or murder in a territory considered pacified, 50 Greeks (male) are to be shot for one murdered German. . . . The decision regarding executions for losses in band combat is made by the competent troop commander. Here also the ratio is 1:50. The prerequisite for the order of execution is indubitable proof that the population of a village has participated in hostile action against the German armed forces. In addition, the villages are to be destroyed." This order supersedes that of 13 September 1943. Numerous killings of hostages and reprisal prisoners, in addition to those enumerated, appear in the record. There are reports to the effect that "all the inhabitants" of named villages and "all men capable of bearing arms" were shot to death. Persons designated as "civilians" were shot on numerous occasions.

The orders for the taking of reprisal measures were clearly unlawful. An order to shoot 50 Greeks for each German killed regardless of circumstances meets the legal objections hereinbefore stated in this opinion. Instead of reprisals against innocent inhabitants being taken as a last resort, they were more often taken in the first instance. Reprisal killings were often carried out against the inmates of hostage camps and not against the population having some relationship with the crime committed. Attacks by armed bands having no connection with the local population were avenged by killing innocent inhabitants who had no possible association with the guilty. Many villages were destroyed and the civilian inhabitants shot without any logical reason at all except to wreak vengeance upon the population generally. According to the reports in evidence, court martial proceedings were not held. The killings were had on the order of the competent field commander, the evidence showing that battalion commanders sometimes gave such orders. The defendant says that as a tactical commander he was too busy to give attention to the matter of reprisals. This is a very lame excuse. The unlawful killing of innocent people is a matter that demands prompt and efficient handling by the highest officer of any army. This defendant, with full knowledge of what was going on, did absolutely nothing about it. Nowhere does an order appear which has for its purpose the bringing of the hostage and reprisal practice within the rules of war. The defendant does not even contend that he did. As commander of the XXII Corps it was his duty to act and when he failed to so do and permitted these inhumane and unlawful killings to continue, he is criminally responsible.

The defendant Lanz is also charged as commander of the XXII Mountain Corps with having ordered or permitted the unlawful execution of Italian officers and soldiers of the surrendered Italian army. He is also specifically charged with ordering troops under his command to execute the captured Italian General Gandin and all officers of his staff. The general situation regarding the collapse of Italy and the surrender of its armies has been set forth in the portion of the opinion dealing with the defendant Rendulic and it will not be repeated here except as necessity requires.

The record discloses that the defendant Lanz knew when he assumed command of the XXII Mountain Corps that Field Marshal Badoglio had succeeded Mussolini as head of the Italian Government and Commander in Chief of the Italian Army. On 8 September 1943, he heard of the armistice which the Italians had signed with the Allies. On the same day, due to the absence of senior officers from Athens, General Alexander Loehr, commander in chief of Army Group E, commissioned the defendant Lanz to negotiate with General Vecchiarelli, the commander in chief of the 11th Italian Army. After much negotiating, General Vecchiarelli surrendered the 11th Army to the Germans on 9 September 1943. The surrender terms were carried out during the following 14 days, without difficulty insofar as troops stationed on the

Greek mainland were concerned. On the islands of Corfu and Cephalonia, however, difficulties arose. These two islands were occupied by one Italian division under the command of General Gandin. The defendant Lanz as commanding general of the XXII Corps demanded that General Gandin surrender his troops and the demand was refused even though General Vecchiarelli had directed him to do so. General Gandin vacillated, contending that his orders were not clear and that he had no right to surrender the division. The situation resulted in fighting between the German and Italian troops on the island of Cephalonia and the eventual surrender of the Italian forces, including General Gandin and his staff, on 21 September 1943.

During this stage of the proceedings, a Fuehrer order arrived directing that the 6,000 or 7,000 Italians of General Gandin's division were to be shot for mutiny. The defendant Lanz refused to carry out this order for the reason that it was neither feasible nor lawful to do so. The Fuehrer order was then modified providing only that the officers were to be shot for mutiny. The defendant objected to the shooting of all officers and advocated that the order apply only to the guilty. The evidence indicates that the defendant Lanz ordered the German commandant of the islands to determine the guilty officers by court martial proceedings. This was done and on 24 September 1943, General Gandin and his staff officers were shot.

A similar situation developed on the island of Corfu. Fighting ensued, the Italians surrendered, and the officers shot after a summary court martial. The record shows that a large number of Italian officers were shot in this manner. One instance shows that on 5 October 1943, 58 Italian officers were shot by troops subordinate to the XXII Corps.

The killing of these Italian officers was clearly unlawful. The evidence of the defendant shows that he believed that their killing was unlawful. While his protests to Army Group E, based on the illegality of the Fuehrer order, were successful in reducing the number of Italians to be subjected to the unlawful order, the fact remains that the killing of the reduced number was just as much a criminal act. That he gave the order to the commandant of Cepholonia to execute the guilty officers only, he readily admits. The Italian soldiers were not *francs-tireurs.* They were still allies of Germany, insofar as their commanding officers then knew, although they had notice that an armistice had been signed with the Allied Powers. If they were prisoners of war by virtue of the surrender of the 11th Italian Army by General Vecchiarelli, it is clear that they were entitled to the protection of the Geneva Convention, 1929, regulating the treatment to be afforded prisoners of war. This was not done in any material respect. The reasoning set forth on the same subject in this opinion as it pertains to the defendant Rendulic applies here and is adopted by reference to the present situation. We are obliged to hold that the killing of the Italian officers was a war crime for which the defendant is responsible.

We find the defendant Lanz guilty on counts one and three.

The defendant Speidel assumed the position of Military Commander Southern Greece in early October 1942, and remained in the position until

Sentences

The reading of the opinion and judgment having been concluded, the portion of the harbor Pyraeus and the adjoining coastal strip, a small section northeast of Athens and the Islands Salamis and Aegina. The balance of the area, including Athens, was controlled by the Italians. Under the second assignment his authority extended over the whole of Greece although such authority was limited to certain functions. He had no tactical or operational tasks in this position, they being in the hands of Army Group E.

As Military Commander Southern Greece, his chief tasks were the maintenance of public peace and order within the area occupied by German forces, the security of German troops and installations, and jurisdiction over crimes committed against the Germans by the population. As Military Commander Greece, his principal tasks were the maintenance of peace and order, the administration of the judicial authority over the population as to crimes and offenses committed against the Germans and their military installations and the handling of negotiations with the Greek Government. As in the case of his previous assignment, all tactical and operational matters were in the hands of Army Group E in Salonika.

Subordinated to the defendant were 7 subarea headquarters [administrative area headquarters] units. On and after 22 December 1943, reprisal measures could be ordered only by divisional commanders after agreement with the competent subarea headquarters. This order, promulgated by General Loehr as Acting Commander in Chief Southeast, provided in part: "The revenge for attacks which are directed against the unit and its installation may be ordered only by a German commander with the disciplinary authority to punish of at least a division commander in accord with the competent administrative subarea headquarters. If an agreement is not reached, the competent territorial commander is to decide. Reprisal measures for losses in the air corps, navy, police, and the OT [Organizationa Todt] are to be ordered principally by the territorial commanders."

That the Military Commander Greece could control the reprisal and hostage practice through the various subarea headquarters which were subordinate to him cannot be questioned. This conclusion is borne out by the testimony of the defendant and charts prepared by him. It is plainly established that all administrative subarea headquarters [administrative area headquarters] and local headquarters of his area of command were subordinated to the Military Commander Greece by the Keitel order of 21 December 1943.

The defendant contends that many of the acts charged against him were committed by or under the direction of the Higher SS and Police Leader, General Schimana. Whether General Schimana was subordinate to the Military Commander Greece insofar as the ordering of reprisal and hostage measures was concerned is directly disputed. We are convinced that the record shows that he was. In this respect the record quite conclusively shows that General Schimana was directly subordinate to Himmler as to matters of discipline, promotions, and matters of similar import. Ordinarily, Himmler insisted that all SS units remain wholly subordinate to him, a matter of which he was very jealous. But in the present instance, the matter is controlled by regulations issued by Fuehrer headquarters under date of 7 September 1943 which in part says [*NOKW–1438, Pros. Ex. 419*]:

> By agreement with the Chief of OKW, the Reich Fuehrer SS and Chief of the German Police appoints a Senior [Higher] SS and Police Leader for the area of Military Commander Greece. The Senior SS and Police Leader is an office of the Reich Fuehrer SS and Chief of the German Police, which is subordinate to Military Commander Greece for the period of its employment in Greece. . . . The military commander is authorized to issue directives to the Senior SS and Police Leader which are necessary to avoid interference with Wehrmacht operations and duties. They take precedence over any other directives. The Senior SS and Police Leader will receive policies and directives for the execution of these duties from the Reich Fuehrer SS and Chief of the German Police. He will carry them out independently, currently, and opportunely, informing the Military Commander Greece in as far as he does not receive any restrictive directives from the latter.

The defendant admits that General Schimana considered himself subordinate to the Military Commander Greece as to the ordering and carrying out of hostages and reprisal killings. That the Senior SS and Police Leader was a member of the staff of Military Commander Greece is shown by the Keitel order of 21 December 1943. The evidence is clear that the defendant is responsible for the execution of these measures except when they were taken during tactical operations on which occasions, of course, the responsibility rests with the tactical superior.

A review of some of the hostage and reprisal measures taken within area of the defendant's command and for which responsibility attaches, will be necessary. On 3 December 1943, the following report was made: "Nineteen Communist reprisal prisoners shot, as revenge for the murder and wounding of Greek police, by the Senior SS and Police Leader in Athens." On 31 December 1943, the defendant reported: "In December on the Peloponnesus 758 people were shot to death, including reprisal operation 'Kalavritha'. In the remaining areas hostages were seized, and to a small extent executions have taken place." On 9 January 1944, it was reported: "By (order of) Senior SS and Police Leader, 30 Communists were shot to death in reprisal for the murder of Greek policeman and for 36 attacks." On 10 January 1944, the Military Commander Greece reported: "50 Communists shot as reprisal measure for murdering two German police." On 13 March 1944, it was reported: "On the highway Sparta-Tripolis, truck convoy attacked. Eighteen Wehrmacht members dead, 25 heavily wounded, 19 slightly wounded, and 6 Greeks wounded. As reprisal, state of emergency for southern Peloponnesus. Shooting of 200 Communist hostages." On 18 March 1944, the defendant reported in part as follows: "Tendency to strikes and partial strikes at the railroad and several plants at the beginning of March were suppressed by energetic military measures; 50 Communists were shot immediately while others who were arrested are awaiting their sentence." While the defendant was absent from his command for almost 2

September 1943. From September 1943, until May 1944, he occupied the position of Military Commander Greece. His first assignment extended to a the action taken by his deputy as shown by the foregoing report. On 22 March 1944, the Military Commander Greece reported: "On the Peloponnesus, five Greeks hanged in reprisal for attack on railroad." On 22 March 1944, the defendant reported: "administrative subarea headquarters [administrative area headquarters] Corinth report 52 hostages in Tripolis and 44 hostages in Sparta were shot as reprisal measure on 21 March." On 1 April 1944, defendant reported: "Up to now—Wehrmacht one dead, 14 wounded. Tracks blocked only for a short while. The execution of 70 Greeks at the locality of the incident has been ordered." On 2 April 1944, defendant reported: "65 Communists in reprisal for railroad sabotage, 10 south La Rissa shot to death at the scene of the incident." On 6 April 1944, defendant reports: "In Verria [Veroia] (60 southeast West Solonika). Fire attack by bandits during roll call of the battalion. Losses of our own—four dead, eleven wounded of which eight are heavily wounded. One hundred and fifty people suspected of belonging to bands shot in Verria as reprisal measures." On 8 April 1944, the defendant reported: "50 Communists shot to death for attack on German soldiers (three dead) North Athens." On 25 April 1944, the defendant reported: "In Tripoli, 12 known Communists shot in reprisal for a murdered Gendarmerie officer." On 26 April 1944, the defendant reported: "Officers of the commander of the Ordnungspolizei [order police] attacked by about 70 bandits while on duty trip on the road Arachova-Amphissa (15 west Levadeia). Major Schulz and Major Krueger dead, Captain Unger and four men missing. Two passenger automobiles and two motorcycles were burned out. Three men found their way to Levadeia. Fifty Communists from Levadeia were shot as reprisal measures. Additional reprisal measures are intended."

That the foregoing killings were excessive in most instances is readily apparent. That no connection existed between the population and the offense committed in many cases is shown. That the reprisal and hostage practice here employed was not one of last resort but one of the first instance in most cases can be seen. The incidents cited show cases where the hostages were taken and killed at a distance from the place of the offense. Court martial proceedings are not mentioned. That the incidents recited, indicating the practice followed, were not in accord with international law is beyond question. The responsibility of the defendant therefore has been established beyond a reasonable doubt.

We find the defendant Speidel guilty on count one of the indictment.

Evidence has been produced in an attempt to show that the Allied armies, or units thereof, engaged in the practice of taking and killing hostages and reprisal prisoners. There is but one instance cited that even resembles a case of shooting in reprisal. As to this, the evidence shows that four persons were shot by Allied forces in Reutlingen, Germany, during the invasion. The official announcement proclaimed, however, that those responsible for the killing of a French soldier had been apprehended and shot. There is no convincing evidence that it was a hostage or reprisal shooting. It is not shown that a single hostage or reprisal prisoner had been killed by Allied forces throughout the course of the late war. It also has been stated in the evidence and argued to the Tribunal that the rules of war have changed and that war has assumed a totalitarian aspect. It is argued that the atom bombings of Hiroshima and Nagasaki in Japan and the aerial raids upon Dresden, Germany in the final stages of the conflict afford a pattern for the conduct of modern war and a possible justification for the criminal acts of these defendants. We do not think the argument is sound. The unfortunate pattern adopted in the Second World War was set by Germany and its allies when hostilities were commenced. The methods of warfare employed at Rotterdam, Warsaw, Belgrade, Coventry, and Pearl Harbor can aptly be said to provide the sources of the alleged modern theory of total war. It is not our purpose to discuss the lawfulness of any of these events. We content ourselves with the statement that they can give no comfort to these defendants as recriminatory evidence.

Throughout the course of this opinion we have had occasion to refer to matters properly to be considered in mitigation of punishment. The degree of mitigation depends upon many factors including the nature of the crime, the age and experience of the person to whom it applies, the motives for the criminal act, the circumstances under which the crime was committed, and the provocation, if any, that contributed to its commission. It must be observed, however, that mitigation of punishment does not in any sense of the word reduce the degree of the crime. It is more a matter of grace than of defense. In other words, the punishment assessed is not a proper criterion to be considered in evaluating the findings of the Court with reference to the degree of magnitude of the crime.

It has been suggested in the course of the trial that an element of unfairness exists from the inherent nature of the organizational character of the Tribunal. It is true, of course, that the defendants are required to submit their case to a panel of judges from a victor nation. It is unfortunate that the nations of the world have taken no steps to remove the basis of this criticism. The lethargy of the world's statesmen in dealing with this matter, and many other problems of international relations, is well known. It is a reproach upon the initiative and intelligence of the civilized nations of the world that international law remains in many respects primitive in character. But it is a matter with which this Tribunal cannot deal, other than in justifying the confidence reposed in its members by insuring to the defendants a fair, dispassionate, and impartial determination of the law and the facts. A tribunal of this character should through its deliberations and judgment disclose that it represents all mankind in an effort to make contribution to a system of international law and procedure, devoid of nationalistic prejudices. This we have endeavored to do. To some this may not appear to be sufficient protection against bias and prejudice. Any improvement, however, is dependent upon affirmative action by the nations of the world. It does not rest within the scope of the functions of this Tribunal.

months prior to 17 March 1944, he appears to have known of and approved Tribunal will now impose sentence upon those defendants who have been adjudged guilty in these proceedings. As the name of each defendant is called, he will arise, proceed to the center of the dock and put on the earphones.

The defendant Wilhelm List will arise.

Wilhelm List, on the counts of the indictment on which you have been convicted, the Tribunal sentences you to life imprisonment. You will retire with the guards.

Walter Kuntze. Walter Kuntze, on the counts of the indictment on which you have been convicted, the Tribunal sentences you to life imprisonment. You will retire with the guards.

Lothar Rendulic. Lothar Rendulic, on the counts of the indictment on which you have been convicted, the Tribunal sentences you to 20 years of imprisonment. It is the order of the Tribunal that you will receive credit upon your sentence for the time already spent in confinement and pending trial, namely, from 13 September 1946. You will retire with the guards.

Ernst Dehner. Ernst Dehner, on the count of the indictment on which you have been convicted, the Tribunal sentences you to 7 years of imprisonment. It is the order of the Tribunal that you receive credit upon your sentence for the time already spent in confinement and pending trial, namely, from 29 December 1946. You will retire with the guards.

Ernst von Leyser. Ernst von Leyser, on the counts of the indictment on which you have been convicted the Tribunal sentences you to 10 years of imprisonment. It is the order of the Tribunal that you receive credit upon your sentence for the time already spent in confinement and pending trial, namely, from 18 December 1946. You will retire with the guards.

Hubert Lanz. Hubert Lanz, on the counts of the indictment on which you have been convicted the Tribunal sentences you to 12 years of imprisonment. It is the order of the Tribunal that you receive credit upon your sentence for the time already spent in confinement and pending trial, namely, from 17 January 1947. You will retire with the guards.

Helmuth Felmy. Helmuth Felmy, on the counts of the indictment on which you have been convicted the Tribunal sentences you to 15 years of imprisonment. It is the order of the Tribunal that you receive credit upon your sentence for the time already spent in confinement and pending trial, namely, from 4 January 1947. You will retire with the guards.

Wilhelm Speidel. Wilhelm Speidel, on the count of the indictment on which you have been convicted the Tribunal sentences you to 20 years of imprisonment. It is the order of the Tribunal that you receive credit upon your sentence for the time already spent in confinement and pending trial, namely, from 13 December 1946. You will retire with the guards.

The defendants *Hermann Foertsch* and *Kurt von Geitner,* have been acquitted, shall be discharged from custody by the Marshal when the Tribunal presently adjourns. They will retire with the guards.

The Tribunal now stands adjourned without day.

THE KRUPP CASE

Nuremberg, July, 1948*

OPINION AND JUDGMENT OF THE UNITED STATES
MILITARY TRIBUNAL AT NUREMBERG
IN UNITED STATES *VS.* ALFRIED KRUPP ET AL.

JUDGE DALY: This Tribunal was established by and under an order issued by command of the United States Military Commander and Military Governor of Germany (U.S.), and the undersigned were designated as the members thereof. As thus constituted the Tribunal entered upon and completed the trial of the case. The indictment was filed with the Secretary General of Military Tribunals on 16 August 1947 and the case was assigned to this Tribunal for trial. A copy of the indictment in the German language was served upon each defendant on 18 August 1947. The defendants were arraigned on 17 November 1947, each defendant entering a plea of "not guilty" to all charges preferred against him. Thirty-four German counsels selected by the twelve defendants were approved and have represented the respective defendants. One defendant was represented by an American attorney, selected by him, in addition to German counsel.

The presentation of evidence by the prosecution in support of the charges was commenced on 9 December 1947, and was followed by evidence offered by the defendants. The taking of evidence was concluded on 9 June 1948. The Tribunal has heard the oral testimony of 117 witnesses presented by the prosecution and the defendants and 134 witnesses have been examined before commissioners appointed under the authority of Ordinance No. 7, of Military Government for Germany (U.S.) establishing the procedure for these trials. One thousand four hundred and seventy-one documents offered by the prosecution have been admitted in evidence as exhibits. One hundred and forty-five documents offered by the prosecution have been marked for identification. Two thousand eight hundred and twenty-nine documents offered by the defendants have been admitted in evidence as exhibits and 318 documents offered by the

**Trial of War Criminals,* Vol. 9, p. 1327 (Washington D.C., 1950).

defendants have been marked for identification. No document marked for identification has been considered unless it was one the contents of which justified us in taking judicial notice thereof.

Ordinance No. 7, referred to above, provides that affidavits shall be deemed admissible. Exercising its right to construe this ordinance, this Tribunal announced at the beginning of the trial that it would not consider any affidavit unless the affiant was made available for cross-examination or unless the presentation of the affiant for cross-examination had been waived, and this ruling has been strictly adhered to.

The Tribunal ruled to the effect that the contents of affidavits made by defendants would only be considered as evidence against the respective affiants and not as against any other defendant unless such affiant or affiants took the witness stand and became subject to cross-examination by the other defendants or their counsel. None of the defendants took the stand to testify upon the issues in this case, and hence such affidavits have only been considered in accordance with the ruling made.

The trial was conducted in two languages with simultaneous interpretations of German into English and English into German throughout the proceedings.

Final arguments of counsel have been concluded and briefs have been filed. Each defendant was given an opportunity to make a statement to the Tribunal in accordance with the provisions of Article XI of Ordinance No. 7 of the Military Government for Germany (U.S.). Two of the defendants availed themselves of it, one in behalf of himself and the other in behalf of himself and the other ten defendants, and their statements were heard by the Tribunal. The briefs and final pleas of defense counsel consist of more than 1,500 pages, and counsel for the defendants consumed 5 days in final arguments. The briefs and arguments covered every conceivable question of law and fact connected with the case. The closing arguments were made on 30 June 1948, and the case was then taken under consideration.

The following named persons, twelve in number, are the defendants:

Alfried Felix Alwyn Krupp von Bohlen und Halbach
Ewald Oskar Ludwig Loeser
Eduard Houdremont
Erich Mueller
Friedrich Wilhelm Janssen
Karl Heinrich Pfirsch
Max Otto Ihn
Karl Adolf Ferdinand Eberhardt
Heinrich Leo Korschan
Friedrich von Buelow
Werner Wilhelm Heinrich Lehmann
Hans Albert Gustav Kupke

The indictment contains four counts, which for convenience may be generally described as follows:

(1) Planning, preparation, initiation, and waging aggressive war.

(2) Plunder and spoliation.

(3) Crimes involving prisoner of war and slave labor.

(4) Common plan or conspiracy to commit crimes against peace.

On 24 February 1948, the prosecution announced that it had completed the presentation of its evidence and rested its case-in-chief. Thereafter, during the session of 5 April 1948, the Tribunal, through the President, said, in part, as follows:

> On March 12 last, the defendants filed a joint motion for an acquittal on the charges of crimes against the peace. We construe this to be a motion for a judgment of not guilty on counts one and four of the indictment on the ground that the evidence is insufficient as a matter of law to warrant a judgment against them on those counts.
>
> After a careful consideration of this motion, the prosecution's reply thereto, and the briefs and the evidence, we have come to the conclusion that the competent and relevant evidence in the case fails to show beyond a reasonable doubt that any of the defendants is guilty of the offenses charged in counts one and four. The motion accordingly is granted and for the reasons stated the defendants are acquitted and adjudged not guilty on Counts one and four of the indictment.

Following this ruling the Tribunal filed an opinion stating the reasons for its conclusion.

In taking the foregoing action with respect to counts one and four, the Tribunal was guided by the rule as stated in one of the most authoritative American texts. This is as follows:

> The defense is not required to take up any burden until the prosecution has established every essential element of crime charged beyond a reasonable doubt. When the prosecution has finished its case, the defendant is entitled to an acquittal if the case of the prosecution is not made out beyond a reasonable doubt. When this is done, then, but not before, can the defendant be called upon for his defense.

Consequently in this judgment only those charges which are contained in counts two and three of the indictment remain for consideration.

Following the unconditional surrender of Germany, the supreme legislative authority in that country has been exercised by the Allied Control Council composed of the authorized representatives of the Four Powers: The United States of America, the United Kingdom of Great Britain and Northern Ireland, the French Republic, and the Union of Soviet Socialist Republics. On 20 December 1945, that body enacted Control Council Law No. 10. The preamble to Control Council Law No. 10 is as follows: . . .

* * *

The Krupp concern, as it is frequently referred to, originated with the business known as Fried. Krupp, founded in 1812. This was changed into a corporation (A.G.) in 1903. It was then known as Fried. Krupp A.G. and was a private, limited liability company. Bertha Krupp, the mother of the defendant Alfried Krupp, owned all but a very few shares of this company. The shares not owned by her were held by others for the purpose of complying with legal requirements, and were kept under careful control. In December 1943 Fried. Krupp A.G. was dissolved and in accordance with provisions of the "Lex Krupp," a special Hitler decree, the defendant Alfried Krupp became the proprietor. Since December 1943, the unincorporated, privately-owned concern, owned and controlled directly, and through subsidiary holding companies, mines, steel, and armament plants, two subsidiary operating companies, the Germania Shipyards at Kiel, and the Grusonwerk machinery factory at Magdeburg. Many mines, collieries, development, research, and other enterprises were conducted by and through many of the subsidiaries.

* * *

The words "Vorstand" and "Direktorium" were used interchangeably in documents in evidence. Both terms refer to the small group of men in the Krupp concern in whom management was centralized. "Direktorium" is the name given to that body after the reorganization in December 1943. There was, in fact, no difference in responsibility and activities within the concern.

In December 1943, pursuant to the provisions of the "Lex Krupp" as stated above, the Fried. Krupp Aktiengesellschaft was converted into the individually owned firm of Fried. Krupp with headquarters in Essen. On the same date 15 December 1943 simultaneously and on establishment of articles of incorporation of the Fried. Krupp, the firm was vested in the sole ownership of the defendant Alfried Krupp von Bohlen und Halbach. Upon registration in the commercial recording office the family enterprise had the name Fried. Krupp, and the branch enterprise Fried. Krupp, Aktiengesellschaft, Friedrich-Alfred-Huette and Krupp-Stahlbau, Fried. Krupp, Aktiengesellschaft thereafter had the trade names of Fried. Krupp, Friedrich-Alfred-Huette and Fried. Krupp, Stahlbau. Thereafter, the defendant Krupp had the name of Alfried Krupp von Bohlen und Halbach, whereas heretofore, his name had been Alfried von Bohlen und Halbach. After the conversion in December 1943 the owner of the family enterprise, Alfried Krupp von Bohlen und Halbach, had the full responsibility and direction of the entire enterprise. To assist him he appointed a business management with the name, "Das Direktorium." The regular and deputy members of the former Vorstand, with the exception of the defendant Loeser, who had resigned, continued to be the regular and deputy members of the Direktorium. Thereafter, they had authority to sign for the firm in place of the owner, and without mention of "Prokura."

The authority to sign for the individually owned firm by the others who were formerly the authorized agents of the Fried. Krupp Aktiengesellschaft was confirmed. No change was made with regard to the subsidiary companies which were continued to be managed as independent legal entities.

Control and management of the subsidiary companies was maintained in a number of ways. At least one member of the Vorstand was on the Aufsichtsrat of each of the principal subsidiary companies. The defendants Krupp, Loeser, and Janssen were members of the Aufsichtsrat at the Germaniawerft and the Grusonwerk, during various periods. The members of the Vorstand of the principal subsidiaries were required to and did submit regular reports of their activities to the parent company at Essen. Financial questions of consequence were decided by the Vorstand of the parent company, including all capital investments in excess of 5,000 Reichsmarks.

The defendant Loeser entered the Krupp firm on 1 October 1937 as a member of the Vorstand. The defendant Krupp became a member of the Vorstand in 1938. The third member was Paul Goerens. In April 1943 the Vorstand was enlarged, and the defendants Erich Mueller, Houdremont, and Janssen also became members, as did one Fritz Mueller. Before that, these four had all been deputy directors, and then deputy Vorstand members. In 1937 the defendant Janssen became deputy director. In 1938 the defendants Eberhardt, Houdremont, Korschan, Ihn, and Erich Mueller became deputy directors. In 1941 Pfirsch who had been a deputy director since 1923 and the defendants Janssen, Korschan, and Mueller were made deputy Vorstand members. In 1943 the defendants Eberhardt and Ihn were made deputy Vorstand members. As previously stated, the regular and deputy members of the Vorstand with the exception of Loeser were made regular and deputy members of the Direktorium when Fried. Krupp A.G. became the private firm Fried. Krupp in 1943.

Until 1943 various phases of activities were divided among the three members of the Vorstand. One field was finance and administration which had been under the direction of the defendant Loeser, and was under the direction of the defendant Janssen after Loeser resigned. Production in the plants was under Goerens, and the design, sale, and development of war material had been under the direction of the defendant Alfried Krupp.

Although each member had his own sphere of activity, the management of the enterprise depended upon the coordinated efforts of the members. This has already been stated, as it was required by the charter of Fried. Krupp, A.G. The coordination of three departments was required on major enterprises.

When the Vorstand was enlarged in April 1943 Alfried Krupp became chairman of the Vorstand, and Goerens became deputy chairman. Houdremont was then put in charge of metallurgy and steel plants, and also in charge of machine plants after November 1943. From April 1943 on, Janssen was in charge of trade, finance, and administration. All of the foregoing were members of the enlarged Vorstand. These defendants continued in these activities when the Vorstand members became Direktorium members in December 1943 at the time Fried. Krupp A.G. became a private firm. The department directors were referred to as "Dezernenten." They had full responsibility for the results achieved by their departments, and apart from their immediate sphere of work, assisted the Vorstand in its capacity as management of the concern. An order issued by the Vorstand, dated 31 January 1942, provided in part as follows:

> The work of the Dezernenten with the plants outside the Gusstahlfabrik will generally be restricted to questions of a basic nature and decisions of considerable importance . . . . It is the plant manager's duty to get in touch with the respective Dezernenten when necessary, while on the other hand, the Dezernenten have to instruct the plant manager accordingly.

The defendants Houdremont, Mueller, Janssen, Pfirsch, Ihn, Eberhardt, and Korschan were all within this class at one time or another. The defendant von Buelow achieved a status which for all practicable purposes was the same as that of a department director.

Count Two—Plunder and Spoliation

All of the defendants except the defendants Lehmann and Kupke are charged with war crimes and crimes against humanity under count two of the indictment. They are accused of having exploited, as principals or as accessories in consequence of a deliberate design and policy, territories occupied by German armed forces in a ruthless way, far beyond the needs of the army of occupation and in disregard of the needs of the local economy.

These acts are alleged to have taken place in France, Belgium, and the Netherlands, Austria, Yugoslavia, Greece, and the Soviet Union; to have been committed unlawfully, willfully, and knowingly; and to constitute violations of the laws and customs of war, of international treaties and conventions, including Articles 46–56 inclusive of the Hague Regulations of 1907, of the general principles of criminal law as derived from the criminal laws of all civilized nations, of the internal penal laws of the countries in which such crimes were committed, and of Article II of Control Council Law No. 10.

* * *

As the records of the Hague Peace Conference of 1899 which enacted the Hague Regulations show, great emphasis was placed by the participants on the protection of invaded territories and the preamble just cited, also known as "Mertens Clause," was inserted at the request of the Belgian delegate, Mertens, who was, as were others, not satisfied with the protection specifically guaranteed to belligerently occupied territory. Hence, not only the wording (which specifically mentions the "inhabitants" before it mentions the "belligerents") but also the discussions which took place at the time make it clear that it refers specifically to *belligerently occupied country.* The preamble is much more than a pious declaration. It is a general clause, making the usages established among civilized nations, the laws of humanity, and the dictates of public conscience into the legal yardstick to be applied if and when the specific provisions of the Convention and the Regulations annexed to it do not cover specific cases occurring in warfare, or concomitant to warfare.

However, it will hardly be necessary to refer to these more general rules.

The Articles of the Hague Regulations, quoted above, are clear and unequivocal. Their essence is—if, as a result of war action, a belligerent occupies a territory of the adversary, he does *not*, thereby, acquire the right to dispose of property in that territory, except according to the strict rules laid down in the Regulations. The economy of the belligerently occupied territory is to be kept intact, except for the carefully defined permissions given to the occupying authority—permissions which all refer to the army of occupation. Just as the inhabitants of the occupied territory must not be forced to help the enemy in waging the war against their own country or their own country's allies, so must the economic assets of the occupied territory not be used in such a manner. . . .

Upon the facts hereinabove found we conclude beyond a reasonable doubt that the defendants Krupp, Loeser, Houdremont, Mueller, Janssen, and Eberhardt are guilty on count two of the indictment. The reasons upon which these findings of guilt are based have been set forth heretofore in the discussion of each specific act of spoliation.

The nature and extent of their participation was not the same in all cases and therefore these differences will be taken into consideration in the imposition of the sentences upon them.

The evidence presented against the defendants Karl Pfirsch, Heinrich Korschan, Max Ihn, and Friedrich von Buelow we deem insufficient to support the charge of spoliation against them as set forth in count two, and we, therefore, acquit Karl Pfirsch, Heinrich Korschan, Max Ihn, and Friedrich von Buelow of count two of the indictment.

Count three of the indictment charges all of the defendants of a violation of Article II, paragraphs 1 (*b*) and (*c*) of Control Council Law No. 10. These provisions are as follows:

> (*b*) *War Crimes.* Atrocities of offenses against persons or property constituting violations of the laws or customs of war, including but not limited to, murder, ill treatment or deportation to slave labor or for any other purpose, of civilian population from occupied territory, murder or ill treatment of prisoners of war or persons on the seas, killing of hostages, plunder of public or private property, wanton destruction of cities, towns or villages, or devastation not justified by military necessity.
>
> (*c*) *Crimes against Humanity.* Atrocities and offenses, including but not limited to murder, extermination, enslavement, deportation, imprisonment, torture, rape, or other inhumane acts committed against any civilian population, or persecutions on political, racial or religious ground whether or not in violation of the domestic laws of the country where perpetrated.

It is also averred that the acts relied upon as constituting violations of these provisions were likewise violations of the laws and customs of war, of the general principles of criminal law as derived from the criminal laws of all civilized nations and of international conventions, particularly of certain specified articles of the Hague Regulations of Land Warfare, 1907, and of the Prisoners of War Convention, Geneva, 1929.

All of the acts relied upon as constituting crimes against humanity occurred during and in connection with the war.

Civilians brought under compulsion from occupied territories and concentration camp inmates and prisoners of war were used in the German armament industry during the war on a vast scale. There is no contention to the contrary. Likewise, the undisputed evidence shows that the firm of Krupp participated extensively in this labor program. According to an analysis, introduced by the prosecution, of the documentary evidence, the whole enterprise consisting of about 81 separate plants within greater Germany employed, between 1940 and 1945, a total of 69,898 foreign civilian workers and 4,978 concentration camp inmates; the great majority were forcibly brought to Germany and detained under compulsion throughout the period of their service, as well as 23,076 prisoners of war.

The principal plant of the concern was the Gusstahlfabrik located in Essen, the headquarters of the enterprise. The Gusstahlfabrik is known in the record as the Cast Steel Factory, the name having been taken from the original factory with which became the nucleus of the Krupp enterprise. However, the name is misleading. It was not a factory but consisted of between 80 to 100 factories all located in Essen. We deem it necessary to deal in detail with this plant only, and for convenience we refer to it upon occasion as the Cast Steel Factory. With one or two exceptions, we need only refer in passing to the subsidiary companies located outside Essen.

It would serve no useful purpose to undertake to specify the number of prisoners of war and foreign civilian workers employed each year in the Cast Steel Factory. Taking, as the defense does, August 1943 as the key date, it is sufficient to say that at that time, of a total number of 70 to 76 thousand workers employed in Essen, 2,412 were prisoners of war and 11,557 were foreign civilian workers.

Under the Hague Regulations of Land Warfare, the employment of prisoners of war must be "according to their rank and aptitude." (Art. 6, para. 1.) Their "tasks shall not be excessive and shall have no connection with the operations of war." (Art. 6, par. 2.)

Article 29, of Geneva Convention, provides "no prisoner of war may be employed at labors for which he is physically unfit." Article 30 stipulates that "the length of the day's work of prisoners of war, including therein the trip going and returning, shall not be excessive and must not, in any case, exceed that allowed for civilian workers in the region employed at the same work. Every prisoner shall be allowed a rest of 24 hours of every week, preferably on Sunday." Article 31, paragraph 1, provides that "labor furnished for prisoners of war shall have no direct relation with war operations. It is especially prohibited to use prisoners for manufacturing and transporting arms or munitions of any kind or for transporting material intended for combat units." By Article 32, it is forbidden to use prisoners of war at unhealthful or dangerous work, and the same article also provides that any aggravation of the conditions of labor by disciplinary measures is forbidden.

In a compilation by the Reich Minister of Labor of the laws governing employment of prisoners of war published in the Reich Labor Gazette, 25 July

1940, there was a provision that "the work to be performed by the prisoners of war must not be directly connected with the operations of war." So far as it appears, this law was never amended or repealed. Keitel seems to have been responsible for an order to the contrary. There is oral testimony of two or three witnesses to the effect that they thought the order was issued on oral instructions from Hitler.

The laws and customs of war are binding no less upon private individuals than upon government officials and military personnel. In case they are violated there may be a difference in the degree of guilt, depending upon the circumstances, but none in the fact of guilt.

Practically every one of the foregoing provisions were violated in the Krupp enterprises. In the early stages of the war, it was sought to evade the provisions of Article 31 of the Geneva Convention and the corresponding provisions of the Hague Regulations as well as the German law above quoted by an interpretation alleged to have been given by the commandant of the prisoner of war camp or some other military authorities. This appears from a memorandum of a Krupp representative who attended a conference of counter-espionage employees of the armament industry of Wehrkreis 6, held at Essen on 5 December 1940. He reported to the officials of the Krupp firm as follows (D-198, Pros. Ex. 848):

> According to international agreement PW's may not be employed in the manufacture and transportation of arms and war material. But if any material cannot be clearly recognized as being part of a weapon, it is permissible to get them to work on it. Responsible for this decision is not the intelligence branch (Abwehrstelle) but the commandant of the PW camp.

This brings to mind the German practices in the First World War in the use of poison gas. By the Hague Convention of 1907 and the Geneva Convention of 1907, it was agreed that the signatories would not use "projectiles," the sole object of which is diffusing of noxious gas. The Germans sought to justify their use of gas by the insistence that in view of the explicit stipulation that "projectiles" are prohibited, the use of gas from "cylinders" was legal and this notwithstanding the effect upon the victim was much worse.

But in the recent conflict all pretense was in time abandoned and by the defense's own evidence, as well as that of the prosecution, it is conclusively shown that throughout German industry in general, and the firm of Krupp and its subsidiaries in particular, prisoners of war of several nations including French, Belgian, Dutch, Polish, Yugoslav, Russian, and Italian military internees were employed in armament production in violation of the laws and customs of war. It is equally clear that in many instances, including employment in the Krupp coal mines, prisoners of war were assigned to tasks without regard to their previous trainings, in work for which they were physically unfit and which was dangerous and unhealthy.

The practice began as early as August 1940. At that time, 185 Belgian and Dutch prisoners of war were employed at the Gusstahlfabrik in Essen. French prisoners of war were employed in armament production as early as

1941 and Russian prisoners of war beginning in March 1942. Polish prisoners of war were employed at ELMAG in 1944 and during the disastrous air raids in the fall of that year, more than 3,000 prisoners were employed in Essen. In the various subsidiaries the practice was likewise pursued. These included the Friedrich-Alfred-Huette, the Bergwerke Essen, the Grusonwerk, the Berthawerk, and the ELMAG. In the various enterprises 22,000 prisoners of war were employed in June 1944.

Russian prisoners of war were discriminated against in every material respect. It was shown before the International Military tribunal, hereinafter referred to as the IMT, and shown here that prior to the attack on Russia, the high Nazi policy makers had determined not to observe international law in the treatment of Russian prisoners of war. The regulations on the subject were signed by General Reinecke on 8 September 1941. They brought a protest from Admiral Canaris. He pointed out in substance that although Russia was not a party to the Geneva Convention, the principles of general international law as to the treatment of prisoners of war were applicable. Continuing, he said:

> Since the 18th century these have gradually been established along the lines that war captivity is neither revenge nor punishment, but solely protective custody, the only purpose of which is to prevent the prisoners of war from further participation in the war. This principle was developed in accordance with the view held by all armies that it is contrary to military tradition to kill or injure helpless people. . . . The decrees for the treatment of Soviet prisoners of war enclosed are based on a fundamentally different viewpoint

The IMT held that this protest correctly stated the legal position. However, it was ignored entirely. The reason is indicated by a note by Keitel, chief of the High Command of the Armed Forces, made on the back of Admiral Canaris' protest. This is as follows:

> The objections arise from the military concept of chivalrous warfare. This is the destruction of an ideology. Therefore I approve and back the measures.

It is well enough to refer just here to the testimony of General Westhoff, who was introduced as a witness by the defendants. He had been a regimental commander on the eastern front, but in February 1943 returned to Germany to join the Armed Forces High Command for prisoners of war affairs. The actual decisions with respect to these matters, he testified, were made by the chief of the Armed Forces High Command. The office of Westhoff dealt with administrative tasks, particularly with the observance of the Geneva Convention. He said that the order relating to the treatment of Russian prisoners of war did not meet with the approval of armed forces in general, and after a struggle they succeeded in having it rescinded and that as a result after December 1942, Russian prisoners of war were treated according to the Geneva Convention. This may have been the official attitude of the competent authorities, but it is abundantly clear that it was not the attitude which prevailed in the Krupp enterprise.

* * *

Conditions at the Krupp prisoners of war camps at the time under consideration were so bad that they came to the attention of the Army High Command. A contemporaneous document from the Krupp files records a telephone call made on 14 October 1942 by the Office of the Chief of the Prisoner of War Department of the Supreme Command of the Armed Forces, to the Krupp firm. The call was to the defendant von Buelow but he seems to have not been available and apparently it was taken by his secretary who made a record of it communicating it to von Buelow. The record is as follows (NIK–12356, Pros. Ex. 904):

> Subject: Telephone call by Colonel Breyer of the High Command of the Armed Forces, Department of PW's, Berlin. Colonel Breyer who wanted to talk to Mr. von Buelow, requested me to pass on the following to Mr. von Buelow:
>
> The High Command of the Armed Forces has lately received from their own offices and recently also in anonymous letters from the German population a considerable number of complaints about the treatment of PW's at the firm Krupp (especially that they are being beaten, and furthermore that they do not receive the food and time off that is due them. Among other things the PW's are said not to have received any potatoes for 6 weeks.) All those things would no longer occur anywhere else in Germany, the High Command of the Armed Forces has already requested several times that full food rations should be issued to the prisoners. In addition if they have to perform heavy work, they must also get corresponding time off, the same as the German workers. Colonel Breyer also informed me that the conditions at Krupp would be looked into either by the Army District Command or by the High Command of the Armed Forces themselves. He had requested General von der Schulenburg on the occasion of a trip to call at Krupp in person concerning this matter; unfortunately this had not been possible. I told Colonel Breyer that I could not judge the conditions but would pass on his information to Mr. von Buelow immediately.

When the foregoing information was communicated to the defendant von Buelow he passed it on to the defendant Lehmann with the advice that he had just had a call from a captain from the General Command Muenster, and that in the course of the conversation,—

> I mentioned the call from Colonel Breyer, and told him that these complaints were certainly not justified. Besides, I was not the proper authority but would pass on the matter to competent officers in our firm. May I request you to take care of everything further.

There were also complaints by army officers charged with the supervision of prisoners of war about conditions in the Krupp enterprise. In January 1943, they again told Eichmeier that the "Oedema cases only existed in Krupp camps."

In June 1943, the official vegetable rations for Russian prisoners of war were less than one-quarter pound per day. In view of this fact, it is quite understandable how the department under the charge of the defendant Kupke reported "that it is impossible to prepare two even moderately satisfying hot meals on one and a half liters out of this quantity."

In the light of the foregoing documents, it cannot be said that the Krupp firm was required by governmental directives to work prisoners of war who, in many instances, were bordering on starvation. The Cast Steel Factory at Essen (Gusstahlfabrik) had officially been declared a military plant exclusively at the disposal of the High Command of the Armed Forces and of the Wehrmacht departments under its command, "which will furnish the plant with detailed instructions." The official directive expressly stated that only these military departments will have authority over this plant.

This was confirmed by Jauch, commander of Stalag VI-F at Bocholt, whose affidavit introduced by the defense has already been referred to. He deposed that (*Lehmann 149, Def. Ex. 1006*) "naturally there were directives for the employment and treatment of prisoners of war which were based on the Geneva Convention. The executory decrees were issued by the High Command of the Armed Forces immediately. Thus the Stalags were only the organs which had to see to it that these directives were obeyed and not violated."

But apart from this evidence it is conclusively shown that the allocation of prisoners of war and their supervision was by the military authorities and, moreover, that requests by a firm for prisoners of war were granted only on condition that those physically unfit would not be put to work until they had been gotten in shape by proper feeding, or whatever measures were necessary.

This is made clear not only by documentary evidence offered by the defense, but also by the defense witness Borchmeyer who, beginning early in 1943, was the office chief of counterintelligence at the Stalag, charged with supervision of prisoners of war camps in that area. Borchmeyer did the best he could to exonerate the defendants and the Krupp firm, but in the light of the contemporaneous documents his efforts must be regarded as futile. He testified that in many instances, because of their poor physical condition, Russian prisoners of war had to be "fed up" and "treated very carefully in regard to food in order to bring them up to strength," and very often this was a long process. But he made it clear that in granting requests for allocation of prisoners of war the Wehrmacht did so with the distinct understanding that it was the obligation of the employer to see that they were in the proper physical condition before putting them to work. With respect to Russian prisoners of war in particular, he testified that "they should be pampered and treated like raw eggs" and he was emphatic in stating that if any prisoners of war were put to work in a physically unfit or undernourished condition it was not the fault of the Wehrmacht but in part at least the fault of the factory to which they had been allocated.

Moreover, he confirmed that the employment of prisoners of war in the Krupp enterprise, particularly in Essen, exposed them to great danger. Anticipating the alleged defense of necessity, hereinafter discussed, it is interesting to note that Borchmeyer testified that he had no fear of reprisals for the policy of "pampering" Russian prisoners of war.

There is much evidence by the defense as to the so-called "pampering" of Russian prisoners of war, by "feeding them up" with extra rations before they were put to work. Such measures seem to have been considered necessary at the most temporarily. The defense introduced a letter from the board of directors of Fried. Krupp, A. G., Essen, dated 26 September 1942, signed by the defendants Ihn and Lehmann, addressed to the Army High Command. In this letter it was pointed out that a recent shift of Russian prisoners of war allocated for essential war work were so weak and undernourished that even with the best intention they were unable to work, and that with the food due them they could not be strengthened enough to work in the near future. It was accordingly asked "whether it might be possible to authorize additional food necessary for a feeding-up campaign" of from 4 to 6 weeks, which would be necessary to get the prisoners of war in condition to work. The letter concluded that "as we are, under the circumstances described, very anxious to employ the Russian prisoners of war in the very near future, we should be most grateful if you would give us your opinion on this matter as soon as possible." (Lehmann 421, Def. Ex. 1186)

A reply to this letter, dated 15 October 1942, was as follows:

> As from 19 October 1942 new food regulations will be in force for Soviet prisoners of war with notable improvement of food allocations for these prisoners of war both in quality and quantity. The procurement of these supplies will make it possible to feed the Soviet prisoners of war adequately and to reestablish the full working capacity of the prisoners. Further provisions for special feeding-up of prisoners should therefore no longer be necessary. [Lehmann 422, Def. Ex. 1187]

Whatever may be said about the inadequacy of official rations prior to October 1942, and the efforts made by the Krupp firm to bring about an increase, there are two determinative facts which are established beyond doubt by contemporaneous documents taken from the Krupp files, some of which are quoted hereinabove. These are (1) that Russian prisoners of war were put to heavy work when, due to undernourishment, they were totally unfit physically, and (2) that not only was there no official requirement that this be done, but it was directly contrary to the orders of the competent officials.

* * *

Law on the Deportation and Employment of Foreign Civilian Workers and Concentration Camp Inmates

It is contended that the forcible deportation of civilians from occupied territory was perfectly lawful. The argument made in this connection by the ostensible leader of defense counsel needs an answer, if for no reason other than to indicate the nature of the principal defenses upon this phase of the case.

The substance of the argument is as follows: "There exists in the Hague Rules of Land Warfare no provision explicitly prohibiting the use of manpower from occupied territories for the purpose of war economy. Article 48 is certainly not conclusive. . . . Reference to international common law is not more conclusive. For the only case in modern history, the conscription of Belgian labor during the First World War has remained a completely open question as regards its admissibility under international law."

It is, therefore, insisted that the prosecution's position with respect to wholesale deportation on a compulsory basis of members of a civilian population of occupied territories "is based on a fundamental misconception of the first rule of war, viz., that measures necessary for achieving the purpose of war are permissible unless they are expressly prohibited, and that methods required for achieving the purpose of war are determined by the development of war into total war, especially in the field of economic warfare."

In principle this is the same argument made in connection with the asserted proposition that the concept of total war operated to abrogate the Hague Rules of Land Warfare. But the reference to the deportation of Belgian labor to Germany during the First World War requires an additional answer, if for no other reason than to keep the record straight. That the crime, on the part of imperial Germany, caused world wide indignation.

The deportations began after the German Supreme Command had issued its notorious order of 3 October 1916, "concerning restrictions of public relief." Shortly prior thereto the Reich Chancellery had declared in an expert opinion that " 'under the law of nations, the intended deportation (Ausschiebung) of idle (arbeitsscheue) Belgians to Germany for compulsory labor can be justified if (*a*) idle persons became a charge of public relief; (*b*) work cannot be found in Belgium; (*c*) forced labor is not carried on in connection with operations of war. Hence, their employment in the actual production of munitions should be avoided.' "

The obvious subterfuge lies in the fact that the measure was ostensibly directed against vagrants to combat unemployment in Belgium as an economic measure. But no one was deceived by this pretense and it was soon abandoned in a manner which indicated an awareness of the illegality of the procedure.

The protests were so wide spread and vigorous that the Kaiser was forced to retreat. These protests were based upon either the general principles of international law and humanity or specifically upon the Hague Regulations. For instance, the United States Department of State protests "against this action which is in contravention of all precedent and of those humane principles of international practice which have long been accepted and followed by civilized nations in their treatment of noncombatants in conquered territory."

The protest of the Netherlands Government pointed out the incompatibility of the deportations with the precise stipulations of Article 52 of the Hague Regulations. It was pointed out by Professor James W. Garner, scholar and author of high repute, that if "a belligerent were allowed to deport civilians from occupied territory, in order to force them to work in his war industries and thereby to free his own workers for military service, this would make illusory the prohibition to compel enemy citizens to participate in operations of war against their own country. 'The measure must be pronounced as an act of tyranny, contrary to all notions of humanity, and one entirely without precedent in the history of civilized warfare.' "

Negotiations through diplomatic and church channels to repatriate the deportees and stop the practice were partially successful. From February 1917, Belgians were no longer deported from the Belgian "Government General" and the Kaiser promised that by 1 June 1917, deportees who would not volunteer to remain in Germany would be repatriated.

Nevertheless, long after the end of the First World War, the unsuccessful effort of the Kaiser's government was to an extent upheld in Germany. A parliamentary commission created by the German Constituent Assembly to investigate charges made against that nation of having violated international law during the war by a majority report submitted 2 July 1926, stating that the deportations had been in conformity with the law of nations and, more particularly, with the Hague Regulations. The report proceeded upon the theory that "the workers in question did not find sufficient opportunity to work in Belgium and that the measure was indispensable for reestablishing or maintaining order and public life in the occupied territory." The Belgian Minister of Foreign Affairs expressed the sentiment of the civilized world when he declared that his country had erred in its belief "that at least on this point, the war policy of the Kaiser's government would no longer find defenders." And it should be noted in this connection that even a minority of the German parliamentary commission above-mentioned found no justification for the practice and upon the other hand, squarely condemned it.

It is apparent, therefore, that learned counsel's contention that "the conscription of Belgian labor during the First World War has remained a completely open question as regards its admissibility under international law," is based upon the fact that a majority of a committee appointed by the parliamentary body of Republican Germany found it to be in accord with the law of nations. We think it must be conceded that this is at least rather thin ground upon which to establish a negation of international customary law. However this may be, it is certain that this action by the majority of the committee of the German body did not operate to repeal the applicable Hague Rules of Land Warfare, particularly Article 52, which in the present case was shown beyond doubt to have been violated. Deportees were not only used in armament production in the Krupp enterprise, but in the latter years of the war the production of armament on a substantial scale reached could not have been carried on without their labor.

This was not only a violation of the Hague Rule of Land Warfare but was directly contrary to the expert opinion of the Reich Chancellery hereinabove referred to which preceded the order of the German Supreme Command of 3 October 1916, for the deportation of Belgians. As above indicated, that opinion, though providing a subterfuge for the illegal conduct, did annex as one of the conditions "that forced labor is not carried on in connection with operations of war. . . . Hence their employment in the actual production of munitions should be avoided."

The law with respect to the deportation from occupied territory is dealt with by Judge Phillips in his concurring opinion in the United States of America *vs.* Milch decided by Tribunal II. We regard Judge Phillips' statement of the applicable law as sound and accordingly adopt it. It is as follows:

> Displacement of groups of persons from one country to another is the proper concern of international law in as far as it affects the community of nations. International law has enunciated certain conditions under which the fact of deportation of civilians from one nation to another during times of war becomes a crime. If the transfer is carried out without a legal title, as in the case where people are deported from a country occupied by an invader while the occupied enemy still has an army in the field and is still resisting, the deportation is contrary to international law. The rationale of this rule lies in the supposition that the occupying power has temporarily prevented the rightful sovereign from exercising its power over its citizens. Articles 43, 46, 49, 52, 55, and 56, Hague Regulations which limit the rights of the belligerent occupant, do not expressly specify as crime the deportation of civilians from an occupied territory. Article 52 states the following provisions and conditions under which services may be demanded from the inhabitants of occupied countries.
>
> 1. They must be for the needs of the army of occupation.
> 2. They must be in proportion to the resources of the country.
> 3. They must be of such a nature as not to involve the inhabitants in the obligation to take part in military operations against their own country.
>
> Insofar as this section limits the conscription of labor to that required for the needs of the army of occupation, it is manifestly clear that the use of labor from occupied territories outside of the area of occupation is forbidden by the Hague Regulations.
>
> The second condition under which deportation becomes a crime occurs when the purpose of the displacement is illegal, such as deportation for the purpose of compelling the deportees to manufacture weapons for use against their homeland or to be assimilated in the working economy of the occupying country. . . .
>
> The third and final condition under which deportation becomes illegal occurs whenever generally recognized standards of decency and humanity are disregard ed. This flows from the established principle of law that an otherwise permissible act becomes a crime when carried out in a criminal manner. A close study of the pertinent parts of Control Council Law No. 10 strengthens the conclusions of the foregoing statements that deportation of the population is criminal whenever there is no title in the deporting authority or whenever the purpose of the displacement is illegal or whenever the deportation is characterized by inhumane or illegal methods. . . .
>
> Article II, paragraph 1(*c*) of Control Council Law No. 10 specifies certain crimes against humanity. Among these is listed the deportation of any civilian population. The general language of this subjection as applied to deportation indicates that Control Council Law No. 10 has unconditionally contended as a crime against humanity every instance of the deportation of civilians. Article II, paragraph 1 (*b*) names deportation to slave labor as a war crime. Article II, paragraph 1 (*c*) states that the enslavement of any civilian population is a crime against humanity. This Law No. 10 treats as separate crimes and different types of crime "deportation" to slave labor and "enslavement." The Tribunal holds that the deportation, the transportation, the retention, the unlawful use and the inhumane treatment of civilian populations by an occupying power are crimes against humanity.

In connection with the subject of deportation of civilians from occupied territory, it is interesting to note that as shown by a document introduced by the defense, General Thoenissen was dismissed from the service by the High Command during World War II because of his "refusal to violate" the laws of war and to deport French workers to Germany.

The deportation of Belgians to Germany also was over the vigorous protests of the military commander in Belgium, General von Falkenhausen. With reference to Sauckel's order introducing a compulsory labor service for the Belgians, he deposed that "this was done against my explicit and constant protest for I had various objections against a compulsory labor allocation and considered it more important to keep the indigenous economy in motion."

That the employment of concentration camp inmates under the circumstances disclosed by the record was a crime there can be no doubt. The conclusion is inescapable that they were mostly Jews uprooted from their homes in occupied territories and no less deportees than many of the other foreign workers who were forcibly brought to Germany. The only difference was that they had to go through all of the horrors of a concentration camp under the supervision of the SS before they finally landed at the firm of Krupp. That these persecutees had been arrested and confined without trial for no reason other than that they were Jews is common knowledge and in fact not controverted. The subject is dealt with exhaustively by the judgment of the IMT and there is no need to add anything to what is there said to show the unspeakable horrors to which these unfortunate people were subjected. However, in the present connection, one or two excerpts from the judgment are pertinent. It is there recited that "the Nazi persecution of Jews in Germany before the war, severe and repressive as it was, cannot compare, however, with the policy pursued during the war in the occupied territories."

After referring to the fact that in the summer of 1941, however, plans were made for the "final solution" of the Jewish question in all Europe, the judgment continues: "Part of the 'final solution' was the gathering of Jews from all German occupied Europe in concentration camps. Their physical condition was the test of life and death. All who were fit to work were used as slave laborers in the concentration camps. . . ." The "final solution" meant extermination.

Under the facts of this case it is obvious from what has been said as to the law that the employment of these concentration camp inmates was also a violation of international law in several different particulars. . . .

Necessity As a Defense

The real defense in this case particularly as to count three, is that known as necessity. It is contended that this arose primarily from the fact that production quotas were fixed by the Speer Ministry; that it was obligatory to meet the quotas and that in order to do so it was necessary to employ prisoners of war, forced labor, and concentration camp inmates made available by government agencies because no other labor was available in sufficient quantities and that, had the defendants refused to do so, they would have suffered dire consequences at the hands of the government authorities who exercised rigid supervision over their activities in every respect.

The defense of necessity was held partially available to the defendants in the case of the United States of America *vs.* Flick, et al., decided by Tribunal IV. There, as here, the defendants were industrialists employing prisoners of war, forced labor, and concentration camp inmates in the production of armament in aid of the war effort. Flick and one of his codefendants were nevertheless found guilty on the charge presently under consideration. This was applicable. The basis of this aspect of the decision appears from the following quoted from the opinion: . . .

The defense of necessity in municipal law is variously termed as "necessity," "compulsion," "force and compulsion," and "coercion and compulsory duress." Usually, it has arisen out of coercion on the part of an individual or a group of individuals rather than that exercised by a government.

The rule finds recognition in the systems of various nations. The German Criminal Code, Section 52, states it to be as follows:

> A crime has not been committed if the defendant was coerced to do the act by irresistible force or by a threat which is connected with a present danger for life and limb of the defendant or his relatives, which danger could not be otherwise eliminated.

The Anglo-American rule as deduced from modern authorities has been stated in this manner:

> Necessity is a defense when it is shown that the act charged was done to avoid an evil both serious and irreparable; that there was no other adequate means of escape; and that the remedy was not disproportioned to the evil. Homicide through necessity, i.e., when the life of one person can be saved only by the sacrifice of another, will be discussed in a subsequent chapter. The issue, it should be observed, is not simply whether a particular life is to be sacrificed in case of necessity, but whether it is right for a person to commit a crime in order to save his life. The canon law prescribes that a person whose life is dependent on immediate relief may set up such necessity as a defense to a prosecution for illegally seizing such relief. To the same general effect speak high English and American authorities. Life, however, can usually only be taken, under the plea of necessity, when necessary for the preservation of the life of the party setting up the plea, or the preservation of the lives of relatives in the first degree.

As the prosecution says, most of the cases where this defense has been under consideration involved such situations as two shipwrecked persons endeavoring to support themselves on a floating object large enough to support only one; the throwing of passengers out of an overloaded life boat; or the participation in crime under the immediate or present threat of death or great bodily harm. So far as we have been able to ascertain with the limited facilities at hand, the application to a factual situation such as that presented in the Nuernberg trials of industrialists is novel.

The plea of necessity is one in the nature of confession and avoidance. While the burden of proof is upon the prosecution throughout, it does not have to anticipate and negative affirmative defenses. The applicable rule is that the prosecution is compelled to establish every essential element of the crime charged beyond a reasonable doubt in the first instance. However, if the accused's defense "is exclusively one of admission and avoidance, or if he pleads some substantive or independent matter as a defense which does not constitute an element of the crime charged, the burden of proving such defense devolves upon him. As a general rule, in matters of defense, mitigations, excuse, or justification, the accused is required to prove such circumstances by evidence sufficient to prove only a reasonable doubt of his guilt. And if the circumstances relied upon are supported by such proof as produces a reasonable doubt as to the truth of the charge against the accused when the whole evidence is considered by the jury, there must be an acquittal." The question then is whether, upon a consideration of the whole evidence, it can be justly said that there is such a doubt.

The defense of necessity is not identical with that of self-defense. The principal distinction lies in the legal principle involved. Self-defense excuses the repulse of a wrong whereas the rule of necessity justifies the invasion of a right.

In the view of German writers the law of necessity involves not the assertion of right against right, but of privilege against privilege. But from the standpoint of the present case, the rule of necessity and that of self-defense has, among others, one characteristic in common which is of determinative significance. This is that the question is to be determined from the standpoint of the honest belief of the particular accused in question. Thus, with respect to the law of self-defense, Mr. Wharton quotes Berner, an authoritative German jurist:

> Whether the defendant actually transcended the limits of self-defense can never be determined without reference to his individual character. An abstract and universal standard is here impracticable. The defendant should be held guiltless (of malicious homicide) if he only defended himself to the extent to which, according to his honest convictions as affected by his particular individuality, defense under the circumstances appeared to be necessary.

Wharton himself says "that the danger of the attack is to be tested, . . . from the standpoint of the party attacked, not from that of the jury or of an ideal person."

We have no doubt that the same thing is true of the law of necessity. The effect of the alleged compulsion is to be determined not by objective but by subjective standards. Moreover, as in the case of self-defense, the mere fact that such danger was present is not sufficient. There must be an actual bona fide belief in danger by the particular individual.

The evidence of the prosecution with respect to particular defendants was sufficient to discharge the burden resting upon it in the first instance. Thereupon the burden shifted to the defendants of going forward with the evidence to show all of the essential elements of the defense of necessity to an extent sufficient to raise a reasonable doubt in the minds of the Tribunal upon a consideration of the whole of the evidence. In this respect the evidence falls short in a vital particular.

Assuming for present purposes the existence of the tyrannical and oppressive regime of the Third Reich which is relied upon as a basis for the application of the rule of necessity, the competent and credible evidence leaves no doubt that in committing the acts here charged as crimes, the guilty individuals were not acting under compulsion or coercion exerted by the Reich authorities within the meaning of the law of necessity.

Under the rule of necessity, the contemplated compulsion must actually operate upon the will of the accused to the extent he is thereby compelled to do what otherwise he would not have done. Thus, as Lord Mansfield said in the case cited in the Flick opinion as giving the underlying principle of the rule invoked:

> Necessity forcing man to do an act justifies him, because no man can be guilty of a crime without the will and intent in his mind. When a man is absolutely, by natural necessity, forced, his will does not go along with the act.

Here we are not dealing with necessity brought about by circumstances independent of human agencies or by circumstances due to accident or misadventure. Upon the contrary, the alleged compulsion relied upon is said to have been exclusively due to the certainty of loss or injury at the hands of an individual or individuals if their orders were not obeyed. In such cases, if, in the execution of the illegal act, the will of the accused be not thereby overpowered but instead coincides with the will of those from whom the alleged compulsion emanates, there is no necessity justifying the illegal conduct. That is this case.

Hence the Flick Case is distinguishable upon the facts. For instance, a determinative factor in that case is indicated by the following from the opinion: "With the specific exception above alluded to and as hereinafter discussed, it appears that the defendants here involved were not desirous of employing foreign labor or prisoners of war."

In the present case the evidence leaves no doubt that just the contrary was true. For instance, we have hereinabove referred to a letter from the board of directors of Fried. Krupp, A.G., Essen, dated 26 September 1942, addressed to the Army High Command, which as noted, concludes as follows (*Lehmann 421, Def. Ex. 1186*):

> As we are, under the circumstances described, very anxious to employ Russian prisoners of war in the very near future, we should be grateful if you would give us your opinion on this matter as soon as possible.

The minutes of a meeting at the penal camp Dechenschule, 14 March 1944, prepared by the defendant von Buelow, furnish another illustration. After reciting that most of the inmates to be confined in that camp would be people guilty of breach of labor contracts who had been apprehended in France by the military authorities, von Buelow concludes, "finally I pointed out to Kriminalrat

Nohles (of the State Police) that the question of labor allocation is decisive for us and that we would like to secure these valuable French workers for ourselves for this reason."

A letter of 18 September 1943, addressed to the employment office in Essen indicates the attitude of the Krupp officials toward the Reich policy of conscription of foreign labor. It is as follows (*NIK–15402, Pros. Ex. 1574*):

> The 1-year contracts of a great number of our French, Belgian, and Dutch workers of the Cast Steel Works will expire within the next 2 months. Since these people are not prepared to renew their contracts we intend to have them conscripted. With reference to the conversation with your Mr. Dieckmann we ask you to consider how the necessary formalities may be best carried out. This applies to about 200 persons.

But long before this the Krupp firm had manifested not only its willingness but its ardent desire to employ forced labor.

In December 1942 and prior thereto the Krupp firm maintained a labor recruiting office in Paris. Their representative was a Mr. Hennig, said to have "the best connections to all German and French departments." Learning that a new draft of bout 265,000 workers was to be made in occupied France during the month of January, the defendant Lehmann made a trip to Paris with a view of seeing that the Krupp firm got a larger share of these workers than was then to be expected. He had Dr. Servatius, Oberregierungsrat of the Regional Land Office [Land Labor Office] Rhineland, go with him. In reporting the result of his efforts, Lehmann said, among other things, "With our aid, our requests were then distributed properly to the various district commanders [Bezirkschefs] and [regional military] field headquarters [Feldkommandaturen]. As much as possible, the selection of the drafted individuals is then also to be undertaken with the help of one of our representatives."

Referring to the possibility of getting skilled workers from unoccupied France, Lehmann, in the same report, stated as follows (*D–196, Pros. Ex. 888*):

> Because of the new political situation in the so far unoccupied part of France, the French government agencies will from now on act energetically at the draft of workers in this region. As one of the first measures, the French railways will transfer to Germany approximately 460 skilled workers. That will be 60 percent of the skilled workers who have been promised to us for some time, but who could not be persuaded to sign the contracts and to leave. The workers will be sent during the first week in January from the various factories to Lyon, where they can be received by our representative and will be conducted to Essen.
>
> In the beginning of January, Mr. Hennig will also try immediately to start on their way to Essen the 210 skilled workers allotted to us from the locomotive factory Fougat, Beziers. On our part we shall try to achieve that these workers will not be considered as part of our January quota since they have been promised to us for some time.

The willing attitude of the Krupp officials toward the employment of concentration camp inmates is indicated by the minutes of a conference held on

5 June 1944 in the office of Ihn. This conference was attended by the defendant Krupp among others. The defendant Ihn prepared the minutes. The following quotation refers to the Friedrich-Alfred-Huette at Geisenheim. It is as follows:

> Mr. Vorwerk, F.A.H., will examine the question as to whether there is any possibility for the F.A.H., to employ any prisoners and convicts. If necessary the Cast Steel Works will try to include this requirement in their request.
>
> Messrs. Guenther, Graefe, and Geisenheim, are negotiating with the concentration camp in their zone. Although no result has been reached in these negotiations so far, Geisenheim will continue to deal with the question on their own. Only if no result is reached will the Cast Steel Works take a hand in the matter.

A copy of the minutes was distributed to the defendants Krupp, Houdremont, Janssen, Mueller, von Buelow, and Kupke, among others.

The efforts of the Krupp concern to expand during the war years also negatives the idea that they were acting under compulsion.

* * *

. . . we deem it not inexpedient to briefly examine the nature of the evidence offered by the defendants to establish the existence of the compulsion or coercion under which they claim to have acted. They introduced several witnesses who testified in general terms that because of the attitude of the Reich authorities, the officials of the Krupp firm had "no possibility of refusing a production quota."

Whatever may have been true with respect to Flick and other industrialists, the witnesses for the defense in the present case made it clear that the defendants acted not from necessity within the meaning of the rule invoked but from what they conceived to be a sense of duty. If it were permissible, as the defense seems to think, to show the subjective attitude of one person by the testimony of another, then that of the defense witness Schieber is typical. Schieber was an SS Brigadefuehrer and high official in the Speer Ministry, which was in charge of the allocation or the fixing of production quotas and seeing that they were met. He was examined about the nature of the coercion upon industrialists. He testified that "what is decisive is the nature in which public opinion was directed. The defamation of such a man who opposed the State. This defamation was so severe that I believe any reasonable man would have seen to it that he avoided it." Asked how "this defamation [would] express itself" he answered, "it would hardly be possible for me to list all these defamations one by one. In general, it was not defamation from above, but from the man's neighborhood, or from the man on the street, the block leader, or the children, for example. You know how difficult from 1943 on, or how severe the leadership of the people, and of industry in the whole State became after 1943." He further testified that "I believe that for the vast majority of

German plant managers, the moral coercion, namely the duty stood in the absolute foreground." And again, "a refusal to meet production programs does not occur in an orderly state which is at war. I am further of the view that when you speak of coercion to production that you might just as well call it a self-evident duty or task to produce." Asked about the Krupp firm in particular, he stated that "it regarded it as a patriotic duty to do what it could in aid of the war effort by meeting these production schedules."

This brings forward another aspect of the rule of necessity which as applied to the facts of this case needs consideration. It will be observed that it is essential that the "act charged was done to avoid an evil both serious and irreparable," and "that the remedy was not disproportioned to the evil." What was the evil which confronted the defendants and what was the remedy that they adopted to avoid it? The evidence leaves no doubt on either score. As said, Speer was the top official in charge of the allocation of production quotas and the ultimate arbiter concerning penalties in case they were not met. He testified as a witness for the defense in the Flick Case. Although he was available he was not offered as a witness in this case. However, under the liberal rules followed in these trials, short excerpts of his testimony in the Flick trial were allowed to be introduced in evidence by the defendants. The excerpts reflect that he was examined with respect to what would have happened to an industrialist prior to the implementation of an order of 6 September 1943, giving the main committee the legal basis for issuing directives to industrial plants. In dealing with the question presently under consideration we need not be concerned with the possibilities after September 1943, because many of the acts charged in the indictment were committed prior to that date, and moreover, so far as appears there were no changes in the attitude of the defendants. So far as the present question is concerned it was the same throughout.

From the excerpts introduced, it appears that Speer was asked and answered as follows:

> Q. Now, if an industrialist should have said, before the promulgation of this law, "The main committee has no legal basis, I shall do what I please." What would have happened then?
>
> A. The industrialist would have lost his plant. He would have lost every possibility of exerting any influence on his plant. Such cases did occur, but not because of a refusal by the industrialist, but merely brought about by the fact that a plant regularly failed to achieve the production required of it. As an example I might mention the replacement of the plant manager of Krupp-Markstaedt, whose position was filled against Krupp's wishes by a Hamburg plant manager.

In the present case, the possibility of "losing a plant" did not exist for any of the defendants except Alfried Krupp and not for him prior to December 1943 when he became owner of the enterprise. None of them had any property interest in the business. The most that any of them had at stake was a job.

So accepting Speer's testimony, the question from the standpoint of the individual defendants resolves itself into this proposition: To avoid losing my job or the control of my property, I am warranted in employing thousands of civilian deportees, prisoners of war, and concentration camp inmates; keeping them in a state of involuntary servitude; exposing them daily to death or great bodily harm, under conditions which did in fact result in the deaths of many of them; and working them in an undernourished condition in the production of armament intended for use against the people who would liberate them and indeed even against the people of their homelands.

If we may assume that as a result of opposition to Reich policies, Krupp would have lost control of his plant and the officials their positions, it is difficult to conclude that the law of necessity justified a choice favorable to themselves and against the unfortunate victims who had no choice at all in the matter. Or, in the language of the rule, that the remedy was not disproportioned to the evil. In this connection it should be pointed out that there is a very respectable authority for the view that the fear of the loss of property will not make the defense of duress available.

But the extreme possibility hinted at, was that Gustav Krupp and his officials would not only have lost control of the plant but would have been put in a concentration camp had they refused to adopt the illegal measures necessary to meet the production quotas. Considering Gustav Krupp's influence and friendship with Hitler and the influence in Germany of the firm in general, it is difficult to conceive of this possibility. The fate of minor industrialists hardly can be regarded as evidence of what would have happened to the officials of the Krupp firm in similar circumstances. Rohland, a witness for the defense, correctly described the situation. He was an industrialist whom Speer made deputy chairman of the Reich Association Iron, one of the most important nationwide economic groups in the war economy of Germany. He became involved in a serious controversy with Sauckel and Ley and the latter threatened him with dire consequences. But he testified that "Speer covered for me completely," and that whether "one who was in serious opposition with the Reich authorities was sent to a concentration camp as a consequence depended very much on the person and on the question of whether the person concerned was directly in touch with someone like Speer."

The firm of Krupp was even better protected than Rohland. It was not only a vital factor in the war effort, but the head of it, Gustav Krupp, was a personal friend of Hitler. Gustav Krupp, not only had contributed large sums of money to the Nazi Party in the campaign which resulted in their rise to power, but played a leading part in bringing to Hitler's support other influential industrialists. Throughout the war years he and the Krupp firm continued to be regarded by Hitler with high favor. If nothing else appeared, this is conclusively shown by the "Lex Krupp," a special decree of Hitler whereby of all industrial firms in Nazi Germany that of Krupp alone was enabled to continue as a family enterprise free from the manifold burdens of a corporate structure. All of the officials of the firm were important in industrial life in Germany and far from lacking influential friends.

Moreover, in all fairness it must be said that in any view of the evidence the defendants, in a concentration camp, would not have been in a worse plight than the thousands of helpless victims whom they daily exposed to danger of death, great bodily harm from starvation, and the relentless air raids upon the armament plants; to say nothing of involuntary servitude and the other indignities which they suffered. The disparity in the number of the actual and potential victims is also thought-provoking.

This phase of the case must not be left without reference to the fact that there is a flat contradiction running throughout the defense of necessity. Upon the one hand it is said that the acts of omission and commission were required by the multitude of directives issued by state authorities which the defendants were bound to obey under penalty of grievous injury. Upon the other hand, it is said that they risked grave danger by violating such directives and even defying the Gestapo in order to mitigate the plight of the victims. There are numerous examples of this for which there is neither time nor space. The record speaks for itself. Three instances, however, may be referred to. The Gestapo issued an order that pregnancy of eastern workers should be interfered with. This was contrary to the law and the ethics of the medical profession. The Krupp doctor did not want to obey the directive, but was afraid to take a stand without the backing of the officials of the firm. The defense claims that he was given this backing unqualifiedly, notwithstanding that throughout this case the power and influence of the Gestapo is held out as being one of the factors which hung over the heads of the defendants.

As a preface to the second instance, we quote from the final plea made by counsel for defendants Krupp and Ihn. After referring to the establishment of the Central Planning Board, and the so-called "tapeworm decree," he states (*Tr. p. 12571*):

> There is only one sentence which is quite clear in this decree. Only one man has the sole responsibility of meeting the requirements of war production, and that man is Speer, and he is also the man who issues very clear instructions prohibiting any considerations of private economy in industry.
>
> It is self-evident that no factory is any longer authorized to engage in peacetime production. But even any planning for peacetime conditions is strictly prohibited. Ruthless action is taken against any managers who disregard this prohibition, the conversion to exclusive war production is enforced by very robust methods.

Yet, the testimony of defense witness Kraus indicates that, whatever may have been true with respect to other industrialists, the officials of the Gusstahlfabrik were not intimidated by the situation described by counsel. During the war, Kraus was a "group chairman" and in December 1944 was appointed a plant director in the Gusstahlfabrik. After having testified that a "considerable peacetime production" was carried on during the early years of the war, he was then examined about such production during the later years. On this topic and with reference to the later years of the war, he was asked and answered as follows:

Q. Please tell us another few branches of peacetime production.

A. Well, we had our appliances production Nos. 1 and 2; we produced chemical containers. We even produced milk cans. Incidentally, whenever these investigation committees came they always objected to that, and we always had great arguments when we had to show what a number of different products we were manufacturing in the Gusstahlfabrik. We were even blamed for producing locomotives, and that was quite a considerable part of our total production.

Q. What about motor vehicles?

A. Yes, we made them too. I know that one of the inspecting commissions tried to close down some of the peacetime production in order to release the workers for war production.

Whatever may be said with respect to the relation to wartime production of the specific items mentioned by the witness, the fact nevertheless remains that it appears from his testimony that the Gusstahlfabrik in the later years of the war was engaged in what the witness said the "investigating committees" considered peacetime production and, so far as appears, nothing was done about it even though the "committees" objected thereto.

The third instance relates to the sale of Reich bonds by the Krupp firm. It was related by Schroeder, head of Krupp's accounting department and a witness for the defense. From his testimony it appears that in 1943 the Krupp officials became convinced that the war was lost and it was necessary to adopt a new policy looking to the post war period. At that time, the firm had accumulated government bonds in the amount of 200 million Reichsmarks, Schroeder said that "we started to sell these gradually so that when the war was nearly over we had only 68 million Reichsmarks in bonds. We did not on purpose sell all of them because that would have been too noticeable and it would have smelled too much of defeatism; therefore, we had to retain a certain amount of bonds." The witness further testified that this was very dangerous and hence was done with great secrecy. He justified the policy upon the theory that the firm had a responsibility toward the workers whose livelihood depended upon them.

Whatever the reason, the sale of these bonds amounted to treason under the laws of the Reich for which the penalty was death. It was the very type of thing which the dread Gestapo, of which so much is said in this case, was supposed to detect and prevent.

It is true that the sale of the bonds was not openly made but if it be conceded that in the case of invididuals so influential and important as the owners and officials of the Krupp firm that the risk was great, it must also be conceded that it was readily incurred whenever they thought there was involved interest of sufficient importance to justify such a course.

Law As to Individual Responsibility

As already said, we hold that guilt must be personal. The mere fact without more that a defendant was a member of the Krupp Directorate or an official of the firm is not sufficient. The rule which we adopt and apply is stated in an authoritative American text as follows:

> Officers, directors, or agents of a corporation participating in a violation of law in the conduct of the company's business may be held criminally liable individually therefor. So, although they are ordinarily not criminally liable for corporate acts performed by other officers of agents, and at least where the crime charged involves guilty knowledge or criminal intent, it is essential to criminal liability on his part that he actually and personally do the acts which constitute the offense or that they be done by his direction or permission. He is liable where his scienter or authority is established, or where he is the actual present and efficient actor. When the corporation itself is forbidden to do an act, the prohibition extends to the board of directors and to each director, separately and individually.

Under the circumstances as to the set up of the Krupp enterprise after it became a private firm in December 1943, the same principle applies. Moreover, the essential facts may be shown by circumstantial as well as direct evidence, if sufficiently strong in probative value to convince the tribunal beyond a reasonable doubt and to the exclusion of every other reasonable hypothesis.

Upon the facts hereinabove found, we conclude beyond a reasonable doubt that the defendants Krupp, Loeser, Houdremont, Mueller, Janssen, Ihn, Eberhardt, Korschan, von Buelow, Lehmann, and Kupke are guilty on count three of the indictment. The reasons upon which these findings of guilt are based have been set forth heretofore in the discussion of the facts under count three.

The nature and extent of their participation was not the same in all cases and therefore these differences will be taken into consideration in the imposition of the sentences upon them. The evidence presented against the defendant Karl Pfirsch we deem insufficient to support the charges against him set out in count three, and we therefore acquit the defendant Karl Pfirsch on count three of the indictment. The defendant Karl Pfirsch having been acquitted upon all counts upon which he was charged, shall be discharged by the Marshal when the Tribunal presently adjourns.

SENTENCES

PRESIDING JUDGE ANDERSON: The Tribunal will now proceed to pronounce sentences on those of the defendants who have been found guilty, and since I am in respectful disagreement with my colleagues about the phase of the matter, I will ask them to perform that task. Judge Daly.

JUDGE DALY: The defendant *Alfried Felix Alwyn Krupp von Bohlen und Halbach* will arise.

On the counts of the indictment on which you have been convicted, the Tribunal sentences you to imprisonment for twelve years and orders forfeiture of all of your property, both real and personal. The same shall be delivered to the Control Council for Germany and disposed of in accordance with the provisions of Article II, paragraph 3 of Control Council Law No. 10. The period already spent by you in confinement before and during the trial is to be credited on the term already stated, and to this end the term of your imprisonment, as now adjudged, shall be deemed to begin on the 11th day of April 1945.

You may be seated.

The defendant *Ewald Oskar Loeser* is not present. He has asked to be excused because of his condition of health, and his request has been granted. The defendant Ewald Oskar Ludwig Loeser, on the counts of the indictment on which he has been convicted, is sentenced by the Tribunal to imprisonment for seven years. The period already spent by him in confinement before and during the trial is to be credited on the term already stated, and to this end the term of imprisonment, as now adjudged, shall be deemed to begin on the 13th day of July 1947.

The defendant *Eduard Houdremont* will arise.

On the counts of the indictment on which you have [been] convicted, the Tribunal sentences you to imprisonment for ten years. The period already spent by you in confinement before and during the trial is to be credited on the term already stated, and to this end the term of your imprisonment, as now adjudged, shall be deemed to begin on the 10th day of September 1945.

The defendant *Erich Mueller* will arise.

On the counts of the indictment on which you have been convicted, the Tribunal sentences you to imprisonment for twelve years. The period already spent by you in confinement before and during the trial is to be credited on the term already stated, and to this end the term of your imprisonment, as now adjudged, shall be deemed to begin on the 10th day of September 1945.

You may be seated.

The defendant *Friedrich Wilhelm Janssen* will arise.

On the counts of the indictment on which you have been convicted, the Tribunal sentences you to imprisonment for ten years. The period already spent by you in confinement before and during the trial is to be credited on the term already stated, and to this end the term of your imprisonment, as now adjudged, shall be deemed to begin on the 10th day of September 1945.

You may be seated.

JUDGE WILKINS: The defendant *Max Otto Ihn* will arise.

On the count of the indictment on which you have been convicted, the Tribunal sentences you to imprisonment for nine years. The period already spent by you in confinement before and during the trial is to be credited on the term already stated, and to this end the term of your imprisonment, as now adjudged, shall be deemed to begin on the 10th day of September 1945.

The defendant *Karl Adolf Ferdinand Eberhardt* will arise.

On the counts of the indictment on which you have been convicted, the Tribunal sentences you to imprisonment for nine years. The period already spent by you in confinement before and during the trial is to be credited on the term already stated, and to this end the term of your imprisonment, as now adjudged, shall be deemed to begin on the 10th day of September 1945.

The defendant *Heinrich Leo Korschan* will arise.

On the count of the indictment on which you have been convicted, the Tribunal sentences you to imprisonment for six years. The period already spent by you in confinement before and during the trial is to be credited on the term already stated, and to this end the term of your imprisonment, as now adjudged, shall be deemed to begin on the 22d day of April 1947.

The defendant *Friedrich von Buelow* will arise.

On the count of the indictment on which you have been convicted, the Tribunal sentences you to imprisonment for twelve years. The period already spent by you in confinement before and during the trial is to be credited on the term already stated, and to this end the term of your imprisonment, as now adjudged, shall be deemed [to begin] on the 10th day of September 1945.

You may be seated.

The defendant *Werner Wilhelm Heinrich Lehmann* will arise.

On the count of the indictment on which you have been convicted, the Tribunal sentences you to imprisonment for six years. The period already spent by you in confinement before and during the trial is to be credited on the term already stated, and to this end the term of your imprisonment, as now adjudged, shall be deemed to begin on the 24th day of September 1945.

You may be seated.

The defendant *Hans Albert Gustav Kupke* will arise.

On the count of the indictment on which you have been convicted, the Tribunal sentences you to imprisonment for two years, ten months, and nineteen days. The period already spent by you in confinement before and during the trial is to be credited on the term already stated, and to this end the term of your imprisonment as now adjudged shall be deemed to begin on the 10th day of September 1945, and it shall end today. If there is any variance between the number of days between the dates, in any event you are to be released this evening.

You may be seated.

THE MINISTRIES CASE
Nuremberg, January, 1948*

Opinion and Judgment of United States Military Tribunal at Nuremberg in United States *vs.* Ernest von Weizsaecker et al.

On 18 November 1947, an indictment . . . was filed with the Secretary General of the United States Military Tribunals at Nuernberg. Generally stated, said indictment, consisting of eight counts, charged the defendants with having committed crimes against peace, war crimes, crimes against humanity, and with having participated in a common plan and conspiracy to commit crimes against peace, all as defined in Control Council Law No. 10, duly enacted by the Allied Control Council on 20 December 1945.

Several, but not all, of the defendants are charged under each of the counts of the indictment. The applicable provisions of Control Council Law No. 10 will hereinafter be referred to and set forth as they relate to each count of the indictment when such counts are reached for discussion and decision.

The indictment was served upon all of the defendants in the German language, more than 30 days before arraignment of the defendants thereunder. On 19 December 1947 the case was assigned to this Tribunal for trial by the Supervisory Committee of Presiding Judges of the United States Military Tribunals in Germany, in conformity with Article V of Military Government Ordinance No. 7, as amended, this Tribunal theretofore having been duly established and constituted, pursuant to said Ordinance No. 7, which ordinance was promulgated by the United States Military Governor of the United States Occupation Zone of Germany on 18 October 1946. The arraignment of the defendants took place on 20 December 1947, at which time all defendants pleaded "Not Guilty" to the charges in the indictment.

Throughout the trial of this case, all of the defendants were represented by German counsel of their own choice. One defendant requested that he also be allowed to retain American counsel to represent him. The request was granted.

* *Trial of War Criminals,* Vol. 14, p. 308 (Washington D.C., 1952).

The presentation of evidence in the case was commenced on 7 January 1948. Final arguments before the Tribunal were concluded on 18 November 1948. The transcript record of the case consists of 28,085 pages. In addition thereto, the prosecution and the defense together introduced in evidence 9,067 documentary exhibits, totaling over 39,000 pages. Generally accepted technical rules of evidence were not adhered to during the trial, and any evidence that, in the opinion of the Tribunal, had probative value was admitted when offered by either the prosecution or the defense. This practice was in accord with that followed by the International Military Tribunal, and as subsequently thereto provided in Article VII of the hereinbefore referred to Military Government Ordinance No. 7. In the interest of expedition the Tribunal, following the practice adopted by the International Military Tribunal, appointed court commissioners to assist in taking both oral and documentary evidence, but many of the principal witnesses and all of the defendants who testified were heard before the Tribunal itself.

In order that any relevant documentary defense evidence of which the defendants had knowledge or which they believed existed might be made available to the defense, the Tribunal in response to various defense motions uniformly ordered that the persons or agencies having possession or custody of such evidence make same available to the defense. This was even true with respect to documentary evidence in possession of the prosecution. Moreover, at the request of a number of the defendants, the Tribunal appointed a German research analyst, of the defendants' choice, for the purpose of making a search of files of the former Reich government, located in the Document Center in Berlin, under Allied control. Such research analyst spent many months in Berlin in this search for defense evidence. The same research expert was further authorized by this Tribunal to visit London for the purpose of research in behalf of the defendants and was, in fact, so engaged for a number of weeks with the cooperation of British authorities. Other representatives were likewise authorized to make search of former Reich government files in Berlin.

In arriving at the conclusions hereinafter reached with respect to the charges against the defendants as contained in the indictment, the Tribunal was undeviatingly adhered to the proposition that a defendant is presumed innocent until proved guilty beyond a reasonable doubt.

During the course of the trial, a motion was made in behalf of all defendants charged in count four of the indictment that said count be stricken. The motion was granted and a formal order in the matter made and filed by the Tribunal.

During the trial from time to time motions were also made in behalf of individual defendants to dismiss counts of the indictment relating to them on the ground that the Tribunal was without jurisdiction to try the defendants on such counts and on the further ground that the evidence adduced by the prosecution was insufficient to sustain the charges. Such motions were denied without prejudice, except in three instances where charges in certain counts of the indictment were dismissed with respect to certain defendants because of a failure of proof. Specific attention to the charges thus dismissed and the defendants affected thereby will be given when the charges involved in such dismissals are reached in the ensuing discussion of the individual counts of the indictment. Like attention will be called to instances wherein the prosecution, during the trial, withdrew certain charges against certain of the defendants.

In the final arguments and briefs of the defendants, the contention that this Tribunal is without jurisdiction in this matter was renewed. In this connection, attention is directed to the fact that a number of United States Military Tribunals of precisely the same type and origin as this one have heretofore had their jurisdiction questioned on similar grounds in the course of their trial of cases involving offenses defined in Control Counsel Law No. 10. (Flick, et al., Case 5; List, et al., Case 7; and Ohlendorf, et al., Case 9.) The statements made in the judgments of such cases in the course of disposing of the attacks made on the jurisdiction of such Tribunals, we deem to be conclusive answers to the challenge here made to this Tribunal's jurisdiction, and we accordingly reject the contention of the defendants that these proceedings should be dismissed because of the Tribunal's lack of jurisdiction.

The record, including briefs of counsel all of which the Court has considered and examined, amounts to approximately 79,000 pages. The evidence of this case presents a factual story of practically every phase of activity of the Nazi Party and of the Third Reich, whether political, economic, industrial, financial, or military.

Hundreds of captured official documents were offered, received, and considered which were unavailable at the trial before the International Military Tribunal (sometimes herein referred to as the IMT), and which were not offered in any of the previous cases before United States Military Tribunals, and the record here presents, more fully and completely than in any other case, the story of the rise of the Nazi regime, its programs, and its acts.

The Tribunal has had the aid of and here desires to express its appreciation and gratitude for the skill, learning, and meticulous care with which counsel for the prosecution and defense have presented their case.

Notwithstanding the provisions in Article X of Ordinance No. 7, that the determination of the International Military Tribunal that invasions, aggressive acts, aggressive wars, crimes, atrocities, and inhumane acts were planned or occurred, shall be binding on the Tribunals established thereunder and cannot be questioned except insofar as the participation therein and knowledge thereof of any particular person may be concerned, we have permitted the defense to offer evidence upon all these matters. In so doing we have not considered this article to be a limitation on the right of the Tribunal to consider any evidence which may lead to a just determination of the facts. If in this we have erred, it is an error which we do not regret, as we are firmly convinced that courts of justice must always remain open to the ascertainment of the truth and that every defendant must be accorded an opportunity to present the facts.

Before considering the questions of law and fact which are here involved, we deem it proper to state the nature of these trials, the basis on which they rest, and the standards by which these defendants should be judged.

These Tribunals were not organized and do not sit for the purpose of wreaking vengeance upon the conquered. Was such the purpose, the power existed to use the firing squad, the scaffold, or the prison camp without taking the time and putting forth labor which have been so freely expended on them, and the Allied Powers would have copied the methods which were too often used during the Third Reich. We may not, in justice, apply to these defendants because they are Germans standards of duty and responsibility which are not equally applicable to the officials of the Allied Powers and to those of all nations. Nor should Germans be convicted for acts or conducts which, if committed by Americans, British, French, or Russians would not subject them to legal trial and conviction. Both care and caution must be exercised not to prescribe or apply a yardstick to these defendants which cannot and should not be applied to others, irrespective of whether they are nationals of the victor or of the vanquished.

The defendants here are charged with violation of international law, and our task is: first, to ascertain and determine what it is; second, whether the defendants have infringed these principles.

International law is not statutory. It is in part defined by and described in treaties and covenants among the powers of the world. Nevertheless, much of it consists of practices, principles, and standards which have become developed over the years and have found general acceptance among the civilized powers of the world. It has grown and expanded as the concepts of international right and wrong have grown. It has never been suggested that it has been codified, or that its boundaries have been specifically defined, or that specific sanctions have been prescribed for violations of it. The various Hague and Geneva Conventions, the Constitution and the Charter of the League of Nations, and the Kellogg-Briand treaties have given definitive shape to limited fields of international law. It can be said that insofar as certain acts are prohibited or permitted by these treaties or covenants, a codification exists and specific rules of conduct prescribed. It does not follow however that they are exclusive, and assuredly it cannot be said that they cover or pretend to cover the entire field of international law.

In determining whether the action of a nation is in accordance with or violates international law, resort may be had not only to those treaties and covenants, but to treatises on the subject and to the principles which lie beneath and back of these treaties, covenants, and learned treatises; and we need not hesitate, after having determined what they are, to apply them to new or different situations. It is by this very means that all legal codes, civil or criminal, have developed.

Aggressive wars and invasions.—The question, therefore, is whether or not the London Charter and Control Council Law No. 10 define new offenses or whether they are but definitive statements of preexisting international law.

That monarchs and states, at least those who considered themselves civilized, have for centuries recognized that aggressive wars and invasions violated the law of nations is evident from the fact that invariably he who started his troops on the march or his fleets over the seas to wage war has endeavored to explain and justify the act by asserting that there was no desire or intent to infringe upon the lawful rights of the attacked nation or to engage in cold-blooded conquest, but on the contrary that the hostile acts became necessary because of the enemy's disregard of its obligations; that it had violated treaties; that it held provinces or cities which in fact belonged to the attacker; or that it had mistreated or discriminated against his peaceful citizens.

Often these justifications and excuses were offered with cynical disregard of the truth. Nevertheless, it was felt necessary that an excuse and justification be offered for the attack to the end the attacker might not be regarded by other nations as acting in wanton disregard of international duty and responsibility. From Caesar to Hitler the same practice has been followed. It was used by Napoleon, was adopted by Frederick the Great, by Philip II of Spain, by Edward I of England, by Louis XIV of France, and by the powers who seized lands which they desired to colonize and make their own. Every and all of the attackers followed the same time-worn practice. The white, the blue, the yellow, the black, and the red books had only one purpose, namely, to justify that which was otherwise unjustifiable.

But if aggressive invasions and wars were lawful and did not constitute a breach of international law and duty, why take the trouble to explain and justify? Why inform neutral nations that the war was inevitable and excusable and based on high notions of morality, if aggressive war was not essentially wrong and a breach of international law? The answer to this is obvious. The initiation of wars and invasions with their attendant horror and suffering has for centuries been universally recognized by all civilized nations as wrong, to be resorted to only as a last resort to remedy wrongs already or imminently to be inflicted. We hold that aggressive wars and invasions have, since time immemorial, been a violation of international law, even though specific sanctions were not provided.

The Kellogg-Briand Pact not only recognized that aggressive wars and invasions were in violation of international law, but proceeded to take the next step, namely, to condemn recourse to war (otherwise justifiable for the solution of international controversies), to renounce it as an instrumentality of national policy, and to provide for the settlement of all disputes or conflicts by pacific means. Thus war as a means of enforcing lawful claims and demands became unlawful. The right of self-defense, of course, was naturally preserved, but only because if resistance was not immediately offered, a nation would be overrun and conquered before it could obtain the judgment of any international authority that it was justified in resisting attack.

* * *

Is there personal responsibility for those who plan, prepare, and initiate aggressive wars and invasions? The defendants have ably and earnestly urged that heads of states and officials thereof cannot be held personally responsible for initiating or waging aggressive wars and invasions because no penalty had been previously prescribed for such acts. History, however, reveals that this view is fallacious. Frederick the Great was summoned by the Imperial Council to appear at Regensburg and answer, under threat of banishment, for his alleged breach of the public peace in invading Saxony.

When Napoleon, in alleged violation of his international agreement, sailed from Elba to regain by force the Imperial Crown of France, the nations of Europe, including many German princes in solemn conclave, denounced him, outlawing him as an enemy and disturber of the peace, mustered their armies, and on the battlefield of Waterloo, enforced their decree, and applied the sentence by banishing him to St. Helena. By these actions they recognized and declared that personal punishment could be properly inflicted upon a head of state who violated an international agreement and resorted to aggressive war.

But even if history furnished no examples, we would have no hesitation in holding that those who prepare, plan, or initiate aggressive invasions, and wage aggressive wars; and those who knowingly participate therein are subject to trial, and if convicted, to punishment.

By the Kellogg-Briand Treaty, Germany, as well as practically every other civilized country of the world, renounced war as an instrumentality of governmental policy. The treaty was entered into for the benefit of all. It recognized the fact that once war breaks out, no one can foresee how far or to what extent the flames will spread, and that in this rapidly shrinking world it affects the interest of all.

No one would question the right of any signatory to use its armed forces to halt the violator in his tracks and to rescue the country attacked. Nor would there be any question but that when this was successfully accomplished sanctions could be applied against the guilty nation. Why then can they not be applied to the individuals by whose decisions, cooperation, and implementation the unlawful war or invasion was initiated and waged? Must the punishment always fall on those who were not personally responsible? May the humble citizen who knew nothing of the reasons for his country's action, who may have been utterly deceived by its propaganda, be subject to death or wounds in battle, held as a prisoner of war, see his home destroyed by artillery or from the air, be compelled to see his wife and family suffer privations and hardships; may the owners and workers in industry see it destroyed, their merchant fleets sunk, the mariners drowned or interned; may indemnities result which must be derived from the taxes paid by the ignorant and the innocent; may all this occur and those who were actually responsible escape?

The only rationale which would sustain the concept that the responsible shall escape while the innocent public suffers, is a result of the old theory that "the King can do no wrong," and that "war is the sport of Kings."

We may point out further that the [Hague and] Geneva Conventions relating to rules of land warfare and the treatment of prisoners of war provide no punishment for the individuals who violate those rules, but it cannot be questioned that he who murders a prisoner of war is liable to punishment.

To permit such immunity is to shroud international law in a mist of unreality. We reject it and hold that those who plan, prepare, initiate, and wage aggressive wars and invasions, and those who knowingly, consciously, and responsibly participate therein violate international law and may be tried, convicted, and punished for their acts.

The "Tu Quoque" Doctrine.—The defendants have offered testimony and supported it by official documents which tend to establish that the Union of Soviet Socialist Republics entered into a treaty with Germany in August 1939, which contains secret clauses whereby not only did Russia consent to Hitler's invasion of Poland, but at least tacitly agreed to send its own armed forces against that nation, and by it could demand and obtain its share of the loot, and was given a free hand to swallow the little Baltic states with whom it had then existing nonaggression treaties. The defense asserts that Russia, being itself an aggressor and an accomplice to Hitler's aggression, was a party and an accomplice to at least one of the aggressions charged in this indictment, namely, that against Poland, and therefore was legally inhibited from signing the London Charter and enacting Control Council Law No. 10, and consequently both the Charter and Law are invalid, and no prosecution can be maintained under them.

The justifications, if any, which the Soviet Union may claim to have had for its actions in this respect were not represented to this Tribunal. But if we assume, *arguendo,* that Russia's action was wholly untenable and its guilt as deep as that of the Third Reich, nevertheless, this cannot in law avail the defendants or lessen the guilt of those of the Third Reich who were themselves responsible. Neither the London Charter nor Control Council Law No. 10 did more than declare existing international law regarding aggressive wars and invasions. The Charter and Control Council Law No. 10 merely defined what offenses against international law should be the subject of judicial inquiry, formed the International Military Tribunal, and authorized the signatory powers to set up additional tribunals to try those charged with committing crimes against peace, war crimes, and crimes against humanity.

But even if it were true that the London Charter and Control Council Law No. 10 are legislative acts, making that a crime which before was not so recognized, would the defense argument be valid? It has never been suggested that a law duly passed becomes ineffective when it transpires that one of the legislators whose vote enacted it was himself guilty of the same practice or that he himself intended, in the future, to violate the law.

Count One—Crimes Against Peace

The defendants von Weizsaecker, Keppler, Bohle, Woermann, Ritter, von Erdmannsdorff, Veesenmayer, Lammers, Stuckart, Darré, Meissner, Dietrich,

Berger, Schellenberg, Schwerin von Krosigk, Koerner, and Pleiger are charged with having participated in the initiation of invasions of other countries and wars of aggression, including but not limited to planning, preparation, initiation, and waging of wars of aggression in violation of international treaties, agreements, and assurances. The invasions and wars referred to and the dates of their initiation are alleged to have been as follows:

Austria	12 March 1938
Czechoslovakia	1 October 1938 and 15 March 1939
Poland	1 September 1939
United Kingdom and France	3 September 1939
Denmark and Norway	9 April 1940
Belgium, Netherlands, and Luxembourg	10 May 1940
Yugoslavia and Greece	6 April 1941
Union of Soviet Socialist Republics	22 June 1941
United States of America	11 December 1941

The prosecution dismissed this count as to the defendants Bohle, von Erdmannsdorff, and Meissner.

* * *

KEPPLER

The defendant, who was a manufacturer, became acquainted with and a follower of Hitler as early as 1927 and acted as the latter's economic adviser. He was a convinced Nazi and still retains a high degree of loyalty toward Hitler believing, as he says, that during the early years at least, Hitler's program was well-intentioned and was fraught with good for the German people, but as the years passed, Hitler, due to illness and strain, changed. When Goering became Plenipotentiary for the Four Year Plan, Keppler lost much, if not all, of his influence on economic matters, at least from a political standpoint, although he remained important in certain fields such as synthetics, fats, oils, and other materials.

In 1936 Keppler was given full authority over the direction of Nazi Party's activities in Austria. From that time on he, as Hitler's direct representative, exercised these functions. The Austrian Anschluss had long been the subject of Hitler's plans of expansion. No secret was made of it. When the Nazi Party expanded into Austria and while outwardly independent of the Reich Nazi Party, it was in fact wholly its creature. Its members and officers took orders from Hitler and held office only so long as they obeyed Hitler. After the unsuccessful Putsch in 1934, in the course of which Dollfuss was murdered, the Party was outlawed in Austria and, as the defendant and his witnesses claim, its members were subjected to discrimination and at times to imprisonment. But it persisted as an underground movement with support, financial and otherwise, from the Nazi Party in Germany. A party which commences an armed revolt and assassinates a head of a state can hardly be regarded as a persecutee if the government thus assaulted takes measures to prevent similar occurrences in the future, and that in this case a recurrence was reasonably to be expected there can be no doubt.

One of the leaders of the Austrian Nazi Party was Leopold, who was strongly of the opinion that forcible measures should be taken.

However, until Hitler felt sure that forcible action against Austria would not bring down upon him Italy as well as the other Western Powers, Leopold's attitude constituted a hazard. Keppler was appointed among other things to prevent the occurrence of that state of affairs. This he did, and Leopold was removed from the scene of action.

During 1937 the defendant Keppler and his assistant, the defendant Veesenmayer, made several trips to Austria, consulted with Party leaders, and directed the activities of the Party there. As a result of Schuschnigg's Berchtesgaden conference with Hitler of 12 February 1938, the Austrian Premier was compelled to appoint Seyss-Inquart a member of the Austrian Cabinet as Minister of the Interior and head of the Security Police, who with others bored from within, and continually increased pressure was brought by Germany and the Party on him and his government until on 9 March 1939 Schuschnigg determined to hold a plebiscite to determine the question of Austria's independence.

This to Hitler was a red flag, and events marched rapidly. Keppler was in Vienna on that date and was immediately called to Berlin, reaching there on 10 March. He there made a report to Hitler, and after this conference, on Hitler's order, he returned to Vienna. There is a dispute in the testimony as to the exact hour of his arrival and as to whether he delivered or reiterated the German ultimatum, namely, that Schuschnigg must resign and Seyss-Inquart be appointed in his place or the German Army would march in. President Miklas testified that Keppler delivered such an ultimatum to him, and Hornbostel of the Austrian Foreign Office testified that during that day he received reports not only of Keppler's and Veesenmayer's arrival at Vienna, but that Keppler had delivered an ultimatum to the Austrian President. We believe and find that he did so, although there is reasonable doubt whether this took place before or after General Muff, German Military Attaché at Vienna, had delivered a like one. But we deem it immaterial which ultimatum was delivered first.

The defendant would have us believe that he acted in a vacuum in this matter and had neither knowledge of nor activity in the unwarranted interference in Austrian affairs. His story, however, is quite incredible. He returned to Berlin to report, and after that, as he was ordered, he flew back to Vienna. He was there during the crucial hours. He admits conferring with Miklas and in fact the record of his telephone conversation with Goering so states. Keppler was in Vienna to do Hitler's will, and it is beyond the realm of possibility that he was not informed before he left Berlin precisely what was to occur and what part he was to play.

Neither Hitler nor the Third Reich had the slightest justification or excuse to interfere in Austrian affairs, particularly in view of the provisions of the Treaty of Versailles and the agreements which the Third Reich entered into with the Austrian state. Hitler's actions became aggressive as soon as he felt that it was safe to do so and as soon as it became clear that there might be a plebiscite which possibly would upset his plans. Resistance by Austria was useless and hopeless, and therefore none was offered when the Wehrmacht poured over the borders and took possession of the Austrian state. But before the army marched in, armed bands of the SS and other Nazi organizations under German direction took possession of the government, arrested its leading officers, and patrolled the streets. In the unlawful invasion of Austria Keppler played an important part, and we find him guilty under count one.

Bohemia and Moravia.—According to the defendant's statement, in December 1938—the exact date being uncertain—Hitler ordered Keppler, according to his statement, to take interest in Slovakian affairs. We think it quite likely that this was due to Hitler's fears that the tension between the Czechs and the Slovaks, which had apparently lessened as can be seen from Hencke's report of 28 December 1938, would disappear. Such a condition was highly unsatisfactory to Hitler's plans to destroy Czechoslovakia. On 7 March 1939 Keppler was present at the Goering conference with Tuka, Durcansky, and other Slovaks. On 11 March 1939 Keppler went to Pressburg, Bratislava, and negotiated with Sidor.

On 12 March Altenburg reported to von Ribbentrop that Keppler had telephoned that the situation in Slovakia was "in a mess," that Seyss-Inquart and Buerckel had been fooled by the people on the other side, and Sidor had apparently been bribed by the Czechs, and one couldn't do anything with him; that at present there was calm in Bratislava, and it would be rather difficult to find new starting points; and that Durcansky's proclamation had indiscreetly already reached foreign correspondents. On the night of 12–13 March 1939 Tiso was visited, and decided to fly to Berlin, and left Vienna at 1 o'clock in company with Keppler. He was received by Hitler at 1915 hours on 13 March, and in the course of that conference Hitler stated that he had been disappointed by the Slovakian attitude and had been faced with the difficult decision whether or not to permit Hungary to occupy it; that he sent Keppler as his Minister to Pressburg [Bratislava], to whom Sidor had declared that he was still a soldier of Prague and would oppose the separation of Slovakia from the Czechoslovakian nation. Hitler stated that he permitted Minister Tiso to come to Berlin in order to make the question clear in a very short time; that it was a matter of indifference to him what happened in Slovakia; and that the question was whether Slovakia wished to conduct her own affairs or not, but he, Hitler, did not wish anything from her; that it was not a question of days but of hours. Hitler stated that if Slovakia wished to make herself independent, he would support this endeavor and guarantee it, and he would stand by his word as long as Slovakia would make it clear that she wished her independence, but if she hesitated or did not wish to dissolve the connection with Prague, he would leave the destiny of Slovakia to the mercy of events for which he was no longer responsible. Tiso replied that Hitler could rely upon Slovakia, but he wished to be excused for the reason that under the impression made by Hitler he could not clearly express his opinion at that moment or could hardly make a decision; that he wished to withdraw with his friend and think the whole question over at his ease, but that they would show that they were worthy of Hitler's care and interest for their country.

On 14 March 1939 Tiso flew back to Bratislava, and Slovakia declared her independence.

On 15 March Hitler summoned the aged and ailing Hacha, President of the Czechoslovakian Republic, to Berlin, and at an early hour of the morning, after threats that Prague would be bombed, Hacha was forced to submit. But German troops had already marched into Czechoslovakia hours before Hacha succumbed to Hitler's threats. The German troops met with some resistance from Czechoslovakian forces, but the Czechs were speedily overcome and the remainder of the Czech state fell. Keppler was present at Hitler's headquarters during the Hacha conference, but claims that he was only there to listen.

The defendant professes to have known nothing about Hitler's plan, although in one of his statements he admits that he thought something of that nature might occur. We are unable to believe him. He played an important part in this matter. The separation of Slovakia from the Czechoslovakian state was an important and an integral part of Hitler's plan of aggression.

Nor did he go to Czechoslovakia merely as an observer. In his own affidavit he admitted that he was assigned in March 1939 to negotiate and conclude a treaty of friendship and defense with Slovakia. We find that the defendant had knowledge of Hitler's plan for aggression against Czechoslovakia, knew that it was indefensible, and that he willingly participated in it. We find him guilty under count one in connection with the aggression against Czechoslovakia.

WOERMANN

In addition to the general charges contained in count one, it is specifically alleged that the defendant Woermann and other defendants named "as high officials of the German Foreign Office played dominant roles in the diplomatic plans and preparations for invasions and wars of aggression, and later participated in the diplomatic phases of the waging of these wars." It is further specifically alleged that members of the German Foreign Office, including the defendants Woermann and von Weizsaecker, were secretly preparing the groundwork for aggression in Czechoslovakia by providing political, military, and financial assistance to the Sudeten German Party, under the leadership of one Konrad Henlein, and inciting that movement to lodge continual demands for the complete separation of the Sudetenland from the Czechoslovakian Republic.

It is further asserted that the defendant Woermann, together with other defendants, particpated in a series of diplomatic and political moves against Poland whereby, in disregard of recent assurances and agreements, the return of Danzig and the Polish Corridor was demanded as a pretext for aggression. Polish counterproposals for the peaceful settlement of German claims were rejected, and an energetic program to mobilize potential allies in the German cause of aggression and to neutralize France and Great Britain as possible opponents was undertaken. It is asserted that the "political propaganda and diplomatic blueprint for this war of aggression was carefully designed" by Woermann and other defendants with a view to shifting the apparent responsibility for the war to the victim. It is apparent that border incidents were staged and alleged acts of terrorism committed by the Poles against German nationals and racial Germans were fabricated and publicized. It is further asserted that all attempts by France, Great Britain, the United States, and other nations to persuade the German Reich to agree to a peaceful settlement of the dispute with Poland were rejected. It is then asserted that in the early hours of 1 September 1939, Germany launched this war of aggression which later involved Great Britain, France, and a great part of the world.

It is further asserted that defendant Woermann and others also participated in the preparation of the aggressions against Norway, Denmark, the Netherlands, Belgium, and Luxembourg, and it is further asserted that defendant Woermann and others participated in the preparation and planning of the attack against the Union of Soviet Socialist Republics on 22 June 1941. It is asserted that Woermann and others, through diplomatic efforts, secured the military support of Rumania and Hungary for such venture. It is further alleged that Woermann and other members of the German Foreign Office, from early 1941, made continuous diplomatic efforts to induce Japan to attack British possessions in the Far East. It is further alleged that Woermann and other defendants, as leading officials of the German Foreign Office, participated in the political development and direction of the occupied territories, particularly those territories wherein puppet governments under the domination of the German Foreign Office had been installed. By the maintenance of continuous diplomatic pressure, intimidation, and coercion, the puppet and satellite governments were compelled to support Germany in the course of its wars of aggression. Further, they participated in the partitioning of certain of the occupied territories, including Yugoslavia, and in the evolution of plans for the final integration of the occupied countries into the orbit of the German Reich after the cessation of hostilities.

Defendant Woermann was Ministerial Director and chief of the Political Division of the Foreign Office in Berlin with the title of Under State Secretary from April 1938 to April 1943.

This defendant testifying before the Tribunal on 6 July 1948 stated (*Tr. p. 11063*):

> I also did and do consider myself responsible for what happened in the Political Division of which I was head even when I did not approve or did not know the individual cases.

The defendant did seek to show that the office of chief of Political Division had decreased in significance so that during the time that he was head thereof it was an office of secondary importance. This however does not square with the facts. The record is replete with evidence of incidents showing that during the times in question Woermann was charged with and energetically carried out important duties and assignments which often involved the exercise of a wide discretion and had a bearing on the plans and policies which were being considered or were in the process of execution.

The defendant also sought to show that he was on unfriendly terms with his chief, von Ribbentrop, from 1938 to 1943, and in his testimony before this Tribunal on 6 July 1948 he alluded to various incidents to support such claim. This, however, is not especially significant for the fact remains that he actually stayed in office under von Ribbentrop from 1938 to 1943—five eventful and critical years. Apparently their differences were not so fundamental as to have prompted Woermann to obstruct the plans or wishes of von Ribbentrop or to cause Woermann to fail in satisfactorily complying with von Ribbentrop's wishes in connection with the carrying out of the aggressive plans and policies of the Nazi regime. That Woermann did actively participate in carrying out the criminal plans and policies of the Reich seems to be amply borne out by the testimony.

It appears that although von Ribbentrop, according to the statement of defendant, had indicated to the defendant that he did not desire to "receive any unsolicited advice" von Ribbentrop did, on 24 July 1941, send a secret wire to Woermann wherein he directed defendant Woermann to carry on a propaganda campaign "on an exact study of the weak spots of the American or English policy."

The evidence discloses that the political division which was under Woermann's charge, as above indicated, gave close attention to the carrying out of von Ribbentrop's wishes in this matter, for in November 1941, Woermann gave detailed instruction to officials in his department with respect to propaganda to be employed. Woermann also sent a secret code telegram to various German missions abroad which contained instructions for putting America in a bad light by means of propaganda therein suggested. The foregoing is of significance as indicating that wide discretionary power was in fact vested in Woermann's office and that he exercised the same to an extensive degree. Reference hereinafter made with respect to the charges against Woermann as they relate to the various countries involved further indicate the wide discretionary power vested in Woermann.

* * *

We come now to a consideration of the charges against Woermann with respect to the aggression against Poland. It is to be observed that on 4 May 1939 Woermann sent a secret telegram to the German Consulate in Bratislava, giving agenda for a military conference to be held between the Slovakian authorities and the Germans. This was obviously a preparation pointing toward Poland, and the defendant in his examination before this Tribunal, while not admitting it to be such, did admit that the Polish question had then come into the foreground. It appears that on 11 May 1939 Woermann transmitted a written order to the German Ambassador in London calling attention to the fact that the "persecution of all classes belonging to the German minorities in Poland, especially in the former Prussian provinces, has for some considerable time been on the increase." He requested in such communication that copies of certain reports inclosed by him, as to such anti-German measures and methods, and further reports of like nature which would in the future be submitted, should be made use of in contacts with the British Government.

On 8 July 1939, Woermann sent a telegram to a number of German foreign missions, requesting that they use certain language and representations with respect to Poland. On 22 August 1939 a memorandum was sent from the Political Division (Woermann's division) setting forth the policies to be followed with respect to England, France, and ten other countries, in case of a Polish-German conflict. The memorandum goes into comprehensive detail of the steps to be taken and representations to be made, as to those countries. In discussing this document during the course of examination before the Tribunal the defendant indicated that he could not remember it, but stated, "some of the things it contains, however, certainly came from the Political Division."

On 21 August 1939 Legation Councillor Heyden-Rynsch and a subordinate of Woermann submitted a memorandum to Woermann for his decision with respect to the measures which the High Command of the Armed Forces (OKW) would institute on the date preceding the invasion of Poland, such measures being news black-outs, closing of the frontier, etc. It appears that on 23 August 1939 Woermann took a very decisive and affirmative step with respect to the Polish aggression in that he sent a top secret telegram to the German Legation in Bratislava, advising the Slovak Government of reports to the effect that Polish operations against the Slovak border might be expected at any time, and that, therefore, to protect Slovakia against surprises, the German Government was requesting the Slovak Government to agree that the commander in chief of the German army might avail himself immediately of the Slovak Army, for the protection of Slovakia's northern border, and that the commander in chief of the German air force be permitted to use the Zipser-Neudorf airfield and, if necessary, that he be permitted to issue a general order to the Slovak air force, forbidding all aircraft to take off. In return for the above "cooperation" requested, the Germans would be willing, first, to safeguard the frontier against Hungary; second, to effect the return of the border territory ceded to Poland in the fall of 1938, in the event that Poland waged war against Germany; and third, to give assurances that, in case Poland waged war against Germany, the Slovak armed forces would not be used outside Slovakia. The wire stated:

> I beg to arrange that the Slovak Government give its assent to abovementioned measures immediately and without loss of time.

Woermann, on the stand, stated that the document "shows that it was not a matter of offensive, but of defensive measure." In view of conditions then obtaining in Slovakia, it was ridiculous to speak of Poland waging war against Germany, and Woermann's attempted explanation becomes farcical. On 28 August 1939, Woermann wrote a secret memorandum stating that Legation Councillor Hoffmann had, on 27 August, called from Bratislava, informing "us" that the Slovak Cabinet had accepted the German request to put all territory at German disposal for the deployment of German troops. The defendant Woermann, on examination on 9 July 1948, stated that when war did break out on 1 September 1939, German troops actually invaded Poland through Czechoslovakia.

It appears from the evidence that the so-called border incidents were being used by Woermann to put the responsibility for the outbreak of the war on Poland. It is significant that on 25 August 1939 defendant Woermann sent a circular telegram to German missions in England and France requesting that all Reich Germans be advised to leave the country by the fastest available means. It further appears that on 28 August 1939 the High Command of the German Navy arranged for the return of all German merchant vessels at foreign ports to home ports, which order was to be transmitted through a telegram bearing Woermann's signature and was to be sent to German missions abroad. It is noteworthy that when Germany finally issued the so-called White Book dealing, among other things, with the war on Poland, defendant Woermann transmitted such White Book to German missions abroad through a circular letter of 7 September 1939. Such letter is in evidence. This circular letter reveals the diplomatic tactics employed and in which Woermann participated in connection with the aggression against Poland. It may be noted therein that one of the methods was to blame England, and that efforts had been made to neutralize Great Britain and France with respect to the Polish matter. Defendant Woermann transmitted a telegram to the German Ambassador in Moscow on 3 September 1939, the contents of which also are significant in revealing the tactics used preparatory to the Polish invasion. It is obvious that defendant Woermann did not in fact believe the representations made in such communications. It also appears that he did not believe the representations which he was making prior to the launching of the invasion of Poland. In testifying before this Tribunal on 9 July 1948, he was asked the following question with respect to the war against Poland (*Tr. p. 11522*):

> Q. In your opinion, at that time what nation or group of nations was responsible for the outbreak of this war?

The defendant answered:

> According to my innermost conviction I held the opinion that a great part was to be attributed to Hitler, but not the exclusive responsibility.

During said examination reference was also made to the following (*Tr. pp. 11522–11523*):

> Q. In this telegram you stated that the full responsibility was on England for the outbreak of the war. Was this theme to serve more or less as official guidance for the Moscow Embassy in their official conversations?

To this question the defendant answered, "Yes."

Further proof of the fact that defendant knew the criminal nature of the aims of the German aggression against Poland appears from a telegram sent by him to the German Embassy at the Vatican on 13 October 1939. In this telegram he states in part:

> There is no question of a return to Poznan in the case of Cardinal Hlond, who is a fierce Polish nationalist. Poznan will in the future undoubtedly form part of the German Reich.

Finally on 6 October 1939, and after Polish military resistance had effectually been crushed, Hitler made a gesture of a peace offer to the Western Powers. On 18 October 1939 defendant Woermann sent a circular telegram to a number of German missions abroad, wherein he instructed such missions as to the line to follow in discussions with respect to such peace offer. In this letter Woermann calls attention to the fact that when the Finnish Foreign Minister had requested the German Minister at Helsinki to inform him, before his departure for Stockholm, whether any other solution for ending the war could be suggested from the German side, the Legation at Helsinki had been given the telegram from the Reich Foreign Minister (*NG–5479, Pros. Ex. 3667*):

> I request you to state in reply to the question of the Finnish Foreign Minister that Mr. Chamberlain has rejected in the most shameless manner the Fuehrer's generous peace offer, and that the matter is now closed as far as we are concerned. I request you not to give any further explanations in the matter. End of instructions to Helsinki. Request that if necessary, you use similar language there.—Woermann

The following postscript appeared on said telegram:

> Berlin, 18 October 1939. Foreign Office. Pol. II 4064 Statement IV. I enclose for your information copy of instructions sent by wire to a number of German missions abroad.

The foregoing references to the evidence adduced in this case, with respect to Poland, would seem to leave very little doubt as to the participation of Woermann in the diplomatic preparations for, and in the execution of the aggression against Poland.

* * *

With respect to the charges against Woermann in connection with the aggression against Greece, it does not appear that the evidence sustains the charges. It appears from the evidence that Woermann had knowledge of the contemplated Italian invasion of Greece, and it appears that Woermann, upon the instructions of the Reich Minister for Foreign Affairs, avoided meeting the Greek Minister who apparently was seeking information with respect to said matter from the German Foreign Office. A consideration of all the evidence adduced with respect to the charges against Woermann in connection with the aggression against Greece does not satisfy the Tribunal beyond reasonable doubt that Woermann's acts in connection therewith constitute such participation as to render him criminally liable therefor.

The Tribunal considers the evidence with respect to the charges against defendant Woermann with respect to Yugoslavia as being entirely inadequate to sustain a finding of guilty. It does appear that Woermann was in the possession of information with respect to activities which would indicate that aggression against Yugoslavia was being contemplated. The evidence, however, does not show that Woermann either initiated or implemented the plans for such aggression.

We come now to the defendant's participation in the aggression against Russia. The Tribunal has examined the evidence with respect to these charges and does not believe that it justifies a finding of guilt against defendant thereunder. Many of the exhibits were of an informational character advising Woermann of what was transpiring. That the plans originated from him or were subsequently furthered or implemented by him, or that he assisted materially in the carrying out of such plans has not adequately been proved to justify a finding of guilt against defendant on this charge.

On the evidence adduced with respect to the charges against Woermann in connection with the aggression against Poland, the Tribunal finds the defendant guilty under count one.

Count Two—Common Plan and Conspiracy

The defendants von Weizsaecker, Keppler, Bohle, Woermann, Ritter, von Erdmannsdorff, Veesenmayer, Lammers, Stuckart, Darré, Meissner, Dietrich, Berger, Schellenberg, Schwerin von Krosigk, Koerner, and Pleiger are charged as leaders, organizers, instigators, and accomplices in a common plan and conspiracy to commit, and which involved the commission of crimes against peace, including war crimes and crimes against humanity.

On motion of the prosecution, the defendants Bohle, von Erdmannsdorff, and Meissner were dismissed from this count.

The Tribunal is of the opinion that no evidence has been offered to substantiate a conviction of the defendants in a common plan and conspiracy, and all the defendants charged therein are hereby acquitted.

Count Three—War Crimes, Murder, and Ill-Treatment of Belligerents and Prisoners of War

Count three charges the defendants von Weizsaecker, Steengracht von Moyland, Ritter, Woermann, Lammers, Dietrich, and Berger with the commission of war crimes, in that they participated, were principals in, accessories to, ordered, abetted, and took a consenting part, and were connected with plans and enterprises involving, and were members of organizations and groups connected with the commission of war crimes, particularly in atrocities and offenses against prisoners of war and members of the armed forces then at war with the Third Reich, or which were under belligerent control of or military occupation by Germany, including, murder, ill-treatment, enslavement, brutalities, cruelties, and other inhumane acts; that prisoners of war and belligerents were starved, lynched, branded, shackled, tortured, and murdered in flagrant violation of the laws and customs of war, and through diplomatic distortion, denial, and fabricated justification, the offenses and atrocities were concealed from the Protecting Powers; that included in the crimes thus mentioned were the following incidents:

a. A policy whereby the civilian population of Germany was urged to lynch English, American, and other Allied fliers who had been forced by military operations to land in Germany, and that those not so lynched were upon capture to be classified as criminals and turned over to the SD for "special treatment," which meant execution, thus circumventing the intervention of Protecting Powers, and as a result of this policy American, English, and other Allied fliers were lynched by the German civilian population, or murdered by the SD;

b. The murder of Allied commando units, even though they had surrendered, and informing the Protective Powers through diplomatic channels that these troops had been killed "in combat";

c. The murder of 50 fliers of the British Royal Air Force who had been captured after escaping from a prisoner-of-war camp;

d. The murder of the French General, Mesny, who was a prisoner of war;

e. Forced marches of American and Allied prisoners of war in severe weather without adequate rest, shelter, food, clothing, and medical supplies, resulting in great privation and death to many thousands of prisoners.

On motion of the prosecution the defendant von Erdmannsdorff was dismissed from this count.

* * *

Ritter

The defendant Ritter's alleged participation in the murder of bailed-out Allied fliers arises from his position as Foreign Office liaison representative with the Wehrmacht. He received Keitel's top secret letter of 15 June 1944, in which the latter stated that for the publication of those cases of capture by the armed forces or the police for special treatment, that is murder by the SD, it was necessary to clearly determine what facts should be regarded as evidence of the criminal action, and established the following, which was to serve also as an instruction to the commander of the reception camp for aviators at Oberursel, namely (*730 PS, Pros. Ex. 1233*)—

> . . . where an investigation disclosed that it would be indicated to separate the offender, . . . or to hand him over to the SD:
>
> (1) Strafing civilians, either individuals or crowds;
>
> (2) Firing on German air crews while suspended in parachutes after having been shot down;
>
> (3) Strafing regular passenger trains;
>
> (4) Strafing military hospitals, hospitals, and hospital trains which are clearly marked with the Red Cross.

Keitel stated that inasmuch as in drafting publications of such actions, protests on the part of the enemy were to be expected, and it was intended that in agreement with the Secret Police, the SD, and the Ob. d. L. (commander in chief, Luftwaffe) until further notice, prior to each publication, agreement should be reached between the OKL West, the Foreign Office, and the SD as to the facts, time, and form of announcement.

The Foreign Office was requested to confirm, before 18 June, its agreement with the definition and with the intended procedure.

On 18 June Ritter telephoned the office of the Supreme Command, stating that the opinion of the Foreign Office could not be made known before the night of the 19th, as Ritter would have to check with Berlin. On 25 June he submitted to the Supreme Command of the Armed Forces a draft of reply which had been submitted to but not yet approved by von Ribbentrop who would be absent for several days.

The draft stated that in spite of obvious objections founded on international law and foreign politics, the Foreign Office was in basic agreement with the proposed measure; that in the examination of the individual cases, a distinction must be made between cases of lynching and "special treatment" by the SD; that "in cases of lynch law" no German agency could be directly responsible, because death would have occurred before the agency was concerned in the matter, and the circumstances would be of such a general nature that it would not be difficult to present the case in a suitable manner when published; that as to "special treatment" by the SD, subsequent publications would be tenable if Germany took this opportunity to declare itself free from the obligations imposed by international agreement which it there still recognized; that when an enemy airman had been captured by the armed forces, or the police, and delivered to a prisoner-of-war camp, he thereby acquired the legal status of a prisoner of war, and the Geneva Prisoner-of-War Convention of 27 July 1929 applied; that any attempt to disguise an individual case by clever wording of publication would be hopeless; that the Foreign Office was unable to recommend a formal repudiation of the Geneva Convention; that an emergency solution would be to prevent the suspected fliers from ever attaining the status of prisoners of war by informing them immediately that they were not regarded as prisoners of war, but as criminals, and delivering them, not to the prisoner-of-war camp, but to authorities competent for the prosecution of criminal acts to be tried by special summary procedure established *ad hoc;* that if, during these proceedings, special circumstances are revealed disclosing that this procedure was not applicable to the particular airman, individual cases might be subsequently transferred to the legal status of prisoners of war and sent to the reception camp.

The memorandum further stated that naturally, even this expedient would not prevent Germany from being accused of violating treaties, nor constitute a safeguard against reprisals upon German prisoners of war, but the proposal would relieve Germany of openly renouncing international agreements or, in individual cases, making excuses which no one would believe; that the alleged offenses under items 2 and 3 of the proposed definition were not legally unobjectionable, but the Foreign Office would be willing to disregard the fact. Finally, the memorandum stated, that the main weight would have to be placed on lynchings and should the campaign be carried out to such an extent that the purpose of deterring enemy fliers was actually achieved, then the strafing attacks by enemy fliers must be exploited for propaganda purposes in a more definite manner than heretofore, if not for home publicity, then certainly for the propaganda effect abroad.

On 29 June Ritter advised General Warlimont of the OKW Operations Staff that the Minister of Foreign Affairs had approved the draft but ordered his liaison officer assigned to the Fuehrer headquarters to present to Hitler the Foreign Office's attitude before the letter was sent to the chief of the Supreme Command of the Armed Forces, and that Hitler's approval of the principles established by the Foreign Office must be obtained.

On 4 July Hitler issued a directive that notice be served by radio and the press that every enemy agent shot down while participating in attacks against small localities without war economic or military value was not entitled to treatment as a prisoner of war, but would be killed as soon as he falls into German hands, but that nothing was to be done at the moment, and the measures of this sort were only to be discussed with the legal section of the OKW and with the Foreign Office.

Tribunal V in Case 12, based on contemporaneous captured documents, found that this program was actually carried out and that the chief of the OKW issued an order stating that it had recently happened that soldiers had protected English and American terror fliers from the civilian population, thus causing justified resentment, and directing that soldiers should not counteract the civilian population in such cases by claiming that enemy fliers be handed over to them as prisoners of war and by protecting them; thus ostensibly siding with the enemy terror fliers.

We have considered Ritter's explanation that the letter from the OKW of 15 June should not have been channeled through him but should have been sent directly to the Foreign Office, and that he did not prepare the Foreign Office reply of 25 June which he transmitted to the chief of the OKW, and that his typewritten signature thereto was due to a mistake of his stenographer's which he corrected by striking a line through it and writing at the head of it the word, "draft" An examination of the document reveals that the typewritten signature is so erased and that the word "draft" is so inserted in longhand. The draft, however, discloses that it was prepared in his office, and bears one of his file numbers. The absence of any of the usual Foreign Office symbols indicating the section of Referat which prepared the draft is significant.

Members of the armed forces of any nation who violate the rules of war are subject to trial and punishment by enemy military authorities either during or after hostilities. Here, however, both the procedures and methods proposed by the Wehrmacht and the Foreign Office were contrary to and in violation of the Hague Rules of Land Warfare. It was the duty of Germany to protect captured soldiers and airmen of the enemy against lunch law. Where a captured enemy is suspected or charged with violation of the rules of war, he has the right to be tried in accordance with those rules. The proposals of the Wehrmacht and of the Foreign Office violated these rights.

We do not regard Ritter as a mere messenger boy. He was selected to occupy a position of considerable delicacy, requiring knowledge and experience. While he did not originate this policy of murder, he implemented it, and although he played a comparatively minor part, it is one which involves criminal responsibility on his part.

We therefore find him guilty under count three with respect to this incident.

* * *

COUNT FIVE—WAR CRIMES AND CRIMES AGAINST HUMANITY; ATROCITIES AND OFFENSES COMMITTED AGAINST CIVILIAN POPULATIONS

The indictment alleges that the defendants von Weizsaecker, Steengracht von Moyland, Keppler, Bohle, Woermann, Ritter, von Erdmannsdorff, Veesenmayer, Lammers, Stuckart, Darre, Meissner, Dietrich, Berger, Schellenberg, Schwerin von Krosigk, Rasche, Kehrl, and Puhl, from March 1938 to May 1945, committed war crimes and crimes against humanity in that they participated in atrocities and offenses, including murder, extermination, enslavement, deportation, imprisonment, killing of hostages, torture, persecutions on political, racial, and religious grounds, and other inhumane and criminal acts against German nationals and members of the civilian populations of countries and territories under belligerent occupation of, or otherwise controlled by Germany, and in the plunder of public and private property, wanton destruction of cities, towns, and villages, and devastation not justified by military necessity.

It is alleged that the Third Reich embarked upon a systematic program of genocide aimed at the destruction of nations and ethnic groups within the German sphere of influence in part by murderous extermination and in part by elimination and suppression of national characteristics with intent to strengthen the German nation and the so-called "Aryan" race at the expense of such other nations and groups by imposing Nazi and German characteristics upon individuals selected therefrom, and by the extermination of "undesirable racial elements"; that portions of the civilian populations of occupied countries, especially in Poland and the occupied eastern territories, were compelled by force to evacuate their homesteads which were sequestered and confiscated by the Reich and their properties, real and personal, were treated as revenue of the Reich, and the so-called "ethnic Germans" were resettled in such lands; that German racial registers were established and legislation enacted defining these classes of "ethnic Germans" and other nationals of occupied territories and the puppet and satellite governments eligible for Germanization; that subsequent acquisition, in some instances of German citizenship, was compelled, and individuals who were forced to accept such citizenship or upon whom such citizenship was conferred by decree became amenable to military conscription, service in the armed forces, and other obligations of citizenship; that failure to fulfill these obligations resulted in imprisonment or death, and the forced Germanization constituted the basis for such punishment; that those classes of persons deemed ineligible and those individuals who refused Germanization were deported to forced labor, confined in concentration camps, and in many instances liquidated; that in the occupied territories the use of judicial mechanisms was a powerful weapon for the suppression and extermination of all opponents of the Nazi occupation and for the persecution and extermination of "races"; special police tribunals and other summary courts were created in Germany and in the occupied territories, and subjected civilians of these occupied countries to criminal abuse, and denial of judicial and penal process; that special legislation was enacted providing summary trial by these special courts and invoking the death penalty or imprisonment in concentration camps for all members of the civilian population of the occupied territories suspected of opposing any of the policies of the German occupation authorities; that persons who committed offenses against the Reich or the German forces in the occupied territories were handed over to the police and taken secretly to Germany for trial and punishment, without notification to their relatives of the disposition of the case; that certain classes of civilians in the occupied territories deemed politically, racially, or religiously undesirable if suspected of having committed a crime were deprived of all legal remedy and turned over to the Gestapo for summary treatment, all for the purpose of creating a reign of judicial terror in the occupied countries in order to suppress all resistance and exterminate undesirable elements; that in the Reich program of "pacification" of the occupied territories through terrorism, the arrest, imprisonment, deportation, and murder of so-called hostages was effected, and Jews, alleged Communists, "asocials," and other innocent members of the civilian population not connected with any acts against the occupying power, were taken as hostages and, without the benefit of investigation of trial, were summarily deported, hanged, or shot; that they were executed or deported at arbitrarily established ratios for attacks by persons unknown on German installations and German personnel in the occupied territories; that through recruitment drives in the occupied territories and puppet and satellite governments, SS units were organized and SS recruits obtained, often by compulsion from among prisoners of war and the nationals of those countries, and assigned to the Waffen SS military divisions, the administration of the SS concentration camp system, and specially constituted penal battalions; that these units engaged in the commission of atrocities and offenses against the civilian populations of occupied and satellite countries; that anti-Jewish activities with each aggression were extended to the incorporated, occupied, or otherwise controlled German-dominated countries; that Austrian, Czechoslovakian, Polish, and other nationals of Jewish extraction were deprived of their civil rights and their property confiscated, tens of thousands thrown into concentration camps and tortured, and many of them murdered; that these measures were followed by barbarous mass killings of people of Jewish extraction and other foreign nationals in the occupied territories in which hundreds of thousands of men, women, and children were exterminated; that the early program for driving out the Jews as pauper *emigrés* was supplanted in 1942 by a program for the evacuation of eleven million European Jews to camps in eastern Europe for ultimate extermination; that they were to be transported to these areas in huge labor gangs, and there the weak were to be killed immediately, and the able bodied worked to death, and thus millions of people of Jewish extraction from Austria, Czechoslovakia, Poland, France, Belgium, the Netherlands, Denmark, Norway, Hungary, Bulgaria, Yugoslavia, Rumania, the Baltic states, the Soviet Union, Greece, Italy, and also from Germany were deported to the eastern extermination areas and murdered.

In addition to these general charges, the indictment alleges the commission of certain specific acts connected with the general program which, it is alleged, were committed by various of the defendants as principals, aiders, cooperators, or abettors. These we will deal with later.

* * *

Foreign Office knowledge of the fate of the Jews in the East.—With typical German thoroughness, not only was the campaign of murder and extermination of Jews in Poland and Russia carried on, but detailed reports were made of these horrible measures. The Foreign Office regularly received reports of the Einsatzgruppen operations in the occupied territories. Many of these were initialed by von Weizsaecker and Woermann. They revealed the clearing of entire areas of the Jewish population by mass murder, and the bloody butchery of the helpless and innocent; the shooting of hostages in numbers wholly disproportionate to the alleged offenses against German armed forces; the murder of captured Russian officials and a reign of terrorism carried on with calculated ferocity; all told in the crisp unimaginative language of military reports.

All this is described in detail in the judgment rendered in Case 9, and it is unnecessary to repeat it again. It suffices to say that many hundreds of thousands of innocent people were murdered without reason or excuse, without trial or opportunity to establish their innocence, and beyond question the Jewish population was the particular object of these murder campaigns.

The prosecution, however, does not contend that the defendants implemented or initiated the crimes committed by the Einsatzgruppen but that they had knowledge of them and they made no objections to their commission. Here the Foreign Office had no jurisdiction or power to intervene. They were in the most part carried on in an area which was still under the jurisdiction of the Wehrmacht. How a decent man could continue to hold office under a regime which carried out planned and wholesale barbarities of this kind is difficult to understand, but there is no evidence of participation on the part of the defendants Woermann and von Weizsaecker.

What is of importance in this case, however, is that the facts disclosed by the records of these crimes disposes of the claim of ignorance of final solution and of the purpose of the deportation of the Jews to the East. Knowing as they did what happened to the Jews when they came under the control of the SS, Gestapo, and police, we find ourselves unable to believe that these defendants had any idea that these deportations ended in anything but the death of these deportees through exhaustion from overwork, starvation, or mistreatment, and by mass murder. The defendants are not men of only ordinary intelligence and understanding. They are educated and trained to official life and experienced in the evaluation of policy, and the motives and acts of parties, officialdom, and of nations, and wholly accustomed to read between the lines of restrained or apparently innocuous language, and from it extract the meaning lying behind the words.

The defendant von Weizsaecker's statement that he thought Auschwitz was merely a camp where laborers were interned, we believe, tells only part of what he knew and what he had good reason to believe. He had access to what was publicly broadcast by the outside world of what was going on there. He was kept informed by his contacts with the Wehrmacht, and the opposition, and with the office of Admiral Canaris, and he knew what happened to the Jews of Poland, of the Baltic states, and of the occupied territories of Russia. Unless he thought that ravening wolves had overnight become meek lambs, he must have realized what the end would be.

It is possible, but we think unlikely, that he was not informed of the exquisite techniques of murder developed in this camp, but that he knew the deported were marked for slave labor and death we have no doubt. This is clearly indicated by the testimony of his own son, Karl von Weizsaecker, and by the testimony of a number of other of his own witnesses, and particularly among those of his Foreign Office associates who, with him, claim that they were members of the underground movement against the Hitler regime. We may mention von Schlabrendorff, Bruns, von Etzdorf, and von Bargen.

Karl von Weizsaecker testified as follows (*Tr. pp. 10028–10030*):

Q. During the war did you also talk to your father about the deportation of Jews and other atrocities?

A. Yes, partly we talked about it generally and partly we discussed specific cases.

Q. Did you and your father know then that the Jews were being killed?

A. Of course, one knew that. The big difficulty was that it was known that such things were happening but that one did not know where and how it happened. . . .

Q. Did your father never consider helping the Jews by open contradiction, that is, by protesting publicly against Hitler's anti-Semitic policy?

A. Well, we discussed that, too, and I can tell you exactly what my father's opinion was on that point. He said,"If one did that, one would become a martyr, but one would certainly not help the Jews by doing it."

* * *

We have stated that the Foreign Office played an important part in these horrors. Through it the arrangements were made whereby the Vichy government of France and the governments of Hungary, Slovakia, Bulgaria, Rumania, and Croatia consented to the deportation of Jews in those territories. Consent was not necessary in occupied France, the Low Countries, Poland, the Baltic states, Denmark, and the occupied Russian territories. There the Jews were merely seized and sent to their deaths. But even here the Foreign Office played an essential part. Among its duties was to ignore, or attempt to quiet, or give evasive and often false answers to the protests or inquiries of other powers. All those who implemented, aided, assisted, or consciously participated in these things bear part of the responsibility for the criminal program.

Lammers

The seizure of power found the defendant Lammers employed as a legal expert in the Ministry of the Interior. He had joined the Nazi Party in February 1932. On 30 January 1933 Hitler appointed him Secretary of State [Staatssekretaer] in the Reich Chancellery, and in August 1934 he was appointed its chief. On 26 November of the same year he was made a Reich Minister without portfolio with the title "Reich Minister and Chief of the Reich Chancellery." On 14 February 1938, he was appointed as executive member of the Secret Reich Cabinet Council, but this council never functioned. On 30 November 1939, 2 months after the Polish invasion, the Ministerial Council for Defense of the Reich was created with Goering as its chairman, and Lammers became one of its executive members.

Among his duties was to present matters to Hitler, sometimes with and sometimes without his own recommendations; to transmit Hitler's decisions on these and other matters to the appropriate Reich Ministries and agencies; to cooperate with the members of the Reich Cabinet and other agencies of the government and the Party; to coordinate and, if possible, reconcile the views and proposals of other ministries with respect to legislation, and to examine, and at times to prepare laws, decrees, and regulations which were under consideration; to ascertain the views and opinions of other ministers in such matters; and to investigate and report and recommend action regarding disputes which might arise between ministers, agencies, and officials.

Although as Reich Minister he had no particular executive functions in the usual sense, both his responsibilities and powers were substantial. Among the reasons which impelled Hitler to raise him to Cabinet rank was that he might become one of the highest Reich authorities possessing the prestige and authority incident thereto, and thereby relieve Hitler of many details and decisions. He was and continued to be one of the most important figures in the Reich government.

* * *

The record contains a number of documentary exhibits which show that Lammers was familiar with and took part in discussions relating to measures against Jews. On 20 July 1942 he stated that Hitler had repeatedly expressed the opinion that applications by part-Jews for status equal to that of Germans had been treated too generously, and in the future they should be allowed only if there were special reasons for exceptional treatment, that is, positive achievements, such as work for the Party in the early days. Lammers requested that future action should be based on Hitler's attitude.

Notwithstanding Lammers' denials, we believe and find that he was informed and knew that the extermination of the Jews was proposed, and that he consciously and willingly participated in measures which were intended for and adapted to that purpose.

Judicial persecution and murder.—The orderly process of the courts and the comparative leniency of the sentences imposed by them irked Hitler, and this fact was conveyed to the Ministry of Justice. Lammers and Schlegelberger conferred, and on 10 March 1941 the latter wrote Lammers enclosing his letter to Hitler. Schlegelberger asked that it be transmitted to Hitler immediately and enclosed a draft of a proposed decree which would enable the public prosecutor to intervene in civil cases, and enable him to file application for the reopening of proceedings if he was of the opinion that new proceedings and a new judgment were necessary in cases deemed of special importance to the national community.

The letter to Hilter is one of cringing servility, in which the writer expressed his earnest intention to install justice with all its branches more and more firmly within the National Socialist State; that there were still judgments which did not entirely comply with the necessary requirements, and in such cases he proposed to take the necessary steps. He calls attention to the fact that Hitler had created the extraordinary plea for nullification of criminal cases, and states that it is desirable to educate the judges more and more to a correct way of thinking, conscious of national destiny, and for this purpose it would be invaluable if Hitler could let Schlegelberger know if a verdict did not meet his approval, inasmuch as the judges were directly responsible to the Fuehrer, and were conscious of their duties, and firmly resolved to discharge them accordingly. Lammers was consulted by Schlegelberger regarding this decree.

On 21 March 1942 after Lammers had consulted with Schlegelberger and Bormann, he suggested to Hitler the issuance of a decree for the alleged simplification of the administration of the law and with Hitler cosigned it. Some of the changes made in the original draft which appear in the final decree were made by Lammers himself. Under it the Minister of Justice, in agreement with Lammers and the Chief of the Party Chancellery, was authorized to implement the decree to take the necessary administrative measures, and in cases of doubt, to decide matters administratively.

Schlegelberger made a suggestion for a decree giving the Ministry of Justice confirmatory rights over every judgment passed, stating that this was a sure way to become master of the insufficient penal measures and legal judgments. Lammers and Bormann consulted and, feeling that Schlegelberger's proposal was insufficient, they determined to hold the matter over until a new Minister of Justice was appointed.

It is perfectly clear that both Bormann and Lammers favored the destruction of the independence of courts, particularly in criminal cases, and that the sentences to be imposed should rest on the uncritical and arbitrary whim of Hitler. The sorry history of this corruption of the judicial process has been set forth in detail in the opinion in the Justice Case, and it is unnecessary to repeat it here. It is sufficient to say that, after examination of the documents and the testimony offered before this Tribunal, we find that those conclusions are fully substantiated, and we agree with the findings therein made.

On 20 August 1942 the defendant cosigned with Hitler a decree reading as follows (*1964-PS, Pros. Ex. 1587*):

> A strong administration of justice is necessary for the fulfillment of tasks of the great German Reich. Therefore, I commission and empower the Reich Minister of Justice to establish a National Socialist administration of justice and to take all necessary measures in accordance with my directives and instructions made in agreement with the Reich Minister and Chief of the Reich Chancellery, and the Leader of the Party Chancellery. He can hereby deviate from any existing law.

Thierack became the new Minister of Justice, and on 27 August 1942 Bormann issued a circular announcing Thierack's appointment, and also that the latter had been appointed Chief of the National Socialist Jurisprudence League and President of the Academy for German Law; and that by these appointments Hitler had united the highest offices in the field of judicial administration of Party and state in the hands of Thierack, and by special decree had empowered the new Minister, in agreement with Lammers and himself, to build up a new [National] Socialist administration of justice in accordance with the guiding rules and directions of the Fuehrer; that the task assigned to Party Member Dr. Thierack was, first of all, a political one, and consisted in bringing justice and the judiciary to the National Socialist idea which could only be attained by closest cooperation with the Party; that should there be complaints by the Party members as to the way justice was administered, they should be presented to Bormann so that he could clear up the situation by confidential negotiations with the Ministry of Justice; and if, on discussion, it would seem absolutely necessary that the problem be brought to the Fuehrer, this would be done by Lammers and himself.

Late in 1942 Thierack was given power to remove recalcitrant judges, and this received Lammers's approval, although it appears that he did so with some misgivings and attempted to impose certain limitations on Thierack's authority.

It was by means of this corruption of the courts of justice that Jews and other enemies and opponents of national socialism were deprived of the ordinary and commonly recognized rights to fair trial and received sentences, including that of death, shockingly disproportionate to the offenses committed.

Lammers was a responsible Reich Minister. He was neither a glorified messenger boy nor a notary public certifying the acts of others. We believe Hitler's reason in raising the head of the Reich Chancellery from the position of State Secretary to that of Reich Minister was to relieve himself of much detail work and many decisions, and to place these functions in the hands of the defendant who, as Reich Minister and Chief of the Reich Chancellery, possessed sufficient rank to interpose and exercise judgment and power.

* * *

Puhl

The defendant Puhl, as the leading executive official of the Reich Bank, is charged with having directed and supervised the execution of an agreement between Funk and Himmler for the receipt, classification, deposit, conversion, and disposal of properties taken by the SS from victims exterminated in concentration camps. There properties, totaling millions of reichmarks in value, included, among other things, gold teeth and fillings, spectacle frames, rings, jewelry, and watches. To insure secrecy, the deliveries from the SS were credited to a fictitious account and the transaction was given a code name. The proceeds were credited to the account of the Reich Treasury under the defendant Schwerin von Krosigk.

Puhl's entire career has been that of a banker. He was first employed in the Reich Bank in 1913, and, except for service in the army during the First

World War, he remained in that organization. He became a director in 1929 and was a senior director in 1932; he was appointed as vice president on 8 August 1940 and remained so until the German surrender in 1945. From 1935 to 1945 he was a member of the Aufsichtsrat (which is, roughly, the supervising board as distinguished from the executive board) of the German Gold Discount Bank. He joined the Nazi Party as early as 1938 although his membership record gives the year as 1937. The defendant asserts that his membership record was antedated.

He served under Schacht, who was acquitted, as well as Funk, who was convicted by the first International Military Tribunal, during their respective periods as president of the bank.

The primary function of the Reich Bank was that of issuing notes; it also had the power to regulate the movement of currency and money transactions, internally as well as abroad, and to insure that the available funds of the German economic system were utilized for the common good and in the interest of national economy; it was under the direct authority of the Fuehrer; it was a public corporate body under corporate law which had a capital of 150,000,000 reichsmarks; and its presidents and directors were under the supervision and control of Hitler, who appointed and could, at will, discharge them. Such was the legal position of the bank under the Reich Bank Law of 1939, which covers the period with which we are here concerned.

On 11 February 1939 Puhl was appointed Funk's deputy for all business in the latter's absence, with the same power to make decisions which Funk possessed under the Reich Bank Law, a position which was superior to that of any other official of the bank. He was the managing vice president, while Lange, the other vice president, was in charge of personnel matters and of safeguarding National Socialist principles in the bank.

Puhl had the comparative rank of a state secretary. In addition to being a member of the Aufsichtsrat of the Gold Discount Bank, in 1944 he became deputy president. This bank was owned and wholly controlled by the Reich Bank.

Action Reinhardt.—No chapter in the law and record of crimes committed during the history of the Nazi regime is so revolting and horrible as the coldly calculated extermination of Jews. Not content with depriving them of the opportunity inherent in all human beings to study, to practice professions, to engage in business in accordance with the individual's nature and talents, they were deprived of their rights of citizenship, subject to senseless degradations, humiliations, and insults, their property in many instances destroyed by Party organized mobs, and finally stolen from them under the euphonius term of "confiscations"; they were deported to the Gaue in the East and finally to extermination camps where they were slaughtered by the million through starvation, shooting, and finally by mass extermination in the gas chambers of Auschwitz and Maidenek, where men and women, girls and youths, the tottering grandfather and the babe in arms, met the same fate. But the Nazi government was not content with this. There were large financial gains to be derived from wholesale murder which could be and were used to wage Germany's wars of aggression. Currency, coins, securities, jewelry, gold watches, gold spectacles, clothing from their bodies, were carefully and systematically collected; the hair was shorn from the heads of the women; and finally the gold from the teeth of the corpses was meticulously removed. The best of the clothing was used to cover the bodies of the members of the master race, the hair for mattresses on which to lay their heads, and the coins, bank notes, jewelry, and gold stored in vaults of the Reich Bank, sold through Berlin pawn shops by the Reich Bank, or sent by the Reich Bank to be melted into bullion.

The defendant contends that stealing the personal property of Jews and other concentration camp inmates is not a crime against humanity. But under the circumstances which we have here related, this plea must be and is rejected. What was done was done pursuant to a governmental policy, and the thefts were part of a program of extermination and were one of its objectives. It would be a strange doctrine indeed, if, where part of the plan and one of the objectives of murder was to obtain the property of the victim, even to the extent of using the hair from his head and the gold of his mouth, he who knowingly took part in disposing of the loot must be exonerated and held not guilty as a participant in the murder plan. Without doubt all such acts are crimes against humanity and he who participates or plays a consenting part therein is guilty of a crime against humanity. The only question we have to decide is whether the defendant Puhl was such a consenting participant as to render him liable to conviction and punishment.

* * *

From the records we draw and make the following findings of fact:

That Puhl was the managing director and vice president of the [Reich] Bank, and that in Funk's absence he exercised all the powers of Funk;

That Funk was seldom in the bank and comparatively seldom exercised his powers as president;

That Puhl, at the time he received the direction from Funk and after he talked to Pohl, knew that what was to be received and disposed of was stolen property and loot taken from the inmates of concentration camps.

We do not believe that at that time he was informed that the grisly dental gold and wedding rings were part of it. However, we think it is fairly established by the record that long before the deliveries were completed he was informed of this. His part in this transaction was not that of a mere messenger of businessman. He went beyond the ordinary range of his duties to give directions that the matter be handled secretly by the appropriate departments of the bank. It is to be said in his favor that he neither originated the matter and that it was probably repugnant to him. He had no part in the actual extermination of Jews and other concentration camp inmates, and we have no doubt that he would not, even under orders, have participated in that part of the program.

But without doubt he was a consenting participant in part of the execution of the entire plan, although his participation was not a major one.

We find him guilty under count five.

* * *

SCHELLENBERG

Schellenberg joined the Party in 1933. In 1934 he became a member of the SD and was assigned to the Office of Domestic Intelligence Service. In 1939 he became Chief of Amt IV-E, which had charge of domestic counterintelligence. In 1941 he was transferred to and became Chief of Amt VI, RSHA, which dealt with foreign intelligence.

The prosecution contends that Schellenberg took an active part in the preparations for the work of the notorious Einsatzgruppen of the East. The record reveals that in the discussion between Mueller, Chief of Amt IV, RSHA, and Quartermaster General Wagner of the Wehrmacht, an impasse arose regarding the use of these corps in the East and their jurisdiction and competence, and Schellenberg, who was a lawyer by profession, was detailed to take up these discussions and attempt to compromise the difference between the Wehrmacht and the RSHA. This he did, and when his final draft of the agreement had been completed Heydrich and Wagner signed it. He asserts that when the two men came to discuss the details of the plan, he was notified to leave the room, and therefore was not informed of the full scope of the activities of these groups, namely, to engage in mass exterminations of the local population and the Jews.

He admits that some time later he attended a meeting in Berlin at which were present counterintelligence officers of the Wehrmacht, but states that this meeting continued over a considerable period and he left several days before it concluded, and he assumed that after he left persons then present were probably informed of the work which the Einsatzgruppen were to carry on.

While we doubt that Schellenberg was as ignorant of the mission of the Einsatzgruppen as he now asserts, the proof that he had knowledge does not convince us to a moral certainty. We therefore give him the benefit of the doubt, and as to this incident we acquit him.

It is also contended that he was deputy to Mueller, Chief of Amt IV, RSHA. While on one or two occasions he signed in that capacity, the record discloses that Mueller had no regular deputy and only when he was absent from his office did one or another of his section chiefs sign communications in his name.

The prosecution further contends that Schellenberg, as Chief of Amt VI, himself, dispatched an Einsatzkommando to White Ruthenia, but we are satisfied that this group dealt with geological and other scientific research and had no connection with crimes against humanity.

Serbian Jews.—While Schellenberg's office was informed of the slaughter of Serbian Jews, it does not appear that Schellenberg took any part in this other than possibly informing Luther, at the latter's request, of Heydrich's return to Berlin, as Luther desired to have a conference with Heydrich regarding the deportation or other disposition of Serbian Jews. The evidence of Schellenberg's guilt is not sufficient, and we acquit him with respect to this incident.

Einsatzgruppen.—Copies of Operational Situation report, No. 128, of the Einsatzgruppen, dated 3 November 1941 (*NO-3157, Pros. Ex. 2058*), were distributed to Schellenberg's group, and to both Aemter IV and VI. It covers approximately 4 months' operations. There the program of murder and extermination is set forth in detail. It callously states that approximately 80,000 persons had been liquidated, describes the objections raised by certain commanders of prisoner-of-war camps, how they were overcome, and of the plans for further operations freed from interference by officers of the Wehrmacht. These and the other reports of the Einsatzgruppen were distributed to Schellenberg's office. His claim that he did not see or paid no attention to particulars in which his office was interested cannot be believed.

We have examined the reports and even the most casual glance would bring out the horrible details. Furthermore, unless we are to assume that his division was so inured to reports of mass murder and that these were no longer deemed worthy of notice and comment, it is inconceivable that his section chiefs would not have called his attention to them. His claim of innocence is wholly incredible. But there is no evidence that he participated directly or indirectly in these atrocities.

Operation Zeppelin.—On 13 October 1941 (*No-3421, Pros. Ex. 2059*) Mueller, Chief of Amt IV, confirmed his telegraphic order regarding the use of Soviet Russians in concentration camps for labor and for the execution of designated Russian prisoners of war.

On 25 October 1941 (*No-3421, Pros. Ex. 2059*) he issued a directive stating that for the purpose of selecting suitable informers of the Russian intelligentsia, delegates of Amt VI, Schellenberg's division, would be assigned to the Einsatzkommandos of the Sipo and SD and, during their activities in the prisoner-of-war camps, these delegates would be subordinated to the leadership of the Einsatzkommandos. In addition, the order made it the duty of these delegates to collect information about political, economic, and cultural conditions in Russian areas not yet occupied, and that Soviet functionaries who were deemed suitable were to be transferred to Berlin and put at the disposal of Amt VI. Both of these documents were distributed to Amt VI and Amt IV. This operation was known as "Operation Zeppelin."

The counsel for prosecution contends that the use of prisoners of war for espionage and other like purposes against their own nation, even if voluntary, is a violation of international law and of the Hague Convention Respecting the Rules and Customs of War. (Art. 6, ch. II [Hague Convention No. IV, 18 Oct 1907]; and Art., ch. VI, Geneva Convention [Prisoner of War Convention,

27 Jul 1929j.) No other authority other than the Articles themselves has been cited to us, and we have been unable to find any. Ordinarily a national of a country, whether or not he is in military service, who gives aid or comfort to the enemy, is a traitor to his country. But we have never before heard it suggested that the enemy who takes advantage of his treason is guilty of a breach of international law. We hold that the cited prohibitions of the Hague Convention prohibit the use of prisoners of war in connection with war operations, and apply only when such use is brought about by force, threats, or duress, and not when the person renders the services voluntarily.

We come now to more serious evidence against Schellenberg with respect to Operation Zeppelin. In a number of instances persons who volunteered were thereafter executed, apparently without trial or notice of any offense of which they were alleged to be guilty. If true, this was a flagrant violation of international law. It appears from the testimony of the witness Smolen that he was a political prisoner at the Auschwitz concentration camp from June 1940 to 1941, and was employed as a "responsible prisoner" in the reception office of the political department of the camp which was not under the jurisdiction of the camp commander, and that this political department had jurisdiction over Block 11 of the camp; that approximately 200 Russians were executed in that block; that these prisoners arrived under escort of SD men; the normal entries regarding them were not made in the records; they were not given the usual prison numbers, and that the documents which they carried bearing their personal data, were immediately delivered to the SD upon their arrival; that these men gave no information about themselves and did not have the slightest idea of the fate which awaited them; that they were killed by a shot in the neck within a few days of their arrival; that the papers for their commitment bore the entry "Zeppelin Geheimnistraeger" the latter term meaning "one in possession of secret information."

A principal cannot be held criminally responsible for isolated criminal acts committed by his criminal subordinates in the excution of the latter's duty, but where there is evidence that this was an official practice, he cannot escape responsibility on the plea of ignorance, inasmuch as such ignorance was in fact nonexistent.

We hold that Schellenberg in fact knew of these practices and is guilty of the crimes as set forth.

* * *

Schwerin von Krosigk

The defendant Schwerin von Krosigk, during the entire Nazi regime, was Reich Minister of Finance and a member of the Cabinet. He was educated at the University of Oxford as a Rhodes Scholar, and he spent many years in the

Ministry of Finance as a civil servant. He faithfully and with complete loyalty served the Weimar republic under several of its presidents. As time passed, his talents were recognized and he finally became director of its budget.

While von Papen was Reich Chancellor, Schwerin von Krosigk was appointed Minister of Finance. This appointment was not made due to any political or party affiliations.

Upon Hitler's seizure of power he was retained in office solely because of his expert knowledge of governmental finance, and not because he was looked upon either as a Party man or as being devoted to or convinced of the principles of national socialism; but we believe because Hitler felt that it was necessary that the Ministry of Finance be put in charge of one who was divorced from the inexperienced, ignorant, and predatory characters who had flocked to the Party; and he desired one who was incorruptible and would be content to carry out the functions of his office without interfering in matters of politics.

Irrespective of our evaluations of his subsequent official actions, in justice it must be said that Schwerin von Krosigk's private life was above reproach. He was and is a man deeply religious in character, devoted to his wife and family, simple in his tastes in life, and wholly free from any desire or ambition to use his official position to enrich himself, a decided contrast to many who held high offices in the Reich.

The evidence clearly shows that he was not a member of Hitler's inner circle, that he was not one of his confidants, and that he came in touch with him but seldom before the war, and even less often afterward. During the course of the years he suffered many conflicts of conscience and was fully aware that measures to which he put his name and programs in which he played a part were contrary and abhorrent to what he believed and knew to be right.

It is difficult to understand what motives or what weaknesses impelled or permitted him to remain and play a part, in many respects an important one, in the Hitler regime. It is one of the human tragedies which are so often found in life. That he could have found or made an opportunity to retire and avoid being made a party to what was done, we have no question. In fact, he is one of the defendants who refused to avail himself of the claim that he was bound to remain in office and could not have retired or resigned had he so desired. He testified that at the time of the Crystal Week Pogrom against the Jews in November 1938 he then and always considered it and the measures which followed it to be a disgrace to the character of the German people.

He states that he remained in the Cabinet to raise the voice of reason and justice; that the events of the Roehm Putsch of June 1934 were a shock to him and emphasized in his mind the dangers inherent in the Nazi regime, but that many people urged him to remain in office so that he could act as a brake to the regime; that among others who held the same idea were some of the chiefs of the bourgeois ministries and old civil servants; that as head of the finance administration he desired his officials should keep their integrity; that the tax administration and other divisions should carry on their tasks with absolute justice; and that he felt as a Minister he could influence laws as they were drafted and after their promulgation exert a "defeating" influence; that in the subsequent years he was able, in certain instances, to help those who were threatened by injustice; that by staying in office he was able to save civil servants from the so-called "purge" law; that in the matter of the billion-mark Jewish fine, he was able to have the funds paid out by the insurance companies for losses incurred during the Crystal Week, and which could not be paid to the Jews themselves, applied upon their respective shares of the national fine.

He testified that he served the Hitler government initially because it was his duty as a civil servant so to do, and later because only from that position was he able to prevent injustices so far as his powers extended, and finally, because he thought it was a manifestation of cowardice to desert a sinking ship; that as he views the matter today in the full view of what he then did not know he deems his behavior politically erroneous, because under a dictatorship all decent and respectable work and all honest efforts must be finally brought under the service of the dictator, but all this comes from after-knowledge, and from the considerations then apparent and known to him, had he again to make the decision he would do as his duty commanded and in the same way.

He asserts that there were no financial considerations which impelled him to remain in office, and that had he resigned he would undoubtedly have had opportunities to obtain positions in the commercial and financial field which would in fact have been greatly to his financial advantage; that while he never became associated with any of the resistance groups because he felt he could be of more service in the capacity in which he served, he was personally and well acquainted with many of its members; that it was not until 1938, when the Crystal Week and the Sudeten crisis arose, that the resistance groups first came into being, and that after the outbreak of the war it was out of the question to resign, as everybody had to work in some position.

We are not inclined to be captious in considering and giving weight to his testimony, although we deem it altogether likely that what he says does not supply all of the lights and shadows regarding his reactions then.

As to many of the decrees, laws, and regulations which bore his name as cosignator, he relies upon the so-called "Federfuehrend" doctrine which may be succinctly stated thus, that where one Minister had jurisdiction over the major problem of the legislation or regulation involved and other departments were more or less incidentally concerned, the legal responsibility rested upon the first and the other cosignators assumed no responsibility for the measures other than those provisions which might immediately affect their jurisdiction, and finally, that the right to intervene or object was limited to questions relating to the propriety or practicability of the measures as it affected their sphere of action.

That the principle as thus stated is oversimplified, and the responsibility of cosigners underemphasized, we have no question, as we find in the record instances where the doctrine was rejected and where the proposed cosigner refused to put his name to the document.

There is a further limitation to this doctrine. Cabinet Ministers had the right to, and in fact did, freely express their views as to proposed legislation. In the early years of the Hitler regime Cabinet meetings were held in which the same right in principle existed. Even when the Cabinet meetings were discontinued, it was the practice, and in fact the invariable rule, that all proposed Reich governmental laws, regulations, and decrees were circulated among the Cabinet Ministers for their objections or suggestions. The defendant Lammers testified that, as to this type of regulation and decree, had a majority of the Cabinet expressed a negative view, Hitler would not have gone contrary to the views of the Cabinet. Lammers stated further, however, that negative views were never expressed and, therefore, the Reich government laws were adopted without dissent. Where the right to object or dissent exists, a majority dissent can only be ascertained if some responsible Minister is the first to register his objections. Under these circumstances one cannot sit supinely by and await the voice of another.

Our attention has not been directed to a single instance in which Schwerin von Krosigk filed his objection or dissent to any proposed Reich government law, regulation, ordinance, or decree which, if enacted, would constitute a crime within the jurisdiction of this Tribunal. Even were we inclined to accept the bald doctrine as of universal application, it could be applicable only to responsibility under German law and is unavailable as a defense to a crime under international law. Furthermore, it cannot be forgotten that, as to the offenses charged under this indictment, we do not deal with the ordinary processes or policies of national law nor even those where there is room for reasonable differences of opinion on political policy.

The offenses charged in this indictment deal with policies which fundamentally violate the common law and understanding of nations, and measures which shocked the consciences of mankind, from which there was, and is, a common revulsion, not limited to those who were or thereafter became political or armed foes of the Third Reich, but among peoples who by choice or necessity remained neutrals. As to those offenses the doctrine of "Federfuehrend" cannot be applied, although it may be considered with other circumstances in mitigation.

In our examination into the defendant's conduct we have endeavored to state and concede as far and as fully and as fairly as possible the foundations of his defense. We now proceed to ascertain and analyze the particulars of his conduct, that we may weigh profession against performance and general benevolence with specific acts. A troubled conscience is not a defense for acts which are otherwise criminal. Nor can we hold that he who signed, cosigned, executed, or administered measures which violate international law, because he thought that acquiescence would enable him to maintain and safeguard the integrity of his department and the career of his officials or even the life or liberty of individuals whose cases came to his attention, but who by his actions condemned the great inarticulate mass to persecution, mistreatment, brutality, imprisonment, deportation, and extermination, escapes responsibility for his conduct.

Schwerin von Krosigk was present at the infamous conference of 12 November 1938 when Goering proposed to levy the billion-mark fine against the Jews. This was shortly after the assassination of von Rath in Paris and the riots and plunderings of the Crystal Week. When the question arose of adopting measures to prevent Jews from realizing on their securities and disposing of their assets, the defendant said (*1816-PS, Pros. Ex. 1441*):

> They have to be taken during the next week at the latest.

When Goering said:

> I shall choose the wording this way, that German Jewry shall, as punishment for their abominable crimes, and so forth, have to make a contribution of one million [billion]—that will work. The pigs won't commit another murder. Incidentally, I like to say again that I would not like to be a Jew in Germany.

Schwerin von Krosigk remarked:

> Therefore, I would like to emphasize what Mr. Heydrich has said in the beginning: That we will have to try to do everything possible by way of additional exports to shove the Jews into foreign countries. The decisive factor is that we don't want the proletariat system [Gesellschaftsproletariat] here. They will always be a terrific liability for us. (Frick: "And a danger.") I don't imagine the prospect of a ghetto is very nice. The idea of the ghetto is not a very agreeable one. Therefore, the goal must be, like Heydrich said, to move out whatever we can.

It is difficult to reconcile this language and the attitude which the defendant now claims he then took.

It was Schwerin von Krosigk who issued the ordinances of 21 November 1938 and of 19 October 1939, the first of which levied an assessment of 20 percent and the second an additional 5 percent on all Jewish property, by means of which the billion-mark fine was extracted, and it is he who issued the detailed instructions to the various Reich offices as to how and by what means payments could and should be made.

Regarding the billion-mark fine, two things are to be observed. First, it was not a fine or penalty for any act done or committed by the individuals who were compelled to pay it, nor was there the slightest ground for the charge that the assassination of von Rath was the result of a general Jewish plot. It was a deliberate confiscation of property and a typical piece of the persecution to which German Jews were subjected. Second, this fine and the proceeds of other confiscations of Jewish property were intended to be and were used for the purpose of rearmament and aggression. This statement was made at a meeting of the Reich Defense Counsel on 18 November 1938. There Goering said (*3575-PS. Pros. Ex. 1068*):

> Very critical situation of the Reich Exchequer. Relief initially through the billion-mark fine imposed on Jewry and through the profits accruing to the Reich in the Aryanization of Jewish enterprises.

The defendant offers, and there is no justification or excuse for these measures.

Financing concentration camps.—As Minister of Finance the defendant furnished the means by which the concentration camps were purchased, constructed, and maintained, but it is clear that he neither originated nor planned these matters, and the funds were provided by him on Hitler's express orders. They were Reich funds and not Schwerin von Krosigk's, and he had no discretion with respect to their disposition. His act in disbursing them for these purposes was actually clerical, and we cannot charge him with criminal responsibility in this matter.

Deportation of Jews to the East.—When the cruel deportation of Jews to the East commenced, the defendant caused the necessary instructions to be given to the senior finance presidents throughout the Reich, who were his subordinates, to confiscate the Jewish property. The Jews were only permitted to have 100 marks and 50 kilograms of luggage apiece. These instructions stated that the administration and utilization of the confiscated property was within the defendant's competency, and he transferred it to the senior finance presidents to perform.

The defendant asserts that by his orders an accurate record of all property thus confiscated was kept, so that at some future time the owners might be able to reclaim it or be reimbursed therefor. Inasmuch, however, as the confiscation was complete and final, the possibility of reclamation or reimbursement could only occur as and when the Nazi regime ceased to exist. We deem his contentions in this respect to be an afterthought and without reality in fact or intention. His instructions spoke not only of deportations which were then imminent, but of deportations which had already taken place, and further, of deportations which were to follow. The confiscations included not only money, securities, jewelry, furniture, clothing, works of art, but also real estate owned by Jews.

In March 1942 the defendant's deputy, by his order, instructed the finance presidents concerning the seizure of Jewish literature, cultural and artistic works, and ordered that they be turned over to the Operational Staff Rosenberg which was the collector and holder of this kind of loot.

On 25 November 1941 the defendant's State Secretary, Reinhardt, cosigned the Eleventh Supplement to the Reich Citizenship Law (*NG–2499, Pros. Ex. 1536*), which deprived all Jews living abroad of their citizenship, as well as those who might in the future take up ordinary residence there. The decree confiscated their property, together with the property of all those Jews who at the time of the enforcement of the decree were stateless if they were formerly Reich citizens. This decree was issued as a result of a conference in the Ministry of the Interior which the defendant attended.

Various other implementary decrees and regulations for the confiscation of Jewish property were from time to time issued or cosigned by the defendant's Ministry of Finance, including those which forfeited the property of Jews who had committed suicide to avoid deportation. This latter regulation was made retroactive to 15 October 1940. The defendant pleads ignorance as to the issuing of some of these documents, particularly the last, and it is not unlikely that in some instances this was true, but that such measures were taken independently by his subordinates without knowing that they were in accord with the policies of his department is, we believe, highly unlikely, if not wholly impossible.

The defendant Schwerin von Krosigk with the defendant Stuckart signed the decree of 2 November 1942 (*NG-180, Pros. Ex. 2453*) forfeiting citizenship and confiscating the property of all Bohemian-Moravian Jews who had established domicile abroad, and the defendant approved the draft of the Terboven Ordinance containing like provisions as to Norwegian Jews.

On 3 October 1939 the defendant Schwerin von Krosigk, together with Frick and von Ribbentrop, signed a decree (*NG-3744, Pros. Ex. 638*) providing for the forfeiture of citizenship of all citizens in the Protectorate who may have "acted in a manner detrimental to the interests of the Reich or which damaged its reputation," as well as those who did not return home when ordered to do so by the Minister of the Interior, and the decree included a forfeiture of their property as well.

On 4 October 1939 the defendant with Frick signed a decree (*NG-3745, Pros. Ex. 635*) which authorized the Reich Protector to sequestrate, for the benefit of the Reich, the property of individuals or associations who fostered tendencies deleterious to the Reich, and the Protector and the Minister of Interior were authorized to determine what tendencies were to be so considered.

On 24 October 1942 Reinhardt, for the defendant Schwerin von Krosigk, and the defendant Stuckart, for the Minister of the Interior, signed a decree conferring jurisdiction on the Proctector, so far as nationals of the Protectorate were concerned, and on the Ministry of the Interior, in all other cases, to determine what activities should be declared "deleterious."

The occupation of Bohemia and Moravia and the formation of the so-called Protectorate were, as we have held, acts of aggression and in violation of international law. The enactment of these decrees was unlawful and was a part and parcel of the original unlawful act and scheme and plan.

It is apparent from the record that the defendant's Ministry of Finance was continually engaged in the work of taking over, disposing of, and realizing on Jewish confiscated property. The number and importance of these transactions and the fact that those engaged therein were responsible officials holding high office in the defendant's ministry, forecloses any possibility that they could have taken place without his knowledge and consent or subsequent confirmation and approval. They were a part, and an important part, of the Jewish persecutions carried on in the Reich and constitute violations of international law and agreements and crimes under count five.

Not only were these confiscations carried on in the Reich and against Jews of German nationality, but they were extended and came to include Jews of all nationalities living in Belgium or the Netherlands, or having fled from thence to occupied France and those who were residents of occupied France. The use to which much of this property was put was to realize foreign exchange for the Reich. They were all without justification, excuse, or legality. The officials of the defendant's ministry participated actively therein. These acts constitute violations of international law and crimes against humanity under count five.

When in June 1944 Himmler made application for the allocation of many millions for the demolition of the Warsaw ghetto, the defendant Schwerin von Krosigk expressed a willingness to make necessary installments on request, but coupled with it the stipulation that Himmler first use the values represented by goods found in the ghetto and inform him how many goods were to be utilized or had been so utilized. Himmler replied that the movable goods thus confiscated had been realized upon and the proceeds paid into the Reich's Main Pay Office in favor of the Ministry of Finance under a special account "Max Heiliger." Into this account was deposited the money and the proceeds of the dental gold extracted from the exterminated inmates of concentration camps and the jewelry and precious stones of which they were robbed. The defendant testifies that he had no knowledge of this account and does not know why it was given a fictitious name. It is to be remembered, however, that approximately 33 tons of dental and other gold alone were shipped to the Reich Bank and credited to this account. That such an acquisition to German gold stocks should not have come to the attention of the Minister of Finance we find it difficult to believe, although it is quite possible that he was not advised of the fictitious name under which the account was carried.

Part of the jewels, gold, and works of art which were seized in Paris from the Rothschild family were turned over to and accepted by the defendant and utilized by his department for Reich purposes. He made some objections to this but these were overcome and he accepted the proceeds which amounted to 1,800,000 marks. This was stolen property to which neither the Reich, the Reich agencies which stole it, nor the Ministry of Finance which accepted it, had the slightest legal claim. It was seized, not because of any wrong done by the owners, but merely because they were Jews.

Final solution.—The defendant was cosigner with Frick, Minister of the Interior; Bormann, Chief of the Party Chancellery; and Thierack, Minister of Justice, of the 13th Regulation under the Reich Citizenship Law. By its provisions criminal acts by Jews were to be punished by the police and not by judgment of the courts; the provisions of the public penal law were no longer applicable to Jews; on death, the property of a Jew was confiscated to the Reich, and only his non-Jewish heirs residing in Germany became entitled to compensation for the loss of their inheritance; the Minister of the Interior, with the concurrence of the higher authorities of the Reich, was empowered to issue the necessary administrative and enforcement regulations and to determine to what extent those provisions should apply to Jewish nationals in foreign countries, and finally the regulation was made applicable to Bohemia-Moravia and to all Jewish citizens of the Protectorate. This regulation was enacted in the midst of the extermination program, and by it the bare shadow of legal form was thrown over the confiscation of property of Jews who were done to death in the East.

The defendant asserts that his only part in the program was to take possession and keep record of the property thus acquired; that Himmler told him the process had been in existence for some months and that he, Schwerin von Krosigk, thought there was nothing he could do, and he "was convinced that the official promulgation would guarantee greater protection under the law than if the police, as heretofore, had handled it anonymously."

This is an explanation which does not explain, and a justification which does not justify. It is difficult to say what comfort it would be to a Jew who was about to be murdered, or to his heirs who were about to be disinherited, to know that he was being robbed according to a tidy governmental regulation and that the receipts of the robbery were to go to the credit of the Reich rather than into the hands and pockets of the executioners.

Germanization program and DUT.—The connection of the defendant Schwerin von Krosigk in this program consists almost entirely of setting aside Reich funds for the purposes mentioned, and which we have heretofore discussed with respect to the defendant Keppler. We find no instance, however, where these things were done at his instigation or other than at a direct order of Hitler. Here again he did not provide or dispose of his own funds nor was he in a position to say whether or not they should be so spent.

It is impracticable, within the compass of this opinion, to recite all of the activities in which the defendant and his department engaged within the purview of the charges alleged in count five. It is clear, however, that notwithstanding the conflicts of conscience which he suffered, and of them we have no doubt, he actively and consciously participated in the crimes charged in count five. Neither the desire to be of service nor the desire to help individuals nor the demands of patriotism constitute a justification or an excuse for that which the evidence clearly establishes he did, although they may be considered in mitigation of punishment.

We find the defendant Schwerin von Krosigk guilty under count five in the particulars set forth.

COUNT SIX—WAR CRIMES AND CRIMES AGAINST HUMANITY, PLUNDER AND SPOLIATION

* * *

COUNT SEVEN—WAR CRIMES AND CRIMES AGAINST HUMANITY; SLAVE LABOR

Count seven charges that defendants von Weizsaecker, Steengracht von Moyland, Woermann, Lammers, Stuckart, Ritter, Veesenmayer, Berger, Darre, Koerner, Pleiger, Kehrl, Puhl, and Rasche committed, during the period from

March 1938 to May 1945, war crimes and crimes against humanity, as defined by Article II of Control Council Law No. 10—

> . . . in that they participated in enslavement and deportation to slave labor on a gigantic scale of members of the civilian population of countries and territories under the belligerent occupation of, or otherwise controlled by, the Third Reich; enslavement of concentration camp inmates, including German nationals; the use of prisoners of war in war operations and work having a direct relation to war operations; and the ill treatment, terrorization, torture, and murder of enslaved persons, including prisoners of war. The defendants committed war crimes and crimes against humanity in that they were principals in, accessories to, ordered, abetted, took a consenting part in, were connected with plans and enterprises involving, and were members of organizations or groups connected with, the commission of war crimes and crimes against humanity.

It is further asserted in this count that the acts and conduct above referred to were carried out as part of the slave-labor program of the Third Reich, with the deliberate purpose to maintain German military power and to weaken the countries and territories occupied by Germany.

It is further asserted that the resources and needs of the occupied countries were completely disregarded in the carrying out of such slave-labor programs, as also were the family honor and rights of the civilian populations involved. It is asserted that frequently the work assigned was of a character which required the laborers to assist military operations against their own countries, and prisoners of war were often compelled to work on projects directly related to war operations. It is asserted that, through such slave-labor program, at least 5,000,000 workers were deported to Germany, and that other inhabitants of occupied territories were conscripted and compelled to work in their own countries to assist the German war economy. It is further alleged that, in many cases, labor was secured through fraud or by drastic and vile methods, including systematic impressment in the streets and by police invasions of homes. There are further allegations to the effect that persons deported were transferred under armed guard, often being packed in trains under cruel and degrading conditions, without adequate heat, food, clothing, or sanitation. It is alleged that millions of persons, including women and children, were subjected to such labor under cruel and inhumane conditions, such as lack of adequate food or shelter, which resulted in widespread suffering and many deaths.

It is asserted that the treatment of slave labor and prisoners of war was based on the principle that they were to be fed, sheltered, and treated in such a way as to exploit them to the greatest possible extent at the lowest possible cost.

During the course of the trial, the charges of this count of the indictment were dismissed, insofar as they relate to the defendant Woermann.

* * *

To recapitulate its conclusions, the Tribunal finds the defendants, hereinafter named, guilty under the counts set opposite their respective names:

VON WEIZSAECKER .... one, five.

STEENGRACHT VON MOYLAND	three, five.
KEPPLER	one, five, six, eight.
BOHLE	eight.
WOERMANN	one, five.
RITTER	three.
VEESENMAYER	five, seven, eight.
LAMMERS	one, three, five, seven, eight.
STUCKART	five, six, eight.
DARRE	five, six, eight.
DIETRICH	five, eight.
BERGER	three, five, seven, eight.
SCHELLENBERG	five, eight.
SCHWERIN VON KROSIGK	five, six.
PUHL	five.
KOERNER	one, six, seven, eight.
PLEIGER	six, seven.
KEHRL	five, six, seven, eight.
RASCHE	six, eight.

[Signed] WILLIAM C. CHRISTIANSON
Presiding Judge

I reserve the right to file later, separate dissenting views as to some convictions.
[Signed] LEON W. POWERS
Judge

[Signed] ROBERT F. MAGUIRE
Judge

SENTENCES

THE MARSHAL: The honorable, the judges of Military Tribunal IV. American Military Tribunal IV is now in session. God save the United States of America and this honorable Tribunal.

There will be order in the Court.

PRESIDING JUDGE CHRISTIANSON: Tribunal IV convened this morning for the purpose of imposing sentences upon those defendants who have been found guilty in this case, Case 11. The Tribunal will now impose sentences upon those defendants who have been adjudged guilty in these proceedings. The Marshal will produce the defendant Ernst von Weizsaecker.

Ernst von Weizsaecker, on the counts of the indictment on which you have been convicted the Tribunal sentences you to imprisonment for 7 years. The period already spent by you in confinement before and during the trial is to be credited on the term stated, and to this end the term of your imprisonment as now adjudged shall be deemed to begin on 25 July 1947. The Marshal will remove the defendant Weizsaecker.

The Marshal will produce before the Tribunal the defendant Ernst Bohle.

Ernst Bohle, on the count of the indictment on which you have been convicted, the Tribunal sentences you to imprisonment for 5 years. The period already spent by you in confinement before and during the trial is to be credited on the term stated, and to this end the term of your imprisonment as now adjudged shall be deemed to begin on 23 May 1945.

The Marshal will remove the defendant Bohle, and the Marshal will produce before the Tribunal the defendant Ernst Woermann.

Ernst Woermann, on the counts of the indictment on which you have been convicted the Tribunal sentences you to imprisonment for a period of 7 years. The period already spent by you in confinement before and during the trial is to be credited on the term stated, and to this end the term of your imprisonment as now adjudged shall be deemed to begin on 15 October 1945.

The Marshal will remove the defendant Woermann and produce the defendant Karl Ritter.

Karl Ritter, on the count of the indictment on which you have been convicted the Tribunal sentences you to imprisonment for 4 years. The period spent by you in confinement before and during the trial is to be credited on the term stated, and to this end the term of your imprisonment as now adjudged shall be deemed to begin on 15 May 1945.

The Marshal will remove the defendant Karl Ritter and produce before the Tribunal the defendant Edmund Veesenmayer.

Edmund Veesenmayer, on the counts of the indictment on which you have been convicted the Tribunal sentences you to imprisonment for a period of 20 years. The period already spent by you in confinement before and during the trial is to be credited on the term stated, and to this end the term of your imprisonment as now adjudged is deemed to begin on 14 May 1945.

The Marshal will remove the defendant Veesenmayer and produce before the Tribunal the defendant Hans Lammers.

Hans Lammers, on the counts of the indictment on which you have been convicted, the Tribunal sentences you to imprisonment for 20 years. The period already spent by you in confinement before and during the trial is to be credited on the term stated, and to this end the term of your imprisonment as now adjudged shall be deemed to begin on 11 May 1945.

The Marshal will remove the defendant Lammers and produce before the Tribunal the defendant Richard Darré.

Richard Darré, on the counts of the indictment on which you have been convicted the Tribunal sentences you to imprisonment for a period of 7 years. The period already spent by you in confinement before and during the trial is to be credited on the term already stated, and to this end the term of your imprisonment as now adjudged shall be deemed to begin on 14 April 1945.

The Marshal will remove the defendant Darré and produce before the Tribunal the defendant Otto Dietrich.

Otto Dietrich, on the counts of the indictment on which you have been convicted the Tribunal sentences you to 7 years. The period already spent by you in confinement before and during the trial is to be credited on the term already stated, and to this end the term of your imprisonment as now adjudged is deemed to begin on 18 August 1945.

The Marshal will remove the defendant Dietrich and produce before the Tribunal the defendant Gottlob Berger.

We must have quiet in the courtroom.

Gottlob Berger, on the counts of the indictment on which you have been convicted, the Tribunal sentences you to imprisonment for a period of 25 years. The period already spent by you in confinement before and during the trial is to be credited on the term stated, and to this end the term of your imprisonment as now adjudged shall be deemed to begin on 7 May 1945.

The Marshal will remove the defendant Berger and produce the defendant Schwerin von Krosigk.

Schwerin von Krosigk, on the counts of the indictment on which you have been convicted, the Tribunal sentences you to a period of 10 years. The period already spent by you in confinement before and during the trial is to be credited on the term already stated, and to this end the term of your imprisonment as now adjudged shall be deemed to begin on 23 May 1945.

The Marshall will remove the defendant Schwerin von Krosigk and produce the defendant Emil Puhl.

Emil Puhl, on the count of the indictment on which you have been convicted, the Tribunal sentences you to imprisonment for 5 years. The period already spent by you in confinement before and during the trial is to be credited on the term stated, and to this end the term of your imprisonment, as now adjudged, shall be deemed to begin on 1 May 1945.

The Marshal will remove the defendant Emil Puhl and produce the defendant Karl Rasche.

Karl Rasche, on the counts of the indictment on which you have been convicted, the Tribunal sentences you to imprisonment for a period of 7 years.

The period already spent by you in confinement before and during the trial is to be credited on the term stated, and to this end the term of your imprisonment as now adjudged shall be deemed to begin on 8 April 1945.

The Marshal will remove the defendant Rasche and produce the defendant Paul Koerner.

Paul Koerner, on the counts of the indictment on which you have been convicted, the Tribunal sentences you to imprisonment for a period of 15 years. The period already spent by you in confinement before and during the trial is to be credited on the term stated, and to this end the term of your imprisonment as now adjudged shall be deemed to begin on 6 May 1945.

The Marshal will remove the defendant Koerner and produce the defendant Paul Pleiger.

Paul Pleiger, on the counts of the indictment on which you have been convicted, the Tribunal sentences you to imprisonment for a term of 15 years. The period already spent by you in confinement before and during the trial is to be credited on the term stated, and to this end the term of your imprisonment as now adjudged shall be deemed to begin on 15 April 1945.

The Marshal will remove the defendant Pleiger and produce the defendant Hans Kehrl.

Hans Kerhl, on the counts of the indictment on which you have been convicted, the Tribunal sentences you to imprisonment for the term of 15 years. The period already spent by you in confinement before and during the trial is to be credited on the term stated, and to this end the term of your imprisonment as now adjudged shall be deemed to begin on 8 June 1945.

The Marshal will remove the defendant Hans Kehrl.

Inasmuch as the defendants Gustav Adolf Steengracht von Moyland, Wilhelm Keppler, Wilhelm Stuckart, and Walter Schellenberg, who have all been convicted in these proceedings, are ill and hospitalized it becomes necessary to impose sentences on them *in absentia.* Each of these defendants, through their counsel, has requested permission to be absent during the imposition of sentence, which requests have been granted. All of these defendants are represented by counsel here today, I believe.

Is Steengracht von Moyland represented here? Yes, I see, by Dr. Haensel.

On the counts of the indictment upon which the defendant *Gustav Adolf Steengracht von Moyland* has been convicted, we sentence him to imprisonment for a term of 7 years. The period already spent by him in confinement before and during the trial is to be credited on the term stated, and to this end the term of imprisonment as now adjudged shall be deemed to begin on 23 May 1945.

We will now impose sentence in the case of Wilhelm Keppler. Wilhelm Keppler's counsel is also present.

On the counts of the indictment upon which this defendant—that is, *Wilhelm Keppler*—has been convicted, the Tribunal sentences him to imprisonment for a period of 10 years. The period already spent by him in confinement before and during the trial is to be credited on the term stated, and to this end the term of his imprisonment as now adjudged shall be deemed to begin on 10 May 1945.

We will now impose sentence in the case of *Wilhelm Stuckart,* who is also represented by counsel here this morning.

In connection with this sentence, the Tribunal wishes to make this statement: Except for a short period of time when he was engaged in presenting his own defense, it has been necessary to excuse the defendant Stuckart from attendance in Court because of illness; he has been hospitalized most of the time, a situation which is expected to continue. His counsel have reported to the Tribunal concerning his physical condition, and they have submitted the report of German medical experts. The Tribunal requested that the United States Army appoint a board of competent Army officers to make a thorough physical examination of the defendant. This was done, and a written report has been submitted which has been filed with the records of this case. It appears that the defendant's physical condition is serious. He suffers from hypertensive cardiovascular disease or high blood pressure, anginal syndrome, and myocardial degeneration of the heart. Neither the American board of physicians nor the German doctors were able to give a favorable prognosis. The defendant is unable to undergo any physical exertion or strain, and must have complete rest and proper medication, and will require more or less constant hospitalization in the future. Under these circumstances, it is not at all unlikely that confinement would be equivalent to the death sentence. We have found the defendant guilty of serious charges, but his degree of guilt is not such as to warrant a sentence of capital punishment, and we are not willing to impose a sentence which in practical effect might entail death. Under these circumstances, the Tribunal is of the opinion that the ends of justice will be met if the sentence which we impose practically coincides with the imprisonment that the defendant Stuckart has thus far undergone. He has been under arrest since 26 May 1945 and has been in continuous custody since that time. The Tribunal therefore sentences this defendant, Wilhelm Stuckart, to imprisonment for a period of 3 years, 10 months, and 20 days. The period already spent by him before and during the trial is to be credited to the term stated, and to this end the term of his imprisonment as now adjudged shall be deemed to begin on 26 May 1945.

We will now impose sentence in the case of *Walter Schellenberg.* Is Walter Schellenberg's counsel here? Yes, I see he is.

On the counts of the indictment on which the defendant Schellenberg is convicted, the Tribunal now sentences him to a term of imprisonment of 6 years. The period already spent by him in confinement before and during the trial is to be credited on the term stated, and to this end the term of his imprisonment as now adjudged shall be deemed to begin on 17 June 1945.

This completed the imposition of sentences.

THE HIGH COMMAND CASE

Nuremberg, October, 1948*

OPINION AND JUDGEMENT OF UNITED STATES
MILITARY TRIBUNAL AT NUREMBERG IN
UNITED STATES *vs.* WILHELM VON LEEB ET AL.

THIS TRIBUNAL is composed of Presiding Judge John C. Young (formerly Chief Justice of the Supreme Court of Colorado), and Associate Judges Justin W. Harding (formerly U.S. District Judge First Division, District of Alaska) and Winfield B. Hale (Justice Tennessee Court of Appeals, on leave of absence).

It was created under and by virtue of Military Government Ordinance No. 7, effective 18 October 1946, adopted pursuant to Control Council Law No. 10, enacted 20 December 1945, in order to give effect to the London Agreement of 8 August 1945, and the Charter issued pursuant thereto for the prosecution of war criminals.

In Nuernberg, on 28 November 1947, in accordance with Ordinance No. 7 (Article III(*a*)), an indictment was lodged against the defendants by Telford Taylor, Brigadier General, U.S.A., Chief of Counsel for War Crimes, acting in behalf of the United States of America. A copy of the indictment in the German language was served upon each defendant at least thirty days prior to arraignment on 30 December 1947, at which time each, in the presence of counsel of his own selection, entered a plea of "not guilty."

The indictment named as defendants:

Generalfeldmarschall (General of the Army) Wilhelm von Leeb, Generalfeldmarschall (General of the Army) Hugo Sperrle, Generalfeldmarschall (General of the Army) Georg Karl Friedrich Wilhelm von Kuechler, Generaloberst (General) Hermann Hoth, Generaloberst (General) Hans Reinhardt, Generaloberst (General) Hans von Salmuth, Generaloberst (General) Karl Hollidt, Generaladmiral (Admiral) Otto Schniewind, General der Infanterie (Lieutenant

* *Trial of War Criminals,* Vol. 11, p. 462 (Washington D.C., 1950).

General, Infantry) Karl von Roques, General der Infanterie (Lieutenant General, Infantry) Hermann Reinecke, General der Artillerie (Lieutenant General, Artillery) Walter Warlimont, General der Infanterie (Lieutenant General, Infantry) Otto Woehler, and Generaloberstabsrichter (Lieutenant General, Judge Advocate) Rudolf Lehmann.

The defendant General Johannes Blaskowitz committed suicide in prison on 5 February 1948, and thereby the case against him was terminated.

THE INDICTMENT

The indictment is in four counts charging (1) crimes against peace; (2) war crimes; (3) crimes against humanity; and (4) a common plan or conspiracy to commit the crimes charged in counts one, two, and three.

Count One—Crimes Against Peace

The first count of the indictment, paragraphs 1 and 2 is as follows:

1. All of the defendants, with divers other persons, including the co-participants listed in Appendix A, during a period of years preceding 8 May 1945, committed crimes against peace as defined in Article II of Control Council Law No. 10, in that they participated in the initiation of invasions of other countries and wars of aggression in violation of international laws and treaties, including but not limited to the planning, preparation, initiation, and waging of wars of aggression, and wars in violation of international treaties, agreements, and assurances.

2. The defendants hold high military positions in Germany and committed crimes against peace in that they were principals in, accessories to, ordered, abetted, took a consenting part in, were connected with plans and enterprises involving, and were members of organizations and groups connected with, the commission of crimes against peace.

Then follow paragraphs 3 to 44, inclusive, covering plans of aggressions, and wars and invasions against Austria, Czechoslovakia, Poland, Great Britain, France, Denmark, Norway, Belgium, The Netherlands, Luxembourg, Yugoslavia, Greece, the U.S.S.R., and the United States of America, and undertook to show the unfolding of these plans of aggression and to particularize the participation of the defendants in the formulation, distribution, and execution thereof.

Count Two—War Crimes

Count two of the indictment, paragraph 45, is as follows:

45. Between September 1939, and May 1945, all of the defendants herein, with divers other persons including the co-participants listed in Appendix A, committed war crimes and crimes against humanity, as defined in Article II of Control Council Law No. 10, in that they participated in the commission of atrocities and offenses against prisoners of war and members of armed forces of nations then at war with the Third Reich or under the belligerent control of or

military occupation by Germany, including but not limited to murder, ill-treatment, denial of status and rights, refusal of quarter, employment under inhumane conditions and at prohibited labor of prisoners of war and members of military forces, and other inhumane acts and violations of the laws and customs of war. The defendants committed war crimes and crimes against humanity in that they were principals in, accessories to, ordered, abetted, took a consenting part in, were connected with plans and enterprises involving, and were members of organizations and groups connected with, the commission of war crimes and crimes against humanity.

Then follows paragraph 46, which in general terms sets out the unlawful acts as follows:

46. Unlawful orders initiated, drafted, distributed, and executed by the defendants directed that certain enemy troops be refused quarter and be denied the status and rights of prisoners of war, and that certain captured members of the military forces of nations at war with Germany be summarily executed. Such orders further directed that certain members of enemy armed forces be designated and treated by troops of the German armed forces, subordinate to the defendants, either as, 'partisans, Communists, bandits, terrorists' or by other terms denying them the status and rights of prisoners of war. Prisoners of war were compelled to work in war operations and in work having a direct relation to war operations, including the manufacture, transport, and loading of arms and munitions, and the building of fortifications. This work was ordered within the combat zone as well as in rear areas. Pursuant to a 'total war' theory and as part of the program to exploit all non-German peoples, prisoners of war were denied rights to which they were entitled under conventions and the laws and customs of war. Soldiers were branded, denied adequate food, shelter, clothing and care, subjected to all types of cruelties and unlawful reprisals, tortured, and murdered. Special screening and extermination units, such as Einsatz groups of the Security Police and Sicherheitsdienst (commonly known as the 'SD'), operating with the support and under the jurisdiction of the Wehrmacht, selected, and killed prisoners of war for religious, political, and racial reasons. Many recaptured prisoners were ordered executed. The crimes described in paragraphs 45 and 46 included, but were not limited to, those set forth hereafter in this count.

This is followed by paragraphs 47 to 58, inclusive, which particularize certain unlawful acts, such as the issuance and execution of the "Commissar Order," the "Commando Order," etc., and the participation of the defendants in the formulation, distribution, and execution of these unlawful plans.

Count Three—Crimes Against Humanity

Paragraph 59 of the indictment, is as follows:

59. Between September 1939, and May 1945, all of the defendants herein, with divers other persons including the co-participants listed in Appendix A, committed war crimes and crimes against humanity as defined in Article II of Control Council Law No. 10, in that they participated in atrocities and offenses, including murder, extermination, ill-treatment, torture, conscription to forced labor, deportation to slave labor or for other purposes, imprisonment without cause, killing of hostages, persecutions on political, racial and religious grounds,

plunder of public and private property, wanton destruction of cities, towns and villages, devastation not justified by military necessity, and other inhumane and criminal acts against German nationals and members of the civilian populations of countries and territories under the belligerent occupation of, or otherwise controlled by Germany. The defendants committed war crimes and crimes against humanity, in that they were principals in, accessories to, ordered, abetted, took a consenting part in, were connected with plans and enterprises involving, and were members of organizations and groups which were connected with, the commission of war crimes and crimes against humanity.

The following paragraphs 60 to 82 set forth generally and particularly the unlawful acts, such as enslavement of the population, plunder of public and private property, murder, etc., and participation of the defendants in the formulation, distribution and execution of these unlawful plans.

Count Four—Conspiracy to Commit Crimes Charged in Other Counts

Paragraphs 83 and 84, are as follows:

83. All the defendants, with divers other persons, during a period of years preceding 8 May 1945, participated as leaders, organizers, instigators, and accomplices in the formulation and execution of a common plan and conspiracy to commit, and which involved the commission of crimes against peace (including the acts constituting war crimes and crimes against humanity, which were committed as an integral part of such crimes against peace) as defined in Control Council Law Number 10, and are individually responsible for their own acts and for all acts committed by any persons in the execution of such common plan or conspiracy.

84. The acts and conduct of the defendants set forth in counts one, two and three of this indictment formed a part of said common plan or conspiracy and all the allegations made in said counts are incorporated in this count.

The trial began 5 February 1948, and the prosecution's case was substantially completed on 5 March at which time a recess was taken until 12 April 1948 to enable counsel to prepare their defense, then resumed and completed on 13 August 1948. Each defendant has been represented by German lawyers of his own selection who have conducted the defense with great ability, energy, and zeal.

A huge mass of evidence has been submitted in behalf of the prosecution and defense. The trial was conducted in two languages—English and German—and all documents submitted were duly translated and given counsel. The defense was also furnished with photostat copies of the original captured documents.

The prosecution's case, including those introduced on cross-examination and rebuttal, was made in part by the introduction of 1,778 documents, the vast majority of which were taken from German records and documents captured by the Allied Armies. The defendants complained that the context of many of these documents was necessary to their proper understanding and evaluation and that other documents would tend to explain or refute any inference of criminality that might be drawn from the documents relied upon by the prosecution. The defendants requested that they be supplied with additional material for their defense specified by them in their application. To this end the Tribunal ordered the Secretary General to procure such thereof as it was possible to procure, and as a result of this order there were procured from Washington 1,503 document folders which filled 37 footlockers. These the defense council and the defendants were permitted to examine and they have used such thereof as they deemed necessary in the presentation of their case either as new evidence or to supplement and explain the documents introduced by the prosecution.

The material used for such purpose by the defendants was taken from 259 different document folders and comprised 2,058 pages which were photostated and used as exhibits in the case. Such material was received at different times. The first shipment from Washington was received on 10 April, and the last on 27 May 1948. The case was not closed for the taking of testimony until 6 August 1948. In addition the defense counsel and the defendants were allowed access to all of the captured records and documents not yet sent over to the United States and still stored in the Court Archives in Nuernberg for the purpose of using such portions thereof as they might deem material. The defendants introduced a total of 2,130 documents and affidavits as exhibits in the presentation of their defense. The transcript of the record contains 10,000 pages.

Insofar as lay within its power, the Tribunal directed and aided in procuring all the witnesses that defense counsel requested, that their testimony might be heard in open court.

One hundred sixty-five witnesses were ordered summoned for the defendants. One hundred five of those summoned it was possible to procure and they were brought to Nuernberg and were available for the defendants to call to the witness stand. Of these only 80 in fact were called by the defendants. That so many of those requested were in fact procured is a tribute to the efficiency and to the cooperation that the administrative officers of the courthouse have rendered in this trial.

At many times during the progress of the case, counsel for the defendants insisted there were many and damaging errors made in the translations of the many documents offered in evidence by the prosecution. The Tribunal repeatedly advised counsel that if any errors had been made and were called to the Tribunal's attention, all efforts would be made to obtain a correct translation.

In the closing statement Dr. Surholt, counsel for the defendant General Reinecke, said:

> The documents must be properly translated, that is, the American translation must convey to the Tribunal the sense of the German text correctly and without omissions. This cannot be said of any of the document books. The English text in the hands of the Tribunal contains such a vast number of mistakes that to correct even the essential points is a task the defense is unable to cope with.

> The reviewing of the document books, arranged by the defense went as far as document books 1–9Q, which is about half of the material. The number of mistakes so far established amounts to 1,936.

And then he gave a few examples of the supposed erroneous translations.

Before the trial ended, the Tribunal again pointed out to counsel the advisability of submitting lists of the translations questioned. Dr. Frohwein, representing the defendant General Reinhardt, submitted a list consisting of thirty-one documents in which there were claimed errors of translation. This list was handed over to the prosecution which agreed to all of the contentions with the exception of three which were left to the decision of the Tribunal. Dr. Mueller-Torgow, for the defendant Hoth, submitted to the Tribunal a list of eighteen documents containing erroneous translations. All were agreed to by the prosecution.

Dr. Leverkuehn, representing the defendant Warlimont, submitted one item which was agreed to by the prosecution. Dr. von Keller, representing the defendant Dr. Lehmann, submitted a list consisting of twelve documents containing alleged errors, all of which were corrected by agreement with the prosecution.

These were the only corrections submitted by any of the counsel and many were of minor, if any, importance. For instance, we notice in one spot there were deleted the words: "These prisoners were shot on the spot after short interrogation." And there was substituted: "These prisoners are shot on the scene of action after short interrogation." At other points, the word "partisan" is deleted and the word "franc-tireur" substituted. In other places, the word "officials" was deleted and the word "functionaries" substituted in lieu thereof. Other criticisms were of more importance but this shows that many were more captious than material.

Such errors and ambiguities as were material and were not cleared up by agreement of counsel were noted and in accordance with proper rules of criminal procedure, any doubts and ambiguities are resolved in favor of the defendants.

A. Control Council Law No. 10.—The preamble to Control Council Law No. 10 reads as follows . . .

Many of the questions in the IMT case are presented in this case. The same unlawful orders, acts, and practices are involved; only the defendants are different. Hitler was the very center of vast expanding concentric rings of influence that touched every person in Germany. The defendants in this case are only one or two steps removed from Goering, Keitel, Jodl, Doenitz, and Raeder, defendants in the IMT case. Much of the evidence introduced in this case was introduced in the IMT hearing. Consequently, the great importance of the judgment of that trial as applying to the issues of law involved in this case, is readily apparent.

Objections During the Trial

The objection has been raised that this Tribunal is not a proper forum in which to try the defendants for the crimes charged. It is said that they were prisoners of war and that they are subject to trial only by a general court martial. We find no merit in such contention.

There is no doubt of the criminality of the acts with which the defendants are charged. They are based on violations of international law well recognized and existing at the time of their commission. True, no court had been set up for the trial of violations of international law. A state having enacted a criminal law may set up one or any number of courts and vest each with jurisdiction to try an offender against its internal laws. Even after the crime is charged to have been committed we know of no principle of justice that would give the defendant a vested right to a trial only in an existing forum. In the exercise of its sovereignty the state has the right to set up a tribunal at any time it sees fit and confer jurisdiction on it to try violators of its criminal laws. The only obligation a sovereign state owes to the violator of one of its laws is to give him a fair trial in a forum where he may have counsel to represent him—where he may produce witnesses in his behalf, and where he may speak in his own defense. Similarly, a defendant charged with a violation of international law is in no sense done an injustice if he is accorded the same rights and privileges. The defendants in this case have been accorded those rights and privileges.

As regards the contention that the defendants are prisoners of war and that the Geneva Convention, Article 63, requires that a prisoner of war be tried by a general court martial, we call attention to the fact that this provision referred to is found in an international agreement, that was entered into, and to which both the United States and Germany were signatories, to protect prisoners of war after they acquire such status and not to extend to them any special privileges or prerogatives with respect to crimes they may have committed before acquiring a prisoner of war status. Such is the reasoning of the Yamashita Case (*327 U.S. 1;66 Sup. Ct. 348*). We think the reasoning sound.

Article 63 of the Geneva Convention provides:

> Sentence may be pronounced against a prisoner of war only by the same courts and according to the same procedure as in the case of persons belonging to the armed forces of the detaining power.

Therefore, say defense counsel, the defendants must be tried by a general court martial since the defendants were prisoners of war taken by the United States, and members in the armed forces of the United States committing crimes are tryable by court martial. But the trial of men in the military forces of the United States by court martial can be only for crimes committed after the accused acquires and during the time he possesses the status of a member of the armed forces of the United States. One who committed murder and thereby violated the law of the state before he was inducted into the military service clearly could not be tried for that crime by a court martial for violating articles of war which did not apply to him when he committed the murder.

Nor do we think it necessary that defendants be discharged as prisoners of war before being brought to trial. Certainly if a man is arrested for violating a municipal traffic ordinance which subjects him only to a civil penalty in a magistrate's court and while he is in custody it is discovered that the day before he committed a murder, there is no violation of any principle of justice in holding him in custody and surrendering him to the officers of a court that has competency to try him for murder.

We are not deciding whether the United States or France or any other nation lawfully could or could not try the defendants in a court martial for a violation of international law. That is not before us. If that may be done, a court martial has not exclusive jurisdiction.

The crimes including the war crimes charged against the defendants are for violations of international criminal law. This Tribunal by Control Council Law No. 10 is vested with authority to try defendants for the crimes charged. That such jurisdiction possibly may be exercised by another military court is also of no consequence. If two courts have concurrent jurisdiction to try the same case the first court that exercises jurisdiction may properly dispose of the case.

The IMT said:

> The jurisdiction of the Tribunal is defined in the Agreement and Charter, and the crimes coming within the jurisdiction of the Tribunal, for which there shall be individual responsibility, are set out in Article 6. The law of the Charter is decisive, and binding upon the Tribunal. . . .
>
> The Tribunal is of course bound by the Charter, in the definition which it gives both of war crimes and crimes against humanity.

What was held by the IMT with respect to the London Agreement and Charter, the basic laws under which it functioned, is authority for a similar holding by this Tribunal with respect to the basic law under which it was set up and under which it functions.

We deem it unnecessary to discuss the objection that Control Council Law No. 10 is in violation of the maxim *nullum crimen sine lege, nulla poena sine lege.* We find it without merit. It has been passed upon so many times by the Nuernberg Tribunals and held without merit, that further comment here is unnecessary.

The further objection was made that one of the nations, namely, the U.S.S.R., cooperated in the promulgation of Control Council Law No. 10 after it had engaged in a war of aggression which is made criminal under the law; this objection also is without merit. The London Agreement and Charter from which Control Council Law No. 10 stems has been approved by 19 nations other than the four signatories thereto. We need not and do not determine whether the charge that one of the signatories of the London Agreement and Charter and Control Council Law No. 10 is guilty of aggressive war for such determination could avail the defendants nothing. Under general principles of law, an accused does not exculpate himself from a crime by showing that another committed a similar crime, either before or after the alleged commission of the crime by the accused.

Various of the defendants by way of objection or motions have raised the question of the sufficiency of the evidence on the part of the prosecution to make out a *prima facie* case of the guilt of the respective defendants. Numbers of these motions were ruled upon during the course of the trial. As to such motions not heretofore ruled upon, the same are denied, in as much as the questions raised by such motions are involved in the final determination of the guilt or the innocence of the defendants. . . .

Controlling Principles in Trial

The proper attitude to be observed in approaching a case of the character of the one before the Tribunal is so well stated by Judge Anderson in his concurring opinion in Case No. 10, the United States *vs.* Alfried Krupp, et al., that we set it forth, omitting only such portions as had particular application to that case, as a statement of the principles that we deem controlling in the approach to the instant case. Therein he said:

> There are certain matters of general application which must be stated in the outset of this investigation. They must be borne in mind throughout the discussion. The first is that this Tribunal was created to administer the law. It is not a manifestation of the political power of the victorious belligerents which is quite a different thing. The second is that the fact that the defendants are alien enemies is to be resolutely kept out of mind. The third is that considerations of policy are not to influence a disposition of the questions presented. Of these there are but two; (*a*) what was the law at the time in question, and, (*b*) does the evidence show *prima facie* that the defendants or any of them violated it. The fourth is that the defendants throughout are presumed to be innocent and before they can be put to their defense, the prosecution must make out a *prima facie* case of guilt by competent and relevant evidence. It is true that the procedural ordinance of the Military Government for Germany (US) provides that, "they [the Tribunals] shall adopt and apply to the greatest possible extent . . . non-technical procedure." But neither the members of this Tribunal nor the people of the nation prosecuting this case regard the presumption of innocence as nothing more than a technical rule of procedure. Nor do they, or we, think it a mere rhetorical abstraction to which lip service will suffice. Upon the contrary, in addition to its procedural consequences, it is a substantive right which stands as a witness for every defendant from the beginning to the end of his trial. . . . The sixth is that it is a fundamental principle of criminal justice that criminal statues are to be interpreted restrictively; that criminal responsibility is an individual matter; that criminal guilt must be personal. The seventh is that the application of *ex post facto* laws in criminal cases constitutes a denial of justice under international law (Quincy Wright: "The Law of the Nuernberg Trial," American Journal of International Law, volume 41, January 1947, p. 53). Hence, if it be conceded that Control Council Law No. 10 is binding on the Tribunal, it nevertheless must be construed and applied to the facts in a way which will not conflict with this view.

To the above we add that the burden rests upon the prosecution to present evidence that satisfies the Tribunal of the guilt of the defendants beyond a reasonable doubt. This rule also we have adhered to in arriving at our judgment. Where there was ambiguity in the testimony or uncertainty as to the defendants' connection with the transactions relied upon to establish their guilt, we have followed the well-recognized principle of criminal law and have accorded to the defendants the benefit of the doubt.

* * *

Superior Orders

Control Council Law No. 10, Article II, paragraphs 4 (*a*) and (*b*), provides:

> 4 (*a*) The official position of any person, whether as Head of State or as a responsible official in a Government Department, does not free him from responsibility for a crime or entitle him to mitigation of punishment.
>
> (*b*) The fact that any person acted pursuant to the order of his Government or of a superior does not free him from responsibility for a crime, but may be considered in mitigation.

These two paragraphs are clear and definite. They relate to the crimes defined in Control Council Law No. 10, Article II, paragraphs 1(*a*), (*b*), and (*c*). All of the defendants in this case held official positions in the armed forces of the Third Reich. Hitler from 1938 on was Commander in Chief of the Armed Forces and was the supreme civil and military authority in the Third Reich, whose personal decrees had the force and effect of law. Under such circumstances to recognize as a defense to the crimes set forth in Control Council No. 10 that a defendant acted pursuant to the order of his government or of a superior would be in practical effect to say that all the guilt charged in the indictment was the guilt of Hitler alone because he alone possessed the law-making power of the state and the supreme authority to issue civil and military directives. To recognize such a contention would be to recognize an absurdity.

It is not necessary to support the provision of Control Council Law No. 10, Article II, paragraphs 4(*a*) and (*b*), by reason, for we are bound by it as one of the basic authorities under which we function as a judicial tribunal. Reason is not lacking.

In as much as one of the reiterated arguments advanced is the injustice of even charging these defendants with being guilty of the crimes set forth in the indictment, when they were, it is said, merely soldiers and acted under governmental directives and superior orders which they were bound to obey, we shall briefly note what we consider sound reasons for the rejection of such a defense.

The rejection of the defense of superior orders without its being incorporated in Control Council Law No. 10 that such defense shall not exculpate would follow of necessity from our holding that the acts set forth in Control Council Law No. 10 are criminal not because they are therein set forth as crimes but because they then were crimes under international common law. International common law must be superior to and, where it conflicts with, take precedence over national law or directives issued by any national governmental authority. A directive to violate international criminal common law is therefore void and can afford no protection to one who violates such law in reliance on such a directive.

The purpose and effect of all law, national or international, is to restrict or channelize the action of the citizen or subject. International law has for its purpose and effect the restricting and channelizing of the action of nations. Since nations are corporate entities, a composite of a multitude of human beings, and since a nation can plan and act only through its agents and representatives, there can be no effective restriction or channelizing of national action except through control of the agents and representatives of the nation, who form its policies and carry them out in action.

The state being but an inanimate corporate entity or concept, it cannot as such make plans, determine policies, exercise judgment, experience fear, or be restrained or deterred from action except through its animate agents and representatives. It would be an utter disregard of reality and but legal shadow-boxing to say that only the state, the inanimate entity, can have guilt, and that no guilt can be attributed to its animate agents who devise and execute its policies. Nor can it be permitted even in a dictatorship that the dictator, absolute though he may be, shall be the scapegoat on whom the sins of all his governmental and military subordinates are wished; and that, when he is driven into a bunker and presumably destroyed, all the sins and guilt of his subordinates shall be considered to have been destroyed with him.

The defendants in this case who received obviously criminal orders were placed in a difficult position, but servile compliance with orders clearly criminal for fear of some disadvantage or punishment not immediately threatened cannot be recognized as a defense. To establish the defense of coercion or necessity in the face of danger there must be a showing of circumstances such that a reasonable man would apprehend that he was in such imminent physical peril as to deprive him of freedom to choose the right and refrain from the wrong. No such situation has been shown in this case.

Furthermore, it is not a new concept that superior orders are no defense for criminal action. Article 47 of the German Military Penal Code, adopted in 1872, was as follows:

> If through the execution of an order pertaining to the service [Dienstsachen], a penal law is violated, then the superior giving the order is alone responsible. However, the obeying subordinate shall be punished as accomplice [Teilnehmer]: (1) if he went beyond the order given to him, or (2) if he knew that the order of the superior concerned an act which aimed at a civil or military crime or offense.

The amendment of this in 1940 omitted the last two words "to him" in paragraph (1) above, and in paragraph (2) changed the words "civil or military crime or offense" to "general or military crime or offense." If this amendment had any effect, it extended rather than restricted the scope of the preceding act.

It is interesting to note that an article by Goebbels, the Reich Propaganda

Minister, which appeared in the "Voelkischer Beobachter," the official Nazi publication, on 28 May 1944, contained the following correct statement of the law:

> It is not provided in any military law that a soldier in the case of a despicable crime is exempt from punishment because he passes the responsibility to his superior, especially if the orders of the latter are in evident contradiction to all human morality and every international usage of warfare.

Orders

A question of general interest to the various defendants in this case involves the criminal responsibility for drafting, transmitting, and implementing illegal orders of their superiors.

For the first time in history individuals are called upon to answer criminally for certain violations of international law. Individual criminal responsibility has been known, accepted, and applied heretofore as to certain offenses against international law, but the Nuernberg trials have extended that individual responsibility beyond those specific and somewhat limited fields.

This Tribunal is therefore charged not only to determine whether certain acts infringe international law, but also whether criminal responsibility attaches to an individual for such infringement, and we must look not only to the international law itself but to fundamental principles of criminal law as generally accepted by the civilized nations of the world for determination of that question. Such has been the principle applied by the Tribunals which have preceded us and we conform to that standard. For a defendant to be held criminally responsible, there must be a breach of some moral obligation fixed by international law, a personal act voluntarily done with knowledge of its inherent criminality under international law.

Control Council Law No. 10 [Article II, paragraph 4 (*b*)] provides that:

> The fact that any person acted pursuant to the order of his government or of a superior does not free him from responsibility of a crime, but may be considered in mitigation.

It is urged that a commander becomes responsible for the transmittal in any manner whatsoever of a criminal order. Such a conclusion this Tribunal considers too far-reaching. The transmittal through the chain of command constitutes an implementation of an order. Such orders carry the authoritative weight of the superior who issues them and of the subordinate commanders who pass them on for compliance. The mere intermediate administrative function of transmitting an order directed by a superior authority to subordinate units, however, is not considered to amount to such implementation by the commander through whose headquarters such orders pass. Such transmittal is a routine function which in many instances would be handled by the staff of the commander without being called to his attention. The commander is not in a position to screen orders so transmitted. His headquarters, as an implementing agency, has been bypassed by the superior command.

Furthermore, a distinction must be drawn as to the nature of a criminal order itself. Orders are the basis upon which any army operates. It is basic to the discipline of an army that orders are issued to be carried out. Its discipline is built upon this principle. Without it, no army can be effective and it is certainly not incumbent upon a soldier in a subordinate position to screen the orders of superiors for questionable points of legality. Within certain limitations, he has the right to assume that the orders of his superiors and the state which he serves and which are issued to him are in conformity with international law.

Many of the defendants here were field commanders and were charged with heavy responsibilities in active combat. Their legal facilities were limited. They were soldiers—not lawyers. Military commanders in the field with far reaching military responsibilities cannot be charged under international law with criminal particpation in issuing orders which are not obviously criminal or which they are not shown to have known to be criminal under international law. Such a commander cannot be expected to draw fine distinctions and conclusions as to legality in connection with orders issued by his superiors. He has the right to presume, in the absence of specific knowledge to the contrary, that the legality of such orders has been properly determined before their issuance. He cannot be held criminally responsible for a mere error in judgment as to disputable legal questions.

It is therefore considered that to find a field commander criminally responsible for the transmittal of such an order, he must have passed the order to the chain of command and the order must be one that is criminal upon its face, or one which he is shown to have known was criminal.

While, as stated, a commanding officer can be criminally responsible for implementing an illegal order of his superiors, the question arises as to whether or not he becomes responsible for actions committed within his command pursuant to criminal orders passed down independent of him. The choices which he has for opposition in this case are few: (1) he can issue an order countermanding the order; (2) he can resign; (3) he can sabotage the enforcement of the order within a somewhat limited sphere.

As to countermanding the order of his superiors, he has no legal status or power. A countermanding order would not only subject him to the severest punishment, but would be utterly futile and in Germany, it would undoubtedly have focussed the eyes of Hitler on its rigorous enforcement.

His second choice—resignation—was not much better. Resignation in wartime is not a privilege generally accorded to officers in an army. This is true in the Army of the United States. Disagreement with a state policy as expressed by an order affords slight grounds for resignation. In Germany, under Hitler, to assert such a ground for resignation probably would have entailed the most serious consequences for an officer.

Another field of opposition was to sabotage the order. This he could do only verbally by personal contacts. Such verbal repudiation could never be of sufficient scope to annul its enforcement.

A fourth decision he could make was to do nothing.

Control Council Law No. 10, Article II, paragraph 2, provides in pertinent part as follows:

> Any person without regard to nationality or the capacity in which he acted, is deemed to have committed a crime as defined in paragraph 1 of this article, if he . . . (*b*) was an accessory to the commission of any such crime or ordered or abetted the same or (*c*) took a consenting part therein or (*d*) was connected with plans or enterprises involving its commission. . . .

As heretofore stated, his "connection" is construed as requiring a personal breach of a moral obligation. Viewed from an international standpoint, such has been the interpretation of preceding Tribunals. This connection may however be negative. Under basic principles of command authority and responsibility, an officer who merely stands by while his subordinates execute a criminal order of his superiors which he knows is criminal violates a moral obligation under international law. By doing nothing he cannot wash his hands of international responsibility. His only defense lies in the fact that the order was from a superior which Control Council Law No. 10 declares constitutes only a mitigating circumstance.

In any event in determining the criminal responsibility of the defendants in this case, it becomes necessary to determine not only the criminality of an order in itself but also as to whether or not such an order was criminal on its face. Certain orders of the Wehrmacht and the German army were obviously criminal. No legal opinion was necessary to determine the illegality of such orders. By any standard of civilized nations they were contrary to the customs of war and accepted standard of humanity. Any commanding officer of normal intelligence must see and understand their criminal nature. Any participation in implementing such orders, tacit or otherwise, any silent acquiescence in their enforcement by his subordinates, constitutes a criminal act on his part.

There has also been much evidence and discussion in this case concerning the duties and responsibilities of staff officers in connection with the preparation and transmittal of illegal orders. In regard to the responsibility of the chief of staff of a field command, the finding of Tribunal V in Case No. 7 as to certain defendants has been brought to the attention of the Tribunal. It is pointed out that the decision as to chiefs of staff in that case was a factual determination and constitutes a legal determination only insofar as it pertains to the particular facts therein involved. We adopt as sound law the finding therein made, but we do not give that finding the scope that is urged by defense counsel in this case to the effect that all criminal acts within a command are the sole responsibility of the commanding general and that his chief of staff is absolved from all criminal responsibility merely by reason of the fact that his commanding general may be charged with responsibility therefore. It is further pointed out that the facts in that case are not applicable to any defendant on trial in this case.

The testimony of various defendants in this case as to the functions of staff officers and chiefs of staff has not been entirely consistent. Commanding generals on trial have pointed out that there were certain functions which they necessarily left to the chiefs of staff and that at times they did not know of orders which might be issued under authority of their command. Staff officers on trial have urged that a commanding officer was solely responsible for what was done in his name. Both contentions are subject to some scrutiny.

In regard to the functions of staff officers in general as derived from various documents and the testimony of witnesses, it is established that the duties and functions of such officers in the German Army did not differ widely from the duties and functions in other armies of the world. Ideas and general directives must be translated into properly prepared orders if they are to become effective in a military organization. To prepare orders is the function of staff officers. Staff officers are an indispensable link in the chain of their final execution. If the basic idea is criminal under international law, the staff officer who puts that idea into the form of a military order, either himself or through subordinates under him, or takes personal action to see that it is properly distributed to those units where it becomes effective, commits a criminal act under international law.

Staff officers, except in limited fields, are not endowed with command authority. Subordinate staff officers normally function through the chiefs of staff. The chief of staff in any command is the closest officer, officially at least, to the commanding officer. It is his function to see that the wishes of his commanding officer are carried out. It is his duty to keep his commanding officer informed of the activities which take place within the field of his command. It is his function to see that the commanding officer is relieved of certain details and routine matters, that a policy having been announced, the methods and procedures for carrying out such policy are properly executed. His sphere and personal activities vary according to the nature and interests of his commanding officer and increase in scope dependent upon the position and responsibilities of such commander.

Since a chief of staff does not have command authority in the chain of command, an order over his own signature does not have authority for subordinates in the chain of command. As shown by the record in this case, however, he signs orders for and by order of his commanding officer. In practice, a commanding officer may or may not have seen these orders. However, they are presumed to express the wishes of the commanding officer. While the commanding officer may not and frequently does not see these orders, in the normal process of command he is informed of them and they are presumed to represent his will unless repudiated by him. A failure to properly exercise command authority is not the responsibility of a chief of staff.

In the absence of participation in criminal orders or their execution within a command, a chief of staff does not become criminally responsible for criminal acts occurring therein. He has no command authority over subordinate units. All he can do in such cases is call those matters to the attention of his commanding general. Command authority and responsibility for its exercise rest definitely upon his commander.

Under normal military procedure a commanding officer signs communications to higher commanders. He also in certain cases signs orders to subordinates which are considered to establish basic policy or whose importance he wishes to emphasize; but the majority of orders issued in a command, as shown by the record, are issued "for" or "by order" and signed only by the chief of staff. All such orders are binding on subordinates. How far a chief of staff can go in issuing orders without previous authorization or without calling them to the attention of his commander depends upon many factors, including his own qualifications, his rank, the nature of the headquarters, his personal relationship with his commander, and primarily upon the personality of the commander. A chief of staff does not hold a clerical position. In the German army chiefs of staff were not used below an army corps. The rank and care with which staff officers were selected show in itself the wide scope of their responsibilities which could, and in many instances undoubtedly did, result in the chief of staff assuming many command and executive responsibilities which he exercised in the name of his commander.

One of his main duties was to relieve his commander of certain responsibilities so that such commander could confine himself to those matters considered by him of major importance. It was of course the duty of a chief of staff to keep such commander informed of the activities which took place within the field of his command insofar at least as they were considered of sufficient importance by such commander. Another well-accepted function of chiefs of staff and of all other staff officers is, within the field of their activities, to prepare orders and directives which they consider necessary and appropriate in that field and which are submitted to their superiors for approval.

As stated heretofore, the responsibility allowed a chief of staff to issue orders and directives in the name of his commander varied widely and his independent powers for exercising initiative therefore also varied widely in practice. The field for personal initiative as to other staff officers also varied widely. That such a field did exist however is apparent from the testimony of the various defendants who held staff positions and in their testimony have pointed out various cases in which they modified the specific desires of their superiors in the interests of legality and humanity. If they were able to do this, the same power could be exercised for other ends and purposes and they were not mere transcribers of orders.

Surely the staff officers of the OKW did not hold their high ranks and positions and did not bask in the bright sunlight of official favor of the Third and Thousand Year Reich by merely impeding and annulling the wishes of the Nazi masters whom they served.

It over-taxes the credulity of this Tribunal to believe that Hitler or Keitel or Jodl, or all three of these dead men, in addition to their many activities as to both military matters and matters of state, were responsible for the details of so many orders, words spoken in conferences, and even speeches which were made. We are aware that many of the evil and inhumane acts of the last war may have originated in the minds of these men. But it is equally true that the evil they originated and sponsored did not spread to the far flung troops of the Wehrmacht of itself. Staff officers were indispensable to that end and cannot escape criminal responsibility for their essential contribution to the final execution of such orders on the plea that they were complying with the orders of a superior who was more criminal.

Commissar Order

This was one of the most obviously malevolent, vicious, and criminal orders ever issued by any army of any time. It called for the murder of Russian political functionaries and, like so much of the evils of the Third Reich, originated in Hitler's fertile brain. As will be shown, it was issued prior to the opening of the campaign against Russia.

On 30 March 1941, Hitler held a conference at Berlin with leaders of the Wehrmacht. Von Leeb was present. At that time, according to the summary contained in General Halder's Diary, Hitler said:

> *Clash of two ideologies.* Crushing denunciation of bolshevism, identified with asocial criminality. Communism is an enormous danger for our future. We must forget the concept of comradeship between soldiers. A Communist is no comrade before nor after the battle. This is a war of extermination. If we fail to grasp this, and though we are sure to beat the enemy, we shall again have to fight the Communist foe 30 years from now. We do not wage war to preserve the enemy.
>
> *War against Russia.* Extermination of the Bolshevist commissars and of the Communist intelligentsia. The new states must be Socialist, but without intellectual classes of their own. Growth of a new intellectual class must be prevented. A primitive Socialist intelligentsia is all that is needed. We must fight against the poison of disintegration. This is no job for military courts. The individual troop commander must know the issues at stake. They must be leaders in the fight. The troops must fight back with the methods with which they are attacked. Commissars and GPU men are criminals and must be dealt with as such. This need not mean that the troops get out of hand. Rather the commander must give orders which express the common feelings of his troops.
>
> This war will be very different from the war in the West. In the East, harshness today means leniency in the future. Commanders must make the sacrifice of overcoming their personal scruples.

This seemed to have caused quite a bit of excitement among those present who, of couse, recognized it as being brutal, murderous, and uncivilized. After Hitler had made his speech and had departed to his inner sanctum, protests were uttered by the commanders to the effect [that] the extermination planned by Hitler would violate their soldierly principles and, further, would destroy discipline. Brauchitsch agreed with them and promised to express their opinion to the OKW and Hitler respectively. He tried through Keitel to obtain a change in the plans but was unable to do so. Subsequently, he lent his approval to the objections made by the field commanders, who, in some instances at least, expressed a negative opinion of the order to their subordinates and tried to avoid its execution as far as they could do so without peril to themselves. One of the means to ameliorate the brutality of the Commissar Order was the issuance by von Brauchitsch of what is known as the "Maintenance of Discipline" order hereafter referred to.

On 6 June 1941, the Commissar Order was issued from the Fuehrer Headquarters as "Top Secret. Transmission only by officer!" and was captioned "Directives for the Treatment of Political Commissars." It was as follows [*NOKW-484, Pros. Ex. 56*]:

In the fight against bolshevism it is *not* to be expected that the enemy will act in accordance with the principles of humanity or of the international law. In particular, a vindictive, cruel, and inhuman treatment of our prisoners must be expected on the part of the *political commissars of all types,* as they are the actual leaders of the resistance.

The troops must realize—

1. In this fight, leniency and considerations of international law are out of place in dealing with these elements. They constitute a danger for their own safety and the swift pacification of the conquered territories.

2. The originators of barbarous Asiatic methods of warfare are the political commissars. They must therefore be dealt with most severely, *at once* and summarily.

Therefore, they are to be liquidated at once when taken in combat or offering resistance.

For the rest, the following directives will apply:

I. *Combat zone.*

(1) Political commissars *who oppose our troops* will be treated in accordance with the, "decree concerning the application of martial law in the Barbarossa area." This applies to commissars of any type and grade, even if they are only suspected of resistance, sabotage, or of instigation thereto.

Reference is made to the "directive concerning the conduct of the troops in Russia."

(2) Political commissars as *organs of the enemy troops* are recognizable by special insignia—red star with interwoven gold hammer and sickle on the sleeves. (For particulars see "The Armed Forces of the U.S.S.R.," High Command of the Armed Forces General Staff of the Army, Qu. IV, Section Foreign Armies East, (II) No. 100/41 Secret of 15 January 1941, Appendix 9d.) They are to be segregated *at once,* e.g., still on the battlefield, from the prisoners of war. This is necessary to prevent them from influencing the prisoners of war in any way. These commissars will not be recognized influencing soldiers, the protection of prisoners of war by international law does not apply to them. They will be liquidated after segregation.

(3) *Political commissars who have not committed, or are not suspected of hostile acts* will not be harmed for the time being. Only after deeper penetration of the country will it be possible to decide whether officials who were left behind may stay where they are or will be handed over to the Sonderkommandos. Preferably the latter should decide on this point. As a matter of principle, in deciding the question whether "guilty or not guilty" the personal impression which the commissar makes of his mentality and attitude will have precedence over facts which may be unprovable.

(4) In cases (1) and (2) a short message (message form) about the incident will be sent: (*a*) by divisional units to divisional headquarters (intelligence officer); (*b*) by troops directly under the command of a corps, an army, an army group or a Panzer group, to the respective headquarters (intelligence officer).

(5) None of the above-mentioned measures must obstruct the operations. Methodical searches and mopping-up actions, therefore, will not be carried out by the troops.

II. In the communication zone commissars who are arrested in the communications zone on account of a doubtful attitude will be handed over to the Einsatzgruppen and/or Einsatzkommandos of the Security Police (Security Service).

III. *Limitations of courts martial and summary courts*—The courts martial and summary courts of the regimental and other commanders must not be entrusted with the execution or the measures as per I and II.

On 8 June 1941, von Brauchitsch sent out a supplement of two additional clauses to be added to the original, viz., to I number (1),

Action taken against a political commissar must be based on the fact that the person in question has shown by a special recognizable act or attitude that he opposes or will in future oppose the Wehrmacht.

To I number (2),

Political commissars attached to the troops should be segregated and dealt with *by order of an officer,* inconspicuously and *outside the proper battle zone.*

On 24 May 1941, however, von Brauchitsch formulated the *Maintenance of Discipline* Order, in which as a supplement to the Fuehrer Order it is said:

Subject: Treatment of enemy civilians and criminal acts of members of the Wehrmacht against enemy civilians

Attacked Fuehrer decree is (hereby) announced. It is to be distributed *in writing* down to the commanders with jurisdiction of their own, beyond that, the principles contained in it are to be made known *orally*.

Supplements to I—I expect that all counterintelligence measures of the troops will be carried out energetically, for their own security and the speedy pacification of the territory won. It will be necessary to take into account the variety of ethnic strains within the population, its over-all attitude, and the degree to which they have been stirred up.

Movement and combat against the enemy's armed forces are the real tasks of the troops. It demands the fullest concentration and the highest effort of all forces. This task must not be jeopardized in any place. Therefore, in general, special search and mopping-up operations will be out of question for the combat troops.

The directives of the Fuehrer concern *serious* cases of rebellion, in which the most severe measures are required.

Criminal acts of a minor nature are, always in accordance with the combat situation, to be punished according to detailed orders from an officer (if possible, a post commander) by resorting to *provisional measures* (for instance, temporary detention at reduced rations, roping-upon a tree, assignment to labor).

The CinC's of the army groups are requested to obtain my approval prior to the reinstatement of Wehrmacht jurisdiction in the pacified territories. The CinC's of the armies are expected to make suggestions in this respect in time.

Special instructions will be issued about the treatment to be given to political dignitaries.

Supplements to II—Under all circumstances it will remain the duty of all superiors to prevent arbitrary excesses of *individual* members of the army and to prevent *in time the troops* becoming unmanageable. It must not come to it that the individual soldier commits or omits any act *he* thinks proper toward the indigenous population; he must rather feel that in every case he is *bound by the orders of his officers*. I consider it very important that this be clearly understood down to the lowest unit. *Timely action* by every officer, especially every company commander, etc., must *help* to maintain discipline, the basis of our successes.

Occurrences with regard to "I" and "II", and which are of special importance, are to be reported by the troops to the OKH as special events.

[Signed] VON BRAUCHITSCH

There are 340 copies of this order which, as noted, had attached a copy of the Fuehrer order. This apparently was given wide distribution, although the original Fuehrer order had a very limited distribution.

It is said the *maintenance of discipline* order was conceived by von Brauchitsch as a means of sabotaging the Hitler order, but it will be noted that in the quoted part of Halder's diary he has Hitler saying, "This need not mean that the troops get out of hand."

It seems to be conceded—if any concession is necessary—that this order was criminal. It has neither defender nor apologist. Instead of a straightforward and manly refusal to execute a criminal order, some of the defendants sought a surreptitious sabotaging and evasion of its enforcement. However, in spite of such rejection or opposition on the part of those in high command, the record contains a large number of reports showing the execution of commissars by units subordinate to various of the defendants, as will be shown in the discussion of the case pertaining to each. This would have been avoided had some of these commanders been sufficiently courageous to have forced the issue. This was not done. It was implemented throughout the army.

It is claimed that on some occasions at least, blown up, exaggerated, or even fictitious figures were given of the number of these functionaries who were murdered. But the cold, hard, inescapable fact remains that many were so executed in utter violation of the laws of war and of humanity.

Can these defendants escape liability because this criminal order originated from a higher level? They knew it was directed to units subordinate to them. Reports coming in from time to time from these subordinate units showed the execution of these political functionaries. It is true in many cases they said they had no knowledge of these reports. They should have had such knowledge. If they had expressed their opposition to and rejection of the Commissar Order, that the reports showing the carrying out of this order would have been shown to them by their subordinates is a conclusion that is inescapable. It was criminal to pass it down to subordinate units. When the subordinates obeyed the order, the superior cannot absolve himself by the plea that his character was so well known that his subordinates should have had the courage to disobey the order which he himself in passing it down showed that he lacked. Such a plea is contemptible and constitutes no defense.

BARBAROSSA JURISDICTION ORDER

The so-called Barbarossa Jurisdiction Order is in a different category from the Commissar and Commando Orders and its consideration is somewhat more complicated. This order was issued by Keitel on 13 May 1941 as "Decree on Exercising Military Jurisdiction in the Area of Barbarossa and Special Measures by the Troops," and reads as follows [*C-50, Pros. Ex. 594*]:

The Wehrmacht's application of its laws (Wehrmachtgerichtsbarkeit) place at *maintaining discipline*.

The vast extent of the operational areas in the East, the fighting methods necessitated thereby and the peculiarity of the enemy give the Wehrmacht courts jobs which—in view of their limited personnel—they can only solve during war operations and until some degree of pacification has been obtained in the conquered area if they limit themselves at first to their main task.

This is possible only if the troops themselves oppose ruthlessly any threat from the enemy population.

For these reasons herewith with following is ordered for the area "Barbarossa" (area of operations, army group rear area, and area of political administration).

I. *Treatment of crimes committed by enemy civilians*

1. Until further order the military courts and the courts martial will not be competent for *crimes committed by enemy civilians.*

2. *Francs-tireurs* will be liquidated ruthlessly by the troops in combat or while fleeing.

3. *Also all other attacks by enemy civilians against the armed forces,* its members, and auxiliaries will be suppressed on the spot by the troops with the most rigorous methods until the assailants are finished (niederkaempfen).

4. Where such measures were not taken or at least were not possible, *persons suspected of the act will be brought before an officer at once. This officer will decide whether they are to be shot.*

Against *localities* from which troops have been attacked in a deceitful or treacherous manner, *collective coercive measures* will be applied immediately upon the order of an officer of the rank of at least battalion etc., commander, if the circumstances do not permit a quick identification of individual perpetrators.

5. It is *strictly forbidden* to *keep* suspects in *custody* in order to put them at the disposal of the courts after the reinstatement of jurisdiction over indigenous inhabitants.

6. The commanders in chief of the army groups can—by agreement with the competent commanders of the Luftwaffe and the navy—*reinstate jurisdiction of the Wehrmacht courts for civilians,* in areas sufficiently pacified.

For the *area of the political administration* this order will be given by the Chief of the OKW.

II. *Treatment of crimes committed against inhabitants by members of the Wehrmacht and its auxiliaries*

1. *With regard to offenses committed against enemy civilians by members of the Wehrmacht* or by its auxiliaries *prosecution is not obligatory,* even where the deed is at the same time a military crime or misdemeanor.

2. When *judging such offenses,* it will be taken into consideration in any type of procedure that the collapse of Germany in 1918, the subsequent sufferings of the German people and the fight against national socialism which cost the blood of innumerable followers of the movement were caused primarily by Bolshevist influence and that no German has forgotten this fact.

3. Therefore the judiciary will decide in such case whether *disciplinary punishment* will be appropriate, or whether *prosecution in court* is necessary. In the case of offenses against indigenous inhabitants the judiciary will order a

prosecution *before the military courts only if the maintenance* of discipline or the security of the forces call for such a measure. This applies for instance to serious deeds due to lack of self-control in sexual matters, which originate from a criminal disposition and which indicates that the discipline of the troops is threatening to deteriorate seriously. Crimes which have resulted in senseless destruction of billets or stores or any other kind of captured material, to the disadvantage of our forces will be judged, as a rule, not less severely.

The *order to start investigation procedure* requires in every single case the signature of the judicial authority.

4. *Extreme caution* is required in judging the credibility of statements made by enemy civilians.

III. *Responsibility of the Troop Commanders*

In as far as they are competent, it is the *personal* responsibility of the troop commanders to see to it—

1. That all officers of the units under their command are instructed in time and in the most emphatic manner about the principles set out under I above.

2. That their legal advisers are informed *in time of* these rules and *of the verbal communications in which the political intentions of the Supreme Command* (Fuehrung) *were explained to the commanders in chief.*

3. That only those sentences will be confirmed which correspond to the political intentions of the Supreme Command (Fuehrung).

IV. *Protection as secret matter*

Once the camouflage is lifted this decree will merely have the classification of *Top Secret.*

It is divided into two main parts: first, it dispensed with court martial jurisdiction over the civilian population and provided that civilians in the occupied areas would be subjected to arbitrary punishment upon the decision of an officer. The second part provided that there was no obligation to prosecute members of the Wehrmacht or its auxiliaries who committed crimes against enemy civilians except in cases involving discipline which were restricted to certain types of offenses.

As to the first phase, court martial jurisdiction of civilians is not considered under international law an inherent right of a civilian population and is not an inherent prerogative of a military commander. The obligation towards civilian populations concerns their fair treatment. Court martial jurisdiction of a military commander and its extent are determined by his superiors. It has been urged in this trial that there is no rule of international law that guerrillas be brought to trial before a court and that this order authorizing their disposition on the arbitrary decision of an officer is therefore not illegal. There may be some doubt that trial before a court is in fact required under international law.

But in considering this order it must be borne in mind that it was not solely applicable to guerrillas and that it is an obligation upon an occupying force to provide for the fair treatment of the civilians within the occupied area. Whatever may be said as to the summary proceedings against guerrillas, the allowing of such summary proceedings in the discretion of a junior officer, in the case of the wide variety of offenses that were left open to him, is considered criminal.

Furthermore, the fourth paragraph of section I above in its most favorable construction is at best ambiguous but the logical inference to be drawn from this section goes further in the opinion of the Tribunal and provides that suspected *francs-tireurs* may be shot, which is also considered illegal.

The fourth paragraph of section I also provides for collective coercive measures to be applied immediately upon the order of an officer of at "least battalion, etc., commander" and is considered illegal in that it places no limitations upon such collective actions whatsoever.

For these reasons the first part of this order is considered illegal and we so find.

With regard to the second aspect of this order, that is the obligation to prosecute soldiers who commit offenses against the indigenous population, this obligation as a matter of international law is considered doubtful. The duty imposed upon a military commander is the protection of the civilian population. Whether this protection be assured by the prosecution of soldiers charged with offenses against the civilian population, or whether it be assured by disciplinary measures or otherwise, is immaterial from an international standpoint. This order in this respect is usbject to interpretation. It surely opened the door to serious infractions of discipline. The German Army was concerned with the discipline of its troops. That discipline could not be maintained without punishment. Unwarranted acts of a soldier against a civilian constituted a breach of discipline. As a matter of fact, practically any offense against civilians could be construed as a breach of discipline. The provisions of the act itself recognize in part this situation. Recognition of this fact in the order was further strengthened by the von Brauchitsch so-called disciplinary order. This order was issued on 21 May 1941, practically coincident with the Barbarossa Jurisdiction Order, and was quoted above in connection with the Commissar Order.

This order was apparently given wide distribution and it is considered not without merit that the military authorities in the issuance of this order had substantially limited section II of the Barbarossa Jurisdiction Order insofar as that order did away with the obligation to prosecute. At any rate, as far as the acts of a soldier against the civilian population were concerned, practically any act might be interpreted as an act against discipline.

This disciplinary order by von Brauchitsch, however, was virtually canceled by certain subsequent orders issued by Keitel which will be hereafter noted in this opinion.

As regards the first part of the Barbarossa Jurisdiction Order, commanders were merely deprived of jurisdiction. It was not a positive order to do some act. It was merely an order which took away part of their powers. It is difficult to see how courts martial could have been established to try civilians under such circumstances and the actions of such courts would have been illegal and futile. As regards the second part of the order, as heretofore stated, it was subject to the interpretation that unwarranted acts against civilians constituted a breach of discipline. The illegal application of the order, therefore, rested to a marked extent with the commanders in the field.

Another provision of this order must be given consideration in this regard. Paragraph 6 of section I provides that the commander in chief of the army groups can by agreement with the competent commanders of the Luftwaffe and the navy "reinstate jurisdiction of the Wehrmacht courts for civilians, in areas sufficiently pacified." While the limitation is placed upon this provision that the areas must be sufficiently pacified before the jurisdiction of the Wehrmacht courts could be reinstated, this provision nevertheless left the door open for commanders in chief of army groups opposed to the arbitrary provisions of the order as to civilians, to take action to eliminate it from their areas. This the record shows none of them did.

This Tribunal does not hold field commanders guilty for a failure to properly appraise the fine distinctions of international law, nor for failure to execute courts martial jurisdiction which had been taken away from them, but it does consider them criminally responsible for the transmission of an order that could, and from its terms would, be illegally applied where they have transmitted such an order without proper safeguards as to its application. For that failure on their part they must accept criminal responsibility for its misapplication within subordinate units to which they transmitted it. And in view of the relation of this order to *francs-tireurs,* it takes the view that while commanding generals might not be able under the provisions of the Barbarossa Jurisdiction Order to establish courts martial to try them, that such commanders were nevertheless responsible, within the areas of their commands, for the summary execution of persons who were merely suspects or those who, from their acts, were not in fact *francs-tireurs* at all, such as the execution of the nineteen-year-old girl who wrote a song derogatory of the German invader of her country.

Commando Order

Following the Dieppe raid, and after drafts and changes had been prepared largely by Warlimont and Lehmann, Hitler issued the following order on 18 October 1942 [*498–PS, Pros. Ex. 124*]:

TOP SECRET

1. For some time our enemies have been using in their warfare methods which are outside the international Geneva Conventions. Especially brutal and treacherous is the behavior of the so-called commandos, who, as is established, are partially recruited even from freed criminals in enemy countries. From captured orders it is divulged, that they are directed not only to shackle prisoners, but also to kill defenseless prisoners on the spot at the moment in which they believe that the latter as prisoners represent a burden in the further pursuit of their purposes or could otherwise be a hindrance. Finally, orders have been found in which the killing of prisoners has been demanded in principle.

2. For this reason it was already announced in an addendum to the armed forces report of 7 October 1942 that in the future, Germany, in the face of these sabotage troops of the British and their accomplices, will resort to the same

procedure, i.e., that they will be ruthlessly mowed down by the German troops in combat, wherever they may appear.

3. I therefore order—

From now on all enemies on so-called commando missions in Europe or Africa challenged by German troops, even if they are to all appearance soldiers in uniform or demolition troops, whether armed or unarmed, in battle or in flight, are to be slaughtered to the last man. It does not make any difference whether they are landed from ships and aeroplanes for their actions, or whether they are dropped by parachute. Even if these individuals, when found, should apparently be prepared to give themselves up, no pardon is to be granted them on principle. In each individual case full information is to be sent to the OKW for publication in the report of the military forces.

4. If individual members of such commandos, such as agents, saboteurs, etc., fall into the hands of the military forces by some other means, through the police in occupied territories for instance, they are to be handed over immediately to the SD. Any imprisonment under military guard, in PW stockades for instance, etc., is strictly prohibited, even if this is only intended for a short time.

5. This order does not apply to the treatment of any enemy soldiers who, in the course of normal hostilities (large scale offensive actions, landing operations and airborne operations), are captured in open battle or give themselves up. Nor does this order apply to enemy soldiers falling into our hands after battles at sea, or enemy soldiers trying to save their lives by parachute after battles.

6. I will hold responsible under military law, for failing to carry out this order, all commanders and officers who either have neglected their duty of instructing the troops about this order, or acted against this order where it was to be executed.

This order was criminal on its face. It simply directed the slaughter of these "sabotage" troops.

The connection of certain defendants with it is treated in the discussion of the individual cases.

Night and Fog Decree

This was another criminal order from Hitler's brain. It was signed by Keitel on 7 December 1941, after prior negotiations with Lehmann and Warlimont, and is as follows [*1733–PS, Pros. Ex. 797*]:

Since the opening of the Russian campaign, Communist elements and other anti-German circles have increased their assaults against the Reich and the occupation power in the occupied territories. The extent and the danger of these activities necessitate the most severe measures against the malefactors in order to intimidate them. To begin with one should proceed according to the following directives.

I

In case of criminal acts committed by non-German civilians and which are directed against the Reich or the occupation power endangering their safety or striking power, the death penalty is applicable in principle.

II

Criminal acts contained in paragraph I will, in principle, be tried in the occupied territories only when it appears probable that death sentences are going to be passed against the offenders, or at least the main offenders, and if the trial and the execution of the death sentence can be carried out without delay. In other cases the offenders, or at least the main offenders, are to be taken to Germany.

III

Offenders who are being taken to Germany are subject to court martial procedure there only in case that particular military concerns should require this. German and foreign agencies will declare upon inquiries on such offenders that they were arrested and the state of the proceeding did not allow further information.

IV

The commanders in chief in the occupied territories and the justiciars, within their jurisdiction, will be personally held responsible for the execution of this decree.

V

The Chief of the OKW will decide in which of the occupied territories this decree shall be applied. He is authorized to furnish explanations, supplements, and to issue directives for its execution. The Reich Minister of Justice will issue directives for the execution within his jurisdiction.

We have heretofore quoted from the judgment of the International Military Tribunal relative to this order and it need not be repeated. The enforcement of this cruel and brutal order cost the lives of many innocent people and untold suffering and misery to their loved ones.

The connection of certain of the defendants with it will be treated in our handling of the cases against them.

There are criminal orders involved in this case, other than those we have specifically mentioned, which we discuss in connection with the case of the defendants to whom they were applicable.

Hostages and Reprisals

In the Southeast Case [Hostage Case], United States *vs.* Wilhelm List, et al. (Case No. 7), the Tribunal had occasion to consider at considerable length the law relating to hostages and reprisals. It was therein held that under certain very restrictive conditions and subject to certain rather extensive safeguards, hostages may be taken, and after a judicial finding of strict compliance with all preconditions and as a last desperate remedy hostages may even be sentenced to death. It was held further that similar drastic safeguards, restrictions, and judicial preconditions apply to so-called "reprisal prisoners." If so inhumane a measure as the killing of innocent persons for offenses of others, even when drastically safeguarded and limited, is ever permissible, under any theory of international law, killing without full compliance with all requirements would be murder. If killing is not permissible under any circumstances, then a killing with full compliance with all the mentioned prerequisites still would be murder.

In the case here presented, we find it unnecessary to approve or disapprove the conclusions of law announced in said judgment as to the permissibility of such killings. In the instance of so-called hostage taking and killing, and the so-called reprisal killings with which we have to deal in this case, the safeguards and preconditions required to be observed by the Southeast judgment were not even attempted to be met or even suggested as necessary. Killings without full compliance with such preconditions are merely terror murders. If the law is in fact that hostage and reprisal killings are never permissible at all, then also the so-called hostage and reprisal killings in this case are merely terror murders.

The responsibility of defendants for any such acts will be considered in our determination of the cases against the individual defendants.

Partisan Warfare

The execution of partisans as *francs-tireurs* is connected with the Barbarossa Jurisdiction Decree in that it involves the treatment of civilians by the occupying and invading forces.

The record in this case contains much testimony and among the numerous exhibits are many documents dealing with so-called partisan warfare. We deem it desirable to make some comment of the law relating thereto before considering the cases of the individual defendants.

Articles 1 and 2 of the Annex to the Hague Convention are as follows:

Article 1

The laws, rights, and duties of war apply not only to armies, but also to militia and volunteer corps fulfilling the following conditions:

1. To be commanded by a person responsible for his subordinates.
2. To have a fixed distinctive emblem recognizable at a distance.
3. To carry arms openly: and
4. To conduct their operations in accordance with the laws and customs of war.

In countries where militia or volunteer corps constitute the army, or form part of it, they are included under the denomination "army."

Article 2

The inhabitants of a territory which has not been occupied, who, on the approach of the enemy, spontaneously take up arms to resist the invading troops without having had time to organize themselves in accordance with Article 1, shall be regarded as belligerents if they carry arms openly and if they respect the laws and customs of war.

A failure to meet these requirements deprives one so failing on capture of a prisoner of war status.

We have a strong suspicion from the record in this case that antipartisan warfare was used by the German Reich as a pretext for the extermination of many thousands of innocent persons. Hitler stated what it seems became the

Wehrmacht policy when he said: "This partisan war again has some advantages for us; it enables us to eradicate everyone who opposes us."

The defendants without exception claim that they executed as partisans only those who were operating as *francs-tireurs* and bandits and who failed to comply with the requirements of the rules of war to constitute them lawful belligerents. They claim there is no evidence adduced by the prosecution that the defendants are guilty of executing any as so-called partisans who complied with the requirements to constitute them lawful belligerents, that is, any who were not in fact *francs-tireurs.* However, we need not on the record before us determine whether this is true or untrue for the evidence shows beyond any question that it was the policy of the Wehrmacht to create classes of partisans by definition in orders and directives and by construction and in this manner they brought within the list of these they prescribed as partisans and shot or hung not only the *franc-tireur,* in fact, but also many other classes that no conceivable reason can be found for so including except as Hitler stated it, "to eradicate all those who oppose us." In a conference called by General Mueller (General for Special Assignments) at Warsaw before the Russian campaign to instruct the judge advocate and intelligence officers of the armies on the meaning and scope of the Barbarossa Jurisdiction Decree, the following was the construction and instruction given:

> One of the two enemies must die; do not spare the bearer of enemy ideology, but kill him.
>
> Every civilian who impedes or incites others to impede the German Wehrmacht is also to be considered a guerrilla (for instance: instigators, persons who distribute leaflets, nonobservance of German orders, arsonists, destroying of road signs, supplies, etc.).
>
> The population is denied the right to take up arms voluntarily. Neither are para-military associations (Komsomoel Osscaviachim) entitled to do so.

The classification certainly is elastic and capable of wide extension. *"Every civilian who impedes or incites others to impede the German Wehrmacht."* taken as a criterion for determining who is a *franc-tireur,* clearly opens the way for arbitrary and bloody implementation. Those falling into the various classifications were summarily executed as partisans and so classified in the reports. There is no warrant in the rules of war or in international law for dealing with such persons as *francs-tireurs,* guerrillas, or bandits. Red Army soldiers in uniform were in some instances shot as so-called partisans. There is, of course, no warrant in international law for such action.

The most vicious classification of the prescribed was that of "partisan suspect." The executions of such were a regular routine and their executions were reported along with those of the so-called partisans.

Suspicion is a state of mind of the accuser and not a state of mind or an act by the one accused. It is a monstrous proposition containing the very essence of license that the state of mind of the accuser shall be the determining factor, in the absence of evidence of guilt, whether the accused shall or shall not be summarily executed. But it is said that when these accused were captured they were interrogated and some were not executed but released or sent to prison camps. But this is no defense for it does not necessarily mean that those who were executed as suspects had been found guilty even by the informal interrogation by an officer; but only that the interrogator *had not had his suspicion that they were guilty removed,* so under the order, they, being still suspected, were executed. This does not amount to even the minimum of judicial protection required before an execution.

The classification of the victims in the numerous reports in the records as partisan suspects is a natural and proper one to be made under the order for execution on mere suspicion of partisan activity. If, as defendants have contended, no suspects were executed until they were lawfully found and adjudged to be guilty, there was no need whatsoever for the distinction made in the classification. We find from the evidence that there were great numbers of persons executed in the areas of various of these defendants, who, under no stretch of the imagination, were *francs-tireurs* and great numbers of others executed solely on suspicion, without any proof or lawful determination that they were in fact guilty of the offenses of which they were suspected. The orders to execute such persons and mere suspects on suspicion only and without proof, were criminal on their face. Executions pursuant thereto were criminal. Those who gave or passed down such orders must bear criminal responsibility for passing them down and for their implementation by the units subordinate to them.

Notwithstanding our strong suspicion that the executions of persons described in the documents as partisans were in a vast number of cases not executions of those whom it was permissible to execute under the rules of war, but a mere cloak under which innocent persons were eradicated, we accord to the defendants the benefit of any possible doubt and determine the question of their criminality on the basis of cases of the type mentioned concerning the criminality of which under both the law and the evidence there can be no doubt.

We shall determine on consideration of the evidence each defendant's guilt or innocence as to such matters charged against him.

* * *

Responsibility of Commanders of Occupied Territories

The defense in this case as to the field commanders on trial has been partially based on the contention that while criminal acts may have occurred within the territories under their jurisdiction, that these criminal acts were committed by agencies of the state with which they were not connected and over whom they exercised no supervision or control. It is conceded that many of these defendants were endowed with executive power but it is asserted that the executive power of field commanders did not extend to the activities of certain economic and police agencies which operated within their areas; that the activities of these agencies constituted limitations upon their exercise of executive power.

In this connection it must be recognized that the responsibility of commanders of occupied territories is not unlimited. It is fixed according to the customs of war, international agreements, fundamental principles of humanity, and the authority of the commander which has been delegated to him by his own government. As pointed out heretofore, his criminal responsibility is personal. The act or neglect to act must be voluntary and criminal. The term "voluntary" does not exclude pressures or compulsions even to the extent of superior orders. That the choice was a difficult one does not alter either its voluntary nature or its criminality. From an international standpoint, criminality may arise by reason that the act is forbidden by international agreements or is inherently criminal and contrary to accepted principles of humanity as recognized and accepted by civilized nations. In the case of violations of international agreements, the criminality arises from violation of the agreement itself—in other cases, by the inherent nature of the act.

War is human violence at its utmost. Under its impact excesses of individuals are not unknown in any army. The measure of such individual excesses is the measure of the people who compose the army and the standard of discipline of the army to which they belong. The German Army was, in general, a disciplined army. The tragedy of the German Wehrmacht and these defendants is that the crimes charged against them stem primarily from its highest military leadership and the leadership of the Third Reich itself.

Military subordination is comprehensive but not conclusive factor in fixing criminal responsibility. The authority, both administrative and military, of a commander and his criminal responsibility are related but by no means coextensive. Modern war such as the last war entails a large measure of decentralization. A high commander cannot keep completely informed of the details of military operations of subordinates and most assuredly not of every administrative measure. He has the right to assume that details entrusted to responsible subordinates will be legally executed. The President of the United States is Commander in Chief of its military forces. Criminal acts committed by those forces cannot in themselves be charged to him on the theory of subordination. The same is true of other high commanders in the chain of command. Criminality does not attach to every individual in this chain of command from that fact alone. There must be a personal dereliction. That can occur only where the act is directly traceable to him or where his failure to properly supervise his subordinates constitutes criminal negligence on his part. In the latter case it must be a personal neglect amounting to a wanton, immoral disregard of the action of his subordinates amounting to acquiescence. Any other interpretation of international law would go far beyond the basic principles of criminal law as known to civilized nations.

Concerning the responsibility of a field commander for crimes committed within the area of his command, particularly as against the civilian population, it is urged by the prosecution that under the Hague Convention, a military commander of an occupied territory is *per se* responsible within the area of his occupation, regardless of orders, regulations, and the laws of his superiors limiting his authority and regardless of the fact that the crimes committed therein were due to the action of the state or superior military authorities which he did not initiate or in which he did not participate. In this respect, however, it must be borne in mind that a military commander, whether it be of an occupied territory or otherwise, is subject both to the orders of his military superiors and the state itself as to his jurisdiction and functions. He is their agent and instrument for certain purposes in a position from which they can remove him at will.

In this connection the Yamashita case has been cited. While not a decision binding upon this Tribunal, it is entitled to great respect because of the high court which rendered it. It is not, however, entirely applicable to the facts in this case for the reason that the authority of Yamashita in the field of his operations did not appear to have been restricted by either his military superiors or the state, and the crimes committed were by troops under his command, whereas in the case of the occupational commanders in these proceedings, the crimes charged were mainly committed at the instance of higher military and Reich authorities.

It is the opinion of this Tribunal that a state can, as to certain matters, under international law limit the exercise of sovereign powers by a military commander in an occupied area, but we are also of the opinion that under international law and accepted usages of civilized nations that he has certain responsibilities which he cannot set aside or ignore by reason of activities of his own state within his area. He is the instrument by which the occupancy exists. It is his army which holds the area in subjection. It is his might which keeps an occupied territory from reoccupancy by the armies of the nation to which it inherently belongs. It cannot be said that he exercises the power by which a civilian population is subject to his invading army while at the same time the state which he represents may come into the area which he holds and subject the population to murder of its citizens and to other inhuman treatment. The situation is somewhat analogous to the accepted principle of international law that the army which captures the soldiers of its adversary has certain fixed responsibilities as to their care and treatment.

We are of the opinion, however, as above pointed out in other aspects of this case, that the occupying commander must have knowledge of these offenses and acquiesce or participate or criminally neglect to interfere in their commission and that the offenses committed must be patently criminal. But regardless of whether or not under international law such responsibility is fixed upon him, under the particular facts in this case, responsibility of the commanders in question rests upon other factors. In this respect we quote certain provisions of the handbook for the general staff in wartime, pertinent to executive power [*NOKW—1878, Pros. Ex. 42*]:

5. The exercising of executive power by military commanders is governed by No. 20–24 of Army Manual 90 (of the army in the field).

6. If a zone of operation is determined, the Commander in Chief of the Army and the commanders in chief of the armies receive at the declaration of a state of defense or at the declaration of a state of war authority for exercising executive power in this territory, without further order (pars. 2 and 9 of the Reich Defense Law).

In other cases, the Fuehrer and Supreme Commander of the Wehrmacht can transfer such authority for exercising executive power to the Commander in Chief of the Army and the commanders in chief of the armies.

7. The executive power comprises the entire state power including the right of issuing laws without prejudice to the independence of jurisdiction. Those persons invested with executive power can decree local orders affecting the territory in which authority for exercising has been turned over to them or transferred to them, set up special courts, and issue instructions to the authorities and offices competent in the territory named, with the exception of the Supreme Reich Authorities, the Supreme Prussian Provincial Authorities, and the Reichsleitung of the NSDAP.

8. The Supreme Reich Authorities, Supreme Prussian Provincial Authorities, and the Reichsleitung of the NSDAP can decree orders for the territory into which executive power has been transferred, only by agreement with the persons invested with executive power. Their right of issuing instructions to the authorities and offices subordinated to them remains intact. Nevertheless the right of issuing instruction by the person invested with executive authority takes precedence.

9. Authority for exercising executive power is incumbent only on the persons invested. It can be transferred further only in as much as an authorization is ordered thereto actually or legally.

Accordingly persons invested with executive power are authorized to entrust subordinated offices with the execution of individual missions.

10. The laws, decrees, etc., which are valid at the transfer of the executive power retain their validity so long as the person invested with executive power encounters no contrary order.

11. The Commander in Chief of the Army regulates the exercising of executive power through the commanders in chief of the armies.

The revision of questions which occur in the exercising of executive power does not fall into the realm of work of the army judges. The civilian commissioner with the High Command of the Army is assigned for that purpose to the Commander in Chief of the Army; the chiefs of the civil administration, to the commanders in chief of the armies. Persons invested with executive power are authorized however, to call in the army judges assigned to them as counselors, especially in the decreeing of legal orders of penal law content.

It is therefore apparent that executive power under German law is the exercise of sovereign powers within an occupied area conferred upon a military commander by the state. The defense has undertaken to minimize to a large extent this wide authority but in view of the above document, it does not appear to be the mere shadow of authority contended. In fact, these provisions fix upon an occupying commander certain responsibilities as to the preservation of law and order within his area.

The contention of defendants that the economic agencies were excluded from their exercise of executive power is disproved by various documents which will hereafter be cited in considering the guilt or innocence of defendants on trial. And regardless of that fact, the proof in this case also establishes a voluntary co-operation of defendants on trial with these economic agencies in the furtherance of their illegal activities.

The defense contends that the activities of the Einsatzgruppen of the Security Police and SD were beyond their sphere of authority as occupational commanders because the state had authorized the illegal activities of these police units and so limited the executive power of the occupational commanders. However, the occupational commanders in this case were bearers of executive power and, one and all, have denied receipt of any orders showing, or knowledge of, a state-authorized program providing for the illegal activities of the Einsatzgruppen.

One of the functions of an occupational commander endowed with executive power was to maintain order and protect the civilian population against illegal acts. In the absence of any official directives limiting his executive powers as to these illegal acts within his area, he had the right and duty to take action for their suppression. Certainly he is not in a position to contend that these activities were taken from his field of executive power by his superiors when he knew of no such action on their part.

The sole question then as to such defendants in this case is whether or not they knew of the criminal activities of the Einsatzgruppen of the Security Police and SD and neglected to suppress them.

It has been urged that all of the defendants in this case must have had knowledge of the illegal activities of the Einsatzgruppen. It has been argued that because of the extent of their murder program in the occupational areas and by reason of the communications available to the high commanders, and the fact that they were in command of these areas, they must necessarily have known of this program. The record in this case shows that some 90,000 so-called undesirable elements were liquidated by Einsatzgruppe D, largely within the area of the 11th Army. It also shows that some 40,000 Jewish women and children were liquidated in Riga which at that time was in the Commissariat Ostland, immediately to the rear of the Army Group North. The Einsatzgruppen and their subordinate units were organized to carry out this program within the operational areas of the army.

It is true that extermination of such a large number of people must necessarily have come to the attention of many individuals, and, also, it is established that soldiers in certain areas participated in some of these executions.

In many respects a high commander in the German Army was removed from information as to facts which may have been known to troops subordinate to him. In the first place, these troops were in many instances far removed from his headquarters. In addition the common soldiers and junior officers do not have extensive contacts with the high commanders and staff officers.

Another factor must also be taken into consideration in connection with the activities of the Einsatzgruppen. This is the dual nature of its functions. On the one hand, it was charged with the criminal liquidation of certain elements; on the other hand it exercised legitimate police activities in connection with the security of the rear communications of the armies, in which capacity it operated largely against guerrillas.

Another factor was the effort made to keep the criminal activities of these police units from the Wehrmacht. In the early stages of the war many of their mass executions, as is shown by the record, occurred under the guise of pogroms instigated by the SIPO and SD but actually carried out by local inhabitants. Racial hatreds and pogroms have been known in Europe for centuries. Pogroms occurred at the time of the Crusades and have recurred in the history of Europe, even in our time. It is established that pogroms were used by Einsatzgruppe A which operated in the area of the Army Group North and in the Commissariat Ostland, as a vehicle for their criminal activities. At times it is shown such pogroms were participated in by local militia which necessarily owed its existence to the German Army.

Another source of information was reports submitted by Einsatzgruppen to army headquarters, but it is noted that such reports concerned mainly activities within their legal sphere of combating partisans and the maintenance of security. However, such reports showed the execution of Jews, gypsies, and others as specific classifications of those liquidated. Reports of the mass murders carried out by these police units, however, were submitted through their own channels to the RSHA in Berlin and were not submitted to army headquarters or through such headquarters.

An army commander has two reliable and extensive official sources of information (1) superior orders, (2) reports of subordinate units.

It is true that no superior orders transmitted to the defendant field commanders show the mass murder program of the Third Reich have been introduced in evidence with the exception of the Commissar Order in which the executing agency was not the SD but the army itself.

Official reports of subordinate units normally furnish a vast amount of information. Reports of individual instances of illegal acts may however not be submitted to higher headquarters if for no other reason than that the suppression of such acts is the province of the subordinate and their occurrence might be a subject for criticism. Also the staff of high operational commands engaged in extensive combat operations is much less likely to bring such matters to the attention of the commander than the staff of a lower command.

Other factors to be considered as to the knowledge of criminal acts of the SIPO and SD by defendants is the time, the localities, the combat situation, the extent of the activities, and the nature of the command.

This, in brief, summarizes the main factors considered and the sources of knowledge appraised in determining the criminal responsibility of the defendants in this case in connection with activities of the Einsatzgruppen of the

SIPO and SD. From this discussion it is apparent we can draw no general presumption as to their knowledge in this matter and must necessarily go to the evidence pertaining to the various defendants to make a determination of this question.

And it is further pointed out that to establish the guilt of a defendant from connection with acts of the SIPO and SD by acquiescence, not only must knowledge be established, but the time of such knowledge must be established.

When we discuss the evidence against the various defendants, we shall treat with great detail the evidence relating to the activities of the Einsatzgruppen in the commands of the various defendants, and to what extent, if any, such activities were known to and acquiesced in or supported by them.

* * *

Wilhelm von Leeb

Field Marshal Wilhelm von Leeb was born in 1876, entered service in 1895, and had various promotions until he became a field marshal in 1040. He was Commander in Chief of Army Group North in the campaign against Russia until 16 January 1942, when he resigned primarily because of interference in technical matters by Hitler and was then placed in the Fuehrer reserve.

The German Army, prior to the establishment of army groups, was based on Heeres or ground forces which were composed of armies and subordinate units. The armies were both administrative and operational. When the army group was established, the staff provided was much smaller than the staff of the subordinate armies, according to the testimony of von Kuechler, one-third or one-half the size of the staff of an army. Judicial authority did not extend through the commander of the army group. He had no representative of the quartermaster general who directly controlled matters of supply. The quartermaster general did not operate directly through the army group but through the armies and army group rear areas where there were representatives of his department on the staff.

A commander of the army group in the early stages of its development had no staff of experts for supervision of prisoner of war affairs which was directly under the quartermaster general and his subordinates. Nor did the economic agencies of the Reich operate through the army group. The armies and commanders of army group rear areas had experts on their staffs to deal with these matters.

During the period of the defendant von Leeb's command of Army Group North the duties imposed upon him were almost exclusively operational and his headquarters and staff were strictly operational in their functions.

Executive power at the beginning of the Russian campaign was conferred directly upon the army commanders and the commanders of the army group rear areas. It was provided, however, that the commander in chief of an army group might issue orders to his subordinates in the field of executive power. In other words, his authority in this field was more in the nature of a right to intervene than a direct responsibility.

This power to intervene followed the general pattern of his command authority over subordinate units. Nevertheless, authority and responsibility as to many administrative matters were directly vested in von Leeb's subordinates. It was common for the OKH and staff officers of the OKH to issue orders directly to these subordinates without such orders always being submitted to army group headquarters for information. In other instances, orders addressed to subordinate units were sent through the army group. In such cases the army group headquarters acted as a forwarding agency, with implementation of orders resulting from their being put into command channels, and not from action on the part of the defendant.

The defendant's army group had moved from East Prussia to Leningrad. He had under his command five to six hundred thousand soldiers. His operations were of great magnitude. They started with the opening of the Russian campaign on 22 June 1941, and his activities terminated officially on 16 January 1942. In this comparatively brief period of time he had moved a great army over a vast territory under the arduous conditions of combat. As stated, his function was operational. Many administrative duties had been left to his subordinate armies and his army group rear area. He and his staff alike would have the right to assume that the commanders entrusted with such administrative functions would see to their proper execution. Under such conditions it must be accepted that certain details of activities within the sphere of his subordinates would not be brought to his attention.

The evidence establishes that criminal orders were executed by units subordinate to the defendant and criminal acts were carried out by agencies within his command. But it is not considered under the situation outlined that criminal responsibility attaches to him merely on the theory of subordination and over-all command. He must be shown both to have had knowledge and to have been connected with such criminal acts, either by way of participation or criminal acquiescence.

Aside from the charge of crimes against peace heretofore disposed of in this opinion, the charges against him relate to the period he was Commander in Chief of Army Group North. We think these charges may be broken down into the following general headings: (1) The Commissar Order; (2) crimes against prisoners of war; (3) The Barbarossa Jurisdiction Order; (4) crimes against civilians; (5) pillage of public and private property; (6) criminal conduct pertaining to the siege of Leningrad. We shall discuss these *seriatim*.

1. The Commissar Order—We have discussed the criminality of the Commissar Order. Von Leeb was present at the meeting held by Hitler in March 1941 when the proposed extermination of the commissars was announced. He considered this to be in violation of international law and, as well, to be stupid in that it tended to defeat its own purpose. He discussed the matter with von

Brauchitsch and lodged a protest with him. Von Brauchitsch assured him he would do all he could to prevent the issuance of the order but notwithstanding this, it was later issued by the OKH. Von Leeb as Commander of Army Group North, and von Bock of Army Group Center, and von Rundstedt of Army Group South were opposed to it. Von Leeb made further protest to von Brauchitsch on the occasion of the latter's visits in July and September 1941 and likewise protested to Keitel on two occasions. Keitel replied he would do his best to obtain a cancellation of the order. Later, pursuant to the objection made by the commanders of the army groups, General Mueller, General for Special Assignments under Commander in Chief of the Army, von Brauchitsch, wrote the OKW on 23 September 1941 as follows:

> It is requested to check on the necessity of the carrying out of the "Commissar" Decree in its present form, considering the development of the situation. Commanders, commanding officers and the troops themselves report that the will to fight on the part of the Russians could be weakened if the commissars, who no doubt are the pillars of the embittered and stubborn resistance, would find it easier to give up the fight, to surrender or to desert.
>
> At present the prevailing situation is such that every commissar faces his death in any case; that is why a large number of them is fighting to the last and also forces the Red Army soldiers to resist stubbornly by the most brutal means.
>
> The combat situation being what it is at present, when here and there the Russian side shows a slight weakening due to the large losses, the diminishing supply of personnel and material, the mixing of units and the indecisiveness of the leadership, a paralysis of the will to fight generally by breaking the resistance of the commissars might have a not inconsiderable success, and under circumstances may save much blood.
>
> The achievement of the goal should be attempted in proper form by all kinds of propaganda by varied means.
>
> *The Commander in Chief of the Army also believes that the above views which have been reported to him personally by all army groups deserve consideration from a military point of view also, and a reconsideration of the treatment of the commissars accorded to them up to now seems expedient to him.*

It will be noted this recommendation is based wholly upon military considerations without any discussion of the moral phase which of course would not have interested Hitler. This recommendation was submitted to Hitler and a notation thereupon was made in Jodl's writing, as follows: "The Fuehrer has refused any change in the decree concerning treatment of Russian commissars issued up to now."

It is apparent that Mueller's letter corroborates von Leeb's testimony regarding the opposition to this order by the commanders in chief of these army groups.

When this order was issued, it was directed by OKH to the armies in these three groups who, however, received copies for informational purposes. In other words, the army group had nothing to do with the passing on of this order to subordinate units beyond the administrative functions of forwarding it to them.

However, in addition to his protests to his superiors, von Leeb discussed this order with subordinate commanders and let them know of his opposition to it. He also mentioned the maintenance of discipline order issued by von Brauchitsch in an effort to thwart as far as he could the enforcement of the Commissar Order.

As a practical purpose, what other action was open to him? He could not revoke this order coming as it did from his superiors, even from the head of the state. Had he undertaken to do so, this would have been a flagrant disobedience of orders. In discussing the resignation, he said:

> . . . In addition, as a commander, I knew that all commanders I talked to were against this order and therefore I hoped that at least it would not be carried out in its full measure, and if I had resigned at that time then I would have saved myself in the cheapest manner possible, but at the same time I would have given up the struggle against Hitler, and for the rest such an application for resignation would probably not have made the slightest impression on Hitler. In addition it would probably have become known why I resigned because I couldn't suddenly say, "I am ill, I can't go on any longer."

He was then asked as to his present impressions about this question, to which he replied:

> I have had ample time and opportunity to think about this order and about what we did at that time under the pressure of responsibility, and here I must admit I don't know even today any better way. At that time as far as it was possible at all, we tacitly sabotaged the order and all depended on our doing it tacitly. I really don't know how we could do it differently today.

This order had been passed down to his subordinate units, the 18th Army under von Kuechler, the 16th Army under Busch, and the 4th Panzer Group under Hoepner. And in spite of von Leeb's attitude, the reports of units in these subordinate commands indicate the murder of many of these functionaries. It may be that in some instances the figures were fictitious or exaggerated, but in spite of this, we find there were many cases of these atrocities. But we cannot find von Leeb guilty in this particular. He did not disseminate the order. He protested against it and opposed it in every way short of open and defiant refusal to obey it. If his subordinate commanders disseminated it and permitted its enforcement, that is their responsibility and not his.

2. Crimes against prisoners of war— . . . We are . . . unable to find from the evidence that the defendant von Leeb was criminally connected with, knew of, or participated in the illegal execution of Red Army soldiers within his area.

3. The Barbarossa Jurisdiction Order—This was a Fuehrer order received by the army group under Leeb's command. There is nothing to show that it was ever directed to subordinate units under him. It has been contended that this was an order pertaining to judicial authority and would not concern an army group and therefore would have been transmitted direct to those commanders who had judicial authority. Examination of the order itself however shows that only in part did it pertain particularly to judicial authority. Basically, it was an order pertaining to the conduct and discipline of troops and of such a nature to be of the highest significance to any officer in command of troops, including the army group commanders. The order itself charges troop officers with the responsibility of informing subordinate officers.

An entry in the war diary of the Army Group North shows that it was transmitted with the OKH order of 1 June 1941 to subordinate units. There is no evidence in the record to show that the defendant von Leeb expressed more than a disapproval of the order and that was on the basis that it threatened the discipline of the army. We must conclude from the evidence that this order was put into the chain of command by von Leeb's action.

It was a criminal order, at least in part. It was further an order that was at best ambiguous in respect to the authority conferred upon a junior officer to shoot individuals who were merely suspected of certain acts. There is nothing to show that in the transmittal of this order, it was in any way clarified or that instructions were given in any way to prevent its illegal application. The evidence establishes that von Leeb implemented this order by passing it into the chain of command. Coming directly through him in the chain of command, it carried the weight of his authority as well as that of his superiors. The record in this case shows that it was criminally applied by units subordinate to him. Having set this instrument in motion, he must assume a measure of responsibility for its illegal application.

4. Crimes against civilians— . . . We are . . . unable to find from the evidence submitted that the defendant von Leeb had knowledge of the murder of civilians within his area by the Einsatzgruppen or acquiesced in such activities.

Nor is it established from the evidence that the defendant participated in the recruitment of slave labor for the Reich. The document relied on in this connection is a report to the effect that in a given period, a number of civilians were sent from the Army Group North to the Reich for labor. Leeb was in command for only a part of the period covered by the report. Furthermore, the document does not establish the involuntary nature of the recruitment.

5. Pillage of public and private property— . . . We do not find any criminality under this phase of the case.

6. Criminal conduct pertaining to the siege of Leningrad—Leningrad was encircled and besieged. Its defenders and the civilian population were in great straits and it was feared the population would undertake to flee through the German lines. Orders were issued to use artillery to "prevent any such attempt at the greatest possible distance from our own lines by opening fire as early as possible, so that the infantry, if possible, is spared shooting on civilians." We find this was known to and approved by von Leeb. Was it an unlawful order?

> A belligerent commander may lawfully lay siege to a place controlled by the enemy and endeavor by a process of isolation to cause its surrender. The propriety of attempting to reduce it by starvation is not questioned. Hence, the cutting off of every source of sustenance from without is deemed legitimate. It is said that if the commander of a besieged place expels the noncombatants, in order to lessen the number of those who consume his stock of provisions, it is lawful, though an extreme measure, to drive them back so as to hasten the surrender.

We might wish the law were otherwise but we must administer it as we find it. Consequently, we hold no criminality attached on this charge.

For the reasons above stated we find this defendant guilty under count three of the indictment for criminal responsibility in connection with the transmittal and application fo the Barbarossa Jurisdiction Order. Under Control Council Law No. 10 it is provided that superior orders do not constitute a defense but may be considered in mitigation of an offense.

We believe that there is much to be said for the defendant von Leeb by way of mitigation. He was not a friend or follower of the Nazi Party or its ideology. He was a soldier and engaged in a stupendous campaign with responsibility for hundreds of thousands of soldiers, and a large indigenous population spread over a vast area. It is not without significance that no criminal order has been introduced in evidence which bears his signature or the stamp of his approval.

We find on the evidence in the record, and for the reasons above stated, the defendant is guilty under count three of the indictment, and not guilty under count two thereof. . . .

Hans Reinhardt

The defendant Reinhardt was born 1 March 1887 at Bautzen in Saxony. He served as a junior officer in World War I and after the war remained with the Reichswehr. As a major general he participated in the invasion of Poland as Commander of the 4th Panzer Division and of Belgium and the Netherlands as Commanding General of the XLI Panzer Corps. With this corps he took part in the invasion of Yugoslavia. Still commanding the XLI Panzer Corps, he entered the campaign against Russia, the corps being subordinated to Army Group North. On 5 October 1941, he was appointed Commander of Panzer Group 3. In March 1942, he was appointed Commander in Chief of the 3d Panzer Army which position he retained until appointed Commander in Chief of Army Group Center on 16 August 1944. Due to differences with Hitler concerning his conduct of operations, he was relieved of this command on 26 January 1945. In 1940, he was promoted to lieutenant general of Panzer Troops and in 1942, to full general. The defendant Reinhardt is charged under all four counts of the indictment. Counts one and four having been disposed of, there remains to be considered the question of his guilt under counts two and three which charge respectively: war crimes and crimes against humanity; crimes against enemy belligerents and prisoners of war, and war crimes and crimes against humanity; crimes against civilians.

The Commissar Order

The Commissar Order was transmitted to Reinhardt by General Hoepner, the commander of Panzer Group 4, and Reinhardt thereafter communicated it orally to his divisional commanders. He testified that when he transmitted it to his divisions, he directed orally that it was not to be carried out. He testified further that General Hoepner was opposed to the order and that he, Reinhardt, protested it to General Hoepner; that General Hoepner protested to the army group under von Leeb and presumably, the protest was carried back from the army group to the Commander in Chief of the [German] Army. Notwithstanding this alleged resistance and repudiation of the order, it appears from the documents that reports of executed commissars shortly began to be sent in from subordinate divisions and that they were sent on by the corps.

The Russian campaign began 22 June 1941. The 269th Infantry Division reported on 9 July to the XLI Corps that 34 Politruks were liquidated. On the same day the XLI Corps reported to Panzer Group 4 a total of 97 Politruks had been executed in the corps area up to 8 July. The balance of 63 liquidated commissars doubtless are chargeable to the three remaining divisions of the corps, the 1st and 6th Panzer Divisions, and the 36th Motorized Division. On 10 July 1941, Panzer Group 4 reported to Army Group North that up to 8 July 1941, 101 commissars had been liquidated. Out of a total of 101 executed Politruks, 97 were liquidated by Reinhardt's XLI Corps, and the balance of 4 by the LVI AK of Panzer Group 4. At the time of the report, Panzer Group 4 consisted only of the XLI AK and the LVI AK. Thereafter, 71 commissars were executed by the 19th of July by Panzer Group 4. We have mentioned that Reinhardt testified that he orally directed that this order not be carried out. A second defense, which is supported by the testimony of two witnesses, Bruns, the intelligence officer of Hoepner's Panzer Group 4 and Mueller, and ADC of Bruns, is to the effect that all of these reports were fictitious. The testimony might be more credible if they had not drawn such fantastic conclusions as that Hoepner clearly expressed his repudiation of the Commissar Order by having Bruns read it to the corps commanders and later that he expressed it by gesticulation. Mueller was more definite as to Hoepner's rejection of the order but it is not possible for the Tribunal to believe in the face of these reports that commissars were not shot pursuant to this order within the area of Reinhardt's command. The order was a criminal order on its face, and one which under the German military regulations and certainly under international law should not have been passed down by either Hoepner or Reinhardt. If international law is to have any effectiveness, high commanding officers, when they are directed to violate it by committing murder, must have the courage to act, in definite and unmistakable terms, so as to indicate their repudiation of such an order. The proper report to have been made from division to army group level when a request was made from the top level to report the number of commissars killed would have been that this unit does not murder enemy prisoners of war.

Counsel for the defendant, in his brief, makes the following statement:

> War has its own laws, even more than peacetime. One of the most incomprehensible laws of war is that certain news spreads through mysterious channels and with unbelievable rapidity over entire fronts, entire armies and whole countries;

that it even spreads from one's own frontline to that of the enemy, and it can never be found out how this was possible. Of course, this also happened with such an extraordinary order as the Commissar Order. Several witnesses testified that it was known among the Russians even at an earlier date than among our soldiers in the front line.

Unless the order had been communicated rather extensively, and as a policy down to low levels and even to the troops, it is difficult to understand how it would sweep the entire Russian front. The obvious explanation for this is that it became known because of its implementation.

That the defense of fictitious reports may itself be fictitious is suggested by the activity report of one of Reinhardt's divisions. The 36th Motorized Division on 3 July 1941 before the need for any fictitious reports was created by a top level inquiry, notes the capture of Latvian and Russian soldiers and that two political commissars were eliminated during the advance. On 4 July, a political commissar who pretended to be a sergeant was eliminated. On 6 July, three commissars were eliminated and on 16 September, a captured Politruk of a Russian rifle regiment was eliminated. It is not quite comprehensible why the shooting of these five commissars on three different days is reported unless the executions actually occurred.

In January 1942, an activity report of the 35th Infantry Division, subordinate to Reinhardt, contains the following:

. . . The reason for the will to fight may be found primarily in the fact that well in advance the enemy learns how the commissars and political leaders are treated when captured by the Germans. The mistake of drawing attention to this has been made even in German propaganda leaflets. It would have been better to keep the treatment of the commissars a secret. It would have sufficed to transport them separately to the rear, to a camp specially established for this purpose by the corps, and to take them to task only then and there.

The Tribunal finds that Reinhardt passed on this criminal order and bears the responsibility for its execution in his area.

The Commando Order

We have discussed this criminal order generally in a preceding part of this opinion. A copy of this order was sent to the 3d Panzer Army. The war diary of this army for 27 October 1942 shows it was received. Reinhardt, at this time, was in command of the 3d Panzer Army. On 28 October, the IX Corps, subordinate to the 3d Panzer Army, notes the order received in its war diary. We take no stock in the defense that this order was not to be effective in the East. That the 3d Panzer Army was of the opinion that it was applicable in the East, appears from the war diary of this army for 18 November 1942, which is several weeks after the receipt of the order. In that war diary it is stated [*NOKW–3482, Pros. Rebuttal Ex. 46*]:

Various difficulties have arisen concerning the execution of the Fuehrer order of 21 October, relative to the shooting of terrorists and groups of bandits. The Pz.

> Army asks the army group to clarify, above all, whether this order Vol. IIb, 30a, merely concerns British terror groups or whether it also applies to the bands in the occupied area. *In this connection, the army group takes the attitude that, until a new OKW decree is published which is in prospect, all bandits are to be shot to death even if they wear uniforms.* Bandits who voluntarily surrender without being forced to do so by their situation will be treated as PW's. An order will be issued to the troops on this subject.

That the army considered the Commando Order of general application is shown by the emphasized portion of the above quotation, that until otherwise advised, the order was to be carried out against men in uniform. Another entry in the war diary of the 3d Panzer Army referring to this same situation reads as follows:

> Until new regulations of OKW are published, bandits who surrender voluntarily without being forced by circumstances, will be treated as PW's. All other bandits, also the uniformed ones, will be shot.
>
> This order will be destroyed after reading, this order will not be passed on in writing.

It was a criminal order, Reinhardt passed it down in the chain of command.

It may be stated as a matter somewhat in mitigation and as showing the personal attitude of the defendant Reinhardt, that in November 1943, he issued an order that parachutists are lawful combatants and are to be treated as prisoners of war. That was at a time when the German Army was not so flushed with success and when it was a little more inclined to soften the treatment meted out to the Russians. The Tribunal has noted it as being a matter proper, at least for consideration, on the question of mitigation. It should further be noted in this connection that it does not appear that Reinhardt, though he received it, ever passed on literally or in substance the notorious Reichenau Order.

Prohibited Labor of Prisoners of War

An order from the commander in chief of the [German] army, providing that mines were to be detected and cleared by Russian prisoners of war in order to spare German blood, was issued on 29 October 1941. This order was transmitted in the area of Army Group North and was implemented in Reinhardt's area. His LIX Corps issued an order [on 2 March 1942] providing [*NOKW-2139, Pros. Ex. 201*]—

> If it is suspected that roads or places are mined, prisoners of war or the local population are to walk in front or clear the mines.

The activity report of the 3d Panzer Army, dated 15 December 1943, notes that there were five prisoners in Dulag 230 who were requested for mine clearing and that Dulag 230 was informed accordingly. A report sent by the LIX Corps to the 3d Panzer Army covering the months of January, February, March, and May 1943 relative to the use of prisoners of war for these months, respectively, shows the following: 246 in supply units, 104 for billet and field fortification construction; 193 in supply units; 25 for billet and field fortifications; 196 in troop supply units, and 183 for billet and field fortifications; 175 in troop supply services; and 11 for billet and field fortifications. On 6 January 1944, the 3d Panzer Army furnished 40 prisoners of war to an SS unit for field fortification work at the front. A report of the 83d Infantry Division in the 3d Panzer Army shows 25 prisoners of war put to work by the 2d Rifle Battalion were killed while working. An activity report of the 3d Panzer Army states that on 4 October 1943, 200 prisoners of war were used on field fortifications. Numerous other documents show the use of prisoners of war on field fortifications and at the front, their use being so general that we conclude it was the policy of the 3d Panzer Army under Reinhardt to use prisoners of war for that purpose.

An order signed by Reinhardt as Commander in Chief of the 3d Panzer Army, dated 18 October 1942, confirms this conclusion in every respect. Under the heading "Labor Allocation of Prisoners of War and Civilians," he states:

> The urgent need for prisoners of war in the zone of operations and for the economy and armament industry at home requires a thorough and planned organization of the labor allocation of prisoners of war.

We do not find all of the above uses of prisoners of war criminal. To use them for field fortifications, loading ammunition, mine clearing, and any other work that is dangerous was clearly prohibited by international law and constitutes a war crime.

* * *

The Tribunal, on all the evidence, finds Reinhardt guilty on counts two and three of the indictment.

RUDOLF LEHMANN

Rudolf Lehmann was born in 1890 at Poznan. After preliminary education, he studied law and received his doctor's degree in 1920 at Marburg. His practice, however, was interrupted by the First World War in which he participated as an officer in the reserve. From then on he followed the career of jurist in various capacities.

In 1925, he became an assistant in the Reich Ministry of Justice and continued in the Ministry in various capacities until 1937. In that year he became presiding judge at the newly created Reich Armed Forces Court which was the highest military court in the German Reich. He sat on the tribunal which was appointed by Hitler to investigate the charges against General Freiherr von Fritsch. He testified that he drew up the verdict in this case. On 15 July 1928, he became Chief of the Legal Department of the OKW, designated in the documents as WR, which position he held until the capitulation of Germany. He held this position as a civil servant. On 1 May 1944, he was given the military title of Generaloberstabsrichter which was in fact a general in the German Army, which corresponds to that of a lieutenant general in the Army of the United States. He was not a member of the Nazi Party or any of its formations. The record does not establish that any honors were conferred upon him by the Nazi Party.

Aside from the charge of crimes against peace, heretofore disposed of in this opinion, we think that charges under counts two and three of the indictment may be disposed of under the following headings: (1) The Commissar Order; (2) The Barbarossa Jurisdiction Order; (3) The Commando Order; (4) Night and Fog Decree; (5) Terror and Sabotage Decrees. These subjects will be discussed in the order herein designated.

1. The Commissar Order—The only connection which the defendant is shown to have had with the issuance of the Commissar Order was an immaterial change in the wording of section 3 as to courts martial and the Tribunal is unable to find from the evidence any criminal connection of the defendant Lehmann with the issuance of this order.

2. The Barbarossa Jurisdiction Order—In this judgment we have previously discussed the legality of the Barbarossa Jurisdiction Order and have found it to have constituted an illegal order. The question now arises as to the criminal connection of the defendant Lehmann therewith.

The defendant Lehmann first received an order concerning this matter sometime in late April of 1941. The early stages of the development of the order are shrouded in obscurity as far as they appear in the documents in evidence. The defendant Lehmann, in his testimony, has given a rather elaborate statement as to what these developments were and his connection therewith. We shall not go into these early developments extensively. From his testimony it would appear that the circumstances of the order as communicated to him by Keitel's adjutant so aroused him that he drew an impracticable order to the effect that legal officers would be dispensed with in the German Wehrmacht and sent into combat service. According to his testimony, his reaction to the communication he received was primarily based upon the effect of the order upon military jurisdiction.

The Barbarossa Jurisdiction Order which was finally produced is an excellent example of the fundamental and essential functions which a staff performs in producing a military order from an original idea. The record discloses conferences, telephone calls, and much correspondence, all independent of Hitler. In this way the details of the order were worked out. Many of these details originated in the minds of various staff officers and some in the mind of the defendant.

In summarizing the generally significant parts of these proceedings, it is shown that on 28 April 1941, the defendant prepared a draft of the Barbarossa Jurisdiction Order. On or about 6 May he received a copy of an order which had been prepared by the OKH, apparently by General Mueller, the General for Special Assignments with the OKH, which embodied certain ideas of Generaloberst Halder, Chief of Staff of OKH. On 9 May the defendant reported to the Chief, WFSt, Department L (Warlimont) concerning certain discussions which he had with General Mueller and General Jeschonnek, and also as to discussions with the chiefs of the legal sections. The defendant had conferences with both General Mueller and General Jeschonnek concerning this matter. As an outgrowth of these activities a final and fourth draft was submitted to Keitel which, with a few minor modifications, was issued over the signature of Keitel and became what is known as the Barbarossa Jurisdiction Order.

In connection with these various conferences and various drafts and the correspondence connected therewith, it is apparent that the defendant's ideas for good or evil became a part of this order as issued. On the favorable side as to these details it can be said that he did not embody in the final draft which he submitted the inflammatory language which was contained in the first draft submitted by the OKH. Furthermore, in his favor in this connection, it is pointed out that that draft provided that inhabitants "who take part *or intend to take part* in the hostilities as guerrillas, etc.," and that in the defendant's final draft the words "or intend" were not included. His final text, however, contained the provisions as to collective punishments which left the door wide open to the decision of an officer of at least the rank of a battalion commander to impose such collective punishments as he saw fit.

This evidence also shows that due to the influence of the defendant the provision was finally inserted in the order to the effect that troops would dispose of all cases and that courts were to have no jurisdiction whatsoever, whereas General Mueller had urged that troops were to dispose of only those clear cases and that doubtful cases were to be left to the jurisdiction of the courts. The defendant's comments on this matter are significant as shown by the document where he states:

> The draft of the army comes very near to our own proposals. The only sentence missing is the provision that the courts of the armed forces have no jurisdiction at all over the indigenous inhabitants. General Halder wished to have this jurisdiction maintained for those cases in which the troops have no time for investigations and for the large number of offenses of minor kinds in which execution by shooting is now justified. I have objections to this, shared by General Jeschonnek.
>
> Once we take this step, we must take it fully. Otherwise it is to be feared that the troops will get rid just of those cases which they consider awkward, namely, the doubtful cases by handing them over to the courts. Thus, the outcome will be contrary to the result we aim at.

In this decision his position was approved by the defendant Warlimont as is shown by the same page of the document. This provision in the order, which obviously was not derived from Hitler, or Keitel, or Jodl, is one of the most vicious parts of the order. The defendant's reasons for this provision appear from the documents and his own testimony to have been that in the event such cases were handed over to the courts, the courts would acquit the defendants for lack of evidence; that those acquittals would bring upon the military courts criticism by Hitler to the effect they were too lenient, as he had done with reference to certain decisions made during the Polish campaign. In other words, it is apparent that, in order to avoid criticism of military courts by the Fuehrer, he was ready to sacrifice the lives of innocent people.

The discussions about the disciplinary features of this order also show the part that a staff officer plays in the final structure of an order. The net result of the entire proceedings as to this order was that Lehmann became the main factor in determining the final form into which the criminal ideas of Hitler were put; that he modified those ideas within his own sphere up to a certain point and placed the whole into an effective military order which was transmitted to the troops and carried out.

Under the record, we find him responsible for criminal connection with, participation in, and formulation of this illegal order.

3. The Commando Order—The Commando Order is another example of the part a staff officer plays in the final structure of a military order. Like the preceding Barbarossa Jurisdiction Order, it cannot be said that the whole of the Commando Order, or the major part of it, is a product of one man's mind. We are not concerned with the question of determining just how far the ideas of any one man are embodied in these orders except insofar as ideas that can be traced to a given defendant show his own state of mind in contributing criminal parts to the criminal whole. The basic criminal offense is in the essential part a staff officer performs in making effective the criminal whole.

This was a criminal order in which the defendant Warlimont, as has been pointed out, was a major factor and the defendant Lehmann's activities were subordinate to a large extent. The defendant was well aware of the criminal nature of this order. This had been pointed out by Admiral Canaris in various telegrams with which he was familiar. He made certain suggestions as to methods which might, by a strained construction, give some appearance of legality and be suitable for publication; constructions which he apparently did not believe himself.

We find no provisions in this order where he contributed to its inherent viciousness but he was one of those responsible for its final production in the form in which this criminal order was transmitted to the army and he was criminally responsible for a part of the vicious product.

4. The Night and Fog Decree—The Night and Fog Decree basically involved legal questions, and in this, as in the Barbarossa Jurisdiction Order, the defendant Lehmann was the major craftsman of its final form. It was the defendant Lehmann who conducted the negotiations whereby the Ministry of Justice was given the task of trying those persons charged under this decree before the Special and, later, the People's Courts, wherein they were deprived of the rudimentary rights which defendants have in the courts of any civilized nation.

His defense as to this charge is not without some merit, in that it was apparently the original idea of Hitler that these unfortunates were to be turned over to the tender mercies of the police for disposition. But for the reason stated above, we find him guilty as a participant of the final production of this terror program.

5. Terror and Sabotage Decrees—On 1 July 1944, from WFSt, Qu. Section, Lehmann received the following communication [*NOKW–2576, Pros. Ex. 823*]:

> Subject: Combating of enemy terrorists in the occupied territories.
>
> On account of events in Copenhagen, the Fuehrer has decreed that court martial proceedings against civilians in the occupied territories must be discontinued with immediate effect. WR is requested to submit suggestions for the draft of an order concerning the treatment of enemy terrorists and saboteurs among the civilian population in the occupied territories by 2 July, 2000 hours.
>
> Policies.
>
> Terror can be countered only by terror, but court martial sentences only create martyrs and national heroes.
>
> If German units or individual soldiers are attacked in any manner, the commander of the unit and/or the individual soldier are bound to take countermeasures independently and, in particular, to exterminate terrorists. Terrorists or saboteurs who are arrested later, must be turned over to the SD.

With this directive before him, he proceeded to make effective the illegal desires of his superiors, which apparently bore fruit in the Terror and Sabotage Decree of 30 July 1944, signed by Hitler. In August 1944, apparently in conjunction with the quartermaster section of the OKW, he participated in the supplemental order enlarging the scope of the original decree. He was therefore in a minor capacity connected with both the order and the supplemental directives.

On the matters above noted and on the record, we find the defendant Lehmann guilty under counts two and three of the indictment.

PRESIDING JUDGE YOUNG: At this time the Tribunal will take a short recess after which the sentences will be pronounced.

SENTENCES

PRESIDING JUDGE YOUNG: One final concluding paragraph was omitted from the reading of the judgment. I shall now read it.

> In the event there shall be any variation between the reading or translation or the stenographic report of the judgment as read and the copy thereof signed and lodged in the office of the Secretary General the latter shall control in all particulars.

The reading of the opinion and judgment having been concluded, the Tribunal will now impose sentences upon those defendants who have been adjudged guilty in these proceedings. Each defendant receiving a sentence for a term of years shall receive credit upon the sentence imposed upon him for such a period or periods of time as he has been in confinement, whether as a prisoner of war or otherwise, since 7 May 1945.

As the name of each defendant is called, he will arise, proceed to the center of the dock and put on the earphones.

Otto Schniewind, the Tribunal having found you not guilty, you will arise and retire with the guards. You will be released as heretofore ordered when the Tribunal presently adjourns.

Hugo Sperrle, having been found not guilty, in accordance with the order heretofore made, will be released when the Tribunal presently adjourns.

The defendant Wilhelm von Leeb will arise.

Wilhelm von Leeb, on the count of the indictment on which you have been convicted, the Tribunal sentences you to three years' imprisonment. You will retire with the guards.

The defendant Georg Karl Friedrich-Wilhelm von Kuechler will arise.

Georg Karl Friedrich-Wilhelm von Kuechler, on the counts of the indictment on which you have been convicted, the Tribunal sentences you to twenty years' imprisonment. You will retire with the guards.

The defendant Hermann Hoth will arise.

Hermann Hoth, on the counts of the indictment on which you have been convicted, the Tribunal sentences you to fifteen years' imprisonment. You will retire with the guards.

The defendant Hans Reinhardt will arise.

Hans Reinhardt, on the counts of the indictment on which you have been convicted, the Tribunal sentences you to fifteen years' imprisonment. You will retire with the guards.

The defendant Hans von Salmuth will arise.

Hans von Salmuth, on the counts of the indictment on which you have been convicted, the Tribunal sentences you to twenty years' imprisonment. You will retire with the guards.

The defendant Karl Hollidt will arise.

Karl Hollidt, on the counts of the indictment on which you have been convicted, the Tribunal sentences you to five years' imprisonment. You will retire with the guards.

The defendant Karl von Roques will arise.

Karl von Roques, on the counts of the indictment on which you have been convicted, the Tribunal sentences you to twenty years' imprisonment. You will retire with the guards.

The defendant Hermann Reinecke will arise.

Hermann Reinecke, on the counts of the indictment on which you have been convicted, the Tribunal sentences you to life imprisonment. You will retire with the guards.

The defendant Walter Warlimont will arise.

Walter Warlimont, on the counts of the indictment on which you have been convicted, the Tribunal sentences you to life imprisonment. You will retire with the guards.

The defendant Otto Woehler will arise.

Otto Woehler, on the counts of the indictment on which you have been convicted, the Tribunal sentences you to eight years' imprisonment. You will retire with the guards.

The defendant Rudolf Lehmann will arise.

Rudolf Lehmann, on the counts of the indictment on which you have been convicted, the Tribunal sentences you to seven years' imprisonment. You will retire with the guards.

THE JALUIT ATOLL CASE

Marshall Islands, December, 1945*

Trial of Rear-Admiral Nisuke Masuda and Four Others of the Imperial Japanese Navy Before United States Military Commission

Outline of the Proceedings

I. The Court

By a Message of 8th October, 1945, the Commander of the Marshalls Gilberts Area requested of the Commander-in-Chief of the Pacific Fleet the authority to convene a Military Commission for the trial of persons accused of War Crimes committed in that area prior to its occupation by United States forces. This authority was duly granted, and, in pursuance thereof, the Commander of the Marshalls Gilberts Area, as Convening Authority, ordered the setting up of a Military Commission on board the United States Naval Air Base at Kwajalein Island "for the trial of such war crime cases as may properly be brought before it." The Military Commission so appointed consisted of the following members, any five of whom were empowered to act: Commodore B. H. Wyatt, U.S.N. (President), Captain C. C. Champion, Jr., U.S.N., Captain J. R. Weisser, U.S.N., Colonel Thomas F. Joyce, Inf., Commander William W. White, U.S.N., Lieutenant-Colonel Basil P. Cooper, F.A., and Lieutenant John A. Murphy, U.S.N.R., and Lieutenant William P. Mahoney, U.S.N.R., as Judge Advocate, either of whom was authorised to act as such.

At the request of the accused, and pursuant to verbal orders from the Convening Authority, Lt. F. J. Madrigan, U.S.N.R., and Lt.-Comdr. Kozo Hirata, I.J.N., acted as Counsel for the accused. Lt. E. F. Field, U.S.N.R., acted as assistant to the Defence Counsel.

A plea to the jurisdiction of the Commission made by the Defence at the outset of the trial was over-ruled by the former, after the Defence and the Prosecution had presented arguments concerning the point (see later).

*_Law Reports of Trials of War Criminals,_ Vol. 1, p. 71 (London, 1947).

II. The Charge and Specification

The accused were Rear-Admiral Masuda, Lieutenant Yoshimura, Ensign Kawachi, Ensign Tasaki, and Warrant Officer Tanaka, all of the Imperial Japanese Navy.

The charge against the five accused, as approved by the Convening Authority, was one of murder. The specification stated that they "did, on or about 10th March, 1944, on the Island of Aineman, Jaluit Atoll, Marshall Islands, at a time when a state of war existed between the United States of America and the Japanese Empire, wilfully, feloniously, with malice aforethought without justifiable cause, and without trial or other due process, assault and kill, by shooting and stabbing to death, three American fliers, then and there attached to the Armed forces of the United States of America, and then and there captured and unarmed prisoners of war in the custody of the said accused, all in violation of the dignity of the United States of America, the International rules of warfare and the moral standards of civilised society."

An objection made by the accused on the grounds that the inclusion in the charge of the words "moral standards of civilised society" was improper and non-legal was over-ruled by the Commission.

The charge as originally drafted contained the word "unlawfully" instead of "wilfully"; the change was authorised by the Convening Authority on the request of the Commission.

Rear-Admiral Masuda did not appear at the trial, and, during its course and on the direction of the Convening Authority, a *nolle prosequi* was entered by the Judge Advocate as to the charge and specification against him. He had committed suicide before the opening of the trial, and had before his death written a statement in which he confessed that he had ordered the execution of the airmen.

III. The Arguments Used by the Prosecution in Support of the Charge and Specification

The Prosecution brought forward a number of witnesses to show that the three American airmen on or about February, 1944, were forced to land near Jaluit Atoll, Marshall Islands, and subsequently became unarmed prisoners of war on Emidj Island, on which was established the Japanese Naval Garrison Force Headquarters under the command of Rear-Admiral Masuda. Approximately one month later, on the orders of Masuda, and without having been tried, the airmen were taken to a cemetery on Aineman, an adjoining island, where they were secretly shot to death and then cremated. Yoshimura, Kawachi and Tanaka had admitted to having killed the prisoners by shooting; one had also used a sword. Tasaki had admitted that, having been in charge of the prisoners, he had arranged their release to the executioners, knowing that they were to be killed. Signed statements to the above effect were produced before the court.

One of the two Judge Advocates, in his opening argument, stated that one of the basic principles which had actuated the development of the laws and customs of war was the principle of humanity which prohibited the employment of any such kind or degree of violence as was not necessary for the purposes of war. Among the many and numerous restrictions and limitations imposed by virtue of this principle was "the universally recognised and accepted rule" provided in Article 23 (*c*) of the 1907 Hague Convention which states: "It is particularly forbidden . . . to kill or wound an enemy who, having laid down his arms, or no longer having means of defence, has surrendered at discretion." If this rule did not suffice, a variety of additional rules had been universally recognised and accepted, protecting prisoners of war from outrages, indignities and punishment.

His colleague relied instead on Article 2 of Part I of the Geneva Convention of 1929 relative to the Treatment of Prisoners of War which states that: "Prisoners of War are in the power of the hostile Government, but not of the individuals or formations which captured them. They shall at all times be humanely treated and protected, particularly against acts of violence, from insults and from public curiosity. Measures of reprisals against them are forbidden."

IV. The Case for the Defence

(i) *The Plea to the Jurisdiction*

The plea, made by the Defence to the jurisdiction of the Commission, was set out in four sections, and may be summarised as follows:

(*a*) The Congress of the United States had not delegated authority to Military Commissions, such as the present, to try enemy nationals for war crimes;

(*b*) The Commission had no jurisidction to try the defendants on charges or specifications founded on laws which were *ex post facto* in that they did not exist at the time of the commission of the acts for which the accused were charged;

(*c*) The "SCAP" rules, issued by command of General MacArthur, by virtue of which the Commission was established and the trial held, violated established rules of United States law, both substantial and procedural. In particular, Section 16 thereof permitted the introduction of hearsay and secondary evidence; and

(*d*) Even if the "SCAP" rules were applicable the venue of the trial was incorrectly laid. Under Section 5 (*b*) of the Rules, trials were to be held in Japan, with the exception that "persons whose offences have a particular geographical location outside Japan may be returned to the scene of their crimes for trial by competent military or civil tribunals of local jurisdiction." Accordingly the trial should have been held either in Japan or in Jaluit, the scene of the alleged crimes.

The Defence finally claimed that the defendants had the power under Section 5 (*b*) to elect to be tried by civil tribunal, and stated that they did so elect.

(ii) *The Defence of Superior Orders*

The accused pleaded not guilty. They admitted their part in the execution of the American Prisoners of War, but claimed as a defence that, as military men of the Japanese Empire, they were acting under orders of a superior authority, which they were bound to obey.

One of the defending Counsel, himself a Lieutenant-Commander in the Imperial Japanese Navy, described the absolute discipline and obedience which was expected from the Japanese forces, and quoted an Imperial Rescript which included the words: "Subordinates should have the idea that the orders from their superiors are nothing but the orders personally from his Majesty the Emperor." The Japanese forces were exceptional among the world's armed forces in this respect and, therefore, he claimed, it was impossible to apply therein "the liberal and individualistic ideas which rule usual societies unmodified to this totalistic and absolutistic military society." The strategic situation was so critical in early 1944 that the characteristic referred to was displayed in the Jaluit unit to an exceptional degree. Furthermore the order was given direct by a Rear-Admiral to "mere Warrant Officers and Petty Officers." If they had refused to obey it, "everyone would have fallen upon them."

As the accused had no criminal intent, it was clear that they had committed no crime.

The other defending Counsel pointed out that the executioners each requested that they should not be assigned the task of carrying out the killing, but when emphatically ordered by Masuda, a man of strong character, they had obeyed, in accordance with their training. Their actions were not of their own volition; they were the will of another.

Tasaki, the custodian of the prisoners of war, who arranged their handing over to the executioners, also merely acted in accordance with the orders of the Rear-Admiral. Certainly the latter had told him why he was to surrender the prisoners, but this fact in no way placed him in the position of a participant in the commission of a crime.

V. The Arguments of the Prosecution Used in Countering the Pleas of the Defence

(i) *Concerning the Jurisdiction of the Court*

The Judge Advocate, in countering the Defence's plea to the jurisdiction of the Commission, began by stating that this jurisdiction had already been upheld. Nevertheless he would reply briefly to the objections raised by the defence.

His arguments, which he arranged so as to meet those of the Defence point by point, were as follows:

(*a*) The power to conduct Military Commissions was part of the executive power of the President of the United States, and was delegated to subordinate commanders. The necessary formalities had in this case been fulfilled.

(*b*) "The statute laws are dated 1929. The laws of humanity also set forth in the specification have no dates, the laws are set back as far as civilisation."

(*c*) The "SCAP" rules had been approved by the Judge Advocate for the United States Navy, and their use was in accordance with the directions of the Commander of the Marshalls Gilberts Area. The Commission was not trying United States citizens but those of a foreign country.

(*d*) A similar objection to the venue of a trial had been over-ruled previously on the grounds that the trial was held as close to the scene of the alleged crime as was convenient. The same applied to the present case.

(ii) *Concerning the Defence of Superior Orders*

Onc of thc two Judge Advocates quoted three authorities with the intention of securing the rejection by the Commission of the plea of superior orders. The Judge Advocate General, he said, had made reference, in Court Martial Orders 212-1919, to the following dictum in *U.S. v. Carr* (25 Fed. Cases 307): "Soldier is bound to obey only the lawful orders of his superiors. If he receives an order to do an unlawful act, he is bound neither by his duty nor by his oath to do it. So far from such an order being a justification, it makes the party giving the order an accomplice in the crime."

In another case, involving the killing of a Nicaraguan citizen by a member of the United States forces, the Judge Advocate stated: "An order illegal in itself and not justified by the rules and usages of war, or in its substance clearly illegal, so that a man of ordinary sense and understanding would know as soon as he heard the order read or given that it was illegal, will afford no protection for a homicide, provided the act with which he may be charged has all the ingredients in it which may be necessary to constitute the same crime in law" (CMO 4-1929).

In the opinion of the Judge Advocate, however, the statement of the law most clearly in point was contained in "the rules promulgated by the Supreme Command of the Allied Powers for use in war crime cases. This body of international law, briefly known as the SCAP rules and adopted by the Commission at the direction of the Judge Advocate General of the Navy, has the following provision applicable to the defence raised by the accused, quoting sub-paragraph (*f*) of paragraph 16:

'The official position of the accused shall not absolve him from responsibility, nor be considered in mitigation of punishment. Further, action pursuant to order of the accused's superior, or of his government, shall not constitute a defence but may be considered in mitigation of punishment if the commission determines that justice so requires.' "

VI. The Evidence

The evidence is not here set out at length, since, in the main, the facts were not disputed, and the case turned essentially on a question of law. The facts derived from an examination of the witnesses for the Prosecution are set out in brief under heading 3 (*supra*). These witnesses comprised a legal officer who had acted as war crimes and atrocities investigator for the Marshalls Gilberts Area, an islander who had witnessed the capturing of the prisoners, one of the captors, a Japanese Lieutenant who had interrogated them, an interpreter who was present during the interrogation, a Japanese truck-driver who had been ordered by Kawachi to take the airmen to the cemetery, the seaman who cremated their bodies, a Japanese Major who testified to the authenticity of Masuda's written statements on the killing of the prisoners, a United States soldier who translated from the Japanese various documents before the Court, and one of the two Judge Advocates in the trial, who testified that the statements by the four accused which were before the Commission had actually been signed by them.

The three accused of having been the actual executioners gave evidence on their own behalf. Tasaki's evidence was given only by way of a signed statement.

VII. The Verdict

All four accused were found guilty.

VIII. The Sentence

Yoshimura, Kawachi and *Tanaka* were sentenced to death by hanging.

Tasaki was sentenced to ten years' imprisonment. His punishment was lighter than that of the others because of the "brief, passive and mechanical participation of the accused."

The proceedings, findings and sentences were approved by the Commander of the Marshalls Gilberts Area, Rear-Admiral Harrill.

Notes on the Case

I. Concerning the Plea to the Jurisdiction of the Commission

Comment upon the plea to the jurisdiction of the Commission made by the

Defence may conveniently be arranged in the same manner as were the remarks of Counsel.

(i) *The Legal Basis of the Commission*

The Defence claimed that no legislative act had ever enabled the holding by such Courts of trials of enemy nationals for war crimes. The contention of the Prosecution was that the authority to hold such trials derived from the executive power of the President.

The same question came before the Supreme Court of the United States in two cases, *Ex Parte Quirin,* 317 U.S.1, and *In the Matter of the Application of General Tomoyuki Yamashita,* No. 61 Miscellaneous and 672, October Term, 1945.

In these cases, the Supreme Court, *per* Mr. Chief Justice Stone, upheld the legality of trials by Military Commissions of enemy combatants for perpetrating war crimes. The Court pointed out that Congress, in the exercise of the power conferred on it by Article I, paragraph 8, cl. 10 of the Constitution to "define and punish Offences against the Law of Nations . . . ," of which the law of war was a part, had, by the statute entitled the Articles of War (1920, amended in 1937 and 1942), recognised the "Military Commission" appointed by military command, as it had previously existed in United States Army practice, as an appropriate tribunal for the trial and punishment of offences against the laws of war. Article 15 declared that "the provisions of these articles conferring jurisdiction upon courts martial shall not be construed as depriving military commissions . . . or other military tribunals of concurrent jurisdiction in respect of offenders or offences that by statute or by the law of war may be triable by such military commissions . . . or other military tribunals." Article 2 included among those persons subject to the Articles of War the personnel of the United States military forces. The Court pointed out, however, that this, as Article 12 indicated, did not exclude from the class of persons subject to trial by Military Commissions "any other person who by the law of war is subject to trial by military tribunals," and who under Article 12 may be tried by Court Martial, or under Article 15 by Military Commission.

Congress had not attempted to codify the laws of war, continued the Chief Justice, but had, by Article 15, incorporated within the pre-existing jurisdiction of Military Commissions created by the appropriate military command "all offences which are defined as such by the law of war, and which may constitutionally be included within that jurisdiction."

The power to convene Commissions of the nature referred to continued after hostilities had ceased, and at least until peace had been "officially recognised by treaty or proclamation of the political branch of the Government."

The conclusion of the Court in the *Yamashita Case* was that the Joint Chiefs of Staff of the American Military Forces were acting legally when, by direction of the President, on September 12th, 1945, they instructed General MacArthur, Commander in Chief, United States Army Forces, Pacific, to proceed with the trial before appropriate military tribunals of such Japanese War Criminals "as have been or may be apprehended."

The opinion of the Supreme Court in *Ex Parte Quirin* was delivered on October 29th, 1942, while that in the *Yamashita Case* was delivered on February 4th, 1946.

The Judge-Advocate prosecuting in the Jaluit Atoll case, in his reply of December 7th, 1945, to the Defence's plea to the jurisdiction of the Commission, did not specify in what "previous case" that jurisdiction had been upheld. The authorities cited above are, however, wholly in line with the decision of the Commission to reject the plea and with the statement of the Prosecution that "The jurisdiction of the military commission to try offences against the law of nations derives from the President of the United States, who, as Commander in Chief of the Armed Forces, exercises the power of military government over territories occupied by our country. His representative in the Pacific, the Commander in Chief of the Pacific Fleet, has, as the deputy military governor, conferred specific authority to convene this commission on the Commander Marshalls Gilberts Area."

It will be noted that the Judge Advocate did not state how far the power of the President in this matter was derived from the Constitution and how far from Congressional legislation. In *Ex Parte Quirin,* the Supreme Court pointed out that the Constitution of the United States conferred on the President the "exeucutive power" (Article II, paragraph 1, cl. 1) and imposed on him the duty to "take care that the Laws be faithfully executed" (Article II, paragraph 3). It also made him the Commander in Chief of the Army and Navy (Article II, paragraph 2, cl. 1). The Court decided, however, that it was not necessary to determine to what extent the President as Commander in Chief had constitutional power to create Military Commissions without the support of Congressional legislation. Nor did the Court in the *Yamashita Case* need to investigate that problem.

(ii) *Ex post facto legislation*

The Judge Advocate's claim that the rules of International Law, with whose infringement the accused were charged, were binding on them at the time of the commission of the alleged war crimes gives rise to no comment. It will be noticed, however, that, for the purpose of refuting the arguments of the Defence on this point, the Judge Advocate made no reference to what may be called the municipal law ingredients included in the charge and specification. Further comment on this inclusion is made later, under heading 2, "Concerning the charge and specification."

(iii) *The legality of the rules applied in the trial*

The Commander of the Marshalls Gilberts Area directed the President of the Commission "to use SCAP Rules governing the trials of War Criminals as a guide, not only for the rules of evidence, but also as a guide for substantive law and procedure on all issues arising in the trial of war criminals." The Defence claimed that these rules violated "established substantive and procedural law known to American jurisprudence." The Judge Advocate, on the other hand, claimed that their use was legal, and secured the concurrence of the Commission on the point.

Here, again, the decision of the Supreme Court in the *Yamashita Case* is relevant. One of the grounds upon which the petitioner sought writs of habeas corpus and prohibition against the Military Commission which tried him was: "that the commission was without authority and jurisdiction to try and convict petitioner because the order governing the procedure of the commission permitted the admission in evidence of depositions, affidavits and hearsay and opinion evidence, and because the commission's rulings admitting such evidence were in violation of the 25th and 38th Articles of War and the Geneva Convention, and deprived petitioner of a fair trial in violation of the due process clause of the Fifth Amendment."

Article 25 prohibits the reception in evidence by a Military Commission of depositions on behalf of the Prosecution in a capital case, while Article 38 empowers the President to prescribe by regulations the procedure for cases before Military Commissions and states that these regulations "shall, in so far as he shall deem practicable, apply the rules of evidence generally recognised in the trial of criminal cases in the district courts of the United States: *Provided*. That nothing contrary to or inconsistent with these Articles shall be so prescribed . . ."

In the opinion of the Supreme Court, however, neither Article was applicable to the trial of an enemy combatant by a Military Commission for violations of the laws of war. Chief Justice Stone, delivering the majority judgment, stated that Article 15 had been added in 1916 to the Articles in order to preserve intact the traditional jurisdiction of "the non-statutory military commission." The Article read: "The provisions of these articles conferring jurisdiction upon courts-martial shall not be construed as depriving military commissions . . . of concurrent jurisdiction in respect of offenders or offences that . . . by the law of war may be triable by such military commissions." Article 2 of the Articles of War enumerated "the persons . . . subject to these articles" and enemy combatants were not included among them. The Court concluded that the benefits of the Articles were not conferred upon such persons, and that the Articles left the control over the procedure in their trials where it had previously been, that is to say with the Military Command. The Commission's rulings on evidence and on the mode of conducting the proceedings were not subject to review by the civil courts but only by the reviewing military authorities. It was therefore unnecessary to consider what, in other situations, the Fifth Amendment might require.

It may be added here that the Supreme Court had already decided in *Ex Parte Quirin* that the Fifth and Sixth Amendments laying down the right to a trial by jury in a civil court for capital crimes did not extend to trials in military tribunals. Since, however, this decision is not relevant to the Masuda trial, it is not analysed in these notes. The *Yamashita Case* is relevant since it shows that a defendant in a trial before a Military Commission is not entitled to object if the rules of evidence applied therein are not those "generally recognised in the trial of criminal cases in the district courts of the United States."

(iv) *The venue of the trial*

The ruling tacitly approved by the Commission on the question of venue gives rise to no comment. No defendant could have reasonably been allowed to plead, for instance, that no liability rested on him had the island on which he had committed his crimes disappeared as the result of a volcanic upheaval.

II. Concerning the Charge and Specification

It will have been noticed that the charge against the prisoners was one of murder and that the specification mentioned both a breach of "the International rules of warfare" and wilful felonious killing "with malice aforethought without justifiable cause, and without trial or other due process." While one Judge Advocate quoted Article 23 (*c*) of the 1907 Hague Convention and made a general reference to related rules of customary International Law, he also recalled that the charge against the accused was one of murder and proceeded to analyse in detail the elements of a definition of murder as "the unlawful killing of a human being with malice aforethought."

His colleague pointed out that the specification had been "patterned carefully after the samples set forth in *Naval Courts and Boards.*" He gave more attention than his colleague to the International Law governing the case, however, and expressed the opinion that the rules of Conventional Law which were the most relevant were the rules laid down in the 1929 Geneva Convention Relative to the Treatment of Prisoners of War, from which he quoted Article 2. It might be argued, he continued, that the Japanese Government was not a signatory to the Convention. Against this, however, he said: "Although Japan has not ratified or formally adhered to the Prisoners of War Convention, it has, through the Swiss Government, agreed to apply the provisions thereof to prisoners of war under its control, and also, so far as practicable, to interned civilians."

Even if Japan were not legally bound, the shooting of unarmed prisoners who are behaving in an orderly fashion is clearly a war crime under customary International Law.

At first sight it may appear that the introduction of the definition of murder, based on Anglo-Saxon rules of Municipal Law, was not strictly justifiable in a case where breaches of International Law on an island under Japanese mandate were alleged. The intention of the Prosecution, however, was not to charge the accused with breaches of United States law *as well as* of International Law. The use of the words in the specification, "all in violation of . . . the

International rules of warfare," as applying to the charge of murder, clearly shows that the introduction of the terms used in United States law was intended merely to amplify and define the specification. In the present state of vagueness prevailing in many branches of the law of nations, even given the fact that there are no binding precedents in International Law, such introduction therein of tested concepts from municipal systems is all to the good, provided that they are recognised to be in amplification of, and not in substitution for, rules of International Law. This is so, even if it involves the use of tautology, inherent in some Common Law definitions, such as is exemplified in the phrase, "wilfully, feloniously, with malice aforethought without justifiable cause . . ." in the specification.

THE ESSEN LYNCHING CASE

Essen, Germany, December, 1945*

Trial of Erich Heyer and Six Others Before British Military Court

Outline of the Proceedings

I. The Court

The Court was convened under the Royal Warrant of June, 1945, and consisted of the following: President: Lieut.-Colonel B. G. Melsom, E. Lancs.; Members: Wing-Commander J. G. C. Barnes, 8501 Air Disarmament Wing, RAF; Major L. E. Dickson, MC, 1 Glasgow Highlanders; Major C. Freeman, MC, 107 Medium Regt. RA.; Legal Member: Captain C. W. E. Shelley, ERE List, Legal Staff, Headquarters British Army of the Rhine. The Prosecutor was Major W. St. J. C. Tayleur, RA, Legal Staff, HQ Lines of Communication. The Defending Officer was Major J. W. Stone, 49 Recce Regiment, in civilian life a solicitor.

II. The Charge

The seven accused were jointly charged with committing a war crime in that they, at Essen-West on the 13th December, 1944, in violation of the laws and usages of war, were, with other persons, concerned in the killing of three unidentified British airmen, prisoners of war.

At the material time, one of the accused, Erich Heyer, had been a Captain in the German army; and the accused Peter Koenen had been a private in the German army.

The rest of the accused were German civilians, inhabitants of Essen.

III. The Case for the Prosecution

The Prosecutor stated that the three captured British airmen had been

**Law Reports of Trials of War Criminals,* Vol. 1, p. 88 (London, 1947).

handed by the German police into the custody of the military unit which was under the command of the accused Hauptmann Heyer. The three airmen were placed by Hauptmann Heyer under an escort consisting of an N.C.O., who was not before the Court, and the accused, Private Koenen.

The Prosecution alleged that Heyer had given to the escort instructions that they should take the prisoners to the nearest Luftwaffe unit for interrogation. It was submitted by the Prosecution that this order, though on the face of it correct, was given out to the escort from the steps of the barracks in a loud voice so that the crowd, which had gathered, could hear and would know exactly what was going to take place. It was alleged that he had ordered the escort not to interfere in any way with the crowd if they should molest the prisoners.

When the prisoners of war were marched through one of the main streets of Essen, the crowd around grew bigger, started hitting them and throwing sticks and stones at them. An unknown German corporal actually fired a revolver at one of the airmen and wounded him in the head. When they reached the bridge, the airmen were eventually thrown over the parapet of the bridge; one of the airmen was killed by the fall; the others were not dead when they landed, but were killed by shots from the bridge and by members of the crowd who beat and kicked them to death.

The allegation of the Prosecution was that there were three stages in the killing, starting with the incitement at the entrance to the barracks, continuing with the beating and finally the throwing over the parapet and shooting. The accused Heyer "lit the match." Each person who struck a blow was "putting flame to the fuel," which was the enraged population, and finally "the explosion" came on the bridge. It was, therefore, the submission of the Prosecution that every person who, following the incitement to the crowd to murder these men, voluntarily took aggressive action against any one of these three airmen, was guilty in that he was concerned in the killing. It was impossible to separate any one of these acts from another; they all made up what is known as a lynching. From the moment they left those barracks, the men were doomed and the crowd knew they were doomed and every person in that crowd who struck a blow was both morally and criminally responsible for the deaths of the three men.

Hauptmann Heyer admittedly never struck any physical blow against the airmen at all. His part in this affair was an entirely verbal one; in the submission of the Prosecution this was one of those cases of words that kill, and he was as responsible, if not more responsible, for the deaths of the three men as any one else concerned.

The Prosecutor expressly stated that he was not suggesting that the mere fact of passing on the secret order to the escort that they should not interfere to protect the prisoners against the crowd was sufficiently proximate to the killing, so that on that alone Heyer was concerned in the killing. The Prosecutor advised the Court that, if it was not satisfied beyond reasonable doubt that he had incited the crowd to lynch these airmen, he was then entitled to acquittal, but if the Court was satisfied that he did in fact say these people were to be shot, and did in fact incite the crowd to kill the airmen, then, in the submission of the Prosecution, he was guilty.

The Prosecution referred to the rule of British law in which an instigator may be regarded as a principal. The same held good in this case if a man incited someone else to commit a crime and that crime was committed. Although the person who incited was not present when the crime was committed, he was triable and punishable as a principal and it made no difference in this respect whether the trial took place under British law or under the Regulations for the trial of war criminals.

Referring to the member of the escort, Private Koenen, the Prosecutor pointed out that his position was somewhat difficult because his military duty and his conscience must have conflicted. He was given an order not to interfere and he did not interfere. He stood by while these three airmen were murdered. Mere inaction on the part of a spectator is not in itself a crime. A man might stand by and see someone else drowning and let him go and do nothing. He has committed no crime. But in certain circumstances a person may be under a duty to do something. In the Prosecutor's submission this escort, as the representative of the Power which had taken the airmen prisoners, had the duty not only to prevent them from escaping but also of seeing that they were not molested. Therefore it was the duty of the escort, who was armed with a revolver, to protect the people in his custody. Koenen failed to do what his duty required him to do. In the Prosecutor's opinion, his guilt was, however, not as bad as the guilt of those who took an active part, but a person who was responsible for the safety of the prisoners and who deliberately stood by and merely held his rifle up to cover them while other people killed them, was "concerned in the killing."

IV. The Evidence

The allegation of the Prosecution that Heyer had ordered the escort not to interfere in any way with the crowd if they should molest the prisoners was proved in evidence, and was also admitted by Heyer himself. It was confirmed by some German witnesses, though not admitted by Heyer, that he made remarks to the effect that the airmen ought to be shot or that they would be shot.

One of the accused, Boddenberg, expressly admitted having hit the airmen with his belt. The part played by each of the others was described by one or more German witnesses.

V. The Verdict

Hauptmann Heyer and Private *Koenen* were found guilty. Two of the accused civilians were acquitted. The other civilians were found guilty.

VI. The Sentences

The Court sentenced *Heyer* to death by hanging, and *Koenen* to imprisonment for five years.

The sentences on the three civilians who were found guilty were as follows:

Johann Braschoss was sentenced to death by hanging,

Karl Kaufer to imprisonment for life, and

Hugo Boddenberg to imprisonment for ten years.

The executions were carried out on March 8th, 1946.

Notes on the Case

There was no Judge Advocate appointed in this case and consequently no summing up in open Court. The considerations as to the facts and as to the law which guided the Court cannot, therefore, be quoted from the transcript in so many words. It is only possible to attempt by inference to derive them from the verdict and from the sentences imposed, having regard to arguments brought forward by Counsel.

As has already been said, the Court found Hauptmann Heyer guilty, from which it follows that the Court accepted the arguments as to the criminal liability of Heyer, set out above.

From the fact that the Court sentenced Peter Koenen to imprisonment for five years, it can be seen that it accepted the Prosecutor's proposition both as to Koenen's guilt and as to the extenuating circumstances which were pointed out in his favour by the Prosecutor himself.

It may be stated in this connection that the Defence did not plead superior orders, either with regard to Heyer or with regard to Koenen, as a circumstance excluding criminal responsibility in a case where the order was illegal.

Two of the accused civilians were acquitted, the Court considering the allegations preferred against them by the witnesses not beyond reasonable doubt.

The other civilians were found guilty because every one of them had in one form or another taken part in the ill-treatment which eventually led to the death of the victims, though against none of the accused had it been exactly proved that they had individually shot or given the blows which caused the death.

The Prosecutor pointed out that the charge alleged that the accused were concerned in the killing of the three British airmen. That was the wording of the charge, but, the Prosecutor added, for the purpose of this trial he would invite the Court to take the view that this was a charge of murder and of nothing other than murder. The allegation would be that all these seven Germans in the dock were guilty either as an accessory before the fact or as principals in the murder of the three British airmen.

This proposition was not accepted by the Court. The legal member pointed out that this was not a trial under English Law. Murder was the killing of a person under the King's peace. The charge here was not murder and if Counsel spoke of murder he was not using the word in the strict legal sense but in the popular sense. As long as everyone realised what was meant by the word "murder" for the purposes of this trial, the legal member did not think there was any difficulty. As to using words like "accessory before the fact" and so on, which are applicable to English law and to felonies, the legal member again saw no objection to that, as long as all concerned knew exactly what they were talking about. They were using the words almost in inverted commas as analogies to English law.

THE ZYKLON B CASE

Hamburg, March, 1946*

TRIAL OF BRUNO TESCH AND TWO OTHERS
BEFORE BRITISH MILITARY COURT

OUTLINE OF THE PROCEEDINGS

I. THE COURT

The Court consisted of Brigadier R. B. L. Persse, as President, and, as members, Lt. Col. Sir Geoffrey Palmer, Bart., Coldstream Gds., and Major S. M. Johnstone, Royal Tank Regt.

Capt. H. S. Marshall was Waiting Member.

C. L. Stirling, Esq., C.B.E., Barrister-at-Law, Deputy Judge Advocate General, was Judge Advocate.

Major G. I. D. Draper, Irish Guards, Judge Advocate General's Branch, HQ. B.A.O.R., was Prosecutor.

Three German Counsel appeared on behalf of the accused. Dr. O. Zippel, Dr. C. Stumme and Dr. A. Stegemann defended Tesch, Weinbacher and Drosihn respectively.

II. THE CHARGE

The accused, Bruno Tesch, Joachim Drosihn and Karl Weinbacher, were charged with a war crime in that they "at Hamburg, Germany, between 1st January, 1941, and 31st March, 1945, in violation of the laws and usages of war did supply poison gas used for the extermination of allied nationals interned in concentration camps well knowing that the said gas was to be so used." The accused pleaded not guilty.

**Law Reports of Trials of War Criminals,* Vol. 1, p. 93 (London, 1947).

III. The Case for the Prosecution

The prosecuting Counsel, in his opening address, stated that Dr. Bruno Tesch was by 1942 the sole owner of a firm known as Tesch and Stabenow, whose activities were divided into three main categories. In the first place, it distributed certain types of gas and gassing equipment for disinfecting various public buildings, including Wehrmacht barracks and S.S. concentration camps. Secondly, it provided, where required, expert technicians to carry out these gassing operations. Lastly, Dr. Tesch and Dr. Drosihn, the firm's senior gassing technician, carried out instruction for the Wehrmacht and the S.S. in the use of the gas which the firm supplied. The predominant importance of these gassing operations in war-time lay in their value in the extermination of lice.

The chief gas involved was Zyklon B, a highly dangerous poison gas, 99 per cent, of which was, prussic acid. The gas was manufactured by another firm. Tesch and Stabenow had the exclusive agency for the supply of the gas east of the River Elbe, but the Zyklon B itself went directly from the manufacturers to the customer.

The contention for the Prosecution was that from 1941 to 1945 Zyklon B was being supplied as a direct result of orders accepted by the accused's firm, Tesch and Stabenow. On that basis, the Zyklon B was going in vast quantities to the largest concentration camps in Germany east of the Elbe. In these same camps the S.S. Totenkopfverbände were, from 1942 to 1945, systematically exterminating human beings to an estimated total of six million, of whom four and a half million were exterminated by the use of Zyklon B in one camp alone, known as Auschwitz/Birkenau. In these concentration camps were a vast number of people from the occupied territories of Europe, including Czechs, Russians, Poles, French, Dutch and Belgians, and people from neutral countries and from the United States. The Prosecutor also claimed that over a period of time the three accused got to know of this wholesale extermination of human beings in the eastern concentration camps by the S.S. using Zyklon B gas, and that, having acquired this knowledge, they continued to arrange supplies of the gas to these customers in the S.S. in ever-increasing quantities, until in the early months of 1944 the consignment per month to Auschwitz concentration camp was nearly two tons.

The accused Weinbacher was a "Procurist"; when Tesch was absent he was fully empowered and authorised to do all acts on behalf of his principal which his principal could have done. His position was of great importance, since his principal would travel on the business of the firm for as many as 200 days in the year.

The case for the Prosecution was that knowingly to supply a commodity to a branch of the State which was using that commodity for the mass extermination of Allied civilian nationals was a war crime, and that the people who did it were war criminals for putting the means to commit the crime into the hands of those who actually carried it out. The action of the accused was in violation of

Article 46 of the Hague Regulations of 1907, to which the German government and Great Britain were both parties.

IV. The Evidence for the Prosecution

Emil Sehm, a former bookkeeper and accountant employed by Tesch and Stabenow, supplied information, regarding the legitimate business activities of the firm and the positions of the three accused therein, which substantially bore out the opening statements of the Prosecutor on these points. He went on to state that in the Autumn of 1942 he saw in the files of the firm's registry one of the reports, dictated by Tesch, which gave accounts of his business journeys. In this travel report, Tesch recorded an interview with leading members of the Wehrmacht, during which he was told that the burial, after shooting, of Jews in increasing numbers was proving more and more unhygienic, and that it was proposed to kill them with prussic acid. Dr. Tesch, when asked for his views, had proposed to use the same method, involving the release of prussic acid gas in an enclosed space, as was used in the extermination of vermin. He undertook to train the S.S. men in this new method of killing human beings.

Sehm had written down a note of these facts and taken it away with him, but had burnt it the next day on the advice of an old friend named Wilhelm Pook, to whom he had related what he had seen.

Dr. Marx, a German Barrister practising since 1934, who was called upon to define the status of a Procurist in German law, said:

> The procurist had the right to act in the name and on behalf of the firm. He is a man who, out of all the others mentioned in the law who have also the right to act on behalf of the firm, has most of these rights. He had the right to act on behalf of the firm and to conclude any transactions or any sort of act on behalf of the firm, and to conclude any transactions or any sort of legal proceedings in which the firm might find itself involved. One can say that anybody who has any sort of transactions with a man who holds the "Procura" and who is called the Procurist is in exactly the same position as if he had had that transaction with the head of the firm."

Erna Biagini, a former stenographer of the firm, who was also in charge of the registry, claimed to have read, in "approximately 1942," a travel report of Dr. Tesch which stated that Zyklon B could be used for killing human beings as well as vermin.

Anna Uenzelmann, a former stenographer of the firm, said that in about June 1942 Tesch, after he had dictated a travel report on returning from Berlin, had told her that Zyklon B was being used for gassing human beings, and had appeared to be as terrified and shocked about the matter as she was.

Karl Ruehmling, who had been a bookkeeper and assistant gassing master with the firm, said that Zyklon B was sent by the concern to the concentration camps at Auschwitz, Sachsenhausen and Neuengamme, but Auschwitz was sent the largest consignments.

Alfred Zaun, who was in charge of the firm's bookkeeping, said that, in his opinion, Auschwitz of all the concentration camps had received the most Zyklon B during the war.

Wilhelm Bahr, an ex-medical orderly at Neuengamme, described a prussic acid course which he had attended in the S.S. Hospital at Oranienburg in 1942, and which Dr. Tesch had conducted. He said that he himself had gassed two hundred Russian prisoners of war in Neuengamme in 1942, using prussic acid gas, but that it was not Dr. Tesch who had taught him the procedure which he had applied.

Perry Broad, who had been a Rottenführer in the Kommandatur of the Auschwitz camp from June 1942 until early 1945, described how persons were gassed there with Zyklon B. The people being gassed, to his knowledge, at Auschwitz and Birkenau were German deportees, Jews from Belgium, Holland, France, North Italy, Czechoslavakia and Poland, and Gypsies.

Dr. Bendel, who had been a prisoner at Auschwitz and had acted as a doctor to the inmates, said that from February 1944 to January 1945 a million people had been killed there by Zyklon B.

The remaining Prosecution witnesses were a member of a British war crimes investigation team, who identified pre-trial statements made by the accused; Wilhelm Pook and his wife; and five more employees of Tesch and Stabenow. The evidence of Pook and his wife supported that of Sehm to a degree, though not in every detail, but the fact that they had discussed the events of 1942 between his and their giving evidence was recognised by the Judge Advocate to be "undoubtedly unfortunate."

The Prosecution, acting in accordance with Regulation 8 (i) (*a*) of the Royal Warrant, submitted to the Court a sworn affidavit in which Dr. Diels, a former high-ranking German government official, stated that it was common knowledge in 1943 in Germany that gas was being used for killing people.

Among various other documents[1] Dr. Tesch's S.S. subscription card was produced before the Court; the Defence pointed out, however, that this did not prove that Dr. Tesch had been an active member of the S.S.

V. The Opening Statements of Defence Counsel

(i) *Counsel for Tesch*

Before calling Tesch to the witness-box, his Counsel stated that he intended to prove to the court, first, that Tesch had no knowledge of the killing of human beings by means of Zyklon B; secondly, that Zyklon B was delivered only for normal purposes of disinfection and for medical reasons; thirdly, that parts of gas chambers were sold only for the purpose of exterminating vermin;

[1]Of the various documents admitted as evidence in the trial (including five affidavits, and the pre-trial statements by all of the accused) the Secretariat of the United Nations War Crimes Commission has only been able to examine an extract from the affidavit of Dr. Diels.

fourthly, that concentration camps got the gas only in amounts which were quite normal in relation to the number of inhabitants, and only for killing vermin; and fifthly, that instruction courses were held only according to the relevant laws and regulations, and again only for the purpose of teaching the method of exterminating vermin.

(ii) *Counsel for Weinbacher*

Dr. Stumme, defending Weinbacher, said that by the evidence which he would call, he would try to prove that Weinbacher had no knowledge of any note or report by Dr. Tesch to the effect that human beings were being killed by poison gas, and that until the capitulation of Germany he never had any reason to believe that Zyklon B was being used for any other purpose than the destruction of vermin.

(iii) *Counsel for Drosihn*

Counsel for Drosihn set out to prove, by the evidence which he called first, that Dr. Drosihn had nothing to do with the business concerning the supply of gas; secondly, that, being on journeys for considerable periods, he had only a very scanty knowledge of the activities of the business; thirdly, that he heard about the gassing of human beings only after the capitulation of Germany; and fourthly, that he never carried out instruction either in concentration camps or for S.S. personnel.

VI. The Evidence for the Defence

(i) *Dr. Tesch*

All three accused gave evidence on oath. Dr. Tesch stated that he had heard nothing and had known nothing about human beings being killed in concentration camps with prussic acid. He denied ever having attended any conference, or having been approached by any official or military authority on the subject, or having written in any document that human beings should be killed by prussic acid. He specifically denied that he had made the remarks referred to by Anna Uenzelmann. He had never been to Auschwitz himself and had had no reason to believe that the camps were incorrectly run.

He did not think that deliveries to Auschwitz were very high because it was a large camp and, further, it "administered more camps in the General Government of Poland." He could not remember Dr. Drosihn ever having instructed S.S. men. Although the witness had paid subscriptions to both the S.S. and the Nazi Party, he had never been an active member of either. He thought that the passage in the travel report which Erna Biagini had read might have been a record of an answer put to him by a pupil.

Drosihn, stated Tesch, was a technical expert and was not concerned with the administration of the firm or the office. Weinbacher, however, had complete control when Tesch was away from the office.

(ii) *Karl Weinbacher*

This accused, giving evidence on oath, said that his work was, briefly, to look after the current business affairs in the absence of Dr. Tesch, seeing to the incoming and the outgoing mail, answering any queries, and confirming any orders received. He read some of Dr. Tesch's travel reports but not all, because there were too many; in particular, he had not read any dealing with the possibility of destroying Jews with Zyklon B. Dr Tesch had not mentioned any such possibility to him, nor had the witness heard during the war that Jews were being gassed. He had never been inside a concentration camp, nor had he received unfavourable reports during the war about such camps. He, too, stated that Drosihn had nothing to do with the business management. He could not agree that the S.S. would necessarily come to Dr. Tesch for advice on the extermination of human beings with Zyklon B, since, although Dr. Tesch was an expert on the use of the gas, there were plenty of books available on prussic acid.

(iii) *Dr. Drosihn*

Drosihn claimed that his part in the activities of the firm consisted in collaborating on scientific issues, being in charge of the gassing, for instance, of ships in Hamburg docks, and examining delousing chambers to see whether they were working correctly. He spent about 150 to 200 days a year in travelling on business. He had been to check the working of the delousing chambers in Sachsenhausen and Ravensbruck and had been to Neuengamme; but had neither been to Auschwitz, nor given instructions to the S.S. in any place. He knew nothing of the size of consignments of gas to Auschwitz. Contrary to Tesch's evidence, the witness claimed to have reported to him once that he had seen happening in the camps things that were contrary to human dignity.

(iv) *The Remaining Defence Witnesses*

Nine other witnesses called by the Defence did not add very substantially to the evidence before the Court. The subjects covered by their remarks included the character of Dr. Tesch, and the extent of general knowledge in Germany concerning the killing of Jews. *Inter alia,* they were called to prove that Zyklon B was widely used for the legitimate purpose of killing vermin. These witnesses were two Medical Officers from Hamburg, a doctor and two chemists employed by the German Hygiene Institute, a retired professor of the same institute, the Manager of the Disinfection Institute of Hamburg, a steno-typist formally employed by Tesch and Stabenow, and Dr. Stumme, one of the Defence Counsel, who gave evidence regarding the German law regarding State secrets.

VII. The Closing Addresses of the Defence Counsel

(i) *Counsel for Tesch*

In his closing address, Dr. Zippel, dealing with the point of law involved, submitted that, since the charge was not one of destroying human life but only of supplying the means of doing so, such action would only be contrary to the laws and usages of war if the means supplied were necessarily intended to kill human beings. To supply a material which also had quite legitimate purposes was no war crime.

Turning to the facts, Counsel claimed that while supplies of Zyklon B to the S.S. were large, it was the duty of the S.S. to see that the state of health in the eastern provinces was kept at a high level, and it was concerned not only with the Wehrmacht itself, but also with the state of health of those parts of the eastern provinces whose population was repatriated to Germany before the entry of Germany into war with Russia. Supplies were not too great to have been used wholly for legitimate purposes. Since 1944 the S.S. had had unlimited permission to use the gas for the destruction of vermin and the prevention of epidemics. He submitted that even in the concentration camps the gas was, at least at the beginning, used only for its legitimate purpose.

Counsel then questioned whether the Zyklon B used at Auschwitz for killing human beings had been supplied by Tesch and Stabenow. The fact that Auschwitz was situated in the district for which the firm were the agents could not be decisive, for other firms were able to supply that district, especially since during the war the boundaries of the districts were not so much respected as before. Further, the S.S. had been active all over the occupied territories during the war and had had various means of securing the gas. So many people were killed by gassing in Auschwitz that the S.S. must necessarily have used sources other than Tesch and Stabenow.

Counsel observed that the witnesses who were called to prove that Dr. Tesch knew about the unlawful use of his gas had given different versions as to how he must or should have known about such use. He proceeded also to throw doubts on the reliability of Sehm, for instance, in view of a statement of his, denied by many other witnesses, that the files of the firm in which he had found the travel report were kept under lock and key. Miss Biagini had denied that she saw anything in this report about a conference with the High Command of the Wehrmacht or any propositions made by Dr. Tesch to this authority. None of the typists who could have typed the travel report in question knew of it or any rumour in the office regarding it. Under the existing war-time regulations of secrecy, it seemed impossible that a man as careful as Tesch should have dictated a report on an interview with the High Command on such a secret matter, placed the report where anyone in the office could read it, as was the case with all travel reports, and then discussed the facts with his employees. Dr. Tesch had been shown to be a fair and honest man, and his concentration on his work explained why he had not heard any rumour which may have circulated Germany concerning the gassing of human beings. Regarding the large supplies of gas to Auschwitz in particular, Counsel submitted that Dr. Tesch was too busy to be expected to know what individual customers bought, and in any case the supply of Zyklon was not as important to the firm as were its gassing activities. Furthermore, Dr. Tesch had regarded Auschwitz as a transit camp needing therefore unusually frequent delousing. Counsel concluded that Dr. Tesch knew nothing of the gassing of human beings either in Auschwitz or Neuengamme.

(ii) *Counsel for Weinbacher*

In his closing address, Dr. Stumme submitted that it had become clear during the trial that Weinbacher did not know that Zyklon B had been used for the killing of human beings. Not one of the witnesses could say really that Weinbacher had any knowledge of a travel report or any observation of Dr. Tesch that human beings had been killed by Zyklon B, or that Dr. Tesch had conversations with Weinbacher on such a subject. Nor had the trial shown that Weinbacher should have had reasonable suspicion, or grounds for suspicion, that Zyklon B had been used for the killing of human beings. Even if Dr. Tesch had written such a travel report as the one alleged, Weinbacher need not have read it, because he was a busy man, and witnesses had shown that many of the travel reports were filed and read by no one. Even Sehm claimed to have come across the particular report by accident, and Miss Biagini because she had to file it. He repeated Dr. Zippel's argument that Dr. Tesch would not write a State secret in a document which all the staff could read. If Sehm had found any other document, it must have been purely by accident; and no such accident had happened to Weinbacher. In connection with the large supplies of gas which were sent to Auschwitz, Counsel pointed out that Weinbacher had stated on oath that he had never had a summary of supplies to a single customer because this was left to the accountants. In any case, it had been shown that the quantity of Zyklon B needed for the killing of human beings was much smaller than that required for the killing of insects. The quantities of Zyklon B needed for killing half a million or even a million human beings stood in such small proportion to the quantities needed for the killing of insects that it would not have been noticed at all. Therefore, there had been no need for Weinbacher to have grown suspicious, since, claimed Counsel, he knew that Auschwitz was one of the biggest camps and a sort of transit camp. Counsel did not think, therefore, that it was correct to assume that the large quantity of Zyklon B going to Auschwitz was any indication of the fact that human beings were being killed there. Supplies for Neuengamme were much lower than those for Auschwitz.

Dr. Stumme did not deal with the law involved, except for stating that Weinbacher, although a procurist, was still only an employee like Sehm and Miss Biagini, against whom no action was being taken, despite the knowledge which they were said to have had.

(iii) *Counsel for Drosihn*

Dr. Stegemann, in his closing address, confined his remarks to what concerned his client exclusively, while claiming the benefit of everything favourable to him which had already been said by the other Counsel. Every witness who was asked had said that the accused had had nothing whatever to do with the firm's business activities. He could not, therefore, for instance, have known of the size of the consignments to Auschwitz. His relatively small salary showed his subordinate position. He was a zoologist, and first technical gassing master to the firm, and spent more than half the year in travelling. When both Tesch and Weinbacher were away, Mr. Zaun had had the power of attorney, not Drosihn.

Both Dr. Tesch and Dr. Drosihn had said that the latter had never instructed S.S. men in the use of Zyklon B, and not even Sehm claimed that he knew anything about the alleged travel report. Drosihn had been away from the office for irregular periods, and was in no position to read Dr. Tesch's travel reports, which were in any case of no interest to him. Counsel denied that there had been general knowledge in Germany before the end of of the war about the gassing of Jews; his client could not therefore have acquired such knowledge from rumours.

VIII. The Prosecutor's Closing Address

In his closing address, the prosecuting Counsel said that the possibility that some firm other than Tesch and Stabenow could have supplied Zyklon B to Auschwitz could be ruled out, as the latter had the monopoly in that area. The essential question was whether the accused knew of the purpose to which their gas was being put. Counsel admitted that the S.S. were under no restrictions as to the use they made of the gas, and that the direct knowledge which was available to Tesch as to that use was of the scantiest, due to the fear and secrecy in which the S.S. worked. He relied for his case on the evidence of Sehm, Miss Biagini and Miss Uenzelmann.

Counsel said that it was unbelievable that Dr. Tesch did not know that anything wrong went on in the concentration camps. Dr. Drosihn had said without hesitation that he saw things there which were not worthy of human dignity, and that he had said so to Tesch. It was also unbelievable that Dr. Tesch had no knowledge of the amounts of gas being supplied to the S.S. and to Auschwitz in particular, by a firm which was wholly his property. In 1942 and 1943 Auschwitz had been the firm's second largest customer. Dr. Tesch had no reason to believe that Auschwitz was a transit camp, and moreover he was too efficient a man to be duped by the S.S. Counsel completed his case against Tesch by casting doubt on his veracity by showing how contradictions existed between his statements and those of other witnesses on certain details unrelated to the main issue.

Dealing very shortly with Weinbacher's position, Counsel contended that all that Tesch knew must, from the nature of the inner organisation of the business, have also been known by Weinbacher. For 200 days in the year he was in sole control of the firm, with access to all the books, able to read the travel reports, indeed compelled to read the travel reports if he was to carry on the business properly during the periods when his principal was away.

Prosecuting Counsel claimed that Drosihn must to some extent have shared the confidence of Tesch and Weinbacher, even although his activities were confined to the technical side of the firm as opposed to the sales and bookkeeping side.

He concluded that, by supplying gas, knowing that it was to be used for murder, the three accused had made themselves accessories before the fact to that murder.

IX. The Summing Up of the Judge Advocate

The Judge Advocate, in summing up the evidence before the Court, pointed out that the latter must be sure of three facts, first, that Allied nationals had been gassed by means of Zyklon B; secondly, that this gas had been supplied by Tesch and Stabenow; and thirdly, that the accused knew that the gas was to be used for the purpose of killing human beings. On points of law he did not think that the Court needed any direction.

After summarising the evidence of the Prosecution witnesses, the Judge Advocate said: "To my mind, although it is entirely a question for you, the real strength of the Prosecution in this case rests rather upon the general proposition that, when you realise what kind of a man Dr. Tesch was, it inevitably follows that he must have known every little thing about his business. The Prosecution ask you to say that the accused and his second-in-command Weinbacher, both competent business men, were sensitive about admitting that they knew at the relevant time of the size of the deliveries of poison gas to Auschwitz. The Prosecution then ask: 'Why is it that these competent business men are so sensitive about these particular deliveries? Is it because they themselves knew that such large deliveries could not possibly be going there for the purpose of delousing clothing or for the purpose of disinfecting buildings?' "

In Weinbacher's case, there was no direct evidence, either by way of conversation or of anything that he had written among the documents of the firm produced during the trial, which formed any kind of evidence specifically imputing knowledge to Weinbacher as to how Zyklon B was being used at Auschwitz. "but the Prosecution," said the Judge Advocate, "ask you to say that, in his case as in Tesch's case, the real strength of their case is not the individual direct evidence, but the general atmosphere and conditions of the firm itself." The Judge Advocate asked the Court whether or not it was probable that Weinbacher would constantly watch the figures relating to a less profitable activity of the firm, particularly since he received a commission on profits as well as his salary.

The Judge Advocate emphasised Drosihn's subordinate position in the firm, and asked whether there was any evidence that he was in a position either to influence the transfer of gas to Auschwitz or to prevent it. If he were not in such a position, no knowledge of the use to which the gas was being put could make him guilty.

X. The Verdict

Tesch and Weinbacher were found guilty.
Drosihn was acquitted.

XI. The Sentence

Counsel for Tesch, pleading in mitigation of sentence, said that if Tesch did know the use to which the gas was being put, and had consented to it, this happened only under enormous pressure from the S.S. Furthermore, had Tesch not co-operated, the S.S. would certainly have achieved their aims by other means. Tesch was merely an accessory before the fact, and even so, an unimportant one.

Counsel for Weinbacher pleaded that the Court should consider the latter's wife and three children; that he as a business employee might have thought that the ultimate use of the gas was Tesch's responsibility; and that if he had refused to supply Zyklon B the S.S. would immediately have handed him over to the Gestapo.

Nevertheless, subject to confirmation, the two were sentenced to death by hanging.

The sentences were confirmed and carried into effect.

Notes on the Case

I. A Question of Jurisdiction: The Nationality of the Victims

The Prosecutor specified a number of Allied countries from which, he claimed, many of the persons gassed had originated. Wilhelm Bahr told how he himself had gassed two hundred Russians. Perry Broad mentioned Jews from Belgium, Holland, France, Czechoslovakia and Poland, among those gassed at Auschwitz. The Judge Advocate, in his summing up, stated that "among those unfortunate creatures undoubtedly there were many Allied nationals."

It was not alleged that British citizens were among the victims.

The British claim to jurisdiction over the case could be based primarily on the fact that by the Declaration regarding the defeat of Germany and the assumption of supreme authority with respect to Germany, made in Berlin on the 5th June, 1945, the four Allied Powers occupying Germany have assumed supreme authority therein. They have, therefore, become the local sovereigns in Germany. There is vested, then, in the United Kingdom authorities, administering the British Zone of Germany, the right to try German nationals for crimes of any kind wherever committed. The claim to jurisdiction is the stronger if, as in the present case, the criminal activities of the accused have been committed in the British Zone of Germany, by German residents of this Zone, although, of course, the crimes to which the accused were alleged to be accessories had their effect outside Germany, in Auschwitz, Poland.

British jurisdiction could further be based on either

(*a*) the general doctrine called Universality of Jurisdiction over War Crimes, under which every independent State has in International Law jurisdiction to punish pirates and war criminals in its custody regardless of the nationality of the victim or the place where the offense was committed; or

(*b*) the doctrine that the United Kingdom has a direct interest in punishing the perpetrators of crimes if the victim was a national of an ally engaged in a common struggle against a common enemy.

II. Questions of Substantive Law

(i) *The crime alleged*

Article 46 of the Hague Convention of 1907, concerning the Laws and Customs of War on Land, on which the case for the Prosecution was based, provides that "Family honour and rights, individual life and private property, as well as religious convictions and worship must be respected." This Article falls under the section heading, *Military Authority over the Territory of the Hostile State,* and was intended to refer to acts committed by the occupying authorities in occupied territory. In the trial of Tesch, the acts to which the accused were allegedly accessories before the fact were committed mainly at Auschwitz, in occupied Poland.

(ii) *Civilians as war criminals*

The decision of the Military Court in the present case is a clear example of the application of the rule that the provisions of the laws and customs of war are addressed not only to combatants and to members of state and other public authorities, but to anybody who is in a position to assist in their violation.

The activities with which the accused in the present case were charged were commercial transactions conducted by civilians. The Military Court acted on the principle that any civilian who is an accessory to a violation of the laws and customs of war is himself also liable as a war criminal.

THE BELSEN TRIAL

Luneburg, Germany, September, 1945*

TRIAL OF JOSEF KRAMER AND FORTY-FOUR OTHERS
BEFORE BRITISH MILITARY COURT

THE CHARGE

THE ACCUSED WERE: Joseph Kramer, Dr. Fritz Klein, Peter Weingartner, Georg Kraft, Franz Hoessler, Juana Borman, Elizabeth Volkenrath, Herta Ehlert, Irma Grese, Ilse Lothe, Hilde Lobauer, Josef Klippel, Oscar Schmitz, Karl Francioh, Fritz Mathes, Otto Calesson, Medislaw Burgraf, Karl Egersdorf, Anchor Pichen, Walter Otto, Franz Stofel, Heinrich Schreirer, Wilhelm Dorr, Eric Barsch, Erich Zoddel, Ignatz Schlomowicz, Vladislav Ostrowski, Antoni Aurdzieg, Ilse Forster, Ida Forster, Klara Opitz, Charlotte Klein, Herta Bothe, Frieda Walter, Irene Haschke, Gertrud Fiest, Gertrud Sauer, Hilda Lisiewitz, Johanne Roth, Anna Hempel, Hildegard Hahnel, Helena Kopper, Antoni Polanski, Stanislawa Starotska and Ladislaw Gura.

All except Starotska were charged with having committed a war crime, in that they "at Bergen-Belsen, Germany, between 1st October 1942 and 30th April 1945 when members of the staff of Bergen-Belsen Concentration Camp responsible for the well-being of the persons interned there, in violation of the laws and usages of war were together concerned as parties to the ill-treatment of certain of such persons causing the deaths of Keith Meyer (a British national), Anna Kis, Sara Kohn (both Hungarian nationals), Hejmech Glinovjechy and Maria Konatkevicz (both Polish nationals), and Marcel Freson de Montigny (a French national), Maurice Van Eijnsbergen (a Dutch national), Jan Markowski and Georgej Ferenz (both Polish nationals), Maurice Van Mevlenaar (a Belgian national), Salvatore Verdura (an Italian national), and Therese Klee (a British national of Honduras), Allied nationals and other Allied nationals whose names are unknown and physical suffering to other persons interned there, Allied nationals and particularly Harold Osmund le

Law Reports of Trials of War Criminals, Vol. 2, p. 1 (London, 1947).

Druillenec (a British national,) Benec Zuchermann, a female internee named Korperova, a female internee named Hoffman, Luba Rormann, Ida Frydman (all Polish nationals) and Alexandra Siwidowa, a Russian national and other Allied nationals whose names are unknown."

Starotska, Kramer, Dr. Klein, Weingartner, Kraft, Hoessler, Borman, Volkenrath, Ehlert, Gura, Grese, Lothe, Lobauer and Schreirer were charged with having committed a war crime in that they "at Auschwitz, Poland, between 1st October 1942 and 30th April 1945 when members of the staff of Auschwitz Concentration Camp responsible for the well-being of persons interned there in violation of the law and usages of war were together concerned as parties to the ill-treatment of certain such persons causing the deaths of Rachella Silberstein (a Polish national), Allied nationals and other Allied nationals whose names are unknown and physical suffering to other persons interned there, Allied nationals, and particularly to Ewa Gryka and Hanka Rosenwayg (both Polish nationals) and other Allied nationals whose names are unknown."

All the accused pleaded not guilty to the charges made against them.

* * *

The Closing of the Case for the Defence

1. *Colonel Smith's Closing Address on Behalf of All the Accused*

. . . The first problem was what is and what is not a War Crime? In every crime one had to consider three elements: the Act, the Perpetrator, and the Victim. In each case the Prosecution had to prove the accused guilty in all three respects. In most cases the last two elements did not matter, but there were some crimes which could be committed by some people only, and certain crimes could only be committed against certain people.

Pursuing his argument along these lines, Counsel asked first what acts constituted war crimes? He directed the attention of the Court to Chapter XIV of the *Manual of Military Law.* That chapter was technically not an authority in the sense in which lawyers understood the word: that is to say, as something which was legally binding. It was not meant for lawyers but for serving officers, as a practical working instruction. He thought, however, that for the most part it was perfectly sound in law. Paragraph 441 of Chapter XIV of the *Manual* which was substantially the same as the relevant provision in the American Basic Field Manual, *Rules of Land Warfare,* said: "The term 'War Crime' is the technical expression for such an act of enemy soldiers and enemy civilians as may be visited by punishment on capture of the offenders. It is usual to employ this term, but it must be emphasised that it is used in the technical military and legal sense only, and not in the moral sense." Paragraph 442, which enumerated four classes of war crimes, in sub-paragraph 1, specified:

"Violations of the recognised rules of warfare by members of the armed forces."

When one read "Violations of the recognised rules of warfare by members of the armed forces" and then read paragraph 443, which gave a long list of examples of violations, it could be seen that they had only one thing in common; they all had something to do with war. They were all concerned with military operations, ending with treatment of the inhabitants of occupied territory. Counsel claimed that when the Prosecutor quoted Paragraph 442 (1) he had overlooked the words "by members of the armed forces".

In its general arrangement, the *Manual* corresponded, broadly speaking, to the rules of warfare attached to the Hague Convention No. IV Relative to the Laws and Customs of War on Land. The greater part of this chapter was devoted to explaining what could and could not be done in actual operations. If the chapter were read as a whole, it could be seen in the right perspective. The only purpose in making a war crime punishable on the individual was to secure legitimate warfare; without this terror hanging over individuals there was no certainty that mere international action on the intergovernmental level would secure legitimate warfare.

Colonel Backhouse had quoted paragraph 383 of the *Manual,* which said: "It is the duty of the occupant to see that the lives of the inhabitants are respected, that their domestic peace and honour are not disturbed, that their religious convictions are not interfered with. . . ." That passage was a paraphrase of Article 46 of the rules attached to the Fourth Hague Convention. He had failed to see that the words "It is the duty of the occupant" refer only to the enemy state. Throughout the Hague Convention the words: "The occupant" were always used in the sense of the enemy state. When it was a question of making a case against individuals these provisions concerning the duties of the occupant were entirely irrelevant. It was the duty of the occupying power to see that everything was done properly in occupied territory; and if the occupying power failed in that duty it had, under Article 3 of the Convention, to make compensation.

It was easy to misunderstand these sections if one did not bear in mind that the primary purpose of the rules was to secure the responsibility of the enemy government, and that it was only in certain exceptional cases, which were carefully defined in the *Manual,* that responsibility rested upon the individual.

These paragraphs were all bound together by the common principle that all the acts cited were directly connected with the operations of war, and the purpose of the punishment of war crimes was to secure the legitimate conduct of the operations of war. In the present trial, however, Counsel submitted that the Court were dealing with incidents, which certainly occurred in time of war, but which had no logical connection with the war whatever. They were done in accordance with what was begun in peace as a peacetime policy and was intended to be carried on as a permanent and long-term aim until its purpose was achieved, the extermination of the unfortunate races involved. The only difference which the war made to this long-term policy was to increase the geographical area over which it could operate. In what way did it assist the security of the British forces to punish someone who had been guilty of misbehaviour in a German concentration camp?

The American Manual was in this respect substantially the same as the British, and there seemed to be a substantial general agreement among the various military manuals as to what a war crime was. They all had this in common, that it must be a crime connected with the prosecution of the war in some way or another, either with hostilities which were still proceeding, or with resistance against occupation in a territory under Military Government.

Counsel referred to the fact that the Court was, under Article 8 (iii) of the Royal Warrant, instructed to take judicial notice of the Laws and Usages of War. He suggested that what he had been trying to define was in fact what every soldier would regard as a war crime.

When a member of the Court pointed out that in modern total warfare between nations everybody was involved, Colonel Smith replied that the point which he had been explaining was a completely different matter from the distinction between combatant and non-combatant. He agreed that the circumstances of modern war made it much more difficult to draw the old distinction between combatant and non-combatant. It was, however, irrelevant whether the perpetrators were combatant or non-combatant. The important point was that whatever was done in these camps had nothing to do with the operations of this war, because it began long before the war and would have continued long after it. Probably the tasks on which the unfortunate people were employed had something to do with the war effort because all work was connected with the war effort, but the accused were not being tried in connection with tasks performed, but with ill-treatment in the camps, which was entirely another matter.

Colonel Smith dealt next with the positions of the perpetrator and the victim. Concerning the perpetrator, he drew the attention of the Court again to paragraph 442 of Chapter XIV of the British *Manual* (which was substantially identical with the provision contained in the American Manual) of which the first sub-paragraph was: "Violations of the recognised rules of warfare by members of the armed forces". Civilians could commit war crimes such as espionage, war treason, and marauding, and a civilian could be guilty of the murder of a prisoner of war, but that was all. If he committed any of these acts he would be committing an act of hostility and an illegitimate act of hostility, for which he could be punished under the second sub-paragraph, but none of the acts charged in the charge sheet before the Court, except possibly one, came under that head.

In one of the few instances charged where the victims were prisoners of war, a British subject who had been captured as a prisoner of war was transferred to the concentration camp. This was a clear international wrong, but the wrong consisted in ceasing to treat him as a prisoner of war, in taking him out of the camp where he was protected by the Geneva Convention, and putting him in a concentration camp where he was exposed to the same treatment as any other inmate. The responsibility rested with those who sent him to Auschwitz or Belsen, but the responsibility of the people at Auschwitz and Belsen was the same in regard to that man as to any other inmate. Counsel did not know whether they even knew he was a prisoner of war. In any case they had no option but to treat him as anyone else. That was why he emphasised the importance of drawing a clear distinction between the responsibility of the German state and the responsibility of the individual in each particular case.

The victims must be Allied nationals. It was no part of the business of the Court to punish crimes committed by one German against another, or to punish Germans for crimes committed against their allies. There were references to Hungarian and Italian victims who were certainly not Allied nationals, even though some of them had changed sides. The words "Allied Nationals" had a definite meaning and related only to those who were nationals of the countries known as the "United Nations".

Among the victims, Poles were, he thought, in the large majority together with some Czechoslovakians and possibly Austrians. Paragraph 443 of the *Manual* included among war crimes the ill-treatment of the inhabitants of occupied territory. The British Government regarded Poland and the greater part of Czechoslovakia as territory occupied by the Germans in the sense of the Hague Convention. Yet what were the accused to do? Should they obey the law of their own country or act upon International Law?

Counsel submitted that wherever there was a conflict between International Law and the law of a particular country it was the duty of the citizen of that country to obey his national law. For that there was overwhelming legal authority from which he selected two cases. The first was that of *Mortensen v Peters* heard in 1906 in the Scottish High Court of Justiciary (8 Sessions Cases, 93; 43 Scottish Law Reports 872). The British Parliament had passed an Act prohibiting certain forms of fishing in the whole of the Moray Firth in Scotland, including a considerable area beyond the recognised limits of territorial waters. A Norwegian fished outside territorial waters, but within the area covered by the Statute. He was convicted in a Scottish Court and the High Court of Justiciary on appeal unanimously held that they were not concerned as to whether the Statute violated International Law or not. The Law of the land, expressed in an Act of Parliament, was binding on the court and they had to uphold the conviction. Counsel commented that if Parliament inadvertently overstepped the limits of International Law that was a matter not for the individual citizen or judge, or policeman, but for discussion between the governments concerned.

The facts of the second case, *Fong Yare Ting v. United States* (93,149 United States Reports 698) heard by the Supreme Court, were that Congress passed legislation restricting Chinese immigration in direct violation of a Treaty with China. The decision was that the provisions of an Act of Congress passed in the exercise of its constitutional authority must, if clear and explicit, be upheld by the Courts, even in contravention of the stipulations in an earlier Treaty.

The attitude of the German Courts was exactly the same. The principle that where there was a conflict between International Law and municipal law the citizen was bound to obey his municipal law did not diminish the responsibility of the State towards the offended State for its failure to make its internal law correspond with its international obligations.

Naturally Great Britain did not recognise the annexation of Poland or of the greater part of Czechoslovakia, but by German law, which Kramer and all the other defendants had to consider, part of the western half of Poland was German territory; it was formally annexed to Germany. The annexation of the western part and the establishment of the so-called "General Government" in the eastern part of German-occupied Poland were both equally permanent; the Polish State, from the German point of view, had ceased to exist, and German law with minor variations was equally applied to both. Every German in those territories, including Auschwitz which was in the annexed part, was bound by German law. It was no longer temporarily under military occupation in the sense of the Hague Convention. German law was applied by German authority, and the Polish State and Polish nation had ceased to exist.

It might be that the annexation was premature. A precise parallel had occurred during the South African War. In May, 1900, about eight months after the beginning of war, the British Government prematurely published a proclamation annexing permanently the Transvaal and the Orange Free State. Would any officer of the Court, if he had been an officer serving in South Africa at that time, have ventured to say to his superior: "I am afraid the Government has been premature in annexing these countries, and I am afraid I cannot obey your orders"? They would, suggested Counsel, have had to obey the articles of the proclamation and leave it to the higher authorities to settle the question in the normal way on the international level.

So far as all the accused were concerned, Auschwitz was Germany, and the people in it were German subjects. They were not German citizens because the citizenship in Germany belonged to a privileged class by virtue of the Nuremberg law of 1935, which restricted German citizenship to pure Germans, but they were subject to the full force of German law, and owed allegiance to Germany. This analysis applied also to Czechoslovakia. The dismemberment of Czechoslovakia was piecemeal but the substance of the matter was the same, and from the point of view of any German that country, except the parts ceded to Hungary or Russia, was German territory either by direct annexation or by a Protectorate; between which there was only a technical difference.

It might be argued by the Prosecution that by the books or by the authorities the alleged acts were not war crimes, but that it was necessary to bring the law up to date. International Law was not static; it was continually developing. It had to adapt itself to meet new situations as they arose. Therefore, the Prosecution might say, something which was not a war crime according to the books and according to the precedents of history was about to be a war crime from the time the Court gave its decision.

Counsel admitted that International Law was not static, but submitted that its development always took the form of the application of accepted principles to new situations and never of a reversal of these principles. For instance, at the beginning of the war Britain had made a proclamation which treated almost everything as contraband. Certain neutrals objected and pointed out, quite rightly, that Britain had never gone so far before. The answer which his Majesty's Government put forward was also perfectly sound. The principle of contraband, however, argued Counsel, was that the belligerent was entitled to stop and capture any cargoes which were going to help its enemy in carrying on the war, and the technical and physical requirements of modern armed forces had brought practically every article of commerce within the principles of contraband.

Did the same principle apply to the present case? Could it be said that some circumstance had arisen which compelled the Court to treat as a war crime something which had nothing whatever to do with the war? The Court was not faced with a new problem. The facts, unfortunately, were not new except in their intensity and atrocity and if it were said that modern International Law ought to punish maladministration in concentration camps in a country conquered, the Court was faced with the fundamental principle that it must not make its law after the event. . . .

The Closing Speech for the Prosecution

Colonel Backhouse next made a general examination of the law involved in the case. He devoted himself largely to the task of answering the points raised by Colonel Smith.

He submitted that Allied nationals could only come into German hands, in an internment or concentration camp, in one of three ways. They could be prisoners of war, and the evidence showed that a number of the internees, particularly Russians, were prisoners of war; or they could be Allied nationals who were living in Germany and were interned, or inhabitants of occupied countries overrun during the war by Germany.

If they were prisoners of war, it was quite sufficient to quote the following passage from Article 46 of the Geneva Convention of 1929, relative to the Treatment of Prisoners of War: "All forms of corporal punishment, confinement in premises not lighted by daylight and, in general, all forms of cruelty whatsoever, are prohibited."

A civilian who was interned was entitled to precisely the same treatment as a prisoner of war. That was not a new doctrine; there existed a ruling of the Judge Advocate General in January, 1918, on the subject, and far from being an arbitrary ruling made with a view to oppressing the Germans, it was a ruling which operated against the British Government in respect of Germans interned in England, making it clear that they had precisely the same rights and were to be treated in precisely the same way as prisoners of war. This ruling was based upon the case of *Ex parte Liebmann* (1916 1 K.B., page 268) where it was laid down that: "An enemy alien subject resident in the United Kingdom who is in the opinion of the executive government a person hostile to the welfare of that country and on that account interned may properly be described as a prisoner of war, although not a combatant or a spy." The Judge Advocate General's comment on the case was that although the annex to the Hague Convention did not expressly deal with or provide for such persons, as their position did not appear to have been contemplated in 1907, they were, nevertheless, entitled to be treated as prisoners of war.

The inhabitants of occupied territories were protected by Article 46 of the Hague Convention which stated: "Family honour and rights, individual life, and private property, as well as religious convictions and worship, must be respected." The *Manual of Military Law,* in chapter XIV, paragraph 383, stated: "It is the duty of the occupant to see that the lives of inhabitants are respected, that their domestic peace and honour are not disturbed, that their religious convictions are not interfered with, and generally that duress, unlawful and criminal attacks on their persons, and felonious actions, as regards their property, are just as punishable as in times of peace."

The Prosecutor denied making any mistake when quoting paragraph 442 of the *Manual.* He left out the words "members of the armed forces", because they were quite immaterial. No one surely could suggest that if a member of the armed forces were put in charge of prisoners and ill-treated them he was guilty of a war crime, and that if, because of the man-power situation, a civilian was put in charge of them instead, and ill-treated them, he was not guilty of a war crime. The whole difficulty arose from the fact that when the Hague Convention was written a military body like the S.S. was not thought of, and it was taken for granted that only a member of the armed forces would guard prisoners of war and would, further, be in a position to ill-treat the inhabitants of occupied countries. The point was, however, completely academic, because Kramer had said: "We were members of the Wehrmacht; as soon as war broke out we became members of the Wehrmacht and I am a member of the armed forces of Germany". The S.S. in the dock were on their own evidence members of the armed forces of Germany.

He agreed that a crime would not be a war crime if it was not connected with war. Where he and Colonel Smith were in complete disagreement was on the question of what was meant by "connected with war". The latter Counsel had argued on the basis that the object of the ill-treatment must be connected with the war effort, whereas, he had argued, this ill-treatment of Jews was going on before the war and would have continued afterwards. The Prosecutor pointed out, however, that what was being complained of in the present trial was ill-treatment of Allied nationals during time of war. Such ill-treatment was not happening before the war and that would not have gone on after the war. Allied nationals were entitled to protection by their Government. The Court was not, of course, concerned with what Germans did to Germans during the war, but it was concerned with the protection of Allied subjects from German ill-treatment during the war. The mere fact that those people came into the hands of the Germans and were interned or imprisoned by them, and that their countries were occupied by the Germans as a result of operations of war, was quite sufficient to turn that ill-treatment into a war crime; it was precisely the type of war crime that was provided against by the Convention. On any other interpretation the Conventions and Regulations themselves would become nonsense. When a prisoner of war was ill-treated by one of his guards that, of course, did not help the war effort, yet if that person was an Allied subject who had come into his guard's hands by operations of war, then if the latter ill-treated him it was a war crime of precisely the type against which the Convention provided.

In any case, was it not quite obvious that the actual internment in Auschwitz or Belsen was done with a view to further a war effort? There were two reasons for interning those people who were so treated. One was the deliberate destruction of the Jewish race. The avowed object of that was to strengthen the home front and to prevent what happened in the previous war. The destruction of Poland was another reason, and that again was an avowed war aim. The gathering into Germany of persons from every country that Germany overran was done with the deliberate intention of weakening that particular country in its effort to resist Germany.

Colonel Smith had suggested that the crime involved was the moving of the prisoner of war from the prisoner-of-war camp into the concentration camp and that anything which happened to him thereafter was thereby excused. The Prosecutor found it difficult to accept the suggestion that if a man were ill-treated in a prisoner-of-war camp that was a war crime, but if the ill-treatment took place outside in the street or in a concentration camp it was not.

Colonel Smith's next point was that the only purpose of the punishment of war crimes was to secure legitimate means of warfare. No extension of the application of a principle was involved in the charges, however, since the offences were, as Counsel had shown, provided against under existing International Law.

Colonel Smith had claimed that the State and not the individual was responsible in International Law, but he admitted that a war crime was one of the exception to that rule. Colonel Backhouse stated that under the Versailles Treaty, which was still in force, it was laid down that: "The German Government recognises the right of the Allied and Associated Powers to bring before military tribunals persons accused of having committed acts in violation of the law and customs of war". The Leipzig trials also recognised that if an individual broke one of the laws and customs of war he could properly be tried and in fact he was in some cases convicted by the Germans for breaches of international agreements.

Colonel Smith's argument on the question of whether the victims were Allied nationals applied, of course, to Poles and certain Czechs only. It had no application, even if accepted, to persons of Russian, French, Dutch, Belgian, Greek, and other nationalities; the Germans made no pretence of annexing their countries. Again, before it was possible to annex a country the war must be ended. Whilst the war was still going on the citizens of the country occupied were entitled to protection under the Convention. The gassing of a Hungarian transport started at about the same time as D-Day. Surely Germany did not think the war was already over on D-Day, in 1944? If it were sufficient for a belligerent to say merely "We have annexed this country", then the Covention could never apply at all. In actual fact the Germans never did such an absurd thing. The only part of Poland which the Germans ever declared annexed was a small piece of Silesia which was taken from them in the previous war by the Poles, and which they said was German. That was the only part they did intend to incorporate into the Reich; the rest of Poland was merely occupied territory. Even if the accused did not know that the victims were Allied nationals, he would still not agree with Colonel Smith's argument. By analogy, if a man assaulted a policeman he could not afterwards say that he did not know the victim was a policeman.

The Prosecutor pointed out that a charge did not become bad if it did not contain the names of the victims. In the *Peleus Trial* and in the *Llandovery Castle Case,* for instance, the victims had not been specifically mentioned in the charges against the accused involved. The charge was required by the Regulations to fall within the Field General Court Martial procedure, and the Field General Court Martial rules stated the charge could be drawn in any ordinary language. It was quite obvious that the accused were not prejudiced in the present case. . . .

The Summing Up of the Judge Advocate

The Judge Advocate began his summing up by pointing out that the Prosecution did not ask the Court to consider whether the taking of Allied nationals to Auschwitz was right or wrong. What they did say was that, when they were there, they should not have been ill-treated or maltreated to an extent that they died or suffered physical hardship. If the Court were satisfied that Allied nationals were taken in the way which had been described, and that they were put in a gas chamber because they were of no use to the German Reich, it seemed to him that a violation of the customs and usages of war had been committed.

In regard to the more general question of ill-treatment or maltreatment, the same difficulties did not arise, because it was not claimed that such treatment was in any way authorised by the German Reich, as it had been suggested might be the case in regard to the gas chambers.

Regarding the plea of superior orders, he advised the Court to follow the law as laid down in Oppenheim's *International Law,* II, p. 452:

> The fact that a rule of warfare has been violated in pursuance of an order of the belligerent Government of an individual belligerent commander does not deprive the act in question of its character as a war crime; netither does it, in principle, confer upon the perpetrater immunity from punishment by the injured belligerent. . . . Undoubtedly, a Court confronted with the plea of superior orders adduced in justification of a war crime is bound to take into consideration the fact that obedience to military orders, not obviously unlawful, is the duty of every member of the armed forces and that the law cannot, in conditions of war discipline, be expected to weigh scrupulously the legal merits of the order received; that rules of warfare are often controversial; and an act otherwide amounting to a war crime may have been executed in obedience to orders received as a measure of reprisals. Such circumstances are probably in themselves sufficient to divest the act of a stigma of war crime. . . . However, subject to these qualifications, the question is governed by the major principle that members of the armed forces are bound to obey legal orders only and that they cannot therefore escape liability if, in obedience to a command, they commit acts which both violate unchallenged rules of warfare and outrage the general sentiment of humanity.

The Court would probably find that the reason why that attitude was adopted by the writer was contained in the next sentence: "To limit liability to the persons responsible for the order may frequently amount, in practice, to concentrating responsibility on the head of the State whose accountability, from the point of view of both international and constitutional law, is controversial."

Questions of Substantive Law

1. *The Sources of Substantive Law Regarding War Crimes*

Colonel Smith claimed that the Military Court trying the accused applied International Law and did not take its substantive law, as distinct from its procedure, either from the Crown or from Parliament. The Court was given its rules of procedure by the Royal Warrant but in deciding cases before it the former was not bound by, for instance, the British *Manual of Military Law.*

It is true that Regulation 1 of the Royal Warrant states: " 'War Crime' means a violation of the laws and usages of war committed during any war in which his Majesty had been or may be engaged at any time since the 2nd September, 1939", and that Regulation 8 (iii) provides that: "The Court shall take judicial notice of the laws and usages of war". It is also true that much substantive law on the matter of war crimes has been created or codified by international agreements such as the Hague Convention No. IV of 1907 (on the rules of land warfare) and the Geneva Prisoners of War Convention of 1929. On the other hand Regulation 9 of the Royal Warrant provides that the punishment of a war crime consists in any one or more of the following: —

(1) Death (either by hanging or shooting);
(2) Imprisonment for life or for any less term;
(3) Confiscation;
(4) A fine.

The Court may also order the restitution of money or property taken or destroyed by the accused. It would not be easy to maintain the proposition that provisions regarding punishment were mere matters of procedure. Further, there are spheres in which International Law is vague, and state practice is a very important source of law. The defence of superior orders is a case in point.

Chapter XIV (*The Laws and Usages of War on Land*) of the British *Manual of Military Law* is intended as a guide for the use of the military forces. It has not therefore the authority as a statement of International Law which attaches to an international treaty.

Such publications, prepared for the benefit of the armed forces of various nations, are frequently used in argument in the same way as other interpretations of International Law, and, *in so far as their provisions are acted upon,* they mould state practice, which is itself a source of International Law.

At another point in his speech Colonel Smith set out to prove that the individual's first allegiance was to his national laws. Counsel's position would seem to be that, whereas the accusing state is bound by International Law on questions of substance, the accused must look first to his own laws. It could be argued, however, that the very fact that a Military Court did administer International Law would preclude an alleged war criminal from pleading on his behalf Municipal Law precedents such as *Mortensen* v. *Peters* and *Fong Yare Ting* v. *United States.*

2. *Responsibility of State and Individual for Breaches of International Law*

Colonel Smith stressed that in International Law the general principle was that the State and not the individual was responsible for breaches of that law. There has not been universal agreement on the extent to which an individual can be held personally liable for breaches of such international agreements as the Hague Convention No. IV (Rules of Land Warfare) and the Geneva Prisoners of War Convention of 1929, according to the strict letter of which the responsibility for breach thereof lies on the State authority to which the perpetrator owes allegiance. The trend of opinion and the practice followed by the Courts, however, has been to make the individual responsible for his acts in breach of international conventions, and this trend was illustrated on a high level by the decision pronounced by the International Military Tribunal at Nuremberg, that certain accused had made themselves criminals by waging war in breach of the terms of an inter-governmental agreement renouncing war undertaken as an instrument of national policy, the Briand-Kellogg Pact. . . .

3. *The Nationality of the Accused*

The Court held five Poles guilty of war crimes against Allied nationals, thus approving the argument of the Prosecution that by identifying themselves with the S.S. the Polish accused had made themselves as guilty as they. The

Court thus acted on the principle that its jurisdiction extended to the trial of Allied nationals alleged to have committed war crimes, their nationality being irrelevant in this connection.

4. *The Nationality of the Victims*

On the 3rd October, Captain Brown objected to part of Dora Almaleh's affidavit and submitted that the facts set out were completely irrelevant. The charge referred to a war crime and to the ill-treatment and death of Allied nationals. Paragraph 3 of the affidavit in question referred to a Hungarian girl and Counsel thought that it was within the knowledge of the Court that a war crime could not be committed by a German against a Hungarian. The Prosecutor made two points in replying. Hungary, he said, left the Axis before April, 1945, and had come on to the Allied side; at that time, therefore, the Hungarians were at least some form of Allies, though Counsel did not know to what extent. A more general point made by the Prosecutor was that what he was trying to prove was the treatment of the Allied inmates of the camp. He thought that he was perfectly entitled to put before the Court evidence of the treatment of other persons in the camp. If there were 10 people and he wanted to prove that one of them was badly treated, in the Prosecutor's submission, he was perfectly entitled to prove that the 10 were badly treated. The treatment of all the inmates in the camp was relevant to show the treatment of any individual inmate.

The Court decided that the paragraph be included in the evidence before the Court.

Colonel Smith claimed that only offenses against Allied nationals could be regarded by the Court as war crimes, and that "Allied nationals" meant nations of the United Nations. The term therefore excluded Hungarians and Italians. As has been seen, the Prosecutor himself in effect disclaimed any intention of charging the accused of crimes against persons other than Allied nationals. Both Prosecution and Defence therefore recognised that, under the Royal Warrant, the jurisdiction of British Military Courts is limited to the trial of war crimes proper and excludes crimes against humanity as defined by Article 6(c) of the Charter of the International Military Tribunal. British Military Courts deal with such crimes only if they are also violations of the laws and usages of war.

A second question relating to the nationality of the victims of atrocities committed in the two camps arose out of Colonel Smith's claim that numbers of them had ceased to be Allied nationals, and had become German subjects, as a result of the annexation of their homelands by Germany. The Prosecutor replied that before it was possible for a country to be annexed the war must be ended. While the war was still in progress the citizens were entitled to the protection of the Hague Convention.

Oppenheim-Lauterpacht, *International Law,* Vol I, fifth edition. p. 450, states that the act of forcibly taking possession of a part of an enemy's territory during the continuance of war, "although the conqueror may intend to keep the conquered territory and therefore to annex it, does not confer a title so long as the war has not terminated either through simple cessation of hostilities or by a treaty of peace. Therefore, the practice, which sometimes prevails, of annexing during a war a conquered part of enemy territory cannot be approved. For annexation of conquered enemy territory, whether of the whole or of part, confers a title only after a *firmly established* conquest, and so long as war continues, conquest is not firmly established. For this reason the annexation of the Orange Free State in May 1900, and of the South African Republic in September 1900, by Great Britain during the Boer War, was premature."

* * *

5. *Civilians As War Criminals*

Colonel Smith assumed that the accused could not be regarded as members of the armed forces. The Prosecutor claimed that the S.S. were members of the German armed forces.

It would be harder to prove that the camp prisoners who were given minor official positions by the authorities were anything more than civilians. In meeting the argument that no war crime could be committed by Poles against other Allied nationals, the Prosecutor said that by identifying themselves with the authorities the Polish accused had made themselves as much responsible as the S.S. themselves. Perhaps it could be claimed that by the same process they could be regarded as having approximated to membership of the armed forces of Germany.

In any case subsequent court decisions have made it quite clear that civilians can commit war crimes. For example, in the *Zyklon B Case* two German industrialists, undoubtedly civilians, were sentenced to death as war criminals for having been instrumental in the supply of poison gas to Auschwitz, knowing of its use there in murdering Allied nationals. Another instance among many is provided by the *Essen Lynching Case* where civilians appeared among persons found guilty of being concerned in the killing of three British prisoners of war. *The Hadamar Trial* provides an example from among the trials held before United States Military Commissions; here the civilian personnel of a medical institution were found guilty of unlawfully putting to death Russian and Polish nationals.

THE OHASHI TRIAL

Rabaul, Territory of New Guinea, March, 1946*

TRIAL OF
SERGEANT-MAJOR SHIGERU OHASHI AND SIX OTHERS
BEFORE AUSTRALIAN MILITARY COURT

OUTLINE OF THE PROCEEDINGS

I. THE CHARGES

SERGEANT-MAJORS Shigeru Ohashi and Yoshifumi Komoda, together with five other members of the Japanese Military Police, were accused of murdering a number of named victims, who were described in the charge as one half-caste and seventeen natives, on 18th September, 1944.

The accused pleaded not guilty.

II. THE EVIDENCE

The evidence showed that during September, 1944, the eighteen victims, who were civilian inhabitants of New Britain then in the occupation of Japan, were beheaded at Vunarima after a summary trial for acts of sabotage and other acts hostile to the Japanese Army and defined as war crimes in the military code. The accused claimed that all the deceased were guilty of a conspiracy against the armed forces of Japan in pursuance of which individual conspirators concealed weapons, stole grenades and rations, blew up a petrol dump and attacked, on one occasion, a Japanese soldier, and on another a Japanese civilian. These allegations were not denied.

Defence evidence, which was unrebutted, showed that the native victims had pleaded guilty to the charges against them after these had been read out to them. All accused were in court at once and were allowed to make their explanations. Two prosecution witnesses were produced to give evidence against them, and the proceedings were interpreted either by the interpreter or

*Law Reports of Trials of War Criminals, Vol. 5, p 25 (London, 1947).

by Komoda. On the other hand, the evidence of the two witnesses was said to have occupied only about four minutes in all, the Court conferred for about ten minutes on the verdict, and ten minutes on the sentence, and the trial as a whole lasted only about fifty minutes. No defending officer was provided for the victims; according to Ohashi's evidence this was "in view of the time element," and the half-caste addressed the Court on behalf of all the accused. The executions began about an hour after the termination of the trial.

General Immamura, Commander-in-Chief of the Japanese Eighth Army Group, who commanded the Rabaul area at the relevant time, said that he declared Vunarima an emergency area in April, 1944, that where inhabitants of an occupied territory were charged with was treason or war rebellion they were under normal conditions sent for trial by court martial, but that "under pressing circumstances unit commanders would have the authority which had been provided by the Emperor to carry it out on their own for the protection of the army."

Later he referred to summary trials in the field, and to the wide discretion accorded to unit commanders not only as to the convening and constitution of the courts but also as to the penalty meted out. He further testified that confirmation of sentence would normally be required and that confirmation by the Provost Marshal should have been sufficient in the circumstances of the case.

In short, General Immamura's evidence was that the Japanese government had directed a summary trial in the field for war criminals under certain operational conditions, and that those conditions existed at Vunarima in September, 1944.

The Provost Marshal, Colonel Kikuchi, stated that he confirmed the finding of the Japanese Tribunal and authorized the execution and that he believed the trial to be a fair and just one.

The evidence of General Immamura and Colonel Kikuchi that in case of emergency a summary trial could be convened instead of a court martial for trial of war crimes as defined by Japanese law was supported by documentary evidence. It was claimed by the Defence witnesses that the emergency justifying such a summary trial was a threatened attack by other natives to rescue the deceased who were then held in custody for investigation of their alleged war crimes against the Japanese, that Lt. Yamada, who was not among the accused, decided to hold the summary trial, that the proper procedure was observed by the Court and that the sentences were confirmed by superior authority before being carried into execution.

The accused Ohashi and Komoda, with their superior officer Lt. Yamada, were members of the summary court which convicted the deceased. Ohashi and Komoda also took part in the execution.

A third accused acted as interpreter during the trial and also took part in the execution.

Four other accused were shown to have taken part in carrying out the orders for the execution of the victims, but not to have been present at their trial or to have had any knowledge of the nature of those proceedings.

III. The Findings and Sentences

Ohashi and *Komoda* were found guilty and sentenced to life imprisonment. The other accused were found not guilty.

The two life sentences were commuted to sentences of imprisonment for two years by the Confirming Officer.

Notes on the Case

I. The Jurisdiction of the Australian Military Court

During his summing up, the Judge Advocate serving with the Australian Military Court which tried the case pointed out that: "The charge is one covered by the War Crimes Act 1945 and the jurisdiction of the Court has been established by the unchallenged evidence of the residence of the natives and the events occurring in an Australian Territory."

The legal basis, jurisdiction, composition and procedure of the Australian Military Courts for the trial of war criminals are further examined in the Annex to this Volume.

II. The Law Binding on the Court

During his summing up, the Judge Advocate set out as follows the rules which the Court was to observe:

1. The War Crimes Act, the Hague Conventions and the judgments of superior British and Australian courts are binding on you.
2. Text books by learned jurist such as Oppenheim, and the Manual of Military Law in its explanatory passages are strongly persuasive and should be followed by this Court unless it is well satisfied to the contrary.
3. You will use in your deliberations your common knowledge and your military knowledge but no other peculiar or expert knowledge any of you may possess. . . .

The explanatory passages of the Australian *Manual of Military Law* were classified by the Judge Advocate as constituting a "strongly persuasive" authority. In so far as it describes the state of international law and does not simply reproduce the text of the Hague and Geneva Conventions, this *Manual* like the British *Manual of Military Law* and the United States Basic Field Manual F.M. 27-10 (*Rules of Land Warfare*), though not a source of law like a statute, prerogative order or decision of a court, is a very authoritative publication.

III. The Status of the Victims

The Judge Advocate advised the Court that:

> By the Laws and Usages of War inhabitants of occupied territories have not only certain rights but owe certain duties to the occupant, who may punish any violation of those duties.
>
> Certain acts if committed by such inhabitants are punishable by the enemy as war crimes.
>
> Amongst such acts are:
>
> (*a*) Illegitimate hostilities in arms committed by individuals who are not members of the armed forces.
>
> (*b*) Espionage and war treason.
>
> The deceased would, being civilian inhabitants of an occupied territory, be guilty of the war crime known as War Rebellion if they rose in arms against the occupant.
>
> War treason includes such acts by private individuals as damage to war material or conspiracy against the armed forces or against members of them.

After stating that the allegations of the accused that the deceased had been guilty of acts of hostility against the Japanese armed forces had not been rebutted and were entitled to be believed, the Judge Advocate continued:

> Their actions rendered the deceased liable to punishment as war criminals.
>
> Charges of war crimes may be dealt with by military courts or such courts as the belligerent concerned may direct.
>
> In every case there must be a trial before punishment and the utmost care must be taken to confine the punishment to the actual offender.
>
> All war crimes are liable to be punished by death.
>
> So far as I have been able to ascertain . . . there is no provision in International Law relating to the composition of such courts or the procedure to be followed at the trials.
>
> The type of trial to which the deceased were entitled was therefore subject to certain fundamental principles of justice, that were directed by Japan."

The advice of the Judge Advocate regarding the rights of the deceased and the decision of the Military Court must therefore be regarded as authorities more particularly on the rights under International Law of alleged war criminals.

Among the acts defined as war crimes in Oppenheim-Lauterpacht *International Law,* Vol. II, Sixth Edition revised, are the following: "(2) All hostilities in arms committed by individuals who are not members of the enemy armed forces, (3) espionage and war treason."

It is later stated that: "Private individuals who take up arms and commit hostilities against the enemy do not enjoy the privileges of armed forces, and the enemy has, according to a customary rule of International Law, the right to treat such individuals as war criminals. But they cease to be private individuals if they organize themselves in a manner which, according to the Hague Convention, confers upon them the status of members of regular forces. Espionage and war treason . . . bear a two-fold character. International Law gives a right to belligerent to use them. On the other hand, it gives a right to belligerents to consider them, when committed by enemy soldiers or enemy private individuals within their lines, as acts of illegitimate warfare, and consequently punishable as war crimes. . . .

"War treason consists of all such acts (except hostilities in arms on the part of the civilian population, spreading of seditious propaganda by aircraft, and espionage) committed within the lines of a belligerent as are harmful to him and are intended to favour the enemy. War treason may be committed, not only in occupied enemy country, or in the zone of military operations, but anywhere within the lines of a belligerent."

The provisions of the Hague Convention which define the limits of the category of persons which "enjoy the privileges of armed forces" (to use the same phrase as the authority just quoted) are those contained in Chapter I (The Status of Belligerent):

Art. 1. The laws, rights, and duties of war apply not only to army, but also to militia and volunteer corps fulfilling all the following conditions:

(1) They must be commanded by a person responsible for his subordinates;
(2) They must have a fixed distinctive sign recognizable at a distance;
(3) They must carry arms openly; and
(4) They must conduct their operations in accordance with the laws and customs of war.

In countries where militia or volunteer corps constitute the army, or form part of it, they are included under the denomination "army".

Art. 2. The inhabitants of a territory not under occupation who, on the approach of the enemy, spontaneously take up arms to resist the invading troops without having had time to organize themselves in accordance with article 1, shall be regarded as belligerents if they carry arms openly, and if they respect the laws and customs of war.

Art. 3 The armed forces of the belligerents may consist of combatants and non-combatants. In the case of capture by the enemy, both have the right to be treated as prisoners of war.

Elsewhere it is said that: "War treason is a comprehensive term for a number of acts hostile to the belligerent within whose lines they are committed; it must be distinguished from real treason, which can only be committed by persons owing allegiance, albeit temporary, to the injured State. War treason can be committed by a soldier or an ordinary subject of a belligerent, but it can also be committed by an inhabitant of occupied enemy territory, or even by a subject of a neutral State temporarily staying there, and it can take place after an arrangement. In any case, a belligerent making use of war treason acts lawfully, although the Hague Regulations do not mention the matter at all."

Of espionage the same authority writes, *inter alia,* that: "No regard is paid to the status, rank, position, or motive of a spy. He may be a soldier or a civilian, an officer or a private. He may be following instructions of superiors, or acting on his own initiative from patriotic motives."

IV. Denial of a Fair Trial

The Judge Advocate further advised the Court that the accused would be entitled to an acquittal if it had been proved that "the deceased had a fair and reasonable trial, that such trial was of the kind directed by Japan and that the accused were authorized to take part in such trial and execution." It was "for the belligerent to decide the form of trial subject to certain fundamental principles of justice."

The Judge Advocate continued:

> I consider these principles to be:
>
> "(*a*) Consideration by a tribunal comprised of one or more men who will endeavour to judge the accused fairly upon the evidence using their own common knowledge of ordinary affairs and if they are soldiers their military knowledge, honestly endeavouring to discard any preconceived belief in the guilt of accused or any prejudice against him.
>
> "(*b*) The accused should know the exact nature of the charge preferred against him.
>
> "(*c*) The accused should know what is alleged against him by way of evidence.
>
> "(*d*) He should have full opportunity to give his own version of the case and produce evidence to support it.
>
> "(*e*) The court should satisfy itself that the accused is guilty before awarding punishment. It would be sufficient if the court believed it to be more likely than not that the accused was guilty.
>
> "(*f*) The punishment should not be one which outrages the sentiments of humanity.
>
> Unless provision is made for observance of all of these principles I do not consider any other form of proceedings which a belligerent might direct would in law really amount to a trial.

The Judge Advocate later added: "Furthermore you should give close attention to the question of good faith in the accused as regards holding the proceedings at all as that has a direct bearing on deciding what was their attitude during the proceedings, keeping in mind of course their relationship towards Lt. Yamada. . . . You will consider whether at such proceedings the deceased did in fact plead guilty and the effect such a plea would have on the minds of the tribunal in arriving at a verdict sentence."

He also pointed out that the executioners would be entitled to the defence of justifiable homicide if it had been shown that each was a "proper officer executing a criminal in conformity with his sentence."

The Court found not guilty those accused who had taken part in the execution of the victims but had not acted as their judges, including the accused who had acted as interpreter. Those found guilty were the two accused who had acted as judges at a trial which, according to the evidence of the Defence themselves, lacked any representation of the accused by Counsel and occupied only about 50 minutes and was followed rapidly by execution of sentence, in which those found guilty by the Australian Military Court participated. It will be noted, however, that the accused were allowed to address the court and pleaded guilty, that the proceedings were interpreted, and, finally, that the sentence passed by the Australian Military Court, as commuted, was a relatively light one.

V. Superior Orders

The Judge Advocate stated that the Court should consider, *inter alia,* the question whether the proceedings against the deceased were "conducted in accordance with the directions given by Japan." He later added: "You should bear in mind that the accused were soldiers, consider what orders were given them, and their duty to obey, also the limited protection afforded subordinates by superior orders as explained in the *Manual of Military Law,* Australian Edition, page 288, para. 443, as amended which I will read out to you."

It seems therefore that the Judge Advocate was willing to concede that the plea of superior orders would afford some limited protection if the acts of the accused were actually conducted as laid down by those orders. The passage from the Australian *Manual of Military Law* to which the Judge Advocate referred is in the same terms as the passage from paragraph 443 of the British *Manual,* which has already been quoted.

THE HOESS TRIAL

Poland, March, 1947*

TRIAL OF OBERSTURMBANNFÜHRER RUDOLF FRANZ FERDINAND HOESS BEFORE SUPREME NATIONAL TRIBUNAL OF POLAND

OUTLINE OF THE PROCEEDINGS

I. THE INDICTMENT

THE ACCUSED Rudolf Franz Ferdinand Hoess, a German subject, was charged with the following crimes:

(1) That from 1st September, 1939, till May, 1945, in the German Reich, and from 1st May, 1940, till September, 1944, on the occupied territory of the Polish State he was a member of the German National Socialist Workers' Party (NSDAP), a criminal organization, which aimed at the subjugation of others nations through planning, organizing and perpetrating crimes against peace, war crimes and crimes against humanity, and also was a member of the S.S., a further criminal organization;

(2) That from 1st May, 1940, till the end of October, 1943, as Commandant of the Auschwitz concentration camp set up by him, and thereafter from December, 1943, till May, 1945, as Head of the D.I. Department of the S.S. Central Economic and Administrative Office, as well as in June, July and August, 1944, as commander of the SS garrison at Auschwitz, in execution of the Nazi system of persecution and extermination of nations in concentration and death camps organized for the purpose, he supervised the application of that system in the Auschwitz concentration camp against the Polish and Jewish civilian population and against other nationals of the territories occupied by Germany, as well as to Soviet prisoners of war, and thereby acting either himself or through the subordinate camp personnel, he deliberately:

*_Law Reports of Trials of War Criminals,_ Vol. 7, p. 11 (London, 1947).

(i) deprived of life: (*a*) about 300,000 camp registered inmates, (*b*) about 4,000,000 people mainly Jews brought to the camp from different European countries to be killed upon their arrival, and therefore not included in the register of the camp inmates, (*c*) about 12,000 Soviet prisoners of war confined in the camp in violation of the Geneva Convention on the treatment of Prisoners of War; all this by asphyxiation in gas-chambers, shooting, hanging, lethal injections of phenol or by medical experiments causing death, systematic starvation, by creating special conditions in the camp which were causing a high rate of mortality, by excessive work of the inmates, and by other methods;

(ii) ill-treated and tortured the inmates physically and morally by various means;

(iii) supervised wholesale robbery of property, mostly jewels, clothes and other valuable articles taken from people on their arrival to the camp, and of gold teeth and fillings extracted from dead bodies of the victims.

II. The Case and Evidence for the Prosecution

The Auschwitz camp occupied the most prominent position among the nine greatest concentration camps established by Nazi Germany. The most inhuman rule prevailed in the camp which caused the loss of life of nearly all inmates. Over four million people from all countries occupied by Germany met with death in the gas-chambers and crematoria installed in the camp. Soviet prisoners of war were the first victims of this extermination campaign. They were followed by Jews who perished in even larger numbers. Poles constituted the largest group of murdered from among the registered inmates of the camp. Among the victims of other nationalties there were: a few Americans and British, and large numbers of Austrian, Belgian, Bulgarian, Chinese, Czechoslovak, French, Greek, Dutch, Spanish, Jugoslav, Lithuanian, Latvian, German, Norwegian, Persian, Rumanian, Swiss, Turkish, Hungarian and Egyptian, and of other nationalities.

The camp was devised as a central concentration camp and was equipped with the largest and most efficient technical installations for the extermination of people. The highest capacity of its gas-chambers amounted to killing of 60,000 people per 24 hours and that of the crematoria to burning of 24,000 bodies per 24 hours.

The Auschwitz concentration camp was also used as a place of confinement of people considered as dangerous to the occupation authorities. Statistical sheets lising the causes of death in the camp contained nine different categories of "criminals" such as "political", "professional", etc., and among them one described "Poles". Thus the latter were considered criminals, merely because of their nationality. This explains why Poles arrested by accident during street raids and not connected with any political activities were nevertheless sent to concentration camps. Soviet prisoners of war constituted a separate group in the camp. They were eliminated from the general prisoners of war camps and brought as "criminals" to the Auschwitz camp.

In the camp, the kind of living quarters, of food and clothing, unsanitary conditions, excessive work, ill-treatment and penalties which prevailed contributed to the death-rate. Medical treatment was completely lacking and illness was the ground on which people were selected for extermination. Simultaneously various means aiming at breaking the moral resistance of the inmates were applied. Their personal dignity was abased. Only a small number of individuals survived owing to exceptional powers of endurance or to fortunate accidents.

The exploitation of the inmates as forced labour took place either in branch camps or in the branches of I.G. Farben Industrie producing synthetic petrol and of Krupp's works active under the firm "Weichsel-Union", and in other factories which had been built in the neighbourhood of Auschwitz by the inmates themselves.

The system applied to the inmates was built on patterns established in other concentration camps, but was perfected by the accused Hoess. He underwent special training in camp duties and practised in this respect in the Dachau and Sachsenhausen concentration camps, before he took over the commandant's duties at Auschwitz.

The accused continued to be in control of all these activities even after he left the post of the camp's commandant. He fulfilled then the functions of Himmler's special plenipotentiary for extermination of Jews and in that capacity he either sent people to Auschwitz or supervised the extermination on the spot.

For his activities on the Auschwitz camp the accused was awarded the German Military Cross, first-class with Swords, and was promoted from the rank of Hauptsturmführer to that of SS Obersturmbannführer. The same decoration was also conferred on SS Hauptscharführer Otto Mohl, who was in charge of the Auschwitz crematoria.

The Indictment enumerated and described in great detail the activities of the accused in the camp and the criminal acts committed therein. It dealt, *inter alia,* with the following subjects: the establishment of the camp and its constant enlargement, its organization, various categories of the inmates, the living conditions, accommodation and food, insufficient medical treatment, exploitation of forced labour, generally inhuman treatment, heavy arbitrary punishment and medical experiments; and further with the methods of extermination, e.g., such as shooting, hanging, the so-called "*Sonderbehandlung*" (special treatment) and "*Sonderaktion*" (gassing and cremating), finally with the gas-chambers and crematoria, and the final "liquidation" of the camp. The Indictment also described in some detail the wholesale robbery of the inmates' possessions and valuables, the value of which amounted to many thousand millions of Reichsmarks at their rate of exchange at the time.

As already stated the people who fell victim of the Nazi extermination system carried out in the camp were Poles, Jews of various nationalities and Soviet prisoners of war. The extermination system applied against the latter was based on a special secret order of the *Amstgruppe D* dated 15th January, 1941, and issued upon directives given by the *Reichsführer S.S. und Chef der Deutchen Polizei,* Heinrich Himmler. According to these directives all Soviet prisoners were to be transferred to concentration camps for extermination, except those who were sufficiently strong to be used as forced labour in the quarries.

Apart from statements given by a large number of witnesses of Polish and other nationalities, former inmates of the camps, and other documentary evidence, the case for the Prosecution rested also on evidence submitted to the Tribunal by the following experts: Mr. Blumenthal Nahman, Director of the Central Jewish Historical Commission in Warsaw, who described the general Nazi policy and system of extermination of Jews and the organization of the concentration and death camps set up for the purpose by the German authorities in the occupied territories; Dr. J. Olbrycht, Professor in the University of Cracow, who described the general conditions in the Auschwitz camp and in particular as regards health, food, hygienics and the system of treatment; Dr. R. Dawidowski, Professor of the Mining Academy in Cracow, who submitted a detailed report on the organization and work of the gas-chambers and crematoria; Dr. E. Kowalski, Assistant-Professor at the University of Cracow, who gave evidence on the medical experiments performed by German doctors on the camp's inmates. Finally, the Tribunal took note of the reports submitted by Professor Robel, expert in toxicology and Professor Romer, expert in geography.

As part of the evidence also a documentary film was projected in the court, showing the camp buildings and establishments.

III. Medical War Crimes

The evidence submitted by Professor Kowalski and other witnesses showed that numerous medical experiments were performed on men and women of non-German origin, mostly Jews, at the Auschwitz concentration camp. They were carried out on orders from the supreme German authorities. The experiments fall into the following groups:

(*a*) castration experiments;
(*b*) experiments intended to produce sterilization;
(c) experiments causing premature termination of pregnancy and carried out on pregnant and child-bearing women;
(*d*) experiments of artificial semination;
(*e*) experiments aimed at cancer research;
(*f*) other experiments.

(A) *Castration experiments.* They were performed on healthy, normal individuals of both sexes, and of different ages and nationalities, mostly Jews, without their voluntary consent.

X-ray treatment was applied to male and female genital organs and in particular to ovaries and testes. Before or after the X-ray application both or only one of the ovaries and testes were removed. Different dosages, usually very large, of X-rays were applied. The results were checked by the histopathological method. This aimed at establishing the fertility or sterility of the persons subjected to the experiments. Also experiments in which small or minimal doses of X-rays were applied took place. These experiments brought about a temporary loss of fertility.

These experiments were carried out by Professor Schumann instructed to this purpose by Himmler. They caused undue suffering, permanent injuries or even death of the individuals concerned. The large dosage of X-rays caused not only complete castration, but also burns and necrosis of parts of the body subjected to X-rays.

Men who were subjected to intensive X-ray treatment and had severe burns of the scrotum and thighs often died. Even if they survived, they were in constant danger of death. They were temporarily or permanently deprived of their fertility and even of their potency. Women subjected to intense X-rays were showing climacteric symptoms related to the atrophy of the ovaries. They soon showed senile changes and died. Even if they survived a temporary or permanent loss of fertility followed. Burns and necroses, the aftermath of X-ray treatment, made the use of genitalia impossible. Castration of women was also carried out by short waves, causing coagulation of the deeper layers of the tissue, severe burns and even death.

German personnel performing experiments often observed from hiding the behaviour of castrated Jewish men and women, who were especially accommodated in common. Thus they wanted to ascertain changes which may have occurred in their libido.

(B) *Experiments intended to produce sterilization.* Sterilization of women was carried out by the pumping of a thick white test fluid, consisting of contrast medium and some unknown chemical agents, into the uterus and tubes. Also sterilizing operations were performed, the uterus, tubes and even sometimes breasts being removed. Women experienced great suffering during test fluid experiments and after them. Usually salpingitis or peritonitis followed which often proved fatal.

These experiments were performed on young and healthy Jewish women of 20–30 years of age, who had regular periods, a not too narrow cervix and who had borne at least one child. After the experiments they often lost their periods. Experiments were repeated from two to six times at intervals of from three to four weeks. In their course an X-ray control was carried on by screening and an X-ray was taken afterwards. The experiments aimed at the obliteration of the tubes. This was to be achieved through the inflammation of the mucous membrane of the uterus and of the tubes. This, in conjunction with the inflammation of the internal genital organs and often of the peritoneum, caused widespread adhesions and fibrothic changes. Men were also sterilized through suture of the vas deferens.

The total number of sterilization experiments was estimated by witnesses at about 3,000 and of the test fluid experiments at about 1,000.

Test fluid sterilization experiments were performed by Professor Clauberg or under his control. He was an eminent German gynaecologist and acted under Himmler's orders. According to one of the witnesses Professor Clauberg admitted that his experiments were of no scientific value. Identical results were previously obtained on animals and were well known to the medical profession. Thus the experiments on women in the Auschwitz camp could not serve any scientific end. In addition they were performed in terrible conditions which often led to chronic illness, permanent injury or even death. Neither the doctors nor the assistant personnel were properly trained for the purpose. Unsterilized instruments and dressings were often used.

(C) *Premature termination of pregnancy and other experiments on pregnant or child-bearing women.* Premature termination of pregnancy was carried out by the emptying of the uterus, injections of Abortus Bangserum or by laparotomy and extirpation of the uterus. Women were ill several weeks after those experiments.

Delivery was provoked by artificially causing contracture of the uterus musculature or by the use of a balloon. About 50 pregnant women were subjected to those experiments. Frequently blood of people suffering from typhus was injected before labour.

(D) *Experiments of artificial insemination.* These were also carried out without the voluntary consent of the subjects concerned. Sperm obtained from Jewish men in the camp was used. In addition to the vaginal method, sperm was directly introduced in the uterus. Such a method was dangerous and caused infection of the female genital organs as sperm obtained through artificial ejaculation cannot be aseptic.

These experiments aimed in certain cases at the checking of results of X-ray castrations, in others on the effects of test fluid injections into the uterus and tubes.

Men and women previously subjected to castration and sterilization experiments were accommodated together. Four hundred men and 250 women were thus put into the same place and results of natural insemination were observed, while in other cases artificial insemination experiments were performed. Another camp for 3,500 of such human "guinea pigs" was also built.

(E) *Experiments aimed at cancer research.* These consisted in excising parts of the uterine body, and the wound was sutured and frozen sections with the excised material made. These experiments aimed at examining early stages of cancer. They were performed not only on older and sick women, but also on young girls. Excisions were also made on completely healthy persons with no suspicion of cancer of the genital organs. Incisions were in fact amputations of the cervical part of the uterus and in each case damage of the submucous layer of the uterine body occurred.

Incisions were carried out on about 120-130 women over 30 years of age, and on many very young girls. Each day about four such experiments were performed and in this connection the uterus was illuminated and photos taken. The material obtained was sent to Dr. Wirths in Hamburg and also examined on the spot. These incisions often caused bleeding, exudative parametrytis and peritonitis. This was due to the circumstance that German doctors performing the operation did not have necessary qualifications and that the experiments were carried out in unclean conditions.

Owing to the removal of an excessive portion of the submucous membrane sexual intercourse was impossible for a certain time. Also the fibratic and scarifying changes caused the obliteration of the cervical channel and thereby relative sterility.

Experiments of transplanting cancerous bodies to the uterus and cervical channel were also carried out. After a certain time the uterus was removed and results of the transplanting observed. As in most cases these experiments were successful, however, victims usually died within one-and-a-half years, or at least temporary illness followed.

(F) *Other experiments.* Fifteen to twenty-one young girls were deprived of their virginity in a brutal manner by SS men, no noxious consequences having been known to follow. Injections of hormones to women were also made and results observed.

IV. The Case for the Defence

During the preliminary investigation conducted by a *juge d'instruction* and during the trial the accused, who was defended by two counsels appointed by the Tribunal, admitted in substance all the facts preferred against him in the indictment. In particular, he admitted that he was a member of the NSDAP and the SS, and that in his capacity as commandant of the concentration camp at Auschwitz and later as chief of D.I. Department of the Central Economic and Administrative Office of the SS he carried out and supervised the extermination of many million Jews and other people. He also admitted that in the course of this action the victims were robbed of all their possessions and valuables.

The accused denied, however, that he personally committed any acts of ill-treatment or cruelty, and questioned the accuracy of the total number of victims killed in the camp, which according to him was much lower than that of about four million submitted in the Indictment. All his questions put forward to witnesses were directed to this end in view. Neither he himself, nor his defence, introduced any evidence or witnesses on his behalf and he entirely relied on those put forward by the Prosecution. His whole defence rested solely on the submission that he was only carrying out orders received from his superiors, and he recognized his entire responsibility for everything that occurred in the camp whether he personally knew it at the time or not.

V. The Judgment of the Tribunal

The Tribunal found the accused guilty of the alleged crimes and sentenced him to death. In addition, the Tribunal pronounced the loss of public and civic rights, and forfeiture of all property of the accused.

There are, however, some important differences between the Indictment and the Judgment, which should be noted. Apart from those which concern the findings of the Tribunal in regard to the accused's membership in the criminal organizations, and which will be described later, these differences are the following:

The Indictment charged the accused with "depriving of life", while the Tribunal described the corresponding offenses as "participation in the murder of . . . ". In the passage relating to the number of people exterminated in the Auschwitz camp, the Tribunal stated that "an undetermined number of people, at least 2,500,000, mainly Jews" were murdered.

The Indictment contained in para. (2) the charge accusing Hoess personally of "ill-treating inmates . . . physically by . . . and morally by . . . ". The wording of the corresponding section of the sentence establishes that the accused "acted to the detriment of civilians, members of the armed forces and prisoners of war by maintaining them in a state of slavery, combined with their confinement in an enclosed camp and with various physical and moral ill-treatment and tortures such as . . ."

Para. (iii) of the Indictment alleged that the accused "supervised wholesale robbery of property", etc. The Tribunal stated in its Judgment that the accused acted to the detriment of persons mentioned above also "by taking part in the wholesale robbery of . . ."

Thus it appears that the Tribunal did not express any explicit view on the question whether the accused did personally ill-treat or tortured any of the inmates, a question which was highly controversial as far as the evidence given by witnesses is concerned, and in addition brought the corresponding charges within the wording of the relevant provisions in force at the time of the trial.

Notes on the Case

I. The Court and the Legal Basis of the Trial

The Court was the Supreme National Tribunal for trial of War Criminals, the jurisdiction and powers of which have been defined in the Decrees of 22nd

January and 17th October, 1946, and in the Decree of 11th April, 1947. The case was tried in Warsaw. The substantive law applied was that laid down in the Decree of 31st August, 1944, *concerning the punishment of Fascist-Hitlerite criminals guilty of murder and ill-treatment of the civilian population and of prisoners of war, and the punishment of traitors to the Polish Nation,* as promulgated in the consolidated text of this Decree on 11th December, 1946.

II. The Nature of the Offences

The acts committed by the accused were crimes in violation of Article 1 para. 1, and Articles 2 and 4 of the Decree mentioned above, the text of which is given in the Annex to this volume. These acts were also in violation of the corresponding provisions of the Polish Civil Criminal Code of 1932 concerning murder, grievous bodily harm, torture and ill-treatment, infringement of personal liberty and appropriation of property (Articles 225, 235, 236, 246, 259 and 278). The Prosecution submitted that the crimes committed against the Soviet prisoners of war were also in violation of the Geneva Convention relative to prisoners of war.

Apart from the provisions of the above Decree already indicated, the Tribunal based its Judgment on Article 5 para. 1 of the said Decree concerning superior orders and duress, the plea of which the Tribunal rejected, and on article 7 concerning additional penalties. The Tribunal also applied the relevant provisions of the Criminal Code dealing with the basic principles of responsibility for criminal acts.

III. Criminal Organizations

(i) *Membership in the NSDAP*

1. The Indictment which, it is presumed, was drafted before the Polish Law on membership of criminal organizations had been enacted, charged the accused Hoess with the membership of the German National Socialist Worker's Party (NSDAP) and of the SS, and described both these organizations as criminal, putting forward specified allegations against the NSDAP alone. The latter was described as an organization which was "planning, organizing and perpetrating crimes against peace, war crimes and crimes against humanity" as means leading to "the subjugation of other nations".

The logical and legal construction of the corresponding passage of the Sentence pronounced by the Tribunal is different. It is stated therein that Hoess was a member of both organizations, but the SS is mentioned first and it alone is explicitly defined as a criminal organization. The activities of both organizations are, however, closely interlinked in the Sentence, and the SS is considered a tool of the NSDAP used for committing war crimes and crimes against humanity. Crimes against peace have thus been omitted in the sentence but the NSDAP is considered as having had criminal aims of subjugating other nations, which are described as a crime in violation of Polish municipal law (Article 4 of the Decree of 31st August, 1944, as amended by the Decree of 11th December, 1946).

Thus the Tribunal had shifted the main emphasis from the NSDAP and put the emphasis on the accused's membership in the SS which alone was also mentioned in the closing speeches of the Prosecution. This was evidently done because the Tribunal could not consider the accused's membership in the NSDAP as criminal in view of the fact that Article 4, para. 3 of the Decree of 1944 lays down the rule that membership of this organization is considered criminal only as regards the leading positions, and the accused did not hold such a position in the Nazi Party.

The question of which leading positions in the NSDAP should be considered as criminal became for some time controversial in Polish legal literature and among the Polish judges. This was in consequence of a general wording of Article 4, para. 3 of the said Decree which says that membership of the NSDAP is considered criminal "as regards *all* leading positions." Thus, for instance, the question arose whether or not the position of an *Ortsgruppenkassenleiter* (Chief Cashier of the NSDAP District Organization) should be considered criminal in the meaning of the above provision. However, the view finally prevailed that only such leading ranks and positions of the NSDAP should be considered as criminal as are enumerated in the Nuremberg Judgment, i.e., the Reichsleitung of the Party, the Gauleiters, the Kreisleiters, and the Ortsgruppenleiters, as well as the Amtsleiters who were heads of offices on the staffs of the Reichsleitung, Gauleitung and Kreisleitung.

This view has been authoritatively upheld by a ruling of the Polish Supreme Court of 28th February, 1948. The Supreme Court gave the following reasons on which it based its decision, namely, that (*a*) the Polish legislation, by enacting the law concerning the membership of criminal organizations, wanted to bring Polish municipal law into line with the developments which have already taken place in international criminal law, in particular, in connection with the Judgment of the Nuremberg Tribunal which was pronounced prior to the Polish enactment in question; and therefore, (*b*) while formulating the provision dealing with the criminality of membership in the NSDAP, the Polish legislator had in view only such positions in that organization as have been recognized as leading by the International Military Tribunal.

(ii) *Concentration Camp As a Criminal Organization*

It will be of some interest, it is thought, to devote some space in this report to another Polish case concerning the Auschwitz concentration camp, in which a number of lesser members of its personnel was tried by the same Tribunal, and to discuss the problem indicated in the above heading.

When discussing the Polish law relating to the membership of criminal organizations it has been pointed out that from the law as laid down in Article 4, paras. 2 and 3 of the Decree of 1944 (the consolidated text of 11th

December, 1946), it is clear that Polish courts are not bound by the fact that certain groups or organizations have not been indicted and adjudicated by the Nuremberg tribunal as criminal within the meaning of the London Charter. It has also been stated there that consequently in such cases the Polish court may declare such groups or organizations to be criminal within the Polish jurisdiction. Such, for instance, was the case in regard to members of the concentration camp staff at Auschwitz.

In this second Auschwitz case, in which forty officials of that camp including Artur Liebehenschel, a successor of Hoess, were tried by the Supreme National Tribunal in Cracow separately and subsequently to the Hoess trial, the Tribunal declared the authorities, the administration and members of the garrison of the Auschwitz camp to be a criminal group, irrespective of whether or not the members of these administrative or military units were at the same time members of the SS or any other organization pronounced criminal by the Nuremberg Tribunal.

In its judgment of 22nd December, 1947, the Supreme National Tribunal give a number of reasons that served as the basis for its declaration. The most important of them can be summarized as follows:

(1) The Nuremberg Judgment does not limit the right of the Polish legislator to decide those acts which were not a subject of the findings of the Nuremberg Tribunal and can be considered as liable to punishment within the Polish jurisdiction, unless they have been explicitly declared as not criminal, as, for instance, the acts of the organization of the SA.

(2) The provisions of the Polish law now in force are not in contradiction to the Nuremberg Judgment. The interpretation of the Polish law cannot be contrary to the explicit text of this Judgment, but on the other hand there is no legal obstacle in the way of supplementing the legal principles established in this Judgment by further principles, if in substance they are not in contradiction with the former.

(3) There is no doubt that the organization of the German concentration camps is a criminal group in the meaning both of the Nuremberg Judgment and of Article 4 of the Decree of 1944, as these camps had been set up with the aim of unlawfully depriving of freedom and health, property and life of individuals and groups of people because of their race (Jews and Gipsies), nationality (Poles and Czechs), religion (Jews) or political convictions (socialists, communists and anti-Nazis). The organization of the German concentration camps thus aimed at committing crimes against humanity, which at the same time were crimes in violation of the penal law of all civilized nations, and also war crimes as regards the acts committed against the Soviet prisoners of war.

(4) By the description "organization of a concentration camp" should be understood the authorities, the administration and the personnel of a camp, with the exception of the inmates who under compulsion were performing various administrative functions. The latter can only be responsible for their personal deeds as they were not members of the criminal organization as it is

understood by the Nuremberg Judgment, namely, they were not bound together by a common aim which was the commission of crimes against humanity. Those people had no ideological ties with the organization of the concentration camps, but had been simply used as tools for the perpetration of certain crimes. This does not protect them from punishment for their personal acts, but they cannot be declared guilty of membership of a criminal organization as of a separate offence.

(5) Article 9 of the Nuremberg Charter states that the International Military Tribunal has the power to declare at the trial of any individual member of any group or organization (in connection with any act of which the individual may be convicted) that the group or organization of which the individual was a member was a criminal organization. Thus, Article 9 gave to the Tribunal the power to declare criminal *any* group or organization, the members of which committed any of the crimes enumerated in Article 6 of the Charter, i.e. crimes against peace, war crimes and crimes against humanity.

(6) The law laid down in Article 9, according to which an international Tribunal may at any time at its discretion increase the number of organizations considered as criminal, has its application in international jurisdiction. As far as the municipal jurisdiction is concerned, the municipal law has priority, and international law is to be applied only subsidiarily. International law is based not only on codifications like the Charter, but also on the judgments of courts like the Nuremberg Judgment.

(7) If therefore, the Charter and the Nuremberg Judgment are both a source of law, of which the former permits any organization to be declared a criminal one, and the latter does not prevent this, there is no legal obstacle for declaring, in accordance with Article 4, para. 2, of the Decree of 1944, as criminal the organization of the concentration camps.

(8) As the Polish legislation and judgments of Polish courts are, of course, not binding outside the Polish territory, the recognition by a Polish court of the Central Administration of the Concentration Camps as a criminal organization in general could raise objections. There is, however, no objection for declaring as criminal the organizations of the concentration camps in Poland, and foremost the organization of the concentration camp at Auschwitz.

In connection with the above declaration of the Supreme National Tribunal, and especially with its paragraphs (3) and (7), it should be pointed out that the Nuremberg Judgment did not include the organization of the concentration camps as such among the organizations declared as criminal, primarily because the Nuremberg Indictment did not ask the Tribunal to make such a declaration in this respect. Nevertheless, the Tribunal did make in its Judgment many references to the concentration camps which it described as a means for systematic commission of war crimes and crimes against humanity. Moreover, the Tribunal expressly stated that "in the administration of the occupied territories the concentration camps were used to destroy all opposition groups". With specific reference to one of the ill-framed concentration camps the Tribunal, quoting the report of the War Crimes Branch of the Judge Advocate's Section of the 3rd U.S. Army, established, for instance, that:

> Flossenburg concentration camp can be described as a factory dealing in death. Although this camp had in view the primary object of putting to work the mass slave labour, another of its primary objects was the elimination of human lives by the methods employed in handling the prisoners. Hunger and starvation rations, sadism, inadequate clothing, medical neglect, disease, beatings, hangings, freezing, forced suicides, shooting, etc., all played a major role in obtaining their object. Prisoners were murdered at random; spite killings against Jews were common, injections of poison and shooting in the neck were everyday occurrences: epidemics of typhus and spotted fever were permitted to run rampant as a means of eliminating prisoners; life in this camp meant nothing. Killing became a common thing, so common that a quick death was welcomed by the unfortunate ones.

One more passage may be quoted from the Nuremberg Judgment. It reads:

> A certain number of the concentration camps were equipped with gas-chambers for the wholesale destruction of the inmates, and with furnaces for the burning of the bodies. Some of them were in fact used for the *extermination of Jews* as part of the "final solution" of the Jewish problem. Most of the non-Jewish inmates were used for labour although the conditions under which they worked made labour and death almost synonymous terms. Those inmates who became ill and were unable to work were either destroyed in the gas-chambers or sent to special infirmaries, where they were given entirely inadequate medical treatment, worse food if possible than the working inmates, and left to die.

When dealing with the criminal aims of the SS, the Nuremberg Tribunal described in detail the activities of the RSHA (ReichsSicherheit HauptAmpt) and the WVHA (Wirtschafts Verwaltungs HauptAmpt). The Tribunal then stated that already since 1934 the SS through the medium of the RSHA was responsible for the central administration of concentration camps, and from 1942, when this administration was taken over under the control of the WVHA, the concentration camps were used as a source of slave labour, for the extermination of "anti-social elements", experiments on human beings and extermination of Jews.

In this way the Nuremberg Judgment established that the concentration camps were an important part of the machinery for the criminal activities of the SS as a whole, and of the WVHA in particular, which was one of the central offices of the SS declared by the Tribunal as a criminal organization. If, in addition, we take into account that the concentration camps were in fact the constituent executive units of the WHVA and were serving its criminal aims in general, and the realization of the plan of exterminating other nations in particular, it may well be said that the Supreme National Tribunal was on strong ground in declaring the concentration camp as a criminal group.

In making the above declaration the Supreme National Tribunal not only based itself on Article 9 of the Nuremberg Charter, bur also applied *per analogiam* the statement of principle made in this connection by the Nuremberg

Tribunal which stated that according to Article 9 "the Tribunal is vested with discretion as to whether it will declare any organization criminal. This discretion is a judicial one and does not permit arbitrary action, but should be exercized in accordance with well settled legal principles . . . If satisfied of the criminal guilt of *any* organization or group, this Tribunal should not hesitate to declare it to be criminal because the theory of 'group criminality' is new . . ."

The Supreme National Tribunal evidently considered that in regard to the concentration camps it is not sufficient, as did the Nuremberg Judgment, to have declared as criminal the three or four principal Nazi organizations, as in point of fact there were many Nazis employed in the administration of every single concentration camp, and responsible in a general sense for the mass criminality committed therein, sometimes in a higher degree than the actual perpetrators, and who were not members of any of the organizations declared as criminal by the Nuremberg Tribunal. Therefore, the Supreme National Tribunal declared the members of the authorities, of the administration and of the garrison of the German concentration camps in occupied Poland as criminal groups in the meaning of Article 4 of the Decree of 1944 (1946). It declared these members to be a criminal *group* and not *organization,* in view of the fact that the above Decree as well as the international enactments use both these descriptions, and the expression "group" is in this case more appropriate from the technical point of view, and because of the etymological character of the word "organization".

It appears that a few words should finally be said as regards criminal knowledge on the part of the members of the concentration camps personnel. It should be recalled that the Nuremberg Tribunal declared criminal the membership of the four organizations (the Leadership Corps of the Nazi Party, the Gestapo, the SD and the SS) on the condition that the members "become or remained members of the organization with knowledge that it was being used for the commission of acts declared criminal by Article 6 of the Charter, or who were personally implicated as members of the organization in the commission of such crimes".

Although the Supreme National Tribunal did not mention in its declaration this particular question, it must be presumed that this Tribunal, having based the declaration on the analysis of the Nuremberg Charter and Judgment, took this requirement as self-evident and did not see the necessity of pointing it out. It would also seem self-explanatory that the first part of the Nuremberg Tribunal's *proviso* is hardly of much importance in the case of concentration camps, as every member of their personnel must have known that these camps were being used for the commission of acts which any ordinary sensible person must have acknowledged as criminal.

IV. Genocide

As it is apparent from the outline of the proceedings the trial of Hoess was another case in which the crimes perpetrated in the Auschwitz camp come within the notion of the crime of genocide. We have already described briefly the concept of this notion in connection with the case of Amon Goeth. As regards the present case it may be mentioned that the Prosecution, after describing the German policy aiming at the extermination of Jews, pointed out that the mass crimes committed in concentration camps were part of the Nazi scheme of exterminating whole nations. In this connection the Prosecution recalled among others that General von dem Bach of the German police, who was a witness in the trial against Governor Fisher, sentenced previously by the Supreme National Tribunal, had testified that during a conference held by Himmler some time before the outbreak of war, the latter explained a plan which aimed at the extermination of some thirty million of the Slav population.

The Supreme National Tribunal dealt in its Judgment only very generally with this type of the Nazi criminality. It stated that the Nazi Party had as one of its aims the biological and cultural extermination of subjugated nations, especially of the Jewish and Slav nations, in order to establish finally the German *Lebensraum* and the domination of the German race. This programme and practice of extermination of entire groups of people and of nations on specific grounds, described as the crime of genocide, the Tribunal defined as an attempt on the most organic bases of the human relationship such as the right to live and the right to existence.

One of the aspects and elements of the German system of extermination put into preliminary execution in the Auschwitz camp were the medical experiments described in some detail in the preceding part of this report.

Even if it could be assumed that the medical experiments carried out at Auschwitz concentration camp were not expected to serve any definite political aims, their criminal character is beyond any doubt. They violated all rules which must be observed when medical experiments are performed on human beings. Special circumstances in which they were performed constitute in addition elements which allow them to be classified as violations of the laws and customs of war and laws of humanity.

Experiments were always carried out under compulsion and in many cases physical violence was used. They were often performed by unqualified doctors and in appalling conditions. They did not serve any scientific purpose. They were performed with unnecessary suffering and injury and without proper protection against the risks of disability or death. The subjects experienced extreme pain and torture, and permanent injury or death followed in many cases. The doctors and the personnel performing experiments did not show any care or give any assistance to persons frequently seriously ill in consequence of the experiments.

Thus all these experiments violated general principles of criminal law as derived from the criminal laws of all civilized nations.

But paramount importance should be attached to the political aspect of the crime. The general scheme of the wholesale experiments points out clearly to the real aim. They were obviously devised at finding the most appropriate means with which to lower or destroy the reproductive power of the Jews, Poles, Czechs and other non-German nations which were considered by the Nazi as standing in the way of fulfilment of German plans of world domination. Thus, they were preparatory to the carrying out of the crime or genocide.

These conclusions seem justified not only by the experiments themselves. They were corroborated by the statements of the accused Hoess himself. He confirmed the existence of plans of wholesale destruction of the Slav nations, and of Poles and Czechs in particular. It is also known that Himmler entrusted Professor Clauberg with experiments which were nothing else but the application in reverse of his successes in the domain of the treatment of sterility. Clauberg himself recognized that his experiments could contribute very little to the progress of science.

The defendant Hoess declared that the experiments of wholesale castration and sterilization were carried out in accordance with Himmler's plans and orders. These aimed at the biological destruction of the Slav nations in such a way that outside appearance of a natural extinction would have been preserved.

The X-ray experiments, particularly in cases when small or minimal dosage of rays was applied, and the setting up of a special mixed camp for about 3,500 men and women in this connection seem to be particularly characteristic. Thus a special breeding place for individuals carrying supposedly hereditary "lethal" genes, which it was hoped could be artificially cultivated among the subjugated nations, seems to have been created. This contention seems, according to Professor Kowalski who gave expert evidence in this trial, to be justified by experiments on animals. It was known from them, said this witness, that X-rays applied in a certain dosage to germinative cells caused hereditary injuries to the latter. Progency born from such cells either could not survive or would carry congenital anomalies. Also X-ray treatment of female genital organs and in particular of the uterus caused injuries, owing to which pregnancy ended in about 42 per cent of cases in miscarriage or premature delivery.

Thus it seems probable that the X-ray experiments aimed at checking on the results obtained on animals and at providing necessary statistical data. These experiments could have determined the X-ray dosage necessary for injuring human hereditary genes. They also aimed at creating conditions in which the injured genes could be multiplied and degenerated progency observed, so that in the end those observations could have been used for political purposes.

Still more typical were Clauberg's sterilization experiments. They all aimed at causing sterility of non-German women. In the opinion of Professor Kowalski, they were of great importance because all other well-known methods of sterilization are difficult, require much time, complicated technique and skilled doctors, and because they could be easily noticed by the persons concerned.

The aim of the German doctors of sterilizing in a wholesale manner non-German women could have been achieved by the discovery of a drug which would easily and surely obliterate the relatively narrow lumen of the tubes, without injuring the mucous membrane of the uterus. Thus periods would continue, internal female genital organs would remain healthy and damage inflicted to the reproductive power of women concerned would remain unobserved. The wholesale application of such a drug, the discovery of which cannot be ruled out, would have paved a way to a demographic policy aiming at a total extinction of nations.

Thus in view of the political directives, issued by the Supreme German authorities, and the character of the experiments performed in Auschwitz on their orders, it seems obvious that they constituted the preparatory stage of one of the forms of the crime of genocide, which was intended to be perpetrated by scientific means.

TRIAL OF SUSUKI MOTOSUKE

Amboina, Netherlands East Indies, January, 1948*

Before Netherlands Temporary Court-Martial

Outline of the Proceedings

I. The Charges

The accused, Susuki Motosuke, was a First Lieutenant of the Japanese Army Engineer Corps, posted with the Hosikikan (Japanese Intelligence Service) in the island of Ceram, Netherlands East Indies.

He was charged with having, between August and November, 1944, that is "in time of war, contrary to the laws and customs of war, intentionally, by abuse of the authority he enjoyed over his subordinates . . . incited the latter" to execute Indonesian natives, subjects of the Netherlands East Indies, whilst knowing that the victims "had not been tried, at any rate in a legal manner."

The Court was requested by the prosecution to find the defendant guilty of the war crime of "murder, committed four times" and to sentence him to the death penalty.

II. Facts and Evidence

According to the evidence admitted by the Court from the prosecution and collected from other sources, the crimes charged were committed in the following circumstances:

In August, 1944, as officer of the Japanese Intelligence Service, the defendant gave orders to subordinates to execute by shooting a Dutch subject by the name of Barends. During the Japanese occupation of Ceram the latter had joined the ranks of the "Gunkes," a corps of "volunteer combatants," composed mainly of Indonesians serving with the Japanese Army. As a Japanese soldier Barends was found guilty of having shot at a Japanese called Yamamoto, and the defendant ordered a summary execution. The execution was carried out in the presence of the accused, who gave the orders to fire to the execution squad.

**Law Reports of Trials of War Criminals,* Vol. 13, p. 126 (London, 1947).

In September, 1944, the defendant ordered the arrest of three Indonesians, by the names of Skalwik, Tarumasele and Mailoa, the last two being school teachers. Skalwik was accused of stealing a rifle from the Japanese; Tarumasele was accused of setting ambushes in the path of retreating Japanese; and Mailoa was charged with shooting at and robbing Japanese. In October, 1944, the accused gave the orders for their execution and again led the firing squad which killed the three Indonesians.

III. Defence of the Accused

While admitting that he gave the orders for the above executions, the accused pleaded not guilty.

Concerning the execution of Barends the defendant referred to the fact that the victim had volunteered to join the Japanese Army and was consequently subject to Japanese military laws and regulations at the time of the execution. The execution was therefore purely an internal matter of the Japanese Army and did not come within the sphere of war crimes. The Court was not competent to try him on this count.

Concerning the killing of the other three victims, the defendant alleged that their execution was lawful as it was made following a sentence of a Japanese Court-Martial (Gunritsu Kaigi), and was ordered by his superior officer, Lieut.-Colonel Hirunoga or Hirunaka.

IV. Findings and Sentence

The Court dismissed the accused's pleas. In the case of *Barends* it decided that there was no war crime but the common law criminal offence of "intentional incitement to murder by abuse of authority," of which the accused was guilty. In respect of the execution of the other three Indonesians it decided that there were no proper trial by Japanese courts and that the accused was guilty of the "war crime of murder."

The accused was sentenced to imprisonment for life.

Notes on the Case

I. The Bearing of the Victim's Nationality Upon War Crimes

One of the most important findings of the Court was that made in the case of the execution of Barends.

The Court was satisfied that Barends had freely joined the Japanese Army in the Netherlands East Indies, and had therefore been in "foreign military service without the permission" of the Dutch Government. As a consequence the Court decided that Barends "was not a Netherlands subject at the time of his execution and therefore no longer a subject of the United Nations." The Court further referred to an official "Explanation of the Legislation drafted with regard to War Crimes," which was released as a supplement to the Netherlands East Indies Decrees and numbered 15031 of 1946. As evidence that war crimes trials were limited to cases involving victims of Allied nationality, the Court observed that, according to the above "Explanation," it was "the intention of the United Nations Commission for the Investigation of War Crimes to undertake the investigation of *war crimes committed against subjects of the United Nations.*" As Barends had lost his nationality by joining the ranks of the Japanese Army, the Court took the view that "it could hardly be alleged that the act committed against him was contrary to the laws and customs of war," and that for this reason in his case no war crime had been perpetrated.

While discarding the charge of having committed a war crime on account of the victim's national status at the time of the crime, the Court decided that the accused was guilty of a common law crime under the terms of the Netherlands East Indies Penal Code. This decision was reached after consideration of the accused's defence that the execution was a purely internal matter of the Japanese Army, and constituted a lawful act under Japanese laws. The accused referred to two provisions of the Japanese Military Penal Code and claimed that, under Article 62 of the Code Barends had been guilty of insubordination, with the use of arms, in the face of the enemy, which offence was punishable, among other penalties, with death. Under Article 22 of the same Code every commander of a military unit was entitled to acts of summary justice, including the imposition of death penalty, and was not liable to punishment for such acts if they were carried out "in cases of necessity for the maintenance of discipline among army units face to face with the enemy." When giving the orders to execute summarily Barends he, the defendant, had proceeded within these powers.

The Court dismissed this plea on the following grounds:

The accused's unit, to which Barends belonged, had "never once been during the whole war face to face with the enemy," as "no Allied landings ever took place on the island of Ceram in war-time." The accused was therefore not entitled to use the powers given in Article 22 of the Japanese Military Penal Code to army unit commanders. In this connection the application of Article 62 of the same Code was, in the circumstances, "reserved to the judiciary" and could not be carried out by the accused on his own authority.

As a result the accused was found guilty of the common law crime of "intentional incitement to murder by abuse of authority," as provided against in Art. 55, para. 2° of the Netherlands East Indies Penal Code. The relevant passages of this Article read as follows:

> The following shall be punished as the authors of a punishable act: They who by gifts, promises, *misuse of authority,* or of the esteem in which they are held, by force, threats, or deceit, or by providing the opportunity, means or information, intentionally incite the act.

The Court's finding that, in the case of Barends, there was, technically, no war crime as the victim was no longer, at the time of the crime, a national of one of the United Nations, deserves special attention. The Court referred to the terms of reference of the United Nations War Crimes Commission. From the way this reference was made it is apparent that the Court took into account the War Crimes Commission's terms of reference as they were originally determined in the first stages of its existence. The subject of whether or not the concept of war crimes applied only to victims of Allied nationality, was considered by the United Nations War Crimes Commission as early as 20th October, 1943, the very day of its establishment at the diplomatic conference in London. The majority had taken the view that it was applicable only to such victims. Soon after this, however, in April, 1944, the question was raised again with regard to reported killings of many Italian hostages by the Nazis after the Armistice with Italy was signed, as well as to offences perpetrated by the Nazis against inhabitants of Hungary, Roumania, and other enemy countries. A proposal was made that, in the circumstances, the concept of war crimes should be applied irrespective of the nationality of the victims or of the place of the crime, as such offences were also deserving of punishment. The principle previously adopted was maintained, but the concept of "Allied" nationals was at the same time interpreted in a wider sense so as to meet the situation created by the fact that, after her capitulation, Italy had been accepted by the Allied Governments as a co-belligerent Power and had fought against the Germans with military units of her own. A number of cases concerning Italian victims of Nazi crimes perpetrated after Italy had become a co-belligerent Power, were considered by the Commission and charges against perpetrators put on record in the Commission's files as *prima facie* evidence of "war crimes." After the end of the war British military courts in Italy conducted as "war crime" trials, proceedings against Nazi officers, such as Field Marshal Kesselring, for the killing of Italian victims. In this manner the rule that the concept of war crimes applied only to "Allied" nationals was relaxed so as to include nationals of a "co-belligerent" Power.

In the trial under review the victim had joined the ranks of the enemy of an Allied nation and had thereby, according to Netherlands East Indies law, become assimilated to an enemy national.

II. Murder As a War Crime

In the case of the other three victims the Court decided that, in view of their national status, the accused was guilty of the "war crime" of murder.

Murder is one of the offences which have been recognised as a criminal violation of the laws and customs of war ever since these violations were defined. It was included on top of the list of war crimes of the 1919 Commission on the Responsibility of the Authors of the War and on Enforcement of Penalties, and was dealt with in the same manner by the United Nations War

Crimes Commission in regard to violations committed during the Second World War. In the Netherlands East Indies legislation it is punishable as a war crime under the terms of Article I of Statute Book Decree No. 44 of 1946.

In this trial the important point is that the accused's guilt was determined in connection with his plea that the execution was lawful as it allegedly took place in consequence of a sentence passed by a Japanese court after trial of the three victims. The Court heard a Japanese witness who, at the time of the alleged trial, was prosecutor of the Japanese court concerned. He testified that some preparations for a trial were undertaken, but could not remember that the case was actually tried. The Court took this as sufficient evidence that the execution "took place without sentence being passed by any competent judge," and that for this reason it was "contrary to the laws and customs of war" and constituted a "war crime."

III. Violations of the Rule of Fair Trial and Other Requisite Lawful Proceedings

The Court's decision that the accused was guilty of a common law crime in the case of Barends, and of the "war crime of murder" in respect of the other victims, was reached after consideration of yet another important point.

The Court investigated the question as to whether the victims had in fact been guilty of any offence against the Japanese authorities, as claimed by the defendant. In both cases it decided that they were.

Thus, for example, in the case of Barends the following was stated in the Judgment:

> The Court . . . deems proved that the accused . . . ordered a number of Indonesians under his command to kill by rifle fire Barends. who was the head of a group of Gunkes and *who had committed a punishable offence.*

In the case of the other three victims the Court stated:

> The Court . . . deems proved that the accused . . . ordered a number of Japanese under his command to kill by rifle fire Tarumasele, Mailoa and Skalwik *who had committed punishable offences.*

These findings are important as they define the true nature of the offences for which the accused was convicted.

In both cases they bring in the foreground the issue of fair trial and of proper exercise of powers vested in members of the authorities of a belligerent State in occupied territory. In both cases the accused's culpability consisted in that, although the victims were guilty of offences and were liable to punishment by the occupying authorities, they were punished in an unlawful manner. It is on account of this lack of lawful proceedings that the executions were criminal, and that the defendant had become guilty of a crime.

The execution of the three Indonesians is a case in point concerning the right of inhabitants of an occupied territory to be tried by an occupation court before being subjected to a penalty. On the other hand, the circumstances of

Barends's death are illustrative of cases in which victims are, technically, not nationals of the State whose territory is occupied, but are nonetheless entitled to the same right of being subjected to lawful proceedings before punishment. In this latter case the Court's decision is the more remarkable as it, technically, concerned an "enemy" subject. The accused's conviction on this course is, therefore, evidence of the jurisdiction of an occupied Power over offences committed in its territory, during the occupation, between members of the occupying authorities themselves. In this respect another remarkable feature is that the rule of fair trial or of any other requisite lawful proceedings was considered and implemented from the viewpoint of the law of the occupying Power, and that the defendant was found guilty on the grounds that he had transgressed his powers under the terms of his own country's law.

In this manner the Judgment in this trial goes deeply into the issue of the obligations of an occupying State to exercise its powers within given standards of justice, and is a confirmation of the principle that the latter includes in the first instance the duty to extend the right of fair trial to inhabitants of occupied territory.

TRIAL OF WILLY ZUEHLKE

Amsterdam, August, 1948*

Before Netherlands Special Court

Outline of the Proceedings

The Accused, Willy Zuehlke, a former German prison warder, was a member of the Waffen-S.S. during the war 1939–1945, and served as such in the German Security Police (Sicherheitsdienst, commonly known as S.D.). In the early stages of the occupation of Holland he was assigned the duty to guard persons detained in the prisons at Havenstraat and Weteringschans. He was there in command of the guards, and remained in office from the beginning of 1941 until September, 1944.

The accused was tried by the Special Court in Amsterdam, found guilty of several offences and sentenced to seven years' imprisonment, with extenuating circumstances.

Both the accused and the Prosecutor appealed to the Special Court of Cassation, which pronounced a judgment of its own. The guilt of the accused was confirmed and his sentence reduced to five years' imprisonment.

I. Proceedings Before the First Court

1. *The Charges*

The charges against the accused included two types of offences: complicity in illegal detentions and ill-treatment of the prisoners.

Under one count charges were made in respect of prisoners of the Jewish race. The accused was charged with having "co-operated in the German policy of humiliation and persecution of the Jews" in that he had:

(*a*) Intentionally "assisted in the illegal detention" of a number of Jews by "keeping and guarding them in illegal detention."

(*b*) Ill-treated Jewish prisoners by "striking them with the hand, fist or any other object suitable for striking," and by kicking them "violently with a

**Law Reports of Trials of War Criminals,* Vol. 14, p. 139 (London, 1947).

shod foot," whereby prisoners "were caused pain and some of them injured"; and also by compelling Jewish prisoners to clean prison corridors with a tooth-brush and thereafter "emptying buckets of water over them."

Under a second count the accused was charged with similar offences against the prisoners irrespective of their race or religion. The part taken by the accused from this wider aspect was described as "co-operation in the maintenance of a policy of terrorism and brutality against defenceless arrestees." The charges included physical ill-treatment of the same nature as in the case of the Jews, and also, as a specific offence, denial of "spiritual aid," that is of the attendance of a priest, in the instance of prisoners sentenced to death prior to their execution.

All offences charged were described as having been committed "contrary to the laws and customs of war and to humanity." The accused was held guilty both as actual perpetrator and as a superior who had "permitted the German guards under his command" to commit similar acts.

Finally, the prosecution included, as a separate punishable circumstance, the fact that the accused was a member of "criminal organisations," the Waffen-S.S. and the Sicherheitsdienst (S.D.).

2. *Facts and Evidence*

The acts charged were substantiated by the testimony of eye-witnesses, who had themselves been prisoners under the accused's guard or who had served as guards under the accused. Their testimony contained the following facts:

On many occasions the accused beat Jewish prisoners with his hands or feet, or with objects such as keys, rubber truncheons and the like. He beat them on the face or the head. Jewish prisoners were ill-treated by him in a far more brutal manner than the other prisoners.

Evidence was also produced to the effect that the offices of a priest had been denied to prisoners sentenced to death.

3. *The Case for the Prosecution*

The prosecutor asked that the accused be found guilty under the terms of Art. 102 of the Netherlands Penal Code. This Article covers acts of persons "who in time of war lend assistance to the enemy or prejudice the State with respect to the enemy," and carries, in the absence of special circumstances specified in the Article, a maximum penalty of imprisonment for fifteen years. The Prosecutor's plea was made with regard to lesser punishments prescribed for the offence of illegal detention (Art. 282 of the Penal Code) and ill-treatment (Art. 300 of the same code.) In the absence of more serious consequences for the prisoner, such as severe bodily injury or death, illegal detention is punishable by a maximum of seven years and six months imprisonment. Similarly, ill-treatment unaccompanied by serious consequences for the victim is punishable by a maximum of two years' imprisonment. No such serious consequences would apply in the accused's case.

4. *The Defence*

The accused pleaded that he had acted upon superior orders and under duress. His contention was that, as a member of the Waffen-S.S., he could not do otherwise than discharge his duties in accordance with orders and methods concerning the custody of prisoners applied by his unit.

5. *Findings and Sentence*

The accused was found guilty on both counts, that is of taking part in the persecution of Jews by illegally detaining and ill-treating them and of taking part in systematic "terrorism and brutality" by ill-treating prisoners altogether. The above offences were described as war crimes and/or crimes against humanity, as defined in Art. 6 (*b*) and (*c*) of the Nuremberg Charter, which constituted at the same time, under Netherlands municipal law, the crime of illegal detention punishable by Art. 282 of the Penal Code, and the crime of ill-treatment punishable Under Art. 300 of the same Code.

The Court could not agree with the prosecution that the offences charged fell within the terms of Art. 102 of the Penal Code. If the latter were to be applied it would mean that the defendant, being an enemy, would have "lent assistance" to himself, and this was not the type of case covered by Art. 102.

The Court could also not agree that punishment could be imposed for the accused's membership of criminal organisations. The reason given was that the Netherlands metropolitan law had not provided for the punishment of such members and that there was consequently no legal basis for conviction on this ground. In addition, such membership did not add to or substract anything from the criminal nature of the acts committed by the accused against the prisoners.

The accused was acquitted of the specific charge that he was guilty of ill-treating prisoners by denying spiritual assistance to those condemned to death. The Court came to the conclusion that it had not been proved that such denial was contrary to the laws and customs of war. In addition, no evidence was to hand that it was the accused's duty to forward requests for spiritual assistance to the authorities concerned, or that such requests would have succeeded in view of the existing regulations.

The accused was sentenced to 7 years' imprisonment with extenuating circumstances. The circumstances taken into account were that the arrests followed by detentions "did not originate with the accused" and that the latter had "stupidly allowed himself to be carried along with the criminal stream of German terrorism, rather than acted with intent on his own initiative." It was also found that the ill-treatment inflicted was not of a "very serious nature" and that, by ill-treating prisoners, the accused had acted "rather on account of his rough nature than driven by the desire to attack his victims."

II. Proceedings Before the Special Court of Cassation

1. *Appeal of the Prosecution*

The Prosecutor appealed on two grounds.

While not raising again the issue as to the applicability of Art. 102 of the Netherlands Penal Code, he complained that the punishment imposed under the combined effect of Arts. 282 and 300 of the Penal Code did not correspond to "the gravity of the criminal actions committed by the accused," so that severer penalty should be imposed.

Objection was also raised in regard to the decision of the first court concerning the accused's membership of criminal organisations. The Court had established the fact that the accused belonged to organisations declared criminal by the International Military Tribunal at Nuremberg, and was wrong in holding the view that such membership was not punishable within the jurisdiction of Netherlands Courts. According to Art. 10 of the Nuremberg Charter members of organisations declared criminal by the Nuremberg Tribunal were liable to prosecution by the "competent national authority," which included Netherlands officers competent for the prosecution of war crimes. Membership of a criminal organisation was in itself a war crime, and therefore fell within the jurisdiction of and was punishable by Netherlands courts.

2. *The Accused's Appeal*

The accused appealed on the following grounds:

That, as was admitted by the first Court itself, the illegal detention of prisoners under the accused's guard had not originated from the accused, but from other German authorities. The fact of having been in charge of the prisoners as a guard could not be regarded as complicity in their being illegally detained.

That the punishment was too severe and did not correspond with the gravity of the offences committed.

3. *The Court's Findings and Sentence*

With respect to the prosecution's appeal the Court concurred with the first Court that the provisions of Netherlands Law applied by it were correctly implemented as to the nature of the offences, and that there was no room for applying Art. 102 of the Penal Code.

It dismissed the plea concerning membership of criminal organisations on the grounds that, in the case tried, such membership was only "a circumstance under which the other acts were committed." There was, therefore, no basis for adjudication on this point as a separate offence.

The accused was found guilty of the offences as established by the first Court, but in view of the mitigating circumstances and the nature of the offences, his sentence was reduced from 7 to 5 years' imprisonment.

Notes on the Case

I. Criminal Nature of Violations of the Laws of War and Its Legal Basis

In its findings concerning the criminal nature of the acts committed by the accused, the first Court entered into the question of the legal basis on account of which such acts were punishable. On this occasion it gave reasons with which the Court of Cassation, whilst concurring with the first Court as to the fact that the acts concerned were criminal, could not agree.

The first Court came to the conclusion that the acts committed were contrary to the laws and customs of war for the following reasons:

(1) The war between Germany and the Netherlands was "an international crime" on the part of Germany. For this reason "everything done by the Germans as members of the occupying authorities, except that which occurred in the normal exercise of the law," was "illegitimate."

(2) Detaining and guarding civilians on account of their race or religion, as well as ill-treating defenceless civilians "were not military operations" and could not, therefore, be justified by the "necessities of war." In virtue of Art. 43 of the Hague Regulations the occupant was, as a rule, under the obligation to respect the laws in force in occupied Holland, and this meant that it was bound to respect the Netherlands Constitution which, in its Art. 4, guarantees protection to persons and property. In virtue of Art. 23 (*h*) of the Hague Regulations, the occupant was not entitled to suspend the right of the Netherlands population to such protection.

(3) The acts committed were contrary to the laws of humanity, as the latter imposed the duty to "grant aid and protection to the defenceless and needy," whereas the accused's conduct could not be reconciled with this principle.

The Court of Cassation dissented from the first Court's opinion that all acts committed by the Germans against the Netherlands civilian population were criminal because of the war of aggression launched and waged by Germany against Holland. It agreed that the said war was an international crime, and added that on account of this fact the Netherlands "would have been authorised to answer" the aggression "with reprisals, even with regard to the normal operation of the laws of war on land, sea and in the air." However, said the Court, "it is going too far to regard as war crimes all acts committed against the Netherlands or Netherlanders by the German forces and other organs during the war, solely on the grounds of the illegal nature of the war launched by the then German Reich." Such acts might be criminal even if the war itself were lawful.

The Court of Cassation dissented also from the reasons given by the first Court under (2) above, and in this connection came to the following conclusions:

The first Court's opinion that the acts committed were criminal because they did not form part of military operations and were thus not justified by the necessities of war, was based upon the erroneous view that the substance of the laws of war was to permit certain acts, whereas it was the opposite which was true: they prohibit certain acts. For this reason the question as to whether or not an act constituted a "military operation" was not decisive for determining whether it represented a war crime or a crime against humanity. This was to be established as an issue in itself in the sense of Art. 6 (*b*) and (*c*) of the Nuremberg Charter.

It was also "not reasonable" to make reference to Art. 43 of the Hague Regulations, in conjunction with the Netherlands Constitution. The Court did not elaborate on this point, but presumably meant that the criminal nature of the acts concerned did not depend on whether they were committed in violation of municipal law, either altered or suspended or not, but on whether they were contrary to the laws and customs of war taken in themselves. On the other hand, the Court explicitly dismissed the argument based on Art. 23 (*h*) of the Hague Regulations, on the grounds that it was meant only to protect rights at civil law and therefore did not apply in this case.

Finally, the Court of Cassation also disagreed with the reason given under (3) above. An act was not a war crime or a crime against humanity because it violated the "moral rule that the defenceless and needy may claim protection and help." It was so on account of its unlawful nature under the laws and customs of war as expressed in Art. 6 (*b*) and (*c*) of the Nuremberg Charter.

Subject to these particular differences of opinion the Court of Cassation agreed with the first Court's findings that the acts tried constituted war crimes and/or crimes against humanity and were punishable under the provisions of the Netherlands law applied by the first Court.

II. Illegal Detention a Crime Against Humanity

The findings of both Courts show that they had found the accused guilty of complicity in illegal detentions, in so far as this applied to prisoners of the Jewish race.

The relevant passages of the first Court's findings were in the following terms:

> "The Court has been convinced and considers legally proved that the accused . . . contrary to the laws and customs of war, . . . :
>
> 1. Co-operated in the German policy of humiliation and persecution of the Jews . . . by:
>
> (*a*) Intentionally assisting in the illegal detention of a number of persons of the Jewish race in that he intentionally kept them illegally confined in the said prisons and guarded them . . ."

The Court of Cassation specified that this fell under the notion of "other inhumane acts committed against any civilian population" before or during the war, as prescribed in the definition of crimes against humanity in Art. 6 (*c*) of the Nuremberg Charter, and as applicable in Netherlands law according to Art. 27 (A) of the Netherlands Extraordinary Penal Law Decree of 22nd December, 1945.

It thus appears that, in this trial, illegal detention was treated as an "inhumane act" on the grounds that it constituted at the same time a case of persecutions on racial or religious grounds, which in itself belongs also to the concept of crimes against humanity as defined in the said Art. 6 (*c*).

The conviction of the accused is an instance of a case in which persons whose part in illegal detentions are purely instrumental are none the less held responsible as accomplices.

III. Denial of Spiritual Assistance a Criminal Offence

When considering the charge that the accused was guilty of denying the services of a priest to prisoners condemned to death, the first Court came to the conclusion that it had "not been proved" that the accused's refusal was "contrary to the laws and customs of war or to [the laws] of humanity." The reason given by the Court was that no evidence was to hand to show that it was "the accused's duty to forward requests for spiritual assistance" to the competent authorities, nor that such requests "would not have been rejected in advance on the basis of the existing regulations."

The Court of Cassation acknowledged that it was within the first Court's powers to decide that the accused could not be held personally responsible on the above grounds, but it made it clear that, in its opinion, denial of spiritual assistance constituted a punishable offence. Its views were expressed in the following terms:

> This Court . . . is of the opinion that the refusal to allow spiritual assistance to someone under sentence of death does . . . in itself definitely constitute a crime, both a war crime and a crime against humanity. However, in the present case the Special Court has passed judgment on grounds which are of a *de facto* nature and for which therefore it remains responsible, that in the given circumstances it was not appellant Zuehlke's duty to further requests for spiritual assistance.

IV. Plea of Superior Orders in Netherlands Law

Unlike the course taken by most countries affected by war crimes during the war 1939–1945, in Netherlands metropolitan special war crimes legislation no specific provision was inserted as to the effect of the plea of superior orders on the personal penal liability of the actual perpetrator of a war crime. The Netherlands common penal law contains a general provision,—Art. 43 of the Penal Code—according to which a subordinate is, in principle, not punishable if the offence was committed in execution of an "official order given him by the competent authority." He is, however, liable to punishment if the official order was given "without competence." But even then, his liability is removed if he had considered "in all good faith" that the order was given "competently," and if his obedience to the order was "within his province as a subordinate."

As reported elsewhere, when the enactment of metropolitan Netherlands war crimes laws was under study, the Special Court of Cassation recommended the adoption of the rule contained in Art. 8 of the Nuremberg Charter. This provided the following:

> The fact that the defendant acted pursuant to order of his Government or of a superior shall not free him from responsibility, but may be considered in mitigation of punishment if the Tribunal determines that justice so requires.

The starting point of the above rule was thus the opposite of the principle expressed in Art. 43 of the Netherlands Penal Code: according to it the subordinate is penally responsible in spite of the orders, and may obtain only mitigation of the punishment according to the merits of the case. Under Art. 43 the subordinate is, on the contrary, not penally responsible, and may be held guilty only in exceptional cases.

When the provisions relating to war crimes were enacted, the above recommendation was not followed up and the rule of Art. 8 of the Nuremberg Charter was not adopted. This made it uncertain as to what was the position created in Dutch municipal law in regard to war crimes committed upon superior orders. There were, among others, two possible interpretations. The omission of a rule similar to that of Art. 8 of the Nuremberg Charter, could have meant that the rule of Art. 43 of the Penal Code was applicable to war crimes in addition to common law offences and, as a rule, had the effect of relieving from penal responsibility the perpetrator acting pursuant to superior orders. Another possible interpretation was that, in the specific instance of war crimes, the rule of Art. 43 was elastic enough to achieve the same ends as those secured under the Nuremberg Charter. Art. 43 made the subordinate punishable if the orders were issued "without competence" and if the subordinate could not be regarded as having followed the orders "in all good faith" as to their "competency." This made it possible to hold the view that no authority or superior was competent to issue criminal orders, and that consequently every such order was given "without competence."

The Zuehlke trial furnished an occasion to Netherlands Courts, including the Court of Cassation, to make known their views on the subject. They ultimately offered a third solution, according to which neither Art. 8 of the Nuremberg Charter nor Art. 43 of the Netherlands Penal Code were binding upon them, but the issue is treated with regard to certain minimum standards of justice which bring about results similar to those expressed in the Charter.

The first Court expressed the opinion that Art. 8 of the Nuremberg Charter, invoked by the prosecution, was not applicable because it did not, as the Court saw it, express a general rule of International Law and could not therefore be implemented as such by Netherlands Courts. The Court's view was that it constituted a special rule limited to the case of the major war criminals with whom the Charter was solely concerned, and consequently did not apply in the case of other, "minor" war criminals, such as the ones tried by Netherlands and other national courts. In this connection the Court took the view that the "exonerating effect" of a superior order was still valid in the sphere of "minor" war criminals and that therefore the accused had a formal legal basis to plead on those grounds. The Court expressed its opinion in the following terms:

> The accused has pleaded that official orders were given him by his superiors.
>
> The chief Prosecutor does not consider this plea to be admissible, himself referring to Art. 8 of the Charter whereby an official order was declared to be non-exculpatory.
>
> This provision, however, . . . has no direct application in the present case, but could apply indirectly if it were to be regarded as a rule concerning a special instance of an express general rule of international criminal law.
>
> It is the opinion of the Court that this is not so, and it cannot be understood why the exonerating effect of an official order, which is recognised in one form or another in practically all national legislations, should not be valid in the sphere of international criminal law.
>
> It must be assumed that its operation has been excluded with regard to the 'major' criminals, because they were considered *a priori* to have wanted to take part in the criminal system of Germany and were, therefore, made individually responsible for the crimes they committed in this system.
>
> Consequently the accused has grounds for his plea.

While recognising in this fashion and for the above reasons the accused's right to plead not guilty on the grounds of superior orders, the first Court came to the conclusion that, in his case, the plea could not exonerate him from the charges. It based its findings in this respect on the opinion that subordinates were under the obligation not to carry out orders relating to "actions forbidden by international law," and that ignorance of the relevant rules did not "carry with it exclusion from penal liability" of the subordinates. The Court was also of the opinion that custody of persons detained on account of their race or religion, as well as ill-treatment of prisoners, did not belong to the "sphere of military subordination"; that the accused must have had "knowledge" of this; and that he was answerable also under German law, according to which subordinates who knew of the criminal nature of the acts ordered remain penally responsible. These views were expressed in the following terms:

> The Court rejects this plea. Indeed . . . there was no need for him [the accused] in the given circumstances to carry out such orders.
>
> An order to commit actions forbidden by international law may not be carried out, and a mistaken idea as to the validity or existence of such prohibitive provisions does not carry with it exclusion from penal liability.
>
> The detention in prison of persons who were incarcerated on the grounds of their origin, or the ill-treatment and humiliation of prisoners, does not belong to the sphere of military subordination.
>
> The accused, who was not only a prison warder by occupation but had also been trained as a non-commissioned officer, must have known this.

> The accused is also punishable according to provisions in force in Germany, which provide that in spite of an official order a subordinate remains criminally responsible if he knows that the order in question aims at the commission of a punishable act.

The Special Court took much the same course, but furnished a more elaborate legal basis for its findings. It discarded Art. 8 of the Nuremberg Charter for the same reason as the first Court, and also Art. 43 of the Netherlands Penal Code. It laid great stress on the relevance of the German law in the accused's specific case, by taking the view that the responsibility of the accused could best be judged in the light of the latter's hierarchical position under the law of his own country. It was held that this was permissible on condition that the German law in this field met the minimum requirements of justice as recognised by civilised nations, and it was found that this was the case with the German rules concerned. It is on this basis that the Court of Cassation reached the same conclusions as the first Court as to the accused's guilt. Its opinion was expressed in the following terms:

> According to Netherlands law the accused has the right to invoke the plea of official orders as a basis for exoneration from penal liability.
>
> This right could be limited or excluded only by the presence of a higher rule of law, and in the absence of a rule of international customary law in force during the Second World War, alone Art. 8 of the [Nuremberg] Charter can be taken into consideration in this case.
>
> This Article, however, does not contain anything before which the Netherlands law . . . should give way.
>
> As appears from the context of the text [of Art. 8] it relates only to the major war criminals for the trial of whom the International Military Tribunal [at Nuremberg] had been set up, and not to the other war criminals, such as is the appellant himself.
>
> The said Art. 8 is also not the expression of a principle of international law of wide purport, to be applied to all war criminals without exception.
>
> All the same, as the Special Court [in the first instance] rightly observes, this provision finds its justification in the exceptional case of the major war criminals within the scope of the German criminal policy.
>
> The judge is therefore called upon to test appellant Zuehlke's plea of official orders under the written and unwritten Netherlands law in force, according to which the trial of the so-called 'localised' crimes committed by 'minor' war criminals takes place pursuant to the Moscow Declaration of 30th October, 1943.
>
> Art. 43 of the [Netherlands] Penal Code, which is also applicable to military men, does not come into consideration for direct application.
>
> The judgment of this Court is indeed . . . that an appeal to the above Article is justified only if the authority of the superior giving the order to the subordinate obeying it is based upon Netherlands law or an international rule of law binding upon Netherlands law.
>
> With the reserve mentioned below, this Court gives its preference to a test under the German law, rather than by an analogous application of Art. 43 of the Penal Code.
>
> Indeed reason requires that penal consequences of hierarchical subordination be judged according to the official framework within which the accused was placed, provided that his national law answers at least the minimum requirements which can be expected of a civilised nation.

International law, upon which the trial of war criminals eventually rests, does not permit account to be taken if the accused's national law is below this standard.

The German law in force during the Second World War did, however, satisfy on this point the minimum requirements.

Art. 47 of the 'Militärstrafgesetzbuch' [German Military Penal Code] of 1872, which was promulgated again—and on this point remained unaltered—by a Decree of the 'Ministerrat für die Reichsverteidigung' [German Ministerial Council for the Defence of the Reich] of 10th October, 1940, . . . reads as follows:

1. If a penal provision is violated in the execution of an official order, the superior giving the order is alone responsible. Nevertheless the subordinate who obeys is liable to punishment as an accomplice:

(1) If he has exceeded the given order;

(2) If he knew that the superior's order concerned an act aimed at the commission of a common or a military crime or offence.

2. If the guilt is small on the part of the subordinate, his punishment can be dispensed with.

From this it follows that an order given in the circumstances described in para. 1 under (2) above, does not exclude the unlawfulness of the subordinate's action.

The Court then made reference to authoritative German writers and to judgments rendered by German courts, which both concurred with the Court's conclusion. The Court ended its findings by considering the accused's position in the light of the extent to which he was compelled to act under superior orders, that is with regard to the presence or absence of duress:

If during the Second World War the doctrine "Befehl ist Befehl" (orders are orders) was sometimes carried out by the German forces to the extreme of its logical consequences for obviously criminal purposes, no longer compatible with the human dignity of the subordinates, there was no legal basis to do so, and an appeal to duress on the part of the subordinate concerned can at the most be admitted if actual requirements concerning such duress were present.

The appellant Zuehlke's plea of duress . . . is rejected on the sufficient grounds that it does not appear that any pressure was brought to bear upon him.

When applying the German law the judge enjoys sufficient discretion to measure the extent of independence left in the face of superior orders according to the importance of the position held by the subordinate concerned.

With his rank of non-commissioned officer and his position of prison guard only a slight degree of freedom of action can be ascribed to appellant.

Within this framework some of the grounds on which the Special Court [in the first instance] rejected the appellant's plea of superior orders remain in any case in force.

Therefore the Special Court has correctly decided that, as the acts with which appellant was charged and which were declared proved, were punishable, so was the appellant himself as their perpetrator punishable, since no grounds for exoneration from punishment have appeared with regard to him.

Apart from the manner in which the plea of superior orders was treated and applied in this trial, the main point of interest from the viewpoint of international law is the attitude taken towards the validity of the principle expressed in Art. 8 of the Nuremberg Charter.

This attitude was that the latter could not be regarded, at least for the time being, as a general rule of international law. This would seem to conflict with the development which took place on the occasion of and after the Second World War, and which was apparent at the time of the trial under review. The position is that, in addition to the Nuremberg Charter, other authoritative documents on the present state of international law, as well as rules of a representative number of nations, have followed the lines of the above Art. 8. Such was the case with the Far Eastern Charter, enacted for the trial of the Japanese major war criminals, and with Law No. 10 of the Allied Control Council for Germany which applies to all categories of war criminals other than those belonging to the class of "major" criminals. Such is also the case with the municipal laws or military manuals issued for the guidance of military personnel of Great Britain, United States, France, China, Canada, Norway, Czechoslovakia, Poland, and even the Netherlands East Indies. This development is evidence that, in the present stage of the advancement of international law as generally understood and as applied by individual nations, the above principle concerning the effect of superior orders upon penal liability for war crimes represents the wider consensus of opinion.

The trial under review illustrates that the differences existing between the principles expressed respectively in Art. 43 of the Netherlands Penal Code and Art. 8 of the Nuremberg Charter, are more of a theoretical than of a practical nature. The former is based upon the principle that, *as a rule,* the subordinate is not guilty when acting upon superior orders he is pledged to obey. The latter is based upon the opposite principle that, again *as a rule,* superior orders do not relieve the subordinate from penal liability and that consequently he is, *as a rule,* liable to punishment as if he had acted without orders. Both, however, operate with exceptions which, in the instance of the Netherlands Penal Code and the German Military Penal Code, bring about practical results similar to those contained in the principle of the Nuremberg Charter. Conversely, the latter makes possible mitigation of punishment which may and in practice do result in freeing the accused from penal responsibility. Whatever the principle chosen as a starting point, the outcome is that cases are tried according to their merits and that justice is done with similar results under either of them.

TRIAL OF GENERALOBERST NICKOLAUS VON FALKENHORST

Brunswick, Germany, July, 1946*

OUTLINE OF THE PROCEEDINGS

THE DEFENDANT, Nickolaus von Falkenhorst, a German national and former Generaloberst in the German army, was tried at Brunswick before a British Military Court sitting with a Judge Advocate. The defendant was charged with nine charges pursuant to Regulation 4 of the Regulations attached to the Royal Warrant for the trial of War Criminals, dated 6th June, 1945. The charges covered the period from October, 1942, to July, 1944, and were as follows:

1ST CHARGE

Committing a war crime in that he at Oslo, in the Kingdom of Norway, when as Commander-in-Chief of the Armed Forces, Norway (Wehrmachtbefehlshaber Norwegen), in an order dated on or about 26th October, 1942, in violation of the laws and usages of war, incited members of the forces under his command not to accept quarter or to give quarter to Allied soldiers, sailors and airmen, taking part in Commando Operations, and, further, in the event of any Allied soldier, sailor or airman taking part in such Commando Operations being captured, to kill them after capture.

2ND CHARGE

Committing a war crime in that he in the Kingdom of Norway, in or about the month of October, 1942, in violation of the laws and usages of war, was responsible as Commander-in-Chief of the Armed Forces, Norway (Wehrmachtbefehlshaber Norwegen), for the handing over by forces under his command to the Sicherheitsdienst (Security Service) of two British Officers and six British Other Ranks, Prisoners of War, who had taken part in Commando Operations, with the result that the said Prisoners were killed.

**Law Reports of Trials of War Criminals,* Vol. 11, p. 18 (London, 1947).

3rd Charge

Committing a War Crime in that in the Kingdom of Norway, in or about the month of November, 1942, in violation of the laws and usages of war, when as Commander-in-Chief of the Armed Forces, Norway (Wehrmachtbefehlshaber Norwegen), was concerned in the killing of fourteen British Prisoners of War.

4th Charge

Committing a War Crime in that he in the Kingdom of Norway, in or about the month of November, 1942, in violation of the laws and usages of war, was responsible as Commander-in-Chief of the Armed Forces, Norway (Wehrmachtbefehlshaber Norwegen), for the handing over by forces under his command to the Sicherheitsdienst (Security Service) of nine British Prisoners of War who had taken part in Commando Operations, with the result that the said Prisoners were killed.

5th Charge

Committing a War Crime in that he in the Kingdom of Norway, in or about the month of January, 1943, in violation of the laws and usages of war, was responsible as Commander-in-Chief of the Armed Forces, Norway (Wehrmachtbefehlshaber Norwegen), for the handing over by forces under his command, to the Sicherheitsdienst (Security Service) of Seaman Robert Evans, a British Prisoner of War who had taken part in Commando Operations with the result that the said Seaman Robert Evans was killed.

6th Charge

Committing a War Crime in that he in the Kingdom of Norway, in or about the month of May, 1943, in violation of the laws and usages of war, was responsible as Commander-in-Chief of the Armed Forces, Norway (Wehrmachtbefehlshaber Norwegen), for the handing over by forces under his command to the Sicherheitsdienst (Security Service) of one officer, one Non-Commissioned Officer and five Naval Ratings, British Prisoners of War, who had taken part in Commando Operations, with the result that the said Prisoners were killed.

7th Charge

Committing a War Crime in that he at Oslo, in the Kingdom of Norway, when as Commander-in-Chief of the Armed Forces of Norway (Wehrmachtbefehlshaber Norwegen), in an order dated 15th June, 1943, in violation of the laws and usages of war, incited members of the forces under his command not to accept quarter or to give quarter to Allied soldiers, sailors and airmen taking part in Commando Operations, and, further, in the event of any Allied soldier, sailor or airman taking part in such Commando Operations being captured, to kill them after capture.

8th Charge

Committing a War Crime in that he in the Kingdom of Norway, in or about the month of July, 1943, in violation of the laws and usages of war, was responsible as Commander-in-Chief of the Armed Forces, Norway (Wehrmachtbefehlshaber Norwegen), for the handing over by forces under his command to the Sicherheitsdienst (Security Service) of one Norwegian Naval Officer, five Norwegian Naval Ratings, and one Royal Navy Rating, Prisoners of War, with the result that the said Prisoners were killed.

9th Charge

Committing a War Crime in that he at Oslo, in the Kingdom of Norway, when as Commander-in-Chief of the Armed Forces, Norway (Wehrmachtbefehlshaber Norwegen), in a document dated 19th July, 1944 in violation of the laws and usages of war, ordered troops under his command to deprive certain Allied Prisoners of War of their rights as Prisoners of War, under the Geneva Convention.

To each of the nine charges the defendant pleaded Not Guilty.

In his opening speech, the Prosecuting Officer claimed that during the relevant period covered by the nine charges, the defendant was the Commander-in-Chief (Wehrmachtbefehlshaber) of the German Armed Forces in Norway, which included the Army, Navy and the Air Force. In this capacity the defendant was directly responsible to the OKW (the Supreme Headquarters of the German Armed Forces) in Berlin.

The facts were that during 1941 and 1942, the Allied Forces made a series of raids on Norwegian shipping and vital installations in the territory of Norway which were known as "Commando Raids." These raids had a certain damaging effect upon the German war effort and to discourage such raids in the future, Hitler himself issued an order dated 18th December, 1942, referred to in this report as the "Commando Order." This order was received by the defendant, who passed it on to the subordinate military units under his command and also distributed it to the naval and air force commanders in Norway in the latter part of October, 1942. A photostat of the original Commando Order was exhibited in the case, and its contents have been set out here as an authentic version of this well-known order:

Paragraph 1

"For some time our enemies have been using in their warfare, methods which are outside the international Geneva Conventions. Especially brutal and treacherous is the behaviour of the so-called Commandos who, as is established, are partially recruited even from freed criminals in enemy countries. Their capture orders divulge that they are directed not only to shackle prisoners but also to kill defenceless prisoners on the spot at the moment in which they believe that the latter, as prisoners, represent a burden in the further pursuance of their purpose or can otherwise be a hindrance. Finally, orders have been found in which the killing of prisoners has been demanded in principle.

Paragraph 2

"For this reason it was already announced in an addendum to the Armed Forces Report of 7th October, 1942, that in the future Germany in the face of these sabotage troops of the British and their accomplices will resort to the same procedure, i.e., that they will be ruthlessly mowed down by the German troops in combat wherever they may appear.

Paragraph 3

"I therefore Order, from now on all opponents brought to battle by German troops in so-called commando operations in Europe or Africa, even when it is outwardly a matter of soldiers in uniform or demolition parties with or without weapons, are to be exterminated to the last man in battle or while in flight. In these cases it is immaterial whether they are landed for their operations by ship or aeroplane or descend by parachute. Even should these individuals on their being discovered, make as if to surrender, all quarter is to be denied them on principle. A detailed report is to be sent to the O.K.W. on each separate case for publication in the Wehrmacht communique.

Paragraph 4

"If individual members of such commandos working as agents, saboteurs, etc., fall into the hands of the Wehrmacht by other means, e.g. through the police in any of the countries occupied by us, they are to be handed over to the S.D. immediately. It is strictly forbidden to hold them in military custody, e.g. in PW camps, etc., even as a temporary measure.

Paragraph 5

"This order does not apply to the treatment of any enemy soldier who in the course of normal hostilities (large scale offensive actions, landing operations and air-born operations) are captured in open battle or give themselves up. Nor does this order apply to enemy soldiers falling into our hands after battles at sea or enemy soldiers trying to save their lives by parachute after battles.

Paragraph 6

"In the case of non-execution of this order, I shall make responsible before the Court Martial all commanders and officers who have either failed to carry out their duty in instructing the troops in this order, or who acted contrary to this order in carrying it out.

Signed Adolf Hitler."

At the end of a supplementary Order issued by the Fuhrer on the same day, namely, 18th October, 1942, Hitler set out to explain to his officers why it had become necessary to issue this Commando Order and this Supplementary Order, and ended with this passage, which constituted an addition to the original order:

> If it should become necessary for reasons of interrogation to spare initially one man or two, then they are to be shot immediately after interrogation.

The prosecution submitted that paragraph 3 was illegal and that it constituted an order to deny quarter to combatant troops.

At the same time that Hitler signed this Order, he issued the supplementary order of the same date already mentioned which was addressed to Commanding Officers only, and in which he stated that the main Order was a counter measure to the partisan activities on the eastern front.

The supplementary order also stated that the system of commando operations was an illegal method of warfare in that if commandos were caught in their operation they immediately surrendered, thereby preserving their lives, and if not so caught, they escaped to neutral countries. The importance of the last paragraph of the supplementary order (quoted above) was stressed by the prosecutor.

The defendant received the Commando Order and the Supplementary Order on or about 24th October, 1942, whereupon he re-issued the order himself. No copy of the actual document so issued by the defendant was available at the trial. The re-issuing of the Commando Order formed the subject matter of the first charge against the defendant.

In the document dated 15th June, 1943, the defendant issued a second document addressed to officers only in which he referred to the original Commando Order of 18th October, 1942, in these terms:

> Saboteurs. . . . I am under the impression that the wording of the above order (the Commando Order) which had to be destroyed, is no longer clearly in mind, and I therefore again bring to particular notice paragraph 3 (above quoted).

In a later passage in the same document appeared the words: "A further order of the Wehrmacht Commander, Norway, Top Secret, of 26.10.42, since destroyed, lays down: 'If a man is saved for interrogation he must not survive his comrades for more than 24 hours.' " The issuing of that document by the defendant was relied upon by the Prosecution to substantiate the 7th charge.

The intervening charges, 2–6 inclusive, and charge No. 8, all dealt with specific instances in which British or Norwegian prisoners of war were killed by German troops in Norway or were handed over to the S.D., with the result that they were killed by that agency. In each case the captured commandos were wearing uniform, with the addition that in the case of those captured and killed as alleged in the third charge, they were wearing skiing clothes underneath their uniforms. Further, in each case the commandos were engaged on attacking targets directly connected with the German war effort.

The 9th charge was in respect of a document which the defendant had issued in July, 1944, and was of a different nature from the Commando Order, being an order whereby certain prisoners of war, e.g. Jews, were not to be held in prisoner of war camps but were to be handed over to the S.D.

The evidence produced in support of these charges by the prosecution consisted of the oral evidence of a former German officer, Major-General von Behrens, who served under the defendant at the relevant time and in whose area of command those victims were killed whose death formed the subject matter of the 3rd charge. There was also the oral evidence of Colonel Scotland, who gave formal evidence as to the statements of the defendant made prior to trial, and expert evidence as to the position of the defendant when Wehrmachtbefehlshaber in Norway. The witness giving this last-mentioned testimony stated, *inter alia,* the following:

> His (the defendant's) duties would be to act as the representative of the O.K.W. to pass on any orders which were issued to him by the O.K.W. and these orders through him would reach all branches of the armed forces in Germany. It was in evidence that the Fuhrer's Commando Order had been received by the defendant from the O.K.W.

On this point the witness was asked the following question and gave the answer stated:

> Q. You know the Fuhrerbefehl which is addressed to Norway. Would it be the duty of the Wehrmachtbefehlshaber to forward that on to everybody, whether of the army, navy or the air force: A. Yes, such an order, coming from the highest authority, his would be the only final channel through which it could reach the armed forces in Norway.

The remaining evidence for the prosecution consisted of documentary evidence in the form of affidavits put in under Regulation 8 (i) (*a*) of the Royal Warrant, most of which dealt with the fate of allied service personnel who were captured on Commando raids and were either shot by the armed forces or handed over to the S.D. and shot by that agency at a later stage.

Although the prosecution did not suggest that any of the victims in the various charges met their death as a result of his direct order, they contended that the evidence showed that the death of the victims or their being handed over to the S.D. and subsequent death was the result of the defendant's re-issuing the Commando Order in October, 1942, and republishing it in 1943, with the amendment to the original order providing that those spared for interrogation should be liquidated within 24 hours.

The prosecution withdrew the fifth charge relating to the victim Seaman Robert Evans in the course of the trial, apparently on the ground that at no time was this prisoner of war in the custody of the German armed forces, but was an S.D. prisoner from the beginning.

The accused was acquitted on charge No. 2, apparently on the ground that the execution of the victims named in that charge was carried out in Germany by the S.D., and also that they were in Wehrmacht custody as long as they were within the defendant's command in Norway.

On all other charges the defendant was found guilty, and sentenced to death. His sentence was, however, commuted to one of life imprisonment.

Notes on the Case

I. The Structure of the Charge Sheet

It will be observed that the nine charges resolve themselves into three groups: (1) charges dealing with the issuing of an illegal order, that is the Commando Order of 1942, its republication in 1943, (2) the charge of issuing the so-called Prisoner of War Order in 1944, (3) the charges claiming that the defendant was concerned in the killing or in the handing over to the S.D. by forces under his command of allied prisoners of war. The defence of the German advocate on this form of the charge sheet is not without interest. He pointed out that the defendant was being accused both of issuing an illegal order, and of being responsible for events that occurred as a direct consequence of his issuing that order. That, he contended, was improper and it was analogous to accusing the defendant in the same charge sheet with incitement to murder, and also with the actual murder that took place as a result of his incitement, and he added that such a charge could not be laid by German law. To this it must be said that the law governing this trial was not German law, but that contained in the Royal Warrant, namely, the laws and usages of war and the Army Act and Rules of Procedure thereto. The point that the Defence was making may be looked upon from one angle as substantive, and from another as procedural. It seems to have been decided that the actual issuing of an illegal order by a responsible Commander can be a war crime in itself although no criminal acts were proved to have arisen as a result of that issuing. The procedural point seems to be that a charge sheet should not charge a defendant with the same thing twice, called by a different name or arising from a different grouping of the same facts. The defence advocate did not elaborate this argument, but it would seem that he was trying to suggest that the method whereby the defendant was accused of being "responsible for the killing" or "concerned in the killing" or "concerned in the handing over to the S.D." was the defendant's issuing of the very orders which form the subject of charges 1 and 8 respectively, so that in effect the defence said that the defendant was being charged with the same set of acts twice over. In any event this argument was not accepted by the court and must be treated as having been decided against the defendant.

II. The Defence of Superior Orders

This aspect of the case can conveniently be considered under four headings: (*a*) Superior orders as a defence to the charge, (*b*) Superior orders purported to be reprisals as a defence to the charges, (*c*) Duress as a defence, and (*d*) Superior orders as a ground for mitigation of sentence after the finding of guilty.

With respect to the defence of duress, this has rarely been pleaded in war crimes trials and indeed was not in this case now under review.

The circumstances in which duress may be pleaded as a defence to a crime by English law is stated in Kenny's *Outlines of Criminal Law,* 15th Edition, page 84, in these terms:

> Duress *per minas* is a very rare defence; so rare that Sir James Stephen, in his long forensic experience, never saw a case in which it was raised. . . . It is, however, clear that threats of the immediate infliction of death, or even of grievous bodily harm, will excuse some crimes that have been committed under the influence of such threats. . . . It certainly will not excuse murder.

Now it is appreciated that in a case such as this, where the order in question emanated from the Fuhrer, who, if he was not always a supreme legal authority in the Reich always represented the supreme physical power, that this may be looked at as a very severe threat, particularly when one studies the last paragraph of the Fuhrer Order of 18th October, 1942, wherein it is stated that officers failing to comply with the order expose themselves to court-martial. Nevertheless, it would appear on the facts that no threat of the immediate infliction of death or even of grievous bodily harm would have been presented to the defendant in this case. No case is yet known in which the plea of duress has been successfully raised as a complete defence to a charge of committing a war crime, although instances have been proved in the course of trials where, in concentration camps, one prisoner has been forced at the point of a pistol of an SS man to commit an atrocity on another prisoner. Such a grouping of facts is very remote from the circumstances of a German Commander-in-Chief such as the present defendant.

With regard to the defence of superior orders alone, this was urged by the defence and it was dealt with by the Judge Advocate in his summing up to the court. He quoted the passage from the British *Manual of Military Law* which has so often been cited in British war crime trials, and which is based on a well-known passage in Oppenheim's *International Law,* Volume II, 6th Edition, pages 452–3. The court in this case decided that this defence was not open to the defendant and they may have arrived at this decision on either of two grounds, as follows:

(*a*) that they were not satisfied that the defendants did not willingly participate in carrying out the Fuhrer's order relating to commandos;
(*b*) that as a matter of law the rule of warfare that was violated by the Fuhrer's order is an unchallenged rule of warfare and that the acts of the defendant violated such a rule of warfare and at the same time outraged the general sentiments of humanity.

The question arises whether it should be shown by the prosecution as a matter of proof that the defendant knew that in passing on the Fuhrer's order he was violating an unchallenged rule of warfare and outraging the general sentiments of humanity, or whether it is the case of ignorance of law being no excuse, and provided the defendant passed on the order with full knowledge of the consequences that would ensue if his order were obeyed, then his knowledge of the legal nature of his acts did not enter into the problem. This amounts to whether the standard laid down in Oppenheim's text book is an objective standard or a subjective standard. In all these points the present case must be taken to have been decided against the defendant, although it is not clear on which ground the court placed emphasis in arriving at its decision since in a military court the Judge Advocate merely proffers advice on points of law to the court and does not give a direction in the way that a Judge does to a jury.

Superior orders becomes a more complicated matter when it is joined with the defence that the superior order relied on purported or was thought by the defendant to have been a measure of reprisal by his own government against the enemy (see Professor Lauterpacht's Article in *British Yearbook of International Law,* 1944). The defendant in this case, through his counsel, appears to have taken the line in defence that on questions of reprisal he, a soldier, was entitled to assume that the appropriate legal considerations had been entered into by his own government, before they launched the order as a reprisal order which he, as a Commander-in-Chief, was being required to carry out. Before this point can be taken to arise, unless a clean case of reprisal has already been made out, it is thought that the defendant must first show that he had valid reason for believing as a matter of fact that the order he was asked to carry out was intended as a reprisal order and if the court is not satisfied on that initial point, which is a question of the court believing the defence or not, then the legal problems do not really arise. Should a defendant establish, as a matter of fact believed by the court, that he really thought that the order of his government was meant to be a reprisal, then the question arises whether, if his government exercised the right of reprisal on inadequate grounds or in bad faith, then to what extent is the defendant exonerated in carrying out such an order if there is no proof that the defendant knew of the inadequate grounds or the bad faith that purported to give rise to the reprisal by his government.

The question whether such a matter should be dealt with on the actual facts or according to the belief of the accused then becomes very important to the defendant. Whereas a matter of military knowledge a senior soldier such as the defendant would be deemed to know the outstanding rules of warfare after some 20 years of senior service, and also as a human being to have knowledge of the accepted standards of humanity, it does not necessarily follow that he would know the exact circumstances in which a right to reprisal may be exercised which is not only a controversial matter among lawyers, in legal text books and other publications, but is a very difficult matter to determine in any specific case of reprisals. Possibly the defendant might be expected to know that great care must be exercised before reprisals are launched, but to that he might well say that those at the source from which this order emanated would have the best legal advice that can be obtained and that, as a military commander in a war, he could not be expected to have to go into such questions.

It would seem that in this case as in others, the defence of superior orders, raised with the question of reprisal, has not been strongly stressed by the defence. It is true that Dr. Müller, the defending counsel in this case, said in his closing address: "In fact, General von Falkenhorst at that time took this measure as a reprisal. . . . I should like to point out that in the beginning it seemed to him as to other officers, to be a measure of reprisal as had been stated by the Fuhrer himself, and, of course he, the accused, was not in the position to verify whether these facts, which have been portended (*sic*) by the Fuhrer were right or not. Whether they were founded or not, he must take them as such as he had got them from the headquarters at Berlin."

In the summing up of the Judge Advocate, no reference can be found to this point, which is only mentioned, as it were, in passing, by the defence, and it may well be that there were no facts upon which the court could find that the defendant really believed that the Fuhrer Order purported to be a reprisal order, notwithstanding the fact that in the preface to the Order itself it stated, though not in specific terms, that it is a reprisal order, and Hitler and Keitel issued it in that form. As is stated above, once it is rejected as a matter of fact that the defence believed it was a reprisal order, then other more controversial matters do not arise. Possibly there is no more difficult subject in the ambit of the law relating to war crimes than a correct application of the principles in a case where reprisal and superior orders are raised by the defence in respect of one and the same order which the defendant is alleged to have carried out. The whole basis of the wrongfulness of disobeying an unlawful order may fall to the ground because a reprisal is defined as "where one belligerent retaliates upon another by means of otherwise than legitimate acts of warfare in order to compel him and his subjects and members of his forces to abandon illegitimate acts of warfare and to comply in future with the rules of legitimate warfare." (Oppenheim, 6th Edition, Revised, page 446.)

Perhaps it is for this very reason that the laws of war demand that there must be a concurrence of a considerable number of factors before an occasion to exercise the right or reprisal arises. Finally, Article 2 of the Geneva Convention of 1929 forbids measures of reprisal being taken against prisoners of war.

III. Commando Operations and Saboteurs

The defence also relied upon the peculiar nature of commando operations and endeavoured to suggest that they really partook of the nature of sabotage, and therefore might be considered as a form of war treason and here the question of uniform worn by people participating in commando operations becomes, it is submitted, of the greatest importance.

It is thought that an examination of the law relating to war treason will show the acts which were carried out during the war as in this case, under the name of "commando operations" would probably constitute war treason if the members of the forces of the belligerent who carried them out operated in disguise or civilian clothes. Oppenheim states in Volume II of his *International Law,* 6th Edition, on pages 454–5:

> War treason consists of such acts (except hostilities in arms on the part of the civilian population, spreading sedition propaganda by aircraft and espionage) committed within the lines of a belligerent as are harmful to him and are intended to favour the enemy. . . . Enemy soldiers—in contradistinction to private enemy individuals—may only be punished for war treason when they have committed the act of treason during their stay within the belligerent's lines under disguise. If, for instance, two soldiers in uniform are sent to the rear of the enemy to destroy a bridge they may not, when caught, be punished for war treason because their act was one of legitimate warfare. But if they exchange their uniforms for plain clothes and thereby appear to be members of the peaceful private population, they may be punished for war treason.

It is suggested that this is the very example that most nearly covers the type of activity committed by the commando troops of the allies during the recent war, as is evidenced in the case now being reviewed.

It will be observed that the question of what is the objective is, for the purpose of the law regarding war treason, not the point, but the question of whether it is committed by members of the armed forces and whether they committed it in uniform. Further, that it is not properly a matter of war crime but of war treason, which nevertheless means that the perpetrators may be tried and punished in the same way as war criminals.

Dr. Müller endeavoured to say that sabotage activity was a development of modern warfare not contemplated by the Hague Regulations of 1907. But the law relating to war treason existed indeed before those regulations, of which one of the most notable cases occurred in 1904, during the Russo-Japanese war, when two Japanese were caught trying to destroy a railway bridge by explosives in Manchuria in the rear of the Russian forces and while they were disguised in Chinese clothes. For this they were tried, sentenced and shot.

It would also seem that the legal advisers of the Fuhrer in the O.K.W. had provided two items of the Fuhrer Order which put it clearly in the category of an illegal order even if it were meant to be an order combatting acts of war treason.

The first provision was that there should be no military courts, for even a war traitor is entitled to a trial, and the second provision was that a commando order was to apply to troops engaged on commando operations whether in uniform or not and therein lay the clear criminality of the order, apparent to every officer who had a working knowledge of the rules of war.

It is not possible to say that troops who engage in acts of sabotage behind the enemy lines are bandits, as Hitler declared them. They carry out a legitimate act of war, provided the objective relates directly to the war effort and provided they carry it out in uniform. The only difficulty in this case on this point lies, in fact, in respect of some of the commando operations which were the subject matter of the charges; the commando troops may have been wearing uniform with skiing clothes underneath, the intention being that they would carry out the sabotage operation in uniform and then proceed to the Swedish boundary in skiing clothes as civilians. It is not necessary to decide this point for the purpose of this case, because the evidence shows that they were captured in uniform, whether or not they were wearing skiing clothes underneath, and were treated as service personnel by the people who captured them. An interesting point would arise if the commando troops, after having destroyed the installations while they were in uniform, had then discarded their uniform and were then in process of flight as civilians when they were caught by the enemy agencies. Should they then be tried as war traitors, or possibly as spies on the ground that they are clandestinely (as civilians) seeking to obtain information concerning the belligerent in the zone of belligerent operations with the intention of communicating it to the other belligerent? That would be a question of fact and if it were proved that the defendants were merely fleeing to a neutral country from the scene of their devastation, espionage would not be in point. Strictly, it would seem that if so caught, as mentioned above, they should be apprehended and upon them satisfying the authorities that they were members of the armed forces who had carried out the sabotage they should be placed in a prisoner of war camp and treated rather as troops of a belligerent army who are fleeing from the scene of operations in disguise. It is not thought that this point has ever been determined in any war crime trial to date.

IV. The Issuing of an Illegal Order with No Proof of Compliance

What is the position where, as in the 9th charge in this case, the accused has been charged with issuing an illegal order, and it is proved either that it was never carried out or that it was impossible to carry it out? This seems to be the circumstances in respect of the order dated 19th July, 1944, whereby certain classes of prisoners of war, namely Jews, were to be transferred to S.D. custody. It was proved that no allied Jewish prisoners were so transferred in

Norway, and in fact all prisoners of war, after temporary transit, were sent to Germany. There were, of course, large numbers of Russian prisoners of war in Norway, but they do not appear to have been the subject matter of this case.

A senior officer, when he issues the order, has done all he can to secure compliance, but the question of whether he, the author, faces trial as a war criminal turns on an accident of whether anybody was able to comply with his order or not. The question of the state of mind of the accused when he issued the order becomes important from the point of view of *mens rea,* because if he knew that the order could not be carried out, then no question of criminality should arise. It is only when he thought that it could be carried out but was surprised to find that it could not or was not, that criminality may occur. The fact that the accused was found guilty on the 9th charge is further evidence that it may occur.

V. The Position of the Defendant as Commander-in-Chief, Norway

This point is purely one of fact and of military knowledge, and it is not thought that for the purpose of this trial it has any legal interest. The court seems to have decided on the evidence as a matter of fact, that the position of the defendant did seem to give him the power to order all three services in Norway and it was proved that the Commando Order and its variations had been passed down by the defendant to the army, navy and air force in Norway.

VI. Denial of Quarter

It will be remembered that in the text of the Commando Order of 1942, allied commando troops were to be denied quarter in battle or in flight and this seems to be a clear and serious contravention of international law.

On the subject of quarter, it is stated on page 270 of Oppenheim's *International Law,* Vol. II, 6th Edition: "But combatants may only be killed or wounded if they are able and willing to fight and to resist capture. . . . Further such combatants as lay down their arms and surrender or do not resist . . . may neither be killed or wounded but must be given quarter. These rules are universally recognised and are expressly encouraged by Article 23 (*c*) of the Hague Regulations, although fury of battle frequently makes individual fighters forget and neglect them."

There are, indeed, certain circumstances in which quarter may be denied as for example as a reprisal for refusal of quarter by the other side. Nowhere in Hitler's explanation to the Commando Order, although he talks in terms of reprisal, does he state that the reason for the Commando Order is that allied troops have denied quarter to German troops. Therefore, it may be taken that the Commando Order was, on the face of it, clearly illegal in this point. The question of denying quarter in flight is a rather more difficult matter, as it will be remembered that the most frequent cause that was given out by the German agencies for the shooting of prisoners of war was "shot in flight" or "shot while trying to escape." That seems to be a question of fact as to whether or not any given prisoner was trying to escape and whether or not shooting was the only way in which the escape could have been prevented. Such circumstances cannot by any stretch of the imagination have been deemed to have arisen in the way in which the commandos in this case met their death.

THE TRIAL OF ALBERT KESSELRING
Venice, February–May, 1947*

OUTLINE OF THE PROCEEDINGS BEFORE A BRITISH MILITARY COURT

I. THE CHARGES

THE ACCUSED was charged with "being concerned in the killing as a reprisal of some 335 Italian nationals," in the Ardeatine Caves (first charge), and with "inciting and commanding . . . forces . . . under his command to kill Italian civilians as reprisals in consequence of which a number of Italian civilians were killed" (second charge).

II. THE EVIDENCE

(i) *Evidence on the first charge*

Most of the evidence was agreed upon by Counsel for the Defence and Counsel for the Prosecution.

The evidence on the bomb explosion in Rosella Street, on the 23rd March, 1944, and on the mass shooting in the Ardeatine Caves, on the 24th March, 1944, was substantially the same as the evidence given with regard to these events in the Mackensen trial. The accused returned from the front to his headquarters on the evening of the 23rd and the events of Rosella Street were reported to him immediately. Then two telephone conversations took place. A staff officer from Hitler's headquarters spoke to Kesselring's chief-of-staff and informed him that the Führer had ordered that as a reprisal for the bomb attack, 10 Italian hostages were to be killed for every German policeman who had died as a result of that bomb attack.

With regard to the second telephone conversation which took place between the head of the SD (Security Service) in Rome and the accused, the evidence for the Prosecution and the evidence for the Defence are at variance. The head of the SD testified that he informed the accused that he had enough persons "worthy of death" to carry out the reprisal. This, he explained, meant

**Law Reports of Trials of War Criminals,* Vol. 8, p. 9 (London, 1947).

persons under sentence of death or charged with offences for which the death penalty could be imposed. The accused maintained that he was informed by the head of the SD in the course of this telephone conversation that he had sufficient persons actually sentenced to death in the prisons of Rome. The accused then issued the following orders to General Mackensen, the commander of the 14th Army, which was one of the armies under the accused's command: "Kill 10 Italians for every German. Carry out immediately."

Later, during the night a second order from the Führer's headquarters was received at Kesselring's headquarters. It repeated the first order and added that "the execution was to be carried out by the SD." This order was passed down to 14th Army by the accused's chief-of-staff, who, also, informed the accused.

The case for the prosecution on this evidence was that the accused had ordered reprisals at the rate of ten to one, which was excessive, and that as he had passed the orders to subordinate army formations, he was responsible for the way in which they were carried out. The case for the defence was that on receiving the news of the bomb attack, the accused had ascertained that there were sufficient persons already sentenced to death to carry out the reprisal without killing innocent people.

The two main arguments of the defence were: (1) that in passing down the order received from the Führer to the 14th Army, the accused had deliberately left out the word "hostages" to avoid any persons not sentenced to death being killed. He thus carried out the orders he was given in the most humane way that was open to him. (2) That the second order charged the SD with the execution and thus freed the accused from all responsibility for carrying out the execution and that therefore after passing on the second order the accused never enquired into the manner in which it was carried out.

The Judge Advocate said: "The Field Marshal's real defence is: 'I never carried out any orders at all, all I did was to pass along the chain of communication, a message to the SD.' "

(ii) *Evidence on the second charge*

On 1st May, 1944, Field Marshal Keitel, as Commander-in-Chief of all German forces, issued an order which gave the accused, as Commander-in-Chief of all German forces in Italy, the overall command and direction in the fight against Italian partisans who had become a serious menace to the security of the German forces in that theatre. For this particular purpose all SS and police forces in Italy, as well as the fighting services, were brought under his command. On the 17th June, 1944, the accused issued an order to his troops concerning "new regulations for partisan warfare," which contained the following passage: "The fight against the partisans must be carried out with all means at our disposal and with the utmost severity. I will protect any commander who exceeds our usual restraint in the choice and severity of the means he adopts whilst fighting partisans. In this connection the old principle holds good, that a mistake in the choice of the means to achieve an objective is always better than failure to act or neglect . . . partisans must be attacked and destroyed."

On 28th June, 1944, the accused issued an appeal to the Italian population over the wireless in which he condemned the method of fighting adopted by the allies in Italy. He alleged that the allied commanders had issued a number of proclamations in which they had incited the Italian population to assail German military posts, attack sentries by stabbing them in the back and to kill as many Germans as possible. He continued: "Up to now I have proved that to me the respect of human principles is a matter of normal logic . . . However, as a responsible commander I can no longer hesitate to prevent by the most repressive means this despicable and mediaeval method of fighting. I give warning that I shall use these means forthwith. Followers of the Allies and subversive elements are warned not to continue the behaviour shown hitherto."

On 1st July, 1944, the accused issued a second order to his troops in which he pointed out that his broadcast announcement was not to be an empty threat. The order said, "where there are considerable numbers of partisan groups a proportion of the male population of the area will be arrested. In the event of acts of violence being committed these men will be shot. The population must be informed of this. Should troops, etc., be fired on from any village, the village will be burned down. Perpetrators or ringleaders will be hanged in public." The order ends with the sentence: "All counter measures must be hard but just. The dignity of the German soldier demands it."

During the months of July and August many punitive actions were carried out by the German forces in Italy, both against the partisans and against the civilian population, in the course of which over a thousand Italians, amongst them women and children, were killed. The prosecution submitted affidavit evidence of over twenty instances of indiscriminate killing of Italians by German troops during the relevant period. On the 21st August, 1944, the accused acknowledged these facts in an order to his troops in which he pointed out that "instances have occurred within the last few weeks which caused the greatest harm to the dignity and discipline of the German armed forces, and which had nothing to do with punitive measures."

On the 24th September, 1944, the accused, in another order to his troops, stated: "The Duce has furnished me with fresh instances which are revolting in the manner in which they have been carried out and are driving even the peaceful elements of the population into the enemy's camp or to the partisans."

Relying on these facts, the Prosecutor said: "the orders of 17th June and 1st July, were contrary to the laws and usages of war. The order of the 17th June was an incitement to the troops under the accused's command to commit excesses, and the prosecution obviously relies on the expression 'I will protect any commander,' etc. I say no more than that this is an *incitement,* but in the order of the 1st July the accused goes further and *orders* his troops to take reprisals and it is not until 24th September that he says 'this must stop.' That is the gravamen of this charge."

The Prosecution further maintained that these orders on the one hand and the atrocities alleged to have been committed by the German troops in Italy on the other were cause and effect and that the accused must therefore be held responsible for the actions of the troops under his command.

The case for the defence was that the orders of the 17th June and 1st July were not illegal and that they, in effect, said to the German forces, "You must be hard, you may do many severe things you must keep within the law." The defence submitted that in the first order the assurance to officers that they would be protected if they attacked partisans was necessary, as in the past commanders had been taken to account for action against partisans as politically undersirable. The re-stating of the "old principle" which for a century had appeared in most training pamphlets for the German army was appropriate in these circumstances.

With regard to the second order, the defence maintained that it outlined the taking of hostages and the infliction of reprisals both of which were legal as everything set out in the order was conditioned by the last sentence, that all measures taken "must be hard, but just." As far as instances of unlawful killings by German troops were concerned, the defence denied some instances altogether, attacking the credibility of the Prosecution's evidence which on this point was predominantly affidavit evidence, and admitting other instances while pleading that they occurred not as a result of the accused's orders but as a result of independent actions by the troops or by local commanders.

The issue which the court had to decide was, therefore, in the words of the Judge Advocate, whether the accused's orders were "a definite incitement to kill Italians or just badly worded orders which were rather carelessly drafted," and whether all or any of the instances of indiscriminate killings of Italians by German troops were a direct consequence of these orders.

III. Findings and Sentences

The accused was found guilty on both charges and sentenced to death by shooting. The sentence was commuted by the confirming officers to one of life imprisonment.

Notes on the Case

I. The Legality of Killing Innocent Persons by Way of Reprisals

In presenting the Prosecution's case on the first charge the Prosecutor conceded that the German authorities were justified in imposing reprisals after the bombing attack in Rosella Street. After quoting some authorities on the subject, he pointed out that whereas there was authority for destruction of property and incarceration of nationals of occupied territory as reprisals, there was no authority for the taking of human life. The defence argued that in extreme circumstances the taking of human life in the course of reprisals was permissible. A commentary on German Military Law, published during the second world war, was quoted by Counsel in this context. The author says: "Hostages are held in a kind of safe custody. They vouch with their lives for the lawful conduct of the opponent. According to the usages of war it must be announced that hostages are being taken and for what purpose. Above all, the taking of hostages has to be brought to the notice of those for whose lawful conduct the hostages are a guarantee. If the event which was to be prevented by the taking of hostages occurs, e.g. if the opponent continues his unlawful conduct, the hostages can be killed." Defence Counsel argued that the first step towards the inflicting of reprisals is the taking of hostages. He said that "any military commander in the course of reprisals is authorised to arrest civilians in case partisans should attack his troops or military establishments. If at a later stage outrages against the troops of the occupying power are committed, prisoners belonging to the group detained as hostages may be killed in the course of reprisals." In support of this proposition Defence Counsel quoted section 358(*d*) of the American *Rules of Land Warfare*. "Hostages taken and held for the declared purpose of ensuring against unlawful acts by the enemy forces or people may be punished or put to death if unlawful acts are nevertheless committed."

The Judge Advocate said in his summing up: "I have come to the conclusion that there seems to be on the part of writers a very deliberate attempt not to come out in the open and answer the very question that the Court wants answered and this is 'Can you shoot, in certain circumstances, an innocent person by way of reprisal'? . . . International Law is generally on a high level. It is about what one belligerent may do to another belligerent, but what Field Marshal Kesselring had to deal with were not countries which were organised with governments but irresponsible people in the main whom he could not negotiate with, people in respect of whom he could not say to responsible leaders 'You must control your followers.' Therefore I do suggest that if there ever were circumstances in which one would have to resort to reprisals if one failed after proper application to find the real culprit that that is the sort of thing in which a reprisal must have been considered appropriate. . . . I have come to the conclusion that there is nothing which makes it absolutely clear that in no circumstances and especially in the circumstances which I think are agreed in this case that an innocent person properly taken for the purpose of a reprisal cannot be executed. I feel that if there is some doubt in the law, the benefit of that doubt must be given to the Field Marshal and therefore I am not prepared to put this case to you on the basis that if you are satisfied that the Field Marshal was deliberately shooting one innocent person by way of reprisal, that that in itself is a war crime of which he should be convicted."

The issues before the court on the first charge were these:

(1) Were the German armed forces, represented by the accused, or the Security Service, represented by the head of the SD in Rome, responsible for the shootings?

(2) Was the shooting of 335 Italians a legitimate reprisal or a war crime?

With regard to the first question, the Judge Advocate advised the court in his summing up, that: "if you feel that it is right on the evidence as a whole that the shooting was clearly the responsibility of the Security Service and that all responsibility had passed from the Wehrmacht, then to my mind you are bound to acquit the accused." It seems then that the court found that the accused bore the responsibility for these shootings.

With regard to the second question, the court found that the shootings constituted a war crime but this finding does not supply an answer to the question whether the taking of human life as a reprisal is permissible or not as the finding of the court could be supported either by holding that the ratio of 10 to 1 was excessive or by the fact that 335 persons were killed instead of 330 as ordered. The Judge Advocate said in his summing up: "whatever you may think about International Law and reprisals, clearly five of these 335 Italians were murdered. That was a war crime and you cannot get away from it. There was no Führer order to cover it and it was quite outside the reprisal."

The issue before the court on the second charge was not merely whether the measures ordered by the accused were legitimate reprisals or not but, as the Judge Advocate pointed out in his summing up: "The charge is a much more serious and grave one and that is that the Field Marshal deliberately and knowingly when he produced the relevant orders, was having them produced in such form that he knew what the results would be and that he intended by bringing these orders into existence, to bring about these results. That is what the Prosecution have to prove on this charge."

Thus, the finding of the court on both charges leaves the question of the legality of killing of innocent persons as a reprisal, open.

II. Hostages and Reprisals

The killings of Italian nationals with which the accused was charged, were in both charges described as reprisals. The shooting in the Ardeatine caves which was the subject of the first charge was no doubt a reprisal and was described as such by the German authorities. The order of the 1st July which forms the main subject of the second charge orders both the taking of hostages (. . . "proportion of the male population of the area will be arrested and in the event of acts of violence being committed these men will be shot") and the infliction of reprisals (. . . "should troops, etc., be fired on from any village, the village will be burned down"). The Prosecution described both parts of the order as reprisals; Defence Counsel treated the taking of hostages as the first step towards inflicting reprisals. The Judge Advocate did not refer to the distinction in his summing up. This distinction was also made in the judgment of the American Military Government Court in the United States *v*. List and others: "For the purpose of this opinion the term 'hostages' will be considered as those persons of the civilian population who are taken into custody for the purpose of guaranteeing with their lives the future good conduct of the population of the community from which they were taken. The term 'reprisal prisoners' will be considered as those individuals who are taken from the civilian population to be killed in retaliation for any offence committed by unknown persons within the occupied area . . . where innocent individuals are seized and punished for a violation of the laws of war which has already occurred, no question of hostages is involved. It is nothing more than an infliction of a reprisal. . . . Throughout the evidence in the present case we find the term 'hostages' applied where a 'reprisal' only was involved."

Professor Lauterpacht points out that the taking of hostages "must not be confused with the still existing practice of seizing enemy individuals for the purpose of making them the object of reprisals."

It is usual to speak of "hostages" in occupied territories when the occupying forces imprison members of the community of the occupied territory announcing at the same time that they will be treated as hostages if the community does not refrain from certain activities against the occupying forces. The term "reprisal" is used in this connection for measures taken by the occupying forces in retaliation for the unlawful conduct of unidentified members of the community of the occupied territory. Thus hostages ae taken *before* the act of illegitimate warfare committed by the enemy whereas reprisals are inflicted *after* such an act.

TRIAL OF KARL BAUER, ERNST SCHRAMECK AND HERBERT FALTEN

Dijon, France, October, 1945*

Outline of the Proceedings Before a French Permanent Military Tribunal

I. The Accused

The Accused were officers of a German unit which was engaged in combats with formations of the "French Forces of the Interior" (F.F.I.), which became the major resistance movement in France during the war of 1939–1945.

Karl Bauer was a colonel, in command of a German column of marines which, in August and September 1944, were retreating before the Allied forces from the area of the Landes and Bordeaux to that of Autun. The other two accused were under Bauer's orders in the same column, Ernst Schrameck being a colonel and Herbert Falten a lieutenant.

II. The Charge

The accused were charged with complicity in murder in that, "by abusing authority and powers," they had "provoked murder in reprisals of three soldiers of the F.F.I." captured as "prisoners of war."

III. Evidence of the Prosecution

According to the evidence submitted by the Prosecution Bauer's column started its retreat on 21 August, 1944. On 8 September it had reached the area of Autun where it met a combined force of French regular troops and an F.F.I. unit. A battle took place, which lasted two days. In the course of the battle three F.F.I. combatants were captured by the Germans, two on the evening of 8 September, and one on the morning of the 9th. They were taken to Bauer's headquarters on 9 September at 11 a.m. Bauer handed them over to Schrameck

**Law Reports of Trials of War Criminals,* Vol. 8, p. 15 (London, 1947).

and ordered that they "be taken away and shot." Schrameck passed the order to Lieutenant Falten, and all three prisoners were shot by a squad under Falten.

The affidavit of a German witness was produced. The latter, Major Spielberg, another officer of Bauer's column, testified that the victims had first been sent to him by Bauer for interrogation. The interrogation had revealed no offence on the part of the prisoners, apart from the fact they had fought for one day against the column in regular combat.

The Prosecution described the three prisoners as having been dressed almost entirely in civilian clothes. According to one witness, however, one of them wore a tricolour strap around the arm, and another had an American helmet. According to another witness, two of the prisoners had tricolour straps, and the third wore a khaki overall.

IV. Defence of the Accused

All the accused pleaded not guilty on account of superior orders.

Bauer invoked express orders issued by Hitler in April 1944 to execute irregular combatants, and thereby implied that such was the status of the prisoners. His plea was contested by the Prosecution. Witness Spielberg was quoted to have stated that Hitler's orders "were known to him," but that "in his opinion, they should not have been applied to prisoners captured among elements against which we had been fighting for a day."

Schrameck referred to orders given him by Bauer, and Falten to those given by Schrameck. The latter contended that Bauer's orders were "categorical" and were thus not "subject to discussion." It was shown that Falten, after taking the prisoners to the place of execution in pursuance of Schrameck's transmission of orders, had gone back to Schrameck to see once more whether he should carry on with the execution. He was told to do so "at once."

V. The Judgment

All the accused were found guilty of the charge. Bauer was sentenced to death. The fact that Schrameck and Falten had acted on Bauer's orders was admitted as an extenuating circumstance, and the two accused were each convicted to five years' imprisonment.

Notes on the Case

I. The Status of Guerrilla Units

The central question in this trial is the status of the three members of the F.F.I. The Tribunal's findings, which coincided with the Prosecution's charges, were that the victims had the status of belligerents as recognised by the laws and customs of war, and that they were thus covered by the rules concerning the treatment of prisoners of war.

This is clearly indicated in the question put by the President of the Court to the judges and in the confirmative answer given by the latter. The question reads as follows:

> Is it established that in the area of Autun, on 9th September, 1944, a murder of three F.F.I. French soldiers, prisoners of war, was committed on the occasion or under pretence of the state of war, but without being justified by the laws and customs of war, by unidentified German marines belonging to a German column in retreat which included Colonels Bauer and Schrameck and Lieutenant Falten?

The judges answered "yes" by a majority vote.

Article 1 of the Regulations respecting the Laws and Customs of War on Land, appended to the IVth Hague Convention, recognises the status of belligerent not only to regular units of the army, "but also to militia and volunteer corps" on four conditions: that they are "commanded by a person responsible for his subordinate"; that they wear a "fixed distinctive sign recognisable at a distance"; that they "carry arms openly"; and that they "conduct operations in accordance with the laws and customs of war."

Article 2 of the same Regulations goes further and extends the above recognition even to civilian combatants under certain circumstances and conditions. These are fulfilled when "inhabitants of a territory not under occupation, on the approach of the enemy, spontaneously take up arms without having had time to organise themselves in accordance with Article 1" of the Hague Regulations. In such cases it is not required that combatants fight under a commander, or that they wear a distinctive sign, such as a uniform. It is sufficient, and at the same time mandatory, that they carry arms openly and respect the laws and customs of war when conducting military operations.

The Prosecution specifically invoked this latter provision, and not that of Article 1 of the Hague Regulations. It stated that "F.F.I. troops had opposed for a day the column of Bauer, together with French regular troops and with the knowledge of the Germans, and had fought the invading troops without having had time to organise themselves."

The implementation of Article 2 of the Hague Regulations requires the presence of two essential elements: that arms were taken up to resist the enemy by inhabitants "of a territory not under occupation," and that this is done by inhabitants who had no "time to organise themselves" by having a commander and wearing distinctive signs.

From this it follows that the concept of what is and what is not an "occupied territory" is also essential. Article 42 of the Hague Regulations provides the following:

> Territory is considered occupied when actually placed under the authority of the hostile army.
>
> The occupation extends only to the territory where such authority has been established and is in a position to assert itself.

The setting up and maintenance of an actual and effective occupying administration makes the difference between occupation and mere invasion. It thus appears that, when the occupant withdraws from a territory or is driven out of it, the occupation ceases to exist. This is clearly so in cases where liberating forces are steadily advancing and gradually regaining control of parts of the occupied territory. But the question arises of the status of smaller parts still *within* the occupied territory, in which the occupant's powers cannot be exercised on account of military operations still in progress. Are the inhabitants of such parts entitled to rise to arms, drive the enemy out, even temporarily, and while doing so, enjoy the rights of belligerents?

According to the facts of the trial as they appear from the indictment, it would seem that there was, in the area of Autun, a situation combining that of a territory being liberated by outside forces and that being freed by local inhabitants. In any case it would appear that the military operations were in full development and that, at the time of capturing the three F.F.I. combatants, the occupant's authority in the area had not yet disintegrated.

If one is to assume that the Tribunal accepted the Prosecution's thesis and applied Article 2 of the Hague Regulations, its decision that the F.F.I. combatants had the status of belligerents and were consequently to be treated as prisoners of war, would contribute to defining the concept of occupied territory. It would appear to be based upon the view that, once control of an occupied territory is disputed by the force of arms, and consequently, already at the stage in which the occupant's authority is at stake, the status of occupation ceases to exist. This would not necessarily mean that the contest may be wholly conducted by local inhabitants who are under the occupant's authority. The main fact of the trial is that the latter were fighting *jointly* with regular French troops, which formed part of the Allied forces who invaded France in June 1944 with the purpose of driving the Germans out of France and other occupied European countries. There is also no indication that the F.F.I. members had resorted to arms prior to their junction with the regular troops, and consequently before at least one portion of their own territory had been, however temporarily, already liberated. It can be observed, of course, that the fact that the F.F.I. members in question were fighting together with the regular troops, which in fact means within their ranks, could have provided grounds for both the prosecution and the Tribunal to establish that they were under proper command, and had thus fulfilled one of the conditions of Article 1 of the Hague Regulations. The fact that some or all of them wore certain military distinctive signs, as alleged by the Prosecution on the basis of witnesses' accounts, could have made possible the application of Article 1 instead of Article 2 of the said Regulations. The whole issue of whether the F.F.I. combatants were or were not in territory "not under enemy occupation," would have then been immaterial.

If, however, Article 2 is accepted as having been applied by the Court the case brings the following features to light in the manner in which Article 2 was implemented:

(*a*) Any part of territory in which the occupant has been deprived of *actual* means for carrying out *normal* administration by the presence of opposing military forces, would not have the status of "occupied" territory within the terms of Articles 2 and 42 of the Hague Regulations. The fact that other parts of the occupied country, as a whole, are under effective enemy occupation, would not affect this situation.

(*b*) Inhabitants of such parts as are described above, when taking up arms against the enemy, would be deemed to have done so "on the approach of the enemy." This would mean not only the resorting to arms in the initial stages of a country's invasion by the future occupant, but in any other stage during or nearing the end of occupation. The enemy's "approach" in contested area, from which the enemy has been or is being driven out, would consist in the combats fought between the two hostile forces in the disputed area.

(*c*) Inhabitants resorting to arms in the above circumstances would enjoy the rights of belligerents. It is immaterial whether they wear civilian clothes or any other kind of dress. The sole conditions are that they carry arms openly and respect the laws and customs of war when fighting. In our case the German witness Spielberg testified that the three F.F.I. men had committed no violations of the laws of war, and from the fact that they were captured while fighting it follows that they carried arms openly.

A word or two should be said regarding the allegation that the F.F.I. combatants "had no time to organize themselves" by having a commander of their own and by wearing military signs such as full uniforms. It has already been observed that, by fighting shoulder to shoulder with regular French troops, it could have been said that they were "commanded by a person responsible for his subordinates." On the other hand, it is a matter of opinion whether objects such as tricolour straps around the arm, helmets or khaki overalls, are sufficiently distinctive signs as required by the Hague Regulations. The F.F.I., as a whole, were an underground but nevertheless a single and well organised body of combatants throughout France, so that, from this point of view, it cannot be said that its members "had no time to organise themselves." They were divided into units, at the head of which stood commanders. Whenever on military duty they wore, as a rule, a French tricolour sign or badge. However, as the operations against the occupant developed and progressed, their ranks were filled by new members, who often had no time either to be placed under proper command, or to wear anything else but plain mufti clothes. This was particularly true of units which grew during the weeks and months that preceded the liberation of the whole of France, between June 1944 and April–May, 1945. It may well be, and it is very likely, that such was precisely the case with the units fighting in the area of Autun. Inhabitants were filling the ranks of F.F.I. combatants and joining regular troops in military operations in continuous streams and waves, and as a unit or units of the F.F.I., as distinct from the regular troops, they may have had no commander of their own in the strict sense of the word. It is probably this position which was meant by the Prosecution when it referred to Article 2 of the Hague Regulations.

II. The Killing of Prisoners of War

Once the status of belligerent was recognised in regard to the F.F.I. combatants, the rule that they were to be treated as prisoners of war, and could not therefore be shot after capture, followed by itself.

Article 4 of the Hague Regulations provides:

> Prisoners of war are in the power of the hostile government, but not of the individuals or corps who capture them.
>
> They must be humanely treated.

The same rule is repeated in Article 2 of the Geneva Convention relative to the Treatment of Prisoners of War, of 1929, which stresses that humane treatment has to be applied "at all times," and that the prisoners have to be "protected, particularly against acts of violence." A specific prohibition to "kill or wound the enemy" who has "laid down his arms" or "no longer has means of defence," and has surrendered, is contained in Article 23 (*c*) of the Hague Regulations.

Uner the terms of Article 2, para. 4, of the French Ordinance of 28 August, 1944, concerning the Suppression of War Crimes, any "putting to death in reprisals" is regarded as premeditated murder as provided against in Article 296 of the French Penal Code. It was submitted by the Prosecution and admitted by the Tribunal that the three F.F.I. prisoners had been shot as a "reprisal," that is in revenge for having fought against the German troops. The Tribunal applied Article 2 of the said Ordinance, and consequently also Article 296 of the Penal Code.

III. The Plea of Superior Orders

As already stressed, the Tribunal dismissed the plea of superior orders in regard to the chief defendant, Bauer, and admitted it as an extenuating circumstance in the case of Schrameck and Falten.

In doing so the court applied the rule that superior orders do not, in themselves, exonerate the perpetrator from responsibility when the orders are illegal, but may be admitted in mitigation of punishment on the merits of each particular case. This rule is generally recognised in contemporary International and Municipal Law, and has been applied in numerous war crimes trials. In instruments of International Law the most authoritative source is Article 8 of the Nuremberg Charter:

> The fact that the defendant acted pursuant to order of his Government or of a superior shall not free him from responsibility, but may be considered in mitigation of punishment if the Tribunal determines that justice so requires.

In French law, the rule is laid down in Article 3 of the Ordinance of 28 August, 1944, concerning the Suppression of War Crimes, in the following terms:

> Laws decrees or regulations issued by the enemy authorities, orders or permits issued by those authorities, or by authorities which are or have been subordinated to them, cannot be pleaded as justification within the meaning of Article 327 of the Penal Code, but can only, in suitable cases, be pleaded as an extenuating or exculpating circumstances.

Article 327 of the French Penal Code provides that if "homicide, wounds and blows" have been ordered by the law and committed under "command" of the proper authority, there is no crime.

Bauer's plea consisted in that there were orders issued personally by Hitler in April 1944, that "partisan" or "guerrilla" combatants should be regarded as rebels and shot after capture.

As was established at the Nuremberg Trial of the German Major War Criminals, orders of this kind existed as early as in 1942. On 18th October, 1942, a directive, authorised by Hitler, was issued to "slaughter to the last man" all members of Allied "commando" units, whether armed or not, even if they surrendered. The Nuremberg Tribunal found all such orders contrary to the laws and customs of war, and consequently criminal in nature. The rejection of Bauer's plea was based upon the rule that he should not have obeyed orders which were of a criminal nature, and it may be noted further that, at the time of the crime, he was under no direct pressure or duress to implement Hitler's orders.

Bauer's personal liability in this case lay in that he originated the crime by giving orders to his subordinates in pursuance of Hitler's instructions. Such responsibility is covered by Article 6, last paragraph, of the Nuremberg Charter:

> Leaders, organisers, instigators, and accomplices participating in the formulation or execution of a common plan or conspiracy to commit any . . . crimes are responsible for all acts performed by any persons in execution of such plan.

In French law, it is covered by Article 4 of the Ordinance of 28th August, 1944, concerning the Suppression of War Crimes:

> Where a subordinate is prosecuted as principal perpetrator of a war crime, and his hierarchical superiors cannot be charged as joint perpetrators, the latter are regarded as accomplices to the extent to which they had organised or tolerated criminal acts of their subordinates.

From this it follows that, if a superior is prosecuted because of orders issued to subordinates, he is held responsible as principal or joint perpetrator, as the case may be.

In our case it would appear that Bauer was found guilty as principal perpetrator, and therefore convicted to death. This resulted from the findings regarding the part played by his two subordinates. By admitting their respective pleas, the Tribunal in fact decided that both were instrumental in the killing of the three F.F.I. prisoners, but bore lesser responsibility. The Tribunal presumably took into account Schrameck's defence that Bauer's orders were "categorical" and left no room for "discussion." It would also appear that it took into consideration the fact that Falten had postponed the execution on his own initiative and gone back to Schrameck to raise once more the issue, thus giving an opportunity for cancelling the order. All these or other considerations were in the powers of the Tribunal which was at liberty to estimate the degree of guilt of each participant in the crime according to the circumstances. By convicting the two to five years' imprisonment each, the Tribunal admitted the plea of superior orders only in mitigation of the punishment, but not in exculpation of guilt, as it was empowered to do under the terms of Article 3 of the Ordinance of 28th August, 1944.

TRIAL OF FRANZ HOLSTEIN AND TWENTY-THREE OTHERS

Dijon, France, February, 1947*

Outline of the Proceedings Before a French Permanent Military Tribunal

I. The Accused

The Accused were members of various German units who took part in a series of crimes against the French population in the area of Dijon in 1944. Some belonged to the Army, and others to the Gestapo and SD (Security Police).

Three accused were present at the trial. They were Franz Holstein, a Major; Georg Major, a Captain commanding "Ost Battalion 654"; and Emil Goldberg, an Adjutant of the S.D. at Châlon-sur-Saône. The remainder twenty-one accused were tried *in absentia* and were the following: Hans Kruger, head of the S.D. at Châlon-sur-Saône; Ludwig Schellaas, Adjutant of the S.D. at Dijon; Klaus Schenevoigt, non-commissioned officer of the S.D. at Dijon; Schirmacher, a Lieutenant commanding the 3rd Company, Ost Battalion 654; Vier, a Colonel, Feldkommandant at Nevers; Eder, Artillery Lieutenant, Ortskommandant at Château-chinon; Verfurt, Lieutenant serving at Autun; Gierszewski, a Lieutenant, commanding the 2nd Company, Ost Battalion, 654; Fuierer, a Lieutenant, commanding the 1st Company, Ost Battalion 654; Lenartz, Adjutant, interpreter of the S.D. at Dijon; Gottlieb Hilgenstohler, sergeant of the S.D. at Châlon-sur-Saône; Runkewitz, sergeant, interpreter of the S.D. at Châlon-sur-Saône; Eugen Knodler, Chief Adjutant of the S.D. at Châlon-sur-Saône; Karl Haeberle, sergeant-major of the S.D. at Châlon-sur-Saône; Hildebrand, deputy O.C. of the German Officer Cadet School at Dijon; Moeckel, Lieutenant, Feldgendarmerie at Autun; Gunther Irmisch, Colonel, head of the Feldkommandantur 669 at Dijon; Hulf, Sturmbannführer of the Gestapo at Dijon; Hefeke, Captain, 2nd Battalion, 5 Kouban Regiment; Albert Hippe, Colonel, O.C. of the German Officer Cadet School at Dijon, and Merck, a Lieutenant serving at Dijon.

**Law Reports of Trials of War Criminals,* Vol. 8, p. 22 (London, 1947).

II. The Facts and Evidence

(i) *Background of the Crimes and Composition of Units Involved*

According to the evidence presented by the prosecution, the accused took part in the combined operations against members of the French resistance movement. The operations were decided upon and planned at a conference held at Dijon under the auspices of General Hederich, Feldkommandant and "Befehlshaber Nord-Ost Frankreich" (G.O.C., North-East, France), in June, 1944. Six of the accused attended in their respective commanding capacities: Irmisch, Hippe, Major, Hulf, Kruger and Verfurt. They were to provide the troops and issue instructions, and all had to take personal part in the operations at the head of their units.

The conference decided that the French resistance movement in the area was to be suppressed and annihilated, and that severe measures were to be taken against them and the population "in reprisals" for their struggle against the occupying authorities or assistance given in this respect. In the light of some of the evidence, such measures were to consist in executing on the spot every member of the resistance, captured with arms, pursuant to Hitler's orders to kill all "terrorists" or "saboteurs"; in the burning down of three farms for every German soldier killed, and of one farm for every German soldier wounded.

The events described by the Prosecution showed that, in carrying out the above instructions, the accused killed a large number of inhabitants, destroyed by fire many buildings in various localities, and pillaged property of the population.

The assignment was conducted and the crimes perpetrated by several columns operating simultaneously in the different areas, and moving from one area to the other. One column was composed of German officer-cadets supplied and commanded personally by Hippe and his deputy, Hildebrand. Another column consisted of Russian quisling troops, Ost Battalion 654, under the command of German officers and N.C.O.'s. The O.C. was Major. The ranks of a third column were filled with members of 5 Kouban Regiment, another Russian (cossack) unit, under Captain Hepeke. In addition, there were detachments of German Feldgendarmes from the Ortskommandantur at Chateau-Chinon, under Lieutenants Moeckel and Eder, and almost the entire personnel of the S.D. at Chalon-sur-Saone, with its head Kruger. In the events of August, 1944, another German officer, Colonel Vier, took an active part as Feldkommandant at Nevers.

(ii) *The Crimes*

The crimes were committed in six different places and their surroundings.

Events at Toulon-sur-Arroux

On 25th June, 1944, two columns left Dijon for Toulon-sur-Arroux. One was composed of the officer cadets and the other of one company of Ost

Battalion 654. The latter arrived at Châlon-sur-Saône at 10 a.m. and was joined by three more companies of the same Battalion The column then headed towards Toulon-sur-Arroux and, when approaching it, deployed in the fields. In a hamlet, Prayes, they shot at farmers who were haymaking. One was wounded and several others were seized and executed on the spot. When the wounded man moved, he was killed by five Germans. He was later identified as one Swedrowski.

The column then surrounded another small locality, St. Eugene, northeast of Toulon-sur-Arroux. They seized two inhabitants, ill-treated them and shot them without investigation or trial. After this the place was looted.

Events at Dun-les-Places

The column regrouped and arrived at Autun at 11 a.m. There they found the first column, with officer-cadets. At this juncture, a third column, that of the Russian Cossacks, 5 Kuban Regiment, arrived from Dôle, via Châlon-sur-Saône. Together with the other two columns, as well as with elements of the Feldgendarmeries, Gestapo and S.D., they all moved the next day, 26th June, towards Dun-les-Places. According to some witnesses the Cossacks column, before arriving at Dun, met detachments of the French resistance movement and shots were exchanged, which did not extend beyond mere skirmishes. According to other witnesses, however, no such encounter took place. When the above combined force arrived at Dun-les-Places, Feldgendarmes and S.D. men arrested a large number of the male population. The arrestees were all taken at their homes, and were locked in the local church. Some were interrogated and all were physically ill-treated. At this point fires were heard in the village and a confusion arose. The Germans contended that shots were fired at them from the church steeple by resistance men. According to other witnesses, the incident was entirely invented by the Germans themselves in order to justify hard measures against the population. At any rate, after this the inhabitants detained in the church were massacred. They were lined up in front of the church and shot by Bren-guns. The massacre was carried out under Kruger's direct orders and supervision. In the early morning, an officer cadet was seen killing off some of those who had survived. Two of the victims, however, who had also survived, had time to flee before the morning, and were later to give full account of the event. Twenty-one inhabitants in all fell as victims on this occasion.

On 27th June, the place was thoroughly pillaged and twelve houses were set on fire and burnt to the ground. On 28th June, at 1 p.m., the Germans left the locality.

Events at Vermot

The third or Cossacks column, under the Command of Hefeke, had left on the 26th June, at about 5 p.m. It went to Vermot, a hamlet 2 kms. north of Dun. When leaving, it took with it six hostages from Dun-les-Places. According to the evidence of the Prosecution, while approaching Vermot, the column met a group of resistance men hidden in the nearby woods. A battle took place which lasted one hour. After the battle the column entered Vermot, and as revenge for the battle, severely ill-treated many inhabitants and pillaged their property. One of the victims, named Petit, had his jaw fractured by a rifle butt, and his grandson had his right arm broken. Petit died of the ill-treatment. In addition, the six hostages were executed. They were all identified. Eleven houses were set on fire and property of the inhabitants was looted. The column left Vermot on 28th June.

Events at Vieux-Dun

According to the accused Major, on 26th June, in the evening, while at Dun-les-Places, he received orders from Hildebrand to proceed with a detachment to Vieux-Dun, another small locality in the area, and search all the woods on the way. He arrived at Vieux-Dun on 27th June, at 8 or 9 a.m. According to a German witness no members of the resistance movement were met or found and no incidents took place. The head of the S.D., Kruger, also came to Vieux-Dun, and in spite of these quiet conditions, had one house set on fire. The village was also pillaged.

Events at Arleuf

Several weeks later, a similar expedition was made on the orders of Vier, Feldkommandant at Nevers, and was carried out by Major. His assignment was to make a general search in the area of Nevers for hidden arms, to execute those found with arms, and to destroy houses from which shots would be fired. Major alleged that the expedition took place as a result of shots which were fired at German soldiers eight or ten days before. On 10th August the detachment arrived at Arleuf and soon several crimes were to be committed. According to a German witness the events took place in the following manner:

A French girl, Mlle. Buteau, had her parents arrested by members of the French resistance movement, and they were taken away. She appealed to Major for help to liberate them, and on this occasion told him that the whole population of Arleuf was in the resistance movement. Major had the locality surrounded by a company under Schirmacher, and gathered one member of every family in a café. He told them if Mlle. Buteau's parents were not returned by the night, he would have the whole village set on fire. The Major despatched two youths to contact men of the resistance and request the return of the Buteaus by 8 p.m.

The crimes took place in the course of these events. At 6.30 a.m., when members of families were being collected, an agricultural worker, Goujon, took fright and tried to escape or hide. He was apprehended and brought to Major, who ordered that he be shot. The man was taken away and executed.

A revolver was found in the house of an old man, Boulle, aged 71. The man and the revolver were brought to Major. The latter fired a shot from the revolver into the ceiling and told Boulle: "For this you are going to be shot." These words were heard by a soldier who instantly took Boulle away and killed him.

A third man was killed in the following circumstances. Several inhabitants were lined up against a wall with their hands up, and were searched by Major's men. At one moment one of the inhabitants, Gantes, moved his right arm down. A soldier moved one or two yards back and killed him with a Bren-gun.

Events at Crux-la-Ville

Several days later an expedition took place under the direct command of Colonel Vier. The purpose was to annihilate units of the resistance movement, which were encamped west of Crux-la-Ville. Major and his men again took part in this operation.

On 15th August, Major and elements of his Battalion attacked a body of resistance men and suffered losses. The following day, after the battle was over, a young resistance combatant, Chermette, who had been captured on the 15th, was taken to a yard and tortured. Over a hundred soldiers watched the torture. The victim was laid on a table and beaten all over his body. After that he was thrown on a heap of refuse and killed by Bren-guns. At 7 p.m., of the same day, soldiers broke into the house of a farmer, Ricard. They found his wife and son working on the cattle and accused the son of being a "terrorist." They shot him on the spot. Another four inhabitants were seized, tortured and killed, bringing the total to six victims. Seven houses were set on fire, one on 15th August and six on 16th August.

III. The Findings and Sentences

Twenty-two accused were found guilty of some of the above offences and two were acquitted for lack of evidence that they had personally perpetrated crimes.

According to the findings the accused could conveniently be classified into three categories: those found guilty as instigators, mainly by issuing orders; those found guilty as perpetrators; and those found guilty as their accomplices.

Irmisch, Hippe, Hulf and *Hildebrand* were found guilty as instigators of the killing of twenty-one inhabitants at Dun-les-Places. *Kruger, Schenevoigt, Lenertz, Hilgenstohler, Runkewitz, Knodler, Hoeberle, Schellhaas,* were found guilty as perpetrators, and *Merck, Goldberg, Eder* and *Moeckel* as their accomplices.

Kruger was found guilty for instigating the arsons at Dun-les-Places, the killing of six hostages at Vermot and the arson at Vieux-Dun. He was also found guilty as perpetrator of the killing of Swedrowski at Toulon-sur-Arroux.

Verfurt was found guilty as perpetrator of the arsons at Dun-les-Places, Hefeke was found guilty of instigating the arsons at Vermot, and of being an accomplice to the killing of the six hostages, the pillage and the ill-treatment of Petit and his grandson, all at Vermot. *Major* was found guilty of instigating the murder of two of the three victims at Arleuf, and the arson at Arleuf. *Vier* was found guilty as instigator of the killing of all the three victims at Arleuf and of the six victims at Crux-la-Ville, and of the arsons at Arleuf and Crux-la-Ville. *Schirmacher* was also held responsible as instigator in the arson at Arleuf and Holstein was found guilty of the arson at Crux-la-Ville as an accomplice.

The two acquitted were *Fuierer* and *Gierszewski.*

All the accused found guilty, except two, were sentenced to death. Holstein and Major were convicted with extenuating circumstances and were sentenced, Holstein to hard labour for 15 years, and Major to hard labour for 20 years.

Notes on the Case

I. The Nature of the Offences

The offences for which the accused were found guilty fall into the following four categories: killing of civilians, which the court described as murders committed as "reprisals"; destruction of property by arson; pillage; and ill-treatment of civilians.

(a) *Killing Civilians as "Reprisals"*

Convictions for murder were made in respect of the killing of the twenty-one inhabitants at Dun-les-Places, the farmer Swedrowski at Toulon-sur-Arroux, the six hostages at Vermot, the three inhabitants at Arleuf, and the six victims at Crux-la-Ville.

In respect of all these killings the court found the accused concerned guilty of murder in that they "deliberately inflicted death" and that all such "wanton homicides were committed in reprisals."

The first part of this finding was based on Article 295 of the French Penal Code which provides:

> Homicide committed deliberately is murder.

The second part was based upon Article 2, para. 4, of the Ordinance of 28th August, 1944, concerning the Suppression of War Crimes, which reads:

> Premeditated murder, as specified in Article 296 of the Penal Code, shall include killing as a form of reprisal.

In this manner the consequence of the finding that all the above killings were committed in "reprisals," was that the accused were found guilty of "premeditated" murder (*assassinat*) and not of ordinary murder (*meurtre*).

That murder, premeditated or not, is punishable as a war crime, has had a long recognition in the laws and customs of war. Its latest expression can be found in the Charter of the International Military Tribunal at Nuremberg (Article 6) and also of that at Tokyo (Article 5). It can also be found in the municipal law of many nations dealing with war crimes, as it emerged during or after the war 1939–45. The main point of interest in this trial, however, is the element of "reprisals" which, under the Ordinance of the 28th August, 1944, had the effect of making the accused guilty of premeditated murder.

The subject of "reprisals" is one of difficulty in International Law. Its limitations are still not well defined, and regarding the rules guiding it one has chiefly to rely on the opinion of learned publicists and on judicial precedents of a differing nature. This gap is particularly felt within the sphere of the laws and customs of war. As stressed by Lord Wright, Chairman of the United Nations War Crimes Commission, no complete "law of reprisals" in time of war has yet developed.

In the theory concerning reprisals in time of peace it is generally agreed that the latter are exceptionally permitted as a means of enforcing International Law. They are then regarded as an answer to international delinquency and as one of several different modes of compulsive settlement of disputes when negotiations or other amicable modes have failed. The development of International Law after the first World War, by the setting up of the League of Nations and, *mutatis mutandis,* of the United Nations, has led some authoritative writers to raise the problem as to whether, after the acceptance of obligations regarding the pacific settlement of international disputes, States are still entitled to resort to compulsive means of settlement between themselves, including reprisals. The opinion has been expressed that "so long as the renunciation of the right of war," as the paramount means of compulsive settlement, "is not accompanied by an obligation to submit disputes to obligatory judicial settlement, and so long as there is no agency enforcing compliance with that obligation and with the judicial decision given in pursuance thereof, *reprisals,* at least of non-forcible character, *must be recognised as a means of enforcing international law.*"

Similar conclusions, though for other reasons, were drawn in regard to reprisals in time of war. It was admitted that "reprisals between belligerents cannot be dispensed with, for the effect of their use and of the fear of their being used cannot be denied."

It would thus appear that, in the present stage of its growth, International Law still recognises reprisals, admittedly within certain conditions and limitations. The problem in time of war, as a learned writer put it, is that "a war crime does not necessarily cease to be such for the reason that it is committed under the guise of reprisals," but that, on the other hand, "as a rule, an act committed in pursuance of reprisals, as limited by International Law, cannot properly be treated as a war crime." It is precisely the limitations within which reprisals are permissible that are still left to be answered with precision sufficient to remove elements of doubt and uncertainty.

In conditions created by a state at war, the question of reprisals arises when one belligerent violates the rules of warfare and the other belligerent retaliates in order to bring about a cessation of such violations. The problem then consists in determining the scope and nature of acts which the retaliating party is deemed entitled to undertake.

In the trial under review the killings, and in fact all the other offences as well, were committed by German occupying authorities against French inhabitants on account of the struggle of members of the French resistance movement. It would appear that the Germans had taken the view that such struggle was in violation of the laws and customs of war, and that the inhabitants were to be victimised as a means of inducing the resistance members to stop their struggle.

According to the general theory regarding reprisals, referred to above, it is required that retaliation is made "in proportion to the wrong done." One trend of opinion, however, gives further definition to this principle and qualifies it by certain limitations. In regard to reprisals in time of peace it is emphasised that "the only acts of reprisals admissible against foreign officials or citizens is arrest; they must be treated not like criminals, but like hostages, and in no circumstances may they be executed, or subjected to punishment." A similar conclusion regarding treatment of civilians is made by certain writers in respect of reprisals in time of war. It is considered that, in any case, reprisals must take place "in compliance with fundamental principles of war," and in this connection it is stressed that this implies "respect for the lives of non-combatants."

This authoritative trend of opinion provides certain indications as to how our problems may be solved. According to it, it would appear that wherever persons are the object of reprisals, their lives are the ultimate limit the retaliating party is not permitted to transgress. On the other hand, the recognition that "foreign citizens" may lawfully be taken as hostages in time of peace, would also apply in time of war to inhabitants of occupied territory, as conditions are then more compelling than in time of peace. A further rule would then follow, that while entitled to take hostages in order to bring about a cessation of violations of the laws of war by the other party, the retaliating party is expected to treat hostages in a humane manner, which in no case may lead to putting them to death. Any such act committed in retaliation for acts for which persons were taken and kept as hostages, would be criminal and would, legally speaking, result in a situation where there was no "reprisal" in the proper sense, but merely arbitrary acts of revenge.

It will be noted that Article 2, para. 4, of the French Ordinance of 28th August, 1944, according to which any "killing as a form of reprisal" constitutes premeditated murder, is fully in line with this school of thought. One of the striking features of the case tried is that no evidence was at hand to show that any of the inhabitants killed was guilty of any violation of the laws and customs of war. There was nothing to show that they belonged to the resistance movement and that, as such, they indulged in the commission of acts prohibited or punishable under the said laws and customs.

The solution furnished by the French Ordinance of 28th August, 1944, is a welcome contribution to the gradual elimination of uncertainty regarding the law of reprisals in time of war, and to the further determination of obligations which lie upon belligerent powers. The fact that it reflects so strikingly the principles formulated by authoritative writers prior to the enactment of the Ordinance, tends to indicate that the course adopted may bear the seeds for a wider agreement among nations in the further development of International Law in this field.

(b) *Destruction of Inhabited Buildings*

Convictions for destruction of buildings were made in respect of the setting on fire of 12 houses at Dun-les-Places, 11 houses at Vermot, 7 houses at Crux-la-Ville, and 1 house each at Vieux-Dun and Arleuf.

The accused concerned were found guilty under the terms of Article 434, of the French Penal Code, which prescribes the heaviest penalty, death, for anybody who "wantonly sets fire to buildings, vessels, boats, shops, works, when they are inhabitated or used as habitations." When the buildings or places are not inhabited or used as habitations, the penalty is hard labour for life.

In International Law, Article 23 (*g*) of the Hague Regulations respecting the Laws and Customs of War on Land, 1907, forbids the "destruction or seizure of enemy property" unless it is "imperatively demanded by the necessities of War." This careful phraseology is usually interpreted to mean that "imperative demands of the necessities of war" may occur only in the course of active military operations. In the case tried there was no evidence to show that, on the few occasions of clashes between the German units involved and the French resistance movement, there was any necessity to set the houses on fire. On the contrary, the evidence was to the effect that the houses were deliberately set on fire as a measure of intimidation for suppressing the activities of the resistance movement in the area.

Another provision of International Law is contained in the general rule of Article 46 of the Hague Regulations, whereby "private property must be respected."

According to the list of war crimes drawn up by the 1919 Commission on Responsibilities, item XVIII, "wanton devastation and destruction of property" is regarded as a violation of the laws and customs of war. Finally, Article 56 of the Hague Regulations, which assimilates "the property of local authorities" to private property, prescribes that "any seizure or destruction of property should be made the subject of legal proceedings," thus presumably signifying both civil and penal proceedings.

Under the terms of Article 1 of the Ordinance of 28th August, 1944, when committed during the war against French citizens, destruction of property by arson, as covered by Article 434 of the Penal Code, is punishable as a war crime when such devastation "was not justified by the laws and customs of war." The Tribunal's findings were that the acts of arson committed were not justified by these laws and customs.

Reflected upon the question of reprisals, this means that, even though the Germans may have carried out destruction as a measure of retaliation for the activities of the resistance movement, their deeds were regarded by the Tribunal as trespassing the limitations of International Law, and, therefore, constituting arbitrary acts of revenge of a criminal nature. The distinction between lawful and unlawful, or legitimate and arbitrary reprisals, was, thus, brought to light once more.

(c) *Ill-treatment of Civilians*

Convictions for ill-treatment were made in regard to the farmer Petit and his grandson at Vermot, and also in regard to five of the six men who were killed at Crux-la-Ville. The five were beaten and tortured before being killed.

The accused concerned were found guilty of "wantonly inflicting blows and wounds" as provided against in Article 309 of the Penal Code. In the case of Petit, who died as a consequence of the ill-treatment, the findings were that the "wantonly inflicted blows and wounds had caused death without intent to inflict it."

According to Article 309, when the ill-treatment has resulted in illness or in a working incapacity for over twenty days, the penalty is imprisonment for from two to five years. If it has resulted in more serious consequences, such as mutilation, amputation, or other permanent infirmities, the penalty is solitary confinement with hard labour for from five to ten years. If ill-treatment has resulted in death which was not intended, as in the case of Petit, the penalty is hard labour for from five to twenty years. Finally, according to Article 311, if none of the above consequences have occurred, the penalty is imprisonment for only from six days to two years.

As in the case of destruction of property, under Article 1 of the Ordinance of 28th August, 1944, the offences covered by the above provisions of the French Penal Code are punishable as war crimes if committed during the war against French citizens and not justified by the laws and customs of war. As already reported in connection with another trial, ill-treatment of civilians, irrespective of whether they are or are not guilty of offences, is explicitly regarded as a war crime and made punishable as such by provisions of both international and municipal law.

(d) *Pillage*

Convictions on the count of pillage were made for the lootings which took place at Dun-les-Places, Vermot and Vieux-Dun.

The accused concerned were found guilty of "pillage committed in gangs by military personnel with arms or open force," as provided against by Article 221 of the Code of Military Justice. The latter makes punishable by hard labour for life "any pillage or damage to food, merchandise or goods, committed by military personnel in gangs either with arms or open force, or with breakages of doors or external closures, or with violence against persons." Pillage in gangs committed in any other circumstances is punishable by solitary confinement with hard labour for from five to ten years. This provision was made applicable by the Ordinance of 28th August, 1944, concerning the Suppression of War Crimes, to cases of pillage committed by enemy occupying authorities in France.

Pillage was recognised as a war crime in the list of the 1919 Commission on Responsibilities, as well as in the Charters of the International Military Tribunals at Nuremberg and Tokyo. Prior to that it was explicitly prohibited by Article 47 of the Hague Regulations.

II. The Personal Guilt of the Accused

As previously stressed, each of the accused was found guilty of some of the above offences in different capacities: as instigator, as perpetrator, or as accomplice other than instigator. Some were found guilty in two or all three capacities, according to the part they took in the commission of the various crimes. The guilt of instigators and other accomplices in French law deserves special attention.

(a) *The Guilt of Instigators*

The offences for which a number of accused were found guilty as instigators include the killing of the twenty-one inhabitants at Dun-les-Places, of the six hostages at Vermot, of the three men at Arleuf, and of the six inhabitants at Crux-la-Ville. They also include the arsons in all these places.

The accused involved were in all cases in command of the men who committed the crimes and were held responsible for either issuing orders to their subordinates or permitting that they commit their misdeeds.

The responsibility of persons in authority over perpetrators and other accomplices, is covered by a general provision of the French Penal Code and also by the Ordinance of 28th August, 1944.

Article 60, para. 1 of Penal Code reads:

> Those who, by gifts, promises, threats, *abuse of authority or powers,* guilty machination, or artifices, provoke an act constituting a crime or a delict, or *give instructions* to commit it, shall be punished as accomplices.

Article 4 of the Ordinance of 28th August, 1944, concerning the Suppression of War Crimes provides:

> When a subordinate is prosecuted as principal perpetrator of a war crime and when his hierarchical superiors cannot be accused as joint perpetrators, they are

treated as accomplices to the extent to which they have organised or tolerated the criminal acts of their subordinates.

The Tribunal applied the provision of the Penal Code and found all those concerned guilty of "provoking" the offence in question "by abuse of authority and powers" or of "giving instructions." The accused found guilty in this capacity were: Irmisch, Hippe, Hulf, Hildebrand, Kruger, Hefeke, Major, Schirmacher and Vier.

The above provisions are based on the same principle as that expressed in Article 6, last paragraph, of the Charter of the International Military Tribunal at Nuremberg. Referring to crimes against peace, war crimes and crimes against humanity, as defined in its previous paragraphs, Article 6 provides:

> Leaders, organisers, instigators and accomplices participating in the formulation or execution of a common plan or conspiracy to commit any of the foregoing crimes are responsible for all acts performed by any persons in execution of such plan.

This rule is to be regarded as evidence of the present state of International Law in the field of personal responsibility for war crimes.

(b) *Guilt of Accomplices Other Than Instigators*

It is a universally recognised principle of modern penal law that accomplices during or after the fact are responsible in the same manner as actual perpetrators or as instigators, who belong to the category of accomplices before the fact. That is a principle recognised equally in the field of war crimes.

It is a matter of comparative interest to pass briefly in review the provisions of the French municipal law under which the accused concerned were found guilty as accomplices other than instigators. Their liability is regulated in Article 60, para. 2 and 3 of the Penal Code, which comprises among accomplices the following two categories:

> Those who have furnished arms, instruments or any other means which have served in the action knowing that they would serve this purpose;
>
> Those who knowingly have aided or assisted the perpetrator or perpetrators of the action in the facts which have prepared or facilitated or in those which have consummated the action.

Most of the accused concerned were found guilty of complicity in the latter capacity, that is for having "aided or assisted in the facts which prepared or facilitated or in those which consummated" the crime involved. Some, however, were also found guilty for supplying the means used in the crime.

THE YAMASHITA CASE

1945–1946

Decision of the United States Military Commission at Manila, December 7, 1945

The Commission has heard 286 persons during the course of this trial, most of whom have given eye-witness accounts of what they endured or what they saw. They included doctors and nurses; lawyers, teachers, businessmen; men and women of religious orders; prisoners of war and civilian internees; officers of the United States Army; officers of the Japanese Army and Navy; Japanese civilians; a large number of men, women and children of the Philippines; and the accused. Testimony has been given in eleven languages or dialects. Many of the witnesses displayed incredible scars of wounds which they testified were inflicted by Japanese from whom they made miraculous escapes followed by remarkable physical recovery. For the most part, we have been impressed by the candour, honesty and sincerity of the witnesses whose testimony is contained in 4055 pages in the record of trial.

We have received for analysis and evaluation 423 exhibits consisting of official documents of the United States Army, the United States State Department, and the Commonwealth of the Philippines; affidavits; captured enemy documents or translations thereof; diaries taken from Japanese personnel, photographs, motion picture films, and Manila newspapers.

The Prosecution presented evidence to show that the crimes were so extensive and widespread, both as to time and area, that they must either have been wilfully permitted by the accused, or secretly ordered by the accused. Captured orders issued by subordinate officers of the accused were presented as proof that they, at least, ordered certain acts leading directly to exterminations of civilians under the guise of eliminating the activities of guerrillas hostile to Japan. With respect to civilian internees and prisoners of war, the proof offered to the Commission alleged criminal neglect, especially with respect to food and medical supplies, as well as complete failure by the higher echelons of command to detect and prevent cruel and inhuman treatment accorded by local commanders and guards. The Commission considered evidence that the provisions of the Geneva Convention received scant compliance or attention, and that the International Red Cross was unable to render any sustained help. The cruelties and arrogance of the Japanese Military Police, prison camp guards and officials, with like action by local subordinate commanders were presented at length by the Prosecution.

The Defence established the difficulties faced by the accused with respect not only to the swift and overpowering advance of American forces, but also to the errors of his predecessors, weaknesses in organisation, equipment, supply with especial reference to food and gasolene, train communication, discipline and morale of his troops. It was alleged that the sudden assignment of Naval and Air Forces to his tactical command presented almost insurmountable difficulties. This situation was followed, the Defence contended, by failure to obey his orders to withdraw troops from Manila, and the subsequent massacre of unarmed civilians, particularly by Naval forces. Prior to the Luzon Campaign, Naval forces had reported to a separate ministry in the Japanese Government and Naval Commanders may not have been receptive or experienced in this instance with respect to a joint land operation under a single commander who was designated from the Army Service. As to the crimes themselves, complete ignorance that they had occurred was stoutly maintained by the accused, his principal staff officers and subordinate commanders, further, that all such acts, if committed, were directly contrary to the announced policies, wishes and orders of the accused. The Japanese Commanders testified that they did not make personal inspections or independent checks during the Philippine campaign to determine for themselves the established procedures by which their subordinates accomplish their missions. Taken at full face value, the testimony indicates that Japanese senior commanders operate in a vacuum, almost in another world with respect to their troops, compared with standards American Generals take for granted.

This accused is an officer of long years of experience, broad in its scope, who has had extensive command and staff duty in the Imperial Japanese Army in peace as well as war in Asia, Malaya, Europe, and the Japanese Home Islands. Clearly, assignment to command military troops is accompanied by broad authority and heavy responsibility. This has been true in all armies throughout recorded history. It is absurd, however, to consider a commander a murderer or rapist because one of his soldiers commits a murder or a rape. Nevertheless, where murder and rape and vicious, revengeful actions are widespread offences, and there is no effective attempt by a commander to discover and control the criminal acts, such a commander may be held responsible, even criminally liable, for the lawless acts of his troops, depending upon their nature and the circumstances surrounding them. Should a commander issue orders which lead directly to lawless acts, the criminal responsibility is definite and has always been so understood. The *Rules of Land Warfare,* Field Manual 27–10, United States Army, are clear on these points. It is for the purpose of maintaining discipline and control, among other reasons, that military commanders are given broad powers of administering military justice. The tactical situation, the character, training and capacity of staff officers and subordinate commanders as well as the traits of character, and training of his troops are other important factors in such cases. These matters have been the principal considerations of the Commission during its deliberations.

General Yamashita, The Commission concludes: (1) That a series of atrocities and other high crimes have been committed by members of the Japanese armed forces under your command against people of the United States, their allies and dependencies throughout the Philippine Islands; that they were not sporadic in nature but in many cases were methodically supervised by Japanese officers and noncommissioned officers; (2) That during the period in question you failed to provide effective control of your troops as was required by the circumstances.

Accordingly upon secret written ballot, two-thirds or more of the members concurring, the Commission finds you guilty as charged and sentences you to death by hanging.

Order of General Douglas MacArthur Confirming Death Sentence of General Tomoyuki Yamashita, February 6, 1946

It is not easy for me to pass penal judgment upon a defeated adversary in a major military campaign. I have reviewed the proceedings in vain search for some mitigating circumstances on his behalf. I can find none.

Rarely has so cruel and wanton a record been spread to the public gaze. Revolting as this may be in itself, its pales before the sinister and far-reaching implication thereby attached to the profession of arms. The soldier, be he friend or foe, is charged with the protection of the weak and unarmed. It is the very essence and reason for his being.

When he violates this sacred trust he not only profanes his entire cult but threatens the very fabric of international society. The traditions of fighting men are long and honorable, based upon the noblest of human traits—sacrifice.

This officer, of proven field merit and entrusted with a high command involving authority adequate to his responsibility, has failed this irrevocable standard; has failed his duty to his troops, to his country, to his enemy, and to mankind; he has failed utterly his soldier faith.

The transgressions resulting therefrom as revealed by the trial are a blot upon the military profession, a stain upon civilization, and constitute a memory of shame and dishonor that can never be forgotten. Peculiarly callous and purposeless was the sack of the ancient city of Manila, with its Christian population and countless historic shrines and monuments of culture and civilization, which, with the campaign conditions reversed, had previously been spared.

It is appropriate here to recall that the accused was fully forewarned as to the personal consequences of such atrocities. On October 24—four days following the landing of our forces in Leyte—it was publicly proclaimed that I would "hold the Japanese military authorities in the Philippines immediately liable for any harm which may result from the failure to accord to prisoners of war, civilian internees or civilian noncombatants the proper treatment and protection to which they of right are entitled."

No new or retroactive principles of law, either national or international, are involved. The case is founded upon basic fundamentals and practices as immutable and as standardized as the most matured and irrefragable of social codes.

The proceedings were guided by that primary rational of all judicial purpose—to ascertain the full truth unshackled by any artificialities or narrow method of technical arbitrariness. The results are beyond challenge.

I approve the findings and sentence of the Commission and direct the Commanding General, Army Forces in the Western Pacific, to execute the judgment upon the defendant, stripped of uniform, decorations and other appurtenances signifying membership in the military profession.

In Re Yamashita*

Mr. Chief Justice Stone delivered the opinion of the Court.

From the petitions and supporting papers it appears that prior to September 3, 1945, petitioner was the Commanding General of the Fourteenth Army Group of the Imperial Japanese Army in the Philippine Islands. On that date he surrendered to and became a prisoner of war of the United States Army Forces in Baguio, Philippine Islands. On September 25th, by order of respondent, Lieutenant General Wilhelm D. Styer, Commanding General of the United States Army Forces, Western Pacific, which command embraces the Philippine Islands, petitioner was served with a charge prepared by the Judge Advocate General's Department of the Army, purporting to charge petitioner with a violation of the law of war. On October 8, 1945, petitioner, after pleading not guilty to the charge, was held for trial before a military commission of five Army officers appointed by order of General Styer. The order appointed six Army officers, all lawyers, as defense counsel. Throughout the proceedings which followed, including those before this Court, defense counsel have demonstrated their professional skill and resourcefulness and their proper zeal for the defense with which they were charged.

On the same date a bill of particulars was filed by the prosecution, and the commission heard a motion made in petitioner's behalf to dismiss the charge on the ground that it failed to state a violation of the law of war. On October 29th the commission was reconvened, a supplemental bill of particulars was filed, and the motion to dismiss was denied. The trial then proceeded until its conclusion on December 7, 1945, the commission hearing two hundred and

*327 U.S. 1 (1946)

eighty-six witnesses, who gave over three thousand pages of testimony. On that date petitioner was found guilty of the offense as charged and sentenced to death by hanging.

The petitions for habeas corpus set up that the detention of petitioner for the purpose of the trial was unlawful for reasons which are now urged as showing that the military commission was without lawful authority or jurisdiction to place petitioner on trial, as follows:

(a) That the military commission which tried and convicted petitioner was not lawfully created, and that no military commission to try petitioner for violations of the law of war could lawfully be convened after the cessation of hostilities between the armed forces of the United States and Japan;

(b) that the charge preferred against petitioner fails to charge him with a violation of the law of war;

(c) that the commission was without authority and jurisdiction to try and convict petitioner because the order governing the procedure of the commission permitted the admission in evidence of depositions, affidavits and hearsay and opinion evidence, and because the commission's rulings admitting such evidence were in violation of the 25th and 38th Articles of War (10 U.S.C. §§ 1496, 1509, 10 U.S.C.A. §§ 1496, 1509) and the Geneva Convention (47 Stat. 2021), and deprived petitioner of a fair trial in violation of the due process clause of the Fifth Amendment;

(d) that the commission was without authority and jurisdiction in the premises because of the failure to give advance notice of petitioner's trial to the neutral power representing the interests of Japan as a belligerent as required by Article 60 of the Geneva Convention, 47 Stat. 2021, 2051.

On the same grounds the petitions for writs of prohibition set up that the commission is without authority to proceed with the trial.

The Supreme Court of the Philippine Islands, after hearing argument, denied the petition for habeas corpus presented to it, on the ground, among others, that its jurisdiction was limited to an inquiry as to the jurisdiction of the commission to place petitioner on trial for the offense charged, and that the commission, being validly constituted by the order of General Styer, had jurisdiction over the person of petitioner and over the trial for the offense charged.

In Ex parte Quirin, 317 U.S. 1, 63 S.Ct. 2, 87 L.Ed. 3, we had occasion to consider at length the sources and nature of the authority to create military commissions for the trial of enemy combatants for offenses against the law of war. We there pointed out that Congress, in the exercise of the power conferred upon it by Article I, § 8, Cl. 10 of the Constitution to "define and punish . . . Offenses against the Law of Nations . . .," of which the law of war is a part, had by the Articles of War (10 U.S.C. §§ 1471–1593, 10 U.S.C.A. §§ 1471–1593) recognized the "military commission" appointed by military command, as it had previously existed in United States Army practice, as an appropriate tribunal for the trial and punishment of offenses against the law of war. Article 15 declares that "the provisions of these articles conferring jurisdiction upon courts-martial shall not be construed as depriving military commissions . . . or other military tribunals of concurrent jurisdiction in respect of offenders or offenses that by statute or by the law of war may be triable by such military commissions . . . or other military tribunals." See a similar provision of the Espionage Act of 1917, 50 U.S.C. § 38, 50 U.S.C.A. § 38. Article 2 includes among those persons subject to the Articles of War the personnel of our own military establishment. But this, as Article 12 indicates, does not exclude from the class of persons subject to trial by military commissions "any other person who by the law of war is subject to trial by military tribunals," and who, under Article 12, may be tried by court martial, or under Article 15 by military commission.

We further pointed out that Congress, by sanctioning trial of enemy combatants for violations of the law of war by military commission, had not attempted to codify the law of war or to mark its precise boundaries. Instead, by Article 15 it had incorporated, by reference, as within the preexisting jurisdiction of military commissions created by appropriate military command, all offenses which are defined as such by the law of war, and which may constitutionally be included within that jurisdiction. It thus adopted the system of military common law applied by military tribunals so far as it should be recognized and deemed applicable by the courts, and as further defined and supplemented by the Hague Convention, to which the United States and the Axis powers were parties.

We also emphasized in Ex parte Quirin, as we do here, that on application for habeas corpus we are not concerned with the guilt or innocence of the petitioners. We consider here only the lawful power of the commission to try the petitioner for the offense charged. In the present cases it must be recognized throughout that the military tribunals which Congress has sanctioned by the Articles of War are not courts whose rulings and judgments are made subject to review by this Court. See Ex parte Vallandigham, 1 Wall. 243, 17 L.Ed. 589; In re Vidal, 179 U.S. 126, 21 S.Ct. 48, 45 L.Ed. 118; cf. Ex parte Quirin, supra, 317 U.S. 39, 63 S.Ct. 16, 87 L.Ed. 3. They are tribunals whose determinations are reviewable by the military authorities either as provided in the military orders constituting such tribunals or as provided by the Articles of War. Congress conferred on the courts no power to review their determinations save only as it has granted judicial power "to grant writs of habeas corpus for the purpose of an inquiry into the cause of the restraint of liberty." 28 U.S.C. §§ 451, 452, 28 U.S.C.A. §§ 451, 452. The courts may inquire whether the detention complained of is within the authority of those detaining the petitioner. If the military tribunals have lawful authority to hear, decide and condemn, their action is not subject to judicial review merely because they have made a wrong decision on disputed facts. Correction of their errors of decision is not for the courts but for the military authorities which are alone authorized to review their decisions. . . .

Finally, we held in Ex parte Quirin, supra, 317 U.S. 24, 25, 63 S.Ct. 9, 10, 87 L.Ed. 3, as we hold now, that Congress by sanctioning trials of enemy aliens by military commission for offenses against the law of war had recognized the right of the accused to make a defense. Cf. Ex parte Kawato, 317 U.S. 69, 63 S.Ct. 115, 87 L.Ed. 58. It has not foreclosed their right to contend that the Constitution or laws of the United States withhold authority to proceed with the trial. It has not withdrawn, and the Executive branch of the government could not, unless there was suspension of the writ, withdraw from the courts the duty and power to make such inquiry into the authority of the commission as may be made by habeas corpus.

With these governing principles in mind we turn to the consideration of the several contentions urged to establish want of authority in the commission. We are not here concerned with the power of military commissions to try civilians. See Ex parte Milligan, 4 Wall. 2, 132, 18 L.Ed. 281; Sterling v. Constantin, 287 U.S. 378, 53 S.Ct. 190, 77 L.Ed. 375; Ex parte Quirin, supra, 317 U.S. 45, 63 S.Ct. 19, 87 L.Ed. 3. The Government's contention is that General Styer's order creating the commission conferred authority on it only to try the purported charge of violation of the law of war committed by petitioner, an enemy belligerent, while in command of a hostile army occupying United States territory during time of war. Our first inquiry must therefore be whether the present commission was created by lawful military command and, if so, whether authority could thus be conferred on the commission to place petitioner on trial after the cessation of hostilities between the armed forces of the United States and Japan.

The Authority To Create the Commission. General Styer's order for the appointment of the commission was made by him as Commander of the United States Armed Forces, Western Pacific. His command includes, as part of a vastly greater area, the Philippine Islands, where the alleged offenses were committed, where petitioner surrendered as a prisoner of war, and where, at the time of the order convening the commission, he was detained as a prisoner in custody of the United States Army. The Congressional recognition of military commissions and its sanction of their use in trying offenses against the law of war to which we have referred, sanctioned their creation by military command in conformity to long established American precedents. Such a commission may be appointed by any field commander, or by any commander competent to appoint a general court martial, as was General Styer, who had been vested with that power by order of the President. 2 Winthrop, Millitary Law and Precedents, 2d Ed., *1302; cf. Article of War 8.

Here the commission was not only created by a commander competent to appoint it, but his order conformed to the established policy of the Government and to higher military commands authorizing his action. In a proclamation of July 2, 1942 (56 Stat. 1964, 10 U.S.C.A. §1554 note), the President proclaimed that enemy belligerents who, during time of war, enter the United States, or any territory possession thereof, and who violate the law of war, should be subject to the law of war and to the jurisdiction of military tribunals.

Paragraph 10 of the Declaration of Potsdam of July 6, 1945, declared that ". . . stern justice shall be meted out to all war criminals including those who have visited cruelties upon prisoners." U.S. Dept. of State Bull., Vol. XIII, No. 318, pp. 137, 138. This Declaration was accepted by the Japanese government by its note of August 10, 1945, U.S. Dept. of State Bull., Vol. XIII, No. 320 p. 205.

By direction of the President, the Joint Chiefs of Staff of the American Military Forces, on September 12, 1945, instructed General MacArthur, Commander in Chief, United States Army Forces, Pacific, to proceed with the trial, before appropriate military tribunals, of such Japanese war criminals "as have been or may be apprehended." By order of General MacArthur of September 24, 1945, General Styer was specifically directed to proceed with the trial of petitioner upon the charge here involved. This order was accompanied by detailed rules and regulations which General MacArthur prescribed for the trial of war criminals. These regulations directed, among other things, that review of the sentence imposed by the commission should be by the officer convening it, with "authority to approve, mitigate, remit, commute, suspend, reduce or otherwise alter the sentence imposed," and directed that no sentence of death should be carried into effect until confirmed by the Commander in Chief, United States Army Forces, Pacific.

It thus appears that the order creating the commission for the trial of petitioner was authorized by military command, and was in complete conformity to the Act of Congress sanctioning the creation of such tribunals for the trial of offenses against the law of war committed by enemy combatants. And we turn to the question whether the authority to create the commission and direct the trial by military order continued after the cessation of hostilities.

An important incident to the conduct of war is the adoption of measures by the military commander, not only to repel and defeat the enemy, but to seize and subject to disciplinary measures those enemies who, in their attempt to thwart or impede our military effort, have violated the law of war. Ex parte Quirin, supra, 317 U.S. 28, 63 S.Ct. 11, 87 L.Ed. 3. The trial and punishment of enemy combatants who have committed violations of the law of war is thus not only a part of the conduct of war operating as a preventive measure against such violations, but is an exercise of the authority sanctioned by Congress to administer the system of military justice recognized by the law of war. That sanction is without qualification as to the exercise of this authority so long as a state of war exists—from its declaration until peace is proclaimed. See United States v. Anderson, 9 Wall. 56, 70, 19 L.Ed. 615; The Protector, 12 Wall. 700, 702, 20 L.Ed. 463; McElrath v. United States, 102 U.S. 426, 438, 26 L.Ed. 189; Kahn v. Anderson, 255 U.S. 1, 9, 10, 41 S.Ct. 224, 226, 65 L.Ed. 469. The war power, from which the commission derives its existence, is not limited to victories in the field, but carries with it the inherent power to guard against the immediate renewal of the conflict, and to remedy, at least in ways Congress has recognized, the evils which the military operations have produced. See Stewart v. Kahn, 11 Wall. 493, 507, 20 L.Ed. 176.

We cannot say that there is no authority to convene a commission after hostilities have ended to try violations of the law of war committed before their cessation, at least until peace has been officially recognized by treaty or proclamation of the political branch of the Government. In fact, in most instances the practical administration of the system of military justice under the law of war would fail if such authority were thought to end with the cessation of hostilities. For only after their cessation could the greater number of offenders and the principal ones be apprehended and subjected to trial.

No writer on international law appears to have regarded the power of military tribunals, otherwise competent to try violations of the law of war, as terminating before the formal state of war has ended. In our own military history there have been numerous instances in which offenders were tried by military commission after the cessation of hostilities and before the proclamation of peace, for offenses against the law of war committed before the cessation of hostilities.

The extent to which the power to prosecute violations of the law of war shall be exercised before peace is declared rests, not with the courts, but with the political branch of the Government, and may itself be governed by the terms of an armistice or the treaty of peace. Here, peace has not been agreed upon or proclaimed. Japan, by her acceptance of the Potsdam Declaration and her surrender, has acquiesced in the trials of those guilty of violations of the law of war. The conduct of the trial by the military commission has been authorized by the political branch of the Government, by military command, by international law and usage, and by the terms of the surrender of the Japanese government.

The Charge. Neither Congressional action nor the military orders constituting the commission authorized it to place petitioner on trial unless the charge preferred against him is of a violation of the law of war. The charge, so far as now relevant, is that petitioner, between October 9, 1944, and September 2, 1945, in the Philippine Islands, "while commander of armed forces of Japan at war with the United States of America and its allies, unlawfully disregarded and failed to discharge his duty as commander to control the operations of the members of his command, permitting them to commit brutal atrocities and other high crimes against people of the United States and of its allies and dependencies, particularly the Philippines; and he . . . thereby violated the laws of war."

Bills of particulars, filed by the prosecution by order of the commission, allege a series of acts, one hundred and twenty-three in number, committed by members of the forces under petitioner's command, during the period mentioned. The first item specifies the execution of "a deliberate plan and purpose to massacre and exterminate a large part of the civilian population of Batangas Province, and to devastate and destroy public, private and religious property therein, as a result of which more than 25,000 men, women and children, all unarmed noncombatant civilians, were brutally mistreated and killed, without cause or trial, and entire settlements were devastated and destroyed wantonly and without military necessity." Other items specify acts of violence, cruelty and homicide inflicted upon the civilian population and prisoners of war, acts of wholesale pillage and the wanton destruction of religious monuments.

It is not denied that such acts directed against the civilian population of an occupied country and against prisoners of war are recognized in international law as violations of the law of war. Articles 4, 28, 46, and 47, Annex to Fourth Hague Convention, 1907, 36 Stat. 2277, 2296, 2303, 2306, 2307. But it is urged that the charge does not allege that petitioner has either committed or directed the commission of such acts, and consequently that no violation is charged as against him. But this overlooks the fact that the gist of the charge is an unlawful breach of duty by petitioner as an army commander to control the operations of the members of his command by "permitting them to commit" the extensive and widespread atrocities specified. The question then is whether the law of war imposes on an army commander a duty to take such appropriate measures as are within his power to control the troops under his command for the prevention of the specified acts which are violations of the law of war and which are likely to attend the occupation of hostile territory by an uncontrolled soldiery, and whether he may be charged with personal responsibility for his failure to take such measures when violations result. That this was the precise issue to be tried was made clear by the statement of the prosecution at the opening of the trial.

It is evident that the conduct of military operations by troops whose excesses are unrestrained by the orders or efforts of their commander would almost certainly result in violations which it is the purpose of the law of war to prevent. Its purpose to protect civilian populations and prisoners of war from brutality would largely be defeated if the commander of an invading army could with impunity neglect to take reasonable measures for their protection. Hence the law of war presupposes that its violation is to be avoided through the control of the operations of war by commanders who are to some extent responsible for their subordinates.

This is recognized by the Annex to Fourth Hague Convention of 1907, respecting the laws and customs of war on land. Article I lays down as a condition which an armed force must fulfill in order to be accorded the rights of lawful belligerents, that it must be "commanded by a person responsible for his subordinates." 36 Stat. 2295. Similarly Article 19 of the Tenth Hague Convention, relating to bombardment by naval vessels, provides that commanders in chief of the belligerent vessels "must see that the above Articles are properly carried out." 36 Stat. 2389. And Article 26 of the Geneva Red Cross Convention of 1929, 47 Stat. 2074, 2092, for the amelioration of the condition of the wounded and sick in armies in the field, makes it "the duty of the commanders-in-chief of the belligerent armies to provide for the details of execution of the foregoing articles [of the convention], as well as for unforeseen cases." And, finally, Article 43 of the Annex of the Fourth Hague Convention, 36 Stat. 2306, requires that the commander of a force occupying enemy territory, as was petitioner, "shall take all the measures in his power to restore, and ensure, as far as possible, public order and safety, while respecting, unless absolutely prevented, the laws in force in the country."

These provisions plainly imposed on petitioner, who at the time specified was military governor of the Philippines, as well as commander of the Japanese forces, an affirmative duty to take such measures as were within his power and appropriate in the circumstances to protect prisoners of war and the civilian population. This duty of a commanding officer has heretofore been recognized, and its breach penalized by our own military tribunals. A like principle has been applied so as to impose liability on the United States in international arbitrations. Case of Jenaud, 3 Moore, International Arbitrations, 3000; Case of "The Zafiro," 5 Hackworth, Digest of International Law, 707.

We do not make the laws of war but we respect them so far as they do not conflict with the commands of Congress or the Constitution. There is no contention that the present charge, thus read, is without the support of evidence, or that the commission held petitioner responsible for failing to take measures which were beyond his control or inappropriate for a commanding officer to take in the circumstances. We do not here appraise the evidence on which petitioner was convicted. We do not consider what measures, if any, petitioner took to prevent the commission, by the troops under his command, of the plain violations of the law of war detailed in the bill of particulars, or whether such measures as he may have taken were appropriate and sufficient to discharge the duty imposed upon him. These are questions within the peculiar competence of the military officers composing the commission and were for it to decide. See Smith v. Whitney, 116 U.S. 167, 178, 6 S.Ct. 570, 576, 29 L.Ed. 601. It is plain that the charge on which petitioner was tried charged him with a breach of his duty to control the operations of the members of his command, by permitting them to commit the specified atrocities. This was enough to require the commission to hear evidence tending to establish the culpable failure of petitioner to perform the duty imposed on him by the law of war and to pass upon its sufficiency to establish guilt.

Obviously charges of violations of the law of war triable before a military tribunal need not be stated with the precision of a common law indictment. Cf. Collins v. McDonald, supra, 258 U.S. 420, 42 S.Ct. 328, 66 L.Ed. 692. But we conclude that the allegations of the charge, tested by any reasonable standard, adequately allege a violation of the law of war and that the commission had authority to try and decide the issue which it raised. Cf. Dealy v. United States, 152 U.S. 539, 14 S.Ct. 680, 38 L.Ed. 545; Williamson v. United States, 207 U.S. 425, 447, 28 S.Ct. 163, 171, 52 L.Ed. 278; Glasser v. United States, 315 U.S. 60, 66, 62 S.Ct. 457, 463, 86 L.Ed. 680, and cases cited.

The Proceedings before the Commission. The regulations prescribed by General MacArthur governing the procedure for the trial of petitioner by the commission directed that the commission should admit such evidence "as in its opinion would be of assistance in proving or disproving the charge, or such as in the commission's opinion would have probative value in the mind of a reasonable man," and that in particular it might admit affidavits, depositions or other statements taken by officers detailed for that purpose by military authority. The petitions in this case charged that in the course of the trial the commission received, over objection by petitioner's counsel, the deposition of a witness taken pursuant to military authority by a United States Army captain. It also, over like objection admitted hearsay and opinion evidence tendered by the prosecution. Petitioner argues as ground for the writ of habeas corpus, that Article 25 of the Articles of War prohibited the reception in evidence by the commission of depositions on behalf of the prosecution in a capital case, and that Article 38 prohibited the reception of hearsay and of opinion evidence.

We think that neither Article 25 nor Article 38 is applicable to the trial of an enemy combatant by a military commission for violations of the law of war. Article 2 of the Articles of War enumerates "the persons . . . subject to these articles," who are denominated, for purposes of the Articles, as "persons subject to military law." In general, the persons so enumerated are members of our own Army and of the personnel accompanying the Army. Enemy combatants are not included among them. Articles 12, 13 and 14, before the adoption of Article 15 in 1916, 39 Stat. 653 made all "persons subject to military law" amenable to trial by courts-martial for any offense made punishable by the Articles of War. Article 12 makes triable by general court martial "any other person who by the law of war is [triable] by military tribunals." Since Article 2, in its 1916 form, 39 Stat. 651, includes some persons who, by the law of war, were, prior to 1916, triable by military commission, it was feared by the proponents of the 1916 legislation that in the absence of a saving provision, the authority given by Articles 12, 13 and 14 to try such persons before courts-martial might be construed to deprive the non-statutory military commission of a portion of what was considered to be its traditional jurisdiction. To avoid this, and to preserve that jurisdiction intact, Article 15 was added to the Articles. It declared that "The provisions of these articles conferring jurisdiction upon courts-martial shall not be construed as depriving military commissions . . . of concurrent jurisdiction in respect of offenders or offenses that by the law of war may be lawfully triable by such military commissions."

By thus recognizing military commissions in order to preserve their traditional jurisdiction over enemy combatants unimpaired by the Articles, Congress gave sanction, as we held in Ex parte Quirin, to any use of the military commission contemplated by the common law of war. But it did not thereby make subject to the Articles of War persons other than those defined by Article 2 as being subject to the Articles, nor did it confer the benefits of the Articles upon such persons. The Articles recognized but one kind of military commission, not two. But they sanctioned the use of that one for the trial of two classes of persons, to one of which the Articles do, and to the other of which they do not apply in such trials. Being of this latter class, petitioner cannot claim the benefits of the Articles, which are applicable only to the members of the other class. Petitioner, an enemy combatant, is therefore not a person made subject to the Articles of War by Article 2, and the military commission before which he was tried, though sanctioned, and its jurisdiction saved, by Article 15, was not convened by virtue of the Articles of War, but pursuant to the common law of war. It follows that the Articles of War, including Articles 25 and 38, were not applicable to petitioner's trial and imposed no restrictions upon the procedure to be followed. The Articles left the control over the procedure in such a case where it had previously been, with the military command. . . .

* * *

Writs denied.

MR. JUSTICE JACKSON took no part in the consideration or decision of these cases.

MR. JUSTICE MURPHY, dissenting.

The significance of the issue facing the Court today cannot be overemphasized. An American military commission has been established to try a fallen military commander of a conquered nation for an alleged war crime. The authority for such action grows out of the exercise of the power conferred upon Congress by Article I, § 8, Cl. 10 of the Constitution to "define and punish . . . Offenses against the Law of Nations. . . ." The grave issue raised by this case is whether a military commission so established and so authorized may disregard the procedural rights of an accused person as guaranteed by the Constitution, especially by the due process clause of the Fifth Amendment.

The answer is plain. The Fifth Amendment guarantee of due process of law applies to "any person" who is accused of a crime by the Federal Government or any of its agencies. No exception is made as to those who are accused of war crimes or as to those who possess the status of an enemy belligerent. Indeed, such an exception would be contrary to the whole philosophy of human rights which makes the Constitution the great living document that it is. The immutable rights of the individual, including those secured by the due process clause of the Fifth Amendment, belong not alone to the members of those nations that excel on the battlefield or that subscribe to the democratic ideology. They belong to every person in the world, victor or vanquished, whatever may be his race, color or beliefs. They rise above any status of belligerency or outlawry. They survive any popular passion or frenzy of the moment. No court or legislature or executive, not even the mightiest army in the world, can ever destroy them. Such is the universal and indestructible nature of the rights which the due process clause of the Fifth Amendment recognizes and protects when life or liberty is threatened by virtue of the authority of the United States.

The existence of these rights, unfortunately, is not always respected. They are often trampled under by those who are motivated by hatred, aggression or fear. But in this nation individual rights are recognized and protected, at least in regard to governmental action. They cannot be ignored by any branch of the Government, even the military, except under the most extreme and urgent circumstances.

The failure of the military commission to obey the dictates of the due process requirements of the Fifth Amendment is apparent in this case. The petitioner was the commander of an army totally destroyed by the superior power of this nation. While under heavy and destructive attack by our forces, his troops committed many brutal atrocities and other high crimes. Hostilities ceased and he voluntarily surrendered. At that point he was entitled, as an individual protected by the due process clause of the Fifth amendment, to be treated fairly and justly according to the accepted rules of law and procedure. He was also entitled to a fair trial as to any alleged crimes and to be free from charges of legally unrecognized crimes that would serve only to permit his accusers to satisfy their desires for revenge.

A military commission was appointed to try the petitioner for an alleged war crime. The trial was ordered to be held in territory over which the United States has complete sovereignty. No military necessity or other emergency demanded the suspension of the safeguards of due process. Yet petitioner was rushed to trial under an improper charge, given insufficient time to prepare an adequate defense, deprived of the benefits of some of the most elementary rules of evidence and summarily sentenced to be hanged. In all this needless and unseemly haste there was no serious attempt to charge or to prove that he committed a recognized violation of the laws of war. He was not charged with personally participating in the acts of atrocity or with ordering or condoning their commission. Not even knowledge of these crimes was attributed to him. It was simply alleged that he unlawfully disregarded and failed to discharge his duty as commander to control the operations of the members of his command, permitting them to commit the acts of atrocity. The recorded annals of warfare and the established principles of international law afford not the slightest precedent for such a charge. This indictment in effect permitted the military commission to make the crime whatever it willed, dependent upon its biased view as to petitioner's duties and his disregard thereof, a practice reminiscent of that pursued in certain less respected nations in recent years.

In my opinion, such a procedure is unworthy of the traditions of our people or of the immense sacrifices that they have made to advance the common ideals of mankind. The high feelings of the moment doubtless will be satisfied. But in the sober afterglow will come the realization of the boundless and dangerous implications of the procedure sanctioned today. No one in a position of command in an army, from sergeant to general, can escape those implications. Indeed, the fate of some future President of the United States and his chiefs of staff and military advisers may well have been sealed by this decision. But even more significant will be the hatred and ill-will growing out of the application of this unprecedented procedure. That has been the inevitable effect of every method of punishment disregarding the element of personal culpability. The effect in this instance, unfortunately, will be magnified infinitely for here we are dealing with the rights of man on an international level. To subject an enemy belligerent to an unfair trial, to charge him with an unrecognized crime, or to vent on him our retributive emotions only antagonizes the enemy nation and hinders the reconciliation necessary to a peaceful world.

That there were brutal atrocities inflicted upon the helpless Filipino people, to whom tyranny is no stranger, by Japanese armed forces under the petitioner's command is undeniable. Starvation, execution or massacre without trial, torture, rape, murder and wanton destruction of property were foremost among the outright violations of the laws of war and of the conscience of a civilized world. That just punishment should be meted out to all those responsible for criminal acts of this nature is also beyond dispute. But these factors do not answer the problem in this case. They do not justify the abandonment of our devotion to justice in dealing with a fallen enemy commander. To conclude otherwise is to admit that the enemy has lost the battle but has destroyed our ideals.

War breeds atrocities. From the earliest conflicts of recorded history to the global struggles of modern times inhumanities, lust and pillage have been the inevitable by-products of man's resort to force and arms. Unfortunately, such despicable acts have a dangerous tendency to call forth primitive impulses of vengeance and retaliation among the victimized peoples. The satisfaction of such impulses in turn breeds resentment and fresh tension. Thus does the spiral of cruelty and hatred grow.

If we are ever to develop an orderly international community based upon a recognition of human dignity it is of the utmost importance that the necessary punishment of those guilty of atrocities be as free as possible from the ugly stigma of revenge and vindictiveness. Justice must be tempered by compassion rather than by vengeance. In this, the first case involving this momentous problem ever to reach this Court, our responsibility is both lofty and difficult. We must insist, within the confines of our proper jurisdiction, that the highest standards of justice be applied in this trial of an enemy commander conducted under the authority of the United States. Otherwise stark retribution will be free to masquerade in a cloak of false legalism. And the hatred and cynicism engendered by that retribution will supplant the great ideals to which this nation is dedicated.

This Court fortunately has taken the first and most important step toward insuring the supremacy of law and justice in the treatment of an enemy belligerent accused of violating the laws of war. Jurisdiction properly has been asserted to inquire "into the cause of restraint of liberty" of such a person. 28 U.S.C. § 452, 28 U.S.C.A. § 452. Thus the obnoxious doctrine asserted by the Government in this case, to the effect that restraints of liberty resulting from military trials of war criminals are political matters completely outside the arena of judicial review, has been rejected fully and unquestionably. This does not mean, of course, that the foreign affairs and policies of the nation are proper subjects of judicial inquiry. But when the liberty of any person is restrained by reason of the authority of the United States the writ of habeas corpus is available to test the legality of that restraint, even though direct court review of the restraint is prohibited. The conclusive presumption must be made, in this country at least, that illegal restraints are unauthorized and unjustified by any foreign policy of the Government and that commonly accepted juridical standards are to be recognized and enforced. On that basis judicial inquiry into these matters may proceed within its proper sphere.

The determination of the extent of review of war trials calls for judicial statesmanship of the highest order. The ultimate nature and scope of the writ of habeas corpus are within the discretion of the judiciary unless validly circumscribed by Congress. Here we are confronted with a use of the writ under circumstances novel in the history of the Court. For my own part, I do not feel that we should be confined by the traditional lines of review drawn in connection with the use of the writ by ordinary criminals who have direct access to the judiciary in the first instance. Those held by the military lack any such access; consequently this judicial review available by habeas corpus must be wider than usual in order that proper standards of justice may be enforceable.

But for the purposes of this case I accept the scope of review recognized by the Court at this time. As I understand it, the following issues in connection with war criminal trials are reviewable through the use of the writ of habeas corpus: (1) Whether the military commission was lawfully created and had authority to try and to convict the accused of a war crime; (2) whether the charge against the accused stated a violation of the laws of war; (3) whether the commission, in admitting certain evidence, violated any law or military command defining the commission's authority in that respect; and (4) whether the commission lacked jurisdiction because of a failure to give advance notice to the protecting power as required by treaty or convention.

The Court, in my judgment, demonstrates conclusively that the military commission was lawfully created in this instance and that petitioner could not object to its power to try him for a recognized war crime. Without pausing here to discuss the third and fourth issues, however, I find it impossible to agree that the charge against the petitioner stated a recognized violation of the laws of war.

It is important, in the first place, to appreciate the background of events preceding this trial. From October 9, 1944, to September 2, 1945, the petitioner was the Commanding General of the 14th Army Group of the Imperial Japanese Army, with headquarters in the Philippines. The reconquest of the Philippines by the armed forces of the United States began approximately at the time when the petitioner assumed this command. Combined with a great and decisive sea battle, an invasion was made on the island of Leyte on October 20, 1944. "In the six days of the great naval action the Japanese position in the Philippines had become extremely critical. Most of the serviceable elements of the Japanese Navy had become committed to the battle with disastrous results. The strike had miscarried, and General MacArthur's land wedge was firmly implanted in the vulnerable flank of the enemy. . . . There were 260,000 Japanese troops scattered over the Philippines but most of them might as well have been on the other side of the world so far as the enemy's ability to shift them to meet the American thrusts was concerned. If General MacArthur succeeded in establishing himself in the Visayas where he could stage, exploit, and spread under cover of overwhelming naval and air superiority, nothing could prevent him from overrunning the Philippines." Biennial Report of the Chief of Staff of the United States Army, July 1, 1943, to June 30, 1945, to the Secretary of War, p. 74.

By the end of 1944 the island of Leyte was largely in American hands. And on January 9, 1945, the island of Luzon was invaded. "Yamashita's inability to cope with General MacArthur's swift moves, his desired reaction to the deception measures, the guerrillas, and General Kenney's aircraft combined to place the Japanese in an impossible situation. The enemy was forced into a piecemeal commitment of his troops." Ibid, p. 78. It was at this time and place that most of the alleged atrocities took place. Organized resistance around Manila ceased on February 23. Repeated land and air assaults pulverized the enemy and within a few months there was little left of petitioner's command except a few remnants which had gathered for a last stand among the precipitous mountains.

As the military commission here noted, "The Defense established the difficulties faced by the Accused with respect not only to the swift and overpowering advance of American forces, but also to the errors of his predecessors, weaknesses in organization, equipment, supply with especial reference to food and gasoline, training, communication, discipline and morale of his troops. It was alleged that the sudden assignment of Naval and Air Forces to his tactical command presented almost insurmountable difficulties. This situation was followed, the Defense contended, by failure to obey his orders to withdraw troops from Manila, and the subsequent massacre of unarmed civilians, particularly by Naval forces. Prior to the Luzon Campaign, Naval forces had reported to a separate ministry in the Japanese Government and Naval Commanders may not have been receptive or experienced in this instance with respect to a joint land operation under a single commander who was designated from the Army Service."

The day of final reckoning for the enemy arrived in August, 1945. On September 3, the petitioner surrendered to the United States Army at Baguio, Luzon. He immediately became a prisoner of war and was interned in prison in conformity with the rules of international law. On September 25, approximately three weeks after surrendering, he was served with the charge in issue in this case. Upon service of the charge he was removed from the status of a prisoner of war and placed in confinement as an accused war criminal. Arraignment followed on October 8 before a military commission specially appointed for the case. Petitioner pleaded not guilty. He was also served on that day with a bill of particulars alleging 64 crimes by troops under his command. A supplemental bill alleging 59 more crimes by his troops was filed on October 29, the same day that the trial began. No continuance was allowed for preparation of a defense as to the supplemental bill. The trial continued uninterrupted until December 5, 1945. On December 7 petitioner was found guilty as charged and was sentenced to be hanged.

The petitioner was accused of having "unlawfully disregarded and failed to discharge his duty as commander to control the operations of the members of his command, permitting them to commit brutal atrocities and other high crimes." The bills of particular further alleged that specific acts of atrocity were committed by "members of the armed forces of Japan under the command of the accused." Nowhere was it alleged that the petitioner personally committed any of the atrocities, or that he ordered their commission, or that he had any knowledge of the commission thereof by members of his command.

The findings of the military commission bear out this absence of any direct personal charge against the petitioner. The commission merely found that atrocities and other high crimes "have been committed by members of the Japanese armed forces under your command . . . that they were not sporadic in nature but in many cases were methodically supervised by Japanese officers and noncommissioned officers . . . that during the period in question you failed to provide effective control of your troops as was required by the circumstances."

In other words, read against the background of military events in the Philippines subsequent to October 9, 1944, these charges amount to this: "We, the victorious American forces, have done everything possible to destroy and disorganize your lines of communication, your effective control of your personnel, your ability to wage war. In those respects we have succeeded. We have defeated and crushed your forces. And now we charge and condemn you for having been inefficient in maintaining control of your troops during the period when we were so effectively besieging and eliminating your forces and blocking your ability to maintain effective control. Many terrible atrocities were committed by your disorganized troops. Because these atrocities were so widespread we will not bother to charge or prove that you committed, ordered or condoned any of them. We will assume that they must have resulted from your inefficiency and negligence as a commander. In short, we charge you with the crime of inefficiency in controlling your troops. We will judge the discharge of your duties by the disorganization which we ourselves created in large part. Our standards of judgment are whatever we wish to make them."

Nothing in all history or in international law, at least as far as I am aware, justifies such a charge against a fallen commander of a defeated force. To use the very inefficiency and disorganization created by the victorious forces as the primary basis for condemning officers of the defeated armies bears no resemblance to justice or to military reality.

International law makes no attempt to define the duties of a commander of an army under constant and overwhelming assault; nor does it impose liability under such circumstances for failure to meet the ordinary responsibilities of command. The omission is understandable. Duties, as well as ability to control troops, vary according to the nature and intensity of the particular battle. To find an unlawful deviation from duty under battle conditions requires difficult and speculative calculations. Such calculations become highly untrustworthy when they are made by the victor in relation to the actions of a vanquished commander. Objective and realistic norms of conduct are then extremely unlikely to be used in forming a judgment as to deviations from duty. The probability that vengeance will form the major part of the victor's judgment is an unfortunate but inescapable fact. So great is that probability that international law refuses to recognize such a judgment as a basis for a war crime, however fair the judgment may be in a particular instance. It is this consideration that undermines the charge against the petitioner in this case. The indictment permits, indeed compels, the military commission of a victorious nation to sit in judgment upon the military strategy and actions of the defeated enemy and to use its conclusions to determine the criminal liability of an enemy commander. Life and liberty are made to depend upon the biased will of the victor rather than upon objective standards of conduct.

The Court's reliance upon vague and indefinite references in certain of the Hague Conventions and the Geneva Red Cross Convention is misplaced. Thus the statement in Article 1 of the Annex to Hague Convention No. IV of October 18, 1907, 36 Stat. 2277, 2295, to the effect that the laws, rights and duties of war apply to military and volunteer corps only if they are "commanded by a person responsible for his subordinates," has no bearing upon the problem in this case. Even if it has, the clause "responsible for his subordinates" fails to state to whom the responsibility is owed or to indicate the type of responsibility contemplated. The phrase has received differing interpretations by authorities on international law. In Oppenheim, International Law (6th ed., rev. by Lauterpacht, 1940, vol. 2, p. 204, fn. 3), it is stated that "The meaning of the word 'responsible' . . . is not clear. It probably means 'responsible to some higher authority,' whether the person is appointed from above or elected from below; . . ." Another authority has stated that the word "responsible" in this particular context means "presumably to a higher authority," or "possibly it merely means one who controls his subordinates and who therefore can be called to account for their acts." Wheaton, International Law (14th ed., by Keith, 1944, p. 172, fn. 30). Still another authority, Westlake, International Law (1907, Part II, p. 61), states that "probably the responsibility intended is nothing more than a capacity of exercising effective control." Finally, Edwards and Oppenheim, Land Warfare (1912, p. 19, par. 22), state that it is enough "if the commander of the corps is regularly or temporarily commissioned as an officer or is a person of position and authority." It seems apparent beyond dispute that the word "responsible" was not used in this particular Hague Convention to hold the commander of a defeated army to any high standard of efficiency when he is under destructive attack; nor was it used to impute to him any criminal responsibility for war crimes committed by troops under his command under such circumstances.

The provisions of the other conventions referred to by the Court are on their face equally devoid of relevance or significance to the situation here in issue. Neither Article 19 of Hague Convention No. X, 36 Stat. 2371, 2389, nor Article 26 of the Geneva Red Cross Convention of 1929, 47 Stat. 2074, 2092, refers to circumstances where the troops of a commander commit atrocities while under heavily adverse battle conditions. Reference is also made to the requirement of Article 43 of the Annex to Hague Convention No. IV, 36 Stat. 2295, 2306, that the commander of a force occupying enemy territory "shall take all the measures in his power to restore, and ensure, as far as possible, public order and safety, while respecting, unless absolutely prevented, the laws in force in the country." But the petitioner was more than a commander of a force occupying enemy territory. He was the leader of an army under constant and devastating attacks by a superior re-invading force. This provision is silent as to the responsibilities of a commander under such conditions as that.

Even the laws of war heretofore recognized by this nation fail to impute responsibility to a fallen commander for excesses committed by his disorganized troops while under attack. Paragraph 347 of the War Department publications, Basic Field Manual, Rules of Land Warfare, FM 27–10 (1940), states the principal offenses under the laws of war recognized by the United States. This includes all of the atrocities which the Japanese troops were alleged to have committed in this instance. Originally this paragraph concluded with the statement that "The commanders ordering the commission of such acts, or under whose authority they are committed by their troops, may be punished by the belligerent into whose hands they may fall." The meaning of the phrase "under whose authority they are committed" was not clear. On November 15, 1944, however, this sentence was deleted and a new paragraph was added relating to the personal liability of those who violate the laws of war. Change 1, FM 27–10. The new paragraph 345.1 states that "Individuals and organizations who violate the accepted laws and customs of war may be punished therefor. However, the fact that the acts complained of were done pursuant to order of a superior or government sanction may be taken into consideration in determining culpability, either by way of defense or in mitigation of punishment. The person giving such orders may also be punished." From this the conclusion seems inescapable that the United States recognizes individual criminal responsibility for violations of the laws of war only as to those who commit the offenses or who order or direct their commission. Such was not the allegation here. Cf. Article 67 of the Articles of War, 10 U.S.C. § 1539, 10 U.S.C.A. § 1539.

There are numerous instances, especially with reference to the Philippine Insurrection in 1900 and 1901, where commanding officers were found to have violated the laws of war by specifically ordering members of their command to commit atrocities and other war crimes. Francisco Frani, G. O. 143, Dec. 13,

1900, Hq. Div. Phil.; Eugenio Fernandez and Juan Soriano, G. O. 28, Feb. 6, 1901, Hq. Div. Phil.; Ciriaco Cabungal, G. O. 188, Jul. 22, 1901, Hq. Div. Phil.; Natalio Valencia, G. O. 221, Aug. 17, 1901, Hq. Div. Phil.; Aniceta Angeles, G. O. 246, Sept. 2, 1901, Hq. Div. Phil.; Francisco Braganza, G. O. 291, Sept. 26, 1901, Hq. Div. Phil.; Lorenzo Andaya, G. O. 328, Oct. 25, 1901, Hq. Div. Phil. And in other cases officers have been held liable where they knew that a crime was to be committed, had the power to prevent it and failed to exercise that power. Pedro Abad Santos, G. O. 130, June 19, 1901, Hq. Div. Phil. Cf. Pedro A. Cruz, G. O. 264, Sept. 9, 1901, Hq. Div. Phil. In no recorded instance, however, has the mere inability to control troops under fire or attack by superior forces been made the basis of a charge of violating the laws of war.

The Government claims that the principle that commanders in the field are bound to control their troops has been applied so as to impose liability on the United States in international arbitrations. Case of Jeannaud, 1880, 3 Moore, International Arbitrations (1898) 3000; Case of The Zafiro, 1910, 5 Hackworth, Digest of International Law (1943) 707. The difference between arbitrating property rights and charging an individual with a crime against the laws of war is too obvious to require elaboration. But even more significant is the fact that even these arbitration cases fail to establish any principle of liability where troops are under constant assault and demoralizing influences by attacking forces. The same observation applies to the common law and statutory doctrine, referred to by the Government, that one who is under a legal duty to take protective or preventive action is guilty of criminal homicide if he willfully or negligently omits to act and death is proximately caused. State v. Harrison, 107 N.J.L. 213, 152 A. 867; State v. Irvine, 126 La. 434, 52 So. 567; Holmes, The Common Law, p. 278. No one denies that inaction or negligence may give rise to liability, civil or criminal. But it is quite another thing to say that the inability to control troops under highly competitive and disastrous battle conditions renders one guilty of a war crime in the absence of personal culpability. Had there been some element of knowledge or direct connection with the atrocities the problem would be entirely different. Moreover, it must be remembered that we are not dealing here with an ordinary tort or criminal action; precedents in those fields are of little if any value. Rather we are concerned with a proceeding involving an international crime, the treatment of which may have untold effects upon the future peace of the world. That fact must be kept uppermost in our search for precedent.

The only conclusion I can draw is that the charge made against the petitioner is clearly without precedent in international law or in the annals of recorded military history. This is not to say that enemy commanders may escape punishment for clear and unlawful failures to prevent atrocities. But that punishment should be based upon charges fairly drawn in light of established rules of international law and recognized concepts of justice.

But the charge in this case, as previously noted, was speedily drawn and filed but three weeks after the petitioner surrendered. The trial proceeded with great dispatch without allowing the defense time to prepare an adequate case. Petitioner's rights under the due process clause of the Fifth Amendment were grossly and openly violated without any justification. All of this was done without any thorough investigation and prosecution of those immediately responsible for the atrocities, out of which might have come some proof or indication of personal culpability on petitioner's part. Instead the loose charge was made that great numbers of atrocities had been committed and that petitioner was the commanding officer; hence he must have been guilty of disregard of duty. Under that charge the commission was free to establish whatever standard of duty on petitioner's part that it desired. By this flexible method a victorious nation may convict and execute any or all leaders of a vanquished foe, depending upon the prevailing degree of vengeance and the absence of any objective judicial review.

At a time like this when emotions are understandably high it is difficult to adopt a dispassionate attitude toward a case of this nature. Yet now is precisely the time when that attitude is most essential. While peoples in other lands may not share our beliefs as to due process and the dignity of the individual, we are not free to give effect to our emotions in reckless disregard of the rights of others. We live under the Constitution, which is the embodiment of all the high hopes and aspirations of the new world. And it is applicable in both war and peace. We must act accordingly. Indeed, an uncurbed spirt of revenge and retribution, masked in formal legal procedure for purposes of dealing with a fallen enemy commander, can do more lasting harm than all of the atrocities giving rise to that spirit. The people's faith in the fairness and objectiveness of the law can be seriously undercut by that spirit. The fires of nationalism can be further kindled. And the hearts of all mankind can be embittered and filled with hatred, leaving forlorn and impoverished the noble ideal of malice toward none and charity to all. These are the reasons that lead me to dissent in these terms.

MR. JUSTICE RUTLEDGE, dissenting.

Not with ease does one find his views at odds with the Court's in a matter of this character and gravity. Only the most deeply felt convictions could force one to differ. That reason alone leads me to do so now, against strong considerations for withholding dissent.

More is at stake than General Yamashita's fate. There could be no possible sympathy for him if he is guilty of the atrocities for which his death is sought. But there can be and should be justice administered according to law. In this stage of war's aftermath it is too early for Lincoln's great spirit, best lighted in the Second Inaugural, to have wide hold for the treatment of foes. It is not too early, it is never too early, for the nation steadfastly to follow its great constitutional traditions, none older or more universally protective against unbridled power than due process of law in the trial and punishment of men, that is, of all men, whether citizens, aliens, alien enemies or enemy belligerents. It can become too late.

This long-held attachment marks the great divide between our enemies and ourselves. Theirs was a philosophy of universal force. Ours is one of universal law, albeit imperfectly made flesh of our system and so dwelling among us. Every departure weakens the tradition, whether it touches the high or the low, the powerful or the weak, the triumphant or the conquered. If we need not or cannot be magnanimous, we can keep our own law on the plane from which it has not descended hitherto and to which the defeated foes' never rose.

With all deference to the opposing views of my brethren, whose attachment to that tradition needless to say is no less than my own, I cannot believe in the face of this record that the petitioner has had the fair trial our Constitution and laws command. Because I cannot reconcile what has occurred with their measure, I am forced to speak. At bottom my concern is that we shall not forsake in any case, whether Yamashita's or another's, the basic standards of trial which, among other guaranties, the nation fought to keep; that our system of military justice shall not alone among all our forms of judging be above or beyond the fundamental law or the control of Congress within its orbit of authority; and that this Court shall not fail in its part under the Constitution to see that these things do not happen.

This trial is unprecedented in our history. Never before have we tried and convicted an enemy general for action taken during hostilities or otherwise in the course of military operations or duty. Much less have we condemned one for failing to take action. The novelty is not lessened by the trial's having taken place after hostilities ended and the enemy, including the accused, had surrendered. Moreover, so far as the time permitted for our consideration has given opportunity, I have not been able to find precedent for the proceeding in the system of any nation founded in the basic principles of our constitutional democracy, in the laws of war or in other internationally binding authority or usage.

The novelty is legal as well as historical. We are on strange ground. Precedent is not all-controlling in law. There must be room for growth, since every precedent has an origin. But it is the essence of our tradition for judges, when they stand at the end of the marked way, to go forward with caution keeping sight, so far as they are able, upon the great landmarks left behind and the direction they point ahead. If, as may be hoped, we are now to enter upon a new era of law in the world, it becomes more important than ever before for the nations creating that system to observe their greatest traditions of administering justice, including this one, both in their own judging and in their new creation. The proceedings in this case veer so far from some of our time-tested road signs that I cannot take the large strides validating them would demand.

I

It is not in our tradition for anyone to be charged with crime which is defined after his conduct, alleged to be criminal, has taken place; or in language not sufficient to inform him of the nature of the offense or to enable him to make defense. Mass guilt we do not impute to individuals, perhaps in any case but certainly in none where the person is not charged or shown actively to have participated in or knowingly to have failed in taking action to prevent the wrongs done by others, having both the duty and the power to do so.

It is outside our basic scheme to condemn men without giving reasonable opportunity for preparing defense; in capital or other serious crimes to convict on "official documents . . . ; affidavits; . . . documents or translations thereof; diaries . . . , photographs, motion picture films, and . . . newspapers" or on hearsay, once, twice or thrice removed, more particularly when the documentary evidence or some of it is prepared ex parte by the prosecuting authority and includes not only opinion but conclusions of guilt. Nor in such cases do we deny the rights of confrontation of witnesses and cross-examination.

Our tradition does not allow conviction by tribunals both authorized and bound by the instrument of their creation to receive and consider evidence which is expressly excluded by Act of Congress or by treaty obligation; nor is it in accord with our basic concepts to make the tribunal, specially constituted for the particular trial, regardless of those prohibitions, the sole and exclusive judge of the credibility, probative value and admissibility of whatever may be tendered as evidence.

The matter is not one merely of the character and admissibility of evidence. It goes to the very competency of the tribunal to try and punish consistently with the Constitution, the laws of the United States made in pursuance thereof, and treaties made under the nation's authority.

All these deviations from the fundamental law, and others, occurred in the course of constituting the commission, the preparation for trial and defense, the trial itself, and therefore, in effect, in the sentence imposed. Whether taken singly in some instances as departures from specific constitutional mandates or in totality as in violation of the Fifth Amendment's command that *no* person shall be deprived of life, liberty or property without due process of law, a trial so vitiated cannot withstand constitutional scrutiny.

One basic protection of our system and one only, petitioner has had. He has been represented by able counsel, officers of the army he fought. Their difficult assignment has been done with extraordinary fidelity, not only to the accused, but to their high conception of military justice, always to be administered in subordination to the Constitution and consistent Acts of Congress and treaties. But, as will appear, even this conceded shield was taken away in much of its value, by denial of reasonable opportunity for them to perform their function.

On this denial and the commission's invalid constitution specifically, but also more generally upon the totality of departures from constitutional norms inherent in the idea of a fair trial, I rest my judgment that the commission was without jurisdiction from the beginning to try or punish the petitioner and that, if it had acquired jurisdiction then, its power to proceed was lost in the course of what was done before and during trial.

* * *

V. The Geneva Convention of 1929.

If the provisions of Articles 25 and 38 were not applicable to the proceeding by their own force as Acts of Congress, I think they would still be made applicable by virtue of the terms of the Geneva Convention of 1929, in particular Article 63. And in other respects, in my opinion, the petitioner's trial was not in accord with that treaty, namely with Article 60.

The Court does not hold that the Geneva Convention is not binding upon the United States and no such contention has been made in this case. It relies on other arguments to show that Article 60, which provides that the protecting power shall be notified in advance of a judicial proceeding directed against a prisoner of war, and Article 63, which provides that a prisoner of war may be tried only by the same courts and according to the same procedure as in the case of persons belonging to the armed forces of the detaining power, are not properly invoked by the petitioner. Before considering the Court's view that these Articles are not applicable to this proceeding by their terms, it may be noted that on his surrender petitioner was interned in conformity with Article 9 of this Convention.

The chief argument is that Articles 60 and 63 have reference only to offenses committed by a prisoner of war while a prisoner of war and not to violations of the law of war committed while a combatant. This conclusion is derived from the setting in which these articles are placed. I do not agree that the context gives any support to this argument. The argument is in essence of the same type as the argument the Court employs to nullify the application of Articles 25 and 38 of the Articles of War by restricting their own broader coverage by reference to Article 2. For reasons set forth in the margin, I think it equally invalid here.

Neither Article 60 nor Article 63 contains such a restriction of meaning as the Court reads into them. In the absence of any such limitation, it would seem that they were intended to cover all judicial proceedings, whether instituted for crimes allegedly committed before capture or later. Policy supports this view. For such a construction is required for the security of our own soldiers, taken prisoner, as much as for that of prisoners we take. And the opposite one leaves prisoners of war open to any form of trial and punishment for offenses against the law of war their captors may wish to use, while safeguarding them, to the extent of the treaty limitations, in cases of disciplinary offense. This, in many instances, would be to make the treaty strain at a gnat and swallow the camel.

The United States has complied with neither of these Articles. It did not notify the protecting power of Japan in advance of trial as Article 60 requires it to do, although the supplemental bill charges the same failure to petitioner in Item 89. It is said that, although this may be true, the proceeding is not thereby invalidated. The argument is that our noncompliance merely gives Japan a right of indemnity against us and that Article 60 was not intended to give Yamashita any personal rights. I cannot agree. The treaties made by the United States are by the Constitution made the supreme law of the land. In the absence of something in the treaty indicating that its provisions were not intended to be enforced, upon breach, by more than subsequent indemnification, it is, as I conceive it, the duty of the courts of this country to insure the nation's compliance with such treaties, except in the case of political questions. This is especially true where the treaty has provisions—such as Article 60—for the protection of a man being tried for an offense the punishment for which is death; for to say that it was intended to provide for enforcement of such provisions solely by claim, after breach, of indemnity would be in many instances, especially those involving trial of nationals of a defeated nation by a conquering one, to deprive the Articles of all force. Executed men are not much aided by post-war claims for indemnity. I do not think the adhering powers' purpose was to provide only for such ineffective relief.

Finally, the Government has argued that Article 60 has no application after the actual cessation of hostilities, as there is no longer any need for an intervening power between the two belligerents. The premise is that Japan no longer needs Switzerland to intervene with the United States to protect the rights of Japanese nationals, since Japan is now in direct communication with this Government. This of course is in contradiction of the Government's theory, in other connections, that the war is not over and military necessity still requires use of all the power necessary for actual combat.

Furthermore the premise overlooks all the realities of the situation. Japan is a defeated power, having surrendered, if not unconditionally then under the most severe conditions. Her territory is occupied by American military forces. She is scarcely in a position to bargain with us or to assert her rights. Nor can her nationals. She no longer holds American prisoners of war. Certainly, if there was the need of an independent neutral to protect her nationals during the war, there is more now. In my opinion the failure to give the notice required by Article 60 is only another instance of the commission's failure to observe the obligations of our law.

What is more important, there was no compliance with Article 63 of the same Convention. Yamashita was not tried "according to the same procedure as in the case of persons belonging to the armed forces of the detaining Power." Had one of our soldiers or officers been tried for alleged war crimes, he would have been entitled to the benefits of the Articles of War. I think that Yamashita was equally entitled to the same protection. In any event, he was entitled to their benefits under the provisions of Article 63 of the Geneva Convention. Those benefits he did not receive. Accordingly, his trial was in violation of the Convention.

VI. The Fifth Amendment.

Wholly apart from the violation of the Articles of War and of the Geneva Convention, I am completely unable to accept or to understand the Court's ruling concerning the applicability of the due process clause of the Fifth Amendment to this case. Not heretofore has it been held that any human being is beyond its universally protecting spread in the guaranty of a fair trial in the most fundamental sense. That door is dangerous to open. I will have no part in opening it. For once it is ajar, even for enemy belligerents, it can be pushed back wider for others, perhaps ultimately for all.

The Court does not declare expressly that petitioner as an enemy belligerent has no constitutional rights, a ruling I could understand but not accept. Neither does it affirm that he has some, if but little constitutional protection. Nor does the Court defend what was done. I think the effect of what it does is in substance to deny him all such safeguards. And this is the great issue in the cause.

For it is exactly here we enter wholly untrodden ground. The safe signposts to the rear are not in the sum of protections surrounding jury trials or any other proceeding known to our law. Nor is the essence of the Fifth Amendment's elementary protection comprehended in any single one of our time-honored specific constitutional safeguards in trial, though there are some without which the words "fair trial" and all they connote become a mockery.

Apart from a tribunal concerned that the law as applied shall be an instrument of justice, albeit stern in measure to the guilt established, the heart of the security lies in two things. One is that conviction shall not rest in any essential part upon unchecked rumor, report, or the results of the prosecution's ex parte investigations, but shall stand on proven fact; the other, correlative, lies in a fair chance to defend. This embraces at the least the rights to know with reasonable clarity in advance of the trial the exact nature of the offense with which one is to be charged; to have reasonable time for preparing to meet the charge and to have the aid of counsel in doing so, as also in the trial itself; and if, during its course, one is taken by surprise, through the injection of new charges or reversal of rulings which brings forth new masses of evidence, then to have further reasonable time for meeting the unexpected shift.

So far as I know, it has not yet been held that any tribunal in our system, of whatever character, is free to receive "such evidence 'as *in its opinion*'" would be "*of assistance* in proving or disproving the charge" or, again as in its opinion, "would have probative value in the mind of a reasonable man"; and, having received what in its unlimited discretion it regards as sufficient, is also free to determine what weight may be given to the evidence received without restraint.

When to this fatal defect in the directive, however innocently made, are added the broad departures from the fundamentals of fair play in the proof and in the right to defend which occurred throughout the proceeding, there can be no accommodation with the due process of law which the Fifth Amendment demands.

All this the Court puts to one side with the short assertion that no question of due process under the Fifth Amendment or jurisdiction reviewable here is presented. I do not think this meets the issue, standing alone or in conjunction with the suggestion which follows that the Court gives no intimation one way or the other concerning what Fifth Amendment due process might require in other situations.

It may be appropriate to add here that, although without doubt the directive was drawn in good faith in the belief that it would expedite the trial and that enemy belligerents in petitioner's position were not entitled to more, that state of mind and purpose cannot cure the nullification of basic constitutional standards which has taken place.

It is not necessary to recapitulate. The difference between the Court's view of this proceeding and my own comes down in the end to the view, on the one hand, that there is no law restrictive upon these proceedings other than whatever rules and regulations may be prescribed for their government by the executive authority or the military and, on the other hand, that the provisions of the Articles of War, of the Geneva Convention and the Fifth Amendment apply.

I cannot accept the view that anywhere in our system resides or lurks a power so unrestrained to deal with any human being through any process of trial. What military agencies or authorities may do with our enemies in battle or invasion, apart from proceedings in the nature of trial and some semblance of judicial action, is beside the point. Nor has any human being heretofore been held to be wholly beyond elementary procedural protection by the Fifth Amendment. I cannot consent to even implied departure from that great absolute.

It was a great patriot who said:

He that would make his own liberty secure must guard even his enemy from oppression; for if he violates this duty he establishes a precedent that will reach himself.

MR. JUSTICE MURPHY joins in this opinion.

HOMMA *vs.* PATTERSON

1946*

MASAHARU HOMMA *vs.* LIEUTENANT GENERAL WILHELM D. STYER, COMMANDING GENERAL, UNITED STATES ARMY FORCES, WESTERN PACIFIC.

MOTION FOR LEAVE to file petition for writ of habeas corpus and writ of prohibition and petition for writ of habeas corpus and writ of prohibition.

On petition for a writ of certiorari to the Supreme Court of the Commonwealth of the Philippines.

Feb. 11, 1946. On motion for leave to file petition for writs of habeas corpus and prohibition and on petition for a writ of certiorari to the Supreme Court of the Commonwealth of the Philippines. The motion for leave to file petition for writ of habeas corpus and writ of prohibition is denied and the petition for writ of certiorari is also denied on authority of Application of Yamashita, and Yamashita v. Styer, 327 U.S. 1, 66 S.Ct. 340. Mr. Justice MURPHY has filed a dissenting memorandum in which Mr. Justice RUTLEDGE concurs. Mr. Justice RUTLEDGE has filed a dissenting memorandum in which Mr. Justice MURPHY concurs.

MR. JUSTICE MURPHY, dissenting.

This case, like In re Yamashita, 327 U.S. 1, 66 S.Ct. 340, poses a problem that cannot be lightly brushed aside or given momentary consideration. It involves something more than the guilt of a fallen enemy commander under the law of war or the jurisdiction of a military commission. This nation's very honor, as well as its hopes for the future, is at stake. Either we conduct such a trial as this in the noble spirit and atmosphere of our Constitution or we abandon all pretense to justice, let the ages slip away and descend to the level of revengeful blood purges. Apparently the die has been cast in favor of the latter course. But I, for one, shall have no part in it, not even through silent acquiescence.

*327 U.S. 759 (1946)

Petitioner, a civilian for the past three and a half years, was the victorious commander of the 14th Army of the Imperial Japanese Army in the Philippines from December 12, 1941, to August 5, 1942. It may well be that the evidence of his guilt under the law of war is more direct and clear than in the case of General Yamashita, though this could be determined only by an examination of the evidence such as we have had no opportunity to make. But neither clearer proof of guilt nor the acts of atrocity of the Japanese troops could excuse the undue haste with which the trial was conducted or the promulgation of a directive containing such obviously unconstitutional provisions as those approving the use of coerced confessions or evidence and findings of prior mass trials. To try the petitioner in a setting of reason and calm, to issue and use constitutional directives and to obey the dictates of a fair trial are not impossible tasks. Hasty, revengeful action is not the American way. All those who act by virtue of the authority of the United States are bound to respect the principles of justice codified in our Constitution. Those principles, which were established after so many centuries of struggle, can scarcely be dismissed as narrow artificialities or arbitrary technicalities. They are the very life blood of our civilization.

Today the lives of Yamashita and Homma, leaders of enemy forces vanquished in the field of battle, are taken without regard to due process of law. There will be few to protest. But tomorrow the precedent here established can be turned against others. A procession of judicial lynchings without due process of law may now follow. No one can foresee the end of this failure of objective thinking and of adherence to our high hopes of a new world. The time for effective vigilance and protest, however, is when the abandonment of legal procedure is first attempted. A nation must not perish because, in the natural frenzy of the aftermath of war, it abandoned its central theme of the dignity of the human personality and due process of law.

MR. JUSTICE RUTLEDGE agrees with these views.

MR. JUSTICE RUTLEDGE, dissenting.

I dissent upon the grounds stated in the dissenting opinions in the Yamashita case, 327 U.S. 1, 66 S.Ct. 340, all of which are exemplified in these applications, and for additional reasons presented by them.

For the first time the Court, by its denial of the applications with the effect of sustaining the commission's jurisdiction, permits trial for a capital offense under a binding procedure which allows forced confessions to be received in evidence; makes proof in prior trials of groups for mass offenses "prima facie evidence that the accused is likewise guilty of that offense"; and requires that the findings and judgment in such a mass trial "be given full faith and credit" in any subsequent trial of an individual person charged as a member of the group. These provisions of the directive ordering the creation of the commission in my judgment vitiate the entire proceeding.

Moreover the time allowed for preparation of the defense was cut from the three weeks given to Yamashita to fifteen days between arraignment and the beginning of trial. Motions at arraignment for 30 days to prepare defense before the trial began and on the opening day of trial for a ten-day continuance, the latter supported by counsel's affidavit of insufficient time, were denied.

Other serious questions, affecting the validity and fairness of the commission's constitution are presented which were not raised in the Yamashita petitions.

I think the motion and petition respectively should be granted and determined on the merits.

MR. JUSTICE MURPHY joins in this opinion.

THE EICHMANN TRIAL
Jerusalem, December, 1961

ATTORNEY-GENERAL OF THE GOVERNMENT OF ISRAEL *vs.* ADOLF EICHMANN

Israel, District Court of Jerusalem. December 12, 1961

(Landau J., President; Halevi and Raveh JJ.)

Supreme Court (sitting as a Court of Criminal Appeal). May 29, 1962.

(Olshan J., President; Agranat J., Deputy President; Silberg, Sussman and Witkon JJ.)

JUDGMENT OF THE DISTRICT COURT

1. ADOLF EICHMANN has been arraigned before this Court on charges of unsurpassed gravity—crimes against the Jewish people, crimes against humanity, and war crimes. The period of the crimes ascribed to him, and their historical background, is that of the Hitler régime in Germany and in Europe, and the Counts of the indictment encompass the catastrophe which befell the Jewish people during that period—a story of bloodshed and suffering which will be remembered to the end of time. This is not the first occasion that the catastrophe has been discussed in court proceedings. It was dealt with extensively by the International Military Tribunal at Nuremberg during the *Trial of the Major War Criminals,* and also at several of the trials which followed. This time, however, it has occupied the central place in the proceedings, and it is this fact which distinguishes the present trial from those which preceded it. Hence also the trend to widen its range, noticed before and during the trial. The desire was felt—readily understandable in itself—to give, within the limits of this trial, a comprehensive and exhaustive historical account of the events of the catastrophe, and, in so doing, to emphasize also the signal feats of heroism of

the Ghetto-fighters, of those who mutinied in the camps, and of the Jewish partisans. Others again sought to regard this trial as a forum to clarify questions of great import, some of which arose from the catastrophe, while others, of long standing, have now re-emerged more acutely because of the unprecedented sufferings which were visited upon the Jewish people and the world as a whole in the middle of the twentieth century. How could this happen in the full light of day, and why was it just the German people from whom this great evil sprang? Could the Nazis have carried out their evil designs without the help given them by other peoples in whose midst the Jews dwelt? Would it have been possible to avert the catastrophe, at least in part, if the Allies had displayed a greater will to assist the persecuted Jews? Did the Jewish people in the lands of freedom do all in their power to rally to the rescue of their brethren and to sound the alarm for help? What are the psychological and social causes of the group-hatred which is known as anti-semitism? Can this ancient disease be cured, and by what means? What is the lesson which the Jews and other nations, as well as every man in his relationship to others, must learn from all this? Other questions arise also, of various kinds, which cannot even be fully enumerated.

2. In this maze of insistent questions, the path of the Court was and remains clear. It must not allow itself to be enticed to stray into provinces which are outside its sphere. The judicial process has ways of its own, laid down by law and immutable, whatever the subject-matter of the trial. Were it not so, the course of law and of procedure would be impaired, whereas it must be adhered to punctiliously since it is in itself of great social and educational significance, and the trial would otherwise resemble a rudderless ship tossed about on the waves.

The purpose of every criminal trial is to investigate the truth of the prosecutor's charges against the accused who is on trial, and, if the accused is convicted, to mete out due punishment to him. Whatever requires clarification to achieve these ends must be examined at the trial, and whatever is foreign to it must be excluded from the proceedings. Not only is any pretension to overstep these limits forbidden to the Court—it would be bound to end in complete failure. The Court does not possess the facilities required for investigating general questions of the kind referred to above. For example, to describe the historical background of the catastrophe, a great mass of documents and evidence has been submitted to us, collected most painstakingly and certainly out of a genuine desire to delineate as complete a picture as possible. Even so, all this material is but a tiny fraction of the extant sources on this subject. According to our legal system, the Court is by its very nature "passive," for it does not itself initiate the bringing of proof before it, as is the custom with a commission of enquiry. In consequence, its ability to describe general events is inevitably limited. As for questions of principle which are outside the realm of law, no one has made us judges of them and therefore our opinion on them carries no greater weight than that of any person who has devoted study and thought to these questions.

These prefatory remarks do not mean that we disregard the great educational value implicit in the very holding of this trial; both for those who live in Zion and for those beyond the confines of this State. To the extent that this result has been achieved in the course of the proceedings, it is to be welcomed. Thus, the evidence given at this trial by survivors of the catastrophe, who poured out their hearts as they stood in the witness box, will certainly provide valuable material for the research worker and the historian, but as far as this Court is concerned all these things are merely a by-product of the trial.

3. Before passing to the case itself, we desire to express our appreciation to counsel for both parties, who laboured in the preparation of this case. The Attorney-General, Mr. Gideon Hausner, and his assistants, Dr. Y. Robinson, Mr. Y. Bar-or, Mr. G. Bach and Mr. Z. Terlo, who helped him in the conduct of the trial, carried an enormous burden on their shoulders to attain complete mastery of the mass of legal and factual material prepared for them by the police investigators who toiled in a manner also deserving of praise. The Attorney-General himself emerged honourably from the dilemma to which we alluded above, and which he, too, certainly felt in its full impact. In spite of a slight deviation here and there from the narrow path which the Court saw it as its duty to set, Mr. Hausner conducted the prosecution in all its stages as a lawyer of the highest professional standards. In his brilliant opening speech, which was eloquent and broad in perspective, and again in his concluding statement, he gave vent also to the profound emotions which stir the heart of the entire people. Similarly, we wish to express our appreciation to counsel for the defence, Dr. R. Servatius, and his assistant, Mr. D. Wechtenbruch. Dr. Servatius, who stood almost alone in this strenuous legal battle, in an unfamiliar environment, always directed himself to the essence of the matter, and refrained from unnecessary controversy over matters which did not seem to him to be essential for the defence of his client. He thereby rendered valuable assistance to the Court. Not even the few discordant notes in his concluding speech could detract from the worthy and serious impression made by his defence as a whole.

4. We must state at the outset the reasons for our ruling (No. 3 of April 17, 1961, Session 6) that we have jurisdiction to try this case. It is the duty of the Court to examine its competence *ex officio* even without the plea being raised by the accused; indeed, even if the accused had consented to be tried by this Court we would not have been entitled to try him unless the law empowered us to do so. The Law which confers on us jurisdiction to try the accused in this case is the Nazis and Nazi Collaborators (Punishment) Law, 5710/1950 (hereinafter briefly referred to as "the Israel Law," "the Law in question" or "the Law").

Section 1 (*a*) of the Law provides:

A person who has committed one of the following offences—

(1) done, during the period of the Nazi régime, in an enemy country, an act constituting a crime against the Jewish people;

(2) done, during the period of the Nazi régime, in an enemy country, an act constituting a crime against humanity;

(3) done, during the period of the Second World War, in an enemy country, an act constituting a war crime;

is liable to the death penalty.

The three above-mentioned classes of crime—a crime against the Jewish people, a crime against humanity, a war crime—are defined in Section 1 (*b*) of the Law.

Section 3 (*a*) provides:

A person who, during the period of the Nazi régime, in an enemy country, was a member of, or held any post or exercised any function in, an enemy organization, is liable to imprisonment for a term not exceeding seven years.

"An enemy organization" is defined in Section 3 (*b*). Section 16 defines the terms "the period of the Nazi régime," "the period of the Second World War," and "an enemy country."

5. In Criminal Appeal 22/52, *Honigman* v. *Attorney-General* (7 Piske Din 296, 303), Justice Cheshin said:

The Law in question is designed to make it possible to try in Israel Nazis, their associates and their collaborators for the murder of the Jewish people . . . and for crimes against humanity as a whole. . . . This particular Law is totally different . . . from all other legislation usually found in the criminal codes. The Law is retroactive and extraterritorial . . .

Indeed, the expressions "in an enemy country," "during the period of the Nazi régime" and "during the period of the Second World War," which define the application of the Law in point of place and in point of time, indicate unequivocally that the crimes are "foreign crimes" and that the law has retroactive application. These two features indeed fall outside the characteristics of ordinary criminal legislation, which generally applies prospectively and not—or at least not only—retrospectively, and territorially and not—or at least not only—exterritorially; but these features necessarily derive from the very object of the Law for the punishment of the Nazis and their collaborators.

* * *

From the point of view of international law, the power of the State of Israel to enact the Law in question or Israel's "right to punish" is based, with respect to the offences in question, on a dual foundation: the universal character of the crimes in question and their specific character as intended to exterminate the Jewish people. In what follows we shall deal with each of these two aspects separately.

12. The abhorrent crimes defined in this Law are not crimes under Israel law alone. These crimes, which struck at the whole of mankind and shocked the conscience of nations, are grave offences against the law of nations itself

(*delicta juris gentium*). Therefore, so far from international law negating or limiting the jurisdiction of countries with respect to such crimes, international law is, in the absence of an International Court, in need of the judicial and legislative organs of every country to give effect to its criminal interdictions and to bring the criminals to trial. The jurisdiction to try crimes under international law is *universal.*

* * *

18. On May 28, 1951, the International Court of Justice gave, at the request of the United Nations General Assembly, an Advisory Opinion on the question of *Reservations to the Convention on Genocide.* The Advisory Opinion said, *inter alia* (p. 23):

> The origins of the Convention show that it was the intention of the United Nations to condemn and punish genocide as "a crime under international law" involving a denial of the right of existence of entire human groups, a denial which shocks the conscience of mankind and results in great losses to humanity, and which is contrary to moral law and to the spirit and aims of the United Nations (Resolution 96 (1) of the General Assembly, December 11th, 1946). The first consequence arising from this conception is that the principles underlying the Convention are principles which are recognized by civilized nations as binding on States, even without any conventional obligation. A second consequence is the universal character both of the condemnation of genocide and of the co-operation required "in order to liberate mankind from such an odious scourge" (Preamble to the Convention). The Genocide Convention was therefore intended by the General Assembly and by the contracting parties to be definitely universal in scope. It was in fact approved on December 9th, 1948, by a resolution which was unanimously adopted by fifty-six States.

19. In view of the repeated affirmation by the United Nations in the resolution of the General Assembly of 1946 and in the Convention of 1948, and also in view of the Advisory Opinion of the International Court of Justice, there is no doubt that genocide has been recognized as a crime under international law in the full legal meaning of this term, *ex tunc;* that is to say, the crimes of genocide which were committed against the Jewish people and other peoples during the period of the Hitler régime were crimes under international law. It follows, therefore, in accordance with the accepted principles of international law, that the jurisdiction to try such crimes is universal.

* * *

27. Learned counsel for the defence has summed up his argument against the jurisdiction of the Israel legislator by stressing (Session 5, pp. 17–20) that under international law there must be a connection between the State and the person who committed the crime and that in the absence of a "recognized linking point" the State has no authority to inflict punishment for foreign offences.

* * *

32. We have already mentioned the view of Grotius on "the right to punish," a view which is also based on a "linking point" between the criminal and his victim. Grotius holds the very commission of the crime creates a legal connection between the offender and the victim such as vests in the victim the right to punish the offender or demand his punishment. According to natural justice, the victim may himself punish the offender, but the organization of society has transferred that natural right to the sovereign State. One of the main objects of the punishment—continues the author of *The Law of Peace and War* (Book 2, chap. 20)—is to ensure that "the victim shall not in future suffer a similar injury at the hands of the same person or at the hands of others" (*ne post hac tale quid patiatur aut ab eodem aut ab aliis*).

Grotius also quotes an ancient authority who said that the punishment is necessary to "defend the honour or authority of him who was injured by the offense so that the failure to punish may not lead to his reproach and indignity", and he adds that what has been said of the attack upon a person's authority applies to the infringement of all his rights. And again: *"Ne ab allis laedatur qui laesus est punitione non quavis, sed aperta atque conspicua quae ad exemplum pertinet obtinetur."*

* * *

Notwithstanding the difference of opinion as to the closeness of the requisite link, the very term "connection" or "linking point" is useful for the elucidation of the problem before us. The question is, what is the special connection between the State of Israel and the offences attributed to the accused, and whether this connection is sufficiently close to form a foundation for Israel's right of punishment regarding the accused. This is no merely technical question but a wide and general one; for the principles of international law are broad universal principles and not articles of an express code.

33. When the question is presented in its widest form, as above, it seems to us that the answer cannot be in doubt. The "linking point" between Israel and the accused (and for that matter any person accused of a crime against the Jewish people under this Law) is striking in the case of "crime against the Jewish people", a crime that postulates an intention to exterminate the Jewish people in whole or in part. Indeed, even without such specific definition—and it must be noted that the draft Law had only defined "crimes against humanity" and "war crimes" (Drafts of Law of the year 5710, No. 36, p. 119)—there was a subsisting "linking point, since most of the Nazi crimes of this kind were perpetrated against the Jewish people; but in the light of the definition of "crime against the Jewish people", the legal position is clearer. "Crime against the Jewish people", as defined in the Law, constitutes in effect an attempt to exterminate the Jewish people, or a partial extermination of the Jewish people. If an effective link (not necessarily an identity) existed between the State of Israel and the Jewish people, then a crime intended to exterminate the Jewish people has an indubitable connection with the State of Israel.

34. The connection between the State of Israel and the Jewish people needs no explanation. The State of Israel was established and recognized as the State of the Jews. The Declaration of the Establishment of the State of Israel of Iyar 5, 5705 (May 14, 1948) (*Official Gazette* No. 1) opens with the words: "Eretz-Israel was the birthplace of the Jewish people"; it dwells on the history of the Jewish people from ancient times until the second World War; it refers to the Resolution of the United Nations General Assembly of November 29, 1947, calling for the establishment of a Jewish State in Palestine; it lays down the "natural right of the Jewish people to be masters of their own fate, like all other nations in their own sovereign State," and proclaims "the establishment of a Jewish State in Eretz-Israel, to be known as the State of Israel." It would appear that there is hardly need for any further proof of the very obvious connection between the Jewish people and the State of Israel: this is the sovereign State of the Jewish people.

* * *

40. By our decision No. 3 of April 17, 1961 (Session 6), we dismissed Counsel's objections to the jurisdiction of the Court and ruled that there was no need to hear the witnesses summoned with reference to his second submission. The following were the reasons for our decision.

41. It is an established rule of law that a person being tried for an offence against the laws of a State may not oppose his trial by reason of the illegality of his arrest or of the means whereby he was brought within the jurisdiction of that State. The courts in England, the United States and Israel have constantly held that the circumstances of the arrest and the mode of bringing of the accused into the territory of the State have no relevance to his trial, and they have consistently refused in all instances to enter upon an examination of these circumstances. . . .

* * *

52. . . . To sum up, the plea of the accused to the jurisdiction of the Court by reason of his abduction from Argentina is basically no more than a plea for immunity by a fugitive offender on the strength of the refuge given him by a sovereign State. This plea does not avail the accused for two reasons. (*a*) According to the existing rule of law there is no immunity for a fugitive offender save in the one and only case where he has been extradited by the asylum State to the requesting State for a specific offence, which is not the offence for which he was being tried. The accused was not surrendered to Israel by Argentina, and the State of Israel is not bound by any agreement with Argentina to try the accused for any other specific offence, or not to try him for the offences being tried in the present case. (*b*) The rights of asylum and immunity belong to the country of asylum and not to the offender, and the accused cannot compel a foreign sovereign State to give him protection against

its will. The accused was a wanted war criminal when he escaped to Argentina by concealing his true identity. Only after he was kidnapped and brought to Israel was his identity revealed. After negotiations between the two Governments, the Government of Argentina waived its demand for his return and declared that it viewed the incident as closed. The Government of Argentina thereby refused to grant the accused any sort of protection. The accused has been brought to trial before the Court of a State which charges him with grave offences against its laws. The accused has no immunity against this trial and must stand trial in accordance with the indictment.

For all the above-mentioned reasons we have rejected the second submission of counsel and his application to hear witnesses on this point.

* * *

[*The Accused's Complicity in the Extermination Operations*]

141. Has the accused's activity in the actual extermination operations, as distinct from his activities in rounding up the Jews and despatching them to the places of extermination, been *proved,* and to what extent? In our view, the question is of only secondary importance, because the legal and moral responsibility of he who delivers up the victim to his death is, in our opinion, no smaller, and may even be greater, than the responsibility of he who kills the victim with his own hands. But the question has been raised and we must deal with it.

* * *

143. The Auschwitz-Birkenau Camp was administered by Division D of the Head Office for Administration and Economy, headed by Glueks, to whom Hoess, the first Commander of the Camp and the person who carried out most of the extermination operations there, was subordinate. The accused argued that he had no influence on what was done inside the Auschwitz Camp. He would despatch transports of Jews to Auschwitz in accordance with the orders he had received, upon information from the said Division D that the camps were able to take in additional Jews. At the same time, he admitted that he visited Auschwitz on about five occasions and that, at the time of the deportations from Hungary, he checked directly with Hoess the reception capacity of the camp (Session 93, at p. 25). He also admitted that on one of his visits to Auschwitz he witnessed with his own eyes the mass burning of bodies on an iron grating inside a pit, 100 or even 180 metres long (T/37, p. 227). . . .

* * *

145. It follows therefore that every trainload of "Transport Jews" reached Auschwitz Camp with its passengers condemned to death under a general order, given in respect of the transport as a whole by the accused's department.

The moment the Jews passed through the Camp gates, they came within the power of the Camp Administration, which had to carry out the death sentence. At the same time, however, it had authority to defer the execution of those fit for work. As time passed, the need grew for exploiting prisoners for the production of arms and other work. This emerges, for example, from a telegram to Himmler signed by Mueller and marked IVB4a, dated December 16, 1942, in which Mueller refers to Himmler's order for increasing the labour force in the concentration camps and reports the despatch of 45,000 Jews to Auschwitz, including persons unfit for work, elderly people and children. He calculates that "if a suitable criterion is used in 'selecting' Jews on their arrival, at least 10,000 to 15,000 labourers will become available" out of the total of 45,000 (T/292). This accords with the statement made by Hoess that the percentage of persons fit for work was approximately 25 per cent.

It has also been proved that the accused was competent to give instructions in advance that a specific transport should not be taken off for immediate extermination but only after some time had elapsed, as determined by him. That happened to a transport from Theresin which was sent to the Families' Camp in Auschwitz with instructions that the people in this transport were to be executed six months later. (See below, chapter on Theresin.)

146. Amongst the Jews who reach Auschwitz Camp as detainees and not as "Transport Jews," were those who had allegedly committed criminal offences such as making telephone calls or contravening the curfew. Of these the witness Raya Kagan, who worked in the Registration Office at Auschwitz, related that they enjoyed better treatment because they were exempted from the selections (Session 70, p. 12). Jews "in protective custody" (*Schutzhaftjuden*) reached the camp by virtue of individual orders issued by section IVC2 of the RSHA, which dealt with protective custody matters (see T/1280 p. 3). In his Statement T/37, p. 163, the accused explained that the substantive examination of these individual cases was made by his section, and that section IVC2 only issued the formal order.

From Exhibit T/103 it appears that matters of release from concentration camps were also within the competence of the RSHA (*ibid.*, p. 9, paragraph II (*f*)). But as Raya Kagan testified, for Jews this was only theoretical, because once he entered Auschwitz a Jew never came out again (Session 70, p. 21; see also the accused's account of his Statement T/37, pp. 223–224).

The accused was not authorized to give orders of his own accord for execution of the death sentence by way of punishment of Jews in Auschwitz and in other concentration camps. Apparently this power was reserved to Himmler himself and to Mueller (see T/202, p. 1 at end). But notification of the carrying out of the execution of Jews was transmitted to the accused's section (T/37, p. 2101).

* * *

162. We now propose to determine more precisely the part played by the

accused in the extermination operations. We have already touched upon this central topic in some of the earlier sections, when describing the background of events, especially in Hungary and Eastern Europe; in other sections, in which we described the expulsions of the Jews and all that was connected therewith in the Reich itself and in the other European countries, the part played by the accused is clearly seen from the very description of activities carried out there by his subordinates. In regard to all these, we have only to summarize and finally determine our conclusions. But we have not yet discussed the status of the accused within the RSHA, the centre from which the extermination operations throughout the length and breadth of Europe were directed, and this we now propose to do. In the course thereof we shall touch upon a further series of events in which the prosecution seeks to prove specific acts by the accused, *i.e.* the introduction of the method of killing by gassing and the supply of gas to the extermination camps.

163. First, let us elucidate the date on which the accused was informed that the order for complete extermination had been given by Hitler, for clearly we cannot place upon him responsibility for participating in the implementation of the "Final Solution" of the Jewish problem except from the moment when he began to act with knowledge that the signal had been given for carrying out the "Final Solution."

The accused contended that Heydrich informed him of the matter orally and that on the same occasion Heydrich sent him to Lublin, to Globocnik, in order to ascertain what stage had been reached by the latter in his preparations for the exterminations. He related that he travelled to Lublin as ordered and there saw the extermination installations in the course of construction and was informed that the Jews would be killed by motor exhaust gases (T/37, p. 172). He mentioned the date of the conversation and the visit in his Statement T/37 at pp. 169/170:

> In June, I think, was the outbreak of war, in June or July, let us say July was the outbreak of war. And apparently about two months later, it could be about three months later, at all events it was at the end of the summer . . . when Heydrich summoned me. I presented myself and he told me . . . "The Fuehrer has ordered the physical destruction of the Jews". . . . And then he said to me: "Eichmann, go to Globocnik in Lublin. . . . The Reichsfuehrer has already given Globocnik appropriate instructions, and see how far he has progressed in the work he has to do."

From the accused's evidence before us, it appears that his visit to Globocnik took place approximately in the middle of September (Session 87, p. 20; see also Session 78, p. 13) and we are prepared to accept this as a fact.

But, contrary to the accused's version, we find that he had been informed of Hitler's order for the physical destruction of the Jews not at the end of the summer of 1941 in the circumstances he has described, but as early as the beginning of that summer.

The accused admitted that he was present at the meeting of members of the Operation Groups which took place in Berlin on the eve of the war against

Russia, *i.e.* in June 1941, but in evidence he denied that the members of the Operation Groups were there told what their task would be; he stated that the discussion concerned questions of organization only (Session 102, pp. 10–11). This evidence, however, is contradicted by the declaration of Walter Blume, in the *Trial of Ohlendorf and Others* (Trial No. 9 of the subsequent trials at Nuremberg). Blume, who was commander of a unit in the Operation Groups, declared (T/306, p. 3) that he was present at that gathering and that Heydrich spoke about the task of the Operation Groups in the extermination of the Jews. Blume's Statement is corroborated by the accused's own Statement (T/37). When Superintendent Less asked him if Hitler's order for extermination had been mentioned at that gathering, he maintained that he did not remember what happened there but added (*supra,* p. 2119):

> I assume that when the discussion opened, they referred to some order . . .

and again, at p. 2121, in answer to a further question about Hitler's order or another order which was given there to the men of the Operation Groups:

> You are absolutely right, Mr. Superintendent, something like this was certainly mentioned.

We find further confirmation that the accused already knew in the summer months of 1941 that an order had been given for the "Final Solution" by mass extermination, in the following:

(*a*) The accused admitted, when cross-examined by the Attorney-General, that he had received reports of the activities of the Operation Groups in the East from the end of June 1941 onwards (Session 102, p. 11) and thus had weekly information about the mass killings of Jews. Is it conceivable that he neither understood nor knew at the time that these activities were being carried out in accordance with an order from above for total extermination?

(*b*) On August 28, 1941, the accused wrote to the Foreign Ministry that the emigration of Jews from German-occupied territories was to be prevented "having regard to the impending final solution of the European Jewish problem *at present in the preparatory stage"* (T/183—our emphasis). It should also be pointed out that, during the very same period, the accused secretly informed Rademacher that the Fuehrer had agreed that the Jews in Germany should be obliged to wear the "Jews' badge" (see Section 82 above).

We have already remarked, when dealing with an earlier stage, that the ruling circles sometimes also called the Madagascar Plan the "final solution", but in time the significance of this term changed. This gradual change in content, while the term itself remained the same, was a convenient camouflage vis-a-vis all those who were not privy to the secret decisions taken from time to time by the top leadership. Thus when the accused stated, for example, in a letter dated March 12, 1941 (T/697), that the emigration of German Jews from Yugoslavia was not desirable "having regard to the final solution of the Jewish problem which is now impending", it is not yet clear what is the "final solution" mentioned here. But when, on August 28, 1941, the words are added that this solution is "at present in the preparatory stage", it is clear that the reference is to the new solution, and that this solution, though at the moment still in the preparatory stage, is none other than total extermination. If, in the same letter, the accused gives as an additional reason that as a result of the emigration of Jews from the occupied areas the possibilities of Jewish emigration from the Reich would be still further limited, it can be assumed that the reference here is to that trickle of emigration which was still being allowed until by Himmler's order the gates were finally closed in October 1941.

(*c*) In his Statement (T/90, p. 1), Hoess says that Himmler informed him in the summer of 1941 (he could not give the exact date) that Hitler had ordered the "Final Solution" of the Jewish problem and that the S.S. would have to carry out the order. It is inconceivable that at that same time this matter was unknown to the accused, who held the same rank as Hoess and was the director of the section for Jewish Affairs in the RSHA.

(*d*) Finally, in the letter of appointment dated July 31, 1941, mentioned above (T/179), Goering ordered Heydrich to submit to him at an early date a plan for implementing the "Final Solution," by way of "deportation," *i.e.* the extermination of the Jews. It can be certainly assumed that immediately upon receipt of this letter Heydrich summoned the official authorized to handle Jewish affairs in the RSHA and gave him the new instructions which ensued therefrom.

164. It follows, therefore, that it was already clear to the accused in the summer of 1941 that everything connected with the expulsion of Jews would finally lead to their physical destruction.

* * *

179. With regard also to the scope of the duties placed within his competence, the accused attempted in his Statement to the police and in evidence before us to reduce his own stature, contrary to the truth. His repeated contention was that he was no more than an official preparing timetables for the trains which carried the deportees to the East from their various countries. There is no doubt that even to obtain the railway trucks required called for much effort in the face of military needs at a time of total war. For this he had a special assistant, Novak, whose duty it was to conduct negotiations with the Railway Administration. But by no means can it be said that the accused's duties ended here. The main work of the accused lay not in obtaining the trucks but in obtaining the Jews with which to fill them, in order to carry them to extermination and everything connected therewith. The nature of this work is not to be discovered by detailing his duties. The purpose was a single one; the duties were many and varied, according to the constantly changing circumstances in any given place. As the accused said in his Statement at p. 2408:

> As far as evacuation was concerned . . . for two reasons it was the duty of IVB4 to set the pace, as it were: first, the clear and determined orders given by the

> Reichsfuehrer S.S. and Head of the German Police to carry out the matter energetically. This was a fixed standing order. Secondly, as I said before, IVB4 was dependent upon means of transport. If there were times when it was easier for IVB4 to obtain the trucks, IVB4, in accordance with the general order from the Reichsfuehrer S.S. and Head of the German Police, had to act vigorously also to have the trucks used to their maximum capacity. This IVB4 did, of course. . . . These were the two hinges on which the whole matter turned.

"To have the trucks used to their maximum capacity"—this, in effect, sums it all up, and there is a vast difference between this and the mere arrangement of timetables. It demanded the creation of all the conditions preliminary to hunting down Jews wherever they lived and assembling them for transportation. At the other end also, attention had to be paid to the "reception" of the transports at their destination, so that the expulsion machine should not be halted midway; and it is clear, for example, that the speeding up of the extermination process facilitated the reception of fresh transports at peak periods, such as the period of the deportations from Hungary to Auschwitz. Thus both the speed and the methods of extermination also became part of the group of interests of the accused and his department.

The accused's key position in everything relating to the expulsion of the Jews from the Reich and the Protectorate stands out boldly from those facts which we have found. This is true of all the European countries in which the Advisers on Jewish Affairs operated and whose activities he used to direct from his place behind the desk in Berlin with the aid of modern means of communication and through his frequent journeys to the focal points of operations throughout the length and breadth of Europe. Thus we have noted his special activity in Hungary. . . .

Legal Analysis of the Findings of Fact in the Light of the Indictment

181. The acts of the accused against the Jewish people have been set out in detail in Counts 1–8 of the indictment. In all these Counts, the accused was charged with offences under Section 1 of the Nazi and Nazi Collaborators (Punishment) Law, 1950. That section defines three crimes for which the punishment is death:

> Crime against the Jewish people—Section 1 (*a*) (1), and with this the accused is charged in Counts 1–4;
>
> Crime against humanity—Section 1 (*a*) (2), and with this the accused is charged in Counts 5–7;
>
> War crime—Section 1 (*a*) (3), and with this the accused is charged in Count 8.

Section 1 (*b*) defines the nature of these three crimes.

* * *

216. The accused's principal defence is that everything he did was in accordance with orders from his superiors. This he regards as full justification for all his deeds. He explains that his S.S. training inculcated in him the idea of blind obedience as the supreme virtue, obedience based on boundless faith in the judgment of the leadership, which would always know what the good of the Reich demanded and give its orders accordingly. At the end of the trial, we heard this argument in its most extreme form from counsel for the defence, as follows:

> The basic principle of all States is loyalty to their leadership. The deed is dumb and obedience is blind. These are the qualities on which the State is founded. Do such qualities merit reward? That depends upon the success of its policy. If a policy is unsuccessful the order will be considered a crime in the eyes of the victors. Fortune will not have served the one who has obeyed and he will be called to judgment for his loyalty. The gallows or a decoration—that is the question. To fail is the abominable crime. To succeed is to sanctify the deed. [Session 114, p. 39]

If in these words counsel for the defence intended to describe a totalitarian régime based on denial of law, as was Hitler's régime in Germany, then his words are indeed apt. Such a régime seeks to turn the citizen into an obedient subject who will carry out every order coming from above, be it to commit injustice, to oppress or to murder. It is also true that under such a régime the criminal who acts in obedience to a criminal leader is not punished but on the contrary earns a reward, and only when the entire régime collapses will justice reach him. But arguments of this kind are not to be heard in any State in the world whose system of government is based on the rule of law. The attempt to turn an order for the extermination of millions of innocent people from a crime into a political act in order thus to exempt from personal criminal responsibility those who gave and those who carried out the order, will not avail. And let not counsel for the defence console us with the promise of a World Government to come when such "acts of State" will pass from the world. We do not have to wait for such a radical change in the relations between nations to bring a criminal to judgment for his personal responsibility for his deeds, which is the basis of criminal jurisdiction the world over.

We have already considered elsewhere in our judgment the defence of "act of State" in international law, and have shown that it cannot avail the accused. At this point we shall add that even according to the positive law of the State of Israel no such defence exists to relieve the accused from responsibility for the crimes he committed, although he committed them at the command of one of the State authorities.

The personal responsibility of a government official for his acts lies at the foundation of the rule of law which we have adopted under the inspiration of the Common Law. As Dicey, *Law of the Constitution,* 10th ed., Ch. XI, p. 326, explains:

> The Minister or servant of the Crown . . . is legally responsible for the act in which he is concerned, and he cannot get rid of his liability by pleading that he

acted in obedience to royal orders. Now supposing that the act done is illegal—he becomes at once liable to criminal or civil proceedings in a court of law.

217. An additional argument, similar in spirit to the previous one, which counsel for the defence hinted at rather than argued explicitly, is that the accused could have relied for his defence upon the laws of war. In his final submissions he said:

> Although war was not declared upon the Jews, yet a close connection exists between the War and the struggle against Jewry. [Session 114, pp. 37–38]

It would have been better had this argument also not been put forward. This only is true, that Nazi propaganda declared the Jews "enemies of the Reich" and for this purpose also exploited Dr. Weizmann's declaration at the Zionist Congress on the eve of the outbreak of the Second World War, that the war of the Western Democracies was the war of the Jewish people (Session 112, p. 81). As the Attorney-General said, would that the Jews under the rule of Hitler had been granted the status and rights of prisoners of war. But this "war" took the form of sending helpless people to be slaughtered by citizens of the State in which they lived, for no reason save that of gratuitous hatred and without any object save that of their very extermination. It is true only that the state of war between Germany and the Allies created convenient conditions for the implementation of the "Final Solution," by enveloping the territory under German rule in a smoke screen which hid much of what was done there from the eyes of the world and made it easier to prepare the slaughter without hindrance.

218. Substantive legal discussion of this subject is only possible within the sphere of the plea of "superior orders." But according to our law, this plea does not relieve the accused of criminal responsibility where the indictment is under the Nazi and Nazi Collaborators (Punishment) Law, 1950. Section 8 of the Law states:

> Sections 16, 17, 18 and 19 of the Criminal Code shall not apply to offences under this Law.

Section 19 (*b*) of the Criminal Code Ordinance, 1936, is the one dealing with "superior orders" and it provides as follows:

> A person is not criminally responsible for an act or omission if he does or omits to do the act in any of the following circumstances, that is to say:—
>
> (*b*) In obedience to the order of a competent authority which he is bound by law to obey, unless the order is manifestly unlawful.
>
> Whether an order is or is not manifestly unlawful is a question of law.

Notwithstanding Section 8 of the Law, importance still attaches to the provisions of Section 19 (*b*) of the Criminal Code in regard also to offences against the Law, because of Section 11 of the Law, which provides:

> In determining the punishment of a person convicted of an offence under this Law, the court may take into account, as grounds for mitigating the punishment, the following circumstances:

(*a*) that the person committed the offence under conditions which, but for Section 8, would have exempted him from criminal responsibility or constituted a reason for excusing the offence, and that he did his best to reduce the gravity of the offence; . . .

In the case, however, of an offence under Section 1, the court shall not impose on the offender a lighter punishment than imprisonment for a term of ten years.

In this respect our Law follows Article 8 of the London Charter under which the International Military Tribunal at Nuremberg was set up, and Article 114 (*b*) of Law No. 10 of the Allied Control Council for Germany, under which courts were set up to try subsequent cases against war criminals. These also reject the plea of "superior orders" as exempting from responsibility, but permit the court to consider the existence of such an order as a ground for mitigation of the penalty.

219. Although the provisions of Section 11 of the Law concern only the last stage of the trial proceedings—the stage of sentence—it is desirable that we find the facts now in that regard since they emerge from the same evidence as was adduced regarding the accused's criminal responsibility.

We therefore have to clarify whether the accused committed the offences in circumstances which might exempt him from responsibility had Section 19 (*b*) of the Criminal Code Ordinance applied here. This necessitates consideration of the question whether the orders upon which the accused acted were "manifestly unlawful".

This concept in Section 19 (*b*) was explained by the District Military Court for the Central District in the matter of *Chief Military Prosecutor* v. *Melinski and Others* (13 Pesakim Mehoziim, p. 90) in the following terms:

> The distinguishing mark of a "manifestly unlawful order" should fly like a black flag above the order given, as a warning saying "Prohibited!" Not formal unlawfulness, hidden or half-hidden, not unlawfulness discernible only by the eyes of legal experts, is important here, but a flagrant and manifest breach of the law, definite and necessary unlawfulness appearing on the face of the order itself, the clearly criminal character of the order or of the acts ordered to be done, unlawfulness piercing the eye and revolting the heart, be the eye not blind nor the heart stony and corrupt—that is the measure of "manifest unlawfulness" required to release a soldier from the duty of obedience upon him and make him criminally responsible for his acts.

The Military Court of Appeal adopted these words in its judgment in the appeal in that case (Pesakim Elyonim, vol. 44, p. 362), and for its part added that our Legislator's solution in Section 19 (*b*) of the problem of the conflict between law and obedience is, as it were, a golden mean between giving complete preference to one of these factors over the other, because

> it recognizes the impossibility of fully reconciling these two values by means merely of formal law, and therefore relinquishes the attempt to solve the problem solely by such means and, as it were, breaks away from pure legal categories, calling in aid the feeling of lawfulness which lies hidden deep within the conscience of every human as such, even if not conversant with the law books. [*ibid.*, p. 410].

The Military Court of Appeal continued (*ibid.*, p. 411):

> This is our law in this regard, and it is not for us as a court of law to question its validity. But it seems to us that this solution, arrived at under the inspiration of notable jurists within the sphere of influence of the English Common Law, is the best that can be achieved and is fully suited to the requirements of a State such as ours, based as it is upon the rule of law.

220. Here we shall add that the rejection of the defence of "superior orders" as exempting completely from criminal responsibility, has now become general in all civilized countries. This rule has also been acknowledged by the General Assembly of the United Nations, being one of the principles of the London Charter and of the judgment in the *Trial of the Major War Criminals* (Resolution of the Plenary Session, No. 55, dated December 11, 1946). Perhaps it is not a vain hope that the more this recognition takes root in the minds of men, the more they will refrain from following captive after criminal leaders, and then the rule of law and order in the relations between nations will be reinforced.

It should be pointed out here that even the jurists of the Third Reich did not dare to set down on paper that obedience to orders is above all else. They did not repeal Section 47 (2) of the German Military Criminal Code, which provides that whoever commits an offence against the criminal law through obedience to an order of his superior is punishable as an accomplice to a criminal act if he knew that the order concerned an act which is a crime or an offence according to general or military law. This provision was applicable also to S.S. men, according to the laws of their jurisdiction.

221. It is self-evident that the accused well knew that the order for the physical extermination of the Jews was manifestly unlawful and that in carrying out this order he engaged in criminal acts on a colossal scale. So to find, we do not have to rely on the word of the accused, because in the terms of Section 19 (*b*) the question whether an order is manifestly unlawful is a question of law, to be decided by the court by objective tests. In any case, we shall also quote his evidence in the matter, which he gave after much evasion and as though it needed a great inner effort on his part to realize such a simple truth.

> Your Honour, President of the Court, since you call upon me to say and give a clear answer, I must declare that I see in this murder, in the extermination of Jews, one of the gravest crimes in the history of humanity.

And in answer to Judge Halevi:

> . . . I already realized at the time that this solution by the use of force was something unlawful, something terrible, but to my regret I was obliged to deal with it in matters of transportation, because of my oath of loyalty from which I was not released.

Not only was the order for physical extermination manifestly unlawful, but also all the other orders for the persecution of Jews for being Jews, even though they were framed in the formal language of legislation and subsidiary legislation, since these were only a cloak for arbitrary discrimination contrary to the basic principles of law and justice. As was said by the Court in Nuremberg which tried the Nazi lawyers (*The Justice Case*) (Green Series, vol. 3, p. 1063):

> But it is alleged that they participated in carrying out a governmental plan and programme for the persecution and extermination of Jews and Poles, a plan which transcended territorial boundaries as well as the bounds of human decency. Some of the defendants took part in the enactment of laws and decrees the purpose of which was the extermination of Poles and Jews in Germany and throughout Europe. . . .
>
> The overt acts of the several defendants must be seen and understood as deliberate contributions towards the effectuation of the policy of the Party and State. The discriminatory laws themselves formed the subject-matter of war crimes and crimes against humanity with which the defendants are charged.

This was not a single crime, but a consecutive series of crimes committed over the course of many years. The accused had more than enough time to reflect on his deeds and to desist from them. But he did not stop, and as time went on he even intensified his activity.

222. From what has been said up to now, the accused's attempt to rely on the superior orders he received as justification for his acts or even in mitigation of his punishment according to Section 11 of the Law, is already doomed to failure. Since the orders were manifestly unlawful, he cannot rely on them. Yet we shall go on to examine what was the inner attitude of the accused to the orders within the framework of which he acted. Did these orders cause him to struggle with his conscience, so that he acted under compulsion from which he saw no escape; or did he act with inner indifference like an obedient automaton; or did he perhaps identify himself in his heart with the contents of the orders. Although it makes no difference as regards convicting the accused, yet the enquiry is important for determining the measure of the accused's moral responsibility for his acts. For this reason the Attorney-General rightly requested that in this regard we draw our conclusions at this stage from the evidence before us.

223. What is in fact the accused's version of the matter? He was verbose both before this Court and in his statements outside the Court, but ultimately we do not find in his words any clear and consistent version. Besides repeating in effect that he acted according to orders and that the oath of loyalty which he had taken as a member of the S.S. and S.D. further fortified his absolute duty to obey every order given to him, he kept on saying that up to a certain moment he was carrying out his duties willingly and with inner rejoicing. Thus it was, he said, as long as he was busy with the Emigration Centres in Vienna and Prague, for he regarded this work as beneficial to both sides—his side and the Jewish side. Such also was his attitude to the Madagascar Plan, on which he laboured so much, for even this was still "a political solution." But when this plan was also shelved, his world crumbled and his inner attitude to his work changed from one extreme to the other. He lost interest in his work and decided to act in future as an ordinary official obeying instructions and no more. Thus

far the version is more or less clear. From here onwards the picture becomes increasingly blurred. How does he describe his reaction to the horrifying sights which from time to time he witnessed during his visits to the East—the slaughter of masses of Jews, men, women and babies, by shooting at the side of their grave pit, the blood spurting from the common mass grave; the loading of Jews into the gas vans in Chelmno; the cremation of bodies there; the transport of Jews into the gas chambers? This is what he said, in his own words, to Mueller on his return from such a journey:

> "Terrible, I tell you, the inferno, I cannot stand this," I told him (T/37, 177). "Please don't send me there. Send someone else, someone more robust (*Jemand robusteren*). Look, I have never been allowed to go to the front. I was never a soldier. . . . They do not collapse. I cannot watch it." I said, "I cannot sleep at night! I have dreams—I cannot carry on this way, Gruppenfuehrer."

Somewhere else in his Statement to Superintendent Less he explains his desire to be transferred to another post, giving as additional reasons the opportunity for promotion and lack of interest in police work as such from the outset, from the very time of his transfer to Berlin in 1939 (T/37, p. 250).

Thus also in evidence, in answer to the Attorney-General (Session 94, pp. 13–14):

> I first referred to him (Mueller) with such a request and asked not to be transferred to Berlin at all because I wanted to remain where I lived with my family. I applied a second time with an urgent request and told him I would not be able to stand it physically, after the service trip to the East, the first trip, and after each trip I would apply. Mueller was well aware of my state of mind after such a trip.

224. It is therefore clear that, according to his contention, he requested a transfer to another post for reasons of convenience, to obtain promotion and also, according to his own words, because physically he was not robust enough to bear all the horrifying sights which he witnessed in the East. But there is not a word here about any inner protest against the extermination of Jews for reasons of conscience. It is true that, when pressed by the Attorney-General, who asked

> And you did not mind acting as the great expediter of death?

he answered:

> I did mind, I minded very much—more than anyone can imagine. That is why from time to time I requested my superior, and repeated my request, that he find me another job, (Session 94, pp. 11–12).

225. But this version, that he asked to be relieved of his post for reasons of conscience, is contradicted by the accused himself. When his counsel asked him:

> It seems from the remarks in the Memoirs taken down by Sassen, as well as now, that you were quite satisfied with the Conference (the Wannsee Conference). Can you express your opinion about this? (Session 79, p.2)

his answer was

> Yes, but the origin of my satisfaction is to be sought elsewhere than in Heydrich's satisfaction. . . . And so, after many efforts (to find other solutions), after the Wannsee Conference I could say to myself that in spite of my wish and not as a result of my own preparations, through no fault of mine and feeling like Pontius Pilate washing his hands of the matter, I could feel that the guilt was not mine, since at this Wannsee Conference the men at the top, the élite, the popes of the empire, laid down the law. And I? I had only to obey.

Let us remember that even before the Wannsee Conference he had already seen what was happening in the East and had begun sending Reich Jews to the slaughter; yet, in spite of this, according to his evidence here, he felt like Pontius Pilate, that is, like a man who could find a way for his conscience to relent. And this, in fact, is his basic contention, that the order sets his conscience free, that blind obedience, in accordance with an oath of loyalty, comes first and stands above all, and that against it the voice of conscience can never be heard. Dr. Grueber, the German priest, one of the just men of this world, who because of his activities on behalf of persecuted Jews was himself thrown into a concentration camp, described to us this type of German, the *Landsknecht:*

> A German *Landsknecht,* as soon as he dons his uniform, puts aside his mind and his conscience, it is said that he deposits them in the cloakroom. (Session 41, p. 76.)

And here, in the evidence of the accused, is the argument in all its nakedness:

> . . . responsibility and the matter of conscience lie with the Heads of the State (Session 88, p. 9).

Later, when cross-examined by the Attorney-General, he retreated somewhat from this extreme position and clung to the most miserable of excuses (Session 95, pp. 33–34):

> To my mind, to break an oath of loyalty is the worst crime and offence that a man can commit.
>
> Q. A crime greater than the murder of six million Jews, amongst them one and a half million children, is that correct?
>
> A. Not that, of course. But I was not engaged in extermination. Had I been occupied in exterminating, had I been ordered to deal with extermination—I believe that I would have committed suicide by shooting myself.

This answer calls to mind some remarks in the same spirit which he noted down in his comments on the article in "Life" magazine, in connection with the activity of Department IVB4:

> We had nothing to do with the atrocities, but dealt with our affairs in a decent way (T/51, second paragraph).

That is to say, had he been ordered to throw the gas container amongst the victims, then his conscience would have been stirred; but since his duty was only to hunt down the victims in the countries of Europe and transport them to the gas chambers, his conscience was at peace and he obeyed orders without hesitation.

226. The Attorney-General submitted that had the accused truly and sincerely wanted to be released from his murderous task, he would have found ways of achieving his desire. He could have asked to be transferred to the front; he could have been evasive under various pretexts, as others were, or he could have stated openly that his heart was not at one with the task assigned to him. In the evidence before us there is ground for these contentions. For instance, Justice Musmanno told about his conversations with Schellenberg who told him that men were released from Operation Groups when it became clear that they were incapable of taking part in murder (Session 39, pp. 77–80). Such a case (concerning a man named Jost) is also mentioned in the Declaration of Best which was submitted in the *Einsatzgruppen Trial* (T/687), and in a Declaration made by Burmeister about the release of Six, a witness for the defence, from the Operation Groups (T/688, pp. 24–26; see also the evidence by Six himself in the present case, p. 8). Himmler's speech at Poznan also implied that whoever showed signs of recoiling from the work of murder could obtain his release (T/1288, p. 151). But we do not intend to go deeply into this matter because, in our opinion, the whole discussion is beside the point, since this kind of question never troubled the accused. He never thought of giving up his important job in the office at the RSHA Centre, to which he had been promoted because he was an expert in a problem wich kept the Third Reich and its leaders so busy. It is possible that he was not at ease when watching the scenes of bloodshed. Perhaps he even spoke to Mueller about it, although it is difficult to accept this as a fact because such a manifestation of weakness would not have been becoming to an S.S. man like him, for whom ruthlessness was one of the principal personal qualities. As we have shown, the accused's version is far from clear in this matter, and in so far as he talked about pangs of conscience his words are hardly creditable, since they are entirely contrary to his true attitude towards his work on the battle front against Jews in all its phases.

227. With this we reach the heart of our discussion of the inner motives which prompted the accused's activities. That he was merciless in all that he did is almost undisputed. One illustration will suffice. When, in connection with the "goods for blood" transaction in Hungary, he was asked what moved him to regard this transaction favourably, he explained that he pursued it because of rivalry with Becher who had been poaching on his preserves in matters of Jewish emigration. He was asked then by his counsel:

> In negotiations with your superiors, did you also speak of the pity which you felt for the Jews and say that they ought to be helped?

And he answered:

> I am giving evidence under oath and I must tell the truth. I did not approach

the matter out of pity. Moreover, I would have fired had I adopted such an attitude (Session 86, p. 16).

In answer to the Attorney-General in the same matter:

Q. Perhaps you agree with me that your heart was not in any event in this whole affair?

A. "I did not contend otherswise. I have already said that this was done for reasons of expediency. I did not say that this was a rescue operation." [Session 103, pp. 18–19.]

That is to say, the possibility never entered into his considerations, that human beings could save their lives in this way. This reveals to us the same block of ice, or of marble, which Dr. Grueber saw before him when he came to the accused on the humanitarian mission he had taken upon himself.

228. The accused tried, however, to convince us that only obedience to orders motivated and guided him in all his activities that it was only blind obedience, "corpse-like" obedience (*Kadavergehorsam*), which silenced his conscience. That is why he represented himself as a minor official, with no opinion of his own on any of the matters with which he had to deal, and lacking all initiative in his work.

We have already discussed this contention in another context, when we examined it from the aspect of the actual deeds done by the accused. Now we repeat that also with regard to his inner attitude to his work, the picture which he has tried to draw for us appears entirely distorted. Although the accused gave such obedience as was required of a good National-Socialist and S.S. man, in whom utter and undeviating obedience was inculcated, that does not mean that he carried out his duties solely because of orders to do so. On the contrary, he performed his duties at every stage because of an inner conviction as well, whole-heartedly and willingly. Let us review briefly the evidence which has led us to this conclusion.

The accused admits that he was a zealous National-Socialist, devoted to his Fuehrer (T/37, p. 325), but contends that he was no anti-Semite. The answer to this contention is found in the words of Dr. Grueber (Session 42, pp. 22–25):

Q. Did you find personal hatred for the Jews on the part of the accused, sharp personal anti-Semitism, or was it National-Socialist fanaticism that you saw in him?

A. It is difficult to distinguish between the two. National-Socialist zeal was always bound up with strong anti-Semitism. These two elements were always bound up together and went hand in hand.

Indeed, this is common knowledge. In Hitler's bogus ideology, the elevation of the German nation to the position of a "master-race" was indissolubly bound up with hatred of the Jews and their degradation to the rank of "sub-humans."

229. It is possible that the accused did not believe in Streicher's crude methods of incitement, for he considered himself an expert in the fight against Jewry, one who had studied the problem thoroughly, and he was so regarded by his superiors. As an expert, he understood that crude methods are not necessar-

ily effective. However, his attempt to argue that he, the expert on Jewish affairs in the Reich Security Main Office, was of all people that "white raven"—a National-Socialist who did not hate Jews—is refutable. Had a man of his kind, who stood in the forefront of the fight against Jews—at first in the battle of ideas and later in the actual struggle—shown the slightest deviation from the anti-Semitic orthodoxy which was demanded from every ordinary member of the Party, he could not have held his position there for even one day. The heads of the S.D. and the Gestapo, with whom he worked, would certainly have very quickly detected any such deviation. But let us quote defence witness Six, who knew the accused closely from the time he worked in the S.D. Head Office, when Six was head of the branch in which the accused worked. In evidence taken in Germany, he said (p. 6):

> Eichmann believed wholeheartedly in National Socialism. . . . I believe that when in doubt Eichmann invariably acted according to the doctrine of the Party in its most extreme interpretation.

230. The evidence before us fully confirms these words. Even today, when noting his observations on the article in "Life," the accused explains his remarks to Sassen as to why Hitler disappointed him (T/48, p. 8):

> I said that the real war agitators were the circles of infernal high finance (*die infernalische Hochfinanz*) of the Western Hemisphere, whose servants are Churchill and Roosevelt, and the puppets, their pawns in this game, are Hitler, Mussolini, Daladier, Chamberlain.

The "circles of infernal finance" were, of course, according to the concepts of the "Protocols of the Elders of Zion," the Jews—that "International Finance Jewry" about whom Hitler spoke in his speech in January 1939 when he threatened to exterminate the Jews. This was the style used by the accused, according to his own words, as late as 1957. So deep was his conviction from past days that the Jews were the enemies of humanity that he reached a new peak in the development of the Nazi mythology: Hitler himself was merely a plaything in the hands of the Jews. Thus he also unhesitatingly adopted the official Nazi doctrine, that the Jews had declared war upon the German Reich and must be exterminated as enemies. As Himmler said in his speech in Posen on October 4, 1943:

> We had the moral right on behalf of our people. It was our duty to exterminate this nation which wanted to exterminate ours. (T/1288, p. 2.)

This doctrine of hatred echoes through the accused's words in the Sassen document, in the part (file 17) written in his own handwriting and to which he confessed (*ibid.*, p. 735):

> The slogan on both sides was: the enemy must be exterminated. And world Jewry . . . had obviously declared war upon the German Reich.

A few lines earlier he made it clear that the Jews had always been the enemies of the German people and not only upon the outbreak of the Second World War, since Hitler had already declared war upon them years earlier (*ibid.*, p. 734).

And again he had a ready explanation. The intention was not actual extermination, for neither the British people nor the French people were exterminated during the war (Session 96, pp. 9–10)—an excuse that is self-defeating.

231. On this soil of hatred for the Jews grew the deeds of the accused, and it is clear that mere blind obedience could never have brought him to commit the crimes which he did with the efficiency and devotion with which he carried them out, had it not been for his fanatical belief that he was thereby fulfilling an important national mission. We have already seen the accused's position within the RSHA establishment, which was a key position in the implementation of the "Final Solution." Although he received his principal orders from above, and these set out the various phases of implementation for him, yet within the general framework he still had much scope to work out the details of implementation entrusted to him. This too was a very considerable and manifold task, taking into account the wide range of activities which were required to round up the Jews in their various countries, to transport them for extermination and to remove the obstacles which sometimes hindered these activities. The accused also controlled a widespread establishment of officials, immediately subject to his discipline, whom he set to work, constantly supervising and spurring them on. All this required a great deal of initiative and continuous independent thought as well as devotion to the task before him.

232. Here we shall mention one more of the accused's arguments which has no foundation, namely, that the Nazi establishment was, as it were, divided into two sections—one consisting of those who gave orders, bearing full responsibility, and the other of those who received orders which they had only to obey, and bore no burden of responsibility. It is well known that in the Nazi régime, based as it was on the principle of leadership, every rank, apart from Hitler himself, both received and gave orders. And, as is common in any hierarchical régime, an order becomes increasingly detailed and elaborated as it passes down from one level to the next. The accused certainly did not act simply as a channel for passing on orders precisely as received. Had it been as he says, had he done his work in a purely routine manner, he would have been removed from office and replaced by another, because the activities of Department IVB4 were far from being routine activities. But it was not so, since the accused was praised by his immediate superior, Mueller, who said of him: "If we had had fifty Eichmanns, we should automatically have won the war" (Session 98, pp. 17–18; T/1432 (6)). We do not believe the accused when he says that this statement referred only to his later activities in preparing his office building for the Battle of Berlin; it was a concise evaluation of all his activities in Mueller's domain.

233. There is abundant evidence of this inner attitude of the accused in his very acts and in his declarations on various occasions, as has been proved to us.

No single case has been brought to our notice in which the accused showed any sign of human feelings in his dealing with Jewish affairs, except for the help which, according to his own words, he extended to the daughter of his uncle (his stepmother's brother), who was half-Jewish, and another Jewish couple on whose behalf the same uncle had intervened (T/37, pp. 114–5). In all his activities the accused displayed indefatigable energy, verging on frenzy, to advance the "Final Solution," both in his general decisions and in his treatment of individual cases of Jews who sought to escape death.

* * *

240. A very clear picture emerges from all that has been said—a picture matching, in our opinion, the evaluation given by Hoess, who wrote of the accused (T/88):

> Eichmann was a man full of vitality, always active, . . . full of vigour. He always had new plans and sought new ideas and improvements. He was untiring. He was like one "possessed" by the Jewish question and the "final solution" which had been ordered. (*Von der Judenfrage und der befohlenen "Endloesung" war er besessen*). . . .
>
> Eichmann was entirely taken up with his task and also convinced that this work of extermination was essential in order to guard the German people in the future against the Jews' desire to exterminate them. (p. 4.)

We shall add here that the accused has never alleged that Hoess bore him any grudge (see, for instance, T/37, p. 391).

This inner attitude obviously contradicts all attempts by the accused to "do his best to reduce the gravity of the consequences of the offence" under Section 11 (*a*) of the Law. There was no desire here to alleviate, but a determined effort to aggravate matters in every respect.

241. We shall sum up this section by holding that the accused put his conscience behind him, as was demanded of him by the régime to which he had devoted and sold himself body and soul. Thus far, Dr. Grueber's description of the *Landsknecht* fits the accused. Thus he sank from one depth to another, until in implementation of the "Final Solution" he reached the infernal nether regions. But it is not to be said of him that his mind also ceased to function or that it functioned only in blind obedience. He believed to the utmost in the National-Socialists' false ideology that the Jews were enemies of the Reich and were to be destroyed without mercy. His hatred was cold and calculated, aimed rather against the Jewish people as a whole than against the individual Jew, and it is for just this reason that it was so venomous and destructive in all its manifestations. To the task he devoted his alert mind, his great cunning and his organizing skill. He acted within the general framework of the orders which were given to him, but within this framework he went to the very limit to bring about the speedy and complete extermination of all Jews in the territories under German rule and influence.

242. In saying all this we do not mean that the accused was exceptional in

his evilness in the régime which had raised him. He was a loyal disciple of a régime which was wholly evil and malicious.

Counsel for the defence devoted his utmost efforts to prove the part played by others in the commission of the crimes with which the accused is charged. In fact, it is not disputed that in all that he did the accused always acted together with others, and that is how he was charged in the indictment. We would not see the complete picture if we placed the responsibility for the entire extermination campaign upon the accused alone. Above him was a summit, beginning with Hitler himself, which initiated the "Final Solution" and gave the basic orders which guided the accused. At the side of the accused and his department were many other elements, all imbued with brazen determination to carry out the Fuehrer's order, each in his own particular field of action—the Ministries of the Interior and Justice, which laid the main formal groundwork for the persecution of the Jews by drafting the definitions which isolated the Jews from the rest of the population and determined precisely who was a Jew, who the issue of a mixed marriage and who a non-Jew, and by enacting laws and regulations aimed at putting the Jews beyond the pale of the law; the Foreign Ministry, which laboured unceasingly to spread the poison of anti-Semitism all over the world and to create conditions for the surrender of the Jews of other countries into German hands in order to be sent to the slaughter; the Ministry of Finance and the Reichsbank, which took part in plundering the property of the victims; the Fuehrer's Chancellery, which was active in operating the system of killing by gas; and also the German Army Command, which tainted itself by co-operating with the S.S. in the extermination of the Jews in the East, in Greece and elsewhere. Not only these, but all the authorities of the Reich and of the National-Socialist Party, at whatever point their sphere of activity touched upon Jewish affairs—they all zealously competed with one another in furthering the common end, namely the total extermination of the Jews, the "enemies of the Reich," by every available means, with efficiency and with speed.

All this, however, does not derogate from the fact that the accused's department in the RSHA was central in carrying out the "Final Solution," and the guilt of the others does not lessen by one jot the personal guilt of the accused.

243. The accused's evidence in this case was not truthful evidence, in spite of his often repeated declarations that he was reconciled to his fate, knowing the gravity of the deeds to which he had voluntarily confessed, and that his only desire now was to reveal the truth in order to correct in the eyes of his people and of the whole world the wrong impression of his activities which had been created during the passage of time. In the course of this judgment we have pointed to various episodes as to which the accused was shown to have lied in his evidence. We now add that his entire testimony was nothing but a sustained and consistent attempt to deny the truth so as to avoid his proper share of responsibility or to minimize it as far as possible. His effort was not

unskilful, due to those qualities in which he had excelled at the time of his actions—an alert mind, the ability to adapt himself to any difficult situation, cunning, and a smooth tongue. But he did not have the courage to confess to the truth, neither about how things actually happened, nor about his inner attitude to the acts he committed. We saw him again and again twisting and turning under the pressure of cross-examination, retreating from complete to partial denial and that only when left with no alternative to admission, but relying always on the fact that in all matters, great or small, he ostensibly acted on explicit orders.

The question remains: Why did the accused confess to Superintendent Less to a number of incriminating matters which *prima facie* it would have been impossible to prove but for his confession, in particular his journeys to the East where he saw the atrocities with his own eyes? We cannot search the depths of the accused's soul now, while he is in detention, to discover what moved him to do so. One may variously speculate to explain these partial admissions, but it would be futile to do so for the purpose of a legal evaluation of his evidence. Suffice it for us to say that these admissions did not in our view add credibility to his evidence before us as regards all those matters in which he was found to be lying.

244. The indictment was drawn in considerable detail. The method generally followed by the Attorney-General was to set out in each Count the essence of the charge in one of the paragraphs of the "particulars of offence," for example, in paragraph (*a*) of the first Count (crime against the Jewish people by killing Jews), in paragraph (*b*) of the third Count (crime against the Jewish people by causing serious physical and mental harm) and in paragraph (*a*) of the seventh Count (crime against humanity by the plunder of property). To this the Attorney-General has added a detailed factual description of part of the acts attributed to the accused. This is particularly evident in the first and seventh Counts. At the same time it is stressed everywhere that the factual description is not exhaustive. Thus in paragraph (*h*) of the first Count a partial description is given of the activities of the "Operation Groups" by specifying the number of their victims during a given period, but it is clear from the opening words "the activities of such groups included the following acts, *inter alia*," etc., that the Attorney-General merely sought to give some examples from among all the activities carried out by the Operation Groups. Again, in the seventh Count various acts of plunder of property are enumerated, but it is stated that these were *among* the activities of the accused.

We do not mean to criticize this way of wording the indictment. On the contrary, in the nature of things the description could not be exhaustive because of the vast range of the activities with the execution of which the accused has, together with others, been charged, while the method of partial specification was enough to inform the accused with greater clarity of the nature of the acts of which he was accused. But as we come now to pronounce judgment on the accused we do not consider ourselves bound by this partial specification in the indictment. We shall adhere to the general framework of the indictment in so far as concerns the description of the statement of offence, and also those parts of the particulars of offence in which a general description of the nature of the offence is given. As regards all other details, however, we base the conviction of the accused on the detailed description of the facts which we have found in this judgment and of which the principal ones have been recapitulated in the section containing the legal analysis of the facts. In the light of this detailed description we will now include in the text of the conviction only that which appears to us essential in each of the Counts of the indictment, in so far as they have been proved before us.

(1) Accordingly, we convict the accused pursuant to the first Count of the indictment of a crime against the Jewish people, an offence under Section 1 (*a*) (1) of the Nazi and Nazi Collaborators (Punishment) Law, 1950, in that during the period from August 1941 to May 1945 in Germany, in the territories of the Axis States, in the areas which were occupied by Germany and by the Axis States and in the territories which were subject to the authority of Germany and the Axis States he, together with others, caused the killing of millions of Jews for the purpose of executing the plan known as "the final solution of the Jewish problem" with intent to exterminate the Jewish people.

We acquit the accused of the charge of a crime against the Jewish people by reason of the acts attributed to him in this Count of the indictment during the period up to August 1941. The criminal acts of the accused until that time (see paragraphs 185, 186 above) will be included in the conviction for crimes against humanity under clause (5) of the conviction (see below).

(2) We convict the accused pursuant to the second Count of the indictment of a crime against the Jewish people, an offence under Section 1 (*a*) (1) of the above-mentioned Law, in that during the period from August 1941 to May 1945, in the territories and areas mentioned in clause (1) of the conviction above, he, together with others, placed millions of Jews in living conditions which were calculated to bring about their physical destruction, for the purpose of executing the plan known as "the final solution of the Jewish problem," with intent to exterminate the Jewish people.

We acquit the accused of the charge of a crime against the Jewish people by reason of the acts attributed to him in this Count during the period up to August 1941.

(3) We convict the accused pursuant to the third Count of the indictment of a crime against the Jewish people, an offence under Section 1 (*a*) (1) of the above-mentioned Law, in that during the period from August 1941 to May 1945 in the territories and areas mentioned in clause (1) of the conviction above, he, together with others, caused serious physical and mental harm to millions of Jews with intent to exterminate the Jewish people.

We acquit the accused of the charge of a crime against the Jewish people attributed to him in this Count during the period up to August 1941.

(4) We convict the accused pursuant to the fourth Count of a crime

against the Jewish people, an offence under Section 1 (*a*) (1) of the above-mentioned Law, in that during the years 1943 and 1944 he devised measures the purpose of which was to prevent childbearing among Jews by his instruction forbidding births and for the interruption of pregnancy of Jewish women in the Theresin Ghetto with intent to exterminate the Jewish people.

We acquit the accused of having committed all the other acts mentioned in the fourth Count of the indictment.

(5) We convict the accused pursuant to the fifth Count of a crime against humanity, an offence under Section 1 (*a*) (2) of the above-mentioned Law, in that during the period from August 1941 to May 1945 in the territories and areas mentioned in clause (1) of the conviction above he, together with others, caused the murder, extermination, enslavement, starvation and deportation of the Jewish civilian population in these countries and in these areas.

We also convict the accused of a crime against humanity, an offence under Section 1 (*a*) (2) of the above-mentioned Law, in that during the period from March 1938 to October 1941 he, together with others, caused the deportation of Jews from their homes in the area of the old Reich in Austria and in the Protectorate of Bohemia-Moravia, by way of forced emigration through the Emigration Centres at Vienna, Prague and Berlin.

We also convict the accused of a crime against humanity, an offence under Section 1 (*a*) (2) of the above-mentioned Law, in that during the period from March 1938 to October 1941 he, together with others, caused the deportation of Jews to Nisco and the deportation of Jews from areas in the East annexed to the Reich and from the Reich area proper into the German Occupied Territories in the East and to France.

(6) We convict the accused pursuant to the sixth Count of a crime against humanity, an offence under Section 1 (*a*) (2) of the above-mentioned Law, in that while carrying out the activities mentioned in Counts 1 to 5 above he persecuted Jews on national, racial, religious and political grounds.

(7) We convict the accused persuant to the seventh Count of a crime against humanity, an offence under Section 1 (*a*) (2) of the above-mentioned Law, in that during the period from March 1938 to May 1945 in the territories and areas mentioned in Count (1) above he, together with others, caused the spoliation of the property of millions of Jews by means of mass terror, linked with the murder, extermination, starvation and deportation of these Jews.

(8) We convict the accused pursuant to the eighth Count of a war crime, an offence under Section 1 (*a*) (3) of the above-mentioned Law, in that he did the acts of persecution, expulsion and murder mentioned in the preceding clauses of the conviction, in so far as these were done during the Second World War, against Jews from among the populations of the countries occupied by Germany and by the other Axis States.

(9) We convict the accused pursuant to the ninth Count of a crime against humanity, an offence under Section 1 (*a*) (2) of the above-mentioned Law, in that during the years 1940 to 1942 he, together with others, caused the

deportation of a civilian population, namely, hundreds of thousands of Poles, from their places of residence.

(10) We convict the accused pursuant to the tenth Count of a crime against humanity, an offence under Section 1 (*a*) (2) of the above-mentioned Law, in that in 1941 he, together with others, caused the deportation of a civilian population, namely, more than 14,000 Slovenes, from their places of residence.

(11) We convict the accused pursuant to the eleventh Count of a crime against humanity, an offence under Section 1 (*a*) (2) of the above-mentioned Law, in that during the period of the Second World War he, together with others, caused the deportation of a civilian population, namely, scores of thousands of gipsies, from Germany and German-occupied areas and their transportation to the German-occupied regions in the East. It has not been proved before us that the accused knew that the gipsies were being transported to extermination.

(12) We convict the accused pursuant to the twelfth Count of a crime against humanity, an offence under Section 1 (*a*) (2) of the above-mentioned Law, in that in 1942 he, together with others, caused the deportation of 93 of the children of the Czech village of Lidice. It has not been proved before us that the accused is guilty of the murder of these children.

(13) We acquit the accused of the charges of membership in hostile organizations under Counts thirteen, fourteen and fifteen, with respect to the period until May 1940, by reason of these offences having become prescribed.

(14) We convict the accused pursuant to the thirteenth Count of membership of a hostile organization, an offence under Section 3 (1) of the above-mentioned Law, in that as from May 1941 he was a member of the organization known as *Schutzstaffeln der* N.S.D.A.P. (S.S.) which was declared a criminal organization by the International Military Tribunal which tried the Major War Criminals, and as a member of such organization took part in acts that were declared criminal in Article 6 of the London Charter of August 8, 1945.

(15) We convict the accused pursuant to the fourteenth Count of membership of a hostile organization, an offense under Section 3 (*a*) of the above-mentioned Law, in that as from May 1941 he was a member of the organization known as *Sicherheitsdienst des Reichsfuehrers SS* (S.D.) which was declared a criminal organization by the International Military Tribunal which tried the Major War Criminals, and as a member of such organization took part in acts declared criminal in Article 6 of the London Charter of August 8, 1945.

(16) We convict the accused pursuant to the fifteenth Count, of membership of a hostile organization, an offence under Section 3 (*a*) of the above-mentioned Law, in that he was from May 1940 a member of the organization known as the *Geheime Staatspolizei,* which was declared a criminal organization by the International Military Tribunal which tried the Major War Criminals, and as a member of such organization took part in acts which were declared criminal in Article 6 of the London Charter of August 8, 1945.

[Report: (1965) 45 Pesakim Mehoziim 3 (in Hebrew).]

Eichmann appealed against conviction and sentence.

TEXT OF JUDGMENT OF THE SUPREME COURT

May 29, 1962

1. The appellant, Adolf Eichmann, was found guilty by the District Court of Jerusalem of offences of the most extreme gravity against the Nazi and Nazi Collaborators (Punishment) Law, 1950 (hereinafter referred to as "the Law") and was sentenced to death.

* * *

3. The appellant has appealed to this Court against both conviction and sentence.

4. The oral and written submissions of learned counsel who supported the appeal, Dr. Servatius, may, in so far as they are directed against conviction, be classified under two heads:

(1) Purely legal contentions, the principal object of which was to undermine the jurisdiction of a court in Israel to try the appellant for the crimes in question;

(2) Factual contentions the object of which was in essence to upset the finding of the District Court that there was no foundation for the defence of the appellant that he played the part of a "small cog" in the machine of Nazi destruction, that in all the above-mentioned chapters of events he functioned as a minor official without any independent initiative, and that nothing but the compulsion of orders and blind obedience to commands from above guided him in carrying out his work at all stages.

With regard to these contentions, counsel for the appellant asked us for leave to produce new evidence at the appeal stage. At the conclusion of argument we decided to refuse this application, and the reasons for our decision are set out below.

5. The District Court has in its judgment dealt with both categories of contentions in an exhaustive, profound and most convincing manner. We should say at once that we fully concur, without hesitation or reserve, in all its conclusions and reasons, because they are fully supported by copious judicial precedents cited in the body of the judgment and by the abundant proof culled and abstracted from the monumental mass of evidence produced to the Court. Moreover, we are bound to observe that were it not for the grave outcome of the decision of the Court which constitutes the subject of the appeal, we would have seen no need whatever to give a reasoned opinion separately and in our own language—as we contemplate doing—since the conclusions of the District Court rest on solid foundations. However, it is not superfluous for us to take this

opportunity to express our appreciation of the immense effort which the learned Judges who tried the case in the Court below expended in the actual conduct of the arduous and wearying proceedings before them. As to the contribution made to this responsible task by the Attorney-General and his assistants, on the one hand, and counsel for the defence, on the other, proper and significant observations have already been expressed in the judgment of the District Court and we cannot but associate ourselves with them.

6. Most of the legal contentions of counsel for the appellant revolve around the argument that in assuming jurisdiction to try the appellant the District Court acted contrary to the principles of international law. These contentions are as follows.

(1) The Law of 1950, which is the only source of the jurisdiction of the Court in this case, constitutes *ex post facto* penal legislation which prescribes as offences acts that were committed before the State of Israel came into existence; therefore the validity of this Law is confined to its citizens alone.

(2) The offences for which the appellant was tried are "extra-territorial offences," that is to say, offences that were committed outside the territory of Israel by a citizen of a foreign State, and even though the Law confers jurisdiction in respect of such offences, it conflicts in so doing with the principle of territorial sovereignty, which postulates that only the country within whose territory the offence was committed or to which the offender belongs—in this case, Germany—has the right to punish therefor.

(3) The acts constituting the offence of which the appellant was convicted were at the time of their commission Acts of State.

(4) The appellant was brought to Israel territory, to be tried for the offences in question, unwillingly and without the consent of the country in which he resided, and this was done through agents of the State of Israel, who acted on the orders of their Government.

(5) The judges of the District Court, being Jews and feeling affinity with the victims of the plan of extermination and Nazi persecution, were psychologically incapable of giving the appellant an objective trial.

7. We reject all these contentions.

The short answer to the first two contentions—and we shall deal with each separately—will be found in paragraph 10 of the judgment:

> The Court has to give effect to a law of the Knesset, and we cannot entertain the contention that this Law conflicts with the principles of international law.

In the opinion of counsel for the appellant, this reply is mistaken since where two legal systems are in conflict it is imperative to give preference to the principles of international law. We do not agree with this view. According to the law of Israel, which is identical on this point with English law, the relationship between municipal law and international law is governed by the following rules:

(1) The principle in question is received into the municipal law and

becomes a part of that law only after it has acquired general international recognition.

> "The municipal Courts of a particular State," said Mr. Justice Dunkelblum in Motion 41/49 (*Shimshon Palestine Portland Cement Factory Ltd.* v. *The Attorney-General,* 4 Pesakim 143, pp. 145, 146), "will recognise the principles of international law and will decide in accordance therewith only if all other civilised peoples have agreed to them, so that it is a necessary assumption that such principles have also been accepted by that State. A principle of international law must therefore be established by sufficient proof to justify the conclusion . . . that it is recognised by the majority of States and widely prevails."

* * *

(2) This, however, only applies where no conflict exists between the provisions of municipal statutory law and a rule of international law. But where such a conflict does exist, it is the duty of the Court to give preference to and apply the laws of the local Legislature (see Israeli and English precedents mentioned in paragraph 10 of the judgment). True, the presumption must be that the Legislature strives to adjust its laws to the principles of international law which have received general recognition. But where a contrary intention clearly emerges from the statute itself, that presumption loses its force and the Court is enjoined to disregard it.

(3) On the other hand, having regard to the above-mentioned presumption, a local statutory provision whose construction is equivocal and whose content does not demand a different construction, must be construed in accordance with the rules of public international law. (*Amsterdam and Others* v. *Minister of Finance,* (1952) 6 Piske Din, 945, 966; Oppenheim, *International Law,* vol. I (8th ed. by Lauterpacht, 1955), p. 41, para. 21*a.*) It should be noted that this rule of construction has no relevance to the present case, since the nature of the Law in question as one which created extra-territorial offences with retroactive effect is not in doubt.

It follows from the second rule that even were counsel for the appellant right in saying that the character as aforesaid of the Law is repugnant to the law of nations, even then this contention could not avail him.

[*Retroactive Penal Legislation in International Law*]

8. We reach the same conclusion according to the first rule as well. For the sake of convenience we shall state the grounds of our conclusions separately in respect of each of the two above-mentioned arguments of counsel for the appellant. As to the first argument, the answer must be that the principle *nullum crimen sine lege, nulla poena sine lege,* in so far as it negates penal legislation with retroactive effect, has not yet become a rule of customary international law:

> There is no rule of general customary international law forbidding the

enactment of norms with retrospective force, so called ex post facto laws. [Kelsen, *Peace through Law* (1944), p. 87.]

There is clearly no principle of international law embodying the maxim against retroactivity of criminal law. [Stone, *Legal Controls of International Conflict* (1959), p. 369].

It is true in many countries the said principle has been embodied in the constitution of the State or in its criminal code, because of the considerable moral value inherent in it, and in such countries the Court may not depart from it by one iota. (See Cr.A. 53/54: *Eshed, Merkaz Zmani L'Tahbura* v. *Attorney-General* (1954) 8 Piske Din 785, 819, 830–832.) But this state of affairs is not universal. Thus in the United Kingdom, a country whose system of law and justice is universally recognized as being of a high standard, there is no constitutional limitation of the power of the Legislature to vest its criminal laws with retrospective effect, and should it do so the court will have no power to deny them this force (Allen, *Law in the Making,* 5th ed., p. 444). Certainly, there too, general recognition prevails of the moral value of the principle embodied in the above-mentioned maxim. But that recognition has become legally effective to the extent only that that maxim constitutes a rule for the construction of statutes, that is to say, where doubt exists as to the intention of the Legislature the court is directed not to construe the criminal statute with which it is dealing so as to include within its purview an act committed prior to its enactment. (*Queen* v. *Griffiths* [1891] 2 Q.B. 145, 148; Allen, *op. cit.,* pp. 443–444.) Similarly, the British Parliament usually avoids passing a criminal statute with retroactive effect, and it will only do so exceptionally where the object of *salus populi* compels the taking of this course (Willes J. in *Phillips* v. *Eyre* (1871) L.R. 6 Q.B. 1, 25, cited in paragraph 7 of the judgment—p. 21, above).

Accordingly, if it is the contention of counsel for the appellant that we must apply international law as it is, and not as it ought to be from the moral point of view, then we must reply that precisely from a *legal* point of view no such rule of international law is to be found; and *ipso facto* the said principle cannot be deemed to be part of the Israel municipal legal order by virtue of international law, but the extent of its application in this country is the same as in England.

As to the *ethical* aspect of the principle, one may indeed agree that the sense of justice generally recoils from punishing a person for an act committed by him for which at the date of its commission he could not have known—since it had not yet been prohibited by law—that he would become criminally liable. But this value judgment cannot be extended to the odious crimes attributed to the appellant, all the more so when dealing with the range and magnitude of their commission as described in the judgment. In such a case the above-mentioned maxim loses its moral value and is deprived of its ethical foundation. One's sense of justice must necessarily recoil even more from the non-punishment of the person who participated in such outrages, for he cannot argue—even as there was no possible prospect for the appellant successfully to argue with regard to his part in the realization of the "Final Solution"—that at the moment of acting he was not aware that he was violating deeply-rooted universal moral values. What Stone wrote (*op. cit.,* pp. 369–370), in repudiating the relevance of the ethical content of the principle of *nulla poena* to the parallel crimes of which the major war criminals were convicted at Nuremberg, is also apposite here:

> . . . the ethical import of the maxim is confronted by the countervailing ethical principles supporting the courts and sentences. Killing, maiming, torturing and humiliating innocent people are acts condemned by the value-judgments of all civilised men, and punishable by every civilised municipal legal system. . . . All this was known to the accused when they acted, though they hoped, no doubt, to be protected by the law of a victorious Nazi State from punishment. If, then, the rules applied at Nuremberg were not previously rules of positive international law, they were at least rules of positive ethics accepted by civilised men everywhere, to which the accused could properly be held in the forum of ethics.

In the absence therefore of a positive rule of international law prohibiting criminal legislation with retroactive effect, and in the absence also of a moral justification for preventing the application of such legislation to the offences which are the subject of this appeal, it follows that the second part of the argument of counsel for the appellant—that the State of Israel did not exist when these offences were committed and its competence to impose punishment therefor is limited to its own citizens—is equally unfounded. We shall see in what follows that the deeds for which the appellant was convicted must be regarded as having been prohibited by the law of nations since "time immemorial," and that from this aspect the enactment of the Law of 1950 was not in any way in conflict with the maxim *nulla poena,* nor did it violate the principle inherent therein. We have confined ourselves here to rejecting the "international" submission of counsel for the appellant on the strength of the first rule mentioned in the preceding paragraph, which governs the relationship between domestic law and the provisions of international law. As already stated, this rule postulates that the above-mentioned principle is not to be deemed to be embodied in municipal law by virtue of international law, and the District Court therefore was not enjoined to pay heed to it. This ground in itself is an adequate reply to the first argument of counsel for the appellant.

9. The same applies to the second argument also. As will be recalled, this argument is to the effect that the enactment of a criminal law applicable to an act committed in a foreign country by a foreign national conflicts with the principle of territorial sovereignty. But here too we must hold that there is no such rule in customary international law, and that to this day it has not obtained general international agreement. Evidence of this is to be found in the Judgment of the Permanent Court of International Justice in the *Lotus* case (*P.C.I.J.*, Series A, No. 10, 1927.) There the majority of the Judges recognized the competence of the State of Turkey to enact a criminal statute covering the negligent conduct of a French citizen while on duty as officer-of-the-watch of a French ship at the time of her collision on the high seas—and therefore outside

Turkey's territorial waters—with a ship flying the Turkish flag. The collision caused the sinking of the Turkish ship and also the death of eight of her passengers who were of Turkish nationality. It was held in that case that the principle of territorial sovereignty merely requires that a State exercise its penal power within its own borders and not outside them; that subject to this restriction every State has a wide discretion as to the application of its laws and the jurisdiction of its courts in respect of acts committed outside the State; and that only in so far as it is possible to point to a specific rule prohibiting the exercise of this discretion—a rule agreed upon by international treaty—is a State prevented from exercising it. That view was based on the following two grounds: (*a*) it is precisely the conception of State sovereignty which demands the preclusion of any presumption that there is a restriction on its independence; and (*b*) even if it is true that the principle of the territorial character of criminal law is firmly established in various States, it is no less true that in almost all such States penal jurisdiction has been extended, in ways that vary from State to State, so as to embrace offences committed outside its territory.

* * *

We would add that even if counsel for the appellant were right in his view that international law prohibits a State from trying a foreign national for an act committed outside its borders, this would not avail his client. The reason for this is that according to the theory of international law, in the absence of an international treaty vesting rights in an individual, that law only recognizes the rights of a State; in other words, assuming that there is such a prohibition in international law, the violation of it is deemed to be a violation of the rights of the State to which the accused belongs and not a violation of the individual's own rights (see Green, *loc. cit.,* p. 512). Thus in the *Molvan* case the Privy Council (as an additional reason for its decision) applied this test also and found that it was not open to the owner of the ship—for reasons which do not concern us here—to claim "the protection of any State nor could any State claim that any principle of international law was broken by her seizure" (*ibid.,* p. 370).

It should be noted—and we shall again revert to this fact with reference to another argument by counsel for the appellant—that it emerges from his own words that his application to the Government of Western Germany to claim the right to try the appellant in Germany was refused.

10. We have thus far stated our reasons for dismissing the first two contentions of counsel for the appellant in reliance upon the rules that determine the relationship between Israel municipal law and international law. Our principal object was to make it clear—and this by way of a negative approach—that under international law no *prohibition* whatsoever falls upon the enactment of the Law of 1950 either because it created *ex post facto* offences or because such offences are of an extra-territorial character. Nevertheless, like the District

Court, we too do not content ourselves with this solution but have undertaken the task of showing that it is impossible to justify these contentions even from a positive approach—that in enacting the said Law the Knesset only sought to set out the principles of international law and embody its aims. The two propositions on which we propose to rely will therefore be as follows:

(1) The crimes created by the Law and of which the appellant was convicted must be deemed today as having always borne the stamp of international crimes, banned by the law of nations and entailing individual criminal responsibility.

(2) It is the peculiarly universal character of these crimes that vests in every State the authority to try and punish anyone who participated in their commission. . . .

The category of "war crime" comprises in essence acts which are prohibited by the laws and customs of war. Accordingly, only acts committed in time of war are included therein, whereas the category of "crime against humanity" embraces—according to the plain meaning of the definition in the Law—inhuman acts as well that were committed during the Nazi period preceding the outbreak of war (September 1, 1939). We attach no practical importance to this distinction, even as we attach no like importance to the finding of the Nuremberg Tribunal that for the purpose of a conviction for the offence of a "crime against humanity" as defined in Article 6 (*c*) of the Charter, it was necessary to prove that it was committed in connection with one of the other two offences therein defined ("crimes against peace" or "war crimes"). The reason for our disregarding these distinctions is that, as emerges from the judgment of the District Court, the misdeeds attributed to the appellant in the Counts on which he was convicted were for the most part perpetrated during the war and in connection with the war. It will be noted—and the Court has dwelt on this fact in paragraph 29 of its judgment—that according to the judgment of the Nuremberg Tribunal Hitler's invasion of Austria also constitutes a "crime within the jurisdiction of the Court" in the sense of Article 6 (*c*) of the Charter, in other words, a "crime against peace" (see also the article by Schwelb on "Crimes against Humanity" in *British Year Book of International Law,* XXIII (1946), pp. 189–205). There is yet another distinction between the two types of crimes. While the acts appertaining to the "crime against humanity" are limited to acts of murder, etc., that were perpetrated among the civilian population, this limitation does not necessarily apply also to the acts belonging to the "war crimes" category (*ibid.,* p. 190). On the other hand, it is clear that many of the acts included in the one category overlap those in the other category, even though it is not imperative that they should all be identical (*ibid.,* pp. 188, 191). Be that as it may, this distinction too loses its force in this appeal, since the Court found (paragraph 206 of its judgment) that "all acts of persecution, deportation and murder in which the accused took part, as we have found in discussing crimes against the Jewish people and crimes against humanity, are *ipso facto* also war crimes within the meaning of Section 1 (*a*) (3) of the Law, as far as they were committed during the Second World War and the Jews who fell victim to these acts belonged to the population of the countries conquered by Germany and the other Axis States". . . .

11. *The first proposition.* Our view that the crimes in question must today be regarded as crimes which were also in the past banned by the law of nations and entailed individual criminal responsibility, is based upon the following reasons:

(*a*) As is well known, the rules of the law of nations are not derived solely from international treaties and crystalized international custom. In the absence of a supreme legislative authority and international codes the process of its evolution resembles that of the common law; in other words, its rules are fashioned piecemeal by analogy with the rules embedded in treaties and custom, on the basis of the "general principles of law recognized by civilized nations" and having regard to vital international needs that compel an immediate solution. A principle which constitutes a common denominator of the legal systems current in many countries must clearly be regarded as a "general principle of law recognized by civilized nations."

* * *

The underlying principle in international law regarding such crimes is that the individual who has committed any of them and who, when doing so, may be presumed to have fully comprehended the heinous nature of his act, must account for his conduct. It is true that international law does not prescribe explicit and scaled criminal sanctions; that there still does not exist either an International Criminal Court or even international penal machinery. For the time being, however, international law surmounts these difficulties—which merely reflect its present retarded stage of development—by authorizing the countries of the world to mete out punishment for the violation of its provisions, which is effected by putting these provisions into operation either directly or by virtue of municipal legislation which has adopted and integrated them. Let us explain this by three illustrations:

(1) The classic example of a "customary" international crime, also mentioned by the District Court, is that of piracy *jure gentium.* A person who has committed this crime, said Judge Moore in his dissenting judgment in the *Lotus* case (p. 70),

> . . . is treated as an outlaw, as the enemy of all mankind—*hostis humani generis*—whom any nation may *in the interest of all* capture and punish. Wheaton defines piracy by law of nations as murder or robbery committed on the high seas by persons acting *in defiance of all law,* and acknowledging obedience to no flag whatsoever.

In the report submitted to the League of Nations by the Committee for the Progressive Codification of International Law, the emphasis was placed on the interests of world trade which are endangered by that offence: "It constitutes a crime against the security of commerce on the high seas." (Quoted from *The Law of Nations* by Briggs, 2nd ed., p. 390.)

* * *

(2) As an example of customary international law an instructive case is that which came before an American Court in 1784, in which a person was tried for threatening to assault the Secretary of the French Diplomatic Mission (*Respublica* v. *De Longchamps*, 1 Dallas 110). In sentencing him to a fine and imprisonment for this offence, Chief Justice McKean of Pennsylvania said:

> The first crime in the indictment is an infraction of the law of nations. This law, in its full extent, is part of the law of this State, and is to be collected from the practice of different nations and authority of writers. The person of a public minister is sacred and inviolable. Whoever offers any violence to him, not only affronts the sovereign he represents, but also *hurts the common safety and well-being of nations:—he is guilty of a crime against the whole world.* . . . You then have been guilty of an atrocious violation of the law of nations.

(3) The last example—one which is closer to our case—is that of a "war crime" in the conventional sense. It will be recalled that the reference here is to a group of acts committed by members of the armed forces of the enemy which are contrary to the "laws and customs of war." These acts are deemed to constitute in essence *international* crimes; they involve the violation of the provisions of customary international law which obtained before the Hague Conventions of 1907, the latter merely "declaring" the rules of warfare as dictated by recognized humanitarian principles. Those crimes entail individual criminal responsibility because they challenge the foundations of international society and affront the conscience of civilized nations. When a belligerent State punishes for such acts, it does so not only because persons who were its nationals—be they soldiers taken prisoner by the enemy or members of the civilian population—suffered bodily harm or material damage, but also, and principally, because they involve the perpetration of an international crime which all the nations of the world are interested in preventing. The article by Lauterpacht on "Law of Nations and Punishment of War Crimes" (in *British Year Book of International Law,* XXI (1944, p. 64) lends support to the above characterization of crimes of this type:

> War criminals are punished, fundamentally, for breaches of international law. They become criminal according to the municipal law of the belligerent only if their action finds no warrant in and is contrary to international law. When, therefore, we say that the belligerent inflicts punishment on war criminals for the violation of his municipal law, we are making a statement which is correct only in the sense that the relevant rules of international law are being applied, by adoption or otherwise, as the municipal law of the belligerent. Intrinsically, punishment is inflicted for the violation of international law.

At p. 65 he emphasizes that the provision of Hague Convention No. IV of 1907 which imposed on a belligerent State which had violated the terms of the Convention the obligation to pay indemnity for physical and material damage, did not exclude the responsibility of the individual to account for any violation by him of the laws of war or "the customary right of States to punish enemy individuals for the violation of rules of war." He adds (*loc. cit.*):

> The Hague Conventions . . . formulate and are largely declaratory of the fundamental rules of warfare as directed by generally recognized principles of humanity. . . . In their broad purpose . . . these international conventions are expressive, in the words of the preamble of Hague Convention No. IV, "*of the principles of the law of nations, derived from usages established among civilized peoples, from the laws of humanity, and from the dictates of public conscience.*"

It was in the spirit of this approach that the United States Supreme Court ruled in *Ex parte Quirin et Al.* (1942), 87 L.Ed. 3, 12, 13) that the accused were criminally liable for acts contrary to the laws of war on the ground that these laws were always recognized and applied as part of the law of nations:

> From the very beginning of its history this Court has recognized and applied the law of war as including that part of the law of nations which prescribes, for the conduct of war, the status, rights and duties of enemy nations as well as of *enemy individuals.* By the Articles of War . . . Congress has . . . exercised its authority to define and punish offenses against the law of nations by sanctioning, within constitutional limitations, the jurisdiction of military commissions *to try persons for offenses which, according to the rules and precepts of the law of nations, and more particularly the law of war, are cognizable by such tribunals.* [Emphasis added.]

The Supreme Court affirmed this view in *In re Yamashita* (1945), . . .

(*c*) In view of the characteristic traits that mark the international crimes discussed above and having regard to the organic development of the law of nations—a development that advances from case to case under the impact of the humane sentiments common to civilized nations and by virtue of the needs vital for the survival of mankind and for ensuring the stability of the world order—it definitely cannot be said that, when the Charter of the Nuremberg International Military Tribunal was signed and the categories of "War Crimes" and "Crimes against Humanity" were defined in it, this merely amounted to an act of legislation by the victorious countries. The truth, as the Tribunal itself said, is that the Charter, with all the principles embodied in it—including that of individual responsibility—must be seen as "the expression of international law existing at the time of its creation; and to that extent (the Charter) is itself a contribution to international law." (I.M.T. (1947), vol. 1, p. 218.) See also the identical view expressed by Court No. III in the American Zone of Germany concerning two of the types of crimes mentioned in Control Council Law No. 10.

> All of the war crimes and many, if not all, of the crimes against humanity as charged in the indictment . . . were . . . (not) violative of pre-existing principles of international law. To the extent to which this is true, C.C. law may be deemed to

be a codification, rather than original substantive legislation (*U.S.* v. *Altstoetter,* T.W.C., vol. 3, p. 966).

* * *

Secondly, and this is most important, the interest in preventing and punishing acts belonging to the category in question—especially when they are perpetrated on a very large scale—must necessarily extend beyond the borders of the State to which the perpetrators belong and which evinced tolerance or encouragement of their outrages; for such acts can undermine the foundations of the international community as a whole and impair its very stability. Evidence of the manifestation of this international concern before the First World War can be found in a series of incidents which occurred during the nineteenth and the beginning of the twentieth centuries and resulted in vigorous diplomatic intervention by various countries on grounds of "humanitarian considerations" in respect of the terrible atrocities initiated or directed by certain other countries against whole sections of their own citizens (see the list of these incidents in the above-mentioned case of *Altstoetter,* at pp. 981–982; also in Greenspan's *The Modern Law of Land Warfare* (1959), p. 438).

Thirdly, the said criticism affects at most the question of penal jurisdiction, with which we shall deal later; but it cannot derogate from the characterization of the crimes concerned as offences against international law by every standard of enlightened humanity.

Fourthly, if, as we are asked to do, we are to regard customary international law as a developing progressive system, then the criticism becomes devoid of value. The reason is that once the International Military Tribunal at Nuremberg decided this question, as it did, the very decision must be seen as a judicial act which establishes a "precedent" defining a rule of the law of nations. In any event it would be unseemly for any other court to disregard such a rule and not to follow it. As Schwelb has said (*op. cit.,* p. 212):

> He would be a bold judge of any national, occupation, or military court, who would decline to be guided by the reasoned judgment of a court composed of four eminent members of the legal profession of the four Great Powers, arrived at after a trial, unique in its history, backed by the authority not only of the four Signatories, but also of nineteen "adherent" States, always provided that the facts—and the law to be applied—are the same.

Fifthly, if any doubt existed as to this appraisal of the Nuremberg Principles as principles that have formed part of the customary law of nations "since time immemorial," two international documents justify it. We allude to the United Nations General Assembly Resolution of December 11, 1946, which "affirms the principles of international law recognized by the Charter of the Nuremberg Tribunal and the Judgment of the Tribunal," and also to the General Assembly Resolution of the same date, No. 96 (1), in which the

General Assembly "affirms that Genocide is a crime under international law."

The outcome of the above analysis is that the crimes set out in the Law of 1950, which we have grouped under the inclusive caption "crimes against humanity," must be seen today as acts that have always been forbidden by customary international law—acts which are of a "universal" criminal character and entail individual criminal responsibility. That being so, the enactment of the Law was not from the point of view of international law a legislative act which conflicted with the principle *nulla poena* or the operation of which was retroactive, but rather one by which the Knesset gave effect to international law and its objectives. For this reason also, therefore, the first contention of counsel for the appellant rests on shaky foundations.

12. *The second proposition.* It will be recalled that according to this proposition it is the universal character of the crimes in question which vests in every State the authority to try and punish those who participated in their commission. This proposition is closely linked with the one advanced in the preceding paragraph, from which indeed it follows as a logical outcome. The grounds upon which it rests are as follows:

(*a*) One of the principles whereby States assume in one degree or another the power to try and punish a person for an offence is the principle of universality. Its meaning is substantially that such power is vested in every State regardless of the fact that the offence was committed outside its territory by a person who did not belong to it, provided he is in its custody when brought to trial. This principle has wide currency and is universally acknowledged with respect to the offence of piracy *jure gentium.* But while general agreement exists as to this offence, the question of the scope of its application is in dispute (see *Harvard Research* (1935), pp. 503 ff.). Thus, one school of thought holds that it cannot be applied to any offence other than the one mentioned above, lest it involve excessive interference with the competence of the State in which the offence was committed. This view is reflected in the following extract from the judgment of Judge Moore in the *Lotus* case (p. 71):

> It is important to bear in mind the foregoing opinions of eminent authorities as to the essential nature of piracy by law of nations, especially for the reason that nations have shown the strongest repugnance to extending the scope of the offence, because it carried with it . . . the principle of universal jurisdiction . . .

What is more (p. 70):

> Piracy by law of nations, in its jurisdictional aspects, is *sui generis.*

A second school of thought—represented by the authors of the draft convention on this subject in *Harvard Research* (p. 559)—agrees, it is true, to the extension of the principle to all manner of extra-territorial offences committed by foreign nationals, but regards it as only an auxiliary principle to be employed in circumstances in which no resort can be had to the principle of territorial sovereignty or to the nationality principle, two principles on which all are agreed. The authors of this draft therefore variously restrict the application of the principle of universal jurisdiction with the object of avoiding opposition by those States who find the need to punish the offender under one of the other two principles mentioned. One of these restrictions—to which we shall revert—is that the State contemplating the exercise of the power in question must first offer the extradition of the offender to the State within whose territory the offence was committed (*forum delicti commissi*). The justification found by this school of thought, as distinct from the first, for adopting the said principle, albeit as a purely auxiliary one, is the consideration that it is calculated to prove useful in circumstances in which the offender is likely to escape punishment if it is not applied.

A third school of thought holds that the rule of universal jurisdiction, which is valid in cases of piracy, is logically applicable also to all such criminal acts of commission or omission which constitute offences under the law of nations (*delicta juris gentium*), without any reservation whatever or at most subject to a reservation of the kind mentioned above. (See the quotation in paragraph 14 of the judgment of the District Court from Wheaton's *Elements of International Law,* 5th English ed. (1916), p. 184; also proposals in this spirit referred to in *Harvard Research,* pp. 555, 562, 563). This view has been opposed in the past because of the difficulty of securing general agreement as to the offences to be included in the above-mentioned class (*ibid.,* pp. 555, 558).

A fourth view is that expressed *de lege ferenda* by Lauterpacht in 1949 in the *Cambridge Law Journal* (vol. 9, p. 348, n. 61):

> It would be in accordance with an enlightened principle of justice—a principle which has not yet become part of the law of nations—if, in the absence of effective extradition, the courts of a State were to assume jurisdiction over common crimes, by whomsoever and wherever committed, of a heinous character.

(*b*) The brief survey of views set out above shows that, notwithstanding the differences between them, there is full justification for applying here the principle of universal jurisdiction since the international character of "crimes against humanity" (in the wide meaning of the term) dealt with in this case is no longer in doubt, while the unprecedented extent of their injurious and murderous effects is not to be disputed at the present time. In other words, the basic reason for which international law recognizes the right of each State to exercise such jurisdiction in piracy offences—notwithstanding the fact that its own sovereignty does not extend to the scene of the commission of the offence (the high seas) and the offender is a national of another State or is stateless—applies with even greater force to the above-mentioned crimes. That reason is, it will be recalled, that the interest to prevent bodily and material harm to those who sail the seas and to persons engaged in trade between nations, is a vital interest common to all civilized States and of universal scope, as was emphasized by the authors of the *Harvard Research* (p. 552):

> The competence to prosecute and punish for piracy was commonly explained by saying that the pirate . . . was the enemy of all alike . . . The competence is

> better justified at the present time upon the ground that the punishable acts are committed upon the seas where all have an interest in the safety of commerce and where no State has territorial jurisdiction. Notwithstanding the more effective policing of the seas in modern times, the common interest and mutual convenience which gave rise to the principle have conserved its vitality as a means of preventing the recurrence of maritime depredations of a piratical character.

This means that it was not the capacity of universal jurisdiction to try and punish the person who committed "piracy" that from a practical point of view justified bestowing upon this act the character of an international crime *sui generis,* but it was the agreed vital interest of the international community that made the exercise of such jurisdiction justifiable.

> *As a result of this attitude of mankind towards these two great public crimes* . . . piracy and the slave trade wherever practised are subject to punishment by any political authority apprehending the persons engaged therein irrespective of their nationality or allegiance. (Lansing, *op. cit.,* p.25.)

It follows that the State which prosecutes and punishes a person for piracy acts merely as the organ and agent of the international community and metes out punishment to the offender for his breach of the prohibition imposed by the law of nations:

> With regard to the pirate, the State punishing him as an organ of the international legal community. For it is international law which the State applies against the pirate. (Kelsen, *op. cit.,* p. 345.)
>
> The prosecution must perforce be conducted in the Courts of the State which has seized the pirate; but the violation of the law invoked is one which concerns the entire Community of Nations, and the prosecuting State is acting, in effect, as agent of all civilized States in vindicating the law common to them all. (Glueck, *op. cit.,* p. 100.)

The above explanation of the substantive basis upon which the exercise of the principle of universal jurisdiction in respect of the crime of piracy rests, justifies its exercise in regard also to the crimes which are the subject of the present case.

(*c*) The truth is—and this further supports our conclusion—that the application of this principle has for some time been moving beyond the international crime of piracy. We have in mind its application to conventional war crimes as well. As we observed in paragraph 11 (*c*) of this judgment, whenever a "belligerent" country tries and punishes a member of the armed forces of the enemy for an act contrary to "the laws and customs of war," it does so because the matter involves an international crime in the prevention of which the countries of the whole world have an interest. Thus, in his article mentioned in the same paragraph, Cowles reviewed a series of cases prior to the Second World War, in which American Military Tribunals tried offenders for war crimes committed within territory which was not at the time under the control of the armed forces of the United States but which was only subsequently reached by them. On the strength of that review, he summarized the position by saying (*loc. cit.,* p. 217):

> Actual practice shows that the jurisdiction assumed by military courts, trying offences against the law of war, has been personal, or universal, not territorial. The jurisdiction exercised over war crimes has been of the same nature as that exercised in the case of the pirate, and this broad jurisdiction has been assumed for the same fundamental reason.

He therefore reached the conclusion (p. 218) that

> . . . under international law, every independent State has jurisdiction to punish war criminals in its custody regardless of the nationality of the victim, the time it entered the war, or the place where the offence was committed.

In his Note on the legal basis of jurisdiction over war crimes in the *British Year Book of International Law*, XXVIII (1951), p. 382, at pp. 390, 391, Baxter stated that the end of the Second World War cases of war crimes were tried by the British Military Tribunal in Germany in which the victims were not British subjects but nationals of Allied countries, and he exemplified:

> In the *Zyklon B* case . . . those killed by poison gas supplied by the accused included Belgian, Dutch, French, Czech, and Polish nationals, and it was not alleged that any British subjects were among the victims. (See the report of this case in *L.R.T.W.C.*, vol. I, pp. 93, 102.)

In this connection mention should also be made of a case which was tried by a British Military Court in Singapore. There the Court, which was composed of *British* officers, sentenced to death a member of the *Japanese* army for unlawfully killing *American* prisoners of war in Saigon (then *French* Indo-China); that is to say, the Court exercised jurisdiction notwithstanding the fact that the scene of the crime was in French territory and the victims were not British subjects (*L.R.T.W.C.*, vol. 1, p. 106).

Although the fact that the victims of the crimes in these cases were nationals of countries in alliance with the prosecuting State derogates in some degree from the universal character of the jurisdiction exercised, nevertheless, on the other hand, the cases indicate that substantial strides were made towards extending the use of the said principle. Baxter indeed concluded, on the basis of these cases and also of those that were tried by the American tribunals in Germany under Control Council Law No. 10, that:

> International law also surmounts the jurisdictional barrier, as municipal law cannot, by recognizing the universality of jurisdiction enjoyed by war crimes tribunals.

Moreover, according to this expert's opinion, even a neutral country has jurisdiction to try a person for a war crime (*loc. cit.*, p. 392). This is also the view of Greenspan (*op. cit.*, p. 503):

> Since each sovereign power stands in the position of a guardian of international law, and is equally interested in upholding it, any State has the legal right to try war crimes, even though the crimes have been committed against the nationals of another power and in a conflict to which that State is not a party.

(The expression "war crimes" in the above extract extends also to "crimes against humanity" and "genocide" in time of war: *op. cit.*, p. 420.)

(*d*) It is here opportune to discuss the limitation upon the exercise of universal jurisdiction imposed by most of those who support this principle, namely, that the State which has apprehended the offender must first offer to extradite him to the State in which the offence was committed (see sub-paragraph (*a*) above). This means that only if the second State does not respond to the offer of extradition may the first State arrogate to itself the jurisdiction to try and punish. The above limitation is based upon the approach implicit in the maxim *aut dedere aut punire*. Counsel for the appellant also took this view and accordingly submitted that so long as the State of Israel had not offered to extradite his client to Germany—the *forum delicti commissi* of many of the crimes attributed to him—it had no right to place him on trial. He further contended that the fact of the appellant's German nationality also obliged Israel to follow the course of offering to extradite him to Germany. As to this, let it be said at once that it cannot assist the appellant, since the requirement of making an offer to extradite the offender to the State of his national origin is supported neither by international law nor by the practice of States (*Harvard Research,* p. 569).

As to the limitation itself in the above sense, we are of the opinion that it has no place in the circumstances of this case. First, as already stated, counsel for the appellant has himself admitted that his application to the Government of West Germany to demand the extradition of his client was refused and therefore an offer in this sense by the Government of Israel could be of no practical use. Secondly—and this is the principal reason for rejecting his submission—the idea behind the above-mentioned limitation is not that the requirement to offer the offender to the State in which the offence was committed was designed to prevent the violation of its territorial sovereignty. Its basis is rather a purely practical one. Normally, the great majority of the witnesses and the greater part of the evidence are concentrated in that State and it is therefore the most convenient place (*forum conveniens*) for the conduct of the trial. This point was taken by Lauterpacht in the continuation of the passage cited in sub-paragraph (*a*) above:

> Territoriality of jurisdiction is a rule of convenience in the sphere of the law of evidence. It is not a requirement of justice or even a necessary postulate of the sovereignty of the State. (*Loc. cit.*, p. 348.)

Baxter too had this meaning of the limitation in mind when he said (*op. cit.*):

> If a neutral State should, by reason of the availability of the accused, witnesses, and evidence, be the most convenient locus in which to try a war crime, there is no reason why that State should not perform that function.

If, therefore, we consider the above-mentioned contention of counsel for the appellant in the light of this practical test, it must be said that the great majority of the witnesses who gave evidence here on the grave crimes attributed to the appellant, especially those against the Jews, are residents of Israel, and, moreover, the bulk of the vast mass of documents produced was previously gathered and is preserved (through the Yad Va-Shem Institute) in the State of

Israel. It should be noted that the appellant himself has relied for his defence on a number of the documents which are in this country and which were made available to him. It is clear therefore that it is the State of Israel—not the State of Germany—that must be regarded as the *forum conveniens* for the conduct of the trial.

We have also taken into consideration the possible desire of other countries to try the appellant in so far as the offences contained in the indictment were committed in those countries or their injurious effects extended thereto. But the practical reason that has justified the holding of the trial here is equally applicable to them. It is to be observed that we have not heard of a single protest by any of these countries against conducting the trial in Israel, and it is reasonable to believe that in face of Israel's exercise of jurisdiction no other State will demand the right to do so itself. What is more, it is precisely the fact that the crimes in question and their effects have extended to numerous countries that drains the territorial principle of all content in the present case and justifies Israel in assuming criminal jurisdiction by virtue of the "universal" principle. For Israel to decide to which particular country the appellant should be extradited would have meant a completely arbitrary choice:

> The allegedly general principle of law entitling a man to be tried where his offences are charged to have been committed is rendered nugatory . . . by the fact that his offences were committed in a great number of places. Application of the territoriality principle in this instance would thus lead to an arbitrary choice. (Helen Silving, *op. cit.*, p. 335.)

It follows that the *aut dedere* rule cannot assist the appellant in the circumstances of this case.

(*e*) Counsel for the appellant has further submitted that under Article 6 of the Genocide Convention a person accused of this crime shall be tried by a court of competent jurisdiction of the State in which it was committed. According to his submission, that article has affirmed the application of the "territorial" principle, and the "universal" principle is therefore implicitly negated. The reply to this contention was given by the District Court in paragraphs 21 *et seq.* of its judgment. It is that Article 6 imposes upon the parties contractual obligations with future effect, that is to say, obligations which bind them to prosecute for crimes of genocide which may be committed within their territories in the future. This obligation, however, has nothing to do with the universal *power* vested in every State to prosecute for crimes of this type committed in the past—a power which is based on *customary* international law.

(*f*) We sum up our views on this subject as follows. Not only do all the crimes attributed to the appellant bear an international character, but their harmful and murderous effects were so embracing and widespread as to shake the international community to its very foundations. The State of Israel therefore was entitled, pursuant to the principle of universal jurisdiction and in the capacity of a guardian of international law and an agent for its enforcement, to try the appellant. That being the case, no importance attaches to the fact that the State of Israel did not exist when the offences were committed. Here therefore is an additional reason—and one based on a positive approach—for rejecting the second, "jurisdictional," submission of counsel for the appellant.

We wish to add one further observation. In regard to the crimes directed against the Jews the District Court found additional support for its jurisdiction in the connecting link between the State of Israel and the Jewish people—including that between the State of Israel and the Jewish victims of the holocaust—and the National Home in Palestine, as is explained in its judgment. It therefore upheld its criminal and penal jurisdiction by virtue also of the "protective" principle and the principle of "passive personality." It should be made clear that we fully agree with every word said by the Court on this subject in paragraphs 31–38 of its judgment. If in our judgment we have concentrated on the international and universal character of the crimes of which the appellant has been convicted, one of the reasons for our so doing is that some of them were directed against non-Jewish groups (Poles, Slovenes, Czechs and gipsies).

13. It will be convenient if at this point we proceed to consider the fourth submission of counsel for the appellant, which is also jurisdictional. It will be recalled that he argued that his client was brought to this country against his will, without the consent of his country of residence (Argentina) and by agents of the State of Israel. Counsel for the appellant has complained to us that the District Court refused to grant his application for the hearing of evidence to prove that the Government of Israel was implicated in the act of abduction, and he repeated his application in this Court.

This submission is unconnected with the preceding two, since it denies the right of the State of Israel to try the appellant for the crimes in question because of the circumstances under which he was brought here, while the others deny such right even if he were to be tried in this country after having arrived here of his own free will. We have no intention of dealing with this contention at any great length, for it has been analysed with great thoroughness by the District Court (paragraphs 41–52 of its judgment). Relying on a long line of local, British, American and Continental precedents, which were cited extensively in its judgment, the District Court reached the following conclusions:

(1) In the absence of an extradition agreement between the State to which a "fugitive offender" has been brought for trial and the country of "asylum" (from which he was removed by force or by strategem)—and even if such an agreement existed between the two countries but the offender was not extradited to the first country in accordance therewith—the Court will not investigate the circumstances in which he was detained and brought into the area of jurisdiction.

(2) This also applies if the offender's contention is that the abduction was carried out by agents of the State prosecuting him, since in such a case the right violated is not that of the offender but the sovereign right of the State aggrieved. In other words, the violation of the right raises a question—either political or one of a breach of international law—between the two countries

concerned and it must therefore find its solution at this international level. It is not, however, justiciable before the Court into whose area of jurisdiction the offender has been brought.

(3) From the point of view of international law the aggrieved State may condone the violation of its sovereignty and waive its claims, including the claim for the return of the offender to its territory, and such waiver may be explicit or by acquiescence.

(4) Only in one eventuality has a fugitive offender a right of immunity, namely, when he has been extradited by the country of asylum to the country requesting his extradition for a specific offence which is not the offence for which he is tried.

(5) The appellant was not extradited to Israel by Argentina and the State of Israel is not bound by any agreement with Argentina to try him for a specific offence or not to try him for the offences involved in this case.

(6) Moreover, following upon the Resolution of the Security Council of the United Nations of June 23, 1960 (Exhibit T/1), the Governments of Argentina and Israel settled the dispute between them when they issued, on August 3, 1960—before the indictment was presented—a joint communiqué (Exhibit T/4) stating that they "have resolved to regard as closed the incident that arose out of the action taken by citizens of Israel, which infringed the fundamental rights of the State of Argentina." This means that Argentina has condoned the violation of her sovereignty and has waived her claims, including that for the return of the appellant. Any violation therefore of international law that may have been involved in this incident has thus been remedied.

(7) The rights of asylum and immunity belong to the country of asylum and not to the offender. It was not for the appellant to force Argentina, a foreign sovereign State, to give him asylum against its will, especially when at the time of entering upon its territory he was a "wanted war criminal," concealed his true identity and resided there subsequently "under an assumed name and on forged papers." It follows therefore that the State of Argentina gave him no asylum or refuge from the outset, while by the declaration of the settlement of the incident and the waiver of the claim for his return, it finally refused to grant him asylum.

(8) In view of the foregoing there was no room for hearing the evidence which counsel for the appellant sought to adduce on the circumstances of the abduction.

* * *

14. The next submission to be considered is that the crimes of which the appellant was convicted were at the time within the definition of Acts of State and that therefore he is absolved from criminal responsibility in respect thereof. The theory of "Act of State" means that the act performed by a person as an organ of the State—whether he was head of the State or a responsible official

acting on the Government's orders—must be regarded as an act of the State alone. It follows that only the latter bears responsibility therefor, and it also follows that another State has no right to punish the person who committed the act, save with the consent of the State whose mission he performed. Were it not so, the first State would be interfering in the internal affairs of the second, which is contrary to the conception of the equality of States based on their sovereignty (see Kelsen, *Peace through Law,* pp. 81 ff.). The contention of counsel for the appellant is therefore that the acts done by his client for the realization of the "Final Solution" had their origin in Hitler's decision to put that plan into effect and consequently they were purely "Acts of State," responsibility for which does not rest on the appellant.

We utterly reject this contention, as did the District Court (paragraph 28 of the judgment). Our reasons are as follows.

(*a*) The concept of "sovereignty," from which the doctrine of "Act of State" derives, is not considered today to be an absolute concept, as was made clear by Kunz in his article, "The Nottebohm Judgment," in *A.J.I.L.,* vol. 54, p. 545:

> Any *a priori* or unlimited political concept of sovereignty must, with inescapable logic, lead to the non-existence of international law as law. Sovereignty is, therefore, essentially a *relative* notion.

This also applies to the "Act of State" doctrine. Even Chief Justice Marshall, who relief on it in *Schooner Exchange* v. *McFaddon* (3 L.Ed. 287), was particularly careful to base it on the sole foundation that the State within whose territory an illegal act was committed on behalf of another State had expressly or impliedly consented to waive its sovereign territorial right to punish for it. What is more, he added the reservation that where implied consent is involved "its extent must be regulated by the nature of the case, and the views under which the parties requiring and conceding it must be supposed to act" (p. 296).

Commenting on this passage, Glueck has observed (in *Harvard Law Review,* vol. 59, p. 426):

> As Marshall implied, even in an age when the doctrine of sovereignty had a strong hold, the non-liability of agents of a State for "acts of State" must rationally be based on an assumption that no member of the Family of Nations will order its agents to commit flagrant violations of international and criminal law.

As to the opinion given in 1841 by the American Secretary of State, Webster, in *In re McLeod,* which is also based on the same doctrine and on which Kelsen relied (*op. cit.,* p. 83), it was pointed out by Quincy Wright (in *A.J.I.L.,* vol. 41, p. 71) that even then it had not gained general recognition:

> This position was disputed by many at the time on the ground that the Government's authority could not confer immunity upon its agents for acts beyond its powers under international law.

(*b*) In any event, there is no basis for the doctrine when the matter pertains to acts prohibited by the law of nations, especially when they are international crimes of the class of "crimes against humanity" (in the wide sense). Of such odious acts it must be said that in point of international law they are completely outside the "sovereign" jurisdiction of the State that ordered or ratified their commission, and therefore those who participated in such acts must personally account for them and cannot shelter behind the official character of their task or mission, or behind the "Laws" of the State by virtue of which they purported to act. Their position may be compared with that of a person who, having committed an offence in the interests of a corporation which he represents, is not permitted to hide behind the collective responsibility of the corporation therefor. In other words, international law postulates that it is impossible for a State to sanction an act that violates its severe prohibitions, and from this follows the idea which forms the core of the concept of "international crime," that a person who was a party to such a crime must bear individual responsibility for it. If it were otherwise, the penal provisions of international law would be a mockery.

> [I]n modern times a State is—*ex hypothesi*—incapable of ordering or ratifying acts which are not only criminal according to generally accepted principles of domestic penal law but also contrary to that international law to which all States are perforce subject. Its agents, in performing such acts, are therefore acting outside their legitimate scope; and must, in consequence, be held personally liable for their wrongful conduct. (Glueck, *loc. cit.*, pp. 427–428.)

This was written before the Nuremberg Tribunal delivered its judgment; and indeed, even before the Second World War the defence of "Act of State" was not regarded as an adequate defence to the charge of an offence against the "laws of war" (a "conventional" war crime). Lauterpacht saw in this a complete answer to the doctrine in question:

> It is universally agreed that in any case persons who have ordered the commission of war crimes are liable to punishment for the violations of rules of warfare. It is clear that in this vital respect the apparently established doctrine breaks down altogether. The law declines, in this matter, to accept the artificial distinction between the State and those acting on its behalf. The fact that the offender acts on behalf of the State is irrelevant. He is bound personally by rules of international law whether he is acting in his personal capacity, in order to satisfy private greed or lust, or as an organ of the State. [63 *Law Quarterly Review* (1947), pp. 442–443.]

In support of this view Glueck (*loc. cit.*, p. 428) cites the case of the German General, Stenger, who was sentenced in 1920 by the Supreme Court in Leipzig for the killing of wounded French soldiers during the First World War. In its judgment the German Court said:

> The lawfulness or unlawfulness of an act of war is determined by the rules of international law. The killing of enemies in war is in accordance *with the will of the State* which wages the war and whose laws are decisive for the question of legality or illegality *only to the extent that it is done under the conditions and within the limits which international law establishes.*

(*c*) Whatever may be the value of the above doctrine in other cases, the principle laid down in Article 7 of the Charter of the International Military

Tribunal at Nuremberg, to which the Tribunal (basing itself also on *Ex parte Quirin*) adhered, is that the doctrine cannot afford a defence in respect of international crimes, particularly those defined in the Charter. To quote the Court:

> The principle of international law which, under certain circumstances, protects the representatives of a State, cannot be applied to acts which are condemned as criminal by international law. The authors of these acts cannot shelter themselves behind their official position in order to be freed from punishment in appropriate proceedings. Article 7 of the Charter expressly declares: "The official position of Defendants, whether as heads of State, or responsible officials in Government departments, shall not be considered as freeing them from responsibility, or mitigating punishment." On the other hand, the very essence of the Charter is that individuals have international duties which transcend the national obligations of obedience imposed by the individual State. He who violates the laws of war cannot obtain immunity while acting in pursuance of the authority of the State if the State in authorizing action moves outside its competence under international law. [*Trial of the Marjor War Criminals* (Nuremberg, 1947), vol. 1, p. 223.]

The principle expressed in these words, which totally negates the "Act of State" plea, is today one of the "Nuremberg Principles" which have become part of the law of nations and must be regarded as having been rooted in it also in the past, as explained in paragraph 11 above (see also Article IV of the Genocide Convention; Principle No. III of the Nuremberg Principles, as formulated by the International Law Commission following upon the United Nations Resolution 177 (II)—report of the Commission on its proceedings, U.N. General Assembly, *Official Records,* 5th Session, Suppl. No. 12A 1316 (1950) p. 12). The result is that this plea, so far as concerns the crimes in question, finds no support in international law and can in no way avail the appellant.

(*d*) Counsel for the appellant proceeded to plead that the acts attributed to his client were committed within the framework of the anti-Jewish decrees of the Nazi régime and the personal orders of Hitler himself—decrees and orders which, for all the injustice they entailed, had at the time the force of law. To this argument there are two replies. First, if any one wishes to entrench himself behind the formal concept of a Nazi "Law," it must be said that the "Final Solution" was at no time embodied in a "Law"—not, indeed, because of any deference on the part of the Nazis to the law which they ostensibly had no wish to violate, but because they were most anxious to conceal their deeds in darkness and not expose them to the civilized world (a fact which also evidences the Nazis' knowledge of the criminality of their deeds). It would appear, moreover, that the dominant tendency in the jurisprudence of West Germany today is to invalidate *ab initio* the discriminatory and destructive decrees of the Nazi régime, to deny them any legal validity from the day they were issued or enforced, and to apply this rule also to the "norms" which were of Hitler's own creation. The view by which West German Courts are guided is expressed in the formula stated by Radbruch (called by the Attorney-General "the greatest positivist in German thought") in his post-war writings (*Rechtsphilosophie* (1950), p. 353):

> Preference should be given to the rule of positive law, supported as it is by due enactment and State power, even when the rule is unjust and contrary to the general welfare, unless the violation of justice reaches so intolerable a degree that the rule becomes in effect "lawless law" and must therefore yield to justice. (Translated by Professor Lon Fuller of Harvard University.)

(See also the article by Silving, p. 344, and the extracts from German judgments therein cited, and the review of these judgments in *Legal Theory* by Friedmann, 4th ed., pp. 310, 311.)

It follows that, according to the said jurisprudence, not only is the present contention of counsel for the appellant completely untenable even in German law, but that also according to the theory of Kelsen (*op. cit.,* note on p. 82) the acts in question cannot be accorded the nature of "Acts of State." However, we need not resort to modern German judgments as support for rejecting this contention. The second and principal reason for our doing so is that the discriminatory and plunderous decrees of that evil State and the murderous edicts of the autocrat who directed its affairs are not laws in the contemplation of international law and can in no manner render these terrible crimes valid or absolve those who participated in committing them from the personal responsibility they bear.

> Hitler's decrees were a protection neither to the Fuehrer himself nor to his subordinates, if in violation of the law of the community of nations. (*U.S.* v. *Altstoetter,* L.R.T.W.C., vol. 3, p. 1011.)

To conclude this aspect of the matter we can do no better than repeat the words of the District Court:

> The very contention that the systematic extermination of masses of helpless human beings by a Government or régime could constitute "an act of State", appears to be an insult to reason and a mockery of law and justice.

The plea of "Act of State" is rejected.

15. Counsel for the appellant coupled with the plea of "Act of State" also that of "obedience to superior orders." He contended that it was the oath of allegiance taken by his client on joining the S.S. organization and the compelling force of Hitler's order to destroy the Jews completely which guided him in acting as he did. At this stage we shall deal with this submission from the legal point of view alone; our main object will, on the one hand, be to distinguish it from the "Act of State" plea and, on the other hand, to clarify its meaning and significance from the viewpoint of international law.

(*a*) The defence of "obedience to superior orders" differs from that of "Act of State" in the following three respects.

(1) While the latter plea means that the criminal act is not to be imputed to the person who committed it but only to the State, the former signifies that though he may be regarded, even in point of law, as the doer of the act, the fact

that he acted under the compulsion of an order of the competent authority, to which he was directly subordinate, serves as his justification.

(2) While the "Act of State" theory gives the mission in question this character only because the *supreme authority* in the State ("the Heads of State," etc.) ordered or authorized it (see Kelsen *op. cit.,* p. 104), this does not necessarily apply to the theory of "superior orders," which seeks to justify the criminal act solely because *the immediate superior* of the perpetrator ordered him to carry it out and the latter was bound to obey.

(3) "Act of State" does not simply mean that the person who performed the mission acted under ministerial direction which left him no margin of discretion; it is the fact alone that the act was performed within the scope of the given authorization which suffices to vest it with that character. On the other hand, the defence that the act was done in obedience to superior orders means *ex hypothesi* that the person who performed it had no alternative—either under the law or under the regulations of the disciplinary body (army, etc.) of which he was a member—but to carry out the order he received from his superior.

It should be noted that we have not as yet dealt with the legal merits of the defence in question, but have dwelt only on the differences existing between it and the other defence. The third difference makes it clear that the "superior orders" doctrine cannot, by its very nature, serve the appellant because, when we come to analyze the facts, it will be found that within the framework of the order to carry out the "Final Solution" the appellant acted independently and even exceeded the duties imposed on him through the service channels of the official chain of command (see paragraphs 16–18 of Part II of this judgment).

(*b*) The question whether the public interest requires that the defence of "superior orders" be recognized, raises the following two difficulties. On the one hand, the good order of the disciplinary body to which the accused belongs demands that he should not disobey his superior officer and should not pause to ponder the legality of the command he has received, lest the purpose for the realization of which he was ordered to act be impaired. On the other hand, the damage that will be caused to the public in consequence of the offence committed by virtue of the order demands that he should obey it not automatically but only if reasonably convinced that the order was lawful. These two conflicting aspects have been aptly summarized by Stephen in his *History of Criminal Law in England* (vol. 1, p. 206):

> The inconvenience of being subject to two jurisdictions, the sympathies of which are not unlikely to be opposed to each other, is an inevitable consequence of the double necessity of preserving on the one hand the supremacy of the law and on the other the discipline of the army.

There is also the personal problem of the soldier himself, when placed in the dilemma that if he disobeys the order of his commanding officer and it later turns out to have been lawful, he will be tried by a court martial, whereas if he obeys the order and it later transpires that it was not lawful, he will be liable to punishment under the general criminal law. This difficulty is likely to be a serious one in view of the fact that the simple soldier is not always capable of deciding on the spot whether the order given was lawful or not:

> It is not easy for any man, still less for the poorly educated soldier, to decide whether an order addressed to him is reasonably necessary for quelling a disturbance . . . To make matters worse for him he is subject to two different jurisdictions. (Glanville Williams, *The Criminal Law,* etc., 2nd ed., p. 297.)

All three difficulties demonstrate that the problem whether it is desirable to sanction this defence depends on the answer to the question whether, and to what extent, the mental state of the accused at the time of the offence ought to be taken into consideration—the fact that he did not then know that the order he carried out was contrary to law. The *via media* solution provided by the general criminal law of this country—in accordance with the tendency of English law (Glanville Williams, *op. cit.,* pp. 297, 298)—is that such defence is admissable where there was obedience to an order not manifestly unlawful (Section 19 (*b*) of the Criminal Code Ordinance 1936; see also the passages from Israel cases cited in paragraph 219 of the District Court's judgment). However, in Section 8 of the Nazi and Nazi Collaborators (Punishment) Law the legislature has provided that the defence of "superior orders"—and the same is true of the defences of "constraint" and "necessity"—shall not apply with respect to the offences covered by the Law, while in Section 11 it has provided that it is permissible, in certain circumstances, to take it into account as a factor in mitigation of sentence. We certainly agree with the view of the District Court that even if it had to decide the case on the basis of the provisions of the general criminal law, it would also have had to reject that defence not only because the order for physical extermination was manifestly unlawful (and all the other orders to persecute the Jews were equally contrary to the "basic ideas of law and justice"), but also because the appellant was fully conscious at the same time that he was a party to the perpetration of the most grave and horrible crimes. Indeed, in paragraph 221 of its judgment the District Court has set out the evidence of the appellant in which he himself admitted this fact:

> Your Honour, President of the Court, since you call upon me to say and give a clear answer, I must declare that I see in this murder, in the extermination of the Jews, one of the gravest crimes in the history of humanity.

And in answer to Judge Halevi:

> . . . I already realized at the time that this solution by the use of force was something unlawful, something terrible, but to my regret I was obliged to deal with it in matters of transportation, because of my oath of loyalty from which I was not released. (Session 95, pp. 35, 36.)

(c) Thus far we have dwelt principally on the juridical significance of the defence in question—on the distinction between it and the plea of "Act of State"—and on the attitude adopted towards it by the legislature. We now wish to answer the question whether the special attitude taken by the legislature in Section 8 of the 1950 Law, which precludes the application of the defence of "superior orders" to the crimes dealt with by the Law, conflicts with the principles of international law.

(1) Our first answer to this question is that until the Second World War there was no agreed rule in the law of nations which recognized the defence of "superior orders," not even with regard to the charge of committing an act contrary to "the laws of war." See Stone, *op. cit.*, p. 362; Schick in *A.J.I.L.*, vol. 41, p. 793; Lord Wright, *History of the United Nations War Crimes Commission* (1948), p. 274.

The answers to the question whether such defence should be admissible at all—and if so, to what extent one may take into account the accused's knowledge or ignorance of the unlawful character of the order or the fact that he was "bound" to know of it—have varied from State to State. This is not the place to deal with them at length (see the review by Greenspan, *op. cit.*, pp. 490 ff.; also Wright, *op. cit.*, pp. 281 ff.). We may, however, mention the principle embodied in the British and American Military Codes of 1914, which lays down that a superior order shall serve as a defence for a member of the armed forces who has committed a war crime in obedience to it, and that the commanding officer responsible for such order shall alone bear criminal responsibility for the former's act. This is the principle known as *respondeat superior,* which conflicted with the provisions of the general criminal law then in force in those countries and was moreover not in accord with the decisions of their courts. In 1944 Glueck (*op. cit.*, pp. 149–150) wrote that the legal position on this issue had not yet crystallized in those countries. Indeed, a little later their military codes were amended and the principle was laid down that a superior order under which a member of the armed forces has acted in contravention of the laws of war would not confer upon him absolute immunity from punishment but that the Court might take such defence into consideration if the order was not obviously unlawful (British amendment). It is also pertinent to add that the relevant provision of German law of the last century, which the Nazis left intact, imposed liability for a breach of the criminal law committed by a person while acting in obedience to an order given him by his superior, on the latter alone, but at the same time specified that the former shall be treated as an accomplice if he knew that the order concerned an act which was a crime or an offence under general or military law (Article 47 (2) of the German Military Law of Criminal Jurisdiction of 1882, cited in paragraph 220 of the judgment of the District Court). That provision appears to have prescribed a sort of subjective test as to the admissibility of the defence of "superior orders," but in its judgment in the *Llandovery Castle* case, which concerned a charge of a war crime committed in the First World War, the Supreme Court of Germany held in Leipzig in 1921 that the accused should be deemed to have had knowledge of the unlawful character of the order he carried out:

> . . . if such an order is *universally known to everybody,* including also the accused, to be without any doubt whatever against the law . . . In the present case it was perfectly clear to the accused that killing defenceless people in the lifeboats

could be nothing but a breach of law. (Quoted from the judgment in *United States* v. *Ohlendorf*, L.R.T.W.C., vol. 4, p. 484.)

We have made passing reference to this test because it too requires that full criminal intent be attributed to the appellant even had he not admitted this fact in evidence. But our main purpose here is to make it clear that in the past no principle recognizing such a defence had crystallized in international law.

(2) There was thus no departure from the provisions of international law—and this will be our second answer to the above question—when Article 8 of the Charter of the International Military Tribunal provided, with respect to the crimes defined therein, that the fact that the accused acted pursuant to an order of a superior shall not free him from responsibility but that the Tribunal may take it into consideration in mitigation of punishment, should it find that justice so requires. It must be understood that this express provision was designed to defeat in advance any attempt by the Nazi criminals so to resort to the plea of *respondeat superior* as to reduce it to an absurdity, in view of the *Fuehrerprinzip* which dominated Nazi Germany and in the last analysis made it possible to identify Hitler alone as the source of the satanic orders in consequence of which the frightful Nazi crimes, including that of the "Final Solution," were committed.

> Had their contention that they acted upon the orders of Hitler been accepted as a valid defence, the rule *respondeat superior* would have served merely as a *reductio ad absurdum* for the purpose of frustrating the law. Upon such a theory it would have been impossible to punish anyone for the crimes of this war. All the perpetrators charged with offences might have made the same defense, and the arch-criminal, Hitler, by committing suicide, made it impossible to inflict punishment upon this earth. (Finch in *A.J.I.L.*, vol. 41, p. 21.)

See also the observation of Justice Jackson in the report submitted by him to the President of the United States in June 1945 (quoted by Lord Wright, *op. cit.*, p. 274):

> "Society as modernly organized cannot tolerate so broad an arch of official irresponsibility."

Here therefore is a most logical reason for rejecting the said defence as relieving from responsibility in cases of this kind. The other reason—that the very commission of the crimes in question demanded the existence of criminal intent in the perpetrator—emerges from the language used by the Nuremberg Tribunal in affirming that Article 8 is part of the law of nations:

> The provisions of this article are in conformity with the law of all nations. That a soldier was ordered to kill or torture in violation of the international law of war has never been recognized as a defense to such acts of brutality, though, as the Charter here provides, the order may be urged in mitigation of the punishment. The true test, which is found in varying degrees in the criminal law of most nations, is not the existence of the order, but whether moral choice was in fact possible. [*Trial of Major War Criminals* (Nuremberg, 1947), vol. 1, p. 224]

This principle also is one of the "Nuremberg Principles" which were confirmed by the United Nations Assembly Resolution of December 11, 1946, and which have become the legacy of civilized countries. If this is so, it must again be held that the provisions of Sections 8 and 11 of the Law of 1950 accord with international law.

(*d*) The last point in this regard with which it is necessary to deal—one touching on the third aspect of the general problem presented above—pertains to the statement at the end of the passage just cited from the Nuremberg Judgment. It was there observed that the true test was not whether a superior order existed but "whether moral choice was in fact possible." In other words, the mere plea of obedience to the order of a superior—as distinct from the plea that he could not avoid committing the crime because he had no "moral choice" to pursue any other course—will not avail the accused. The Tribunal did not specify what it meant by the expression "moral choice." It may be that its intention was to take into consideration circumstances which placed the accused under the threat of having to pay with his life if he disobeyed the criminal order (see Greenspan, *op. cit.,* p. 493, especially n. 334; Levontin, *Myth of International Security,* pp. 260–261). If this interpretation is correct—and we do not decide this—then it must be understood that the Tribunal meant to sanction the defence of "constraint" or "necessity." As stated, the applicability of these defences as relieving from responsibility in respect of the offences the subject of the Law of 1950 has been excluded by Section 11 thereof. But even had the Law permitted the accused to rely on the defence that in carrying out the order to commit the crime he was acting in circumstances of "constraint" or "necessity," he would still not succeed unless the following two facts were proved: (1) that the danger to his life was imminent; (2) that he carried out the criminal task out of a desire to save his own life and because he saw no other possibility of doing so. The American Tribunal IIA which applied Control Council Law No. 10 also insisted on these two conditions (*United States* v. *Ohlendorf,* L.R.T.W.C., vol. 4, p. 480):

> The threat, however, must be imminent, real and inevitable. . . . The test to be applied is whether the subordinate acted under coercion or whether he himself approved of the principle involved in the order. If the second proposition be true, the plea of superior orders fails. . . . When the will of the doer merges with the will of the superior in the execution of the illegal act, the doer may not plead duress under superior orders.

As will be seen below, neither of the said conditions has been met in this case. But we stress in particular the non-fulfilment of the second condition because each of the said two defences goes to the question of the *motive* that urged the accused to carry out the criminal act—the motive to save his own life—and also because the District Court relied in the main on its finding that the appellant performed the order of extermination of all times *con amore,* that is to say, with full zeal and devotion to the task. We shall also justify this finding of the Court when we come to examine the contentions of counsel for the appellant as to facts.

16. We must answer briefly the argument of counsel for the appellant that the judges of the District Court—and he advanced the same contention with reference to the Judges of this Court—were psychologically incapable of trying the case of his client objectively.

Like the District Court, we too reject this argument, and the reply which that Court gave in so doing is also our reply:

> As to the accused's apprehensions regarding the background to the hearing of this trial, we can do no more than reiterate what holds good for every judicial system worthy of the name, that the judge, when dispensing justice in a court of law, does not cease to be a human being, with human emotions and human passions. Yet he is enjoined by the law to overcome these emotions and passions, for were it not so, no judge would ever be fit to try a criminal case which evokes deep feelings and revulsion, such as treason or murder or any other serious crime. It is very true that the memory of the Holocaust shakes every Jew to the depths of his being, but once this case has been brought before us it is our duty to subdue even these emotions as we sit in judgment. We shall abide this duty. (Decision No. 3, Session 6, April 17, 1962.)

The learned Judges did indeed abide their duty fully and to the end.

* * *

17. The facts set out above also constitute a decisive rebuttal of learned counsel's third plea, that the appellant was acting on orders from his superiors. We here refer to the factual aspect of the plea, for the legal aspect has already been dealt with in section I, paragraph 15, of this judgment.

In point of fact, the appellant did not receive orders "from above" at all; he was the high and mighty one, the commander of all that pertained to Jewish affairs. He ordered and commanded, not only without orders from his superiors in the hierarchy of the service, but also at times completely contrary to such orders, as already shown above. The following illustrates how far he was possessed by the concept of the "Final Solution" and to what extent he attempted to surpass even his "illustrious masters." In April 1945, about a month before Germany's complete collapse, when even the Reichsfuehrer S.S., in quest of an alibi for himself, had already begun to consider "more humane methods" of persecuting the Jews, he—Eichmann—was still uneasy about these methods and only with deep regret and emotional self-restraint did he comply with Himmler's instruction, as he told the representative of the International Red Cross (T/865). It is clear that the *idea* of the "Final Solution" was not his own but the Fuehrer's. Yet that idea might not have assumed so satanic and infernal a manifestation—in the blood of millions of tortured and martyred Jews—but for the thorough planning, the zeal, the fanatical enthusiasm and the insatiable bloodthirstiness of the appellant and those who did his bidding. We do not minimize even by one jot the terrible guilt that rests on the heads of many, many others; no one who lent the least assistance—active or passive, direct or indirect—to Nazi gangsterism in Europe, is to be exculpated. But here in this trial we are concerned with the appellant's individual guilt, and as to him it has been proved with unchallengeable certainty that he took his place not only among those who were active in but also those who activated the implementation of the "Final Solution", the total extermination of the Jews of Europe. The appellant was no petty killer in this undertaking, but took a leading part and had a central and decisive role.

18. Thus the fourth submission of counsel for the appellant, the plea of "necessity" falls to the ground. He (the appellant) was not coerced into doing what he did and was not in any danger of his life, since, as we have seen above, he did far more than was demanded or expected of him by his superiors in the chain of command. No one would have taken him to task, and he would certainly not have been brought to the gallows, had he—to give one example—based himself on the consent of Hitler and Ribbentropp to the emigration to Sweden and Switzerland of a few score thousand Jews (see paragraph 16 (*e*) above) and not undermined the proposal so wickedly and guilefully. As we have seen above, he was lavish in such "volunteer acts." In the upper echelons of their organization, the Nazis did not need the services of those who acted like unwilling ciphers. That would have impaired operational efficiency, and they had no shortage of zealous followers, people with unshaken nerve, in other words people lacking all human feeling. This is proved by the thousands of arch-murderers, the members of the Operation Units and execution squads, who operated in Riga, Minsk, Kiev (Babi Yar) and other places and wiped out about a million Jews by shooting—isolated, individual shooting at point blank range—without hesitation or failure of nerves (see the statement of Otto Ohlendorf at Nuremberg, T/312). Had the appellant exhibited at any stage the slightest displeasure or heart-searching or even mere lack of enthusiasm for the implementation of the "Final Solution," his superiors would willingly have relieved him of his post and replaced him by some other person more "qualified" than he. Thus on October 4, 1943, Himmler delivered a long address in Posen in which he said, *inter alia:*

> If anyone thinks that he cannot undertake to carry out an order (given him) he must say honestly: "I cannot undertake this task, please relieve me of it." Then, in most cases, the order would probably be: "You must nevertheless carry this out." Or (the commander) might think. "This man's nerves are shaken, he is weak," in which case he would be told, "All right, you had better resign." (T/1288.)

The appellant never displayed any remorse or weakness or sapping of strength or weakening of will in performing the task he had untertaken. He was "the right man in the right place," and he carried out his unspeakably horrible crimes with genuine wholehearted joy and pleasure, to his own gratification and the satisfaction of all his superiors. Here certainly were not present the conditions of "necessity" mentioned in Section 18 of the Criminal Code Ordinance, and the appellant would be liable to the death penalty under Section 1 of the Law for the Punishment of Nazis and Nazi Collaborators, 1950, even if the defence under Section 18 of the Ordinance had not been taken away by Section 8 of the Law in respect of offences set out in that Law. All the more so now that this defence has been excluded. For no one has even as much as suggested that the appellant "did his best to reduce the gravity of the consequences" of the offence or that he did what he did with intent "to avert . . . consequences more serious than those which resulted from the offence" (sub-sections (*a*) and (*b*) of Section 11 of the Law).

There was here therefore neither any "necessity" within the meaning of Section 18 of the Ordinance, nor any "extenuating circumstances" within the meaning of Section 11 of the Law, and the appellant deserves the punishment to which he was sentenced by the District Court.

THE SENTENCE

In deciding to affirm both the judgment and the sentence passed upon the appellant, we know only too well how utterly inadequate the sentence of death is as compared with the millions of unnatural deaths he decreed for his victims. Even as there is no word in human speech to describe deeds such as the deeds of the appellant, so there is no punishment under human law sufficiently grave to match the appellant's guilt.

But our knowledge that any manner of dealing with the appellant would not be comparable and any penalty or punishment inflicted on him would be inadequate—dare not move us to mitigate the punishment. Indeed, there can be no sense in sentencing to death, under the Law for the Punishment of Nazis and Nazi Collaborators, one who had killed a hundred people, while setting free, or merely keeping under guard and in security, one who had killed millions. When, in 1950, the Israel Legislature provided the maximum penalty laid down in the Law, it could not have envisaged a criminal greater than Adolf Eichmann, and if we are not to frustrate the will of the legislature we must impose on Eichmann the maximum penalty prescribed by Section 1 of the Law, that is the penalty of death.

The fact that the appellant—by a variety of ruses, such as escape, hiding, false papers, etc.—succeeded in evading the death sentence that awaited him, in company with his fellows, at Nuremberg, cannot stand him in good stead here, when at long last he answers to the law before an Israel Court of Justice.

We have therefore decided to dismiss the appeal as to both conviction and sentence, and to affirm the judgment and the sentence of the District Court.

[Report: (1962) 16 Piske Din, p. 2033 (in Hebrew).]

[Eichmann was hanged on May 31, 1962]

THE SHIMODA CASE

Tokyo, December, 1963

RYUICHI SHIMODA ET AL. *vs.* THE STATE

THE FACTS.—The plaintiffs, Japanese nationals, were all residents either of Hiroshima or of Nagasaki when atomic bombs were dropped on these cities by bombers of the United States Air Force in August 1945. Most of the members of their families were killed and many, including some of the plaintiffs themselves, were seriously wounded as a result of these bombings. The plaintiffs jointly brought the present action against the defendant, the State, for damages on the following grounds: (*a*) that they suffered injury through the dropping of atomic bombs by members of the Air Force of the United States of America; (*b*) that the dropping of atomic bombs as an act of hostilities was illegal under the rules of positive international law (taking both treaty law and customary law into consideration) then in force, for which the plaintiffs had a claim for damages; (*c*) that the dropping of atomic bombs also constituted a wrongful act on the plane of municipal law, ascribable to the United States and its President, Mr. Harry S. Truman; (*d*) that Japan had waived, by virtue of the provisions of Article 19 (*a*) of the Treaty of Peace with Japan of 1951, the claims of the plaintiffs under international law and municipal law, with the result that the plaintiffs had lost their claims for damages against the United States and its President; and (*e*) that this waiver of the plaintiffs' claims by the defendant, the State, gave rise to an obligation on the part of the defendant to pay damages to the plaintiffs.

The plaintiffs' cause of action was based, more specifically, on the provisions of Article 1 of the State Redress Law, which was applicable to the case of injury to a private person through an unlawful act of a government official; on the provisions of Article 20 of the Constitution, which provided for the obligation to pay just compensation in every case of expropriation of private property by the State for public use; and finally, on unlawful infringement of the rights of the plaintiffs through the omission of the defendant to take appropriate measures for recovery of compensation.

Held: that the action must fail on the merits. The aerial bombardment with atomic bombs of the cities of Hiroshima and Nagasaki was an illegal act of hostilities according to the rules of international law. It must be regarded as indiscriminate aerial bombardment of undefended cities, even if it was directed at military objectives only, inasmuch as it resulted in damage comparable to that caused by indiscriminate bombardment. Nevertheless, the claimant as an individual was not entitled to claim damages on the plane of international law, nor was he able, as a result of the doctrine of sovereign immunity, to pursue a claim on the plane of municipal law. In these circumstances, the plaintiffs had no rights to lose as a result of the waiver contained in Article 19 (*a*) of the Treaty of Peace with Japan.

The Court said: "I. *Evaluation of the act of bombing according to international law.*—(1) Whether an atomic bomb as a so-called nuclear weapon is permitted in international law or not is no doubt an important and very difficult question of international law. In the present case, however, the point at issue is whether the act of atomic bombing of Hiroshima and Nagasaki by the United States is to be regarded as illegal in the light of positive international law then in force. It will suffice here therefore to consider this point only.

"(2) As a preliminary for judging how the act of atomic bombing referred to above is to be estimated in positive international law, we will begin by considering what are the rules of international law that have come into existence among modern States with regard to warfare, especially acts of hostilities, since the latter half of the nineteenth century.

Listed chronologically, the following may be cited as relevant to the present case:

In 1868—St. Petersburg Declaration renouncing the use, in time of war, of explosive projectiles under 400 grammes weight.

In 1899—Convention relative to the laws and customs of war on land, concluded at the First Hague Peace Conference, and its annex, Regulations respecting the laws and customs of war on land.

Declaration concerning the prohibition of the use of bullets which expand or flatten.

Declaration concerning the prohibition of the launching of projectiles and explosives from balloons.

Declaration concerning prohibition of the use of projectiles the object of which is the diffusion of asphyxiating or deleterious gases.

In 1907—Convention relative to the laws and customs of war on land, which was concluded at the Second Hague Peace Conference (the revision of the Convention of the same name concluded at the First Hague Peace Conference).

Declaration concerning the prohibition of the launching of projectiles and explosives from balloons.

In 1922—Treaty relating to the use of submarines and noxious gases in warfare.

In 1923—Draft Rules of air warfare.

In 1925—Protocol for the prohibition of the use of asphyxiating, poisonous or other gases and bacteriological methods of warfare.

"(3) The rules contained in these instruments do not include any provisions directly touching upon the atomic bomb, a new weapon which appeared during the Second World War. On the strength of this fact, the defendant State argues that the question of violation of positive international law cannot arise, since the use of an atomic bomb was not expressly prohibited by positive international law inasmuch as there was neither a customary rule of international law nor treaty law prohibiting its use at that time.

"It can naturally be assumed that the use of a new weapon is legal as long as international law does not prohibit it. However, the prohibition in this context is to be understood to include not only the case where there is an express rule of direct prohibition, but also the case where the prohibition can be implied *de plano* from the interpretation and application by analogy of existing rules of international law (customary international law and treaties). Further, the prohibition must be understood also to include the case where, in the light of principles of international law which are at the basis of these positive rules of international law, the use of a new weapon is deemed to be contrary to these principles, for there is no reason why the interpretation of rules of international law should be limited to literal interpretation, any more than the interpretation of rules of municipal law.

" (4) An argument is also advanced that a new weapon by its very nature cannot be subject to the regulation of international law at all, but the argument is as much unfounded as the one just referred to. Any weapon the use of which is contrary to the customs of civilized countries and to the principles of international law should *ipso facto* be deemed to be prohibited even if there is no express provision in the law; the new weapon may be used as a legal means of hostilities only if it is not contrary to the principles of international law.

"Against this, some may argue that the invention and use of new weapons has always been objected to in various quarters, but that they have soon come to be regarded merely as more advanced weapons, and their prohibition has become altogether meaningless as with the progress in technology they turned out to be effective means of waging hostilities. This is testified by past history, and the atomic bomb is no exception.

"It is undeniable that often in the past although a new weapon was objected to, at its first appearance, in various interested quarters, it nevertheless came to be regarded as lawful with the advance of civilization and the development of science and technology. This may perhaps have been due to the fact that international law was still in an undeveloped state, that feelings of hostility, were so strong against the enemy or the heathen, or else that the progress of weapons in general was so gradual. This, however, has not always been the case, as is evident from the existence of the Treaties prohibiting the use of dum-dum bullets and poisonous gases, referred to above. Thus, for a weapon to be legal it is not enough that it is a new weapon; and a new weapon must naturally be subjected to the examination of positive international law.

"(5) The next step is to examine the rules of international law of that time, relevant to the act of atomic bombing.

"The first question which arises is whether the act of atomic bombing is permissible under the rules of law respecting aerial bombardment, since such act constitutes aerial bombardment performed by military aircraft as an act of hostilities.

"No general treaty respecting aerial bombardment has been concluded. However, according to the customary rules generally recognized in international law concerning hostile acts, there is a distinction between a defended city and an undefended city with regard to bombardment by land forces, and between a defended area and an undefended area with regard to bombardment by naval forces. While indiscriminate bombing of a defended city or a defended area is permissible, in regard to an undefended city or an undefended area only bombardment directed at combatants and military installations (military objectives) and not against non-combatants and non-military installations (non-military objectives) is permissible. Bombardment in breach of this principle is necessarily regarded as an illegal act of hostilities. The existence of such a principle is beyond doubt in view of the following provisions: Article XXV of the Hague Regulations respecting war on land, which provides that 'the attack or bombardment, by whatever means, of towns, villages, dwellings, or buildings which are undefended is prohibited'; Article I of the Convention concerning bombardment by naval forces in time of war, adopted at the Hague Peace Conference of 1907, which provides that 'the bombardment by naval forces of undefended ports, towns, villages, dwellings, or buildings is forbidden . . . ; and Article II, which lays down that among the above-mentioned objects against which bombardment is prohibited are not included 'military works, military or naval establishments, depots of arms or war *matériel,* workshops or plant which could be utilized for the needs of the hostile fleet or army, and the ships of war in the harbour.'

"(6) With regard to air warfare, the 'Draft Rules of Air Warfare [of 1923]' provide in Article 24 as follows:

(1) Aerial bombardment is legitimate only when directed at a military objective—that is to say, an object of which the destruction or injury would constitute a distinct military advantage to the belligerent.

(2) Such bombardment is legitimate only when directed exclusively at the following objectives: military forces; military works; military establishments or depots; factories constituting important and well-known centres engaged in the manufacture of arms, ammunition, or distinctively military supplies; lines of communication or transportation used for military purposes.

(3) The bombardment of cities, towns, villages, dwellings, or buildings not in the immediate neighborhood of the operations of land forces is prohibited. In cases where the objectives specified in paragraph (2) are so situated that they cannot be bombarded without the indiscriminate bombardment of the civilian population, the aircraft must abstain from bombardment.

(4) In the immediate neighbourhood of the operations of land forces, the bombardment of cities, towns, villages, dwellings, or buildings is legitimate provided that there exists a reasonable presumption that the military concentration

> is sufficiently important to justify such bombardment, having regard to the danger thus caused to the civilian population. . . .

It is also provided, in Article 22, that 'aerial bombardment for the purpose of terrorizing the civilian population, of destroying or damaging private property not of military character, or of injuring non-combatants, is prohibited.' Thus the Draft Rules of Air Warfare prohibit targetless aerial bombardment; establish the principle of military objectives; and, on the basis of the distinction between areas in the immediate vicinity of the operations of land forces and other areas, provide that indiscriminate aerial bombardment against the former is permitted while against the latter the aerial bombardment of military objectives only, is permitted. These provisions might appear too strict in expression in comparison with those concerning bombardment by land and naval forces, but what is meant by them is thought to be the same as the distinction between the defended city (area) and the undefended city (area). Although the Draft Rules of Air Warfare cannot be described as part of positive law as they have not yet come into effect as a treaty, students of international law regard them as authoritative on the law of air warfare. Some States adopt the substance of the Rules as a code for the activities of their armed forces, and their essential provisions were formulated in line with the rules of international law and practice then in force. It can therefore be said that the prohibition of indiscriminate aerial bombardment of an undefended city and the principle of military objectives contained therein are rules of customary international law in view of the fact that these are also found in common in the rules of land and sea warfare. Further, whereas the distinction between land, sea, and air warfare is based on the place of hostilities and their purpose, there would seem to be ample ground for the view that the laws and regulations respecting land warfare may apply by analogy to the aerial bombardment of a city, since in effect the latter is no more than bombardment on land.

"(7) What, then, is the distinction between a defended city and an undefended city? In principle, a defended city is a city which resists an attempt at occupation by land forces. A city even with defence installations and armed forces cannot be said to be a defended city if it is far away from the battlefield and is not in immediate danger of occupation by the enemy. Since there is no military necessity for indiscriminate bombardment, only bombing of military objectives there is permissible. However, indiscriminate bombardment is permissible on grounds of military necessity against a city which resists an attempt at occupation by the enemy, since in that case an attack based on the distinction between military objectives and non-military objectives is of little military effect and cannot effect and cannot achieve the intended purpose. Thus it can be concluded that it is a generally recognized principle of international law respecting air warfare that indiscriminate aerial bombardment going beyond the aerial bombardment of military objectives is not permissible in regard to an undefended city.

"Of course it is possible that the aerial bombardment of a military objective will result also in the destruction of non-military objectives or in casualties to non-combatants: this is not unlawful as long as it is an inevitable result incidental to the aerial bombardment of a military objective. Nevertheless, it remains true that aerial bombardment directed at a non-military objective or without distinction between military objectives and non-military objectives (the so-called 'blind aerial bombardment of an undefended city') is not permissible in the light of the principle enunciated above.

"As already stated, the power of destruction and damage of the atomic bomb is tremendous, and even such a small-scale bomb as the one dropped on Hiroshima and Nagasaki discharges energy equivalent to 20,000 tons of conventional bombs. It is clear that the explosion of an atomic bomb of such power of destruction will bring about the almost complete destruction of a medium-sized city, to say nothing of the distinction between military objectives and non-military objectives. Thus, the aerial bombardment with an atomic bomb of an undefended city, if not of a defended city, should be regarded as tantamount to a blind aerial bombardment and as such contrary to international law of the time.

"(8) It is beyond dispute that Hiroshima and Nagasaki were not cities which were resisting an attempt at occupation by land forces at that time. It is also clear from what has been stated that neither of these cities fell within the definition of a defended city, since they were not in immediate danger of occupation by the enemy, even though both were defended with anti-aircraft and other guns against air raids, and had military installations. Further, it was well known that some 330,000 civilians in Hiroshima and some 270,000 civilians in Nagasaki had their homes there, even though both cities also had what may be called military objectives, such as armed forces, military installations and munitions factories. In these circumstances, it is proper to conclude that the aerial bombardment with an atomic bomb of both Hiroshima and Nagasaki was an illegal act of hostilities under international law as it existed at that time, as an indiscriminate bombardment of undefended cities. This is so since aerial bombardment with an atomic bomb, even if its target is confined to military objectives, brings about the same result as a blind aerial bombardment because of the tremendous destructive power of the bomb.

"(9) Against this conclusion is advanced the argument that war in those days had the character of so-called 'total war,' in which it was difficult to distinguish between combatants and non-combatants or between military objectives and non-military objectives, and that the principle of military objectives was not always maintained during the Second World War.

"It is difficult to deny that the concept of a military objective, though prescribed by various expressions in these treaties, is not necessarily static in content but may change with time, and its scope tends to be enlarged under conditions of total war. Nevertheless, the distinction between a military objective and a non-military objective cannot be said to have completely disappeared. For example, schools, churches, temples, shrines, hospitals and private houses cannot be classed as military objectives, even under conditions of total war. If the concept of total war were to be taken to imply that everyone who is a national of a belligerent State is a combatant, and that all means of production are means of injuring the enemy, there would arise the necessity to destroy the whole population and all the property of the enemy, and it would be meaningless to distinguish between a military objective and a non-military objective. However, this concept of total war has been propounded in recent times simply to point to the fact that the outcome of a war is not decided only by armed forces and weapons, but that other factors—mainly economic factors—such as energy, resources, productive capacity of industry, food stuffs, and trade, and human factors including the general population and the labour force, also have a far-reaching effect on the method and the potential of war. Thus the concept of total war has not been propounded as consisting of a mere failure to distinguish between combatants and non-combatants, etc., as has been argued; nor, indeed, has there been any case of that kind. Accordingly, it is wrong to claim that the distinction between a military objective and a non-military objective has disappeared under the situation of a total war.

"(10) During the Second World War, it was sometimes found impossible to identify each individual military objective for attack in a place where munitions factories and military installations were concentrated in a comparatively small area, and where defence installations against air raids were very strong. In such a case aerial bombardment of the whole area took place, and some hold the view that this practice may be regarded as lawful. Such aerial bombardment, called target-area bombardment, may be regarded as lawful even if it goes beyond the principle of military objectives, since the destruction of non-military objectives is small in proportion to the large military interests or necessity involved. However, the doctrine of target-area bombardment cannot apply to the cases of Hiroshima and Nagasaki, since both cities clearly could not be said to be areas where such military objectives were concentrated.

"(11) Again, the atomic bombing of both Hiroshima and Nagasaki is believed to be contrary to the principle of international law prohibiting means of injuring the enemy which cause unnecessary suffering or are inhuman. It goes without saying, however, that it is not permissible to extend this argument so as to prove that the atomic bomb must necessarily be prohibited because it has characteristics different from other conventional weapons in the inhumanity of its effects.

"For the international law of war is not formulated simply on the basis of humanitarian feelings. It has as its basis both considerations of military necessity and effectiveness and humanitarian considerations, and is formulated on a balance of these two factors. To illustrate this, an example often cited in the textbooks may be given, of the provisions of the St. Petersburg Declaration of 1868 prohibiting the use of projectiles under 400 grammes which are either explosive or charged with combustible or inflammable substances. The reason for the prohibition is explained as follows: such projectiles are small and just powerful enough to kill or wound only one man, and as an ordinary bullet will do for this purpose, there is no overriding need for using these inhuman weapons. On the other hand, the use of a certain weapon, great as its inhuman result may be, need not be prohibited by international law if it has a great military effect.

"When looked at from this angle, the question is whether the act of atomic bombing falls under 'the employment of poison or poisonous weapons' prohibited by Article 'xxiii (*a*) of the Hague Regulations respecting war on land, or under the prohibitions provided for in the Declaration of 1899 prohibiting the use of projectiles the sole object of which is the diffusion of asphyxiating or deleterious gases, or the Protocol of 1925 prohibiting the use in war of asphyxiating, poisonous and other gases and bacteriological methods of warfare. With regard to this point, there is as yet no agreement among international lawyers on the difference between poisons, poisonous gases, bacteria, etc., on the one hand, and atomic bombs, on the other. However, in view of the fact that the St. Petersburg Declaration provides that '. . . considering that the use of a weapon which increases uselessly the pain of people who are already placed out of battle and causes their death necessarily is beyond the scope of this purpose, and considering that the use of such a weapon is thus contrary to humanity . . .' and that Article XXIII (*e*) of the Hague Regulations respecting war on land prohibits the employment of such 'arms, projectiles, and material as cause unnecessary injury,' it can safely be concluded that besides poisons, poisonous gases and bacteria, the use of means of injuring the enemy which cause injury at least as great as or greater than these prohibited materials is prohibited by international law. It is doubtful whether the atomic bomb with its tremendous destructive power was appropriate from the viewpoint of military effect and was really necessary at that time. It is indeed a fact to be regretted that the atomic bombing of the cities of Hiroshima and Nagasaki took away the lives of tens of thousands of citizens, and that among those who have survived are those whose lives are still imperilled owing to its radioactive effects even now after eighteen years. In this sense it is not too much to say that the sufferings brought about by the atomic bomb are greater than those caused by poisons and poisonous gases; indeed the act of dropping this bomb may be regarded as contrary to the fundamental principle of the law of war which prohibits the causing of unnecessary suffering.

"II. *Evaluation of the act of bombing according to municipal law.*— If, as has been shown at length above, the act of atomic bombing of Hiroshima and Nagasaki was contrary to international law, the next question is whether it also constituted an unlawful act according to the municipal law of Japan and of the United States of America.

"(1) With regard to Japan, the Imperial Constitution in force at the time when the atomic bombs were dropped contains no express provisions on the relationship between international law and the municipal law of Japan. It was believed, however, that customary international law was part of its municipal law, and that treaties had the force of law in its municipal law by promulgation. Accordingly, there is sufficient ground for the view that inasmuch as the act of atomic bombing is contrary to international law, it also constitutes an unlawful act in the municipal law of Japan.

"(2) With regard to the United States, it is known that treaties are the supreme law of the land in accordance with Article 6, paragraph 2, of the Constitution of the United States, and that customary international law is also part of the law of the land. Such being the case, it would seem to be a fair assumption that an act contrary to international law constitutes an unlawful act in the municipal law of the United States.

"(3) Be that as it may, it is of little use to examine further in the abstract the question whether an act of atomic bombing is contrary to the municipal law of Japan and the United States, since the question whether an act violates municipal law, on the one hand, and the question whether the responsibility for the violation can be placed on some person or the question as to what court may be seised for the purpose of pursuing the responsibility, on the other hand, are two different categories of questions which must be treated separately. A concrete question is solved only when these latter questions are considered. This point will be touched upon below, where the question of responsibility for acts contrary to international law is dealt with.

"III. *Claims of individuals for damages.*—(1) It is an established principle of international law that a belligerent who causes damage to the other belligerent by acts of hostilities contrary to international law is under an obligation to make compensation to the latter for the damage.

"Since it is not disputed that the act of atomic bombing on Hiroshima and Nagasaki was a regular act of hostilities performed by an aircraft of the United States Army Air Force, and that Japan suffered damage from this bombing, it goes without saying that Japan has a claim for damages against the United States in international law. In such a case, however, responsibility cannot be imputed to the person who gave the order for the act, as an individual. Thus in international law damages cannot be claimed against President Truman of the United States of America who ordered the atomic bombing, as it is a principle of international law that the State must be held directly responsible for an act of a person done in his capacity as a State organ, and that that person is not held responsible as an individual.

"(2) May the individual who suffered injury by an act contrary to international law then have a claim for damages in international law against the State which caused the injury?

"When discussing this point, the first question to consider is whether an individual can be a subject of rights in international law. The traditional view limits the subjects of rights in international law to States, on the ground either that international law is a law for regulating the relations of States, or that international law is established on the basis of agreement among States. However, even if international law has hitherto been concerned chiefly with regulating the relations between States, it does not follow that therefore an individual cannot become a subject of rights in international law; and the status of a subject for creating norms of international law has nothing to do with the status of a subject of rights in international law. The view is also put forward that an individual may not be a subject of rights because international law does not always possess the force of law within a State. This view is not acceptable, since it is possible in theory that international law may accord to the individual the status of a subject, even when it does not have the force of law within a State. Thus, an examination of the fundamental character of international law does not lead us to the conclusion that by its very nature only a State can be the subject of rights in international law.

"(3) Can, on the contrary, an individual always be a subject of rights in international law? The question of an individual being a subject of international law arises when international law (mainly treaties) prescribes rights and duties for an individual. In such a case, there are found two conflicting views in the doctrine of international law: the view that an individual acquires *ipso facto* rights and duties in international law if international law prescribes rights and duties for the individual, and the view that an individual cannot be said to acquire rights and duties in international law unless there is a means through which the individual can assert these rights or be bound by these duties in his name on the plane of international law. This conflict arises from a difference of views on the subject of international law and, indeed, of law in general. The Court is of the view that, speaking in the abstract, for a person to be a subject of rights or of law implies that he must be able to assert his rights and to be bound by duties in his own name. Accordingly, in order for a person to be a subject of rights in international law, he must be able to assert his rights and be bound by his duties in his own name. That being so, the Court regards the latter view as the correct one.

"An examination from this angle of treaties which recognized individuals as subjects of international law in this sense will reveal the following: as examples in which an individual was entitled to appear as a party before an international tribunal can be cited the treaty for the establishment of an international Prize Court adopted at the Hague Peace Conference of 1907, the treaty for the establishment of the Central American Court of Justice concluded by five Central American countries in 1907, and the economic clauses of the Versailles Treaty and other peace treaties concluded at the end of the First World War (Treaty of St. Germain-en-Laye, Treaty of Trianon, Treaty of Lausanne and Treaty of Neuilly-sur-Seine). The treaty for the establishment of an International Prize Court is a special case in that it was not ratified, and so did not become part of positive international law, and that it was concerned with a court of appeal from the decrees of national prize courts. Again, the treaty for the establishment of the Central American Court of Justice was in force for only ten years among five Central American countries. For these reasons, these two treaties are not suitable for the consideration of the general question here at issue.

"On the other hand, the Versailles Treaty and other peace treaties provided for the establishment of mixed arbitral tribunals to deal with cases concerning property rights of nationals of the Allied and Allied and Associated Powers were given the right to bring cases directly against the German Government, before mixed arbitral tribunals, for compensation for the damage suffered in respect of their property, rights, and interests within German territory as a result of the application of wartime emergency measures or of transfer measures of the German Government. Moreover, they could bring cases before mixed arbitral tribunals in their own names, quite independently of the will of their home Governments. In this case, therefore, individuals can be said to be subjects of rights in international law. The view has been expressed on the strength of this example that individuals have come to be recognized in general as subjects of rights in international law. This view, however, cannot be accepted, because in this case the object of compensation was limited to the damage to property, rights, or interests within German territory resulting from the application of wartime emergency measures or transfer measures of the German Government and did not extend to all the damage caused by the conduct of the war by Germany, and also because the right to claim damages was open only to nationals of the Allied and Associated Powers, and not to nationals of the defeated States. Further, the mixed arbitral tribunals were *ad hoc* tribunals established separately by each of the victorious Powers and Germany. The most important point is the fact that they were all based on concrete provisions of the treaties concerned. The case therefore is not a sufficient ground for the view that individuals have come to be recognized in general as subjects of rights in international law, and a procedure for asserting such rights on the level of international law has been guaranteed. The Court deems it proper to conclude that individuals become subjects of rights in international law only in so far as they are recognized as such in concrete cases by treaties, as seen in the example of mixed arbitral tribunals.

"(4) The plaintiffs argue that an individual has a claim in international law, since the right of the individual can be exercised by his home Government. However, if what is meant by this argument is that the State exercises the right of an individual on the level of international law in his name, as his agent on his behalf, there is no such rule in international law nor is there any ground in international law to justify this argument.

"It is true that a State is entitled in international law to demand from another State reparations for the damage caused to its nationals in the name of the State on behalf of its nationals. This is what is widely known as diplomatic protection. Diplomatic protection is an act flowing from the right of the State itself to give protection to its own nationals, and the claim for damages is asserted not as the claim of an individual but as that of the State itself. And the State exercises the right of diplomatic protection in its own judgment and in its own name, not in its capacity as agent of its national. Borchard and others call this phenomenon 'immersion of the individual's claim into the State's claim.' In this case, the State is completely free from interference of its nationals as to how and what it claims, or how it settles the claim. The State need not claim compensation for all the damage caused to its nationals, and it freely decides as it pleases the manner in which it distributes any compensation obtained. Therefore there is no room in such a case for regarding the individual as a subject of rights in international law.

"(5) It has now become clear from what has been said above that there is in general no way open to an individual who suffers injuries from an act of hostilities contrary to international law to claim damages on the level of international law, except for the cases mentioned above. Accordingly, the question left to the individual is whether he can ask for redress before a municipal court of one or both of the belligerent States. However, redress before a Japanese court is impossible, because the position of an individual who brings an action before a Japanese court against the State in question as defendant, in this case the United States, is subjected to an established principle of international law that a sovereign State is not subject to the jurisdiction of the civil courts of other States, a principle which is recognized in Japan (Court of Cassation, Case No. (ku) 218 of 1928, Decision of December 28, 1928; 7 *Collection of Judicial Precedents Concerning Civil Affairs* 1128.

"(6) Is redress possible, on the other hand, before the courts of the United States?

"With regard to this point, questions of both procedural and substantive law arisc, such as whether the courts of the United States have jurisdiction, or whether the plaintiffs as foreigners have the *locus standi* to bring an action. In short, however, the conclusion in substantive law is that the plaintiffs cannot make the United States or President Truman liable for the responsibility for an act which is unlawful according to the law of the United States.

"In the law of the United States, the doctrine of sovereign immunity has consistently been applied since the nineteenth century. It is the principle that the State does not incur liability for damages for unlawful acts of its officials committed in the performance of their duties, similar in effect to the principle in England that 'the King can do no wrong.' This doctrine of sovereign immunity is variously explained in case-law and legal theories: that it is based on political considerations imposed out of necessity, that it is unthinkable *for all the subjects to commit an unlawful act* (*sic*), or that what the State does must be lawful. The doctrine of sovereign immunity is applied not only to the State but also to the highest executive organs of the State, including the President, and it is held that these organs do not incur liability as individuals for their unlawful acts committed in the performance of their duties. It is true that, as the plaintiffs contend, the English doctrine that 'the King can do no wrong' has not been adopted as such by the United States, and how the doctrine of sovereign immunity, quite similar to the English doctrine, has come to be applied in the United States is not well known. Nevertheless, there is no denying the fact that the doctrine of sovereign immunity is generally applied in the United States. Great as the atomic bomb may be in its destructive power, as alleged by the plaintiffs, one cannot believe that it has succeeded in destroying this doctrine.

"Since the Second World War, the United States has enacted the Federal Tort Claims Act, and has come to accept the liability of the State for damage arising from its unlawful acts. The Act, however, contains many exceptions, for example, that the State is not liable when an executive organ of the State has performed a discretionary function, that it is not liable for acts of hostilities by the Army or the Navy, and that claims which arise in foreign countries are excluded. These exceptions in themselves will exclude the possibility of a claim for damages against the United States or President Truman for an unlawful act in the law of the United States. It is self-evident that this conclusion is not affected according to whether the case is brought at the time of the atomic bombing or after the enactment of the Federal Tort Claims Act.

"(7) What has been stated above with respect to the case where an individual brings a claim in international law before the municipal courts of Japan or the United States applied with equal force to the case where an individual brings a claim for damages before the courts of Japan or the United States on the ground that the act constitutes a tort under the law of Japan or the United States. There is no need to repeat the conclusion that the individual cannot ask for redress before the courts of Japan or the United States with respect to his claim under municipal law.

"IV. *Waiver of claims in the Peace Treaty with Japan.*—(1) The greater part of the conclusion as to this case may already be clear from what has been stated above. However, all the questions have not yet been studied. It remains to be examined how the rights and duties arising out of the state of war between Japan and the United States are dealt with by the treaties existing between both countries, and especially how the claims of individuals under international law are dealt with in the Treaty.

"(2) Article 19 (*a*) of the Treaty of Peace with Japan, which was signed at San Francisco on September 8, 1951, and came into force on April 28, 1952, provides:

> Japan waives all claims of Japan and its nationals against the Allied Powers and their nationals arising out of the war or out of actions taken because of the existence of a state of war, and waives all claims arising from the presence, operations or actions of forces or authorities of any of the Allied Powers in Japanese territory prior to the coming into force of the present Treaty.

It would seem clear that the 'claims of Japan' which were waived by these provisions include all the claims which Japan has on the basis of treaties and customary international law. Accordingly, there is no doubt that claims such as those for compensation for damage caused to Japan by illegal acts of hostilities are included.

"(3) What then does 'claims of [Japanese] nationals' mean? The defendant contends that inasmuch as Japan and Japanese nationals are different subjects of law, Japan cannot waive the rights of its nationals, and that accordingly what has been waived in these provisions is nothing else but the right of Japan to give diplomatic protection with regard to the rights of individuals.

"But this view cannot be accepted. The right of diplomatic protection, as already stated, is an inherent right of a State. Accordingly, it is to be included in the 'claims of Japan' for the purposes of Article 19 (*a*). Moreover, while the 'claims of Japanese nationals,' as a general expression, appear to imply substantive rights, the right of diplomatic protection is thought to be no more than a procedural right, even though in many cases the State takes up the rights of its own nationals under the municipal law of the other State through invoking the right of diplomatic protection.

"(4) As for the contention that a State cannot waive the claims of its nationals, who are different subjects of law, the contention would surely be justified if the claims of nationals referred to meant the rights of its nationals under international law. However, it must be pointed out that a State has the power to waive the claims of its nationals under municipal law. A State has, as a function of its sovereignty, the power to create, modify and extinguish rights and duties of its nationals in accordance with the due process of its municipal law; it is therefore possible in theory for a State to undertake, as against another State, to waive the rights of its nationals which have such character in relation to the State, setting aside the question of the propriety of such an undertaking. This is evident also from the provisions of Article 14 (*a*) 2 (I) of the Peace Treaty, in which Japan recognizes that the Allied Powers shall have the right to dispose of property of Japanese nationals within the territory of the Allied Powers (the so-called overseas assets). And it will be easily understood that the object of waiver in this case is the rights of Japanese nationals under the municipal law.

"(5) In the light of this examination, it appears natural to interpret the term 'claims of Japanese nationals' waived by Article 19 (*a*) as including the claims of Japanese nationals against the Allied Powers and their nationals under the municipal laws of Japan and of the Allied Powers. The opinions of experts submitted to the Court unanimously conclude that the 'claims of Japanese nationals' refer to the rights of Japanese nationals themselves. Moreover, that the Japanese Government itself regarded them as referring to the rights of Japanese nationals is seen from the statement to the same effect made in the House of Representatives by the then Director of the Treaties Bureau of the Ministry of Foreign Affairs.

"(6) The plaintiffs contend that in 'claims of Japanese nationals' are included claims of nationals under international law as well. However, as already stated, the claim of an individual under international law comes to be recognized only in so far as it is specifically provided for in a treaty, with the *locus standi* and other procedural guarantees for asserting the claim recognized on the international level. The Peace Treaty with Japan of course does not recognize such procedural guarantees. Again, if, as contended by the plaintiffs, the claims of Japanese nationals under international law were to be included in the Peace treaty with Japan, one would be forced to the conclusion that the claims of Japanese nationals for damages under international law were recognized constitutively by the provisions of this Treaty only to be waived at the same time by the same Treaty. It is, however, not natural to assume that a special technique of this kind was employed in the Treaty, nor is there any necessity to resort to such a technique. There is no case in history prior to the Peace Treaty with Japan in which claims of individuals for damages under international law were recognized. In these circumstances, the Peace Treaty with Japan did not recognize the claims of Japanese nationals for damages under international law, nor did it waive such claims. What was waived by Article 19 (*a*) of the Peace Treaty with Japan were claims of Japanese nationals under the municipal laws of Japan and of the Allied Powers.

"V. *The defendant's responsibility for the waiver of claims.*—The plaintiffs allege that they have lost their claims for damages, under both international law and municipal law, against the United States and President Truman through the waiver of these claims by the defendant. It has been shown above that claims under international law, if any, were not the object of the waiver in the provisions in question; and the claims under municipal law which were the object of waiver in these provisions could not arise in the present case, as has already been explained in detail. Such being the case, the plaintiffs had no rights to lose, and therefore there is no reason for regarding the defendant State as legally responsible to the plaintiffs for an unlawful act."

COURT-MARTIAL OF WILLIAM L. CALLEY, JR.

Fort Benning, Georgia, March, 1971

INSTRUCTIONS FROM THE MILITARY JUDGE TO THE COURT MEMBERS IN UNITED STATES *vs.* FIRST LIEUTENANT WILLIAM L. CALLEY, JR.

YOU HAVE NOW HEARD all the evidence and listened to the argument of counsel. Following these instructions, this court will recess and you will retire to the deliberation room where you will deliberate and vote separately on each specification to determine whether L. Calley is guilty as charged, guilty of one of the lesser offenses, or not guilty. Each of you must resolve the ultimate issue of guilt or innocence of each specification in accordance with the law and the evidence admitted in court. As I told you initially, it is my duty to instruct you on the law. It is your duty to determine the facts, apply the law to those facts and determine the guilt or innocence of LT. Calley.

You must bear in mind that under the law LT. Calley is presumed to be innocent of the charges against him. The fact that someone may have preferred charges against him, or the fact that charges have been referred to this court for trial is not evidence, and may not be considered by you for any purpose whatsoever. The burden of proof is and always remains upon the government to prove each and every element of the offenses charged beyond a reasonable doubt.

Counsel for both sides have argued the law and the facts to you. Their argument is not evidence and is merely designed to assist you in arriving at your ultimate decision. I must caution you that I and I alone will tell you what the law is in this case and you are required to take the law from me and from no other source. Further, you must base your decision on the facts as you remember hearing them in open court. Moreover, testimony that has been stricken will not be considered by you for any purpose, and you must not speculate on what the evidence might have been when I sustained an objection or when matters were discussed out of your sight and hearing. First I will give you some preliminary matters, then the elements of the offenses charged; then, the applicable law reasonably raised by the evidence. In the latter connection I may, by the way of example, summarize some but not all of the evidence and tell you how the law applies to that particular evidence. The fact that I may highlight certain evidence gives it no greater weight than any other testimony or evidence in this case. My sole purpose is to explain what the law is in regard to that evidence and how that law should be applied. Lastly, in these instructions I will explain voting and other procedural matters.

Of necessity these instructions will be lengthy and in some areas may be complex. After I read them in open court, you will each be provided with a written copy. However, I want it clearly understood that if there is any doubt as to the meaning of any part of the instructions while you are deliberating you must return to open court and ask your questions of me so that I may clarify the matter.

LT. Calley is charged with four specifications alleging premeditated murder in violation of Article 118 of the Uniform Code of Military Justice. These offenses are alleged to have occurred on the same date in the village of My Lai (4), but each specification alleges a separate offense, and proof that LT. Calley committed one offense may not be considered as proof that LT. Calley committed any other alleged offense. Each offense is separate and distinct from all of the other alleged offenses, and you must be satisfied beyond a reasonable doubt separately as to the elements of each offense. I will give the elements of each major offense separately. Since there are certain lesser included offenses reasonably raised by the evidence, I will give the lesser included offense elements as to the first specification only, when they are identical with the lesser included offenses of the other specifications. However, you are instructed that they will apply with equal effect to each specification and you will consider the lesser included offenses separately as to each specification as I will explain later.

As I go through these instructions there initially may be some confusion in your minds as to certain matters. For example, in the elements of the offense I will use language that suggests that you must find the deaths to have been personally accomplished by LT. Calley. Later on in the instructions I will explain the law regarding principals and how any counselling, or commanding, or procuring of killings by LT. Calley, if such be the case, should be viewed by you. As I have said, these instructions will be lengthy and it is impossible to cover all aspects of the law in a few concise sentences. Thus I want to caution you at the outset that no one part of these instructions is more important than any other part and that they must be considered by you in their entirety.

As to the four specifications, each alleges that the victims were occupants of the village of My Lai (4). The term "occupant" is surplusage. For the purpose of this trial the word "occupant" is defined as any oriental human being, other than personnel of Task Force Barker, who was physically present in the village of My Lai (4) on 16 March 1968.

The specifications also allege that killings were accomplished by means of rifle. There may be some evidence that some of the victims were killed by machine gun or other hand-held or crew-served weapon. Once again, for the purpose of this trial, the weapon used is immaterial; but in order to convict LT. Calley of any offense, you must be satisfied beyond a reasonable doubt that the killings were done by LT. Calley or by ground troops who acted pursuant to the counsel, command, or procurement of LT. Calley. Obviously, any deaths caused by aircraft, artillery or ground troops acting independently of LT. Calley or pursuant to orders from sources other than LT. Calley cannot in any way be attributed to LT. Calley.

To assist the defense in their pretrial preparation, early in these proceedings I required the Government to file a Bill of Particulars. As to both specifications under the Charge, the Government's theory of this case was then, and is now, that LT. Calley either personally killed or caused others to kill the oriental human beings as alleged. Further, it is the Government's theory that the killings alleged in Specification 1 occurred in the southern portion of My Lai (4) and that they occurred before the killings alleged in Specification 2, which the Government contends occurred in the vicinity of the eastern edge of My Lai (4). Additionally, it is the contention of the Government that the killing of the male oriental human being alleged in Specification 1 of the Additional Charge was done by LT. Calley personally and occurred after the multiple killing alleged in Specification 2 of the Charge. The Government also contends that the death alleged in Specification 2 of the Additional Charge was done by LT. Calley personally, and after the killing of the male oriental human being. The Government's Bill of Particulars identifies the crimes charged and thereby fixes their limits; and is thus relevant to your deliberations in those respects and in several others.

A multiple killing of not less than seventy oriental human beings is alleged in Specification 2 of the Charge. When in your deliberations you begin determining the number of individuals killed by LT. Calley or at his direction in the vicinity of the eastern edge of My Lai (4), if you get that far in your deliberations, you may not count as victims any human being killed after the alleged killing of the male oriental human being whose death is charged in Specification 1 of the Additional Charge. In fact, not only is the burden upon the government to prove beyond a reasonable doubt the number of charged victims killed in the eastern portion of My Lai (4), but the Government must also prove beyond a reasonable doubt that any victim found to have been killed as alleged in Specification 2 of the Charge was killed before the offense involving the male oriental human being. Charged victims which you find to have been later killed, if any, cannot be included in any finding of guilty on Specification 2 of the Charge.

The elements of Specification 1 of the Charge are:

1. That an unknown number, but not less than thirty oriental human beings, males and females of various ages, whose names are unknown, occupants of the village of My Lai (4), are dead.

2. That their death resulted from the act of the accused, by means of shooting them with a rifle, on or about 16 March 1968, in the village of My Lai (4), Quang Ngai Province, Republic of Vietnam.

3. That the killing of the not less than thirty oriental human beings as I described them in the first element, by LT. Calley, was unlawful; and

4. That, at the time of the killings, LT. Calley had a premeditated design to kill.

The elements of Specification 2 of the Charge are:

1. That an unknown number but not less than seventy oriental human beings, males and females of various ages, whose names are unknown, occupants of the village of My Lai (4), are dead.

2. That their death resulted from the act of the accused by means of shooting them with a rifle, on or about 16 March 1968, in the village of My Lai (4), Quang Ngai Province, Republic of Vietnam.

3. That the killing of not less than seventy oriental human beings, as I have described them in the first element, by LT. Calley was unlawful; and

4. That, at the time of the killings, LT. Calley had a premeditated deisgn to kill.

With regard to these two specifications only, you note that not less than thirty and not less than seventy oriental human beings are alleged as having been killed. The following instruction applies to both specifications under Charge I and to all lesser offenses of these two specifications that I will later instruct you upon:

In all instances where multiple deaths are alleged, two-thirds of you must be convinced beyond a reasonable doubt that the same oriental human beings are dead. For example, in connection with the alleged killings in the eastern portion of My Lai (4), three of you must be satisfied that oriental human beings in the north portion of the ditch were killed by LT. Calley but other dead human beings in the south portion were not, and three of you might be satisfied that human beings in the south portion were killed by LT. Calley but that individuals in the north portion were not. Thus two-thirds of you would not be agreed as to the same deaths. Therefore, I reiterate, that two-thirds of you must be satisfied beyond a reasonable doubt that the same identical oriental human beings are dead, and that they were killed by LT. Calley. Additionally, if you are satisfied beyond a reasonable doubt that LT. Calley is guilty of killing at least one, but not all of the oriental human beings as alleged, then you must modify your findings so that each accurately reflects the number of oriental human beings killed by LT. Calley as to which two-thirds of you have no reasonable doubt. The rule as to identity of victims remains the same, of course.

You will note that the elements of both Specifications 1 and 2 of the Charge require you to find, in order to convict, that the deaths, if any, resulted from the act of the accused; you are advised that a person who actually commits an offense—here, causing death by shooting another person, with the intent which the law deems culpable—is called a principal. Likewise any person who counsels, commands, or procures another to commit an offense that is subsequently perpetrated in consequence of such counseling, command, or procuring is also a principal and is just as guilty of the offense as he would have been had he actually perpetrated the offense himself. His presence at the scene where the offense is committed is not essential.

The term "counsel" means to advise, recommend, or encourage. The term "command" imports an order given by one person to another, who, because of the relationship of the parties, is under an obligation or sense of duty to obey the order. The term "procure" means to bring about, cause, effect, contrive, or induce. When the act counseled, commanded or procured by a person is actually done, the person who counseled, commanded, or procured is chargeable as a principal with all results that could have been expected to flow as a probable consequence from the act.

In this case the Government has introduced evidence that LT. Calley ordered Mr. Meadlo to "waste" a group of Vietnamese that Mr. Meadlo has testified he was guarding, and that LT. Calley and Mr. Meadlo thereafter shot the people. This is the offense charged as Specification 1 of the Charge. LT. Calley admits giving an order somewhat similar to the one to which Mr. Meadlo has testified, but denies personal participation in the shooting described by Mr. Meadlo and others. LT. Calley also testified that he gave the order at a location different from that where the Government has sought to place it, and that he has no knowledge of whether the group of people that he testified he ordered moved or "wasted" were actually killed. There are other conflicts in the evidence as to whether this event occurred at all and if so, where; and I will instruct you in a few moments on the role that location must play in your deliberation on this Specification. In accordance with my instructions on principals, however, I advise you that only if two-thirds of you are satisfied beyond reasonable doubt that charged victims died as the result of the same act or acts by LT. Calley—as a result of the alleged conversation with Mr. Meadlo, or by his own actions, or a combination of both, and that these acts made him a principle, may you consider the other elements of the offense charged in Specification 1 to determine guilt or innocence.

Similarly, in connection with Specification 2 of the Charge, you have heard conflicting evidence concerning LT. Calley's role in the killing of Vietnamese that allegedly were shot in a ditch on the eastern side of My Lai (4). In order to convict LT. Calley of all or a portion of the deaths as charged, two-thirds of you must be convinced beyond reasonable doubt that the victims included in any finding of guilty died as a result of the same act or acts by LT. Calley, and that these acts made him a principal as I have defined that term.

You must also find beyond reasonable doubt that, at the time of any act which you find to have made LT. Calley a principal, he had the intent required by law, as stated in the elements of the offense and defined in these instructions. If you do not find that, beyond a reasonable doubt, then the act is not counseling, commanding, or procuring as required by law.

Both specifications of the Additional Charge require the personal action by LT. Calley as charged.

The elements of Specification 1 of the Additional Charge are:

1. That one oriental male human being, whose age and name is unknown, an occupant of the village of My Lai (4), is dead.

2. That his death resulted from the act of the accused by means of shooting him with a rifle on or about 16 March 1968, in the village of My Lai (4), Quang Ngai Province, Republic of Vietnam.

3. That the killing of the unknown male oriental human being, as I have described him in the first element, by LT. Calley, was unlawful; and

4. That at the time of the killing, LT. Calley had a premeditated design to kill.

The elements of Specification 2 of the Additional Charge are:

1. That one oriental human being, approximately two years of age, whose name and sex is unknown, an occupant of the village of My Lai (4), is dead.

2. That the death of this oriental human being resulted from the act of the accused by means of shooting that oriental human being with a rifle, on or about 16 March 1968, in the village of My Lai (4), Quang Ngai Province, Republic of Vietnam.

3. That the killing of this oriental human being, as I have described that person in the first element, by LT. Calley, was unlawful; and

4. That at the time of the killing LT. Calley had a premeditated design to kill.

Those are the elements that the Government must prove to your satisfaction beyond a reasonable doubt in order for you to convict LT. Calley of premeditated murder. If you are not satisfied beyond a reasonable doubt that the Government has proven each and every element of the principal offense charged in each specification, you of course must acquit him of that charged offense. However, you must then determine if the evidence has established LT. Calley's guilt beyond a reasonable doubt as to one of the lesser offenses. The lesser included offenses applicable to all four specifications are, in order of their seriousness, unpremeditated murder, and voluntary manslaughter.

The first three elements of unpremeditated murder are exactly the same as those given previously in the premeditated murder instructions, and they apply to each offense charged. Only the last element is different.

I will cover them again only as to the first specification of Charge I, but they apply equally to all specifications except, of course, the identity of the alleged victims is different.

The elements of unpremeditated murder are:

1. That an unknown number but not less than thirty oriental human beings, males and females of various ages, whose names are unknown, occupants of the village of My Lai (4), are dead.

2. That their deaths resulted from the act of the accused by means of shooting them with a rifle on or about 16 March 1968, in the village of My Lai (4), Quang Ngai Province, Republic of Vietnam.

3. That the killing of not less than thirty oriental human beings, as I have described them in the first element, by LT. Calley, was unlawful; and

4. That at the time of the killing LT. Calley had an intent to kill.

The elements of the offense of voluntary manslaughter as to each specification of the Charge are identical to those I have just given you concerning unpremeditated murder and I will repeat them only as to the 1st Specification; but, once again, you are instructed that the elements of voluntary manslaughter apply equally to all four of the specifications, except that the identity of the alleged victims is different in each specification.

The elements of voluntary manslaughter are:

1. That an unknown number but not less than thirty oriental human beings, males and females of various ages, whose names are unknown, occupants of the village of My Lai (4), are dead.

2. That their death resulted from the act of the accused by means of shooting them with a rifle on or about 16 March 1968, in the village of My Lai (4), Quang Ngai Province, Republic of Vietnam.

3. That the killing of not less than thirty oriental human beings, as I have described them in the first element, by LT. Calley, was unlawful; and

4. That at the time of the killing LT. Calley had an intent to kill.

The offense of voluntary manslaughter is committed when a person with intent to kill, unlawfully kills a human being in the heat of sudden passion caused by adequate provocation.

Now let me explain how these three offenses, premeditated murder, unpremeditated murder, and voluntary manslaughter, differ from and are similar to one another. They are similar in this respect:

1. The first three elements of each crime are identical.

2. Element 3 of each of these offenses requires that the Government prove that the killings were unlawful. You are instructed that the killing of a human being is unlawful when it is done without legal justification or excuse, and this instruction applies to premeditated murder, unpremeditated murder, and voluntary manslaughter. One of the matters raised by the defense is that these killings were done pursuant to orders, and that the killings are therefore lawful. I will cover this matter in greater detail later on.

The offenses differ in this respect. The last element of the premeditated murder instruction is: "That at the time of the killing LT. Calley had a premeditated design to kill." The phrase "premeditated design to kill" means formation of a specific intent to kill and consideration of the act intended to bring about death; here, that LT. Calley intended to bring about the death of his victim or victims, and that he considered his act or acts intended to bring about death, if any, prior to doing them. It is not necessary that the "premeditated design to kill" shall have been entertained for any particular or considerable length of time, but it must precede the killing. When a fixed design to kill has been deliberately formed, it is immaterial how soon afterward it is put into execution.

The last element of unpremeditated murder is, "That at the time of the killing the accused had an intent to kill" his victim or victims. This intent need not exist for any particular time before the commission of the act causing death, or previously existed at all. It is sufficient that it existed at the time of the act of the accused which caused the death.

The distinction between premeditated murder and unpremeditated murder is contained in the last element of the offenses as I have defined the terms used in that element. Hence, if you are satisfied beyond a reasonable doubt that LT. Calley had the premeditated design to kill as I have explained that term, together with all the other elements of the offense, you may find him guilty as charged. However, if you are not satisfied beyond a reasonable doubt that he had the premeditated design to kill but you are satisfied beyond a reasonable doubt that he had an intent to kill as I have explained that term, you must find him not guilty of premeditated murder, but you may find him guilty of unpremeditated murder, if you are satisfied beyond a reasonable doubt as to all other elements of that offense.

Voluntary manslaughter is the unlawful killing of a human being, with an intent to kill, but in the heat of sudden passion caused by adequate provocation. You are advised that an act which would otherwise be murder constitutes only the lesser offense of voluntary manslaughter if this act was done in the heat of sudden passion, caused by adequate provocation. The law recognizes that a man may be provoked to such an extent by circumstances that he may kill before he has time to control himself. While the law does not excuse the homicide because of this passion, it does not hold him guilty of murder. To be adequate, the provocation must be such as would excite uncontrollable passion in the mind of a reasonable man and the killing must be committed under and because of that passion. Consequently, in order to find the accused guilty of murder, either premeditated or unpremeditated, you must be satisfied beyond a reasonable doubt that the alleged killing was not done in the heat of sudden passion caused by adequate provocation.

You have heard the testimony that the village of My Lai (4) was under combat assault when it was initially entered, and you have heard testimony concerning the history of Company C, 1/20th Inf, Americal Division, and its other combat operations against the enemy. You have heard about the combat losses sustained by Task Force Barker and their inability to actually find and fix the enemy. You have also heard testimony concerning LT. Calley's role in these operations. These facts standing alone, or in conjunction with other facts, may reduce one or more of the charged offenses to that of voluntary manslaughter if you find, under the standards set out herein, that the killings occurred, but that LT. Calley was at the time of the killings in a state of fear, rage or passion and that this state was caused by adequate provocation. However, you are further instructed that if a sufficient cooling time elapses between the provocation and the killing to permit a reasonable man to collect his wits and regain self control so as not to kill, the provocation will not reduce murder to voluntary manslaughter, even if the passion of the accused persisted throughout the killing.

Even if you find a sufficient cooling time, any passion found should still be considered in connection with those offenses as I have told you requires a "premeditated design to kill," which phrase was defined previously. At the time of the alleged killings, LT. Calley must have possessed sufficient mental capacity to entertain a "premeditated design to kill." An accused may not be found guilty of premeditated murder if, at the time of the killing, his mind was so befuddled by fear, rage, passion or any other condition that he could not or did not premeditate. The fact that the accused's mind may have been befuddled by rage, fear, passion or any other condition at the time of the alleged killings does not necessarily show that he was deprived of his ability to premeditate or that he in fact did not premeditate, but this, like all other issues, is a question that must be resolved by you. I will cover the matter of capacity to premeditate in greater detail subsequently. I call your attention to it now to acquaint you with the connection between a provoked passion and "premeditated design." If you find provoked passion in this case, but are satisfied beyond a reasonable doubt that a sufficient cooling off time had elapsed between the provocation and killing to permit a reasonable man time to collect his wits and regain self control so as not to kill, then the question presented for your determination is whether in light of the evidence of the accused's passion, he in fact entertained a premeditated design to kill at the time of the killing. Unless you are satisfied beyond a reasonable doubt that the accused entertained a premeditated design to kill as charged in each of the four specifications, you must find him not guilty of each specification to which such reasonable doubt exists; however, you may in this situation find him guilty of unpremeditated murder, provided you are satisfied beyond a reasonable doubt as to the elements of that offense.

I have talked at some length about the differences between premeditated murder and the lesser included offenses of unpremeditated murder and voluntary manslaughter. One of the elements of each, you will remember, is an intent to kill. I have defined that above. In connection with Specifications 1 and 2 of the Charge, which allege the deaths of multiple victims, you are further advised that when an individual, with intent to kill, acts, by commanding, counseling, or procuring, to bring about the death of a certain person or persons, and his act is one which makes him a principal, and further, his act of commanding, counseling, or procuring does bring about the death of a person toward whom he had no specific intent to kill, if the death of that victim is a result which could have been expected to flow as a probable consequence from his counsel, command, or procurement, he is liable for the death as if he had committed it himself. The degree of guilt—premeditated murder, unpremeditated murder, or voluntary manslaughter—is determined by his state of mind at the time he did the act causing death. Consequently, if you are satisfied beyond a reasonable doubt that one or more of the alleged victims is dead and that this death resulted from the counsel, command, or procurement of LT. Calley, with intent to kill some specific person or persons other than the person or persons actually killed, you may find LT. Calley guilty of the homicide of the charged victim or victims actually killed, even if those deaths were not specifically intended, if the deaths were a result which could have been expected to flow as a probable consequence of the counseling, commanding, or procuring. Again, the degree of guilt is determined under the rules I have given you in connection with the charged offenses and lesser included offenses of Charge I, and the reasonable doubt standard applies.

There is one other lesser offense that is reasonably raised by the evidence. Specification 2 of the Additional Charge, alleging the killing of a child, has as a lesser offense the offense of assault with intent to commit murder. Mr. Sledge testified that LT. Calley, following the alleged killing of the man at the ditch, picked up a child that was running away from the ditch area. Mr. Sledge said that LT. Calley threw the child back into the ditch and then fired his weapon in the direction of the child. There is no direct evidence tending to show that LT. Calley hit the child with a bullet. There was testimony that two children were alive in the ditch at one point in time and that later one of them was dead and the other was then evacuated from the ditch by a helicopter pilot. There is no testimony of any witness other than Mr. Sledge that LT. Calley shot at this child and LT. Calley has denied the incident in its entirety. Accordingly, if you find that this offense occurred as related by Mr. Sledge, but you are not satisfied that the child was actually killed, you could consider the offense of assault with intent to commit murder, a lesser included offense.

The elements of that offense are:

1. That on or about 16 March 1968 in the village of My Lai (4), Quang Ngai Province, Republic of Vietnam, LT. Calley attempted to do bodily harm to one oriental human being, approximately two years of age, whose name and sex is unknown.

2. That he did so by shooting at this described person.

3. That such act was done with unlawful force or violence.

4. That, at the time, LT. Calley intended to commit murder; and

5. That under the circumstances the conduct of LT. Calley was of a nature to bring discredit upon the armed forces. As to this offense it is not necessary that murder was in fact committed. However, the specific intent of LT. Calley to commit murder is a necessary element of this included offense. An assault is an attempt with unlawful force or violence to do bodily harm to another, whether or not the attempt is consummated. An act of force or violence is unlawful if done without legal justification or excuse. The instructions here given concerning the offense of unpremeditated murder, to include the elements of the offense of unpremeditated murder (except death of the victim), intent, superior orders, and so on apply to this assault offense as well. I emphasize that the only way you can convict LT. Calley of this included

offense is if you are satisfied beyond a reasonable doubt that LT. Calley specifically intended to murder the described victim by shooting at him but missed or merely wounded him, and are satisfied beyond reasonable doubt of the other elements of the offense.

As I previously instructed you, you must find the facts, and apply the law, as I give it, to the facts found. I now want to set out some of the questions which you must resolve in this case.

The government contends that the first killing occurred in the southernly portion of the village, in the vicinity of the intersection of the North-South trail. The government has offered direct and circumstantial evidence that LT. Calley ordered killed, and himself killed people at that time and place. Prosecution Exhibit 12A was offered in evidence as the picture of the persons killed by Mr. Meadlo and LT. Calley, acting personally or through directions given his subordinates, at that location. On the other hand, Mr. Meadlo states that these killings did occur prior to the killings at the ditch, but he does not know exactly where in relation to the intersection of the North-South trail and he did not identify Prosecution Exhibit 12A. Mssrs. Conti, Dursi, and Sledge place this incident in the southern portion of the village, on or near a main trail, but are not in complete agreement on the details of the incident, and none identified 12A as a photograph of the scene. Mr. Haberle, who testified that he took the photo, said that he observed a group alive in that general location from a distance, but that all he found in the area photographed were the bodies shown in 12A. LT. Calley denies personally shooting anyone in conjunction with Mr. Meadlo prior to the incident at the ditch, although he does admit seeing Mr. Meadlo with a group of Vietnamese at the Southeasterly portion of the village and admits telling Mr. Meadlo to get rid of them. Here is the problem confronting you: First, you must determine whether the killings charged in Specification 1 of the Charge occurred prior to the incident at the ditch as the government alleges. Then if you decide that they did occur, you must determine if they occurred at the time and place as alleged by the government. In short, if you are not satisfied beyond a reasonable doubt that the killings occurred in the southern portion or near the southern edge of the village, in the vicinity of the North-South trail intersection, but instead conclude that they occurred elsewhere in the village, LT. Calley cannot be found guilty of Specification 1 of the Charge. However, in this case you might still consider this evidence in connection with LT. Calley's state of mind and intent to kill the persons at the ditch, if you are satisfied beyond a reasonable doubt that the ditch offense, Specification 2 of the Charge, occurred. As to the offense allegedly involving the male oriental human being, Specification 1 of the Additional Charge, the government has offered evidence, both direct and circumstantial, that LT. Calley butt stroked and then shot this man in the head, blowing part of his head away. LT. Calley admits the butt stroking an individual of similar description, but denies the shooting. If you are not satisfied beyond a reasonable doubt that LT. Calley shot and killed this man, he must be acquitted of this specification.

Both the issue of premeditation and of the intent to kill must be resolved by you. The state of mind of a person ordinarily cannot be proved by direct evidence unless, for example, that person has made a statement about his intentions. In this case, LT. Calley has testified about his state of mind on 16 March 1968. This evidence may be corroborated or contradicted by other evidence in the record. Direct evidence, as I have previously stated, is not the only evidence available to you. The intent of LT. Calley may also be proved by circumstantial evidence, that is, by facts and circumstances in evidence. For example, the testimony of some witnesses that LT. Calley not only ordered the killing of unresisting Vietnamese but participated, as well, in the killings, and the testimony that LT. Calley shot and killed an unresisting woman near the ditch after the alleged offenses occurred, if you find that this later killing actually occurred, are some evidence bearing on the issue of LT. Calley's state of mind and intent. The evidence of events at My Lai (4) is also circumstantial evidence bearing on the issues of his state of mind and intent at the time of the offenses. As I said before, proof of one offense is not proof that LT. Calley committed any other offense, and before you decide the issue of state of mind or intent you must first reach a determination that the killings did in fact occur. Of course, you must consider all the evidence in arriving at your determination, and the weight, if any, to be given an inference of LT. Calley's state of mind and intent must depend upon the circumstances attending the proved facts which give rise to the inferences, as well as all the other evidence in this case.

You are advised that there are two types of evidence from which you may find the truth as to the facts of this case. They are called direct evidence and circumstantial evidence. Direct evidence is that evidence which tends directly to prove or disprove a fact in issue. Circumstantial evidence is that evidence which tends directly to prove or disprove not a fact in issue, but a fact or circumstance from which, either alone or in connection with other facts, one may, according to the common experience of mankind, reasonably infer the existence or nonexistence of another fact which is in issue.

There is no general rule for contrasting the weight of circumstantial evidence and direct evidence. The assertions of an eyewitness may be more convincing than contrary inferences that may be drawn from certain circumstances. Conversely, an inference drawn from one or more circumstances may be more convincing than the contrary assertion of an eye witness.

There are certain instances, as in this case, where direct evidence and circumstantial evidence may be intertwined. For example, testimony by a witness that he observed LT. Calley shooting Vietnamese in the village of My Lai or who testified that he heard LT. Calley tell others to kill Vietnamese at My Lai, would be direct evidence. As I explained earlier, one of the elements of the offenses of premeditated murder, unpremeditated murder, and voluntary manslaughter is proof of intent on the part of LT. Calley. This same testimony, which would be direct evidence of certain facts, might also constitute circumstantial evidence of LT. Calley's intent at the time of the alleged offenses. This is also true on the issue of premeditation.

An element of each of the offenses charged which the government must prove beyond reasonable doubt is the fact of death of the victims. Like other elements of the offenses, it may be proved both by direct and circumstantial evidence. You have heard testimony from various individuals that the people they saw appeared dead. You have heard other testimony about the nature of the wounds. Dr. Lane, a pathologist, testified concerning the effects of the M-16 projectile on the human body, indicating that it fragments under certain conditions and may not pass through the victim in such instances. Again, each of you must determine what inferences may logically be drawn from the evidence, applying your common sense and experience.

You have heard the testimony of Dr. Crane and Dr. Hamman, witnesses for the defense, and Dr. Edwards, Dr. Jones, Dr. Johnson, Dr. Lane, and Captain Horne, witnesses for the government, on psychiatry, pathology, and surveying. These persons are known in law as expert witnesses because they are more qualified in their respective fields of psychiatry, pathology, and surveying than ordinary men. You are advised that there is no rule of law that requires you to give controlling significance to their testimony merely because of their qualifications as expert witnesses. In fact, with regard to the testimony of the psychiatrists, the testimony of the expert witnesses for the defense may be in conflict with the expert witnesses for the government. You should, however, consider, with due regard for their qualifications, the testimony of each of these witnesses and give such weight thereto as in your fair judgment it reasonably deserves in the light of all the circumstances, including your own common knowledge and observations.

Further, Dr. Crane, one of the defense psychiatrists, and Dr. Lane, the pathologist who appeared for the government, were asked and gave answers to hypothetical questions. An expert witness in answering a hypothetical question assumes as true every asserted fact stated in the question. Therefore, if you find that the evidence fails to establish the truth of the asserted facts in an hypothetical question, you cannot consider the answer of the expert to that hypothetical question, and must disregard it in your deliberations on the merits of the case. In determining whether the asserted facts have been established you should look to the substance of the facts asserted in the question and not merely to their form.

As I have said before, the offense of premeditated murder requires proof beyond reasonable doubt that at the time of the act causing death LT. Calley entertained a premeditated design to kill. I have defined that term previously. Both Dr. Crane and Dr. Hamman testified for the defense that LT. Calley, in their professional opinion, did not have the capacity on 16 March 1968 to premeditate. The government's psychiatrists, Doctors Johnson, Jones, and Edwards, testified that LT. Calley did have the mental capacity to premeditate on 16 March.

Following this testimony I told you that you would ultimately have to decide the question of mental capacity, and I also admitted some additional evidence for the limited purpose of assisting you in arriving at your decision on this issue. Testimony was admitted concerning the shooting of a woman, allegedly shot by LT. Calley while she was walking along a paddy dike near the ditch at My Lai (4), and there was also testimony about the shooting of a man by a well several weeks prior to the 16 of March. Both of these matters, if you are convinced that they occurred, may be considered by you on the issue of mental capacity. You have also heard considerable testimony concerning LT. Calley's background. The law recognizes that an accused may be sane and yet, because of some underlying mental impairment or condition, be mentally incapable of entertaining a premeditated design to kill. You should therefore consider, in connection with all other relevant facts and circumstances, all evidence tending to show that LT. Calley may have been suffering from a mental impairment or condition of such consequence and degree that it deprived him of the ability to entertain the premeditated design to kill required in the offense of premeditated murder. The burden of proof is upon the government to establish the guilt of LT. Calley beyond a reasonable doubt. Unless, in light of all the evidence, you are satisfied beyond a reasonable doubt that LT. Calley, on 16 March 1968, in the village of My Lai (4), at the time of each of these alleged offenses, was mentally capable of entertaining, and did in fact entertain, the premeditated design to kill required by law, you must find him not guilty of each premeditated murder offense for which you do not find premeditated design. You may, however, find LT. Calley guilty of any of the lesser offenses in issue, provided you are convinced beyond a reasonable doubt as to the elements of the lesser offense to which you reach a guilty finding, bearing in mind all these instructions.

During the rebuttal testimony there was some evidence indicating that the accused was involved in some way in an incident that took place prior to March 16, 1968. At that time it appears that a Vietnamese in the vicinity of a well was shot and might have been killed. This testimony concerns an alleged event which was known to the government but was not made the basis of a charge before you, and it has been admitted only for a limited purpose. You are therefore instructed that the accused's failure to take the stand and deny the incident is not an admission of guilt of that event and therefore is not usable to support the charges and specifications. On the contrary, in considering this evidence, if you find it clear and convincing, you must view it only for whatever tendency it may have, if any, to prove or disprove that on March 16, 1968, LT. Calley had the capacity to form a premeditated design to kill, and for whatever tendency this evidence may have, if any, to prove that LT. Calley knew or did not know that any order you find to have been given him was illegal.

You are reminded that LT. Calley is charged only with four specified acts of murder. During his testimony he recounted that he shot two men in a house at My Lai (4). Were he on trial for those offenses, the law would deem those justifiable, and thus not criminal in nature. I cannot think of any presently, but there may be other evidence which you might construe as indicating that LT.

Calley committed some dereliction or offense not charged. You may not infer from any such evidence that LT. Calley has an evil disposition or criminal propensity, and that he, therefore, committed the offenses charged.

The final determination as to the weight of the evidence and credibility of the witnesses in this case rests solely with you. In determining the weight and value to be given to the testimony which you have heard, you should carefully scrutinize the testimony given, the circumstances under which each witness has testified, and every matter in evidence which tends to indicate the witness' intelligence, the acuteness of his memory, his apparent candor, his appearance and deportment, his demeanor on the witness stand, his friendships and prejudices and his character as to truth and veracity. For example, there is some evidence before you that Mr. Conti has a bad reputation for truth and veracity, some evidence that Mr. Conti used marihuana immediately before the assault on My Lai (4), and some evidence of misconduct by him at My Lai (4), allegedly terminated by LT. Calley. Mr. Conti denied using marihuana and denied the misconduct. Other witnesses were also questioned about these matters. All this testimony should be considered in connection with Mr. Conti's credibility. Mr. Sledge testified that he was convicted of a Peeping Tom offense and given a two year sentence when he was seventeen. Sentences exceeding one year are normally felonies. In any event, this is a matter that may affect his credibility. Captain Medina has testified that he is under charges for offenses allegedly occurring about the same time and place as the alleged offenses we are trying here. Moreover, Captain Medina has testified that he is charged with some of the same offenses as LT. Calley. These are matters that may affect his credibility. Mr. Meadlo, Captain Kotouc, Mr. Boyce, and Sgt Shields received testimonial immunity before they testified at this trial. The grant of testimonial immunity to a witness means that nothing contained in that witness' testimony before this court can be used against him, nor may any evidence discovered as a result of his testimony here be used against him should he be tried subsequently for a similar offense. False testimony given under a grant of immunity is still the proper subject of perjury charges, however. The involvement of these individuals in the events at My Lai (4), necessitating a grant of immunity to compel their testimony, may be a matter affecting credibility, and may be considered by you.

Both the government and the defense have shown you, on a number of occasions, that witnesses have made statements out-of-court that were inconsistent with their in-court testimony. This, too, is a matter which may affect that witness' credibility. As I have explained several times during the course of this trial, you must ask yourselves three questions in connection with the alleged prior inconsistent statement made by a witness out-of-court: first, did he make the statement?; second, is it inconsistent with his in-court testimony?; and third, if it is, do you believe him any the less for it? I again want to caution you, however, that unless adopted by the witness in court as truthful, the prior statement is no evidence of the truth of the matters stated. It only tends to show that at some prior time the witness spoke inconsistently with his in-court testimony.

You may also consider the relationship each witness may bear to either side of the case, the manner in which each witness might be affected by the verdict, and the extent to which, if at all, each witness is either supported or contradicted by other evidence. You should consider the probability of each witness' testimony, the opportunity the witness had to observe and to be informed as to the matters respecting which he gave testimony, and the inclination of the witness to speak the truth or otherwise as to matters within his knowledge.

These instructions on credibility apply to all witnesses in this case, including LT. Calley, and the witnesses called at your request. As I have told you repeatedly the final determination as to the weight of the evidence and the credibility of the witnesses is a matter for your exclusive determination. There are inconsistencies and discrepancies in the testimony of many of the witnesses, and there are variances between the witnesses as to some of the events. This is true for both the government and defense witnesses. It may or may not cause you to discredit that testimony. In weighing the effect of an inconsistency or discrepancy, consider whether it pertains to a matter of importance or an unimportant detail and whether it results from innocent error or willful falsehood. Where conflict appears in the testimony, it is your function to resolve it and to determine where the truth lies. It is not necessarily the number of witnesses called in support of a particular issue, but it is the force, effect, and convincing character of the testimony given which will be your guide in weighing and giving due credit to the testimony.

During the trial of this case witnesses have testified who may be viewed by the law as accomplices. You may consider as an accomplice any person who has testified in this case and whom the evidence indicates was culpably involved in the crimes with which the accused has been charged or in closely related crimes which were committed by the witness in the assault on and through My Lai (4). Your attention is called to this aspect of the law to alert you to a matter specifically affecting a witness' credibility, that is, his motive to falsify his testimony in whole or in part, because of self-interest which may be present under the circumstances. Many present at My Lai (4) on 16 March 1968 could, in law, be considered as aiding, abetting, or voluntarily participating in the over-all operation that has resulted in the charges against the accused. Some have admitted killing Vietnamese persons in the same village and in the same time-frame as those charged against the accused. You are further advised that the testimony of all persons whom you consider, on the basis of the evidence to be an accomplice to any act that the accused is charged with, is of doubtful trustworthiness and should be considered with great caution, and given only such weight as you deem it deserves. In determining the credibility of an accomplice, you should consider the part played in any act charged against the accused and those acts committed by the witness. Whether they participated in any shooting or in the rounding up of Vietnamese they knew were likely to be shot; whether they gave any order that resulted in acts charged against the accused; whether they shot any Vietnamese knowing it was wrongful; and whether any witness was, in fact, an accomplice presents a question of fact for your determination. Thus accomplices might include, but would not be limited to, any witness who shared the criminal intent or purpose that is attributed to the accused, or was his superior officer and ordered the accused to commit the alleged offenses, or aided, encouraged, or participated in the killing of unresisting Vietnamese in My Lai (4) on the day in question. As I say, you must resolve the facts of this case, and thus it is you who must determine who are accomplices. Assess the degree to which their testimony is corroborated by other evidence, and even then you must proceed with great caution.

In this case the testimony of Mr. Daniel Hill, Sergeant Nguyen Ding Phu, Sergeant Duong Minh, Major General Nguyen Van Toan, and Mr. Ta Linh Vien were read to you by way of deposition. Depositions are an authorized means whereby the testimony of a witness who is unavailable to appear at the trial in person, is recorded prior to trial and then read to you gentlemen at the trial. Deposition testimony may be corroborated, attacked, contradicted, or explained in the same way as testimony actually given by a witness in person. Once again, you are the sole judges of the weight, if any, that you will accord this testimony. Unlike the documentary evidence admitted during this trial, because a deposition is actually the testimony of a witness, you may not take it with you while deliberating. However, if you desire to hear again any testimony contained in any of the depositions, it will reread to you, in the same manner as the testimony of the other witnesses.

You have viewed the photograph, Prosecution Exhibit 12A. The government has offered it as a photographic representation of all or a portion of the persons allegedly killed as charged in Specification 1 of the Charge. You may not consider it as any evidence of the number of persons who died as alleged in Specification 1 of the Charge, or as any evidence that such persons actually are dead, unless and until you find beyond reasonable doubt that the incident described in the testimony of Meadlo, Conti, Sledge, and Dursi actually occurred and that 12A depicts the bodies of people actually shot or ordered shot by LT. Calley. If you are not satisfied that this picture depicts bodies of people actually shot or ordered shot by LT. Calley, the picture still may be relevant and have some probative value to corroborate or contradict LT. Calley's testimony, if you find it accurately represents a scene at My Lai (4) on 16 March 1968. If such is the case, it might be used to assist you in determining what orders were actually given C Company by Captain Medina, or it might be helpful in evaluating Captain Medina's testimony, or the testimony of various witnesses concerning the radio transmissions between Captain Medina and LT. Calley. These are all matters for your exclusive determination. If you do find it to be a picture depicting people shot by or at the direction of LT. Calley, you should consider the testimony of the witnesses who stated that among the bodies depicted were one or more individuals shot by a member of the command group.

We next come to the area of acts done in accordance with the orders of a superior. If, under my previous instructions, you find that people died at My Lai (4) on 16 March 1968, as charged—which would include a finding that LT. Calley caused their deaths—you must then consider whether LT. Calley's actions causing death were done pursuant to orders received by him. There is considerable evidence in the record on this point.

Captain Medina, you will recall, testified that he told his assembled officers and men that C Company had been selected to conduct a combat assault on My Lai (4), which intelligence indicated was the current location of the 48th VC Battalion; that they would probably be out-numbered two to one; that they could expect heavy resistance; that they would finally get an opportunity to engage and destroy the battalion which they had been chasing unsuccessfully, and which was responsible for all the mines, booby-traps and sniper fire they had received. He recalled telling his personnel that "innocent civilians or non-combatants" would be out of the village at market by the time of the assault; and that they had permission to, and were ordered to destroy the village of My Lai (4) by burning the hootches, killing the livestock, destroying the food crops, and closing the wells. He testified that he recalled being asked whether women and children could be killed, and that in response to that question he instructed his troops to use common sense, and that engagement of women and children was permissible if women or children engaged or tried to harm the American troops. He denied saying that everything in the village was to be killed.

LT. Calley testified that he attended the company briefing and that Captain Medina instructed the company to unite, fight together, and become extremely aggressive; that the people in the area in which they had been operating were the enemy and had to be treated like enemy; that My Lai (4) was to be neutralized completely; that the area had been prepped by "psy war" methods; that all civilians had left the area and that anyone found there would be considered to be enemy; that everything in the village was to be destroyed during a high speed combat assault; and that no one was to be allowed to get in behind the advancing troops. Subsequent villages, through which they would be maneuvering enroute to the primary assault on the 48th VC Battalion at Pinkville or My Lai (1), were to be treated in the same manner. He testified that at a platoon leaders' briefing after the company briefing, Captain Medina reemphasized that under no circumstances would they allow anyone to get behind them, and that nothing was to be left standing in these villages. LT. Calley also testified that while he was in the village of My Lai (4), on the eastern side, he twice received orders from Captain Medina: first to "hurry and get rid of the people and get into position that [he] was supposed to be in;" and thereafter, to stop searching the bunkers, to "waste the people," and to move his troops out onto the defensive perimeter as Captain Medina had ordered. Captain Medina denied giving any such orders.

A number of other witnesses have also testified about the terms used by Captain Medina in issuing the assault order to his platoon leaders and troops on 15 March; about their actions done in response to these orders; about radio transmissions remembered—and not remembered—occurring during the operation; and about other matters that may have a bearing on what orders, if any, were issued LT. Calley. I have not summarized all this evidence, but you should consider it all. As I have previously stated, it is your recollection of the evidence, not mine, that governs. On the basis of all the evidence you have heard, you should determine what order, if any, LT. Calley acted under when he caused the deaths of any or all of the alleged victims, if he did cause their deaths. As I previously stated, you do not reach the question of orders unless you have found one or more of the charged victims dead—or in the case of Specification 2 of the Additional Charge, have found that charged victim to be dead or to have been assaulted—*and*, under my previous instructions, have found the deaths to have been caused or assault to have been committed in that one case, by LT. Calley. As I also previously instructed you, for the death of an individual to be termed murder or manslaughter under our law, the killing must have been done without justification or excuse. To convict LT. Calley, you must also reach that conclusion. Thus you must consider the legality or illegality of any acts done by LT. Calley resulting in the death of charged victims, and the legality or illegality of any order which you find him to have been acting pursuant to and in accordance with, during your deliberations on guilt or innocence. I will again give you the law. You must apply it to the facts.

The conduct of warfare is not wholly unregulated by law. Nations have agreed to treaties limiting warfare; and customary practices governing warfare have, over a period of time, become recognized by law as binding on the conduct of warfare. Some of these deal with the propriety of killing during war. The killing of resisting or fleeing enemy forces is generally recognized as a justifiable act of war, and you may consider any such killing justifiable in this case. The law attempts to protect those persons not actually engaging in warfare, however; and limits the circumstances under which their lives may be taken.

Both combatants captured by and noncombatants detained by the opposing force, regardless of their loyalties, political views, or prior acts, have the right to be treated as prisoners until released, confined, or executed, in accordance with law and established procedures, by competent authority sitting in judgment of such detained or captured individuals. Summary execution of detainees or prisoners is forbidden by law. Further, it is clear under the evidence presented in this case, that hostile acts or support of the enemy North Vietnamese or Viet Cong forces by inhabitants of My Lai (4) at some time prior to 16 March 1968, would not justify the summary execution of all or a part of the occupants of My Lai (4) on 16 March, nor would hostile acts committed that day, if, following the hostility, the belligerents surrendered or were captured by our forces. I therefore instruct you, as a matter of law, that if unresisting human beings were killed at My Lai (4) while within the effective custody and control of our military forces, their deaths cannot be considered justified, and any order to kill such people would be, as a matter of law, an illegal order. Thus if you find that LT. Calley received an order directing him to kill unresisting Vietnamese within his control or within the control of his troops, that order would be an illegal order.

The question does not rest there, however. A determination that an order is illegal does not, of itself, assign criminal responsibility to the person following the order for acts done in compliance with it. Soldiers are taught to follow orders, and special attention is given to obedience of orders on the battlefield. Military effectiveness depends upon obedience to orders. On the other hand, the obedience of a soldier is not the obedience of an automaton. A soldier is a reasoning agent, obliged to respond, not as a machine, but as a person. The law takes these factors into account in assessing criminal responsibility for acts done in compliance with illegal orders.

The acts of a subordinate done in compliance with an unlawful order given him by his superior are excused and impose no criminal liability upon him unless the superior's order is one which a man of ordinary sense and understanding would, under the circumstances, know to be unlawful, or if the order in question is actually known to the accused to be unlawful.

To reach this issue of "superior orders" during your deliberations, you must first have concluded, as I have outlined above, that one or more of the charged victims died, or that the alleged victim in Specification 2 of the Additional Charge was assaulted, as a result of the accused's actions. You must next determine whether the actions which you have found LT. Calley to have committed, if any, were done in accordance with and pursuant to the orders which he testifies that he received from Captain Medina.

The record contains substantial evidence bearing on the question of the order given. You have heard the testimony of LT. Calley, Captain Medina, and others as to the orders that LT. Calley was given. I have recounted part of this previously. There is also circumstantial evidence that you may find relevant. For example a number of witnesses have testified that there were bodies scattered throughout the village, from west to east. Other witnesses testified that when they discovered that there was light or no resistance, they ceased firing and began to gather and move the occupants of the village as on previous search and clear operations. There is evidence that this was labeled a search and destroy operation. There is evidence also that artillery was to be placed close to or on the village. Other witnesses have testified about the actions of the gunships, and of the members of all three platoons and the headquarters element. Various radio-telephone conversations on the day of the assault have been recounted, and you have heard testimony from all of Captain Medina's RTO's and from Mr. Sledge, who was one of LT. Calley's RTO's. LT. Calley's other RTO, whom LT. Calley has testified was carrying the company-push radio, was later killed in combat. You have also heard LT. Calley's testimony that Captain Medina's two radio calls, on which he testified he acted, were transmitted to him while he was on the eastern side of the village, and that he was never south of the village at the area that has been referred to here as the intersection of the North-South and East-West trails.

As I have mentioned a number of times, I am only calling your attention to some of the evidence to give you an indication of the variety of matters you might consider in resolving these questions. The evidence, as we are all aware, is voluminous; and you must decide what portions of it are relevant and credible to determine the issues presented to you. In determining what order, if any, LT. Calley acted under, if you find him to have acted, you should consider all the matters which he has testified reached him and which you can infer from other evidence that he saw and heard. Then, unless you find beyond a reasonable doubt that he was not acting under orders directing him in substance and effect to kill unresisting occupants of My Lai (4), you must determine whether LT. Calley actually knew those orders to be unlawful.

Knowledge on the part of any accused, like any other fact in issue, may be proved by circumstantial evidence, that is by evidence of facts from which it may justifiably be inferred that LT. Calley had knowledge of the unlawfulness of the order which he has testified he followed. In determining whether or not LT. Calley had knowledge of the unlawfulness of any order found by you to have been given, you may consider all relevant facts and circumstances, including LT. Calley's rank; educational background; OCS schooling; other training while in the Army, including Basic Training, and his training in Hawaii and Vietnam; his experience on prior operations involving contact with hostile and friendly Vietnamese; his age; and any other evidence tending to prove or disprove that on 16 March 1968, LT. Calley knew the order was unlawful. If you find beyond reasonable doubt, on the basis of all the evidence, that LT. Calley actually knew the order under which he asserts he operated was unlawful, the fact that the order was given operates as no defense.

Unless you find beyond reasonable doubt that the accused acted with actual knowledge that the order was unlawful, you must proceed to determine whether, under the circumstances, a man of ordinary sense and understanding would have known the order was unlawful. Your deliberations on this question do not focus solely on LT. Calley and the manner in which he perceived the legality of the order found to have been given him. The standard is that of a man of ordinary sense and understanding under the circumstances.

Think back to the events of 15 and 16 March 1968. Consider all the information which you find to have been given LT. Calley at the company briefing, at the platoon leaders' briefing, and during his conversation with Captain Medina before lift-off. Consider the gunship "prep" and any artillery he may have observed. Consider all the evidence which you find indicated what he could have heard and observed as he entered and made his way through the village to the point where you find him to have first acted causing the deaths of occupants, if you find him to have so acted. Consider the situation which you find facing him at that point. Then determine, in light of all the surrounding circumstances, whether the order, which to reach this point you will have found him to be operating in accordance with, is one which a man of ordinary sense and understanding would know to be unlawful. Apply this to each charged act which you have found LT. Calley to have committed. Unless you are satisfied from the evidence, beyond reasonable doubt, that a man of ordinary sense and understanding would have known the order to be unlawful, you must acquit LT. Calley for committing acts done in accordance with the order.

Throughout these instructions I have used the term "reasonable doubt." The words "reasonable doubt" themselves furnish the best definition. Those words mean exactly what they say. It is a reasonable doubt arising from the evidence or from the lack of evidence after you have considered all the evidence in this case. You are thus instructed:

First, that LT. Calley must be presumed to be innocent until his guilt is established by legal and competent evidence beyond reasonable doubt;

Second, if there is reasonable doubt as to the guilt of LT. Calley, the doubt shall be resolved in favor of LT. Calley and he shall be acquitted;

Third, if there is reasonable doubt as to the degree of guilt, the finding must be in the lower degree as to which there is no reasonable doubt. Thus if you have reasonable doubt as to LT. Calley's guilt of the offense of premeditated murder, you must find him not guilty of that offense, but you may then consider the lesser offenses instructed upon. If a reasonable doubt exists in your mind as to the principal offense and the lesser included offenses then LT. Calley must be acquitted. Needless to say, your findings must be in the lower degree as to which you have no reasonable doubt.

Fourth, that the burden of proof to establish the guilt of LT. Calley beyond reasonable doubt is upon the Government. In this regard, I emphasize that if I have made some grammatical error in these instructions which may be interpreted as shifting the burden of proof to LT. Calley it is my grammar and not the law which is in error. The burden of proof never shifts to him. The burden of proof to establish the guilt of LT. Calley beyond reasonable doubt is and always remains upon the Government.

Defined further, the term "reasonable doubt" means, not a vague, speculative, imaginary doubt, but just such a doubt as would cause you, as reasonable men, to hesitate to act in matters of importance to you. The real question is whether after hearing the evidence, and from the evidence and the instructions on the law which I have given you, you have or have not an abiding belief, amounting to a moral certainty, that LT. Calley is guilty. If you have such a belief so formed, it is your duty to convict. If you do not have such a belief so formed it is your duty to acquit.

The rule as to reasonable doubt extends to every element of the offense charged and the lesser offenses. The fact that there is some evidence, either direct or circumstantial, or both, tending to establish an essential element of an offense does not preclude the existence of a reasonable doubt with respect to that element.

I want to caution you that only matters properly before you as a whole may be considered. You must not be influenced by any knowledge not based upon the evidence, by opinions not properly in evidence, or by motives of partiality, favor, or affection. In short, your decision in this case must be based solely on the evidence properly before you and the law as I have given it to you.

In weighing the evidence you are expected to utilize your common sense and your knowledge, gained during your civilian and military experience, of human nature and the ways of the world.

I have told you this repeatedly and I want to reemphasize it: The final determination as to the weight of the evidence and the credibility of the witnesses in this case rests solely with you. I don't believe that I have done this, but if I have made any comment or in any manner seemed to indicate my opinion as to the guilt or innocence of LT. Calley, you must disregard it, as you and you alone have the independent responsibility of deciding the ultimate issue as to the guilt or innocence of LT. Calley in accordance with the law as I have given it in these instructions, the evidence admitted in court, and your own conscience.

I will now cover the procedural rules that will be followed in your voting on the findings.

As has already been the case during arguments, from this time until you reach your findings you will be sequestered. You will be permitted to communicate with no one other than the three bailiffs during the time you are sequestered. If there is anything you need for your personal comfort, within reason, they will obtain it for you. Of course, you must not discuss this case at any time in their presence. There may be questions concerning the law that arise during your deliberations which you feel need clarification, or you may have questions concerning the evidence, including particular testimony. Any such questions must be answered or resolved by me in open court. Thus, if you will write out your question or write out what particular portion of testimony you want reread, place it in a sealed envelope and give it to the bailiff, he in turn will give it to me, and I will go over it with the counsel. As soon thereafter as possible, we will have you return to open court and provide the information you are seeking. You may set your own hours for deliberations and the bailiffs will be available to transport you to and from the court room as you see fit. However, please bear in mind that you must avoid becoming overtired; and also bear in mind that, absent a special request, I will not have all the court personnel immediately available during an evening deliberation session. Thus, if you have questions or want portions of the record reread, please reserve those matters for the hours of 0830 to 1630, if you can do so.

As I have previously instructed you, you may discuss the case only in the deliberation room and then only when all of you are present. All of the exhibits will be left in the deliberation room and no exhibit may be removed from there without specific authorization from me. I have already provided each of you, and the bailiffs, with additional instructions governing your conduct while deliberating. Follow those carefully.

As to the actual voting, each of you have an equal voice and vote in deliberating upon and deciding all questions pertaining to the guilt or innocence of LT. Calley. Needless to say, seniority of rank may not be employed in any manner. Judging from my observations of you gentlemen there is no danger of that occurring, but I do want to clearly point out that you each individually represents a separate, independent vote.

Additionally, you should have a full and free discussion among yourselves before any ballot is cast.

Voting on the findings must be accomplished by secret written ballot and each of you is required to vote. The order in which the several charges and specifications are to be voted on should be determined by the president, Colonel Ford, subject to objection by a majority of the court. Voting on the specifications under each charge must precede voting on that charge. Captain Salem is the junior member, and as such, it will be his function to collect and count the votes. This count will be checked by the president, Colonel Ford, who will immediately announce the results of the ballot to the rest of you. At no time will you be permitted to say how you or any other member of this military jury has voted.

It takes the concurrence of two-thirds of you to find LT. Calley guilty of any offense charged. Since there are six members, in order to convict LT. Calley of any offense, four of you would have to vote guilty. After you have fully discussed the evidence and these instructions among yourselves, I suggest that you first vote on Specification 1 of the Charge. If less than four of you vote for a finding of guilty, a finding of not guilty of the offense of premeditated murder results; but you should then repeat the process as to each of the lesser included offenses in descending order of their seriousness. If less than four of you vote for a finding of guilty as to any lesser included offenses, then LT. Calley is not guilty of Specification 1 of the Charge.

You should then repeat this same process in connection with each of the other specifications.

The law permits you to reconsider any finding before it is formally announced in open court. You may also reconsider any finding of guilty on your own motion at any time before you have announced a sentence, if you reach a finding of guilty in this case. If a reballot is proposed by any member of the court, the question of whether or not to reballot on the findings shall be determined by a separate secret written ballot. A reballot shall be taken on a prior "not guilty" finding only when a majority of the court—in this case, four of you—votes in favor of reballot on that finding. A reballot on a prior "guilty" finding shall be taken if more than one-third of you favor reballoting—in this case, three of you.

You may have to modify your findings by exception and substitution to reflect any verdict of guilty of a lesser included offense in connection with any specification. Such a finding would result, of course, if two-thirds of you agree that the government has proved beyond a reasonable doubt the material elements of a lesser included offense though it has not discharged its burden of proof as to the material elements of a charged offense, as I have instructed you earlier. Thus, and only as an example, if in Specification 1 of the Charge two-thirds of you are convinced beyond a reasonable doubt that LT. Calley is guilty of voluntary manslaughter, you would except from the finding on this specification the words "with premeditation, murder" and substitute therefore the words "willfully and unlawfully kill."

You may also have to modify your findings by exception and substitution if two-thirds of you are agreed beyond a reasonable doubt that an offense has been committed under either Specification 1 or 2 of the Charge, but the number of victims to which two-thirds of you are agreed is less than the number alleged in either Specification 1 or 2 of the Charge. You must modify your findings as to each specification of the Charge, if necessary, to reflect the number of persons which two-thirds of you, pursuant to my earlier instructions in this regard, are agreed beyond a reasonable doubt were killed by LT. Calley.

As to voting on the charges: If you find LT. Calley guilty only of premeditated or unpremeditated murder on any specification of a charge, then no modification of the charge as to that specification is necessary. You must find him, of the charge as to that specification, guilty of a violation of Article 118. However, if you find him, under any specification of a charge, guilty of voluntary manslaughter, then as to that finding he is guilty of a violation of Article 119. Likewise, if you find him guilty, under Specification 2 of the Additional Charge, of assault with intent to commit murder, you must of necessity find LT. Calley, of the Additional Charge, as to Specification 2, not guilty of a violation of Article 118, but guilty of a violation of Article 134.

Of course, it should be noted, that if you acquit LT. Calley of all the charges and specifications, no modification of any sort is necessary.

At the conclusion of my instructions and just prior to the time you retire to deliberate, I will give you a FINDINGS WORKSHEET. This WORKSHEET lists all the Charges and Specifications and all lesser included offenses included thereunder, as well as all of the possible findings you might reach in this case as to specifications. It also provided a form for findings on the charges. This WORKSHEET also contains possible findings by exception and substitution as to each offense included under each specification. It should assist you in implementing all the instructions I have given you on the offenses charged and the material elements of those offenses, and assist you in putting your findings in proper form.

If during your deliberations you have any difficulty with either the instructions or the WORKSHEET, please ask for clarification. Colonel Ford, before you announce the findings of the jury in open court, I will ask you to show me the WORKSHEET so that I can assure myself that your findings are in proper order.

COURT-MARTIAL OF ERNEST L. MEDINA

Fort McPherson, Georgia, September, 1971

INSTRUCTIONS FROM THE MILITARY JUDGE TO THE COURT MEMBERS IN UNITED STATES *vs.* CAPTAIN ERNEST L. MEDINA

YOU HAVE NOW HEARD all the evidence and listened to the argument of counsel. Following these instructions, this court will recess and you will retire to the deliberation room where you will deliberate and vote separately on each specification to determine whether Captain Medina is guilty as charged, guilty of one of the lesser offenses, or not guilty. Each of you must resolve the ultimate issue of guilt or innocence of each specification in accordance with the law and the evidence admitted in court. As I told you initially, it is my duty to instruct you on the law. It is your duty to determine the facts, apply the law to those facts and determine the guilt or innocence of Captain Medina. . . .

Evidence has been presented which gives rise to the issue of whether the actions of Captain Medina in interrogating a suspected prisoner of war was in accordance with established interrogation procedures and therefore justifiable and lawful. I have advised you that the fourth element of these offenses which you must find beyond reasonable doubt is that the offer of force or evidence was done unlawfully. In this regard, you are again advised that an act of force and violence is unlawful if done without legal justification or excuse. Evidence has been presented to you which indicates that the alleged victim was a person detained by combat forces of the United States and who was suspected of having engaged in activities hostile to our forces. Captain Medina is charged with committing offenses against that person while interrogating him. You are advised that with respect to persons detained by United States forces as suspected hostiles in the Republic of Vietnam before, on or about 17 March 1968, and thereafter, the law of nations contained in the Geneva Convention forbids and did forbid the inflicting of any physical or mental torture, or any other form of coercion on them to secure from them information of any kind whatsoever. The law permits the interrogation of such detainees or suspected persons in an attempt to secure information useful to our own or friendly military forces. During such interrogations certain strategems and ruses may lawfully be used, such as using threatening tones of voice, or even threatening words amounting to a verbal threat of death. However, suspected persons must be treated humanely and those who refuse to answer questions may not be threatened by the use of actual violence, insulted or exposed to unpleasant or disadvantageous treatment amounting to physical abuse of any kind.

In implementing the provisions of the Geneva Conventions, to which the United States is a signatory, the United States Army has issued certain regulations and directives with respect to intelligence interrogations which were in force on 16–17 March 1968. These regulations and directives authorize and make lawful the use of harsh and abusive language toward a suspected enemy detainee believed to possess information useful to US Forces. These directives further authorize the interrogator to threaten violence in an attempt to get such information; that is, the interrogator may threaten physical violence only, but may not threaten by use of physical violence against the detainee. The same regulations and directives provide that an interrogator must observe the provisions of the Geneva Conventions which prohibit any form of coercion as a legal method of obtaining information.

Considering the evidence that Captain Medina allegedly fired his M-16 rifle twice over the head of a suspected, high-ranking enemy detainee during an interrogation being conducted by Captain Medina to obtain information in accordance with a field manual authorizing the threat of violence, together with the provisions of the Geneva Conventions granting humane treatment of such detainees, I advise you that unless you are satisfied beyond reasonable doubt that the alleged offer of force or violence was unlawful, that is, without legal justification in that it exceeded a threat of violence, then you must acquit the accused of the two Specifications of Charge II and Charge II. The burden is, as always, upon the prosecution to establish to your satisfaction beyond a reasonable doubt that the alleged offer of force or violence was without legal justification and therefore unlawful. I now call your attention to the Specification of the additional Charge and the additional Charge, both as modified to allege the offense of involuntary manslaughter in violation of Article 119, Uniform Code of Military Justice. Before stating the elements of that offense, I believe it to be prudent and necessary to state certain preliminary matters. As I understand the issues and theories of the prosecution and defense, the specific issues for your determination are represented by the opposing parties to be as follows:

The following statements are prosecution representations and not my conclusions as to the state of the evidence but the prosecution alleges that Captain Medina was the company commander of Charlie Company, 1st Battalion, 20th Infantry of the 11th Brigade. As company commander Captain Medina had briefed the men of his company, assigned them specific missions and dispatched them on a combat assault described as a search-and-destroy mission, into the village of My Lai (4) at about 0730 hours on 16 March 1968. The prosecution alleges that the accused was on the ground in and about the village of My Lai (4) from shortly after 0730 hours, 16 March 1968, until after Charlie Company moved from the village of My Lai (4) into a night laager position in the afternoon of 16 March 1968, as well as thereafter. The prosecution also alleges that Captain Medina was in radio contact throughout the operation with his platoons. It is contended that the accused was aware almost from the beginning of the operation that the units of his company were receiving no hostile fire and in fact early in the morning ordered his men to conserve ammunition. The prosecution also contends that some time during the morning hours of 16 March 1968, the accused became aware that his men were improperly killing non-combatants. It is contended that this awareness arose because of the accused's observations, both by sight and hearing, and because of the conversation between Sgt. Minh and the Accused. The prosecution contends this time of awareness on the part of the accused was at least at some time between 0930–1030 hours, 16 March 1968, if not earlier. The contention is further made that the accused, as Company Commander, had a continuing duty to control the activities of his subordinates where such activities were being carried out as part of an assigned military mission, and this became particularly true when he became aware that the military duties were being carried out by his men in an unlawful manner. The prosecution contends that Captain Medina, after becoming aware of the killing of noncombatants by his troops, declined to exercise his command responsibility by not taking necessary and reasonable steps to cause his troops to cease the killing of noncombatants. It is further contended by the prosecution that after the accused became aware of these acts of his subordinates and before he issued an order to cease fire, that a number of unidentified Vietnamese civilians were killed by his troops. The contention is made that Captain Medina did not issue a cease fire order until late in the morning and that when a cease fire order was in fact given, that the troops did cease their fire. It is the prosecution's contention that the accused was capable of controlling his troops throughout the operation, but that once learning he had lost control of his unit, he declined to regain control for a substantial period of time during which the deaths of unidentified Vietnamese civilians occurred. It is finally the prosecution's contention that as a commander the accused, after actual awareness, had a duty to interfere he may be held personally responsible because his unlawful inaction was the proximate cause of unlawful homicides by his men.

Contrary to the theory of the prosecution, the defense alleges that Captain Medina never became aware of the misconduct of his men until too late and immediately upon suspecting that his orders were being misunderstood and improper acts occurring, he ordered his men to cease fire. The accused contends that even though he was on the ground he stayed with his command post west of the village for tactical reasons and never saw any evidence of suspicious or unnecessary deaths until immediately prior to the cease fire order. He contends that he was aware of an artillery prep and double coverage of helicopter gunships, and that it was likely that some noncombatants might be killed by such protective fires. He believed that noncombatants, and particularly the women and children, would not be in the village on that particular morning. He contends that though he saw a few bodies near the vicinity of the village of My Lai (4), he believed these to be the results of the artillery and gunship fire. The accused contends that though he became aware that his troops were out of control, by the time of this awareness, the deaths had all occurred and it was too late to prevent what had occurred; but as soon as he became aware he did issue a cease fire order. He asserts that though there was some degree of volume of fire throughout the morning, he was aware that his men were under orders to kill the livestock in My Lai (4) and in the initial stages of the operation his men were advancing toward and through what he believed to be an area heavily infested with a well-armed enemy and his men were laying down a suppressive fire.

In relation to the question pertaining to the supervisory responsibility of a Company Commander, I advise you that as a general principle of military law and custom a military superior in command is responsible for and required, in the performance of his command duties, to make certain the proper performance by his subordinates of their duties as assigned by him. In other words, after taking action or issuing an order, a commander must remain alert and make timely adjustments as required by a changing situation. Furthermore, a commander is also responsible if he has *actual* knowledge that troops or other persons subject to his control are in the process of committing or are about to commit a war crime and he wrongfully fails to take the necessary and reasonable steps to insure compliance with the law of war. You will observe that these legal requirements placed upon a commander require actual knowledge plus a wrongful failure to act. Thus mere presence at the scene without knowledge will not suffice. That is, the commander-subordinate relationship alone will not allow an inference of knowledge. While it is not necessary that a commander actually see an atrocity being committed, it is essential that he know that his subordinates are in the process of committing atrocities or are about to commit atrocities.

Furthermore you are advised that the conduct of warfare is not wholly unregulated by law. Nations have agreed to treaties limiting warfare; and customary practices governing warfare have, over a period of time, become recognized by law as binding on the conduct of warfare. Some of these deal with the propriety of killing during the conduct of war activities. The killing of resisting or fleeing enemy forces is generally recognized as a justifiable act of war, and you may consider any such killing justifiable in this case. The law attempts to protect those persons not actually engaging in warfare, however, and limits the circumstances under which their lives may be taken.

Both combatants captured by and noncombatants detained by the opposing force, regardless of their loyalties, political views, or prior acts have the right to be treated as prisoners until released, confined, or executed in accordance with law and established procedures, by competent authority sitting in judgment of such detained or captured individuals. Summary execution of detainees or prisoners is forbidden by law. Further, it is clear under the evidence presented in this case, that hostile acts or support of enemy North Vietnamese or Viet Cong forces by inhabitants of My Lai (4) at sometime prior to 16 March 1968, would not justify the summary execution of all or a part of the occupants of My Lai (4) on 16 March 1968, nor would hostile acts committed that day, if, following the hostility, the belligerents either surrendered or were captured, and thus were under the control of our forces. I, therefore, instruct you, as a matter of law, that if unresisting human beings were killed at My Lai (4) while within the effective custody and control of our military forces, their deaths cannot be considered justified.

Considering the theories of the two parties and the general statements of legal principles pertaining to military law and customs and the law of war, you are now advised that the following is an exposition of the elements of the offense of involuntary manslaughter, an offense alleged to be in violation of Article 119 of the *Uniform Code of Military Justice*.

In order to find the accused guilty of this offense, you must be satisfied by legal and competent evidence beyond reasonable doubt, of the following four elements of that offense:

(1) That an unknown number of unidentified Vietnamese persons, not less than 100, are dead;

(2) That their deaths resulted from the omission of the accused in failing to exercise control over subordinates subject to his command after having gained knowledge that his subordinates were killing noncombatants, in or at the village of My Lai (4), Quang Ngai Province, Republic of Vietnam, on or about 16 March 1968;

(3) That this omission constituted culpable negligence; and

(4) That the killing of the unknown number of unidentified Vietnamese persons, not less than 100, by subordinates of the accused and under his command, was unlawful.

You are again advised that the killing of a human being is unlawful when done without legal justification.

Culpable negligence is a degree of carelessness greater than simple negligence. For purposes of making the distinction between the two, you are advised that simple negligence is the absence of due care, that is an omission by a person who is under a duty to exercise due care, which exhibits a lack of that degree of care for the safety of others which a reasonable, prudent commander would have exercised under the same or similar circumstances. Culpable negligence, on the other hand, is a higher degree of a negligent omission, one that is accompanied by a gross, reckless, deliberate, or wanton disregard for the foreseeable consequences to others of that omission; it is an omission showing a disregard of human safety. It is higher in magnitude than simple inadvertence, but falls short of intentional wrong. The essence of wanton or reckless conduct is intentional conduct by way of omission where there is a duty to act, which conduct involves a high degree of likelihood that substantial harm will result to others.

As to the offense of involuntary manslaughter, you are advised that the omission of the accused must not only constitute culpable negligence but it must also be a proximate cause of the death or deaths. In this regard, the deaths of the unknown number of unidentified Vietnamese persons, not less than 100, must have been the natural and probable consequence of the accused's alleged culpable omission. That is, if Captain Medina had ordered his men to stop shooting noncombatants after he became aware that such was occurring, no deaths or further deaths would have occurred, and that such deaths were not the result of an independent intervening cause in which the accused did not have knowledge, and which he could not have foreseen. If it appears that the alleged culpable omission of the accused was not the proximate cause of the deaths of the unknown number of unidentified Vietnamese persons, not less than 100, but that another cause intervened over which the accused had no knowledge or control, and but for which death would not have occurred, such intervening cause is a good defense to the charge of involuntary manslaughter. To put this rule in evidentiary perspective, there has been expert evidence offered that because of experiences of the men of Charlie Company prior to the day of 16 March 1968, and because of the pressures of the combat assault, Captain Medina could have experienced difficulty in maintaining control over his men. There has also been evidence offered to the contrary, tending to indicate that his subordinates were responsive to Captain Medina's orders. The burden is upon the Government to establish beyond reasonable doubt that there was no such independent intervening cause, but that the accused's alleged culpable negligence was a proximate cause of the deaths of the unknown number of unidentified Vietnamese persons, not less than 100. Consequently, unless you are satisfied beyond reasonable doubt that the alleged victims' deaths were not the result of the unresponsiveness of the men of Charlie Company to Captain Medina's orders, but was proximately caused by the accused's alleged culpably negligent omission, you must acquit the accused of the Additional Charge and its Specification.

I have repeatedly referred to an unknown number "not less than 100" as being the number of unidentified victims in this Specification. In relation to this number of victims or any lesser number of victims, you are advised that four of you five members must be convinced beyond reasonable doubt that the same unidentified Vietnamese persons are dead. At this time I reiterate to you my limiting instruction as to the pictures admitted as evidence and as to the over-all testimony of the shooting of noncombatants. You will recall I stated that you could consider the pictures as some evidence of a circumstantial nature, together with all the other competent evidence admitted, for the purpose of determing whether or not the accused became aware that his men were killing noncombatants prior to the conclusion of the operation of 16 March 1968 at My Lai (4). I stated that you could not consider any picture as evidence of a death or deaths attributable to the accused unless you were satisfied by legal and competent evidence beyond reasonable doubt that such picture represented some evidence of a shooting that occurred in point of time after the accused became aware that his men were killing noncombatants and before his men ceased such acts pursuant to his orders, assuming you so find. This limitation equally applies to verbal evidence of the killing of noncombatants which did occur or might have occurred prior to the time the accused is alleged to have become aware his men were killing noncombatants.

With this limitation in mind, I call to your attention that there has been testimony from different witnesses tending to indicate that one or more noncombatants may have been shot at several different locations at differing times or by different persons. Thus three of the five members might be satisfied that one or more Vietnamese persons or a specific number were shot at a first location established by the evidence at a point in time after the accused became knowledgeable and before he acted but other Vietnamese persons at a second and different location in the same time frame were not shot, while another combination of three of you might be satisfied that one or more Vietnamese persons of a specific number were shot at the second location, but that the Vietnamese persons at the first location were not within the time frame. Thus two-thirds of you, that is, four of five members, would not be agreed as to the same deaths. Therefore, I reiterate, that four of five of the members must be satisfied beyond reasonable doubt that the same identical one or more Vietnamese persons are dead. Additionally, if you are satisfied beyond reasonable doubt that Captain Medina is responsible for the death of at least one, but not all of the unidentified Vietnamese persons as alleged, then you must modify your findings so that it accurately reflects that specific number of Vietnamese persons as to which at least four of you have no reasonable doubt, or if you are satisfied beyond reasonable doubt that there was more than one but that the ultimate number is unknown, then you should indicate that findings by excepting the words and figures "not less than 100" and substituting therefor the words and figure "more than one."

I have advised you that knowledge by Captain Medina that the men of Charlie Company were unlawfully killing non-combatants is necessary to establish the commission of the offense of involuntary manslaughter. You are instructed that you cannot convict the accused of this offense unless you have been satisfied beyond reasonable doubt that he had such knowledge. However, this required knowledge on the part of the accused, like any other fact, may be proved by circumstantial evidence; that is by evidence of facts or circumstances from which it may be justifiably inferred that the accused had such knowledge. In this regard you must consider all relevant facts and circumstances. I will now outline for your consideration the significant evidentiary factors bearing upon this as offered both by the defense and the prosecution. Of course, this does not purport to be a total delineation of all the evidence on this issue nor is my recollection controlling upon you, as you have been previously instructed. It is your recollection of the evidence upon which you must rely and not the statement of the evidence or the factors bearing upon knowledge as I might recall them. In this case the defense has offered in substance the following information that tends to reflect that the accused did not have any knowledge that his men were killing non-combatants unlawfully. First of all, Captain Medina himself denies having knowledge that his men were killing non-combatants until immediately prior to the time he gave a cease fire order. Other factors include information that had been passed to him by the S-2, Captain Kotouc, and Colonel Barker concerning intelligence that this would be a heavily defended assault and that his troops, that is, the troops of Charlie Company would be facing a Viet Cong battalion and that Charlie Company would be outnumbered approximately two to one. On the morning of the assault itself, information has been offered tending to indicate that reports from helicopters and other sources came to the attention of Captain Medina indicating that Viet Cong persons were fleeing the village and that Viet Cong being stopped and shot possessed weapons. Information has also been submitted that Captain Medina overheard a report that the landing zone itself and its supporting aircraft had received hostile fire and the LZ was hot. In addition the evidence offered by the defense reflects that the accused was only in the village at one time prior to the Carter Medivac and then only for a distance of some 75 yards. Also you should consider the excursion of the accused to the area south of the village prior to returning to the Carter Medivac site. You should also recall evidence that the village had limited visibility due to ground vegetation and trees restricting the vision of persons for any distance within the village. Orders had been issued by Captain Medina and from higher authority to kill the livestock, thereby accounting for the continued firing by his troops in the absence of any known enemy resistance. You should consider the report that Lt. Calley made to the accused that there had been a body count of 69 VC KIA indicating that there were armed enemy. And finally you should consider that the artillery and gun ship preparatory fires would probably have inflicted casualties indicating that bodies seen by Captain Medina outside the village were the result of such preparatory fire rather than by his own men. These are the factors offered by the defense as tending to indicate the accused was not possessed of any knowledge that his troops were killing unlawfully non-combatants.

On the other hand the Government has offered evidence tending to indicate that early in the operation the accused became aware that there was no active resistance and that there was no hostile fire, indicating that the Viet Cong battalion was not in the village. In spite of the absence of hostile fire the Government offers evidence indicating that there was a continued volume of fire by the men of Charlie Company. The accused, aware of the volume of fire, it is contended by the Government, ordered his men to conserve ammunition reflecting further that the accused was aware that there was no enemy resistance. The Government submits that the absence of hostile fire, Lt. Calley's report that a helicopter pilot had landed and complained about the way he, Lt. Calley, was conducting the operation, and a body of 69 from Lt. Calley show that Captain Medina was aware of the activities of his troops. The Government offers evidence that it is possible that a boy was shot in his presence and Captain Medina indicates that a boy was shot in his presence. The Government asks you to consider the pile of bodies of the north-south trail that gave rise to knowledge on the part of the accused that unnecessary deaths were occurring. The Government requests you to recollect the statements made to Mr. Brisentine concerning the state of the accused's knowledge. Lastly, the Government asks you to consider that there were no communication failures between the command group and the platoons. Again, this is not intended to be a complete summary of all the evidence either on behalf of the defense or on the behalf of the Government but these are the evidentiary factors recalled by the Military Judge which you may consider along with all the other facts and circumstances of this case giving rise to a possible knowledge of the activities of Charlie Company by the accused. The weight, if any, to be given such an inference of the accused's knowledge must, of course, depend upon the circumstances attending the proved facts which give rise to the inference, as well as all the other evidence in the case. It is for you to make this determination.

INDEX

H

I

J

N

O

S

X Y Z